# MONEY, BANKING and FINANCIAL MARKETS

Lloyd B. Thomas
Kansas State University

THOMSON
SOUTH-WESTERN

Australia · Canada · Mexico · Singapore · Spain · United Kingdom · United States

THOMSON
SOUTH-WESTERN

**Money, Banking, and Financial Markets**

Lloyd B. Thomas

**VP/Editorial Director:**
Jack W. Calhoun

**VP/Editor-in-Chief:**
Dave Shaut

**Acquisitions Editor:**
Mike Worls

**Sr. Developmental Editor:**
Trish Taylor

**Sr. Marketing Manager:**
John Carey

**Production Editor:**
Cliff Kallemeyn

**Sr. Technology Project Editor:**
Peggy Buskey

**Technology Project Editor:**
Pam Wallace

**Sr. Manufacturing Coordinator:**
Sandee Milewski

**Art Director:**
Tippy McIntosh

**Production House:**
Graphic World, Inc.

**Printer:**
RR Donnelley
Willard, OH



Printed in the United States of America
1 2 3 4 5 08 07 06 05

Package ISBN: 0-324-17673-2

Book-only ISBN: 0-324-32282-8

Library of Congress Control Number:
2004114017



For more information
contact South-Western,
5191 Natorp Boulevard,
Mason, Ohio 45040.
Or you can visit our Internet site at:
http://www.swlearning.com

*To Sally*

# ABOUT THE AUTHOR

Lloyd B. Thomas, Jr., is Professor and Head of the Department of Economics at Kansas State University. He received a B.A. and M.A. in economics from the University of Missouri and a Ph.D. in economics from Northwestern University. Professor Thomas has published in numerous economics journals, primarily in the areas of macroeconomic policy, monetary economics, and international finance. Most recently, his research has focused on the accuracy and rationality of survey measures of inflation expectations and other forecasts of inflation. He is the author or coauthor of five previous textbooks, several of which have been published in multiple editions.

Recognized as an excellent teacher, Professor Thomas has won numerous teaching awards. His teaching interests lie chiefly in the areas of money and banking, monetary theory and policy, and principles of economics. Professor Thomas has gained teaching experience at numerous universities, including Northwestern University, the University of California at Berkeley, Florida State University, the University of Delaware, the University of Idaho, Indiana University at Bloomington, and Adelaide University in Australia. For fun, he enjoys running and playing tennis.

# BRIEF CONTENTS

# CONTENTS

# PREFACE

Students come to undergraduate money and banking courses with widely differing backgrounds, majors, and objectives. Money and banking instructors place varying degrees of emphasis on monetary theory, institutions, and policy. This textbook reflects my view that the money and banking course should be the most interesting and timely course in an economics or finance curriculum, and that it should be of considerable value to students with diverse backgrounds and interests. In addition, *Money, Banking, and Financial Markets* should help instructors teach more easily, regardless of academic focus.

This textbook will provide students with a solid grasp of the fundamental topics, principles, and issues traditionally covered in the money and banking course that are *not* thoroughly covered in other courses in the curriculum. This book seeks to minimize any overlap with intermediate macroeconomics courses. Instead, it aims to provide clear and up-to-date coverage of such fundamental topics as the nature and role of money, financial institutions and markets, and banking structure and regulation. *Money, Banking, and Financial Markets* provides an unusually thorough treatment of Federal Reserve instruments, strategies, and policy transmission, the determinants of interest rates, stock prices, foreign exchange rates, and the nation's money supply. Compared to other leading money and banking texts, this one seeks to cover fewer topics, but to cover those selected topics more clearly and effectively.

This is a policy-oriented text. It provides a thorough explanation of the relevant analytical framework, keyed closely to economic policy issues. We pay greater-than-normal attention to the instruments of Federal Reserve policy and the difficulties involved in conducting monetary policy in uncertain economic environments. Separate chapters (12 and 13) cover the institutional makeup of the Federal Reserve System and the European Central Bank. The challenges confronting discretionary conduct of monetary policy and the "rules versus discretion" debate are thoroughly covered. The text features unprecedented coverage and analysis of the Taylor Rule (chapter 24), analyzing its strengths and weaknesses both in formulating monetary policy prospectively and in evaluating policy retrospectively. Modern views of the transmission mechanism of monetary policy—the myriad ways in which monetary policy influences economic activity—are thoroughly covered in Chapter 23. Because more than 20 nations have now adopted inflation-targeting central bank regimes, an entire chapter (25) provides unprecedented coverage of this topic. In short, this text covers monetary policy in more depth than any existing money and banking text.

*Money, Banking, and Financial Markets* provides a solid theoretical framework. Students sometimes find economic theory dull or difficult to understand. But an economic theory, after all, is simply a rigorous explanation of an economic phenomenon. The loanable funds model of interest rates and the various theories of the term structure of interest rates are carefully developed in chapters 5 and 6. We invoke the present value framework to explain stock, bond, and other asset pricing in chapters 5 and 7. Chapter 8 presents theories of long-run and short-run exchange rate determination. Following a brief chapter on the principles of deposit expansion and contraction, we set forth the monetary base—money supply multiplier framework for understanding money supply determination in chapters 15 and 16. Chapter 20 develops the aggregate demand and aggregate supply framework; this chapter also includes a thorough analysis of the Phillips curve hypothesis and the factors that cause the natural rate of unemployment to fluctuate over time. Chapter 22 provides a comprehensive discussion of the theory of money demand and velocity. Chapter 23 analyzes the transmission of monetary policy, including an in-depth discussion of the "money view" and the "credit view."

The book adopts a mainstream analytical approach in which *both* monetary and fiscal policies significantly influence economic activity, and leaves debates about the various theoretical paradigms that diametrically contradict one another to intermediate macroeconomics courses.

While this text does not skimp on economic theory, it develops the relevant theory only to shed light on important economic events and developments. We surround theory with examples from current events and economic history. For example:

- As soon as we present the analytical framework for understanding how to price shares of stock in chapter 7, we discuss the 1990s' run-up of stock prices, the ensuing crash, and the contentious issue of whether central banks should intervene to head off stock market bubbles.
- Immediately after developing the Fisher hypothesis—which links nominal interest rates to expected inflation—in chapter 5, we test the theory by examining bond yields and inflation rates in a cross section of 14 nations.
- As soon as we examine the purchasing power parity (PPP) theory of exchange rates in chapter 8, we provide a graph illustrating the actual and PPP U.S.-Australia exchange rates over a 30-year period. This presentation enables students to observe that purchasing power parity is strictly a *long-run* theory of exchange rate determination.
- As soon as chapters 15 and 16 develop the monetary base—money supply multiplier framework, we use the framework to analyze the fundamental causes of the contraction of the U.S. money supply in the Great Depression and the Federal Reserve's role in that catastrophe (chapter 17).
- Immediately after chapter 20 discusses the aggregate supply-aggregate demand model, we use the framework to analyze the most important macroeconomic developments of the past 75 years (emphasizing those of the past decade).

Given this approach, students develop the attitude that economic theory is interesting and valuable in understanding contemporary economic events.

## DISTINGUISHING FEATURES OF THIS TEXT

Reviewers consistently remarked on the clarity of the writing style, the timeliness of the topics discussed, and the thorough coverage of recent developments. Such developments include the post-1995 acceleration of productivity, the unusual nature of the 2001 recession and the "jobless recovery" of 2002–2004, the 2003 Federal Reserve change in discount window procedures, the corporate and mutual fund scandals of 2002–2004, and recent changes in the list of the nation's 10 largest banks. Instructors will note several distinguishing features of this textbook vis-a-vis alternative texts.

**Empirical Orientation.** More than any other money and banking text, this book provides students with a feel for a multitude of key monetary and financial variables, via tables and time-series graphs. More than 70 graphs illustrate how such variables as exchange rates, bond yields, the currency ratio, the money-supply multiplier, velocity of money, stock prices, and inflation rates have behaved over a period of years. Other figures show the price-earnings ratios of the S&P 500 stock market index; the fed funds rate vs. that indicated by the Taylor Rule both in the U.S. and in Japan; actual and potential GDP; the high correlation between money market yields in the U.S. and Germany, and other economic phenomena. Many of these illustrations are unique—they do not appear in other money and banking texts. While the interest rate chapter of a leading money and banking text includes only one time-series graph featuring interest rates or yields, this one includes seven such graphs. Students gain a feel for the magnitude and behavior over time of the variables under discussion.

**Substantive Exhibits.** Numerous reviewers commented on the substantive and unique nature of the boxed exhibits. This book includes more than 50 exhibits that cover such topics as the "tech wreck" of 2000–2002, the economics of ATMs, the growth of internet banking, an evaluation of the Gramm-Leach-Bliley Act, the 2004 enlargement of the European Union, and salaries of top Federal Reserve officials. Other exhibits discuss Irving Fisher's genius and versatility; recent trends in U.S. productivity growth; a brief history of money market mutual funds; the demise of the reserve requirement tax; bandwagon phenomena in exchange rate movements, and oil prices as aggregate supply shocks. Both instructors and student readers will find these exhibits superior to those in other texts.

**Emphasis on the Worldwide Applicability of Concepts and Economic Phenomena.** The more we study economics, the more we become aware of the sense that "we are in this together." In the age of the Internet, information travels around the world instantaneously. This text emphasizes the high degree of correlation between asset prices, business cycle developments, and other economic phenomena in the United States and in other nations. This point is driven home by time-series graphs illustrating the co-variation of interest rates, stock prices, and other phenomena across countries. Students come to appreciate the worldwide nature of macroeconomic and financial developments, which enhances the value of the analytical tools that help us understand these phenomena.

**Entire Chapter on the Stock Market.** As the number and percentage of American families owning stocks has increased and knowledge of the superior long-term performance of equities has become widespread, interest in the stock market has increased apace. Students are keenly interested in the stock market. Chapter 7 is devoted entirely to the stock market, providing a framework for understanding the factors determining the prices of stocks. The chapter also looks at various stock market indexes and discusses the various measures of stock valuation. We analyze the risk inherent in stocks relative to government bonds and discuss the equity risk premium anomaly and the phenomenon of mean reversion in stock prices.

**Unique Chapter on the Great Depression.** The economics profession has seen a remarkable resurgence of interest in the Great Depression in the past decade or two. This tragic episode presents an excellent case study of monetary policy gone awry. This text devotes a full chapter (17) to the causes of the contraction of the money supply in the early 1930s, the role of the Federal Reserve in that experience, and the ongoing debate over whether monetary policy is rendered impotent in an environment of deflation.

**Unique Chapter on Inflation Targeting.** In recent years, inflation rates in industrial nations have declined to the lowest levels in half a century. This reduction is due, in part, to the fact that more than 20 nations have implemented inflation targeting monetary policy regimes. We include a full chapter (25) that analyzes the cases for and against inflation targeting and looks at the contentious issue of whether the Federal Reserve should implement such a regime.

## PEDAGOGICAL FEATURES

This work contains a number of features designed to enhance the effectiveness of this book as a teaching instrument.

- **Part Openers** for each of the six sections of the text outline the importance of and relationships among the topics covered in each section.

- **Definitions of Key Terms** appear in the margins as the terms are introduced, as well in the textual discussion.
- A **glossary** of all key terms is compiled in alphabetical order at the end of the book.
- More than 50 **boxed exhibits** provide interesting background on various economic and financial relationships, events, and developments.
- **International Perspectives** boxes provide a global perspective on key topics and empirical economic phenomena. These boxes provide discussion of such topics as the worldwide decline in inflation since 1990, the synchronization of economic phenomena across countries, and the use of the Taylor Rule to evaluate the Bank of Japan's contribution to deflation in the past decade.
- A **From the Financial News** feature introduces students to financial tables from daily newspapers, covering such topics as the yield curve, stock prices, foreign exchange rates, and weekly Federal Reserve data.
- A **Your Turn** feature gets students into active mode by posing questions that test their understanding of various formulas and concepts as the ideas are introduced. Answers appear at the end each chapter.
- More than 70 time-series **figures** introduce students to a multitude of macroeconomic and financial data.
- **Chapter summaries** review key points developed in each chapter.
- **Study Questions** at the end of each chapter test students' understanding of the most important concepts and principles discussed in the chapter.
- An **Additional Reading** feature at the end of each chapter points instructors (as well as highly motivated students) to classic literature as well as recent articles on major topics.
- **URLs** are provided with each time-series figure so that students may access original data and check to see how the pertinent variables have changed most recently.

## Supplementary Materials

The **Study Guide,** written by Professor Alan Grant of Eastern Illinois University, provides an overview of each chapter and a variety of measures to increase student learning. Each Study Guide chapter supplies a variety of questions for students, including matching, true-false, fill in the blank, multiple choice, and problems. Answers are provided at the end of each chapter.

A **Test Bank** written by Amanda Freeman, Alan Grant, and Lloyd Thomas provides some 1900 multiple choice examination questions, or an average of about 75 questions per chapter. Lloyd Thomas has contributed about 50 percent of these questions and has reviewed all other questions for quality.

An **Instructor's Manual,** written by Professor Robert Guell of Indiana State University includes sample course outlines, answers to end-of-chapter questions, and teaching hints for each chapter. Instructor's Manual chapters are keyed directly to PowerPoint Software presentations.

**Power Point Presentation Software,** also prepared by Professor Robert Guell of Indiana State University, illustrate the key concepts and principles presented in each chapter.

**Thomas Textbook Support Web Site (http://thomas.swlearning.com)** provides instructional materials for professors, including the Instructor's Manual, Test Bank, and PowerPoint Presentation Software via a password-protected section of the site that is not accessible to students. Approximately 10 online quizzing questions for students are also available at this site.

## Thomas Xtra! Web Site (http://thomasxtra.swlearning.com/)

Thomas Xtra!, available to be packaged with the textbook, provides access to a robust set of online learning tools for students. Please ask your Thomson sales representative for more information. Thomas Xtra! contains these key features:

- **Interactive E-Lectures.** Difficult concepts from each chapter are explained and illustrated via Flash-animated tutorials.
- **Xtra! Quizzing.** In addition to the open-access chapter-by-chapter quizzes found at the Thomas Product Support Web site, (http://thomas.swlearning. com), Thomas Xtra! offers students the opportunity to practice for midterms and finals by taking extensive interactive quizzes.
- **Economic Applications.** EconNews Online, EconDebate Online, EconData Online, and EconLinks Online help to deepen students' understanding of theoretical concepts through hands-on exploration and analysis of the latest economic news stories, policy debates, and data.

**TextChoice** is a custom format of Thomson Learning's online digital content that provides the fastest, easiest way for you to create your own learning materials. You may select content from hundreds of best-selling titles, choose material from our numerous databases, and add your own material. http://thomsoncustom.com.

**Ecoursepacks** Create a customizable, easy-to-use, online companion for any course with eCourse packs. ECourse packs give educators access to current content from thousands of popular, professional, and academic periodicals, including NACRA and Darden cases, and business and industry information from Gale. You can easily add your own material—even collecting a royalty if you choose. http://ecoursepacks.swlearning.com.

**ExamView** *ExamView Computerized Testing Software* contains all of the questions in the Test Bank. ExamView is an easy-to-use test creation package compatible with both Microsoft Windows and Macintosh client software. You can select questions by previewing them on the screen, selecting them by number, or selecting them randomly. Questions, instructions, and answers can be edited, and new questions can easily be added. You can also administer quizzes online—over the Internet, through a local area network (LAN), or through a wide area network (WAN).

**MarketSim** MarketSim, by Tod Porter at Youngstown State University, is an online simulation designed to help students in microeconomics classes better understand how markets work, by having students take on the roles of consumers and producers in a simulated economy. In the simulations, students "make" and "accept" offers to buy and sell labor and goods asynchronously via the Internet.

**CNN Economics Video** CNN video segments bring the real world right to students' desktops by using the CNN Principles of Economics Video Updates. This video provides current stories of economic interest, and the accompanying integration guide provides a summary and discussion questions for each clip. The video is produced in cooperation with Turner Learning Inc.

Contact your local Thomson Learning/South-Western sales representative about obtaining these support materials.

## ACKNOWLEDGEMENTS

The author is indebted to many individuals who have contributed substantially to the development of this project over the past three years. Foremost among those to whom I am indebted is Professor Alan Grant of Eastern Illinois University, whose contribution to this project over the years has been enormous. Al carefully critiqued two versions of every chapter, contributed numerous end-of-chapter Study Questions, pointed me to relevant journal articles, and is responsible for chapter 10 on banking structure and regulation. In addition, he contributed hundreds of questions for the Test Bank, wrote the Study Guide for this text, and has generally been a tremendous colleague in the development of this entire project. Professor Robert Guell of Indiana State University did a meticulous job of putting together the PowerPoint and Instructor's Manual ancillaries for this project. Professor Ronnie J. Phillips of Colorado State University reviewed the entire manuscript and provided a multitude of constructive suggestions. Amanda Freeman, a Ph.D. student at Kansas State University and a money and banking instructor, made a major contribution to this project during the final year of its development. In addition to carefully proofreading and critiquing each chapter, she checked all URLs and references for accuracy, put together the Test Bank, and served as an extremely able and invaluable resource for the author. Professor Mark Wohar of the University of Nebraska–Omaha, through numerous phone calls and e-mails, provided important prodding and encouragement to bring this work to fruition. My colleague and a veteran money and banking teacher, Michael Oldfather, critiqued several chapters and also contributed by sharing his extensive knowledge of the business, structure, and regulation of commercial banking. Numerous conversations with colleagues Patrick Gormely, Wayne Nafziger, and Roger Trenary also added value to the final product. Many graduate and undergraduate students at KSU contributed in a variety of ways. Jared Wirths and Jared Dressman are responsible for developing the multitude of time-series graphs in this book. Boaz Nandwa, Daniel Nibarger, Shane Sanders, Jamie Stamatson, and Danhua Wu also contributed in such ways as checking references, contributing study questions, supplying the author with pertinent literature, and reading the page proofs. Kristi Smith and Susan Koch helped with manuscript preparation and typing of tables.

I am greatly indebted to numerous individuals at Thomson Learning/South-Western. At the top of the list is my Senior Development Editor, Trish Taylor. Trish expertly handled the myriad challenges of coordinating the development of the text with that of the Study Guide, Instructor's Manual, Test Bank, PowerPoint slides, and other ancillary materials. I am also indebted to Trish for being a stickler about efficiency in writing style, for prodding me to revise the manuscript conscientiously in response to constructive suggestions from reviewers, and for calmly dealing with an author of rather volatile temperament. I am indebted to production editor Cliff Kallemeyn for coolly dealing with numerous glitches and roadblocks, carefully implementing needed corrections, and delivering the end product in excellent condition. I am grateful to Tippy McIntosh for the outstanding design of this book, including the spectacular cover. Senior Technology Product Editor Peggy Buskey brought her expertise to bear in creating a superior package of electronic supplements. Senior Acquisitions editor Mike Worls and Senior Marketing Manager John Carey supplied important encouragement and counsel during the development of this work.

Most of all, I am grateful to my wife (Sally), daughter (Elizabeth Thomas Horn), and mother (Marianne Moon Thomas) for their encouragement, support, and loyalty.

Numerous reviewers made constructive suggestions and contributed materially to the final product. These include:

Burton Abrams (University of Delaware)
Richard Boylan (University of Alabama)
Charles Britton (University of Arkansas)
Stacy Brook (University of Sioux Falls)
Jim Butkiewicz (University of Delaware)
Miles Cahill (College of Holy Cross)
Thomas Carroll (University of Nevada–Las Vegas)
Catherine Chambers (Central Missouri State University)
Martin Cherkes (Princeton University)
Dal Didia (Jackson State University)
Chris Erickson (New Mexico State University)
David Flynn (University of North Dakota)
James Gale (Michigan Technological University)
Ralph Gamble (Fort Hays State University)
Ron Gilbert (Texas Tech University)
Ismail Genc (University of Idaho)
Dipak Ghosh (Emporia State University)
Wafica Ghoul (Davenport University)
Rik Hafer (Southern Illinois University–Edwardsville)
Bradley Hobbs (Florida State University)
Jon Hooks (Albion College)
Thomas Ireland (University of Missouri–St.Louis)
Art Janssen (Emporia State University)
Nancy Jianakoplos (Colorado State University)
Bryce Kanago (University of Northern Iowa)
Shawn Kantor (University of Arizona)
Elizabeth Sawyer Kelly (University of Wisconsin–Madison)
Kathy Kelly (University of Texas-Austin)
Benjamin Kim (University of Nebraska–Lincoln)
Todd Knoop (Cornell College)
Sungkyu Kwak (Washburn University)
B. Starr McMullen (Oregon State University)
Ed Merkel (Troy State University)
Michael Oldfather (Kansas State University)
Douglas Pearce (North Carolina State University)
Mark Perry (University of Michigan–Flint)
Ronnie Phillips (Colorado State University)
Scott Redenius (Bryn Mawr College)
Prosper Raynold (Miami University of Ohio)
Russell Rhine (St. Mary's College of Maryland)
Joseph Santos (South Dakota State University)
Edward Sattler (Bradley University)
Donald Scarry (Rutgers–The State University of New Jersey)
Elizabeth Schmitt (SUNY–Oswego)
Paul Storer (Western Washington University)
Robert Tokle (Idaho State University)
Karen Vorst (University of Missouri–Kansas City)
John Wassom (Western Kentucky University)
Mark Wohar (University of Nebraska–Omaha)
Gil Wolpe (Newbury College)
Robert Wright (University of Virginia)
Shu Wu (University of Kansas)
Bill Yang (Georgia Southern University)
David Zalewski (Providence College)

# Part ONE

In this opening section, we introduce several important concepts that we will discuss throughout this course. Chapter 1 overviews the role that money, banks, financial markets, and the central bank play in a nation's economy. Key financial markets include the stock market, the bond market, and the foreign exchange market. Current and expected economic conditions profoundly influence these markets and the prices that are determined in them. These prices, in turn, affect spending decisions and thereby influence economic phenomena such as employment, output, and the nation's price level. Chapter 2 examines the nature, functions, and evolution of money. In addition, chapter 2 introduces the idea of central banks. Central banks control the quantity of money in their nations. A rapid increase in the money supply results in inflation, whereas a severe contraction in the money supply leads to deflation and hard times. The United States and other countries have devised several alternative measures of money supply, and there is no clear consensus about which measure is best.

Chapter 1

# MONEY, BANKING, AND FINANCIAL MARKETS—AN OVERVIEW

Money, banking, and financial markets represent a dynamic and exciting area of study. In recent years, we have witnessed:

- the development of important new financial markets and instruments;
- the removal of trade barriers;
- an increased integration of financial markets and economic activity worldwide;
- the adoption of a single currency by a dozen European nations; and
- a major consolidation of the U.S. banking industry as the number of U.S. commercial banks declined from more than 14,000 in 1980 to fewer than 8,000 today.

Further, since the mid-1990s, the United States has experienced a tremendous run-up of stock prices (1995–2000). 2001 and the early years of the twenty-first century followed with a bursting of the stock market "bubble" and an ensuing dramatic decline in the price of hundreds of technology and other stocks. Stock price volatility appears perhaps most clearly by the NASDAQ system and the changes in this market for smaller firms. The NASDAQ stock market index increased nearly 100 percent in a single year (1999) and then proceeded to lose more than three-fourths of its value (peak to trough) from 2000 to 2002. In aggregate, U.S. stockholders lost approximately $7 trillion (nearly half) of their stock market wealth during this 2-year period.

The 1990s witnessed optimistic talk of a "new economy"—an economy in which national output and living standards would rise more quickly than in the previous quarter century. This "new economy" would also feature low inflation and relatively mild, occasional economic downturns. The acceleration in **productivity**—output per hour of work—that began in 1995 continued through the 2001 recession and beyond, lending credibility to the "new economy" view. Indeed, world economic history shows that productivity growth is the predominant source of rising living standards like those predicted for the U.S. in the 1990s.

**productivity**
output per hour of work

In the early part of the new millennium, however, a series of shocks hit the U.S. economy, impairing consumer and business confidence and thereby hindering economic activity. The first shock: The stock market bubble burst after March 2000. The second shock: Terrorists attacked both New York City and Washington, DC, on September 11, 2001. Then, in the spring and summer of 2002, a wave of accounting scandals hit. U.S. corporations—and their auditors—reported fraudulent profits, which damaged ordinary Americans' confidence in the integrity of America's capital markets. The nation's elected officials scurried to create remedies. Disclosure in late 2003 of unethical (and in some cases illegal) mutual fund activities that enriched mutual fund managers at the expense of American investors furthered investor unease. To combat the ensuing economic weakness and rising unemployment, the Federal Reserve reduced interest rates 13 times from 2001 to 2003, dropping short-term interest rates to the lowest levels in nearly half a century.

Although you may be aware of these and more recent events, you probably do not fully understand their ramifications for U.S. financial markets and economic activity. As you carefully read this text, you will become increasingly aware of the consequences that important financial, macroeconomic, and international economic phenomena play in your own economic lives. For example, you will understand the causes and consequences of changes in the nation's money supply and level of interest rates, stock prices, and exchange rates. You will learn about the functions of various financial institutions and markets. You will gain a keen appreciation for the nature and role of the U.S. central bank, the Federal Reserve System, and the sources of its great power. Furthermore, you will emerge from this course with a grasp of the fundamental causes of important economic developments. Changes in unemployment and inflation occur over the course of the business cycle and the Federal Reserve combats such adverse economic developments. You will gain exposure to debates that rage among economic and financial experts.

This introductory chapter provides a brief overview of some of the key financial markets, players, and topics that we will cover in depth throughout this course. You will quickly discover that, in addition to being interesting and important, this subject matter has a direct bearing on your daily life, your material well-being, and your future job prospects.

## MONEY AND BANKING: KEY ELEMENTS

Four key elements play an important role in the U.S. (and other nations') economic environment today:

- Money,
- Financial intermediaries (especially banks),
- Interest rates, and
- Government budget deficits (or surpluses).

Each of these elements appears frequently in this book. Here, we sketch briefly the nature and importance of each element.

### Money

People often define money as the stock of items widely used to pay for goods and services. More specifically, **money,** or the **money supply,** includes all currency and coins in circulation outside of financial institutions and government coffers, together with checking accounts owned by individuals and business firms in depository institutions (commercial banks, savings and loan associations, mutual savings banks, and credit unions). These checking accounts, currency, and coins constitute M1, our narrowest measure of the nation's money supply. We discuss broader measures of money (M2 and M3) in Chapter 2. This text aims to provide a clear explanation of the causes and consequences of changes in a nation's money supply.

**money (money supply)**
all currency and coins in circulation outside of financial institutions and government coffers, together with the checking accounts in depository institutions owned by individuals and business firms

**What Determines the Money Supply?** In Part 4, we will see that many factors affect week-to-week and longer-term fluctuations in the nation's money supply. The most important player in this process—the **central bank**—clearly steers the *trend* or *long-run* behavior of a country's money supply. In the United States, the central bank also controls short-term interest rates and is known as the **Federal Reserve System,** or simply the **Fed.** By implementing policy tools, the Fed and other nations' central banks conduct **monetary policy.** Monetary policy involves decisions

**central bank**
a nation's monetary authority or agency charged with conducting monetary policy and other duties

**Federal Reserve System (Fed)**
the central bank of the United States, charged with conducting monetary policy and other duties associated with our financial system

**monetary policy**
measures implemented by the central bank that influence the availability of credit, the level of interest rates, and the money supply in the nation

and actions that influence the availability of credit, the level of interest rates, and the nation's money supply. For example, when the U.S. economy experiences a period of recession or very sluggish economic activity and rising unemployment (such as during 2001–2003), the Fed will attempt to stimulate economic activity through monetary policy actions. In 2001–2003, the Fed used its policy tools to make bank loans more easily available to the public. "Easier money" results in falling interest rates and a rising money supply, developments that boost aggregate expenditures for goods and services. Such "easy money" thereby works to counteract the weakness in the economy.

On the other hand, when the economy suffers from excessive growth of expenditures and unacceptably high levels of inflation, the Federal Reserve implements measures that restrain aggregate spending. The Fed uses its policy tools to reduce both credit availability and to contract the money supply: It pushes up short-term interest rates. For example, in 1999 and early 2000, the U.S. economy reached full employment and appeared to be on the threshold of an undesirable increase in the inflation rate. As a result, the Fed boosted interest rates and restrained the growth of bank credit and the money supply. Parts 4 through 6 of this book provide an in-depth analysis of the Federal Reserve System and the conduct of U.S. monetary policy.

Figure 1-1 shows how the U.S. money supply (M1) has behaved in recent years. In mid-2004, it stood at approximately $1,300 billion (1.3 trillion), divided rather evenly between checking accounts and currency. This amounts to some $4,500 per person (approximately $15,000 per family). If this strikes you as too high a figure for the typical family, you are right! The figures are skewed by the fact that businesses held a large portion of the nation's money supply. Just as you and I hold money (checking accounts and currency) to finance upcoming purchases of goods and services and other transactions, firms maintain money balances to pay for materials,

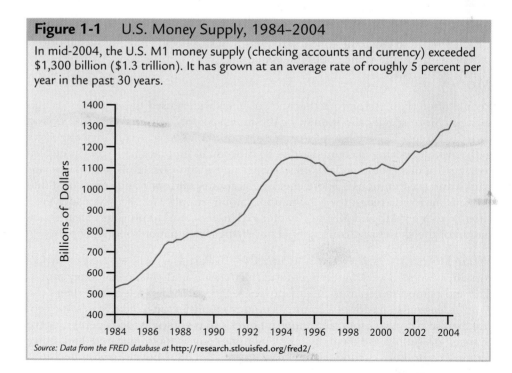

**Figure 1-1** U.S. Money Supply, 1984–2004

In mid-2004, the U.S. M1 money supply (checking accounts and currency) exceeded $1,300 billion ($1.3 trillion). It has grown at an average rate of roughly 5 percent per year in the past 30 years.

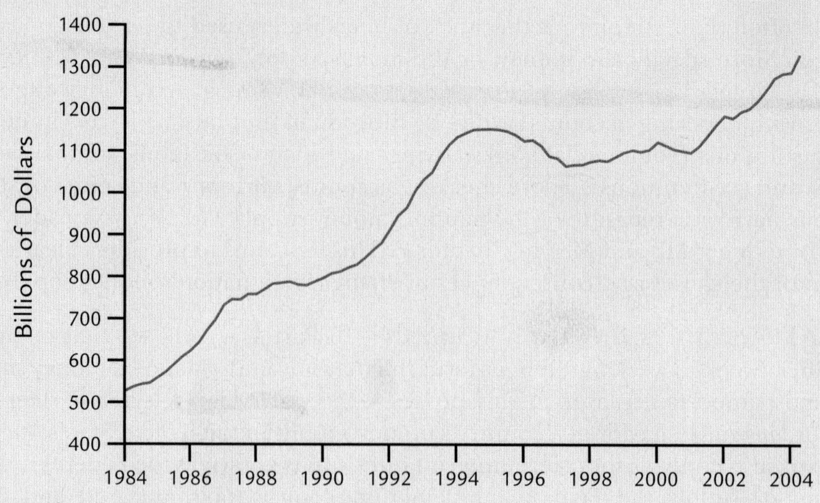


*Source: Data from the FRED database at* http://research.stlouisfed.org/fred2/

meet payrolls, and so forth. Thousands of business firms hold large checking accounts in depository institutions, and these accounts all are included in the various measures of the nation's money supply. In addition, large amounts of cash are used to finance transactions in the U.S. *underground economy,* that is, to finance illegal activities such as drug purchases. Most significantly, U.S. currency is considered a "hard currency," acceptable as payment in many foreign nations, including numerous central and eastern European nations and in Latin America. Although accurate data are not available, many economists believe that perhaps half of the currency component of the U.S. money supply actually resides outside of U.S. borders.

**Money, Inflation, and Deflation.** When a nation's money supply increases for a sustained period at a substantially more rapid rate than the country's capacity to expand output of goods and services, inflation occurs. **Inflation** is a persistent or continuing increase in a nation's general price level. Inflation results fundamentally from excessive growth of aggregate expenditures for goods and services. Rapid expansion of a nation's money supply typically leads to rapid growth in expenditures, thereby resulting in inflation. History teaches us that in every historical episode of severe inflation, both in the United States and abroad, the nation's money supply has grown rapidly.

**inflation**
persistent or continuing increase in a nation's general price level

Figure 1-2 illustrates the relationship between the average money growth rate and the average inflation rate for a cross section of nations from 1988 to 2002. Countries with very high money growth rates systematically experienced relatively high inflation rates. Each listed country that experienced average inflation rates in

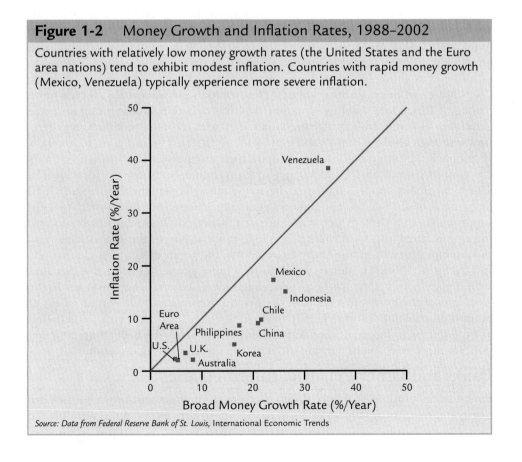

**Figure 1-2** Money Growth and Inflation Rates, 1988–2002

Countries with relatively low money growth rates (the United States and the Euro area nations) tend to exhibit modest inflation. Countries with rapid money growth (Mexico, Venezuela) typically experience more severe inflation.

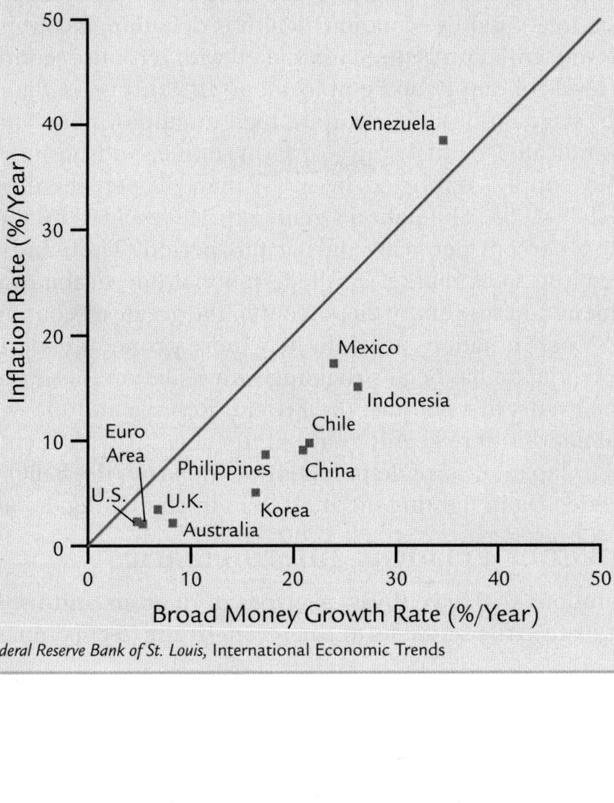


*Source: Data from Federal Reserve Bank of St. Louis,* International Economic Trends

excess of 10 percent per year also exhibited money growth rates of more than 20 percent per year. Note, however, that although the relationship between money growth and inflation is positive and fairly strong, it is far from a perfect correlation. Other factors besides money growth influence price levels, and this consideration is especially pertinent in countries with modest rates of inflation. If you use U.S. data for the past 20 years (an era of low inflation) and plot the money growth rate each year versus inflation in the following couple of years, you would observe very little correlation. In other words, the U.S. inflation in the past 20 years has not been tightly linked with money growth.

**inflation targeting**
monetary policy strategy in which a central bank specifies an explicit range within which it pledges to maintain the rate of inflation

Nations have become increasingly aware that inflation arises from central banks' tendency to expand the money supply at excessive rates. Approximately 20 nations have thus implemented **inflation targeting** programs in the past 15 years. Under inflation targeting, central banks announce explicit ranges within which they pledge to maintain the rate of inflation. The banks then conduct policies with the predominant objective of achieving that goal. For example, in 1993, the Reserve Bank of Australia set an inflation target range of 2 to 3 percent per year, and it has generally maintained inflation within that range. Canada, Israel, Mexico, New Zealand, Spain, and the United Kingdom also target inflation. Today, inflation rates are unusually low in many nations, partly because of inflation targeting. We add the caveat "only partly" because, as we noted above, the correlation between money supply growth and inflation rate growth is not perfect, particularly during periods of low inflation.

The U.S. Federal Reserve has not implemented inflation-targeting. Some economists criticize the Federal Reserve for its failure to act, but the Fed has successfully maintained inflation within acceptable bounds in the past couple of decades (review Figure 1-2). As long as the public strongly believes in a central bank's resolve to maintain inflation at very low rates, the central bank may not have to implement an explicit inflation-targeting regime. Chapter 25 provides an in-depth discussion of inflation targeting.

**deflation**
persistent or continuing *decline* in a nation's general price level

Although we generally hear about inflation and its perils, perhaps an even more damaging threat to a nation's economic health is **deflation,** a continuing *decline* in general price levels. Inflation is often associated with a robust economy and therefore with high levels of output and employment. In contrast, deflation is generally accompanied by stagnant or falling output, high unemployment, and severe financial distress as indicated by high rates of farm, home, and business foreclosures. The U.S. money supply contracted by more than 30 percent during the Great Depression of 1929–1933. The nation's general price level fell by about 25 percent (approximately 6 percent per year) during this period. Thousands of banks and businesses failed, the stock market crashed, national output fell dramatically, and the unemployment rate rose above 20 percent in the greatest economic catastrophe in U.S. history. Modern nations are definitely more prone to experience inflation than deflation, but Japan has been struggling with deflation for several years. In the early part of the twenty-first century, the Federal Reserve and the central banks of other industrial nations were keenly aware of the need to avoid a cycle of deflation as experienced by Japan. Fear of deflation is due in part to the belief that monetary policy is more effective in fighting inflation than in combating deflation.

**banks**
institutions that accept various types of deposits and use the funds primarily to grant loans and purchase relatively safe debt instruments

## Banks and Other Financial Intermediaries

**Banks** are institutions that accept various types of deposits and use the funds primarily to grant loans. We use the term *banks* generically to encompass not only the commercial banks in which many people maintain checking accounts but also other depository institutions such as savings and loan associations, mutual savings banks, and credit unions. In earlier times, the activities and functions of commercial banks and of other depository institutions were quite distinct. However, the distinction has diminished as a result of deregulatory financial legislation implemented in the 1980s. Today the various depository institutions are more homogeneous in nature. For example, all of these institutions are authorized to issue checking accounts and make loans; therefore, we consider all of them to be "banks."

Our interest in the behavior of banks is generated by the intimate role of banks in the money supply and credit creation processes. As we will see in Chapter 14, when banks extend new loans, money is created in the form of new checking accounts. When bank lending is reduced, bank customers write checks to pay off the loans. The money supply declines as aggregate funds in bank checking accounts decrease. The Federal Reserve System utilizes certain policy tools, discussed in Part 5, to strongly influence the ability and willingness of banks to make loans. The Fed retains full responsibility for the trend or longer-run behavior of the money supply but not necessarily for its week-to-week gyrations. We are particularly interested in studying the nature and behavior of banks because banks are the conduit for the Fed's implementation of U.S. monetary policy.

Banks rank as the most important of our **financial intermediaries**—institutions that serve as "middlemen" for transfer of funds from the millions of individual households, business firms, and other entities with surplus funds to those who borrow in order to purchase consumer goods or invest in real assets such as houses, business plants, and equipment. Financial intermediaries promote economic efficiency by gathering the savings from millions of individual households and other surplus units and making the funds available in appropriate denominations and maturities to deficit-spending units. This process raises the nation's living standards. Financial intermediaries transfer funds from savers to borrowers, improving the well-being of both savers and borrowers. Banks and other financial intermediaries are important sources of financial innovations that have expanded the range of alternatives open to both savers and borrowers. Parts 2 and 3 of this text analyze the nature and economic function of financial intermediaries, the instruments they deal with, the markets in which they conduct business, and the regulatory environment in which they operate.

**financial intermediaries**
institutions that serve as middlemen for the transfer of funds from individuals, businesses, and other entities with surplus funds to those who borrow

## Interest Rates

The **interest rate** is the cost of borrowing (or the return from lending), expressed as a percent per year. It is a key economic variable that plays an important role in consumers' decisions to purchase durable goods such as cars and houses and influences construction of new business plants and commercial buildings. The **real interest rate,** the interest rate adjusted for expected inflation, is particularly significant. (If your government bond yields 5 percent per year and you expect inflation to be 3 percent per year, your expected real interest rate on the bond is 2 percent per year.) The real interest rate influences consumption and investment expenditures and the way in which wealth is redistributed between borrowers and lenders. If real interest rates are unusually high, lenders benefit at the expense of borrowers. If real rates are abnormally low, borrowers benefit at the expense of lenders.

**interest rate**
cost of borrowing (or the return from lending), expressed as a percent per year

**real interest rate**
interest rate after adjusting nominal interest rate for expected inflation

Although we speak of "the" interest rate, a multitude of interest rates (or yields) prevail at any given time. Financial instruments differ in their risk, time to maturity, tax treatment, and other characteristics that influence interest rates. At any given time, we observe different interest rates on home mortgages, passbook savings accounts, certificates of deposit, municipal bonds, U.S. government bonds, corporate bonds, and other financial instruments. Typically, the interest rates on various financial instruments move in tandem, influenced by Federal Reserve policies, the business cycle, the outlook for inflation, and other factors.

The Federal Reserve can alter *short-term* interest rates by influencing the availability of loans through banks. However, factors other than Federal Reserve policy powerfully affect interest rates, and the Fed has very limited ability to directly influence *long-term* interest rates. The media and the public sometimes incorrectly attribute to the Federal Reserve responsibility for interest rate movements that, in reality, are caused by changes in the inflation outlook, changes in business cycle conditions, and other considerations.

**prime loan rate**
key interest rate posted by large U.S. banks, used as a benchmark for setting bank lending rates

Figure 1-3 illustrates the movement of the **prime loan rate** and the yields on 3-month U.S. Treasury securities and short-term corporate debt (90-day commercial paper) in recent years. The prime loan rate is a key interest rate posted by large U.S. banks. It is used as a benchmark for setting a multitude of bank lending rates to small businesses, consumers, and other borrowers.[1] The Federal Reserve can control the short-term interest rates shown in the figure. Indeed, the Fed deliberately engineered the sharp rate decline from 2001 to 2003 to bolster the economy during the 2001 recession (recessions in the figure are designated by shaded areas) and in the period of sluggish economic activity following the recession.

In competitive financial markets, interest rates are established by market forces of supply and demand for loans. Interest rates are among the most important variables you will encounter in this course. Chapters 5 and 6 provide a comprehensive analysis of interest rates.

**Figure 1-3** Prime Loan Rate and Other Short-Term Rates

The prime rate is a benchmark interest rate set by large U.S. banks. It changes frequently, triggering changes in loan rates charged to bank customers whose loan rates are linked to the prime rate. (Shaded areas are periods of recession.)

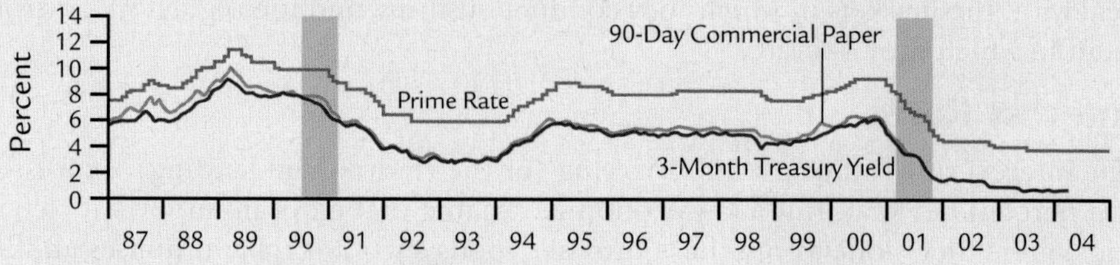

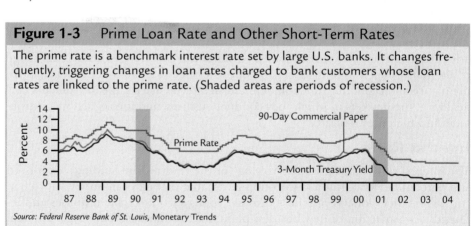

*Source: Federal Reserve Bank of St. Louis,* Monetary Trends

[1] The *prime rate* sometimes is defined as the rate banks charge their biggest and best customers, that is, large and highly stable corporations. Technically, this definition is not precisely correct because corporations often obtain big loans from large banks at rates *below* the prime rate. However, the overwhelming majority of bank borrowers are charged a rate above the prime. For example, home improvement loans may be set at 3 percentage points above the prime rate, high-quality commercial real estate loans at 1 percentage point above the prime, and credit card loans at 10 percentage points above prime. These other bank loan rates typically change in lockstep when the prime rate changes. It is best to think of the prime rate as a *benchmark* interest rate.

## INTERNATIONAL PERSPECTIVES

### Worldwide Synchronization of Economic Phenomena

The more you study macroeconomic and financial market developments, the more impressed you are with the high degree of synchronization of the phenomena in countries around the globe. When you look at various macroeconomic and financial data, you typically see a very strong correlation between what is happening in the United States and what is transpiring in the United Kingdom, European nations, Canada, Australia, and other nations. This is true whether you look at stock prices, short-term interest rates, inflation rates, growth rates of real GDP, or other important variables.

This striking correlation is partly due to the tendency for the waves of positive and negative sentiment that drive important variables such as consumer expenditures, investment spending, stock prices, and so forth, to be in effect worldwide. The correlation also is partly due to the causal links between one nation's economy and that of other nations. If the United States falls into recession, U.S. demand for foreign goods and services declines significantly, and the U.S. weakness spreads to many other countries. Stock prices and interest rates around the world tend to quickly fall as information portending likely U.S. economic softness is released.

International transmission of information is amazingly fast with the advent of the Internet. Waves of psychology that affect U.S. financial markets simultaneously influence European, Asian, Australian, and other markets worldwide. For example, when the fraudulent reporting

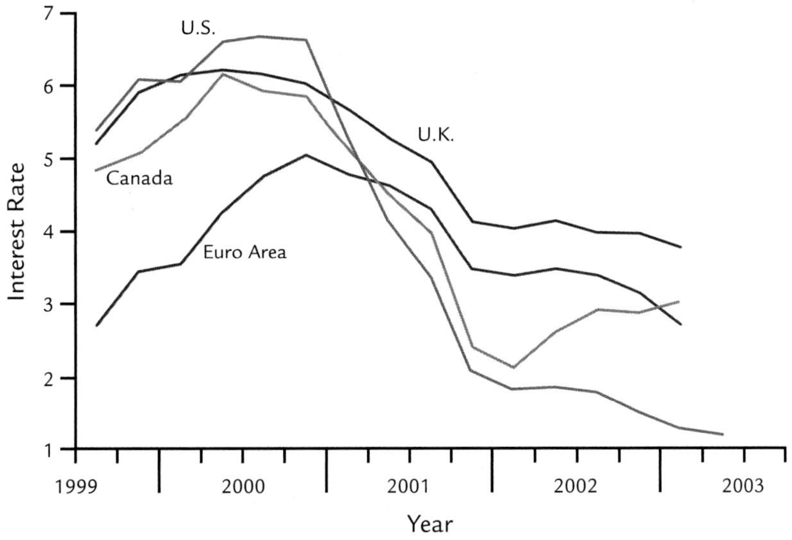

INTERNATIONAL PERSPECTIVES —*continued*

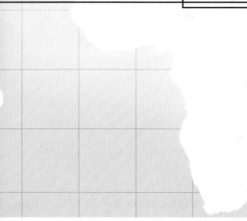

of profits by U.S. corporations and the accounting firms that audit them sprang to the forefront of U.S. news in the spring and summer of 2002, stock markets throughout the world experienced a severe sell-off.

The accompanying figure illustrates one example of this interconnectedness: the worldwide nature of the decline in short-term interest rates during the global economic slowdown from 2001 to 2003. Similar correlations across countries are apparent if you look at growth rates of real GDP, unemployment rates, and indexes of stock prices. The moral: If you read in the news that the Federal Reserve is leaning toward boosting interest rates to ward off incipient inflation in an excessively robust U.S. economy, the chances are high that other central banks around the world will experience the same inclination.

## Federal Budget Deficits

**budget deficit**
annual amount by which federal government expenditures exceed tax revenues

**national debt**
stock of government debt outstanding; cumulative sum of past budget deficits less past surpluses

Since 1969, the U.S. government has exhibited a budget surplus in only 4 years: 1998, 1999, 2000, and 2001. Budget deficits prevailed in all other years. The federal government's **budget deficit** is the annual amount by which federal government expenditures exceed tax revenues. The **national debt** is the cumulative sum of past budget deficits less past surpluses. The budget deficit has important economic ramifications because it must be financed by issuing debt. To gain a perspective on the magnitude of the federal budget deficit (or surplus), it is best to view the deficit relative to the nation's gross domestic product, that is, as a percentage of the value of aggregate output and income in the nation. Figure 1-4 illustrates the budget surplus (positive numbers) or deficit (negative numbers) as a percentage of GDP since 1960.

From 1960 to 1980, the budget deficit averaged less than 1 percent of GDP. Traditionally, the United States exhibited *large* budget deficits only in times of war. However, major income tax cuts in the early 1980s, coupled with a doubling of national defense expenditures between 1980 and 1987 and an unwillingness to reduce entitlement expenditures (social security, Medicare, and so forth), ushered in a new era of enlarged deficits in the 1980s. The nation's budget deficit increased from an average of $36 billion per year during the 1970s to an average of $185 billion per year from 1980 to 1995.

The deficit-to-GDP ratio declined sharply from 1993 to 2000, largely due to a very long and powerful economic expansion that strongly enhanced federal tax receipts. During President Bill Clinton's time in office (January 1993–January 2001), the federal budget position swung from an inherited deficit of $290 billion in 1992 to a *surplus* of $236 billion in 2000. However, very large deficits have reemerged due to federal income tax cuts enacted in 2001, 2002, and 2003, the 2001 U.S. recession, and the budgetary consequences associated with the aftermath of the tragic events

**Figure 1-4** Federal Government Budget Surplus (Deficit) Relative to GDP, 1960–2004

The U.S. federal budget position deteriorated from the early 1960s to the 1980s. The deficit reached 5 percent of GDP in 1992. It then declined continuously for about 8 years and increased sharply after 2000.

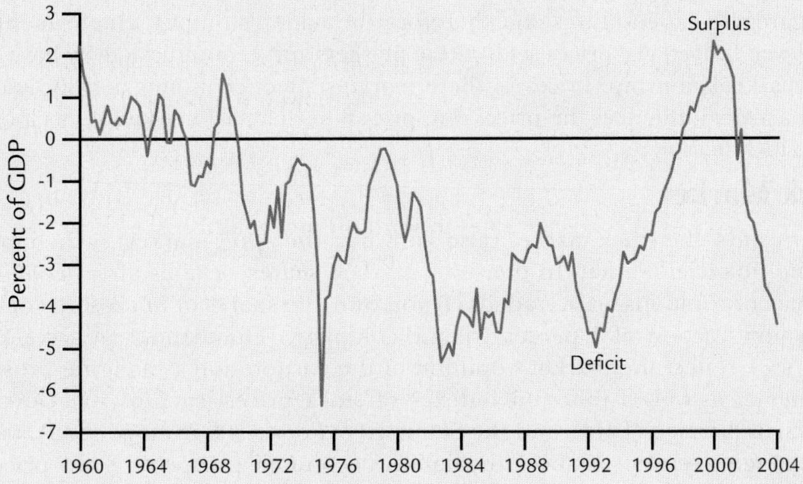


*Source: Data from the FRED database at* http://research.stlouisfed.org/fred2

of September 11, 2001, and the U.S. intervention in Iraq. Barring legislative action to significantly raise taxes or slow the growth of federal expenditures, U.S. budget deficits likely will continue for a long time.

Economists disagree about the economic consequences of government budget deficits. In countries with politically fragile or corrupt governments, large deficits often are associated with severe inflation, largely because politically subservient central banks are forced to assist in financing deficits by printing money. Large deficits lead to rapid money growth, which causes inflation. Most economists believe that in countries with strong and stable democratic governments, such as the United States and European nations, larger deficits are much less likely to result in severe inflation but may result in higher interest rates. Higher interest rates may compromise investment spending on new plants, equipment, and technology, thereby slowing long-run growth in living standards. This is the primary manner in which large and persistent budget deficits are believed to impose costs on future generations. Such deficits may cause future living standards to be lower than they otherwise would be.[2]

[2] The impact of deficits on future living standards is a very complicated issue. Clearly, this impact depends on the *source* of the deficit. For example, deficits resulting from increased government expenditures on education and scientific research or from enactment of tax incentives for investment expenditures likely will have more favorable effects on future living standards than deficits resulting from increased federal subsidies to farmers for limiting production. Deficits due to a fundamental, continuing mismatch between revenues and expenditures may be more detrimental than deficits due to a temporary decline in economic activity during a recession. Thus, *cyclical* deficits are thought to be less damaging than *structural* deficits. Indeed, larger (cyclical) federal budget deficits incurred during recessions tend to reduce the severity of economic downturns and contribute favorably to long-term growth of living standards by moderating the decline in private investment expenditures during recessions. Thus, economists view cyclical deficits more favorably than structural deficits.

# KEY FINANCIAL MARKETS

The stock market, the bond market, and the foreign exchange market are three crucial financial markets for study in any money and banking course. These markets are important because the prices set in these financial markets importantly affect aggregate expenditures and therefore the nation's output, employment, and price level. In fact, the prices set in these markets and economic activity have a two-way causal relationship. Prices in these markets affect economic activity, and economic activity influences the prices that prevail in financial markets. Let's look first at the stock market.

## Stock Market

**shares**
claims of ownership in individual corporations held by stockholders

In many ways, the stock market (also known as the *equity* market) is the most fascinating financial market. In the stock market, **shares**—claims of *ownership* in individual corporations—are traded. (If you own 100 shares of Microsoft stock, you own a tiny fraction of 1 percent of the company.) Fluctuations in a company's stock price reflect the market's opinion of the corporation's changing prospects. Movements in widely followed indexes of stock prices, such as the Dow-Jones Industrials Average (DJIA) and the Standard & Poor's 500 Average (S&P 500), reflect changing sentiment about the nation's economic prospects. Stock prices are an important barometer indicating collective perceptions about future economic conditions.[3]

Stock prices can be volatile, which helps to explain the public's fascination with the stock market. As millions of Americans learned firsthand during the past decade, you can lose (or earn) a lot of wealth in a hurry in the stock market! Figure 1-5 shows the movements in the S&P 500 Stock Average in the past half century. A *logarithmic scale* is used to plot stock prices because stock prices increased more than 50-fold over this time. Given the logarithmic scale, changes in the *slope* of trends in stock prices in the graph are interpreted as changes in the *growth rate* of stock prices. For example, the graph indicates that stock prices increased more rapidly from 1995 to 1999 than in any other 5-year period since 1950.

As indicated in the figure, U.S. stock prices appreciated strongly from 1950 to 1965, fluctuated without trend from 1966 to 1982, and increased dramatically from 1982 to 1999 before falling sharply in 2000 to 2002. Over the full half-century period illustrated in the figure, the S&P index increased at an average rate of approximately 7.5 percent per year.

Stock prices have important macroeconomic ramifications, influencing both consumption and investment expenditures. Stocks constitute an important portion of people's wealth. Nearly 50 percent of collective U.S. stock market wealth simply evaporated when the stock market plummeted during the severe bear market from 2000 to 2002. Conversely, the wealth of some 50 million American households owning stocks in direct holdings or through retirement plans and pension funds increased dramatically during the long bull market that began in 1982. These

[3] However, the stock market is not a particularly good *predictor* of future economic conditions. Stock prices can change dramatically without foretelling any significant change in economic activity. The DJIA fell 522 points on October 19, 1987 (losing about 22 percent of its value in a single day), but its fall was not followed by a decline in economic activity. Stock prices fell sharply from January to October 2002, but economic activity continued to expand. Economist Paul Samuelson, poking fun at the poor predictive performance of stock prices, once quipped that the stock market had "correctly signaled nine of the last five recessions."

**Figure 1-5** U.S. Stock Prices, 1950–2004 (Standard & Poor's 500 Index)

Stock prices ter … )-1965 and 1982–1999. Bo … par stock mar- ket performanc …

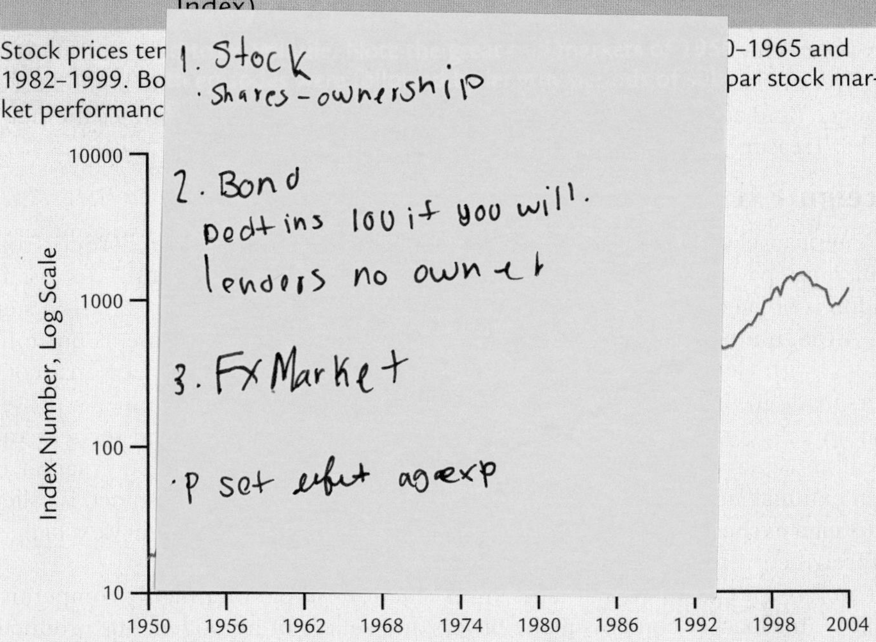


*Source: Data from Robert Shiller's Web site at* http://aida.econ.yale.edu/~shiller/data

changes in wealth alter consumer expenditures, thereby influencing macroeconomic variables such as GDP and the nation's unemployment rate. The support provided to consumption spending by the dramatic increase in stock values from 1995 to 2000 is one reason the United States was able to avoid a recession during the record-length, decade-long economic expansion from 1991 to 2001.

Stock prices may also influence investment spending on plants and equipment. The level of stock prices determines the amount and cost of funds firms can obtain by issuing new shares of stock. When stock prices are relatively high, many corporations issue new shares. They then use the proceeds to finance plant expansions, equipment purchases, and new research and development. The booming stock market of the 1990s helps explain the surge in corporate investment expenditures on information technology and other capital goods. This robust investment spending helps account for the resurgence of U.S. productivity growth—growth in output per hour of work—that commenced in the mid-1990s. The stock market and its ramifications are analyzed in depth in Chapter 7.

## Bond Market

A **bond** is a debt instrument—an IOU—issued by a corporation, government, or government agency. It is a contractual agreement that the issuer will make a stream of interest payments to the lender (bond buyer) on specified future dates and return the principal at maturity. Unlike stocks, which are claims of ownership or equity, bonds are instruments through which lenders (or creditors) make funds available to borrowers (or debtors). Bondholders are *lenders,* whereas stockholders are *owners.*

**bond**
long-term debt instrument issued by a corporation, government, or government agency; a contractual agreement to make certain payments at specified future dates

**foreign exchange market**
market in which national currencies such as dollars, yen, euros, and pesos are traded for one another

**foreign exchange rate**
price at which one country's currency exchanges for foreign currency

**fixed exchange rates**
international financial arrangement in which exchange rates are pegged or held constant by direct government intervention in the foreign exchange market

In the bond market, interest rates (or yields) are determined by the market forces of supply and demand. The bond market is a very active market. It is of special interest for study in this course because the Federal Reserve conducts its monetary policy chiefly by purchasing and selling U.S. government bonds (and shorter-term Treasury securities) and because interest rates (or yields) in the bond market influence (and are influenced by) economic activity. Figure 1-6 illustrates the yields on U.S. Treasury and corporate bonds since 1960.

## Foreign Exchange Market

An American electronics retailer that imports Sony video cassette recorders from Japan must pay for the equipment in Japanese currency—in yen. A tourist in London is obliged to pay the hotel bill and taxi driver in British currency—in sterling. A U.S. mutual fund specializing in German stocks must purchase its portfolio of stocks with German currency—in euros. A Mexican importer of personal computers made in the United States or a Japanese importer of U.S. lumber must settle up in U.S. currency—in dollars. Thus, foreign trade in goods and services and in real and financial assets leads to trade in national currencies. The market in which national currencies such as dollars, yen, euros, and pesos are traded is called the **foreign exchange market.** The price at which one country's currency exchanges for foreign currency is the **foreign exchange rate.**

The foreign exchange market is an excellent example of a highly competitive market. This market contains many buyers and sellers of homogeneous products, that is, national currencies. For many years, exchange rates were fixed. They were pegged or held constant by direct government intervention in the foreign exchange market. World trade was based on a system of **fixed exchange rates.** For

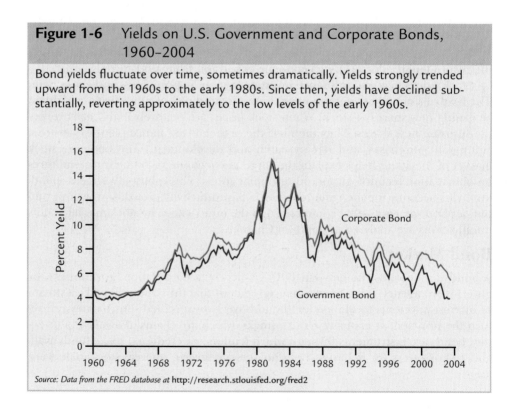

**Figure 1-6** Yields on U.S. Government and Corporate Bonds, 1960–2004

Bond yields fluctuate over time, sometimes dramatically. Yields strongly trended upward from the 1960s to the early 1980s. Since then, yields have declined substantially, reverting approximately to the low levels of the early 1960s.

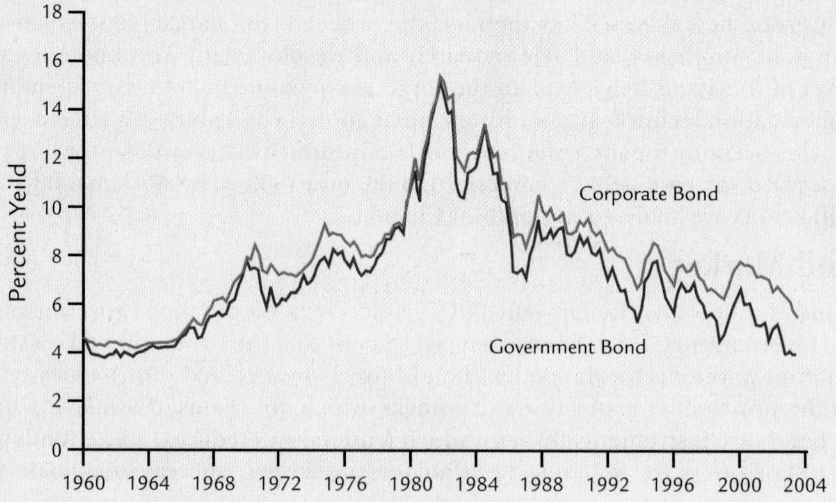


*Source: Data from the FRED database at* http://research.stlouisfed.org/fred2

**Figure 1-7 Exchange Rate of the U.S. Dollar, 1975–2004 (Index Number, 1973 = 100)**

Exchange rates fluctuate continuously. The U.S. dollar appreciated strongly during 1981–1985 and 1995–2002. It depreciated during 1985–1995 and in 2003. These changes have important consequences for Americans.

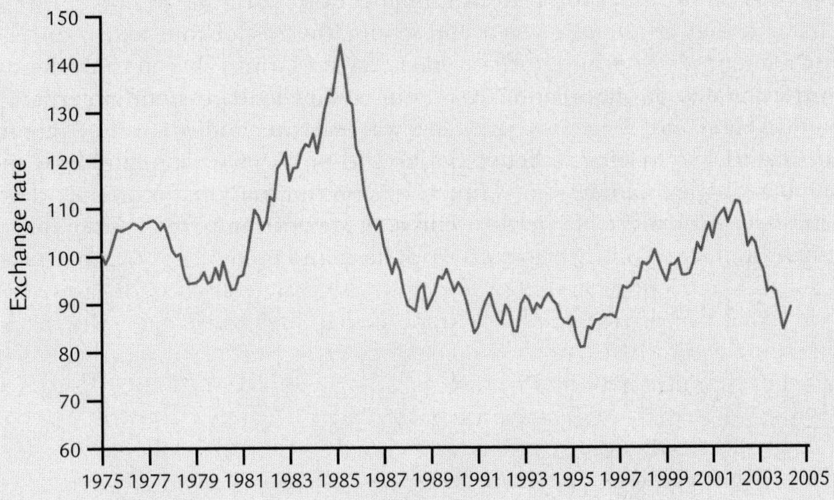


*Source: Data from the FRED database at* http://research.stlouisfed/org/fred2

more than 30 years, however, exchange rates of major nations have been allowed to change continuously each day in response to the market forces of supply and demand, albeit with occasional government intervention to influence the exchange rate. This system is known as **floating exchange rates.**

**floating exchange rates**
international financial arrangement in which exchange rates are allowed to change continuously in response to the market forces of supply and demand, with occasional government intervention

Figure 1-7 shows an index of the average exchange rate of the U.S. dollar against foreign currencies of major industrial nations. The exchange rate, expressed as units of foreign currency per dollar, has fluctuated substantially in recent years. When the dollar experiences **appreciation**—rises in value (as from 1995 to 2001)—the cost of goods produced in the United States increases to foreign buyers. Conversely, foreign products become cheaper in the United States because the dollar buys more units of foreign currencies. U.S. manufacturing and agricultural firms find it more difficult to compete in world markets, but U.S. consumers benefit from cheaper foreign goods and services. The U.S. **trade deficit**—the excess of the dollar value of U.S. imports over the dollar value of U.S. exports—rises. In 2004, the U.S. trade deficit was running at a rate of approximately $500 billion per year.

**appreciation**
an increase in value of one nation's currency relative to another currency

**trade deficit**
excess of the dollar value of U.S. imports over the dollar value of U.S. exports

The tables are turned when the dollar experiences **depreciation**—declines in value against foreign currencies. U.S. exports increase and U.S. imports decline as U.S. goods become more affordable in foreign markets and foreign products become more expensive in the United States. The U.S. trade deficit decreases, that is, the deficit moves in the direction of a surplus.

**depreciation**
a decrease in value of one nation's currency relative to another currency

Fluctuations in the exchange rate have important consequences for you personally and for the U.S. economy. In Chapter 8, we will analyze the causes and consequences of exchange rate changes. International economic and financial considerations are of pervasive significance throughout this course; therefore, international economic developments and their implications are woven into almost every chapter of this book.

## SUMMARY

Money, banking, and financial markets are important and exciting subjects characterized by rapid change. In this text, we focus on a multitude of principles and issues that are intimately related to ongoing news developments and are likely to influence your future job prospects and material well-being. Developments such as trade and banking legislation, financial innovations, the business cycle, changes in stock prices, and Federal Reserve monetary policy actions influence your part-time job prospects while you are in school, the cost of your loans, and the returns earned on your savings. As you study these phenomena, your ability to digest and interpret economic news will improve, and you will be in a much better position to understand contemporary monetary, financial, and international economic developments. This course stands to be of considerable value to you. Work hard and enjoy!

## KEY TERMS

productivity
money (money supply)
central bank
Federal Reserve System (Fed)
monetary policy
inflation
inflation targeting
deflation
banks
financial intermediaries
interest rate
real interest rate
prime loan rate
budget deficit
national debt
shares
bond
foreign exchange market
foreign exchange rate
fixed exchange rates
floating exchange rates
appreciation
trade deficit
depreciation

## NOTE TO STUDENTS AND INSTRUCTORS

Each remaining chapter of this book is followed by a list of Study Questions and a discussion of recommended Additional Reading materials that provide other perspectives on the topics discussed in the chapter. Here, at the end of the first chapter, we simply list some sources of important data and other information that you may wish to tap throughout the course. Most of these sources are available free of charge on the Internet. Your library likely will have many of these items on hard copy. The periodicals published by the Board of Governors and the 12 district Federal Reserve Banks are available on the Internet, and hard copies often are available on request, free of charge.

- The Federal Reserve System has an excellent Web site with lots of useful information, available at http://www.federalreserve.gov. The Board of Governors of the Federal Reserve System publishes a quarterly *Federal Reserve Bulletin* that includes information on recent monetary policy and financial developments. Your library will have hard copies, and the bulletin is available on the Federal Reserve Web site. The *Annual Report* of the Board of Governors of the Federal Reserve System contains a convenient summary of the year's monetary policy deliberations and actions, along with lots of data. It is available on the Federal Reserve System Web site. The *Annual Report* of the Federal Reserve Bank of New York contains an excellent discussion of each year's monetary and financial developments. It is available on the New York Federal Reserve Bank's Web site at http://www.ny.frb.org/. Each of the 12 district Federal Reserve Banks publishes a bimonthly or quarterly *Review* that contains interesting and timely articles.

- Other informative publications are the *Economic Report of the President* (available at http://w3.access.gpo.gov/eop/), which is published annually in February by the U.S. Government Printing Office, and the *Annual Reports* issued by the Federal Deposit Insurance Corporation and the International Monetary Fund. They are available at http://www.fdic.gov/ and http://www.imf.org/, respectively. The U.S. Treasury publication *Treasury Bulletin* contains a wealth of statistical information on various aspects of public debt, fiscal operations, and international finance. It is available at http://www.ustreas.gov/.
- Major sources of international financial data are *International Financial Statistics,* which is published monthly by the International Monetary Fund, and *International Economic Trends,* which is published quarterly by the Federal Reserve Bank of St. Louis, with an annual edition each July. Other good sources of data relevant to this course are *Monetary Trends, National Economic Trends,* and *U.S. Financial Data,* all published by the St. Louis Fed. These publications are available on the St. Louis Fed Web site at http://research.stlouisfed.org/ (click on "Publications" and scroll down to desired publication).
- Almost any monetary, financial, and other U.S. economic data you might need are available at the Federal Reserve Bank of St. Louis, Federal Reserve Economic Data (FRED) Web site at http://research.stlouisfed.org/fred2/. You might want to bookmark this important site. A good source of global financial data is http:// www.globalfindata.com/. Robert Shiller's Web site at http://aida.econ.yale.edu/~shiller/ data is a convenient location for stock market data.
- For timely and well-written articles on recent developments, see *Current Issues in Economics and Finance,* initiated in 1995 by the Federal Reserve Bank of New York and published quarterly and available at the New York Fed bank's Web site.
- In general, you can find articles on financial and monetary developments almost daily in *The Wall Street Journal.* In particular, this publication features extensive daily stock, bond, Treasury bill, and foreign exchange rate quotations. Each Friday, the *Wall Street Journal* publishes an article that outlines recent movements of monetary variables and Federal Reserve actions.
- An outstanding source for in-depth and relatively sophisticated analyses of numerous topics is *The New Palgrave Dictionary of Money and Finance,* edited by Peter Newman, Murray Milgate, and John Eatwell. It was published in 1992 by Macmillan Reference Limited, London, and Grove Dictionaries Inc., New York.
- To glimpse the kind of research that occupies the frontiers of monetary economics and finance, pick up a recent issue of *The Journal of Money, Credit, and Banking, The Journal of Monetary Economics,* the *Journal of Finance,* or *The Journal of International Money and Finance* at your library.

Chapter 2

# MONEY: ITS NATURE, FUNCTIONS, AND EVOLUTION

A famous individual once remarked that the lack of money is the root of all evil. Although this clearly is an overstatement (and an incorrect use of the word "money"), the statement has been literally true for several historical episodes. In the Great Depression of the 1930s, a sharp contraction of the quantity of money in numerous countries contributed importantly to the depth of the economic disaster. However, *too much* money has been the root of all evil in other historical episodes, such as the runaway inflation of the 1990s in Russia.

In one sense, money (or the money supply) is unimportant. The level of a nation's living standard is determined by the capacity of the nation's people to produce goods and services. If development and implementation of new technologies were to quickly double the amount of goods and services that we collectively produce, our collective real income and standard of living would double. However, if we were to suddenly double the amount of money (currency in circulation and checking accounts) in the nation, we would not be better off. Our ability to produce goods and services would not be enhanced, and our living standards would not rise. Indeed, the inflation unleashed by excessive expansion of the money supply would be highly detrimental to the nation's well-being.

In another sense, money is extremely important. Money facilitates the process of exchange, allowing the economy to operate more efficiently and raising living standards higher than they otherwise would be. A society with an appropriate quantity of money can avoid the polar extremes of deflation and depression on the one hand and severe inflation on the other. Money helps maintain an environment that allows economic activity to flourish. Irresponsibly or incompetently managed money can cause enormous damage to a society. Prudently managed money can be a positive force contributing to the stability of economic variables—prices, income, and employment—that affect each of us. In this chapter, we examine the nature, functions, and evolution of money. We also look at the various measures of money used today by our central bank, the Federal Reserve System.

## NATURE AND FUNCTIONS OF MONEY

Money is a fascinating subject that has occupied the minds of profound thinkers and of numerous crackpots. Analysis of the management and economic influence of the nation's money constitutes an important portion of this book and this course. Who determines the amount of money, and how? How do changes in the quantity of money affect economic activity? Why does excessive growth of money cause inflation? Could the Federal Reserve have prevented the Great Depression of the 1930s? Should the agencies responsible for the nation's money supply be allowed to implement discretionary policies as they see fit, or should they be governed by rules that prohibit discretionary actions? These questions will be covered later. First, some preliminaries are in order. To begin, we address the questions, "What is money?" and "What are the functions of money?"

## Meaning of Money

People often define **money** as anything that is generally acceptable as payment for goods and services or for settlement of debt. This definition is behavioral, not legal. This definition emphasizes the element of confidence involved in the concept of money. Put simply, money is what we believe others will accept as payment. Our willingness to accept a given item as payment is contingent on the belief that the item will retain its value or purchasing power and will continue to be acceptable. This confidence relies, in turn, on reasonably strict limits on the supplies of the item being used as money. Historically, many different things—whale teeth in Fiji, leather in France, stones on the island of Yap, tobacco and whiskey in the American colonies, and numerous types of metallic coins—have served as money because people had confidence in the value of these items and were willing to accept them as payment.

**money**
anything that is generally acceptable as payment for goods and services or for settlement of debt; most commonly defined to include currency, coins, and checking accounts in depository institutions

Traditionally, economists have defined money to include all currency (coins and paper bills) held by the public, together with demand deposits and other checking deposits in commercial banks and thrift institutions (savings and loan associations, mutual savings banks, and credit unions). Because practically all payments are made by currency exchange or by transfer of deposit balances via check or electronic (wire) means, the economists' definition of money fits our conceptual notion of money as items that are "generally acceptable" for payment.

What about credit cards? Credit cards essentially postpone payment for a few days or months. They are a credit arrangement and as such do not constitute money. Actual payment is made later, when the customer transfers checking account funds to the credit card company by issuing a check. Credit cards reduce an individual's need to hold money balances at any given time by synchronizing the receipt of income with the expenditure of funds. Rather than influencing the *supply* of money, credit cards alter the need or willingness to hold money—what economists call the *demand* for money.

The U.S. government has decreed coins and paper currency to be **legal tender**—coins and paper currency cannot lawfully be refused as payment for goods and services or for discharge of debts. No merchant or creditor can demand payment in another form if the payer wishes to make payment in legal tender. Checking accounts in commercial banks and other depository institutions are *not* classified as legal tender. However, banks are required to redeem checking account deposits in legal tender (currency) upon the depositor's request. Although the status of legal tender guarantees an item will be accepted as money, historically many items without the status of legal tender have served as money. In other words, having the status of legal tender is *sufficient* but not *necessary* for an item to be considered money. Today, the transfer of checking account balances among individuals, firms, and other entities is the most important means of making transactions. Of the total dollar value of all transactions made in the United States each year, an estimated 1 percent is made with currency and an overwhelming 99 percent is made by transfer of checking account balances.

**legal tender**
money that cannot lawfully be refused as payment for goods and services or for discharge of debts; consists of currency and coins

## Distinctions Among Money, Wealth, and Income

Misstatements about money are pervasive. You can ask a friend if she has any money. In reality, you want to know if your friend is carrying *currency,* a specific type or component of money. It is commonplace in everyday conversation to confuse money with *wealth* or *income*.[1] Even professional economists are guilty of stating incorrectly that Bill Gates has a lot of "money" (instead of wealth) or that baseball star Alex Rodriguez earns a lot of "money" (instead of income). Money, wealth, and income all are expressed in terms of dollars, but each has a distinctly different meaning.

Money consists of certain items held by people because the items have unique properties. Money is a *stock* of assets (measured at a given point in time) exhibiting certain characteristics. The items that should be included in this stock are debatable, as we will note later in this chapter. The most traditional definition of money limits the stock of assets to currency in circulation plus the public's bank deposits that may be transferred by check or electronic means.

**wealth**
the value of assets, including money stock and other financial and real assets, minus the value of liabilities

**Wealth** also is a stock concept, measured at a given point in time. Wealth encompasses the money stock as well as the value of many other financial and real assets. The *narrow* money stock—currency and checking deposits—constitutes less than 2 percent of the nation's total wealth. Even the *broader* measures of money, discussed later in this chapter, make up less than 10 percent of all wealth. The bulk of our wealth consists of our homes, autos, farms, bonds, shares of stock, and life insurance.

**income**
flow of earnings, measures as dollars per unit of time

In contrast, **income** is a *flow* of dollars per unit of time, for example, $2,000 per month or $24,000 per year. Income consists of wages and salaries, dividends, interest, and other forms of payment. Because income is paid in dollars, an individual's money balances may roughly equal the income of the paycheck period when the paycheck is first deposited in the bank. At other times, an individual holds only a small portion of monthly income in the form of paper currency, coins, and checking accounts.

The amount of money a person customarily maintains is a matter of discretion and varies within the constraints of the individual's assets or wealth. The portion of wealth held in the form of money depends on the rate of return expected from nonmoney assets (stocks, bonds, etc.), as well as on other factors. An individual may hold a very small amount of money at any given time, even if he or she earns $1 million per year. Technically, it is possible (though unlikely) for a blue-collar worker to have more money than an NBA basketball star.

An individual can increase or decrease money holdings (within the constraints of wealth) at will, but the nation's supply of money is not controlled by the collective actions of the public but by the Federal Reserve System, the central bank in the United States. This is an important and intriguing aspect of money.

## Functions of Money

The role of money seems so obvious that we tend to take it for granted. In reality, the economic contributions of money include beneficial aspects that you most likely have never considered. Money serves three important functions: it acts as a *medium of exchange* or *means of payment,* as a *standard of value* or *unit of account,* and as a *store of value*. To understand the role and functions of money, consider the operation of an economic system in the absence of money, that is, in a **barter economy**—an economy in which goods and services are traded directly for one another.[2]

**barter economy**
economy in which goods and services are traded directly for one another

[1] The opening sentence of this chapter contains a statement by George Bernard Shaw. He appears to be confusing money with something else. Can you identify what he is confusing money with?

[2] Barter and monetary economies have existed in the same time period and within the same country. Even in ancient societies in which barter was the predominant basis for exchange of goods, some commodity—whether corn, stones, or some metallic substance—was commonly singled out for use as money.

**Medium of Exchange or Means of Payment.** Consider the process of exchange in a barter situation. An individual wheat farmer attempting to purchase a given commodity (e.g., a personal computer [PC]) requires the following information:

1. Who is offering PCs and on what terms?
2. Which of the individuals offering PCs desires to purchase wheat?

The major obstacle to exchange in this barter situation is the need for the individual who produces wheat and wants to purchase a PC to locate a PC producer who wants wheat. This barter-economy requirement of a *double coincidence of wants* in order for exchange to occur implies a time-consuming, socially inefficient search process. In a primitive society such as a self-sufficient farming community in which each family produces its own food, clothing, and shelter, no medium of exchange is needed. Money likely does not exist because it is not needed. However, as society evolves and people become more specialized and more dependent on goods and services produced by others, the amount of time devoted to exchange in a barter economy becomes a huge drag on the society, imposing large costs. In a barter economy, the time devoted to the *exchange* of goods and services may exceed the time allocated to the *production* of goods and services.

The introduction of money as a medium of exchange effectively eliminates the requirement of a "double coincidence of wants." The farmer seeking to buy the PC does not need to locate a PC producer who wants wheat. The farmer sells wheat for dollars, which then can be used to purchase a PC. Money used as a medium of exchange allows purchases and sales of goods and services to be made independently of one another. The purchase of one good no longer requires a simultaneous sale of another, as in a barter economy. As a medium of exchange, money greatly increases the efficiency of the economic system and the scope of specialization and division of labor, thus raising living standards. Indeed, money serving this function is a necessary precondition in the transformation of a primitive society of relatively self-sufficient families into a society of interdependent, highly specialized units.

Historically, money was introduced early in the evolution of primitive societies. An increase in the degree of specialization and division of labor usually brings about the introduction of money serving as a medium of exchange. Use of money, in turn, reduces the time and resources devoted to exchange, further expanding the scope for specialization and division of labor. Clearly, use of money as a medium of exchange is a necessary condition for supporting today's population sizes and living standards. Table 2-1 lists some items that have been used as media of exchange by various societies over the centuries.

**Table 2-1 Some Items That Have Served as Money**

| | | |
|---|---|---|
| Tobacco | Corn | Copper |
| Whale teeth | Salt | Brass |
| Tortoise shells | Leather | Bronze |
| Woodpecker heads | Knives | Nickel |
| Cigarettes | Whiskey | Silver |
| Cattle | Stones | Gold |
| Horses | Iron | |

**Standard of Value or Unit of Account.** Money is used as a measuring rod or yardstick in assessing the relative value of various goods and services. Just as we use
nd miles per hour to measure weight, distance, and speed, we use
euros to measure the value of a pizza, house, gallon of gasoline, or
h have in mind the price, expressed in dollars, of dozens of items
rchase (or contemplate purchasing). By expressing the value of
many goods and services in terms of one common denominator—
reatly simplify economic life.
his point, consider a barter economy. Without money serving as a
each item brought to market bears a certain value in relation to
items. Even with a relatively limited number of commodities, the
nge rates (prices) among different items becomes cumbersome.
ears ago an aboriginal Australia produced four goods: A (apples),
C (coconuts), and D (didgeridoos). Without money serving as a
he value of each of these four goods is expressed relative to *each*
with four goods, Australian aborigines have six exchange rates
nber: A/B, A/C, A/D, B/C, B/D, and C/D. Such an extremely
ty can get by nicely without the use of money, so money likely did
rly centuries of aboriginal Australia. However, as the number of
s in a society increases, the number of prices increases rapidly.
This is illustrated in the following expression:

Barter Economy Calculation

$$R_B = \frac{N(N-1)}{2} \qquad (2\text{-}1)$$

where $R_B$ is the number of different prices or exchange rates in a barter economy, and N is the number of different goods and services in the economy.[4] There are $N(N-1)/2$ different prices in a barter economy. Table 2-2 shows how the number of prices or exchange rates in a barter economy and in a money economy increases as the number of goods and services increases. The table indicates the cumbersome nature and inefficiency of such an exchange system for a society with a multitude of goods and services.

The first two columns illustrate the relationship between the number of items (N) and the number of different price ratios in a barter economy ($R_B$), as calculated using Equation 2-1. The third column indicates the number of prices for the same number of items in a money economy. In a primitive society with only a few commodities, the barter system is manageable. With 10 commodities, we need to consider 45 exchange ratios, or prices. With 1,000 various goods and services—which is still an unsophisticated economy by modern standards—the number of exchange ratios is nearly half a million! Imagine entering a general store that offers for sale each of the 1,000 different items available in this (relatively primitive) nation. Because no unit of account such as the dollar is serving as a measuring stick,

---

[3] One fundamental difference between the nature of the "yardsticks" used to measure weight, distance, and speed and those used to measure the value of goods and services is that the units of account for the first group are absolute constants; they do not change over time. One liter is exactly the same volume today as it was 100 years ago. The same cannot be said for the U.S. dollar, the Japanese yen, the Mexican peso, or other national currencies. The value of a unit of currency in terms of goods and services fluctuates over time as the price level changes. Nevertheless, at any point in time, a nation's currency serves as a measuring rod in ascertaining the value of thousands of individual goods and services.

[4] In this case, there are N different items. Each item has a price expressed in terms of each other $(N-1)$ item. Hence, the numerator of our expression is $(N)(N-1)$. Because half of the prices are redundant (e.g., A/B is the reciprocal of B/A), it is clear that there are $N(N-1)/2$ different prices in a barter economy.

**Table 2-2** Number of Prices in Barter and Money Economies

| | Number of Prices | |
|---|---|---|
| Number of Commodities (N) | Barter Economy ($R_B$) | Money Economy ($R_M$) |
| 3 | 3 | 3 |
| 10 | 45 | 10 |
| 1,000 | 499,500 | 1,000 |
| 1,000,000 | 499,999,500,000 | 1,000,000 |

the price tag for each item contains 999 different prices. For example, a new wristwatch might be priced at 20 cans of oil, 31 loaves of bread, 14 tubes of toothpaste, and so forth. In most cases, the price tag would be larger than the item to be purchased!

In a barter economy, you need to be aware not only of the exchange ratio between the item offered and the item needed but also of a host of other exchange ratios.[5] When money as a unit of account is introduced into an economy of 1,000 commodities, only 1,000 prices exist—one for each of the 1,000 commodities quoted in terms of the common denominator or unit of account, for example, dollars. Information and transactions costs of exchange are reduced. As a result, the volume of production, exchange, and per capita income rise. Money is a highly productive social innovation!

**YOUR TURN**

**a.** Suppose a primitive society produces only six goods. If the society is a barter economy, how many different prices or exchange ratios would there be? If the society were a money economy, how many prices would there be? Name your six goods and list each exchange rate to double check the results provided via Equation 2-1.

**b.** Now suppose the same society produces 10,000 goods. How many prices would there be if the economy were based on barter? On money?

**Store of Value.** A function of money that is closely allied with the medium-of-exchange function is that of a temporary abode of purchasing power, otherwise known as the *store-of-value function*. In a barter economy, the purchase of any item implies a simultaneous sale of another item. Likewise, the sale of any good or service necessitates a corresponding purchase of another good or service. Use of money allows purchases and sales independent of one another. Today, most of us sell our labor services for income. Because this income is received at discrete, rather

[5] Suppose that in a barter economy an individual brings good A (axes) to the market and seeks to exchange them for good B (bread). The individual should check not only the exchange ratio between axes and bread but also of a multitude of combinations of exchange ratios involving other goods. For example, he might receive more bread by trading axes for lumber and then lumber for bread than by bartering axes directly for bread. However, the scenario can easily become much more complicated. To maximize material well-being in a barter economy, an individual should devote much time and effort to the details of exchange. In this case, activities that are profitable for an individual are a huge waste of resources for a society.

## Exhibit 2-1 The Euro—A Single Currency for European Nations

Imagine taking a vacation drive across an America in which each state uses a different currency. Assume the Pennsylvania currency is the guilder, the Minnesota currency the kroner, and so forth. In each state in which you have a meal, buy gas, or sleep in a motel, you have to exchange the currency of your home state (or another state) for the relevant state's currency. Consider the inconveniences and costs of such an arrangement. Anyone wishing to make any kind of a transaction involving a party in another state would incur similar costs.

Western Europe consists of a set of nations whose collective geographic area is much smaller than the United States. It is a region whose collective population and level of GDP are similar to those of the United States. For centuries, travel and the conduct of commerce within Europe were complicated by the separate forms of money in each country. The Italians used the lira, the Germans used marks, the French used francs, and so forth. In the latter part of the twentieth century, members of the 15-country European Union (Austria, Belgium, Germany, Greece, Finland, France, Ireland, Italy, Luxembourg, the Netherlands, Portugal, Spain, Sweden, Denmark, and the United Kingdom) spoke seriously about establishing a single currency for the entire region. The idea was to create an integrated and unified market like that in the United States.

Euro denominations.

Today, all of these countries except Denmark, Sweden, and the United Kingdom have abandoned their traditional currencies in favor of a common currency—the euro. The 12-country transition to the euro came in stages. The 1991 Treaty on European Union, held in the Dutch city of Maastricht, set forth a timetable for transition to the common currency. Each nation was required to meet specified rigorous conditions prior to adopting the euro. For example, each country was required to lower its budget deficit to less than 3 percent of GDP and its inflation rate to a low rate similar to that prevailing in Germany. At the beginning of 1999, exchange rates of countries entering the monetary union were fixed against the euro, governments began issuing their debt in euros, and the euro became the new unit of account for electronic and checking transactions. In early 2002, euros began circulating as media of exchange in each country, along with the nation's traditional currency. By the summer of 2002, the traditional currencies were withdrawn from circulation in each country, and the transition was complete.

When we look back in 20 years, will the move to the single currency be considered a success? Optimists believe that a single currency will (1) eliminate the transactions costs associated with exchanging different currencies, (2) promote integration of the various European economies, and (3) enhance efficiency by inducing countries to institute reforms removing anticompetitive rigidities in labor markets and other areas. These reforms will move the nations further toward free-market capitalism. European political clout in world affairs may increase, and the euro may come to rival the dollar as the premier currency in world markets.

**Exhibit 2-1** The Euro—A Single Currency for European Nations—*cont'd*

Skeptics argue that implementation of the common currency has thrown together countries of diverse financial traditions and growth prospects. Some of the economically weaker countries that adopted the euro may have placed themselves at a disadvantage by sacrificing two important tools of policy. First, the nations have given up independent use of monetary policy because the European Central Bank now conducts monetary policy for the region as a whole. Second, because all 12 nations have the same currency, individual nations have given up the ability to assist their export industries and stimulate economic activity through depreciation of their national currency on the foreign exchange market. Largely for these reasons, Denmark, Sweden, and the United Kingdom have not adopted the euro. Given the disadvantages, skeptics fear that some European nations will prosper while others stagnate.

lengthy intervals that do not coincide with our more continuous flow of expenditures, we need to store purchasing power over time. One way to store purchasing power through time is to hold money.

Money is not unique as a store of value. In an economy with developed financial institutions, many financial assets serve as means of storing wealth through time. Examples include various types of savings and time deposits, government and corporate bonds, short-term securities, common stocks, and other financial instruments. The U.S. government now issues an *indexed bond* that guarantees a return that will beat inflation, thereby serving as a reliable store of value. Various "real" assets, such as land and other real estate, antiques, jewelry, paintings, and gold and silver, serve as vehicles for storing wealth over time. Advantages of real assets over money as means of storing wealth include the higher interest rate than can be obtained from money and the prospect of price appreciation over time.[6]

**Table 2-3** Real Rates of Return on Various Assets

| Period | Money* | Gold | Treasury Bills | U.S. Government Bonds | AAA Corporate Bonds | Common Stocks |
|---|---|---|---|---|---|---|
| 1926–1976 | −2.4% | 1.5% | 0.0% | 0.8% | 1.5% | 6.6% |
| 1976–2003 | −4.5 | −0.7 | 2.1 | 3.8 | 4.6 | 7.8 |
| **1926–2003** | **−3.0** | **0.9** | **0.7** | **1.7** | **2.5** | **7.0** |

*Assumes interest rate paid on money was zero throughout. Because inflation averaged 3.0 percent per year during 1926–2003, the inflation-adjusted rate of return on money was -3.0 percent per year.

*Sources: Data from Global Financial Data at* http://www.globalfindata.com *and Federal Reserve Bank of St. Louis, FRED database at* http://research.stlouisfed.org/fred2/

[6] If you define money narrowly to include currency, demand deposits, and other checkable deposits in depository institutions, only the third category pays interest. Currency and coins do not pay interest, nor do regular demand deposits in depository institutions. Other checkable deposits pay interest, but the rate paid is low relative to other interest rates in the economy. Using this definition of money, then, only about one fourth of money pays interest, and even that portion pays a relatively low rate.

; the *real* or *inflation-adjusted* rate of return earned from money and ts over the past 80 years. Note that over the full 1926–2003 period int), all nonmoney assets outperformed money as a store of value. ere most effective, returning 7 percent annually after inflation. Long- d government bonds, short-term Treasury bills, and gold also served f value, although the returns from gold and Treasury bills barely cov- ney depreciated in real terms at an average annual rate of 3 percent d (4.5 percent in the more recent 27-year period). With 3 percent in- ses half its value in approximately 24 years. If money does not retain her assets, why do people hold it as a store of value? The answer lies costs associated with converting money into other assets and then con- ts back into money in time to finance impending expenditures.

ness of money as a store of value depends on the behavior of the period of falling prices (deflation) such as the early 1930s, money its store-of-value function. Because the real value of wealth held in the form of money rises in proportion to the decline in the level of prices, people who hold money in rare episodes of deflation benefit from the general redistribution of wealth from debtors to creditors. In periods of substantial inflation such as the 1970s, however, money fails to effectively serve the store-of-value function. Inflation imposes a tax on money; the annual tax rate is the difference between the inflation rate and the interest rate paid on money, if any.

**liquidity**
relative ease with which an asset can be converted into money without significant commissions or other charges, inconvenience, and risk of loss of principal

The magnitude of the costs of converting an asset into money is encompassed in a very important concept known as **liquidity.** Liquidity is the relative ease with which an asset can be converted into money (i.e., "liquidated") without significant commissions or other charges, inconvenience, and risk of loss of principal. Money is the ultimate in liquidity; it is ready to spend at a moment's notice. Liquidating other financial assets, ranging from passbook savings accounts to common stocks, involves various transactions costs, inconveniences, and risks. These assets suffer from varying degrees of *illiquidity*—that is, lack of liquidity. People hold some portion of their wealth in the form of money because it is liquid, even though money is inferior to other financial and real assets as a store of value. As we will see in Part 6, the nature of the decision-making process associated with holding money as a store of value importantly influences monetary theory and policy.

In a sense, the store-of-value function and the medium-of-exchange function of money are inseparable. This truth is illustrated by historical episodes of *hyperinflation,* for example, Russia, Poland, Ukraine, and Bulgaria in the 1990s. When the rate of inflation advanced beyond certain thresholds, individuals and firms frantically attempted to rid themselves of money because its value was deteriorating rapidly. In other words, the store-of-value function of money had broken down. At the same time, merchants refused to accept payment in money, insisting instead on payment in goods and services. Thus, the breakdown in the store-of-value function of money led to the collapse of the medium-of-exchange function. The money economy broke down, and economic exchange reverted to a system of barter. Depression and chaos inevitably ensued. Money must function reasonably effectively as a store of value for it to be widely accepted as a medium of exchange.

## EVOLUTION OF MONEY AND THE PAYMENTS SYSTEM

Our payments system and the nature and use of money evolved over centuries. Thousands of years ago, metallic coins replaced items such as stones, leather, and corn and circulated as money in numerous civilizations. Later, coins were heavily supplemented with more convenient paper currency. Still later, checks were used to transfer account balances in depository institutions in payment for goods and services. Today, our payments system continues to evolve. Our paper-oriented system is being increasingly replaced with forms of electronic money. In the following sections, we trace the evolution of our payments system, beginning with the earliest coins.

## Full-Bodied or Commodity Money

In ancient civilizations, certain substances that were visually attractive, durable, divisible, and available in relatively small quantities naturally emerged as money—they became widely used as media of exchange. Thousands of years ago, societies began using as money metallic substances, such as bronze, iron, and copper, with the desired qualities. These early monies were **full-bodied money (commodity money)**—that is, money whose value is approximately the same whether it is used as money (in exchange for goods and services) or for nonmoney purposes (as a commodity). The forces of supply and demand assure this equality of value. For example, gold coins worth more for their metallic (nonmoney) content than as money would be melted down. The coins would be used for their nonmoney functions and disappear from circulation. This reallocation of use reduces gold's value as a commodity and increases its value as money. The process would continue until the two values were equal. Conversely, gold coins worth more as money than as a commodity would be withdrawn from industrial use and sold for use as metallic coins. In this way, the forces of supply and demand ensure that the value of gold as money never deviates markedly from its value as a commodity. Money's alternative use as a commodity inspired confidence in coins and assured their acceptability as media of exchange.

**full-bodied money (commodity money)** form of money whose value is approximately the same whether it is used as money or for nonmoney (commodity) purposes

Metallic coins were widely used in ancient civilizations. Initially, iron and copper predominated. However, payment with coins became inconvenient as coin values decreased with major increases in metal supply (coins of convenient value were too heavy). Then silver, which was much scarcer, became popular as money. Until a couple of hundred years ago, gold could not serve effectively as money because of the scarcity of gold; the coins would have been too small. However, gold coins of sufficient size became possible due to increased gold supplies from major worldwide discoveries in the nineteenth century.

## Representative Full-Bodied Money

Societies became more affluent and more dependent on exchange with increasing specialization and division of labor. As the trends accelerated during the industrial revolution, which began in the eighteenth century, the exclusive use of coins as media of exchange became increasingly inconvenient. The weight and size of coins made them cumbersome to transport, store, and use in transactions involving large amounts of money. Imagine making a down payment on a new house with coins! For convenience, coins were supplemented with paper currency, initially backed 100 percent by the valuable metals. Paper money that attests to an ownership claim on a commodity such as gold or silver is referred to as **representative full-bodied money.** The more convenient paper currency circulates in place of the commodity, which is held in safekeeping.

**representative full-bodied money** paper money that attests to an ownership claim on a commodity such as gold or silver

This form of money was first introduced in England during the sixteenth century, although paper money was invented by the Chinese more than 500 years earlier. Originally, the paper notes in England were issued by private firms called goldsmiths. Essentially the notes were warehouse receipts acknowledging rights to a certain number of gold or silver coins, collectable on demand by the bearer of the note. Notes quickly became as acceptable a medium of exchange as coins themselves because the notes could be exchanged for a fixed quantity of metal coins on demand. This form of money circulated as gold certificates in the United States between 1900 and 1933. Bearers of gold certificates were entitled to redeem the certificates in gold coins at the U.S. Treasury. Silver certificates, a form of paper currency redeemable at the U.S. Treasury in silver, also circulated in the United States for many years.

## Fiat or Credit Money

Representative full-bodied money is 100 percent "backed," that is, the money is fully redeemable in a commodity such as gold or silver. However, does money need to be backed 100 percent, or even 25 percent, by a commodity in order to effectively perform its functions? Does it need to be backed by a commodity at all? Some individuals disagree based on historical experience, but the logical answer to this question is no. If we can receive goods and services in exchange for our money, and if the monetary system is stable and functions effectively, who cares how much gold (or other substance) is available to "back" our money? Today our money is "backed" by our implicit faith and confidence that government will limit the quantity of money so that the purchasing power of a dollar does not decline appreciably in a given week, month, or year. Given this faith, money can serve its functions quite effectively without any commodity backing.

**fiat money (credit money)**
form of money that derives its value by fiat or government decree rather than through its value as a commodity

Money that derives its value by fiat or government decree rather than through its value as a commodity is called **fiat money (credit money).** The genesis of this type of money can be traced back some 400 years. English goldsmiths issued warehouse receipts—paper notes entitling the bearer to gold or silver on demand—in exchange for gold or silver. The goldsmiths soon realized that they did not need to back their notes fully in gold. Normally, in any week or month, the public requested only a small percentage of the total paper notes outstanding be redeemed in gold. Therefore, the goldsmiths began to issue notes in amounts above and beyond the value of gold and silver held in safekeeping. They loaned the notes to businesses and other worthy borrowers, earning a nice profit in the form of interest income. Furthermore, some of the benefits were returned to the gold owners in the form of reduced service charges for safeguarding the precious metals. These paper notes can be considered a forerunner of our modern fractional reserve banking system—whenever a goldsmith issued a note without receiving gold in exchange, money was created. The rigid link between precious metals and the nation's money supply had been broken.

Today, all our paper currency and coins are fiat or credit monies. The link between gold and the money supply has been totally severed. The value of the U.S. dollar springs from its widespread acceptability (which, in turn, is based on implicit confidence that government will not issue excessive amounts of money), not from the material from which it is made. In fact, a $20 or $100 dollar bill contains only a few cents worth of paper, printing inks, and other materials. A quarter contains less than 10 cents worth of nickel and copper. The fiat money system has several advantages. (1) Fiat money costs the government considerably less to produce than full-bodied money. Fewer of the nation's resources are used to produce money, freeing up these resources for more socially productive uses.[7] (2) In principle, the

[7] To estimate the savings involved in a fiat money system, suppose our GDP currently is $12,000 billion ($12 trillion) per year and our money supply is $1,200 billion ($1.2 trillion). Suppose that we require a 4 percent annual increase in the money supply to support 4 percent GDP growth. This means an increase of $48 billion in the first year (4% × $1,200 billion) or a cost of approximately 0.4 percent of our nation's GDP. In a commodity money system, producing $48 billion of new money costs approximately $48 billion. To produce this money, we would produce $48 billion less of other goods and services. This illustrates the waste of resources in a commodity money system. In a fiat money system, $48 billion of money costs very little to produce.

quantity of money in circulation can be determined by rational human judgment rather than by the vagaries of mining discoveries. A disadvantage of the fiat money system is possible severe inflation due to excessive amounts of money issued by a corrupt government.

## Checking Accounts

The introduction of checking accounts and the use of checks were important innovations in the evolution of the payments process. Checks permit payment through balance transfers at depository institutions. Checking accounts first became popular after the Civil War because the federal government placed a 10 percent tax on bank notes issued by state-chartered banks. People using checking accounts no longer need to carry large amounts of paper currency. Without checks, you might have to pay your bills by hand-delivering currency to the phone company, your landlord, or the insurance company because sending currency through the mail is risky. Paying for occasional big-ticket items, such as a new automobile, would be even more awkward.

Checks allow us to make sizable transactions without carrying large amounts of currency. The transportation costs of moving currency are eliminated, thereby increasing economic efficiency. Demand deposits up to $100,000 are insured by the Federal Deposit Insurance Corporation. These deposits are safer than currency because currency must be stored and can be lost or stolen. Unlike currency, checks are safe to send through the mail because checks have no value until they are endorsed. They also provide a useful record of transactions for income tax and other purposes.

A payments system based on checks has drawbacks, however. (1) Most importantly, the checking account system is expensive. Check processing in the United States costs more than $5 billion per year. (2) Checks require extra time for transit. (3) Funds from a check you deposit in your account may not be available to spend for several days.

## Electronic Money

Three major innovations in payments media made since the time of exchange based on barter are commodity money, including metal coins; fiat paper money and token coins; and checking accounts. A fourth innovation now well underway is implementation of an **electronic money system**—a system in which money is stored electronically on cards or in computer accounts. This system has the potential to substantially reduce the use of currency, coins, checks, and credit cards, thereby increasing the efficiency of the payments system.

**electronic money system**
a system in which money is stored and transferred electronically via cards and computer accounts

Technological advances in electronic data processing, information retrieval, and communications systems have made it technically feasible to implement a comprehensive communications system in which deposit balances can be transferred instantaneously anywhere in the nation. In a fully implemented electronic money system, a nationwide computer network would monitor the credits and debits of individuals, firms, and governmental units as transactions occur. The potential benefits of such a system lie in its efficiency. The huge costs associated with our current paper-oriented checking system would be sharply reduced. Billions of dollars now spent handling checks could be saved. Further gains would accrue to the extent that electronic money replaces credit cards. Credit cards are a relatively inefficient system, involving excessive paperwork for the transfer of information and for billing. The costs are not billed directly to credit card users but are paid by the merchants who accept credit cards. Ultimately, the costs are shifted onto consumers-at-large through higher prices. Because the costs levied on credit card users are below the true costs to society, use of credit cards is excessive. The system is inefficient. The same is true for checks. In a fully implemented electronic money system, the true cost of transferring funds would be greatly reduced, and this benefit would manifest itself in higher living standards.

**Early Forms of Electronic Money.** The transition to electronic money has been underway for a couple of decades. Today, almost all large wholesale financial transactions are made electronically. For example, the Federal Reserve has a payment system known as *Fedwire.* Through this telecommunications system, thousands of financial institutions that maintain accounts at Federal Reserve banks wire funds to each other, circumventing the use of checks and permitting instantaneous transfer of large amounts of funds. In the private sector, telecommunications systems known as CHIPS *(Clearing House Inter-bank Payments and Settlements)* and *SWIFT (Society for Worldwide Inter-telecommunications Financial Transfers)* allow banks to transfer funds internationally via electronic impulse. Nonfinancial corporations, securities dealers, money market funds, and other major players frequently wire funds through these systems. Fewer than 1 percent of the *number* of transactions in the United States but more than 85 percent of the *dollar value* of transactions is conducted by wire. In other words, almost all multimillion-dollar transactions are made electronically.

Other forms of electronic payment have been in place for several years. Many employers pay salaries by wiring funds directly into employees' checking accounts. Individuals pay certain recurring bills (utility, mortgage, and so forth) electronically, either automatically by preauthorized agreement with their bank or via personal computer each month as bills come due.

**Newer Forms of Electronic Money.** Electronic money—money that is stored and transferred electronically—appears in several forms, including debit cards, stored value cards, electronic cash, and electronic checks. A **debit card** looks like a credit card but is fundamentally different. With a debit card, an individual pays for an item by transferring funds electronically and *immediately* from the client's bank account to that of the merchant. At a retail store or restaurant, for example, the debit card is swiped through a card reader, which quickly verifies that the transaction has been consummated (assuming sufficient funds in the bank account). A PIN (personal identification number), typically known only to the card owner, provides some security in the event the card is lost or stolen. Companies such as Visa and MasterCard issue debit cards, as do many banks. A **stored value card** differs from a debit card in that it is loaded with a predetermined amount of money, for example, $200. The owner uses the card for various everyday transactions, gradually spending down the balance before replenishing the card at the bank. Some of the newer stored value cards, known as *smart cards,* contain a computer chip that allows the owner of the card to load new funds onto the card from a checking account via a personal computer or an ATM (automated teller machine). These cards have gained some popularity in the United States but are used much more widely in Europe and other countries.

**debit card**
card with which an individual pays for an item by transferring funds electronically and *immediately* from his/her bank account to the merchant's bank account

**stored value cards**
cards loaded with a predetermined amount of money; used to make payments

**electronic cash (e-cash)**
form of money that facilitates payment for items purchased over the Internet

**Electronic cash (e-cash),** which is associated with electronic commerce, facilitates payment for items purchased over the Internet. An individual sets up a bank account in which the bank transfers e-cash to the individual's personal computer via the Internet. When the individual buys a new camera through a retailer's Web site, she instructs her computer to transfer the requisite funds from her computer to the retailer's computer. Before shipping the camera, the retailer arranges by

# INTERNATIONAL PERSPECTIVES

## Differing Use of Payments Instruments Across Countries

You are well aware of the widespread use of credit cards and checks in the United States and the increasing use of electronic means of payment. What might be news to you is that the use of various payments instruments differs dramatically across countries. The following table indicates, per capita, the number of checks written, credit card transactions conducted, direct electronic debits levied against checking accounts, and various other forms of electronic payments made in the United States and six other nations in 2000.

The average U.S. inhabitant writes 180 checks per year compared with five or fewer in Germany, the Netherlands, Sweden, and Switzerland. The discrepancy in credit card use is almost as large. Americans use credit cards more than 15 times as frequently as Germans, Dutch, and Swedes. Only Canada even remotely resembles the United States in its use of socially inefficient checks and credit cards. Studies indicate that the United States could save tens of billions of dollars annually by switching from checks and credit cards to electronic payments.

Europeans (especially Scandinavians) use electronic means of payment more than Americans. In Germany, Holland, and Sweden, where use of cell phones and the Internet is much more pervasive than in the U.S., five to 10 times as many payments are made via direct electronic debit of checking accounts than by checks and credit cards combined. Europeans are accustomed to making payments online, via debit cards, or by automatic recurrent payments prearranged with their financial institutions. Question: In the years ahead, how quickly will Americans converge to the payments habits of their heavily wired friends across the Atlantic?

**Use of Noncash Payments Instruments in Various Countries (Number of Transactions per Inhabitant in 2000)**

| Country | Checks | Credit Cards | Direct Debits | Other Paperless Credit Transfers* |
|---|---|---|---|---|
| Canada | 54 | 41 | 14 | 19 |
| Germany | 5 | 4 | 67 | 87 |
| The Netherlands | 1 | 4 | 53 | 72 |
| Sweden | 0 | 2 | 10 | 81 |
| Switzerland | 2 | 10 | 6 | 76 |
| United Kingdom | 45 | 27 | 34 | 31 |
| United States | 180 | 74 | 7 | 13 |

*Includes government and central bank wire transactions.

*Source: Data from Bank for International Settlements, Committee on Payments and Settlements Systems in Selected Countries at* http://www.bis.org/publ/cpss49.pdf

computer for the electronic transfer of funds from the buyer's to the retailer's bank account. This form of money is growing very slowly in the United States. Most consumers continue to pay for Internet purchases with a credit card or debit card. **Electronic checks** are similar to regular checks except that the process is electronic, circumventing the costly procedure of physically processing and transporting checks. Essentially, the Internet buyer instructs her computer to issue a "check" and send it electronically to the retailer. The retailer forwards the check electronically to its own bank, which arranges for electronic transfer of funds from the buyer's to the retailer's bank account. Some organizations, such as departments of state governments, now use electronic checks because of the lower cost relative to traditional paper checks.

**electronic checks**
form of checks that are processed electronically, circumventing the costly procedure of physically processing and transporting checks

**Factors Slowing the Transition to Electronic Money.** A couple of decades ago, some writers suggested that with the advent of electronic money, currency and paper checks would be obsolete within a generation or two. Clearly, this has not happened. Although electronic money is potentially more efficient than our paper-oriented checking system, several factors create resistance to comprehensive implementation of a full-blown electronic money system. (1) Tens of thousands of small businesses are reluctant to invest in the requisite e-money technology given Americans' unwillingness to embrace electronic money wholeheartedly. Many people are satisfied with our current system. (2) Checks provide a convenient receipt and a record of payment that people find useful. (3) Our paper check system gives rise to *float,* but an electronic money system does not. In other words, an electronic system does not provide consumers the benefit of delaying payment for a day or two if bank account funds are temporarily low. (4) More importantly, many individuals are wary about outsiders' access to personal information in the mysterious world of cyberspace. (5) Perhaps even more daunting, certain legal and security problems inherent in the use of electronic money must be resolved. Who is responsible if someone accesses your account PIN number and steals your money? Widely publicized stories of computer fraud raise the specter of unscrupulous individuals transferring huge sums from others' accounts to their own. Thus, widespread implementation of electronic money probably is contingent on further breakthroughs in the developing field of computer security. Until then, currency and traditional paper checks will be around for quite some time.

## MEASURES OF THE MONEY SUPPLY

Because a nation's money supply influences the country's output, income, and price level, reasonably accurate measures of the money supply must be tabulated and published on a regular basis. Today, many industrial nations use fairly standard measures of money. In fact, each country typically reports several measures of money, differentiated by the type of deposits (and close substitutes for deposits) included. One measure of money, sometimes known as the *transactions* or *narrow* measure, consists of currency in circulation plus checking accounts in depository institutions used for everyday expenditures. Broader measures of money add checkable accounts that are used predominantly as savings rather than transactions vehicles plus certain other liquid financial assets.

The Federal Reserve currently publishes several different measures of the U.S. money supply. These measures, sometimes known as the *monetary aggregates,* include

M1, M2, and M3. Table 2-4 gives the magnitude of the U.S. monetary aggregates and their components as of June 2004.

## Narrow Definition of Money (M1)

Traditionally, many economists have preferred the narrow or transactions measure of money, **M1.** M1 includes only currency, demand and other checking accounts in depository institutions, and traveler's checks. The M1 measure of money may be most appropriate if you emphasize the medium-of-exchange function of money, that is, if you view money as consisting strictly of things widely used as means of payment. Even if you define money this narrowly, some judgment calls are necessary. What about balances in money market mutual funds (MMMFs)? As we will discuss in Chapter 3, MMMF balances can be transferred by check, albeit only in amounts above some minimum such as $250 or $500. What about money market deposit accounts (MMDAs) in depository institutions (i.e., interest-bearing accounts) that allow limited check-writing privileges? What about credit lines in brokerage accounts, such as the Merrill Lynch Cash Management Account, which permit account holders to write checks against the value of stocks and bonds in the accounts? Lines of credit can easily be used to make payment. The Federal Reserve has judged that MMMFs and MMDAs are used more as saving vehicles than as means of payment;

**M1**
narrow or transactions measure of money, which includes only currency, demand deposits and other checking accounts in depository institutions, and traveler's checks

**Table 2-4** Federal Reserve Measures of the Money Supply, June 2004

| Monetary Aggregate and Component | Dollar Value (in Billions) |
|---|---|
| **M1:** | $1,336 |
| Currency[1] | 677 |
| Demand deposits[2] | 322 |
| Other checkable deposits[3] | 329 |
| Traveler's checks | 8 |
| **M2:** | 6,293 |
| M1 | 1,336 |
| Savings deposits at all depository institutions and money market deposit accounts (MMDAs)[4] | 3,408 |
| Money market mutual fund shares (retail) | 757 |
| Small time deposits at all depository institutions[5] | 792 |
| **M3:** | 9,293 |
| M2 | 6,293 |
| Large time deposits at all depository institutions[6] | 1,014 |
| RPs and Eurodollars (both overnight and term) | 874 |
| Money market mutual funds shares (institutions) | 1,112 |

[1]Coins and paper currency outside the Treasury, Federal Reserve banks, and depository institutions.
[2]Non-interest-bearing checking accounts at banks.
[3]Interest-bearing checking accounts of the following types: NOW (negotiable order of withdrawal accounts), ATS (automatic transfer system) accounts, credit union share draft accounts, and demand deposits at thrift institutions.
[4] MMDAs (Money market deposit accounts) are interest-bearing accounts at depository institutions, on which a limited number of checks can be written each month.
[5]Time deposits issued in denominations of less than $100,000.
[6]Time deposits issued in denominations of $100,000 or more.
*Source: Federal Reserve Board Release H6 at http://www.federalreserve.gov/releases/h6/*

therefore, these accounts are excluded from M1 (but not from the broader money supply measures). The Fed excludes credit lines in brokerage accounts from all measures of money. You can see, however, that the line of demarcation is fuzzy between items included and those excluded from M1.

Until the 1980s, the narrow M1 measure of money consisted only of currency, non–interest-bearing demand deposits, and traveler's checks. However, the definition became obsolete with financial innovations and deregulation. Prior to the 1980s, banks were generally prohibited from paying interest on checking accounts. As market interest rates increased in response to rising inflation in the 1970s, savings institutions in New England developed a new instrument, known as a *negotiable order of withdrawal (NOW) account.* NOW accounts are interest-bearing savings ac-

## Exhibit 2-2 Staying Ahead of Counterfeiters

One of the most reliable and enduring lessons of economics is that opportunities to earn easy profits almost certainly will be exploited, whether or not they are legal. Scalping of football tickets and smuggling of cocaine are well-known examples. Counterfeiting of a nation's currency is another example. In 2001, an estimated $47 million of counterfeit money was printed in the United States, up approximately 20 percent from 1 year earlier. Until recently, a state-of-the-art personal computer, a digital scanner, and a good inkjet printer often sufficed for the dedicated counterfeiter. The Secret Service estimates that almost 40 percent of U.S. counterfeit currency circulating domestically in 2001 was produced by computers, up from less than 1 percent in 1995. Governments around the world have stepped up efforts to check the increasing volume of counterfeit money facilitated by the declining cost of producing counterfeit money.

The United States, which has more paper currency in circulation than any other country, began stepping up anticounterfeit efforts in 1996. The Treasury Department's Bureau of Engraving and Printing began inserting a tiny thread into new paper money, along with other measures intended to raise the cost of counterfeiting. Take a look at one of the series 2004 20-dollar bills, on which the picture of Andrew Jackson faces up. Hold the bill up to the light. Note the vertical line with tiny, barely legible lettering embedded about three quarters of an inch from the left-hand side of the bill and the several images embedded within the bill. These features are extremely difficult for counterfeiters to duplicate.

Australia has long been plagued by counterfeiting. Recently it aggressively attacked the problem by introducing paper currency containing a thin but prominent plastic sheath. This transparent window in the currency is impossible to copy with an inkjet printer. In fact, Australia now licenses currency-making technology being used by Mexico, Taiwan, and more than 10 other nations. The U.S. Treasury has conducted tests using various forms of plastic for possible future use.

In 2001, Canadian police exposed a counterfeiting ring that had printed more than 40,000 Canadian $100 bills using a computer scanner and an inkjet printer. Canada is considering using a newly invented paper currency composed of an extremely thin layer of plastic embedded between two layers of paper. The developer of the new currency believes it will be used worldwide in the near future. In any event, it is clear that the agencies responsible for producing legitimate national currencies must hustle to stay one step ahead of the counterfeiters.

counts on which a limited number of checks may be written. In 1981, deregulatory legislation authorized nationwide issuance of NOW and *automatic transfer service (ATS) accounts*. ATS accounts are savings accounts that are transferred automatically by the bank's computer to a customer's checking account as needed to prevent overdrawing the account as checks clear.

Today, banks are permitted to pay interest on checking accounts. Accordingly, the "other checkable deposits" component of M1 consists of interest-bearing checking accounts held by individuals and nonprofit organizations in depository institutions. (Corporations and other profit-oriented firms are prohibited from owning interest-bearing checking accounts in depository institutions.) As indicated in Table 2-4, currency makes up about half of M1. Demand deposits and other checkable deposits each constitute approximately one-fourth of M1; traveler's checks contribute less than one percent of the total. Hereafter, we ignore traveler's checks when we discuss the composition of M1. Thus, M1 is defined as DDO + $C^P$, that is, demand deposits and other checkable deposits in depository institutions (DDO) plus currency held by the nonbank public ($C^P$).

## Broader Measures of Money: M2, M3

Although the M1 money supply measure conforms to the criterion that money includes only *transactions funds*—funds actually used to make payment—the broader measures of money (M2 and M3) have garnered increasing attention from central bankers and economists in the past 25 years. In conducting monetary policy over the past decade or two, the Federal Reserve has placed higher priority on M2 than on M1. The broader measures are appropriate if you emphasize the store-of-value rather than the medium-of-exchange function of money. However, once you admit into the measure of money items that are not actually media of exchange, the line of demarcation between money and nonmoney assets becomes ambiguous and difficult to establish.

Assets can be classified based on *liquidity*, the ease and convenience with which they can be converted into the medium of exchange. Three considerations determine an asset's liquidity: how easily and quickly it can be sold; the costs of selling it (transactions costs); and the stability and predictability of its price. An asset that can be sold quickly at a low transactions cost is not very liquid if the owner is *reluctant* to sell because the price of the asset has changed significantly since purchase. There is a continuum of liquidity among assets, ranging from highly liquid passbook savings accounts to highly illiquid real estate and antique cars.

Passbook savings accounts are extremely liquid. They can be converted quickly to media of exchange (cash or checking accounts) by a trip to the bank or ATM or by the touch of a computer keyboard. The transactions costs are not significant. The principal or value in the account is known with certainty in advance. Houses and vintage automobiles are at the other extreme of the liquidity continuum. Selling such real assets at a price near fair market value often requires several months and large commissions. What about government bonds, corporate bonds, and common stocks? Bonds are considered relatively liquid. The bond market is active, transactions costs are fairly low, and bond prices, especially short-term bond prices, are relatively stable.[8] Common stocks are less liquid than bonds. Although both stocks and bonds can be quickly and easily sold, stock prices are more variable

[8] We will demonstrate in Chapter 3 that for any given change in market yields, the relative change in a bond's price varies directly with its length of time to maturity. Longer-term bonds exhibit larger price fluctuations than shorter-term bonds and therefore are less liquid.

**M2**
broad measure of money, which includes M1 and several highly liquid financial assets such as savings deposits, money market mutual fund shares owned by individuals, and other instruments

**M3**
very broad measure of money, which includes M2 and several additional liquid instruments

than bond prices.[9] For these reasons, individuals may be unwilling to sell their shares of stock quickly or on short notice.

The Fed now publishes two broad measures of money, M2 and M3, defined and measured in Table 2-4. These monetary aggregates are constructed by combining assets of comparable liquidity levels. In constructing **M2,** certain highly liquid assets are added to M1. MMMF shares owned by individuals (retail MMMFs) are close substitutes for demand deposits and are included in M2. In fact, some economists would prefer to include the funds in M1. Savings deposits, small time deposits, and money market deposit accounts in banks are quite liquid and are included in M2. Note that M2 is almost five times as large as M1. **M3** is constructed by adding certain slightly less liquid financial assets to M2. M3 includes M2 plus large time deposits ($100,000 and above), repurchase agreements and Eurodollar deposits, and MMMF shares held by institutions.

People who emphasize the broader money measures point out that many highly liquid financial assets are easily substitutable for the narrow money measure, M1. Savings and time deposits in banks can easily be converted to cash or demand deposits with little inconvenience and forgone interest. Even though the deposits cannot be used to make payments directly, the public regards them as almost equivalent to the narrow measures of money. Several other financial instruments also can be converted to money with minimal cost and effort. Examples include money market mutual fund shares and large time deposits.

## Which Measure Is Most Useful?

Economists who advocate the use of broader measures of money point out that the paramount motive for defining and measuring the money supply is to monitor and control its magnitude. This should help stabilize economic activity or at least prevent abrupt changes in the money supply that might damage the economy. The definition of money should be based on empirical evidence instead of being limited only to items used to make payment. Items having the strongest influence on aggregate expenditures should be included in the money supply measure. The best measure of money is that measure that best tracks nominal GDP, real output, and the price level. The medium of exchange is not necessarily the measure of money most closely associated with these key economic variables.

Because financial technology changes over time, the measures of money should not be regarded as fixed and immutable. To a large extent they are a matter of judgment. Milton Friedman and Anna Schwartz, leading exponents of this view, have made the point eloquently:

> The definition of money is to be sought for not on grounds of principle but on grounds of usefulness in organizing our knowledge of economic relationships. "Money" is that to which we choose to assign a number by specified operations; it is not something in existence to be discovered, like the American continent; it is a tentative scientific construct to be invented, like "length" or "temperature" or "force" in physics.[10]

This concept of money raises the strong possibility that the group of assets constituting our "best" measure of money likely will evolve over time. Because of innovative financial practices ushered in by record-level interest rates and liberalization of regulatory practices in the late 1970s and early 1980s, the Federal Reserve replaced

[9] Other things being equal, assets with greater price variability are less liquid because people are less willing to sell them. If an asset's price has risen since its purchase, its sale necessitates payment of capital gains taxes. If an asset's price has fallen, an individual may not be willing to acknowledge a mistake and accept a loss.
[10] Milton Friedman and Anna Schwartz, *Monetary Statistics of the United States* (New York: National Bureau of Economic Research, 1970), 137.

older money measures with the current measures. We will revamp our measures of the money supply periodically as long as new financial developments continue to loosen the link between traditional money measures and economic activity.

Economists agree that the behavior of M1, M2, and M3 has important implications for aggregate expenditures, nominal GDP, and the price level. However, consensus about which measure is best is lacking. If the three measures always moved in unison over time (were scalar multiples of each other), the Fed would not be forced to choose among them. Unfortunately, Figure 2-1 shows this is not always the case. The monetary aggregates are plotted on a *logarithmic scale,* so you can interpret differences in *slopes* as differences in *growth rates* of the aggregates. The growth rates of the three monetary aggregates sometimes move in different directions. For example, M1 growth declined sharply after 1994 whereas M2 and M3 growth rates increased.

## Weighted Measures of Money

The existing monetary aggregates (M1, M2, and M3) give equal weight to each of the items included. For example, M2 gives the same weight to passbook savings accounts and MMMF shares as to currency held by the public and demand deposits in banks. This lack of discrimination is a shortcoming because different financial assets likely do not influence expenditures in exactly the same way. Just as the consumer price index places a larger weight on houses than on candy bars, our money supply measures should place more weight on components strongly influencing aggregate expenditures (such as demand deposits and currency) than on items less closely linked to aggregate expenditures (such as small time deposits). If we knew that demand deposits and currency possessed exactly twice the influence on economic activity as MMMF shares and four times the influence as passbook savings accounts and small time deposits, we could define the money supply as follows:

$$\mathbf{M = DDO + C^{P} + 0.50\,(MMMF) + 0.25\,(SD + TD).}$$

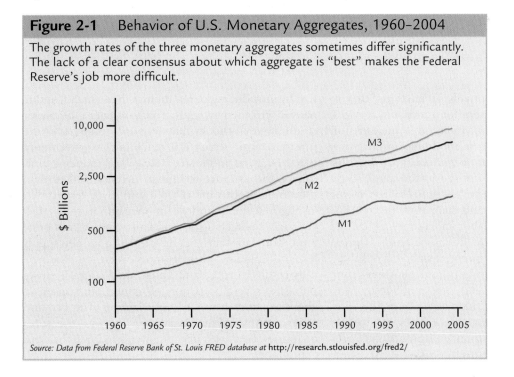

**Figure 2-1** Behavior of U.S. Monetary Aggregates, 1960–2004

The growth rates of the three monetary aggregates sometimes differ significantly. The lack of a clear consensus about which aggregate is "best" makes the Federal Reserve's job more difficult.

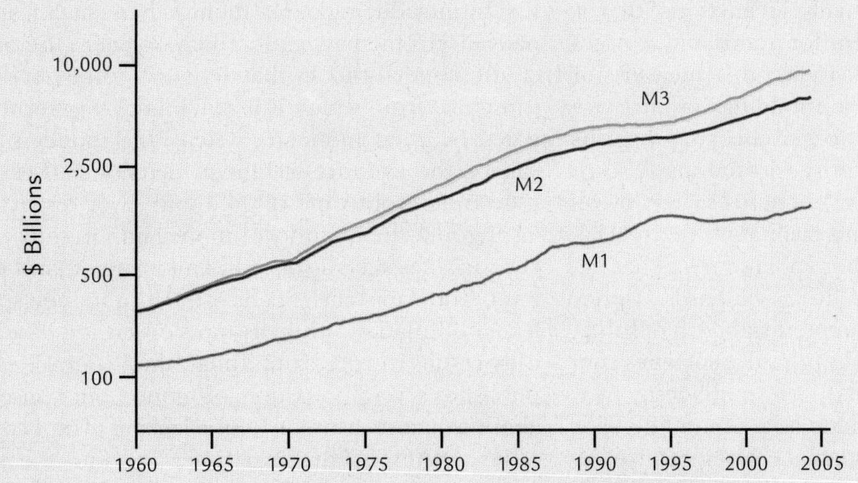


*Source: Data from Federal Reserve Bank of St. Louis FRED database at* http://research.stlouisfed.org/fred2/

**divisia aggregates**
weighted measures of money used to predict changes in price level and output of goods and services; may eventually replace our current measures of money

However, given the current state of knowledge and economists' uncertainty regarding the appropriate weights of the various components in our money measure, all items are weighted equally. The Federal Reserve is working on the problem. Experimentation with **divisia aggregates**—weighted measures of money—indicate weighted aggregates can be superior to existing monetary aggregates in predicting changes in the nation's price level and output of goods and services. In the future, the Fed may replace the current measures of money with new measures based on weighted averages of the various components.

## SUMMARY

Money is defined conceptually as anything that is widely acceptable as payment for goods and services or as repayment of debt. Today, this measure of money consists of the public's holdings of currency and coins and demand and other checking deposits in banks and other depository institutions. Use of money (as opposed to barter) benefits society by reducing transactions costs and facilitating the specialization and division of labor, phenomena that increase efficiency and boost living standards. Money serves as a medium of exchange, a standard of value, and a store of value. Money in primitive societies consisted only of substances that were highly esteemed and possessed significant value as a commodity. For centuries, precious metals such as copper, bronze, silver, and gold served as money. Transactions costs were reduced and economic efficiency was enhanced first by introducing paper money, then checks, and finally electronic payments. Today, societies use fiat or credit money—money that derives its value not by the substance from which it is made but by government edict. In a fiat monetary system, the money supply can be the product of human decision rather than the random outcome of gold and silver discoveries. Changes in the quantity of money importantly affect key variables such as output, employment, and price level. Too rapid an expansion of the money supply leads to inflation, whereas too slow an increase typically results in recession. Today, the Federal Reserve publishes several measures of money, but consensus about which measure is best is lacking. The Fed and other economists are experimenting with measures of money that use different weights for its various components.

## YOUR TURN ANSWERS

PAGE 23

**a.** In a barter economy, each good must be expressed in units of each other good. Hence, there are 6 × 5 = 30 exchange rates. However, half of the exchange rates are redundant, being the reciprocal of another exchange rate (if one bushel of wheat costs 10 loaves of bread, then one loaf of bread costs 0.1 bushel of wheat). Hence, there are (6 × 5)/2 or 15 different price ratios in this barter economy. In a money economy, there would be only six prices because the price of each good would be expressed in units of the nation's standard of value, for example, dollars.

**b.** In a barter economy with 10,000 different goods, there would be (10,000 × 9,999)/2 different exchange rates, or 49,995,000 prices. In a money economy, there would be only 10,000 prices.

# KEY TERMS

money
legal tender
wealth
income
barter economy
liquidity
full-bodied money (commodity money)
representative full-bodied money
fiat money (credit money)
electronic money system
debit card
stored value card
electronic cash
electronic checks
M1
M2
M3
divisia aggregates

# STUDY QUESTIONS

1. Carefully explain the meaning of the following concepts: money, income, and wealth.
2. Critique the following statements: "Doctors earn more money than engineers," and "Barry Bonds has more money than George Bush."
3. Are credit cards money? Explain why or why not.
4. What do we mean by "legal tender"? Is all money legal tender? Is all legal tender money?
5. Focusing on the standard-of-value and medium-of-exchange functions of money, analyze the benefits to society when money is introduced into a barter economy.
6. "Money served more effectively as a store of value in the 1990s than in the 1970s." What does this true statement imply about price level behavior in the two decades? Explain.
7. "When the store-of-value function of money collapses, so does the medium of exchange function." Do you agree or disagree? Explain.
8. In 1980, the U.S. consumer price index increased 12.5 percent. Which function of money was most jeopardized in 1980? Explain by examining the effects of this event on the usefulness of each of money's three functions.
9. Explain how the introduction of money eliminates the requirement for a double coincidence of wants in order for exchange to take place.
10. Is the money supply important to the economic health of a nation? Why do we care about the money supply? Why does the Federal Reserve publish three different measures of the money supply?

11. Historically, which of the following assets—money, gold, Treasury bills, U.S. government bonds, corporate bonds, and common stocks—has been most effective as a store of value? Which has been least effective?

12. Explain the distinction between full-bodied money and fiat or credit money. What are the advantages and disadvantages of each?

13. Give three examples of electronic money in the United States today. What would be the benefits of a comprehensive electronic money system? What obstacles inhibit the implementation of such a system in the United States?

14. Both money market mutual funds (MMMFs) and money market deposit accounts (MMDAs) permit transfer of funds by check, yet neither is included in the Federal Reserve's narrow money measure, M1. Should MMMFs and MMDAs be included in M1? Explain.

15. Calculate your personal M1 holdings today. Are they larger or smaller than your monthly income?

16. Define the concept of liquidity. Rank the following assets according to their liquidity (most liquid to least liquid).

   **A.** Used car
   **B.** Funds in Dreyfus Liquid Assets (a money market mutual fund)
   **C.** $1,000 in a passbook savings account
   **D.** $1,000 in a 1-year certificate of deposit at your bank
   **E.** 400 shares of IBM stock
   **F.** Expected inheritance from your 65-year-old grandfather

# ADDITIONAL READING

- Good general discussions of money are found in the two Palgrave dictionaries edited by Peter Newman, Murray Milgate, and John Eatwell: *The New Palgrave Dictionary of Money and Finance* (New York: Groves Dictionaries, Inc., 1992) and *The New Palgrave Dictionary of Economics* (London: Macmillan Press, Ltd., 1987). On the history of money, see Arthur Nussbaum, *A History of Money* (New York: Columbia University Press, 1957) and Paul Einzig, *Primitive Money,* second edition (New York: Oxford University Press, 1966).
- A classic article outlining the development of money in a prisoner of war camp is R.A. Radford, "The Economic Organization of a Prisoner of War Camp," *Economica,* November 1945, pp. 189–201. An early discussion on measuring money is William Barnett, Edward Offenbacher, and Paul Spindt, "New Concepts of Aggregate Money," *Journal of Finance,* May 1981, pp. 497–505. A more recent paper on the same subject is K. Alec Chrystal and Ronald MacDonald, "Empirical Evidence on the Recent Behavior and Usefulness of Simple Sum and Weighted Measures of the Money Stock," Federal Reserve Bank of St. Louis *Review,* March/April 1994, pp. 73–109 (see also the following comments by Charles Nelson).
- On the use of credit cards in the United States, see "Credit Cards: Use and Consumer Attitudes, 1970–2000," *Federal Reserve Bulletin,* September 2000, pp. 623–634. Good articles on electronic money include Stuart Weiner, "Electronic Payments in the U.S. Economy: An Overview," Federal Reserve Bank of Kansas City *Economic Review,* Fourth Quarter, 1999; Loretta Mester, "The Changing Nature of the Payments System: Should New Players Mean New Rules?" Federal Reserve Bank of Philadelphia *Business Review,* March/April 2000, pp. 3–26; and "Electronic Bill Presentment and Payment—Is It Just a Click Away?" Federal Reserve Bank of Chicago *Economic Perspectives,* Fourth Quarter 2001, pp. 2–14.
- On the prospects for the United States moving toward electronic money, see David Humphrey, Lawrence Pulley, and Jukka Vesala, "The Check's in the Mail: Why the United States Lags in the Adoption of Cost-Saving Electronic Payments," *Journal of Financial Services Research,* 2000, No.1, pp. 17–39, and Kenneth Kuttner and James McAndrews, "Personal On-Line Payments," Federal Reserve Bank of New York *Economic Policy Review,* December 2001, pp. 35–50.

# Part TWO

Financial instruments and markets increase the range of outlets for surplus funds. They reduce the cost of obtaining funds for deficit-spending units such as business firms. Highly developed financial markets contribute to economic efficiency and growth. Interest rates are influenced by the business cycle, inflation expectations, Federal Reserve policy, and other factors. Interest rates, in turn, influence important economic decisions such as expenditures on consumer durable goods and investment projects and the flow of financial capital across national borders. Fluctuating stock prices reflect society's changing sentiment about the nation's economic prospects. Stock market swings influence aggregate expenditures and economic activity. The exchange rate, determined in the highly competitive foreign exchange market, directly influences the price of a nation's goods, services, and assets around the world.

Chapter 3

# FINANCIAL MARKETS AND INSTRUMENTS

A fundamental lesson of elementary economics is the crucial role of saving and investment in a nation's growth and development. Consider the primitive world of Robinson Crusoe and his friend Friday, characters in the book *Robinson Crusoe* by Daniel Defoe. Marooned on a deserted island, Crusoe and Friday are confronted with the basic fact of economic life—a shortage of goods and services relative to wants. Without adequate equipment, Crusoe and Friday are forced to obtain food by the most primitive techniques. Their method of catching fish is so inefficient that obtaining adequate nourishment occupies almost their entire day. To extricate themselves from their hand-to-mouth existence, Crusoe and Friday invest in capital equipment—a fishing net. The investment enhances their productivity in obtaining food, freeing up time to produce nonfood items and possibly even enjoy some leisure activities. The investment boosts their command over goods and services, that is, it increases their standard of living.

To find time to produce the capital good (the fishing net), Crusoe and Friday first must catch more fish than they consume in a given day. This act of *saving* enables them to transfer economic resources (labor) from the production of *consumer goods* (fish) to the production of *investment goods* (fishing net). Once Crusoe and Friday invested in the fishing net, they were on their way toward the "good life."

This elementary example illustrates the fundamental importance of saving and investment in any economy. Because capital goods wear out or depreciate over time, a nation must generate and transfer a significant flow of saving into investment goods just to maintain the nation's capital stock and preserve existing living standards. The nation then must sustain a healthy flow of saving and investment to provide for *rising* living standards. As a general rule, the greater the proportion of current output saved and invested, the more rapid a nation's rate of long-term economic growth.

## FINANCIAL MARKETS AND THE FLOW OF FUNDS

Unlike the Robinson Crusoe example, decisions to save and decisions to invest are typically made by different individuals and groups. Millions of U.S. households and thousands of U.S. firms engage in saving. A different and smaller group of individuals and firms purchase investment goods. To realize investment goals, the savings of the masses must be transferred to investors in capital goods. A key function of financial institutions and markets is to facilitate the transfer of funds from savers to investors.

Financial markets and institutions do not just transfer funds from household savers to investors in capital goods. Thousands of business firms, many state and local government units, and foreign entities, as well as households seek outlets for surplus funds in U.S. financial markets. Many borrowers besides businesses seek funds to finance investment expenditures. At some point, almost every household and individual is a deficit spender or borrower. For example, you might be one of the millions of students taking out student loans. Later, you likely will borrow when you buy your first home. State and local governments often borrow to finance capital expenditures such as new roads and schools. In most years, the federal government spends more than it takes in, issuing bonds to finance the budget deficit. That is, the federal government is typically a borrower. Foreign firms and governments often turn to U.S. financial markets to obtain funds.

Table 3-1 indicates the total cumulative debt incurred by various deficit-spending units (other than financial institutions) in the United States in 1976 and 2003. The data are arranged by the economic sector (government, household, business, etc.) of the debt issuer (borrower). Keep in mind that the figures refer to gross rather than net debts of various sectors. For example, U.S. households had $9,401 billion ($9.401 trillion) of outstanding debt at the end of 2003. However, they also owned a very large amount of bonds, savings accounts in banks and other depository institutions, and other types of debt instruments. That is, the household sector and the other sectors are *creditors* as well as *debtors*. The table indicates only the debt side of the ledger. The table also indicates the average annual growth rate of total debt issued by each sector over the 27-year period.

**Table 3-1** Debt Owed by U.S. Nonfinancial Sectors

| Sector | Amount Outstanding ($ Billion) | | Average Annual Growth Rate (Percent) |
|---|---|---|---|
| | End of 1976 | End of 2003 | |
| U.S. government* | 513 | 4,033 | 7.9 |
| State and local governments | 238 | 1,560 | 7.2 |
| Households | 826 | 9,401 | 9.4 |
| Farms and unincorporated businesses | 323 | 2,439 | 7.8 |
| Nonfinancial corporations | 608 | 4,986 | 8.1 |
| Total | 2,508 | 22,299 | 8.4 |
| *Memo:* | | | |
| 1. Market value of nonfinancial sector corporate equity | 935 | 15,473 | 11.0 |
| 2. Gross domestic product (nominal) | 1,885 | 11,271 | 6.8 |

*Net debt of federal government, excluding debt owned by U.S. government accounts.
*Source: Federal Reserve System,* Flow of Funds Accounts, *release Z.1 at* http://www.federalreserve.gov/releases/Z1

The U.S. household sector is the largest (and fastest growing) debtor, followed by nonfinancial corporations (AT&T, Microsoft, etc.) and the federal government. The total market value of outstanding equity (shares of stock) issued by nonfinancial corporations is more than twice the market value of outstanding debt issued by the same corporations (see item 1 under "Memo"). Total nonfinancial sector debt in the United States expanded 8.4 percent per year over the quarter century. Household sector debt increased somewhat faster. Total debt and the debt of all five sectors increased faster than the nation's gross domestic product over the period.

Financial markets and institutions bring together the issuers of debt and equity (deficit units) with those seeking attractive outlets for available funds (surplus units). The mechanism of surplus fund transfer through financial markets to deficit-spending units is illustrated in Figure 3-1.

The surplus units (savers/lenders) are positioned in the left-hand portion of the figure. The group includes millions of individual households, many firms, various levels of government on some occasions, and foreign entities lending in the United States. The deficit-spending units (whose annual receipts are insufficient to cover expenditures) are shown in the right-hand portion of the figure. The group includes certain households, state and local governments in some periods, the federal government in most periods, large numbers of business firms, and foreign entities borrowing in the United States. Almost all individuals, firms, and governments bor-

**Figure 3-1** Transfer of Funds from Surplus to Deficit-Spending Units via Direct Credit Markets and Financial Intermediaries

Households and other surplus units (left) make their funds available to deficit-spending units (right) either directly, by purchasing financial instruments issued by deficit spenders (top), or indirectly, by purchasing secondary claims issued by financial intermediaries (bottom).

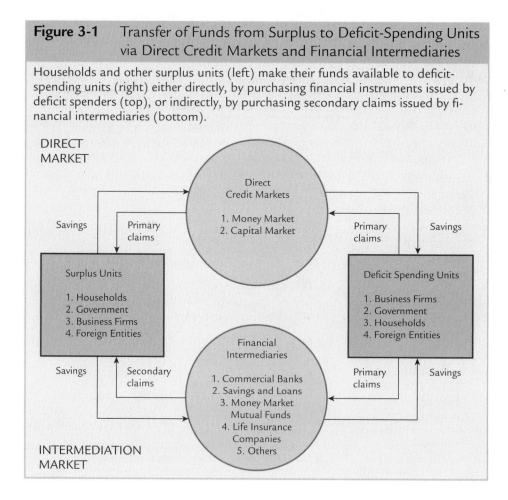

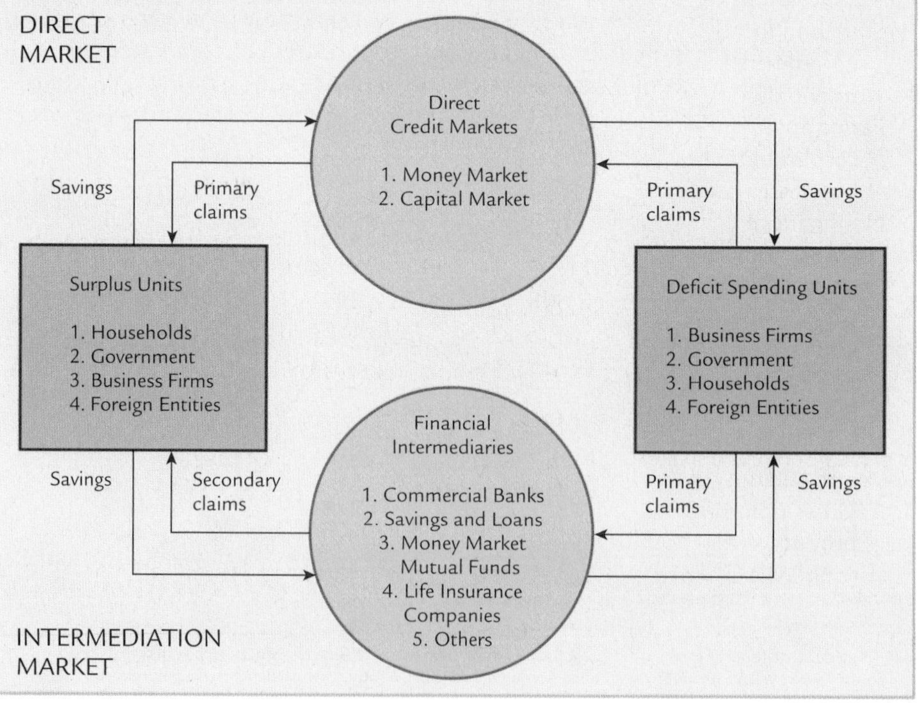

row occasionally. Taken collectively, firms and governments typically are net deficit spenders; households typically are net surplus units. In recent decades, foreign entities have been net surplus units, lending more than borrowing in U.S. markets.

The diagram shows that the savings generated by the surplus units (savers/lenders) are made available to the deficit-spending units (borrowers/spenders) through two avenues: *direct credit markets* and *indirect credit markets* via financial intermediaries. In the direct credit market, deficit-spending units issue financial claims, such as shares of stock, bonds, and other debt instruments, which are sold directly to surplus units by brokers and dealers. **Brokers** act as customers' agents, charging a commission to locate security buyers or sellers. **Dealers** hold inventories of securities and stand ready to buy or sell at quoted bid and ask prices. Dealers do not charge a commission. Their income derives from a spread between the *ask* price (dealer's selling price) and the *bid* price (dealer's buying price). The top part of the figure illustrates this flow of claims, known as *primary claims,* issued by deficit spenders and sold via the direct credit market to savers/lenders in exchange for the savings.

**brokers**
individuals acting as customers' agents, locating a security buyer or seller and charging a commission for the service

**dealers**
holders of inventories of securities who stand ready to buy or sell at quoted bid and ask prices

The indirect credit market involves financial intermediaries such as banks, money market mutual funds, and life insurance companies. These institutions are financial middlemen (hence the term *intermediary*), shown at the bottom of the figure. In **financial intermediation,** some of the primary claims issued by deficit-spending units (bonds, mortgages, and so forth) are sold to financial intermediaries rather than directly to surplus units. Financial intermediaries hold the primary claims as investments; the primary claims are assets of the intermediaries. The intermediaries then issue *secondary claims* on themselves to fund the purchase of the primary claims; the secondary claims are liabilities of the intermediaries. These secondary claims—savings deposits, life insurance policies, and money market mutual fund shares—are sold to the surplus units (savers). A **financial intermediary** is an institution that issues secondary claims to obtain funds and uses the proceeds to purchase primary claims. This act transfers funds from society's savers/lenders to borrowers/spenders. For example, a commercial bank issues you a savings account and then lends the proceeds to a local farmer to purchase a new tractor. In this case, the bank is a "middleman" between you and the farmer. In the United States, most funds flowing from savers to deficit spenders are channeled through financial intermediaries (bottom loop of Figure 3-1).

**financial intermediation**
flow of funds from savers to deficit spenders by way of financial intermediaries

**financial intermediary**
institution that obtains funds by issuing secondary claims and uses the proceeds to purchase primary claims, thereby transferring funds from society's savers/lenders to borrowers/spenders

In the remainder of this chapter, we focus on the top part of the figure. We examine the direct credit markets—the money market and the capital market—and the financial instruments traded in these markets. We devote special attention to the U.S. government securities market—the market through which the Federal Reserve System conducts monetary policy and one of the most active financial markets in the world. Chapter 4 provides an analysis of financial intermediation and a discussion of the various types of U.S. financial intermediaries.

## ATTRIBUTES OF FINANCIAL INSTRUMENTS

Before we discuss the various financial markets and instruments, background information about financial instruments is useful. Three key attributes or characteristics of any financial instrument are liquidity, risk, and yield. These attributes importantly influence the decision making of individuals and firms allocating financial wealth among money, stocks, bonds, and various other financial instruments. We briefly describe each attribute and discuss the relationship of the three attributes.

## Liquidity

As defined in Chapter 2, *liquidity* is the ease with which an asset can be converted into money (bank checking accounts and currency) on short notice. A financial instrument must possess three prerequisites to be considered highly liquid. First, the instrument must be easily convertible to cash. Second, the cost of converting (transactions costs) must be reasonably low. Third, the principal or price of the instrument must remain relatively stable over time. Highly developed secondary markets in which financial instruments can be easily bought and sold contribute strongly to liquidity.

Common stocks are less liquid than short-term U.S. government securities. Both instruments are conveniently sold in easily accessible markets, but stock prices vary considerably more over time than government securities. Money-market (short-term) instruments with their greater price stability typically are more liquid than capital market (long-term) instruments.

**default risk**
risk that issuer of debt instrument will not make interest payments or pay back the face value when the instrument matures

**market risk**
risk that the price of a financial instrument will fluctuate

**yield**
rate of return on an asset, expressed as a percentage per year

**current yield**
yield computed as the annual payment from the instrument (in dollars) divided by the price or initial principal

**yield to maturity**
average annual return including any capital gain or loss realized at maturity when the face value of the bond is redeemed

## Risk

The risk in a financial instrument derives from the possibility that its owner may be unable to recover the full value of funds originally invested. Risks can be divided into two types: default and market.

**Default risk** is the risk of not receiving contractual interest payments in a timely fashion or not recovering the principal due to financial impairment of the instrument's issuer. The U.S. government has the constitutional authority to tax or even print money to meet its financial obligations; corporations do not. Thus, U.S. government bonds carry lower default risk than corporate bonds. Savings accounts have lower default risk than municipal or corporate bonds because the Federal Deposit Insurance Corporation insures savings deposits in commercial banks, up to $100,000 per account. Corporate and municipal bonds do not offer similar safety features. Corporate bonds have lower default risk than corporate equities because bondholders are paid before stockholders if the corporation has severe financial problems.

**Market risk** is the risk of fluctuation of the price of the financial instrument. If you are forced to sell the instrument on short notice, you may not recover the original principal. A passbook savings deposit in a commercial bank has less market risk than a long-term marketable government or corporate bond. You can cash in a savings account on short notice without losing principal. This is not true for marketable bonds, whose prices fluctuate continuously with changes in market interest rates. Common stocks have more market risk (as well as default risk) than corporate bonds because stock prices are more variable from day to day and month to month.

## Yield

The **yield** is the rate of return on an asset, expressed as a percentage per year. The yield is computed as the yearly return on the instrument (in dollars) divided by the price, or initial principal. This is the **current yield.** An alternative measure, the **yield to maturity,** is sometimes used for bonds. The yield to maturity considers any capital gain or loss realized at maturity, when the face value of the bond (usually $1,000 or $10,000) is redeemed. For a bond purchased below face value, the yield to maturity—the average rate of return over the life of the instrument—exceeds the current yield. For a bond purchased above face value, the yield to maturity is lower than the current yield because a capital loss is realized at maturity. We illustrate these yield concepts later in this chapter when we discuss the market for U.S. government securities.

### Liquidity, Risk, and Yield: Their Relationship

The three attributes of a financial instrument (liquidity, risk, and yield) are systematically related. Liquidity and yield are inversely related. Investors typically accept a lower yield for increased liquidity. Passbook savings accounts have lower yields than 3-year certificates of deposit, which are relatively illiquid because banks penalize depositors for cashing in a CD before maturity. Risk and yield are positively related. Most investors are *risk averse,* that is, they require higher returns for taking greater risk. Corporate bonds have higher yields than U.S. Treasury bonds because corporate bonds have greater default risk. Liquidity and risk are inherently related. More liquid financial instruments are less risky because they can be converted to cash on short notice at a price close to the original purchase price. Long-term bonds, which exhibit greater price fluctuations than short-term bonds, are less liquid and more risky than short-term bonds.

## CLASSIFICATION OF FINANCIAL MARKETS

Financial markets can be classified by several criteria: debt versus equity, primary versus secondary, organized versus over the counter, cash versus derivative, and money versus capital. We discuss the various classifications to provide important institutional background information.

### Debt Versus Equity Markets

A **debt instrument** is an issuer's contractual agreement to pay a particular amount of money (principal or face value) at a specified future date. Most arrangements include the issuer's (borrower's) agreement to pay a specific stream of interest payments (most commonly semiannually). Examples of debt instruments include all forms of U.S. government securities, corporate bonds, municipal bonds, mortgages, and several short-term money market instruments issued by banks and other businesses. These debt instruments are actively traded in financial markets. **Equities** are financial claims giving an owner the right to share the net income of the corporate issuer. The main equity instruments are common stocks issued by corporations.

For buyers of securities (surplus units), debt instruments with a contractual claim on the issuer are safer than equities. In case of corporation insolvency, owners of corporate debt instruments (bondholders) have a priority claim over owners of equity instruments (stockholders) for the corporation's income and assets. Bondholders are paid first. On the other hand, stockholders possess ownership claims and benefit from a firm's earnings growth; holders of bonds and other debt instruments do not. In the middle of 2004, the aggregate market value of outstanding equities in the United States was approximately \$15 trillion (\$15,000 billion). The aggregate value of outstanding debt instruments was even larger at approximately \$22 trillion.

**debt instrument**
contractual agreement by the issuer to pay a specific amount of money (principal or face value) at a specified future date; contract may include periodic interest payments as well

**equities**
financial claims representing ownership in a business entity; gives bearer the right to share in the net income of issuer

**primary market**
market in which newly issued securities are exchanged

**secondary market**
market in which securities are traded after they have been issued

### Primary Versus Secondary Markets

A **primary market** is a market for brand new issues. A **secondary market** is a market for exchange of previously issued (secondhand) securities. The media cover primary markets less than secondary markets, and the public is more familiar with sec-

**investment bank**
institution specializing in providing information and counsel to companies on finance-related issues

ondary markets. When a corporation issues new bonds or shares of stock, the company engages an **investment bank**—an institution specializing in providing information and counsel to companies on finance-related issues, such as the choice between issuing debt and issuing stock. If the firm issues new debt, the investment bank provides counsel on the appropriate coupon rate, maturity of the bond or other debt instrument, and other pertinent matters. If the firm issues new equity (shares of stock), the investment bank *underwrites* the securities; that is, it stands ready to purchase the entire issue and then sell the shares to the public. Several investment banking firms sometimes pool their resources and jointly underwrite a large offering of new shares, thus spreading the risk. When the U.S. Treasury issues new debt, it conducts sealed bid auctions. The chief bidders are banks, pension funds, life insurance companies, and other large organizations. Average U.S. individuals are seldom involved in these primary market transactions.

Americans are more familiar with secondary markets. The New York Stock Exchange and the U.S. government securities markets are examples of secondary markets. When an individual calls a broker to buy stocks or bonds or when a large money-center bank purchases marketable government securities in the secondary market for its investment portfolio, corporations or the government are not supplied with new funds. The institutions receive new funds only when securities are first offered in the primary market. In the secondary market, the buyer purchases an existing equity or debt instrument from other parties. Well-functioning secondary markets are critically important to the viability of primary markets. The secondary market provides *liquidity* to financial instruments, making the instruments attractive to prospective buyers and enhancing the ability of firms and governments to attract funds through new issues. Few individuals or firms purchase newly issued stocks and bonds in the absence of healthy and efficient secondary markets. Firms use the continuing flow of information about stock prices and bond yields provided by the second market to decide whether to issue new bonds or shares of stock.

## Organized Exchanges Versus Over-the-Counter Markets

After a security is issued, it can be traded in a secondary market either through an organized exchange or "over the counter" (OTC)—a system of computer contacts among various dealers who stand ready to buy or sell out of their inventory. The OTC market has become increasingly competitive in recent years. Today, it is not appreciably inferior to the organized exchanges in terms of information flow and efficiency. The New York Stock Exchange, American Stock Exchange, and other organized exchanges provide a physical meeting place and communications facilities where exchange member brokers and dealers can conduct transactions. The brokers and dealers are linked through various communications devices to other brokers, dealers, firms, and individuals throughout the nation. Buy and sell orders are transmitted through this network to the floor of the exchange, where transactions are conducted. The bulk of trading on organized exchanges is in shares issued by relatively large corporations. Shares of smaller companies normally are traded OTC.

The dominant portion of the *value* of all outstanding corporate stock consists of corporate stocks traded on the exchanges. However, the shares of only a small *number of firms,* that is, a minority of corporations, are traded on the exchanges. The equities issued by the great majority of corporations and most of the debt instruments issued by corporations, the U.S. government, and state and local governments are traded OTC. Some dealers and brokers specialize in specific types of securities. For example, U.S. government securities are traded OTC by 40 dealers specializing in those instruments. OTC markets include municipal bond, negotiable certificate of deposit, and foreign exchange markets.

## Cash Versus Derivative Markets

Financial markets can be classified according to whether payment and receipt of the security occur at the outset or settlement and delivery of the instrument are deferred to a later date. The **cash market** involves transactions in which the buyer pays the seller up front for an asset. If you purchase shares of Wal-Mart stock or a corporate bond, you deal in the cash market and make payment immediately. In the **derivative market,** trades are arranged currently and the terms are locked in, but settlement and delivery of the instrument occur at a specified future date. Derivative instruments *derive* their value from the value of the underlying asset. Derivatives include financial futures and options. **Financial futures** involve the purchase of (and payment for) a financial instrument at a specified future date, at a price determined *in advance.* **Options** are contracts providing an owner the right (option) to buy or sell a financial asset (e.g., shares of stock or financial futures) at a specified price and time period.

Financial futures markets have proliferated and such markets now exist for many of the financial instruments discussed later in this chapter. For example, a large bank anticipating future cash needs might use a financial futures contract. The bank arranges today to borrow federal funds (deposits at the Federal Reserve owned by another bank) for delivery and payment 30 days later in order to lock in the cost of funds in advance. The bank protects itself against a potential increase in the federal funds rate over the next 30 days (Exhibit 3-1). In another scenario, the bank expects a large income tax rebate in 90 days and wants to invest the funds in U.S. government bonds. If the bank anticipates declining interest rates (and corresponding increase in bond price) over the next 3 months, it can buy the bonds in

**cash market**
transactions in which the buyer pays the seller for the asset up front

**derivative market**
trades that are arranged currently with locked-in terms, but settlement and delivery of the instrument are made at a specified future date

**financial futures**
purchase of (and payment for) a financial instrument at a specified future date, at a price determined *in advance*

**options**
contracts that give the owner the right to buy or sell a financial asset at a particular price within a specified time period

### Exhibit 3-1 Financial Futures Contracts

Financial futures contracts have proliferated in recent years. A variety of interest rate futures contracts in U.S., British, European, and other nations' government securities now are traded, as are future contracts in federal funds, municipal bonds indexes, and other debt instruments. In addition to the popular interest rate futures, major U.S., British, and Japanese stock market indexes are traded in futures markets, as are currency contracts for Japanese yen, Swiss francs, and other foreign currencies. Most financial futures are traded on either the Chicago Mercantile Exchange or the Chicago Board of Trade. Key information is provided daily in the "Money and Investing" section of *The Wall Street Journal.* The following table, taken from the March 2, 2004, issue of the *Journal,* indicates key data for some interest rate futures contracts as of March 1, 2004.

Contracts call for delivery of (and payment for) securities on the last day of the month indicated in the table. Data (in order) include the opening, high, low, and closing price for the day, the change in price from the previous day's close, the high and low price since contract inception, and the open interest, that is, the number of contracts outstanding. Note the popularity of Treasury note and bond futures and federal funds futures, as indicated by the amount of open interest in the contracts.

*continued*

## Exhibit 3-1 Financial Futures Contracts—*cont'd*

Consider the quotations for the 30-day federal funds futures, traded in minimum blocks of $5 million. To calculate the federal funds rate implied by these contracts, subtract the prices from 100. On March 1, 2004, the federal funds rate implied on the September 2004 contract (using the settlement price) is 1.18 percent. This figure is sharply lower than the highest rate experienced since the inception of the contract, 1.78 percent (100 − 98.22). On March 1, 2004, a large bank anticipating the need to borrow or lend federal funds (bank reserve deposits at the Federal Reserve) at the end of September 2004 could lock in a rate of 1.18 percent. Because the spot federal funds rate on March 1 was 1.0 percent, the futures rate of 1.18 percent indicates market participants' view that the chances were high the Federal Reserve would increase the federal funds rate to 1.25 percent by September (the Fed normally increases rates in increments of 0.25 percent). Pick up a recent issue of *The Wall Street Journal* and note the variety of financial futures contracts now available.

### Interest Rate Futures

**Treasury Bonds** (CBT)-$100,000; pts 32nds of 100%

| | | | | | | | | |
|---|---|---|---|---|---|---|---|---|
| Mar | 114-02 | 114-20 | 113-20 | 113-26 | −2 | 116-23 | 101-00 | 233,956 |
| June | 112-18 | 113-07 | 112-06 | 112-12 | −2 | 116-15 | 104-00 | 382,058 |
| Sept | 110-31 | 111-03 | 110-28 | 110-31 | −2 | 111-23 | 101-25 | 803 |

Est vol 225,329; vol Fri 391,486; open int 617,117, +6,929.

**Treasury Notes** (CBT)-$100,000; pts 32nds of 100%

| | | | | | | | | |
|---|---|---|---|---|---|---|---|---|
| Mar | 115-14 | 16-005 | 115-04 | 15-095 | −2.5 | 116-10 | 106-29 | 451,809 |
| June | 113-30 | 14-105 | 113-20 | 13-255 | −2.5 | 14-105 | 107-13 | 873,415 |

Est vol 744,741; vol Fri 990,490; open int 1,330,017, −55,629.

**5 Yr. Treasury Notes** (CBT)-$100,000; pts 32nds of 100%

| | | | | | | | | |
|---|---|---|---|---|---|---|---|---|
| Mar | 113-26 | 114-00 | 113-18 | 13-215 | −3.0 | 19-215 | 09-145 | 349,194 |

Est vol 436,430; vol Fri 539,498; open int 1,019,061, −3,580.

**2 Yr. Treasury Notes** (CBT)-$200,000; pts 32nds of 100%

| | | | | | | | | |
|---|---|---|---|---|---|---|---|---|
| Mar | 07-262 | 07-272 | 107-23 | 107-25 | −1.2 | 07-272 | 106-02 | 88,309 |

Est vol 39,565; vol Fri 52,344; open int 238,814, +287.

**30 Day Federal Funds** (CBT)-$5,000,000; 100 - daily avg.

| | | | | | | | | |
|---|---|---|---|---|---|---|---|---|
| Mar | 99.000 | 99.000 | 98.995 | 98.995 | ... | 99.160 | 98.740 | 48,049 |
| Apr | 99.00 | 99.00 | 99.00 | 99.00 | ... | 99.17 | 89.96 | 75,451 |
| May | 98.99 | 98.99 | 98.98 | 98.99 | ... | 99.79 | 98.40 | 48,813 |
| June | 98.98 | 98.98 | 98.98 | 98.98 | ... | 98.99 | 98.38 | 37,203 |
| July | 98.94 | 98.94 | 98.93 | 98.93 | −.01 | 98.95 | 98.20 | 41,510 |
| Aug | 98.88 | 98.89 | 98.87 | 98.87 | −.01 | 98.89 | 98.24 | 10,592 |
| Sept | 98.82 | 98.82 | 98.81 | 98.82 | −.01 | 98.90 | 98.22 | 17,317 |

Est vol 7,014; vol Fri 18,969; open int 355,603, +3,011.

**10 Yr. Interest Rate Swaps** (CBT)-$100,000; pts 32nds of 100%

| | | | | | | | | |
|---|---|---|---|---|---|---|---|---|
| Mar | 112-29 | 112-31 | 112-19 | 112-22 | −4 | 113-05 | 107-20 | 21,757 |

Est vol 5,860; vol Fri 19,969; open int 41,509, +960.

**10 Yr. Muni Note Index** (CBT)-$1,000 x index

| | | | | | | | | |
|---|---|---|---|---|---|---|---|---|
| Mar | 106-02 | 106-05 | 105-28 | 106-02 | 3 | 106-05 | 99-21 | 2,645 |

Est vol 193; vol Fri 1,248; open int 3,155, +267.
Index: Close 106-04; Yield 4.243.

the futures market today, locking in the price and yield of the bonds to be received in 90 days. Futures trading in Treasury bonds, federal funds, and other financial instruments is conducted on the Chicago Board of Trade. Clearly, hedging against price changes in cash markets is an important motive for derivative transactions.

## Money Versus Capital Markets

**money market**
market in which *short-term* debt instruments—those with maturities less than 1 year—are traded, typically in massive quantities

**capital market**
market in which *long-term* securities issued by government and private concerns are exchanged

The **money market** is a market for trade of *short-term* debt instruments—those with maturities less than 1 year. Typically massive quantities are traded. Money market instruments, issued by governments, banks, and other private firms, are characterized by high liquidity and relatively low default risk. The **capital market** is a market for exchange of *long-term* securities issued by government and private concerns. Both debt and equity instruments are traded in the capital market. Capital market instruments often carry greater default and market risks than money market instruments. In compensation, however, these long-term instruments typically provide a higher return than money market instruments.

Business firms typically use the money market to obtain working capital, that is, funds to cover short-term operating expenses. Firms normally use the capital market to obtain funds for long-term investment in plants, equipment, and technology. That is, they issue bonds and equities to finance projects with long-term payoffs.

# INSTRUMENTS OF MONEY AND CAPITAL MARKETS

Money market instruments are debt instruments with original maturities of less than 1 year. Capital market instruments have original maturities of 1 year or longer. Examples include long-term instruments such as bonds and mortgages. Common stocks (equities) have potentially unlimited maturities and are classified as capital market instruments.

## Money Market Instruments

The chief instruments traded in the money market are commercial paper, negotiable certificates of deposit, U.S. Treasury bills, repurchase agreements, Eurodollars, federal funds, and banker's acceptances. Table 3-2 gives the dollar amount of these money market instruments outstanding at the end of 2003 and the average annual growth rate of the outstanding amount from 1980 to 2003.

**commercial paper**
short-term promissory notes issued by major corporations to attract funds for day-to-day business needs

**Commercial Paper.** **Commercial paper** consists of short-term promissory notes (IOUs) issued by major corporations to attract funds for day-to-day business needs. Nonfinancial corporations such as Ford Motor, finance companies such as General Motors Acceptance, public utilities such as Duke Power, and bank holding companies such as Citigroup are the main issuers of commercial paper. Only well-known firms with impeccable credit ratings—about 1,200 of the nation's two million business firms—can borrow in this market. The magnitude of the typical new issue is more than $100 million. Commercial paper is sold directly or through dealers to a wide range of buyers investing large amounts of cash for brief periods. Primary buyers include various financial institutions and nonfinancial corporations looking for an attractive, low-risk outlet for surplus funds. The instruments

**Table 3-2** Principal Money Market Instruments

| Type of Instrument | Amount Outstanding as of December 31, 2003 ($ Billion) | Average Annual Growth Rate (Percent) 1980-2003 |
|---|---|---|
| Commercial paper | 1,289 | 12.1 |
| Negotiable certificates of deposit | 1,233 | 6.2 |
| U.S. Treasury bills | 929 | 6.7 |
| Repurchase agreements | 356 | 9.4 |
| Eurodollars | 212 | 6.7 |
| Federal funds | 146 | 10.6 |
| Banker's acceptances | 25 | −10.7 |

*Sources: Federal Reserve System,* Flow of Funds Accounts, *release Z.1 at* http://www.federalreserve.gov/releases/Z1, *Economic Report of the President, and U.S. Treasury Bulletin*

are low in default risk and provide a significantly higher rate of return than ultra-safe Treasury bills.

Commercial paper is a very old money market instrument in England and Europe. It has become increasingly popular in the United States in recent decades. Major corporations issue commercial paper as an alternative to borrowing from banks. Large companies have increasingly turned to the commercial paper market as a source of funds in the past couple of decades. In 2004, the volume of commercial paper outstanding was more than $1,200 billion ($1.2 trillion), growing at a phenomenal rate of more than 12 percent per year over the past quarter century.

**certificate of deposit (CD)**
a form of deposit that stipulates that the bearer will receive annual interest payments of a specified amount plus a lump sum equal to the original principal at maturity

**Negotiable Certificates of Deposit.** A **certificate of deposit (CD)** is a receipt issued by a bank for deposit of funds. The receipt stipulates that the bearer will receive annual interest payments of a specified amount plus a lump sum equal to the original principal at maturity. CDs initially were relatively illiquid and unattractive because banks assess a significant penalty to redeem CDs prior to maturity. In the early 1960s, a secondary market for trade of large CDs in denominations of $100,000 and above was established. The CDs are traded prior to maturity through a network of dealers. Because the CDs are "negotiable," that is, tradable in secondary markets prior to maturity, they are **negotiable CDs.**

**negotiable CDs**
large CDs that can be traded through a network of dealers prior to maturity

Large banks often issue negotiable CDs to attract additional funds for loan expansion. The volume of negotiable CDs outstanding is volatile, expanding significantly when credit demands escalate and/or the Federal Reserve implements restrictive policies. Negotiable CDs are purchased by major lenders needing temporary investment outlets for large amounts of cash, typically $1 million or more. The primary buyers of negotiable CDs are corporations, money market mutual funds, government institutions, charitable organizations, and foreign buyers.

**Treasury bills**
short-term IOUs issued by U.S. government, traded at a discount from face value in a well-developed secondary market

**U.S. Treasury Bills.** **Treasury bills** are a form of short-term government debt. Treasury bills are highly popular because of their safety and liquidity. They constitute approximately 25 percent of the marketable federal debt of the United States. The U.S. Treasury issues new Treasury bills in 3-month, 6-month, and 12-month maturities at weekly sealed bid auctions. The proceeds refinance maturing issues and finance ongoing budget deficits. The principal bidders are government security dealers, banks, money market mutual funds, other corporations, and individuals willing to invest $10,000 or more. More than $40 billion worth of maturing Treasury bills are "rolled over" or refinanced in the average week. Once issued, Treasury bills are traded through a network of dealers in an active and highly efficient secondary market. The volume of daily trading activity in this market is enormous, approximately ten times that of the New York Stock Exchange. Thus, U.S. Treasury bills are considered the most liquid debt instrument in the world.

**repurchase agreement**
short-term loan from a corporation or other large entity with temporarily idle funds to a commercial bank, securities dealer, or other financial institution

**Repurchase Agreements.** A **repurchase agreement,** also known as a *repo* or *RP,* is a short-term loan (often overnight) from a corporation or other large entity with temporarily idle funds to a commercial bank, securities dealer, or other financial institution. Most commonly, a large corporation with $100 million or more that will not be needed for a few days lends the money to a major bank by "buying" a large block of government securities from the bank.[1] The bank agrees to "repurchase" the securities on the date the corporation needs the funds (typically in 1 to 14 days), at a price sufficiently above the initial price. The bank provides to the corporation a rate of return

[1] The term *repurchase agreement* is a misnomer in that ownership of the securities never actually changes hands. The bank retains ownership of the securities, merely using them as collateral for the loan.

about 0.25 percentage point below the current federal funds rate. Banks, security dealers, and others borrowing in this market find it a useful source of funds. The RP market has grown dramatically in the past 25 years because of almost universal aggressive cash management by large corporations, state and local governments, and other large organizations. Total RPs outstanding exceeded $350 billion in 2004.

**Eurodollars.** The term **Eurodollar** refers to deposits (generally time deposits) in foreign banks or U.S. bank branches in foreign countries (not necessarily in Europe), in denominations of U.S. dollars rather than local currencies such as euros or Swiss francs. Eurodollars developed after World War II, when the U.S. dollar became widely accepted in international markets. To the extent that U.S. dollars are accepted abroad, merchants and others avoid costly foreign exchange transactions by maintaining Eurodollar deposits for use in foreign transactions. Eurodollars are considered a money market instrument because U.S. banks needing funds can borrow Eurodollars from foreign banks or branches of U.S. banks in foreign cities. U.S. firms seeking investment outlets can lend in this market when rates payable on Eurodollars are attractive. Banks turned to the Eurodollar market for funds when they could not obtain funds through traditional channels. This phenomenon was triggered by statutory interest rate ceilings on various time deposits (including CDs) in the United States, which were later abolished. More than $200 billion in Eurodollar funds were borrowed abroad in 2004.

**Eurodollar**
deposits in foreign banks or U.S. bank branches in foreign countries, in denominations of U.S. dollars rather than local currencies

**Federal Funds.** **Federal funds** are unsecured loans (usually overnight) in the form of deposits at the Federal Reserve Banks, made between depository institutions. Regulations require banks and thrift institutions to maintain a certain portion of their deposit liabilities in the form of **reserves**—cash or deposits at a Federal Reserve Bank. Depository institutions failing to meet the requirements are penalized. Banks keeping excessive funds on deposit at the Federal Reserve penalize their profits because deposits at the Fed do not earn interest.

A very active market in federal funds developed after World War II. Typically, relatively large banks borrow deposit balances at the Federal Reserve from other banks. Banks with reserves insufficient to meet the Federal Reserve's requirements borrow or "buy" federal funds; banks with reserves more than sufficient to meet requirements lend or "sell" federal funds. Federal funds are traded through the Fed's wire system, and the minimum unit is $1 million. The interest rate for the transaction—the **federal funds rate**—is a sensitive and widely publicized money market rate. The Federal Reserve directly controls the federal funds rate in conducting monetary policy.

**federal funds**
unsecured loans, in the form of deposits at the Federal Reserve Banks, made between depository institutions

**reserves**
cash on hand and deposits at the Federal Reserve maintained by depository institutions

**federal funds rate**
rate of interest prevailing on overnight loans between banks of deposits at the Federal Reserve

**Banker's Acceptances.** Banker's acceptances are a form of credit used for centuries in other countries and for more than 90 years in the United States. A **banker's acceptance** is a bank draft (a check) generally written by a business firm. It is payable at a specific future date and is stamped "accepted" by a major bank. Banker's acceptances are sometimes used by little-known U.S. firms desiring to import foreign products for sale in the United States. A company not well known to foreign exporters draws a bank draft that is marked "accepted" by a well-known U.S. bank, essentially substituting the bank's higher credit rating for its own. The bank charges the firm a modest fee for this service. The bank requires the firm to deposit the funds stipulated on the draft no later than the instrument's maturity date. The U.S. importer sends the check (banker's acceptance) to the foreign company, providing assurance of payment on the instrument's maturity date.

A banker's acceptance stamped "accepted" by a reputable bank is virtually risk free and therefore highly marketable. A foreign exporter may sell a banker's ac-

**banker's acceptance**
check, generally written by a business firm, payable at a specific future date and stamped "accepted" by a major bank

ceptance immediately upon its receipt rather than waiting until the maturity date for payment. Because these instruments constitute an agreement to pay a specified amount *in the future,* banker's acceptances are sold at a discount from face value, like U.S. Treasury bills. Banker's acceptances are traded through dealers in a secondary market. Some prospective buyers regard banker's acceptances as substitutes for commercial paper and U.S. Treasury bills.

## Capital Market Instruments

The *capital market* derives its name from the fact that funds obtained for financing long-term capital expenditures are typically obtained through this market. Thus, the *capital market* involves long-term debt and equity instruments. The most important capital market instruments include corporate stocks (equities) and bonds, mortgages, U.S. Treasury bonds and notes, U.S. government agency securities, and state and local government bonds. Table 3-3 indicates the various capital market instruments, the amount of each instrument outstanding at the end of 2003 and the average annual growth rate of each instrument from 1980 to 2003.

**common stocks**
ownership claims against a firm's real capital assets; entitles owner to share in profits of the firm

**Common Stocks.** **Common stocks** are ownership claims against a firm's real capital assets. Unlike debt instruments, stocks have no maturity date. Common stocks are outstanding for as long as the corporation is in business. Shares of stock are traded by brokers in organized stock exchanges and OTC markets. Stock of any corporation with more than 300 stockholders can be traded OTC. Large corporations meeting certain standards of size and stability can apply to the Securities and Exchange Commission for listing on an organized stock exchange, such as the New York Stock Exchange or the American Stock Exchange.

The preponderant portion of stock transactions is made in secondary markets. The annual magnitude of new stock issues typically is considerably less than 1 percent of the existing total value of stock outstanding, varying considerably with eco-

**Table 3-3** Principal Capital Market Instruments

| Type of Instrument | Amount Outstanding as of December 31, 2003 ($ Billion) | Average Annual Growth Rate (Percent) 1980-2003 |
|---|---|---|
| Corporate equities | 15,473 | 12.4 |
| Residential mortgages | 7,685 | 8.9 |
| Corporate bonds | 3,582 | 9.8 |
| U.S. Treasury bonds and notes | 2,646 | 8.3 |
| State and local government bonds | 1,899 | 8.5 |
| Commercial and farm mortgages | 1,588 | 6.9 |

*Sources: Federal Reserve System,* Flow of Funds Accounts, *release Z.1 at* http://www.federalreserve.gov/releases/Z1, *U.S. Treasury Bulletin, and Economic Report of the President*

nomic and financial conditions. When stock prices are depressed, as in 2001 to 2002, firms move away from issuing new stock; in fact, they may buy back existing shares. When stock prices are high, firms issue new shares. The increasing valuation of real capital assets, reflected by rising share prices, induces firms to expand investment expenditures. For this reason, a healthy stock market is important for capital formation and economic growth processes.

**corporate bonds** long-term debt claims against a corporation's assets, claims that may or may not be secured by mortgages and other assets

**Corporate Bonds.** **Corporate bonds** are debt claims against a corporation's assets. The claims may or may not be secured by mortgages and other assets. Each year, new corporate bond issues substantially exceed new stock issues even though the total value of corporate bonds outstanding is less than one fourth the value of stocks (Table 3-3). This puzzle is explained by the fact that bonds mature (stocks do not) and the fact that many bonds have *call features* permitting the issuer to recall (or buy back) the bond prior to maturity. Corporate stocks are *perpetuities*—they have no maturity date. Corporate bonds generally have original maturities of 10 to 30 years and are traded OTC in a market that is "thin" compared with the U.S. government securities market. Many corporate bonds have call features that benefit the issuing corporation. Some corporate bonds are convertible into a specified number of shares of common stock of the company. This feature "sweetens" the bond for potential buyers and allows the corporation to borrow at a lower interest rate. Buyers of corporate bonds—life insurance companies and private pension funds—primarily are institutions that do not require highly liquid assets but need stable and predictable flows of income.

**municipal bonds** long-term debt instrument representing a claim on a city or county

**Municipal Bonds.** Like corporations, state and local governments and other political subdivisions must finance capital investment projects such as schools, bridges, airports, and subways. Roughly two thirds of these capital expenditures are financed by **municipal bonds.** In 2004, some $1,700 billion ($1.7 trillion) of municipal bonds were outstanding, including more than one million different bonds issued by 90,000 political subdivisions in the United States. New issues of municipal bonds are purchased by investment bankers and then resold to commercial banks, property and casualty insurance firms, and high-income individuals. The municipal bond market is thin because of the limited number of participants. The number of dealers handling a given issue is limited, and many dealers hold small inventories.

Years ago, Congress ruled that interest income earned from municipal bonds is not taxable by the Internal Revenue Service. As a result of the tax-free interest status, yields on municipal bonds are slightly lower than yields on U.S. government bonds and considerably lower than yields on corporate bonds. Municipal bond purchase is advantageous only for investors in high tax brackets. Commercial banks, typically in the 34 percent corporate income tax bracket, are important buyers and today own more than half of the municipal bonds outstanding.

**U.S. Government Notes and Bonds.** U.S. Treasury notes and bonds are popular instruments because of the efficient, well-organized market in which they are traded and because of their absence of default risk. Major purchasers include individuals, life insurance companies, private pension funds, government trust funds, and state and local government retirement funds. We discuss these instruments in depth later in this chapter.

**U.S. Government Agency Bonds.** These long-term bonds are issued by government agencies such as the Federal Housing Administration (to provide subsidized housing for low-income families) and the Farm Credit System Financial

Assistance Corporation (to provide loans to financially impaired farmers). The bonds typically are guaranteed by the U.S. government. U.S. government agency bonds are reasonably close substitutes for U.S. government bonds and are purchased by many of the same entities that buy ordinary government bonds.

**mortgage**
long-term loan financing the purchase of real property, secured by a lien on that property

**Mortgages.** A **mortgage** is a long-term loan financing the purchase of real property, secured by a lien on that property. Traditionally, mortgages carry interest rates that are fixed over the life of the mortgage. Variable rate mortgages have been available for more than 25 years. Since the 1930s, mortgage payments have been *amortized*—part of each regular payment pays the interest and part repays the principal. At maturity the debt is extinguished, and the property is owned free and clear. As indicated in Table 3-3, the mortgage market is the largest debt market in the U.S. capital market. Today, more than $7,000 billion ($7 trillion) in residential mortgages is outstanding. Other types of mortgages finance business property and farms. Savings and loan associations (S&Ls), mutual savings banks, and commercial banks are the chief mortgage lenders (issuers of mortgages).

Americans believe that home ownership is a high social priority. To subsidize home buyers, the federal government became heavily involved in the mortgage market after World War II. Three government agencies improve the mortgage market, assisting the market when credit is tight and interest rates are high. The Federal National Mortgage Association (FNMA, or "Fannie Mae"), the Government National Mortgage Association (GNMA, or "Ginnie Mae"), and the Federal Home Loan Mortgage Company (FHLMC, or "Freddie Mac") issue bonds and use the proceeds to provide funds to the mortgage market.

**mortgage-backed security**
financial instrument that splits the financing and servicing of mortgages; banks package groups of mortgages, which are sold in security form to large investors

**Mortgage-Backed Securities.** Individual mortgages have different risks, maturities, and interest rate. Thus, they not are not well adapted for trade on secondary markets. Prior to the 1980s, individual S&Ls, mutual savings banks, and commercial banks that issued mortgages typically held them until maturity. In those days, more than 80 percent of the mortgages outstanding were owned by these institutions. A new instrument introduced and guaranteed by Ginnie Mae, known as the **mortgage-backed security,** now dominates the residential mortgage market. This instrument permits splitting the financing and servicing of mortgages. A commercial bank or S&L packages a group of mortgages into a standard $5 million or $10 million package and sells it to a large investor, typically a pension fund or life insurance company. The bank or S&L collects the monthly mortgage payments from individual households and passes them on to the pension fund or life insurance company. Ginnie Mae guarantees these "passthrough" payments to the buyer of the mortgage-backed security, making the security almost free of default risk. Today, more than 80 percent of mortgages made by banks and S&Ls are packaged and sold as mortgage-backed securities. This revolutionary development has improved the efficiency of the mortgage market and contributed to lower mortgage rates for homeowners.

## U.S. GOVERNMENT SECURITIES MARKET

The U.S. government securities market warrants special attention because of its importance to commercial banking and Federal Reserve policy. The Federal Reserve implements monetary policy predominantly by purchasing and selling U.S. government securities through a network of government securities dealers. Other active participants in this market include both financial and nonfinancial firms, pension and retirement funds, individuals, and foreigners. The volume of transactions conducted in the U.S. government securities market is enormous, typically exceeding $100 billion per day.

## Kinds of U.S. Government Securities

Several types of U.S. government securities, both marketable and nonmarketable, are outstanding. Table 3-4 shows the composition of the U.S. government debt at the end of 2003.

Slightly more than half of the gross public debt (approximately $7,000 billion [$7 trillion] in early 2004 and rising rapidly) is marketable and actively traded. Prices and transactions are quoted daily in the major newspapers. About 40 government securities dealers, associated with New York commercial or investment banks, hold inventories and stand ready to buy or sell these securities. Government securities dealers do not charge a commission or brokerage fee for their service. They earn income by maintaining a slightly higher price received ("asked" price) than price paid ("bid" price). Due to the enormous volume of government securities transacted daily, dealers can earn a high income based on a remarkably small spread between their bid and asked prices.

Dealers buy and sell four types of marketable U.S. government securities: Treasury bills, Treasury notes, Treasury bonds, and inflation-indexed bonds and notes known as *treasury inflation-protected securities (TIPS)*. Treasury bills are short-term debt instruments with original maturities of 3 months to 1 year. **Treasury notes** have original maturities of 1 to 10 years. **Treasury bonds** have original maturities of 10 to 40 years. As Table 3-4 shows, about 80 percent of marketable U.S. government debt is in the form of Treasury bills and notes. The U.S. Treasury practices federal *debt management,* that is, it determines the maturity structure of newly issued government debt. Because large amounts of federal debt mature each month and the federal government currently is running a budget deficit, the U.S. Treasury issues new debt each week. We now discuss several types of marketable and nonmarketable U.S. government securities.

**Treasury notes**
IOUs issued by the U.S. government that have an original maturity of 1 to 10 years

**Treasury bonds**
IOUs issued by the U.S. government that have original maturity of 10 to 40 years

**Table 3-4 U.S. Government Debt Outstanding by Type of Security December 31, 2003**

| Type of Security | Amount of Debt ($ Billion) |
|---|---|
| Marketable | 3,575 |
| Treasury bills | 929 |
| Treasury notes | 1,906 |
| Treasury bonds | 564 |
| Inflation-indexed bonds and notes | 176 |
| Nonmarketable | 3,423 |
| Government account series* | 3,007 |
| Savings bonds and notes | 204 |
| Other | 212 |
| **Total public debt** | **$6,998** |

*Held only by U.S. government agencies and trust funds.
*Source: Economic Report of the President, February 2004, Table B-87*

## **Exhibit 3-2** Who Holds the National Debt?

When the U.S. government runs a budget deficit, it issues new Treasury bills, notes, and bonds. The stock of government debt outstanding—the national debt—increases. In 2004, the rapidly expanding U.S. national debt moved above the $7 trillion ($7,000 billion) mark. Who owns all these bills, notes, and bonds? Ownership of U.S. government debt is divided among government, private sector, and foreign entities. Numerous U.S. government trust funds are legally bound to invest only in U.S. government securities. The largest is the Federal Old-Age and Survivors Insurance Trust Fund (Social Security), which alone owns more than 10 percent of the national debt. Altogether, about 20 such government funds hold more than 40 percent of the debt (see accompanying figure). The Federal Reserve's large portfolio of government securities (more than $700 billion in 2004), accumulated over the years to provide for an expanding U.S. money supply, constitutes another 10 percent of the debt.

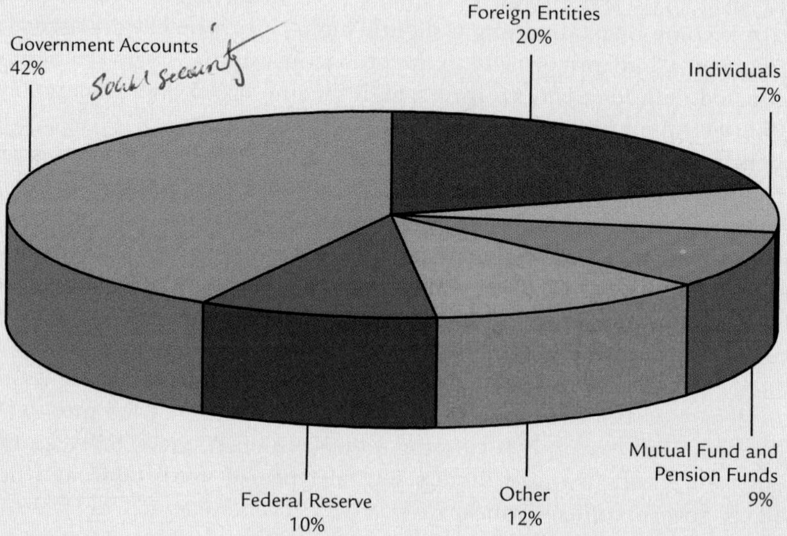


U.S. individuals own about 7 percent of the debt *directly*, split between U.S. savings bonds and other government securities. U.S. individuals account for a considerably larger share of the debt *indirectly*, holding claims issued by money market mutual funds, pension funds, and other financial intermediaries that invest in government securities. Pension funds and mutual funds hold a significant portion. Foreign entities (central banks, commercial banks) today own approximately 20 percent of the debt, up sharply from only 3 percent in the 1950s and about 14 percent in 1990.

Proceeds from a federal budget *surplus* are used to retire a portion of the national debt. Toward the end of the twentieth century, a booming U.S. economy stimulated federal tax revenues and produced budget surpluses of more than $100 billion per year in 1999 and 2000. Economists at the Federal Reserve and elsewhere worried that the entire national debt would be paid off within a few decades, prompting several questions. What will conservative bond buyers invest in if risk-free government securities no longer exist? How will the Fed conduct monetary policy in the absence of an active Treasury securities market? Not to worry! In 2001, a major tax cut, the events of September 11 and its aftermath, and a national recession joined forces to bring back large deficits. In your lifetime, it is unlikely you will see the national debt as small as it is today.

**Treasury Bills.** These popular instruments are issued in 91-day (13-week), 182-day (26 weeks), and 1-year maturities. The large number of outstanding Treasure bills implies a correspondingly large runoff (number of bills maturing) each month. The U.S. Treasury auctions off large quantities of newly issued Treasury bills each week. The Treasury bills are sold on a competitive basis via sealed bids. Once issued, Treasury bills are traded in a highly competitive secondary market. The market in Treasury bills maturing within 6 months is quoted daily in *The Wall Street Journal* and many other major newspapers. Table 3-5 shows the spectrum of Treasury bills outstanding as of August 4, 2004. The securities mature on the dates indicated, when the purchaser (lender) receives the specified principal or face value, for example, $1,000.

On August 4, 2004, a prospective investor could choose from Treasury bills maturing each week from August 12, 2004, through February 3, 2005. Buyers can tailor their purchases of Treasury bills so that the securities reach maturity when the proceeds are needed to meet planned expenditures, an attractive feature of the Treasury bills market.

Treasury bills are conventionally quoted in annual rates of return—discount rates and yields—rather than prices. This form of quotation is convenient for thousands of market participants who quickly compare the returns on Treasury bills with returns on alternative investments. Consider the first security listed in Table 3-5: the Treasury bill maturing in 7 days (August 12, 2004), quoted as "bid" 1.16 percent, "asked" 1.15 percent, and "asked yield" 1.17 percent. Treasury bills are sold at a discount from face value of $1,000. The return derives from the difference between the price paid and the $1,000 guaranteed at maturity. The relationship among the discount rate (r), the price (P), and the number of days to maturity is as follows:

$$\text{(3-1)} \quad r = \frac{1{,}000 - P}{1{,}000} \times \frac{360}{\textit{days to maturity}}$$

**Table 3-5** Market for U.S. Treasury Bills as of August 4, 2004

**Treasury Bills**

| MATURITY | DAYS TO MAT | BID | ASKED | CHG | ASK YLD |
|---|---|---|---|---|---|
| Aug 12 04 | 7 | 1.16 | 1.15 | ... | 1.17 |
| Aug 19 04 | 14 | 1.23 | 1.22 | -0.01 | 1.24 |
| Aug 26 04 | 21 | 1.25 | 1.24 | ... | 1.26 |
| Sep 02 04 | 28 | 1.32 | 1.31 | 0.02 | 1.33 |
| Sep 09 04 | 35 | 1.27 | 1.26 | -0.01 | 1.28 |
| Sep 16 04 | 42 | 1.29 | 1.28 | -0.01 | 1.30 |
| Sep 23 04 | 49 | 1.32 | 1.31 | -0.03 | 1.33 |
| Sep 30 04 | 56 | 1.33 | 1.32 | -0.02 | 1.34 |
| Oct 07 04 | 63 | 1.35 | 1.34 | ... | 1.36 |
| Oct 14 04 | 70 | 1.34 | 1.33 | -0.02 | 1.35 |
| Oct 21 04 | 77 | 1.40 | 1.39 | -0.01 | 1.41 |
| Oct 28 04 | 84 | 1.41 | 1.40 | -0.01 | 1.42 |
| **Nov 04 04** | **91** | **1.46** | **1.45** | ... | **1.48** |
| Nov 12 04 | 99 | 1.46 | 1.45 | -0.01 | 1.48 |
| Nov 18 04 | 105 | 1.48 | 1.47 | ... | 1.50 |
| Nov 26 04 | 113 | 1.50 | 1.49 | ... | 1.52 |
| Dec 02 04 | 119 | 1.51 | 1.50 | ... | 1.53 |
| Dec 09 04 | 126 | 1.53 | 1.52 | 0.01 | 1.55 |
| Dec 16 04 | 133 | 1.54 | 1.53 | 0.01 | 1.56 |
| Dec 23 04 | 140 | 1.56 | 1.55 | -0.01 | 1.58 |
| Dec 30 04 | 147 | 1.36 | 1.35 | -0.19 | 1.38 |
| Jan 06 05 | 154 | 1.43 | 1.42 | -0.18 | 1.45 |
| Jan 13 05 | 161 | 1.65 | 1.64 | ... | 1.68 |
| Jan 20 05 | 168 | 1.68 | 1.67 | ... | 1.71 |
| Jan 27 05 | 175 | 1.70 | 1.69 | ... | 1.73 |
| **Feb 03 05** | **182** | **1.72** | **1.71** | ... | **1.75** |

*Source:* The Wall Street Journal, *August 5, 2004*

In this formula, the annual rate of return, known as the *discount rate (r)*, equals the gain on the asset relative to its face value of $1,000, that is, (1,000 – P)/1,000 multiplied by a factor that crudely *annualizes* the gain (360/days to maturity). If a U.S. Treasury bill maturing in 60 days sells for $995, its discount rate is $5/$1,000 × 360/60, or 3 percent.[2]

We can compute the discount rate using Equation (3-1), given the price of the Treasury bill and days to maturity. Treasury bills are conventionally quoted in discount rates rather than prices. We can rearrange Equation (3-1) to calculate the price of a Treasury bill as follows:

$$P = \$1000 - \frac{\$1000\ (r)\ (\text{days to maturity})}{360} \tag{3-2}$$

Solving for the asked price of the first Treasury bill quoted in Table 3-5 at an asked discount rate of 1.15 percent: P = $1,000 – [1,000 (0.0115) 7]/360 = $999.776.

We can easily check the validity of our calculation by substituting our answer of $999.776 back into Equation (3-1) and ascertaining whether we obtain the quoted rate of 1.15 percent. Check this out!

To get an idea about the transactions costs in U.S. Treasury bills, compute the dealer's *bid* price using the *bid* discount rate quoted on the same security (1.16 percent). The price is $999.774. On a $1,000 transaction, the spread between the dealer's bid and asked price is only about a fifth of a penny! Transactions costs in U.S. Treasury bills are virtually nil, a key factor contributing to their high liquidity and popularity.[3] Major players conducting multimillion dollar transactions in the Treasury bill market, such as banks and money market mutual funds, enjoy phenomenally low transactions costs.

**YOUR TURN**

**a.** A Treasury bill with 36 days to maturity is priced at $998. Calculate its discount rate.

**b.** A Treasury bill with 80 days to maturity is quoted at a discount rate of 0.031 or 3.1 percent. Calculate its price.

One more demonstration confirms the great liquidity and popularity of Treasury bills. Based on the data in Table 3-5, a graph relating the price of Treasury bills to days remaining to maturity is illustrated in Figure 3-2.

The time to maturity, measured in days, is shown on the horizontal axis. The market price, computed from the asked discount rates of selected issues quoted in Table 3-5, is shown on the vertical axis. Note that at any point in time (in this case, August 4, 2004), the market price of a Treasury bill is closely (and inversely) related to the time to maturity. The nearer the maturity date, the higher the

[2] The alert reader sees two peculiarities in this calculation and Equation (3-1). First, contrary to conventions of financial terminology, we know there are 365 days in 1 year. Second, it seems more useful to compute the rate of return based on P, the purchase price of the Treasury bill, rather than its face value of $1,000. Incorporating these considerations, the yield on a Treasury bill is Y = [(1,000 – P)/P] × 365/days to maturity. The yield column in Table 3-5 is calculated using this formula. The quoted yield of 1.17 percent on the August 12 Treasury bill applies this formula, using the asked price of the bill.

[3] The bid asked price spread increases as the maturity date lengthens, primarily because the market is thinner, that is, the trading volume is lower. For example, the bid and asked prices on the January 13, 2005, maturity Treasury bill quoted in Table 3-5 are $992.621 and $992.666. In this case, the spread is 4 cents on the $1,000 transaction. Check the spread on the February 3, 2005, issue.

**Figure 3-2** Treasury Bill Price Versus Time to Maturity August 4, 2004

Treasury bills with shorter times to maturity sell at higher prices. Once issued, a Treasury bill gradually appreciates in price until it reaches face value ($1,000) at maturity.

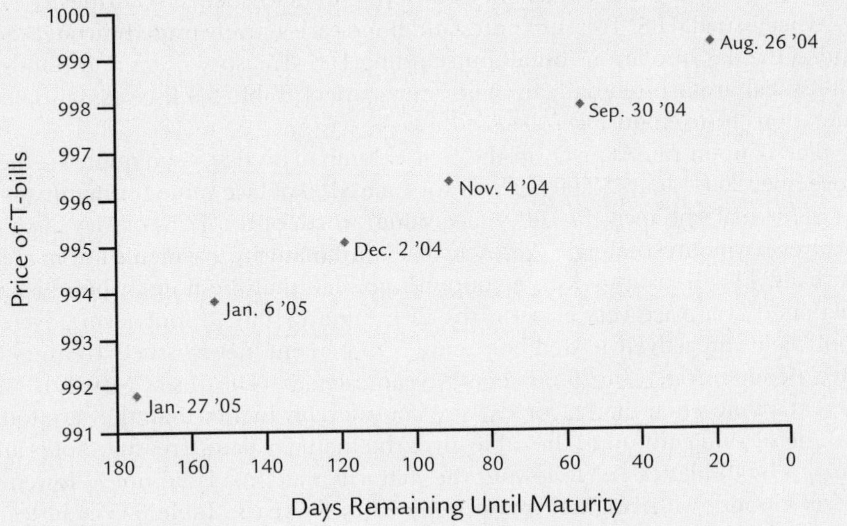

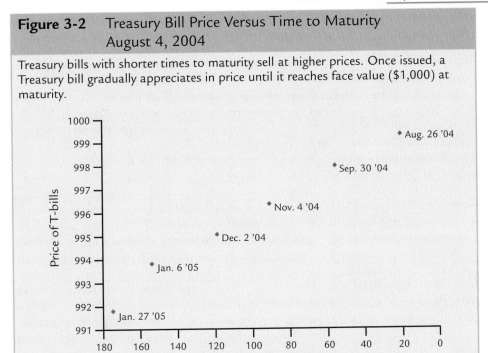

*Source: Calculated from data in Table 3-5*

price. To provide a given yield, a Treasury bill *must continually rise in price* as the maturity date approaches. Otherwise, the yield rises continually as the maturity date approaches.[4]

Because the price of any 91-day or 182-day U.S. Treasury bill almost inevitably rises each week as the Treasury bill approaches maturity, the risks to owners of Treasury bills are about as close to zero as possible. The default risk is nil because the U.S. government can tax, borrow, or print money to pay its creditors. Market risk is extremely low due to the mechanism illustrated in Figure 3-2. If you purchase a newly issued 91-day Treasury bill and are forced to sell it 30 days later, odds are extremely good that the Treasury bill appreciated in price. Only a phenomenal upsurge in market interest rates in the 30 days following its purchase prevents an appreciation in price. This virtual absence of risk, together with the extremely low transactions costs, explains the popularity of Treasury bills as an investment outlet for commercial banks, money market mutual funds, and corporations with surplus funds to invest for short periods. Individuals can purchase Treasury bills in minimum denominations of $10,000 through their district Federal Reserve Bank.

**Treasury Notes and Bonds.** Treasury notes have original maturities of 1 to 10 years; bonds are longer-term instruments. Notes and bonds are issued through three methods: auction, exchange, and subscription. Some notes and bond are *auctioned off* in the same way as Treasury bills. In an *exchange,* the Treasury offers own-

[4] Suppose a U.S. Treasury bill with 60 days to maturity is priced at $995. Using the formula in Footnote 2, the yield is about 3 percent: $5/$995 × 365/60. Suppose the same Treasury bill remains priced at $995 after 30 days. Its yield then is about 6 percent: $5/$995 × 365/30. Market forces of supply and demand prevent this occurrence by bidding the price up toward $997.50.

ers of existing maturing notes and bonds a choice of several new issues. In a *subscription,* the public is notified of the *coupon rate* (annual yield based on its face value) and other pertinent features of a new issue. By a specified date, investors must subscribe for their desired amounts, which are sold to them at face value. If the amount the public subscribes for exceeds the amount offered by the Treasury, as is commonly the case, each subscriber is allocated a pro rata share of the amount requested. Commercial banks often subscribe to newly issued securities.

Once issued, U.S. Treasury notes and bonds are actively traded through dealers. End-of-the-day quotations on all outstanding U.S. Treasury notes and bonds (over 200 issues) are printed daily in major newspapers. Table 3-6 lists a small sample of quotations from August 4, 2004.

The coupon rate is given in the first column. The first issue quoted—the 2s of November 2004—pays $2.00 per year for each $100 of face value (or maturity value). An individual who owns $10,000 (face value) worth of the 7.25s of May 2016 bonds receives payments totaling $725 each year until maturity. Payments are made semiannually. The Treasury selects a coupon rate such that the note or bond is initially auctioned at a price very close to the face value ($100). If long-term government bond yields on actively traded bonds are 5.25 percent, newly issued Treasury bonds have a coupon rate of 5.25 percent. We can infer that the 10s of May 2010 were issued at a time when market yields were considerably higher than they are today.

The second column of the table gives the maturity date. Treasury notes are designated by the letter "n" following the maturity date. An issue not followed by an "n" is a bond, with original maturity of 10 to 40 years. Table 3-6 includes three Treasury notes and three Treasury bonds. The third and fourth columns list the dealers' bid and asked prices. In the bond market convention, the figures to the right of the colon refer to 32nds rather than 100ths. The 106:04 bid price for the 10s of May 2010 indicates a price of $106 4/32, or $106.12 per $100 face amount. Column 5 indicates the change in bid price relative to the previous day's closing bid price, measured in 32nds of a dollar. On August 4, 2004, three securities decreased in price and three remained unchanged.

Note that all six securities in Table 3-5 are quoted at prices above the face value payable at maturity ($100). All of these bonds sell at a *premium* because

**Table 3-6 Selected U.S. Treasury Notes and Bonds August 4, 2004**

| Coupon Rate | Maturity Date (Month, Year) | Bid* | Asked* | Bid Change** | Percent Yield |
|---|---|---|---|---|---|
| 2.00 | November 2004n*** | 100:04 | 100:05 | . . . | 1.45% |
| 7.50 | February 2005n | 103:00 | 103:00 | −1 | 1.73 |
| 4.75 | November 2008n | 105:02 | 105:03 | . . . | 3.46 |
| 10.00 | May 2010 | 106:04 | 106:05 | −2 | 1.95 |
| 7.25 | May 2016 | 122:24 | 122:25 | . . . | 4.71 |
| 5.375 | February 2031 | 103:00 | 103:00 | −1 | 5.17 |

*Figures immediately following a colon represent 32nds.
**Change in bid price from previous day's closing price, in 32nds.
***An "n" following the maturity date indicates the issue is a note. Other issues are bonds.
*Source:* The Wall Street Journal, *August 5, 2004*

market yields on the day the prices were quoted (August 4, 2004) were very close to their lowest levels in more than 30 years. The coupon rate, set at the date when each of the bonds was issued, exceeded competitive yields prevailing in the market in August 2004. Market forces had bid up the prices of the bonds above face value. Buyers were willing to pay (and sellers insisted on receiving) more than the face value for the right to receive these attractive annual coupon payments, which were established in times of significantly higher market yields. If market yields at any point are *higher* than the yields when a security was issued, the market dictates a price *below* the $100 face value, and the bond sells at a *discount* from face value.

Now we discuss yields on U.S. Treasury notes and bonds. The two relevant yield concepts mentioned earlier in this chapter—current yield and yield to maturity—apply to all types of notes and bonds: government, corporate, and municipal. The *current yield* is the annual payment (coupon) divided by the price. Stated algebraically, the current yield is as follows:

$$(3\text{-}3) \qquad Y_c = \frac{R}{P}$$

where $Y_c$ is the current yield, R is the annual coupon payment in dollars, and P is the market price.

Using the 5.375s of February 2031 in Table 3-6 and the "asked" quotation gives a current yield of $5.375/$103.00, or 5.22 percent. Because the market price is above face value ($100), the current yield of 5.22 percent is below the coupon rate of 5.375 percent. The current yield may be relevant to an individual purchasing a long-term security for annual income only. This individual may not be concerned about a potential capital gain or loss to be realized at a distant maturity date. Because the current yield does not consider the gain or loss that will accrue at maturity, it is a poor measure of the average annual return earned over the years if the note or bond is held to maturity.

To account for capital gain or loss realized at maturity, you must calculate the *yield to maturity*—the average yield over the life of the security if it is held to maturity. In some cases, appreciation or depreciation in the market price of a security constitutes a considerable portion of the average annual yield earned over the life of an asset. A very crude measure of the yield-to-maturity is expressed as follows:

$$(3\text{-}4) \qquad Y_m = \frac{R + (C/N)}{P}$$

where $Y_m$ is yield to maturity, R is the annual coupon payment in dollars, C is the capital gain (+) or loss (−) realized at maturity, N is the number of years remaining to maturity, and P is the current price of the security. The distinguishing consideration in this equation is the C/N component, which is the average annual capital gain (or loss, if C is negative) received over the remaining life of the security. Let us illustrate by returning to the 5.375s of February 2031. Given the current "asked" price of $103.00, a capital loss of $3.00 will be realized at maturity, about 27 years in the future. Using Equation (3-4), $Y_m = [5.375 + (-3.00/27)]/\$103.00 =$ 5.11 percent, a yield fairly close to that reported in the table.[5]

[5] The alert reader sees a shortcoming of our formula for yield to maturity. Because the gain or loss at maturity comes in the future, you should discount it to calculate the present value of the gain or loss. The present value of the loss of $3.09 to be incurred 27 years in the future is considerably less than $3.09. Hence, the 5.17 percent yield reported in the table exceeds our estimate of 5.11 percent.

The owner holding the security to maturity receives an average annual capital loss of about $0.11 (per $100 face value) in addition to the annual coupon of $5.375. The calculated yield to maturity is 5.11 percent per year. Because a capital loss will be incurred at maturity, the yield to maturity is less than the current yield of 5.22 percent. Any note or bond purchased *below* face value ($100) has a yield to maturity higher than its current yield because a capital gain will be realized at maturity.

**YOUR TURN**

The U.S. Treasury 5.5s of August 2029 are quoted at an asked price of 102:08. Assuming the bond matures exactly 24 years from today, compute both its current yield and its yield to maturity. Why is the yield to maturity lower than the current yield?

**Treasury Inflation-Protected Securities.** About 5 percent of the marketable U.S. government debt is in the form of securities designed to protect investors against inflation. The bonds, first offered by the U.S. Treasury in 1997, are called *TIPS,* an acronym for *treasury inflation-protected securities.* TIPS pay income each year based on the coupon rate; in addition, the principal is indexed to the nation's consumer price index (CPI). If you buy $10,000 worth of a newly issued TIPS bond with a 2.5 percent coupon rate and the CPI rises 4 percent in the first year, you receive the coupon payment of $250 and your principal automatically rises to $10,400. The unusually low inflation rate in recent years has limited the popularity of TIPS. (On TIPS, see "From the Financial Pages.")

## Nonmarketable Government Debt

As indicated in Table 3-4, a substantial portion of government debt is issued in forms other than marketable bills, notes, and bonds. The dominant portion of the nonmarketable debt is the government account series, of which more than $3,000 billion was outstanding in 2004. These securities are sold only to the approximately 20 government agencies and trust funds, such as the Federal Old Age and Survivors Insurance Trust Fund (Social Security Trust Fund), the Federal Employee Retirement Fund, and the Bank Insurance Fund, which are legally mandated to invest only in U.S. government securities.

U.S. savings bonds, designed for individual investors, are nonmarketable in that they cannot be traded to others through financial markets. However, they can be redeemed for cash prior to maturity through commercial banks and other financial institutions. The U.S. Treasury currently offers two types of savings bonds: series EE bonds and HH bonds. Series EE bonds are offered in denominations ranging from $25 to $10,000. They are *appreciation bonds,* like U.S. Treasury bills. For example, a $25 bond appreciates to $50 after several years. A series EE bond can be cashed in 6 months after it is issued, at a redeemable cash value based on the length of time the bond is held. Series HH bonds are *income bonds* sold in denominations of $500, $1,000, and $5,000, and $10,000. They pay interest only, that is, they do not appreciate. Interest income earned on Series EE and HH savings bonds is not subject to state or local income tax.

## FROM THE FINANCIAL PAGES

### Treasury Inflation-Protected Securities (TIPS)

U.S. Treasury bonds are considered the safest securities in the world. They are virtually devoid of default risk. In an important sense, however, traditional government bonds are a very risky investment. Suppose your grandparents purchased a newly issued 10-year Treasury bond in 1970, such as the 5s of 1980. The bond paid annual interest in the amount of $5 per $100 face value, a rate that matched the going yield of 5 percent per year. Unfortunately, the 1970s was a decade of unusually high inflation. The U.S. price level doubled between 1970 and 1980. If your grandparents purchased $10,000 of these bonds in 1970, the principal returned to them in 1980 was worth only $5,000 in purchasing power. In this case, your grandparents made a poor investment. Bonds can be a very bad investment in times of unexpectedly high inflation.

More than 2 decades ago, several nations including Australia, Israel, and the United Kingdom were struggling with inflation. Each nation issued government bonds to protect investors from inflation. The principal in the bonds was indexed to keep pace with the nation's price index. The U.S. trailed other countries in this action, finally issuing a 10-year indexed bond known as treasury inflation-protected securities (TIPS) in January 1997. Pertinent information on TIPS is quoted each day in *The Wall Street Journal.* The following table is taken from the August 5, 2004, issue.

**Inflation-Indexed Treasury Securities**

| RATE | MAT | BID/ASKED | CHG | *YLD | ACCR PRIN |
|---|---|---|---|---|---|
| 3.375 | 01/07 | 107-02/03 | −8 | 0.452 | 1194 |
| 3.625 | 01/08 | 109-16/17 | −4 | 0.812 | 1171 |
| 3.875 | 01/09 | 111-28/29 | −5 | 1.120 | 1153 |
| 4.250 | 01/10 | 115-01/02 | −5 | 1.379 | 1124 |
| 3.500 | 01/1 1 | 111-22/23 | −6 | 1.580 | 1087 |
| 3.375 | 01/12 | 111-14/15 | −7 | 1.726 | 1065 |
| 3.000 | 07/12 | 108-22/23 | −9 | 1.816 | 1052 |
| 1.875 | 07/13 | 99-19/20 | −7 | 1.921 | 1030 |
| 2.000 | 01/14 | 100-10/11 | −7 | 1.960 | 1022 |
| 2.000 | 07/14 | 100-01/02 | −6 | 1.993 | 1003 |
| 2.375 | 01/25 | 99-23/24 | ... | 2.390 | 1003 |
| 3.625 | 04/28 | 121-26/27 | ... | 2.409 | 1169 |
| 3.875 | 04/29 | 127-08/09 | −2 | 2.403 | 1151 |
| 3.375 | 04/32 | 121-02/03 | −3 | 2.363 | 1066 |

*Yield to maturity on accrued principal.

Note the second issue in the table: the 10-year bond issued in January 1998, now trading in the secondary market until it matures in January 2008. Guaranteed annual returns on this bond consist of two components: the *coupon rate* or the rate of interest paid on the original principal of $1000, shown in the left-hand column (3.625 percent), and *compensation* for the annual rate of increase in the consumer price index. The compensation accrues as principal appreciation each year. If you bought this bond in January 1998 at a face value of $1,000 and the consumer price index increased 2 percent in the following 12 months, your principal was marked up to $1,020. In addition, you received interest of $3.625 each year per $100 face value purchased, so your total return the first year was 5.625 percent. As of August 2004, the accrued principal on the bond reached $1,171 (right-hand column). This is an average increase of about 2.3 percent per year, the average annual rate of U.S. inflation from January 1998 to August 2004. Owning these bonds protects the investor from inflation but with one significant drawback. The increase in principal each year due to inflation is not paid out to the bondholder until maturity yet is treated by the IRS as current income for federal income tax purposes. Bondholders needing current income to meet ongoing expenses likely will not be interested in these bonds.

# SUMMARY

The key economic function of financial markets is to transfer funds from households and firms having surplus funds (savers/lenders) to households, firms, and units of government needing access to funds (spenders/borrowers). Some of the bonds and other instruments issued by spenders/borrowers are sold directly to savers/lenders. Others instruments are sold to financial intermediaries such as banks, life insurance companies, and money market mutual funds. The financial intermediaries, in turn, issue claims such as savings accounts, life insurance policies, and shares and sell them to the ultimate savers/lenders. The instruments issued by the spenders/borrowers are classified as money market instruments or capital market instruments. Money market instruments—commercial paper, negotiable CDs, and Treasury bills—have maturities of 1 year or less. Capital market instruments—share of stock, mortgages, and bonds—have maturities in excess of 1 year. The various financial market instruments can be evaluated based on criteria of risk, yield, and liquidity. Riskier securities typically provide a higher yield to compensate risk averse lenders for the additional risk. Instruments with greater liquidity typically provide a lower yield but less market risk than less liquid instruments. The U.S. government securities market is one of the most highly developed and efficient markets in the world. This market is of special interest in this course because the Federal Reserve conducts monetary policy predominantly by buying and selling U.S. government securities through a network of dealers.

## YOUR TURN ANSWERS

PAGE 60

**A.** The discount rate is $[(\$1{,}000 - \$998)/\$1{,}000] \times 360/36 = 0.02$, or 2 percent.

**B.** The price is $\$1{,}000 - [\$1{,}000(.031)(80)]/360 = \$993.11$.

PAGE 64

The current yield is \$5.50/\$102.25, or 5.38 percent. The yield to maturity is $[\$5.50 - \$2.25/24]/\$102.25 = 5.29$ percent. The yield to maturity is lower than the current yield because the principal will decline from its purchase price of \$102.25 to \$100 at maturity. A capital loss will accrue at maturity.

# KEY TERMS

brokers
dealers
financial intermediation
financial intermediary
default risk
market risk
yield
current yield
yield to maturity
debt instrument
equities
primary market
secondary market
investment bank
cash market
derivative market
financial futures
options

money market
capital market
commercial paper
certificate of deposit (CD)
negotiable CDs
Treasury bills
repurchase agreement
Eurodollar
federal funds
reserves
federal funds rate
banker's acceptance
common stocks
corporate bonds
municipal bonds
mortgage
mortgage-backed securities
Treasury notes
Treasury bonds

# STUDY QUESTIONS

1. Explain the distinction between transferring funds from lenders to borrowers via the direct credit market and through financial intermediaries via the indirect credit market.

2. Discuss the relationship between liquidity and risk in a financial instrument; between risk and yield; and between liquidity and yield.

3. Why is a corporate bond considered less liquid than a U.S. Treasury bill? Why are common stocks considered less liquid than long-term U.S. government bonds?

4. Explain the characteristics that make U.S. Treasury bills popular short-term investment outlets for banks and other corporations.

5. "If you buy a 91-day Treasury bill and sell it 30 days later, the odds are better than 100 to 1 that you will sell it for more than you paid for it." Do you agree or disagree? Explain.

6. What is the distinction between the current yield and the yield to maturity of a bond?

7. List and define five instruments of the U.S. money market.

8. What is the price of a Treasury bill that exhibits a discount rate of 4 percent if it matures in 360 days? 90 days? 30 days?

9. Calculate the price of a Treasury bill that matures in 30 days if it has an "asked" discount rate of 7 percent. How does your answer change if the "asked" discount rate is 9 percent? Can you explain the difference in price intuitively?

10. Consider your answer to Question 9. Your friend Richard "The Brain" tells you that the bid rate on a given Treasury bill is 6 percent and the asked rate 6.2 percent. Is your friend as bright as his name suggests? Why or why not?

11. A corporate bond with a coupon rate of 6 percent matures in 5 years. Its price is currently $115 (per $100 face amount).
    - **A.** Calculate the current yield on this bond.
    - **B.** If this bond is held to maturity, will its holder realize a gain or loss at maturity? How much will the gain or loss be? Divide the gain or loss by the number of years to maturity to calculate the average annual gain/loss.
    - **C.** Calculate the yield to maturity on this bond.

12. You are considering purchasing an IBM coupon bond and want to look up relevant price and yield information. However, your friend Elmo spilled ketchup on the price quotation. All you can see is that the coupon rate is 6.5 percent and the asked yield is 5.3 percent.
    - **A.** Does this bond sell at a premium or discount to face value? Explain.
    - **B.** Is the current yield higher or lower than 6.5 percent? Explain.

13. Suppose a Sears coupon bond sells at a discount from face value.
    - **A.** Is the coupon rate higher or lower than the current yield? Explain.
    - **B.** Is the yield to maturity greater or lower than the current yield? Explain.
    - **C.** How do your answers change if the bond sells for a premium?

mply trade *second-hand* secu- issuer receives nothing in this ore, secondary markets play no capital formation process. They are a sideshow." Evaluate this statement.

it a coincidence that the ten most highly developed countries in the world all have well-developed secondary markets for securities whereas the ten poorest do not? Explain.

**16.** A. Rank the following assets based on liquidity (most liquid to least liquid).

**A.** Shares of stock in a newly formed biotech company
**B.** Shares of IBM stock
**C.** AT&T 20-year bonds
**D.** Commercial paper issued by IBM
**E.** U.S. Treasury bills
**F.** 20-year U.S. Treasury bonds

B. Rank the same assets by the rate of return you require to purchase each (from highest to lowest). Is your ranking correlated with your ranking for part A? Explain.

**17.** Pick up a recent copy of *The Wall Street Journal* and turn to the "Interest Rate Futures" box in the "Money and Investing" section. After reviewing Exhibit 3-1, calculate the federal funds rate in the most distant month listed (use "settle" price). Now, compare this with the current spot fed funds rate. What does the futures fed funds rate imply about the market's expectation about the future spot fed funds rate?

# ADDITIONAL READING

- On the money market and the instruments traded therein, see Timothy Cook and Robert LaRoche (ed.), *Instruments of the Money Market,* 7th edition (Federal Reserve Bank of Richmond, 1993) and Marcia Stigum, *The Money Market,* 3rd edition (Homewood, Illinois: Dow-Jones Irwin, 1990).
- A study of the U.S. government securities market is Dominique Dupont and Brian Sack, "The Treasury Securities Market: Overview and Recent Developments," *Federal Reserve Bulletin,* December 1999, pp.785–806. For a more recent work that assesses various measures of liquidity of U.S. government securities, see Michael J. Fleming, "Measuring Treasury Market Liquidity," Federal Reserve Bank of New York *Economic Policy Review,* September 2003, pp. 83–105.
- For a wealth of data on both marketable and nonmarketable U.S. government securities, see *The Treasury Bulletin,* published quarterly by the U.S. Treasury and available on the Web at http://www.ustreas.gov/.
- On the commercial paper market, see Mitchell Post, "Evolution of the Commercial Paper Market since 1980," *Federal Reserve Bulletin,* December 1992, pp. 879–891.

# Chapter 4

# FINANCIAL INTERMEDIATION

Figure 3-1 in Chapter 3 illustrates the flow of funds from surplus units (savers/lenders) to deficit-spending units (borrowers/spenders). Funds can be channeled from savers/lenders to borrowers/spenders either directly, through the sale of money and capital market instruments to the savers/lenders, or indirectly, through financial intermediaries. This chapter discusses *financial intermediation*—the flow of funds from savers to borrowers via financial intermediaries.

The money and capital market instruments discussed in Chapter 3—U.S. government securities, commercial paper, corporate and municipal bonds, mortgages, and so forth—are *primary claims* issued by the ultimate deficit-spending units, chiefly corporations and government. Financial intermediaries—banks, life insurance companies, and mutual funds—issue their own *secondary claims* to attract the funds of individuals and firms. Examples include savings deposits, life insurance policies, and mutual fund shares. Financial intermediaries use the funds attracted through these secondary claims to purchase the primary claims issued by deficit-spending units.

## ECONOMIC BASIS FOR FINANCIAL INTERMEDIATION

To fully understand the role of financial intermediaries in our economy, try to imagine a world without them. Begin by assuming there are no financial institutions or markets—no banks, money market mutual funds, or stock markets. Now suppose you have $10,000 cash saved for a rainy day. You want a return on your money so that the principal will grow. Unfortunately, your choices are extremely limited because there are no financial institutions or markets.

Meanwhile, your neighbor Joe, an enterprising recent high-school graduate, is embarking on a second year in his lawn-care service. Last year he earned $8,000 from the business, using only an inexpensive, residential-grade lawnmower and a few other inexpensive tools. If he could obtain $10,000 to purchase a commercial-grade 42-inch Snapper mower, he could take on several large projects, earn 20 percent per year on his investment, and boost his income appreciably. Unfortunately, Joe finds it difficult to get a loan because there are no financial institutions. He is prevented from moving up the ladder of economic success by the absence of developed financial institutions and markets.

You, Joe, and society at large are penalized by the absence of financial institutions. If you (the saver) could somehow get your funds to Joe (the prospective borrower), you and Joe both could benefit. You could split the 20 percent return from his purchase of a state-of-the-art lawnmower. In a world without financial intermediaries, you can lend directly to Joe, but such an arrangement is risky and unlikely to occur.

### Risks and Costs in the Absence of Intermediation

Joe learns of your desire to earn interest on your savings. He approaches you for a direct loan. He offers to pay you 10 percent per year on the loan, suggesting that

**asymmetric information**
condition in which two parties to a transaction have differing information about the intentions of the other party and the likely risks involved

**adverse selection**
condition in which people who are most undesirable from the other party's viewpoint are the ones most likely to seek to engage in a transaction

**moral hazard**
risk that one party to a transaction will undertake activities that are undesirable from the other party's viewpoint

the two of you split the 20 percent return on the lawnmower. However, you are reluctant to lend the money to Joe because of **asymmetric information,** the condition in which two parties to a transaction have unequal knowledge about each other. Joe has a better understanding of his intentions, the lawn-care business, and the likely risks and returns associated with that business than you do. Asymmetric information gives rise to two problems that reduce your willingness to lend to Joe. These problems are *adverse selection* and *moral hazard.*

**Adverse Selection and Moral Hazard.** **Adverse selection** is the problem a lender faces in distinguishing low-risk from high-risk loan applicants *before* making a loan. In general, persons who are most undesirable as borrowers are most likely to pursue a transaction. In this case, individuals with the highest probability of experiencing financial problems search most aggressively for loans. Such individuals more likely need to borrow than do highly prudent and conservative individuals and are willing to pay relatively high interest rates to obtain funds. You may be unwilling to lend to Joe, not knowing his financial history or personal characteristics and being aware of the principle of adverse selection.

The second problem associated with asymmetric information, **moral hazard,** occurs *after* a transaction is made (for example, after purchasing insurance or taking out a loan). Moral hazard is the risk that one party to a transaction will undertake activities that are undesirable from the other party's viewpoint. Moral hazard arises with loans because the debt contract allows the borrower to keep any and all income earned exceeding the fixed payments specified in the loan agreement. In an attempt to reap a high return, the borrower may take on high-risk ventures inconsistent with the best interests of the lender. Once you make the loan to Joe, how can you be sure that he won't catch the next plane to Las Vegas and roll the dice in an effort to run your \$10,000 up to \$1 million? Because Joe will lose only *your* \$10,000 but has a chance to gross \$1,000,000 from this risky venture (\$990,000 of which he gets to keep), he has an incentive to engage in risky or "immoral" (from your perspective) activities with your money. You may not be willing to loan your hard-earned money to Joe because you cannot be sure he will not take undue risk with your funds and because you are aware of the principle of moral hazard.

A major rationale for the existence of financial intermediaries is their superior ability to deal with asymmetric information and the associated problems of adverse selection and moral hazard. Financial institutions such as commercial banks, thrift institutions, and finance companies specialize in assessing the credit risks of prospective borrowers. Financial institutions have access to private information such as the loan applicant's income, assets, liabilities, and credit history. They are better equipped than you and I are to monitor the borrower's activities after the loan is made. With these advantages, financial institutions are better positioned to make rational loan decisions. Financial intermediaries reduce the potential problems associated with asymmetric information.

Now, consider a world *with* financial intermediaries. You deposit your funds in a bank or thrift institution savings account or buy commercial paper issued by a finance company, earning 6 percent annual interest in the process. Joe approaches the bank or the finance company and is granted a loan at 12 percent interest. Joe comes out ahead because he earns 20 percent on his new Snapper but pays only 12 percent on his loan. You earn 6 percent on your savings, so you are happy, too. The 6 percent rate is lower than the 10 percent rate you might have earned directly from Joe, but the lower default risk (virtually zero on a federally insured bank deposit) on your loan to the financial intermediary more than compensates you for your lower rate of return. Even if Joe's business goes bankrupt, you are not affected.

In this example, the financial intermediary facilitates the flow of funds from a saver (you) to a borrower (Joe). Economic efficiency improves, and both Joe and you are better off. From society's viewpoint, welfare is enhanced. The nation's capital stock increases (new mower is purchased), boosting productivity and living standards. A net gain to society accrues from the existence of the intermediary. Viewed in this light, financial intermediaries are seen not as opportunistic "middlemen" but as socially beneficial organizations contributing materially to the economic process.

**Transactions Costs.** Another important problem associated with asymmetric information, **transactions costs,** involves the money and time needed for financial transactions. An important element in transactions cost is *search cost.* In the absence of financial intermediaries, Joe spends considerable time searching for someone who will lend him $10,000 at a reasonable interest rate. The time and money you spend before deciding to lend to Joe represent additional transactions costs. For example, you spend significant time evaluating the financial viability of the lawn-care business. If you decide to lend to Joe, you might pay a lawyer $300 to draw up a sound loan contract that will protect you. From society's vantage point, these transactions costs are a waste of scarce resources. By pooling the funds of many individual savers and dealing with numerous prospective borrowers, financial intermediaries can exploit economies of scale that increase efficiency. For instance, a bank or finance company uses a standard loan contract drawn up by the bank attorney for use in hundreds of loans. Officials of these institutions are trained to efficiently evaluate prospective borrowers. By reducing transactions costs in this way, financial intermediaries benefit both savers and deficit spenders.

**transactions costs**
value of money and time needed for financial transactions

The problem of matching individual borrowers' needs with those of lenders cannot be overestimated. Many features of financial instruments issued by deficit-spending units are incompatible with the preferences of individual surplus units. In other words, borrowers and lenders have different needs. One borrower (a municipality) needs access to $20 million for 25 years to build a new high school. Another (an individual) needs a 30-year, $150,000 loan to purchase a new home. On the other hand, an individual saver has $900 to lend for 1 year. Another (a large firm) has $80 million to lend for 60 days. Brokers, dealers, and investment bankers can often mesh the needs of individual borrowers and individual lenders directly, through money and capital market transactions. However, the predominant portion of funds transferred today is channeled through financial intermediaries.

## Benefits of Intermediation

Financial intermediation benefits both surplus and deficit-spending units. The process of financial intermediation benefits society at large, that is, it increases economic efficiency and raises living standards.

**Benefits to Savers.** Financial intermediaries provide certain obvious benefits to surplus units (savers). By pooling the funds of thousands of individuals, intermediaries can overcome obstacles that stop savers from purchasing primary claims directly. Some of these obstacles are lack of financial expertise, lack of adequate information, limited access to certain financial markets, absence of many financial instruments in sufficiently small denominations, and regressive transactions costs.[1]

[1] Brokerage fees in common stocks are highly regressive. Fees can amount to 3 percent or more of the principal for transactions up to $1,000 but only about 0.2 percent or less for transactions greater than $10,000,000. Most bonds cannot be purchased in units less than $1,000. Negotiable CDs and commercial paper come in minimum denominations of $100,000 and $1,000,000, respectively. From the perspective of the typical American household, many of these denominations are prohibitively large.

Another extremely important consideration for the individual saver is the desire for *diversification*—spreading the risk—which financial intermediaries achieve by pooling the funds of thousands of savers. Financial intermediaries have sufficient funds to acquire the large variety of claims needed to adequately diversify assets and substantially reduce risk. An individual may be unwilling to purchase an individual corporate stock or bond with a 2 percent probability of default, but he or she may be quite willing to invest in a mutual fund or pension fund that holds 200 stocks or bonds, each having a 2 percent default probability. An individual may be unwilling to invest in a single mortgage (i.e., lend to a new home buyer) for the same reason you are unwilling to lend to Joe, but he or she may be quite willing to own a share of a large package of mortgages or a certificate of deposit in a bank or savings and loan association holding thousands of similar mortgages.

**Benefits to Deficit Units.** Financial intermediaries also provide substantial benefits to borrowers/spenders. Intermediaries broaden the range of instruments, denominations, and maturities an institution can issue, significantly reducing transactions costs. In the absence of insurance companies and other intermediaries, municipalities and corporations would be greatly inconvenienced if they had to issue bonds in $100 units to attract funds directly from hundreds of thousands of individual savers. They also would suffer if, in the absence of financial intermediaries, they could not market securities maturing in more than 5 years. Imagine the chaotic state of affairs if, in the absence of financial intermediaries, each household seeking a mortgage on a new home first had to locate an individual or business that would lend the desired amount at an acceptable interest rate and maturity. By reducing transactions costs and dealing more effectively with the problem of asymmetric information, financial intermediaries increase economic efficiency, boost economic activity, and elevate living standards.

We now turn to an analysis of the specific types of financial intermediaries in the United States.

## CLASSIFICATION AND GROWTH OF FINANCIAL INTERMEDIARIES

Several types of U.S. financial intermediaries exist, each with certain unique characteristics. However, all financial intermediaries share one characteristic—all issue (secondary) claims against themselves to the public. They use the funds obtained to purchase the (primary) claims issued by deficit-spending units. Financial intermediaries are classified into three categories: depository institutions, contractual savings institutions, and investment-type intermediaries. Table 4-1 lists the principal *sources* of funds (liabilities) of various institutions in each intermediary category and each institution's primary *uses* of funds (that is, the assets of each type of intermediary).

### Depository Institutions

Depository institutions are a critically important financial intermediary. Their share of total assets of all intermediaries has declined sharply in the past 20 years. The depository institution category includes commercial banks, savings and loan associations, mutual savings banks, and credit unions. The latter three sometimes are combined and referred to as *thrift institutions* or *thrifts.*

Depository institutions issue checking, savings, and time deposits. They then use the funds to make various types of loans and to purchase securities. The deposits issued by these institutions have no market risk because the principal does not fluctuate in nominal value as do stocks and bonds. (For example, your savings account

**Table 4-1 Principal Assets and Liabilities of Financial Intermediaries**

| Type of Intermediary | Principal Liabilities (Sources of Funds) | Principal Assets (Uses of Funds) |
|---|---|---|
| Depository Institutions | | |
| Commercial banks | Deposits | Mortgages, loans, government securities |
| Savings and Loan Associations | Deposits | Mortgages, government securities |
| Mutual savings banks | Deposits | Mortgages, government securities |
| Credit unions | Deposits | Consumer loans |
| Contractual Savings Institutions | | |
| Life insurance companies | Premiums | Corporate bonds, mortgages |
| Fire and casualty insurance company | Premiums | Bonds, stocks, government securities |
| Private pension funds and government retirement funds | Employee and employer contributions | Corporate stocks and bonds |
| Investment Intermediaries | | |
| Mutual funds | Shares | Stocks, bonds |
| Finance companies | Shares, bonds, commercial paper | Consumer and business loans |
| Money market mutual funds | Shares | Money market instruments (Treasury bills, commercial paper) |

never declines in nominal value unless you withdraw funds. If you have $1,000 in the account now, you will have $1,000 plus interest later.) In practice, these deposits can be withdrawn on very short notice, in most instances on demand. As a result of their high liquidity, most deposits issued by these institutions are included in one or more of the various measures of the U.S. money supply (see Chapter 2). Figure 4-1 shows the uses of funds attracted by depository institutions. (You can refer back to this figure as we outline the nature of each of the deposit-type intermediaries.)

**Commercial Banks.** Commercial banks are the largest and most important of all the financial intermediaries. Compared with other intermediaries, banks have historically been the most diversified in their activities. Their liabilities (sources of funds) are predominantly demand deposits, savings accounts, and time deposits. Assets (uses of funds) are distributed among mortgages, government securities, business (commercial) loans, consumer loans, and other items (Figure 4-1). The share of commercial bank assets constituted by mortgages has increased appreciably in the past 2 decades, while the share allocated to consumer and business loans has fallen as bank loan customers increasingly turned to other fund sources.

A commercial bank receives its operating charter from either the federal government or the state in which it operates. Commercial banks are regulated and supervised by a variety of organizations, including the Federal Reserve System, the

**Figure 4-1** Allocation of Funds (Assets) of Depository Institutions on December 31, 2003

Depository institutions use their funds principally to make business, consumer, and mortgage loans and to purchase securities.

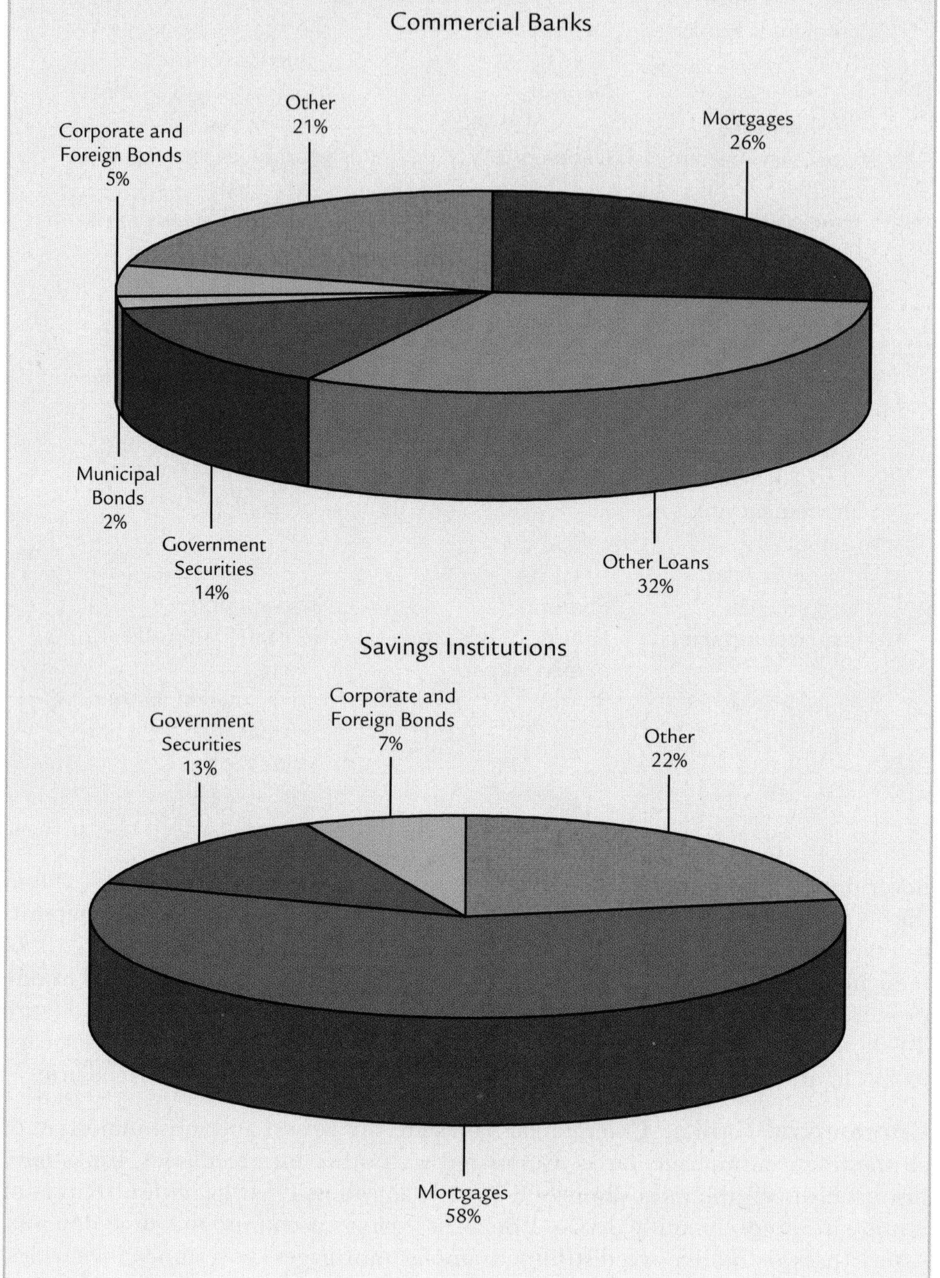

**Figure 4-1** Allocation of Funds (Assets) of Depository Institutions on December 31, 2003—*cont'd*

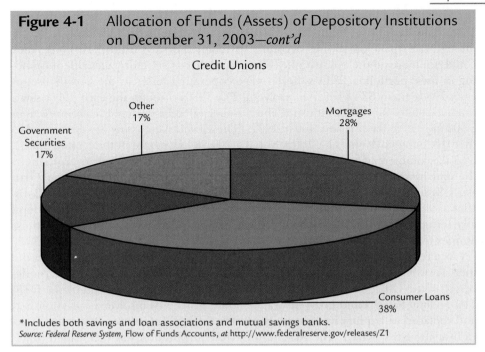

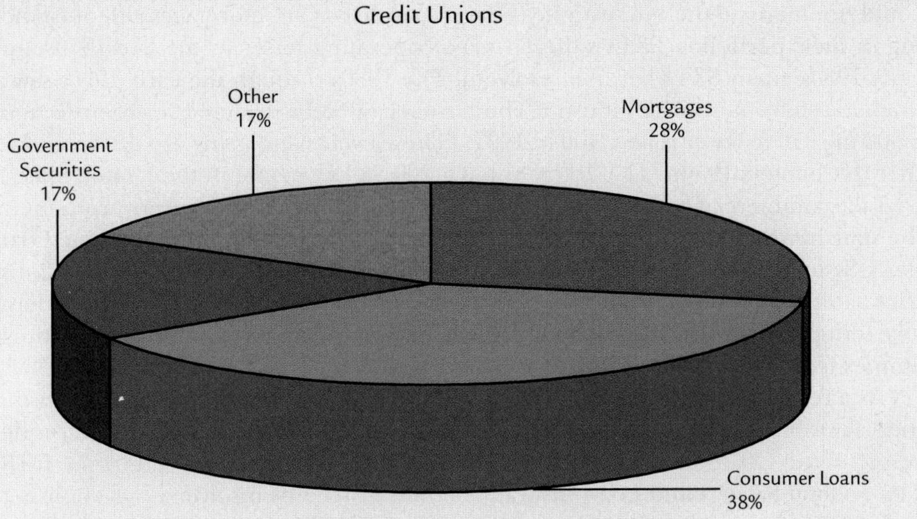


*Includes both savings and loan associations and mutual savings banks.
*Source: Federal Reserve System,* Flow of Funds Accounts, *at* http://www.federalreserve.gov/releases/Z1

Comptroller of the Currency, the Federal Deposit Insurance Corporation (FDIC), and state banking commissions. This text places special emphasis on the nature and behavior of commercial banks because of the banks' important role in the money supply process. Chapter 9 discusses commercial banking. Chapter 10 examines the structure, evolution, and regulation of the banking industry.

**Savings and Loan Associations.** Savings and loan associations (S&Ls) originally were known as "building and loan associations." S&Ls were first formed on the East Coast in the 1830s by groups of people fostering home ownership. The individuals in a group pooled their savings and made loans to a few members (sometimes selected by lottery) for home purchases. Beginning in the 1930s, the federal government contributed to widespread home ownership by establishing the Federal Housing Administration (FHA) to insure mortgages and encouraging the issue of amortized mortgages by S&Ls. In an **amortized mortgage,** part of each monthly payment reduces the principal so that the home is owned free and clear after 15 or 30 years.[2]

**amortized mortgage** mortgage in which part of each monthly payment reduces the principal so that the home is owned free and clear after a period of 15 or 30 years

Home ownership expanded rapid immediately after World War II. Between 1945 and 1965, total assets of S&Ls increased twentyfold. In 1930, only about one third of American households were homeowners. Today, approximately two thirds of households own their own home. S&Ls grew with the postwar boom in home mortgages.

Traditionally, S&Ls are highly specialized. They obtain funds by issuing passbook savings accounts and time deposits and use the funds mostly to grant long-term mortgage loans (review Figure 4-1). S&Ls borrow short-term to finance long-term mortgages, so they are vulnerable when market forces drive interest rates sharply higher. In the late 1970s and early 1980s, a sustained increase in inflation in the

[2] Earlier types of mortgages involved periodic payment of interest only. At the end of the loan period, the homeowner failed to increase equity in the home. Such arrangements made it difficult for most Americans to ever own their home free of debt.

United States (followed by restrictive monetary policy actions designed to combat it) produced dramatically higher interest rates. S&Ls were forced to sharply raise the interest rates paid on savings accounts to retain their depositors. However, they could not increase the interest rates charged on fixed-rate mortgages still outstanding in their portfolios. S&Ls suffered major operating losses in the late 1970s and early 1980s; many S&Ls became insolvent. The 1980s through the early 1990s saw a dramatic shakeout of the industry. The number of S&Ls declined from more than 3,900 in 1970 to fewer than 1,400 in 1992. (These events and issues are discussed further in Chapters 10 and 11.) Today about 1,200 S&Ls operate in the United States.

Like commercial banks, S&Ls are chartered by either the federal government or the state in which they operate. Most S&Ls are members of the Federal Home Loan Bank System (FHLBS), which was established in the 1930s. The FHLBS has 12 district banks and is supervised by the Office of Thrift Supervision (OTS), the federal chartering agency for S&Ls. The OTS sets minimum capital requirements and examines federally chartered S&Ls.

As a result of the thrift industry crisis of the 1980s, a number of changes in the industry were legislated in 1989. The Federal Home Loan Bank Board (the predecessor of the Office of Thrift Supervision) was abolished and replaced by the OTS. The Federal Savings and Loan Insurance Fund, which was insolvent, was abolished and replaced with a new insurance agency, the Savings Association Insurance Fund (a branch of the FDIC). The Resolution Trust Corporation was established to administer the closing and merging of insolvent thrift institutions. Congress established the Resolution Funding Corporation (RFC) to issue government-insured bonds to finance the cleanup, avoiding the embarrassment of paying for the losses out of general tax revenues. Total cost of the S&L bailout was estimated at approximately $140 billion. (Chapter 11 examines the S&L fiasco in more detail.)

**Mutual Savings Banks.** Mutual savings banks (MSBs) were established in the early nineteenth century to encourage saving by working-class Americans. Like S&Ls, MSBs obtain funds by issuing savings and time deposits and use the funds primarily to invest in mortgages. Unlike S&Ls, MSBs operate in only 16 of the 50 states; only three of the states are west of the Mississippi River. Over 90 percent of all MSB assets are held in New York, Massachusetts, and the New England states (half in Massachusetts alone). At one time, the total assets of MSBs were far greater than those of S&Ls. MSBs did not join S&Ls in the westward expansion of the U.S. economy, so MSB assets today are only about one fourth those of S&Ls. Approximately 90 percent of the roughly 400 MSBs operating today were established prior to 1900.

All MSBs are chartered by the 16 states permitting these organizations. Traditionally the state authorities severely limit the types of assets MSBs can acquire. Eligible assets include mortgages, U.S. government securities, and high-grade corporate securities. Legislation passed in 1980 allows MSBs, as well as S&Ls and credit unions, to diversify their asset holdings and requires them to abide by reserve requirements set by the Federal Reserve System. Deposits of the majority of MSBs are insured by the FDIC up to $100,000 per account. Deposits in MSBs not insured by the FDIC typically are insured by state insurance funds.

**Credit Unions.** Credit unions (CUs)—relatively small, consumer-oriented saving and lending institutions—were established in the early 1900s to provide loans for working-class people and provide them an alternative to dealing with loan sharks. CUs are organized by groups of individuals, such as labor unions, universities, or members of a particular firm or occupation. CUs issue time deposits ("shares") to members and use the funds chiefly to lend to other members. Loans usually are granted for home improvements or durable goods purchases (cars, furniture). CUs issue mortgages and modestly diversify their portfolios by investing about one sixth of their assets in U.S. government securities. Profits earned by CUs are exempt from federal income taxes, allowing CUs to offer attractive interest rates relative to banks and other thrift institutions. Because assets are predominantly short-term consumer loans and short-term government securities rather than long-term mortgages, CUs avoided the severe financial problems experienced by S&Ls and MSBs in the late 1970s and early 1980s, when short-term interest rates increased dramatically.

Like MSBs, CUs are "mutuals," that is, they are owned and run by the members (depositors). Advantages of CUs derive from low overhead expenses. Members sometimes work for the institution without pay, and time and space are commonly furnished by the employer. CUs are chartered by either the federal government or the state. The National Credit Union Administration (NCUA) issues federal charters, examines CUs, and sets minimum capital requirements. Deposits of roughly 97 percent of the nation's approximately 10,000 CUs are insured up to $100,000 per account by the National Credit Union Share Insurance Fund. Although CUs tend to be quite small—over half of CUs currently have less than $40 million in deposits—total assets of CUs have grown more rapidly than assets of other depository institutions during the past 30 years.

Table 4-2 indicates the total assets of the various types of depository institutions, contractual savings institutions, and investment intermediaries at the end of 2003 and the growth rate of each type of intermediary from 1970 to 1990 and 1990 to 2003. Total assets of commercial banks are nearly four times as large as the combined total assets of S&L associations, MSBs, and CUs and constitute about 25 percent of total assets of all financial intermediaries.

## Contractual Savings Institutions

Contractual savings institutions obtain funds under long-term contractual arrangements. They invest the funds predominantly in the capital market, that is, in long-term equity and debt instruments. Contractual savings institutions include various types of insurance companies, private pension funds, and state and local government retirement funds. These institutions enjoy relatively stable inflows of funds because of agreements requiring regular payments from policyholders and pension fund participants. Because both the inflows and outflows of funds from these institutions are relatively stable and predictable, liquidity typically is not a high priority in the asset management of these institutions. Figure 4-2 shows the uses of funds (the assets) of three types of contractual savings institutions.

A fundamental growth source of contractual intermediaries is the public's desire to make financial provisions for old age. Increasing life expectancy, rising medical care costs, and growing recognition that social security benefits unlikely will be sufficient for retirement needs have increased the public's demand for various types of retirement funds and life insurance policies. Total assets of contractual savings institutions have grown more rapidly than those of depository institutions, both over the past 35 years and in the more recent period (Table 4-2).

**Life Insurance Companies.** Life insurance companies issue life insurance policies. More than two thirds of the proceeds are invested in corporate bonds and equities. On the surface, life insurance companies appear to be totally different from depository institutions such as S&Ls and MSBs, but they are similar in some respects. Life insurance premiums constitute a continuing source of funds, as do savings inflows for savings institutions. Holders of some life insurance policies own a potentially liquid asset with a fixed nominal value, which is legally convertible to

**Table 4-2 Growth Rates and Total Assets of Financial Intermediaries on December 31, 2003**

| Intermediary | Average Annual Growth Rate (%) 1970–1990 | 1990–2003 | Total Assets on December 31, 2003 ($ Billion) |
|---|---|---|---|
| Depository Institutions | | | |
| Commercial banks | 10.1 | 6.7 | $7,812 |
| Savings institutions* | 10.3 | −0.3 | 1,475 |
| Credit unions | 13.6 | 8.6 | 617 |
| Contractual Savings Institutions | | | |
| Life insurance companies | 10.2 | 8.2 | 3,823 |
| Other insurance companies | 12.8 | 5.4 | 1,043 |
| Private pension funds | 13.1 | 9.4 | 4,194 |
| State and local government pension funds | 14.0 | 8.3 | 2,284 |
| Investment Intermediaries | | | |
| Mutual funds | 13.9 | 17.5 | 4,665 |
| Finance companies | 11.6 | 6.9 | 1,381 |
| Money market mutual funds | 41.3** | 12.4 | 2,016 |

*Savings and loan associations, mutual savings banks, and federal savings banks.
**1974–1990
*Source: Federal Reserve System,* Flow of Funds Accounts, *at* http://www.federalreserve.gov/releases/Z1

cash on demand. That is, many life insurance policies have a specified cash surrender value that increases over time; policyholders can obtain that cash on request.

The fundamental difference between life insurance companies and depository institutions is the customers' perception of the products. Policyholders regard insurance more as a source of protection than as a source of liquidity. Consequently, they view the cash value of their policies as untouchable except in extreme emergency. Savings accounts in depository institutions are not considered in the same manner, being routinely tapped to purchase a new stereo, finance the family vacation, or pay for college expenses. Thus, the asset structure of life insurance companies requires less liquidity than that of depository institutions, explaining their large holdings of stocks and bonds. Life insurance companies typically are regulated by the state insurance commissioner. Only a tiny portion of their assets are in the form of cash and demand deposits. In 2004, some 2,000 life insurance companies operated in the United States, with assets totaling about $4 trillion.

**Fire and Casualty Insurance Companies.** Fire and casualty insurance companies sell protection against loss resulting from fire, theft, accident, natural disas-

**Figure 4-2** Allocation of Funds (Assets) of Contractual Savings Institutions on June 30, 2004

Because liquidity is a lower priority for contractual savings institutions than stability and growth of income, these institutions invest heavily in bonds and stocks.

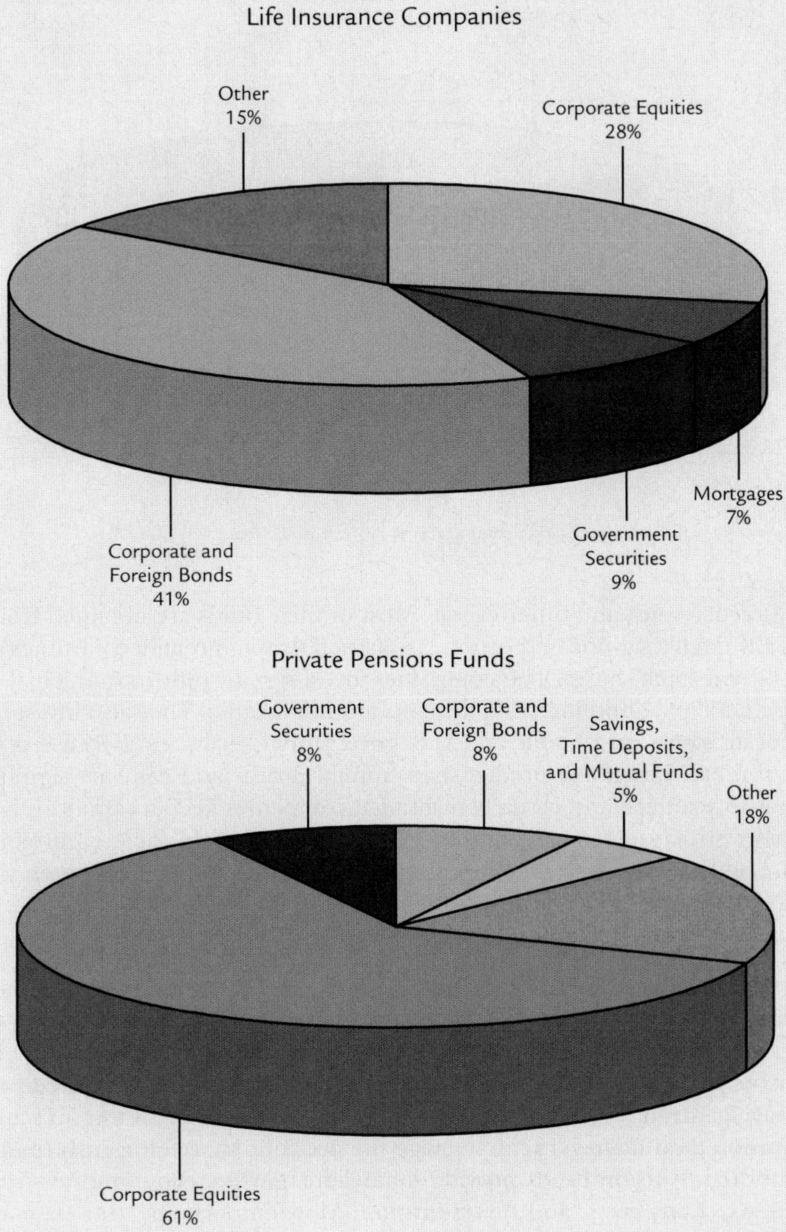

**Figure 4-2** Allocation of Funds (Assets) of Contractual Savings Institutions on June 30, 2004—*cont'd*

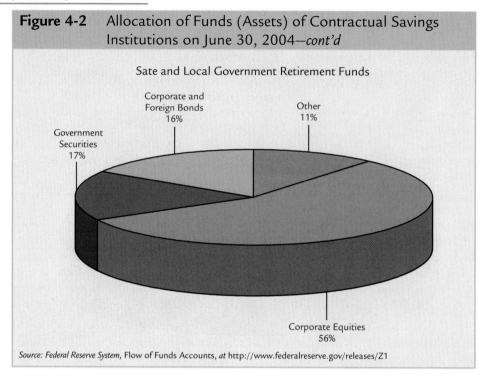

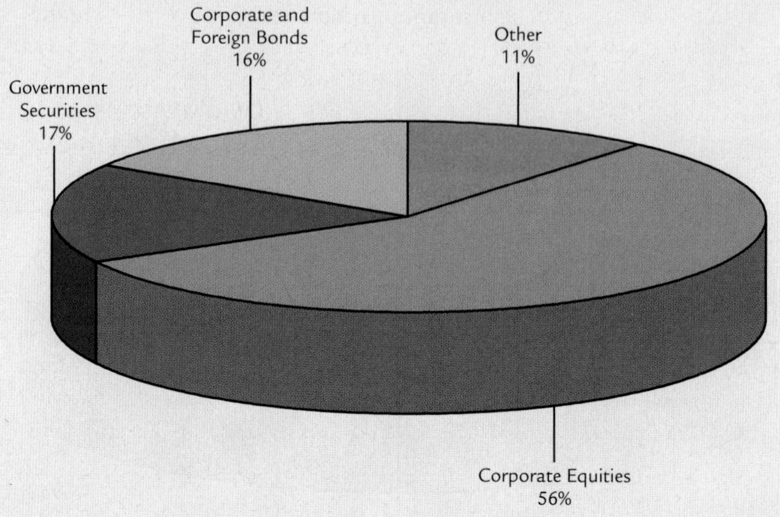


*Source: Federal Reserve System,* Flow of Funds Accounts, *at* http://www.federalreserve.gov/releases/Z1

ter, malpractice suits, and other events. Most of their funds are obtained from premiums, although a significant portion is obtained through retained earnings and issuance of new stock shares. The companies invest significantly in municipal bonds because municipal bond interest payments are not taxable. They also invest heavily in corporate stocks and bonds and U.S. government securities. Because property losses are more difficult to predict than human deaths and can vary significantly from year to year, fire and casualty insurance companies keep a significantly more liquid asset structure than do life insurance companies. In 2004, approximately 3,900 fire and casualty insurance companies operated in the United States, with total assets of approximately $1 trillion. The companies are regulated by state insurance commissioners.

**Private Pension Funds and Government Retirement Funds.** The public's desire for financial security in retirement has led to remarkable growth in various types of retirement funds. Saving for retirement can be accomplished in two ways: through personal saving initiatives and through employer-sponsored pension plans. Saving through employer-provided funds have several distinct advantages. First, pension fund managers can manage the portfolio more efficiently than a typical individual. Pension funds provide financial expertise, economies of scale, reduced transactions costs, and diversification. More importantly, the tax code encourages employees and employers to contribute to pension plans. Income contributed directly to a retirement fund is nontaxable, that is, contributions are tax deductible. Income is taxed upon distribution at retirement.[3]

[3] A major advantage of saving through private pension funds and government retirement funds is that income that accrues to the fund (contributions and earnings therefrom) is nontaxable by federal and state governments, that is, income that is taxed if placed in a personal saving program compounds tax-free in private pension plans and government retirement programs. In addition, the employer's matching contribution is tax-deductible to the employer. Hence, the tax code not only provides strong incentives for individuals to save through pension programs, it also provides employers incentives to expand retirement benefits in lieu of wage and salary hikes.

The majority of major corporations, state and local governments, and other organizations today offer employee retirement programs. Employers withhold the funds from workers' paychecks and send the funds, sometimes with matching contributions, to a pension or retirement fund. The retirement fund invests the contributions in corporate stocks and bonds and U.S. government bonds. The employee receives a lump sum or a regular monthly income at retirement. Because monthly contributions by employees and employers substantially exceed monthly benefits paid out to retirees, pension funds have a relatively large and stable pool of funds to invest each year. With more than $6 trillion in assets in 2004, private pension funds and government pension funds held approximately one fourth the value of publicly traded corporate equities and bonds outstanding.

## Investment-Type Financial Intermediaries

Investment-type intermediaries include (stock and bond) mutual funds, finance companies, and money market mutual funds. The benefits to investors include low transactions costs (obtained by buying in large blocks), financial expertise and experience supplied by mutual fund management, and increased diversification relative to that feasible for a typical individual. Growth of total assets of mutual funds and money market mutual funds has exploded in the past 35 years (Table 4-2).

**Mutual Funds.** Mutual funds pool the funds of many individuals in order to purchase a diversified portfolio of stocks and/or bonds. You can choose from mutual funds with various objectives, including long-term growth of capital, high current income, or capital preservation. Particular mutual funds can emphasize technology, health care, natural resource, utility, or emerging growth stocks. Other funds specialize in international stocks, holding shares in corporations in countries such as China, Brazil, Latin America, Europe, Japan, and other countries.

Two broad categories of mutual funds specialize in common stocks: *open-end funds* and *closed-end funds*. An open-end fund has the right to issue additional shares at its discretion. When you buy an open-end fund, you purchase a pro rata share of a portfolio. Shares can be redeemed at any time at their net asset value—the value of the shareholder's portion of the portfolio. A closed-end fund cannot issue additional shares, and the owner cannot redeem the shares at market value from the fund itself. Instead, the shares in the fund are traded like common stocks in a secondary market (over the counter or through one of the stock exchanges). Open-end funds can be further classified as *no-load* or *load* funds. A no-load fund does not levy an upfront charge, although it typically charges an annual fee of 0.5 to 1.5 percent of total assets. A load fund charges a fairly stiff fee up front—typically 4 to 8 percent of the total value of the transaction. No annual fee is charged thereafter.

Americans' perceived need to provide for their retirement years and the tremendous stock market boom of the last 2 decades of the twentieth century have led to increased investment in mutual funds. Total assets of mutual funds increased at a phenomenal average rate of approximately 15 percent per year from 1970 to 2003. Figure 4-3 indicates the growth in total assets of mutual funds since 1984 and the allocation of assets between stocks and bonds. Bonds constituted the majority of mutual fund assets from 1985 to 1993. The stock portion increased sharply in the past 15 years.

Mutual funds are regulated by the Securities and Exchange Commission (SEC). The SEC enforces reporting and disclosure regulations for mutual funds and guards investors against fraudulent practices by mutual fund managers. The 2003 disclosure of widespread unethical (and sometimes illegal) industry practices suggesting that many fund managers were more interested in their own financial welfare than that of their customers rocked the public's confidence in mutual funds.

**Figure 4-3** Growth and Composition of Mutual Fund Assets

Mutual fund assets have grown dramatically since the early 1980s. Today, more than 70 percent of mutual fund assets are in stocks. Less than 30 percent are in bonds.

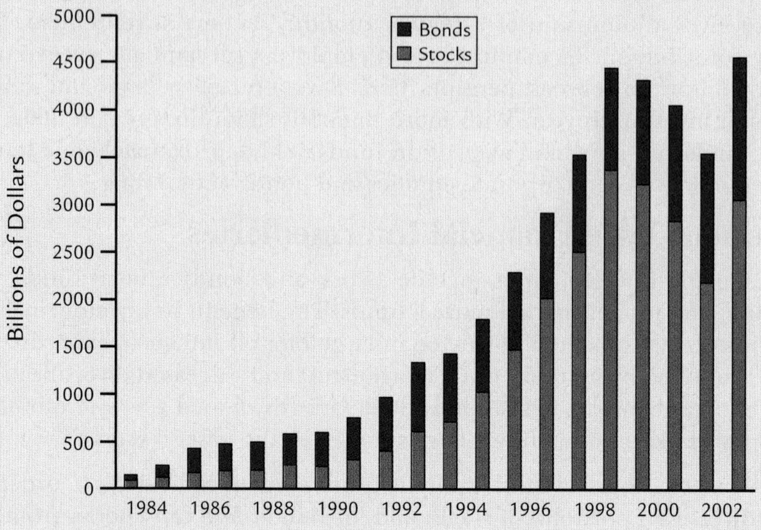

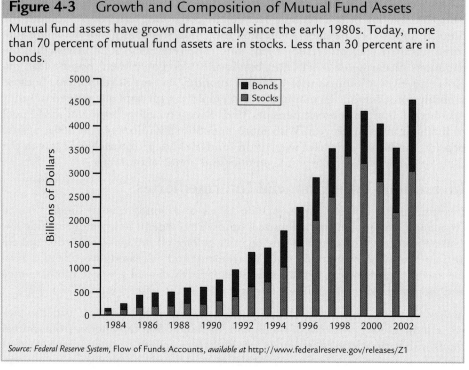

*Source: Federal Reserve System,* Flow of Funds Accounts, *available at* http://www.federalreserve.gov/releases/Z1

**Finance Companies.** Finance companies obtain funds by issuing commercial paper, borrowing from banks, and issuing shares of stock. They use the funds to make small loans to individuals and businesses. They gather and monitor information allowing them to estimate potential borrowers' default risk. Finance companies typically charge higher interest rates than banks because finance company customers tend to have higher default risks than bank borrowers. Unlike commercial banks, finance companies obtain funds in large blocks and lend in small amounts. The development of the commercial paper market has given finance companies an advantage over commercial banks. As a result, finance companies have maintained their share of the intermediation market while that of commercial banks has declined. Because finance companies do not issue deposits, regulatory authorities impose few regulations on them beyond disclosure requirements and efforts to prevent fraud. The asset structure of finance companies is largely unregulated.

Finance companies can be divided into three categories. *Sales finance companies,* which usually are associated with a large corporation, finance the sale of its products. For example, the General Motors Acceptance Corporation conveniently provides auto loans for cars sold by General Motors. *Consumer finance companies,* such as Household Finance Corporation, make small loans to households for furniture and appliance purchases and home improvements. *Business finance companies* make loans to small businesses, often by purchasing the business' accounts receivable at a discount from face value. Finance companies actively purchase expensive equipment (such as airplanes) and lease the equipment to businesses. Total assets of all finance companies were approximately $1,300 billion ($1.3 trillion) in 2004.

**Money Market Mutual Funds.** Money market mutual funds (MMMFs) are relatively new institutions that blossomed during the period of escalating interest rates in the late 1970s (Exhibit 4-1). These funds issue "shares," which are essentially interest-bearing deposits. The yield payable on MMMF shares changes daily in response to market forces.[4] Customers can write checks on their deposits, although MMMFs typically require that checks be in amounts of at least $250 or $500. A minimum deposit from $1,000 to $20,000 usually is required to open an account.

MMMFs pool the funds of thousands of depositors and purchase large blocks of liquid money market instruments, such as commercial paper, U.S. Treasury bills, repurchase agreements, and negotiable CDs. Unlike deposits in banks and thrift institutions, MMMF shares are not insured. However, they are relatively safe because MMMFs invest in instruments of very low default risk. Some MMMFs invest entirely in U.S. Treasury bills, making their shares virtually free of default risk. Yields currently payable by each of the approximately 1,250 MMMFs, total assets, and average maturity of assets of each MMMF are published each Thursday in *The Wall Street Journal*.

MMMFs are investment-type intermediaries, but they clearly have some characteristics of depository institutions. MMMF shares are highly liquid and can be transferred by check. MMMF shares outstanding are included in M2 and M3, the broader measures of the U.S. money supply. Interest earned on MMMF shares normally is taxable. Several MMMFs specialize in short-term municipal bonds, with interest earned nontaxable by the IRS. Total assets of MMMFs grew explosively in the 1970s and 1980s (Table 4-2) and amounted to more than $2 trillion in 2004. Figure 4-4 shows the allocation of money market mutual fund assets at the end of 2003.

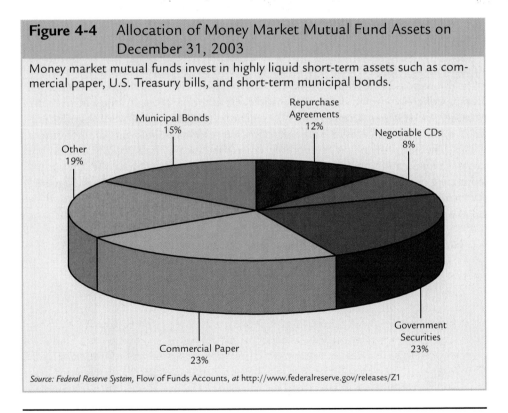

**Figure 4-4** Allocation of Money Market Mutual Fund Assets on December 31, 2003

Money market mutual funds invest in highly liquid short-term assets such as commercial paper, U.S. Treasury bills, and short-term municipal bonds.

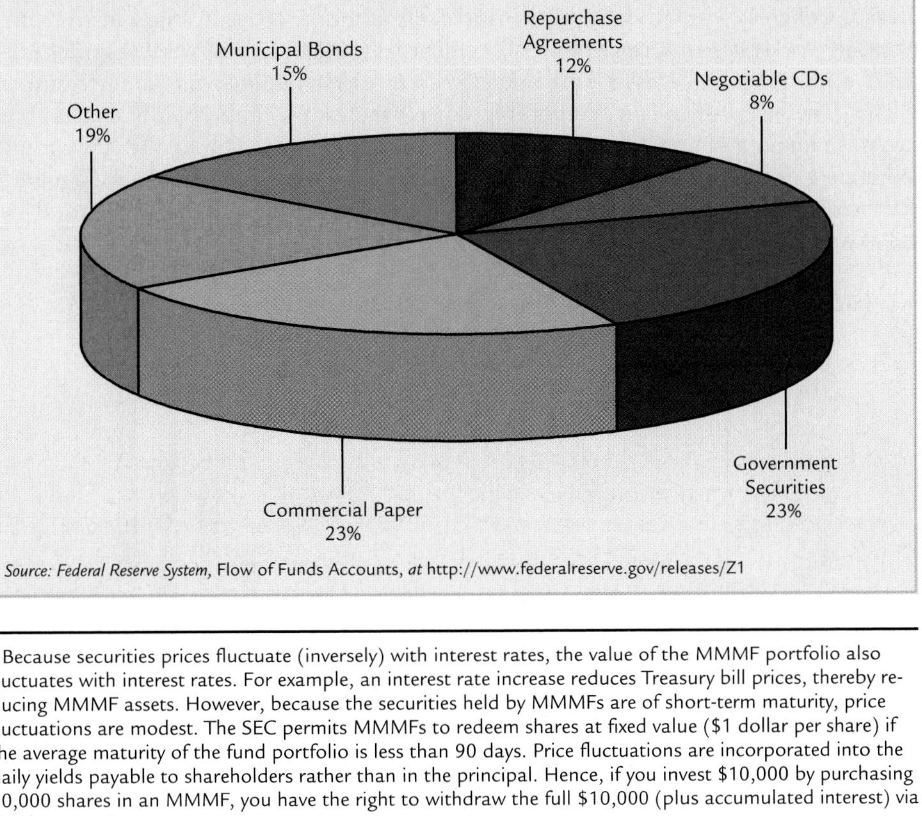


*Source: Federal Reserve System,* Flow of Funds Accounts, *at* http://www.federalreserve.gov/releases/Z1

[4] Because securities prices fluctuate (inversely) with interest rates, the value of the MMMF portfolio also fluctuates with interest rates. For example, an interest rate increase reduces Treasury bill prices, thereby reducing MMMF assets. However, because the securities held by MMMFs are of short-term maturity, price fluctuations are modest. The SEC permits MMMFs to redeem shares at fixed value ($1 dollar per share) if the average maturity of the fund portfolio is less than 90 days. Price fluctuations are incorporated into the daily yields payable to shareholders rather than in the principal. Hence, if you invest $10,000 by purchasing 10,000 shares in an MMMF, you have the right to withdraw the full $10,000 (plus accumulated interest) via check at any time.

## Exhibit 4-1 Brief History of Money Market Mutual Funds

The emergence of money market mutual funds (MMMFs) in the 1970s is an excellent example of how government regulations and powerful market incentives lead to financial innovations. Before the 1980s, banks and thrift institutions were governed by statutory interest rate ceilings. The interest rates banks and thrifts could pay depositors on savings and time deposits were capped. In addition, banks are subject to reserve requirements, forcing them to hold a portion of their deposit liabilities in the form of cash and non-interest-bearing deposits at the Federal Reserve. These two regulations led to the emergence of MMMFs.

The first MMMF, established in 1971, provided the public a viable alternative to bank deposits. Total MMMF shares outstanding were limited for several years because market interest rates generally stayed below the ceiling rates payable by depository institutions. Bank depositors had little incentive to move funds out of banks. In the late 1970s, yields on money market instruments such as Treasury bills and commercial paper moved above 10 percent in response to escalating inflation and restrictive Federal Reserve policy measures. The 10 percent yield was far above the 5.5 percent statutory ceiling rate on saving and time deposits in banks and thrift institutions. Customers of depository institutions pulled funds from savings and time deposits and invested in high-yielding MMMF shares. Total assets of MMMFs soared, rising from less than \$4 billion in 1977 to \$220 billion by the end of 1982, a figure about three times as large as total assets of ordinary (stock) mutual funds at the time.

Depository institutions reacted first by lobbying Congress to level the playing field by imposing reserve requirements and other restrictions on MMMFs. However, this proved politically impossible because MMMFs had become very popular in the country. Instead, Congress granted depository institutions authority to issue a new instrument, the *money market deposit account (MMDA)*. Similar to MMMF shares, MMDAs offer limited check-writing privileges and are not subject to reserve requirements or interest rate ceilings. The new instrument temporarily slowed the exodus into MMMF shares, but MMMFs remain an important player in U.S. financial markets. During the 15-year period ending in December 2003, MMMF shares expanded at a remarkable average rate of approximately 14 percent per year and today account for about 8 percent of total assets of all financial intermediaries.

Money Market Mutual Funds Shares Outstanding, 1975–2003

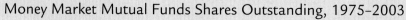

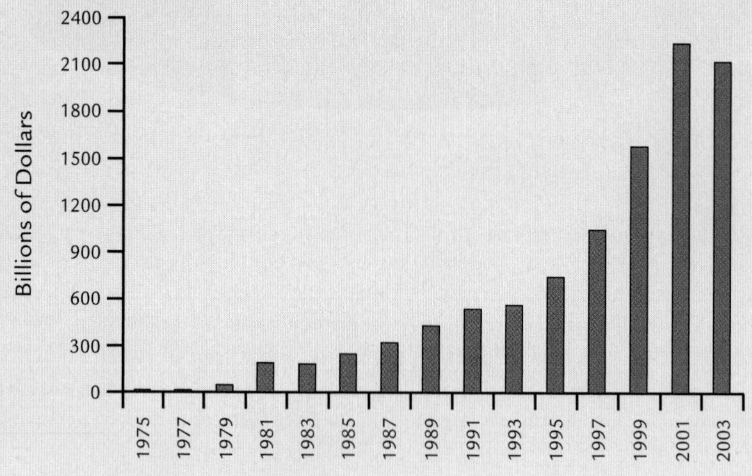

# GOVERNMENT REGULATION OF THE FINANCIAL SYSTEM

Relative to other sectors of the U.S. economy, the financial system is heavily regulated. The same generalization is true in other nations around the world. What is the rationale for extensive government regulation of financial intermediaries and financial markets? Government regulations aim to (1) increase the flow of information to prospective financial market participants, (2) strengthen the stability of the nation's financial system, and (3) improve the central bank's ability to control the nation's money supply and credit conditions.

## Increasing the Availability and Accuracy of Information

All participants in the nation's financial system must have access to timely and accurate information. Without such information, making financial decisions is extremely difficult. Earlier in this chapter we noted that asymmetric information in financial markets suggests that prospective lenders may be troubled by *adverse selection* and *moral hazard* problems, thus impairing the workings of financial markets. The principle of adverse selection suggests that the more risky (and sometimes even corrupt) individuals or firms most aggressively seek to obtain funds by selling securities to the public and likely offer what appear to be the most attractive terms, that is, the highest yields, highest dividends, and so forth. After a firm gains access to funds by borrowing or selling securities to the public, the firm can engage in risky activities that are at odds with the interests of the lenders or investors. To the extent that these problems become severe, people withdraw their funds from financial markets and financial intermediaries, voiding the considerable potential benefits these markets and institutions provide to society. In extreme instances, the financial system might even seize up, with legitimate borrowers unable to get access to funds. In principle, the problems of adverse selection and moral hazard can be reduced by government regulations ensuring the disclosure of reliable, accurate, and timely information to the public about the financial condition of firms.

The Securities and Exchange Act of 1933, which followed the stock market crash of 1929 and the associated revelation of fraud and corruption in the U.S. financial sector, created the **Securities and Exchange Commission (SEC).** The SEC aims to prevent many of the abuses that occurred before 1933, such as insider trading of stocks, bonds, and other financial instruments, and failure of corporations to clearly and honestly disclose key financial information. Today, corporations are required to file periodic reports of their assets, liabilities, sales, and profits. The reports must be audited by accounting firms to verify their authenticity. Numerous cases of apparent fraud, accounting irregularities, and corruption in the U.S. corporate sector that came to light in 2001 and 2002 (e.g., Enron, WorldCom, and Tyco), along with allegations of insider trading, jeopardized the perceived integrity of U.S. financial markets and institutions. The episodes suggest that the regulatory authorities' objective of transparent and accurate reporting by U.S. corporations of their true financial condition remains elusive (Exhibit 4-2).

**Securities and Exchange Commission (SEC)** government organization charged with preventing financial abuses such as insider trading of stocks, bonds, and other financial instruments, and failure of corporations to clearly and honestly disclose key financial information

## Ensuring the Stability of Financial Intermediaries

The principle of asymmetric information suggests that managers of depository institutions and other financial intermediaries know better than their customers the true financial condition of their institutions. Most bank depositors cannot accurately assess their bank's financial condition. If customers doubt the financial condition of their bank or the financial system in general, they can withdraw funds

**banking panic**
waves of systemic bank runs that lead to contraction of bank lending and economic contraction

from depository institutions. A **banking panic** occurs if many bank customers withdraw their funds, forcing healthy as well as impaired banks to close. A banking panic can result in large economic costs, including a contraction in credit available to legitimate borrowers, a decline in the nation's output and income, and an increase in unemployment throughout the nation. Governments impose regulations to reduce exposure to banking panics. Regulations include restricting entry into the banking business, limiting activities banks are allowed to engage in, requiring periodic disclosure of accurate information, and implementing deposit insurance.

**Restricting Entry.** The Comptroller of the Currency and individual state banking and insurance commissions have established stringent criteria for opening up a new financial intermediary. Unlike starting a lawn-care business or an auto repair shop, opening a new bank or other financial intermediary requires a charter from the federal government or the state in which the institution is located. The intermediary must meet rigorous standards to obtain a charter. Individuals failing to establish a strong record of personal character and financial probity likely will not be granted a charter.

**Restrictions on Activities.** Financial panics are triggered by public perceptions of possible severe financial problems in financial institutions and markets. Financial intermediaries are heavily restricted in the types of assets they are allowed to acquire, thus promoting safety. U.S. commercial banks and other depository institutions, unlike those in Japan and certain other countries, are generally prohibited from buying shares of stock. Life insurance companies are permitted to own only limited quantities of shares of stock. Savings institutions are prohibited from owning stocks and other assets perceived to be risky, although earlier regulations constraining such institutions to invest almost entirely in mortgages have been relaxed.

**Requiring Periodic Disclosure.** Financial intermediaries are subject to stringent disclosure requirements. Banks are required to submit balance sheets to regulatory authorities regularly and to publish their balance sheets periodically in hometown newspapers. The timely flow of information reduces uncertainty and encourages institutions to make prudent financial decisions, contributing to the stability of the financial system.

**Provision of Deposit Insurance.** Insurance of deposits against a financial institution's failure enhances the public's willingness to entrust funds to banks and other financial institutions. The insurance promotes financial intermediation and its associated benefits to society and reduces the likelihood of financial panics. The FDIC was established in 1934 following the banking panic and ensuing collapse of the banking system and U.S. economy in the early 1930s. The FDIC insures each deposit in a federally insured commercial bank or mutual savings bank (98 percent of all institutions) up to $100,000 against failure of the institution. Other types of depository institutions also carry deposit insurance. The Savings Association Insurance Fund (SAIF) provides deposit insurance for S&Ls, and the National Credit Union Share Insurance Fund insures CU depositors.

## Improving Monetary Control

Depository institutions are subject to *reserve requirements*—stipulations requiring these institutions to maintain reserves (cash and deposits at the Federal Reserve) amounting to no less than a specified percentage of their deposit liabilities. As we learn in Part 4, reserve requirements enhance the Federal Reserve's ability to control the quantity of money in circulation and influence general credit conditions. Because the quantity of money, in turn, influences economic activity and the nation's price level, the Federal Reserve is granted this authority to set and enforce reserve requirements. Prior to the 1980s, the reserve requirements set by the Federal Reserve applied only to commercial banks that were members of the Federal Reserve System. Nonmember banks and savings institutions were not subject to the Fed's reserve requirements. Because of the increasing perception that the Fed's ability to control the money supply and credit conditions was endangered, legislation enacted in 1980 (The Monetary Control Act) extended reserve requirements to all commercial banks, S&Ls, and MSBs. Deposit insurance reduces system exposure to possible panics and the resulting contraction in the quantity of money, enhancing the Federal Reserve's ability to influence economic activity.

Table 4-3 indicates some of the most important regulatory agencies in the U.S. financial system and outlines the nature of the regulations that each agency applies.

**Table 4-3 Principal U.S. Financial System Regulatory Agencies**

| Regulatory Agency | Subject Regulated | Type of Regulation |
|---|---|---|
| Securities and Exchange Commission (SEC) | Organized exchanges and financial markets | Requires disclosure of information, restricts insider trading |
| Commodities Futures Trading Commission (CFTC) | Markets | Sets regulations for trading in futures markets |
| Federal Reserve System (FRS) | Depository institutions | Sets reserve requirements, examines Federal Reserve member banks |
| Office of the Comptroller of the Currency (OCC) | Federally chartered commercial banks | Charters and examines federally chartered banks, restricts types of assets they can hold |
| Federal Deposit Insurance Corp (FDIC) | Commercial banks, savings and loan associations, and mutual savings banks | Examines insured banks, restricts assets they can hold, provides deposit insurance of $100,000 per deposit |
| State banking and insurance commissions | Depository institutions chartered by states | Charters and examines state-chartered banks, restricts assets they can hold, imposes restriction on branching |
| Office of Thrift Supervision (OTS) | Savings and loan associations | Examines savings and loan associations, restricts types of assets they can hold |
| National Credit Union Administration (NCUA) | Credit unions chartered by federal government | Examines federally chartered credit unions, restricts types of assets they can hold |

# CHANGING NATURE OF FINANCIAL INTERMEDIATION

**Glass-Steagall Act**
law mandating the separation of commercial banking and investment banking

After the Great Depression of the 1930s, Congress implemented a host of measures promoting a highly specialized financial system. The measures locked financial intermediaries into specific activities, protected them from economic hardship, and generally reduced competition both within and across industries. Commercial banks were set up to accept deposits and issue short-term loans. Statutory ceilings on interest rates payable to depositors and legal restrictions on bank branching reduced the scope for competition. Thrift institutions were prohibited from making business or consumer loans; they were forced to specialize in long-term fixed-rate mortgages. Life insurance companies were made to issue policies and purchase corporate bonds; they were forbidden to hold significant amounts of corporate stock. In 1933, the **Glass-Steagall Act** (also known as the *Banking Act of 1933*) mandated the separation of commercial banking and investment banking. Commercial banks were forbidden to underwrite corporate stocks and bonds or to hold common stocks in their portfolios. Investment banks were forbidden to accept household deposits or to make business loans.

Financial institutions traditionally were highly specialized. Families would go to different institutions for a mortgage, a checking account, brokerage services, and a car loan. In the 1950s, the typical middle-class family held a savings account in a bank or thrift institution and a life insurance policy containing saving provisions (that is, a whole life policy). Only 15 percent of the labor force participated in a private pension plan. Only very wealthy families held stocks and bonds.

In recent decades, financial innovations, changing public preferences, rising living standards, and a sustained movement toward deregulation of the financial sector have produced major changes in the nature of financial intermediation. Table 4-4 indicates the changes in shares of total assets of financial intermediaries held by various types of intermediary from 1960 to 2003.

The sharp decline in the relative importance of depository institutions in the intermediation process and the corresponding increase in the relative importance of both contractual savings institutions and investment intermediaries are especially prominent. The shares of aggregate U.S. financial intermediary assets owned by commercial banks, savings institutions, and life insurance companies have declined sharply, while the asset shares of private pension funds and government retirement funds, mutual funds, and money market mutual funds have increased rather dramatically. We discuss these changes in the next two sections.

## Emergence of Retirement Funds and Mutual Funds

Most noteworthy in Table 4-4 (and Table 4-2) is the very strong growth of private pension funds, state and local government retirement funds, mutual funds, and money market mutual funds. Altogether, the share of total financial intermediary assets contributed by these four types of institutions increased from less than 13 percent in 1960 to 21 percent in 1980 and approximately 44 percent in 2003. In recent decades, these institutions have dramatically stepped up competition for household savings, a phenomenon that has forced many financial institutions to adapt and engage in new activities in order to survive.

Private pension plans, state and local government retirement plans, and mutual funds have dramatically altered the allocation of household savings. In the early 1950s, U.S. households held only 6 percent of their total financial assets in pension funds and only 1 percent in mutual funds. By the end of 2003, those figures were

**Table 4-4 Share of Total Assets of All Financial Intermediaries from 1960 to 2003 (in Percent)**

| | 1960 | 1980 | 2003 |
|---|---|---|---|
| Depository institutions | | | |
| Commercial banks | 38.6% | 36.7% | 27.6% |
| Savings and loan associations and mutual savings banks | 19.0 | 19.6 | 5.2 |
| Credit unions | 1.1 | 1.6 | 2.2 |
| Total | 58.7 | 57.9 | 35.0 |
| Contractual Savings Institutions | | | |
| Life insurance companies | 19.6 | 11.5 | 13.0 |
| Property and casualty insurance companies | 4.4 | 4.5 | 3.5 |
| Private pension funds | 6.4 | 12.5 | 13.8 |
| State and local government retirement funds | 3.3 | 4.9 | 7.6 |
| Total | 33.7 | 33.4 | 38.0 |
| Investment Intermediaries | | | |
| Mutual funds | 2.9 | 1.7 | 14.8 |
| Finance companies | 4.7 | 5.1 | 4.5 |
| Money market mutual funds | 0.0 | 1.9 | 7.7 |
| Total | 7.6 | 8.7 | 27.0 |
| Grand Total | 100 | 100 | 100 |

*Source: Federal Reserve System,* Flow of Funds Accounts, *at* http://www.federalreserve.gov/releases/Z1

18 percent and 7 percent, respectively. The same period saw a major shift of household assets away from *direct* ownership of stocks and savings accounts and life insurance and toward *indirect* ownership of stocks and bonds through mutual funds and pension funds. From 1952 to 2003, the portion of household financial assets consisting of direct equity holdings declined from 32 percent to 12 percent and the life insurance portion declined from 12 percent to 2 percent. Households also reduced their relative holdings of bonds and savings deposits.

Life insurance companies have benefited from the increased role of private pension programs. As the demand for life insurance policies was outpaced by the increasing role of pension and mutual funds, life insurance companies adapted by moving heavily into pension fund asset management. The dramatic increase in the relative importance of pension funds and mutual funds has put pressure on commercial banks, thrift institutions, and investment banks. The declining role of individual investors in the stock market (individuals directly held 91 percent of corporate stocks in 1952 and only 36 percent in 2003) has challenged brokerage houses traditionally catering to individual investors. In the next section we examine the effects of these changing events on commercial banks and thrifts.

## Declining Role of Commercial Banks and Thrift Institutions

The phenomenal growth of pension and mutual funds and money market mutual funds has adversely affected commercial banks and thrift institutions. Money market mutual funds squeeze bank profitability by raising the cost of bank funds and reducing the returns earned on bank assets. First, the added competition for depositors forces banks to increase interest rates paid on deposits to prevent an exodus of funds into MMMFs. The remarkable growth of MMMFs (Exhibit 4-1) boosts the commercial paper market (note in Figure 4-4 that MMMFs hold more commercial paper than any other asset). MMMFs provide a major outlet for commercial paper, encouraging large corporations to issue commercial paper rather than borrow from banks. Small businesses increasingly borrow from finance companies, which in turn issue commercial paper to obtain funds. The rise of the commercial paper market reduces business demand for bank loans, forcing banks to look for other ways to maintain a high rate of return on assets.

The growth of mutual funds, private pension funds, and state and local government retirement funds creates a large demand for high-yielding mortgage-backed securities. The successful marketing of these "securitized" mortgages in the 1970s led to the securitization of consumer loans in the mid-1980s. Individual loans made by banks and finance companies are increasingly bundled (securitized) and sold off in large blocks to life insurance companies, pension funds, and other buyers looking for a stable and relatively high income. This confluence of events put downward pressure on bank profits in the 1980s and early 1990s, although profits have recovered strongly since then.

Squeezed by higher costs of funds, lower returns, and declining market share, banks are forced into new endeavors. Banks now invest a larger share of their funds in mortgages. The demise of Glass-Steagall resulted from enactment of the **Gramm, Leach, Bliley Financial Services Act of 1999**—a law stating that commercial banks can underwrite and distribute securities, sponsor mutual funds, and sell insurance products. (Chapter 10 analyzes the structure and evolution of the commercial banking industry). For a time, thrift institutions were authorized to expand into consumer and business loans, but the large losses they suffered in the late 1980s led to new restrictions and a renewed emphasis on mortgage lending.

**Gramm, Leach, Bliley Financial Services Act of 1999**
law that repealed the Glass-Steagall Act, thereby removing the separation of the banking and securities industries

## Exhibit 4-2 Repeal of Glass-Steagall: Was It Wise?

Prior to the Great Depression of 1929 to 1933, underwriting of new securities and their distribution to the public in the United States commonly was performed not only by investment banks but also by commercial banks and life insurance companies. No "fire walls" separated investment banking activities from commercial or life insurance activities. In the Great Depression, commercial banks had many loans outstanding to corporations experiencing severe financial difficulties. Some of the commercial banks apparently underwrote new security issues for corporations that had debts outstanding to these same banks. The potential conflict of interest in this situation is obvious. Some banks allegedly sold newly issued securities issued by insolvent (or nearly insolvent) client firms to an unwary public and allowed the proceeds to be used to repay the bank loans. In other words, the banks allegedly duped the public into buying worthless securities in order to save the banks from their own bad loans.

Two possible remedies existed: mandate full disclosure to the public of the financial condition of firms issuing securities, or legally separate commercial banking from investment banking. An aroused Congress enacted both. Under the sponsorship of Senator Carter Glass of Virginia and Representative Henry Steagall of Alabama, Congress passed the Banking Act of 1933, otherwise known as the *Glass-Steagall Act*.

*continued*

## Exhibit 4-2 Repeal of Glass-Steagall: Was It Wise?—*cont'd*

This act mandated the legal separation of firms conducting commercial banking from those conducting investment banking. (Investment banks favored this split because they were losing market share to affiliates of commercial banks.) For example, the renowned banking firm J.P. Morgan soon became two separate companies: J.P. Morgan Bank (the commercial bank) and Morgan Stanley (the investment bank). In addition, the Securities Act of 1933 mandated full disclosure of information to the public.

The Glass-Steagall Act put U.S. banks at a competitive disadvantage because foreign banks operating in the U.S. were not governed by its strictures and few countries had followed the depression-era move by the U.S. separating commercial banking from investment banking. The act also denied the country the potential benefits of scale economies and other efficiencies resulting from combining the two types of banks. Stimulated by financial innovations and profit incentives, U.S. commercial and investment banks found ways to circumvent the restrictions of Glass-Steagall. In the 1970s and 1980s, investment banks encouraged large corporations to issue securities (commercial paper, bonds, equities) rather than borrow from commercial banks. Large commercial banks encroached on investment bankers' turf by executing corporate mergers and helping find buyers for new corporate debt issues. In 1987, the Federal Reserve Board granted approval to commercial banks to underwrite new issues of commercial paper and securitized (packaged) mortgages. In 1989 and 1990, J.P. Morgan became the first commercial bank granted authority by the Federal Reserve Board to underwrite corporate bonds and stocks. Several other large bank holding companies were granted similar authority shortly thereafter. Finally, Congress effectively repealed the Glass-Steagall Act by enacting the Gramm-Leach-Bliley Financial Services Act of 1999. This act permits insurance companies and securities firms to purchase commercial banks and permits commercial banks to underwrite securities and engage in insurance and real estate activities.

Critics of the removal of the "fire walls" soon found ammunition to use against the Gramm-Leach-Bliley Act. In 2002, two of the largest U.S. banks—Citigroup and J.P. Morgan Chase—reportedly facilitated illicit actions by Enron and WorldCom, two disgraced corporations that recently declared bankruptcy in the midst of charges of corruption and fraud. Both banks had lucrative investment banking arrangements with Enron and WorldCom, and both allegedly helped Enron hide more than $8 billion in debt from the public. The two banks made large loans to the companies, allegedly as payoffs for the coveted investment banking fees. For example, Citigroup loaned nearly $5 billion to Enron over a period of years. The bank shifted most of the risk onto other parties through complicated derivatives transactions. Several pension funds that purchased WorldCom bonds in 2001 filed lawsuits against the two banks (who underwrote the bonds) for ignoring blatant accounting shenanigans at the company. (The fraudulent accounting also went unreported by the disgraced and now defunct accounting firm, Arthur Andersen). At a minimum, removal of the fire walls and the emergence of esoteric derivative instruments suggest that the critical banking function of dealing with moral hazard problems is in jeopardy. Why would a bank have incentive to monitor its loans if it can unload the risk via arcane derivatives transactions?

## Benefits and Costs of Institutional Change

The remarkable growth in the role of private pension funds, state and local government retirement funds, mutual funds, and money market mutual funds in the nation's intermediation process must be regarded on balance as a positive development. This growth has simultaneously increased the range of investment outlets for individuals and firms with surplus funds and expanded the range of alternatives open to deficit spenders. In this way, it has enhanced the efficiency of financial intermediation.

The reallocation of funds among the various financial intermediaries, coupled with the demise of Glass-Steagall, could work to increase financial instability in the future. The increasing portion of assets held in the relatively volatile shares of stock via pension and mutual funds (and the corresponding declining share held in more stable life insurance policies and deposits in banks and thrift institutions) means that "wealth effects" associated with changes in stock prices may be larger than in the past. In this event, output and employment could become more unstable. The increased competition due to growth of mutual funds and pension funds can increase the vulnerability of commercial banks and thrift institutions to future shocks, such as a collapse of oil prices. We have not yet experienced the effects of the demise of Glass-Steagall and its firewalls separating commercial banking from investment banking. Many banks and thrifts failed in the late 1980s and early 1990s, but depository institutions' earnings and balance sheets have strengthened dramatically since then. Today banks are relatively healthy, with failures running at very low levels in the past 10 years.

The financial system established in the early post-Depression era was designed to stabilize financial intermediaries. However, it inhibited competition and prevented the flow of household savings to the best opportunities. Ultimately, it raised the economic cost of intermediation. Today, many legal restraints have been removed. Competition from MMMFs, the commercial paper market, and securitization ties depository institutions' loan rates more closely to money and capital market rates. Household savings flow more readily to their best opportunities, improving the efficiency of the intermediation process.

# SUMMARY

Financial intermediaries are institutions that facilitate the transfer of funds from households, businesses, and other entities with extra funds (savers/lenders) to businesses, governments, and other entities requiring more funds (borrowers/spenders). Financial intermediaries are better equipped than households and other lenders to grapple with the problem of asymmetric information in financial markets. These intermediaries issue such claims as savings deposits, insurance policies, and "shares" to obtain funds. The funds are used to purchase the bonds, stocks, mortgages, and other instruments issued by deficit spenders. Financial intermediaries include depository institutions (commercial banks, savings institutions, and CUs), contractual savings institutions (insurance companies and various pension and retirement funds), and investment intermediaries (mutual funds, finance companies, and money market mutual funds). The share of the intermediation market constituted by depository institutions and insurance companies has declined sharply over the past 40 years, while the share contributed by various retirement funds, mutual funds, and money market mutual funds has increased dramatically. This shift has contributed to dynamic change among the financial intermediaries, forcing various institutions to adapt in order to remain financially viable.

# KEY TERMS

asymmetric information
adverse selection
moral hazard
transactions costs
amortized mortgage
Securities and Exchange Commission
banking panic
Glass-Steagall Act
Gramm, Leach, Bliley Financial Services Act of 1999

# STUDY QUESTIONS

1. If information between lender and borrower were not asymmetric, would the problem of adverse selection still exist? Could a moral hazard problem still exist? Explain.

2. Why might you be unwilling to lend directly to your neighbor? Why might you be more willing to lend to your neighbor than to a lawn-mowing enterprise in Cleveland?

3. Explain how the emergence of financial intermediaries reduces the problems of adverse selection and moral hazard. Does it *eliminate* those problems?

4. Observers have noted that when bank loan rates are very high, the number of "bad loans" increases appreciably. Explain how this can be related to the problem of adverse selection. What could banks do to reduce this problem?

5. Joe Average has an average life—an average job, average home, 2.5 kids, a dog, and a Ford in the garage. He dreams of becoming rich some day and is secretly withholding a portion of his income to invest each month. Describe the difficulties and potential problems Joe will encounter if he tries to invest his funds in the direct credit market. Explain how financial intermediaries can reduce those problems.

6. As a small saver, it probably makes little difference whether you take your money to a commercial bank, a savings and loan association, or a credit union. However, if you want to borrow $4,000 to repair your car, the institution you approach can make a big difference in your chances of getting the loan. Examine Figure 4-1 and explain how these depository institutions are different from one another.

7. Explain the fundamental reasons that private pension funds have experienced rapid growth in the past 25 years.

8. Explain why Aetna Crop Insurance Company maintains a larger share of its assets in short-term government securities than Northwestern Mutual Life Assurance Company.

9. Framing your discussion in the context of the advantages of transferring funds through *intermediaries* rather than *directly* to society's deficit-spending units, discuss the factors that contributed to the rapid growth of mutual funds (that buy common stocks) over the last 25 years. What are some of the implications of the rapid growth in mutual funds?

10. Explain the circumstances that triggered the dramatic growth of money market mutual funds in the late 1970s and early 1980s.

11. From your personal vantage point as a lender of funds, what are the advantages of placing your funds in a money market mutual fund instead of a bank? The disadvantages?

12. "Because they are not subject to reserve requirements, money market mutual funds have been granted an unfair advantage over commercial banks." Based on the nature of the two types of institutions, do you agree or disagree? Explain.

13. Could money market mutual funds be categorized as depository institutions rather than as investment intermediaries? Explain.

14. Explain the effects of financial intermediation on market efficiency and overall societal welfare.

## ADDITIONAL READING

- For more in-depth discussions of the various financial intermediaries, see George G. Kaufman, *The U.S. Financial System: Money, Markets, and Institutions,* 7th edition (New York: Prentice-Hall, 2000).
- For analysis of the evolution of financial institutions, see Thomas Simpson, "Developments in the U.S. Financial System since the mid-1970s," *Federal Reserve Bulletin,* January 1988, pp. 1–13, and Anthony Santomero, "The Changing Structure of Financial Intermediaries: A Review Essay," *Journal of Monetary Economics,* September 1989. An excellent early article is Benjamin Friedman, "Postwar Changes in American Financial Markets," in Martin Feldstein, ed., *The American Economy in Transition* (Chicago: University of Chicago Press, 1980).
- A good source on changes in financial intermediaries and their implications for Federal Reserve policy is Federal Reserve Bank of Kansas City, *Changing Capital Markets: Implications for Monetary Policy,* 1993. A more recent source is H. Franklin Allen and Anthony Santomero, "What Do Financial Intermediaries Do?," *Journal of Banking and Finance,* 2000, pp. 271–294.
- A lucid analysis of the causes and consequences of the increasing role of pension and mutual funds in the intermediation process is Gordon Sellon, "Changes in Financial Intermediation: The Role of Pension and Mutual Funds," Federal Reserve Bank of Kansas City *Economic Review,* Third Quarter, 1992, pp. 53–70.
- An excellent source on the controversial Glass-Steagall Act is George Benston, *The Separation of Commercial and Investment Banking: The Glass-Steagall Act Revisited and Reconsidered* (New York: Oxford University Press, 1990).

# Chapter 5

# INTEREST RATE DETERMINATION

In Chapters 3 and 4 we outlined the instruments and markets involved in the transfer of funds from surplus units (lenders) to deficit-spending units (borrowers). We looked at the role of financial intermediaries in the U.S. economy. In this chapter we analyze the forces determining interest rate levels in financial markets.

Interest rates rank among the most crucial variables in macroeconomics and in the practical world of finance. Interest rate changes importantly influence many economic phenomena, including the level of consumer expenditures on durable goods, investment expenditures on plants, equipment, and technology, and the way wealth is redistributed between borrowers and lenders. Interest rates influence the prices of key financial assets such as stocks, bonds, and foreign currencies. On an individual level, interest rates determine monthly payments on car loans and home mortgages. Interest rates determine income earned on savings accounts, certificates of deposit, various types of bonds, and money market mutual fund shares.

An interest rate can be the price paid for borrowing funds, expressed as a percent per year. Alternatively, an interest rate can be the price received for lending of funds. In this chapter, we use the terms *interest rate* and *yield* interchangeably. Many different interest rates or yields exist, for example, rates on mortgages, U.S. Treasury bills, commercial paper issued by corporations, bank certificates of deposit, and bonds issued by corporations, municipalities, and the U.S. government. If lenders considered all of these instruments as perfect substitutes for one another, the interest rate or yield on all would be the same. Clearly this is not the case in the real world. Differences among various instruments in default risk, liquidity, tax considerations, and time to maturity account for the many interest rates or yields existing at any given time.

At the outset you must distinguish between the nominal interest rate and the real interest rate. The **nominal interest rate** is the actual interest rate unadjusted for inflation. The **real interest rate** is the nominal interest rate adjusted for inflation—the difference between the nominal interest rate and the inflation rate. If the nominal or actual interest rate is 7 percent and the inflation rate is 4 percent, the real interest rate is 3 percent. You can think of the real interest rate as the actual interest rate that would prevail in a hypothetical world of zero inflation. We analyze real interest rates later in this chapter. For now, we focus on nominal interest rates.

**nominal interest rate**
actual interest rate unadjusted for inflation

**real interest rate**
interest rate after adjusting the nominal interest rate for inflation

For analysis purposes, economists speak of "the" interest rate. We take the yield on a hypothetical debt instrument having neither default risk nor market risk as "the" interest rate, that is, our benchmark interest rate representative of interest rates in general. In the United States, the U.S. Treasury bill most closely approximates this ideal. Various other debt instruments are less liquid and involve greater default risk than Treasury bills. Their yields typically move in tandem with the Treasury bill yield, differing by a margin sufficient to compensate lenders for the greater default risk and inferior liquidity. "From the Financial Pages" indicates how yields on various financial instruments differ at given points in time.

## FROM THE FINANCIAL PAGES

Each weekday, *The Wall Street Journal* publishes a column, "Money Rates," which reports the current interest rates (or yields) on a large number of U.S. and foreign debt instruments. Among the many interest rates or yields included are the prime rate set by large U.S. banks, the federal funds rate, and the rates on commercial paper, certificates of deposit, Treasury bills, and money market mutual fund shares (Merrill Lynch Ready Assets Trust). A quick glance at this newspaper column gives you an overview of yields currently available to households and other prospective lenders. The following column shows the yields available on August 5, 2004. Note that the yields on this date were unusually low. How do yields today compare with the ones reported here?

# Money Rates

Thursday, August 5, 2004

The key U. S. and foreign annual interest rates below are a guide to general levels but don't always represent actual transactions.

### Commercial Paper

Yields paid by corporations for short-term financing, typically for daily operation

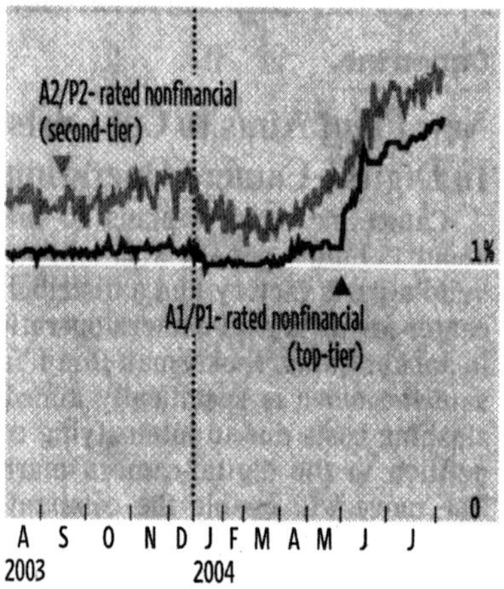


Source: Federal Reserve

**Prime Rate:** 4.25% (effective 07/01/04). The base rate on corporate loans posted by at least 75% of the nation's 30 largest banks.

**Discount Rate (Primary):** 2.25% (effective 06/30/04).

**Federal Funds:** 1.375% high, 1.250% low, 1.250% near closing bid, 1.375% offered. Effective rate: 1.30%. Source: Prebon Yamane (USA) Inc. Federal-funds target rate: 1.250% (effective 06/30/04).

**Call Money:** 3.00% (effective 07/01/04).

**Commercial Paper:** Placed directly by General Electric Capital Corp.: 1.43% 30 to 32 days; 1.50% 33 to 62 days; 1.57% 63 to 87 days; 1.64% 88 to 117 days; 1.71% 118 to 153 days; 1.80% 154 to 179 days; 1.88% 180 to 207 days; 1.95% 208 to 238 days; 2.02% 239 to 270 days.

**Euro Commercial Paper:** Placed directly by General Electric Capital Corp.: 2.04% 30 days; 2.07% two months; 2.08% three months; 2.10% four months; 2.12% five months; 2.15% six months.

**Dealer Commercial Paper:** High-grade unsecured notes sold through dealers by major corporations: 1.47% 30 days; 1.56% 60 days; 1.64% 90 days.

**Certificates of Deposit:** 1.47% one month; 1.65% three months; 1.94% six months.

**Bankers Acceptances:** 1.42% 30 days; 1.51% 60 days; 1.61% 90 days; 1.70% 120 days; 1.81% 150 days; 1.90% 180 days. Source: Prebon Yamane (USA) Inc.

**Eurodollars:** 1.48% - 1.45% one month; 1.58% - 1.55% two months; 1.66% - 1.63% three months; 1.75% - 1.71% four months; 1.85% - 1.81% five months; 1.90% - 1.87% six months. Source: Prebon Yamane (USA) Inc.

**London Interbank Offered Rates (Libor):** 1.5625% one month; 1.7100% three months; 1.9500% six months; 2.3600% one year. Effective rate for contracts entered into two days from date appearing at top of this column.

**Euro Libor:** 2.07963% one month; 2.11888% three months; 2.18325% six months; 2.34425% one year. Effective rate for contracts entered into two days from date appearing at top of this column.

**Euro Interbank Offered Rates (Euribor):** 2.077% one month; 2.116% three months; 2.186% six months; 2.344% one year. Source: Reuters.

**Foreign Prime Rates:** Canada 3.75%; European Central Bank 2.00%; Japan 1.375%; Switzerland 2.31%; Britain 4.75%.

**Treasury Bills:** Results of the Monday, August 2, 2004, auction of short-term U.S. government bills, sold at a discount from face value in units of $1,000 to $1 million: 1.465% 13 weeks; 1.735% 26 weeks. Tuesday, August 3, 2004 auction: 1.335% 4 weeks.

**Overnight Repurchase Rate:** 1.26%. Source: Garban Intercapital.

**Freddie Mac:** Posted yields on 30-year mortgage commitments. Delivery within 30 days 5.66%, 60 days 5.74%, standard conventional fixed-rate mortgages: 2.875%, 2% rate capped one-year adjustable rate mortgages.

**Fannie Mae:** Posted yields on 30 year mortgage commitments (priced at par) for delivery within 30 days 5.76%, 60 days 5.83%, standard conventional fixed-rate mortgages; 3.50%, 6/2 rate capped one-year adjustable rate mortgages. Constant Maturity Debt Index: 1.663% three months; 1.908% six months; 2.293% one year.

**Merrill Lynch Ready Assets Trust:** 0.75%.

**Consumer Price Index:** June, 189.7, up 3.3% from a year ago. Bureau of Labor Statistics.

*Source:* The Wall Street Journal, *August 6, 2004*

In this chapter we use a simple analytical framework to analyze the behavior of "the" interest rate. We use this framework to analyze the effects of factors such as expected inflation, Federal Reserve policy, the business cycle, and federal budget deficits (or surpluses) on interest rates. We sketch the causes of major swings in U.S. interest rates over the past 40 years. We discuss measurement of inflation expectations and analyze *real* or *inflation-adjusted* interest rates. Chapter 6 explores the effect of term-to-maturity on interest rate levels—*the term structure of interest rates.*

## PRESENT VALUE: INTEREST RATES AND SECURITY PRICES

We begin with a general framework that demonstrates how financial markets specifically price financial assets expected to provide a future flow of payments. The framework demonstrates the relationship between price and yield of assets and helps you understand intuitively why the prices of bonds, Treasury bills, stocks, and other assets fluctuate from day to day.

### Concept of Present Value

Suppose you place $1,000 in a certificate of deposit in your hometown bank today. The certificate of deposit pays 5 percent interest. In 1 year, your $1,000 earns $50 interest, growing to $1,050. The *future value* (FV) of your $1,000 is $1,050 after 1 year. Your *present value* (PV) or principal of $1,000 grows to its future value of $1,050. In terms of simple arithmetic:

$$\text{(5-1)} \quad \mathbf{FV = PV\ (1 + i), \text{ that is, } \$1{,}050 = \$1{,}000\ (1.05).}$$

In this expression, the future value (FV) 1 year from now ($1,050) equals the present value ($1,000) times 1.05, that is, $1,000 times one plus the interest rate. Conversely, to determine the present value (PV) of a future sum (FV) to be received in 1 year, divide both sides of Equation (5-1) by (1 + i) to solve for PV:

$$\text{(5-2)} \quad \mathbf{PV = \frac{FV}{(1 + i)}, \text{ that is, } \$1{,}000 = \frac{\$1{,}050}{1.05}.}$$

The present value of $1,050 to be received 1 year from now, given a 5 percent interest rate, is $1,050/(1.05), or $1,000. More generally, for any asset that will generate a *stream* of *n* future annual payments, consider the **present value formula,** expressed in Equation (5-3).

**present value formula**
formula expressing the value today of the right to receive a payment or stream of payments in the future

$$\text{(5-3)} \quad \mathbf{PV\ (\text{or Price}) = \frac{R_1}{(1 + i)} + \frac{R_2}{(1 + i)^2} + \frac{R_3}{(1 + i)^3} + \cdots + \frac{R_n}{(1 + i)^n}.}$$

In the equation, PV is the present value of the asset. Assuming markets are rational and appropriately price the asset, the market price is the same as PV. $R_1$, $R_2$, $R_3$, ··· $R_n$ indicate the payments (in dollars) currently expected from the asset 1, 2, 3, ··· n years from now. *i* is the interest rate used to discount the future returns (discussed shortly).

Every financial asset promises to produce a stream of payments in future years. The payments are designated $R_1$, $R_2$, $R_3$, ··· $R_n$. Some types of securities involve only one payment to be received in 1 year ($R_1$) or 30 years ($R_{30}$). An example of the former is a 1-year Treasury bill. An example of the latter is a 30-year **zero coupon bond**—a bond that provides no annual payments but returns a specific principal (say $1,000) at maturity in 30 years. Most corporate, municipal, and U.S. government bonds are

**zero coupon bond**
bond that provides no annual payments but agrees to return a specific principal at maturity

**coupon bonds**
bonds that promise a finite series of constant annual or semi-annual payments for 10, 20, or 30 years and repayment of principal at maturity

**present value**
value *today* of payments to be received in the future

**coupon bonds.** They promise a finite series of constant annual or semi-annual payments for 10, 20, or 30 years and repayment of the principal at maturity.

Bonds and other debt instruments involve payments to be made in the *future.* The face amount of these anticipated future payments must be discounted to properly evaluate their **present value**—the value *today* of payments to be received in the future. An instrument calling for a one-time payment of $1,050 in 1 year is worth $1,000 today if the interest rate is 5 percent. This is true because an individual who places $1,000 in an interest-bearing account today receives exactly $1,050 in 1 year.

Figure 5-1 shows how the present value of a fixed claim of $1 payable in the future depends on both the interest rate used to discount the dollar payment and the number of years in the future the dollar is to be received. The figure indicates that the present value of $1 to be received in 10 years drops from 61 cents to 39 cents to 25 cents as the interest rate rises from 5 percent to 10 percent to 15 percent. If you use a (very high) 15 percent interest rate to discount future payments, the present value of $1 to be received in 20 years is only about 6 cents!, that is, $\$1/(1.15)^{20} = \$0.06$. Conversely, 6 cents grows to approximately $1 after 20 years given an annual interest rate of 15 percent, that is, $(1.15)^{20} \times \$0.06 = \$0.98$.

**YOUR TURN**

A zero coupon government bond pays $1,000 at maturity in 30 years.

**a.** If competitive yields in the marketplace on similar instruments are 7 percent, calculate the present value (and current price) of the bond.

**b.** If yields rise to 8 percent, what happens to the price of the bond?

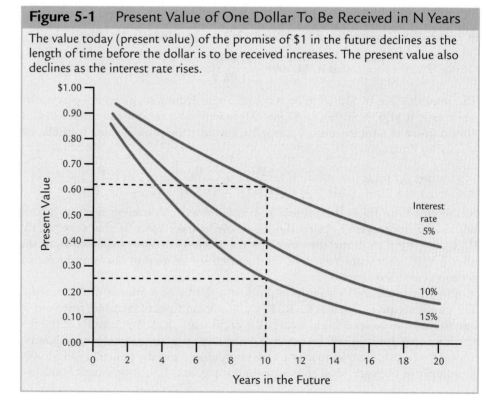

**Figure 5-1** Present Value of One Dollar To Be Received in N Years

The value today (present value) of the promise of $1 in the future declines as the length of time before the dollar is to be received increases. The present value also declines as the interest rate rises.

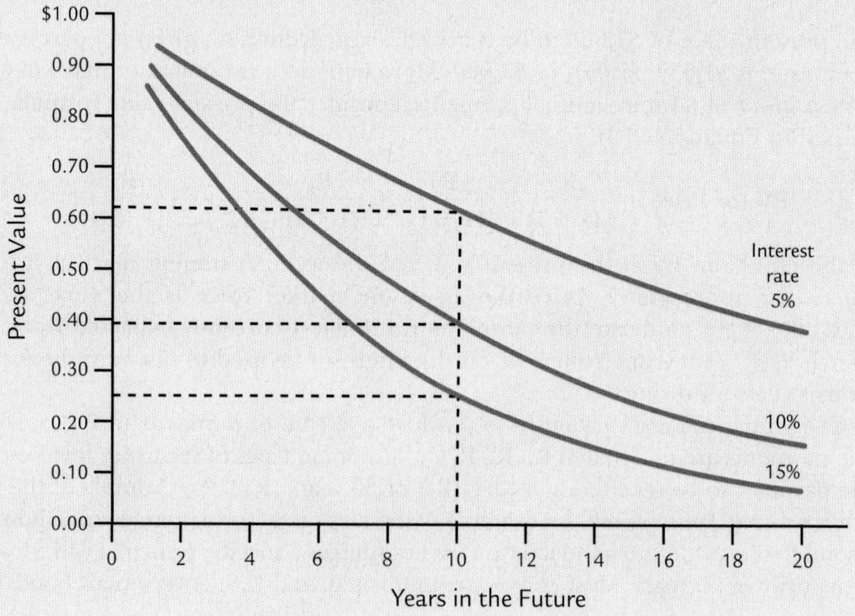

## Interest Rates and Security Prices

In the "Your Turn" problem, an *increase* in market yields (interest rates) is associated with a *decrease* in zero coupon bond prices. This inverse relationship between interest rates and prices applies to all debt instruments. An increase in interest rates reduces bond prices; a decrease in interest rates increases bond prices. Consider a bond paying a series of annual "coupons" or annual payments, designated C's, and the principal or face value at maturity, designated F, after n years. The general present value formula expressed in Equation (5-3) now is more specific, as indicated in Equation (5-4):

$$\text{(5-4)}\qquad \mathbf{PV} = \frac{C_1}{(1+i)} + \frac{C_2}{(1+i)^2} + \frac{C_3}{(1+i)^3} + \cdots + \frac{(C_n + F)}{(1+i)^n}.$$

$C_1, C_2, C_3, \cdots C_n$ represent the payments (annual "coupons") at the end of years 1, 2, 3, $\cdots$ n. F represents the face value of the bond, to be redeemed when the bond matures at the end of year n. The i in the denominators represents the prevailing interest rate or yield on comparable securities in the market.

You can use formulation 5-4 to calculate the market price of a bond, given the coupon payments and the current market yield. Suppose a bond with 4 years to maturity provides an annual coupon payment of $50 and that market yields on comparable instruments are 5 percent. Assume the bond repays the principal of $1,000 at maturity. The market valuation (and price) of this instrument can be calculated as follows:

$$\mathbf{PV} = \frac{\$50}{1.05} + \frac{\$50}{(1.05)^2} + \frac{\$50}{(1.05)^3} + \frac{(\$50 + \$1{,}000)}{(1.05)^4} = \$1{,}000.$$

If yields on comparable instruments are 5 percent, the market prices this instrument at $1,000. If the bond were priced at less than $1,000, its yield would exceed 5 percent. Other securities would be sold in order to purchase this bond, bidding its price up (and yield down). If this bond were priced at more than $1,000, its yield would fall short of 5 percent. Market participants would sell the bond to buy alternative securities yielding 5 percent. This action would bid the bond price back down to $1,000.

Suppose instead that yields on comparable instruments are 6 percent. No one would be interested in the bond at a price of $1,000. The present value and price of the bond would be less than $1,000. Specifically,

$$\mathbf{PV} = \frac{\$50}{1.06} + \frac{\$50}{(1.06)^2} + \frac{\$50}{(1.06)^3} + \frac{(\$50 + \$1{,}000)}{(1.06)^4} = \$965.34.$$

Because the current market interest rate or yield on comparable securities is used to discount the fixed stream of payments from a debt instrument, placing a value or price on it, it is clear that the price and yield of a debt instrument are inversely related. The higher the price, the lower the yield, and vice versa. The lower the price, the higher the yield, and vice versa. Falling interest rates indicate rising bond prices. Rising interest rates indicate falling bond prices.

## LOANABLE FUNDS MODEL OF INTEREST RATES

**loanable funds model**
model in which the supply and demand for funds determine the interest rate

To analyze the behavior of interest rates, we now develop a relatively simple and highly useful framework called the **loanable funds model.** Economists and financial analysts use the model to forecast interest rates. In this model, the interest rate is the price paid for the right to borrow and use loanable funds. Borrowers, society's deficit-spending units, issue claims or IOUs (bonds, notes, etc.) to finance expenditures in excess of funds currently on hand. These actions constitute a *demand for funds.* When AT&T issues new bonds to finance research and development expenditures, it is *demanding* funds. On the other side of the market, lenders seek to purchase financial instruments, that is, to *supply* loanable funds to the market. If you purchase a new AT&T bond, you are *supplying* funds to the market.

## Market for Loanable Funds

Table 5-1 indicates that individual households, business firms, governmental units, and foreign entities participate on both sides of the market for loanable funds. Households are major suppliers of funds through personal saving. However, they are demanders of funds through consumer credit purchases and home mortgages. Business saving is a source of funds. Business investment in plants, equipment, and inventories creates a demand for funds. State and local governments use temporarily idle cash to purchase federal government bonds and other IOUs, supplying funds to the market. On the other hand, federal (or state and local) government deficits produce a demand for funds as the government issues new bonds and related instruments. Foreign lending in the United States is a source of U.S. funds. Foreign borrowing in the United States represents a demand for U.S. funds.

If we look at the categories of borrowers and lenders on an actual *net* basis and assume (accurately) that the federal government is running a budget deficit, the supply of loanable funds typically comes from three sources: personal saving, bank loans (strongly influenced by the Federal Reserve), and foreign lending in the United States. Collectively, personal saving by households normally exceeds household buying on credit, making the household sector a net supplier of funds. On the other hand, aggregate business saving typically is outstripped by business investment, rendering the business sector a net demander of funds. In the past 40 years, the federal government budget has been in deficit about 90 percent of the years, making the federal government a demander of funds in most years. In recent years, foreign lending in the United States has exceeded foreign borrowing here (this could change in the future). On a *net* basis, demanders of loanable funds (suppliers of bonds and other debt instruments) include the business and government sectors.

Just as the quantity of wheat supplied and demanded in the market responds to the price of wheat, the quantity of loanable funds supplied and demanded depends on the price of loanable funds, that is, the interest rate. This principle is illustrated in Figure 5-2.

In the figure, $S_{LF}$ and $D_{LF}$ represent the supply and demand curves for loanable funds. The appearances (slopes) of these curves can be explained intuitively by as-

**Table 5-1 Individual Sources of Supply and Demand for Loanable Funds in the United States**

| Sources of Supply | Sources of Demand |
|---|---|
| Personal saving | Household credit purchases |
| Business saving | Business investment spending |
| Government budget surplus | Government budget deficit |
| Bank loans | Foreign borrowing in the United States |
| Foreign lending in the United States | |

**Figure 5-2** Interest Rates and Supply and Demand for Loanable Funds

Interest rates are determined in financial markets by supply and demand for loanable funds. Changes in interest rates are produced by shifts in supply and demand curves.

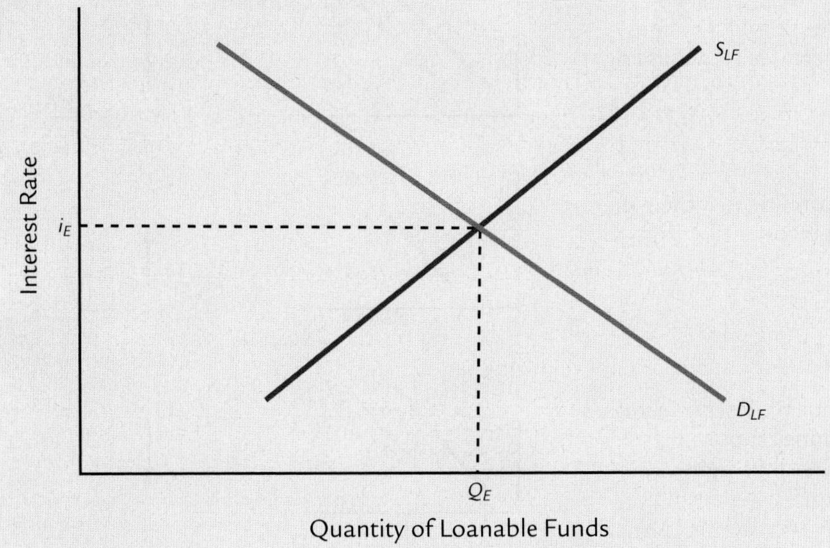


sessing the interest-rate responsiveness of the individual sources of supply and demand for funds.

The supply curve of loanable funds is an upward-sloping function of the interest rate. Classical (pre-1930s) economists regarded the interest rate as a measure of the incentive to abstain from current consumption. That is, they viewed the interest rate as the reward for saving. Individuals who save substitute future consumption for current consumption. The higher the interest rate, the greater the amount of future consumption gained by abstaining from current consumption, that is, by saving. A high interest rate counteracts the human trait of **time preference**—the propensity for people to prefer current consumption over future consumption—to want things *now*—and encourages saving.[1]

**time preference**
human propensity to exhibit preference for current consumption over future consumption

According to econometric studies, household saving does not respond strongly to interest rate changes. This lack of response suggests a very steep or nearly vertical supply curve in Figure 5-2. However, other forces are working to make the quantity of funds supplied fairly responsive to the interest rate. For example, bank lending (and the money supply) varies directly with interest rates because profit-maximizing banks more aggressively seek out and grant loans as rates rise. When foreign interest rates are held constant, an increase in U.S. rates attracts foreign funds to U.S. financial markets because an enormous pool of financial capital

[1] Suppose you have $20,000 of accumulated savings and are considering buying today a new Ford priced at $20,000. Suppose as an alternative you postpone the purchase and can earn 2 percent on a 20-year government bond, with car prices remaining constant over time. Your $20,000 grows to $29,719 after 20 years, allowing purchase of a fancier car. If you earn 5 percent per year, your $20,000 grows to $53,066 in 20 years, possibly permitting purchase of a Mercedes at that time. The *opportunity cost* (value of the alternative choice you give up) of spending the $20,000 today rather than saving it increases as the interest rate rises. A rational and forward-looking individual likely saves more when interest rates are higher.

**Table 5-2 Examples of Events Shifting the Supply and Demand for Loanable Funds**

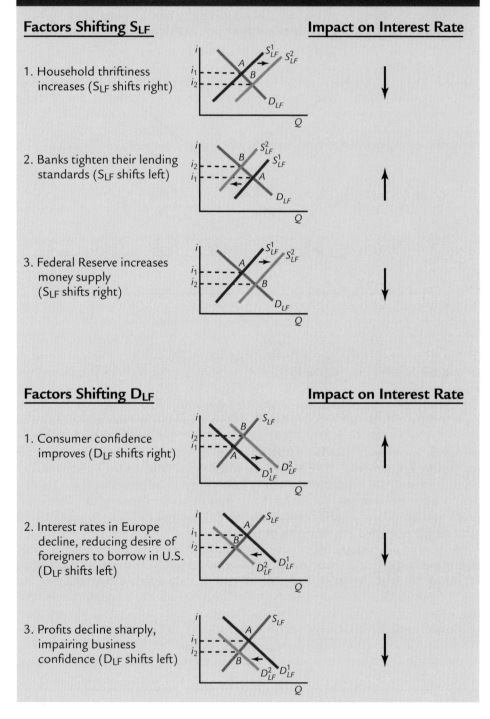

**Factors Shifting $S_{LF}$** — **Impact on Interest Rate**

1. Household thriftiness increases ($S_{LF}$ shifts right)

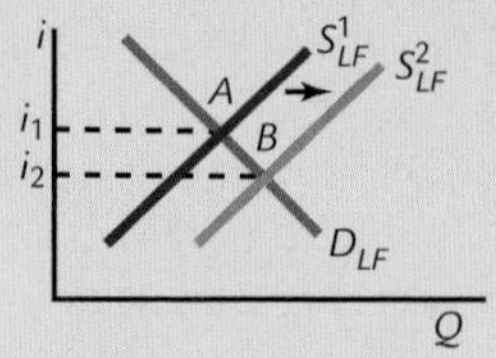


Impact on Interest Rate: ↓

2. Banks tighten their lending standards ($S_{LF}$ shifts left)

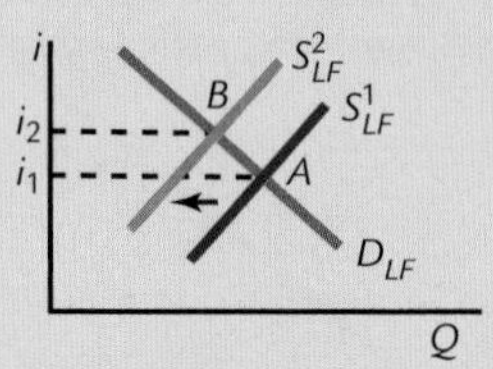


Impact on Interest Rate: ↑

3. Federal Reserve increases money supply ($S_{LF}$ shifts right)

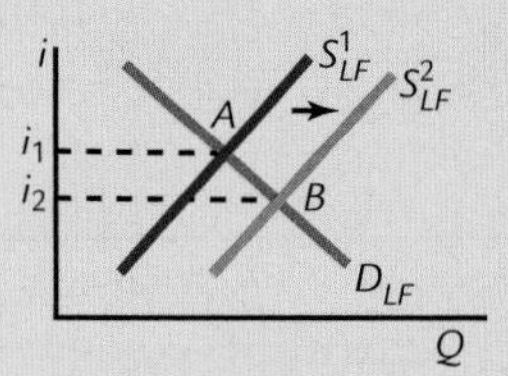


Impact on Interest Rate: ↓

**Factors Shifting $D_{LF}$** — **Impact on Interest Rate**

1. Consumer confidence improves ($D_{LF}$ shifts right)

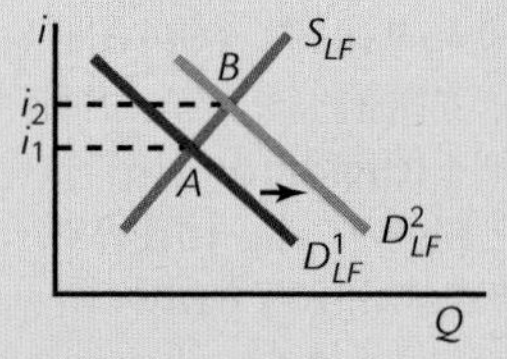


Impact on Interest Rate: ↑

2. Interest rates in Europe decline, reducing desire of foreigners to borrow in U.S. ($D_{LF}$ shifts left)

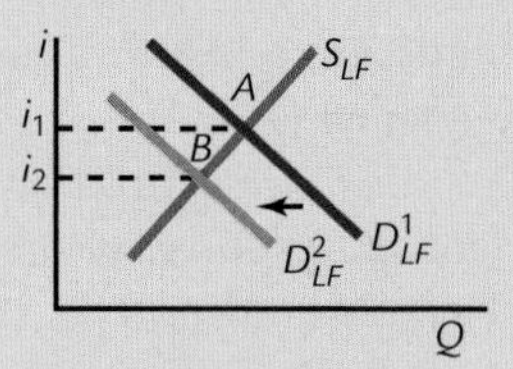


Impact on Interest Rate: ↓

3. Profits decline sharply, impairing business confidence ($D_{LF}$ shifts left)

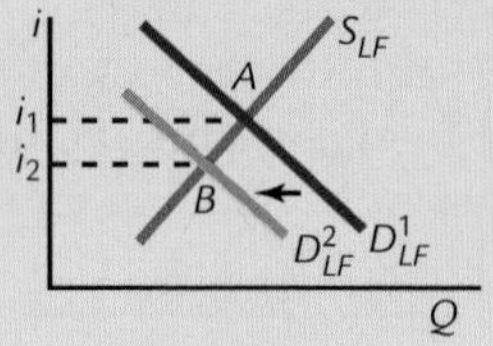


Impact on Interest Rate: ↓

can be transferred easily and instantaneously between countries in response to yield incentives. For these reasons, we draw the $S_{LF}$ curve as upward sloping.

The demand curve for loanable funds is downward sloping: lower interest rates stimulate expenditures on items financed through borrowing. A decline in car loan rates reduces monthly payments, thereby increasing affordability of cars and the quantity of car loans demanded. Other examples of interest-sensitive expenditures contributing to the downward slope of the demand curve in Figure 5-2 include other durable goods purchases, new home purchases, and investment in plants, equipment, inventories, and nonresidential real estate. Lower interest rates in the United States when interest rates in other countries are held constant induce foreigners to increase borrowing in the United States.

## Factors Shifting Supply and Demand for Loanable Funds

According to the loanable funds model, the interest rate moves to the equilibrium level—the level that equates the quantity of loanable funds supplied with the quantity of loanable funds demanded. In Figure 5-2, equilibrium occurs at $i_E$. Any factor producing a shift in the position of the supply curve or demand curve changes the equilibrium interest rate. An increase in demand (rightward shift of the demand curve) or a reduction of supply (leftward shift of the supply curve) increases interest rates. An increase in supply (rightward shift of the supply curve) or a decrease in demand (a leftward shift of the demand curve) decreases interest rates.

Return to the list of factors in Table 5-1. What specific factors would exert downward pressure on interest rates? An increase in personal saving resulting from demographic changes or increasing thriftiness would increase the supply of loanable funds, causing interest rates to decline. So would an increase in business saving resulting from cost-cutting measures on the part of firms. Federal Reserve actions increasing the availability of loans through banks boost the supply of funds and reduce interest rates. Increased political and economic instability in foreign nations increases worldwide preference for U.S. financial assets, boosting supply of funds. On the demand side of the market, a decline in business and consumer confidence due to events such as the terrorist attacks of September 11, 2001, reduce demand for loanable funds and exert downward pressure on interest rates. A decline in foreign interest rates that reduces the willingness of foreigners to borrow in the United States also decreases interest rates. Table 5-2 illustrates the effects of several specific events that shift the supply and demand curves for loanable funds, thereby altering interest rates.

# FUNDAMENTAL DETERMINANTS OF INTEREST RATES

A multitude of factors initiate shifts in the supply or demand for funds, producing changes in interest rates. Four particularly important forces affecting interest rates are inflation expectations, Federal Reserve policy, the business cycle, and the state of the federal budget, that is, the magnitude of government budget surplus or deficit. We examine each of these fundamental forces driving interest rates.

## Inflation Expectations

Interest rates rise when expected inflation increases. Interest rates fall when expected inflation declines. The loanable funds framework easily explains the propensity for interest rates to vary directly with the magnitude of inflation expectations, as demonstrated in Figure 5-3.

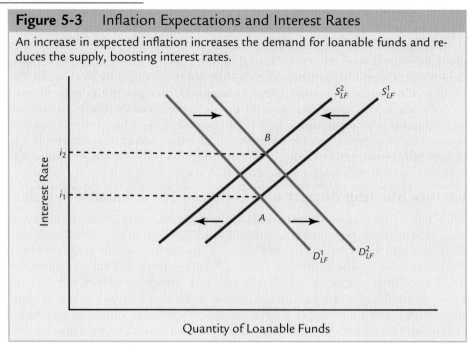

**Figure 5-3** Inflation Expectations and Interest Rates

An increase in expected inflation increases the demand for loanable funds and reduces the supply, boosting interest rates.

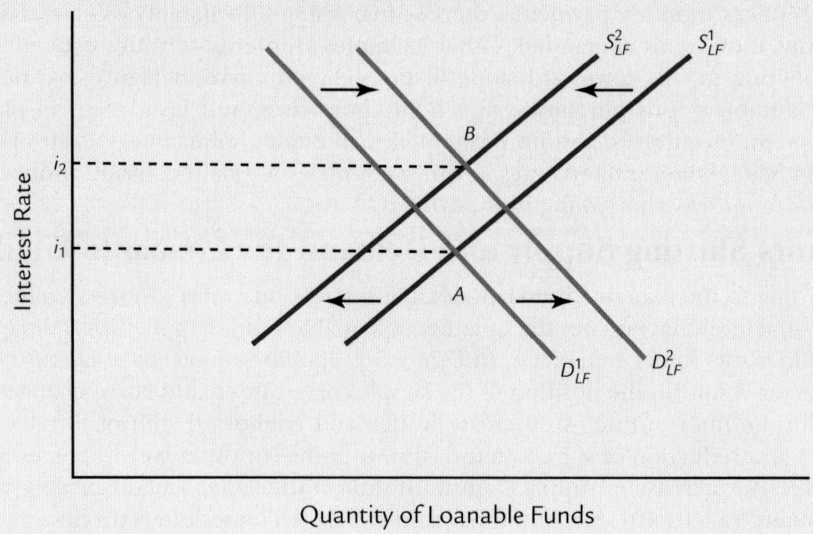


Suppose inflation has been relatively subdued for several years, approximately 2 percent per year for the past decade. The supply and demand curves for loanable funds are represented by $S^1_{LF}$ and $D^1_{LF}$ in Figure 5-3, with the equilibrium at *A*. The equilibrium interest rate is $i_1$.

Now suppose the inflation rate escalates to 5 percent per year, and the public expects the higher inflation rate to continue for some time. The supply curve of loanable funds shifts leftward, the demand curve shifts rightward, and the equilibrium interest rate increases.

Development of prospects for continuing inflation of 5 percent reduces the supply of funds, shifting the supply curve leftward from $S^1_{LF}$ to $S^2_{LF}$. At each and every possible interest rate, the willingness to lend funds is reduced because the real value of the principal loaned out is expected to erode more rapidly. Lenders reconsider the alternatives to lending. Some former lenders elect instead to purchase shares of common stock, gold and other precious metals, real estate, or other real assets believed to be effective hedges against inflation. For these reasons, the supply of loanable funds decreases (shifts leftward). At each possible interest rate, lending is less attractive now that expected inflation has increased.

At the same time, the increase in expected inflation raises the demand for loanable funds. At each and every interest rate, the willingness to borrow is stimulated, shifting the demand curve rightward from $D^1_{LF}$ to $D^2_{LF}$. The real value of the debt incurred is expected to decline more rapidly, *benefiting* borrowers (debtors). The *real* value of projects built or goods purchased with borrowed funds remains constant during inflation, while the real burden of debt is reduced by higher prices. Inflation reduces the burden of debt, making it more attractive to borrow.[2] An in-

[2] Consider an extreme case. In the German hyperinflation of the early 1920s, an individual who took out a multimillion deutsche mark 5-year loan in 1920 at 10 percent interest to buy a large farm could pay off the loan in 1925 with a sum of money that would not even purchase a loaf of bread. The borrower then owned the farm free and clear, having given up almost no real purchasing power to obtain it.

crease in expected inflation tends to increase the rate of homebuilding, household credit purchases, and investment in plants, equipment, and inventories at each possible interest rate. The demand curve for loanable funds in Figure 5-3 shifts rightward when expected inflation increases.

Given the reduction in supply and the increase in demand for loanable funds induced by the increase in expected inflation, the equilibrium moves from *A* to *B* in the figure. The equilibrium price of loanable funds—the interest rate—rises. Assuming the existence of competitive financial markets unrestricted by controls, the interest rate in Figure 5-3 rises from $i_1$ to $i_2$. The effect of a change in expected inflation on interest rate levels is the **Fisher effect,** named for Irving Fisher, the great American economist who pioneered the theory linking expected inflation and interest rates (see the exhibit on Irving Fisher in Chapter 22).

**Fisher effect**
tendency for interest rates to be positively related to the level of inflation expectations

**Fisher Hypothesis.** A formulation linking nominal (actual) interest rates and expected inflation is given in Equation (5-5).

$$\text{(5-5)} \quad \mathbf{i = r + \beta\pi^e.}$$

**Fisher hypothesis**
strong form of this theory asserts that interest rates move one-for-one with the magnitude of expected inflation; the weak form states that expected inflation significantly influences interest rates

In this equation, i is the nominal (actual) interest rate, r is the real interest rate, that is, the interest rate prevailing in a sustained era of zero inflation, and $\pi^e$ is the expected rate of inflation. The coefficient $\beta$ indicates the extent to which nominal interest rates adjust to each one percentage-point increase in the expected inflation rate. This framework indicates that nominal or actual interest rates (i) change due to changes in real rates (r) or expected inflation ($\pi^e$). If the real interest rate (r) remains constant over time and $\beta = 1$, then changes in expected inflation ($\pi^e$) account entirely for movements in nominal interest rates (i). In reality, both the real interest rate and expected inflation change over time, producing changes in nominal interest rates.

The **Fisher hypothesis,** in its strong form, asserts that $\beta = 1$, that is, interest rates move one-for-one with the magnitude of expected inflation. The weak form of the Fisher hypothesis states that $\beta$ is positive and significant, that is, expected inflation significantly influences interest rates. If the real rate (r) stays constant at 2 percent and expected inflation increases from 3 to 8 percent, nominal interest rates increase from 5 to 10 percent in the strong version of the Fisher hypothesis. This is known as the **inflation neutrality** case. The increase in interest rates compensates fully for the increase in expected inflation and neutralizes the potential effect of higher inflation on real wealth distribution between lenders and borrowers.

**inflation neutrality**
condition in which inflation is fully anticipated and compensated for by economic agents, attenuating the potential redistributive effects of inflation

Actually, the real interest rate changes over time. Classical economists argued that the fundamental forces driving real interest rates were the marginal productivity of capital and the rate of time preference. The **marginal productivity of capital** is the rate of return expected by firms from purchase of an additional unit of capital goods such as new computer hardware and software. Given other factors that influence real interest rates, if marginal productivity of capital increases, firms increase borrowing to purchase capital equipment (demand for funds shifts rightward), thereby raising real interest rates. The **rate of time preference** is the *extent* to which people prefer present goods over future goods. If the rate of time preference increases so that people more strongly desire present goods over future goods, household saving rates decline. This phenomenon shifts the supply curve of funds leftward, thereby raising real interest rates. Other factors producing changes in real interest are Federal Reserve policies, changes in the position of the federal government budget, and business cycle conditions. Therefore, changes in nominal in-

**marginal productivity of capital**
rate of return expected by firms from purchase of an additional unit of capital goods

**rate of time preference**
extent to which people prefer present consumption over future consumption

terest rates often reflect factors other than changes in expected inflation. Furthermore, $\beta$ may not be precisely equal to one.[3] Nevertheless, economists agree that inflation expectations powerfully influence the level of interest rates, *especially long-term rates.* If $\beta$ is not equal to one, it certainly is positive and not dramatically different from one in magnitude.

Because inflation expectations are significantly influenced by the recent course of actual inflation, long-term interest rates tend to be positively correlated with the actual recent rate of inflation. Figure 5-4 illustrates the yield on 10-year U.S. government bonds, plotted against the 12-month U.S. inflation rate since 1960. The dramatic upward trend of U.S. bond yields from 1965 to 1980 is attributable principally to the rising trend of inflation (and inflation expectations) in that period. The decline in inflation after 1980 was responsible for much of the following decline in bond yields. If the inflation rate increases appreciably in the next 2 years, it is almost certain that long-term interest rates also will increase.

**Empirical Evidence on the Fisher Hypothesis.** Empirical research designed to measure the size and statistical significance of $\beta$ in Equation (5-5)—that is, the response of interest rates to a change in expected inflation—indicates that the sensitivity of interest rates to inflation increased sharply in the post–World War II era. Before the 1940s, financial markets did not respond to inflation in the systematic manner suggested by the Fisher hypothesis. This is perhaps attributable to

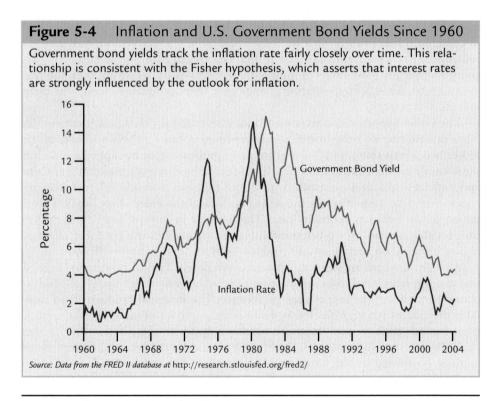

**Figure 5-4** Inflation and U.S. Government Bond Yields Since 1960

Government bond yields track the inflation rate fairly closely over time. This relationship is consistent with the Fisher hypothesis, which asserts that interest rates are strongly influenced by the outlook for inflation.

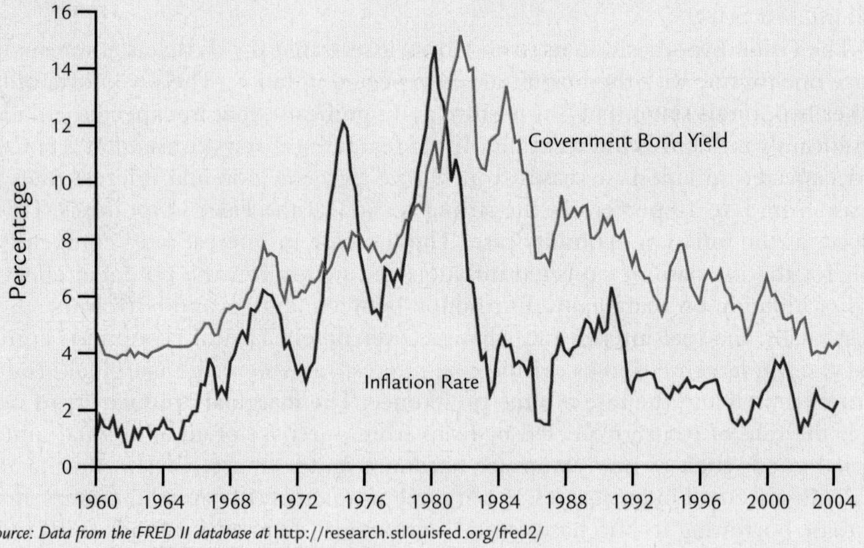


*Source: Data from the FRED II database at* http://research.stlouisfed.org/fred2/

[3] Beta, the coefficient relating the expected inflation rate to the interest rate, may not be precisely one. Its value depends on the elasticities of the supply and demand curves for loanable funds (Figure 5-2) and the magnitude of the shifts in the curves in response to changes in expected inflation. You can argue that $\beta$ should be greater than one, because nominal interest income is taxable to the lender and tax-deductible to the borrower. To preserve a given *real after-tax* return in the face of increased inflation, the lender must receive an increase in pre-tax yield greater than the increase in the inflation rate. The borrower can afford to pay an increased interest rate greater than the increase in the inflation rate and still preserve a given real after-tax interest cost.

**Figure 5-5** Government Bond Yields and Inflation Rates in 18 Nations

Countries experiencing high inflation tend to experience high interest rates. Countries with modest inflation typically exhibit lower interest rates. This fact is consistent with the Fisher hypothesis.

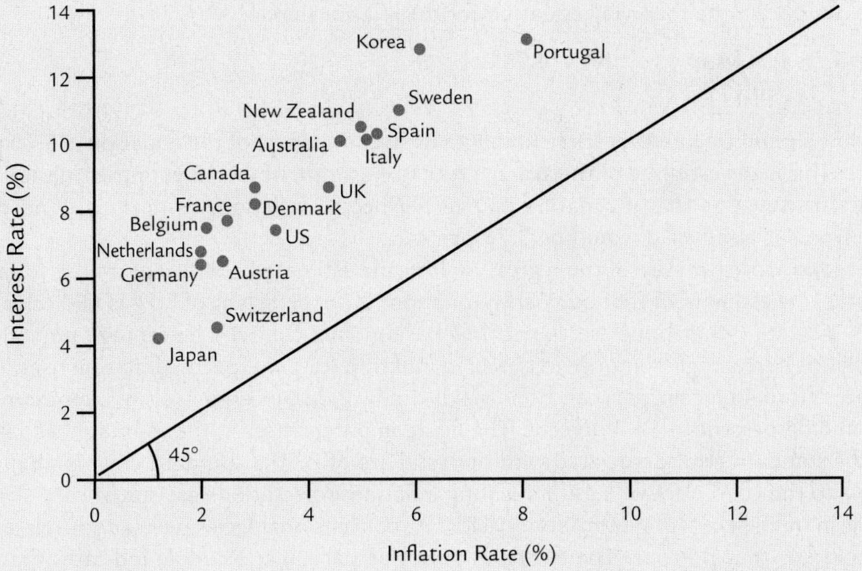


*Source: Computed from data in International Monetary Fund,* International Financial Statistics *at* http://ifs.apdi.net/imf/

the fact that the U.S. price level was approximately the same in the early 1940s as in the 1770s. In other words, there was little or no net inflation from the origin of the United States until the 1940s. Periods of inflation were followed by periods of *deflation*—falling prices. In the inflation-conscious era of the past 50 years, the U.S. consumer price index increased more than sixfold, and interest rates have exhibited a definite sensitivity to the outlook for inflation.

Figure 5-5 illustrates the relationship between inflation rates and long-term interest rates across 18 nations from 1990 to 2000. The average inflation rate and the average long-term government bond yield experienced over the decade are plotted for each country. The graph provides a crude international test of the Fisher hypothesis that interest rates move closely with expected inflation. The figure clearly shows a positive relationship between inflation and interest rates. Nations with very high inflation rates (Portugal, Korea, Sweden) experienced high bond yields. Countries with relatively low inflation (Japan, Germany, Switzerland) exhibited low bond yields.

In the figure, the vertical distance between each point plotted and the 45-degree line indicates the difference between the average government bond yield and the average inflation rate for each country, that is, the distance measures the average *real* interest rate over the decade. In all instances, the nominal interest rate exceeds the inflation rate, that is, the real interest rate is positive. The real rate ranges from about 2 percent in Switzerland to about 4 percent in Korea, Canada, Australia, and New Zealand. In general, the graph strongly supports the view that expected inflation exerts a powerful effect on interest rates. (See Exhibit 5-1 for an econometric analysis of the relationship illustrated in the figure.) We will see, however, that inflation expectations is only one of several important forces that influence interest rates.

## **Exhibit 5-1** Estimating the Relationship between Expected Inflation and Interest Rates

From the data illustrated in Figure 5-5 we can conduct a very simple, crude test of the Fisher hypothesis. Suppose we wish to estimate the simple model of the form $i = r + \beta\pi^e$ for this cross section of nations. If we fit a regression line to the points in the figure, we obtain the following equation for the relationship:

$$\mathbf{i = 3.78 + \underset{(0.17)}{1.14}\,\pi^e} \qquad \mathbf{R^2 = 0.78}$$

How should we interpret these findings? First, the *intercept* of the equation is 3.78 percent. This is the estimate of the average real interest rate of the 18 countries in the sample. This suggests that if a nation had zero expected inflation, its nominal (and real) government bond yield would be 3.78 percent.

Second, note the *slope* of the regression line, the estimated coefficient on the $\pi^e$ term, that is, the estimate of $\beta$ of our Fisher equation. This coefficient of 1.14 is fairly close to 1.0, indicating that bond yields rise 114 basis points (or 1.14 percentage points) for each one percentage point rise in expected inflation ($\pi^e$). If expected inflation rises from 2 percent to 4 percent per year, bond yields rise by 2.28 percentage points, for example, from 6.06 percent to 8.34 percent. The figure in parentheses in the estimated equation is the standard error associated with our estimate of $\beta$. The standard error is small relative to the coefficient of 1.14, indicating inflation expectations are statistically significant in influencing long-term bond yields. At conventional levels, we cannot reject the hypothesis that $\beta$ is 1.0. The evidence from this particular example indicates that we cannot reject either the weak form or the strong form of the Fisher hypothesis.

Finally, note that $R^2$ is 0.78. Variation in inflation rates across countries accounts statistically for 78 percent of the variation in government bond yields across the same countries. In other words, the points plotted in the figure cluster closely about the regression line.

This model is overly simplistic and naïve. Other variables influencing nominal interest rates besides expected inflation must be added to the model. Nevertheless, even this simple model reminds us of the powerful role of inflation expectations in long-term interest rate determination.

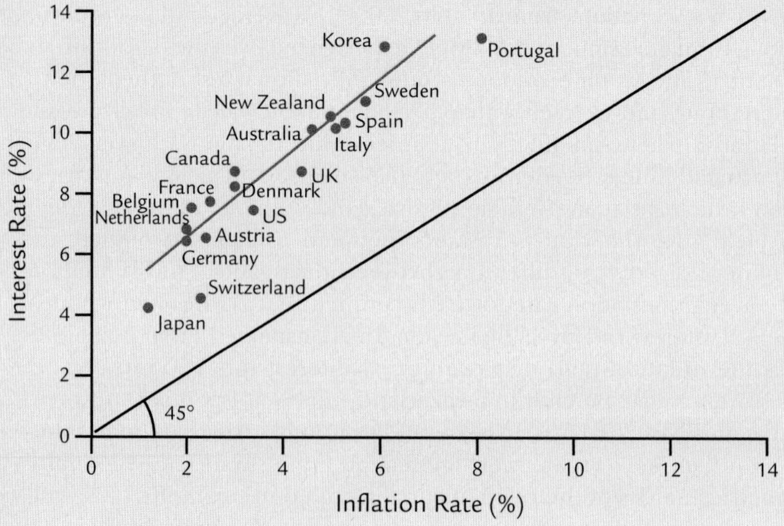

## Federal Reserve Policy

The Federal Reserve uses certain policy tools to influence the availability of loans through banks and the nation's money supply. When banks expand loans, the money supply rises. When banks reduce loans, the money supply falls. This process is analyzed in depth in Parts 4 and 5. Because bank loans are an important component of the supply of loanable funds, Federal Reserve policy actions initiate shifts in the supply curve of loanable funds ($S_{LF}$) in Figure 5-2.

To stimulate the economy, the Fed implements measures encouraging banks to expand loans, thereby boosting the money supply. The supply curve of loanable funds shifts rightward, reducing interest rates. To restrain economic activity, the Fed implements actions forcing banks to reduce lending. The money supply falls and the supply curve of loanable funds shifts leftward, driving up interest rates. The Federal Reserve has considerably more direct influence on short-term interest rates than on long-term rates. The latter are more strongly influenced by the outlook for inflation and budget deficits and the expected rates of return from investment in capital goods (marginal productivity of capital). In the past when inflation was particularly severe and deemed by financial market participants to be closely associated with money growth, the *announcement* of a sharp increase in the money supply boosted inflation expectations and ignited an *increase* in long-term interest rates via the Fisher effect.

## Business Cycle

Interest rates exhibit a strong cyclical pattern, rising during the expansion phase of the business cycle and falling during periods of economic contraction (recession or depression). This *pro-cyclical* pattern—the tendency for interest rates to be positively correlated with the strength of economic activity—is most evident in short-term interest rates and is illustrated in Figure 5-6.

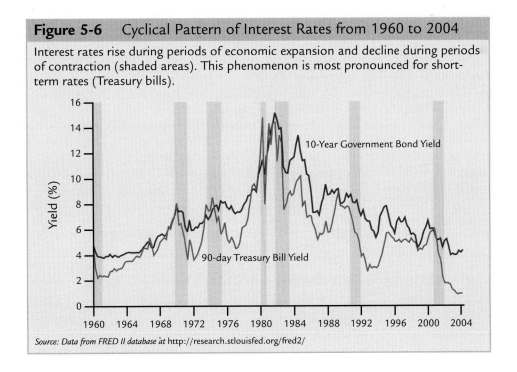

**Figure 5-6** Cyclical Pattern of Interest Rates from 1960 to 2004

Interest rates rise during periods of economic expansion and decline during periods of contraction (shaded areas). This phenomenon is most pronounced for short-term rates (Treasury bills).

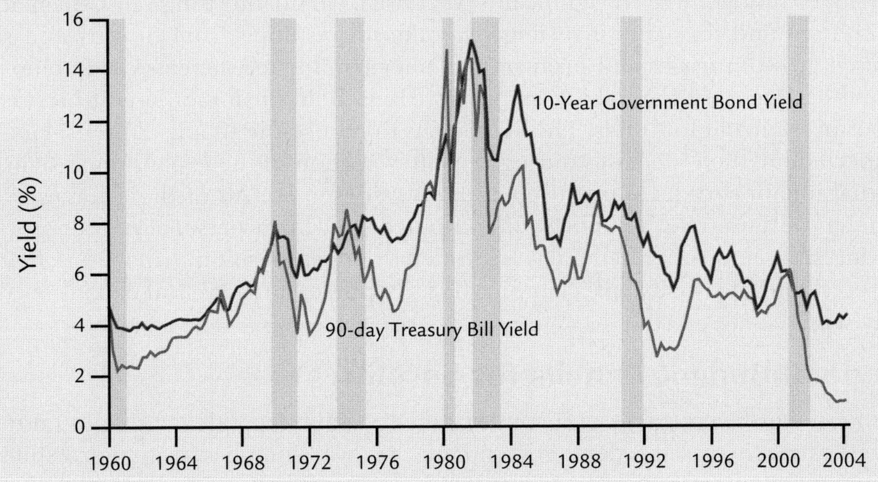


*Source: Data from FRED II database at* http://research.stlouisfed.org/fred2/

Figure 5-6 shows the pattern of yields on short-term and long-term U.S. Treasury securities since 1960, a period encompassing seven full business cycles (recessions are shaded in the figure). Interest rates typically decline during recessions and increase during economic expansion. This cyclical pattern is especially pronounced for short-term yields (Treasury bills). Long-term rates normally exhibit a pro-cyclical pattern but are less variable than short-term yields, exhibiting considerably less amplitude over the course of the business cycle.

The loanable funds framework can explain the pro-cyclical pattern of interest rates. During periods of economic expansion, the demand for funds grows rapidly as business and consumer borrowing escalates. Inflationary pressures typically increase as economic activity strengthens, pulling up interest rates through the Fisher effect. The Fed may restrict the availability of funds to counteract inflation as the economy strengthens. All three forces tend to pull up interest rates. The opposite occurs during recessions. The demand for funds drops as businesses and consumers retrench and inflationary pressures diminish. The Federal Reserve more aggressively increases the supply of loanable funds. These three forces often combine to bring interest rates down during periods of recession.

This overview is broadly valid, simplifying a more complex process. In the early phase of cyclical expansion—the first 1 or 2 years—upward pressure on interest rates is very mild or nonexistent. Credit demands rise modestly as firms borrow to increase inventories and bolster working capital. However, several forces work to hold down and even depress interest rates in the first 1 or 2 years of economic expansion. The federal budget deficit declines because of rising tax revenues during expansion. On the supply side of the market, reduced unemployment and income growth increase personal saving. Business profits and retained earnings respond positively to economic expansion. Because the economy continues to exhibit considerable unemployment and excess capacity in the initial years of the expansion, the Federal Reserve increases the supply of funds through stimulative policy actions. Inflation expectations typically reach a cyclical low in the early phase of the economic expansion. On balance, interest rates experience little or no upward pressure in the first 1 or 2 years of expansion.

In the later phase of cyclical expansion, the upward pressure on interest rates becomes increasingly pronounced. Business investment expenditures (and demand for funds) increase significantly because of high and rising rates of capacity utilization and the natural feeling of optimism resulting from healthy and sustained growth in sales and profits. Consumer confidence increases as unemployment declines and job stability improves. Household buying on credit increases, boosting demand for funds. The Fed begins to reduce the supply of funds. Finally, expected inflation increases during the latter portion of the expansion as signs of actual inflationary pressures become more widespread. All of these forces overwhelm the favorable influences of continued growth in personal and corporate saving and improving federal government budget position (smaller deficits). Interest rates increase appreciably in the later phase of the cyclical expansion (review Figure 5-6).

## Federal Budget Deficits (or Surpluses)

Other things being equal, an increase in the federal budget deficit should raise interest rates. Increased federal government borrowing implies a rightward shift in the demand curve for loanable funds. Interest rates must rise unless the supply curve is horizontal. Moreover, announcement of a larger budget deficit may arouse inflation expectations, pulling up interest rates via the Fisher effect. Many econo-

# INTERNATIONAL PERSPECTIVES

## International Synchronization of Interest Rate Movements

Interest rate movements in the United States typically are accompanied by similar movements in other nations. The accompanying figure illustrates the high correlation between short-term market yields in Germany and the United States over the past quarter-century. Interest rates in both nations spiked from 1980 to 1981, trended downward through 1986 or 1987, increased in the late 1980s, and came down in the worldwide recessions of the early 1990s and early 2000s. A similar pattern occurred in France, England, Australia, and other industrial nations. What forces synchronize interest rate movements across countries?

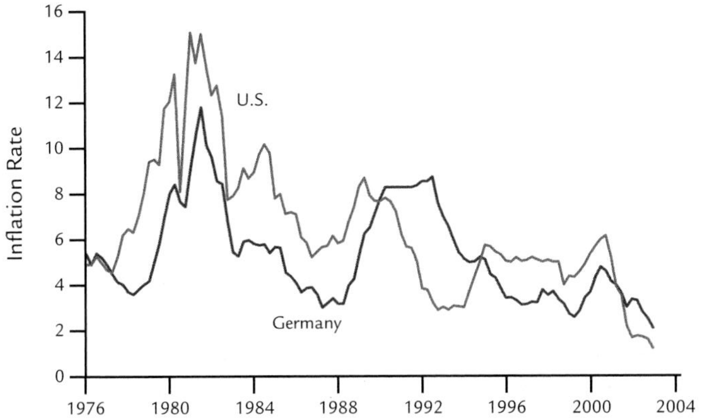


First, many of the forces influencing U.S. interest rates are experienced simultaneously by other nations. The recession that hit the United States in 2001 was essentially worldwide in scope. Interest rates fell in almost all countries. The 1979 oil price shock that pushed up inflation in the United States had a similar effect in Germany and other nations, leading to higher interest rates. Business cycles tend to be transmitted internationally. For example, a contraction in economic activity in the United States reduces U.S. demand for imported products, and the spillover dampens economic activity abroad. Because business cycles tend to be worldwide in scope and because interest rates fluctuate systematically over the business cycle in each country, you expect interest rate swings to be synchronized across countries. Because inflationary pressures often are worldwide in scope, the Fisher effect produces similar interest rate movements in many countries.

Finally, because an enormous pool of funds can be quickly transferred across national borders to the country offering the most attractive yields, interest rate movements are propagated across countries. An increase in interest rates in the United States reduces the supply of funds available in Germany as German funds flow to the United States. Interest rates in Frankfurt therefore rise in sympathy with rates in New York. A yield decline in New York pulls down German yields because the supply curve of loanable funds in Frankfurt shifts rightward in response to the increasing relative attractiveness of German financial instruments. For all of these reasons, interest rate movements in the United States are highly correlated with interest rate movements abroad.

mists agree that bigger deficits lead to higher interest rates,[4] but this is a contentious issue in the economics profession. Economists who do not believe budget deficits significantly influence interest rates advance two explanations in support of their view. One involves the worldwide scope of the market for loanable funds. The other involves the hypothesized tendency for changes in government budget deficits to trigger attenuating changes in the nation's private saving rate.

The first reason for questioning the proposition that U.S. budget deficits strongly influence interest rates is that the size of the U.S. deficit, sometimes enormous in an absolute sense, has been small in relation to the total pool of worldwide financial capital. Financial markets around the world have become increasingly integrated, so the market is virtually worldwide in scope. As interest rates in the United States begin to rise in response to heavier federal borrowing, the quantity of funds available to meet the government's demand rises sensitively as foreign institutions increase lending in the United States. The supply curve of loanable funds in the U.S. market (Figure 5-2) is elastic—almost horizontal—with respect to the interest rate. This sensitive supply response limits the upward pressure on U.S. rates resulting from increased federal borrowing associated with larger U.S. budget deficits.

The second explanation advanced by economists who are skeptical about the importance of budget deficits involves the alleged relationship between the federal budget deficit and saving behavior of individuals. Suppose the public is *forward-looking* and *rational*—individuals consider all available information when making consumption and saving decisions. The public correctly recognizes that larger budget deficits today imply either higher future taxes or lower future government benefits. Individuals increase current saving rates when they see larger deficits coming, protecting themselves and their heirs from future belt-tightening. Because household saving is a fundamental source of supply of funds, the supply curve of loanable funds shifts rightward when budget deficits increase. The effect of the government's increased demand for funds on interest rates is neutralized. Given certain strong assumptions about rational behavior and accurate foresight, interest rates are unaffected by larger budget deficits.

**Ricardian equivalence proposition**
theory that asserts that agents anticipate future tax liabilities associated with larger budget deficits and increase their saving rates to compensate

This position is the **Ricardian equivalence proposition** (named after David Ricardo, a nineteenth-century British economist). It hypothesizes that an increase in budget deficits due to an increase in government appropriations or a tax cut is *equivalent* to a future increase in taxes. Supporters of this proposition emphasize that it is consistent with rational behavior. A larger deficit today implies greater future interest expenditures to finance the enlarged stock of government debt and therefore higher future tax rates. In response, perceptive and rational individuals increase their saving rates today. Critics of the Ricardian equivalence proposition regard it as unrealistic. They point out that few individuals make the kind of calculations assumed by the adherents of the proposition, and most measures of private saving rates declined in the 1980s and early 1990s when deficits grew considerably larger. Professional financial market participants believe that larger deficits or larger expected future deficits significantly raise interest rates. Academic economists are divided on this issue.

[4] It is important to distinguish between a *structural deficit*—one that arises due to a fundamental mismatch between government expenditures and revenues even when the economy is at full employment—and a cyclical deficit—one that arises because a weak economy reduces government revenues and increases "safety net" expenditures. An increase in a structural deficit much more likely will be accompanied by higher interest rates than an increase in a cyclical deficit resulting from a weakening economy.

## MAJOR INTEREST RATE MOVEMENTS FROM 1960 TO 2004

We now use our loanable funds framework to sketch the forces accounting for major swings in long-term U.S. interest rates over the past four decades. Figure 5-7 illustrates the pattern of yields on 10-year U.S. government bonds and AAA- and BAA-rated corporate bonds over the long period.

The figure shows that 1960 to 1965 was a stable period for U.S. financial markets and interest rates. Inflation was subdued and bond yields were relatively low. This period of low and stable interest rates was followed by a long period of substantial fluctuations in interest rates. Why?

First, interest rates persistently increased from 1965 to 1981 as strong growth of demand for funds outstripped growth in the supply of funds. The powerful acceleration of inflation from 1965 to 1980 increased interest rates through the Fisher effect. Escalation of military expenditures on the Vietnam War from 1966 to 1969 overheated the economy, starting the inflation ball rolling. An economic boom fueled by the natural forces of the business cycle and the Federal Reserve's excessive monetary stimulus created a major increase in inflation in the late 1970s. Dramatic increases in oil prices in 1973 and 1979 contributed to the most severe episode of peacetime inflation in U.S. history from 1978 to 1980. The increase in inflation was followed by a dramatic spike in interest rates in 1980 and 1981 as the Federal Reserve pushed short-term interest rates sharply higher in an ultimately successful effort to eradicate severe inflation.

In the 1980s and early 1990s, interest rates came down a long way from their peaks of the early 1980s. The rate of inflation (and therefore expected inflation) declined sharply after 1980. Inflation came down more quickly than economists or

**Figure 5-7** Yields on Bonds in the United States from 1960 to 2004

Bond yields generally trended upward from the early 1960s until 1981. They then trended downward, reaching levels in recent years not seen since the early 1960s.

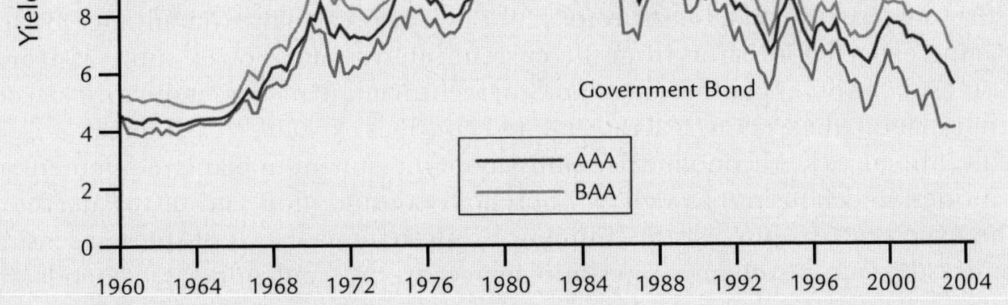

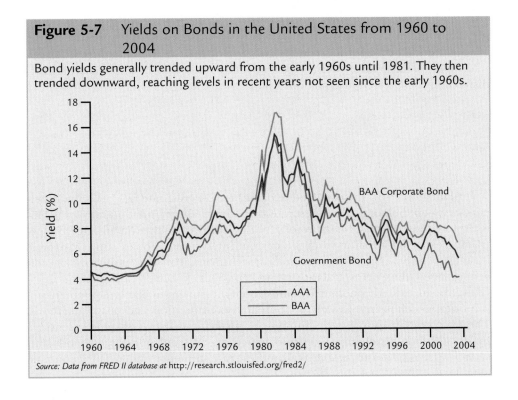


*Source: Data from FRED II database at* http://research.stlouisfed.org/fred2/

households expected, declining from 12.5 percent in 1980 to around 4 percent within 2 years. The eradication of severe inflation *gradually* pulled down bond yields because expectations of inflation lagged behind the actual (rapidly declining) rate of inflation. Economic activity remained less than robust in the United States and in other countries during and immediately after the severe worldwide recession of 1981 to 1983. Decreased economic activity contributed to lower bond yields. Rising actual and expected future budget deficits after 1981 helped maintain moderately high bond yields throughout the 1980s. Except for a temporary surge in the late 1980s, the U.S. inflation rate remained around 2 to 3 percent per year from 1983 to 2004. This favorable development kept bond yields much lower after 1990 than in the late 1970s and the 1980s.

The recession of 1990 to 1991, the unusually sluggish economic recovery that followed the recession, and the Federal Reserve's aggressive easing of monetary policy from in 1992 and 1993 resulted in significant further declines in *short-term* interest rates. *Long-term* rates throughout most of the 1990s remained above the very low levels of the period from 1960 to 1966. A remarkably good inflation performance coupled with rising budget *surpluses* in the last few years of the twentieth century exerted downward pressure on bond yields. In the first few years of the twenty-first century, sluggish economic activity coupled with extremely low inflation contributed to very low bond yields. By 2003 and 2004, bond yields had come full circle over a 40-year period! Government bond yields returned to the low levels of the early 1960s. However, a dramatic increase in the federal budget deficit during 2002 to 2004 increased the prospects for higher bond yields in the second half of the decade.

## REAL INTEREST RATES: EX ANTE VERSUS EX POST

You are acutely aware by now of the important distinction between *nominal* and *real* interest rates as a result of inflation. With inflation, real interest rates are lower than nominal rates. It is important to distinguish between two different concepts of real interest rates: the *expected* or *ex ante* real rate and the *realized* or *ex post* real rate. This distinction is expressed in Equations (5-6) and (5-7).

$$\mathbf{r}_{\text{ex ante}} = \mathbf{i} - \pi^e. \tag{5-6}$$

$$\mathbf{r}_{\text{ex post}} = \mathbf{i} - \pi. \tag{5-7}$$

**expected (ex ante) real interest rate ($r_{\text{ex ante}}$)** difference between nominal interest rate and *expected* inflation rate

In Equation (5-6), the **expected (ex ante) real interest rate ($r_{\text{ex ante}}$)** is the difference between the nominal interest rate (i) and the *expected* inflation rate ($\pi^e$). This is the key *forward-looking* measure of real rates. It is calculated in advance by subtracting expected inflation from the current interest rate. For example, if a small business bent on expansion faces an 8 percent bank loan rate and expects 4 percent inflation, the ex ante real rate is 4 percent. This expected real interest rate crucially influences key economic decisions about investment in plants, equipment, inventories, and housing, as well as household consumption and saving decisions. The expected real interest rate influences international flows of interest-sensitive funds, impacting exchange rates and hence exports and imports of goods and services. The *expected* or *ex ante* real interest rate influences important economic decisions.

**Table 5-3 Ex Ante and Ex Post Real Interest Rates in the United States**

| Period | Treasury Bill Yield (%)* | Expected Inflation (%)** | Ex Ante Real Actual Interest Rate (%) | Actual Inflation (%)*** | Ex Post Real Interest Rate (%) |
|---|---|---|---|---|---|
| 1961–1970 | 4.7 | 3.4 | 1.3 | 3.0 | 1.7 |
| 1971–1980 | 7.6 | 7.2 | 0.4 | 8.8 | −1.2 |
| 1981–1990 | 9.3 | 4.9 | 4.4 | 4.1 | 5.2 |
| 1991–2000 | 4.9 | 3.9 | 1.0 | 2.7 | 2.2 |
| 2001–2003 | 2.2 | 2.5 | −0.3 | 2.1 | 0.1 |
| Average, 1961–2003 | 6.3 | 4.7 | 1.6 | 4.5 | 1.8 |

*Average 1-year Treasury bill yield.
**Average expected inflation rate (CPI) from Michigan Survey.
***Average actual (CPI) inflation rate.
*Source: Data from FRED database at* http://research.stlouisfed.org/fred2/

In Equation (5-7), the **realized (ex post) real interest rate ($r_{ex\ post}$)** is the difference between the interest rate and *realized* inflation ($\pi$). It is calculated only *in retrospect,* that is, *after the fact.* In the case of the small business facing the 8 percent loan rate, suppose inflation turns out to be 6 percent. The ex post real rate is 2 percent instead of the expected 4 percent. The ex post real rate does not influence economic decisions, but it reveals information about the *outcome* of various decisions. Because realized inflation and expected inflation often differ, ex ante and ex post real interest rates frequently differ. This is illustrated in Table 5-3, which shows average ex ante and ex post real rates on U.S. Treasury bills during various 10-year intervals in recent decades.

**realized (ex post) real interest rate ($r_{ex\ post}$)** difference between nominal interest rate and *realized* inflation rate

## Ex Ante and Ex Post Real Rates in the United States

When calculating ex ante real interest rates, we face the problem of finding a suitable measure of inflation expectations. Economists draw inferences about inflation expectations by several methods—results of surveys of households and economists, forecasts made by macroeconomic models, and indicators derived from financial market phenomena. In Table 5-3, we use the median expected inflation rate (consumer price index) of the approximately 500 households participating each month in the Michigan Survey as our measure of expected inflation.

The table indicates that from 1971 to 1980, the Treasury bill yield averaged 7.6 percent and expected inflation of households averaged 7.2 percent. The average ex ante real Treasury bill yield during the decade was a meager 0.4 percent. Households buying Treasury bills expected to earn 0.4 percent after inflation. Because inflation turned out to be even higher than expected (8.8 percent versus the expected 7.2 percent), the ex post real Treasury bill yield was a *negative* 1.2 percent. Buying Treasury bills in the 1970s was a poor decision, partly because inflation was more severe than expected.

## Exhibit 5-2 Surveys of Inflation Expectations

You can draw inferences about inflation expectations from information in surveys of professional economists or of households. Several surveys of inflation expectations are available in the United States. The oldest is the Livingston Survey of professional economists, which dates back to 1946. The Livingston Survey and the Survey of Professional Economists (which began in 1981) are conducted by the Federal Reserve Bank of Philadelphia (http://www.phil.frb.org/). Another well-known survey of inflation expectations is the University of Michigan survey of households, which commenced in 1948 (http://www.sca.isr.umich.edu/main.php). The consensus (mean) 1-year-ahead consumer price index inflation forecasts and ensuing actual inflation rates of the Livingston Survey respondents and ensuing actual inflation rates are shown in the figure below.

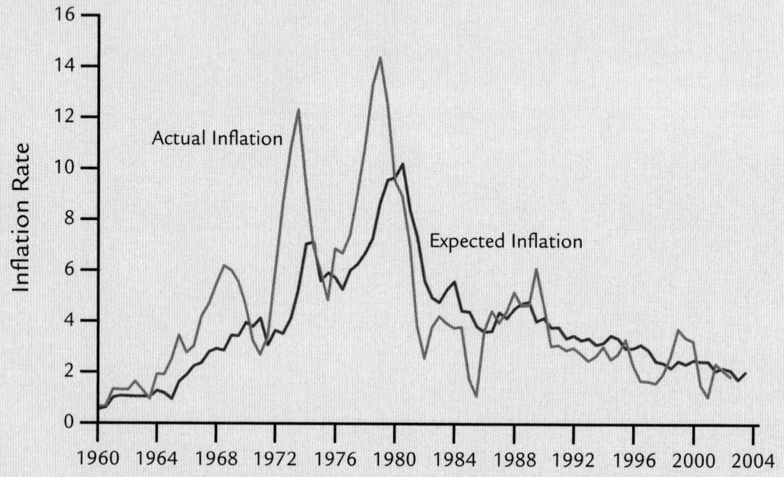


Several characteristics of inflation forecasting performance are noteworthy. First, while the U.S. inflation rate was ratcheting upward from the mid-1960s to 1980, economists persistently underestimated inflation. When inflation declined precipitously after 1980, the forecasts typically were too high—economists overestimated inflation. Second, turning points in inflation forecasts often lag behind turning points in actual inflation. These two facts suggest that past inflation (among other things) significantly influences economists' forecasts. Finally, when inflation trended strongly downward from 1990 to 2003, professional economists overestimated inflation (as did almost all econometric models). Studies demonstrate that inflation forecasts tend to be *unbiased* over long periods of time. In other words, significant forecasting errors are made in the short run, but positive and negative forecast errors tend to average out pretty close to zero over a very long period of time.

From 1981 to 1990, Treasury bills were a great investment. The average nominal yield was 9.3 percent. Because inflation expectations of households averaged 4.9 percent during this decade, the expected real return was 4.4 percent. Because inflation was lower than expected in this decade (4.1 percent versus the expected 4.9 percent), the ex post real rate earned on Treasury bills was 5.2 percent—an unusually high rate. The table indicates that over 10-year intervals, inflation expectations have sometimes been significantly off the mark, causing ex ante and ex post real rates to differ considerably. Over the full 43-year period, however, the average expected inflation rate (4.7 percent per year) was very close to the average realized rate (4.5 percent per year). The ex post and ex ante real Treasury bill yields were very similar, both averaging slightly less than 2 percent over the full period, as indicated in the bottom row of the table.

## Two Measures of Ex Ante Real Interest Rates

The measure of real interest rates influencing economic decisions is the *expected* or *ex ante* real rate. In the remainder of this chapter, we focus on this measure of real rates. Two conceptual measures of ex ante real interest rates exist: one ignores income taxes; the other considers income taxes. The two measures are defined in Equations (5-8) and (5-9).

$$\mathbf{r} = \mathbf{i} - \pi^{e} \tag{5-8}$$

$$\mathbf{r}_{at} = \mathbf{i}\,(1 - \mathbf{t}) - \pi^{e}. \tag{5-9}$$

Equation (5-8) is the standard calculation of the real interest rate, as described previously. If Linda earns 10 percent interest on Treasury bills and expected inflation is 4 percent, her expected real rate is 6 percent. This measure of real rates ignores income taxes. Equation (5-9) expresses the real *after-tax* rate, $r_{at}$, where t is the income tax rate. Given the same circumstances but acknowledging that Linda is in a marginal income tax bracket of 30 percent (t = 0.30), her expected real after-tax return is 3 percent. After taxes, her *nominal* return is 7 percent, that is, 10 percent times (1 − 0.30). Subtracting the expected inflation rate of 4 percent from this after-tax nominal return of 7 percent, we calculate the expected real after-tax interest rate to be 3 percent. Given that we live in a world of income taxes, rational individuals base decisions about borrowing and lending on expected real after-tax interest rates.

**YOUR TURN**

Suppose you want to buy a 3-year Treasury note paying 6 percent interest. Assuming you are in a 25 percent income tax bracket (federal, state, and local combined) and you expect inflation to average 3 percent annually over the next 3 years, calculate your expected real after-tax yield on this Treasury note.

Table 5-4 shows how r and $r_{at}$ differ, given various nominal interest rates and the assumptions that expected inflation is 4 percent and the income tax rate is 30 percent. Using the formulas in Equations (5-8) and (5-9), check the center and right-hand columns of the numbers in the table to confirm that you understand the distinction between the real interest rate and the real after-tax interest rate. The real after-tax rate is always lower than the simple real rate. When nominal interest rates are relatively high, the difference between r and $r_{at}$ is relatively large.

## Historical Behavior of Expected Real Interest Rates

The expected real interest rate is not constant over time. Factors other than inflation expectations influence interest rates, changing expected real interest rates. As we discussed earlier, classical economists believed that the marginal productivity of

**Table 5-4 Relationship Between Nominal Interest Rate and Two Measures of Real Interest Rates***

| Nominal Interest Rate (i) (%) | Real Interest Rate (r) (%) | Real After-Tax Interest Rate ($r_{at}$) (%) |
|---|---|---|
| 5 | 1 | −0.5 |
| 8 | 4 | 1.6 |
| 10 | 6 | 3 |
| 14 | 10 | 5.8 |

*Assumes expected inflation is 4 percent and marginal income tax rate is 30 percent.

capital and the rate of time preference were important factors influencing expected real interest rates. Expected real interest rates are boosted by increases in the expected marginal productivity of capital and the rate of time preference. Other important factors include expected budget deficits, actual and expected central bank policy, and developments related to the business cycle.

Figure 5-8 illustrates the actual Treasury bill yield from 1960 to 2004, the expected real Treasury bill yield (r), and the expected real after-tax Treasury bill yield for an individual in a 30 percent income tax bracket ($r_{at}$). As indicated in the figure and in Table 5-3, real rates were considerably higher in the 1980s than in the 1970s. The increase in real interest rates was dramatic in the early 1980s. Like the 1960s, real rates in most of the 1990s were intermediate between those of the 1970s and

**Figure 5-8 Treasury Bill Yield and Two Measures of Real Yields***

Real interest rates fluctuate over time. Rates were unusually low in the 1970s and 2000s and unusually high in the 1980s.

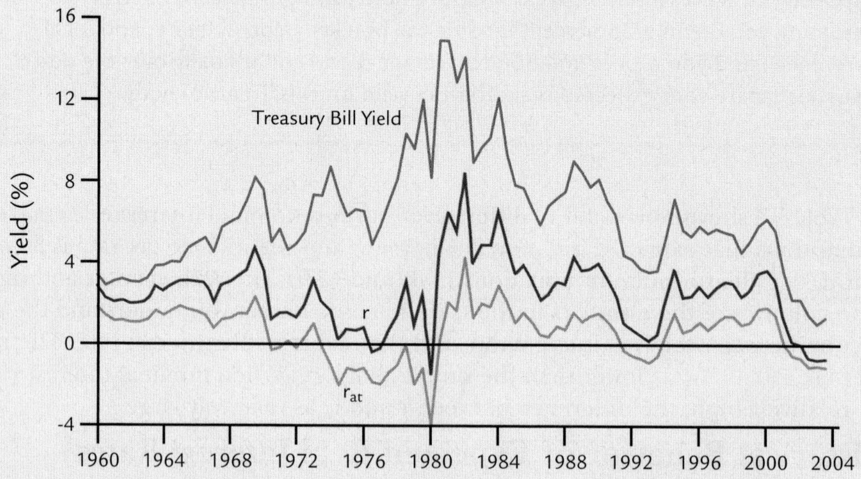

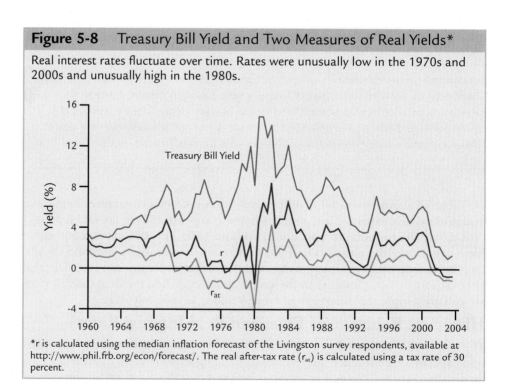

*r is calculated using the median inflation forecast of the Livingston survey respondents, available at http://www.phil.frb.org/econ/forecast/. The real after-tax rate ($r_{at}$) is calculated using a tax rate of 30 percent.

1980s. From 2000 to 2004, real rates frequently were negative as the Federal Reserve maintained nominal rates at very low levels to boost the sluggish U.S. economy. Why were real interest rates higher in the early 1980s than in earlier and later periods?

**High Rates of the 1980s.** At least four explanations for the abnormally high real interest rates of the 1980s have been proposed. First, following the very high inflation in the 1970s, the Federal Reserve slammed on the brakes in the early 1980s, dramatically boosting short-term interest rates to bring down inflation. The Fed maintained its restrictive posture for a lengthy period. Second, major buildup in national defense expenditures and a series of income tax cuts in the early 1980s led to large federal budget deficits after 1981. The demand curve for funds shifted rightward, pushing up nominal and real yields. Third, pro-business legislation implemented by the new Reagan administration (cuts in business taxes, deregulatory actions, and so forth) increased the expected returns from capital expenditures, boosting business firms' demand for funds. Real energy prices declined in the 1980s after rising sharply in the 1970s. Because capital goods are energy intensive, the decline in prices signaled firms to increase investment expenditures. This development boosts demand for funds, increasing real interest rates. For all of these reasons, the 1980s witnessed unusually high real interest rates.

**Low Real Rates of the 1970s and 2000s.** In contrast to the 1980s, several factors conspired to keep real interest rates low in the 1970s. First, monetary policy was relatively stimulative in the 1970s. High inflation, high business taxes, very high real energy prices, and low rates of technological innovation kept the expected returns from capital goods low, holding down the demand for funds and keeping ex ante real interest rates relatively low. Also, relatively small budget deficits prevailed in the 1970s.[5]

In the remarkable period from 1995 to 2000, technological innovations in information systems, telecommunications, and other areas led to a sharp increase in expected returns from capital. Investments in computer hardware and software, telecommunications equipment, and other equipment increased dramatically. Normally, this cycle produces very high real interest rates. However, a major swing from large federal budget deficits to large surpluses inhibited the upward pressure on real rates. The Federal Reserve maintained a stimulative monetary policy mode despite a booming economy because inflation stayed low due to surging productivity and a strong U.S. dollar internationally. Figure 5-8 indicates that real rates were at moderate positive levels in the 1990s. Following the boom of the late 1990s, a recession occurred in 2001. Demand for capital equipment declined sharply, resulting in a contraction in business demand for funds. The September 11, 2001, terrorist attacks further eroded consumer and business confidence, reducing demand for funds. Faced with a weakened economy, the Federal Reserve pushed short-term nominal interest rates down to the lowest levels in 45 years. For these reasons, the United States exhibited negative real rates during much of 2001 to 2004.

[5] In the figure, our measures of expected real Treasury bill yields were sometimes *negative* in the 1970s. How can this be explained? In a period of high inflation and considerable uncertainty, expected real returns on Treasury bills can be negative. Inflation in the 1970s averaged more than 7 percent per year. A negative 1 or 2 percent real return on Treasury bills is better than a negative 7 percent real return you earn holding cash or a non-interest-earning checking account.

## SUMMARY

Interest rates are among the most important economic variables, influencing a broad array of key economic decisions and outcomes. Interest rates are set in competitive financial markets and are driven by fundamental forces such as the outlook for inflation, Federal Reserve policy, the posture of federal government budgetary policy, and forces of the business cycle. The Federal Reserve has great influence over short-term interest rates but little immediate or direct influence over long-term rates. Long-term rates are dominated by the medium- and longer-term outlook for inflation and federal budget deficits and expected rates of return on capital. The Fed's main influence on long-term interest rates derives from its influence on the inflation outlook. The real interest rate is the interest rate that would prevail in an economy with no inflation. Modern economies almost always exhibit some inflation. To calculate the expected real interest rate you must subtract the expected inflation rate from the nominal or actual interest rate. The expected real interest rate influences business decisions about expenditures on plants, equipment, inventories, and technology and household decisions on home buying, consumption, and saving. The expected real interest rate strongly influences the flow of funds internationally, impacting the U.S. dollar exchange rate vis-à-vis other nations. Expected real short-term interest rates were unusually low in the 1970s and early 2000s and abnormally high in the 1980s.

## YOUR TURN ANSWERS

Page 98

**A.** The expression for the bond's present value is $PV = \$1{,}000/(1 + 0.07)^{30}$. The price of the bond is $131.37.

**B.** The price of the bond is now $PV = \$1{,}000/(1 + 0.08)^{30}$. The price of the bond falls to $99.38. An increase in yields means that bond prices fall.

Page 117

Using Equation (5-9), the real after-tax yield is (6 percent × 0.75) minus 3 percent, or 1.5 percent. Given the 6 percent pre-tax nominal return, the after-tax nominal return is 4.5 percent (6 percent × 0.75). Subtracting 3 percent expected inflation from the after-tax nominal return of 4.5 gives the expected real after-tax yield of 1.5 percent.

## KEY TERMS

Nominal interest rate
Real interest rate
Present value formula
Zero coupon bond
Coupon bonds
Present value
Loanable funds model
Time preference
Fisher effect
Fisher hypothesis
Inflation neutrality
Marginal productivity of capital
Rate of time preference
Ricardian equivalence proposition
Ex ante (expected) real interest rate
Ex post (realized) real interest rate

# STUDY QUESTIONS

[illegible] ply and de- [illegible] the supply [illegible] mand

[illegible] diagram [illegible] ected in- [illegible] tes.

[illegible] al estate [illegible] ment of [illegible] ther [illegible] happen to nominal interest rates? To real interest rates?

4. Suppose, in 2008, a new president considered strongly "pro-labor" and "anti-business" is elected. Given other factors influencing ex ante real rates, what effect would you expect the announcement of this election to have on ex ante real interest rates? Explain.

5. In October 1979, with inflation raging at rates in excess of 10 percent per year, the Federal Reserve announced the adoption of a new set of procedures that signaled to the public a movement to a more restrictive monetary policy posture. If credible with the public, what effect would this announcement have on long-term interest rates? Explain.

6. In 2003, Congress enacted a major income tax cut extending over the following decade. Using the loanable funds framework and holding other factors influencing interest rates constant, analyze the effect this would have on interest rates.

7. Explain all of the forces you can think of that typically reduce interest rate levels during the contraction (recession) phase of the business cycle.

8. Using *The Wall Street Journal* or the most recent data on the FRED database (http://research.stlouisfed.org/fred2/), look up the recent 1-year Treasury bill yield. Now, assuming you expect 3 percent inflation and are in a marginal income tax bracket of 25 percent, calculate the real after-tax yield you would expect to earn on this security over the next year.

9. Assume that political instability increases dramatically in Asian countries. What impact would this have on U.S. interest rates? Explain.

10. Why do interest rates rise more slowly in the first half than in the second half of an economic expansion? Explain by examining the role of business and consumer confidence, inflation expectations, and Federal Reserve policy.

11. Interest rates strongly tend to move pro-cyclically, typically rising during periods of cyclical expansion. Following the recession that began in the summer of 1990, a business cycle trough occurred in March 1991, and the longest expansion in U.S. history (exactly 10 years) ensued. Yet long-term interest rates were lower near the end of the expansion (in early 2001) than at the very beginning (early 1991) (review Figure 5-6). Explain how this could have occurred. What factors could have counteracted the normal tendency for long-term interest rates to increase during cyclical expansion?

12. All economists agree that an increase in government budget deficits increases the demand for loanable funds (shifts the demand curve rightward), but some argue that larger deficits do not significantly raise interest rates. How can this be possible? Explain.

# ADDITIONAL READING

- A comprehensive treatment of all aspects of interest rates together with citations of relevant literature is provided in James C. Van Horne, *Financial Market Rates and Flows,* 6th edition (Englewood Cliffs, NJ: Prentice-Hall, 2001).
- On the theory of interest rates, a classic treatment is Irving Fisher, *The Theory of Interest Rates* (New York: Macmillan, 1930), reprinted by Augustus M. Kelley in 1955 and 1961. On surveys of inflation expectations, see Lloyd B. Thomas, "Survey Measures of Expected U.S. Inflation," *The Journal of Economic Perspectives,* Fall 1999, pp. 125–144.
- For analyses of the effects of inflation expectations on interest rates, see James Wilcox, "Why Were Interest Rates so Low in the 1970s?," *American Economic Review,* March 1983, pp. 44–53, and Lawrence Summers, "The Non-adjustment of Nominal Interest Rates: A Study of the Fisher Effect," in James Tobin, ed., *Macroeconomics, Prices and Quantities* (Washington: Brookings Institution, 1983), pp. 201–241.
- Another important paper investigating the Fisher effect is William J. Crowder and Mark Wohar, "Are Tax Effects Important in the Long-Run Fisher Relation: Evidence from the Municipal Bond Market," *Journal of Finance,* February 1999, pp. 307–317.
- The Ricardian equivalence proposition is set forth in Robert Barro, "The Ricardian Approach to Budget Deficits," *The Journal of Economic Perspectives,* Spring 1989, pp. 37–54.
- A good review of the various studies of the effect of budget deficits on interest rates is provided in Preston J. Miller and William Roberds, "How Little We Know About Deficit Policy Effects," Federal Reserve Bank of Minneapolis *Quarterly Review,* Winter 1992, pp. 2–11.
- Two more recent studies reporting evidence that actual or expected long-term interest rates are positively associated with expected future deficits are Vincent Reinhard and Brian Sack, "The Economic Consequences of Disappearing Government Debt," *Brooking Papers on Economic Activity,* 2000, No. 2, pp. 163–209, and Thomas Laubach, "New Evidence on the Interest Rate Effects of Budget Deficits and Debt," Federal Reserve Board *Finance and Economics Discussion Series,* May 2003.

# Chapter 6

# TERM STRUCTURE AND RISK STRUCTURE OF INTEREST RATES

In Chapter 5 we developed a framework for analyzing the behavior of nominal and real interest rates. We used the framework to understand the influence of factors such as expected inflation, the business cycle, government budget deficits, and Federal Reserve policy on interest rate levels. We examined the distinction between nominal and real interest rates, emphasizing the importance of expected real rates in many economic processes. Two other factors significantly influence both nominal and real interest rates: a financial instrument's length of time to maturity and its *default risk.* Default risk is the risk that the lender will not recover the original principal and/or all of the stipulated interest payments due to insolvency of the debt instrument's issuer. This chapter examines the roles of term to maturity and default risk in interest rate determination.

## TERM STRUCTURE OF INTEREST RATES

A financial instrument's length of time to maturity contributes importantly to its yield. For analysis, suppose we hold constant all factors governing interest rates or yields except length of time to maturity. That is, suppose we choose securities of equal default risk, tax treatment, and marketability—securities differing only in time to maturity—and compare their yields. The relationship *at a given point in time* between the length of time to maturity and the yield on a security is the **term structure of interest rates.** The graphical depiction of this relationship is the **yield curve.**

**term structure of interest rates**
relationship *at a given point in time* between the length of time to maturity and the yield on a security

**yield curve**
graphical depiction of the term structure of interest rates

For each yield curve, the length of time to maturity is on the horizontal axis and the yield on the vertical axis. A set of points is plotted, corresponding to the yields on various maturities of a particular type of bond on a given day. The graph indicates that on May 15, 1981, 1-year bonds were yielding approximately 16.5 percent, 5-year bonds about 15 percent, and 30-year bonds roughly 14 percent. The yield curve or term structure of interest rates is a snapshot rather than a moving picture. The yields shown in Figure 6-1 are for U.S. Treasury securities; a similar figure can be constructed for corporate or municipal bonds. We can eliminate default risk and focus attention on relatively marketable securities by confining our graph to U.S. government securities.[1]

[1] U.S. government securities are free of default risk because the U.S. government has the constitutional authority to tax or, if necessary, to print money to meet its financial obligations. All maturities of U.S. government securities are relatively liquid, although the short-term market is more active and has lower transactions costs than the long end. Hence, short-term Treasury securities are the most liquid.

**Figure 6-1** Yield Curves Prevailing on Selected Dates

The yield curve is a snapshot of the yields available on securities of differing maturities at a given point in time. The shape and position of the yield curve change continuously over time.

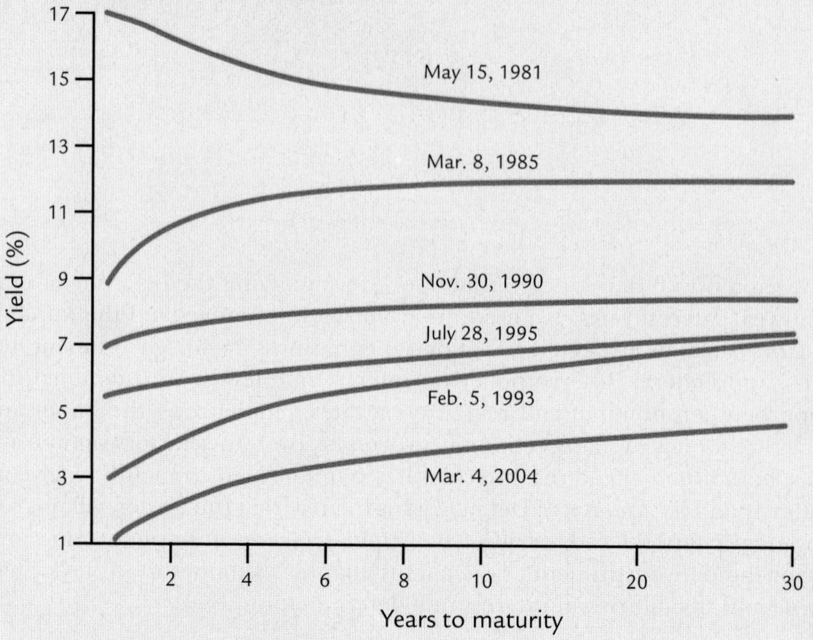

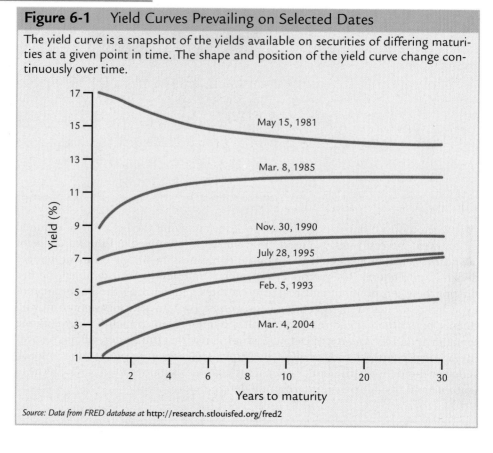

*Source: Data from FRED database at* http://research.stlouisfed.org/fred2

We see from the figure that both the level and shape of the yield curve change significantly over time. Historically, upward-sloping or ascending yield curves are much more common than downward-sloping or descending patterns. From 1979 to 1981, when yields were at post–Civil War highs, the downward-sloping pattern predominated. In March 1985 the yield curve was almost flat for maturities beyond 4 years. In March 2004, when yields were unusually low, the yield curve was quite steep. On average, the gap by which long-term yields exceed short-term yields diminishes (and sometimes becomes negative) as interest rates rise. That is, the yield curve is flatter (and sometimes downward sloping) when interest rates are relatively high. The yield curve normally is steeper when interest rates are low. Note the strongly upward-sloping yield curve of March 4, 2004, when short-term interest rates were at 45-year lows, and the descending yield curve of May 15, 1981, when interest rates were extremely high. We provide explanations for these tendencies as we discuss the theories of term structure.

Figure 6-2 summarizes the various patterns of the yield curve.

The perfectly flat yield curve in panel A is extremely improbable, although yield curves approaching it have occurred (note the curve for November 30, 1990, in Figure 6-1). The ascending or upward-sloping yield curve in panel B is the most common. The downward-sloping or inverted yield curve in panel C sometimes occurs when interest rates are considerably higher than normal. The humped yield curve in panel D is more common. What determines the shape of the yield curve?

## FROM THE FINANCIAL PAGES

### Treasury Yield Curve

Each issue of *The Wall Street Journal* contains a graph showing the yield curve for U.S. Treasury securities at the end of the previous day, 1 month earlier, and 1 year earlier. A quick look at this graph provides much information. The graph shown here was published on Friday, March 5, 2004.

Examination of the graph allows prospective lenders to compare the returns available on safe government securities of various maturities. On March 4, 2004, lenders could earn approximately 1 percent on maturities ranging from 1 to 6 months, about 3 percent on 5-year maturities, and just under 5 percent on long-term Treasury bonds (30-year maturity). In March 2004, the yield curve was quite flat for maturities ranging from 1 to 6 months and quite steep beyond that. In fact, the yield curve was unusually steep. The spread between the long-term bond yield and the 1-month Treasury bill yield was not far from record levels. By the time you finish this chapter, you will understand why the yield curve was so steep. Take a look at today's *The Wall Street Journal* and note how the yield curve has changed relative to the one shown here.

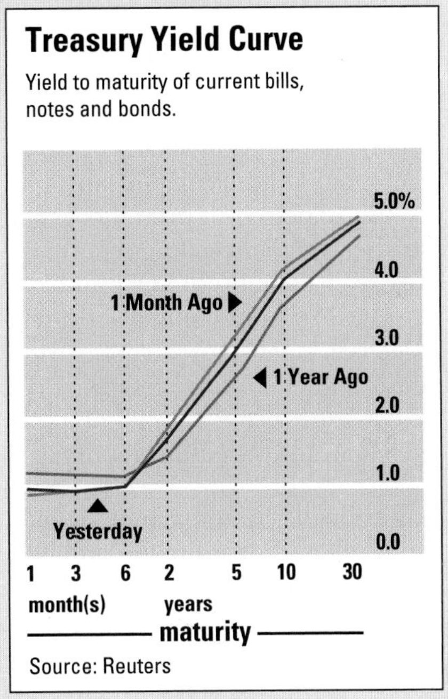


**Figure 6-2** Patterns of the Yield Curve

The yield curve assumes one of four general shapes: flat (A), ascending (B), descending (C), or humped (D). The most common is the ascending or upward-sloping pattern (B).

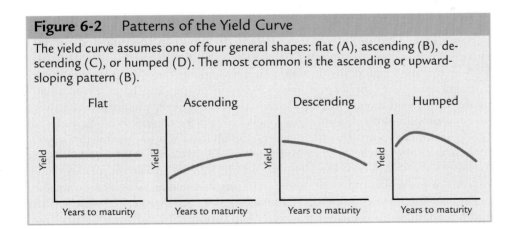

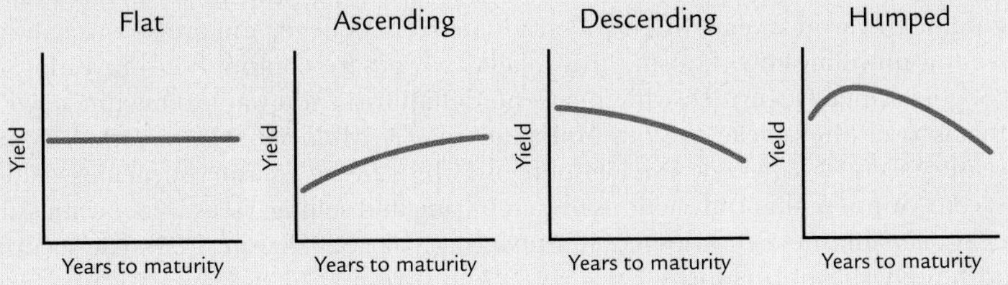

# THEORIES OF TERM STRUCTURE

We examine four different theories of the term structure of interest rates—pure expectations theory, liquidity premium theory, segmented markets theory, and preferred habitat theory. The theories attempt to explain the shape of the yield curve at any point in time and the changes in shape over time.

## Pure Expectations Theory

In this theory, current expectations of financial market participants toward future interest rates is the crucial determinant of the current term structure of interest rates. According to the **pure expectations theory,** market forces dictate that the yield on a long-term security of any particular maturity equals the geometric mean (the average) of the current short-term yield and successive future short-term yields currently expected to prevail over the life of the long-term security. If transactions costs in buying and selling securities are zero, the investor earns the same average return over the long run by purchasing a long-term bond and holding the bond to maturity as by purchasing a short-term bond and "rolling it over"—reinvesting the proceeds in a new short-term security each period. In this theory, market forces produce a yield curve or term structure that equalizes expected returns among alternative maturities for any planning period or investment horizon.

**pure expectations theory**
theory in which market forces dictate that the yield on a long-term security of any particular maturity equals the geometric mean (the average) of the current short-term yield and successive future short-term yields currently expected to prevail over the life of the long-term security

The pure expectations theory is based on the following assumptions:

1. Investors desire to maximize holding period returns—the returns earned over their relevant planning horizon.
2. Investors have no institutional preference for particular maturities. They regard various maturities as perfect substitutes for each other.
3. Transactions costs associated with buying and selling securities are zero. Hence, investors will always swap maturities in response to perceived yield advantages.
4. Many investors form expectations about the future course of interest rates and act aggressively on those expectations.

If these assumptions are valid, the term structure of interest rates reflects only expectations about future interest rates. Nothing else affects the shape of the yield curve.

You can understand the intuition underlying the pure expectations theory through a simple example. You have $20,000 in savings and hope to buy a late-model used car in 2 years when you graduate from college. You are a conservative investor, unwilling to risk losing this wealth, so you are committed to investing in U.S. government securities, which have no default risk. You want to maximize your returns over the 2-year period. You read in *The Wall Street Journal* that 1-year Treasury securities currently yield 4 percent, while 2-year Treasury securities yield 6 percent. Suppose that transactions fees in buying and selling Treasury securities are negligible. You must choose between investing your $20,000 in the 2-year security and holding it until maturity (strategy 1) and investing in the 1-year security and reinvesting the proceeds a year from now when the security matures (strategy 2).

The optimal choice depends on your expectation of the yield on 1-year Treasury securities 1 year from now. If you believe the yield will be the same as it is today—4 percent—you are better off buying the 2-year bond, which yields 6 percent. If you expect 1-year Treasury yields to rise to 10 percent in the next year, you are better off with strategy 2. Your return would average approximately 7 percent annually [(4 percent + 10 percent)/2] rather than the 6 percent per year currently available on the 2-year bond. You would have more funds at the end of 2 years than with strategy 1, permitting you to purchase a nicer car.

**Implicit Forward Interest Rate:** Two-Year Investment Horizon. Some implicit **forward interest rate**—rate on 1-year securities 1 year in the future—can leave you indifferent between the two strategies. Consider the following expression:

**forward interest rate** hypothetical future short-term interest rate that equalizes average returns earned on a long-term security and a succession of short-term securities

$$\mathbf{R_1 + {}_{t+1}r_1 = 2R_2.}$$

$R_1$ and $R_2$ are the yields available today on 1-year and 2-year Treasury securities, respectively. The term ${}_{t+1}r_1$ is the implicit forward rate that balances the equation—the hypothetical 1-year rate that, if prevailing 1 year from now, makes your two investment alternatives produce the same average return over the 2-year period. Given that both $R_1$ and $R_2$ are known today (4 percent and 6 percent, respectively), it is easy to calculate the implicit forward rate:

$$\mathbf{{}_{t+1}r_1 = 2R_2 - R_1.}$$

In the example of saving for a car, the implicit forward rate that equalizes returns for the two strategies is 8 percent: 2 × 6 percent − 4 percent. The average return earned via strategy 2 is the simple arithmetic mean of 4 percent and 8 percent, that is, 6 percent, which matches the return you earn by purchasing the 2-year bond and holding it to maturity.

With compound interest—both principal and interest are reinvested each year—we modify the analysis slightly. Consider the following expression:

$$\text{(6-1)} \quad \mathbf{(1 + R_1)(1 + {}_{t+1}r_1) = (1 + R_2)^2.}$$

In this formula, each dollar invested in a 1-year bond at yield $R_1$ is compounded after 1 year at the implicit 1-year forward rate (${}_{t+1}r_1$) to earn the same rate of return currently available on 2-year bonds, $R_2$. Solving for the implicit forward rate, we obtain:

$$\text{(6-2)} \quad {}_{t+1}r_1 = \mathbf{\frac{(1 + R_2)^2}{(1 + R_1)} - 1 = \frac{(1.06)^2}{1.04)} - 1 = 1.0804 - 1 = .0804, \text{ or } 8.04 \text{ percent.}}$$

The 1-year forward rate that makes you indifferent between the two strategies is slightly more than 8 percent. According to the pure expectations theory of term structure, the implicit rate of 8.04 percent is the market's expectation of the yield that will prevail 1 year from now on 1-year Treasury securities.[2]

To confirm the theory, assume instead that the market expects interest rates on 1-year securities will be less than 8 percent 1 year from now. Investors can accumulate more wealth over the 2-year period using strategy 1—buying and holding the 2-year bond. Investors sell their 1-year securities to purchase 2-year securities. The price of 1-year bonds is bid down, raising its yield. The price of 2-year bonds is bid

[2] Economists evaluate this theory by testing whether the forward rate is an unbiased measure of the market's expectation of future short-term rates. The theory hypothesizes that the forward rate is equal to the expected future interest rate. Thus, the pure expectations theory is sometimes known as the *unbiased expectations theory.* Consider the regression equation $i^e = a + bi^f$, where $i^e$ is the expected future interest rate, $i^f$ is the forward rate prevailing today, and a and b are parameters. In a regression model, if a and b are estimated to be 0 and 1, respectively, then $i^f$ is an unbiased estimate of $i^e$, that is, on average, the forward rate equals the expected future rate. Such an empirical finding supports the pure expectations theory. In practice, the theory is difficult to test because existing measures of the market's expectations of future interest rates are subject to shortcomings.

up, reducing its yield. $R_1$ rises above 4 percent and $R_2$ falls below 6 percent. Activity continues to boost 1-year yields and reduce 2-year yields until expected returns from the two strategies are equalized.

If investors believe that 1 year from now 1-year yields will exceed 8 percent, they will sell 2-year bonds and purchase 1-year bonds. Activity drives up $R_2$ and drives down $R_1$ until returns expected over the 2-year period are equalized. The pure expectations theory is based on the intuitively plausible notion that market forces produce a term structure that leaves investors motivated to maximize returns indifferent among maturities. This term structure is the *only* equilibrium term structure; any other term structure produces incentives for lenders and borrowers to switch maturities, altering the shape of the yield curve.

Looking at Equation (6-1), you see that if expected future short-term rates ($_{t+1}r_1$) exceed current short-term rates ($R_1$), then $R_2$ must exceed $R_1$. In other words, if interest rates are expected to rise, then longer-term interest rates today will exceed shorter-term interest rates—the yield curve is upward sloping. Conversely, if $R_2$ exceeds $R_1$, then $_{t+1}r_1$ must exceed $R_1$. An upward-sloping yield curve indicates market consensus that yields will increase.

On the other hand, if $_{t+1}r_1$ is lower than $R_1$, then $R_2$ is lower than $R_1$. If the market expects rates to fall, the yield curve today is downward sloping. Conversely, if $R_1$ exceeds $R_2$, then $_{t+1}r_1$ is smaller than $R_1$. A downward-sloping yield curve indicates market consensus that interest rates will fall.

**Implicit Forward Rate:** 20-Year Investment Horizon. As we extend the planning horizon and the range of maturities beyond 2 years, we use Equation (6-3) to obtain the implicit forward rate:

$$(6\text{-}3)\qquad (1 + {}_tR_L)^n = (1 + {}_tR_1)(1 + {}_{t+1}r_1)(1 + {}_{t+2}r_1)\ldots(1 + {}_{t+n-1}r_1).$$

The R's represent yields available *today* on long-term bonds ($_tR_L$) and short-term (1-year) bonds ($_tR_1$). The investor can buy and hold a long-term bond (say 20-year maturity) or buy a short-term security and reinvest the proceeds each year. The lowercase r's again represent the implicit forward interest rates—the hypothetical interest rates that balance the equation. The subscripts preceding the actual and implied rates refer to the year (t is today, t + 1 is 1 year from now, and so forth). The subscripts following the rates refer to the number of years to maturity of the instrument (L is long-term—20 years in this example, and 1 is 1 year). The variable n is the number of years in the planning horizon or the investor's holding period—20 years in this example.

Suppose an investor is considering investing in government securities over a 20-year period, beginning today. From Equation (6-3), some implicit future pattern of short-term interest rates (r's), combined with today's yield on 1-year bonds ($_tR_1$), causes $1 invested today to grow to the same sum in 20 years ($n = 20$) as accumulates by purchasing the 20-year bond today and holding the bond to maturity. According to the pure expectations theory, the implicit rates are *unbiased estimates* of the market's expectation of future interest rates.

The intuition underlying this theory is straightforward. Rational investors desire to maximize holding-period returns. Suppose the holding period is 20 years. If investors believe they can accumulate more wealth in a 20-year period by purchasing the 20-year bond and holding the bond to maturity, market participants sell short-term bonds and buy long-term (20-year) bonds. The action pushes up short-term yields and bids down long-term yields until the advantage of the 20-year bond no longer exists. On the other hand, if investors believe they can accumulate more wealth over 20 years by buying the 1-year bond and reinvesting in 1-year bonds for 19 consecutive years, market participants immediately begin selling long-term bonds and purchasing short-term securities. Again, any initial advantage is bid away as long-term yields are pushed up and short-term yields are pressured downward. The pure expectations theory is appealing because it is based on the plausible notion that investors aim to maximize their returns over their planning horizons.

If we rearrange Equation (6-3) to solve for ${}_tR_L$, we obtain the following expression:

$$(6\text{-}4)\qquad {}_tR_L = \sqrt[n]{(1 + {}_tR_1)(1 + {}_{t+1}r_1)(1 + {}_{t+2}r_1)\ldots(1 + {}_{t+n-1}r_1)} - 1$$

This formula states that the current long-term bond yield (${}_tR_L$) is the geometric mean or average of the current 1-year bond yield (${}_tR_1$) and future 1-year bond yields (r's) currently expected to prevail over the life of the long-term bond. This is the essential meaning of the pure expectations theory.

From Equation (6-4), if the r's exceed ${}_tR_1$, then ${}_tR_L$ must exceed ${}_tR_1$. That is, if investors believe short-term interest rates will be higher in the future, the yield curve today is upward sloping. Long-term yields are higher than short-term yields. On the other hand, if the r's are lower than ${}_tR_1$, then ${}_tR_1$ must exceed ${}_tR_L$. If investors think interest rates will decline in the future, the yield curve is downward sloping or inverted. In the pure expectations theory, an ascending yield curve indicates market consensus that interest rates are headed upward. A downward-sloping or inverted yield curve indicates economic agents expect lower interest rates. A flat yield curve indicates a consensus that future yields will remain the same as current yields.[3] In the pure expectations theory, *nothing except the outlook for interest rates* affects the shape of the yield curve.

**YOUR TURN**

Suppose the yield curve currently is perfectly flat—yields are the same on U.S. securities of all maturities. The U.S. economy is operating very close to full employment. The president unexpectedly announces U.S. involvement in a major foreign war. Assume you believe in the pure expectations theory.

**a.** As a personal investor with $100,000 to invest in U.S. government securities today, how would you allocate your funds between long-term and short-term securities?

**b.** What would happen to the shape of the yield curve after the market digests the announcement of war?

## Liquidity Premium Theory

A second theory of term structure, the **liquidity premium theory,** accepts the basic intuition underlying the pure expectations theory of term structure but adds one major amendment. Because long-term bonds entail greater *market risk*—risk of ap-

**liquidity premium theory**
theory asserting that the long-term interest rate equals the average of current and expected future short-term interest rates plus a premium to compensate lenders for market risk

[3] The humped yield curve illustrated in Figure 6-2(D) is rationalized by proponents of the pure expectations theory as follows. Suppose investors believe that interest rates are above normal now, will rise in the short term, and then come down. This belief causes borrowers (issuers of debt instruments) to concentrate on intermediate-range offerings rather than long-term and very-short-term debt instruments. Lenders are motivated to purchase either long-term or very short-term bonds. Such behavior produces the humped yield curve.

preciable fluctuation in a security's price—than short-term securities, long-term yields include a premium compensating investors for higher risk. The premium for increased market risk is a **term premium.**

**term premium**
additional yield embedded in long-term debt instruments to compensate lenders for market risk

The volatility of bond prices increases with length of time to maturity. Long-term bonds are riskier than short-term bonds because investors may have to sell their assets prior to maturity, exposing themselves to possible losses. Table 6-1 shows the price that 1-year, 10-year, and 30-year zero coupon bonds (with face value of $1,000) will sell for in three different interest-rate scenarios.[4]

The table documents the well-known fact that higher interest rates (i) are synonymous with lower bond prices (read laterally across each row of the table). More importantly, note that for any given change in interest rates, long-term bond prices exhibit relatively greater price fluctuations than short-term bonds. For example, if yields rise from 6 percent to 8 percent, the 1-year bond price falls from $943 to $926, a decline of less than 2 percent. On the other hand, the 30-year bond price falls from $174 to $99, a decline of more than 40 percent. This result demonstrates that market risk in bonds increases with length of time to maturity.

Investors (bond buyers) who are risk averse must be compensated (through a premium in the yield) for the greater market risk inherent in long-term bonds.[5] According to the liquidity premium theory, the long-term interest rate is the average of the current and expected future short-term yields *plus a term premium* compensating the investor for the additional market risk inherent in long-term securities. Equation (6-5) expresses the liquidity premium theory of the term structure.

$$\mathbf{tR_L} = \sqrt[n]{(1 + {}_t\mathbf{R}_1)(1 + {}_{t+1}\mathbf{r}_1)(1 + {}_{t+2}\mathbf{r}_1)\ldots(1 + {}_{t+n-1}\mathbf{r}_1)} - 1 + \mathbf{TP} \quad (6\text{-}5)$$

In this theory, the long-term rate *exceeds* the average of current and expected future short-term rates by a term premium (TP) that is a positive function of the length of time to maturity of the longer-term bond. Because TP is positive and increases with term length, the liquidity premium theory asserts that the normal yield

**Table 6-1 Impact of Interest Rate Fluctuations on Zero Coupon Bond Prices**

| Maturity (Years) | Price (Dollars) | | |
|---|---|---|---|
| | i = 4% | i = 6% | i = 8% |
| 1 | 962 | 943 | 926 |
| 10 | 676 | 558 | 463 |
| 30 | 308 | 174 | 99 |

[4] Recall from Chapter 5 that the general formula relating the price to the yield of a zero coupon bond is $PV = \$1,000/(1 + i)^n$, where i is the yield, PV is the present value and price of the bond, and n is the number of years to maturity. The same principle relating price responsiveness to interest rate changes across maturities applies to coupon bonds, but the formula relating price and yield is more complicated. Hence, we use zero coupon bonds in this illustration.

[5] If borrowers (issuers of debt) are risk averse, they generally prefer to borrow in the long-term market. Borrowing short term and refinancing frequently by issuing new debt expose borrowers to the risk of future interest rates increases. To avoid this prospect, risk-averse borrowers prefer to borrow long term and lock in the interest rate. The predisposition to borrow long to avoid the risk of future interest rate increases contributes to the predominance of ascending yield curves. That is, the behavior of risk-averse borrowers reinforces the behavior of risk-averse lenders. Both parties contribute to the general prevalence of an upward-sloping yield curve.

**Figure 6-3** Term Structure Patterns in Pure Expectations (PE) and Liquidity Premium (LP) Theories

(a) Interest rates expected to rise. (b) Interest rates expected to remain constant. (c) Interest rates expected to fall.
The liquidity premium theory implies a more steeply upward-sloping (or less steeply downward-sloping) yield curve than the pure expectations theory.

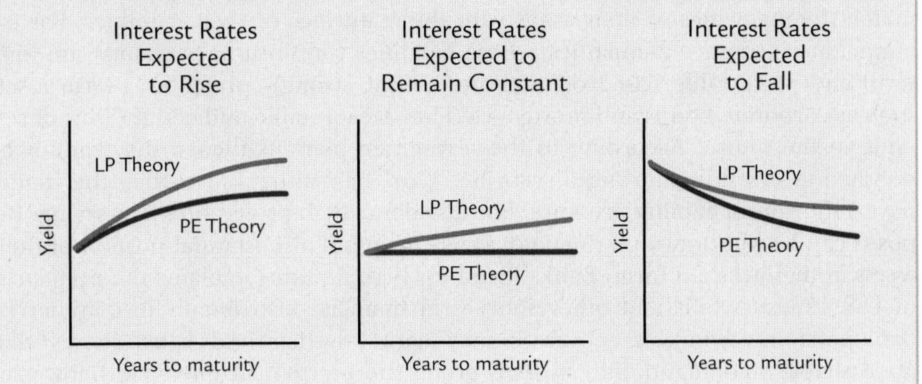

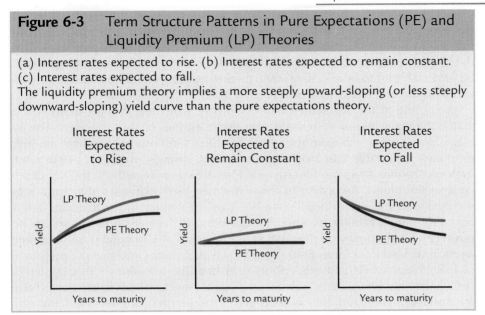

structure is ascending or upward sloping. In other words, the yield curve will slope upward even if agents expect future interest rates will be the same as today's rate. The yield curve will slope downward only if market participants agree that interest rates will come down *considerably* in the future.

Figure 6-3 illustrates the implications for the shape of the yield curve of the liquidity premium theory relative to the implications of the pure expectations theory. Regardless of the outlook for interest rates, the liquidity premium theory implies higher long-term yields than does the pure expectations theory. When yields are expected to remain constant, the pure expectations implies a flat yield curve but the liquidity premium theory implies a modestly upward-sloping yield curve. When yields are expected to rise, the pure expectations theory implies an upward-sloping yield curve but the liquidity premium theory implies an even steeper yield curve. When yields are expected to fall, the pure expectations theory implies a downward-sloping yield curve but the liquidity premium theory implies a more gently downward-sloping or perhaps even a flat or modestly upward-sloping yield curve. Exhibit 6-1 illustrates the relevance of the theory of term structure to an important real-world policy issue—how the U.S. Treasury manages the maturity structure of U.S. debt.

## Segmented Markets Theory

A third theory of term structure, the **segmented markets theory,** asserts that securities of different maturities are very poor substitutes for one another. The theory disputes the second assumption underlying the pure expectations theory. The segmented markets theory instead asserts that various lenders and borrowers have a strong preference for particular maturities. From the lender's viewpoint, short-term securities possess liquidity and great stability of principal (that is, price stability). Thus, short-term securities have low market risk. On the other hand, long-term securities provide stability of income over time. A lender locks in a fixed annual income for many years by buying a long-term bond. Thus, a lender preferring income stability over principal stability clearly prefers long-term bonds. A lender who values protection of principal over long-term stability of income clearly prefers short-term securities.

**segmented markets theory**
theory that borrowers and lenders are committed to particular maturities, unwilling to switch in response to yield considerations

Borrowers also have clear-cut preferences. Firms borrowing to finance inventories prefer short-term loans. Families buying homes prefer long-term fixed rate mortgages to avoid the risk of rising mortgage rates (and monthly payments) after the home is purchased. Municipalities and corporations financing long-term capital projects prefer to borrow long term, thereby assuring continuous access to funds and locked-in interest costs in advance.

According to the segmented markets theory, firms are strongly motivated to match the maturities of their assets with the maturities of their liabilities. For example, life insurance companies, whose liabilities (life insurance claims) are long term and predictable based on mortality tables, strongly prefer long-term assets such as corporate bonds and mortgages. They seek a stable and certain flow of revenue in the future. According to the segmented markets theory, they cannot be tempted to invest in short-term securities. Commercial banks, on the other hand, have a short-term liability structure. Because demand deposits and many savings deposits can be withdrawn on demand, banks maintain a substantial portion of their assets in highly liquid form. Banks' need for high liquidity explains the popularity of U.S. Treasury bills and other short-term financial instruments in commercial bank portfolios. Similarly, because money market mutual funds issue "shares" that are cashable on demand, they strongly prefer short-term instruments with low market risk, such as Treasury bills, commercial paper, and negotiable CDs.

Segmented markets theorists conclude that securities of different maturities cannot be substituted for one another in response to perceived yield advantages. Each maturity sector of the market is viewed as almost totally cemented off from other maturity sectors (hence the term *segmented markets theory*). Because of low substitutability, yields in any maturity sector are determined strictly by supply and demand conditions in that sector, with minimal influence from conditions in other maturity sectors. The flow of funds from one maturity to another in response to interest rate incentives is minimal and almost nonexistent.

Segmented markets theory implies that corporate and U.S. Treasury debt management decisions significantly influence the shape of the yield curve. If firms and the government are currently issuing predominantly long-term debt, the yield curve is relatively steep (large supply of long-term bonds implies low bond prices and high bond yields). If firms and the government are issuing principally short-term debt, short-term yields are high relative to long-term yields. In the segmented markets theory, Treasury debt management is a potential tool of economic policy influencing the yield curve. Suppose the Treasury wants to raise short-term interest rates to attract foreign capital to the United States and strengthen the dollar in foreign exchange markets. Suppose the Treasury also wants to reduce long-term interest rates to bolster domestic investment in plants, equipment, and new technology. The Treasury then issues only short-term debt, pushing up short-term yields and reducing long-term yields, effectively twisting the yield curve (Figure 6-4). The Federal Reserve contributes to twisting of the yield curve by simultaneously selling short-term securities and buying long-term bonds.[6] The Treasury's influence over the yield curve is not possible if the pure expectations theory or its variant, the liquidity premium theory, is valid. In those theories, expectations of future interest rates dominate the shape of the yield curve.

**preferred habitat theory**
theory that borrowers and lenders have strong preferences for particular maturities but may be induced to switch if expected benefits are large

## Preferred Habitat Theory

The **preferred habitat theory** combines elements of the other three theories of term structure; it is a hybrid theory. Its proponents hypothesize that borrowers and

[6] The Fed and Treasury collaborated in the early 1960s, attempting to twist the yield curve in this manner. No consensus on whether the effort succeeded exists in the empirical literature.

## Exhibit 6-1 Managing the National Debt

The U.S. Treasury manages the federal debt. Because about one third of the nation's marketable government debt is in maturities of 1 year or less, each year the Treasury issues more than $1 trillion ($1,000 billion) of new marketable securities to refinance maturing Treasury bonds, notes, and bills. The Treasury finances additional borrowing in years of budget deficits (about 40 of the past 44 years).

The Treasury faces choices regarding maturities of new debt issues. Should it issue short-term or long-term debt? An important consideration in making this decision is the desire to minimize the interest expense incurred by government over many years.

In 1993, shortly after taking office, the Clinton administration proposed that the Treasury stop issuing long-term bonds and instead fund the debt entirely through short-term Treasury bills. The proposal looked attractive to many observers. In February 1993, the yield curve was unusually steep (review Figure 6-1). Short-term yields were around 3 percent, while 30-year bond yields were approximately 7 percent. In the near term, the Treasury could produce savings for the Treasury (and taxpayers) by issuing only short-term Treasury bills. Given these yields, if the Treasury issued $1,000 billion ($1 trillion) in new debt in 1993, the government would incur about $40 billion less interest expense in the first year alone by funding all of its borrowing requirement in the short-term sector rather than in 30-year bonds.

But what about interest expense in later years? Remember that the pure expectations theory states that the yield on long-term securities is simply the average of the current short-term yield and the short-term yields currently expected to prevail in the future. If market expectations are correct, the ultimate cost to the Treasury over many years is the same irrespective of the maturity of the newly issued debt. The Treasury initially saves taxpayers money by shortening debt maturity, but the Treasury loses the gain when it refinances in periods of higher interest rates. In this theory, the Clinton administration's proposal saves money over the long run only if the market is wrong about future interest rates and the Treasury is wiser than the market. Proponents of the pure expectations theory likely regard the proposal as short sighted and politically motivated.

If the liquidity premium theory is valid, the proposal saves taxpayers money over the long term. In this theory, because long-term rates are higher *on average* than short-term rates, cost savings result from reducing the average maturity of the nation's debt. In 2004, the average maturity of the marketable U.S. government debt was approximately 5 years.

lenders have strong preferences for particular maturities, as assumed in the segmented markets theory. Thus, the yield curve does not conform strictly to the predictions of the pure expectations or liquidity premium theory. However, the preferred habitat theory does not accept the proposition that expectations play no role in the term structure. Institutions change from their preferred maturities or habitats if expected additional returns gained by deviating from the original maturities or habitats become sufficiently large. For example, banks and money market mutual funds lengthen the maturities of their assets if fund managers expect returns from long-term securities will exceed those on short-term Treasury bills by a large enough margin. That is, they purchase some intermediate-term or long-term bonds. If the excess returns expected from buying short-term securities become large enough, life insurance companies no longer limit themselves to long-term securities market, instead placing a portion of their portfolio in shorter-term instruments.

# INTERNATIONAL PERSPECTIVES

## Inflation Targeting, Inflation Expectations, and the Yield Curve in Australia

Inflation rates around the world surged in the 1970s, largely due to the dramatic increase in oil prices and inappropriate budgetary and monetary policies conducted in many countries. For the full decade of the 1970s, inflation rates in the United States and Australia averaged 7.6 percent and 10.3 percent per year, respectively. The United States "bit the bullet" in the early 1980s, eradicating severe inflation through the Federal Reserve's protracted policy of extremely high interest rates. The Reserve Bank of Australia (RBA) was not as aggressive in attacking inflation. While U.S. inflation averaged 4.9 percent per year in the 1980s, Australia inflation averaged 8.3 percent per year.

Part of the cure for inflation is achieving public confidence in the authorities' anti-inflation proclamations. If a central bank gains credibility in its anti-inflation campaign, the cost of reducing inflation (in terms of lost output and higher unemployment) is reduced. Largely for this reason, many central banks have implemented *inflation targeting regimes* in the past 15 years. In an inflation targeting regime, the central bank declares its primary objective—to maintain inflation within a specific, relatively narrow band of low inflation rates. The first country to implement inflation targeting was the Reserve Bank of New Zealand in 1990. The RBA followed suit in 1993. Today, more than 20 central banks—including those in Canada, Israel, Korea, Sweden, and the United Kingdom—use inflation targets. (Chapter 25 is devoted to inflation targeting.)

One indicator of the early benefits of an inflation targeting regime is the impact of the announcement of the new regime on the term structure of interest rates. A policy initially effective in reducing long-term inflation expectations is reflected in lower long-term interest rates and a flatter yield curve. The data below indicate the term structure in Australia both immediately *before* and 10 months *after* March 1993, when the RBA announced its overriding priority was maintaining inflation within a band of 2 to 3 percent.

| Period | 90-Day Treasury Bill Yield (%) | 5-Year Treasury Bond Yield (%) | 10-Year Treasury Bond Yield (%) |
|---|---|---|---|
| February 1993 | 5.69 | 7.26 | 7.98 |
| December 1993 | 4.72 | 6.17 | 6.68 |

In the 10 months following implementation of the new regime, the yield curve flattened somewhat. Short-term rates fell 97 basis points (largely due to a weak economy and near-term stimulative actions by the RBA). The 10-year bond yield fell by 130 basis points. Flattening of the yield curve is consistent with the view that the RBA's announcement of the new regime reduced long-term inflation expectations.

**Figure 6-4** Twisting the Yield Curve

In the segmented markets theory, the Treasury and the Federal Reserve can change the shape of the yield curve by altering supply and demand for securities of various maturities.

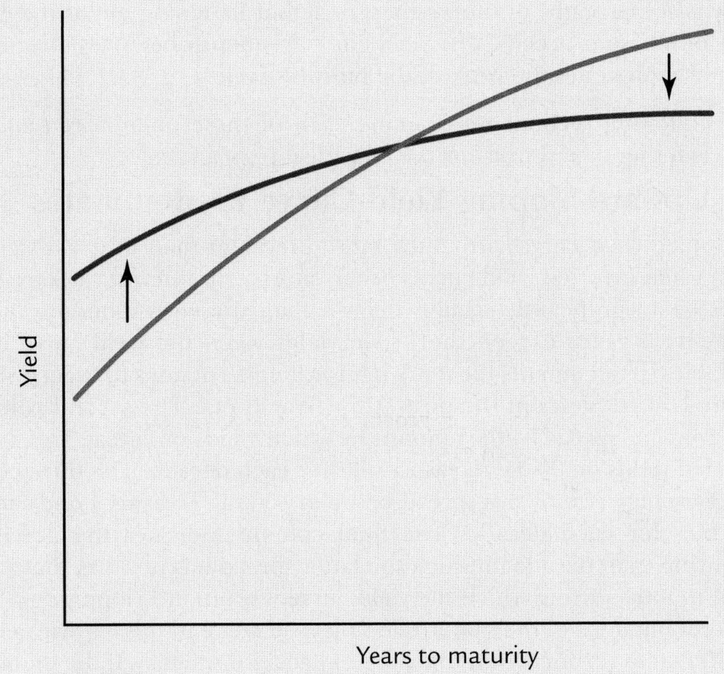


The preferred habitat theory is based on the realistic notion that agents and institutions accept greater risk in return for additional expected returns. In accepting elements of both the segmented markets and pure expectations theories yet rejecting their extreme polar positions, the preferred habitat theory moves closer to explaining real-world phenomena. In the preferred habitat theory, both market expectations and institutional factors emphasized in the segmented markets theory influence the term structure of interest rates.

## TERM STRUCTURE THEORIES: HOW WELL DO THEY EXPLAIN THE FACTS?

The validity and usefulness of any theory hinge on the theory's ability to explain real-world phenomena. The *facts* that any useful term structure theory must explain include the following empirical regularities in the term structure of interest rates:

1. The yield curve is upward sloping most of the time. On average, long-term yields are significantly higher than short-term yields.
2. The yield curve typically shifts up and down over time rather than twisting or rotating about some point along the curve. In other words, when short-term yields are rising, yields on securities in adjacent maturities (including long-term bonds) are rising. When short-term yields fall, intermediate and long-term yields fall. Short- and long-term yields seldom move in opposite directions.

3. While both short-term and long-term interest rates exhibit a pro-cyclical pattern, short-term yields exhibit considerably greater amplitude over the business cycle than long-term yields. Short-term yields fall faster than long-term yields in recessions and rise faster than long-term yields during economic expansions. The yield curve exhibits a regular cyclical pattern, sloping steeply upward near the low point (trough) of the business cycle but flattening out as the economic expansion phase proceeds. The yield curve frequently becomes inverted as the economy approaches the peak of the business cycle.

In the following sections we examine each of these phenomena and explain how well each theory accounts for the empirical regularities.

## Fact 1: Upward-Sloping Yield Curve Predominates

Upward-sloping yield curves are much more prevalent than inverted yield curves. In periods when inverted yield curves occur, short-term interest rates exceed long-term rates by a significantly smaller margin than the corresponding margins by which long-term yields exceed short-term yields when the yield curve is upward sloping. Table 6-2 documents the tendency for long-term rates to exceed short-term rates in the United States in the post–World War II era. The second column indicates the average "spread"—the amount by which yields on 5-year Treasury securities exceeded yields on 90-day Treasury bills for each decade. The third column indicates the average size of this spread between 30-year Treasury bonds and 90-day Treasury bills for each decade. The final column indicates the percentage of months during each decade in which the latter spread was positive, that is, the percentage of months during which the yield curve was upward sloping.

The predominance of the upward-sloping yield curve in this 54-year period is extremely difficult to reconcile with the pure expectations theory. If the theory is valid, upward-sloping and downward-sloping yield curves would occur with approximately the same frequency. Instead, the yield curve was upward sloping 88 percent of the time over the long period (right-hand portion of the table). According to the pure expectations theory, this outcome occurs only if people regard interest rates as consistently below normal levels (88 percent of the time) and therefore persistently expect rates to be higher in the future. Such an asymmetrical and biased expectation is inconsistent with the theory of rational expectations, which asserts that people do

**Table 6-2 Average Yield Spreads on U.S. Government Securities from 1950 to 2003**

| Decade | 5-Year—90-Day Spread (%) | 30-Year—90-Day Spread (%) | Percent of Months Ascending* (%) |
|---|---|---|---|
| 1950s | +0.67 | +1.04 | 98 |
| 1960s | +0.59 | +0.56 | 73 |
| 1970s | +0.92 | +1.10 | 73 |
| 1980s | +1.20 | +1.74 | 87 |
| 1990s | +1.38 | +2.10 | 100 |
| 2000–2003 | +1.29 | +2.50 | 100 |
| 1950–2003 | +0.98 | +1.41 | 88 |

*Percentage of months in which 30-year bond yield exceeded 3-month Treasury bill yield.
*Source: Data from FRED database at* http://research.stlouisfed.org/fred2

not repeatedly make the same mistake—that is, *on average,* people do not expect interest rates to increase. Hence, the strong predominance of the upward-sloping yield curve is incompatible with the pure expectations theory of term structure.

The pure expectations theory implies that on average the yield spread should be zero over a long period of years. In each of the six decades listed, average yields on both 5-year and 30-year bonds exceeded short-term Treasury bill yields. On average, the 5-year yield exceeded the bill yield by 98 basis points (0.98 percentage points) over the 54-year period, while the 30-year bond yield exceeded the bill yield by 141 basis points. (Most of the upward slope in the yield curve comes in the first 5 years of the maturity structure.)

The liquidity premium theory implies a premium in long-term yields to compensate for risk and is consistent with the facts reported in Table 6-2. The theory developed in response to the observed tendency of the yield curve to be upward sloping most of the time. The segmented markets theory emphasizes institutional preferences for various maturities by lenders and borrowers and is consistent with the facts shown in the table. The preferred habitat theory accepts portions of all other term structure theories and is compatible with these facts.

## Fact 2: Yields of Various Maturities Typically Move in the Same Direction

Most times, when short-term yields are falling, intermediate and long-term yields also are declining. When short-term rates are rising, long-term rates usually are rising. In other words, the yield curve typically shifts upward or downward each week or month rather than twisting or rotating about some point along the yield curve.

The pure expectations theory and its close relative, the liquidity premium theory, easily explain this empirical regularity. Suppose short-term yields are pushed up by aggressive Federal Reserve sales of short-term securities. Because these theories consider the various maturities as close substitutes for one another, rising short-term yields trigger a chain of reactions. Lenders sell some of their longer-term bonds to purchase the newly attractive short-term securities. Borrowers issue more longer-term securities to avoid the suddenly increased cost of short-term borrowing. These actions by lenders and borrowers push up long-term yields and reduce short-term yields, quickly transmitting some of the initial increase in short-term rates to longer-term maturities. The yield curve shifts upward.

Because the liquidity premium theory and preferred habitat theory are essentially modifications of the pure expectations theory, they also explain the tendency for long-term and short-term rates to move together over time. However, the segmented markets theory has serious problems accounting for the shifting yield curve. Because the theory regards the various maturities as poor substitutes for each other, its proponents do not expect increasing short-term yields triggered by Federal Reserve actions to be transmitted to other maturities. Instead, the yield curve would show an isolated blip (increase in yield) in the maturity sector in which the Fed is selling securities. In the segmented markets theory the yield curve shifts only by chance, for example, if an event (other than interest rate expectations) triggers a simultaneous decrease in demand for all maturities (shifting the entire yield curve upward). The fact that the yield curve is relatively smooth most of the time suggests a high degree of substitutability among maturities, casting doubt about the validity of the segmented markets theory.

## Fact 3: Yield Curve Exhibits a Regular Cyclical Pattern

Short-term and long-term interest rates move pro-cyclically over the course of the business cycle—rising during expansions and falling during recessions. However, short-term rates exhibit much greater amplitude than long-term rates over the cycle, implying that the yield curve also has a regular pattern over the course of the business cycle. Figure 6-5 illustrates these empirical regularities. The figure shows the yields on 10-year and 90-day U.S. government securities and their differential over the most recent 30-year period. Periods of recession are shaded.

At the trough of a recession (shaded areas) and in the early portion of an economic expansion (unshaded), the yield curve is strongly upward sloping, that is, long-term yields substantially exceed short-term yields. As a nation's output expands during the second half of the expansion, short-term interest rates increase more strongly than long-term rates. The yield curve flattens as the economy approaches the peak of a cycle. Often, a few months before the peak, short-term rates move above long-term rates. The yield curve becomes inverted or downward sloping. During the ensuing recession, the pattern is reversed. Short-term rates fall

The Countercyclical nature of the spread. $(i_{10} - i_{90\text{-day}})$ = The Spread

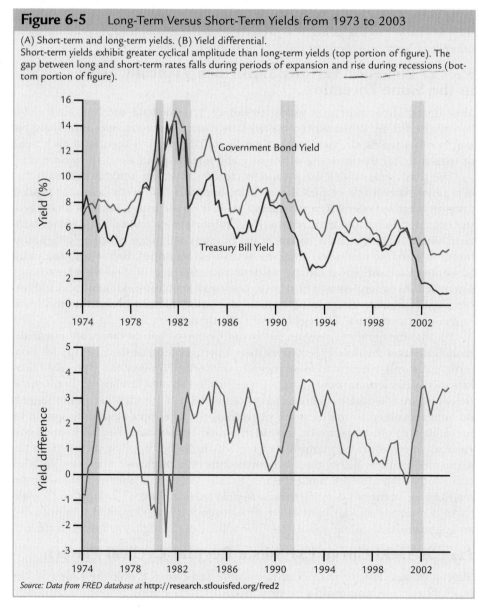

**Figure 6-5** Long-Term Versus Short-Term Yields from 1973 to 2003

(A) Short-term and long-term yields. (B) Yield differential.
Short-term yields exhibit greater cyclical amplitude than long-term yields (top portion of figure). The gap between long and short-term rates falls during periods of expansion and rise during recessions (bottom portion of figure).

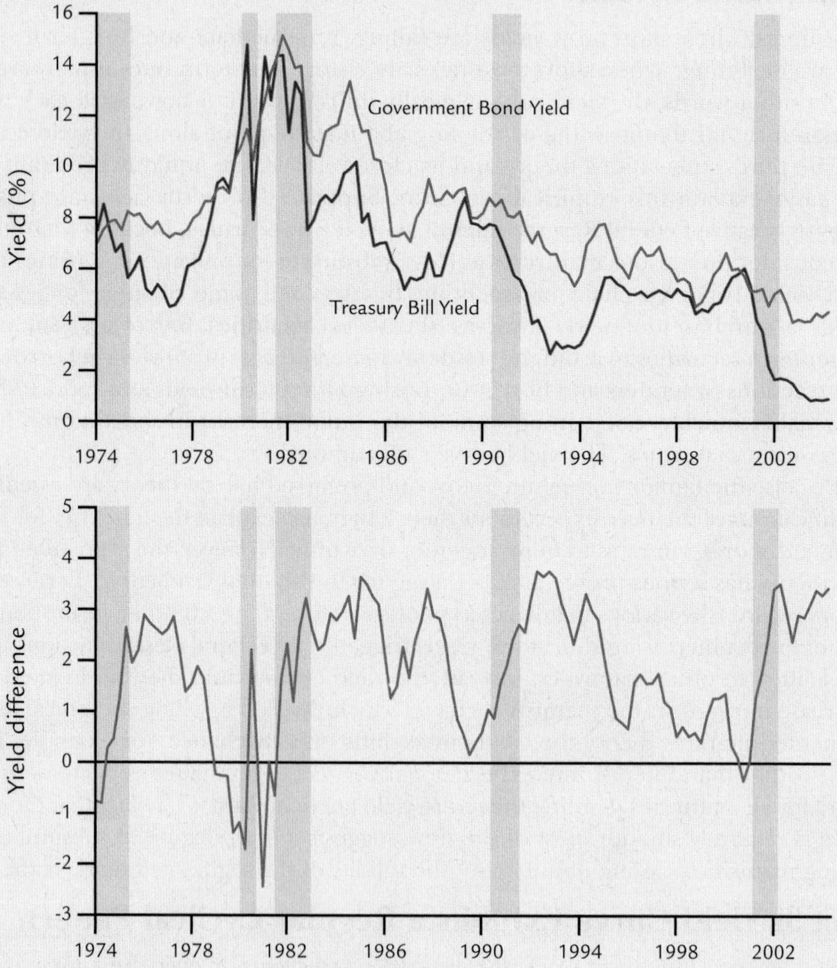


*Source: Data from FRED database at* http://research.stlouisfed.org/fred2

more sharply than long-term rates. As the economy nears the trough (low point) of the recession, the yield curve assumes a strongly ascending pattern. Long-term rates are sharply higher than short-term rates.

The pure expectations theory and its hybrids easily explain the cyclical pattern of the yield curve. Sophisticated financial market agents are well aware of the historic propensity for interest rates to move pro-cyclically—to rise during expansion and fall during recession. During an expansion, interest rates rise as the economy picks up steam and approaches full employment. Wise market participants realize this is a normal phenomenon. They expect interest rates will fall as soon as the economy weakens again. Investors take actions that flatten or invert the yield curve. When the economy is strong and near the peak of the cycle, investors sell short-term securities to purchase long-term bonds, locking in the more attractive long-term yields. As the economy moves into recession and approaches the trough of the cycle, savvy financial market participants recognize that interest rates are abnormally low and likely will rise in the future. Because investors adjust their strategies accordingly (selling long-term bonds and purchasing short-term maturities), the yield curve takes a strongly ascending pattern.

The segmented market theory's explanation for the cyclical pattern of the term structure is not as neat as that of the pure expectations theory, but it is plausible. According to the segmented market theory, loan demand at banks increases as the economy expands in a cyclical upswing. At the same time, however, the Fed tightens its monetary posture. Banks are forced to sell off short-term securities for funds needed to accommodate rising loan demand. Heavy selling pushes Treasury bill prices down and yields up, flattening and possibly inverting the yield curve. In recessions, loan demand at banks plummets and the Federal Reserve eases credit conditions. Banks are awash with funds. Because loan demand is down and banks have an institutional bias against long-term bonds, banks pump their excess funds into Treasury bills, pushing up Treasury bill prices and lowering yields. The yield curve becomes strongly upward sloping. In the segmented markets theory, the residual role of Treasury bills in bank portfolios partly accounts for the cyclical behavior of the yield curve.

Most theories of the term structure of interest rates encounter difficulty explaining some of the empirical regularities observed in interest rate phenomena. The pure expectations theory utterly fails to explain why yield curves are predominantly upward sloping. The segmented markets theory cannot account for the persistent tendency for yields of various maturities to move together. The preferred habitat theory is more versatile in accounting for these empirical regularities. The theory acknowledges borrowers and lenders have certain institutional preferences for specific maturities, and it attributes a powerful influence to expectations in determining the term structure of interest rates.

Now that we understand the role of term to maturity on interest rate levels, we conclude our discussion of interest rates by examining the role of default risk on yield levels.

## RISK STRUCTURE OF INTEREST RATES

A *default* is failure of the security issuer to fully meet the terms of the contractual agreement. For a debt instrument such as a bond, default refers to the borrower's failure to make scheduled interest payments as stipulated or failure to redeem the bond at face value at maturity. Degrees of loss to the lender in a bond default vary, ranging from delay in interest payment to total loss of interest and principal.

## Exhibit 6-2 Can the Term Structure of Interest Rates Forecast Macroeconomic Phenomena?

Information about likely future economic conditions is valuable to individuals and business firms. Corporations pay large sums of money to purchase economic forecasting services. Unfortunately, such services are notorious for lack of accuracy. Some observers suggest that a much cheaper (virtually free) yet equally reliable source of information about future economic conditions is contained in the term structure of interest rates. Can the term structure be used to forecast the future course of interest rates and real gross domestic product?

In most term structure theories, a strongly upward-sloping yield curve indicates marketplace consensus that interest rates will move higher. A downward-sloping or inverted yield curve indicates the market expects interest rates will fall. Because interest rates tend to fall in recession, an inverted yield curve may be a harbinger of recession. A strongly upward-sloping yield curve suggests a considerable period of economic expansion lies ahead.

Several conditions are necessary for the yield curve to function reliably as a forecasting tool. First, the shape of the yield curve must be heavily influenced by expectations about future interest rates, as hypothesized in all theories of term structure except the segmented markets theory. Second, the consensus expectation about the future course of interest rates must be broadly correct. If the yield curve is to be helpful in forecasting real output as well as interest rates, interest rates must be strongly correlated with cyclical conditions—that is, they must move in a systematic fashion over the business cycle.

Assume that interest rates and real economic activity have been very high in recent months. Suppose the market widely believes that the economy will enter a recession soon and therefore interest rates will fall. Through the forces discussed in this chapter, the yield curve will become inverted. If the economy falls into recession next year and interest rates decline during recession (as they almost always do), the inverted yield curve correctly signaled both the recession and the decline in interest rates.

Let us look at the historical record of the past 40 years to see how well the yield curve has signaled the future course of economic activity. The period from 1965 to 2004 witnessed six recessions. In all six instances the yield curve was inverted (with 1-year bond yields exceeding 30-year bond yields) at some point in the year immediately preceding the onset of the recession. In four of the six instances, the yield curve was inverted in the *month* preceding the downturn. The Federal Reserve Bank of Cleveland reported that at least some segment of the yield curve was downward sloping in the year preceding 13 of the 17 cyclical downturns occurring between 1910 and 1994. The strongly upward-sloping yield curves of March 8, 1985, and February 5, 1993, correctly signaled the long periods of economic expansion that lay ahead (review Figure 6-1).

The term structure is not a foolproof indicator of future economic conditions, but it is a useful and cost-free source of information. Look at the yield curve in today's edition of *The Wall Street Journal.* What does the yield curve suggest about the likely strength of economic activity in the next few years?

A premium compensating the lender for default risk is embedded in the yields of risky securities. The premium's magnitude varies widely among different securities. Conceptually, the premium's magnitude is estimated by taking the difference between the yield on a risky security and the yield on a security free of default risk but similar in other respects (maturity, tax treatment, and so forth). For example, to estimate the yield premium on 90-day commercial paper, look at the difference between the paper yield and the 90-day Treasury bill yield. To estimate the yield premium on a corporate bond, calculate the difference between the corporate bond yield and the yield on a U.S. government bond of comparable maturity.[7] The spread between the yields on securities with and without default risk is the **risk premium.** A risk premium is built into the yield of a bond with default risk. An increase in the market's perception of the magnitude of this risk increases the risk premium.

**risk premium**
additional yield contained in financial instruments to compensate lenders for default risk

Prospective bond buyers require information on the default risk of various bonds. Two investment advisory services, Moody's and Standard and Poor's, provide quality ratings of corporate and municipal bonds in the United States. Table 6-3 compares the rating schemes. Bonds with a Moody's rating of Baa or above are considered investment grade. Bonds with lower ratings are considered **junk bonds.**

**junk bonds**
bonds judged to have a high risk of default, rated Ba or lower by Moody's

Figure 6-6 compares yields on long-term U.S. government bonds and Moody's Baa-rated corporate bonds over the past 30 years. You can consider the yield differential between the two (bottom line in figure) as a measure of the default risk in Baa corporate bonds. Periods of recession are shaded.

The magnitude of the gap between yields on these bonds increases during recessions and other periods of financial distress. For example, the risk premium was extremely high during the Great Depression of the 1930s. The risk premium was low and relatively stable during the tranquil period of the 1950s and early 1960s (not shown). The risk premium increased during the severe recessions of 1973 to 1975 and 1981 to 1982 as corporate financial distress escalated sharply. Risk premiums trended downward modestly through most of the economic boom of the 1990s before increasing near the end of the decade. Risk premiums increased again in the 2001 recession and its aftermath, including the period following the terrorists' attacks of September 11, 2001, and the corporate scandals of 2002 (note the 2002 spike).

We can illustrate analytically the behavior producing a change in risk premiums. Figure 6-7 shows the initial supply and demand for loanable funds in both the risky and default-free bond markets. The left-hand portion of the figure shows the market for default-free securities (U.S. government bonds). The right-hand portion shows the riskier market (corporate Baa bonds). Remember that the supply curve

**Table 6-3** Bond Ratings of Investment Advisory Services

| Moody's | Standard & Poor's | Interpretation |
|---|---|---|
| Aaa | AAA | Highest quality |
| Aa | AA | High quality |
| A | A | Upper medium quality |
| Baa | BBB | Medium quality |
| Ba | BB | Lower medium quality |
| B | B | Speculative grade |
| Caa | CCC | Poor quality |
| Ca | CC | Highly speculative grade |
| C | | Extremely poor quality |
| | D | In default |

[7] The tax treatment of the two bonds differs slightly. Interest earned on U.S. government bonds is nontaxable by state governments but taxable by the federal government. Income earned on corporate bonds is taxable by both the federal and state governments. This difference implies that even if a corporate bond has no default risk, the market places a slight premium in corporate bond yields to compensate for the taxable status of corporate bonds relative to U.S. government bonds.

**Figure 6-6** Yields on Corporate Baa Bonds and U.S. Treasury Bonds from 1973 to 2003

A bond's default risk is indicated by the difference between its yield and the yield on a risk-free bond. The difference widens during recessions and other periods of financial distress.

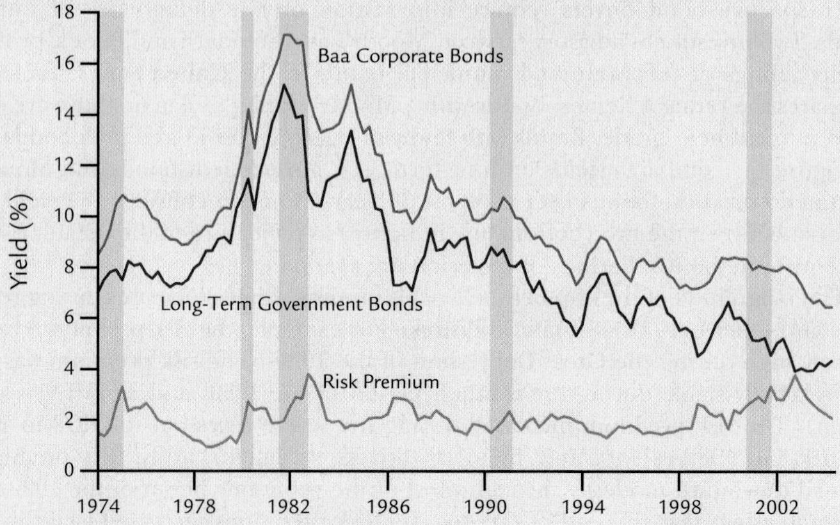


*Source: Data from FRED database at* **http://research.stlouisfed.org/fred2**

**Figure 6-7** Analysis of Changing Risk Premiums

When perceived default risk increases, lenders redirect funds from risky markets to risk-free markets. This action increases the yield differential, that is, the risk premium in corporate bonds.

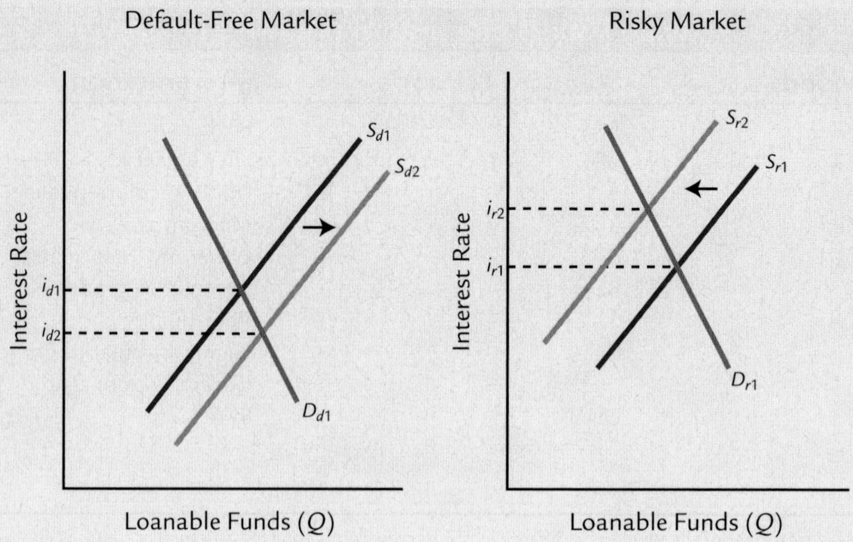

originates from surplus units seeking to lend funds to earn interest. The yields initially prevailing in the default-free and risky markets are $i_{d1}$ and $i_{r1}$, respectively. The initial risk premium in corporate bonds is the difference, $i_{r1} - i_{d1}$.

Suppose a major U.S. corporation shocks financial markets by announcing a dramatic deterioration in its financial condition, raising the specter of potential insolvency. The psychological effect of this announcement significantly impacts the bond markets, including upward revision in the risk premium required by investors on yields of corporate bonds, particularly of firms without outstanding credit ratings. In Figure 6-7, we ignore any shifts in the demand curve for loanable funds (behavior by borrowers) and focus on the behavior of lenders.[8] Because lenders are now more conscious of possible default, they seek to upgrade the quality of their portfolios. The supply of funds offered in the default-free market (government bonds) increases from $S_{d1}$ to $S_{d2}$, while the supply of funds offered in the risky market decreases from $S_{r1}$ to $S_{r2}$. Lenders reallocate funds to safer markets, resulting in a simultaneous increase in yields on medium-grade and lower-grade corporate bonds and a decrease in yields on government bonds. The risk premium increases to $i_{r2} - i_{d2}$.

This analysis explains the tendency for risk premium fluctuation over the course of the business cycle. The yield spread increases in recessions and decreases during economic expansions. In recessions, more firms experience financial problems as business sales and profits decline. As financial distress increases, lenders divert funds from corporate bonds to government bonds, and the risk premium increases. During an economic recovery, sales and profits increase. Firms experience fewer financial problems, and business failures decline. Lenders become more willing to purchase medium-grade and lower-grade corporate bonds, and the risk premium narrows.

## SUMMARY

The term structure of interest rates is the relationship between the length of time to maturity of a debt instrument and its yield, with all other factors influencing yields held constant. Graphical depiction of the term structure is the *yield curve*. Several theories of term structure exist. The pure expectations theory singles out the role of expected future interest rates and excludes other factors in explaining the term structure. The liquidity premium theory accepts the pure expectations theory with the added caveat that long-term yields contain a term premium compensating lenders for the greater market risk inherent in long-term bonds. The segmented markets theory emphasizes institutional factors limiting borrowers and lenders' willingness to substitute among different maturities in response to perceived yield advantages. The preferred habitat theory accepts elements of the other three theories but rejects the two polar viewpoints—that only expectations or only institutional factors determine the term structure. Real-world empirical regularities confronting term structure theories include the following: the yield curve is typically upward sloping; yields on bonds of different maturities usually move together over time; and short-term yields exhibit greater amplitude over time than long-term yields. The preferred habitat the-

[8] The supply of loanable funds corresponds to a demand for bonds. An increase in the supply of loanable funds implies an increase in demand for bonds.

ory—a hybrid theory that accepts a portion of each of the other theories—more closely accords with these facts than the other three theories. Bonds and other debt instruments have varying degrees of default risk. The difference between the yield on a risky bond and a risk-free bond reflects the magnitude of perceived default risk. The difference typically increases in recessions and other times of financial distress and decreases during periods of stability and prosperity.

## YOUR TURN ANSWERS

PAGE 129

**A.** You expect inflation will increase. Interest rates will rise in the coming months and perhaps years due to the Fisher effect. Long-term bond prices likely will fall significantly with time. To avoid exposure to potential capital losses in long-term bonds, you invest all your funds in the short-term market.

**B.** The announcement of war produces a consensus that both inflation and interest rates are headed higher for the foreseeable future. Thousands of investors sell long-term bonds, forcing bond prices down and yields up. Many investors seek a safe haven in short-term Treasury securities, pushing security prices up and yields down. The yield curve quickly changes from a flat to an upward-sloping pattern.

## KEY TERMS

term structure of interest rates
yield curve
pure expectations theory
forward interest rate
liquidity premium theory
term premium
segmented markets theory
preferred habitat theory
risk premium
junk bond

## STUDY QUESTIONS

1. Look for the daily report entitled "Treasury Yield Curve" in the most recent issue of *The Wall Street Journal*. Note the change in the yield curve over the last 4 weeks (shown in the same figure). What recent developments can you think of explain this change?

2. Suppose a constitutional amendment outlawing budget deficits is (unexpectedly) passed by Congress and ratified by the states. Suppose the budget deficit is mandated to be phased out over the next 5 years. In the context of term structure theories emphasizing the role of expectations, what would be the implication of the announcement of this legislation for the shape of the yield curve? Explain.

3. Suppose the Federal Reserve attempts to twist the yield curve by simultaneously selling Treasury bills and purchasing long-term bonds. In which theory (or theories) will the Fed be successful? In which theory (or theories) will the Fed be unsuccessful? Explain.

4. Suppose you read in the paper that the yields available today on 1-year, 2-year, and 3-year Treasury bonds are 6 percent, 7 percent, and 6.5 percent, respectively. According to the pure expectations theory of term structure, what does the market believe 1-year bond yields will be 1 year from now? Two years from now?

5. In your view, why is the yield curve usually upward sloping?

6. Suppose that, instead of being risk averse, both borrowers and lenders are actually *risk lovers*—that is, they prefer risk. According to the liquidity premium theory, what would be the normal shape of the yield curve?

7. Suppose a series of mergers reduces competition among security dealers in the financial markets, causing transactions costs in financial markets to rise sharply. What would this imply for the:
   **A.** Validity of the pure expectations theory?
   **B.** Shape of the yield curve?

8. Interest rates were much more volatile in the 1970s than in the 1990s and 2000s. What is the implication for the average gap between long-term and short-term yields on Treasury securities in those decades:
   **A.** According to the pure expectations theory?
   **B.** According to the liquidity premium theory?

9. Under what conditions would a flat yield curve exist in the:
   **A.** Pure expectations theory?
   **B.** Liquidity premium theory?
   **C.** Segmented markets theory?

10. Treasury bills are issued in minimum denominations of $10,000. Longer-term government notes and bonds are issued in minimum denominations of $1,000. What would have been the likely impact of the advent of money market mutual funds in the 1970s on the term structure of interest rates in the segmented markets theory? In the pure expectations theory?

11. On a
lowe
tury
minu
perio
on yo
ture,
facts?
sprea

12. Assum
pure e
Suppo
and 5-y
cent, 6 pe
are the likely ... for economic activity in the nation in the next few years? Explain.

13. If you knew that a severe recession due to a major decline in consumer confidence was coming next year, would you be better off holding 30-year U.S. Treasury bonds or 90-day Treasury bills? Would you be better off holding 30-year U.S. Treasury bonds or 30-year Baa corporate bonds? Explain.

14. Suppose yield spreads between corporate Baa bonds and U.S. Treasury bonds increase sharply in the next month. What information does this increase give about the market's opinion of the outlook for the economy?

## AL READING

t survey of the theory of term structure, h copious citations of the literature, read 5 of James C. Van Horne, *Financial Markets and Flows,* 4th edition (Englewood Cliffs, NJ: entice Hall, 1998). A rigorous and somewhat mathematical review of term structure is Chapter 13 of Benjamin Friedman and Frank Hahn, *Handbook of Monetary Economics* (Amsterdam, North Holland: 1990), written by Robert Shiller. An enlightening historical discussion of the term structure in the United States, complete with voluminous data, is provided in Sidney Homer and Richard Sylla, *A History of Interest Rates,* 3rd edition (Rutgers, NJ: Rutgers University Press, 1991, pp. 394–409).

- The pure expectations theory was originally developed by Irving Fisher nearly 100 years ago in "Appreciation and Interest," which is reprinted in *Publication of the American Economics Association, XI* (August 1986). Seminal papers setting forth the segmented markets theory and the preferred habitat theory, respectively, are J. M. Culbertson, "The Term Structure of Interest Rates," *Quarterly Journal of Economics,* November 1957, pp. 489–504, and Franco Modigliani and Richard Sutch, "Innovations in Interest Rate Policy," *American Economic Review,* May 1966, pp. 178–197. Other useful papers on term structure include Alan Garner, "The Yield Curve and Inflation Expectations," Federal Reserve Bank of Kansas City *Economic Review,* September/October 1987, and Peter Abken, "Innovations in Modeling the Term Structure of Interest Rates," *Economic Review,* Federal Reserve Bank of Atlanta, July/August 1990, pp. 2–27.
- A study reporting that the yield curve is a good predictor of real economic activity is Arturo Estrella and Gikas Hardouvelis, "The Term Structure as a Predictor of Real Economic Activity," *Journal of Finance,* June 1991, pp. 555–576. An excellent survey of the predictive power of the yield curve is contained in Ben Bernanke, "On the Predictive Power of Interest Rates and Interest Rate Spreads," *New England Economic Review,* November/December 1990, pp. 51–68. A widely cited early paper on default risk is Lawrence Fisher, "Determinants of Risk Premiums on Corporate Bonds," *Journal of Political Economy,* June 1959, pp. 217–237.

# Chapter 7

# THE STOCK MARKET

## INTRODUCTION

For millions of Americans, the most fascinating of all markets is the U.S. stock market. Interest in stocks (also known as *equities*) has grown the past couple of decades. The increased interest in stock is partly attributable to stocks' superior performance relative to bonds, real estate, and other personal investment vehicles over long periods. Over the past 100 years, total returns from stocks have averaged approximately 10 percent per year. In the last 18 years of the twentieth century (1982–2000), the average U.S. stock yielded—including stock price appreciation and dividend reinvestment—an incredible compounded average return of nearly 18 percent per year! The "rule of 72" indicates that anything growing 18 percent annually doubles in 4 years.[1] One thousand dollars invested in the Standard and Poor's (S&P) 500 stock index in June 1982, with dividends reinvested, appreciated to approximately $20,000 by early 2000. Relative to historic norms, the 1982 to 2000 stock market performance was clearly an aberration. This high-return period was followed by a severe decline in the price of most technology and other stocks from 2000 to 2003. Most Americans are optimistic about the long-run prospects for the stock market.

### Long-Term Stock Market Behavior

Figure 7-1 illustrates the behavior of the S&P 500 index, the stock market index favored by most economists, from 1900 to early 2004. A logarithmic scale is used because the index grew enormously over the long period. You can interpret changes in the *slope* of trends in the figure as changes in the trend *growth rate* of stock prices. The figure indicates stock prices trended only modestly upward from 1900 to the end of World War II (1945). The postwar increase in stock prices has been sustained and powerful. Two major "bull markets"—extended periods of above-normal growth of stock prices—occurred after World War II. The first bull market extended from the late 1940s through the mid-1960s. The second extended from 1982 through the end of the twentieth century. After the second bull market, the S&P 500 index declined by approximately 50 percent from August 2000 to February 2003. The run-up of stock prices from 1925 to 1929 and the ensuing "Great Crash" of 1929 to 1933 are also prominent in the figure.

Stock returns have outpaced returns from other assets not just in the period after 1982 but also over extremely long periods. Table 7-1 shows the annual average returns from stocks, 10-year U.S. government bonds, 1-month Treasury bills, and gold from 1926 to 2003, both before and after adjustment for inflation.

---

[1] The "rule of 72" states that the number of years required for anything to double is approximately equal to 72 divided by the annual growth rate. If your income rises 6 percent per year, your income will double in approximately 12 years. If your savings account pays 3 percent interest, your balance will double in approximately 24 years.

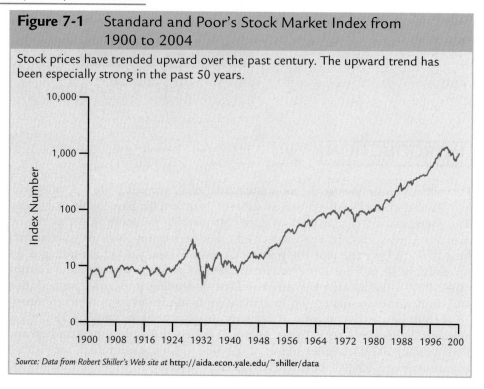

**Figure 7-1** Standard and Poor's Stock Market Index from 1900 to 2004

Stock prices have trended upward over the past century. The upward trend has been especially strong in the past 50 years.

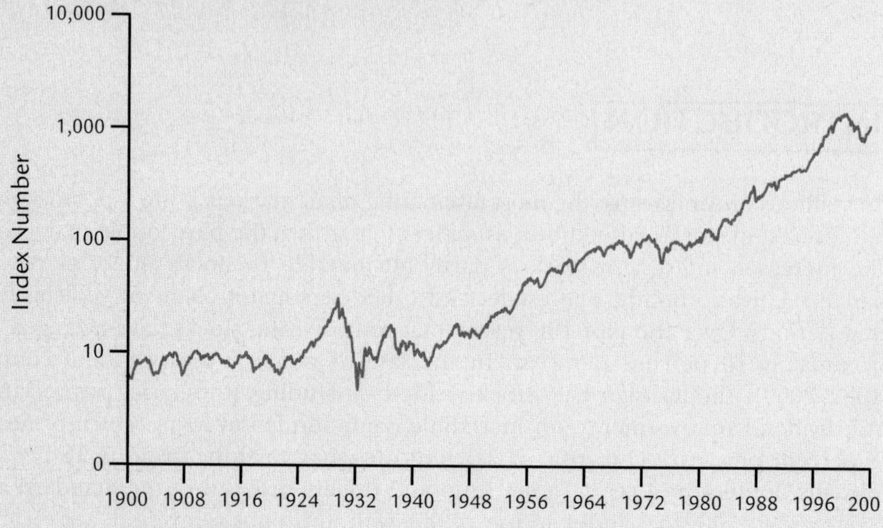


*Source: Data from Robert Shiller's Web site at* http://aida.econ.yale.edu/~shiller/data

Before adjustment for inflation, stocks returned an average of more than 10 percent per year over 75 years, twice the rate of return from government bonds and almost three times the return from Treasury bills and gold. After adjusting for the 3 percent average annual inflation rate of 1926 to 2003, the *real* return from stocks averaged 7.4 percent per year, dramatically exceeding the real returns from the other three assets.

## Stock Prices as a Barometer of Economic Sentiment

A nation's stock market serves as a barometer of public sentiment about the nation's economic prospects. The strong performance of U.S. stocks since the early 1980s reflects optimism about the future of the U.S. economy. In the 22-year period

**Table 7-1** Historic Returns from Stocks, Bonds, Treasury Bills, and Gold: Average Annual Compounded Rates of Return from 1926 to 2003

| | Stocks (S&P 500) | 10-Year Government Bonds | 1-Month Treasury Bills | Gold |
|---|---|---|---|---|
| Nominal | 10.4 | 5.2 | 3.6 | 3.6 |
| Real* | 7.4 | 2.2 | 0.6 | 0.6 |

All figures are given as percent.
*Inflation rate of the consumer price index averaged 3.0 percent per year from 1926 to 2003.
*Source: Calculated from data in Global Financial Data at* http://globalfindata.com

beginning in 1983, the U.S. suffered only two recessions, and these were among the shortest and mildest on record. An economic expansion that began in early 1991 ran a full decade—a record for longevity. The economy became more stable, as indicated by a decline in the variability of output. Inflation generally trended downward after 1989, and unemployment remained relatively low. Beginning in the mid-1990s, the growth rates of U.S. productivity and living standards increased. Several factors sparked this favorable development, including the revolution in telecommunications and information technology, opening up of foreign markets and the increase in worldwide competition, and ongoing restructuring of American industry. Many economists expect the higher growth rate will be sustained for years to come, although this issue is debatable.

The public's confidence in the Federal Reserve's ability to prevent severe economic downturns and promote sustained economic expansions has been high in recent years. At times, however, expectations for an economy's performance in general and for corporate profits in particular can become detached from reality. The last few years of the twentieth century and of the 1920s are examples of this phenomenon (review Figure 7-1). In the 5-year period from the beginning of 1995 to the end of 1999, broad indexes of U.S. stock prices tripled. The NASDAQ stock index, which is dominated by technology stocks, rose from 1,000 in 1996 to more than 5,000 in early 2000. After the mid-1990s, a few observers spoke of a speculative "bubble" in the U.S. stock market—that is, stock prices far above prices warranted by economic conditions and prospects. Discussions in academic circles and within the Federal Reserve centered on whether the central bank should intervene to deflate perceived "bubbles" before they become grossly excessive. While Fed chairman Alan Greenspan famously spoke of "irrational exuberance" in 1996, the Federal Reserve did not aggressively act to slow the advance of stock prices because the condition of the overall economy did not warrant restrictive actions. With the benefit of hindsight, it is apparent that individuals who advanced the "bubble" hypothesis in the late 1990s were correct. Their views were vindicated by the dramatic sell-off of technology and other stocks during 2000 to early 2003. We discuss the issue of asset price bubbles and the appropriate Federal Reserve response to them later in this chapter.

## CONNECTION BETWEEN STOCK PRICES AND ECONOMIC ACTIVITY

The link between stock prices and economic performance reflects causation running in both directions. The nation's economic performance influences the nation's stock market. People pay higher prices for stock shares as companies' sales and profits increase. However, stock prices also influence macroeconomic activity. For example, economists believe that two critical components of aggregate expenditures—consumption spending and investment spending—are influenced by stock prices.

### Stock Prices and Consumption Spending

Consumption spending, composing two thirds of aggregate expenditures, is influenced by *wealth* and by household income. If income remains constant, an increase in stock prices stimulates current consumption spending through the **wealth effect**—the effect of changes in individuals' net worth on their consumption and saving decisions. Over the past 15 years, stock market wealth owned by U.S. households in personal portfolios and retirement accounts increased by more than $8,000 billion ($8 trillion)! The nation's measured saving rate has declined in the

**wealth effect**
effect of changes in individuals' net worth on their consumption and saving decisions

past 25 years partly because of the wealth effect. The saving-to-disposable income ratio has declined and the consumption-to-disposable income ratio has increased. According to national income accounts data, the portion of personal disposable income saved by the average American household declined from more than 10 percent from 1980 to 1982 to less than 2 percent from 2000 to 2003. Rising wealth created through higher stock and home prices reduced many families' perceived need to save current income. The burst of consumption spending helped propel aggregate spending and sustain the record-length economic expansion from 1991 to 2001. The wealth effect clearly has a potential downside. A sharp drop in stock prices can result in an economic downturn if households react by cutting back severely on consumption spending.

## Stock Prices and Investment Spending

Investment spending involves expenditures by firms on new plants, equipment, software, and technology. Investment spending is much smaller in total than consumption spending but is considerably more variable than consumption spending. Investment spending has critical implications for the nation's long-term economic growth. Investment spending increases the nation's capital stock and our capacity to produce goods and services. In the long run, economic growth is determined by the expanded capacity to produce. Given other factors influencing investment expenditures (such as interest rates and federal tax policy), an increase in stock prices boosts investment expenditures. Greater investment stimulates economic activity in the near term, and the resulting increase in the nation's capital stock enhances long-term economic growth.

Firms must use retained profits, issue debt (borrow), or issue new shares of stock (issue equity) to finance new investment expenditures. Many rapidly growing firms having insufficient retained profits to finance desired investment expenditures issue debt or new shares of stock. Each option has drawbacks and advantages. Issuing debt increases the firm's *leverage* and annual interest expenses, increasing the firm's exposure to financial distress and potential insolvency should conditions unexpectedly worsen. On the positive side of the ledger, corporate interest expenditures on debt are tax deductible while dividend payments to stockholders are not. A disadvantage of issuing new shares is that the portion of the company held by existing owners is reduced. If Microsoft issues new shares of stock to the public in an amount equal to the already-existing number of shares (doubles the number of shares outstanding), then the pro rata share of the company owned by Bill Gates and other original stockholders is halved. This process is known as *dilution.* Firms are understandably reluctant to dilute existing owners' share of the company (and their influence over important decisions). Higher stock prices enable companies to raise more revenue per share of stock issued, which counteracts the disadvantages associated with dilution. The major portion of business investment is financed through debt, but issuance of stock is another important source of funds. Like a decline in interest rates, an increase in stock prices reduces the **cost of capital**—the cost of raising funds to finance capital expenditures. At the margin, higher stock prices entice firms to issue additional shares of stock and use the proceeds to finance investment expenditures. Thus, changes in stock prices influence investment spending and economic activity in the near term.

**cost of capital**
cost of raising funds to finance capital expenditures

## Virtuous and Vicious Cycles

Chapter 3 explained that an efficient and healthy secondary market in which shares of stock are traded provides liquidity for prospective shareholders. This makes it feasible for corporations to issue new shares of stock. A vibrant and upward-trending stock market contributes to capital formation and the nation's real economic performance. With hindsight, the United States became happily engaged in a **virtuous cycle** of improving economic performance and rising stock prices in the last decade of the twentieth century.

**virtuous cycle**
cycle in which expanding economic activity and rising stock prices lead to increased investment expenditures, thereby further expanding economic activity

In a virtuous cycle, expanding economic activity and rising stock prices lead to increased investment expenditures. This boosts the nation's capital stock and the capacity to produce goods and services, which in turn accommodates strong growth in demand for goods and services without an increase in the nation's underlying inflation rate. The rising productivity induced by the increase in the amount of capital goods per worker increases living standards and expands corporate profits. At the same time the nation's price level remains relatively stable. Given a favorable inflation environment, the Federal Reserve maintains relatively low interest rates. The stimulus to economic activity results in greater tax revenues flowing into government coffers, reducing the federal budget deficit (or increasing the surplus). The improving budgetary picture and the accommodative Federal Reserve policy (made possible by continued low inflation) contribute to low real interest rates, with the attendant positive effect on investment spending. Given the superb economic environment, foreign demand for U.S. stocks and other assets increases, strengthening the U.S. dollar in foreign exchange markets. A rising dollar reduces the cost of imported goods and further contributes to low U.S. inflation. The stock market responds positively to this confluence of favorable events, leading to additional investment spending. And so the virtuous cycle continues.[2]

What sorts of events eventually end a virtuous cycle? Any number of unforeseen shocks can unravel a virtuous cycle and derail a sustained economic expansion. For example, a sharp increase in oil prices, like the increases in 1973 and 2004, raises production costs and acts like a tax increase. Increased expenditures on gasoline and energy bills necessitate cutbacks in other household and business expenditures. Major political or military developments can provide a negative shock to consumer and business confidence. Consumption and/or investment expenditures are reduced, leading to a recession. The U.S. recession of 1990 to 1991 is commonly attributed to a sudden drop in consumer confidence initiated by Saddam Hussein's confiscation of Kuwaiti oil fields in early 1990. The terrible events of September 11, 2001, negatively impacted public confidence, which contributed to the sluggishness of the U.S. economy in the ensuing couple of years. If U.S. stock prices decline sharply for any reason, the attendant decline in wealth and consumer and business confidence could provoke an economic slowdown or downturn. The Federal Reserve became concerned about high and rising stock prices after the mid-1990s for this reason. To the extent that stocks become overvalued, the possibility of a sharp and potentially damaging decline in stock prices becomes an increasingly worrisome prospect.

[2] In contrast, in much of the 1970s and early 1980s, the United States appeared mired in a *vicious* cycle of declining stock prices—relatively weak investment spending, slow productivity growth, high inflation, a falling dollar, and expanding budget deficits. Inflation and interest rates were rising; investment spending and productivity growth were sluggish. All of these factors justified weak stock prices, further inhibiting investment spending and growth of real output and profits, thereby validating and exacerbating the poor stock market performance. In the 7-year period from the beginning of 1973 to the end of 1979, $1 invested in the S&P 500 stock market index declined in value to 44¢ after adjustment for inflation.

# MEASURING STOCK MARKET PERFORMANCE

Millions of individual investors are interested in how the "market" is doing. They listen to the news on the radio on the way home from work or watch the evening news on television. Quite a few individuals, some contemplating retirement, sneak a look at stock prices on their computer monitor on "company time" during the day. Individuals owning mutual funds or retirement accounts are interested in how their assets are performing. Numerous indexes of stock market performance convey information about stock prices. Each of the stock market indexes serves as a benchmark for a particular segment of the overall universe of common stocks.

## Characteristics of a Good Stock Market Index

A good stock market index possesses several characteristics. Most importantly, it quickly conveys information to a large number of investors about how their stocks are generally performing. The stocks included in the index and the weights given to the stocks represent the stocks and weights applicable to a significant group of investors. Second, the index encompasses a sufficient number of companies such that developments unique to one or two companies do not exert an unduly large effect on the index. Other factors held constant, a larger number of stocks in the index better reflects overall market performance. Third, as the prices of individual stocks change over time, each stock's relative importance in a representative investor's portfolio changes. If the price of your shares of Microsoft rose over the years while your K-Mart stock tanked, then a larger percentage of your total portfolio is invested in Microsoft today than in the past. The weight accorded to Microsoft in the stock index should have increased relative to that of K-Mart for the index to reflect the overall change in a typical investor's financial standing. A good stock market index changes the weights given to individual stocks frequently in response to changing **market capitalization**—the market value of the aggregate shares of stock outstanding for each company in the index. Finally, the index considers the trading frequency of stocks included in the index. An index that includes a large number of infrequently traded stocks fails to accurately reflect market performance, especially over short time intervals, because the price of a non-traded stock remains constant while the price of a stock being traded changes continuously.

**market capitalization**
market value of the aggregate shares of stock outstanding of a corporation or a universe of corporations

## U.S. Stock Market Indexes

Several alternative stock market indexes are available in the United States. The appropriate choice of index depends on your purpose in using a stock market index and the composition of your stock portfolio. We briefly describe the nature of several of the most popular indexes of U.S. stock prices. The most famous and widely quoted index is the Dow Jones Industrial Average (DJIA). The DJIA has some important shortcomings, and several other indexes better represent the broad market than does the Dow.

**Dow Jones Industrial Average(DJIA).** This venerable and widely reported index is a simple *unweighted* average of the prices of 30 very large, actively traded U.S. stocks. Originally developed in 1896 as a 12-stock index, the DJIA was expanded to encompass 30 stocks in 1928. Today, the aggregate market capitalization of the companies included in the DJIA amounts to approximately 25 percent of the value of the roughly 3,000 stocks traded on the New York Stock Exchange (NYSE). The term *industrial* in the DJIA is a misnomer. The index includes corporations engaged in communications, retailing, and services; it is not limited to "industrial" companies. The DJIA includes long-standing blue chips such as AT&T, Coca-Cola, Eastman Kodak, General Motors, IBM, and Proctor & Gamble. The companies included in the DJIA change to reflect the changing nature and structure of the U.S. economy, although the total number of companies included remains fixed at 30. In the past few years, Intel, Home Depot, Honeywell International, Microsoft, and Wal-Mart have been added to the index, while Allied Signal, Chevron, Goodyear, Sears, and Union Carbide have been dropped. Because the index includes only very large, highly capitalized companies and the index is unweighted, its performance can fail to accurately reflect the behavior of the stock market as a whole.[3] The continued popularity of the DJIA stems more from habit and inertia than from its quality as a reflector of performance of stocks owned by a typical investor.

**Standard and Poor's 500 Index (S&P 500).** As the name suggests, this index includes 500 U.S. corporations; therefore it is much broader than the Dow. Like the Dow, the S&P 500 emphasizes the largest U.S. corporations. The stocks included in the S&P 500 account for about 70 percent of the total market value of all U.S. stocks. Unlike the DJIA, which takes a simple average of the prices of the 30 companies, the S&P 500 weights the individual companies by their market capitalization. If the market capitalization of Microsoft is ten times larger than that of Sherwin Williams, a one percentage point increase in Microsoft stock exerts ten times the influence on the S&P 500 index as a one percentage point increase in Sherwin Williams stock. Economists and Wall Street professionals prefer the S&P 500 to the DJIA for several reasons—the S&P 500 includes far more companies than the DJIA but excludes many small and seldom-traded NYSE companies and the S&P 500 weights the individual components by their market capitalization.

**New York Stock Exchange Composite Index.** This index includes all of the approximately 3,000 stocks listed on the NYSE. It is a much broader index than the DJIA or the S&P 500, but it includes many companies that are neither actively traded nor well known. Most market professionals prefer the S&P 500 because of its greater emphasis on larger and more actively traded stocks.

**National Association of Securities Dealers Automated Quotations (NASDAQ).** Stocks included in this popular index are "unlisted" and are traded "over the counter" through a network of dealers rather than on an organized exchange like the NYSE. The 1971 formation of the NASDAQ (National Association of Security Dealers Automated Quotations) fundamentally altered the over-the-counter market by accelerating the dissemination of stock price information. The NASDAQ index is a broad-based indicator of prices in the unlisted securities market. The index includes about 4,900 of the roughly 5,500 stocks traded over the counter. Many newer and smaller companies do not meet requisite standards for earnings, number of stockholders, or market capitalization to qualify for listing on major stock exchanges like the NYSE. Instead, smaller companies are traded "over

---

[3] The DJIA is calculated by adding up the prices of the 30 component stocks and dividing by a number that originally was 30 but has been adjusted downward over the years to allow for stock splits and other factors. The divisor and a listing of the 30 stocks encompassed in the index are published each day in *The Wall Street Journal.* Because relatively mature and slower-growing companies (Sears, Union Carbide) are replaced with more dynamic and rapidly growing firms (Microsoft, Intel) over time, the DJIA probably is *biased upward,* that is, it likely overstates the growth rate of the entire universe of large cap stocks. A similar bias may pertain to the S&P 500 index.

the counter." Most stocks quoted on the NASDAQ have traditionally been smaller, less well known, and less widely held than those traded on the exchanges. However, this image of the NASDAQ has changed as a result of the enormous success in the past 20 years of companies such as Microsoft and Intel, which now are included in the DJIA as well as the NASDAQ. Many high-tech companies that have been very successful in recent years are traded on the NASDAQ. Therefore, this index has become more commonly watched in the past 10 to 15 years. At the end of 2003, about one sixth of total U.S. stock market capitalization was contributed by NASDAQ stocks.

**exchange traded funds (ETFs)** instruments designed to track a particular stock market index or sector; can be purchased by individual investors like shares of stock

**Other Stock Market Indexes.** The American Stock Exchange (ASE) traditionally was dominated by gold, silver, and other natural resource stocks. More recently, the innovative and popular *index shares* ("i shares") or **exchange traded funds (ETFs)** have been traded on the ASE. ETFs are relatively new instruments that were introduced in 1993. Some track a particular U.S. stock market index, such as the DJIA, S&P 500, or NASDAQ 100. Some ETFs are consistently on the "most active" list of ASE stocks traded each day. Other ETFs track particular sectors, such as health care or energy, or markets in foreign countries. Some ETFs track U.S. government bond prices. Owning an ETF enables an individual with modest savings to achieve broad diversification in stocks. ETFs have certain advantages over mutual funds. (Exhibit 7-1 discusses these instruments.) Finally, the Russell 1000, 2000, and 3000 indexes were introduced in 1984. The Russell universe of stocks includes the nation's largest 3,000 corporations, as measured by market capitalization. The Russell 1000 includes only the largest 1,000 corporations. The Russell 2000 includes the smallest 2,000 corporations of the Russell universe. The Russell 2000 has become the most popular indicator of the "small cap" universe of stocks. In 2004, the market capitalization of the average Russell 2000 stock was approximately $700 million, in contrast to the roughly $80 billion and $20 billion for the average Dow Jones and S&P 500 stock, respectively.

### Exhibit 7-1 Help for Small Players: Discount Brokerages, Online Trading, and Exchange Traded Funds

Ownership of stocks traditionally has been limited to upper-class households. Even today, the distribution of stock ownership is highly skewed. The wealthiest 10 percent of U.S. households owns more than 80 percent of the value of all stock held by U.S. households. However, several innovations make stock accumulation feasible for many middle-class Americans. Innovations include discount brokerage firms, online trading with heavily discounted fees, and stock index mutual funds and related innovations known as exchange traded funds (ETFs).

Brokerage fees were extremely regressive until recent years. The fee as a percentage of the value of a transaction was very high and often prohibitive for small transactions. Major brokerage firms such as Merrill Lynch typically imposed a minimum transactions fee of about $35. An individual seeking to buy $350 worth of Microsoft stock faced an exorbitant 10 percent transactions cost. The advent first of discount brokerage firms such as Schwab and later of online trading accounts with heavily discounted fees sharply reduced the regressivity of brokerage fees. Today, an individual can purchase stocks online from a variety of firms and incur transactions costs that are less than 30 percent of the nondiscounted fees charged by full-service brokerage firms. This new

**Exhibit 7-1** Help for Small Players: Discount Brokerages, Online Trading, and Exchange Traded Funds—*cont'd*

competition has forced traditional brokerage houses to reconsider their fee arrangements and offer alternatives to their customers.

Perhaps the most fundamental proposition of finance is that diversification reduces risk. Traditionally, the difficulty of acquiring a diversified portfolio discouraged small investors from investing in stocks. An individual with $2,000 of savings could not feasibly acquire shares in ten different companies. The proliferation of no-load mutual funds and (more recently) ETFs—baskets of securities that trade like individual stocks—dramatically changed the landscape for the small investor. Mutual funds offer the small investor a chance to own a pro rata share of a diversified portfolio, thereby sharply reducing risk. Mutual funds that track major stock market indexes are available. For example, the Vanguard 500 replicates the S&P 500 index and has more than 2.5 million shareholders.

Mutual funds have some clear disadvantages. Management fees typically run at least 1 percent of the principal per year. Mutual funds buy and sell stocks frequently because of inflows and outflows of investor funds. When a mutual fund sells an appreciated stock, the investor must pay taxes on the realized capital gain even if the mutual fund's value declined during the year. In late 2003 the industry was rocked by scandal, with the revelation that many mutual funds had engaged in trading practices (some illegal) that enriched management at the expense of long-term investors.

ETFs are like some mutual funds in that they mirror the performance of a specific stock market sector or a major index. Whereas mutual funds are purchased through a management company, ETFs are traded on the stock exchanges and can be purchased online or through discount brokers for $20 or less. Unlike mutual funds, ETFs are traded and quoted continuously throughout the day. Most ETFs are listed on the ASE. Several ETFs appear daily on the "most active list" of shares traded on the ASE. The first ETF was the Standard and Poor's Depository Receipts (SPDRs, more commonly known as *Spiders*), introduced in 1993 to replicate the S&P 500 stock index. Very quickly, *Diamonds* and the popular *Qubes* (the stock's symbol is QQQ) were instituted to track the DJIA and NASDAQ 100 indexes, respectively. Other ETFs track specific sectors, such as pharmaceuticals, biotechnology, energy, technology, or indexes in foreign countries. Other ETFs replicate the performance of large-cap, mid-cap, or small-cap stocks.

The average minimum investment requirement for the 125 ETFs available at the end of 2003 was about $2,000. An ETF has advantages over a mutual fund—the ETF has lower management fees, and the decision to incur tax liability lies with the individual investor rather than the mutual fund manager. Continuous trading in ETFs eliminates the trading scandals that have marred the reputation of mutual funds. The great diversification and low annual costs (typically less than 0.20 percent of the principal per year) made possible by ETFs are boons to the small investor. The emergence of discount brokerage firms, online trading, no-load mutual funds, and ETFs is partly responsible for the fact that approximately 50 percent of Americans are now invested in the U.S. stock market.

## Historical Performance of Various Stock Market Indexes

Table 7-2 indicates the performance in recent decades of the DJIA, S&P 500, NYSE, and NASDAQ market indexes. Average annual compounded growth rates over various periods are shown for each index. The indexes track each other rather closely over lengthy periods of several decades.

**Table 7-2 Average Annual Rates of Change of Major U.S. Stock Market Indexes**

| Period | DJIA | S&P 500 | NYSE | NASDAQ* |
|---|---|---|---|---|
| 1960s | 3.3 | 5.5 | 5.9 | N/A |
| 1970s | −0.4 | 0.5 | 0.6 | N/A |
| 1980s | 11.5 | 12.1 | 11.9 | 12.4 |
| 1990s | 15.4 | 15.2 | 13.1 | 20.0 |
| January 2000–June 2004 | −0.9 | −4.2 | −4.4 | −10.4 |
| 1955–2003 | 6.7 | 7.1 | 7.0 | N/A |
| 1971–2003 | 7.9 | 7.8 | 7.8 | 9.5 |
| 1982–2003 | 11.7 | 10.4 | 10.1 | 10.9 |

All figures are given as percent.
*The NASDAQ Index originated in 1971.
*Source: Economic Report of the President at* http://w3.access.gpo.gov/eop/

The NASDAQ index, initiated in 1971, is relatively new. The table indicates that the other three indexes exhibited relatively similar growth rates over long periods. For example, in the period from 1955 to 2003, the average annual growth rate of the three indexes ranged from 6.7 to 7.1 percent. Since its 1971 inception, the volatile NASDAQ has risen faster than the other indexes. In the period from 1971 to 2003, the NASDAQ increased at an average compounded rate of 9.5 percent per year, while the other indexes reported average gains of somewhat less than 8 percent per year. In the 1990s, the NASDAQ index climbed 20 percent per year as the technology bubble developed. However, the NASDAQ took a tremendous hit in 2000 to 2003. All of the indexes declined in the first four and a half years of the twenty-first century, largely a reflection of the bubble that developed in the late 1990s.

## Importance of Dividend Reinvestment

The total return from a stock includes both the appreciation (or depreciation) in the price of the stock and the dividends (if any) received from the stock. Stock market indexes aim to capture the change in prices of broad categories of stocks but ignore the returns earned from dividends. In the past, a program of continual reinvestment of dividends, over a long period of time, contributed an important portion of the total return from stocks. Suppose your parents invested $1,000 in the S&P 500 universe of stocks in the year 1980. If they spent the dividends rather than reinvesting them in additional shares, their investment would have grown to approximately $10,000 by the year 2000. If they had reinvested all dividends, their investment would have grown to approximately $15,000. About one third of the increase in stock market wealth would have been attributable to dividend reinvestment. An important moral of this story is that you must be careful in concluding—based on the relative performance of different indexes such as DJIA, S&P 500, NASDAQ, and Russell 2000—that you are better off investing in one index rather than another. The **dividend yield**—the annual dividend expressed as a percentage of the price of the stock—has been much higher over the years for companies included in the DJIA and S&P 500 than for stocks included in the NASDAQ

**dividend yield**
annual dividend expressed as a percentage of the stock's price

and Russell 2000. This consideration has become less important as dividend yields on common stocks trended strongly downward during the past quarter century.[4]

## STOCK MARKET: RISK AND RETURNS

Financial market scholars have compiled indexes of stock prices going back about 200 years. One dollar invested in a "representative" stock in 1802 appreciated to approximately $6 million by the year 2004. This seems amazing, if not unbelievable, but the amount represents a compounded rate of return of approximately 8 percent per year. Such is the astonishing power of compound interest over very long periods! Even though the U.S. price level has increased roughly 14-fold since 1802, the *purchasing power* of $1 invested in stocks in 1802 still would have grown to more than $400,000 today. On the other hand, $1 invested in U.S. government bonds in 1802 would be worth about $700 today, assuming reinvestment of interest earned and adjustment for inflation. One dollar invested in gold would be worth only about $1.25.

Stocks have yielded higher rates of return for investors than bonds over most periods of U.S. history, but stocks are considered riskier than bonds. In the event of corporate financial exigency and possible insolvency, bondholders have a prior claim over stockholders on remaining assets of the firm. In any large universe of stocks, some companies inevitably experience severe financial problems and become insolvent. Other companies remain solvent but fail to meet expectations. Their share prices lose a major portion of their value (see Exhibit 7-2). Holding a portfolio consisting of only a few stocks is risky. However, potential stockholders can circumvent this problem by adequate diversification in the stock portfolio. You can purchase a number of stocks from a variety of industries. If you do not have insufficient funds to purchase numerous stocks from different industries, you can diversify by buying shares in a mutual fund or by purchasing a pro rata share of an entire universe of stocks via "index shares" or exchange traded funds (review Exhibit 7-1).

U.S. government bonds are assumed to be free from default risk. The federal government has constitutional authority to tax or print money if necessary to meet the government's financial obligations. In what sense is a well-diversified collection of stocks riskier than long-term government bonds? The answer lies in the greater volatility of stock prices over bond prices. Stocks exhibit relatively large price fluctuations, especially over *short periods*. For example, in the 12 months beginning in March 2000, the average NASDAQ stock lost more than two thirds of its value. Figure 7-2 shows *backward-looking* average annual total rates of return from government bonds and S&P 500 stocks over each 2-year period since 1903. The initial observation plotted in the figure indicates that stocks and bonds returned approximately negative 5 percent and 3 percent per year, respectively, from the end of 1901 to the end of 1903. The last observation plotted shows that the total return from stocks from the end of 2001 to the end of 2003 was approximately negative 2 percent per year while bonds returned (positive) 8 percent per year in the same period.

---

[4] Note in Figure 7-1 the difference between the behavior of the S&P 500 in the most recent 25 years and in the first half of the twentieth century. The superior price appreciation in the more recent period significantly overstates the difference between the total returns from stocks in the two periods because dividend yields were much higher in the first half of the century than in the more recent period.

**Figure 7-2** Two-Year Backward-Looking Average Annual Rates of Return: S&P 500 Stocks and Long-Term Government Bonds from December 31, 1903, to December 31, 2003

Over 2-year periods, returns from stocks have been much more variable than returns from bonds. Stock returns have more frequently been negative. In the short run, stocks are riskier than bonds.

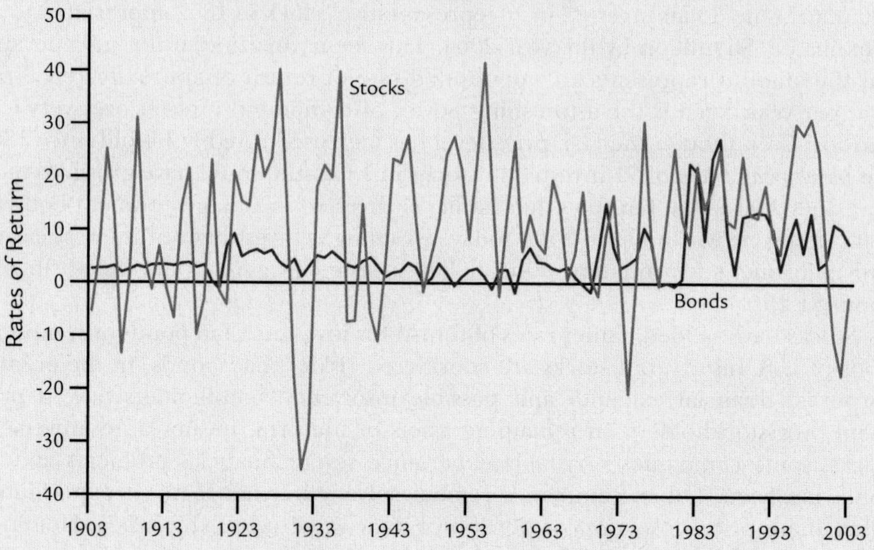


*Source: Data from Global Financial Data web site at* **http://globalfindata.com**

Stock returns are much more variable than bond returns over 2-year horizons. The figure indicates several episodes of significantly *negative* returns from stocks over 2-year periods. Government bonds seldom exhibited negative returns, and the few negative episodes involved very modest losses. If you had purchased the S&P 500 stock index at the end of 2000, you would have lost approximately 17 percent per year over the next 2 years. Government bonds would have returned about 10 percent per year over the same interval. If you have a short, 2-year planning horizon (e.g., parents investing funds to help pay for a high school student's impending college expenses), stocks are clearly riskier than bonds.

As you increase the planning time horizon significantly beyond 2 years, the conclusions regarding stocks versus bonds change substantially. Consider a 10-year horizon (e.g., parents preparing for a third-grader's college expenses). No episodes of negative average total returns from S&P 500 stocks have occurred since the 1929 to 1939 period. In the past 100 years, bonds outperformed stocks in very few 10-year periods. Finally, consider a very long planning horizon of 30 years (e.g., 35-year-old worker planning for retirement). Figure 7-3 indicates backward-looking average annual rates of return from stocks and bonds over consecutive rolling 30-year periods. Viewed from this *long-term* perspective, stocks appear much less risky.

Compare the variability of stock returns in Figures 7-2 and 7-3. The variability is much lower in Figure 7-3. The average annual returns from stocks have not been lower than 4 percent per year in any 30-year period in the past century. Returns have ranged from a low of around 5 percent per year (1903–1933) to a high of

**Figure 7-3** 30-Year Backward-Looking Average Annual Total Rates of Return: S&P 500 Stocks and Long-Term Government Bonds from December 31, 1903, to December 31, 2003

In the context of a 30-year horizon, stock returns look a lot more stable. In the past century, stocks have outperformed bonds over every 30-year period.

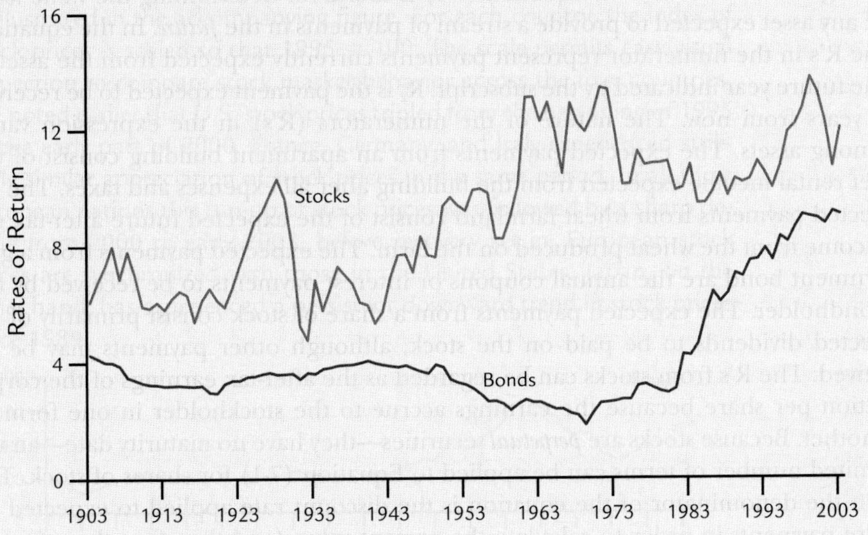


*Source: Global Financial Data Web site at* **http://globalfindata.com**

slightly less than 14 percent per year (1969–1999). Adjusting these returns for inflation, the range of 30-year average *real* returns is significantly smaller. Perhaps most importantly, in the past century, *bonds have not outperformed stocks in any single 30-year period.*[5] The public's growing recognition of the facts illustrated in Figure 7-3 helps account for the increasing popularity of stocks in the past couple of decades. Investors may have overestimated the *long-term* risk of owning a well-diversified portfolio of stocks in earlier times.

## WHAT DETERMINES THE PRICE OF A SHARE OF STOCK?

Chapter 5 introduced the concept of present value in the context of bond prices. The present value formula also is useful for understanding stock prices. The value of a share of stock is a function of the flow of future dollar payments expected from

[5] Note the rising and unprecedented level of 30-year average rates of return from bonds since the early 1980s. What accounts for this increase? From the early 1960s through the end of the 1970s, both inflation and interest rates trended upward and were extremely high by 1980. Therefore, bond prices were extremely low in 1980. As inflation trended downward in the 1980s and 1990s, interest rates also declined (via the Fisher effect), producing a sustained increase in bond prices. Bondholders in the 1980s and 1990s not only received their annual interest payments from bonds but also reaped gains from rising bond prices. Total rates of return were unusually high in those years. Given the low prospect today of further major declines in long-term interest rates (and corresponding increases in bond prices), high rates of return from government bonds over lengthy periods likely will not be available in the near future.

## Indicators of Stock Market Valuations

Several yardsticks are used to determine warranted or appropriate levels of stock prices, providing analysts with clues used to infer whether stocks are generally overvalued or undervalued at any point in time. Some of the popular measures include price/earnings ratios and dividend yields associated with broad stock market indexes, the price-to-book ratio, and the ratio of the market capitalization of the entire stock market to some aggregate measure of economic activity such as gross domestic product (GDP). When the ratios deviate markedly from historic norms, many analysts believe that stocks are incorrectly priced, that is, stocks are generally overvalued or undervalued. We briefly discuss a few of the popular indicators.

**price/earnings (PE) ratio**
ratio of the price of a share of stock to the current annual earnings per share achieved by the corporation

**mean reversion**
tendency to ultimately revert to long-term averages

**Price/Earnings Ratios.** Perhaps the most popular indicator and long-standing measure of stock valuations is the **price/earnings (PE) ratio**—the ratio of the price of a share of stock to the current annual earnings per share achieved by the corporation. The PE ratio varies widely among stocks. If Cisco Systems' stock sells at $20 and the company's annual profits are $0.50 per share, the PE ratio is 40. If Chase Manhattan Bank earns $4 per share and the company's stock is selling at $40, the PE ratio is 10. Many factors influence the PE ratio of individual stocks. A very important factor is the expected future growth rate of earnings of the company. Cisco stock exhibits a higher PE ratio than Chase Manhattan because Cisco is expected to grow more rapidly. The PE ratio can be computed for broad stock market indexes such as the S&P 500, DJIA, and NASDAQ. Traditionalists believe these PE ratios exhibit **mean reversion**—the tendency to ultimately revert to long-term averages. Analysts believe stocks are overvalued if PE ratios of broad stock market indexes are considerably higher than longer-term norms. Unusually low PE ratios suggest that stocks are undervalued. The history of PE ratios for the S&P 500 universe of stocks since 1900 is illustrated in Figure 7-5. The horizontal line depicts the

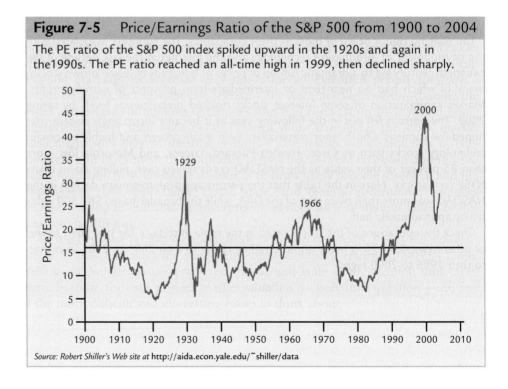

**Figure 7-5** Price/Earnings Ratio of the S&P 500 from 1900 to 2004

The PE ratio of the S&P 500 index spiked upward in the 1920s and again in the1990s. The PE ratio reached an all-time high in 1999, then declined sharply.

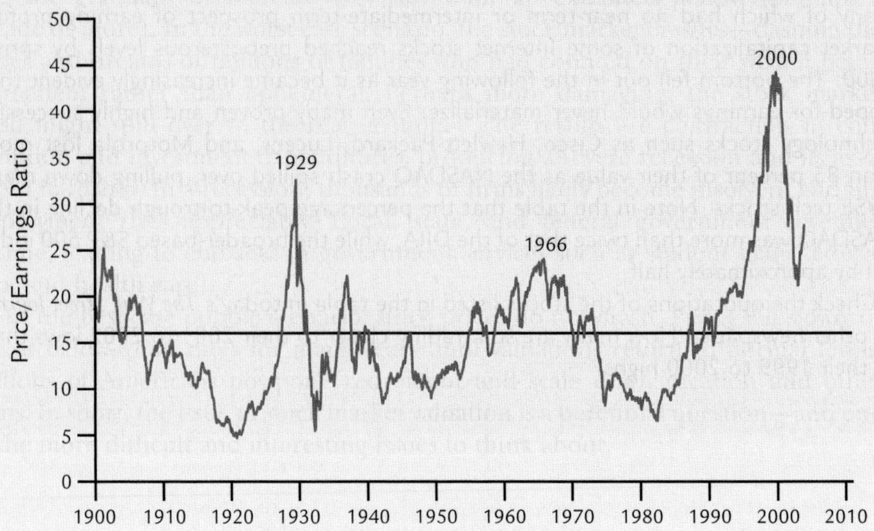


*Source: Robert Shiller's Web site at* http://aida.econ.yale.edu/~shiller/data

100-year S&P 500 average PE ratio of about 16. Analysts placing strong credence in this indicator argue that stocks were overvalued in the late 1920s, the mid-1960s, and the late 1990s and undervalued from 1915 to 1925, 1940 to 1955, and the major portion of the 1970s and 1980s.

**Dividend Yields.** Dividend yield is the annual dividend per share expressed as a percentage of the current price of the stock. If Chase Manhattan stock pays an annual dividend of $1 per share and exhibits a price of $40, the dividend yield is 2.5 percent. A *lower* dividend yield indicates a *higher* stock price relative to the dividend. Analysts traditionally regarded unusually low dividend yields associated with broad stock market indexes as evidence of stock overvaluation. However, this conclusion can be rejected for good reason. Dividend yields today are much lower than 30 years ago. Over the years, the U.S. tax code increased corporations' incentive to use profits for stock buyback or investment in new plants, equipment, and technology rather than dividend payments to stockholders. Dividend recipients were taxed at the relatively high federal marginal income tax rates, which climbed as high as 70 percent in the 1960s and 1970s. Long-term capital gains have been taxed at lower rates but not unless or until the stock shares were sold. Individuals typically have been better off (after taxes) receiving a dollar's worth of appreciated stock than a dollar of dividend income. Largely because of the tax benefit, companies increasingly bought back stock shares (thereby retiring shares and boosting earnings per share) and reinvested profits, enhancing the growth of earnings per share rather than paying out profits as dividends. Legislation in the 1990s reducing capital gains tax rates stimulated incentives further. However, legislation in 2003 reduced the top tax rate on dividend income to 15 percent, which coincides with the top rate on capital gains. Corporations now may increase dividend payments in response to the lower dividend tax rate. In short, changing federal tax policy and other factors have rendered the dividend yield an unreliable benchmark of stock market valuations.

YOUR TURN

Assume Citigroup stock sells for $50 per share, earns profits of $4.00 per share, and pays an annual dividend of $1.20 per share. Calculate Citigroup's PE ratio and dividend yield.

**price-to-book ratio** ratio of the price of a share of stock to the book value of the company

**Other Indicators of Market Valuation.** The **price-to-book ratio** is the ratio of the price of a share of stock to the *book value* of the company, that is, the residual value of the corporation per share after the company liquidates all assets and pays off all debts. The price-to-book ratio increased sharply above historic norms in the late 1990s, suggesting to some analysts that stock prices were too high. Another indicator is the ratio of aggregate stock market capitalization to the nation's GDP. This ratio also increased substantially in the 1990s, sending the same signals about stock valuations as the PE ratio and the price-to-book ratio. Individuals placing high credence in the traditional benchmarks argue that U.S. stocks were overvalued in the late 1990s and early part of the twenty-first century. Individuals believing stocks were priced correctly argue that traditional benchmarks become unreliable with changing tax policy, institutions, and economic environment. For example, if interest rates are lower or stocks are less risky today because of a more stable economic environment or other reasons, the discount rate i used to compute stock val-

## FROM THE FINANCIAL PAGES

### Buying Common Stocks

Suppose you are considering buying shares of Wal-Mart stock. To find its current price and other relevant information, turn to the financial pages of any major newspaper. On August 11, 2004, *The Wall Street Journal* revealed the following information about Wal-Mart stock and corresponding information on thousands of other stocks for the previous day's trading activity.

| YTD % CHG | 52-WEEK HI | 52-WEEK LO | STOCK (SYM) | DIV | YLD % | PE | VOL 100s | CLOSE | NET CHG |
|---|---|---|---|---|---|---|---|---|---|
| -5.5 | 49.49 | 40.35 | Wachovia **WB** | 1.60 | 3.6 | 12 | 22074 | 44.02 | 0.46 |
| -17.3 | 27.28 | 18.45 | WadlRed A **WDR** | .60 | 3.1 | 20 | 2781 | 19.40 | 0.39 |
| -1.6 | 37.82 | 29.83 | Walgreen **WAG** | .21f | .6 | 28 | 17103 | 35.80 | 0.56 |
| -1.8 | 61.31 | 50.50 | WalMart **WMT** | .52 | 1.0 | 24 | 70834 | 52.11 | 0.74 |
| -0.7 | 14.06 | 9.05♣ | WalterInd **WLT** | .12 | .9 | dd | 938 | 13.26 | 0.23 |

Reading from the left, the first column gives the percentage change in the price of Wal-Mart shares in the year to date (the stock was down 1.8 percent). The next two columns reveal the high and low prices of Wal-Mart stock over the previous 52 weeks. Wal-Mart shares traded within a range from $61.31 to $50.50. The next column indicates the symbol for Wal-Mart—WMT. The following two columns provide the annual dividend ($0.52 per share) and the dividend yield (1.0%), which is calculated by dividing the annual dividend by the current price of the stock. The next column indicates that the current price/earnings (PE) ratio of Wal-Mart is 24. The following column reveals that the volume of shares of Wal-Mart traded on August 10 was 7,083,400. The final two columns indicate the closing price of Wal-Mart on August 10, 2004, and the net change in price from the previous day's closing price. Wal-Mart closed on August 10 at $52.11 per share, up 74¢ on the day.

To decide whether any particular stock is a sound investment, obtain as much information about the company's prospects for the next several years as you can. The fact that Wal-Mart's PE ratio of 24 was pretty much in line with the overall market's average PE in August 2004 indicates market consensus that Wal-Mart will experience moderate but not sensational growth. Fifteen years ago, when Wal-Mart's growth prospects seemed almost boundless, the stock exhibited a PE above 40. Check Wal-Mart's price in today's paper and see how it has performed since August 10, 2004.

ues today should be lower now. Lower discount rates imply that indicators such as PE and market capitalization/GDP ratios should legitimately be higher today than historic norms. In this view, nothing about the past norms of the various indicators is sacrosanct.[8] The "normal" or "appropriate" level of the various valuation ratios changes over time.

[8] An interesting hypothesis is that prospective stock market investors prior to the 1990s overestimated the risks of owning stocks, applying too large a discount rate in valuing the expected payments from stocks. Hence, stock prices were allegedly too low before the 1990s. In this view, the dramatic increase in stock prices in the 1990s was largely due to the gradual realization that stock prices had been too low. As the public realized that stocks were less risky than previously believed, the discount rate decreased and stock prices increased. See the book by Glassman and Hassett in *Additional Reading* at the end of this chapter.

# SHOULD THE FEDERAL RESERVE REACT TO PERCEIVED BUBBLES IN ASSET MARKETS?

Speculative bubbles ultimately collapse. When prices in equity or real estate markets collapse, spillover effects adversely impact the real economy. For example, after the Japanese bubbles in stock and real estate markets popped in the late 1980s, the country experienced a 15-year period of economic stagnation and heightened financial distress. If a central bank quickly recognized and gently let the air out of a bubble in its early stages of development, would the economy benefit? Should a wise central bank "lean against the bubble" and pop the bubble in its early stage in the interest of economic stability? The issue is contentious. The Federal Reserve practices a *laissez faire* or "hands-off" policy toward asset price bubbles. Policy activists argue that central bank intervention can be beneficial, but the Federal Reserve and most economists oppose central bank intervention in asset pricing. In this view, the Federal Reserve cannot recognize speculative bubbles in timely fashion. Monetary policy is a blunt instrument for controlling asset prices, and central bank intrusion into this domain can be counterproductive. We examine the pros and cons of central bank intervention for preventing large asset price bubbles.

## Arguments for Federal Reserve Intervention Against Bubbles

Excessive increases in asset prices—principally of stocks and real estate—lead to instability in economic activity. An important avenue is through bank lending. If asset prices increase sharply, the value of available collateral for bank loans increases. Borrowers can acquire additional debt that later proves extremely costly. When the bubble inflating asset values bursts, collateral levels decline dangerously relative to loans outstanding, resulting in elevated financial distress among borrowers. More individuals and firms become insolvent and bank failures increase. Most of the large banks operating today in Japan are technically insolvent because of bad loans resulting from the popping of Japan's enormous bubble of the 1980s. A bubble in stock prices artificially reduces the cost of capital and contributes to excessive business confidence. The spillover effect contributes to excessive corporate investment expenditures. The extreme buildout of fiber optic cable during the U.S. telecommunications boom of the 1990s is an example. The inevitable popping of the bubble leads to a severe contraction in investment spending, with its attendant negative consequences for economic activity.

Individuals advocating "leaning against the bubble" believe the various benchmark measures of valuation are reliable. They believe the Federal Reserve can recognize bubbles as they develop. A red flag goes up if stock prices rise appreciably faster than the trend for a prolonged period and the amount of bank credit incurred to buy stock also increases rapidly. The Fed should take notice. If the indicators of speculative activity are accompanied by major increases in price/earnings, price/book, and aggregate market capitalization/GDP ratios to levels appreciably above historic norms, policy activists believe the Fed should be prepared to take action. (A bubble's existence is finally confirmed when taxi drivers and doctors begin dispensing advice on which stocks to buy and the volume of student "day trading" activity on the Internet surges.) In this view, the Fed should intervene to slow or stop the rise in asset prices.

## Arguments for the Federal Reserve's *Laissez-Faire* Approach

Advocates of a *laissez faire* central bank approach to asset prices make two major points. First, expecting the Federal Reserve to reliably identify asset price bubbles as they develop is unrealistic. To assume otherwise is to assume the Fed is more perceptive than the collective judgment of market participants. Furthermore, the Federal Reserve conducts monetary policy principally to maintain economic stability, not manage asset prices. Monetary policy is a very blunt instrument for dealing with bubbles. If the Fed increases interest rates sharply to deflate an incipient bubble, the Fed is likely to destabilize the economy. By letting itself get diverted from its main responsibility, the Fed may do more damage than good.

A sustained and powerful increase in stock prices seldom, if ever, occurs without some element of justification. Note in Figures 7-1 and 7-5 that stock prices and PE ratios increased dramatically in the late 1920s and late 1990s. In both periods, there was legitimate reason to suspect that ongoing developments were about to result in acceleration in growth rates of productivity, living standards, and corporate profits. In the 1920s, mass production of automobiles, construction of roads, widespread electrification of homes, and other innovations suggested an impending era of great prosperity. Similarly, the development of information technology and the buildout of the Internet in the 1990s promised to radically increase the efficiency of information processing and dissemination, boosting growth rates of productivity and living standards.

To gain perspective on the "lean against the bubble" debate, put yourself in Fed Chairman Greenspan's position in 1997 or 1998 as stock prices were escalating rapidly. With the ongoing high rates of corporate restructuring and the rise of the Internet, expectations were high for enhanced performance of the U.S. economy in the years ahead. Many of the principal indicators of stock market valuations should legitimately move above historic norms. For example, if profits are expected to rise more rapidly than in the past, the market PE and market capitalization/current GDP ratios should be higher than past norms.

The notion that we were in a "new economy," in which unusually high rates of growth of output, productivity, and profits were forthcoming, became widespread in the mid-to-late 1990s. Investors revised upward the expected payments from stocks (the R's). Considerable optimism seemed warranted. Table 7-3 indicates several key measures of U.S. economic performance in the 28 years immediately prior

**Table 7-3 Signs of the "New Economy" after 1994**

| Period | Investment*/ GDP | Growth Rate Real GDP | Growth Rate Productivity** | Average Inflation Rate | Average Unemployment Rate |
|---|---|---|---|---|---|
| 1966–1994 | 7.5 | 3.0 | 1.6 | 5.6 | 6.5 |
| 1995–1999 | 9.0 | 3.8 | 3.1 | 2.4 | 4.9 |

All figures are given as percent.
*Investment in equipment and software.
**Non-farm business sector.
*Source: Data from FRED database at* http://research.stlouisfed.org/fred2

to the beginning of 1995 and in the ensuing 5-year period extending through the end of the twentieth century. In the latter period, the share of the nation's output devoted to investment in equipment and software increased significantly. Productivity growth, a crucial variable, and real GDP growth jumped sharply. Inflation and unemployment on average were lower in the latter period. The strong stock market performance after 1994 appeared to be a rational response to the unfolding improvement in U.S. macroeconomic performance.

To conduct a successful policy of "leaning against the bubble," the Federal Reserve needs to determine not only that stocks are overvalued but also by *how much.* As noted earlier, stock prices increase because expected payments from stocks (the R's) increase or the discount rate i used to calculate the value of expected payments decreases. A relatively small decrease in the equity risk premium comprising part of the discount rate can produce a relatively large increase in stock prices. To determine how much of an increase in stock prices is warranted, the Fed must calculate not only the increase in the forthcoming payments from stocks (the true R's) but also the amount (if any) by which the risk premium in stocks declined after the early 1990s. This is a daunting—if not impossible—task. Critics of the "lean against the bubble" approach believe you cannot expect the Fed to pinpoint how much of an ongoing increase in stock prices is warranted.

Monetary policy is clearly a blunt instrument for letting air out of bubbles. The Federal Reserve's principal policy instrument is short-term interest rates. To reduce stock prices, the Fed increases short-term rates. How much does the Fed increase short-term interest rates to produce a 25 percent decline in stock prices? No economist can answer this question. If a speculative bubble develops, expected rates of return from stocks substantially exceed market interest rates. A very large rate hike may be needed to bring down stock prices significantly. Overall macroeconomic conditions might not justify *any* interest rate hike. A sharp rate increase aimed at slowing the advance of stock prices can easily trigger a recession. Furthermore, it is difficult to stick a pin in a balloon and let out only 25 percent of the air. If the Fed raises interest rates substantially, stock prices can fall considerably more than anticipated. In short, attempting to prick a bubble can be counterproductive. Not many economists are comfortable with the idea.[9]

## Tendency for Mean Reversion in Returns from Stocks

Historically, returns from stocks strongly tend to exhibit *mean reversion,* that is, returns regress toward long-run average rates of return. Lengthy periods of above-normal returns typically have been followed by extended periods of subnormal returns, that is, returns tend to even out over long periods of time. This is demonstrated in Table 7-4, which shows nominal and real rates of return from stocks over each decade of the past 80 years.

If you add the average annual percentage appreciation of stock prices and the dividend yield, you obtain the total nominal return from stocks. Subtracting the inflation rate yields the *real* return (right-hand column of the table). Note that the extremely high returns earned from stocks in the 1920s were followed by unusually

[9] The Fed has authority to change *margin requirements*—the percentage of the value of stock being purchased that must be supplied by an investor's own funds. With a 50 percent margin requirement, an individual purchasing $100,000 of stock must put up at least $50,000 in cash. If the Fed raises margin requirements, fewer speculators engage in heavily leveraged purchases of stock. Some observers believe the Fed should have raised margin requirements in the 1990s to counter speculative activity and to signal the Fed's concern about rising stock prices. Such a move might have slowed the advance of stock prices without necessitating an unwarranted increase in interest rates. The Fed opted not to use this tool.

**Table 7-4 Nominal and Real Returns from S&P 500 Stocks over Various Periods, % per Year**

| Period | Appreciation of Stock Prices (S&P Composite) | Dividend Yield | Total Return from Stocks* | Inflation Rate** | Real Return from Stocks*** |
|---|---|---|---|---|---|
| 1920s | 9.2% | 5.1% | 14.3% | −1.8% | 16.1% |
| 1930s | −5.3 | 5.2 | −0.1 | −1.7 | 1.6 |
| 1940s | 3.0 | 5.6 | 8.6 | 5.6 | 3.0 |
| 1950s | 13.6 | 4.8 | 18.4 | 2.1 | 16.3 |
| 1960s | 4.4 | 3.2 | 7.6 | 2.7 | 4.9 |
| 1970s | 1.6 | 4.2 | 5.8 | 7.4 | −1.6 |
| 1980s | 12.6 | 4.2 | 16.8 | 5.1 | 11.7 |
| 1990s | 15.3 | 2.4 | 17.7 | 2.9 | 14.8 |
| 2000–2003 | 0.0 | 1.4 | 1.4 | 2.4 | −1.0 |
| 1920–2003 | 5.9 | 4.2 | 10.1 | 2.8 | 7.3 |

All figures are given as percent.
*Total return from stocks is the sum of appreciation of stock prices and dividend yield.
**Consumer price index is used to calculate inflation rate.
***Real return from stocks is the difference between total return from stocks and the inflation rate.
*Source: Calculated from data on Robert Shiller's Web site at* http://aida.econ.yale.edu/~shiller/data *and the FRED database at* http://research.stlouisfed/org/fred2

low returns in the 1930s and 1940s. The abnormally low returns were followed by terrific returns in the 1950s, which in turn were followed by subnormal returns in the 1960s and 1970s. This latter episode of poor stock market performance was followed by the tremendous returns of the 1980s and 1990s. If this pattern continues, you should observe below-average returns from stocks in the first decade or two of the twenty-first century.

## SUMMARY

A nation's stock market performance is an indicator of the market's sentiment about the country's economic prospects. Stock price behavior influences expenditures on consumption and investment goods and thereby feeds back to influence the nation's actual economic performance. The U.S. stock market produced very high rates of return from 1948 to 1965 and again from 1982 to 2000. However, past episodes of unusually strong stock market performance have been surrounded by periods of poor returns from stocks. On average over the past century, stocks have returned about 10 percent per year in nominal terms and 7 percent per year after adjusting for inflation. These stock market returns have appreciably exceeded the returns from other assets such as government bonds, Treasury bills, and real estate. Stock prices depend on future payments expected from stocks and the discount rate applied to future payments to determine their present value. Both the expected payments from stocks and the discount rate are sensitive to ongoing developments and are continually revised by market participants in response to economic news. These developments result in substantial changes in stock prices from year to year. On rare occasions, stock prices move sharply above levels warranted by fundamental conditions, a phenomenon known as a *stock market bubble.* Standard benchmarks of market valuation suggest that the U.S. stock market became significantly overvalued in the late 1920s and late 1990s. Some analysts criticized the Federal Reserve for not slowing the tremendous advance of stock prices in the 1990s. However, determining the appropriate level of stock prices at any point in time and pinpointing just how much of an increase in stock prices is warranted are extremely difficult. The Federal Reserve is not well equipped to reliably influence stock prices. For these reasons, most economists support the Federal Reserve's position that the central bank not use monetary policy to attempt to influence stock prices.

### YOUR TURN ANSWERS

Page 167

Citigroup's PE ratio is calculated as $50/$4.00, or 12.5. Its dividend yield is $1.20/$50, or 2.4 percent.

## KEY TERMS

- wealth effect
- cost of capital
- virtuous cycle
- market capitalization
- exchange traded funds (ETFs)
- dividend yield
- equity risk premium
- price/earnings (PE) ratio
- mean reversion
- price-to-book ratio

# STUDY QUESTIONS

1. Explain the ways in which stock market performance feeds back to influence economic activity. Outline the essential elements of the "virtuous cycle" mechanism discussed in this chapter.

2. Analyze the shortcomings of the Dow Jones Industrials Average (DJIA) as a measure of the performance of stocks held by the typical American investor.

3. Suppose the NASDAQ index increases 7 percent annually over the next decade while the S&P 500 increases 6 percent annually. On average are you better off holding NASDAQ stocks than S&P 500 stocks? Explain.

4. Dividend yields are much lower today than they were 25 years ago. Does this imply that stocks have become more overvalued (or less undervalued) than formerly? Explain.

5. Consider two corporations, SGC (slow growth corporation) and RPG (rapid growth corporation). Assume both companies currently earn $1 dollar per share. Assume earnings per share of SGC are expected to grow 6 percent annually while those of RPG are expected to grow 20 percent annually. Using the present value formula and a discount rate of 6 percent for both corporations, calculate the present value of the first four annual payments expected from each company. Explain why RPG will sell at a higher PE ratio today than SGC.

6. Inflation and interest rates were much higher in the 1970s than they are today. What justifications account for the different price/earnings (PE) ratio of the S&P 500 index today compared to the 1970s? Should the PE today be higher or lower than in the 1970s? Explain.

7. Using the framework of the present value equation expressed in Equation (7-1), explain three types of events that can cause the S&P 500 index of stocks to decline in the next year.

8. Using the present value equation expressed in Equation (7-1), analyze the impact of the following events on the S&P 500 stock market index:
   A. Congress cuts the corporate income tax rate from 34 percent to 28 percent.
   B. Crude oil prices surge to $60 per barrel (ignore the effect on stock prices of oil companies).
   C. The Federal Reserve reduces interest rates by a full percentage point.
   D. The index of leading economic indicators falls sharply.
   E. A major U.S. corporation unexpectedly files for Chapter 11 (bankruptcy) protection.

9. Note in Table 7-4 that earlier periods of abnormally high stock market returns (1920s and 1950s) were followed by extended periods of very low returns. Stocks yielded very high returns in the 1980s and 1990s. Now, check Robert Shiller's Web site at http://aida.econ.yale.edu/~shiller/data to find the behavior of the S&P 500 index since the end of 1999. How has the S&P 500 index performed relative to its 1950 to 1999 average appreciation of 9.5 percent per year?

10. Take a position either that stocks in the S&P 500 index are generally overvalued today or that they are not overvalued. Marshal as much intellectual ammunition as you can to defend your position (a brilliant answer could win you a Nobel Prize).

11. Review Table 7-3, which indicates signs of the "new economy" from 1995 to 1999. Using the most recent issue of the *Economic Report of the President* (at http://w3.access.gpo.gov/eop/) or other sources (FRED database), update the table with post-1999 data. Do your new figures more closely resemble the figures from 1966 to 1994 or 1995 to 1999? Do your findings confirm or refute the "new economy" hypothesis? Explain.

12. Turn to the financial section of your newspaper and note the current price/earnings (PE) ratios of Microsoft and General Motors. What explains the difference in the PE ratios of these stocks?

# ADDITIONAL READING

- If you have time to read just one book about the stock market, read Jeremy J. Siegel's highly informative *Stocks for the Long Run,* 3rd edition (New York: McGraw-Hill, 2002). Another classic book is Burton Malkiel, *A Random Walk Down Wall Street,* 8th edition (New York: W.W. Norton, 2003).
- The view that stocks were greatly overvalued in the late 1990s is set forth in *Irrational Exuberance* by Robert J. Shiller (Princeton, NJ: Princeton University Press, 2000). A journal article by two eminent financial economists essentially foretelling the stock market crash of 2000 to 2002 is John Campbell and Robert Shiller, "Valuation Ratios and the Long-Run Stock Market Outlook," *Journal of Portfolio Management,* Winter 1998, pp. 11–26. The view that stocks were irrationally *undervalued* prior to the 1990s is set forth in *Dow 36,000* by James K. Glassman and Kevin A. Hassett (New York: Three Rivers Press, 2000). On the various stock market indexes, see Peter Fortune, "A Primer on U.S. Stock Price Indices," *New England Economic Review,* November/December 1998.
- To understand the fundamentals underlying returns to be expected in the stock market, see John Golob and David Bishop, "What Long-Run Returns Can Investors Expect from the Stock Market?," Federal Reserve Bank of Kansas City *Economic Review,* 1997, Volume 3, pp. 5–20. On price/earnings ratios and subsequent market performance, see Pu Shen, "The P/E Ratio and Stock Market Performance," Federal Reserve Bank of Kansas City *Economic Review,* 2000, Volume 4, pp. 23–36.
- For a discussion of stock market bubbles, an excellent source is the collection of articles in William Hunter, George Kaufman, and Michael Pomerleano, eds., *Asset Price Bubbles: The Implications for Monetary, Regulatory, and International Policies* (Boston: MIT Press, 2003). The Federal Reserve's position on bubbles is given in a speech by Federal Reserve Board Governor Ben Bernanke, "Asset Price 'Bubbles' and Monetary Policy" (October 15, 2002), available on the Board of Governors' Web site at http://www.federalreserve.gov.
- Finally, for highly enjoyable bedtime reading about a traumatic period of U.S. history, see John Kenneth Galbraith, *The Great Crash, 1929* (Boston: Houghton Mifflin, 1961).

# Chapter 8

# THE FOREIGN EXCHANGE MARKET

Nations engage in international trade in goods and services for the same reason individuals engage in domestic trade—to expand material well-being through the specialization and division of labor. An individual can try to be self-sufficient and produce all the goods and services she needs. Alternatively, an individual can enhance her standard of living and the nation's standard of living by specializing in a narrow range of tasks in which she is most proficient and trading for goods and services. All nations attain higher levels of income and consumption, that is, higher living standards, when the principle of comparative advantage extends beyond national borders. Specialization and trade raise living standards. This holds true at all levels: individual, state, regional, and national. Transactions in financial and real assets also extend beyond national borders as investors take advantage of the benefits of diversification, searching worldwide for assets with the most attractive prospective returns.

Just as incentives exist for individuals in a given locality to engage in the exchange of goods and services and for geographic regions of a country to conduct interregional trade, a natural incentive exists for nations to engage in international economic transactions. No *natural* barriers to international trade exist, except for transportation costs. However, various *institutional* barriers cause the volume of world trade to fall short of the level that would maximize the living standards of the nations involved. Among these barriers are different currencies, languages, and financial, cultural, and legal institutions. Various national economic policies impede the free flow of goods, services, and capital among nations. Tariffs, quotas, and foreign exchange controls are examples.

## FOREIGN EXCHANGE MARKETS AND RATES

When a Kansas City grocery store chain purchases a shipment of oranges from a Florida citrus grove owner, both parties to the transaction prefer to deal in the same currency—U.S. dollars. This conformity of preferences does not exist when a U.S. importer purchases a shipment of Japanese Nikon cameras. The U.S. importer prefers to pay in dollars while the Japanese producer wants to receive payment in yen. By the same token, a Japanese importer of U.S. lumber prefers to make payment in yen while the U.S. lumber producers want payment in dollars.

### Foreign Exchange Market

**foreign exchange market**
market in which national currencies are exchanged

The **foreign exchange market** is the market in which such national currencies as dollars, yen, pesos, euros, and Swiss francs are exchanged. The foreign exchange market is not an organized market with fixed hours like the New York Stock Exchange or the Chicago Board of Trade. The foreign exchange market is an over-the-counter market. The primary communication instrument is the computer. The market has developed rapidly in the past quarter century. The volume of activity has escalated dramatically in response to the growth in volume of world trade in goods and services and especially the expansion in **international capital flows**—the acquisition of financial and real assets across national borders. Total worldwide foreign exchange market transactions in 2004 were more than $2 trillion *per day*. More than 90 percent of transactions are associated with capital flows. Among the most important financial centers are New York, London, Tokyo, Paris, Frankfurt, Hong Kong, and Zurich.

**international capital flows**
acquisition of financial and real assets across national borders

The *direct* or *immediate* participants in the foreign exchange market include U.S. commercial banks with deposits in foreign branch banks or foreign correspondent banks, and foreign banks. Several hundred dealers (mostly banks) maintain inventories of major foreign currencies as bank deposits in foreign correspondent banks. The denominations are yen in Tokyo; Australian dollars in Sydney; euros in Frankfurt, Rome, and Paris; and so forth. A dealer selling a foreign currency is selling deposits it owns in a foreign commercial bank. A dealer buying a foreign currency is buying additional deposits in a foreign bank. In other words, the foreign exchange market involves buying and selling bank deposits rather than physical currency and coins. Foreign exchange dealers do not charge a commission. A bid and ask spread provides income for foreign exchange dealers as with U.S. government securities dealers.

Who are the *ultimate* participants in the foreign exchange market? First are the thousands of large and small import/export firms in the United States and their foreign counterparts, who buy or sell foreign currencies in connection with their businesses. Second are all the tourists and other travelers around the world who want foreign currencies. For example, Americans want euros to finance vacations in Italy or France, and Japanese businessmen need dollars to travel in the United States. Third are financial entities such as private pension and government retirement funds and money market mutual funds in one country seeking to purchase financial instruments such as CDs, bonds, and shares of stock in another country. The Federal Reserve and U.S. Treasury often conduct transactions in the foreign exchange market, as do corresponding agencies in other countries.

## Foreign Exchange Rate

The price at which one nation's currency is exchanged for another nation's currency is the **foreign exchange rate.** An exchange rate exists between each pair of nations that engage in trade and do not use the same currency. Table 8-1 indicates the name and symbol of the currency unit of six foreign industrial nations. It also indicates the exchange rate against the U.S. dollar of each country in January of 1974, 1984, 1994, and 2004. Each exchange rate is quoted as the number of units of foreign currency per U.S. dollar. The exchange rates in the table can be interpreted as the value of 1 U.S. dollar expressed in units of foreign currency. For example, in early 2004, 1 U.S. dollar was worth 1.35 Australian dollars, 0.56 British pounds, and 107 Japanese yen. Note that international currency values are reciprocal. If 1 U.S. dollar is worth 0.56 British pounds, then the pound is worth $1.79 U.S. The bottom row of the table indicates the trade-weighted U.S. exchange rate index—the index of the *average* value of the U.S. dollar against the currencies of the major industrial countries the U.S. trades with.

**foreign exchange rate**
price at which one nation's currency is exchanged for another nation's currency

As Table 8-1 indicates, exchange rates vary considerably over time. In early 2004, for example, the U.S. dollar was worth more Australian dollars, British pounds, and Canadian dollars than in 1974. The dollar experienced **appreciation** against these currencies over the long period—that is, the U.S. dollar increased in value, expressed in units of these currencies per U.S. dollar. On the other hand, in 2004 the U.S. dollar was worth *fewer* Japanese yen and Swiss francs than in 1974. The U.S. dol-

**appreciation**
condition in which a unit of a nation's currency buys more units of other nations' currency

**Table 8-1 Foreign Exchange Rates versus U.S. Dollar for Selected Currencies**

| | | Units of Foreign Currency per U.S. Dollar in January | | | |
|---|---|---|---|---|---|
| **Country** | **Currency Unit** | **1974** | **1984** | **1994** | **2004** |
| Australia | Dollar ($) | 0.67 | 1.10 | 1.44 | 1.35 |
| Britain | Pound (£) | 0.45 | 0.71 | 0.67 | 0.56 |
| Canada | Dollar (C$) | 0.99 | 1.25 | 1.32 | 1.33 |
| Japan | Yen (¥) | 298 | 234 | 111 | 107 |
| Norway | Krone (NKr) | 5.97 | 7.88 | 7.51 | 6.70 |
| Switzerland | Franc (S Fr) | 3.36 | 2.24 | 1.47 | 1.25 |
| Trade-weighted index* | | 105.8 | 122.6 | 89.1 | 84.5 |

* Trade-weighted index of major currencies against U.S. dollar (March 1973 = 100).
*Source: Data from Federal Reserve Bank of St. Louis FRED II database at* http://research.stlouisfed.org/fred2

**depreciation**
condition in which a unit of a nation's currency buys fewer units of other nations' currency

lar experienced **depreciation** against the Japanese yen and Swiss franc from 1974 to 2004. If one currency appreciates against a second currency, then by definition the second currency depreciates against the first. In the first two rows of the table, the U.S. dollar appreciated against the Australian dollar and the British pound over the long period, so the Australian dollar and the British pound depreciated against the U.S. dollar. Over the past 30 years, the Japanese yen and the Swiss franc have been "strong currencies," while the Australian and Canadian dollars have been "weak currencies." The U.S. dollar falls into the "intermediate-to-strong" category. The U.S. dollar has appreciated against many currencies over the past 30 years but has depreciated against several foreign currencies.

Figure 8-1 illustrates the exchange rate of the U.S. dollar against one relatively weak currency (Canadian dollar) and one relatively strong currency (Japanese yen) over the past 30 years. These exchange rates are expressed as units of foreign currency per U.S. dollar. The U.S. dollar trended upward (appreciated) against the Canadian dollar over the long period but trended downward (depreciated) against the Japanese yen. This is equivalent to saying that the Canadian dollar depreciated against the U.S. dollar while the Japanese yen appreciated against the U.S. dollar.[1] In this chapter we present a framework explaining why these exchange rate changes have occurred.

## Fixed and Floating Exchange Rates

**floating exchange rates**
exchange rates that change in the marketplace from day to day

Since the early 1970s, international trade has been based on **floating exchange rates**—that is, most large industrial nations permit exchange rates to change in the

[1] Exchange rates are reciprocal and can be quoted either as units of foreign currency per unit of domestic currency or as units of domestic currency per unit of foreign currency. To avoid confusion, focus on the currency in the denominator of the quotation. If the U.S.-Japan exchange rate moves from 120 yen/$ to 130 yen/$, the dollar *appreciates*—it is worth more units of yen—and the yen *depreciates* against the dollar. If the U.S.-euro exchange rate moves from $1.15/euro to $1.20/euro, the euro appreciates—it is worth more dollars—and the dollar depreciates against the euro.

**Figure 8-1** U.S. Exchange Rate Against Canada and Japan

Over a long period of years, the U.S. dollar has appreciated against the Canadian dollar but depreciated against the Japanese yen.

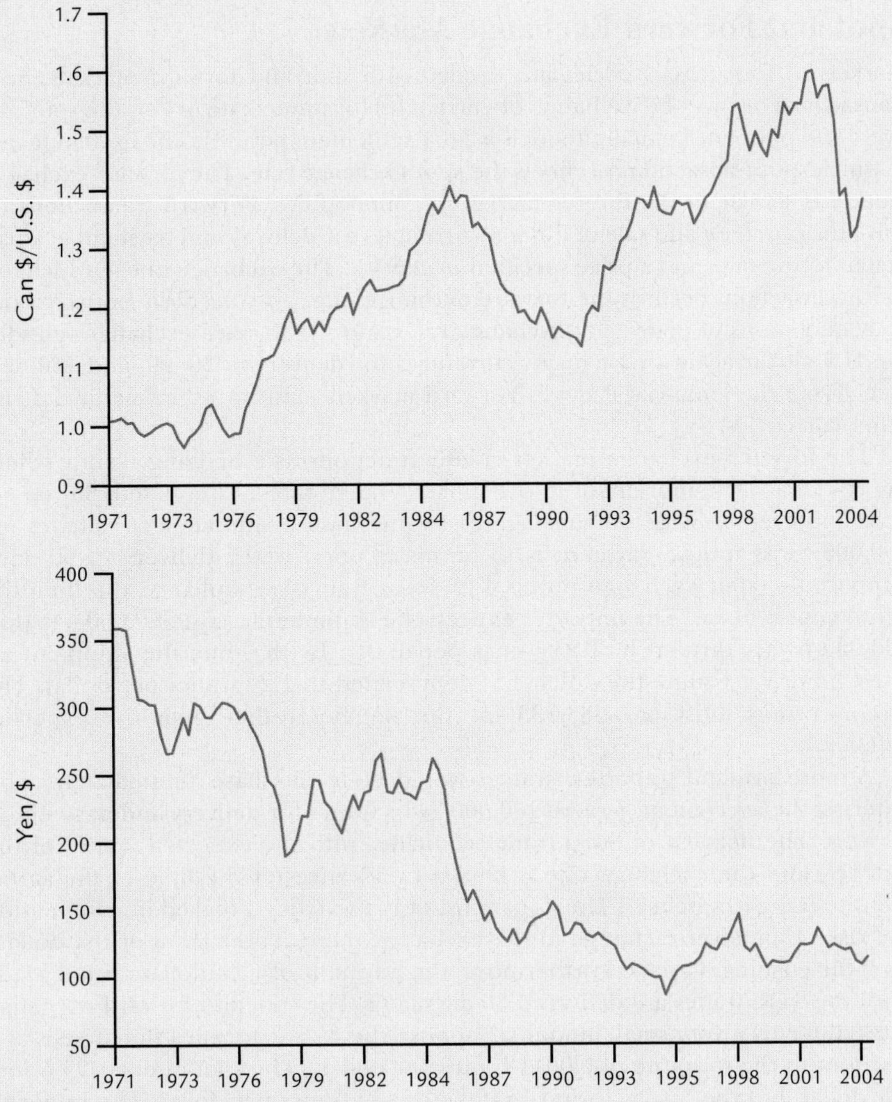

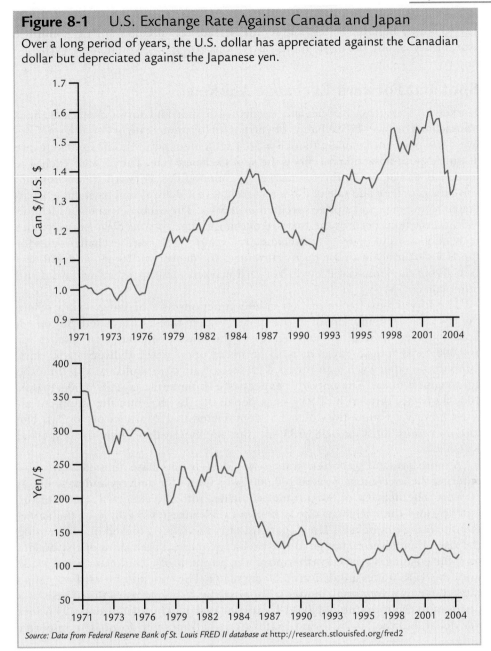

*Source: Data from Federal Reserve Bank of St. Louis FRED II database at* http://research.stlouisfed.org/fred2

marketplace from day to day and continuously throughout the day. Before the 1970s, governments adhered to an agreement in which each country's central bank intervened aggressively in foreign exchange markets to *fix* or *peg* its exchange rate at a predetermined level. Each nation was required to maintain the exchange rate at a specific level unless and until the nation demonstrated to the **International Monetary Fund (IMF)** that the exchange rate level was inappropriate and unsustainable. The exchange rate was adjusted and re-pegged at a new level only with IMF approval. This system was dubbed the **adjustable-peg (Bretton Woods) ex-**

**International Monetary Fund (IMF)** organization created in 1944 for the purpose of creating a stable international monetary order

**adjustable-peg (Bretton Woods) exchange rate system** agreement in which each country's central bank intervenes aggressively in foreign exchange markets to *fix* or *peg* its exchange rate at a predetermined level

**change rate system.**[2] The adjustable-peg exchange rate system collapsed in the early 1970s, mostly because of the highly diverse rates of inflation among countries. World trade among the major industrial nations now is based on floating exchange rates.

## Spot and Forward Exchange Markets

**spot transactions**
exchange of currencies for immediate or "on the spot" delivery and payment

**spot exchange rate**
exchange rate at which spot transactions take place

**forward transactions**
purchase and sale of foreign currencies for delivery and payment at a particular future date and a price specified in advance

**forward exchange rate**
exchange rate at which forward transactions take place

Markets in foreign currencies are divided into spot and forward markets. **Spot transactions** involve the exchange of currencies for immediate or "on the spot" delivery and payment (actually, there is a 2-day settlement period). The exchange rate at which spot transactions occurs is the **spot exchange rate.** The forward exchange market is similar to the futures market in commodities. **Forward transactions** involve the purchase and sale of foreign currencies for delivery and payment at a particular future date and a price specified *in advance.* The exchange rate at which forward transactions occur is the **forward exchange rate.** *The Wall Street Journal* carries daily quotations of many spot exchange rates and the forward exchange rates for the U.S. dollar against four major currencies for delivery in 30, 90, and 180 days (see "From the Financial Pages"). Forward markets exist for other maturities and other currencies.

The forward exchange market chiefly functions as a hedging facility where the risk of adverse movement in the spot exchange rate is eliminated. Suppose a U.S. importer of Swiss watches agrees to purchase a shipment of watches for 100,000 Swiss francs. Payment is to be made upon watch delivery in 30 days. Suppose the spot exchange rate is 1.25 Swiss francs per dollar at the time the agreement is made. The importer expects the shipment to cost $80,000—that is, 100,000 francs divided by 1.25 francs per dollar. By the time the shipment arrives, however, assume the dollar has depreciated to 1.20 francs per dollar. The importer now must pay $83,333 for the watches rather than the expected $80,000.[3]

A more prudent importer strategy would be to purchase, immediately upon entering the agreement, *forward* 100,000 Swiss francs for delivery and payment in 30 days. The delivery of Swiss francs coincides with the expected arrival of the watches, and the exchange rate is known in advance (at the time of the agreement to buy the watches). The dollar cost of the watches is locked in, eliminating the risk of an adverse change in the exchange rate (depreciation of the dollar) over the ensuing 30 days. Furthermore, the payment of U.S. dollars is not made until the Swiss francs are delivered 30 days later. The spot and forward exchange rates differ by a very small amount. Suppose the 30-day forward dollar sells at a discount to the spot rate of 0.0011 francs per dollar.[4] The spot rate is 1.25 francs per dollar, but the 30-day forward rate is 1.2489 francs per dollar. The importer

---

[2] This system was established at an important conference of major industrial nations held in 1944 at Bretton Woods, New Hampshire. The aim of the conference was to establish a new post-World War II international trade and monetary order. The International Monetary Fund and the World Bank also were created at the conference.

[3] Of course, the importer could purchase 100,000 francs on the spot market immediately upon entering into the agreement to buy the watches and hold the francs until the watches arrive or invest the francs in time deposits in Swiss banks for 30 days. These are costly choices involving loss of interest on the funds, inconvenience, and transactions costs for arranging with Swiss banks to earn interest on the funds for 30 days.

[4] Note in "From the Financial Pages" that on August 12, 2004, the dollar sold at a forward discount of 0.0012 francs (1.2550–1.2538).

## FROM THE FINANCIAL PAGES

### Exchange Rate Quotations

U.S. exchange rates with more than 40 foreign nations are quoted each day in *The Wall Street Journal* and other major newspapers. Exporters, importers, tourists, and individuals responsible for investing funds—managers of banks, mutual funds, and pension portfolios—find this information useful. In the table below, exchange rates for Wednesday August 11 and Thursday August 12, 2004, are shown. In the case of Japan, Thursday's rate is quoted two ways: 0.009020 dollars per yen and its reciprocal, 110.86 yen per dollar. Because we are generally interested in the exchange value of the *dollar,* we use the second notation. Note that the dollar *depreciated* Thursday against the yen, falling from 110.90 yen to 110.86 yen. Besides these *spot* rates, quotations of *forward* exchange rates—rates for future delivery and payment—are provided for four U.S. trading partners: Canada, Japan, Switzerland, and the United Kingdom.

Source: Reuters

**Exchange Rates** August 12, 2004

The foreign exchange mid-range rates below apply to trading among banks in amounts of $1 million and more, as quoted at 4 p.m. Eastern time by Reuters and other sources. Retail transactions provide fewer units of foreign currency per dollar.

| | U.S. $ EQUIVALENT | | CURRENCY PER U.S. $ | |
|---|---|---|---|---|
| **Country** | **Thu** | **Wed** | **Thu** | **Wed** |
| **Argentina** (Peso)-y | .3320 | .3306 | 3.0120 | 3.0248 |
| **Australia** (Dollar) | .7150 | .7145 | 1.3986 | 1.3996 |
| **Bahrain** (Dinar) | 2.6525 | 2.6525 | .3770 | .3770 |
| **Brazil** (Real) | .3295 | .3295 | 3.0349 | 3.0349 |
| **Canada** (Dollar) | .7518 | .7549 | 1.3301 | 1.3247 |
| 1-month forward | .7515 | .7546 | 1.3307 | 1.3252 |
| 3-months forward | .7510 | .7540 | 1.3316 | 1.3263 |
| 6-months forward | .7504 | .7534 | 1.3326 | 1.3273 |
| **Chile** (Peso) | .001555 | .001562 | 643.09 | 640.20 |
| **China** (Renminbi) | .1208 | .1208 | 8.2781 | 8.2781 |
| **Colombia** (Peso) | .0003825 | .0003832 | 2614.38 | 2609.60 |
| **Czech. Rep.** (Koruna) | | | | |
| Commercial rate | .03896 | .03884 | 25.667 | 25.747 |
| **Denmark** (Krone) | .1648 | .1642 | 6.0680 | 6.0901 |
| **Ecuador** (US Dollar) | 1.0000 | 1.0000 | 1.0000 | 1.0000 |
| **Egypt** (Pound)-y | .1605 | .1616 | 6.2301 | 6.1900 |
| **Hong Kong** (Dollar) | .1282 | .1282 | 7.8003 | 7.8003 |
| **Hungary** (Forint) | .004931 | .004937 | 202.80 | 202.55 |
| **India** (Rupee) | .02166 | .02160 | 46.168 | 46.296 |
| **Indonesia** (Rupiah) | .0001082 | .0001079 | 9242 | 9268 |
| **Israel** (Shekel) | .2204 | .2204 | 4.5372 | 4.5372 |
| **Japan** (Yen) | .009020 | .009017 | 110.86 | 110.90 |
| 1-month forward | .009032 | .009029 | 110.72 | 110.75 |
| 3-months forward | .009058 | .009057 | 110.40 | 110.41 |
| 6-months forward | .009107 | .009104 | 109.81 | 109.84 |
| **Jordan** (Dinar) | 1.4104 | 1.4104 | .7090 | .7090 |
| **Kuwait** (Dinar) | 3.3920 | 3.3921 | .2948 | .2948 |
| **Lebanon** (Pound) | .0006605 | .0006603 | 1514.00 | 1514.46 |
| **Malaysia** (Ringgit)-b | .2632 | .2632 | 3.7994 | 3.7994 |
| **Malta** (Lira) | 2.8733 | 2.8672 | .3480 | .3488 |
| **Mexico** (Peso) | | | | |
| Floating rate | .0875 | .0876 | 11.4273 | 11.4194 |
| **New Zealand** (Dollar) | .6583 | .6545 | 1.5191 | 1.5279 |
| **Norway** (Krone) | .1477 | .1467 | 6.7705 | 6.8166 |
| **Pakistan** (Rupee) | .01702 | .01698 | 58.754 | 58.893 |
| **Peru** (new Sol) | .2934 | .2935 | 3.4083 | 3.4072 |
| **Philippines** (Peso) | .01796 | .01796 | 55.679 | 55.679 |
| **Poland** (Zloty) | .2765 | .2772 | 3.6166 | 3.6075 |
| **Russia** (Ruble)-a | .03416 | .03417 | 29.274 | 29.265 |
| **Saudi Arabia** (Riyal) | .2667 | .2667 | 3.7495 | 3.7495 |
| **Singapore** (Dollar) | .5831 | .5840 | 1.7150 | 1.7123 |
| **Slovak Rep.** (Koruna) | .03060 | .03050 | 32.680 | 32.787 |
| **South Africa** (Rand) | .1558 | .1611 | 6.4185 | 6.2073 |
| **South Korea** (Won) | .0008639 | .0008654 | 1157.54 | 1155.54 |
| **Sweden** (Krona) | .1331 | .1327 | 7.5131 | 7.5358 |
| **Switzerland** (Franc) | .7968 | .7923 | 1.2550 | 1.2621 |
| 1-month forward | .7976 | .7931 | 1.2538 | 1.2609 |
| 3-months forward | .7992 | .7947 | 1.2513 | 1.2583 |
| 6-months forward | .8020 | .7974 | 1.2469 | 1.2541 |
| **Taiwan** (Dollar) | .02933 | .02942 | 34.095 | 33.991 |
| **Thailand** (Baht) | .02409 | .02408 | 41.511 | 41.528 |
| **Turkey** (Lira) | .00000068 | .00000068 | 1470588 | 1470588 |
| **U.K.** (Pound) | 1.8229 | 1.8291 | .5486 | .5467 |
| 1-month forward | 1.8178 | 1.8240 | .5501 | .5482 |
| 3-months forward | 1.8081 | 1.8141 | .5531 | .5512 |
| 6-months forward | 1.7951 | 1.8009 | .5571 | .5553 |
| **United Arab** (Dirham) | .2723 | .2723 | 3.6724 | 3.6724 |
| **Uruguay** (Peso) | | | | |
| Financial | .03440 | .03430 | 29.070 | 29.155 |
| **Venezuela** (Bolivar) | .000521 | .000521 | 1919.39 | 1919.39 |
| **SDR** | 1.4692 | 1.4668 | .6806 | .6818 |
| **Euro** | 1.2262 | 1.2217 | .8155 | .8185 |

Special Drawing Rights (SDR) are based on exchange rates for the U.S., British, and Japanese currencies. Source: International Monetary Fund.

a-Russian Central Bank rate. b-Government rate. y-Floating rate.

Most foreign exchange market participants obtain less favorable rates than those quoted here. The rates in the table are for multimillion-dollar transactions conducted by dealers. The rates are wholesale exchange rates. An individual or small business needing to buy or sell foreign currency usually makes such transactions through a hometown bank or a credit card company such as Visa or MasterCard. Customers pay the retail rate—that is, they pay a premium (obtain less favorable rates) relative to the quoted wholesale rates.

can lock in the cost of the shipment at $80,070, insuring against a depreciation of the dollar for only $70.[5]

Other market participants enter into forward exchange transactions. Any individual, firm, or organization intending to make or receive payment in foreign currency on a future date can hedge against adverse movement in the dollar exchange rate through a forward transaction. A U.S. money market mutual fund expecting to receive interest payments 90 days hence on high-yielding German 90-day CDs can hedge by selling the prospective euro interest proceeds forward for dollars. Foreign exchange speculators also take advantage of the forward market. Foreign exchange speculators typically are firms that alter the *timing* of foreign exchange transactions to profit from expected movements in exchange rates. Suppose the U.S.–Japan exchange rate is 110 yen per dollar and speculators expect the dollar will appreciate to 115 yen over the next 6 months. A Japanese speculator can buy dollars in the spot market and wait for them to appreciate, investing the funds in U.S. Treasury bills or bank CDs in the meantime. Alternatively, the speculator can purchase dollars for 180-day forward delivery and payment. Because the forward dollars are purchased for approximately 110 yen, the speculator anticipates immediately selling the dollars upon delivery 180 days later in the spot market at a price appreciably above the initial spot and forward prices. In either case, the speculator earns a profit. But the forward route is advantageous because no funds except a small "earnest money" deposit are needed upon entering the forward transaction. Successful speculation in the forward market can produce a positive return with little or no funds invested.

## Importance of the Exchange Rate

A country's exchange rate level has important national economic implications. The exchange rate in conjunction with domestic prices determines the cost of U.S. products in foreign nations, thereby influencing U.S. exports. A Dell computer costs 25 percent more in France if the dollar exchanges for 1 euro rather than 0.80 euros. By the same token, the exchange rate determines the cost of everything Americans purchase from the rest of the world. A 40,000-yen DVD player in Japan costs $400 in the United States if the exchange rate is 100 yen per dollar. If the exchange rate is 125 yen per dollar, the DVD player costs only $320 in the United States. Largely because of such considerations, disputes between nations have occasionally erupted over aggressive government foreign exchange market intervention for the purpose of influencing the exchange rate. Later in this chapter, we examine in more detail the consequences of exchange rate changes. First we examine the factors determining the exchange rate level and the forces that change the level over time.

**YOUR TURN**

Suppose you want to purchase a Japanese-made Sony CD player. Its price in Japan is 30,000 yen. Neglecting transportation costs, taxes, and so forth, how does the CD's cost to you differ if the exchange rate is 150 yen compared to 100 yen per dollar? As a consumer, are you better off with a weak dollar or a strong dollar?

[5] The true cost of this hedge is much lower than $70. As we discuss later in this chapter, the fact that the forward dollar sells at a discount to the spot dollar reflects higher interest rates in the United States than in Switzerland. An importer purchasing forward rather than spot francs can invest the funds in the more attractive U.S. financial instruments for 30 days, offsetting most or all of the $70 cost of the hedge.

# EXCHANGE RATE DETERMINATION

The foreign exchange market is an excellent example of a highly competitive market. The market consists of many buyers and sellers of a homogeneous product—a national currency. Each buyer and seller is small relative to the total market, so no single buyer or seller appreciably influences the exchange rate. In a system of **freely floating exchange rates,** governments do not intervene in the foreign exchange market—exchange rates are driven entirely by free market forces. Like prices in the soybean market and other auction markets, the impersonal forces of supply and demand determine the exchange rate. In a **managed float** (the system in place today), governments occasionally intervene to prevent exchange rate movements perceived to be excessive or strongly at odds with the national interest. Today, the volume of such activity is small relative to the total amount of private activity in the market.

**freely floating exchange rates**
system in which governments do not intervene in the foreign exchange market, permitting exchange rates to be driven entirely by free market forces

**managed float**
system in which governments intervene to prevent exchange rate movements perceived to be excessive or strongly at odds with the national interest

Consider the determination of the U.S.–Japan exchange rate illustrated in Figure 8-2. In this analysis, we explain the value of the U.S. dollar. The units on the vertical axis are expressed as yen per dollar—the price of the U.S. dollar expressed in yen. The units on the horizontal axis are the quantity of dollars per period. The supply and demand curves indicate the flow of dollars supplied and demanded per period at each possible exchange rate. In the figure, the supply and demand curves intersect, determining an equilibrium exchange rate of 120 yen per dollar.

What are the forces behind the supply and demand curves for dollars shown in the figure? The demand curve for dollars stems from Japanese buyers of U.S. goods and services, U.S. financial assets (shares of stock, bonds, and certificates of deposit), and real U.S. assets such as office buildings, banks, factories, and land. Japanese buyers needing to pay for these items in dollars demand U.S. dollars, sell-

**Figure 8-2** U.S.-Japanese Exchange Rate

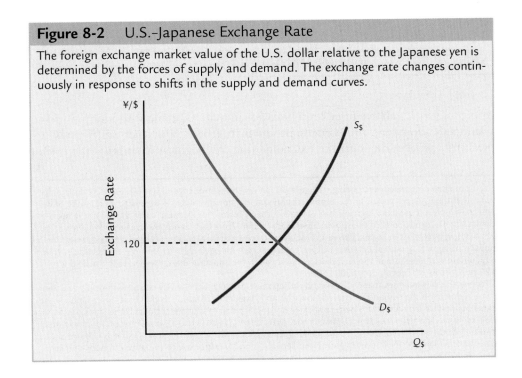

The foreign exchange market value of the U.S. dollar relative to the Japanese yen is determined by the forces of supply and demand. The exchange rate changes continuously in response to shifts in the supply and demand curves.

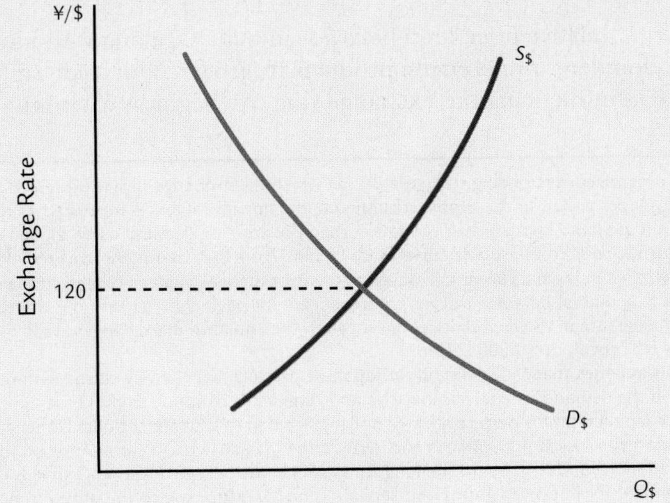

ing yen in exchange. The demand curve in Figure 8-2 is downward sloping because, *holding all other factors constant,* a decline in the price of the U.S. dollar makes everything in the United States cheaper to Japanese buyers, stimulating purchases. For example, if the dollar depreciates from 120 yen to 100 yen, the price in Japan of a \$3 U.S. bushel of wheat declines from 360 yen to 300 yen. For a Japanese tourist, a \$200 San Francisco hotel room drops in price from 24,000 yen to 20,000 yen.

The supply curve in Figure 8-2 originates from Americans seeking to purchase Japanese goods and services, financial assets, and real assets. Americans needing to pay for the items in yen sell dollars to obtain yen and finance the transactions. The supply curve for dollars corresponds to a demand curve for yen.[6] The supply curve in the figure slopes upward because, *holding all other factors constant,* an increase in the value of the dollar (measured in yen) reduces the price of Japanese items in the United States. A Nikon camera selling for 90,000 yen in Tokyo costs an American \$600 if the dollar exchanges for 150 yen. The same camera costs \$900 if the dollar only fetches 100 yen. A stronger dollar reduces the cost of Japanese items to Americans, so we respond by supplying more dollars to finance increased purchases.[7]

Price changes in competitive markets are precipitated by shifts in supply and demand curves. Numerous factors shift the supply and demand curves of Figure 8-2 and thus change the U.S.–Japanese exchange rate. Fundamental factors producing exchange rate changes include changes in price levels, output, and income levels and real interest rates in the countries involved. Changes in consumer preferences, development of new products, and changes in productivity can initiate changes in supply and demand curves in foreign exchange markets, producing changes in exchange rates. Imposition of tariffs, quotas, and other forms of trade barriers produce exchange rate changes. Speculators' anticipation of changes in fundamental factors strongly influences exchange rates from day to day. For purposes of discussion, we divide our analysis of exchange rate determinants into factors that influence exchange rates in the long run and those that influence exchange rates in the short run.

## LONG-RUN EXCHANGE RATE DETERMINANTS

In the long run, relative price level behavior in nations, along with innovation and product development, preferences, productivity growth, and trade restrictions, are powerful forces influencing the exchange rate. We begin by examining the role of

---

[6] You can draw a figure corresponding to Figure 8-2, in which the exchange rate is expressed as dollars per yen rather than yen per dollar. In the hypothetical figure, the horizontal axis is measured as quantity of yen, and the supply and demand curves are in yen rather than dollars. The demand curve for yen in the hypothetical figure corresponds to the supply curve of dollars in Figure 8-2, that is, Americans sell dollars to buy yen for item purchases in Japan. The supply of yen in the hypothetical figure is related to the demand for dollars in Figure 8-2, that is, Japanese sell yen to buy dollars for payments made in the United States. The equilibrium exchange rate in the hypothetical figure, given the equilibrium exchange rate in Figure 8-2 of 120 yen/\$, is its reciprocal, or \$0.00833/yen.

[7] Technically, this assumes that U.S. demand for Japanese products is relatively elastic with respect to the price in dollars. If the demand is relatively inelastic and Americans continue to purchase approximately the same quantity of Japanese items despite a lower dollar price due to a stronger dollar, Americans pay fewer dollars. In the short run, the supply curve is negatively sloped because people do not respond immediately and fully to the more favorable price. In the long run, economists believe the supply curve is upward sloping because U.S. demand for imported goods and services is highly responsive to the price of goods and services in dollars.

**Figure 8-3** Relative Price Level Behavior and Exchange Rates

An increase in the price level in Japan relative to the price level in the United States increases the demand for dollars, reduces the supply of dollars, and causes the dollar to appreciate against the yen.

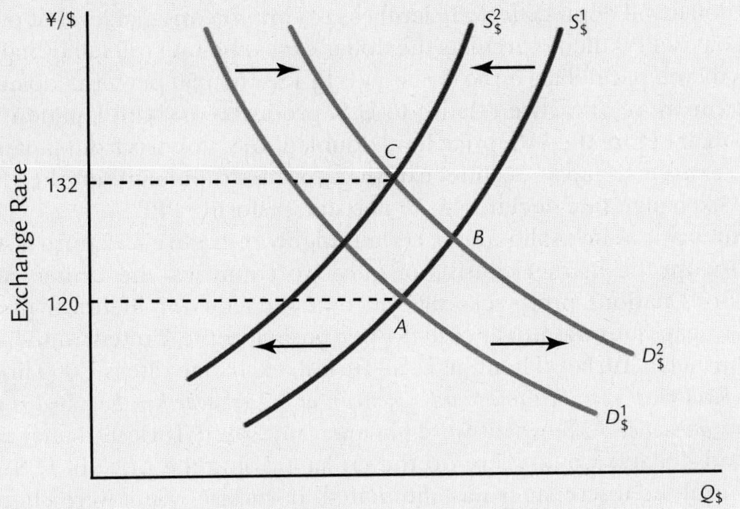

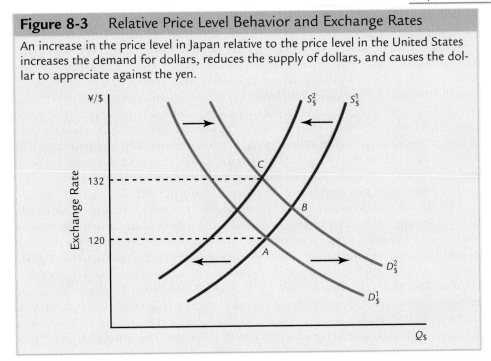

price level behavior. We discover that nations with chronically high inflation are weak currency nations—their currencies *depreciate* over the years against currencies of nations experiencing lower inflation.

## Relative Price Level Behavior

Assume the U.S.–Japanese exchange rate is 120 yen per dollar. The supply and demand curves for dollars ($S^1_\$$ and $D^1_\$$) intersect at point *A* in Figure 8-3. Assume the price level increases 10 percent in Japan but remains constant in the United States. At each and every exchange rate, U.S. goods and services now are relatively more attractive to both Japanese and Americans. The increased desire of Japanese to purchase U.S. goods shifts the demand curve for dollars from $D^1_\$$ to $D^2_\$$. The *increase* in demand moves the equilibrium to point *B* in the figure, indicating an appreciation of the dollar (depreciation of the yen). Also, because Japanese goods now look relatively *less* attractive to Americans at each possible exchange rate, the desire to import from Japan is reduced, and the supply curve of dollars shifts leftward from $S^1_\$$ to $S^2_\$$. The *decrease* in supply indicates a further appreciation of the dollar, with the new equilibrium at point *C* in the figure. The exchange rate reaches 132 yen per dollar. Japanese inflation has produced a depreciation of the yen and a corresponding appreciation of the dollar.

The analysis suggests that countries with relatively high inflation can expect depreciation of their currencies in the long run. The two countries in Table 8-1 exhibiting the most rapid inflation from 1974 to 2004, Australia and Britain, experienced substantial depreciation of their currencies against the dollar. The two countries exhibiting the lowest inflation, Japan and Switzerland, witnessed their currencies *appreciate* considerably against the dollar over the 30-year interval. Mexico (not shown in the table) experienced extremely high inflation rates over a good portion of 1974 to 2004. The peso lost more than 99 percent of its exchange market value against the U.S. dollar.

**purchasing power parity (PPP) theory** theory postulating that exchange rates adjust *completely* to offset the effects of different rates of inflation in two countries

**Purchasing Power Parity Theory.** Building on the preceding analysis, the **purchasing power parity (PPP) theory** postulates that exchange rates adjust *completely* to offset the effects of different rates of inflation in two countries. If the U.S.–Japan exchange rate initially is in equilibrium at 120 yen per dollar and the U.S. price level doubles while Japanese prices remain constant, PPP theory predicts that the dollar will depreciate sufficiently to restore the original level of purchasing power. That is, PPP theory predicts the dollar exchange rate will fall by half (50 percent), to 60 yen per dollar. If the dollar falls by less than 50 percent, Japanese products become more attractive relative to U.S. products—to both Japanese and U.S. buyers—than before the U.S. price level doubled. U.S. imports from Japan increase and U.S. exports to Japan decline, exerting downward pressure on the U.S. dollar until the exchange rate declines by 50 percent, restoring PPP.[8]

PPP theory is always valid under certain highly restrictive and unrealistic conditions. Suppose the market consists of only two countries, the United States and Turkey. Both nations produce only one homogeneous or identical product for export—wheat. Suppose wheat costs $4 per bushel in the United States and 4,000 lire per bushel in Turkey. Then the U.S.–Turkish exchange rate is 1,000 lire per dollar. *The wheat must cost the same to an American or a Turk whether the wheat is purchased at home or abroad.* If U.S. wheat were cheaper, increased Turkish demand for U.S. wheat (and dollars) would drive up the dollar (raising the price of U.S. wheat in Turkey) until the discrepancy was eliminated. If Turkish wheat were cheaper, U.S. demand for Turkish wheat would drive down the dollar, boosting the price of Turkish wheat in the U.S. until the discrepancy was eliminated. This principle is the **law of one price.** If U.S. wheat rises to $8 per bushel while Turkish wheat remains at 4,000 lire, the dollar depreciates from 1,000 lire to 500 lire. Wheat buyers in both Turkey and the United States then are indifferent to whether they purchase wheat in the United States or Turkey. This example reflects the basic intuition behind PPP. (For an appreciation of the limited applicability of the law of one price, see Exhibit 8-1, which discusses the price of Big Macs around the world.)

**law of one price** principle that a homogeneous good's price will be the same whether purchased at home or abroad if free trade and zero transactions costs prevail

## Exhibit 8-1 Price of Big Macs Around the World

The law of one price states that, under free trade conditions, an identical good produced and consumed in two countries does not differ in price by more than the cost of transportation. The exchange rate and the price of the good gravitate to levels where the price of the good (when converted at that exchange rate) is similar in the two countries. The accompanying table shows the price of a Big Mac in the United States and seven foreign countries in June 2004 (column 2). The table indicates the exchange rate of each country (and the euro area) with the United States in June 2004, expressed as units of foreign currency per dollar (column 3).

*continued*

[8] PPP theory implies that inflation does not impair a nation's long-run competitive position in world trade if freely floating exchange rates prevail. The exchange rate is predicted to move and compensate for inflation differences among countries, leaving each nation's products relatively unchanged in price in foreign markets. If U.S. prices double so that the price of an American Buick increases from $35,000 to $70,000 but the dollar falls from 1 euro to 0.5 euro, the Buick continues to sell for 35,000 euros in Europe. Suppose in Europe, where the price level remains unchanged, a Mercedes continues to sell for 80,000 euros. The depreciation of the U.S. dollar to half a euro raises the price of the Mercedes in the United States from $80,000 to $160,000—the same percentage increase in price as the Buick and other U.S. goods. According to PPP theory, floating exchange rates allow countries with chronically high inflation to remain competitive in world trade.

## Exhibit 8-1 Price of Big Macs Around the World—*cont'd*

The price of a Big Mac abroad and the actual exchange rate allow us to compare the 2004 price of foreign Big Macs in U.S. dollars (column 4) with the U.S. Big Mac price of $2.89. Foreign Big Mac prices ranged from a high of $4.96 in Switzerland to a low of $1.27 in China. Column 5 reports the implied purchasing power parity (PPP) exchange rate, calculated by dividing the foreign price of a Big Mac (shown in column 2) by the U.S. price of $2.89. The implied PPP rate is the exchange rate that makes the U.S. cost of a foreign Big Mac equal to the U.S. price of $2.89. If Big Macs are cheaper abroad (in U.S. dollars) than in the United States, the actual exchange rate (foreign currency/$) is higher than the implied PPP rate and the U.S. dollar is overvalued (relative to PPP). If Big Macs are more expensive abroad, the actual exchange rate is below the PPP rate and the U.S. dollar is undervalued.

This simple example suggests that in June 2004, the dollar was overvalued relative to five of seven foreign currencies. The dollar was undervalued against the British pound and the Swiss franc. These findings suggest that for an American, neglecting airfare, travel is considerably cheaper in China and Mexico than in the United States and considerably more expensive in Switzerland. To solidify your understanding of the law of one price, ask yourself why it does not apply to Big Macs.

| Country | Price of Big Mac | Actual Exchange Rate (Foreign Currency/$) | U.S. Dollar Price of Big Mac | Implied PPP Exchange Rate | Percent Implied Over-valuation (+) or Under-valuation (−) of U.S. Dollar |
|---|---|---|---|---|---|
| Australia | A$3.25 | 1.44 | 2.26 | 1.12 | +28 |
| Britain | £1.85 | 0.55 | 3.36 | 0.64 | −14 |
| Canada | C$3.15 | 1.37 | 2.30 | 1.09 | +26 |
| China | Yuan 10.5 | 8.27 | 1.27 | 3.63 | +127 |
| Japan | ¥260 | 110 | 2.36 | 90 | +22 |
| Mexico | Peso 23.5 | 11.4 | 2.06 | 8.13 | +40 |
| Switzerland | S Fr 6.30 | 1.27 | 4.96 | 2.18 | −42 |
| United States | $2.89 | — | 2.89 | — | — |

Adapting this framework to the real world, we must recognize that many products are not homogeneous. When the dollar depreciates and imported Volvos become more expensive relative to Fords, Americans continue to purchase Volvos (though presumably in fewer numbers) because of perceived quality differences, brand loyalty, and force of habit. A nation's price level includes many nontradable goods and services, whereas only tradable items are strictly relevant to PPP. The prices of tradable and nontradable goods do not necessarily move together over time. PPP theory seems to account well for major exchange rate movements during severe inflations. When the U.S. price level doubled in the 1970s, the dollar depreciated sharply against the currencies of low-inflation countries like Germany and

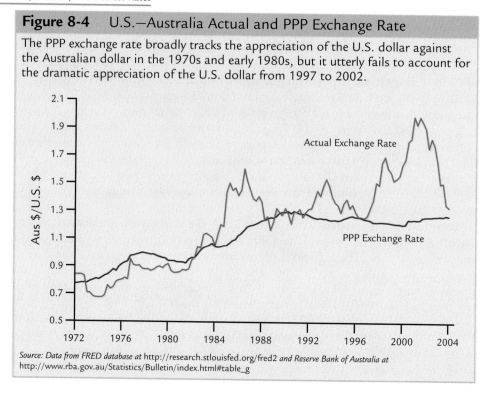

**Figure 8-4** U.S.–Australia Actual and PPP Exchange Rate

The PPP exchange rate broadly tracks the appreciation of the U.S. dollar against the Australian dollar in the 1970s and early 1980s, but it utterly fails to account for the dramatic appreciation of the U.S. dollar from 1997 to 2002.

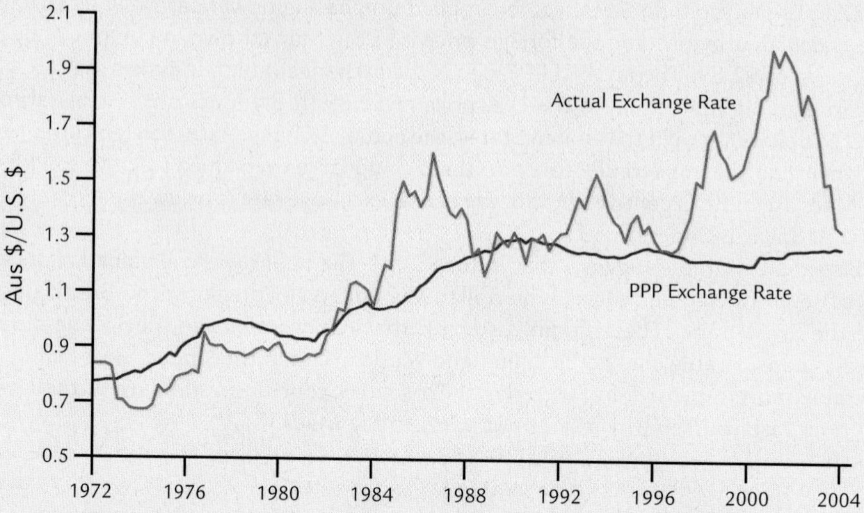


*Source: Data from FRED database at* http://research.stlouisfed.org/fred2 *and Reserve Bank of Australia at* http://www.rba.gov.au/Statistics/Bulletin/index.html#table_g

Switzerland. In the 1970s and 1980s, Australia experienced considerably higher inflation than the United States. The Australian dollar depreciated sharply against the U.S. dollar (the U.S. dollar appreciated against the Australian dollar). In the low-inflation world environment of the past 10 to 15 years, however, PPP theory does not adequately explain exchange rate movements.

Figure 8-4 provides a crude test of PPP theory. The figure illustrates the actual U.S.–Australian exchange rate since 1972 and the hypothetical exchange rate that maintains purchasing power parity, that is, the PPP exchange rate. The actual exchange rate is assumed to reflect PPP in 1973. The figure demonstrates the extent to which price level behavior in the two countries account for exchange rate changes since 1973.

As indicated in the figure, PPP predicts that the U.S. dollar should have appreciated over the long period (Australian inflation exceeded U.S. inflation), and it did. However, during two major episodes—the mid-1980s and 1997 to 2002—the U.S. dollar became considerably *overvalued* relative to the PPP criterion. From 1996 to 2002, the U.S. dollar appreciated from about 1.25 Australian dollars to nearly 2 Australian dollars. PPP suggests the exchange rate should have remained approximately constant in that period (the two countries had almost identical inflation rates from 1996 to 2004). The U.S. dollar fell sharply from 2002 to 2004 but remained slightly overvalued *vis-a-vis* the Australian dollar based on PPP in early 2004. PPP theory fails to account for short-term to intermediate-term (up to a decade long) movements in exchange rates. PPP theory more adequately accounts for extremely long-run exchange rate trends.

## Other Long-Run Exchange Rate Determinants

Other factors influencing long-term exchange rate developments include changes in preferences, product development, changes in productivity behavior, and imposition of tariffs and quotas. We briefly look at each factor.

**Preferences and Product Development.** Exchange rates are influenced by the demand for various products. The demand, in turn, depends on people's preferences. If Seattle's Boeing Company develops a worldwide reputation for producing the safest, most efficient aircraft, a strong preference for Boeing planes develops worldwide. The preference increases the demand for dollars as foreign countries buy more planes, causing the dollar to appreciate. On the other hand, Japanese companies stimulate Americans' preference for Sony electronic products through advertising and other measures, causing the yen to appreciate against the dollar (and the dollar to fall against the yen).

Nations induce increased demand for their products by developing desirable new products or by making major improvements to existing products. The increased demand results in appreciation of the nation's currency. When Silicon Valley engineers initiated vast improvements in the power and efficiency of personal computers, demand increased and the U.S. dollar became stronger. By the same token, if U.S. innovation and product development lags behind that of other nations, the dollar depreciates over the long run. In sum, entrepreneurs cause a nation's currency to appreciate over the long run by developing attractive new products and stimulating worldwide preferences for a nation's existing products.

**Productivity Behavior.** Productivity behavior—changes in output per hour of work—is a major force influencing production costs and product prices. Countries that experience rapid productivity growth are able to hold down production costs and prices. They become increasingly competitive in world markets and their currencies appreciate over time. Countries that lag in productivity growth experience a long-run depreciation of their currencies. The long-run depreciation of the British pound against the U.S. dollar is an example. The British pound has lost nearly two thirds of its value against the dollar in the past 55 years due to slower productivity growth and higher inflation. (In 1948, the exchange rate was $4.86 per pound. Check the current quote of less than $2.00 per pound.)

**Tariffs and Quotas.** **Tariffs** are taxes on imported goods. **Quotas** are restrictions a nation imposes on the volume of imported goods. No tariffs or quotas exist under *free trade.* Let's return to our basic supply and demand model (Figure 8-2) to illustrate. Suppose the U.S. imposes a $100 tax on each Japanese TV set imported into the United States. Imported TVs are now less attractive at the margin. U.S. buyers purchase fewer TVs (and yen), and thus sell fewer dollars in the foreign exchange market. Imposition of the tariff shifts the supply curve of dollars leftward, causing the dollar to appreciate. Similarly, if the U.S. puts a quota on steel imports from Japan (as the Bush administration did in 2002), the supply curve of dollars shifts left, causing the dollar to appreciate.

**tariffs**
taxes on imported goods

**quotas**
nation's restrictions on the volume of imported goods

## Long-Run Exchange Rate Determinants: Summary

Table 8-2 summarizes the *long-run* determinants of exchange rates. Exchange rate movements observed from *day to day* and *month to month* usually are triggered by other factors.

# SHORT-RUN EXCHANGE RATE DETERMINANTS

We discussed a theory of long-run exchange rate determination. From the theory we understand why the U.S. dollar today exchanges for fewer than half as many Japanese yen and Swiss francs as the dollar did in 1974 and why the dollar buys

**Table 8-2 Long-Run Exchange Rate Determinants**

| Factor | Change in Factor | Impact on U.S. Dollar |
|---|---|---|
| Price level behavior | U.S. price level increases | Dollar depreciates |
| Preferences | Preference for U.S. goods increases | Dollar appreciates |
| Product development | Japan develops state-of-the-art high-resolution TV screen | Dollar depreciates |
| Productivity | U.S. productivity growth rises | Dollar appreciates |
| Tariffs | U.S. places tariffs on imported steel | Dollar appreciates |
| Quotas | U.S. places quotas on imported cars | Dollar appreciates |

about twice as many Australian dollars (review Table 8-1). However, to understand why exchange rates move sharply in a given day, week, or month, we look to factors other than relative price level behavior, preferences, innovation and product development, and productivity trends. Such factors cannot account for daily and weekly exchange rate movements. We need a framework equipped to demonstrate why exchange rates change so much in the short run.

To understand short-run exchange rate behavior, we must recognize that foreign exchange market activity is dominated by *asset demand*—demand for financial instruments and deposits in various countries—rather than demand for goods and services. In 2004, the total value of world imports and exports of goods and services accounted for less than 2 percent of the total value of all foreign exchange transactions. The overwhelming portion of exchange market transactions is attributable to capital flows. In today's economy, capital is highly mobile. The currencies of the major industrial nations are very close substitutes for one another. With computer technology and low foreign exchange market transactions costs, dollar deposits in New York can be transformed instantaneously and almost without cost into yen deposits in Tokyo, euro deposits in Paris or Rome, pound deposits in London, and so forth. Any perceived advantage of investing funds in Frankfurt immediately triggers an increase in demand for German deposits and hence in the German currency—the euro.

## Expected Returns from Investing at Home and Abroad

Consider a U.S. institutional investor with $100 million to invest in interest-bearing commercial bank CDs. The investor is willing to transact in any financial center, such as New York, London, Frankfurt, Hong Kong, and so forth. The interest rates available on domestic and foreign CDs are designated $i_D$ and $i_F$, respectively. If the funds are invested in New York CDs, no foreign exchange transactions are involved. The expected return is simply $i_D$. If the investor transfers the funds to a German bank in Frankfurt, the investor knows that the exchange rate will change between the day the funds are invested and the later date on which the funds are repatriated (returned) to the United States. To calculate the expected returns from investing in Frankfurt, the investor considers the prospective appreciation or depreciation of the U.S. dollar while the funds are earning interest in Germany. Suppose the institutional investor can earn 8 percent per year interest on a 1-year German CD but expects the dollar to appreciate (the euro to depreciate) by 3 percent during the year. When the German CD proceeds (principal plus interest) are converted back into dollars, a 3 percent exchange rate loss is expected. It costs 3 percent more euros to buy a dollar now than 1 year earlier when the funds were invested in Germany. The expected return from investing in German securities is only about 5 percent—that is, 8 percent minus 3 percent.[9] Consider the following expression:

$$R_F = i_F - \frac{(ER^e_{t+1} - ER_t)}{ER_t} \quad (8\text{-}1)$$

where $R_F$ is the expected rate of return from investing abroad, $i_F$ is the foreign interest rate (the rate on 1-year German CDs), $ER_t$ is the actual (spot) exchange rate in the current period (t) expressed in euros per dollar, and $ER^e_{t+1}$ is the exchange rate expected to prevail in 1 year when the CD comes due and the German deposits are converted back into U.S. deposits.

The expression states that the expected return from investing in foreign assets is equal to the foreign interest rate minus the expected percentage appreciation of the U.S. dollar (or depreciation of the euro) during the next year. If you can earn 3 percent interest on German CDs but expect the euro to appreciate (dollar to depreciate) by 6 percent during the year, the expected return ($R_F$) is 9 percent. In this case, the U.S. investor expects to earn a 3 percent return in euros and to gain another 6 percent from the dollar's depreciation.

## Interest Parity Condition

Capital is highly mobile and investors seek to maximize their returns. Interest rates and exchange rates tend strongly to align so that *expected* returns equalize across countries. In other words, in equilibrium, $i_D = R_F$. Expected returns in the U.S. and Germany are equalized. If we use Equation (8-1) and set $R_F$ equal to the expected return on domestic deposits ($i_D$), we obtain:

$$i_D = i_{Fjt} - \frac{(ER^e_{t+1} - ER_t)}{ER_t} \quad (8\text{-}2)$$

This expression, the **interest parity condition,** is based on the simple notion that, in a world of capital mobility, expected returns on assets equalize across countries. In equilibrium, interest rates and exchange rates align so that traders cannot expect to profit by switching currencies. The idea seems intuitively plausible. Suppose that investors expect to receive a higher return in Germany than in the United States. The demand for German assets (and demand for euros) increases, causing the euro to appreciate and the dollar to depreciate. Given the expected future exchange rate, the decline in the dollar increases the expected future *appreciation* of the dollar (or reduces the expected depreciation), reducing $R_F$, the expected net return earned from German CDs. Depreciation of the dollar continues until the expected advantage of investing in Germany is eliminated. If investors believe they can earn more by investing in New York, the supply of dollars offered by Americans to purchase currency (euros) falls and the demand for dollars by foreigners rises, causing the dollar to appreciate. Given the expected future exchange rate, exchange rate appreciation reduces expected future appreciation, boosting $R_F$. The process continues until interest parity is achieved—that is, until $i_D = R_F$.

**interest parity condition**
condition in which, in a world of capital mobility, expected returns on assets are equal across countries

[9] Suppose the exchange rate is 1 euro per dollar and the dollar is expected to appreciate by 3 percent to 1.03 euros. The $100 million initially exchanges for 100 million euros and earns 8 million euros interest during the year. The 108 million euros converted back into dollars at 103 euros per dollar at the end of the year fetches only $104,854,400. The rate of return on the original $100 million investment is only 4.85 percent per year.

# Part THREE

Commercial banks and other depository institutions play a key role in a nation's financial system. These institutions are intimately involved in the creation of money and credit. They provide benefits to both lenders and borrowers, and contribute to economic efficiency and growth. The U.S. banking system is unique in its structure. While other nations have only a few large banks with numerous branches, the United States has approximately 7,500 separately owned banks. However, the U.S. banking system has been undergoing consolidation. Today there are only about half as many banks today as existed 20 years ago. First the savings and loan industry and then the commercial banking industry went through extremely difficult times in the 1980s and early 1990s. More than 1,200 commercial banks and about one third of the nation's S&Ls failed in this period. Much of the problem can be attributed to a flawed regulatory system, coupled with severe macroeconomic instability in the 1970s and early 1980s. As a result of this experience, the regulatory structure has been redesigned, and new measures have been implemented to reduce incentives for risk taking by depository institutions. Today, these institutions are in robust financial condition.

# Chapter 9

# COMMERCIAL BANKING

Depository institutions play a key role in channeling funds from savers (surplus units) to borrowers and investors (deficit units). Depository institutions obtain funds mainly by issuing checking, saving, and time deposits and use the proceeds to grant loans to home buyers, businesses, and consumers. Commercial banks are the dominant player among depository institutions. Commercial banks are the oldest and most diversified of all financial intermediaries. In 2005, commercial banks had some $8 trillion ($8,000 billion) in total assets—more than 75 percent of the total assets of all depository institutions (commercial banks, savings and loan associations, mutual savings banks, and credit unions) combined.

Our interest in banks stems from their dominant role among financial intermediaries and their special role in the money supply process. An important portion of the claims that banks issue (checking and savings accounts) count in our money supply measures (M1, M2, and M3). Commercial banks create money by lending and purchasing securities. Commercial banks are the primary conduit through which Federal Reserve policy influences the nation's money supply and credit conditions. For these reasons, commercial banking warrants special attention.

Banks play a key role in the economy, so a financially healthy banking sector is essential to the nation's economic well-being. In the past 25 years, banks have been challenged by financial innovations, deregulation, and globalization. In the process, commercial bank profitability has fluctuated significantly. The banking industry suffered hard times in the late 1980s and early 1990s but recovered strongly through the late 1990s. In the early years of the twenty-first century, the banking industry is in robust condition. However, a few huge money center banks experienced problems related to the collapse of Enron and WorldCom and to large loans made to Latin American nations experiencing severe economic problems.

In Chapter 10, we examine the structure and evolution of the U.S. banking industry. In this chapter we look at the business of banking. To understand commercial banking we start with the commercial bank *balance sheet,* which indicates the sources (liabilities) and uses (assets) of bank funds. We see how banks earn profits and examine the principles governing management of bank assets and liabilities. We look at the concepts of bank liquidity and capital adequacy and learn why some banks become insolvent.

## COMMERCIAL BANK BALANCE SHEET

Banks, like other business enterprises, aim to earn profits. Banks earn profits principally by obtaining funds at relatively low interest rates and then lending the funds or investing in securities at higher interest rates. The "spread" between the rate banks pay for funds and the rate they earn—typically 3 to 4 percentage points—fluctuates and importantly influences bank profits. Bank fees for services have played an increasing role in overall bank profits in recent years.

The most efficient way to learn about the business of banking is to examine a typical bank's balance sheet. The **balance sheet** of any entity (individual, business firm, or government) is a statement of its assets, liabilities, and net worth at a given point in time. A bank's **assets** indicate what the bank *owns,* or claims the bank has on external entities (individuals, firms, governments, and other banks). A bank's **liabilities** indicate what the bank *owes,* or claims external entities have on the bank. A fundamental and simple accounting identity is the following:

**balance sheet**
statement of assets, liabilities, and net worth at a given point in time

**assets**
indications of what is owned or claims on external entities

(9-1) **Assets − Liabilities = Net worth**

or

(9-2) **Assets = Liabilities + Net worth.**

**liabilities**
indications of what is owed or claims that external entities have on a bank or other entity

A bank's **net worth** is a residual item calculated by subtracting total liabilities from total assets. In banking terminology, net worth is known as **capital accounts (capital).** Capital accounts are the value of the bank owners' residual claim on the bank's assets—that is, bank capital is the owners' equity in the bank. The item is listed on the right-hand side of the balance sheet, below total liabilities, so that the two sides of the balance sheet are always equal. From Equation (9-1), net worth or bank capital is the difference between total bank assets and total bank liabilities. From Equation (9-2), total bank assets equals total bank liabilities plus net worth or capital.

**net worth**
amount by which total assets exceed total liabilities

**capital accounts (capital)**
net worth of a bank, or value of the bank owners' residual claim on the bank's assets

You can view the bank balance sheet as a statement of the sources and uses of bank funds. Banks obtain funds by issuing demand, savings, and time deposits, by borrowing funds from other banks or the public, and by obtaining equity funds from bank shareholders (owners) through capital accounts. Banks use the funds to grant loans, invest in securities, purchase equipment and facilities, and hold *reserves*—currency on hand and deposits at the Federal Reserve. These are the banks' assets. Loans and securities constitute the banks' *earning assets* and account for more than 80 percent of total bank assets. The interest earned from loans and securities generates the major portion of commercial banks' revenues. The revenues cover the cost of bank operations and provide a profit for the banks' owners. Figure 9-1 illustrates the sources and uses of commercial bank funds.

Table 9-1 shows the collective balance sheet of all U.S. commercial banks in June 2004. Each item on the balance sheet is expressed as a percentage of total bank assets, which were about $7,700 billion ($7.7 trillion) in June 2004. To understand banking and how the Federal Reserve influences credit conditions and short-term interest rates, you must understand the bank balance sheet. We examine bank liabilities (sources of bank funds), bank assets, and then bank capital.

## COMMERCIAL BANK LIABILITIES

Bank liabilities are obligations banks incur, primarily for obtaining funds to make loans and purchase securities. Bank liabilities include various types of deposits, other forms of bank borrowing, and other liabilities. Your bank deposit, which is an asset to you, is a liability of your bank. You have a claim on the bank—the bank owes you the amount in your account. Bank deposits are divided into two categories: transactions deposits and non-transactions deposits. We examine the various types of deposit in each category, beginning with transactions deposits.

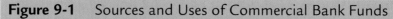

**Figure 9-1** Sources and Uses of Commercial Bank Funds

Commercial banks obtain funds by accepting deposits, borrowing from nondeposit sources, and issuing equity claims (bank capital). Banks use the funds mainly to make loans and purchase securities.

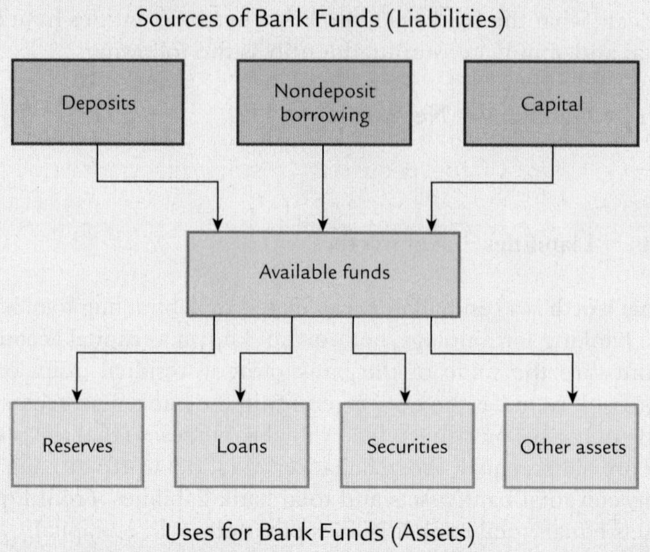


**Table 9.1** Balance Sheet of all U.S. Commercial Banks in June 2004 (items expressed as percentage of total assets)

| Assets (Uses of Funds) | | Liabilities (Sources of Funds) | |
|---|---|---|---|
| Cash Assets: | 4.5% | Deposits: | 65.4% |
| Vault cash | 0.7 | Transaction deposits | 8.7 |
| Deposits with Federal Reserve banks | 0.2 | Non-transaction deposits | 56.7 |
| Deposits with other banks and cash items in process of collection | 3.6 | Borrowings | 19.7 |
| | | Other Liabilities | 6.7 |
| Loans: | 59.6 | Total Liabilities | 91.8 |
| Real estate | 31.0 | | |
| Business | 11.4 | Capital Accounts | 8.2 |
| Consumer | 8.4 | | |
| All other | 8.8 | | |
| Securities: | 25.0 | | |
| U.S. government | 15.4 | | |
| State, local, and other government | 9.6 | | |
| Other Assets | 10.9 | | |
| Total Assets | 100 | Total Liabilities and Capital | 100 |

Items are expressed as percentage of total bank assets.
*Source: Federal Reserve Bulletin and Board of Governors Statistical Release H.8 at* http://www.federalreserve.gov

## Transactions Deposits

**Transactions (checkable) deposits** are deposits on which checks can be written with unlimited checking privileges. Transactions deposits are payable on demand—you can walk into your bank or go to an ATM and withdraw funds from your checking account at any time. You also can order your bank to transfer funds to a third party simply by writing a check or authorizing an automatic payment. Transactions deposits are the lowest-cost source of funds for banks. Transactions deposits include **demand deposits,** which are non–interest-bearing checking accounts, and other types of interest-bearing checking deposits. Interest-bearing checking accounts include **negotiable order of withdrawal (NOW) accounts** and **automatic transfer service (ATS) accounts.** Individuals and non-profit organizations can hold both demand deposits and other types of checkable deposits. Regulations prohibit banks from issuing NOW or ATS accounts to business firms. Profit-oriented business firms are not allowed to hold interest-bearing checking accounts in banks.[1]

**transactions (checkable) deposits**
deposits on which checks can be written with unlimited checking privileges

**demand deposits**
deposits that can be withdrawn in currency or transferred to a third party at the initiative of the owner

### NOW Accounts.

From the 1930s to the early 1980s, federal law generally prohibited depository institutions from paying interest on checking accounts. The prohibition had little effect at the time because market interest rates were low. As money market yields increased sharply in the late 1960s and especially in the 1970s, interest prohibition became a problem for depository institutions. Banks experienced **disintermediation**—active withdrawal of funds from depository institutions by customers searching for higher yields elsewhere. In 1972, after 2 years of litigation, savings banks in Massachusetts were authorized to consider a check a "negotiable order of withdrawal." The accounts on which the checks were written—*NOW accounts*—were not considered demand deposits and thus not subject to the regulations prohibiting interest payment. A NOW account is equivalent to an interest-bearing savings account on which checks can be written. Lobbyists for commercial banks won an early ruling prohibiting the spread of NOW accounts beyond New England, but in 1980 the Depository Institutions Deregulation and Monetary Control Act (DIDMCA) authorized nationwide issuance of NOW accounts by commercial banks and thrift institutions.

**negotiable order of withdrawal (NOW) accounts**
interest-bearing savings account, on which limited check writing privileges are permitted

**automatic transfer service (ATS) accounts**
type of account in which funds are automatically transferred from savings account to checking account as checks are presented for payment

### ATS Accounts.

At about the same time NOW accounts were legalized nationwide, a similar instrument—the ATS account—was authorized. With an ATS account, a bank customer with a large amount of funds maintains a minimal checking account balance and holds additional funds in an interest-bearing savings account. As checks drawn on the checking account are presented for clearance, the bank's computer automatically transfers sufficient funds from the individual's savings account to the checking account, permitting the checks to clear and maintaining the minimum checking account balance. The accounts are sometimes referred to as *sweep accounts.* Like the NOW account, the ATS account is essentially an interest-bearing checking account. In 2004, demand deposits and interest-bearing

**disintermediation**
active withdrawal of funds from depository institutions by customers searching for higher yields elsewhere

[1] Banks circumvent the prohibition of interest payments on corporate checking accounts through *repurchase* agreements, discussed later in this chapter. Banks are prohibited from paying explicit interest to business firms on checking accounts, but the deposits are not a free source of funds for banks. Banks pay *implicit interest* on the accounts. For example, banks routinely provide check-clearing services and send monthly statements to all depositors. Banks frequently provide corporate depositors with services such as payroll preparation and foreign currency transactions. Many banks grant below-market rate loans to corporate customers maintaining large demand deposit balances. Some banks even calculate the total amount of free services provided to corporate customers. Banks typically make this calculation by applying an appropriate interest rate to the average balance held by the corporation.

"other checkable deposits" (NOW and ATS accounts) were of approximately equal magnitude. Each accounted for roughly half of total transactions deposits.

## Non-transactions Deposits

Non-transactions deposits are interest-bearing deposits on which no or only a limited number of checks can be written. Passbook savings accounts, small consumer-type time deposits or certificates of deposits (CDs), money market deposit accounts (MMDAs), and large negotiable CDs in minimum denominations of $100,000 are in this category. Non-transactions deposits are the largest source of bank funds today. Non-transactions deposits account for six times as many bank funds as transactions deposits (review Table 9-1).

**Passbook Savings Accounts.** Passbook savings accounts have been popular with American households for generations. Transactions and accrued interest are recorded in a small blue or green book (the passbook). Passbook savings accounts have no specific denomination. Any amount of funds can be added to or withdrawn from the account at any time. Passbook savings accounts are highly liquid for depositors. In practice, savings can be withdrawn on request without penalty, although technically a bank may require 30 days advance notice. Passbook savings accounts once were a major source of bank funds but have declined in popularity, largely because of attractive new instruments available to the public through financial innovations.

**Small Certificates of Deposit (CDs up to $100,000).** Small consumer CDs or time deposits are issued in specific maturities, typically ranging from 3 months to 5 years. Stiff penalties in the form of loss of accrued interest are levied for withdrawal prior to maturity. Banks pay a higher interest rate on time deposits because they are less liquid and less likely to be withdrawn than passbook savings accounts. Time deposits are a more costly source of funds to banks than passbook savings accounts. The longer the CD maturity, the higher the interest rate banks pay. Small CDs are a very important source of bank funds today.

**money market deposit accounts (MMDAs)**
interest-bearing deposits with limited check writing features that permit banks to compete with money market mutual funds

**Money Market Deposit Accounts (MMDAs).** **Money market deposit accounts (MMDAs)** are interest-bearing deposits. In 1982 the Depository Institutions Act authorized MMDAs, thus allowing banks to compete with money market mutual funds. MMDAs offer limited check-writing privileges (no more than six transactions per month, including pre-authorized automatic or other transfers, and no more than three transactions involving checks). The yield payable fluctuates with interest rates prevailing in the market. Compared to money market mutual fund shares, MMDAs have the advantage of FDIC insurance up to $100,000 per account.

Because MMDAs are less likely to be withdrawn and are not subject to reserve requirements, banks offer a higher interest rate on MMDAs than on NOW and ATS accounts. Demand deposits, NOW accounts, and ATS accounts are included in the Federal Reserve's narrow measure of money (M1), but MMDAs are not (they are included in M2 and M3). The Federal Reserve considers MMDAs more as savings accounts than as vehicles for financing everyday expenditures despite their check-writing feature.

**Negotiable CDs.** Large negotiable CDs are issued in minimum denominations of $100,000. The CDs typically are purchased by corporations and money market mutual funds as alternatives to short-term government securities. Negotiable CDs are issued in specific maturities and are a reliable source of funds for the large banks issuing them. Negotiable CDs are not redeemable by the issuing banks prior to maturity. The CDs can be traded in an active secondary market and therefore are considered highly liquid by owners. The volume of negotiable CDs fluctuates with economic conditions. When credit demands escalate during a strong economic expansion, the volume of negotiable CDs outstanding increases as banks aggressively seek funds. As economic activity softens and demand for bank loans decreases, the volume of negotiable CDs outstanding declines.

## Non-deposit Borrowing

Commercial banks obtain funds from their deposit customers and borrow funds from the Federal Reserve System, other banks, and other entities. Loans made by the Federal Reserve to commercial banks are *discount loans.* The interest rate charged to banks on discount loans is the **discount rate.** The loans typically are made for a short period (often 1 day). Banks can borrow funds overnight from other banks in the form of deposits at the Federal Reserve in the **federal funds market.** The interest rate payable on such loans is the **federal funds rate.** Banks can borrow continuously and in any amount in the federal funds market and can use the funds to grant loans or purchase securities.

**discount rate**
interest rate charged on loans made by the Federal Reserve to commercial banks

**federal funds market**
market in which banks borrow funds overnight from other banks in the form of deposits at the Federal Reserve

**federal funds rate**
interest rate payable on loans in the federal funds market

Banks borrow from other corporations through repurchase agreements (RPs). In an RP, a bank borrows the corporate customer's checking account, typically on an overnight basis, and pays a competitive interest rate for the privilege. U.S. banks also borrow eurodollars—dollar-denominated deposits held by foreign banks or foreign branches of U.S. banks. Most U.S. commercial banks, including almost all large banks, are organized as *bank holding companies.* These banks (which hold more than 90 percent of aggregate commercial bank deposits) borrow by issuing commercial paper or corporate bonds. These fund sources have become increasingly important in recent years. For commercial banks collectively, the ratio of non-deposit bank borrowing to total bank liabilities increased from 2 percent in 1960 to about 20 percent today.

## Other Bank Liabilities

The "other liabilities" category is relatively small. The category includes accounts payable—invoices that have not yet been paid. The category also includes, on an accrual basis, regular payments that are due on a future date—accrued wages and salaries, other payroll expenses, accrued taxes, and other accrued expenses.

## Changing Sources of Bank Funds

Figure 9-2 illustrates the changing sources of bank funds since 1960. The figure indicates the shares of bank funds contributed by transactions deposits, passbook savings and small time deposits, large negotiable CDs, and non-deposit forms of borrowing.

The portion of total bank funds obtained through transactions deposits has declined from about 60 percent in 1960 to less than 10 percent today. As a result of the declining relative importance of these low-cost transactions deposits and the increasing relative importance of higher-cost sources of funds, banks pay more for funds relative to money market yields today than they paid in the 1950s and 1960s. In the past 40 years, consolidation of the banking industry and the increasing share of total bank deposits held by relatively large banks organized as holding companies led to a sharp increase in the share of bank funds obtained through non-deposit sources. In particular, the commercial banking industry is increasingly obtaining funds by issuing commercial paper and corporate bonds.

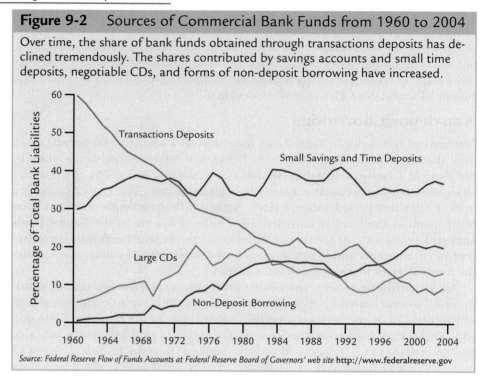

**Figure 9-2** Sources of Commercial Bank Funds from 1960 to 2004

Over time, the share of bank funds obtained through transactions deposits has declined tremendously. The shares contributed by savings accounts and small time deposits, negotiable CDs, and forms of non-deposit borrowing have increased.

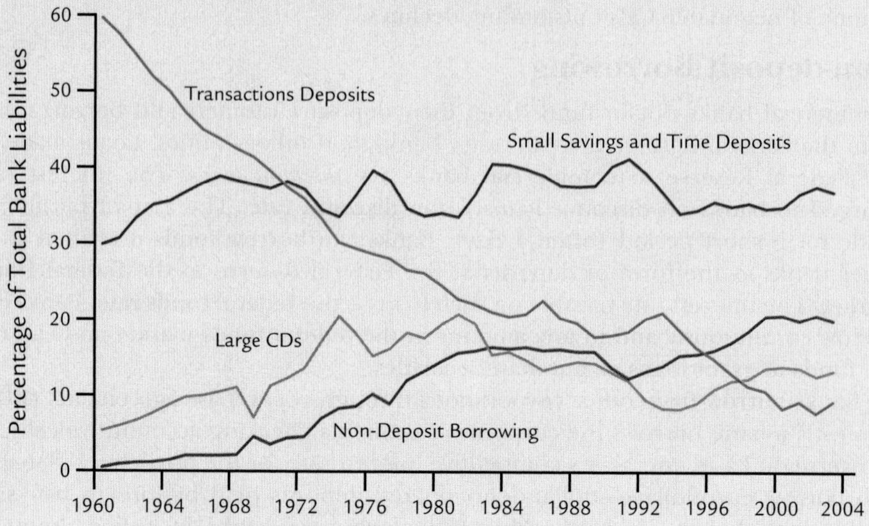


*Source: Federal Reserve Flow of Funds Accounts at Federal Reserve Board of Governors' web site* http://www.federalreserve.gov

## COMMERCIAL BANK ASSETS

Commercial banks use their funds primarily to purchase income-earning assets. On the aggregate commercial bank balance sheet shown in Table 9-1, bank assets are divided into four categories: cash assets, loans, securities, and other assets. Approximately 85 percent of total bank assets are *income-earning assets*—that is, loans and securities.

**legal reserves (reserves)** currency and coins in the bank plus the bank's deposit balance at the Federal Reserve

**reserve requirements (required reserve ratios)** percentage figure that depository institutions are required to hold in reserves to support deposit liabilities

Acquisition of earning assets by commercial banks is constrained by Federal Reserve regulations requiring banks to maintain a certain percentage of their deposit liabilities in the form of non-interest-earning **legal reserves (reserves).** A bank's reserves include currency and coins in the bank plus the bank's deposit balance at the Federal Reserve. The regulations mandating the holding of reserves are **reserve requirements (required reserve ratios).** Reserve requirements apply only to transactions deposits (demand deposits, NOW accounts, and ATS accounts), although in the past reserve requirements also were levied against savings and time deposits and occasionally against other bank liabilities. Chapter 18 discusses reserve requirements in detail. Here we only emphasize that reserve requirements modestly limit the portion of a bank's funds that can be used to make loans and purchase securities.

### Cash Assets

Cash assets provide banks with the funds to meet reserve requirements and the liquidity to help meet the potential withdrawal of deposits and accommodate new loan demand. The cash assets category includes currency and coins (called *vault cash* because the funds are placed in the bank vault after business hours), deposits with Federal Reserve banks, deposits with other banks, and cash items in the process of collection (see Table 9-1). Banks keep currency and coins on hand to meet (a) the public's demand for them and (b) reserve requirements. Besides helping meet reserve requirements, bank deposits with Federal Reserve banks facilitate check clearing through the Federal Reserve's check collection system.

Collectively, commercial banks hold large demand deposit balances in other banks. The deposits derive from the system of *correspondent banking,* in which smaller banks maintain deposits in larger banks in return for a variety of services. Services include check collection, investment counsel, and assistance with transactions in securities and foreign currencies. The correspondent banking system extends to the nation's smaller banks the expertise and economies of scale enjoyed by large banks. The smaller banks maintain deposit balances with the larger correspondent banks in compensation for services rendered.

"Cash items in the process of collection" refers to the dollar value of checks recently deposited in commercial banks but not yet credited to the recipient banks' deposit accounts with the Federal Reserve. The item corresponds to an item included in the "other liabilities" category on the liability side of the balance sheet, indicating the value of checks deposited in banks that will be *debited* later against other banks on which the checks were written.

As a share of total bank assets, cash assets have declined from approximately 20 percent some 50 years ago to less than 5 percent today. Declining cash assets has contributed favorably to bank profitability. A large and steady reduction in the portion of total bank liabilities contributed by deposits subject to reserve requirements, periodic reductions in reserve requirements over the years, and competitive pressures to maintain bank profitability account for the relative decline in cash assets.

## Loans

Loans are the largest single source of income for banks, providing more than 50 percent of total bank revenue today. Bank loans, unlike securities, often involve a personal relationship between banker and borrower. Types of bank loans include (in order of magnitude) real estate, business, and consumer loans. Banks consider loans to be less liquid than other assets. Banks typically cannot cash in loans before the loans come due, unlike securities, which can be sold at any time. Loans have a higher default risk than other bank assets. Loans yield the highest rate of return among bank assets in compensation for lower liquidity and higher risk.

**Real Estate Loans.** Real estate loans include long-term mortgages on residential and business properties, short-term loans to building contractors, and home equity loans. Real estate loans are relatively illiquid. Some real estate loans involve both interest rate risk and default risk. Banks issuing and holding fixed-rate mortgages are at risk when interest rates rise significantly after the loans are made. The default risk in real estate loans derives from a possible decline in values of the real estate used as collateral for the loans. During the late 1980s and early 1990s, many U.S. banks suffered major losses on commercial real estate loans and became insolvent. Banks now reduce the risk in real estate (and other) loans by issuing variable-rate mortgages and, more importantly, by packaging individual mortgages and other loans in *securitized* form. **Securitization,** an important financial innovation, involves the transformation of illiquid assets such as individual mortgages and car loans into highly marketable capital market instruments. Banks bundle a large number of individual mortgages or car loans into standardized packages and sell the packages to institutions such as life insurance companies, pension funds, and

**securitization**
transformation of illiquid financial assets into highly marketable capital market instruments

mutual funds. The banks originating the individual mortgages and car loans collect monthly interest and principal payments, which the banks "pass through" (after deducting a fee for the service) to the package buyer.

**Business Loans.** Banks have a comparative advantage in making business loans relative to other financial intermediaries such as life insurance companies. Banks are equipped to deal with the problem of asymmetric information involved in business borrowing. Banks' familiarity with corporate and other business depositors allows them to evaluate and monitor prospective borrowers. Banks consider business loans to be high-priority items. A large portion of demand deposit balances today are held by business firms. Bankers feel they must accommodate reasonable loan requests from established businesses in order to retain the deposit accounts and maintain a reputation as a reliable source of funds. Small and mid-sized banks lend heavily to local businesses.

Many banks extend a *line of credit* to their business customers. This arrangement guarantees a business firm access to short-term bank loans. The bank makes a *loan commitment* to the firm, typically allowing the firm to borrow on demand. In exchange for this valuable privilege, the customer must maintain a *compensating balance,* usually a non–interest-bearing checking account averaging perhaps 10 percent of the line of credit. A compensating balance raises the cost of the arrangement to the business customer and compensates the bank for the costs involved in guaranteeing a source of funds ready at all times on short notice.

Business loan demand exhibits a marked *pro-cyclical* pattern, rising during economic expansions and declining during recessions. During economic expansions, banks obtain funds to accommodate rising business loan demand by selling short-term U.S. government securities, issuing negotiable CDs, and increasing nondeposit borrowing. During economic downturns when business loan demand declines, banks use the proceeds of loan repayments to purchase short-term government securities, pay off holders of maturing negotiable CDs, and reduce other forms of bank borrowing.

**Consumer Loans.** Banks grant loans to individuals, commonly known as *consumer loans,* through several arrangements. Many consumer loans are for durable goods, such as automobiles. Other loans finance ongoing consumption, such as credit card purchases. Consumer loans are especially suitable for banks, which can take advantage of information they have about the financial condition of their depositors and other prospective borrowers.

Credit card loans and bank overdraft arrangements granting on-the-spot consumer loans that prevent check bouncing are sometimes known as *instant credit lines.* These loans, ushered in by the record-keeping efficiency of computer technology, are automatic lines of credit to consumers. The first credit card was issued in 1952 by the Franklin Bank of New York. A credit card, such as VISA or MasterCard, gives the customer a preauthorized line of credit from the bank issuing the card. Customers use the card to obtain cash advances from the thousands of banks and ATMs accepting the card. Overdraft privileges provide automatic credit when customers write checks in excess of demand deposit balances. The bank grants a loan to the customer in the amount of the overdraft by debiting the customer's credit card or making an automatic direct loan.

Credit card loans are extremely profitable for banks. First, the bank issuing the card pays the store or seller of the good an amount involving a discount of 1 to 3 percent of the transaction value. The interest rates charged on credit card balances often are extremely high. As a result, banks typically earn a *gross* return on credit

**Exhibit 9-1** Changing Composition of Bank Loans

The shares of total commercial bank loans constituted by real estate, business, and consumer loans have changed considerably over the past 30 years. As illustrated in the accompanying figure, the role of business (commercial) loans and consumer loans has declined, while the relative importance of real estate loans has increased sharply, especially since the mid-1980s. Today, real estate loans account for about half of total commercial bank loans. Business loans and consumer loans (including credit card loans) account for approximately 20 percent and 15 percent, respectively.

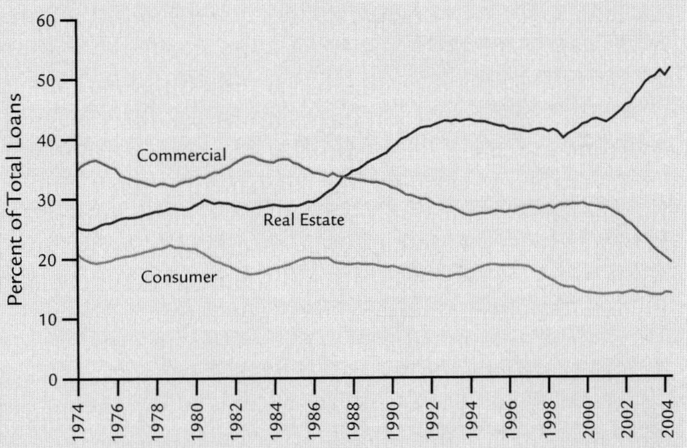


The decline in the relative importance of business loans in bank loan portfolios is largely due to the development of the commercial paper and junk bond markets as sources of funds for corporations. Large, financially stable companies increasingly borrow at appreciably lower interest rates by avoiding the "middleman" (banks) and directly marketing their paper to money market mutual funds and other buyers. Less stable corporations increasingly tap the junk bond market as a source of funds. The expanding role of real estate loans can be partly explained by the decline in corporate borrowing from banks, which stimulated banks to search for alternative earning assets. The trend partly derives from the advent of securitization of mortgages, which makes real estate loans more liquid, less risky, and much more attractive to banks.

card loans more than 10 percentage points higher than interest rates on U.S. Treasury bills. The costs of bank funds, bill processing, and writing off bad credit card loans must be subtracted from the gross return. Given that bank loan losses on customer credit card balances have averaged less than 3 percent in recent years, credit card loans are clearly an attractive source of income for banks.

**Other Loans.** Other types of bank loans include loans to financial institutions; loans to dealers, brokers, and individuals to carry stocks; loans to farmers; and "federal funds sold." "Federal funds sold" refers to commercial bank deposits at the Federal Reserve loaned to other banks. Its counterpart, "federal funds purchased," is included in the liability item "Borrowings" in Table 9-1. Exhibit 9-1 discusses the changing composition of bank loans since 1974.

## Securities

Securities are an important item on the bank balance sheet. Securities account for about one fourth of bank assets and contribute approximately 15 percent of bank income. The item consists almost entirely of debt instruments because banks are not permitted to purchase shares of corporate stock.[2] Among the securities or "investments" banks hold are U.S. government and government agency securities and state and local government bonds.

U.S. government and agency securities are highly liquid because of the well-developed and active market in which they are traded. U.S. Treasury securities have virtually zero default risk because they are issued by the federal government. However, these securities are subject to *market risk*—the risk of falling prices resulting from rising interest rates. Most securities held by banks have short maturities, so the prices of securities change only modestly in response to fluctuating market interest rates. The market risk, for example, in U.S. Treasury bills is quite minimal, as we demonstrated in Chapter 3. Longer-term government securities have appreciable market risk.

State and local government securities offer a potential tax advantage to banks. Interest income earned on the securities is nontaxable by the IRS (and by the state government if the bond is issued by state or locality in which the bank resides). However, these securities are riskier than U.S. government securities because state and local governments occasionally default on their obligations. In the past 20 years, the portion of total commercial bank assets allocated to state and local government bonds has declined significantly. Federal tax legislation in the 1980s and 1990s reduced marginal tax rates for banks and other corporations, making the tax-free status of interest income on state and local government bonds a less compelling reason to buy these bonds.

Figure 9-3 illustrates the trend in the ratio of bank loans to total assets and the ratios of bank holdings of U.S. Treasury securities to total assets and municipal

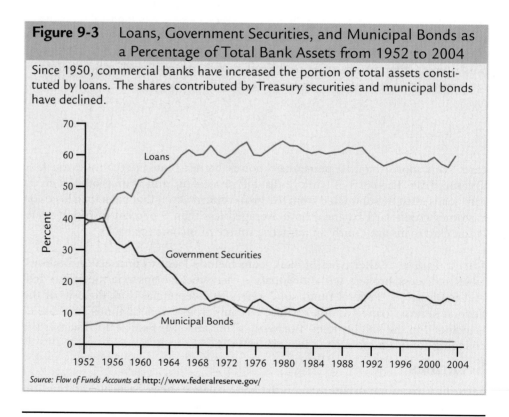

**Figure 9-3** Loans, Government Securities, and Municipal Bonds as a Percentage of Total Bank Assets from 1952 to 2004

Since 1950, commercial banks have increased the portion of total assets constituted by loans. The shares contributed by Treasury securities and municipal bonds have declined.

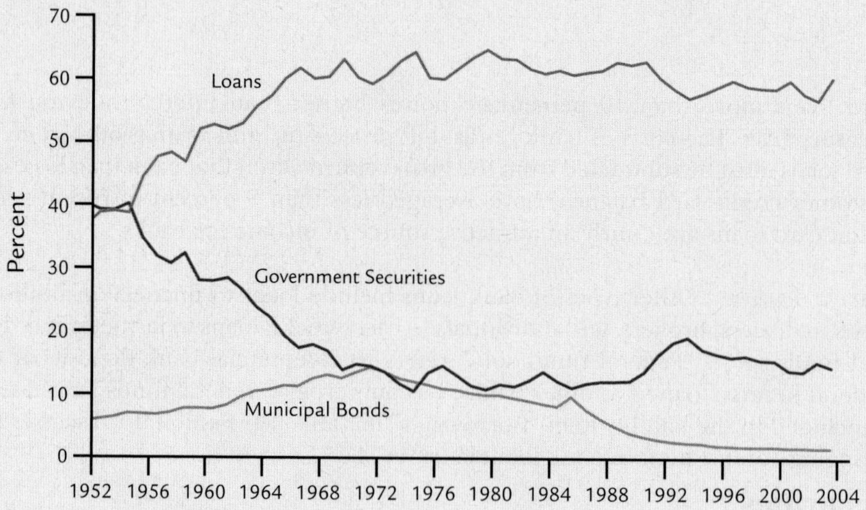


*Source: Flow of Funds Accounts at* http://www.federalreserve.gov/

[2] Many commercial banks buy stocks, but only for trusts, estates, and pension funds they manage for their clients. Banks are not permitted to purchase corporate stocks or corporate bonds for the bank's own portfolio.

bonds to total assets over the past half century. The ratios of Treasury securities to total assets and of municipal bonds to total assets have trended downward, while the loans to total assets ratio has risen. Several factors explain these trends—the increasing cost of bank funds and the resulting need for banks to increase their average rate of return on assets, the long-term increase in the demand for bank loans (especially real estate loans), and the availability to banks of alternative sources of liquidity other than short-term government securities. Banks today obtain funds by issuing negotiable CDs, borrowing in the federal funds market, and, for those banks organized as bank holding companies, issuing commercial paper. Banks with access to these fund sources need not hold as many liquid assets as in earlier times.

### Other Assets

Other bank assets include the physical assets of the bank, such as bank buildings, computers, data processing equipment, automatic teller machines, and furniture. Accounts receivable and the collateral that banks repossessed from borrowers in default are included in this category.

## COMMERCIAL BANK CAPITAL ACCOUNTS

Listed beneath "other liabilities" on the aggregate bank balance sheet in Table 9-1 is bank capital, or capital accounts. The difference between total assets and total liabilities, it is the bank's *net worth*—the owners' equity stake in the bank. Bank capital derives from the issue of shares of bank stock and from *retained earnings*—profits earned by the bank that are not paid out to the stockholders (owners). In June 2004, the aggregate capital accounts of all U.S. commercial banks was 8.2 percent of total bank assets (review Table 9-1).

Bank capital is a cushion protecting the bank's owners from potential insolvency due to contraction in the value of the bank's total assets. **Bank insolvency** occurs when the value of a bank's total assets falls below the value of the bank's total liabilities—that is, when the bank's capital accounts become negative. When this imbalance occurs, regulatory authorities either close the bank or arrange for new owners and managers to take over the bank. The original owners lose their equity stake in the bank.

**bank insolvency**
state of financial condition in which the value of a bank's total assets is less than the value of the bank's total liabilities

Consider the hypothetical balance sheet of the Bank of Muddy Gap (Wyoming) before and after the regulatory authorities force the bank to write off $600,000 worth of bad loans to ranchers. Before the bad-loan write-off, the bank had $11 million of total assets and $10.5 million of total liabilities, so its capital was (positive) $0.5 million.

When the bank writes off bad loans (right-hand balance sheet), the banks' loans and total assets decrease by the amount of the write-off. Given no change in the bank's total liabilities in this example, the bank's capital account also decreases by the amount of the write-off ($0.6 million). Because the bank's capital accounts are now negative (−$0.1 million), the bad-loan write-off places the Bank of Muddy Gap into insolvency. The regulatory authorities close the bank or sell the bank to new owners. (Exhibit 9-2 discusses how banks use *loan loss reserves* to provide a contingency fund against bad loans.)

Frequently, a bank's capital becomes *significantly* negative by the time regulatory authorities take action. The authorities then must compensate an existing bank to take over the failed bank. Hence, bank capital is a cushion protecting the FDIC against potential losses, thereby protecting U.S. taxpayers. Bank capital also is a cushion protecting depositors with accounts in excess of $100,000 (the FDIC in-

**Bank of Muddy Gap (Before Loan Write-off)**

| Assets | | Liabilities | |
|---|---|---|---|
| Cash assets | $1.0m | Deposits | $10.0m |
| Loans | 7.0 | Other liabilities | 0.5 |
| Securities | 2.0 | Total liabilities | 10.5 |
| Other assets | 1.0 | Capital | 0.5 |
| Total assets | 11.0 | Total liabilities and capital | 11.0 |

**Bank of Muddy Gap (After Loan Write-off)**

| Assets | | Liabilities | |
|---|---|---|---|
| Cash assets | $1.0m | Deposits | $10.0m |
| Loans | 6.4 | Other liabilities | 0.5 |
| Securities | 2.0 | Total liabilities | 10.5 |
| Other assets | 1.0 | Capital | −0.1 |
| Total assets | 10.4 | Total liabilities and capital | 10.4 |

All values are given as million dollars.

surance coverage limit). We discuss how banks manage bank capital later in this chapter.

## COMMERCIAL BANK MANAGEMENT

Commercial banks are business firms. Like all firms, banks strive to earn a solid profit. The object of commercial bank management is to earn robust profits while maintaining an extremely low exposure to possible insolvency. To protect against insolvency, a commercial bank takes precautionary measures ensuring that the value of its assets exceeds the value of its liabilities *at all times.* A bank becomes insolvent if, at any point in time, losses from securities, defaulted loans, or other investments depress the value of the bank's assets below the value of the bank's liabilities.

A bank is considered solvent if the bank can, in an orderly manner—perhaps over several weeks—sell all its assets and obtain sufficient revenues to meet its liabilities. Bank solvency must be distinguished from bank *liquidity,* which is a bank's ability to *immediately* meet currency withdrawals, check clearings, withdrawals of CDs, and legitimate new loan demand while abiding by existing reserve requirements. Banks employ skillful *liquidity management* and *capital management* to maintain financial viability. In the remainder of this chapter, we discuss these management tools and the techniques of *liability management.*

### Liquidity Management

Let's begin our discussion of liquidity management by illustrating how currency withdrawal and check clearing affect the bank's balance sheet and the bank's reserve position. To illustrate this, we use **T-accounts**—statements of the *change* in the balance sheet resulting from a given event. The T-account conveniently illustrates the *change* in the balance sheet rather than the total balance sheet before and after the event.

**T-accounts**
a device showing the change in the balance sheet resulting from a given event

Suppose a customer withdraws $200 in cash from a savings account at the Bank of Medicine Bow, Wyoming. The T-account indicates the balance sheet change as follows:

**Bank of Medicine Bow**

| | | | |
|---|---|---|---|
| Cash | −200 | Savings deposits | −200 |

## Exhibit 9-2 Loan Loss Reserves

Occasionally you read that a bank has increased its *loan loss reserves* or reserves for bad loans. Don't confuse loan loss reserves with the reserves banks maintain on the asset side of their balance sheet—that is, cash plus deposits at the Federal Reserve. Loan loss reserves are an entirely different animal, recorded on the right-hand side of the balance sheet in the capital accounts.

Under U.S. tax law, banks can build up reserves for future loan losses from their flow of current income. Loans later declared uncollectable can be charged against this account so that bad-loan write-offs do not sharply reduce the bank's reported current income in the year the losses are taken. When a bank loan is written off, the bank's balance sheet shows equal deductions to bank assets (in the form of loans) and to capital accounts (in the form of the bank's stock of loan loss reserves).

When a bank anticipates writing off a substantial amount of bad loans over the next couple of years, the bank typically sets aside considerable loan loss reserves from the current year's profits. The bank takes this action for several reasons. First, the bank signals the anticipated future losses in advance and seeks to assure the public that the bank can easily handle them. The bank hopes to gain credibility even as it acknowledges its bad judgment in granting the loans. Second, in setting aside additional loan loss reserves, a bank reduces its current reported profits, thereby reducing its current tax liability. Because deferring taxes is advantageous, moving tax write-offs from the future to the present is beneficial to the bank.

In the late 1980s and early 1990s, many bank loans turned into bad loans. As the accompanying figure shows, banks set aside a large amount of loan loss reserves during 1989, 1990, and 1991.

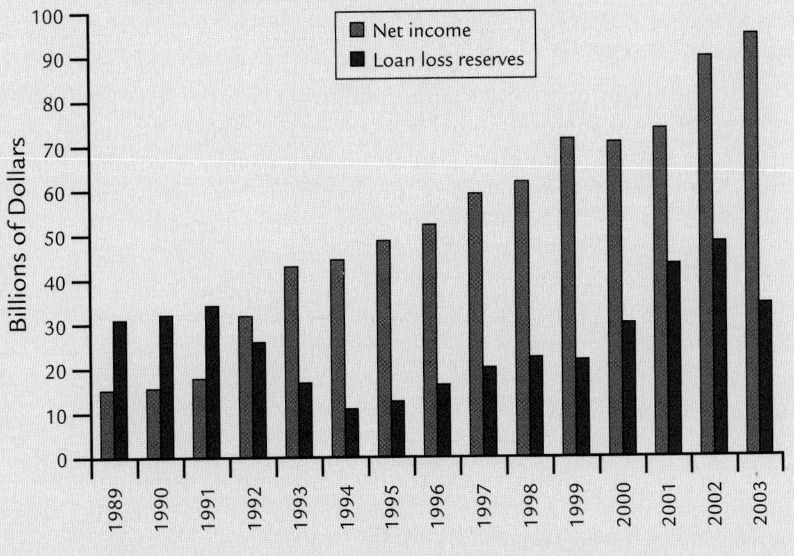


In those years, loan loss provisions exceeded bank net income. The increased provision for loan losses penalized reported bank profits in those years but contributed to the robust profits reported in subsequent years. The banking industry has prospered in the early years of the twenty-first century. Collective net income of commercial banks from 1999 to 2003 was more than five times larger than that reported from 1987 to 1991.

The bank simply presents the customer $200 in currency and debits the savings account by $200. The bank's *reserves* (cash plus deposit at the Federal Reserve) decline by $200 because the withdrawal of currency from a bank reduces bank reserves dollar for dollar. Unless the bank was holding **excess reserves**—reserves above the required amount—the bank now is short on reserves. The bank must obtain additional reserves in order to abide by the Fed's reserve requirements.

**excess reserves**
depository institution reserves (cash and deposits at Fed) above the required amount

A similar situation results when a check written by a bank customer clears. Suppose a customer of the Bank of Medicine Bow writes a $12,000 check to a discount N.Y. brokerage firm for payment of newly purchased shares of stock. The Bank of Medicine Bow, like all banks, maintains deposits at the Federal Reserve. The Fed clears the check by debiting the Bank of Medicine Bow's deposit account at the Fed and crediting the account of the N.Y. bank of the brokerage firm. When the check is processed and cleared, the T-account of the Bank of Medicine Bow appears as follows:

| Bank of Medicine Bow | | | |
|---|---|---|---|
| Deposit at Federal Reserve | −12,000 | Demand deposits | −12,000 |

How does this happen? The brokerage firm deposits the check in its account in a N.Y. commercial bank, which sends the check to the Federal Reserve. The Fed debits the reserve account of the Bank of Medicine Bow by $12,000, credits the reserve account of the brokerage firm's New York bank by $12,000, and sends the check back to the Bank of Medicine Bow. The Bank of Medicine Bow then debits the customer's demand deposit account by $12,000. Importantly, the Bank of Medicine Bow loses reserves in the amount of the check ($12,000) and must replenish its reserves, unless the bank initially had excess reserves.[3]

To recap, withdrawal of currency and/or clearing of checks written on a bank reduce the bank's reserves by the amount of the transaction. On the other hand, deposit of currency into a bank account and/or clearing of checks deposited into a customer's account increase the bank's reserves dollar for dollar. According to the law of averages, withdrawals and deposits approximately cancel out so that a bank's reserves remain roughly constant over a given week or month. However, banks sometimes experience appreciable short-term fluctuations in their reserve positions.

The critical questions facing bank management are the following: How severe is the bank's exposure to appreciable reserve losses of the type illustrated, and what actions must the bank take in the event of a large loss of reserves? If a bank is minimally exposed to large reserve losses or can recover potential reserve losses easily without incurring major costs, the bank is in sound financial condition even with a relatively small capital account. On the other hand, if a bank is exposed to large deposit outflows and can obtain reserves only at substantial cost, the bank can find itself in serious trouble even with a relatively large capital account. Banks exhibiting higher risk need larger capital accounts. We now examine the trade-off between bank liquidity and bank risk.

[3]The dollar amount of required reserves declines because of the reduction in demand deposits in the Bank of Medicine Bow, so the bank need not recover the full $12,000 worth of reserves lost. With a 10 percent reserve requirement, required reserves decline by $1,200. The bank needs to obtain only $10,800 worth of new reserves—that is, $12,000 − $1,200.

**Liquidity–Risk Trade-off.** To see the importance of liquidity management, consider the following (simplified) balance sheet of Imprudent Bank. Assume the reserve requirement for deposits is 10 percent.

| Imprudent Bank | | | |
|---|---|---|---|
| **Assets (millions of dollars)** | | **Liabilities (millions of dollars)** | |
| Reserves (cash + deposits at the Federal Reserve) | 40 | Deposits (DDO) | 400 |
| Marketable securities | 10 | Capital accounts | 40 |
| Loans | 390 | | |
| Total assets | 440 | Total liabilities and capital | 440 |

Imprudent Bank, with reserves of $40 million, just meets the 10 percent reserve requirement established by the Fed. The bank holds checking deposits (DDO) of $400 million, so the required reserves are $40 million (10% × $400 million). The bank has no excess reserves. The bank also holds $10 million in marketable U.S. government securities and $390 million worth of loans. Imprudent Bank allocated an extremely high proportion (almost 90 percent) of its total assets to loans because loans provide a higher rate of return than securities. The right-hand side of the balance sheet indicates that the bank has capital in the amount of $40 million, representing a relatively high capital to total assets ratio of 9.1 percent.

Suppose rumors circulate that a large portion of Imprudent Bank's loans is in trouble due to severe problems in the real estate sector, to which Imprudent Bank made large loans. Some depositors with more than $100,000 (the FDIC insurance ceiling) in their accounts withdraw their deposits. Suppose depositors withdraw 5 percent of the bank's total deposits, or $20 million, by writing checks on the demand deposits and moving the funds to safer banks. The new balance sheet for Imprudent Bank after the checks clear is as follows:

| Imprudent Bank | | | |
|---|---|---|---|
| **Assets (millions of dollars)** | | **Liabilities (millions of dollars)** | |
| Reserves | 20 | Deposits (DDO) | 380 |
| Marketable securities | 10 | Capital accounts | 40 |
| Loans | 390 | | |
| Total assets | 420 | Total liabilities and capital | 420 |

Imprudent Bank's reserves have dropped to $20 million, but its required reserves are now $38 million (10% × $380 million).[4] The bank is $18 million short on reserves. The bank can sell off its marketable securities to gain an additional $10 million of reserves, but it still would be $8 million short of reserves needed to meet the Fed's reserve requirement.

The Bank must attempt to gain $8 million of additional reserves, either by reducing loans or obtaining funds through the liability side of the balance sheet. Both options are difficult and costly. Imprudent Bank may have difficulty borrowing funds because of the widespread rumors of its troubled loans. Would you lend to a

[4] When the customers of Imprudent Bank write checks for $20 million, the Federal Reserve clears the checks by debiting Imprudent Bank's reserve account by $20 million (and crediting the reserve accounts of the banks in which the checks are deposited by $20 million).

bank you suspect will fail? Bank loans are relatively illiquid assets—they are contractual agreements that typically cannot be called in before they come due. The bank can sell its loans to other banks. However, because of information problems (the bank knows its customers better than other banks do), the bank likely sells the loans at a discount to their true value—that is, at prices significantly lower than the amounts of outstanding loans. In doing so, the bank takes a loss—a dollar-for-dollar hit against its capital account. This loss, added to the bad loans (assuming the rumors were true), increases the likelihood that the bank will become insolvent and subsequently closed or sold to new owners.

Imprudent Bank was too aggressive. The bank took big risks to achieve the greater short-run profitability associated with a high loan to total assets ratio. In the next section, we consider the trade-off between bank liquidity and profitability.

**Liquidity–Profitability Trade-off.** Now consider the balance sheet of Prudential Bank, a highly conservative and cautious institution.

| Prudential Bank | | | |
|---|---|---|---|
| **Assets (millions of dollars)** | | **Liabilities (millions of dollars)** | |
| Reserves | 50 | Deposits (DDO) | 400 |
| Marketable securities | 190 | Capital accounts | 40 |
| Loans | 200 | | |
| Total assets | 440 | Total liabilities and capital | 440 |

This hypothetical bank is extremely conservative and risk averse. In fact, the bank is *excessively* concerned about liquidity. Prudential Bank has exactly the same amount of liabilities and capital as Imprudent Bank but has a much more liquid asset structure. Prudential Bank has \$10 million in excess reserves (\$50 million − 10% × \$400 million) and a huge portfolio of marketable securities. It has lots of *secondary reserves*—excess reserves and interest-bearing liquid assets that can be quickly and conveniently converted to actual reserves (cash and deposits at the Fed).[5]

Suppose the rumors about bad loans that brought down Imprudent Bank circulate about Prudential Bank as well. Depositors withdraw \$20 million, but Prudential Bank still has \$30 million left in reserves. The bank's required reserves are now \$38 million, but the bank is short by only \$8 million. The bank can easily liquidate a small portion of its marketable securities, obtaining enough funds to meet the reserve requirement. Prudential Bank does not have to sell off any loans. Prudential Bank clearly is in a better position to handle the bad-loan rumor than Imprudent Bank was. If necessary, Prudential Bank can write off as much as 20 percent of its loan portfolio and still remain solvent. In contrast, write-offs of slightly more than 10 percent of Imprudent Bank's loans would bankrupt that institution.

This example illustrates the trade-off between bank liquidity and bank profitability. Prudential Bank, in its obsession to minimize risk, penalized its own profits by maintaining a large amount of excess reserves (which earn no interest) and an unusually low ratio of loans to total assets. (Remember that loans earn a higher rate of return for banks than securities). Contrast this with Imprudent Bank. In its single-minded quest for profits, Imprudent Bank maintained an illiquid and highly risky asset structure, with almost 90 percent of its assets in loans. In normal and good times, Imprudent Bank earns a higher profit than Prudential Bank. However, Imprudent

[5] Secondary reserves of a bank are defined to include excess reserves, short-term U.S. government securities, federal funds sold (loaned to other banks), and certain other highly liquid earning assets.

Bank is significantly exposed to possible insolvency if a significant portion of its assets turns sour. Almost all real-world banks maintain a balance sheet somewhere between the extremes exhibited by Imprudent Bank and Prudential Bank.

**Indicators of Bank Liquidity.** Several indicators of the liquidity of a particular bank or the commercial banking system exist. One indicator is the ratio of bank loans to total assets and the corresponding ratio of securities to total assets. A lower ratio of loans to total assets and a higher ratio of Treasury securities to total assets indicates a more liquid banking system. Another indicator is the ratio of cash assets to total assets. A higher ratio, given other factors indicates a more liquid banking system.

Indicators point to a decline in bank liquidity over the past 50 years. Bank loans as a percentage of total assets have increased from 35 percent in the early 1950s to approximately 60 percent today (review Figure 9-3). Treasury securities have declined from about 40 percent of total assets in the 1950s to less than 15 percent today.[6] On the other hand, the *need* for a highly liquid bank asset structure has also declined for at least two reasons. First, the share of total bank deposits constituted by demand deposits and other checkable deposits has declined sharply over the past 45 years, from more than 60 percent in 1960 to less than 10 percent today. With a larger share of bank funds coming from savings and time deposits, which have lower turnover rates, a typical bank needs less liquidity in its asset structure today than formerly. Second, since 1960, banks have increasingly turned to the liability side of the balance sheet to obtain funds when needed. In the next section, we turn to the topic of bank liability management.

**YOUR TURN**

Considering the balance sheets of two banks, HC Bank and LC Bank, answer the following:

**a.** Calculate the capital to total assets ratio of each bank.

**b.** Which bank exhibits a more liquid asset structure? Explain.

**c.** Over time, which bank likely will exhibit more variability in its deposits and reserves?

**d.** Which bank would cause more concern to the banking regulatory authorities?

**HC (High Capital) Bank**

| Assets (millions of dollars) | | Liabilities (millions of dollars) | |
|---|---|---|---|
| Cash assets | 10 | Demand deposits | 80 |
| Short-term securities | 5 | Savings deposits | 15 |
| Long-term bonds | 25 | Small time deposits | 5 |
| Loans | 70 | Capital accounts | 10 |
| Total assets | 110 | Total liabilities and capital accounts | 110 |

[6] To the extent that the decline in the cash ratio reflects lower reserve requirements, bank liquidity is not reduced. The required portion of a bank's reserves cannot be used to meet currency withdrawals or adverse check clearings. These reserves are not a source of liquidity—they must be maintained (on average) to meet reserve requirements. Only excess reserves and other items the bank can sell off willingly and easily to raise funds are considered liquid assets. A significant portion of the decline in the ratio of cash items to total assets reflects periodic reductions in reserve requirements over the years.

| LC (Low Capital) Bank | | | |
|---|---|---|---|
| **Assets (millions of dollars)** | | **Liabilities (millions of dollars)** | |
| Cash assets | 20 | Demand deposits | 30 |
| Short-term securities | 25 | Savings deposits | 20 |
| Long-term bonds | 25 | Small time deposits | 50 |
| Loans | 35 | Capital accounts | 5 |
| Total assets | 105 | Total liabilities and capital accounts | 105 |

## Liability Management

Before the 1960s, most commercial banks took their liabilities (sources of funds) as given. Prohibitions on the payment of interest on checking accounts and the statutory ceilings on interest rates payable on savings and time deposits prevented banks from competing aggressively for deposits. Furthermore, the federal funds market was relatively underdeveloped, and negotiable CDs and repurchase agreements had not yet been conceived. Other than mounting advertising and marketing campaigns, a bank could do little to gain additional funds at its own discretion. Banks passively accepted deposits and then decided how to allocate the funds among cash assets, loans, and securities. Banks practiced asset management but not liability management.

Starting in the 1960s, banks began watching for good lending opportunities and then find the funds to finance these loans. Today, a large bank with a profitable lending opportunity can obtain funds through several techniques. One is to "buy" federal funds—that is, borrow the reserve deposits of other banks at the Federal Reserve. Another is to issue negotiable CDs at whatever interest rate is required to attract funds. Banks also can issue repurchase agreements or borrow Eurodollars (dollar-denominated deposits in European or Caribbean banks or foreign branches of U.S. banks). Large banks organized as holding companies can obtain funds through the commercial paper market. Even mid-sized and relatively small banks practice liability management today. They borrow either through the federal funds market or by bidding for *brokered deposits*—pieces of large CDs that have been broken down into fully insurable $100,000 blocks for placement through money brokers. They also can borrow from the Federal Home Loan Bank and through private placements. Liability management has become pervasive among U.S. commercial banks, both large and small.

Today, many large banks target a desired growth rate of total assets. The banks then search for profitable lending opportunities and practice aggressive liability management, obtaining the funds to make the loans needed to achieve the targeted growth. Banks find liability management desirable because it permits them to make profitable loans that they otherwise would have to turn down. Liability management thus contributes strongly to bank profits. The growth of bank liability management is indicated by the increase in volume of bank negotiable CDs outstanding from $31 billion to more than $900 billion between 1965 and 2004. In the same period, the volume of federal funds purchased and bank security RP agreements outstanding also increased sharply.

Dangers are inherent in aggressive liability management. Bank assets typically have longer maturities than bank liabilities, so banks can suffer severe losses if in-

**Exhibit 9-3** Demise of Continental Illinois Bank

In May 1984, the huge $42 billion Continental Illinois Bank experienced a massive "run." The run was not the old-fashioned type, with customers lined up for blocks waiting to get their money. Continental Illinois, the largest bank in the Midwest and the nation's eighth largest in 1984, was a money center bank, like Citigroup and J.P. Morgan Chase. Its financial base consisted of huge deposits held by large corporations, money market mutual funds, and other multimillion dollar accounts. Such funds can be transferred electronically in seconds.

What caused the run on Continental Illinois? A little perspective is helpful. In the late 1970s, the bank fatefully decided to target a very high rate of growth. From 1977 to 1981, its loans expanded at a rate of 22 percent per year. Unfortunately, because Illinois law then prohibited banks from operating more than three branches, Continental lacked a large-scale, rapidly growing consumer deposit base. The bank aggressively purchased funds through liability management to finance its loan growth. The bank issued a huge amount of negotiable CDs, including more than $12 billion to foreign investors. In addition, the bank's asset structure was highly illiquid. The bank's loan to deposit ratio was 79 percent, in contrast to 67 percent for other money center banks and 56 percent for all U.S. banks at the time. Continental was taking big risks, using highly volatile sources of funds to finance an illiquid and risky asset structure.

Continental Illinois had large problem loans outstanding in the energy and agriculture sectors and major loans to troubled Latin American countries. The collapse began when the bank was forced to absorb large losses on energy-related loans it had purchased from the failed Penn Square Bank of Oklahoma City. Because most of Continental's deposits were in the form of huge CDs, only about $4 billion of its $29 billion of deposits were covered by FDIC insurance. As rumors circulated about other bad loans on Continental's books, depositors with large accounts panicked, and the stampede was on. Money market funds, U.S. corporations, and foreign customers withdrew their funds when their multimillion dollar CDs matured. In a few weeks the bank lost $10 billion, or about one third of its deposits.

Without massive aid, Continental would have failed immediately, possibly triggering a run on other banks. But the regulatory authorities did not wait. They implemented an unprecedented relief scheme involving an infusion of $2 billion of capital from federal banking agencies, a credit line of $5.5 billion from a consortium of 24 major U.S. banks, and an extended loan of $5 billion from the Federal Reserve. The FDIC waived the $100,000 insurance ceiling so that all depositors were fully covered (even this action failed to fully stem the run, as some depositors doubted the viability of the FDIC insurance fund). The FDIC, unable to find a suitable merger partner, was forced to purchase about $5 billion of questionable loans from the bank in exchange for 80 percent ownership of the bank. The FDIC later sold its portion of the bank (which no longer exists) to other banks.

terest rates rise sharply or the yield curve becomes inverted. If unfavorable rumors about a bank's financial condition circulate, a bank's sources of funds dry up quickly as large depositors cut and run. This phenomenon contributed to the failure of the huge Continental Illinois Bank in 1984, as customers holding multimillion dollar blocks of negotiable CDs withdrew the funds as the CDs matured (see Exhibit 9-3).

Despite Continental Illinois's experience, some banks act as if liquid funds can be borrowed as needed, almost without limit. The banks see little need to hold relatively low-yielding short-term marketable securities. However, the huge cash shortages experienced in recent years by some banks clearly indicate that liquidity needs cannot be ignored. In fact, the regulatory authorities may close a bank because of liquidity problems, even though the bank is technically solvent. In 1991, the Federal Reserve closed the $10 billion Southeast Bank of Miami when the bank failed to obtain sufficient cash to repay its loans from the Fed.

Liability management practices complicate the Federal Reserve's task. For example, the Fed sometimes implements a restrictive monetary policy to reduce aggregate expenditures in periods of excessively strong economic activity. If banks scramble to issue additional liabilities to fund surging loan demand, the Fed's ability to control aggregate expenditures is weakened. In the past, the Fed has occasionally imposed reserve requirements on certain managed liabilities to curb banks' attempts to circumvent the Fed's efforts to restrain bank credit growth.

## Capital Management

As indicated earlier, bank capital provides a bank with a financial cushion such that transitory adverse developments will not cause the bank to become insolvent. Essentially, bank capital protects large uninsured depositors and the FDIC insurance fund. Bank capital also protects bank managers and owners from their own mistakes. If a bank has substantial capital, reasonable investment mistakes can be made without wiping out owners' equity and terminating managers' careers.

Banks are exposed to various types of risk. First is *default risk*—the risk that a loan (or the interest thereon) will not be repaid or that a municipality will default on its bonds. Second is *interest rate risk*—the risk that interest rates will rise after securities have been purchased, depressing the price of the securities. Because bank assets typically have longer maturities than liabilities, rising interest rates increase the cost of funds without commensurately increasing the return earned on assets, impairing bank profits. Third, banks are subject to *liquidity risk*—the risk that depositors will withdraw their funds. Fourth, banks conducting business across national borders are exposed to *foreign exchange rate risk*—the risk that exchange rates will move in ways that cause bank losses. Fifth, banks making loans and investments abroad are exposed to *political* or *country risk*—the risk that a bank's funds or assets outside the United States will be confiscated or otherwise immobilized and prevented from returning to the United States. Finally, as evidenced by scandals at some of the largest U.S. banks, banks are increasingly subject to *management risk*—the risk that certain bank employees, in an age of highly esoteric (and little understood) financial instruments, will engage in activities involving enormous risk.[7]

Some of these risks can be hedged, at a cost, through derivatives and other financial instruments; other risks cannot. Banks knowingly take legitimate risks in order to earn an attractive rate of return. One of the most fundamental principles of finance is that, on average, riskier investments are associated with higher expected rates of return. A bank that is exceedingly risk averse earns a low rate of return on bank capital and alienates customers by denying them legitimate loans.

[7] Barings, a venerable British bank, became insolvent in 1995 because of the activities of a rogue trader employed by the bank. Nicholas Leeson, who gambled in derivatives with the bank's funds, lost more than $1 billion before his activities were exposed. Because the losses he ran up exceeded the bank's capital, he bankrupted the institution. Evidence suggests that upper bank management was aware of Leeson's activities but failed to stop them because his speculations prior to 1995 had contributed favorably to the bank's profits.

The predominant cause of bank insolvency is bad loans. Loans that appear sound when they are first made are sometimes rendered bad by changing economic conditions. For example, when oil prices collapsed in late 1985, thousands of loans made by banks in the "oil patch"—Texas, Oklahoma, Louisiana, and so forth—went into default as the dramatic decline in oil revenues rippled through the economies of these states, closing businesses and throwing people out of work. Hundreds of banks in these states failed in the following few years.

If other factors are held constant, a higher bank capital ratio (capital/assets) implies a lower risk of insolvency. On the other hand, a higher bank capital ratio implies a *lower* rate of return on capital earned by the bank's owners (the owners' equity is the capital account). Consider the following identity:

$$\text{(9-3)} \qquad \frac{\textbf{Earnings}}{\textbf{Capital}} = \frac{\textbf{Earnings}}{\textbf{Total assets}} \times \frac{\textbf{Total assets}}{\textbf{Capital}}$$

The left-hand side of the expression is the percentage rate of return earned by the bank's owners on their capital or equity in the bank. It is the *rate of return on equity* or *rate of return on capital.* The first expression on the right-hand side is the rate of return on total assets. It is an indicator of the bank's efficiency because it shows the profits earned per dollar of assets. The final expression, the ratio of total assets to capital, is the **equity multiplier.** The equity multiplier is simply the reciprocal of the bank's capital accounts to total assets ratio, expressing the amount of *leverage* applied to the rate of return on total assets. A high capital to assets ratio represents a *low* equity multiplier; a low capital to assets ratio implies a *high* equity multiplier.

**equity multiplier**
ratio of financial institution's total assets to capital; indicates magnitude of leverage applied to the rate of return on assets

Suppose a bank earns an annual profit of 1 percent on its total assets, approximately the average rate earned by U.S. banks over the past 20 years. If the bank has a capital to total assets ratio of 5 percent (an equity multiplier of 20), Equation (9-3) indicates that the owners will earn a rate of return on capital of 20 percent per year (1% × 20). Alternatively, if the capital to total assets ratio is 10 percent (indicating an equity multiplier of 10), the rate of return on capital will be only 10 percent per year (1% × 10). To bank management, a higher capital to total assets ratio has both advantages and disadvantages. A higher ratio reduces the risk of insolvency but also reduces the rate of return earned by the bank's owners. The bank must grapple with the clear trade-off between short-run profitability and the risk of insolvency. If a bank reduces its capital to assets ratio (increases leverage), it increases the rate of return on capital but also increases the bank's exposure to potential insolvency.

Figure 9-4 shows the rates of return U.S. banks have earned on total assets and on capital over the past 35 years. These rates of return have been higher in the past decade than in earlier times. Throughout the 10-year period ending in 2004, insured U.S. commercial banks earned an exceptionally high rate of return on total assets of more than 1.1 percent per year.

The preceding analysis suggests that for each bank some optimal ratio of capital to total assets exists. The optimal ratio depends on the nature of the bank's assets and liabilities and varies with economic conditions. For example, when a period of financial distress appears likely, a prudent bank takes steps to increase its capital ratio. A bank increasing its capital to assets ratio has three choices. First, the bank can increase retained earnings by reducing dividend payments to the bank's owners. Second, the bank can issue new shares of stock. Third, the bank can shrink its total assets by selling securities and reducing loans, using the proceeds to reduce bank borrowings or other liabilities. Unlike the first two alternatives, the third op-

**Figure 9-4** Rates of Return earned by U.S. Commercial Banks from 1968 to 2003

In the past 35 years, rates of return on commercial bank assets and capital have averaged roughly 0.9 percent per year and 12 percent per year, respectively. These rates have increased sharply since the 1990 to 1991 recession.

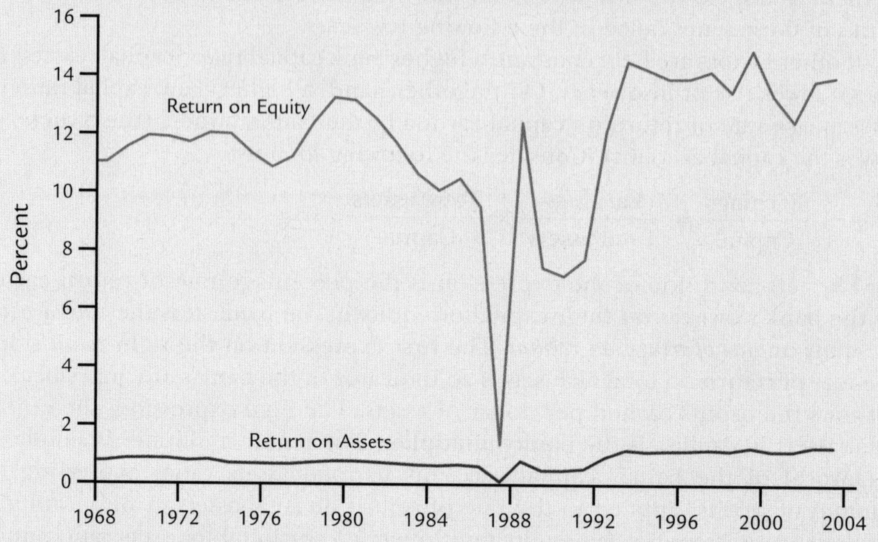


*Source: Data from Board of Governors of Federal Reserve System, Flow of Funds Accounts at* http://www.federalreserve.gov/releases, *click on Z.1 (historical data)*

tion does not increase actual bank capital. However, it does increase the ratio of capital to total assets by reducing the total bank assets.

In the early 1990s, many banks used the third option in the wake of financial distress, anemic bank profits, and depressed stock prices. Major U.S. banks suffered large loan losses in the late 1980s and early 1990s. The number of bank insolvencies soared from 6 per year, on average, from 1960 to 1979 to 150 per year from 1984 to 1992. Regulatory authorities reacted by imposing strict capital standards, which forced thousands of banks to increase their capital ratios. These banks reduced lending to bolster their capital ratios and comply with the new federal standards, creating a *capital credit crunch* in the process. Bank loans became unusually difficult to obtain as thousands of banks tightened their lending standards. Since then, robust profits earned by banks from 1992 to 2004 have further increased bank capital ratios. Even though banks experienced some problems during 2001 and 2002, they are in much stronger financial condition today than they were in the 1980s and early 1990s. From 1995 to 2004, U.S. commercial banks failures averaged only 5 per year.

In closing, it is clear that negative externalities are associated with bank failures—that is, the cost to society of a bank failure exceeds the cost borne by the failed bank. When a bank fails, large depositors and the FDIC insurance fund frequently incur losses (banks are seldom closed before the capital accounts become significantly negative). Also, the community incurs costs from resulting disruptions in credit flows. For these reasons, the capital to total assets ratio deemed optimal by the typical bank is lower than the optimal ratio from society's viewpoint. Most economists support regulatory authorities' imposition of binding capital standards on banks. We have more to say on this issue in Chapter 11.

# SUMMARY

Commercial banks, as the preeminent type of financial intermediary, are key players in the U.S. financial system. Banks take in funds by issuing deposits, borrowing from sources other than depositors, and obtaining equity funds from their owners. Banks use the funds primarily to extend loans to businesses, home buyers, consumers, and other borrowers and to purchase federal, state, and local government securities. A sound banking system is essential to the nation's economic health. To maintain financial viability, banks practice liquidity management and capital management. Although highly liquid assets such as Treasury bills provide relatively low rates of return, banks hold T-bills as protection against the cost of adjusting to deposit and currency outflows and the accompanying loss of reserves. A higher capital to total assets ratio reduces the rate of return on equity for bank owners but provides a larger cushion that reduces the risk of bank insolvency. In the past quarter century, U.S. banks have been challenged by macroeconomic shocks, financial innovations, globalization, and other events. In the 1980s and early 1990s, banking industry financial condition deteriorated, and more than 1,000 commercial banks failed. However, both the income statements and balance sheets of U.S. commercial banks have strengthened appreciably in the past decade.

## YOUR TURN ANSWERS

Page 221

**a.** HC Bank has a capital ratio of 9.1 percent. LC Bank has a capital ratio of 4.8 percent.

**b.** LC Bank has a much more liquid asset structure. It holds twice as many cash assets and five times as many short-term (relatively liquid) securities as HC Bank. It has only half as many loans, which are relatively illiquid (because banks cannot convert loans to cash until the loans come due).

**c.** HC Bank likely will exhibit a more variable deposit structure and greater variability in bank reserves over time. Eighty percent of its total deposits are demand deposits, as opposed to 30 percent for LC Bank. HC Bank has only one tenth the amount of small time deposits as LC Bank (small time deposits have much lower turnover or withdrawal rates than demand deposits).

**d.** Even though HC's capital ratio is nearly twice as high as LC's, the regulatory authorities are likely to be more critical of HC Bank. HC Bank's assets are more heavily weighted with loans, and it finances those assets with a more volatile liability structure than LC Bank does. As a result, HC Bank is much more likely to encounter liquidity problems. (Its holdings of cash and short-term securities are only one-third that of the LC Bank.) A much higher percentage of HC's assets is subject to market risk and default risk. It has twice as many loans (which are subject to default risk) as LC Bank does.

# KEY TERMS

balance sheet
assets
liabilities
net worth
capital accounts (capital)
transactions (checkable) deposits
demand deposits
negotiable order of withdrawal (NOW) accounts
automatic transfer service (ATS) accounts
disintermediation
money market deposit (MMDAs) accounts
discount rate
federal funds market
federal funds rate
legal reserves (reserves)
reserve requirement (required reserve ratio)
securitization
bank insolvency
T-accounts
excess reserves
equity multiplier

# STUDY QUESTIONS

**1.** List three sources and three uses of commercial bank funds.

**2.** Why have "cash items" and "securities" decreased as a proportion of total bank assets over the past 40 years? What has taken their place, and why? Explain.

**3.** What is meant by a bank's capital accounts? Suppose Hometown Bank has total assets of $800 million and capital accounts of $35 million. Suppose the regulatory authorities tell the bank it must increase its capital to total assets ratio to 5 percent. Explain the options open to Hometown Bank.

**4.** This Christmas, you decide to buy your true love a partridge in a pear tree. After consulting with several garden centers, you make your purchase by writing a check for $150. The garden center promptly deposits your check in its bank.

**A.** Using T-accounts, show the effect of this transaction on your bank and on the garden center's bank (after your check is processed and cleared by the Federal Reserve).

**B.** What happens to your bank's reserves? To the reserves of the garden center's bank?

**C.** Assuming the reserve requirement is 10 percent and your bank is not holding excess reserves, what is the level of excess reserves in your bank after the transaction?

**D.** List four possible methods your bank can use to remedy its reserve deficiency.

**5.** "The ratio of capital accounts to total assets is only one of many factors indicating the financial condition of a commercial bank." Evaluate this statement.

**6.** Your bank has total assets of $220 million and a capital to total assets ratio of 7 percent. You learn that your bank's entire $20 million loan package to Central American nations will be written off as bad loans. Will your bank survive this crisis? Explain.

**7.** Explain the difference between bank solvency and bank liquidity.

**8.** From the point of view of an asset manager of a commercial bank, discuss the trade-offs among the objectives of safety, liquidity, and profitability.

**9.** What is meant by the term *liability management*? Discuss the instruments banks use in liability management. What are the advantages and potential pitfalls of aggressive liability management for commercial banks?

**10.** Why does the volume of negotiable CDs outstanding rise and fall with economic expansion and contraction, respectively?

11. A large bank in your community has been invited to participate in an attractive large syndicated loan arrangement, but your bank does not have enough excess reserves to meet the terms of the agreement. How might your bank raise the funds to participate in the deal
    A. Through asset management?
    B. Through liability management?

12. Why might the FDIC and commercial bank stockholders have different opinions about the merits of a commercial bank maintaining a high capital accounts ratio? Discuss the trade-offs involved. Illustrate the trade-off with a numerical example.

13. Bill's Bank and Ted's Bank have dramatically different liability structures. Bill's bank, located in an affluent neighborhood, raises funds primarily by issuing small time deposits to neighborhood residents. Ted's bank, located in a working-class neighborhood, issues mostly checking accounts to its customers. How might you expect the portfolio of assets held by Bill's bank to differ from that held by Ted's bank? Explain.

14. Community Bank has total assets of $600 million, total liabilities of $564 million, and earned profits this year of $6 million. Calculate Community Bank's
    A. Rate of return on total assets
    B. Equity multiplier
    C. Rate of return on capital

## ADDITIONAL READING

- Each year in the Spring issue, the *Federal Reserve Bulletin* publishes an article entitled "Profits and Balance Sheet Developments at U.S. Commercial Banks," providing information for the previous calendar year. An excellent text devoted entirely to commercial banking is Peter Rose, *Commercial Bank Management,* 5th edition (Boston: McGraw-Hill, 2002).
- On bank failures and related issues, consult the Federal Deposit Insurance Corporation, *Annual Report of the FDIC,* published each year in April. It is available at the FDIC Web site at http://www.fdic.gov.
- An excellent journal article on banking is Allen Berger, Anil Kashyap, and Joseph Scalise, "The Transformation of the U.S. Banking Industry: What a Long Strange Trip It's Been," *Brookings Papers on Economic Activity,* 1995, No. 2, pp. 55–218.
- Pertinent articles in the regional Federal Reserve Bank publications include Kenneth Spong and Richard Sullivan, "The Outlook for the U.S. Banking Industry: What Does the Experience of the 1980s and 1990s Tell Us?" Federal Reserve Bank of Kansas City *Economic Review,* 1999:4 and Nicola Cetorelli, "Competition Among Banks: Good or Bad?" Federal Reserve Bank of Chicago *Economic Perspectives,* 2001:2.
- A wealth of data on commercial bank income and balance sheets is contained in Federal Deposit Insurance Corporation, *Statistics on Banking* at http://www.fdic.gov.

Chapter 10

# THE BANKING INDUSTRY: ITS EVOLUTION, STRUCTURE, AND REGULATION

The function of the banking system is the same in all countries—to collect and pool the funds of savers and channel those funds to borrowers. How this function is accomplished differs substantially across countries. The U.S. banking system has unique characteristics.

The U.S. banking system differs from the system of other industrialized countries in its structure and in the scope of activities in which banks are permitted to engage. The number of banks in the United States (nearly 8,000) stands in sharp contrast to the number in other industrialized nations. Germany has only about 300 banks, Japan has fewer than 100, and both England and Canada have fewer than 50. Traditionally, U.S. banks have been severely restricted in the range of activities in which they can engage and the services they can offer. These distinguishing limitations resulted from a web of regulatory legislation ostensibly designed to protect depositors from exploitation and insulate depositors from risk. In this chapter, we examine the effectiveness of these regulations in achieving their goals and analyze the effect of these regulations on consumers. We explore the regulatory environment's implications for *efficiency*—the ability of the banking system to provide services at the lowest possible cost. First, however, we pose an important and interesting question: Why is the U.S. banking system so different from those of other nations?

## EARLY HISTORY AND EVOLUTION OF U.S. BANKING

The forces that shaped our banking system are rooted in the U.S. struggle for independence from Great Britain in the late eighteenth century. The critical issues the founding fathers faced when forming our fledgling government are mirrored in the decisions that shaped our banking system.

In the nation's early years, a heated debate raged over the form the federal government should take. The initial attempt to form a federal government resulted in the Articles of Confederation, under which the new nation was organized as a loosely linked group of highly independent states. According to the Articles, the federal government had little power—the government's chief role was settling disputes among the states. The founding fathers, ultimately dissatisfied with the government produced by the Articles of Confederation, struggled bitterly to redefine the federal government's role. One prominent school of political thought, the Federalists, advocated a strong central government. The Federalists, led by Alexander Hamilton, envisioned a nation built on commerce and industry. In contrast, the Democratic-Republican Party (commonly referred to as the *Anti-*

*Federalists),* led by Thomas Jefferson, envisioned a rural, agrarian society with the states retaining political power.

Given the importance of commerce and industry in the United States today, you may have trouble understanding why Jeffersonian democrats so strongly favored an agricultural society with a distinctly limited role for the federal government. The reason was readily apparent at the time. Prior to the revolution, Americans had suffered under the concentrated political and economic power of Great Britain. Fear of living in an America with such concentration of power fueled the fires of Anti-Federalist thought.

## Bank of the United States

The debate between Federalists and Anti-Federalists greatly influenced the banking industry in its early years. Until the 1790s, banks were chartered not by the federal government but by individual state legislatures. Banks were forbidden from operating across state lines. Following the 1789 enactment of the U.S. Constitution, a compromise between Federalist and Anti-Federalist positions, Hamilton began a concentrated effort to form a nationally chartered bank—the Bank of the United States. Hamilton's reasons were twofold. First, the states had accumulated large debts during the Revolutionary War, debts that were to be assumed by the newly formed federal government. Hamilton believed that a nationally chartered bank could best hold this debt and manage the federal government's financial operations. Second, a vibrant industrial society requires a strong and stable financial sector. Hamilton envisioned a nationally chartered bank as the foundation of such a system. Central to this belief was the need for an official, uniform U.S. currency. At the time, U.S. money existed as notes issued by individual banks. Hamilton hoped a large national bank monopolizing the issue of the nation's currency would eliminate the risks of economic instability inherent in the variety of notes issued by state-chartered banks.

Jefferson advocated a strict interpretation of the Constitution, arguing that only the states could charter banks because the power to charter banks was not specifically granted to the federal government. In contrast, Hamilton maintained that the federal government could assume any powers not specifically prohibited by the Constitution. Hamilton prevailed, and in 1791 the **Bank of the United States** was established and granted a 20-year charter. The new bank was given the exclusive right to branch across state lines. Branching was so widespread that by the time the charter for the Second Bank of the United States (the first bank's successor) expired in 1836, the Second Bank controlled one third of all deposits in the U.S. banking system.

**Bank of the United States**
first national bank chartered in the United States

Jefferson's mistrust of the concentration of financial power was well founded. The Bank of the United States quickly caused difficulty for state-chartered banks. The Bank refused to accept their banknotes or accumulated large quantities of banknotes and presented them to the banks for redemption in gold all at once. Such acts can drive financially sound but illiquid banks into insolvency. The Bank of the United States also was accused of partisanship. The Bank allegedly discriminated against Anti-Federalists in granting loans and extended preferential treatment to commercial and industrial customers over agricultural customers.

Many state-chartered banks enjoyed virtual monopolies prior to national banking. Not surprisingly, the state banks mounted strong opposition when the Bank of the United States' charter came up for renewal in 1811. Appealing to populist sentiment, state banks claimed that national banking was siphoning funds from the country to the city, aiding industry at the expense of agriculture. Opponents of the

Bank of the United States staved off renewal of the Bank's charter until 1816, when a new charter was granted in hopes that a national bank could repair the financial havoc that followed the War of 1812. By the time Populist president Andrew Jackson refused to renew the Second Bank's charter in 1836, the lessons of national banking, real or perceived, were apparent: major concentration of financial power should be opposed. Given the prevalence of the view opposing concentration of financial power, many states adopted strict limits on branching, both across and within state borders. Some states outlawed branching altogether, allowing banks to operate out of one, and only one, office. Such **unit banking** provisions remained on the books in several states until the 1980s.

**unit banking**
system in which a bank is permitted to have only one office, with no branching permitted

## Free Banking Era

**Free Banking Era**
period from 1836 to 1863, characterized by minimal supervision of banking activity

Dissolution of the Bank of the United States ushered in the **Free Banking Era**—a period of little supervision of banking activities. Anyone willing to meet the lenient conditions imposed by state chartering bodies could organize a bank. The number of banks increased and banknotes proliferated.[1] The new system relieved many of the problems associated with national banking but created others. So many individual banks issued notes (paper currency), supposedly redeemable in gold, that distinguishing between genuine and counterfeit notes was difficult. Many banks, known as *wildcat banks,* located their offices in obscure and remote places to hinder the public's efforts to redeem their notes in gold. Notes of faraway banks and banks considered unsafe often circulated at a discount from face value. Merchants maintained books showing the currencies of different banks to establish the authenticity of notes received in trade and to determine the value at which they should be honored. Bank failures were common, although many failures resulted from systemic problems rather than fraud or mismanagement.

## National Banking Act of 1863

**National Banking Act of 1863**
legislation allowing the charting of national banks, thereby facilitating issuance of a uniform currency

The free banking era ended abruptly with passage of the **National Banking Act of 1863.** The impetus for this banking act was twofold. First, the obvious problems of free banking prompted sentiment for legislative reform. Second, the federal government needed a market for the new debt issued to finance the Civil War (1861–1865). The National Banking Act of 1863 allowed the federal government to charter national banks, thereby facilitating issuance of a uniform currency.[2] National banks were required to back their banknotes more than 100 percent with interest-bearing federal government bonds deposited with the Comptroller of the Currency. Note holders were to be repaid in full from these bonds if a national bank failed. The notes, being uniform and safe, were accepted at par value throughout the nation. General acceptance of the banknotes reduced the information costs associated with banknote use, thereby increasing economic efficiency.

Congress levied a high tax on state-bank-issued banknotes as an additional revenue source. Some hoped that the tax, coupled with the uniform acceptability of national banknotes, would drive state banks out of business and eliminate competition faced by national banks. However, the state banks responded swiftly. The state

---

[1] The checking account had not yet been developed. Banks were permitted, within specified limits, to issue their own banknotes (paper currency) whenever they issued a loan. The system operated much like the early English system, in which goldsmiths issued gold certificates with only fractional backing in gold. The effect of the issuance of such notes was the same as occurs today when banks make loans—money is created.

[2] National banks were required by law to redeem the notes of other national banks at par value. This requirement enhanced the public's faith and confidence in the currency and helped maintain the value and acceptability of the notes.

banks developed demand deposit accounts as a substitute for taxable banknotes. Demand deposits were an important financial innovation that helped state banks maintain their deposit bases in the face of strong competition from their federally chartered counterparts. As a result of the survival of state banks, the United States developed a **dual banking system** that remains intact to this day. Today, about one fourth of all commercial banks are national banks, chartered by the Comptroller of the Currency. The remaining three fourths of commercial banks are state banks, chartered by the individual states.

**dual banking system** system in which both the federal government and state governments have authority to charter banks

## REGULATION OF THE U.S. BANKING SYSTEM

Relative to other industrialized countries, our dual banking system and the historical restrictions on the banks' authority to operate multiple branches produced a large number of small banks. The business of banking is critically different from other forms of commerce. Bank activity is intimately related to the nation's credit conditions, money supply, price level, and general macroeconomic conditions. It is natural to ask two questions: Who is acting as watchdog over this powerful group of institutions? And how closely are our banks being monitored and supervised?

In the United States, several regulatory bodies supervise banks. In many cases, the responsibilities of the regulatory agencies overlap. The regulatory agencies include individual state banking commissions, the Comptroller of the Currency, the Federal Reserve System, and the Federal Deposit Insurance Corporation. Each of the agencies seeks to foster a healthy and stable banking industry. When the public's confidence in the banking sector is undermined, the willingness of savers to entrust their funds to financial intermediaries declines, stifling the flow of funds to borrowing units such as households and small businesses. Government enacts regulations intended to bolster the financial health of banks, and the trust depositors place in banks. This promotes the economic benefits that stem from financial intermediation.

### Aspects of Bank Chartering and Regulation

Despite recent easing of restrictions on how and where banks can operate (discussed later in this chapter), banks are still subject to numerous regulations. Beyond the general goal of fostering a healthy banking sector, the regulations are directed toward two specific objectives. First, bank regulation is designed to limit bank failures. As we learned in Chapter 4, important asymmetries in information inhibit the transfer of funds from lenders to borrowers. Borrowers have more information about their intentions and prospects than do lenders. Banks and other financial intermediaries reduce the informational asymmetries inherent in transfers of funds from savers to borrowers, but important information asymmetries nevertheless exist between banks and their depositors. In particular, banks have information about the quality and condition of their own loan portfolios that is unavailable to the typical depositor. Even a *rumor* of deteriorating bank financial condition (whether or not well founded) can touch off a costly panic. One rationale for bank regulation is to reduce the consequences of information asymmetry by assuring the public that banks do not expose depositors to excessive and unwarranted risk. Regulations clearly protect depositors and banks from the potentially disastrous consequences of unfounded rumors of ill health.

A second rationale for bank regulation is to ensure that banks have sufficient liquidity to meet currency withdrawals and adverse check clearings. As we indicated in Chapter 9, the majority of bank assets are loans. Loans are relatively illiquid—most loans cannot be called prior to maturity, and only a limited portion of bank loans can be sold in secondary markets. Because most of a bank's assets are relatively illiquid, unexpected withdrawals can force a bank to either quickly sell assets (often at a loss) or tell depositors that their deposits cannot be fully honored (possibly touching off a bank run). To guard against these adverse outcomes, regulatory authorities require banks to hold liquid assets above their required reserves as a cushion against unanticipated withdrawals. Such liquid bank assets are sometimes called *secondary reserves.*

**Comptroller of the Currency**
government agency within the Treasury Department charged with chartering, supervising, and examining national banks

**bank charters**
official authorizations to open and operate banks

**Chartering.** Individual state banking commissions and the **Comptroller of the Currency** are responsible for issuing **bank charters**—official authorizations to open and operate banks. Individuals seeking to open a state bank apply for a charter with the appropriate state banking commission. Individuals seeking to open a national bank apply to the Office of the Comptroller of the Currency, an agency of the U.S. Department of Treasury. Each of these agencies retains some supervisory responsibility over the banks they charter.

When evaluating the application for a new charter, the regulatory agency typically considers the qualifications of the bank's proposed management, the quantity of capital contributed by the prospective owners, and the bank's potential to achieve and maintain profitability. Prior to the initial deregulation of the banking sector in the early 1980s, chartering bodies often considered how a new bank would impact the profitability of existing banks. Regulators often denied the charter if they believed the new bank would impose significant hardship on the community's other banks. This practice restricted competition and enabled the survival of inefficient and poorly managed banks. Today, regulatory authorities typically do not consider the competitive threat a new bank poses to existing banks when evaluating requests for bank charters, especially for national banks.

**Supervision and Examination.** In addition to state banking commissions and the Comptroller of the Currency, two other agencies examine and supervise banks—the Federal Reserve System and the Federal Deposit Insurance Corporation.

The Federal Reserve System was created in response to the disastrous financial panics that swept the nation between 1863 and 1913. As we learned in Chapter 9, a run on a solvent but illiquid bank can force the bank to close its doors. In the years before the Federal Reserve was created, many banks protected themselves from bank runs by forming groups called *clearinghouses.* Clearinghouses spread the pressures created by an individual bank run across all of the clearinghouse members. In the clearinghouse system, members with adequate liquid funds provided temporary funds to fellow members experiencing severe unanticipated withdrawals.

The clearinghouse system could effectively assist with a run on an individual member bank, but it could not handle major *systemic* shocks adversely impacting many members simultaneously. The clearinghouse required access to an external source of liquid funds. In response to the dramatic Panic of 1907, lawmakers considered the need for a "lender of last resort"—an entity that could provide liquidity to the banking system as a whole in the event of widespread panic. Discussions culminated in the Federal Reserve Act of 1913, which created our nation's central bank. The Federal Reserve initially was charged with two responsibilities: to provide the banking system with emergency reserves when necessary and to issue a uniform fiat currency—the Federal Reserve Note. The notes would coexist with the gold certificates, silver certificates, and coins issued by the U.S. Treasury. Every national bank was (and still is) required to be a member of the Federal Reserve System.

Since its inception, the Federal Reserve has shouldered much of the responsibility for stabilizing the banking system. However, as we will see in Chapter 17, the Fed abdicated that responsibility during the critical years of the Great Depression from 1929 to 1933. During the Great Depression, a rash of bank failures rocked the nation, prompting strong legislative reform of the banking system in 1933 and 1934. The *Banking Act of 1933* created a deposit insurance system administered by the newly created Federal Deposit Insurance Corporation (FDIC). In this system, the Bank Insurance Fund pays depositors of a failed bank the value of their deposits. By law, every national bank and any state bank that is a member of the Federal Reserve System must purchase FDIC insurance. Only state banks that are not Federal Reserve members can decline deposit insurance coverage. Today, only a few hundred small state banks are not FDIC insured.

Regulations governing banks' asset quality and liquidity aim to prevent undesired consequences of information asymmetries by bolstering depositor confidence. The goal of our federal deposit insurance program is the same. Deposit insurance ensures depositors they can recover their funds in the event of bank failure, greatly reducing the public's incentive to withdraw funds from banks suspected of experiencing financial problems.

The Federal Reserve System, the Federal Deposit Insurance Corporation, the Comptroller of the Currency, and state banking commissions share responsibility for supervising and examining our nation's banks. Supervision and examination of a bank entails assessment of the bank's overall financial condition, verification of compliance with all relevant regulations, an audit ensuring that the bank is not misrepresenting its financial condition, and assessment of the riskiness of the bank's asset portfolio. Bank examiners often arrive unannounced to thwart banks' attempts to conceal the true nature of their activities and condition.

Examiners apply a standardized rating system—the **CAMELS system**—to assess a bank's overall financial condition. CAMELS is an acronym for the six categories evaluated: C (capital adequacy), A (asset quality), M (management), E (earnings), L (liquidity), and S (sensitivity to risk). The sensitivity to risk category has become an important focal point over the past few years, given the increasing latitude in the types of assets banks can hold and the activities in which they can engage. Banks hold assets characterized by varying degrees of default risk and market risk. A sudden decline in the value of a bank's assets can extinguish the bank's capital, rendering the bank insolvent. The regulatory authorities' focus on risk sensitivity escalated rapidly following the collapse of Barings Bank in England. Both risk sensitivity and risk management practices are now a standard part of bank evaluation.[3]

**CAMELS system** acronym indicating the six categories evaluated to assess a bank's overall financial condition: C (capital adequacy), A (asset quality), M (management), E (earnings), L (liquidity), and S (sensitivity to risk)

Bank examiners have a great deal of authority. A low CAMELS score can prompt examiners to force a bank to make fundamental balance sheet changes, including divestiture of risky assets and writing off of underperforming loans. If a bank's financial condition becomes sufficiently troubling, the regulators can declare the bank a *problem bank* and order frequent examinations, or they can order the bank to close its doors.

---

[3] Barings, one of England's oldest and most prestigious banks, was driven into insolvency when rogue trader Nicholas Leeson used bank funds to purchase volatile Japanese stock market futures, which fell sharply following the Kobe earthquake. Within a few weeks, Barings had lost over $1 billion, wiping out all of the bank's capital.

**Overlapping Regulatory Authority.** Supervision of bank activity can have a great deal of duplication. For example, a nationally chartered bank can be subject to supervision by the Office of the Comptroller of the Currency (the chartering body), the Federal Reserve System (of which the bank is required to be a member), and the FDIC (whose insurance it must carry). To avoid costly duplicate activities, the agencies often divide responsibility and accept the assessments of the other regulatory bodies for aspects of supervision under their purview. As a general rule, the *de facto* responsibility for supervision and examination is divided along the following lines. Because national banks are chartered by the Comptroller of the Currency, the Comptroller retains responsibility for national bank supervision and examination. State banks that are members of the Federal Reserve System, although chartered by state banking commissions, are supervised and examined by the Federal Reserve. State banks that carry FDIC insurance but are not Federal Reserve members are supervised and examined by the FDIC. State banks that do not carry FDIC insurance are supervised and examined by state banking authorities. The Federal Reserve retains responsibility for supervising the activities of *bank holding companies*—firms that own a controlling interest in one or more banks but do not directly engage in banking. Finally, because of its vested financial interest, the FDIC conducts on-site examinations of the institutions it insures, even though this measure involves duplication of effort.[4]

Numerous proposals for consolidating the supervisory and examination authority of our bank regulators have been suggested. These proposals aim to eliminate the costly duplication of bank supervision and possible confusion that would allow a wayward bank to slip through the cracks of supervision. A consolidation can prevent a great deal of confusion, level the playing field by holding all banks to the same standards, and eliminate costly duplication of effort by our current supervisory agencies. The most recent consolidation proposal in 1994 would have created a Federal Banking Commission with regulatory authority over all federally insured institutions (leaving state banking commissions to examine only about 350 small state banks without FDIC insurance). Federal Reserve Chairman Alan Greenspan objected strenuously to such centralization of responsibility on two grounds. First, Greenspan felt that one large supervisory body would impede the flow of information to agencies with a vested interest in the health of the banking sector. Because the banking sector plays an important role in the nation's overall economy and the Federal Reserve requires timely information to implement monetary policy, Greenspan argued that the Fed needed to retain its role in bank supervision. Second, Greenspan claimed that reducing duplication of examinations by centralization would eliminate an important system of checks and balances. He argued that a problem bank was less likely to slip through the cracks if two or more independent agencies performed separate examinations of that bank.

The 1994 proposal was rejected by Congress. However, the practical arrangements made by our bank regulatory authorities to avoid excessive duplication and the FDIC's charge to perform regular double-checks have provided a relatively secure safety net at reasonably low cost. Any proposals to consolidate responsibility for bank supervision and examination likely will not be enacted in the near future, even though passage of the Gramm-Leach-Bliley Act in 1999 greatly broadened banks' range of permissible activities and raised considerable interest in ensuring adequate supervision over banks. Discussions about these issues will resurface as financial integration continues in the United States.

[4] FDIC examination is one of the provisions of the Federal Deposit Insurance Corporation Improvement Act (FDICIA), which was enacted after the banking crisis of the late 1980s.

## STRUCTURE OF CONTEMPORARY AMERICAN BANKING

Today, our banking system consists of approximately 7,700 commercial banks. A substantial number of these banks operate with multiple branches, and many of these branches cross state lines. Because of this widespread branching, a vacationer from Anchorage, Alaska, can have unrestricted access to her account and a full range of banking services while she is traveling as far away as Key West, Florida.

The banking industry has undergone substantial consolidation. Well over 14,000 banks existed in 1984. Figure 10-1 indicates the steady decline in the number of commercial banks since 1984.

The total number of commercial banks declined by approximately 6,600 from 1984 to 2003. Figure 10-2 illustrates the annual number of new bank charters, the annual number of bank mergers, and the net change in the number of banks operating in the United States each year from 1960 to 2003. During the period from 1986 to 2004, the total number of banks declined at an annual rate of approximately 400 per year. As indicated in the figure, the sharp decline in the number of banks can be attributed predominantly to mergers among existing institutions. You may be one of the millions of depositors whose banks changed names due to mergers. Consolidation and interstate branching are commonplace today but were severely restricted a few years ago. The recent changes have finally put to rest more than 200 years of efforts to restrict banking competition across geographic lines. The restrictions began in 1791 with the chartering of the original Bank of the United States—the only bank allowed to branch across state lines at the time—and continued until about a decade ago.

**Figure 10-1** Total Number of FDIC-Insured Commercial Banks from 1984 to 2003

The number of commercial banks has fallen nearly in half since 1984.

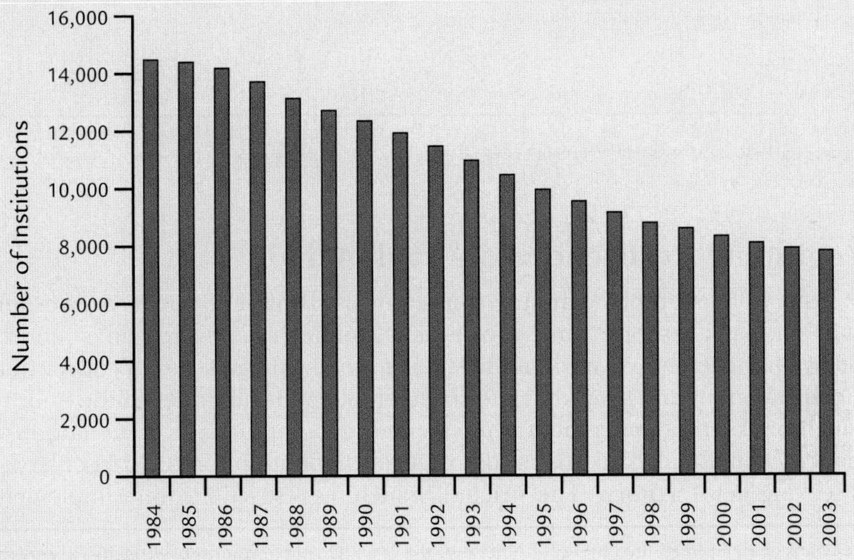

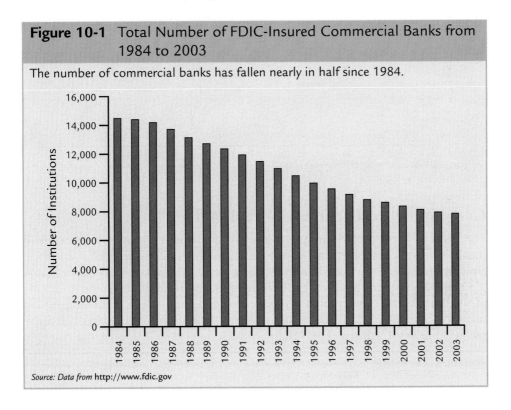

*Source: Data from* http://www.fdic.gov

**Figure 10-2** New Bank Charters, Bank Mergers, and Change in the Number of U.S. Commercial Banks from 1960 to 2003

Since the mid-1980s, the number of bank mergers have sharply exceeded the number of new bank charters. The number of banks declined by about 400 per year.

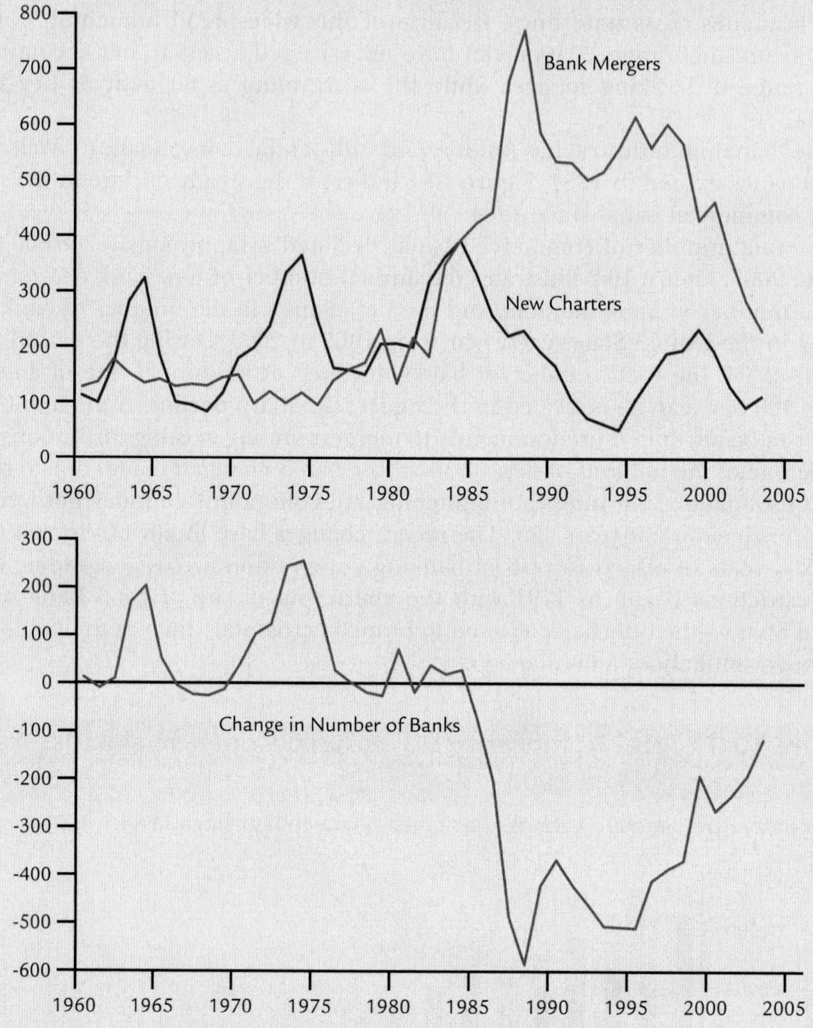


*Source: Data from* http://www.fdic.gov

## Geographic Restrictions on Bank Activity

The history of geographic banking restrictions is a unique picture of government regulation, bank response, and government counterresponse to banks' efforts to circumvent the letter and spirit of the law. Inspired by the mistrust of concentration of financial power and swayed by the considerable political power of the multitude of small banks, the government implemented geographic and branching restrictions protecting small banks from "destructive competition" on the part of larger rivals seeking new territory.[5] The strictest branching restrictions were implemented

[5] Small banks have been granted other subsidies over the years. One important subsidy is the lower reserve requirements levied on small banks throughout our nation's history. Because reserve requirements essentially are a tax on banks that reduces profitability, the lower reserve requirements levied on smaller banks helps them compete against the larger banks that enjoy economies of scale and other advantages.

in the populist, agrarian states of the Midwest and the deep South. Coupled with the regulatory authorities' policy of denying charters to new banks that posed a competitive threat to existing banks, branching restrictions assured small banks a captive market of depositors and a low-cost source of funds.

Until recently, restrictions on branch banking existed at both the federal and state levels. At the federal level, legislation restricting branching originated with the **McFadden Act** (1927). The McFadden Act prohibited national banks from operating outside their home state and compelled banks to abide by state regulations on *intra*state branching. State branching restrictions took a variety of forms. Many states allowed statewide branching, in which banks could operate an unlimited number of offices within state borders. Other states adopted **limited branching** restrictions, which limited banks to a certain number of offices. The most restrictive form of limited branching was *unit banking,* which permitted each bank only one office. Kansas, the last of the unit banking states, finally relaxed its restrictions in 1986.

**McFadden Act**
legislation prohibiting national banks from operating outside their home state and compelling banks to abide by state regulations on intrastate branching

**limited branching**
restrictions limiting banks to a certain number of offices

## Banks' Response to Geographic Restrictions

One of the most reliable predictions of economics is that imposing regulations elicits compensatory responses from the entities on which the regulations are imposed. Commercial banks have displayed great ingenuity in circumventing geographic restrictions on their activities. Here we discuss three banking industry responses: bank holding companies, non-bank banks, and electronic banking.

**Bank Holding Companies.** The first bank response to geographic restrictions was creation of the **bank holding company**—a corporation that owns a controlling interest in one or several banks but is itself not a bank. Until the middle of the twentieth century, bank holding companies could acquire many banks, including banks in different states. One organization could operate multiple banks as branches of a single bank. The popularity of the bank holding company form of corporate organization and its effectiveness in circumventing branching restrictions prompted passage of the **Bank Holding Company Act of 1956,** which prohibited such expansions unless state law permitted interstate acquisitions. However, this act contained a "grandfather clause" that allowed existing multi-bank holding companies to continue their operations.

**bank holding company**
corporation that owns a controlling interest in one or several banks but is itself not a bank

**Bank Holding Company Act of 1956**
legislation prohibiting bank branching via acquisition of banks by bank holding companies

**Non-bank Banking.** The Bank Holding Company Act of 1956 stopped one means of circumventing branching restrictions, but creative bankers quickly found another loophole to exploit. The Bank Holding Company Act of 1956 defined a bank as an entity that accepts deposits and makes commercial loans. The logical reaction of enterprising bankers was to divide commercial banks into two separate entities. They set up "non-bank banks" that accepted deposits but did not make loans, and "non-bank offices" (also known as *loan production offices)* that made loans but did not accept deposits. Funds were channeled from one entity to the other through a controlling parent organization.

Growth of non-bank banking was so rapid that regulatory authorities were pressured into restricting this activity. However, legislative response was slow in coming. The loophole was not closed until enactment of the Competitive Equality in Banking Act of 1987. As with the Bank Holding Company Act, existing institutions were grandfathered in but were given limited opportunities for future growth.

**Electronic Banking.** The third response to branching restrictions was the development of an electronic banking system. As a college student, you are familiar with the automatic teller machine (ATM). Electronic banking struggled early in its

## Exhibit 10-1 Economics of the Ubiquitous ATM

The past decade brought many dramatic changes to the banking industry, perhaps none more visible to consumers than the proliferation of ATMs. ATMs were created by commercial banks to circumvent branching restrictions and reduce costs of providing banking services. The law originally regarded the ATM as a separate bank branch unless the ATM was located on bank premises. Exemptions to this rule were granted to banks that joined regional or national networks. By the 1980s, more than 150 regional networks and two large national networks had been created.

ATMs have been around for decades, but most have been installed since 1995. Between 1995 and 2001, ATMs in service rose from 100,000 to over 275,000. Estimates put today's figure at 400,000 and rising. What factors are responsible for this phenomenal growth?

One important factor contributing to ATM growth is the substantially decreased costs of installing and maintaining ATMs. Stand-alone units that can be wheeled into any location with a power outlet and a phone jack now cost less than $10,000. The cost of servicing and maintaining ATMs is less than $1,000 per month. In response to low ATM costs, banks now distribute ATMs in non-bank locations such as airports, shopping malls, and convenience stores.

A second important factor in the growth and dispersion of ATMs is *surcharging.* Surcharges are fees paid directly by the cardholder to the ATM owner at the time of the transaction, appreciably increasing ATM profits. Surcharging is a relatively new practice. Until a hotly contested lawsuit was decided in 1996, ATM owners who wanted to be a member of the two major national networks were forbidden from imposing surcharges. Prior to surcharging, ATM revenues came from *interchange fees* paid by the cardholder's bank to the ATM owner. Without surcharging, an ATM must generate about 4,000 transactions per month in order be profitable. Addition of a surcharge lowers the break-even number of transactions to between 400 and 1,200 per month, making placement of ATMs in less-trafficked locations feasible.

The final factor responsible for rapid industry growth is consolidation of network providers. Cardholders of a bank that is a network member can access their accounts through any ATM under the network's umbrella. In turn, the network assesses the cardholder's bank a *switching fee* every time a transaction is carried over a network. Over the past 20 years, many of the 150 regional networks disappeared or were gobbled up by their competitors. Today only about 40 networks remain. Ironically, network consolidation increases the power of ATM owners and the convenience of ATM users through what economists call *network effects.* Network effects exist when a service becomes more valuable the more it is used, thus encouraging ever-increasing numbers of adopters. One network serving a community is more valuable than two networks serving the same area. Each ATM owner wants connections to as many cardholders as possible, and each cardholder wants his/her card accepted at as many ATMs as possible. Consolidation of regional networks has greatly extended the reach of the surviving networks, making ATM use more convenient and ATM deployment more profitable.

Transformation of the ATM industry has been too dramatic and too recent to safely predict what the future holds, but many prospective changes bode well for consumers. First, banks likely will use ATM accessibility and pricing as important dimensions of competition. Second, maturity in ATM provision may result in greater market saturation and lower surcharges. Average monthly transactions per machine have already fallen from a high of 7,000 per month in 1992 to fewer than 4,000 today. Surveys report that three quarters of all cardholders arrange their affairs to avoid ATM surcharges, and the decline in per-machine usage should keep surcharges in check. Finally, as network effects increase, consumers will find their accounts accessible at an ever-growing number of locations. Given an increasingly competitive banking sector in general, these three factors suggest we will receive greater banking service at a price that more fully reflects the service's true cost.

development. Several states resisted installation of ATMs, claiming that an ATM owned by a bank legally constituted a branch of that bank. After all, an ATM offers a considerable range of banking services—access to accounts for withdrawals, acceptance of deposits, and extension of loans through credit cards. Regulators permitted exemptions for ATMs owned by other businesses and ATMs allowing access to a network of multiple institutions (such as VIA or CIRRUS). Banks quickly formed electronic networks and used them to establish a presence in markets previously unavailable to them.

## Removal of Restrictions

Banks' efforts to circumvent branching restrictions is strong testament to the banks' desire to expand their scale of operations. Intense lobbying for removal of branching restrictions began in the 1970s. The efforts began to bear fruit in the early 1980s when several New England states authorized full interstate branching. The push toward consolidation received an unfortunate boost in the late 1980s and early 1990s when thousands of banks, especially those in oil-producing states such as Texas, Louisiana, and Oklahoma, found themselves in dire financial straits. Federal regulators did not close the troubled banks; instead, they encouraged more stable institutions to purchase the floundering banks. To increase the pool of willing buyers, regulators made exceptions to the law, granting out-of-state institutions permission to purchase impaired banks.

### Riegle-Neal Interstate Banking and Branching Efficiency Act of 1994.

When lawmakers were satisfied with the weight of accumulated experience with branch banking, they removed the remaining federal restrictions on interstate branching. The **Riegle-Neal Interstate Banking and Branching Efficiency Act of 1994** revoked the rights granted states to determine branching laws for banks operating within individual states. Beginning in September 1995, bank holding companies were allowed to acquire banks anywhere in the nation. By June 1997, bank holding companies were allowed to convert banks in various states into branches of a single interstate bank.

**Riegle-Neal Interstate Banking and Branching Efficiency Act of 1994**
act revoking the rights granted states to determine branching laws for banks operating within individual states

**Exhibit 10-2** Growth of Internet Banking

In the space of a single hour, Joe Cool deposits his paycheck, pays his bills, transfers money from his savings account to his checking account, makes an extra car payment, balances his checkbook, and refinances his home mortgage. Ten years ago this flurry of activity would have required several trips to the bank. This increased efficiency was made possible by the explosive growth of the Internet and the accompanying growth of Internet banking. Assisted by financial management software such as Quicken, online banking picked up steam in the late 1990s. By 2003, more than 3,000 banks offered their customers facilities for online transactions and more than 2,500 were in the planning stages. Some 24 million users were banking online in 2002, and another 24 million users are projected by 2005.

Online banking typically offers three types of services: bill consolidation and payment, fund transfer among accounts, and loan applications. Many non-bank financial services providers specialize in one or more of these services. Online mortgage providers such as Quickenmortgage.com experienced phenomenal growth, bolstered by falling long-term interest rates during the first few years of the new millennium. The number of visits to one online mortgage provider's Web site grew from 35,000 per month to over 500,000 as homeowners eager to refinance their mortgages grew tired of long lines at their banks.

*continued*

**Exhibit 10-2** Growth of Internet Banking—*cont'd*

Banks have quickly jumped on the online bandwagon. Banks recognized the value to consumers of banking at home and worried about losing their customers to online providers. Banks quickly established their own transaction sites and, in the process, found that Internet banking offered significant cost advantages. A bank transaction completed over the Internet costs the bank just 1¢ to process, while ATM and teller transactions cost 27¢ and $1.07, respectively. To maximize this cost savings, many banks offer their customers enticements to bank online. Several banks that allow customers to bank electronically at no cost now charge up to $3 for a teller transaction.

Initially banks believed Internet banking would reduce their fixed costs. An online system enables a bank to complete more transactions with fewer offices. Many early online banks were exclusively Web based, with no brick-and-mortar facilities. As banks gained experience, however, they discovered that most customers prefer the convenience of "bricks-and-clicks" banking—a system that couples the convenience of banking at home with the assurance that a local office is nearby for more complicated transactions and personal service.

Web banking has important implications for the *scale* of bank activity. With the Internet, any bank can open a branch within each customer's home, making the idea of branching restrictions both obsolete and virtually unenforceable. In retrospect, had Riegle-Neal not been passed, many brick-and-mortar banks would have been at a competitive disadvantage relative to their online counterparts. With removal of branching restrictions and growth of the Internet, banks can compete for a nationwide pool of deposits, bringing consumers more choice at lower cost. As more consumers become confident in online banking, banks likely will be able to reduce their physical facilities, leading to important efficiency gains.

Online banking has implications for the *scope* of bank activity. Online financial services may neutralize many of the potential benefits Gramm-Leach-Bliley portended for banks. Online comparison shopping for insurance, loans, and brokerage services through specialized providers has become so easy that the consumer appeal of one-stop shopping at bank branches has all but disappeared. To remain competitive with specialized providers, banks must cross-market services aggressively on their Web sites and sell consumers on the convenience of conducting all financial activity through one portal.

The growth of online banking creates a more competitive banking environment, ameliorating concerns that bank consolidation comes at consumer expense. Fewer chartered banks exist today than at any time in the past hundred years, yet the typical bank consumer has far more choices as to where she does her banking. The consumer does not pay for this convenience. The enhanced competitive environment, coupled with the lower variable costs of Web-based banking, means the online consumer gets the best of all worlds—greater choice at lower cost, and all from the comfort of home.

**Banking Industry Consolidation and Forces Driving Consolidation.** The structure of the U.S. banking industry has changed dramatically, especially after the mid-1980s. One interesting outcome is that lessening of branch banking restrictions did not result in many new branch openings. Rather, freedom to operate branch banks has manifested primarily as bank purchases of existing institutions. Such consolidation is almost completely responsible for the disappearance of more than 2,700 banks since passage of Riegle-Neal in 1994.[6] These developments are illustrated in Figure 10-3, which shows the decline in the number of unit banks and the increasing number of institutions with branches over the past 40 years.

*See footnote on page 243*

**Figure 10-3** Total Number of U.S. Commercial Banks, Unit Banks, and Banks with Branches from 1960 to 2003

Relative to the 1960s, unit banking has declined dramatically while the number of banking institutions with branches has increased.

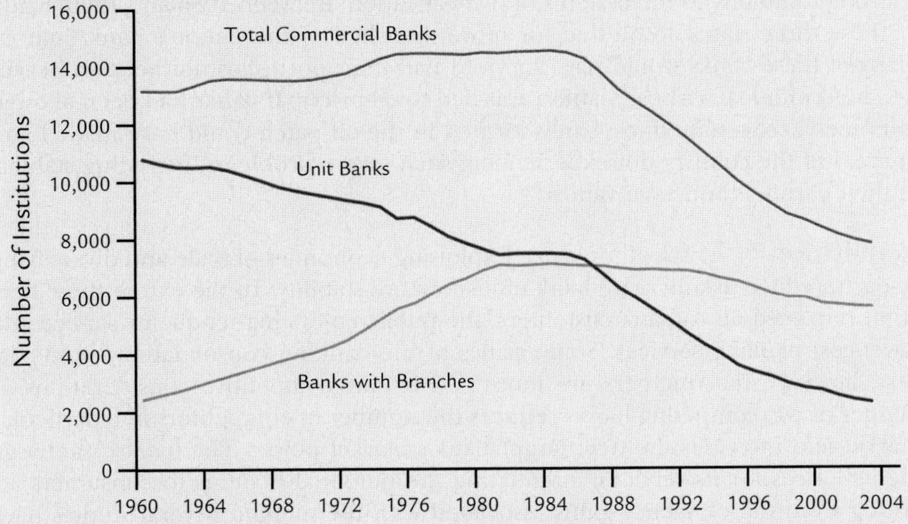

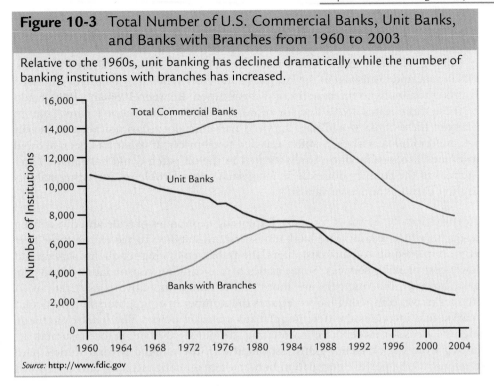

*Source:* http://www.fdic.gov

**Economies of Scale in Banking.** What lies behind the urge to merge and consolidate? Clearly, powerful economic forces are at work, and perhaps the most compelling is **economies of scale** in banking services. Economies of scale exist when the average cost of providing a unit of bank service declines as more units of the service are provided. Given the substantial *fixed costs* in banking (for example, the costs of maintaining and staffing bank facilities, processing information, and reporting to and complying with regulators), a bank holding company may more efficiently run two branches of the same bank rather than two banks functioning independently. Legislation permitting banks to create single institutions from a series of state-by-state affiliates substantially reduces the regulatory burden and eliminates many costs being duplicated at each bank prior to consolidation. Furthermore, cost savings may be associated with providing brick-and-mortar banking facilities. When two banks in close proximity merge, one of the banking facilities can be eliminated without a great loss of service to the customers of either bank.[7]

**economies of scale**
economies formed when the average cost of providing a unit of bank service declines as more units of the service are provided

[6] Only 44 banks failed from 1995to 2003. Clearly, consolidation has been responsible for the enormous decline in the number of chartered institutions. The reduction in the number of chartered banks does not indicate a decline in the number of banking facilities. The restructuring of banking has resulted in fewer banks but more branch offices. The net impact has been positive-the total number of bank offices exceeded 73,500 in 2002, the highest ever.

[7] Past studies of bank efficiency suggest that economies of scale exist for bank size up to about $125 million in deposits. Between $125 and $400 million of deposits, banks' average costs remain fairly constant; above $400 million, average costs rise-that is, dis-economies of scale exist. These early estimates are inapplicable today for two reasons. First, the estimates were based on data from a period with a more restrictive regulatory environment. Dis-economies of scale may exist when a bank with a geographically restricted deposit base tries to attract more deposits, but such dis-economies may disappear when restrictions are lifted and the bank gains access to a nationwide base of deposits. Second, electronic banking has changed the nature of bank costs but as a new phenomenon was not considered in early studies. Some economists suggest that merging of two very large banks is evidence of economies of scale in banking.

**Asset Diversification.** A second force prompting bank consolidation is the benefit to a bank of having a geographically diversified portfolio of assets. Banks with offices in more than one region can lend to a variety of customers, avoiding the trap of putting all their eggs in one basket. The epidemic of bank failures in Texas, Oklahoma, and Louisiana in the late 1980s and early 1990s after oil prices collapsed is strong testimony to the benefits of diversification. Between 1986 and 1990, banks in these three states accounted for more than half of the nation's bank failures. Many of these banks would have survived had their portfolios not been so heavily weighted with loans whose viability was tied to oil prices. If banks had been allowed to branch across state lines, banks located in the oil patch could have made loans in areas of the country not experiencing such severe problems, providing stability to their earnings and asset values.

**Acquisition of Market Power.** Exploiting economies of scale and diversifying assets to reduce risk increase bank efficiency and stability. To the extent these benefits are passed on to bank customers, the public enjoys higher-quality service and lower-cost banking services. Some critics of the banking consolidation trend suggest, however, that mergers are motivated by anti-competitive considerations. A merger of two competing banks reduces the number of competitors in a particular market and increases the new, larger bank's market power. The bank can charge higher prices for its services, attenuating the potential benefits to consumers accruing from the efficiency gains associated with the merger. Several studies have demonstrated a positive correlation between market concentration and the spread between interest rates charged for bank loans and interest paid on deposits. Surveys conducted by the Federal Reserve indicate that large multi-state banks charge substantially more for bank services.

The regulations of the past and the regulatory actions authorizing new bank charters created a banking industry in which banks were partially insulated from competition. Removal of restrictions opens the door for mergers that may increase concentration of market power, but that freedom also facilitates openings of new banks or more branches of an existing bank. When a merger between competitors results in consumer exploitation, the profits received by that entity may attract new competitors. Some economists believe the mere *threat* of entry by potential competitors substantially limits anti-competitive behavior. One study reports that the banking industry is becoming more competitive despite growing concentration in banking, and that consumers can expect to receive net benefits from the wave of mergers in recent years. Another study compares banking efficiency during heavily and lightly regulated time periods and reports that banks' unit costs were 21 percent higher during the regulated period than during the unregulated period.[8] If the banking sector becomes more competitive, some of the cost savings due to deregulation likely will be passed on to consumers.

Consider the potential of greater market power for banks to charge higher loan rates and pay lower deposit rates to customers and the substantially higher fees for services larger banks now charge. You can conclude that most consumers will be best served by the continued existence of small banks providing alternatives to large institutions. Critics of deregulation suggest that a banking industry characterized by larger banks places small banks at a competitive disadvantage and chokes off lending to consumers and small businesses. Some studies document a

[8] See the articles by Cetorelli (1999) and by Evanoff (1998) cited in *Additional Reading* at the end of this chapter.

substantial contraction in total bank lending to small businesses as the bank consolidation trend unfolded. The studies suggest this trend will continue as the extra layers of management and control at larger organizations reduce the autonomy of local lending officers and impede relationship-based lending to typical noncorporate borrowers.

Supporters of bank consolidation argue that the focused lending practices of large banks leave plenty of room for consumer, mortgage, and small business lending by small banks. Advocates suggest small banks will expand their lending to fill voids in the lending areas created by merger of financial institutions. Without action by small banks, voids demonstrate the need for a new institution. Thus, increases in lending and new charters likely fill the performance gaps left in the wake of bank consolidation. Empirical evidence of bank lending to small businesses in markets with heavy merger activity generally confirms these effects.

## Size Distribution of U.S. Commercial Banks

Given the number of bank mergers and the growth of large banking institutions, you can easily overlook the fact that over half of the nation's banks are quite small, collectively holding less than 3 percent of the nation's aggregate bank deposits. Table 10-1 shows the distribution of banks by size. More than 94 percent of all U.S. banks have less than $1 billion in assets. Only 1 percent of the nation's banks have more than $10 billion in assets. These few behemoths own more than 70 percent of total assets in the banking system.

Several studies point to the continued viability of small banking institutions. The growth of both deposits and assets has been greater at small banks than at medium and large banks in each year of a recent 15-year period. However, small banks are limited to a smaller geographic deposit base and pay relatively more for their deposits than do large banks. Why would small banks be willing to pay more for the deposits necessary to fund their asset growth? Small banks can offer more for deposits than large banks because the funds typically earn more for small banks. On balance, the performance of small banks relative to their larger counterparts has been robust. On several measures of bank performance, including net interest margin and rate of return on assets, small banks have met or exceeded the numbers posted by their larger counterparts. Studies confirm the existence of a vibrant community banking sector that fills an important need—lending to local small businesses and households.

**Table 10-1** Size Distribution of Insured U.S. Commercial Banks on December 31, 2002

| Bank Size (Assets) | Number of Banks | Share of All Banks (%) | Share of All Bank Assets (%) |
|---|---|---|---|
| Less than $100 million | 4,168 | 52.9 | 3.0 |
| $100 million–$1 billion | 3,314 | 42.0 | 12.3 |
| $1 billion–$10 billion | 325 | 4.1 | 13.2 |
| More than $10 billion | 80 | 1.0 | 71.5 |
| Total | 7,887 | 100.0 | 100.0 |

Source: Federal Deposit Insurance Corporation, *Statistics on Banking*

# SCOPE OF MODERN BANKING

**investment banks** institutions that underwrite new securities issues and trade existing issues

During most of U.S. history, banks focused on traditional banking activities—accepting deposits and making loans. This focus changed during the First World War, when commercial banks became heavily involved in the securities business. The banking system distributed war bonds, which many banks purchased for their investment portfolios. Gradually, commercial banks acted as **investment banks**—institutions that underwrite new securities issues and trade existing issues.

Some 9,000 banks—fully one third of the nation's banks—failed during the Great Depression from 1929 to 1933. Senator Carter Glass, with the support of other influential politicians, blamed investment bankers for the calamity. Senator Glass's attack on investment banking was three-pronged. First, he noted that institutions holding a sizable portion of their assets in equity securities are inherently vulnerable to a stock market collapse. Second, he revealed that many banks allowed customers to use equity securities as collateral for bank loans, further increasing banks' exposure to market risk. Finally, he charged banks with widespread abuse of privilege that fueled speculation and destabilized the banking industry. The alleged abuses included conflicts of interest, stock price manipulation, and misrepresentation of facts to unwary customers. (Many of these early abuses are similar to those committed in the past 5 to 10 years.)

## Glass-Steagall Act

**Banking Act of 1933 (Glass-Steagall Act)** legislation separating commercial banking from investment banking, and separating banking from industry

Riding a wave of popular sentiment, legislation sponsored by Senator Glass was quickly passed into law. This legislation, the **Banking Act of 1933** (commonly referred to as the **Glass-Steagall Act**), contained the following four major provisions:

1. Commercial banking was legally separated from investment banking. Firms that had been engaged primarily in commercial banking generally chose to remain commercial banks. Firms whose predominant business involved investment banking typically chose to remain investment banks. Some firms split their functions by spinning off one of their services. For example, J.P. Morgan, a predominantly commercial banking enterprise, spun off Morgan-Stanley, one of the nation's most prominent investment banks.
2. Commercial banks were prohibited from underwriting and distributing stocks, bonds, and other securities, except for government bonds and general obligation municipal bonds.
3. Banking was separated from other types of commercial enterprises, such as industrial and insurance firms. This provision stemmed from a general fear of concentration of financial power. Were the industries not separated, banks could favor their industrial affiliates and attempt to drive their competitors out of the market.
4. Banks were permitted to purchase only certain types of approved debt instruments (principally U.S. government and municipal bonds).

To stabilize the banking sector and to assure banks low-cost sources of funds, the Glass-Steagall Act also contained provisions for federal deposit insurance, prohibited the payment of interest on demand deposits, and set statutory interest rate ceilings for time deposits and savings deposits.

In retrospect, the essential purpose of Glass-Steagall is clear. The Act attempted to remedy by legislation the problems caused by information asymmetries between banks and their depositors. The act assured depositors that their banks would not engage in certain risky activities. For example, following enactment of Glass-Steagall, depositors knew their banks would not hold portfolios of volatile equity securities, a sudden decline in the value of which could drive the bank into insolvency. Bank trust customers took comfort in the removal of conflicts of interest between the securities and banking divisions. (One criticism of pre–Glass-Steagall banking is that banks often placed low-quality securities they had underwritten in their clients' trust accounts while reserving better-quality issues for sale to the public.)

## Response to Glass-Steagall

The Glass-Steagall Act drew a sharp line in the sand between commercial banking and investment banking. This line was not crossed for several decades. However, beginning in the 1970s, banks began to experiment with activities beyond those traditionally permissible.

**Securities Underwriting.** Commercial banks began engaging in securities underwriting. Glass-Steagall limited banks to underwriting only those securities backed by the taxing power of government (U.S. and municipal government bonds). In 1988, however, the Supreme Court empowered the Federal Reserve to authorize commercial banks to underwrite high-quality debt such as industrial revenue bonds, commercial paper, and pass-through securities backed by consumer debt. In 1989, the Fed gave banks limited power to underwrite corporate bonds, provided several conditions were met—the underwriting was done by an affiliated subsidiary of a bank holding company, the subsidiary did not have access to insured deposits, and revenue from underwriting would not exceed a certain percentage of its total revenues. Finally, in 1990, bank holding companies were authorized to underwrite new issues of equity (common stock).

**Brokerage Services.** Commercial banks began providing brokerage services. Traditionally, bank holding companies were barred from offering investment advice and transacting securities purchases and sales. In 1983, bank holding companies were permitted to operate discount brokerage facilities that could make securities transactions but could not offer investment advice. Beginning in 1987, banks and bank holding companies were allowed to offer full brokerage services to their customers.

**Mutual Funds.** In the early 1980s, commercial banks began competing with non-bank financial services firms on another front—management and marketing of mutual funds. As interest rates skyrocketed in response to severe inflation in the 1970s, commercial banks—prohibited by the Glass-Steagall Act from offering competitive interest rates—were unable to compete with money market mutual funds for depositors' dollars. A strong bank lobbying effort resulted in phase-out of interest rate ceilings and authorization of the *money market deposit account (MMDA)*. The MMDA permits banks to compete directly with money market mutual funds by offering market rates of interest coupled with limited check-writing privileges. By the 1990s, the competition with mutual funds was even more direct. Banks were permitted to create, manage, and market their own proprietary mutual funds and to market mutual funds managed by other financial services companies.

**Provision of Banking Services by Investment Banks.** These forays into investment-oriented territory were initiated by commercial banks and permitted banks to offer more and better services to their clients. However, the efforts to circumvent Glass-Steagall were not limited to the commercial banking side of the Glass-Steagall firewall. Investment banks and other financial services firms worked just as eagerly to provide traditional banking services to their clients. The creation of money market mutual funds is one example. Investment banks also competed directly with commercial banks by opening and operating non-bank offices, which technically were not classified as banks but served many of the same functions.

## Removal of Glass-Steagall Restrictions

The lobbying effort to remove *all* Glass-Steagall restrictions intensified as inroads into previously forbidden territory progressed. Both commercial and investment banks argued that they were unable to compete in global markets with their less-restricted foreign peers because of Glass-Steagall restrictions. Regulatory sentiment began tilting in favor of rescinding Glass-Steagall given several developments—new academic evidence that the securities activities of banks bore little or no responsibility for the banking collapse during the Great Depression, and encouraging results of recent actions allowing banks greater latitude in their activities. The pressure to remove Glass-Steagall restrictions reached a climax with the 1998 merger of Citicorp and Travelers Group—a financial services conglomerate that owned both an insurance affiliate and the Salomon Smith Barney investment bank. Even though the merger would result in an illegal combination of commercial and investment banking enterprises, the Federal Reserve cleared the application in 1998 under the proviso that any prohibited businesses would be sold off within 5 years. In other words, Citicorp and Travelers gambled that Congress would remove Glass-Steagall restrictions by the time the 5-year deadline was reached, and the merger was quickly consummated.

**Gramm-Leach-Bliley Financial Services Modernization Act.** In retrospect, Citicorp and Travelers gambled well. Within 1 year, Glass-Steagall restrictions were removed by the **Gramm-Leach-Bliley Financial Services Modernization Act of 1999.** This legislation allowed securities and insurance firms to purchase banks and permitted banks to participate in securities, insurance, and real estate activities. The act also delineated supervisory responsibilities for these activities. Adhering to a "functional" approach to regulation, state insurance commissions continued to regulate insurance activities, the Securities and Exchange Commission and state securities regulators continued to regulate investment activities, and federal and state banking regulators regulated bank activities.

**Gramm-Leach-Bliley Financial Services Modernization Act of 1999**
legislation allowing securities and insurance firms to purchase banks and permitting banks to participate in securities, insurance, and real estate activities

**Motives for Removing Glass-Steagall Restrictions.** The lobbying efforts that culminated in passage of Gramm-Leach-Bliley were primarily motivated by **economies of scope.** Economies of scope exist when greater efficiency is achieved by one firm providing a group of services rather than separate specialized firms providing those services. Banks and financial services companies argued that economies of scope exist in the industry because *information* is the key component of credit and lending decisions, and information is costly to obtain. Once information is acquired, perhaps through a longstanding relationship between bank and client, the information should be fully utilized to meet *all* of the client's financial needs. Integrated financial firms providing a full range of services can tailor specific financial solutions. In addition, the services can be provided at lower cost because integration eliminates duplication of costly information gathering and monitoring processes. Increasing the scope of bank operations allows banks to diversify their revenue sources, providing greater stability to the banking industry. Finally, "one-stop shopping" greatly increases consumer convenience.

**economies of scope**
economies formed when greater efficiency is achieved by one firm providing a group of services rather than separate specialized firms providing those services

# INTERNATIONAL PERSPECTIVES

## Combining Banking and Industry

The U.S. banking system differs from that of its foreign peers in one dimension—the United States has far more banks than Japan, England, Germany, and Canada combined. However, banking in foreign countries differs in many other respects. Foreign banks engage in activities and maintain industry ties that are forbidden to their U.S. counterparts.

Japanese banking in many ways echoes the organization of Japanese industry. Unlike the United States, where antitrust concerns traditionally discouraged the formation of huge firms, Japan's economy is organized around just six major industrial concerns, or keiretsu. These huge conglomerates are highly diversified and vertically integrated. Collectively the conglomerates account for about half of the country's sales of primary products and heavy machinery. In the post-World War II era, Japanese firms were prohibited from marketing their securities abroad and issuing lower-grade bonds. The conglomerates became dependent on bank loans as the primary means of financing investment expenditures and quickly developed bank affiliates to meet their credit needs. At one point, these banks became so large that each of the six affiliate banks occupied a position among the world's 10 largest banks.

The German banking system developed as a universal banking system, in which banks are permitted to carry out a wide variety of financial and nonfinancial activities. Similar systems exist in France, Luxembourg, and the Netherlands. Universal banks generally provide highly diversified financial services and typically own substantial equity stakes in commercial firms. Deutsche Bank, for example, owns a substantial equity stake in Daimler-Chrysler. Many observers point to the strong link between banking and industry as partly responsible for the rapid postwar development of Japan and Germany. Evidence suggests that ready access to bank credit permits firms with ties to commercial banking to grow faster than would otherwise be possible. Also, long-term relationships between banks and industrial concerns result in greater sharing of information that makes evaluating and monitoring loans more accurate and less costly.

Other students of the subject have more critical views of combining banking and industry. As critics of Gramm-Leach-Bliley emphasize, potential conflicts of interest are inherent in such relationships. Commercial firms' dependence on bank loans apparently retards the development of capital markets, which is detrimental to the economy as a whole. Critics also worry that in a system where only a few large banks control most of a country's deposits, the ties between banks and industry will choke off credit to consumers and small businesses. Yet both Japan and Germany maintain active small-bank sectors. In Japan, the largest banks are allowed to make only long-term loans; shorter-term loans are the exclusive province of other banks. Both nations maintain extensive systems of credit cooperatives serving the needs of consumers and small businesses.

## INTERNATIONAL PERSPECTIVES —*continued*

Japanese and German banks have not been immune to crisis. In the 1990s, a collapsing Japanese real estate market left banks holding billions of dollars of nonperforming loans. Regulators adopted a policy of forbearance, allowing the banks to continue operating even though they were technically insolvent. By 1998 the Japanese government passed a $500 billion bailout package, but the measure came too late to save several of the largest banks. Many European banks also encountered trouble in the 1990s as they faced increased competition from rapidly developing securities markets. France's largest bank, Credit Lyonnais, received a $10 billion bailout in 1995. BfG Bank, a German bank, needed a large capital infusion from its parent company because of losses in 1992.

Japan has taken the first steps toward rebuilding its struggling banking sector. Japan has allowed several of its largest banks to fail, has undertaken a massive effort to shore up its remaining banks, and (ironically) has passed legislation similar to Glass-Steagall to erect firewalls between commercial and investment banks. The German banking sector has been more stable but still faces challenges as the European Union (EU) integrates banking across member nations and EU-wide branching becomes a reality. Increased competition from other European banks and the rapidly developing European securities markets indicate leaner times ahead. In many respects, regulators in Japan and Germany are facing the same challenges the United States faced a decade ago—how to restructure and regulate in a way that fosters a strong and liquid banking sector but does not expose depositors to excessive risk. Whether these challenges will be met remains to be determined.

**Arguments Against Removing Restrictions.** Opponents of Gramm-Leach-Bliley argued against the bill on several grounds, many reminiscent of popular sentiment in 1933 when Glass-Steagall was enacted. Critics of the proposed legislation pointed to the difficulty of monitoring and assessing risk, especially in a world of increasingly complex derivatives and other modern financial instruments these organizations could potentially hold. Critics argued that the safety net of federal deposit insurance places taxpayers at risk by exposing them to risky activities. Finally, critics argued that the growth of financial conglomerates reduces quality of service to consumers and small businesses.

**Banks' Response to Repeal of Glass-Steagall.** The full impact of Gramm-Leach-Bliley has yet to be experienced; accordingly, the response by banking organizations is not yet complete. The extent of financial integration during the first few years of Gramm-Leach-Bliley has been less than expected. Most large banks have elected to become *financial holding companies* (as is now required in order to offer the new financial services), but few have actually purchased or merged with existing financial services firms. Rather, most of the banks have used their new status to reorganize and provide legitimacy to the activities they had been pursuing via loopholes in existing law. Only a few large banks have acquired securities firms, and none has acquired an insurance carrier. Citicorp quickly sold the insurance branch of Travelers after their 1998 merger. Small banks also have shown interest in exploring the potential of Gramm-Leach-Bliley, although the first steps have been tentative. About 400 banks with assets under $1 billion have reorganized as financial holding companies, but some observers suspect these banks are more interested in selling insurance and purchasing equity in smaller businesses than in becoming full-service financial organizations.

## FUTURE SHAPE OF BANKING

Regulations of the past have greatly influenced our contemporary banking industry. Restrictive regulations created the proliferation of small banks, each operating out of a single bank office. Reluctance to charter new institutions in communities already served by a few banks and reluctance to allow branch banking created an environment that insulated banks from competition. Many inefficient and poorly managed banks survived under these protections, often at the expense of the customers they served.

Removal of restrictions on the scale and scope of banking has strongly impacted our banking industry and will continue to have an impact in the future. Riegle-Neal has spawned thousands of bank mergers, creating a handful of financial behemoths in the process. Table 10-2 shows the total assets of each of the ten largest U.S. banks

**Table 10-2** Ten Largest U.S. Commercial Banks as of December 31, 2003

| Bank | Headquarters | Assets ($ Billion) | Share of All Commercial Bank Assets (%) |
|---|---|---|---|
| Citicorp | New York, NY | 1,317 | 17.4 |
| Bank of America | Charlotte, NC | 820 | 10.8 |
| JP Morgan Chase | New York, NY | 801 | 10.6 |
| Wachovia | Charlotte, NC | 411 | 5.4 |
| Wells Fargo | San Francisco, CA | 397 | 5.2 |
| MetLife | New York, NY | 337 | 4.5 |
| Bank One | Chicago, IL | 320 | 4.2 |
| Fleet Boston | Boston, MA | 200 | 2.6 |
| U.S. Bancorp | Minneapolis, MN | 192 | 2.5 |
| Sun Trust Banks | Atlanta, GA | 125 | 1.7 |
| Total | | $4,920 | 65.0 |

*Source: American Banker at* http://www.americanbanker.com/rankings.html

as of December 31, 2003. These ten banks collectively control about $5,000 billion in assets, or about two thirds of the assets of all 7,700 commercial banks in the U.S. economy!

Merger activity has slowed as major players have established the nationwide banking structure they desire, but the urge to merge is still strong. Gramm-Leach-Bliley opened the door for banks to provide a full range of financial services to their customers—large corporations, small businesses, and households. Banks have been slow to exploit the full latitude granted to them by Gramm-Leach-Bliley, but you can be sure that momentum will build in the next few years.

What, then, will our banking sector look like when this process of consolidation is complete? Will we have a few hundred banks? A few thousand? Or, like Canada and England, just a few dozen? Research suggests that U.S. banking likely will retain its unique shape, the influences of our banking history only partially tempered by the urge to consolidate. Extrapolation of evidence from states with liberal branching laws suggests that we will have a few thousand banks—a few very large banks with hundreds of billions of dollars of assets and focused lending policies and smaller, more traditional community banks specializing in consumer, home, and small business lending.

The market share of large banks has been growing and is expected to increase. However, studies indicate our economy is maintaining a strong and active sector of smaller community banks meeting the needs of households and small businesses. Possible curtailment of credit to small businesses as the banking industry becomes more concentrated is of concern, but studies indicate small banks often fill voids left by their larger counterparts. Gramm-Leach-Bliley permits small banks to underwrite private equity issues, giving small firms greater access to equity capital and reducing their dependence on bank loans. On balance, small businesses have more options than ever before.

At the beginning of the twentieth century, about three fourths of all U.S. financial assets were held in banks. Over the past hundred years, that fraction has declined to about one fourth. As financial markets developed, borrowers found more direct avenues to tap the funds of savers, reducing banks' dependence on customer deposits and loans as the predominant source of income and increasing reliance on fees charged for provision of other services. The Riegle-Neal and Gramm-Leach-Bliley Acts allowed banks to participate in more direct credit channels, offering their clients a broader range of services on a nationwide basis. Bank regulators face a critical challenge in the coming years—how to balance the necessity of ensuring the safety and soundness of the financial system against the need and desire of financial companies to innovate, earn profits, and adapt to changing economic conditions.

## SUMMARY

The United States has a dual banking system—some banks receive their operating charter from the federal government while others get their charter from the state in which the bank is domiciled. Banks are regulated because the FDIC (hence the taxpayers) insures bank deposits and because bank failures often involve large negative externalities. Bank regulations aim to reduce risk-taking and the incidence of bank failures and to ensure that banks maintain reasonable standards of liquidity. Bank supervision in the United States involves a complex system in which four entities—the Federal Reserve, the Federal Deposit Insurance Corporation, the Comptroller of the Currency, and 50 separate state banking agencies—play a sometimes overlapping role. Legislation enacted over the years in response to populist distrust of the concentration of financial power has led to a unique banking system in the United States where a very large number of separate banks coexist (27,000 in 1920 and 7,500 even today). The U.S. system contrasts with systems in other nations, where only a few hundred or fewer banks exist, each having many branches. Powerful forces work strongly to consolidate the banking industry. These forces include economies of scale, the desire to gain increased diversification of assets, and the desire of bank managers to gain increased market and political power. The *scope* of permissible bank activities has come full circle in the past 75 years. Prior to the Great Depression, commercial banks and investment banks could be legally combined. But widespread allegations of conflicts of interest, self dealing, and bank fraud during the 1929 to 1933 debacle led to the enactment of the Glass-Steagall Act, which imposed firewalls separating the two types of institutions. Beginning in the 1970s, various maneuvers increasingly enabled banks to circumvent the intent of this Act, and the Gramm-Leach-Bliley Act of 1999 effectively rescinded remaining Glass-Steagall restrictions. The Gramm-Leach-Bliley Act permits U.S. banks to compete on a more even footing with foreign banks. It is too early to determine whether abolition of Glass-Steagall was a wise move or one we will regret.

## KEY TERMS

Bank of the United States
unit banking
Free Banking Era
National Banking Act of 1863
dual banking system
Comptroller of the Currency
bank charters
CAMELS system
McFadden Act
limited branching
bank holding company
Bank Holding Company Act of 1956
Riegle-Neal Interstate Banking and Branching Efficiency Act of 1994
economies of scale
investment banks
Banking Act of 1933 (Glass-Steagall Act)
Gramm-Leach-Bliley Financial Services Modernization Act of 1999
economies of scope

# STUDY QUESTIONS

1. "Because the U.S. has so many more banks than other nations, the U.S. banking industry clearly must be more competitive and offers more benefits to consumers." Analyze this statement.

2. What is the "dual banking system" and why did it develop?

3. Explain the cycle of banking regulation, bank response, and banking re-regulation that characterizes the history of branch banking in the United States.

4. What have been the two main purposes of U.S. banking regulation? Were the McFadden Act and the Glass-Steagall Act consistent with these two main purposes? Explain.

5. What is the CAMELS system, and which of its components has been the subject of recent focus?

6. Which regulatory agency examines and supervises each of the following companies:
   **A.** First National Bank
   **B.** Farmer's State Bank (FDIC insured)
   **C.** Hometown State Bank (not FDIC insured)
   **D.** Wells Fargo, a bank holding company

7. Why were the founding fathers so firmly opposed to big banks? What legislation originated from their viewpoint?

8. Why might the FDIC have more interest in maintaining supervisory power over banks than the Comptroller of the Currency or the Federal Reserve does?

9. Which recent piece of financial legislation drew on economies of scale as a rationale for its enactment? Which drew on economies of scope?

10. Distinguish between economies of scale and economies of scope. Which more likely will be the driving force behind a merger between two banks? Between a bank and another financial services company?

11. "The main function of deposit insurance is *not* to reimburse depositors when their bank fails." Do you agree or disagree? Explain.

12. Discuss the potential costs and potential benefits of unrestricted interstate branch banking.

13. Analyze the potential costs and potential benefits of the Gramm-Leach-Bliley Act.

14. The wave of bank mergers in the past decade has resulted in substantial industry consolidation. Will this consolidation stifle competition in banking?

## ADDITIONAL READING

- A number of fine books detail the history of the U.S. banking system, including Benjamin Klebaner's *Commercial Banking in the United States: A History* (Hinsdale, IL: Dryden Press, 1974). For an opposing perspective on the free banking era, consult Arthur Rolnick and Warren Weber, "The Free Banking Era: New Evidence on Laissez-Faire Banking," *American Economic Review,* 1983, pp. 1080–1091.
- Recent history of the banking industry, its implications for consumers and the macroeconomy, and the future of banking are discussed in Allen Berger, Anil Kashyap, and Joseph Scalise, "The Transformation of the U.S. Banking Industry: What a Long, Strange Trip It's Been," *Brookings Papers on Economic Activity,* 1995, No. 2, pp. 55–218. Historical rationales for the Glass-Steagall Act are presented and debated in "The Underwriting of Commercial Bank Affiliates Prior to the Glass-Steagall Act: A Reexamination of Evidence for Passage of the Act," *Journal of Banking and Finance,* 1994, p. 351.
- The sensitivity of bank performance to the regulatory environment is explored by Douglas Evanoff in "Assessing the Impact of Regulation on Bank Cost Efficiency," *Federal Reserve Bank of Chicago Economic Perspectives,* Second Quarter 1998, pp. 21–32.
- Nicola Cetorelli examines the competitive implications of bank consolidation in "Competitive Analysis in Banking: Appraisal of the Methodologies," *Federal Reserve Bank of Chicago Economic Perspectives,* First Quarter 1999, pp. 2–15.
- Timothy Hannan compares the pricing power of large and small banks in "Retail Fees of Depository Institutions, 1994–1999," *Federal Reserve Bulletin,* 2001, pp. 1–11. The viability of small banks is explored in William Basset and Douglas Brady's "The Economic Performance of Small Banks, 1985–2000," *Federal Reserve Bulletin,* 2001, pp. 719–728.
- Finally, James Barth, R. Dan Brumbaugh, Jr., and James Wilcox examine the provisions of Gramm-Leach-Bliley in "The Repeal of Glass-Steagall and the Advent of Broad Banking," *Journal of Economic Perspectives,* Spring 2000, pp. 191–204.

# Chapter 11

# THE ECONOMICS OF BANKING REGULATION AND DEPOSIT INSURANCE

In Chapters 4 and 9, we outlined the nature of our nation's depository institutions and their role in the financial system. In Chapter 9, we analyzed the sources and uses of bank funds, the constraints on bank acquisition of earning assets, and the types of risks to which banks are exposed. We discussed the nature and functions of capital accounts and the trade-off between risk and short-term returns earned by depository institutions. The analyses apply equally to thrift institutions, such as savings and loan associations (S&Ls) and mutual savings banks, as well as commercial banks.

In this chapter, we provide an economic analysis of the regulatory apparatus governing bank behavior in the United States and other nations today. We explore how this regulatory structure evolved in response to major banking crises over the course of U.S. history. We illustrate the analysis by examining in-depth two important case studies: the U.S. S&L disaster of the 1980s that cost U.S. taxpayers some $150 billion, and the dramatic increase in commercial bank failures in the late 1980s and early 1990s. We analyze the underlying economic forces that caused these S&L and commercial bank failures and assess the role of the regulatory apparatus and the deposit insurance system in contributing to the problems. We discuss how appropriate design of regulatory policies and deposit insurance can minimize future recurrences of the S&L and commercial bank problems of the past 25 years. We also examine how past regulatory failures are reflected in the current framework of banking regulation and deposit insurance.

One key lesson of this chapter is that the financial system is not static. The financial system is in a continual state of evolution, driven by financial innovations, economic shocks, and other events. Look at Table 11-1, which indicates examples of major financial legislation enacted in the United States in the past 100 years, beginning with the Federal Reserve Act of 1913. Analysis of this table indicates that a recurring pattern—severe problems arise occasionally and lead to the imposition of "solutions" in the form of legislation. The solutions typically resolve the initial problem, but they also produce adverse consequences not foreseen by the legislation's supporters. A few examples are illustrative.

The Federal Reserve Act (1913) created our central bank. The act was instrumental in preventing macroeconomic disruptions resulting from systemic banking panics (with the glaring exception of the early 1930s). Together with the Employment Act of 1946 and other forces, the Federal Reserve Act built an inflationary bias into the U.S. economy. The Banking Act of 1933 sought to bolster the financial condition of the nation's banks (which had been impaired in the Great Depression) by prohibiting payment of interest on checking accounts and placing statutory ceilings on interest rates payable on savings and time deposits. But these restrictions created problems and were removed in the 1980s to avoid bankrupting

**Table 11-1 Key Twentieth-Century Financial Legislation**

| |
|---|
| **Federal Reserve Act (1913)** |
| Created the Federal Reserve System |
| **Banking Acts of 1933 (Glass-Steagall) and 1935** |
| Created the Federal Deposit Insurance Corporation (FDIC) |
| Restricted checkable deposits to commercial banks |
| Prohibited interest payments on checkable deposits |
| Placed interest rate ceilings on savings and time deposits |
| Separated commercial banking from the securities industry |
| **Depository Institutions Deregulation and Monetary Control Act of 1980 (DIDMCA)** |
| Phased out deposit rate ceilings |
| Authorized negotiable order of withdrawal (NOW) and automatic transfer service (ATS) accounts nationwide for commercial banks and thrifts |
| Broadened permissible activities of thrift institutions |
| Imposed uniform reserve requirements on all depository institutions |
| Increased FDIC deposit insurance from $40,000 to $100,000 per account |
| **Depository Institutions Act of 1982 (Garn–St. Germain Act)** |
| Further broadened the permissible range of activities of thrift institutions |
| Authorized depository institutions to issue money market deposit accounts |
| Granted FDIC and Federal Savings and Loan Insurance Corporations (FSLIC) emergency powers to merge troubled thrifts and banks |
| **Financial Institutions Reform, Recovery, and Enforcement Act of 1989 (FIRREA)** |
| Abolished the FSLIC and Federal Home Loan Bank Board |
| Created the Office of Thrift Supervision (OTS) to regulate thrifts |
| Created the Resolution Trust Corporation (RTC) to resolve insolvent thrifts |
| Provided funds to resolve failures of thrift institutions |
| Reimposed restrictions on S&L activities |
| Increased insurance premiums for depository institutions |
| **Federal Deposit Insurance Corporation Improvement Act of 1991 (FDICIA)** |
| Recapitalized the FDIC |
| Established provisions for prompt resolution of impaired depository institutions |
| Increased capital requirements for banks and thrifts |
| Limited brokered deposits |
| Moderated "too big to fail" policy |
| Mandated that the FDIC establish risk-based deposit insurance premiums |
| Increased the Federal Reserve's authority to supervise foreign banks in the United States |
| **Gramm-Leach-Bliley Financial Services Modernization Act of 1999** |
| Overturned Glass-Steagall; eliminated the separation of commercial banking from investment banking and other activities |

thousands of depository institutions. The Banking Act of 1933 also implemented federal insurance of bank deposits to reduce exposure to socially disastrous banking panics and achieved its goal. However, deposit insurance facilitated bank risk-taking by reducing depositors' incentives to monitor their banks' behavior. The Garn–St. Germain Act of 1982 broadened the range of permissible activities of the thrift industry, allowing asset diversification and decreasing vulnerability to macroeconomic shocks. However, the legislation also triggered a massive increase in risk taking by the industry, contributed to hundreds of S&Ls insolvencies, and led to enactment of the Financial Institutions Reform, Recovery, and Enforcement Act of 1989 (FIRREA). The Gramm-Leach-Bliley Financial Services Modernization Act of 1999 authorized banks to dramatically expand their *scope* of operations, permitting U.S. banks to compete on a level playing field with their foreign peers. A good exercise is seeing if you can forecast adverse consequences that will result from this legislation.

## LIMITING THE CONSEQUENCES OF ASYMMETRIC INFORMATION

To design banking regulations and deposit insurance you first must recognize the problems in the banking sector caused by *asymmetric information*. Because of asymmetric information, banks have more information about their activities and the risks they are taking than do bank depositors, government officials, and regulators. The existence of asymmetric information leads to the problems of *moral hazard* and *adverse selection*. The moral hazard problem manifests as banks' propensity to take on more risk than is socially optimal in order to reap high rates of return. An example of the adverse selection problem is the tendency for free-wheeling, and sometimes unscrupulous individuals to seek entry into the banking industry. These individuals gain potential access to funds and, because of asymmetric information in banking, their risky and illicit activities are less likely to be detected than in other sectors. Another example of adverse selection is the tendency for depositors to place funds in the riskiest banks (if deposits are fully protected against potential loss by deposit insurance or government policy preventing certain banks from failing), which typically pay the highest interest rates.

As we indicated in Chapter 9, *negative externalities* are associated with bank failures. A bank failure can disrupt the local economy and trigger a run on other banks, producing adverse macroeconomic consequences such that the collective costs to society substantially exceed the costs incurred by the failed bank. Thus, a major objective of banking regulations and deposit insurance is reducing bank failures. The United States and other nations have established a "safety net" intended to sharply reduce the incidence of bank failures.

### Government Safety Net for Bank Depositors: FDIC Insurance and Other Measures

Before the Banking Act of 1933 created our system of federal deposit insurance, banking panics occurred periodically in the United States. Major banking panics occurred in 1873, 1884, 1893, 1907, and from 1929 to 1933. The panics reflected *contagion effects*—failure of one bank in a region led to runs on other banks in the area. The public rushed to withdraw cash from uninsured bank deposits. Bank reserves declined, forcing banks to reduce their loans. Essential credit was cut off from legitimate borrowers and the nation's money supply declined, resulting in damaging contraction of economic activity. Failure of a few banks touched off banking panics that led to failure of other banks, which in turn produced adverse macroeconomic consequences resulting in additional bank failures. Following the panic of 1907, the Federal Reserve Act created our nation's central bank. A key mission of the new central bank was to be a "lender of last resort," that is, to provide cash (reserves) to the banking system in times of panic. The lender of last resort function, performed effectively, prevents banking panics from forcing our nation's banks to drastically reduce lending. The adverse macroeconomic repercussions of banking panics are greatly reduced, and the stability of the U.S. economy is increased accordingly. As we will document in Chapter 17, the Federal Reserve utterly failed to perform this "lender of last resort" function in the early 1930s. Many economists hold the Federal Reserve largely responsible for the collapse of the banking system and, indeed, for the Great Depression.

As a result of the economic disaster of the early 1930s, the Federal Deposit Insurance Corporation (FDIC) was created to insure bank deposits. Individuals suspecting bank failure might not withdraw cash from their accounts if the deposits are fully insured. Hence, deposit insurance aims to eliminate systemic banking panics and their associated adverse economic consequences. The central bank's need to perform its "lender of last resort" function also is reduced. Deposit insurance thus constitutes a major part of the government safety net for depositors. Roughly 9,000 banks in the United States failed from 1929 to 1933. After implementation of FDIC insurance, fewer than 600 banks failed over the next 40 years. The other component of the safety net involves authorities acting directly to prevent failure of certain banks.

## Challenges Created by the Government Safety Net

The government safety net is critical for preventing destructive, systemic banking panics. However, a safety net likely exacerbates the problems of moral hazard and adverse selection in the banking industry. Depositors no longer have strong incentives to monitor their banks to inhibit bank risk taking (moral hazard) and dissuade entry into the field by irresponsible individuals (adverse selection). Banking authorities—facing a special dilemma in the case of huge banks whose failure can trigger nationwide and even worldwide repercussions—have adopted a **too big to fail policy.** In this policy, the FDIC stands ready to take extreme measures that prevent large banks from failing and their depositors from losing money.[1] The policy increases the moral hazard problem by providing large banks with incentives to take on more risk than they otherwise would, so special efforts are needed to monitor the activities of our largest banks.

**too big to fail policy** regulatory policy of systematically bailing out very large, troubled financial institutions whose failure might touch off major financial market repurcussions

The potential adverse consequences of the too big to fail policy have become increasingly important given the increasing size, scope, and complexity of our mammoth banking organizations resulting from financial consolidation. Such consolidation was stimulated by the Riegle-Neal Interstate Banking and Branching and Efficiency Act of 1994 and the Gramm-Leach-Bliley Financial Services Modernization Act of 1999. One problem resulting from consolidation of the banking industry is the increased *number* of very large banks whose failure can cause systemic problems. More banks are encompassed under the government's "too big to fail" umbrella and therefore are motivated to engage in increased risk. Perhaps even more important is the increasing *scope of activities* of large banks, which implies the safety net must extend to activities such as insurance and securities underwriting. Applying the safety net to nontraditional banking activities can lead to increased risk taking in these areas as well. For these reasons, banking regulatory authorities have faced substantially more challenges in the past decade.

---

[1] Shortly after the massive Continental Illinois Bank failed in 1984, the U.S. Comptroller of the Currency testified before Congress that the government regarded the 11 largest U.S. banks to be "too big to fail."

## REGULATORY MEASURES INTENDED TO LIMIT BANK RISK TAKING

Because the existence of government's banking safety net increases the problems of moral hazard and adverse selection, banking regulations must compensate by effectively limiting risk taking in the banking industry. Banking regulations can contribute to this objective in several ways. Regulations include restrictions on the types of assets banks are permitted to hold, mandatory diversification of bank assets, capital requirements and disclosure requirements, rigorous bank chartering standards, and careful supervision and examination of banks.

### Restricting Types of Eligible Bank Assets, Requiring Diversification, and Mandating Bank Capital Requirements

Even without the government safety net, which motivates increased risk taking, unregulated banks would likely take on more risk than is optimal from society's vantage point. Riskier ventures provide higher average expected returns. The existence of the safety net exacerbates the risk-taking problem, so regulations on banks are essential. Banks are not allowed to hold risky assets such as shares of stock or corporate bonds. Bank's earning assets (other than loans) historically have been limited to U.S. government securities and municipal bonds. Risk is inversely related to diversification. The more diversified a bank's portfolio of assets, the less risk it incurs. Diversification of bank assets is fostered by regulations imposing limits on the share of a bank's loans that can be made to any individual borrower. In addition, liquidity standards ensure that a portion of bank assets are held in relatively low-risk liquid assets such as short-term government securities, federal funds sold, and excess reserves.

If a bank has little of its owners' equity or capital at stake, the bank's incentive to take risk is high because little is lost if things go wrong. Regulatory authorities' imposition and enforcement of strict capital requirements strongly reduce the moral hazard problem in banking. A bank's incentive to take risk is reduced to the extent that more of the bank owners' wealth is at stake. Today, three separate types of capital requirements exist. The first is simply the ratio of bank capital to total assets, sometimes known as the *leverage ratio*.[2] In the CAMELS bank evaluation framework discussed in Chapter 10, a bank's leverage ratio must exceed 5 percent for the bank to be classified as "well capitalized." Additional restrictions, including more frequent bank examinations, are placed upon the bank if the bank's leverage ratio drops below 5 percent, and especially if the ratio drops below 3 percent. Prior to the spectacular failure of the Continental Illinois Bank in 1984 and the demise of hundreds of S&Ls in the late 1980s, the leverage ratio was the only form of capital requirement imposed on U.S. banks.

In the past 15 years, regulators have imposed two additional types of capital requirements on banks. Beginning in 1992, separate risk-based capital requirements have been levied on certain *off-balance-sheet* activities judged to be particularly risky. Such activities include trading positions in futures and options, interest-rate swaps, and other derivatives. In 1998, a third form of capital requirement for the nation's

[2] Recall from our discussion in Chapter 9 that the reciprocal of a bank's capital to total assets ratio is the multiplier through which a bank's rate of return on total assets is converted into a rate of return on capital or owners' equity. A rate of return on total assets of 1 percent implies a rate of return on capital of 10 percent if the bank's capital to total assets ratio is 10 percent or a rate of return on capital of 20 percent if the capital to total assets ratio is 5 percent. Hence the term *leverage ratio*. A low capital to total assets ratio implies a high leverage ratio.

largest banks—supervised by the Federal Reserve—resulted from the consolidation of the U.S. banking industry and the increased scope of activities in which banks can engage. Huge banks now must use their own risk models to estimate the maximum amount they can lose over a 10-day period through trading in derivatives and other risky instruments and then maintain additional capital in the amount of three times the estimated potential loss. Imposition of the two more recent forms of capital requirements reflects the authorities' heightened concern about the potential risks taken by our largest banks in today's wide-open banking environment.

## Banking Supervision and Examination and Disclosure Requirements

Regular examinations allow regulators to detect whether banks are complying with capital requirements and other standards. Thus, the examinations reduce moral hazard. As indicated, the authorities evaluate banks' performance based on the CAMELS criteria (capital, asset quality, management quality, earnings, liquidity, and sensitivity to risk). An inferior CAMELS rating can lead regulators to require a bank to change its behavior or even to close. By reducing bank risk-taking through rigorous conduct of the CAMELS system, the authorities reduce adverse selection problems. Knowledge that the authorities are rigorously limiting risk-taking opportunities reduces the propensity for "high-rollers" to enter the industry.

Certain disclosure requirements are imposed on banks to facilitate evaluation of bank condition. Banks are required to meet conventional accounting standards and publicly disclose pertinent information about the bank's balance sheet and risks incurred by the bank. Each commercial bank is required to file a quarterly *call report* indicating the bank's assets, liabilities, capital, income, dividends paid, and certain activities such as foreign exchange operations.

Bank examinations are conducted on a regular basis, occasionally unannounced. Examiners look at the bank's books to see if the bank is meeting various standards. Examiners can require banks to sell risky assets and write off bad loans. Examiners deeming a bank's capital to be insufficient or detecting other serious problems can declare the bank a "problem bank," a classification that triggers more frequent examinations and other sanctions.

In the past, bank supervision and examination focused almost entirely on quality of bank assets and whether the bank was meeting capital requirements and restrictions on types of assets the bank can own. Regulatory authorities in the United States and elsewhere now place more emphasis on bank management's ability to control risk because of increased *scope* of bank activities and increased possibility of incurring huge losses in a short period through trading of derivatives and other activities. Beginning in 1996, the Federal Reserve and the Comptroller of the Currency have implemented risk assessment evaluations of banks they supervise and examine. Examiners' evaluation of management (the "M" in CAMELS) now includes the quality of a bank's internal controls to prevent fraud and other illicit activities, the quality of the bank's risk monitoring system, and the extent of effective oversight of bank activity provided by the bank's top management and board of directors.

## Granting of Bank Charters and Restrictions on Competition in Banking

Prospective owners of a new bank must apply for a charter from the Comptroller of the Currency (national banks) or the state banking authorities (state banks). The chartering authorities carefully evaluate the quality of prospective management, the proposed amount of initial capital of the bank, and the prospective earnings of the bank. The authorities can use the evaluation to minimize the adverse selection problem by blocking charter requests from individuals deemed to be dishonest, incompetent, or excessively aggressive.

Greater competition in banking reduces profits. In response, bankers may increase risk taking to achieve desired profit levels. The United States and other countries have traditionally imposed various barriers to competition in banking, partly to prevent this bank reaction. U.S. examples include widespread restrictions on branching, restrictions on bank charters in cases where more liberal chartering would appreciably reduce profits of existing banks, and prevention of non-banks from engaging in traditional banking activities. Unfortunately, actions that reduce competition in banking hurt consumers by raising costs and reducing quality of bank service. The banking authorities face a dilemma when measures inhibiting banking competition at once reduce moral hazard problems and harm consumers. With passage of the Riegle-Neal Act of 1994 and the Gramm-Leach-Bliley Act of 1999, U.S. policy has clearly moved away from restricting competition in banking.

## EVENTS LEADING UP TO THE S&L DISASTER OF THE 1980S

We now turn to our two case studies of major crises in the U.S. financial system. First, we analyze the S&L crisis of the 1980s. We then turn to the problems experienced by the commercial banking sector in the late 1980s and early 1990s. Finally, we outline general principles underlying deposit insurance, examine the systems currently in place, and discuss the systems' prospects for minimizing future recurrence of costly financial crises.

In the 1980s, about half of the nation's S&Ls were forced to close their doors. The nation's taxpayers shelled out $150 billion to clean up the mess. What happened? We need to distinguish two separate crises that struck the S&L industry. The first crisis resulted from the macroeconomic forces of severe inflation and deep recession. These forces impaired S&L income statements and balance sheets in the late 1970s and early 1980s. The second and more damaging post-1981 set of forces resulted from the response of Congress, the Reagan Administration, and the regulatory authorities to the initial hardship in the industry. Their responses severely compounded the crisis. We make the argument that government policy decisions were largely responsible for the S&L fiasco.

### Origins and Operations of the S&L Industry

**Federal Home Loan Bank Board (FHLBB)** organization established by Congress to regulate the savings and loan industry

**Federal Savings and Loan Insurance Corporation (FSLIC)** subsidiary of the FHLBB created to insure savings and loan deposits

The S&L concept was fundamentally flawed from the outset. In retrospect, it is surprising that the S&L disaster did not occur sooner. The government fostered S&Ls in the 1930s to encourage home ownership by the masses of middle-class Americans. Congress established the **Federal Home Loan Bank Board (FHLBB)** to regulate the S&Ls and the FHLBB's subsidiary—the **Federal Savings and Loan Insurance Corporation (FSLIC)**—to insure S&L deposits. The S&Ls issued short-term savings deposits to the public and used the proceeds to grant 20- and 30-year mortgages to local home buyers at interest rates guaranteed to remain constant over the life of the mortgage.

Clearly, an S&L loses money if interest rates paid to depositors rise above the average interest rate earned on the institution's portfolio of mortgages. If the situation persists for a lengthy period, the S&L's capital is wiped out, rendering the institution insolvent. In "borrowing short and lending long," S&Ls were inherently vulnerable to episodes of rising interest rates. They also were vulnerable to episodes of inverted yield curves—periods in which short-term yields exceed long-term yields. Government regulations prevented S&Ls from diversifying their assets, instead requiring S&Ls to confine their assets predominantly to fixed-rate mortgages.

For nearly four decades, the S&L industry was stable and prosperous. Life was simple in those low-inflation, stable times. Outsiders enviously joked about the "3-6-3" lifestyle enjoyed by S&L managers—that is, borrow at 3 percent, lend at 6 percent, and head out to the golf course at 3 p.m.! From the 1930s to the mid-1960s, interest rates were relatively low and stable. The yield curve was almost always upward sloping. In other words, long-term yields were higher than short-term yields. Interest rates then trended upward from the mid-1960s through the mid-1970s, but the increase was mild and gradual enough so that the S&Ls did not suffer major problems. Then, in the late 1970s, all hell broke loose!

## Escalation of Inflation and Interest Rates in the 1970s

The U.S. inflation rate averaged less than 3 percent per year from 1935 to 1969 but averaged more than 7 percent per year in the 1970s. As rising inflation exerted upward pressure on interest rates in the late 1970s (through the Fisher Effect and the Federal Reserve's response to higher inflation), the rates moved sharply above the statutory ceiling rates the thrifts were permitted to pay depositors. To avert a severe episode of *disintermediation,* the regulatory bodies authorized banks to issue *money market certificates*—new instruments issued in $10,000 denominations that permitted banks and thrifts to match the yield on 6-month Treasury bills. Some time later, the Depository Institutions Deregulation and Monetary Control Act of 1980 (DIDMCA) phased out the interest-rate ceilings over a 6-year period ending in March 1986.

The regulatory changes allowed S&Ls to stave off disintermediation. However, the changes did not address the fundamental problem—the fact that S&L assets were overwhelmingly composed of fixed-rate mortgages, the bulk of which were issued several years ago and had many years left to run. Fixed-rate mortgages are contractual agreements specifying that the S&L cannot increase the interest rate charged on fixed-rate mortgages already outstanding.[3] Assume that thrift institutions require a 1 percent "spread"—the difference between the average yield earned on assets and the average cost of obtaining funds—to meet operating expenses and remain profitable (actual S&L spreads in recent years have ranged from 3 to 4 percent). Suppose that the average return on the existing portfolio of mortgages is 7 percent. If S&Ls are forced to pay more than 6 percent to obtain funds, they incur losses. An increased cost of funds, payable to *all* depositors, can potentially be shifted only onto *new* home buyers.

Because the S&Ls' asset structures in the late 1970s were heavily weighted with relatively low-interest-rate mortgages issued several years earlier, the average return on the mortgage portfolio could take several years to pull up by a full percentage point. An S&L could not quickly pull up the average return on its mortgage portfolio by dramatically raising interest rates on *new* mortgages. Periods of sharply rising interest rates clearly pose serious problems for S&Ls given their asset structure. Again, federal regulations in place in the 1970s required S&Ls to invest most of their funds in fixed-rate mortgages.

---

[3] Federally chartered S&Ls were first authorized to issue adjustable rate mortgages (ARMs) in the spring of 1981. The rate on an ARM is adjusted periodically (typically once per year) in line with changes in a benchmark interest rate such as the yield on 1-year Treasury notes.

The financial problems thrift institutions encountered prior to 1982 did not result from interest-rate ceilings on deposits but rather from the forces that exerted strong upward pressure on interest rates and the institutional structure of thrift institutions.[4] The high interest rates of the 1970s and early 1980s derived from several factors. Most important were excessively expansionary macroeconomic policies that contributed to rising inflation in the late 1960s and later and two dramatic oil price hikes (1973 and 1979) that fueled the fires of inflation through the 1970s. Figure 11-1 illustrates the relationship between the interest rate earned by S&Ls on new mortgages and the yield on U.S. Treasury bills, which we use as a proxy for the yield S&Ls must pay depositors to remain competitive with money market mutual funds (and thus prevent depositors fleeing the S&Ls in favor of money market mutual funds).

## Squeeze on S&Ls' Profits: Cyclical and Structural Causes

The figure illustrates the dramatic upsurge of short-term interest rates from 1977 to 1981. Although the rate on new mortgages also increased sharply, the positive gap between the mortgage rate and the Treasury bill yield was severely reduced for several years beginning about 1978. The figure significantly *understates* the severity of the problem faced by S&Ls inasmuch as the average yield earned on an S&L's *portfolio of mortgages* lags sluggishly behind the rate on *new mortgages* illustrated in the figure. In 1981, for example, the spread between the yield earned on assets and the cost of funds for the entire S&L industry was *negative* 0.8 percent.

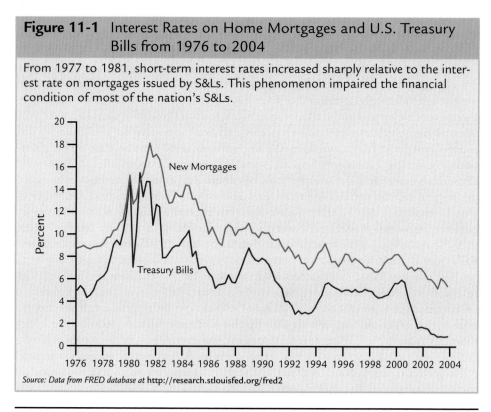

**Figure 11-1** Interest Rates on Home Mortgages and U.S. Treasury Bills from 1976 to 2004

From 1977 to 1981, short-term interest rates increased sharply relative to the interest rate on mortgages issued by S&Ls. This phenomenon impaired the financial condition of most of the nation's S&Ls.

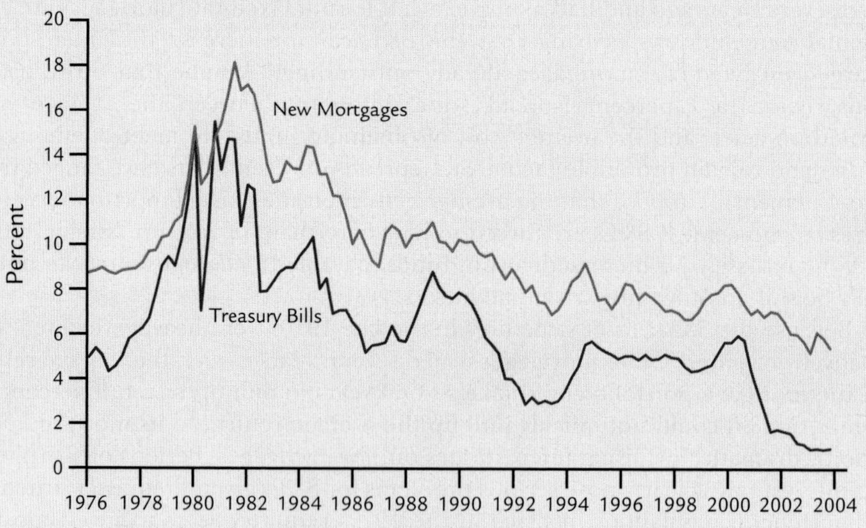


*Source: Data from FRED database at* **http://research.stlouisfed.org/fred2**

[4] If interest-rate ceilings had been maintained through the 1980s rather than phased out by DIDMCA, massive outflows of funds from thrifts to money market mutual funds likely would have bankrupted thousands of S&Ls. The S&Ls would have been forced to liquidate mortgages at low prices to obtain funds to pay depositors. The losses on mortgages would have depleted capital, rendering the S&Ls insolvent.

Because of the phenomenon illustrated in the figure and the losses associated with loan defaults in the severe 1981 to 1982 recession, the S&L industry experienced huge operating losses in 1981 and 1982. Industrywide net operating losses were $6 billion in 1981 and $5 billion in 1982. Approximately 85 percent of the nation's S&Ls lost money in 1981, and nearly 70 percent lost money in 1982. In the figure, however, short-term yields decreased sharply after 1981, and the normal spread between mortgage rates and Treasury bill rates reasserted itself during the remainder of the 1980s and thereafter. The figure suggests that if the S&Ls had stayed with their conservative posture of limiting themselves to mortgage lending, they likely would have "muddled through" and regained their financial strength during the mid-1980s. Instead, a new element—big-time risk taking—came into play and became a decisive force in the S&L fiasco (more on that later).

In addition to the short-term problem caused by the rapid escalation of interest rates from 1977 to 1981, the S&L industry faced longer-term structural problems as a result of financial innovations. Increasing competition from the newly established money market mutual fund industry in the late 1970s meant that S&Ls were forced to pay more for their deposits than formerly. Financial innovations also squeezed S&Ls on the asset side of their balance sheets. Securitization of mortgages caused pension funds and life insurance companies to significantly increase their demand for these mortgage instruments, thereby reducing mortgage rates. These forces benefited consumers but produced a structural reduction in the S&L spread. This phenomenon signaled a contraction of the S&L industry independent of the short-term crisis caused by surging interest rates. Some economists then questioned the need for a separate S&L industry. About one fourth of the 3,200 S&Ls operating in the 1970s—some 800 institutions—were gone by the end of 1982.[5] Some were closed down while others merged with stronger institutions. Estimates indicate that the net worth of the industry declined from approximately $32 billion in 1979 to only $4 billion by the end of 1982, before rebounding.[6]

## GOVERNMENT RESPONSE TO THE S&L PROBLEMS OF THE EARLY 1980s

The U.S. government's response to the financial problems the S&Ls encountered in the early 1980s consisted of three principal elements: deregulation, forbearance (permitting insolvent S&Ls to continue operating), and inadequate funding for supervision of the deregulated and financially impaired industry. In hindsight, the government's response, especially when coupled with the existence (indeed *expansion*) of federal deposit insurance coverage, was very costly to the nation.

### Deregulation

The initial heavy losses suffered by the S&Ls in the early 1980s were essentially caused by government policies that handcuffed the S&Ls from the very beginning. The restrictive government policies and the very large increases in inflation and interest rates from 1965 to 1981 led to legislation allowing S&Ls to compete on a level

[5] Today fewer than 1,500 S&Ls exist in the United States, down from some 3,900 in 1970.

[6] In December 1981, the low point of S&Ls' valuation, a widely quoted estimate, put the net worth of the S&L industry at negative $100 billion. The figure was derived by estimating the value of S&L assets when interest rates were at all-time peak levels (and bond and mortgage prices were at corresponding lows). The 1980 to 1981 spike in interest rates temporarily put the net worth of the S&L industry at all-time low (negative) levels. Two years later, after interest rates had fallen sharply, the increase in bond and mortgage values returned the net worth of the industry to a positive level.

**Depository Institutions Act of 1982 (Garn–St. Germain Act)**
act accelerating deregulation of the S&Ls by authorizing them to engage in additional activities and compete with money market mutual funds

playing field. In 1982, Congress enacted the **Depository Institutions Act of 1982 (Garn–St. Germain Act)** (review Table 11-1). This act accelerated the deregulation of S&Ls by authorizing them to issue money market deposit accounts with no interest ceilings in order to compete with money market mutual funds. More significantly, the act broadened the permissible range of activities of S&Ls by authorizing them to make loans to consumers, businesses, and the commercial real estate sector.

To ensure that institutions under state control were not disadvantaged relative to federally chartered S&Ls, several state legislatures took extreme measures to deregulate their state-chartered thrifts. The S&Ls in Texas, California, and Florida were almost totally deregulated. These institutions were permitted to invest in junk bonds, windmill farms, and real estate ventures in the desert. A large portion of the losses incurred by the S&L industry involved state-chartered institutions in Texas, California, and Florida. Most economists had long advocated deregulation of the financial sector, but Garn–St. Germain could not have been implemented at a more inopportune time. Garn–St. Germain was enacted when the moral hazard problem was at peak levels—when most of the S&Ls in the United States were technically insolvent and therefore eager to engage in increased risk taking.

Had Congress deregulated the thrift institutions a decade earlier when the industry's financial condition was robust, the entire S&L fiasco might have been avoided. In 1971, the Hunt Commission (a bipartisan group appointed by President Richard Nixon) recommended a series of measures to deregulate the nation's depository institutions. The commission recommended elimination of interest-rate ceilings payable by depository institutions. The commission also recommended that S&Ls be permitted to engage in a wider range of lending activities and issue adjustable-rate mortgages. At that time, the thrift industry was quite prosperous and did not support deregulation of interest rates payable on deposits. In addition, the public did not embrace adjustable-rate mortgages. Unfortunately, Congress bowed to these political winds and ignored the Hunt Commission's recommendations until it was too late.

## Forbearance, Deposit Insurance, and Risk Taking

The regulatory authorities did not close down or mandate mergers of insolvent S&Ls with financially sound institutions. Instead, the regulatory authorities let the troubled institutions continue operating in the hopes that better economic times would restore the S&Ls to solvency. This policy was given the pleasant name "forbearance." Closing or merging all S&Ls that were technically insolvent in 1982 or 1983 would have exhausted the entire insurance fund of the FSLIC. Substantial taxpayer assistance would have been needed and the competence of the regulatory authorities and their congressional overseers questioned. So, our government opted to let most of the insolvent S&Ls continue operating. In each year in the critical period from 1983 through 1989, more than 300 insolvent S&Ls (known as *zombies*) were open and doing business (Figure 11-2).

To practice forbearance, the regulatory authorities liberalized the accounting standards of the S&L industry. Even with the more lenient accounting standards in place, the authorities reduced capital standards as industry conditions deteriorated in the early 1980s. The minimum ratio of capital to total assets S&Ls were required to maintain was lowered from 5 percent to 4 percent in 1980 and to 3 percent in 1982. This lower requirement increased the moral hazard problem. With less equity at stake, S&Ls managers rationally decided to take on more risk.

Deposit insurance also contributes to the moral hazard problem. When potential losses are fully covered by insurance, insured depositors have less incentive to guard

**Figure 11-2** Estimated Number of Insolvencies and Insolvencies Resolved at FSLIC-Insured Institutions

The number of insolvent S&Ls in operation increased dramatically after 1981. The government was slow to resolve these insolvencies by closing or merging failed S&Ls.

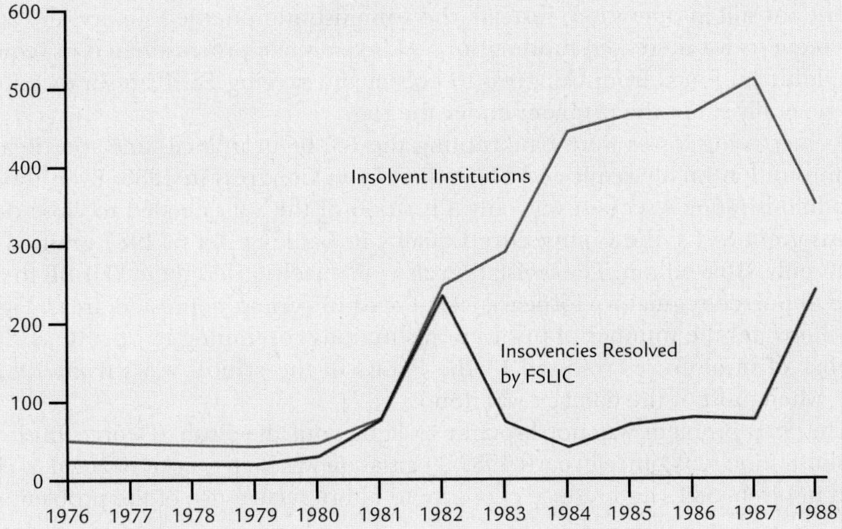


*Source: FDIC*

against the event insured against, and so the event is more likely to occur. For example, if an individual has theft insurance, he or she has less incentive to install an expensive alarm system in the home or car. Thus, theft insurance coverage increases the amount of theft that occurs. Similarly, depositors who are insured against commercial bank or S&L failure no longer have an incentive to watch the institution for prudent behavior. By raising federal deposit insurance from $40,000 to $100,000 per account in 1980, Congress inadvertently signaled thousands of additional depositors that they could safely ignore the activities of their S&L or commercial bank.

Perhaps more importantly, the increase in deposit insurance coverage triggered a socially costly financial innovation known as *brokered deposits*. Brokerage firms such as Merrill Lynch took multi-million dollar blocks of funds, broke them down into fully insured $100,000 lots, and sold them to depository institutions as CDs. By paying a slightly higher interest rate than its peers, an insolvent S&L could attract a large amount of these brokered funds, which the S&L could use in an effort to grow (or gamble) itself out of insolvency. In this way, funds gravitated to the most financially precarious S&Ls (the adverse selection problem). By increasing deposit insurance coverage, Congress probably increased the number of S&L and bank failures.

As thousands of S&Ls became financially impaired in the early 1980s, they had powerful incentives to take additional risks, aiming for higher returns that would strengthen their financial condition. The most severely impaired institutions had the most incentive to take long risks. An insolvent S&L has no downside risk. Because none of the owners' equity is at stake, the situation becomes a "heads we win, tails the government loses" proposition. Increased risk taking is a highly predictable phenomenon in such circumstances, and the public must ask why the regulatory authorities permitted it.

**Financial Institutions Reform, Recovery, and Enforcement Act of 1989 (FIRREA)** legislation abolishing both the FHLBB and the FSLIC and creating The Office of Thrift Supervision, The Bank Insurance Fund, and The Savings Association Insurance Fund

**Office of Thrift Supervision (OTS)** organization created as a bureau within the Treasury Department to replace the FHLBB

## Inadequate Funding for S&L Supervisors and the FSLIC

In view of the moral hazard and adverse selection problems, it is unfortunate that the Reagan administration and the regulatory authorities (the FHLBB and the FSLIC) did not move aggressively to close the insolvent S&Ls or at least impose strong surveillance on the activities of the *zombie* institutions—S&Ls that were insolvent but still in operation. Instead, the administration denied supervisory agencies' requests for increased funding for S&L examiners, procrastinated in requesting additional funds from Congress to bolster the sagging FSLIC insurance fund, and generally swept the problem under the rug.

As increasing losses were bankrupting the FSLIC insurance fund, the Reagan Administration finally requested $15 billion from Congress in 1986. Even though the administration's request was only a fraction of the sum needed to close down the insolvent S&Ls, the Competitive Equality in Banking Act of 1987 granted the FSLIC only $10.8 billion. The legislation also perversely ordered the FHLBB to continue to pursue regulatory forbearance, at least in certain depressed areas. Figure 11-2 illustrates the number of insolvent institutions continuing to operate and the number of insolvencies resolved by the FSLIC in the critical years from 1982 to 1988, when most of the damage was done.

The S&L problem was not brought to light until the Bush (George Bush Sr.) Administration took office in early 1989. Legislation was then quickly enacted to close down insolvent S&Ls and reduce exposure to future recurrence of the problem.

# FINANCIAL INSTITUTIONS REFORM, RECOVERY, AND ENFORCEMENT ACT OF 1989 (FIRREA)

**Bank Insurance Fund (BIF)** insurance fund created by FIRREA for commercial banks

**Savings Association Insurance Fund (SAIF)** insurance fund created by FIRREA for thrift institutions

**Resolution Trust Corporation (RTC)** temporary institution created by FIRREA that managed and resolved insolvent thrift institutions and liquidated assets of failed institutions

The **Financial Institutions Reform, Recovery, and Enforcement Act of 1989 (FIRREA),** enacted in August 1989, was the most comprehensive piece of legislation affecting the thrift industry since the 1930s (review Table 11-1). The act abolished both the FHLBB and the FSLIC, both of which had demonstrated ample actions warranting their termination. The **Office of Thrift Supervision (OTS)** replaced the FHLBB and was created as a bureau within the Treasury Department. The FDIC took over the regulatory functions formerly held by the FSLIC. Two new insurance funds were created: the **Bank Insurance Fund (BIF)** for commercial banks and the **Savings Association Insurance Fund (SAIF)** for the thrift institutions. FIRREA also created the **Resolution Trust Corporation (RTC),** a temporary institution that managed and resolved insolvent thrift institutions and liquidated assets of failed institutions. By the time the RTC closed its doors for good at the end of 1995—1 year ahead of schedule—the RTC had disposed of 747 bankrupt or ailing S&Ls and recovered most of the $450 billion worth of thrift institution assets it inherited from failed institutions.

Rather than putting the cost of the cleanup on budget, Congress created the **Resolution Funding Corporation (RFC),** which issued bonds to cover the cleanup costs. FIRREA sharply boosted insurance premiums for remaining depository institutions to rebuild the insurance funds. FIRREA also rolled back some of the deregulatory measures implemented in the 1982 Garn–St. Germain Act. FIRREA mandated that thrifts hold at least 70 percent of their assets in mortgages and other housing-related instruments and restricted commercial real estate loans to no more than four times an institution's capital. S&Ls were no longer allowed to acquire junk bonds, and all existing holdings were required to be liquidated by

1994. Core capital requirements were increased from 3 percent to 8 percent, and provisions were made for thrifts to eventually abide by the same risk-based capital requirements as commercial banks. Troubled thrifts were no longer allowed to acquire brokered deposits, and some egregious accounting gimmicks were eliminated. Provisions allowing equity investments by S&Ls were tightened. Finally, the regulatory authorities were granted powers to order S&Ls to abandon certain risky operations.

**Resolution Funding Corporation (RFC)** establishment created by Congress to issue bonds to cover the expenses of financial institution reform

## SUMMARY: ROLE OF MORAL HAZARD AND ADVERSE SELECTION IN THE S&L FIASCO

An efficient summary of the basic forces that created the S&L disaster is as follows. A whole series of events conspired to dramatically increase the moral hazard and adverse selection problems in S&Ls. This, in turn, was responsible for much of the ultimate $150 billion loss to taxpayers. First, a series of "historical accidents"—or at least events beyond the control of S&Ls—placed the industry into a weakened state. The historical accidents include the dramatic increases in inflation and interest rates from 1978 to 1981 and the ensuing severe recession triggered by the Federal Reserve's powerful (and successful) efforts to eradicate the inflation. The sharp decline in farm product prices (and therefore farm values) and the collapse of oil prices in the mid-1980s also were instrumental. All of these events impaired the financial condition of depository institutions, increasing the moral hazard problem. The industry's appetite for risky ventures was stimulated.

The moral hazard problems were exacerbated by the untimely deregulation of the financial system and a series of financial innovations. Both of these events boosted the capacity of depository institutions to engage in risk taking. Among the financial innovations that expanded the scope for risk taking were the development of financial futures, swaps and other derivatives, and the advent of junk bonds. The permissive supervisory environment of the 1980s and the existence of deposit insurance added fuel to the fire of the moral hazard problem. The 1980 increase (to $100,000) in federal deposit insurance coverage stimulated the adverse selection problem as depositors were given powerful incentives to transfer funds from conservative and sound S&Ls to the most troubled and risky institutions paying the highest interest rates.

A particular type of moral hazard problem, known as the **principal-agent problem,** explains the regulatory authorities' response to the crisis. In the principal-agent problem, a conflict of interest between one individual (the principal) and another who is employed to act on behalf of the principal (the agent) results in a different outcome than would have occurred if the principal acted alone. In this case, the principals are the taxpayers. Congress and the regulatory authorities—the FHLBB, the FSLIC, and the state regulatory bodies—can be regarded as the agents of the taxpayers. Unfortunately, the incentives of the agents differ from those of the principals. The principals' (taxpayers') overriding incentive is to minimize S&L (and taxpayer) losses. However, the predominant incentives of the regulatory authorities are to escape blame for incompetent performance and to protect their own careers. The regulatory authorities are influenced primarily not by the taxpayers but by those who more directly affect their careers—the politicians. The regulatory authorities, responding to their incentives, basically gutted capital requirements and implemented the policy of forbearance. Some politicians—who are also agents of the taxpayers—responded to their own set of incentives. In at

**principal-agent problem** moral hazard problem that occurs when those in control (agents) act in their own interest rather than the interest of the owners or the public (principals)

## Exhibit 11-1 Culprits in the S&L Hall of Blame

Perhaps because of selective treatment by the news media and the natural tendency to look for simple answers to complicated problems, people tend to underestimate the complexity of the forces that resulted in the S&L disaster of the 1980s. Blame for the disaster, which cost American taxpayers some $150 billion, often focuses on a single cause, such as fraudulent behavior by S&L managers. In reality, many culprits share the blame for the S&L fiasco.

*S&L Crooks.* Deregulation of the financially impaired industry and the emasculated financial condition of supervisory agencies triggered the adverse selection problem. High rollers and unscrupulous characters entered the S&L industry. In some instances, these crooks looted depositors' funds to purchase airplanes and posh vacation homes. But the role of fraud has been exaggerated. Most studies indicate that fraud was responsible for only 10 to 15 percent of the cost of the S&L cleanup.

*Congress.* In 1982 Congress passed the Garn-St. Germain Act, which deregulated the S&Ls. The *timing* of the legislation, coming when half the S&Ls were technically insolvent, was terrible. In addition, several members of Congress who had received large campaign contributions from S&Ls made extraordinary efforts to slow regulators who tried to shut down insolvent S&Ls.

*Regulatory Authorities.* Because closing insolvent S&Ls in the early 1980s would have bankrupted the FSLIC and wrecked the careers of many government bureaucrats, regulatory authorities implemented their costly policy of forbearance—that is, they let insolvent S&Ls continue to operate in hopes the institution would recover. In doing so, authorities engaged in the same activity as the impaired S&Ls—gambling. The authorities gambled that the industry would be bailed out by improving economic conditions. The FSLIC also disguised the deteriorating condition of its insurance fund from Congress and the public.

*Big Accounting Firms.* By law, government regulators must shut down insolvent depository institutions. But insolvency is a gray area—it depends on how various assets of an institution are valued. Accounting firms engaged in "creative accounting"—that is, they cooked the books (much as they did in more recent corporate scandals involving WorldCom, Enron, and others), allowing insolvent S&Ls to keep operating.

*The Reagan Administration.* The administration's large income tax cuts, unaccompanied by expenditure cuts, ushered in an era of huge budget deficits, which helped keep interest rates unusually high from 1981 to 1986. The administration was overzealous in its pursuit of deregulation, confusing the general merits of deregulation with the propriety of permitting a deregulated and insolvent industry to go unsupervised. Finally, the administration acquiesced in a cover-up of the problem. The S&L problem was brought out into the open only in 1989, after President George H.W. Bush Sr. was inaugurated.

*The Federal Reserve.* The Fed's expansionary monetary policy stance, coupled with two dramatic oil price increases, led to escalating inflation in the late 1970s, which pulled up interest rates through the Fisher Effect and helped create the initial S&L crisis. To fight inflation the Fed tightened its policy dramatically after September 1979, contributing to the severity of the 1981 to 1982 recession. Many borrowers defaulted on loans. The double whammy of high interest rates and severe recession crippled the S&L industry and set the stage for the mistakes that followed.

*The Deposit Insurance System.* Depositors who were insured against losses had an incentive to place their funds in the riskiest, most financially impaired S&Ls (another example of adverse selection), which were paying the highest interest rates. The 1980 increase in

**Exhibit 11-1** Culprits in the S&L Hall of Blame—*cont'd*

deposit insurance coverage from $40,000 to $100,000 increased the ability of S&Ls to attract "hot money" through brokered deposits. That ability, in turn, encouraged risk-taking among S&Ls.

*The S&L Industry.* Even honest S&L executives share some blame. S&Ls made major campaign contributions in return for favors such as postponing needed increases in deposit insurance premiums, easing capital requirements, and delaying removal of management of insolvent S&Ls. Also, many S&L managers were not prepared to function effectively in the new, more wide-open financial environment of the 1980s.

*The Economics Profession.* Economists are acutely aware of the merits of competitive markets, and many wholeheartedly supported the deregulation of the S&Ls. Few economists recognized the dangers of fraud and unhealthy risk taking in a industry that was in a weakened state and in which budgets of supervisory authorities were woefully inadequate. Most economists supported the removal of interest-rate ceilings but neglected to consider the possibility that high-rolling S&L managers would bid funds away from conservative, safe institutions.

least one instance politicians obstructed regulatory authorities' efforts to close down an insolvent S&L that had made hefty campaign contributions.[7] Like the regulators, our elected officials generally procrastinated and attempted to sweep the problem under the rug in hopes the problem would go away or at least be announced on someone else's watch. Any serious reform of our financial system must address the principal-agent problem.

## ESCALATION OF COMMERCIAL BANK FAILURES IN THE 1980S

In the 1980s and early 1990s, the U.S. commercial banking industry was adversely impacted by some of the same macroeconomic shocks and financial innovations that impaired the S&Ls. The number of banks on the regulatory authorities' "problem list" increased sharply from the early 1980s through the end of the decade. The capital position of thousands of banks deteriorated as bad loans were written off and banks increased their reserves for loan losses. These conditions increased the moral hazard problem. In the 1980s, commercial banks took increased risks (albeit less extreme) of the sort that contributed to the S&L disaster. Altogether, some 1,387 FDIC-insured commercial banks failed from 1983 to 1992.

[7] The infamous "Keating five" scandal involved five U.S. senators who had collectively received $1.3 million in contributions from Charles H. Keating, Jr., head of the Lincoln Savings and Loan Association. Keating, who had been accused of fraud by the SEC in 1979 for earlier incidents, had been breaking rules and speculating extravagantly with depositors' money in the mid-1980s. His S&L bought junk bonds, speculated in currency futures, and paid Keating's family more than $30 million from Lincoln's funds. The senators went to bat for Keating in 1987, complaining to top regulators that they were being unreasonable. In September 1987, the FHLBB took the case out of the jurisdiction of the San Francisco examiners who had been closing in on Keating. While Keating was speculating wildly with government-insured deposits and looting the S&L, Lincoln's books were not examined for nearly a year. When Lincoln was finally closed in 1989, its costs to taxpayers exceeded $2.5 billion. In 1992 Keating was convicted of numerous counts of fraud and other charges and served a term in prison. The senators were excused with a mild slap on the wrist.

## Adverse Effect of Financial Innovations and Regulatory Actions

Banks prospered from the end of the Great Depression until the mid-1970s, partly because of the protection afforded by regulations. Restrictions on branch banking protected thousands of local banks from encroachment on their turf. Prohibition of interest payments by banks on demand deposits and interest-rate ceilings on time deposits during periods of economic stability assured banks of a healthy spread between the interest rates they earned on assets and their cost of funds. The cheapest source of bank funds—demand deposits—was the dominant source of bank funds through the 1960s.

All of these elements gave way in the 1970s and 1980s, negatively impacting banks' ability to earn profits. Restrictions on branching were eased, stimulating competition. Financial innovations accelerated in the 1960s and 1970s, negatively impacting bank profits on both sides of the bank balance sheet. On the liability side, the development of money market mutual funds forced banks to pay more than they had previously to retain depositors' accounts. The innovation of repurchase agreements essentially meant banks were now paying interest to corporate depositors, formerly an interest-free source of bank funds. The portion of total bank funds raised through the cheapest source—demand deposits—declined steadily over the years, from around 60 percent in the 1950s to around 10 percent today. Market interest rates ratcheted upward from the mid-1960s until the early 1980s. The statutory interest rate ceilings, which had earlier boosted bank profits, triggered disintermediation and were totally removed by 1986. Removal of rate ceilings increased the cost of bank funds. Large foreign banks—particularly Japanese banks with access to the massive low-cost pool of Japanese savings—began to provide formidable competition for U.S. banks.

On the asset side of the balance sheet, financial innovations also hurt banks. The development of the commercial paper market was instrumental in reducing corporate demand for bank loans, traditionally a key source of bank profits. The burgeoning market in money market mutual funds stimulated growth of the commercial paper market by providing a rapidly growing source of demand for this paper. Corporations' cost of borrowing in the commercial paper market decreased, encouraging firms to tap the commercial paper market in lieu of borrowing from banks. The junk-bond market also hurt banks as former lower-quality business borrowers issued low-grade bonds to obtain funds rather than borrowing from banks.

## Economic Instability and Commercial Bank Financial Condition

In addition to these structural changes, unstable macroeconomic conditions contributed powerfully to banks' financial problems in the late 1970s and 1980s. As interest rates increased sharply in the 1970s and early 1980s, the cost of bank funds escalated. Banks had to earn higher interest rates on their assets in order to maintain their "spread." Banks faced with declining bank loan demand by businesses sought out higher yielding (and riskier) loans and investments. Banks faced with contraction in their spread deliberately reduced their capital ratios to maintain high rates of return on capital. Banks increased their portfolio risk by making large loans in the agriculture and energy sectors and by making massive loans to less developed countries (LDCs). All three areas—agriculture, energy, and LDCs—ran into severe problems in the 1980s.

LDCs have traditionally relied heavily on earnings from the export of raw materials to meet interest payments on loans from U.S. banks. The severe worldwide

## Exhibit 11-2 Geographic Implications of S&L and Commercial Bank Failures

An interesting issue surrounding the S&L and commercial bank failures of the 1980s and early 1990s is the *geographic* impact of the costs. The depository institutions' debacle, coupled with associated costs to U.S. taxpayers, produced a redistribution of wealth from north to south.

The accompanying map shows the number of bank failures (top figure) and S&L failures (bottom figure) for each state from 1982 to 1994. The line on the map that extends from San Francisco to Washington, DC, splits the nation north and south. Of the 2,573 institutions that failed in this period, more than 2,000, or approximately 80 percent, were located in the 24 states constituting the southern half of the country. Texas alone accounted for 782 failures, or 30 percent of all the commercial bank and S&L failures in the country. The cost of the failures was borne by U.S. taxpayers, and the divisiveness of the issue is indicated by the title of one article entitled "Looting the North for Texas' Benefit."

Many of the bad loans made by banks and S&Ls financed construction of shopping centers, office buildings, apartment buildings, and homes across the Sun Belt, especially in Texas. When hard times hit the region, due largely to the collapse of oil prices, many tenants of the properties were unable to pay their rent. Building owners not receiving rent from their tenants could not make payments on their loans and defaulted. Heavy loan defaults bankrupted the S&Ls and commercial banks, and the repossessed properties were resold at discounted prices. The government made good on the deposit insurance and paid other financial institutions hefty sums to take over the insolvent institutions. Taxpayers throughout the nation picked up the tab. The glut of properties depressed southern real estate values for a time, but in the long run the presence of the buildings benefited the Sun Belt at the expense of the rest of the country. Houston, for example, mounted a marketing campaign in the 1990s to attract business to the city. A chief selling point—some of the lowest-cost office space in the United States. What the marketing campaigns did not mention, of course, was why rents were so low and who paid for the buildings.

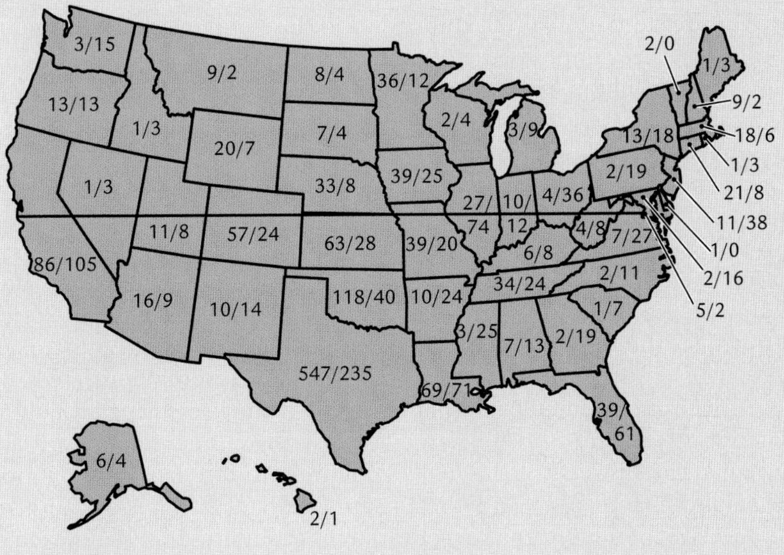

**Figure 11-3** U.S. Commercial Bank Failures from 1935 to 2003

U.S. commercial bank failures, which averaged only five per year from 1945 to 1981, escalated to more than 130 per year from 1983 to 1992 before declining sharply.

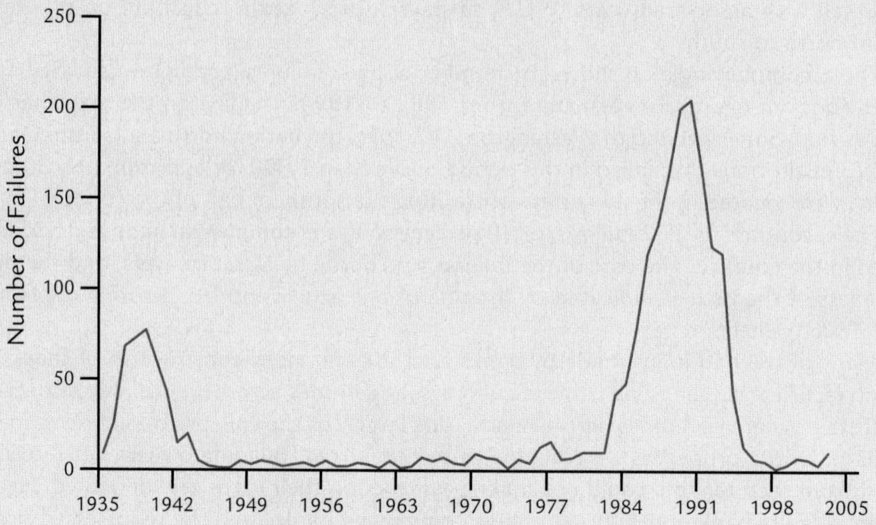

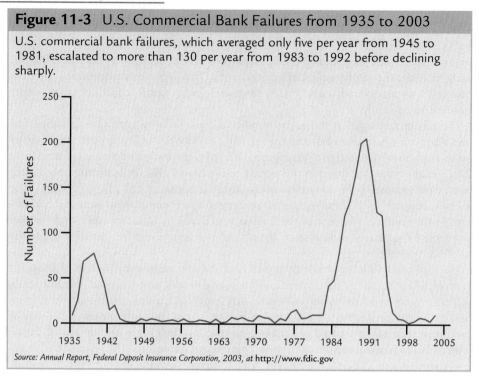

*Source: Annual Report, Federal Deposit Insurance Corporation, 2003, at* http://www.fdic.gov

recession of 1981 to 1983 depressed both the volume of exports and the price of raw materials. As a result of lower raw material prices and sharply reduced volume of exports, many LDCs were unable to meet the (rising) interest expense on their U.S. bank loans. Several huge U.S. money center banks had loans outstanding to LDCs in amounts significantly larger than their capital accounts. U.S. regulatory authorities adopted its "too big to fail" policy to prevent financial panic triggered by failure of money center banks. The policy indicated the FDIC would take extreme measures to ensure depositors or creditors did not lose money when a large bank became insolvent. An example is the 1988 bailout of the First Republic Bank of Dallas, which cost $3 billion. As discussed earlier, a widespread perception that a "too big too fail" policy is in place increases the moral hazard problem as large banks are signaled to increase risk taking.

Back-to-back recessions in the early 1980s produced an increase in loan defaults at banks, reducing banks' capital. Banks in the Midwest were hit hard by severely depressed agricultural land prices and by impairment of import-competing industries, such as automobiles, due to the dramatic appreciation (and resulting overvaluation) of the U.S. dollar in foreign exchange markets in 1983 and 1984. When the price of oil fell sharply near the end of 1985, banks in states such as Texas, Louisiana, and Oklahoma that depend heavily on oil for income were severely impacted. Bank branching restrictions prevented banks in these states from diversifying broadly away from the energy sector. Nine of the ten largest banks in Texas merged or were closed because of financial distress, attributable largely to the collapse of oil prices. Increased volatility played a role in the upsurge of bank failures because most bankers had never experienced the sort of variability of interest rates and exchange rates characteristic of the 1970s and early 1980s. Many bankers had not yet learned hedging techniques to reduce or eliminate such risks.

A decline in real estate prices in several U.S. cities in the late 1980s and early 1990s bankrupted many real estate developers and left banks holding empty office buildings and other real estate as collateral. In the same period, banks increased their exposure to risky loans. For example, banks financed leveraged buyouts of firms by other investors. Many of the buyouts (and bank loans) ran into trouble. As a result of these forces, bank failures escalated in the 1980s and early 1990s to a rate more than 20 times the rate experienced from 1945 to 1981. The number of banks that failed in each year from 1935 through 2003 is illustrated in Figure 11-3.

Following the mild and brief U.S. recession of 1990 to 1991, improving economic conditions aided the financial condition of commercial banks. Interest rates (and the cost of funds) remained low during the following decade. Rising output and income prior to the 2001 recession boosted demand for bank loans. The number of banks on the "problem list" fell sharply. The number of bank failures plummeted from 158 in 1990 and 105 in 1991 to an average of less than six per year in the next 15 years.

## FEDERAL DEPOSIT INSURANCE

Federal deposit insurance was implemented in 1934 to protect small depositors and to end banking panics and their disastrous repercussions. Bank runs likely would not occur if the masses of depositors were protected against loss in the event of bank failure. FDIC insurance has served its intended function. Gone are the old-fashioned banking panics in which hundreds of depositors fearing their banks would run out of money lined up at the teller windows. Unfortunately, however, deposit insurance facilitates the propensity of banks to take excessive risk (the moral hazard problem) and encourages regulatory authorities to delay closure of insolvent institutions (the principal-agent problem).

To the extent that deposit insurance eliminates the incentive of depositors to monitor the activities of their banks, deposit insurance also boosts incentives of banks to increase their risk exposure by deliberately reducing their capital ratios and increasing the riskiness of their asset structure. By eliminating the prospect of banks incurring the wrath of thousands of depositors who lose their savings due to regulatory authorities' failure to immediately close insolvent institutions, deposit insurance reduces bank regulators' incentive to quickly shut down such institutions. In these ways, deposit insurance contributed to the moral hazard and principal-agent problems of the 1980s and early 1990s. Incentives must be aligned correctly to limit moral hazard, adverse selection, and principal-agent problems. As we indicate shortly, legislation enacted in the 1990s has moved in that direction.

Before turning to actual and proposed changes in the federal deposit insurance system, a brief overview of the system implemented in 1934 is in order. Table 11-2 illustrates some important aspects of FDIC insurance.

Table 11-2 and Figure 11-4 illustrate the limits of FDIC insurance coverage since its inception. At the beginning of 1934, insurance coverage started at $2,500 per depositor, increased 6 months later to $5,000, and increased five more times over the years to its current level of $100,000.[8] Coverage has increased more rapidly than the nation's price level over the past 70 years, as indicated by "real coverage" in Figure

[8] Coverage increased to $10,000 in 1950, $15,000 in 1966, $20,000 in 1969, $40,000 in 1974, and $100,000 in 1980. Coverage pertains to each depositor in each bank. A wealthy individual can insure millions of dollars of deposits by opening $100,000 accounts in numerous banks and by using different deposit account names in each individual bank (account in single name, joint name, trust account name, and so forth).

**Table 11-2 Key Aspects of FDIC Insurance from 1934 to 2003**

| End of Year | Insurance Coverage Per Depositor ($) | Total Deposits in Insured Banks ($ Billion) | Insured Deposits in Insured Banks ($ Billion) | Percent Insured | Insurance Fund ($ Billion) | Insurance Fund/ Insured Deposits (%) | Premium (Cents per $100 of Deposits) |
|---|---|---|---|---|---|---|---|
| 1934 | 5,000* | 40 | 18 | 45 | 0.29 | 1.61 | N.A. |
| 1940 | 5,000 | 65 | 27 | 41 | 0.50 | 1.86 | 8.3 |
| 1950 | 10,000 | 168 | 91 | 54 | 1.24 | 1.36 | 3.7 |
| 1960 | 10,000 | 260 | 150 | 58 | 2.22 | 1.48 | 3.7 |
| 1970 | 20,000 | 545 | 350 | 64 | 4.38 | 1.25 | 3.6 |
| 1975 | 40,000 | 876 | 569 | 65 | 6.72 | 1.18 | 3.6 |
| 1980 | 100,000 | 1,324 | 949 | 72 | 11.02 | 1.16 | 3.7 |
| 1985 | 100,000 | 1,974 | 1,503 | 76 | 17.96 | 1.19 | 8.3 |
| 1990 | 100,000 | 2,540 | 1,929 | 76 | 4.04 | 0.21 | 12.0 |
| 1995 | 100,000 | 2,576 | 1,952 | 76 | 25.45 | 1.30 | ** |
| 2003 | 100,000 | 4,090 | 2,548 | 62 | 33.46 | 1.31 | ** |

*Initial coverage of $2,500 was increased to $5,000 on July 1, 1934.

** Since 1993, the FDIC has used a risk-based system that charges higher premium rates to institutions judged to pose higher risks to the insurance fund.

*Source: Federal Deposit Insurance Corporation, Annual Report, 2003*

**Figure 11-4** Nominal and Real FDIC Deposit Insurance Coverage from 1934 to 2004

FDIC insurance coverage has been increased several times over the years (shaded areas). Adjusted for inflation, coverage has trended upward slightly since 1934.

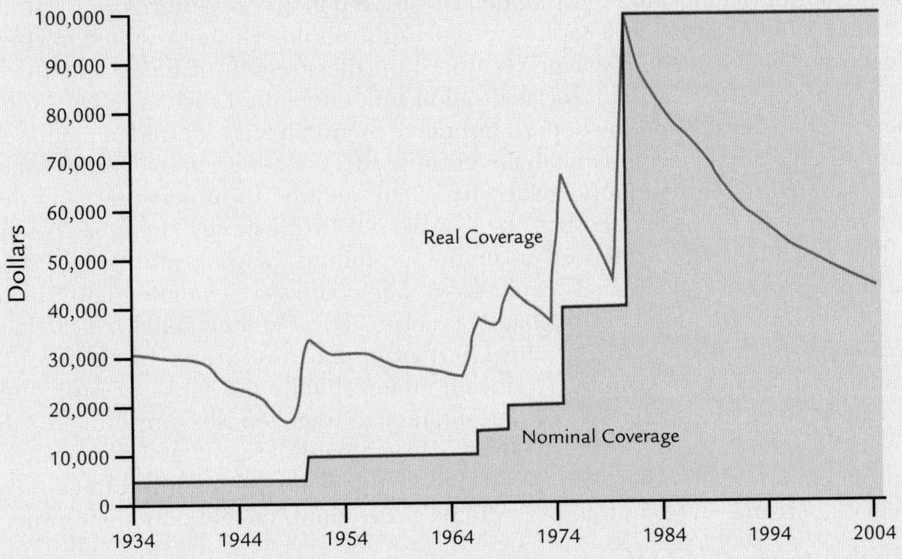


*Source: FDIC*

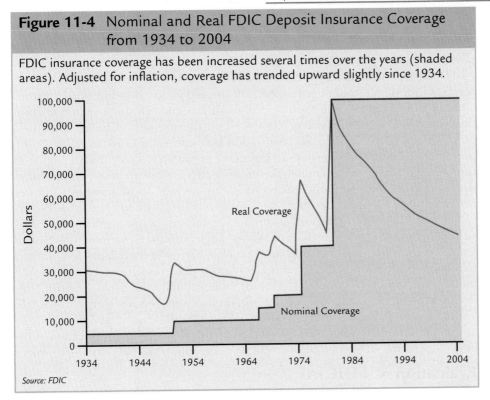

11-4, which deflates the nominal FDIC coverage by the consumer price index. Using 1980 (when coverage was boosted from \$40,000 to \$100,000) as the base year, real coverage today is only slightly higher than \$40,000. Because of the contribution of deposit insurance to the moral hazard problem, some economists advocate rolling back actual coverage to \$40,000 or perhaps even \$20,000. In real terms, the proposals place coverage at lower levels than at any time in the FDIC's history.

Table 11-2 indicates that the percentage of total deposits in the nation's insured banks covered by FDIC insurance increased from 41 percent in 1940 to 62 percent in 2003. Today, some 99 percent of all depositors are covered (not shown). The FDIC's insurance fund increased persistently over the years through the mid-1980s before declining in the later portion of that decade. The fund dropped precipitously in 1990 and 1991 in response to the surging cost of resolving failed banks and became negative before it was recapitalized by Congressional appropriations. Through the mid-1990s the fund was bolstered by sharply reduced bank failures and higher deposit premiums. By 1995, improving financial conditions in the banking system restored the fund to a very strong level, and the insurance fund was sufficiently robust that insurance premiums were reduced to zero in 1996 for banks exhibiting strong capital positions. By 2004, fewer than 10 percent of the nation's insured banks were being charged for FDIC insurance coverage.

## Federal Deposit Insurance Corporation Improvement Act of 1991 (FDICIA)

One of the important provisions of the 1989 FIRREA mandated the U.S. Treasury to conduct a comprehensive study of the federal deposit insurance system and submit proposals for reform. The study was completed in 1991 and led to enactment

**Federal Deposit Insurance Corporation Improvement Act of 1991 (FDICIA)** legislation that recapitalized the nearly insolvent FDIC and redesigned the federal deposit insurance system with the intent of minimizing taxpayer exposure to future losses

of the **Federal Deposit Insurance Corporation Improvement Act of 1991 (FDICIA).** The act had two primary purposes: to recapitalize the nearly insolvent FDIC and to redesign the federal deposit insurance system with the intent of minimizing taxpayer exposure to future losses.

FDICIA restricted access of certain banks to brokered deposits, limited the "too big to fail" principle, and required the FDIC to step in quickly and vigorously when a bank's capital fell below a certain (positive) threshold. The act resulted in classification of banks into five categories, based on the strength of their capital positions. Under FDICIA, a bank's classification influences the activities in which it is permitted to engage and the deposit insurance premium it is required to pay. "Well-capitalized" banks having capital significantly in excess of required capital standards are classified in group 1. Such banks are allowed to underwrite securities. Brokered deposits purchased by these banks are FDIC insured. These banks were subject to relatively low deposit insurance premiums (waived entirely in 1996). Group 2 banks are "adequately capitalized." Such banks are extended fewer benefits than group 1 banks. Group 3 banks are classified as "undercapitalized" and are treated more stringently than group 1 and group 2 banks. Group 4 ("significantly undercapitalized") and group 5 ("critically undercapitalized") banks are prohibited from paying higher than average interest rates to attract deposits. Any brokered deposits they purchase are not FDIC insured. Such banks are charged higher insurance premiums than other banks. In fact, Group 5 banks—those with capital ratios below 2 percent—are required by law to be closed down or sold off to new owners.

## Evaluation of FDICIA

FDICIA initiated the first fundamental change in the deposit insurance system since the FDIC's inception in 1934. To what extent will the FDICIA fix the moral hazard and adverse selection problems inherent in our bank regulatory system? We argue that the FDICIA goes a long way toward curing the system's ills but it may not go quite far enough. First, the act increases the percentage of bank depositors who have an incentive to monitor their bank. It does this primarily by eliminating insurance on brokered deposits (except for brokered deposits purchased by solidly capitalized banks) and by moderating the "too big to fail" policy. Banks, in determining the risk they decide to undertake, now must be concerned with the possibility of losing more depositors. Riskier banks, to compensate depositors for greater risks, now must pay more than safe banks to purchase brokered deposits.

The FDICIA implements strong incentives for banks to reduce risk taking and thereby should reduce taxpayer losses. A bank whose capital falls is granted fewer privileges and becomes subject to more rigorous regulation and higher insurance premiums. Forcing extremely undercapitalized banks to close as soon as their capital to total assets ratio falls below 2 percent (rather than waiting until the ratio is negative) should be especially important in reducing future taxpayer losses. Mandatory prompt corrective action should reduce the principal-agent problem associated with regulators and politicians. Because FDICIA requires prompt corrective actions, regulatory forbearance, which dramatically increased moral hazard incentives for banks, is no longer an option.

Banks that take on higher risk by reducing capital ratios or by purchasing riskier assets are now subject to higher insurance premiums. Thus, risk-based insurance premiums reduce the moral hazard problem. Unfortunately, an important inherent shortcoming of risk-based deposit insurance premiums is the difficulty in assessing the degree of bank risk taking. A bank can increase its capital ratio but still prevent its overall risk level from declining by simultaneously un-

# INTERNATIONAL PERSPECTIVES

## Deposit Insurance Systems in Other Countries

Today, most industrial nations have deposit insurance systems. The U.S. system, established in 1934, is the oldest system in operation. Norway's system, established in 1961, is the second oldest. Many nations did not establish deposit insurance until the 1970s or 1980s, but today more than 35 nations have such systems in place.

The United States has one of the highest deposit insurance coverage levels (behind only Norway and Italy). Many nations charge no premium and have no insurance fund. Instead, they assess insured members as losses occur. Such a system provides an incentive for banks to keep an eye on one another to see that regulations are complied with. Other nations (Argentina, Chile, Italy, Ireland, and the United Kingdom) have coinsurance. For example, in England depositors pay 25 percent of any loss up to the ceiling level; insurance covers the remaining 75 percent. By increasing the incentive for depositors to monitor their banks, coinsurance systems are designed to reduce moral hazard problems.

Among countries that have deposit insurance, membership is voluntary in one fourth; membership is mandatory in all the other countries. Systems are administered in one of three ways. In some countries insurance is sponsored and administered by the government; in an approximately equal number of countries insurance is conducted via private insurance companies; in a few nations, insurance is administered jointly through public and private arrangements. Increasing worldwide integration of financial markets has stimulated a movement toward standardization of insurance systems across countries.

### Aspects of Deposit Insurance in Various Countries

| Country | Year Established | Maximum Amount Covered (in U.S. Dollars) | Membership (Voluntary or Compulsory) | Administered by |
|---|---|---|---|---|
| Canada | 1967 | 44,000 | Compulsory | Government |
| France | 1980 | 81,000 | Voluntary | Private insurance |
| Germany | 1966 | 30% of bank's liable capital per customer | Voluntary | Private insurance |
| Italy | 1987 | 634,000 (coinsurance) | Voluntary | Private insurance |
| Japan | 1971 | 95,300 | Compulsory | Private insurance |
| Norway | 1961 | Unlimited | Compulsory | Joint (private and government) |
| Spain | 1977 | 12,400 | Voluntary | Government |
| United Kingdom | 1982 | 30,900 (coinsurance) | Compulsory | Government |
| United States | 1934 | 100,000 | Compulsory | Government |

*Source: Reforming Federal Deposit Insurance (Washington, DC: Congressional Budget Office, 1990)*

dertaking more risky loans or other activities. These risks are not easy to measure. Loans that appear safe when made often appear risky only after economic conditions change.

## Other Proposed Reforms of Deposit Insurance

Most economists believe that FDICIA is a socially beneficial piece of legislation. Some economists would prefer more radical efforts to address the problems of moral hazard and adverse selection. We discuss a few of these proposals.

**Elimination of Deposit Insurance.** A radical approach is to simply eliminate deposit insurance. All depositors would then have a powerful incentive to monitor banks and make sure their funds are deposited in strong and prudent institutions. Increased depositor scrutiny might impose discipline on banks, forcing them to keep risk in moderation. Unfortunately, the same types of problems that led to the original implementation of deposit insurance in the 1930s would be unleashed. Banks could be subject to runs—lines of frightened depositors trying to protect their wealth. Economists believe deposit insurance has contributed on balance to increased economic stability since the Great Depression. In addition, many economists do not believe depositors are capable of evaluating the risk their bank engages in. Certain key information, such as examiners' reports, are confidential and not available to depositors. Clearly, hundreds of thousands of individual depositors spending significant time monitoring their banks is a misallocation of society's resources. However, large depositors might be able to efficiently evaluate banks, particularly larger banks whose operations are analyzed by Standard and Poor's and other advisory services.

**Reducing the Limits of Coverage.** As indicated in Figure 11-4, the magnitude of deposits per customer covered by FDIC insurance has outpaced inflation. Suppose we reduced the deposit insurance ceiling to $25,000. Depositors who currently have between $25,000 and $100,000 in their accounts would now be given an incentive to monitor the risk their bank is taking. This might impose some measure of discipline on bank risk taking. However, if depositors are risk averse and are poorly informed, implementation of this proposal could result in occasional runs on suspect banks, perversely destabilizing the system.

**Coinsurance.** This proposal makes deposit insurance more like most forms of medical and hazard insurance, in which the insured pays an up-front deductible amount or a certain percentage of the cost. Suppose only 90 percent of each depositor's funds (up to $100,000) is insured. All depositors would now have an incentive to keep an eye on their bank. Again, however, this measure suffers the same potential drawbacks as reducing limits of coverage or totally eliminating insurance coverage.

**Abolishing the Too Big to Fail Policy.** FDICIA limits the "too big to fail" policy, but many critics think the act does not go nearly far enough. The Treasury, Fed, and FDIC still have authority to implement "too big to fail" and bail out uninsured depositors. Knowing about the possible bailout, big banks likely are not adequately influenced in their decision to take risk by fear of defection of large depositors. On the other side of the argument, allowing a large bank to fail could have major ripple effects that are extremely costly. Proponents argue that, in spite of its unfairness, the government unfortunately has no alternative to preventing failure of our huge money-center banks.

**Go to Private Deposit Insurance.** Advocates of private deposit insurance argue that, unlike the case with government insurance, private insurance companies would have full incentive to carefully monitor any bank whose deposits it is insuring. They would charge appreciably higher insurance rates to banks that engage in high-risk activities. Critics of this proposal ask who would bail out the private insurance company if it fails. A private insurance company likely would not have the resources to repay depositors in the event of large losses. Bank runs would become more prevalent if the public did not believe the insurance would be viable in the event their bank failed. The runs on state-insured Ohio and Maryland S&Ls in 1985, at a time when there were no runs on federally insured institutions in the same states, seem to support this view.

## SUMMARY

In the 1980s, both the S&L and the commercial banking industries were buffeted by severe financial problems, and major shake-outs occurred in both industries. Thousands of S&Ls and banks failed. Because of financial innovations, deregulation, and a series of historical accidents, the problems of moral hazard and adverse selection increased dramatically in the 1980s, resulting in huge losses to the industries and ultimately to U.S. taxpayers. The financial problems were triggered by unstable macroeconomic conditions—rising inflation and interest rates in the 1970s, followed by the most severe economic downturn (1981–1982) since the Great Depression. Because S&Ls were set up to borrow short-term funds to finance long-term mortgages, they were inherently susceptible to episodes of sharply rising interest rates. As interest rates increased dramatically in the late 1970s and early 1980s, S&Ls experienced huge losses. Both politicians and regulators are subject to the principal-agent problem. Because politicians and regulators were driven by incentives other than minimizing losses for taxpayers, they responded to the S&L crisis by removing restrictions on acquisition of risky assets, relaxing capital standards, and implementing the disastrous policy of forbearance. These actions allowed insolvent institutions to remain open. Because financially impaired S&Ls predictably responded by increasing their risk taking, these government actions sharply increased the ultimate cost to taxpayers. Important legislation was later implemented to reduce the chances of a recurrence of major losses to taxpayers. The legislation reinstated restrictions on S&L activities, increased capital standards for commercial banks and S&Ls, and redesigned both capital requirements and federal deposit insurance premiums to reduce incentives of depository institutions to engage in risk.

Chapter 12

# THE FEDERAL RESERVE SYSTEM: ITS STRUCTURE AND FUNCTIONS

One of the most crucial institutions in any nation is the central bank. More than 150 nations around the world have a central bank. The central bank in the United States is known as the *Federal Reserve System,* or simply the *Fed.* In this chapter we discuss the origin, structure, and functions of the Federal Reserve System.

Central banks are different from private banks where you keep your money. Central banks, unlike private banks, are not concerned about making profits. Most central banks do not issue checking and savings accounts to the public or make loans to individuals and non-bank business firms. Central banks are government or quasi-government institutions that provide services and strive to achieve goals perceived to be in the nation's broad economic interest. For example, a chief goal of central banks in industrial nations historically has been price level stability.

A natural question to ask is "In which of the three branches of government is the Federal Reserve System located?" The correct answer is "none." The Fed's relationship with the government is complicated. Technically, the Federal Reserve is a private corporation owned by private banks that are members of the Federal Reserve System. In reality, the Federal Reserve is influenced little by the member banks. The Fed operates more like a government agency accountable to Congress, yet the Fed's day-to-day operations are independent of both the legislative and executive branches of government. The Federal Reserve is a complex organization that is essentially part of—and yet detached from—the government.

## ORIGIN OF THE FEDERAL RESERVE SYSTEM

In some nations, such as England, the central bank evolved from a private commercial bank over a long period. In other nations, such as the United States, the central bank was originally established solely as a central bank. The Federal Reserve System is much younger than the central banks in many industrial nations. The central banks in England (Bank of England) and France (Bank of France) were established in 1694 and 1800, respectively. The Federal Reserve System was established in 1913.

Two early experiments with establishing a central bank in the United States failed. The experiments included the First Bank of the United States (1791–1811) and the Second Bank of the United States (1816–1836). Congress initially granted each of these banks a 20-year charter but refused to renew the charter when it expired. The reason for Congress' charter refusal derives from the widespread public view that the banks were vested with excessive financial power. The United States has a history of populist sentiment that includes profound distrust of both the federal government in Washington and the concentration of financial power in few hands. The public, particularly in small towns and rural areas, widely suspected that a central bank would be controlled by—and operated in the interests of—Wall Street and New York bankers. The public's mistrust was the chief reason the United States did not have a central bank between 1836 and 1913.

In the half century prior to the legislation creating the Federal Reserve System in 1913, nationally chartered banks were regulated by provisions of the National Banking Act of 1863. In this regime, smaller commercial banks held cash and deposits in other larger commercial banks. The cash and deposits in the larger bank constituted the smaller bank's **legal reserves,** or simply **reserves.** Banks were required to maintain a certain portion of their deposit liabilities in the form of reserves. Banks in New York, Chicago, and St. Louis were classified as Central Reserve City Banks. Banks in approximately 50 other cities were classified as Reserve City Banks. All other commercial banks were classified as Country Banks. Country Banks held reserves in the form of cash and deposits at Reserve City Banks. Reserve City Banks held reserves in the form of cash and deposits in Central Reserve City Banks. The larger banks often earned interest on the funds deposited by smaller banks by investing the funds in loans to stock brokers, known as *call loans.*

**legal reserves (reserves)**
cash and deposits that a bank places in a larger bank (formerly) or Federal Reserve (today)

This system had several problems. In general, the system lacked flexibility. In a **fractional reserve banking system,** each bank maintains only a small percentage of its deposit liabilities in the form of reserves—that is, cash and deposits in other banks. If a seasonal or panic-induced withdrawal of currency from banks occurs, pressure converges on the larger banks as small banks draw down their deposits to obtain cash for their customers. As we demonstrate in the next chapter, in the absence of a central bank, banks *collectively*—that is, the banking *system*—cannot recover lost reserves when the public withdraws currency. Without help from a central bank, the banking system can recover from a reserve deficiency only through painful and destructive multiple contraction of deposits. Historically, panics in the nation's financial markets ensued when larger banks were forced to call in their loans to brokers. Farmers, businesses, and others who relied on bank loans to conduct their economic affairs were cut off from essential bank credit. As the nation experienced urbanization and industrialization in the late nineteenth and early twentieth centuries and the financial sector became more important to the country's overall economic development, periodic financial breakdowns increased the cost to the nation of being without a central bank. Major banking and financial market panics occurred in 1857, 1873, 1884, 1893, and 1907. The panic of 1907 finally triggered Congressional action that established the Federal Reserve System. The Fed was created by the **Federal Reserve Act,** which was signed into law by President Woodrow Wilson in December 1913.

**fractional reserve banking system**
system in which each bank maintains only a small percentage of bank deposit liabilities in the form of reserves

**Federal Reserve Act**
legislation establishing the Federal Reserve System

An institution that could provide a flexible amount of reserves to the banking system as needed to promote stability was conspicuously missing before 1913. The absence of a viable **lender of last resort** that could provide temporary cash reserves to the banking system in time of crisis—when the psychological force of panic can trigger a monetary and financial collapse—was particularly costly to the nation.[1] Other factors contributed to creation of the Federal Reserve System—the need to provide adequate supervision of the nation's banks, improve the check collection

**lender of last resort**
provider of temporary cash reserves to the banking system in times of crisis

[1] Unfortunately, as we see in Chapter 17, the existence of a central bank such as the Federal Reserve does not guarantee that the "lender of last resort" function will be provided. To the great detriment of the nation, the Federal Reserve failed to serve this function when it was sorely needed in the 1930s.

system, provide for currency issue, and establish an agency to serve as banker for the U.S. Treasury.

The Federal Reserve Act, like the U.S. Constitution, is an interesting compromise among diverse forces and interests. The act achieved a delicate balance and diffusion of power in three different areas: (1) between the government and the private sector; (2) among the various geographic regions of the nation and between rural and urban interests; and (3) among bankers, the non-bank business sector, and the rest of society. In the early twentieth century, before the Federal Reserve Act was enacted, urban business leaders favored a highly centralized organization whose purpose was stabilizing the nation's price level. Rural interests lobbied for a highly decentralized, government-managed central bank dedicated to making loans with favorable terms. The Federal Reserve Act achieved decentralization by establishing 12 **district Federal Reserve banks,** each with significant autonomy. The act fostered centralization through creation of a Board of Governors in Washington, DC, which was to share power with the 12 district Federal Reserve Banks. Although legislation in the 1930s significantly changed the organization of the Federal Reserve, many of the original features are intact today. For example, the 12 regional Federal Reserve banks and the Board of Governors in Washington remain. However, the 1930s legislation shifted a significant amount of power away from the 12 district Federal Reserve banks to the Board of Governors.

**district Federal Reserve banks**
one Federal Reserve bank exists for each of the 12 Federal Reserve districts in the United States

Today, the Federal Reserve is responsible for stabilizing the nation's economy by changing interest rate levels and the money supply, but the Fed was not originally conceived with such a broad and challenging mandate. In the early part of the twentieth century, deliberate efforts to manage economic activity were not considered appropriate or desirable. The massive responsibility today accorded to the Federal Reserve System evolved based on experience, development of macroeconomic analysis, and legislation. The Employment Act of 1946 and the Full Employment and Balanced Growth Act of 1978 (The Humphrey Hawkins Act) charge the federal government with keeping the economy operating at high levels of output and employment. Thus, the Federal Reserve is essentially charged with maintaining prosperity and reasonable price level stability. The Fed's *original* functions were more basic—to serve as a lender of last resort to the banking system, issue currency, improve on the check collection process, serve as banker or fiscal agent for the U.S. Treasury, and improve supervision and examination of the nation's banks.

## BALANCE SHEET AND INCOME STATEMENT OF THE FEDERAL RESERVE SYSTEM

The keys to understanding the nature and role of the Federal Reserve System are two important financial statements—the *balance sheet* and the *income statement.* We begin by examining the Fed's balance sheet.

### Balance Sheet of the Federal Reserve System

Table 12-1 presents the consolidated balance sheet of the 12 Federal Reserve banks—a snapshot indicating the assets, liabilities, and capital accounts of the Federal Reserve at a given point in time (June 17, 2004). The Fed's assets are things the Fed owns and claims the Federal Reserve has on outside entities. The Fed's liabilities are debts the Fed owes or claims outside entities have on the Federal Reserve. The Federal Reserve's capital accounts are simply the difference between its total assets and total liabilities. We begin with the Fed's assets.

**Table 12-1 Consolidated Balance Sheet of the 12 Federal Reserve Banks on June 17, 2004**

| Assets ($ Billion) | | Liabil. and Capital ($ Billion) | |
|---|---|---|---|
| Gold certificate accounts | 11.04 | Federal Reserve notes | 690.61 |
| Special Drawing Rights accounts | 2.20 | Deposits | |
| Coins | 0.74 | A. Banks | 19.21 |
| Loans to depository institutions | 0.17 | B. U.S. Treasury | 7.07 |
| U.S. Treasury securities | 704.17 | C. Foreign and other | 0.37 |
| Cash items in process of collection | 6.80 | Deferred availability cash items | 7.28 |
| Assets denominated in foreign currency and other assets | 38.64 | Other liabilities | 20.45 |
| | | Total liabilities | 744.99 |
| | | Capital accounts | 18.77 |
| **Total assets** | 763.76 | **Total liabilities and capital** | 763.76 |

*Source: Federal Reserve Release H4.1 at* http://www.federalreserve.gov/releases/h41/

**Federal Reserve Assets.** As indicated in the table, the Fed's assets include gold and Special Drawing Rights (SDR) certificate accounts, coins, loans to depository institutions, U.S. government securities, cash items in the process of collection, assets denominated in foreign currencies, and other assets.

The Fed's gold certificate account is historically interesting but is not currently significant. For each dollar's worth of gold the U.S. Treasury owns, the Fed holds $1 in gold certificates. In the past when the Treasury acquired additional gold, it issued a corresponding value of gold certificates to the Federal Reserve. The Fed compensated the Treasury by making a bookkeeping entry—crediting the Treasury's deposit account at the Federal Reserve (liability side of the Fed's balance sheet). A law required that the paper currency issued by the Fed (Federal Reserve notes) be backed by gold certificates. This requirement placed constraints on the amount of currency the Fed was authorized to issue.[2] As the volume of Federal Reserve notes required to accommodate a growing economy increased and the U.S. gold stock diminished, the gold certificate requirement was reduced and then eliminated in 1968.[3] The final vestige of the gold standard was abandoned.

The SDR account is similar to the gold certificate account. SDR certificates are the Fed's claims against SDRs, which are issued by the International Monetary Fund (IMF) and held by the U.S. Treasury (and other governments). SDRs are issued by

[2] This aspect of a gold standard—its rigid constraint on the quantity of money—is the source of its appeal and the source of its shortcomings. Modern-day advocates of a gold standard emphasize the long-term stability of the price level that would exist under a gold standard, owing to the natural limits placed on the nation's money stock. Critics charge that a gold standard handcuffs the central bank by preventing the bank from increasing the money supply to boost economic activity in times of economic stagnation or recession.

[3] Until the U.S. "gold window" was closed in 1971, foreign governments that had accumulated dollars by running balance of payments surpluses vis-à-vis the United States were entitled at their discretion to convert the dollars into gold at the U.S. Treasury at the official gold price of $35 per ounce. By 1971, U.S. gold stock, which stood at $25 billion (half the gold in the world) in 1949, had diminished to around $11 billion. In 1971 the U.S terminated the right of foreign governments to convert their dollars to gold. Since then, the U.S. gold stock has been quite stable at around $11 billion (valued at the official government price of $42.22 per ounce). Because the government's official gold price has been dramatically lower than the free market price for more than 25 years, little or no gold has been sold to the Treasury in recent times.

the IMF to help finance expanding international trade. When the Treasury acquires additional SDRs from the IMF, the Treasury issues SDR certificates to the Federal Reserve. The Fed then compensates the Treasury by crediting the Treasury's deposit account at the Federal Reserve.

The relatively small item "coins" consists of Treasury-issued coins that are currently held by the 12 district Federal Reserve banks. The Fed banks hold coins to accommodate coin requests by depository institutions (banks), which respond to the public's demand for coins. A bank needing additional coins contacts its district Fed bank, which sends out the coins via armored truck and charges the bank's deposit account at the Fed (liability side of the Fed balance sheet).

**discount loans (discounts and advances)**
loans made by the Federal Reserve to depository institutions

Loans made by the Federal Reserve to depository institutions are known as **discount loans,** or **discounts and advances.** Discount loans are discussed in detail in Chapter 18. Banks initiate these very short-term loans in response to reserve deficiencies resulting from unexpected net check clearings against banks' reserve deposits at the Fed and to the public's currency withdrawals.

**open market operations**
buying and selling of government securities by the Fed to influence bank lending, interest rates, and the nation's money supply

The most important item on the asset side of the Federal Reserve's balance sheet is the system's holdings of U.S. government securities, which constitute more than 90 percent of the Fed's total assets. As we emphasize later, the primary tool of Federal Reserve policy is **open market operations**—the buying and selling of government securities to influence bank lending, interest rates, and the nation's money supply. The Fed's massive government security portfolio accumulated gradually over the years in response to the Fed's measures to expand the nation's money supply and accommodate a growing economy.

*Cash items in the process of collection* refers to the value of checks the Fed currently is processing but for which the Fed has not yet collected payment. The Fed collects on these checks by debiting the reserve account of the depository institutions on which the checks are written (right-hand side of the Fed's balance sheet). The cash items are an asset to the Fed—they are the Fed's prospective claim against the depository institution. The Fed will exercise the claim within the next couple of days by debiting the institution's deposit account at the Fed.

The item *assets denominated in foreign currencies* consists chiefly of foreign government bonds—bonds denominated in currencies such as euros, yen, and Swiss francs. The foreign assets provide the Federal Reserve with potential ammunition for supporting the exchange value of the U.S. dollar when the Fed deems it essential. In times of excessive and unwarranted weakness of the U.S. dollar, the Fed liquidates these interest-earning foreign assets for foreign currencies, which are used to purchase U.S. dollars in the foreign exchange market. Finally, *other assets* of the Federal Reserve include items such as the Fed's physical facilities—its buildings, furniture, equipment, computers, and fleet of automobiles.[4]

**Federal Reserve Liabilities.** The dominant liability on the Fed's balance sheet is Federal Reserve notes—the paper money issued by the Fed. This item constitutes more than 90 percent of total Federal Reserve liabilities. The Fed issues this currency in response to public demand, as manifested by withdrawal of currency from depository institutions and ATMs. A bank that is running low on paper currency contacts the Fed, which issues the notes and sends them to the depository institution in an armored truck. The Federal Reserve charges the bank for this currency by debiting the bank's deposit account at the Fed.

[4] In 2004, approximately $17 billion (almost half) of the "denominated in foreign currency and other assets" consisted of assets denominated in foreign currencies.

Various organizations maintain deposits at the Federal Reserve. Commercial banks and other depository institutions hold a large portion of their legal reserves in this form to meet the Fed's reserve requirements and to facilitate check clearing through the Federal Reserve. When a customer deposits a check at a commercial bank, the Fed processes the check, marks up the bank's reserve account at the Fed, and deducts the account of the bank on which the check was written. If you write a check to a store to pay for a pair of shoes, the Fed processes the check by debiting your bank's deposit at the Fed and crediting the deposit of the store's bank.

As we indicated earlier, the Federal Reserve serves as a banker for the U.S. Treasury. The Treasury pays for the bulk of its expenditures through checks written on its account at the Federal Reserve. The Treasury regularly replenishes the account by transferring funds from its accounts in commercial banks, known as **tax and loan accounts.**[5] Foreign central banks and other international organizations such as the World Bank and the IMF also maintain checking accounts at the Federal Reserve. These outside organizations use their Federal Reserve accounts to make payments in the United States. The Fed processes checks written by these organizations by debiting the international organization's account at the Fed and crediting the accounts at the Fed of the U.S. banks where the checks are deposited.

**tax and loan accounts**
deposits held by the U.S. Treasury in commercial banks

*Deferred availability cash items* corresponds to *cash items in the process of collection* on the asset side of the Fed's balance sheet. Deferred availability cash items represent the aggregate value of checks the Fed is processing and will soon credit the accounts of the depository institutions that received the checks. These banks have a claim on the Fed—in a day or two, the Fed will make a bookkeeping entry marking up the banks' reserve accounts. The difference between "cash items in the process of collection" and "deferred credit items" is the **Federal Reserve float.**[6] Float is positive slightly more often than not because the Fed tends to credit the account of the bank where a check is deposited a day or so before it debits the account of the bank on which the check is written. (Float is discussed in more detail in Chapter 15.)

**Federal Reserve float**
difference between "cash items in the process of collection" and "deferred availability cash items"

**Federal Reserve Capital Accounts.** The capital accounts of the Federal Reserve System consist of the difference between its total assets and total liabilities. A major portion of the Fed's capital accounts derives from capital paid in—that is, the equity the owners of the Federal Reserve have invested in the Fed. The remainder comes from funds the Fed transfers from its net income to "surplus," a component of the capital accounts.

Technically, the Federal Reserve is "owned" by the approximately 2,900 commercial banks that are members of the Federal Reserve System. Each member bank is required to purchase shares of stock in the Federal Reserve in the amount of 6 percent of the bank's own capital and surplus. In return, the Fed pays the bank a 6-percent dividend on the shares. Private institution (member bank) "ownership" of the Fed is a manifestation of the prevalent distrust of government that influenced the writers of the Federal Reserve Act. It is a highly unique form of ownership in

[5] Government deposits in commercial banks originate from the receipt of federal tax payments and from the proceeds of government bond sales to the public (hence the name "tax and loan accounts"). These monies are initially deposited by the Treasury in commercial banks (in the Treasury tax and loan accounts) and later transferred to the Treasury account at the Federal Reserve to be spent.

[6] This concept is analogous to another type of float that you may be familiar with. You may have written a check a day or so before you had adequate funds in your account to cover it, knowing it would take at least a day for the check to be presented to your bank. If so, you have engaged in "playing the float."

that member banks "own" the Fed but do not significantly influence the Fed's operations or policies. Indeed, the Fed would be unable to perform its chief functions in a satisfactory manner if the member banks had influence over the Fed.

## Federal Reserve Earnings and Expenses

On the Federal Reserve's balance sheet for June 17, 2004, the total value of interest-earning U.S. government securities held by the Fed was more than $700 billion. This represents approximately 10 percent of the gross national debt of the United States government. The Fed does not conduct its policies with the deliberate intention of earning a large profit, but a natural by-product of the Fed's huge portfolio of Treasury securities is a very large annual income. Table 12-2 indicates the sources and disposition of the income of the 12 Federal Reserve banks for 2001, 2002, and 2003.

Table 12-2 indicates that the predominant source of Federal Reserve income—interest earned on U.S. government securities—was approximately $30 billion in 2001 and somewhat less in 2002 and 2003 (because of decreased yields on government securities). Other sources of income (primarily fees collected for services provided and interest earned on foreign securities) added to the Fed's gross income. After deducting operating expenses and making other accounting adjustments (chiefly for losses or gains incurred on foreign currency transactions), the Fed's net income was approximately $28 billion in 2001, $26 billion in 2002, and $23 billion in 2003. What does the Fed do with all these profits? In 2003, the Fed allocated $520

**Table 12-2 Earnings and Expenses of the 12 Federal Reserve Banks ($ Billion)**

| | 2001 | 2002 | 2003 |
|---|---|---|---|
| Income from | | | |
| Interest on government securities | 30.52 | 25.53 | 22.60 |
| Loans to depository institutions | 0.01 | 0.002 | 0.001 |
| Foreign securities | 0.33 | 0.27 | 0.26 |
| Priced services | 0.93 | 0.92 | 0.89 |
| Other | 0.08 | 0.04 | 0.08 |
| **Total** | **31.87** | **26.76** | **23.83** |
| Net expenses* | 2.72 | 2.86 | 3.52 |
| Additions to income** | −1.12 | 2.15 | 2.70 |
| **Net income** | **28.03** | **26.05** | **23.01** |
| Disposition of income | | | |
| Dividends paid to member banks | 0.43 | 0.48 | 0.52 |
| Transferred to surplus account | 0.52 | 1.07 | 0.47 |
| **Payment to U.S. Treasury** | **27.08** | **24.50** | **22.02** |

* Includes current expenses of the Federal Reserve banks and assessments by the Board of Governors for the Board's expenditures and the cost of currency.

** In 2001, the Federal Reserve incurred losses of approximately $1.12 billion on foreign exchange market transactions and U.S. Treasury and agency bond transactions. In 2002 and 2003, the Fed made gains on such transactions.

*Source: Board of Governors of Federal Reserve System Annual Report, 2001, 2002, 2003 at* http://www.federalreserve.gov/

million for payment of dividends to the member banks that own the Fed; transferred $470 million to the Fed's surplus account (part of its capital accounts) to match the capital paid in by member banks; and turned over the remaining $22.02 billion to the U.S. Treasury. Because more than 90 percent of the interest income paid by the Treasury to the Federal Reserve on the Fed's security portfolio is typically given back to the Treasury, the portion of the national debt the Treasury sells to the Federal Reserve is financed almost without cost to the Treasury.[7]

The unique financial status of the Federal Reserve—the fact that the Fed possesses its own internal source of funds and its resulting lack of dependence on Congressional appropriations—is a key source of the Fed's political independence. In recent decades, some members of Congress have criticized the Federal Reserve as operating without appropriate constraints. Some legislators who frequently take issue with the Fed's policies dislike the Fed's financial (and political) independence and want to tighten the Fed's accountability to the democratic process. Some legislators have suggested that the Fed be required to turn over *all* its revenues to the Treasury and submit annual budget requests to Congress, as government agencies do. Needless to say, the Fed vigorously defends its financial status and political independence, pointing to the fact that the Fed's operating expenditures are typically only 10 percent of gross income. We will discuss this issue in detail later when we examine the case for a politically independent central bank.

## STRUCTURE OF THE FEDERAL RESERVE SYSTEM

The key units of the Federal Reserve System are the Board of Governors, the Federal Open Market Committee, the 12 district Federal Reserve banks (with a total of 26 branches), and some 2,900 member banks. These units and their interrelationships are sketched in Figure 12-1. Refer to this organizational chart as we discuss the structure of authority within the Federal Reserve System and the historic rationale for its existing organization. We begin with the most important element of the Federal Reserve System—the Board of Governors.

### Board of Governors

The seven-person **Board of Governors** (originally known as the *Federal Reserve Board)* is the heart of the Federal Reserve System. The Board of Governors' major responsibilities include setting reserve requirements (within Congressionally established limits); reviewing and "*determining*" the discount rate levels set by the 12 individual district Federal Reserve banks; and serving as voting members on the important **Federal Open Market Committee (FOMC).** The FOMC formulates the basic stance of monetary policy, buying and selling securities to influence credit availability, short-term interest rates, and monetary conditions throughout the nation. Thus, the Board of Governors dominates the monetary policy decision-making process.

The Board of Governors establishes bank supervision and examination procedures and evaluates applications for bank mergers and acquisitions. The Board sets

**Board of Governors**
seven-person board that dominates the conduct of monetary policy; this board sets reserve requirements and the discount rate, and constitutes the voting majority of the Federal Open Market Committee

**Federal Open Market Committee (FOMC)**
committee responsible for formulating the general posture of monetary policy; consists of the seven members of the Board of Governors and the 12 presidents of the district Federal Reserve banks

[7] This situation raises a potential conflict of interest. To save money, the Treasury (located in the executive branch of government) might pressure the Federal Reserve into buying large blocks of the national debt. As we learn later, this results in rapid expansion of the nation's money supply, provoking severe inflation. Such a potential conflict of interest on the government's part is a major reason why the Fed was originally established with safeguards preventing undue influence by the Treasury, the Congress, and the president.

**Figure 12-1** Organization of the Federal Reserve System

The complex formal structure of the Federal Reserve System reflects distrust of both government and concentration of financial power.

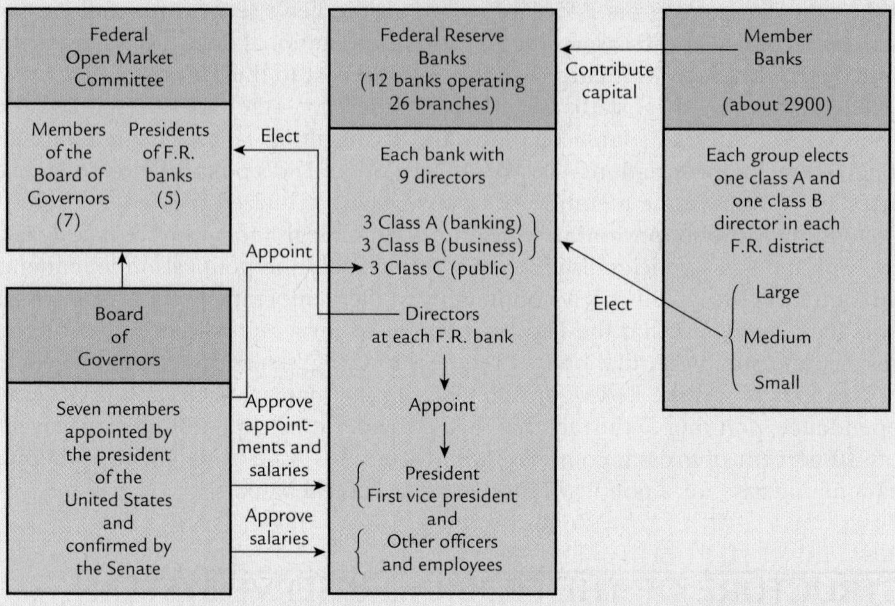

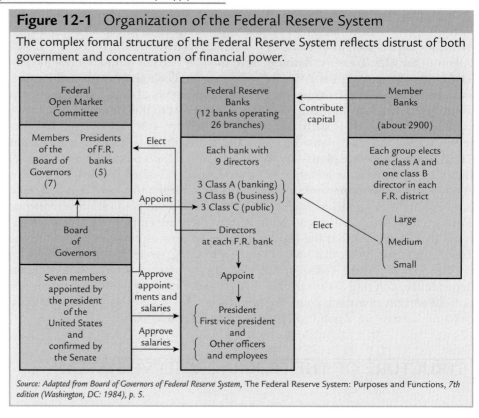

*Source: Adapted from Board of Governors of Federal Reserve System,* The Federal Reserve System: Purposes and Functions, *7th edition (Washington, DC: 1984), p. 5.*

**margin requirements**
percentage of the value of securities purchase that the buyer must pay for using his/her own funds, as opposed to borrowed funds

**margin requirements**—the percentage of the value of the securities purchase that the buyer must pay for using his/her own funds, as opposed to borrowed funds—for stock and bond purchases by the public. The Board of Governors influences the actions of the 12 district Federal Reserve banks. The Board's influence stems from the fact that the Board reviews the budgets of the individual Federal Reserve banks and determines the salaries of bank officers.

Each member of the Board of Governors is appointed by the U.S. president for one 14-year term, subject to confirmation by the U.S. senate. Not more than one of the seven Board members can come from any one of the 12 Federal Reserve districts—a feature implemented to assure geographic dispersion of power. Board members cannot be reappointed after serving a full term.[8] Once appointed, a Board member cannot be fired by the president over policy disagreements. Appointments are overlapping—that is, staggered so that one Board member's term expires on January 31 of even-numbered years. The staggered appointments are intended to prevent the president from "stacking" the Board with individuals sympathetic to the president's political objectives. The rationale for the staggered terms and the long, nonrenewable appointments of Board members is twofold—to reduce the susceptibility of monetary policy to political influence by the executive

[8] A Board member may, however, serve a total of more than 14 years by first serving as a replacement for someone who fails to fill out a full term and then accepting a new 14-year term. An obscure technicality enables a governor to resign just before the end of the term and be reappointed to a new term. This situation happened only once, permitting William McChesney Martin to serve 28 years on the Board (1942-1970). In the past 60 years, only three individuals (including Alan Greenspan) have served more than 14 years on the Board of Governors.

**Exhibit 12-1** Alan Greenspan: Chairman of the Board of Governors, 1987–2006

© Jay Mallin/Bloomberg News/Landor

The chair of the Board of Governors of the Federal Reserve System is commonly viewed as the second most powerful individual in the United States. The chair of the Board greatly influences the nation's powerful monetary machinery, helping to set interest rate levels and ultimately influencing unemployment and inflation rates. The chair sets the agenda for meetings of the Board of Governors and presides over meetings of the Federal Open Market Committee—the group that meets eight times annually in Washington, DC, to decide on the basic stance of monetary policy. The chair also communicates and negotiates with key Congressional committees, the Secretary of the Treasury, and the U.S. president; supervises the huge staff of professional economists and advisors who work for the Board; and communicates current Federal Reserve policy through appearances before Congressional committees, speeches, and public statements.

Alan Greenspan was appointed chairman of the Board of Governors of the Federal Reserve in 1987 by President Ronald Reagan. He was reappointed to additional 4-year terms as chairman by President George H.W. Bush Sr. (1992), President Clinton (1996 and 2000), and President George W. Bush Jr. (2004). Greenspan is only the seventh individual to occupy that crucial seat since 1934. Greenspan graduated *summa cum laude* from New York University in 1948 and received a Ph.D. from NYU in 1977. In the interim, he compiled an impressive record in consulting and government service. From 1954 to 1977 he was CEO of Townsend-Greenspan, an economic consulting firm in New York. In the late 1970s he was a member of the President's Council of Economic Advisors in the Nixon and Ford administrations, serving as chairman of the Council during the troubled years from 1974 to 1977. Greenspan chaired the important National Committee on Social Security Reform from 1981 to 1983 and served as a consultant to both the U.S. Treasury and the Board of Governors in the early 1970s. A keen student of business cycle statistics, Greenspan is famous for spending long hours poring over the data to help formulate his position on the appropriate thrust of monetary policy.

branch of government and to instill a "long view" into management of the nation's money and credit machinery.[9]

The U.S. president appoints a chair of the Board of Governors to a 4-year term. The chair's term is not synchronized with the U.S. president's term, although proposals to do so have frequently been made. The chair of the Board of Governors

[9] In recent times, few members of the Board of Governors have served full 14-year terms. In fact, in the past 35 years fewer than half the Board members have served longer than 5 years on the Board. Recently, Board members have stepped down to accept lucrative positions from Wall Street firms offering salaries that are sometimes ten times those paid for service on the Board of Governors. As a result of the early departure of Board members, President Reagan appointed seven Governors by the end of his second term (1989); President Clinton made four appointments to the Board in his first term (1993-1997); and President George W. Bush made four appointments in his first two years in office (2001 and 2002).

can be reappointed to additional 4-year terms within the limits of the overall term on the Board. Alan Greenspan was appointed to a fifth term as chair in early 2004 (see Exhibit 12-1). The chair of the Board of Governors is potentially an extremely powerful figure. The chair's power derives from his or her influence over nominations to the Board, the attitudes and voting behavior of other members of the Board and the FOMC, and public opinion through testimony before Congressional committees, speeches, and public statements.

## Federal Open Market Committee

The FOMC meets eight times annually (approximately every 6 weeks) at the Board of Governors headquarters in Washington, DC, to chart the course of Federal Reserve policy in general and open market operations in particular. These meetings are attended by the seven members of the Board of Governors, the presidents of the 12 district Federal Reserve Banks, a key advisor to each district Federal Reserve Bank president, and key staff of the Board of Governors and FOMC. At the meeting, FOMC members voice their opinions regarding current economic conditions and the appropriate course of monetary policy. Staff members project the course of output, employment, and inflation that can ensue given various policy stances implemented by the Fed.

**FOMC directive**
formal statement indicating the intended conduct of monetary policy until the next meeting of the Federal Open Market Committee, and voted on by the FOMC

When the members reach a consensus, an **FOMC directive** is drafted indicating the desired conduct of monetary policy until the next FOMC meeting. The directive specifies the level at which a key short-term interest rate (the federal funds rate) is to be maintained until further notice. The directive is then put to a formal vote. Although the seven members of the Board of Governors and the 12 Federal Reserve district bank presidents attend the FOMC meetings and participate in the discussion, only the Board members and *five* of the 12 presidents are allowed to vote at a given meeting. The New York Federal Reserve Bank president is a permanent voting member of the FOMC. The remaining 11 Fed bank presidents alternate as voting members, with four exercising voting privileges in any given year.

**manager of the System Open Market Account**
officer of the Federal Reserve Bank of New York responsible for carrying out, through a network of government security dealers, the open market transactions needed to meet the specifications outlined in the Federal Open Market Committee directive

When the directive is approved by a formal vote, it is issued to the **manager of the System Open Market Account,** who is an officer of the Federal Reserve Bank of New York. The officer is responsible for carrying out, through a network of government security dealers, the open market transactions needed to meet the specifications outlined in the FOMC directive. (This process is examined in detail in Chapter 18.)

Because open market operations are the foremost instrument of Federal Reserve policy, the importance of the FOMC is obvious. The FOMC also conducts occasional operations in the foreign exchange market to stabilize the exchange value of the U.S. dollar *vis-à-vis* other currencies. A schematic outline of the structure of authority within the Federal Reserve System is shown in Figure 12-2. Study this graph to cement your understanding of our discussion in the next several pages.

## Twelve Federal Reserve Banks

The decentralized organization of the Federal Reserve System, with 12 district banks instead of one central bank, is unique. Other nations have a single central bank. Historically, Americans have been wary of the concentration of power and authority in a few hands—especially those of eastern establishment bankers. When the Federal Reserve Act was under discussion, many legislators from western and southern states favored a decentralized structure of central banking authority. Some members of Congress, representing the populist element, suggested that 50

**Figure 12-2** Chain of Authority within the Federal Reserve System

The Board of Governors sets reserve requirements and the discount rate. The Board makes up the majority of the voting members of the important FOMC.

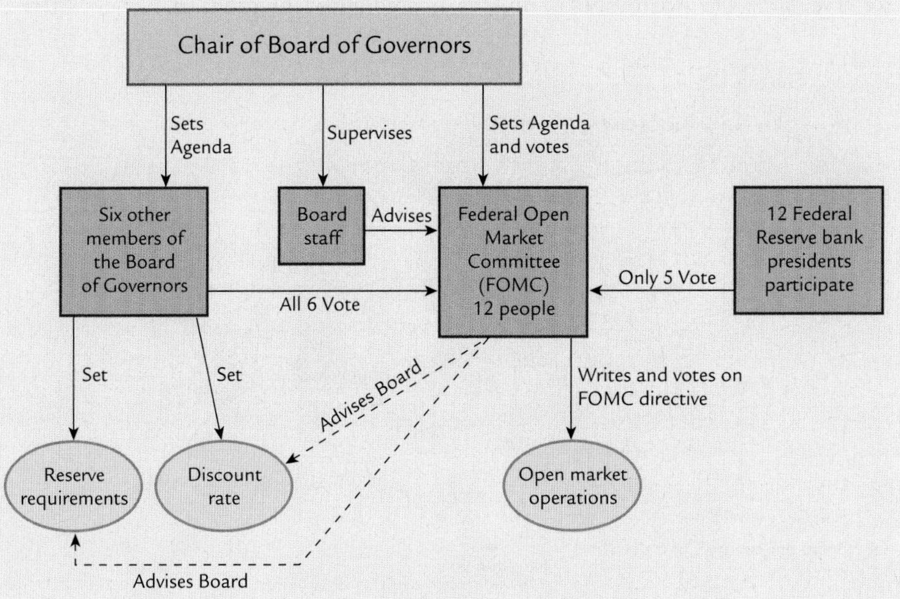


or more autonomous, regional Federal Reserve banks would be appropriate. The legislators held that regional variations in financial conditions required different financial policies for different parts of the country. Other legislators, particularly those in the east, desired to follow the traditional model of a single central bank. The resulting compromise produced the network of 12 regional Federal Reserve banks that we know today.

Figure 12-3 shows the geographic boundaries of the 12 Federal Reserve Districts and the cities in which each of the 12 district Fed banks are located. The figure also shows the location of the Board of Governors in Washington, DC.

The 12 district Federal Reserve banks perform the following functions:

1. Issue new currency and withdraws old or damaged currency from circulation
2. Clear checks
3. "Establish" the discount rate for the district, administer the discount window operation (setting the criteria for bank borrowing), and make loans to banks in the district
4. Examine state-chartered banks in the district that belong to the Federal Reserve System
5. Conduct research on regional/national economic issues and Federal Reserve monetary policy and publish the findings.[10]

Technically, each district Federal Reserve Bank is an incorporated institution, owned by the Federal Reserve member banks of the district and governed by a nine-

[10] Federal Reserve *Reviews* are published by each of the 12 district banks. The *Reviews* typically are published four times annually and are written for the educated lay public. Subscriptions are available free of charge. For the Web site of each Federal Reserve bank, see the list at the end of this chapter in Additional Reading.

**Figure 12-3** The 12 Federal Reserve Districts and Locations of the District Federal Reserve Banks

The nation is divided into 12 Federal Reserve districts, each with its own Federal Reserve bank. The Board of Governors is located in Washington, DC.

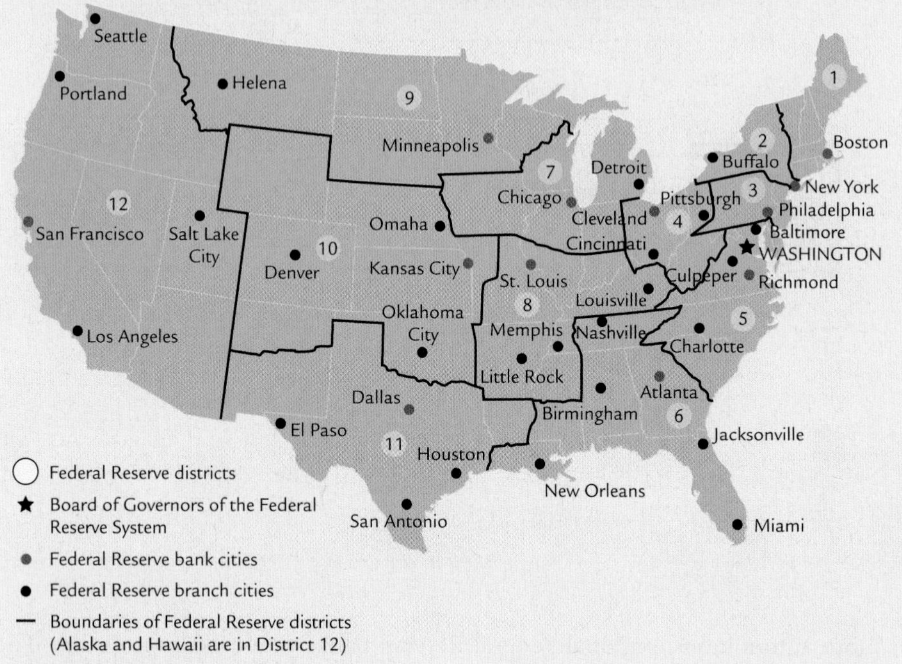


*Source: Federal Reserve Bulletin*

person board of directors. The directors elect the district Federal Reserve bank president, thereby influencing the composition of the important FOMC. The nine directors are grouped into three classes, each with three members (review Figure 12-1). Class A directors are professional bankers elected by the member banks of the district. Class B directors typically are prominent business leaders (from industry, commerce, or agriculture); they also are elected by the member banks. Class C directors represent areas other than the banking and business sectors; They are appointed by the Board of Governors in Washington. The Board of Governors designates two of these Class C directors to serve as chair and deputy chair of the board of directors of the district Federal Reserve banks.

The historical rationale for the three-tier structure of the board of directors of the district Fed banks is to ensure representation of the various constituencies influenced by monetary policy. Class A directors look out for the interests of bankers; Class B directors protect the interests of the non-bank business community; and Class C directors supposedly represent the general public. Proposals increasing the number of class C directors have been made occasionally. Sentiment in favor of reducing the influence of bankers (Class A directors) on monetary policy also has been expressed. Such influence presents a potential conflict of interest because monetary policies that are appropriate for the nation as a whole sometimes differ from the policies that are most favorable for commercial bank profits. As previously mentioned, bankers elect six of the nine directors, who in turn select the president of each Federal Reserve bank. These presidents participate in the crucial FOMC policy deliberations.

Bankers' influence on monetary policy can be reduced by revoking the voting privileges of district Federal Reserve bank presidents on the FOMC. This revocation of voting power would mean the FOMC consists solely of the Board of Governors.[11]

## Member Banks

In 2005, approximately 40 percent of the nation's approximately 7,700 commercial banks were members of the Federal Reserve System. All national banks (approximately 2,000), chartered by the Comptroller of the Currency, must belong to the system. Banks chartered by individual states wishing to join the Federal Reserve System must meet certain requirements—that is, the banks must abide by the Fed's regulations concerning mergers, establishment of branches, maintenance of capital standards, and numerous other matters. Fewer than 1,000 of the approximately 5,800 state-chartered banks currently belong to the Federal Reserve System.

The benefits of Federal Reserve membership include participation in the selection of six of the nine directors of the district Fed bank and perhaps an element of prestige. The most significant deterrents to membership have been strict supervision and regulation by Federal Reserve authorities and, until the 1980s, the higher reserve requirements applicable to member banks. Reserve requirements are a form of taxation levied on banks—the Fed requires banks to hold more of bank assets in non–interest-earning form (as cash and deposits at the Fed) than would be needed in the absence of reserve requirements. Because member banks were once subject to higher reserve requirements than nonmembers, member banks were placed at a disadvantage. During the late 1960s and 1970s, as inflation and interest rates ratcheted upward (thus raising the opportunity cost of holding reserves), the percentage of banks that chose to be members of the Federal Reserve System declined steadily. The Depository Institutions Deregulation and Monetary Control Act of 1980 (DIDMCA) leveled the playing field and stopped the erosion of Federal Reserve membership by requiring all depository institutions to abide by uniform reserve requirements set by the Federal Reserve, regardless of bank membership status.[12]

**YOUR TURN**

What features in the structure of the Federal Reserve System spread power between the government and the private sector? What features spread power among the various geographic regions of the country?

## Allocation of Power within the Federal Reserve System

Since the early 1930s, power has resided more with the Board of Governors in Washington than with the district Federal Reserve banks. For example, each district Federal Reserve bank president is formally appointed by the district's nine-person

[11] In reality, the directors of the district Fed banks are less influential than they appear to be. Typically, only one candidate is nominated as district Federal Reserve bank president, and that nominee is put forward by the Board of Governors in Washington or by the officers of the district Fed bank itself. Hence, the directors simply "rubber stamp" a nominee they had no influence in nominating.

[12] DIDMCA reduced both the costs and benefits of membership in the Federal Reserve System. As a result, the proportion of the nation's banks belonging to the Federal Reserve has not changed significantly in recent years. DIDMCA removed the chief cost of belonging to the Federal Reserve System by equalizing reserve requirements for all depository institutions. The Fed reduced the benefits of membership by permitting nonmember depository institutions to borrow from the Federal Reserve and by providing nonmembers access to other Fed services previously denied to them.

board of directors, but the Board of Governors in Washington retains veto power over these choices and often even initiates the nominations for these positions. In addition, the discount rate is set by each district Federal Reserve bank but is subject to "review and determination" by the Board of Governors. In essence, the Board of Governors determines the discount rate. Finally, in the early days, each Federal Reserve bank was authorized to purchase government securities at its own discretion. Today, decisions concerning such transactions are made in Washington by the FOMC for the system as a whole. The securities are apportioned among the 12 district Federal Reserve banks based on the share of each Fed bank's total assets in the total assets of all 12 Fed banks.

The Board of Governors determines the salaries of the president and other officers of the 12 district Federal Reserve banks. The Board has the authority to remove a district bank president in the event of incompetence or willful obstruction of Federal Reserve policy. (Exhibit 12-2 discusses the salary structure of top Federal Reserve officials.) For practical purposes, we regard the Board of Governors and

## Exhibit 12-2 Salaries of Top Federal Reserve Officials

The accompanying table shows the annual salaries of the members of the Board of Governors of the Federal Reserve System and the presidents of the 12 Fed district banks as of December 31, 2003. The number of officers and the average salaries of officers for each district Federal Reserve bank are given.

Several items are noteworthy. First, note the rather wide range of salaries of the presidents of the district Fed banks. Salaries ranged from a high of $341,900 for the San Francisco Fed bank president to a low of $231,500 for the Cleveland Fed bank president. The salary differences reflect regional variations in the cost of living (especially housing), experience, and other factors. Note also that the 12 district Fed banks employ almost 1,000 officers at an average salary of more than $139,000 per year. The 267 officers of the Federal Reserve Bank of New York earn an average salary of $171,000.

More important, note that the chairman of the Board of Governors, arguably one of the two most powerful individuals in the United States, earns less than *any* of the 12 district Federal Reserve bank presidents and only about *half* the salary earned by the San Francisco bank president. The chairman of the Board of Governors earns less than the division heads of the Board's own staff and approximately 140 officers of the Federal Reserve Bank of New York. The relatively low pay of members of the Board of Governors helps to account for the fact that the typical (median) Board member in the past 35 years has served only approximately 5 years of the 14-year term before departing. Of 39 individuals appointed to the Board from 1970 to 2004, only eight served more than half of the 14-year term, and only two appointees since 1952 have served as long as 14 years. When Paul Volcker and Wayne Angell left the Board in 1987 and 1994, respectively, each reputedly was offered a salary in the $1 million range by a Wall Street firm. Even Alan Blinder's salary increased when he left the Board (after serving less than 2 years) in 1996 to return to his position in academia as professor of economics at Princeton.

| Board of Governors | Salary |
|---|---|
| Chairman | $171,900 |
| Other Board members | $154,700 |
| Division heads of Board staff | $185,000* |

the FOMC as the governing units of the Federal Reserve System. Today, the district Federal Reserve banks are little more than branches.

Among the 12 district Fed banks, the Federal Reserve Bank of New York has always held a preeminent position. The New York Fed owns about 40 percent of the total assets of the Federal Reserve System. It physically carries out open market operations on behalf of the system and occasional foreign exchange market transactions to stabilize the dollar's value. The New York Fed has its finger on the pulse of the major financial markets, which are located in New York. The New York Fed bank president is the only district Fed bank president with continuous voting privileges on the FOMC. Finally, the New York Fed handles the system's dealings with foreign central banks and international institutions.

An early study on the *de facto* shares of power wielded by the various elements within the Federal Reserve System estimated the chair of the Board of Governors maintains 45 percent of the power and the staff of the Board of Governors—highly trained professional economists—holds another 25 percent. The other six mem-

**Exhibit 12-2** Salaries of Top Federal Reserve Officials—*cont'd*

What accounts for the relatively parsimonious salaries of Board members *vis-à-vis* other high Federal Reserve officials? The answer lies in the fact that the salaries of Board members are established by federal statute while the salaries of all other Fed officers are set by the Federal Reserve itself. In other words, Congress is responsible for the low salaries of members of the Board of Governors.

Presidents and other officers of 12 Federal Reserve district banks

| District | Federal Reserve Bank | President's Salary | Officers' Salary | Number of Officers |
|---|---|---|---|---|
| 1 | Boston | $258,600 | $142,139 | 71 |
| 2 | New York | 310,000 | 171,263 | 267 |
| 3 | Philadelphia | 235,300 | 136,700 | 54 |
| 4 | Cleveland | 231,500 | 129,533 | 61 |
| 5 | Richmond | 252,300 | 131,853 | 79 |
| 6 | Atlanta | 281,000 | 142,396 | 81 |
| 7 | Chicago | 283,800 | 139,729 | 88 |
| 8 | St. Louis | 238,000 | 127,551 | 78 |
| 9 | Minneapolis | 264,500 | 137,520 | 44 |
| 10 | Kansas City | 258,800 | 132,834 | 74 |
| 11 | Dallas | 249,800 | 128,887 | 54 |
| 12 | San Francisco | 341,900 | 153,798 | 72 |
| | **Average** | **$267,125** | **$139,517** | **85** |

* Salaries of the staff of the Board of Governors are not public information. However, salaries of the four division heads (Research and Statistics, Monetary Affairs, International Finance, and Banking Supervision) are known to exceed the salary of the chairman of the Board of Governors.

bers of the Board of Governors control 20 percent of the power, leaving only 10 percent for the 12 district Federal Reserve banks and their presidents.[13] The chair of the Board of Governors wields disproportionate power for the reasons we mentioned earlier. Of course, the distribution of power within the Federal Reserve changes over time and depends strongly on the personality, reputation, and forcefulness of the chair of the Board of Governors, the skills and professional competence of the other six members of the Board, and other factors.

## QUESTION OF FEDERAL RESERVE INDEPENDENCE

The Federal Reserve System enjoys considerable independence from the executive and legislative branches of government relative to central banks in many other nations. The Fed's independence was created deliberately by the authors of the Federal Reserve Act and was further strengthened by legislation in the 1930s. The independence derives in part from the lengthy, nonrenewable 14-year terms of the members of the Board of Governors, which reduces the influence of the executive branch of government over Board member decisions. No Board member need curry favor with the president because Board members cannot be reappointed to a second full term or dismissed by a president over disagreements about the appropriate conduct of monetary policy.

Perhaps even more significant is the fact that the Fed's operating revenues are derived from the Fed's portfolio of securities rather than from Congressional appropriations. Other government agencies must submit annual budget requests to Congress. Such a request procedure inevitably permits Congress to influence an agency's behavior. The Fed has not only remained financially independent of Congress, but at one time the Fed even flaunted its independence by refusing to submit to an audit by the General Accounting Office.[14] With regard to day-to-day conduct of monetary policy, the Fed traditionally has occupied the enviable position of taking orders from no one. In numerous instances the Fed has implemented policy actions that were received with open irritation by the president and Congress.

The Federal Reserve's independence is commonly overstated, however. In reality, both the president and Congress have influence over the Fed. The Fed, reluctant to oppose the views of the person selected by the whole nation, strongly prefers to act in a manner consistent with the president's wishes. Also, the Fed is frequently involved in Congressional legislation concerning bank regulation and other matters, so the Fed needs to remain in the president's good graces and have the president's support. The Fed's independence *vis-à-vis* Congress is especially tenuous. The U.S. Constitution gives ultimate authority to govern the money creation process to the legislative branch of government. The Constitution does not mandate a central bank. Congress created the Fed in 1913, altered it significantly in the 1930s, and retains authority to further modify or even abolish it. The Fed is subject to all U.S. laws, including the Employment Act of 1946 and the Humphrey Hawkins Act of 1978. Hence, the Fed's independence from the legislative branch clearly is conditional and fragile. In the end, the Federal Reserve is accountable to Congress and is acutely aware of being so. (The factors motivating Federal Reserve behavior are discussed in Exhibit 12-3.)

---

[13] Sherman Maisel, *Managing the Dollar* (New York: Norton, 1973).

[14] Today, most of the Fed's operations are thoroughly audited by the General Accounting Office. However, the Fed has vigorously and successfully resisted any audit of Fed operations in the foreign exchange market and other international dealings.

## **Exhibit 12-3** What Motivates the Fed—The Public Interest or Bureaucratic Empire Building?

We described the Federal Reserve as a benevolent organization, dedicated solely to the public interest. The Fed serves as a lender of last resort, supervises and regulates banks, controls inflation, and smooths the ups and downs of the business cycle. With these actions the Fed ostensibly is motivated entirely to serve the nation's best interests. Such is the traditional view of the Fed—the *public interest view.*

Public choice economists suggest an alternative explanation for the forces motivating the Federal Reserve and other bureaucracies. In the view of public choice economists, just as consumers seek to maximize utility and business firms strive to maximize profit, the Federal Reserve is motivated to pursue actions that maximize *its own welfare*. The welfare of the Federal Reserve, like that of any bureaucracy, is directly related to the Fed's *power*—the size and strength of the Fed's empire. In this view, the Fed consistently acts to maximize its own welfare rather than the nation's welfare as a whole.

To test this cynical theory of Federal Reserve behavior, you need to specify the theory's predictions about Fed behavior and compare those predictions with the Fed's actual behavior. Predictions include the following: the Fed will strive to maintain its financial autonomy, fight any proposal that reduces its authority or the scope of its responsibilities, and avoid or minimize conflict with those having authority to change the nature of the Federal Reserve—that is, Congress.

Examples of Fed behavior consistent with these predictions exist. The Federal Reserve has repeatedly and effectively fought Congressional proposals to change the Fed's unique financial status. At one time the Fed even refused to submit to an audit of Fed books by the government watchdog, the General Accounting Office. When the Clinton Administration proposed collapsing the nation's four separate and overlapping banking supervisory agencies (the Federal Reserve, FDIC, Comptroller of Currency, and individual state organizations) into a single new regulatory authority in the interest of efficiency, the Fed resisted vigorously (and won the battle). The Fed supported the proposal to permit banks to expand into investment banking and other activities, which culminated in enactment of the Gramm-Leach-Bliley Act in 1999. This act led to expansion of the scope of Federal Reserve responsibility—an increase in the Fed's empire. In appearances before Congressional committees, the Fed chairman seems exceptionally deferential and patient, even when queries and statements by members of Congress appear inappropriate or preposterous. Such demeanor on the part of the Fed chairman likely aims to minimize conflict between the Fed and Congress.

On numerous occasions the Fed has bowed to Congressional pressure by keeping interest rates artificially low. The Fed chairman is an acknowledged expert at "obfuscation"—the art of making deliberately ambiguous statements that are virtually impossible to decipher or interpret. In the 1970s, when Congress required the Fed to specify and justify in advance the Fed's targets for money growth rates, the Fed responded by specifying a multitude of targets (for M1, M2, M3), perhaps to minimize potential criticism. If the Fed missed one target, it would likely hit another. The Federal Reserve is notoriously secretive, although in the past decade it has taken steps to become more transparent. Many economists believe such tactics do little except protect the Fed from criticism. Studies have shown that, economic conditions being the same, the Fed is less likely to raise interest rates in election years.

The view that the Fed is motivated predominantly by self-interest seems harsh. Clearly, the Fed is dedicated to providing a stable, long-run economic climate. A more charitable interpretation of the Fed's behavior might be the following. When no serious conflict with the public interest exists, the Fed acts according to the theory of bureaucratic behavior. When serious conflict exists, the Fed likely will act as it is supposed to act—in the public interest.

## Case for Federal Reserve Independence

The case for an independent central bank derives from the view that executive or legislative branch control of the central bank would result in favoritism based on party affiliation, patronage, and other political considerations. More significantly, political control of the Fed likely would introduce an "easy money" bias into monetary policy, stimulating the nation's propensity for inflation (see *International Perspectives*). The argument—politicians love to spend money but hate to levy taxes to pay for the expenditures. The resulting tendency to run budget deficits means the government must frequently borrow. A politically expedient but highly inflationary method for the government to finance deficit spending is to sell bonds to a subservient Federal Reserve. This process is equivalent to printing money to finance government expenditures. The Fed has long been regarded as the guardian of price level stability, providing checks and balances against excesses of government budgetary policy. Advocates of an independent central bank believe an appreciable reduction in the Fed's independence would exacerbate the U.S. economy's tendency for inflation.

The short terms of the U.S. president and Congress and the associated frequency of elections make the considerations for Fed independence more acute. Supporters of an independent central bank emphasize the need for continuity of monetary policy. Politicians tend to be myopic, looking only as far ahead as the next election. If the central bank is subservient to the executive or legislative branch of government, monetary policy may be dictated by short-term political needs of incumbent politicians rather than legitimate long-term objectives such as price level stability. Monetary policy influences output and employment more quickly than it influences the inflation rate. Therefore, politicians might implement policies that boost economic activity as elections approach, even though such measures may necessitate a post-election recession engineered to bring down inflation resulting from the pre-election economic stimulus. Most economists believe such a "stop-go" policy is the worst prescription for the nation's economic health. In sum, supporters of an independent Federal Reserve emphasize that monetary policy is simply too important and potentially subject to abuse to entrust to politicians.

## Case Against Federal Reserve Independence

Critics of Federal Reserve independence argue that, in a democracy, any agency responsible for monetary policy should be accountable to the electorate, but the Federal Reserve is not sufficiently accountable. If the Fed were made part of the executive branch, the administration in power could be held accountable for the overall conduct of macroeconomic policy, including monetary policy. Poor performance could be penalized through the democratic process by "throwing the rascals out."

Another frequently voiced criticism of the Fed's independent status is the need for various elements of national economic policy to be coordinated rather than allowed to run at cross purposes. Lack of coordination is a distinct possibility given that government expenditure and tax policy—*fiscal policy*—is determined by the executive and legislative branches but monetary policy is set by the independent Federal Reserve. The Reagan Administration clashed openly with the Fed in 1981 and 1982, when tax cuts aimed at stimulating production and employment were countered by very high interest rates resulting from the Fed's restrictive policies aimed at reducing inflation.

Finally, critics of the Fed's independence argue that the Federal Reserve has not used its independence effectively over the years. The Fed presided passively over

# INTERNATIONAL PERSPECTIVES

## Central Bank Independence and Economic Performance

Advocates of a politically independent central bank believe an independent bank is more conducive to favorable economic performance, as indicated by a relatively stable price level. A well-known study discovered a significant inverse (negative) association across nations between the degree of independence of central banks and the average magnitude of inflation experienced over the years. Professors Alberto Alesina and Laurence Summers of Harvard University ranked the central banks of industrial nations on the criterion of independence, using a scale from 1 to 4. The most independent central banks were ranked 4, while the least independent central banks were ranked 1. The rankings were established based on the following criteria—extent to which government officials maintain seats on the board of directors of the central bank, extent to which the central bank is required to help finance government budget deficits, prevalence of informal contacts between officials in the executive branch and the central bank, and formal relationship between the central bank and the government.

We now update the original study by computing the average inflation rate (CPI) experienced by each of the 17 countries from 1971 to 1994. The findings are illustrated in the accompanying figure. Countries whose central banks were judged to be highly independent typically exhibited relatively low inflation rates. For example, the two nations with the most

Relationship Between Central Bank Status and the Inflation Rate from 1971 to 1993

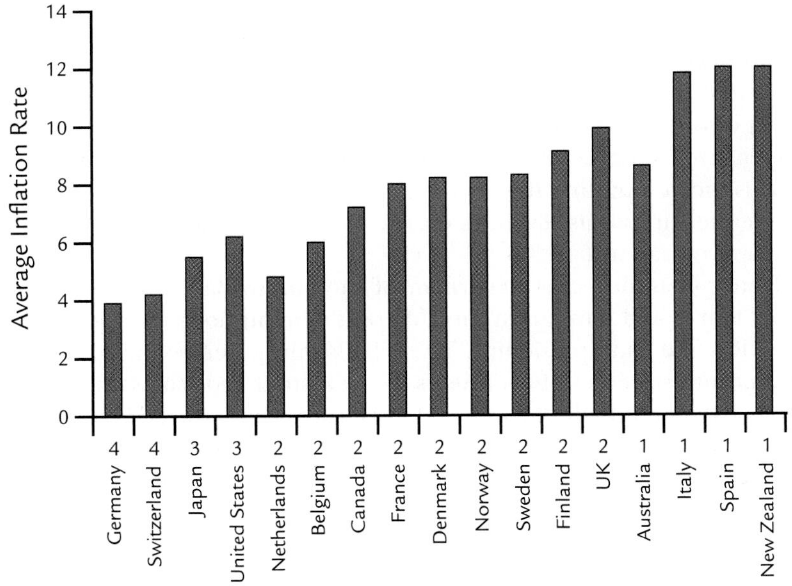

# INTERNATIONAL PERSPECTIVES —*continued*

independent central banks, Germany and Switzerland, experienced the lowest rates of inflation among the 17 nations. Countries with the least independent central banks (for example, Spain and New Zealand) consistently experienced relatively high rates of inflation.

Were the low inflation rates enjoyed by such nations as Germany and Switzerland purchased at the cost of relatively high unemployment rates? The answer is no. Germany, Switzerland, and Japan experienced lower unemployment rates on average over the 22-year period than high-inflation nations such as Italy and England. Since 1993, Australia and New Zealand (and other nations) have taken measures to make their central bank more independent, and inflation in these countries today is far lower than the (earlier) rates illustrated in the figure.

the collapse of the financial system in the early 1930s; contributed substantially to inflationary pressures in the 1940s, the late 1960s, and the late 1970s; and hit the monetary brakes too hard in the severe recession of the early 1980s. The rejoinder to this argument, of course, is that the Fed has learned from its past mistakes and is a far more effective institution today. No major Federal Reserve policy mistakes are evident in the past 15 to 20 years.

Attacks on the Fed's independence come in spurts but are particularly virulent when interest rates are unusually high. One example is the early 1980s, when the Fed pushed interest rates to extremely high levels, hoping to break the back of severe inflation that had been building for 15 years. Various proposed reforms to reduce the Fed's autonomy were seriously discussed at that time. Today, any proposed reforms affecting the Fed's independence seem modest. One proposal is to make the 4-year terms of the chair of the Board of Governor and of the U.S. president coterminous so that the president—upon taking office—can appoint a new Board chair. The term of office of Board members also could be shortened, particularly given the propensity of appointees to serve only a portion of the 14-year term. More radical proposals include putting the Secretary of the Treasury on the FOMC and requiring the Fed to turn all its revenues over to the Treasury and be financed by Congressional appropriations.

In 1993, Henry Gonzalez, then chairman of the House Banking Committee, presented a bill that would have given the U.S. president authority to appoint the district Federal Reserve bank presidents. The bill also proposed reducing the private banks' input into selection of presidents of the district Fed banks and requiring the Fed to make more timely and detailed disclosures about the Fed's policy decisions. So far, only the last proposal has received serious consideration. The Fed has moved (albeit gingerly) in the direction of *transparency*—that is, reducing its historic propensity to be unnecessarily secretive. In 1995, the Fed began announcing major changes in FOMC decisions shortly after the FOMC meeting rather than with the previous 6-week lag. Detailed transcripts of FOMC meetings now are made available to the public 5 years after meetings (previously the details of the meetings were *never* made public). Most economists applaud these moves but argue that the Fed should move farther in the direction of transparency or openness.

Since 1978, the Federal Reserve has been required to confer with Congressional committees twice annually regarding the Fed's intended monetary policy posture. The Fed's testimony is made available to the public. Such dialogues pave the way for intelligent discussion of monetary policy without encroaching on the Fed's independence. In recent years, many nations have implemented measures making their central bank more independent. The European Central Bank is today considered the most independent central bank in the world, as we discuss in Chapter 13. Nevertheless, the Federal Reserve remains one of the more independent central banks today (see *International Perspectives*).

## SUMMARY

A central bank is an organization charged with many tasks. The most important and difficult task is conducting monetary policy—that is, influencing the nation's credit conditions and interest rates and controlling the nation's money supply. The U.S. central bank, established nearly 100 years ago, is known as the Federal Reserve System (or the Fed). By determining key items on its own balance sheet, the Fed can influence availability of credit, interest rates, and the nation's money supply. The most important units in the Federal Reserve System are the Board of Governors and the Federal Open Market Committee. These groups make the important decisions about monetary policy. Because Federal Reserve policies strongly influence the nation's economy, the founders of the Federal Reserve established numerous safeguards limiting the influence of the executive and legislative branches of government on the conduct of monetary policy. However, students of central banking disagree about the extent to which a central bank should be independent of government in a democracy.

## YOUR TURN ANSWERS

PAGE 299

Power is vested in the government inasmuch as the U.S. president appoints the members of the Board of Governors (and designates the chair), the profits of the Fed revert to the Treasury, and the Fed must report and defend its monetary policy objectives periodically before Congressional committees. Power resides in the private sector inasmuch as the presidents of the 12 district Federal Reserve banks are selected by private citizens (directors of the 12 district Fed banks) and the 12 Fed banks are "owned" by the private commercial banks that are members of the Federal Reserve System. Geographic representation derives from the fact that there are 12 district Federal Reserve banks spread throughout the nation and that not more than one member of the Board of Governors can come from any one of the 12 districts.

# KEY TERMS

legal reserves (reserves)
fractional reserve banking system
Federal Reserve Act
lender of last resort
district Federal Reserve banks
discount loans, or discounts and advances
open market operations
tax and loan accounts
Federal Reserve float
Board of Governors
Federal Open Market Committee (FOMC)
margin requirements
FOMC directive
manager of the System Open Market Account

# STUDY QUESTIONS

1. Discuss the problems that led to creation of the Federal Reserve System.
2. Explain why the following items are listed on the asset side of the Federal Reserve's balance sheet:
   A. Loans to depository institutions
   B. Cash items in process of collection
   C. U.S. government securities
3. Explain why the following items are listed on the liability side of the Federal Reserve's balance sheet:
   A. Depository institution deposits at the Federal Reserve
   B. Deferred availability cash items
4. Who owns the Federal Reserve? Explain the nature of this ownership.
5. Explain how the Federal Reserve is financed.
6. Discuss the composition of the Federal Open Market Committee. How do members obtain their positions, and what is the rationale for this method of selecting them? In your view, should any changes be made in those procedures? Explain.
7. "The Board of Governors is the core of the Federal Reserve System." Evaluate this statement.
8. Carefully analyze the merits of the case for a central bank's independence from the legislative and executive branches of government.
9. Is there any reason for maintaining 12 separate Federal Reserve banks today? Why might this arrangement have made more sense in 1913 than it does today?
10. Go to the Internet (http://www.federalreserve.gov/bios/) and find out who are the current seven members of the Fed's Board of Governors and what are their backgrounds. How many of the members have Ph.D. degrees in economics?
11. Why do you suppose the president of the New York Fed maintains a permanent seat on the FOMC while the other 11 district Federal Reserve bank presidents serve on an alternating basis? Is this justified?
12. Can you think of any reason why the state of Missouri has two Federal Reserve district banks yet the entire western third of the United States has only one (in San Francisco)?
13. Can you think of any proposals that would increase the Fed's accountability without seriously infringing on the Fed's autonomy?
14. What measures exist today to hold the Fed accountable for its actions?
15. The theory of bureaucratic behavior suggests that the Fed will take actions that maximize its own power rather than act in the national interest. Can you marshal any evidence to support this claim? To counter it?

**16.** Consider two major pieces of financial legislation of the past quarter century: the Depository Institutions Deregulation and Monetary Control Act (DIDMCA) of 1980 and the Gramm-Leach-Bliley Financial Services Modernization Act (1999). The Federal Reserve supported both legislations. How can the Fed's support be reconciled with:

   **A.** The theory of bureaucratic behavior?
   **B.** The public interest theory?

**17.** Whom do you believe should be the highest paid official in the Federal Reserve System? How many people in the system actually earn more than the chair of the Board of Governors? Why does this occur?

## ADDITIONAL READING

- For a discussion of the events leading up to the creation of the Federal Reserve, see James Parthemos, "The Federal Reserve Act of 1913 in the Stream of Monetary History," *Economic Review,* Federal Reserve Bank of Richmond, July/August 1988, pp. 19–28. On the structure of the Federal Reserve System, see Chapter 1 of *The Federal Reserve System: Purposes and Functions,* 8th edition (Washington, DC: Board of Governors, 1994), available on the Board of Governors' Web site (see below).
- For a discussion of the role of political considerations on the conduct of monetary policy, see Steven M. Roberts, "Congressional Oversight of Monetary Policy," *Journal of Monetary Economics,* August 1978, pp. 543–556. An evaluation of the power of the chair of the Board of Governors is presented in Edward J. Kane, "The Impact of a New Federal Reserve Chairman," *Contemporary Policy Issues,* January 1988, pp. 89–97. Good sources on the factors that motivate Fed behavior include John T. Wooley, *Monetary Politics: The Federal Reserve and the Politics of Monetary Policy* (Cambridge: Cambridge University Press, 1984) and Thomas Mayer, ed., *Political Economy of American Monetary Policy* (New York: Cambridge University Press, 1990).
- Political pressures facing the Fed are discussed in Thomas Havrilesky, *The Pressures on American Monetary Policy* (Boston: Kluwer Academic Publishers, 1993). A classic article that constructs indexes of central bank independence for industrial nations and then examines the relationship between these rankings and several measures of national economic performance is Alberto Alesina and Lawrence H. Summers, "Central Bank Independence and Macroeconomic Performance: Some Comparative Evidence," *Journal of Money, Credit, and Banking,* May 1993, pp. 151–162.
- The minutes and policy directives of each FOMC meeting are collected each year in the *Annual Report,* Board of Governors of the Federal Reserve System, available on the Board's Web site. Interesting and informative recent books dealing with the Fed include Martin Mayer, *The Fed: The Inside Story of how the World's Most Powerful Financial Institution Drives the Markets* (New York: Plume, Penguin Group, 2001) and Bob Woodward, *Maestro: Greenspan's Fed and the American Boom* (New York: Simon and Schuster, 2000).

- Finally, an interesting article detailing why a member of the Board of Governors (Alan Blinder) stepped down after only 2 years of service to return to academia is John Cassidy, "Fleeing the Fed," *New Yorker,* February 19, 1996, pp. 38–46.

*Note:* Each of the 12 district Federal Reserve banks publishes quarterly *Reviews* that present their research findings. You can read the *Reviews* and find other pertinent information at the following Web sites:

| | |
|---|---|
| Federal Reserve Bank of Atlanta | http://www.frbatlanta.org/ |
| Federal Reserve Bank of Boston | http://www.bos.frb.org/ |
| Federal Reserve Bank of Chicago | http://www.chicagofed.org/ |
| Federal Reserve Bank of Cleveland | http://www.clevelandfed.org/ |
| Federal Reserve Bank of Dallas | http://www.dallasfed.org/ |
| Federal Reserve Bank of Kansas City | http://www.kc.frb.org/ |
| Federal Reserve Bank of Minneapolis | http://www.minneapolisfed.org/ |
| Federal Reserve Bank of New York | http://www.ny.frb.org/ |
| Federal Reserve Bank of Philadelphia | http://www.phil.frb.org/ |
| Federal Reserve Bank of Richmond | http://www.rich.frb.org/ |
| Federal Reserve Bank of St. Louis | http://www.stlouisfed.org/ |
| Federal Reserve Bank of San Francisco | http://www.frbsf.org/ |

The Board of Governors Web site is http://www.federalreserve.gov/

# Chapter 13

# THE EUROPEAN CENTRAL BANK

Central banks have existed for more than 300 years. The world's first central bank was the Swedish Riksbank, established in 1668. The venerable Bank of England opened its doors in 1694. By 1800, both Spain and France had central banks. In spite of these early central bank origins, only about 20 central banks were in operation around the world when the Federal Reserve System was created in 1913. In the early post–World War II era, a large number of formerly colonized countries became independent nations, leading to a major increase in the number of central banks. The collapse of the Soviet Union in the 1990s resulted in central bank establishment by numerous former Soviet republics. Today, more than 150 central banks exist worldwide.

The two most prominent central banks today (and the two most *important* in terms of the gross domestic product of countries involved) are the Federal Reserve System and the European Central Bank (ECB), which was formed in 1998. In Chapter 12, we examined the organization and structure of the Federal Reserve and looked at the features that facilitate the Fed's operation as an independent entity within government. In this chapter, we examine the origin, structure, and nature of the new ECB. We pay special attention to the differences in structure and organization between the ECB and the Federal Reserve System.

## MOVEMENT TOWARD ECONOMIC UNIFICATION OF EUROPE

More than 50 years ago, leaders of western European nations spoke seriously about the potential benefits of moving toward economic and political unification of Europe. In the unification, tariffs, passport controls, impediments to migration of workers and financial capital, and other barriers inhibiting economic integration among European nations would be dismantled. Europe would emerge as a unified entity, much like the 50 states constituting the United States. At the time, each European country had its own language, laws, forms of money (francs, lire, marks, etc.), tariffs, and other trade barriers. Each country had its own central bank that conducted monetary policy and other traditional central bank functions. Imagine the inefficient state of affairs if each of the 50 states in the United States had a different currency, central bank, set of interest rates, and tariff policy toward imports from other states. European leaders have long been aware of the potential shift in the global balance of economic and political power if western European nations emerged as a single economic and political bloc. In recent decades, Europe has steadily moved toward this unification goal.

### Road to Monetary Union and Establishment of the ECB

First we trace the steps along the road that ultimately led to western Europe's establishment of a **monetary union**—the adoption of a single currency by a group of countries. This road led to adoption of the **euro**—the new single currency—by 12 western European nations and establishment of a single central bank that conducts monetary policy collectively for the group of countries constituting the monetary union. Today, 12 western European nations constitute the **Economic and Monetary**

**monetary union**
adoption of a single currency by a group of countries

**euro**
single currency used by 12 western European nations

# EUROPEAN CENTRAL BANK

**European System of Central Banks (ESCB)** organization consisting of the European Central Bank and the individual central banks of the European Monetary Union nations

The Maastricht Treaty established the institutional framework for conduct of monetary policy in the EMU. This treaty created the **European System of Central Banks (ESCB),** which is composed of the new ECB and the individual central banks of the 12 EMU member nations. The ESCB is patterned after two major central banks: the Federal Reserve System and the German Bundesbank. The ECB, headquartered in Frankfurt, Germany, was established on June 1, 1998, and opened for business on January 1, 1999.

## Structure of the ECB

**Governing Council** committee that makes European Central Bank monetary policy decisions

**Governors** heads of the central bank of the 12 individual nations making up the Economic and Monetary Union

ECB monetary policy decisions are made by the **Governing Council,** which consists of an **Executive Board** and 12 **Governors.** The governors are the heads of the central bank of the 12 individual nations constituting the EMU. The Governing Council is the main decision-making body of the ECB. The council meets monthly in Frankfurt to formulate the monetary policy for the entire euro area. The Governing Council of the ECB has a similar function as the Federal Open Market Committee (FOMC) of the Federal Reserve System. Just as the FOMC conducts monetary policy in the United States, the Governing Council conducts monetary policy for the 12 EMU nations. The structures of the FOMC and the Governing Council are similar in some ways.

**Executive Board** six-person board that participates on the Governing Council of the European Central Bank in formulating monetary policy

**Council of Economics and Finance Ministers (ECOFIN)** group consisting of the finance ministers of each of the European Union member countries; group initiates the Executive Board appointment process

**Executive Board.** This important group is analogous to the Board of Governors of the Federal Reserve System but has considerably less power than the Board of Governors. The Executive Board consists of six members: a president, a vice president, and four additional members.[4] The Maastricht Treaty specifies that Executive Board members must be persons of recognized standing and professional experience in central banking and monetary policy. The Executive Board appointment process is initiated by the **Council of Economics and Finance Ministers (ECOFIN),** which consists of the finance ministers of each of the EU member countries. The individuals recommended by ECOFIN for membership on the Executive Board are reviewed by the European Parliament and the Governing Council of the ECB. Governments of all member countries of the euro area must agree on the nominee before Board appointment is confirmed.

Each Executive Board member is appointed for an 8-year, nonrenewable term (patterned after the German Bundesbank structure). In conformity with the Federal Reserve System, the terms of Executive Board members are staggered to minimize clustering of new appointees. This staggering provides stability and continuity in monetary policy. Executive Board members work full time for the ECB in Frankfurt. The president of the Executive Board is also president of the Governing Council and is referred to as President of the ECB. This structure is similar to that in the Federal Reserve, where the Chairman of the Federal Reserve Board of Governors is also chairman of the FOMC.

The President of the ECB is chosen from among respected central bankers in the 12 EMU member countries. Unlike the Federal Reserve Chairman, whose term is only 4 years (renewable within the 14-year full term on the Board of Governors), the Executive Board President's appointment is for 8 years but cannot be renewed.

[4] A short biographical sketch of each member of the Executive Board is available at http://www.ecb.int/ecb/orga/decisions/eb

After a contentious debate leading up to the establishment of the ECB, Wim Duisenburg, a respected central banker from the Netherlands, became the first president of the ECB. In the terms of the compromise that allowed Duisenburg's selection, Duisenburg agreed to step down after fulfilling about half of the normal 8-year term. In May 2003, Duisenburg was replaced by Jean-Claude Trichet of France.

**Governors of the National Central Banks.** Each of the participating EMU nations (currently 12) has an independent central bank. The top officer of each of these central banks is the *governor.* The Maastricht Treaty requires that the governors of each nation's central bank be selected by their respective national government and that the duration of the governors' terms be no less than 5 years. The length of a governor's term is determined by each member country, with the stipulation that the term must be at least 5 years. The terms among the 12 EMU countries vary from 5 to 8 years. Eight of the 12 EMU countries allow renewal of governors' terms.

The role of the governors of the national central banks in EMU monetary policy is analogous to that of the presidents of the 12 district Federal Reserve banks in the Federal Reserve System. However, the governors in the ECB have considerably more influence over monetary policy in Europe than do the corresponding presidents of the 12 district Fed banks in the United States. ECB governors account for 12 of the 18 votes of the Governing Council, while presidents of the 12 district Federal Reserve banks account for only 5 of the 12 votes of the FOMC. Thus, while the Board of Governors constitutes the majority of the voting members of the FOMC, the Executive Board accounts for only one third of the votes of the Governing Council in the ECB.[5] The Executive Board members are not consulted about or have veto power over appointment of national central bank governors. The Executive Board does not control the salaries of national central bank governors or the budgets of the national central banks.

The features of the Executive Board stand in contrast to the Federal Reserve, where the Board of Governors has veto power over nominations for district Federal Reserve Bank presidents and controls the salaries of the officers of the 12 district Federal Reserve Banks. Power in the Federal Reserve System is much more centralized in the Board of Governors than in the corresponding Executive Board in the ECB.

## "Ownership" of the ECB and Disposition of Profits

As we indicated in Chapter 12, the private commercial banks that are members of the Federal Reserve System technically "own" (without appreciably influencing) the U.S. central bank. Each member bank must subscribe to shares of capital stock in the Federal Reserve in the amount of 6 percent of the bank's own capital accounts. The Fed first meets operating expenses and pays out a very small portion of its profits as dividends on the capital shares to member commercial banks. Then the

---

[5] Recall that the president of the New York Fed is a permanent voting member of the Federal Open Market Committee. The other 11 district Fed bank presidents alternate as voting members, with only four voting at any given time. Hence, the seven-person Board of Governors accounts for 7 of the 12 FOMC votes. Recognizing that the number of countries belonging to both the EU and EMU likely will increase in the future and desiring to prevent erosion of the Executive Board's relative power in the conduct of monetary policy, the Governing Council of the ECB agreed in December 2002 that the number of national central bank governors exercising a voting right on the Governing Council should not exceed 15. Hence, when the number of national central bank governors exceeds 15, a rotation system of voting takes effect, as is the case today in the Federal Open Market Committee.

Federal Reserve turns over its remaining profits to the U.S. Treasury. The Treasury thus receives well over 90 percent of the Federal Reserve's gross profits.

The national central banks of the 25 EU member nations technically "own" the ECB. In 2004, total ECB capital stock stood at five billion euros. Each EU nation's central bank must subscribe to capital shares in the ECB in an amount that depends on the nation's GDP and population. Given this criterion, in 2004 Germany accounted for almost 25 percent of the ECB capital, while France owned the second largest portion—a bit more than 15 percent. Of EU countries not currently members of the EMU, the United Kingdom had the largest portion—almost 15 percent of total ECB subscribed capital. National central banks of EMU members pay in 100 percent of their subscribed capital, while central banks of EU countries that are not members of the EMU pay in only 5 percent of their subscribed capital.[6]

Unlike the Federal Reserve, the ECB pays out at least 80 percent of its net profits to its owners—the national central banks representing the 25 EU nations. The ECB retains 20 percent of its profits and pays out the remainder to the individual national central banks in proportion to their paid-in capital shares. These national central banks share their profits (or losses) with their respective governments according to individual national laws governing each nation's central bank.

## Issue of Political Independence

An independent central bank is relatively immune from the government's influence on monetary policy. Central bank independence is important because the economic conditions that make politicians happy (and re-electable) are low interest rates and a booming economy—conditions sometimes inconsistent with price stability. Incumbent politicians seeking popular support and re-election often pressure central banks to implement expansionary policies creating a robust economy in the near term, even when such policies lead to inflation in the longer term. Numerous nations around the world have implemented measures increasing the independence of their central banks in the past 15 years. These measures likely account in part for the decreased inflation rates in most countries during this period.

ECB independence from political influence from governments is important because economic conditions across the 12 EMU nations vary much more widely than do economic conditions across the 50 individual states constituting the United States. Suppose the Irish economy is booming and prices are rising sharply but Germany is experiencing stagnant output and slowly falling prices. Clearly, the governments of Germany and Ireland will have different opinions about appropriate ECB monetary policy. Ireland would prefer a restrictive monetary policy, while Germany would prefer a highly expansionary policy. Neither the German nor Irish government should be capable of exerting undue influence on ECB monetary policy.

The ECB is widely believed to be the most independent central bank in the world, largely because the ECB, unlike other central banks, is truly a *supranational* organization. The ECB does not report to any national government. The statutes defining ECB independence derive from an international treaty (the Maastricht Treaty) rather than from any nation's law. Unanimous agreement of its signatories (the governments of the 15 EU nations that signed the treaty) is required to change the treaty. Altering the ECB's independent status would be at least as difficult as changing the status in the EMU country having the most rigorous safeguards to independence prior to the euro's advent (probably Germany or Switzerland).

---

[6] Voting status on the Governing Council is independent of subscribed capital in the ECB. The principle of "one country, one vote" prevails. This policy initially caused apprehension in larger countries such as Germany.

In contrast, the Federal Reserve System was created by Congress, which has authority to amend or revoke the original Federal Reserve Act. (In fact, the Federal Reserve Act has been amended several times.) The Fed knows that Congress can easily amend the Federal Reserve Act, so the Federal Reserve cannot ignore political considerations in conducting monetary policy and other responsibilities. In contrast, the Governing Council is aware of the obstacles confronting those attempting to modify the ECB's independent status, so the Governing Council can better resist political pressures that might impinge upon its conduct of monetary policy.

The ECB's defining statutes are unequivocal in stating that the EU is constitutionally required to accept ECB policies without any interference or meddling on the part of EU member states or other entities. The Maastricht Treaty explicitly constrains the influence of the national governments in the conduct of ECB policy as follows:

> When exercising powers and carrying out the tasks and duties conferred upon them by this Treaty and the Statute of the ESCB, neither the ECB, nor a national central bank, nor any member of their decision-making bodies shall seek or take instructions from Community institutions or bodies, from any government of a Member State or from any other body. The Community institutions and bodies and the governments of the Member states shall undertake to respect this principle and not to seek to influence the members of the decision-making bodies of the ECB or of the national central banks in the performance of their tasks.[7]

The prohibition on ECB lending to the government of any EU nation is important to the issue of independence. The ECB cannot buy new bonds issued by governments of EU member nations. Historically, a primary source of inflation in many nations has been large central government budget deficits financed by central bank purchasing of newly issued debt. This process is known as *monetization* of government deficits—essentially printing money to finance government. Such actions are ruled out by the strictures prohibiting the ECB from buying newly issued government bonds.

Other factors contribute importantly to ECB independence. Like the Federal Reserve, the ECB does not depend on legislative bodies for operating funds. Like members of the Federal Reserve Board of Governors, the ECB Executive Board appointees serve one lengthy, nonrenewable term, and the term is staggered.[8] Executive Board members cannot be dismissed over disagreements about the conduct of monetary policy; they can be dismissed only for serious misconduct or incapacitation.

## Central Bank Accountability

Some critics of central bank independence argue that independence is inconsistent with the principles of a democratic society. After all, a central bank is a very powerful institution, capable of exerting major influence over people's lives. Critics of central bank independence believe that public policy should be made by elected officials. Accountability is often seen as a necessary counterbalance to central bank independence. In other words, an accepted *quid pro quo* for granting central bank independence is the requirement that the central bank be held accountable.

To whom should a central bank be accountable? In principle, a central bank should be accountable to the public. In a democracy, elected representatives should

[7] Maastricht Treaty, Article 107.

[8] Among the key decision-making officers of all the central banks of industrialized nations in the world, members of the Board of Governors of the Federal Reserve have the longest terms (14 years), while the Fed Chairman's term is the shortest (4 years). The President of the ECB's term is 8 years (nonrenewable) both as President and as a member of the Executive Board. The brevity of the Federal Reserve Chairman's term may increase the Chairman's susceptibility to political pressure in the event the individual desires reappointment.

be charged with holding the central bank accountable. The U.S. Constitution gives the Congress responsibility for regulating the creation of money. Because Congress has the authority to amend or abolish the Federal Reserve Act and because members of Congress are representatives of the people, the Federal Reserve should be accountable to Congress. The original Federal Reserve Act has been amended several times, partly to increase the Fed's accountability. Congressional legislation enacted in 1977 requires the Federal Reserve to state its goals and to consult with Congressional committees twice each year about the Fed's goals and progress toward meeting those goals. In 1978, Congress again amended the Federal Reserve Act to require the Board of Governors to submit a written report to Congress prior to the Fed Chairman's biannual appearance before Congressional committees. This report must overview recent economic conditions and relate the FOMC's economic forecast to the administration's forecast.

In the euro area, the ECB is not accountable to any individual government. A natural entity to which the ECB should be accountable is the European Parliament, which represents the European public. However, the Parliament has little authority over the ECB. Congress can change the laws governing the Federal Reserve, but the European Parliament does not have authority to change the laws governing the ECB. Changes can result only by unanimous agreement of all the countries that signed the Maastricht Treaty. The Parliament can require members of the Executive Council of the ECB to testify before its committees, but it has no such authority over national central bank governors, who maintain considerable influence in ECB monetary policy decisions. Unlike the U.S. Senate, which can veto the U.S. president's nominations to the Board of Governors, the Parliament is not empowered to veto appointments to the Executive Board of the ECB. Perhaps because of the absence of any unique entity governing the ECB, the Maastricht Treaty requires the ECB to report annually on monetary policy of the current year and the past year to the European Parliament and to several other European commissions and councils.

For what should a central bank be accountable? The central bank should be accountable for the goals established for the central bank by government. The mandated goals of the Federal Reserve are price stability and high employment, neither of which is precisely defined by Congress. Reasonable people differ on what constitutes price stability and what constitutes full or high employment. Furthermore, these two policy goals often are in short-run conflict. For example, a sharp increase in oil prices increases inflation and unemployment in the near term. In this case, the central bank cannot maintain price stability and high employment simultaneously. Short-run conflicts make accountability ambiguous when the central bank is charged with multiple goals. Accountability is enhanced when the central bank is given a *single* goal and when that goal is expressed in precise terms.

In contrast to the Federal Reserve, the ECB is charged with a single goal—maintenance of price stability. The ECB also may desire to achieve other goals sought by EMU member countries, such as maintaining high employment. However, in case of conflict, the ECB's top priority is clearly stated—price stability—and that goal of price stability is precisely defined. The Governing Council of the ECB defines price stability as an inflation rate of less than 2 percent per annum over the "medium term," as measured by a price index reflecting prices in the euro area as a whole. The fact that the ECB is responsible for achieving a single and precisely defined goal increases the ECB's accountability. Greater accountability, in turn, enables granting of substantial independence to the ECB.

The issue of whether government should conduct an audit of central bank financial operations is contentious. On the one hand, the public has a right to know how the central bank spends its money because the central bank is a public agency. On the other hand, central banks argue that a government audit inevitably leads to government meddling in monetary policy. Government can harass or intimidate the Fed by using its authority to audit the financial statements of the Board of Governors and the district Federal Reserve banks. Perhaps government can even require the Federal Reserve to submit to Congressional control over the Fed's budget. The Federal Banking Act of 1978 authorized the General Accounting Office (GAO) to conduct a very limited audit of the Federal Reserve but exempted from GAO audit all aspects related to monetary policy. Restrictions on auditing of the ECB are even more rigorous. Very limited auditing of the books of the ECB and the national central banks is permitted, and these audits are conducted only by external firms recommended by the ECB.

## Central Bank Transparency

To enhance central bank accountability and credibility, a central bank must be transparent. *Transparency* refers to the ease and clarity with which the public can observe and understand the policy actions and intentions of the central bank. Holding a central bank accountable is difficult if the viewpoints and intentions of the central bank are not clear. Transparency provides the tools that enable the public to hold the central bank accountable. Transparency requires that the *goals* of the central bank be made clear. The ECB is more transparent than the Federal Reserve in this aspect because the ECB has a single and unambiguously defined goal. But transparency also requires that policy decisions and the reasons behind the decisions be communicated clearly to the public. The Federal Reserve is more transparent than the ECB in this aspect.

After each meeting of the FOMC of the Federal Reserve System, the FOMC issues a press release announcing any change (or absence thereof) in the short-term interest rate controlled by the Fed. The release overviews current economic conditions and explains the reasons for any policy change in the context of these conditions. In recent years this release has included the vote of the FOMC and the names of FOMC members who voted for and against the approved policy action. On the Thursday after the *following* FOMC meeting (about 6 weeks later), the Federal Reserve releases the minutes of the meeting. The minutes provide the public with a more detailed picture of the FOMC's views about ongoing and prospective economic conditions and the reasons for changes in monetary policy (if any) implemented in the meeting. The minutes do *not* reveal the discussion or views expressed by the individual members of the FOMC, except for FOMC members who dissented from the committee's decision. The Fed also releases meeting transcripts after 5 years.

After each meeting of the ECB Governing Council, the ECB issues a very brief press release announcing any change in monetary policy. (Examples of typical press releases of the FOMC and the Governing Council are provided in Exhibit 13-3.) Unlike the Federal Reserve, the President of the ECB then gives a press conference, discussing the policy decision in the context of ongoing economic developments and the ECB's assessment of prospective economic conditions. The ECB publishes a lengthy monthly bulletin that discusses policy decisions and analyzes economic conditions in the euro area.[9] However, unlike the FOMC, the Governing Council does not release meeting minutes. No formal vote is taken in Governing

[9] The ECB's bulletin and the press releases and transcripts of the press conference can be accessed at the ECB's Web site at http://www.ecb.int/.

## Exhibit 13-3 Press Releases Following Policy Meetings of the FOMC and Governing Council

**Federal Reserve Press Release**
**Release Date: June 25, 2003**

The Federal Open Market Committee decided today to lower its target for the federal funds rate by 25 basis points to 1 percent. In a related action, the Board of Governors approved a 25 basis point reduction in the discount rate to 2 percent.

The Committee continues to believe that an accommodative stance of monetary policy, coupled with still robust underlying growth in productivity, is providing important ongoing support to economic activity. Recent signs point to a firming in spending, markedly improved financial conditions, and labor and product markets that are stabilizing. The economy, nonetheless, has yet to exhibit sustainable growth. With inflationary expectations subdued, the Committee judged that a slightly more expansive monetary policy would add further support for an economy which it expects to improve over time.

The Committee perceives that the upside and downside risks to the attainment of sustainable growth for the next few quarters are roughly equal. In contrast, the probability, though minor, of an unwelcome substantial fall in inflation exceeds that of a pickup in inflation from its already low level. On balance, the Committee believes that the latter concern is likely to predominate for the foreseeable future.

Voting for the FOMC monetary policy action were Alan Greenspan, Chairman; Ben S. Bernanke; Susan S. Bies; J. Alfred Broaddus, Jr.; Roger W. Ferguson, Jr.; Edward M. Gramlich; Jack Guynn; Donald L. Kohn; Michael H. Moskow; Mark W. Olson; and Jamie B. Stewart, Jr.

Voting against the action was Robert T. Parry. President Parry preferred a 50 basis point reduction in the target for the federal funds rate.

**ECB Press Release**
**Release Date: June 3, 2004**

At today's meeting the Governing Council of the ECB decided that the minimum bid rate on the main refinancing operations and the interest rates on the marginal lending facility and the deposit facility will remain unchanged at 2.00%, 3.00% and 1.00% respectively.

The President of the ECB will comment on the considerations underlying these decisions at a press conference starting at 2:30 p.m. today.

*Source: Web sites of Board of Governors of Federal Reserve at* http://www.federalreserve.gov/ *and the European Central Bank at* http://www.ecb.int/.

Council meetings. The European Parliament has passed several resolutions in recent years asking the ECB to publish the minutes of the Governing Council meetings. The Parliament also has asked the Governing Council to conduct formal votes on policy proposals and to summarize the vote in the published minutes, without indicating member names. The ECB's stated position has been that publication of meeting minutes and vote summaries would inhibit the presentation of viewpoints in Governing Council meetings and cause council members to vote based on national considerations rather than the interests of the euro area as a whole. Critics charge that the ECB's relatively secretive approach hinders the public's credibility in the ECB.

Transparency is enhanced by public knowledge of the central bank's economic forecast because such knowledge provides a guide to likely future policy actions. The Federal Reserve communicates its forecasts to the public in two ways. First, the Fed's biannual reports to Congress indicate forecast ranges for inflation, unemployment, and output for the current year and the following year. Second, since early 2000, the FOMC's press release has included a statement on the Fed's view about the "balance of risks" facing the economy. The statement indicates the Fed's view about whether higher inflation or higher unemployment constitutes the greater risk to the economy in the near future (note the wording in the third paragraph of the Federal Reserve press release of June 25, 2003 in Exhibit 13-3). Initially, the ECB did not reveal its forecasts. However, beginning in December 2000, the ECB has provided general economic forecasts in its *Monthly Bulletin.*

## SUMMARY

Europe has undertaken an important and interesting economic experiment with the adoption of a single currency by 12 nations, whose monetary policy is now determined collectively by a new central bank—the ECB. This central bank, which opened in 1999 when the euro was introduced, was modeled on the Federal Reserve System and the German Bundesbank. The ECB is widely acknowledged to be the most independent central bank in the world. The ECB's independence was deliberately instilled by the representatives of EU nations who met in Maastricht, the Netherlands, to draw up the treaty establishing the ECB. This legal independence of the ECB stems from many factors. The two most important factors for the ECB's independence—(1) the ECB is not accountable to any government or dependent on government for funding, and (2) the ECB's independent status can be modified only by unanimous vote of the EU nations that signed the original Maastricht Treaty. The power structure within the ECB is more decentralized than that in the Federal Reserve. Considerably more power resides in the 12 governors of the national central banks in the euro area than in the 12 presidents of the district Federal Reserve Banks in the United States. However, the structure of a central bank is not static. Just as the Federal Reserve has evolved over the years, the structure and distribution of power within the ECB may change in response to experience. Table 13-1 summarizes a few of the important comparative features of the Federal Reserve System and the ECB.

**Table 13-1 Comparative Features of Federal Reserve System and European Central Bank**

| Aspect | Federal Reserve | European Central Bank |
|---|---|---|
| Legal basis for existence | Federal Reserve Act; amendable by Congress | European Community Treaty, as amended by Maastricht Treaty; amendable only by unanimous agreement of signatories of Treaty |
| Ownership of central bank | Member commercial banks (each bank pays in capital in proportion to bank's own capital) | Member nations' central banks (each nation's central bank pays in capital in proportion to nation's gross domestic product and population) |
| Distribution of central bank profits | 6 percent dividend payment to own ers (member banks); remainder paid to U.S. Treasury | 20% to European Central Bank reserve fund; 80% to the national central banks |
| Mandated goals | High employment and price stability; no precise definition of these terms | Price stability, defined as less than 2 percent inflation over the medium term |
| Financial independence | Yes | Yes |
| Functional independence | Yes | Yes |
| Appointment of key officials | Board members: appointed by U.S. president and approved by Senate<br>District bank presidents: appointed by Board of Directors of district Fed Bank | Executive board members: appointed by heads of state<br>Governors: appointed according to respective national laws |
| Term of office of key officials | Board member: 14 years<br>Chair and Vice Chair: 4 years<br>District Federal Reserve Bank presidents: 5 years | Executive Board: 8 years<br>President and Vice President: 8 years<br>Governors: at least 5 years |

## KEY TERMS

monetary union
euro
Economic and Monetary Union (EMU)
European Central Bank
Treaty of Rome
European Union (EU)
Treaty on Monetary Union (Maastricht Treaty)
convergence criteria
European System of Central Banks
Governing Council
Executive Board
Governors
Council of Economics and Finance Ministers (ECOFIN)

# STUDY QUESTIONS

1. Do you believe the Federal Reserve or the European Central Bank is more susceptible to political influence in the conduct of monetary policy? Explain.

2. Important differences exist between the organization and institutional makeup of the Federal Reserve and the European Central Bank in terms of the issue of independence. What are these differences, and why do they matter?

3. "The Board of Governors is more powerful within the Federal Reserve System than is the Executive Board within the ECB." Do you agree or disagree? Explain.

4. The ECB seems to be more secretive in its communications with the public than is the Federal Reserve. Is there any justification for this discrepancy?

5. The Federal Reserve once adamantly refused to submit to an audit of Fed books by the government watchdog, the General Accounting Office. What justification is there, if any, for the Federal Reserve's position? Explain.

6. Suppose oil prices sharply increase worldwide, to $75 dollars per barrel. Over the following 2 years, will the United States or the euro area more likely experience a greater increase in inflation? Explain.

7. Go to the ECB Web site at http://www.ecb.int/ and find out whether the number of EMU member countries remains at 12 and the number of EU countries remains at 25.

# ADDITIONAL READING

- Two excellent sources that analyze the 1990s movement toward the monetary union in Europe are Christopher Taylor, *EMU 2000? Prospects for European Monetary Union* (London: Royal Institute for International Affairs, 1995) and Paul De Grauwe, *Economics of Monetary Union* (Oxford: Oxford University Press, 2000). A highly readable source that is a good primer on the EMU is Christian N. Chabot, *Understanding the Euro: The Clear and Concise Guide to the New Trans-European Economy* (New York: McGraw-Hill, 1999).
- An excellent source that compares the structure and independence of the European Central Bank to that of the Federal Reserve is Patricia S. Pollard, "A Look Inside Two Central Banks: The European Central Bank and the Federal Reserve," Federal Reserve Bank of St. Louis *Review,* January/February 2003, pp. 11–30. A broad overview of the ESCB is provided in Mark Wynne, "The European System of Central Banks," *Economic Review,* Federal Reserve Bank of Dallas, 1999, No. 1, pp. 2–13.
- Also see Marvin Goodfriend, "The Role of a Regional Bank in a System of Central Banks," Federal Reserve Bank of Richmond *Economic Quarterly,* Winter 2000, pp. 7–25. Finally, for a scholarly analysis of the evolution of the institutional, behavioral, and legislative aspects of central banking in 20 major industrial nations over the past 50 years, see Pierre Siklos, *The Changing Face of Central Banking* (Cambridge, England: Cambridge University Press, 2002).

Chapter 14

# THE DEPOSIT EXPANSION PROCESS: THE SIMPLE ANALYTICS

In Chapter 12 we outlined the structure of the Federal Reserve System, which ultimately controls the nation's money supply and short-term interest rates. In Chapter 9 we discussed several aspects of commercial banking, skipping over the depository institutions' role in the money supply process. In this chapter, we analyze how depository institutions—commercial banks, savings and loan associations, mutual savings banks, and credit unions, hereafter called *banks*—influence the money supply through their lending and investing activities. We sketch the mechanism by which the Federal Reserve influences credit conditions and the growth rate of the money supply. We examine the money supply process in more depth in Chapters 15 and 16.

## BANKS AND CREATION OF BANK DEPOSITS

An important aspect of banking stems from how bank actions influence credit availability and the money supply. These variables importantly affect crucial macroeconomic variables such as output, employment, and the nation's price level. We begin by illustrating the effect of bank lending and investing activities on the money supply, that is, on monetary aggregates such as M1 and M2. We use the T-account to illustrate the process. A T-account indicates the *change* in a depository institution's balance sheet resulting from a given event. Suppose your hometown bank lends $10,000 to a local shoe store owner so that she can increase her inventories. Hometown Bank's T-account summarizes the changes in its balance sheet as follows:

**Hometown Bank**

| | | | |
|---|---|---|---|
| Loans | +10,000 | Demand deposits | +10,000 |

Hometown Bank added a new loan to its assets and created new money—an increase in its demand deposits. The monetary aggregates (M1, M2, M3) increase by the loan amount because demand deposits are included in all money supply measures. The nation's money supply expands by $10,000 as soon as the loan is granted.

The shoe store merchant did not take out the $10,000 loan so that she could leave the funds in a checking account. When she purchases a new shipment of shoes, a $10,000 check drawn on her account at Hometown Bank is sent to the shoe manufacturer in St. Louis. After the shoe manufacturer deposits the check in a St. Louis bank and the check clears, demand deposits in the Hometown Bank return to their original, pre-loan level. However, demand deposits in the St. Louis bank increase $10,000. The T-accounts of the two banks appear as follows:

| Hometown Bank | | | | St. Louis Bank | | | |
|---|---|---|---|---|---|---|---|
| 1. Loans | +10,000 | Demand deposits | +10,000 | | | | |
| 2. Deposits at Federal Reserve | −10,000 | Demand deposits | −10,000 | 2. Deposits at Federal Reserve | +10,000 | Demand deposits | +10,000 |

Note that the $10,000 created by Hometown's loan is still in the banking system. As long as Hometown's loan is outstanding, the U.S. money supply remains elevated by $10,000. The Federal Reserve clears the check by making a bookkeeping transaction. The Fed transfers $10,000 from Hometown Bank's Federal Reserve deposit account to the St. Louis Bank's Fed deposit account (Step 2 in the T-accounts).

In the unlikely event the merchant requests the loan in the form of currency rather than as a bookkeeping entry (a demand deposit), the result is the same—M1, M2, and other monetary aggregates expand by $10,000. Because the currency granted to the merchant comes from the bank's cash (bank cash is not included in the money supply while the cash is in the bank), the monetary aggregates increase as soon as the cash is given to the borrower.[1] The main point can be easily summarized. Whenever banks increase their loans—whether in the form of currency or in the form of a demand deposit entry on the banks' books—the money supply increases by the loan amount.

The same result occurs whenever a bank purchases securities from the public or from security dealers. Suppose Hometown Bank purchases $200,000 of U.S. government securities from a N.Y.C. dealer. Hometown Bank sends a $200,000 check drawn on its account with the Federal Reserve. After the security dealer deposits the check in a N.Y. bank and the Fed processes and clears the check, the balance sheet changes are as follows:

| Hometown Bank | | | New York Bank | | | |
|---|---|---|---|---|---|---|
| U.S. government securities | +200,000 | | Deposit at Fed | +200,000 | Demand deposits | +200,000 |
| Deposit at Fed | −200,000 | | | | | |

When the dealer deposits the check in its N.Y. bank, the money supply rises by $200,000.[2] The Federal Reserve handles the transfer of funds between the two banks by making two bookkeeping entries: one crediting the Fed account of the N.Y. bank

[1] The narrow measure of the money supply, M1, equals DDO + $C^P$. The latter variable, currency in the hands of the public, includes only currency and coins *outside* of depository institutions, the Treasury, and the Federal Reserve. Currency and coins held in banks are *not* included in $C^P$. Hence, when Hometown Bank grants the loan to the merchant in the form of currency, $C^P$ rises. The various money supply measures (M1, M2, etc.) also increase.

[2] The check written by Hometown Bank does not reduce demand deposits in Hometown Bank because the check was drawn by the bank itself from its Federal Reserve account. Hometown Bank's Federal Reserve account (not included in the money supply) is reduced by $200,000, but deposits in Hometown Bank are not reduced.

by $200,000 and another debiting the Fed account of the Hometown Bank by $200,000. The point is clear. When a bank purchases securities from a member of the non-bank public—any entity other than the Treasury, the Federal Reserve, or another bank—the money supply is boosted by the amount of the transaction.

These two examples demonstrate that banks create demand deposits (and money) whenever banks expand their earning assets in the form of loans and securities. Because bank loans and securities earn interest and are profitable, you are naturally inclined to ask: Are depository institutions limited in the amount of money they can create by making loans and purchasing securities? The answer lies in legal reserve requirements, which limit bank acquisition of earning assets. Depository institutions are required by law to maintain *reserves*—cash and deposits at the Federal Reserve—in amounts not less than a specified percentage of the banks' demand deposit liabilities.[3]

At this point, we should review the key concepts of reserves, reserve requirements, required reserves, and excess reserves. *Reserves* are cash in banks plus deposits at the Federal Reserve. The **reserve requirement** is a percentage figure set by the Federal Reserve, applicable to demand deposits in banks. **Required reserves** are the dollar amount of reserves a bank is required to maintain or exceed. The dollar number is calculated by multiplying the reserve requirement percentage by the amount of demand deposits outstanding in a bank. **Excess reserves** are the difference between reserves and required reserves. If reserves exceed required reserves, banks have positive excess reserves.

**reserve requirement**
percentage figure set by the Federal Reserve, applicable to demand deposits in banks

**required reserves**
dollar amount of reserves a bank is required to maintain, calculated by multiplying the percentage reserve requirement by the amount of demand deposits

**excess reserves**
difference between reserves and required reserves

When Hometown Bank makes a loan or purchases securities, the bank loses reserves in the amount of the transaction (review the previous T-accounts). Once a bank has no excess reserves, it cannot afford to lose any reserves. Hence, any bank is limited in the amount of loans it can make or securities it can purchase by the amount of excess reserves it has on hand. However, we will demonstrate that the *banking system* can generate new loans or security purchases by a *multiple* of the excess reserves in the system. The key to this puzzle resides in the following fact—an *individual bank* loses reserves when it grants a loan or purchases a security, but the *banking system* does not lose reserves.

## Multiple Expansion of Bank Deposits

A fractional reserve banking system requires that banks maintain only a small portion of their demand deposit liabilities in the form of reserves (cash and deposits at the Fed). Any new reserves added to the banking system can support deposits that are a *multiple* of the amount of the new reserves. Suppose banks run up against the reserve requirement constraint. That is, suppose banks have no *excess reserves*—no more reserves than the amount the banks are required to hold to meet the Fed's reserve requirements. Therefore, banks cannot make additional loans or buy additional securities—they cannot create any additional money. Now, suppose explorers discover a sunken ship off the Florida coast. The sunken ship contains $5 million in coins. If the coins are placed in a checking account in a Florida bank (Bank A), the T-account effect is as follows:

**Bank A**

| | | | |
|---|---|---|---|
| Currency and coins | +5 million | Demand deposits | +5 million |

[3] Even in the absence of reserve requirements, banks would be motivated to maintain a reasonable quantity of reserves to avoid illiquidity. Depository institutions likely would maintain fairly sizable reserve-to-deposit ratios (though smaller than they currently maintain) even if no explicit reserve requirements existed.

Now, to demonstrate the phenomenon of multiple deposit expansion, we make the following assumptions:

1. Each bank in the nation desires to rid itself of all its excess reserves. That is, each bank continues to acquire earning assets (loans and securities) until the bank runs up against the reserve requirement constraint—until the bank has zero excess reserves.
2. The public's demand for currency ($C^P$) is independent of the amount of demand deposits held. Therefore, changes in demand deposits induce no change in demand for currency by the public.
3. The legal reserve requirement for all demand deposits in all banks is 10 percent.

Due to Assumption 3, Bank A finds itself with excess reserves of $4.5 million.[4] Remember that when a bank makes loans or buys securities, the bank loses reserves in the amount of the transaction. Hence, each bank is limited in its ability to lend and purchase securities by the amount of its excess reserves. Suppose Bank A uses its excess reserves to grant loans to real estate developers. Initially, the bank makes the funds available through bookkeeping entries. The bank credits the demand deposit accounts of the real estate developers. The developers do not leave the funds in their checking accounts. The developers use the $4.5 million to purchase land from individuals who bank with Bank B. The T-account transactions of Banks A and B are as follows:

| Bank A | | | | Bank B | | | |
|---|---|---|---|---|---|---|---|
| 1. Currency and coins | +5 million | Demand deposits | +5 million | | | | |
| 2. Loans | +4.5 million | Demand deposits | +4.5 million | | | | |
| 3. Deposit at Fed | −4.5 million | Demand deposits | −4.5 million | 3. Deposit at Fed | +4.5 million | Demand deposits | +4.5 million |

In Step 1, Bank A receives the initial $5 million deposit in coins from the sunken ship. In Step 2, the bank grants loans of $4.5 million. In Step 3, the checks written by the real estate developers against Bank A are cleared through the Federal Reserve. Two pairs of bookkeeping entries are made. In the first entry, the Fed transfers $4.5 million (bookkeeping account) from Bank A's account at the Fed to Bank B's account. In the second entry, Bank A debits the demand deposit accounts of the real estate developers by $4.5 million, and Bank B credits the land sellers' demand deposit account by the same amount.

When we net out the effects of these three steps on Bank A's balance sheet, Bank A's final result is reserves up by $0.5 million, loans up by $4.5 million, and demand deposits up by $5 million. In granting loans of $4.5 million, Bank A has used up its original $4.5 million in excess reserves and created $4.5 million of demand

[4] Note the T-account of Bank A. Because demand deposits have increased by $5 million and the percentage reserve requirement is 10 percent, the dollar amount of required reserves has increased by 10% × $5 million, or $ 0.5 million. Because the bank gained $5 million of reserves from the coin deposit, the bank's excess reserves initially are up by $4.5 million.

deposits, which now reside in Bank B. But the deposit expansion process has only begun! Bank B, which received both demand deposits and reserves in the amount of $4.5 million, now has $4.05 million of excess reserves.[5] Following Assumption 1, suppose Bank B rids itself of all excess reserves by purchasing U.S. government securities from a N.Y. securities dealer. After Bank B's check is deposited in a N.Y. bank (Bank C) and is processed, the T-accounts look like this:

**Bank B**

| | | | |
|---|---|---|---|
| 1. Deposit at Fed | +4.5 million | Demand deposits | +4.5 million |
| 2. U.S. government securities | +4.5 million | | |
| Deposit at Fed | −4.05 million | | |

**Bank C**

| | | | |
|---|---|---|---|
| | | | |
| 2. Deposit at Fed | +4.05 million | Demand deposits | +4.05 million |

Bank B pays for the securities with a $4.05 million check written on its Federal Reserve account. As soon as the check is deposited in Bank C, the money supply rises by $4.05 million. The Fed completes the transfer of funds from Bank B to Bank C by debiting $4.05 million from Bank B's account with the Fed and crediting Bank C's account by the same amount.

Bank B retains the demand deposit account ($4.5 million) of the people who sold the land to the developers. Bank B also has acquired U.S. securities in the amount of $4.05 million and pays for them with an equal deduction to its Federal Reserve deposit account. Thus, Bank B's final position is Federal Reserve account up by $0.45 million, portfolio of government securities up by $4.05 million, and demand deposits up by $4.5 million. Bank B participated in the money supply process. It received a new demand deposit of $4.5 million and purchased securities in the amount of $4.05 million, thereby creating the same amount of demand deposits in another bank (Bank C). Keep in mind that total reserves in the banking system are *not* increasing. Total reserves are simply being shuffled from banks that are lending and buying securities to other banks in the nation.

You now can grasp the emerging pattern. Bank C is now in a position similar to the positions Banks A and B were in. Bank C has received new reserves in the full amount of its new deposits, but it is required to maintain only 10 percent of those funds in the form of reserves. Bank C can now grant loans and/or purchase securities in the amount of its excess reserves, $3.645 million. In granting loans or buying securities, Bank C creates demand deposits in the amount of $3.645 million in yet another bank (Bank D).

Given our three assumptions, the resulting pattern of multiple deposit creation and rearrangement of reserves in the chain of banks is shown in Table 14-1

The initial coin deposit of $5 million *directly* increases deposits by $5 million. More significantly, after bank lending and investing, the deposit produces an additional $45 million dollars in demand deposits. The total expansion in deposits is 10 times the initial $5 million injection of reserves in the banking system resulting from the coin deposit. Stated another way, the *induced* expansion of deposits *beyond*

[5] Because demand deposits in Bank B increase by $4.5 million, required reserves increase by $0.45 million. Actual reserves increase by $4.5 million, so excess reserves are up by the difference, $4.05 million.

**Table 14-1 Creation of Deposits and Disposition of Reserves**

| Bank | Change in Deposits | Disposition of Reserves |
|---|---|---|
| A | +5,000,000 (original deposit of coins) | +500,000 |
| B | +4,500,000 | +450,000 |
| C | +4,050,000 | +405,000 |
| D | +3,645,000 | +364,500 |
| E | +3,280,500 | +328,050 |
| ⋮ | ⋮ | ⋮ |
| Total | $50,000,000 | $5,000,000 |

the direct deposit of $5 million is 10 times the initial amount of excess reserves ($4.5 million), or a total of $45 million. The $5 million of reserves initially placed in Bank A is scattered throughout the banking system. Each bank along the line rids itself of all its excess reserves, and each bank's final result is an increase in actual reserves equal to 10 percent of the increase in its deposits.

If we lump all banks together and look at the T-account for the banking system as a whole, the effects of the entire operation are easily summarized:

**All Depository Institutions**

| | | | |
|---|---|---|---|
| Currency and coins | +5 million | Demand deposits | +50 million |
| Loans and investments | +45 million | | |

The initial injection of $5 million in cash reserves remains in the banking system and can support $50 million in new demand deposits. Of the $50 million, $5 million is *directly* attributable to the coin deposit. The remaining $45 million results from aggregate expansion in bank loans and security holdings. The formula for the maximum expansion of deposits is as follows:

$$\textbf{Induced Expansion of Deposits} = \textbf{Initial Excess Reserves} \times \frac{\mathbf{1}}{\textbf{\% Reserve Requirement.}}$$

In this example, the induced expansion of deposits = $4,500,000 × 1/10% = $45,000,000.

Remember that the assumptions we make are rather *unrealistic*. In the real world, banks deliberately hold some excess reserves as a precaution against unexpected currency withdrawals by depositors, unexpected adverse check clearings against banks' deposits at the Fed, and other factors. Also, the public's demand for currency increases as demand deposits increase, so the real-world deposit expansion multiplier is smaller than the simple multiplier developed here. The true deposit expansion multiplier is considerably less than 10:1. (A more sophisticated and realistic expression for the money supply multiplier is developed in Chapter 16.)

**YOUR TURN**

Suppose the reserve requirement for all banks is 20 percent and the nation's banks initially have no excess reserves. Suppose you find $1 million of old currency in your grandmother's attic and deposit it into her bank checking account. Calculate:

**A.** The change in reserves in your grandmother's bank

**B.** The change in required reserves in your grandmother's bank

**C.** The change in excess reserves in your grandmother's bank

**D.** The maximum amount by which your grandmother's bank can expand its loans

**E.** The maximum amount the entire banking system can expand its loans

**F.** The potential expansion in the nation's deposits resulting from the initial deposit in your grandmother's bank

**G.** The potential expansion in M1

## Multiple Contraction of Deposits

Just as injection of new reserves into the banking system touches off a multiple expansion of deposits (and hence money), withdrawal of reserves from the banking system precipitates a multiple *contraction* of deposits. The United States in the early 1930s painfully experienced this contraction process, which played a major role in the Great Depression (examined in depth in Chapter 17).

Let us retain the three assumptions we made earlier and suppose that the banking system just meets the reserve requirement—that is, the banking system has no excess reserves. Now, suppose customers of Bank Q obtain $7 million in currency by drawing down their bank demand deposits. The impact of their cash withdrawal on Bank Q is:

**Bank Q**

| | | | |
|---|---|---|---|
| Cash | −7 million | Demand deposits | −7 million |

Given the 10 percent reserve requirement, Bank Q's required reserves decline by $0.7 million but actual reserves are off by the full $7 million. Bank Q's reserves are deficient (required reserves exceed reserves) by $6.3 million. Bank Q (and the aggregate banking system) initially exhibits excess reserves of *negative* $6.3 million.

An individual bank can obtain reserves and alleviate its reserve deficiency by selling securities or reducing bank loans in the amount of the reserve deficiency. Thus, Bank Q can alleviate its reserve deficiency by selling $6.3 million in securities, demanding repayment of $6.3 million worth of loans, or combining the two actions. However, Bank Q is simply shifting its reserve deficiency to another bank, Bank R. The individuals or firms that purchased Bank Q's securities or repaid Bank Q's loans wrote their checks on their accounts in Bank R. Bank R then becomes deficient in reserves and must liquidate loans or securities, thereby shifting the hot potato to another bank, Bank S. Ultimately, the T-account of the whole banking system appears as follows:

**All Banks**

| | | | |
|---|---|---|---|
| Currency and coins | −7 million | Demand deposits | −70 million |
| Loans and investments | −63 million | | |

The initial \$7 million currency withdrawal produces a \$70 million contraction in demand deposits. The currency withdrawal causes a \$7 million direct reduction in deposits. In addition, the currency withdrawal touches off a contraction of loans and security holdings by depository institutions totaling \$63 million, which produces an identical reduction in demand deposits.[6]

The key to understanding this process lies in the following fact. Each bank recovers its lost reserves by liquidating securities or loans, but the reserves of the *entire banking system* do not increase. Selling securities and reducing bank loans merely transfer reserves from one bank to another. The only banking *system* remedy for a reserve deficiency is reducing the amount of *required reserves* by the amount of the reserves shortage, which can be accomplished only by triggering a much larger contraction of deposits. In a fractional reserve banking system with a 10 percent reserve requirement, demand deposits must decline by \$10 to achieve a \$1 reduction of required reserves.

In short, the banking system cannot control its own reserves. In terms of aggregate reserves, the banking system is at the mercy of the public and the Federal Reserve. The public influences reserves by depositing or withdrawing currency from banks. The Federal Reserve System influences reserves by buying and selling securities in the open market and by lending to banks. Thus, the Federal Reserve dominates the amount of reserves in the banking system. We now briefly discuss the Fed's role in determining the aggregate reserves in the banking system.

## HOW THE FEDERAL RESERVE GETS A GRIP ON THE MONEY SUPPLY

At the beginning of this chapter, we looked at an example in which reserves were added to the banking system by deposit of coins found in a sunken ship. The example was a bit atypical, to say the least! In reality, the Federal Reserve controls the aggregate amount of reserves at any given time and the growth in reserves over time. Many factors outside of the Federal Reserve's influence trigger fluctuations in bank reserves. One factor is fluctuations in the public's demand for currency. However, the Fed has unlimited authority to purchase or sell government securities in the open market, so the Fed can easily swamp the influence of these outside forces and control the supply of reserves in the banking system.

Bank reserves consist of cash in banks plus deposits maintained by banks at the Federal Reserve. Whenever the Fed purchases securities in the open market, the Fed pays for the securities by writing a check on itself and presenting the check to the seller. The check recipient deposits the check in a depository institution, which makes a bookkeeping entry showing that the seller's demand deposit account has increased by the amount of the check. The Federal Reserve pays off the depository institution by crediting the bank's Federal Reserve account (a bookkeeping entry). In this way, Federal Reserve security purchases inject an equivalent amount of reserves into the nation's banking system.[7] If the Fed purchases \$900 million of secu-

---

[6] Let R, r, and D represent reserves, the percentage reserve requirement, and deposits, respectively. Then $R = r(D)$, and $\Delta R = r(\Delta D)$. Solving for the change in deposits, we get $\Delta D = \Delta R/r$. The final change in deposits equals the change in reserves times the reciprocal of the reserve requirement (that is, $1/r$). In this example, $\Delta D = -\$7$ million $\times$ $10 = -\$70$ million.

[7] This holds true unless the Fed buys securities directly from the U.S. Treasury, in which case bank reserves are unaltered. Such activity is restricted by regulations governing the Federal Reserve. When the Fed buys securities from individuals, firms, or depository institutions, reserves are increased on a dollar-for-dollar basis.

rities from the public, the T-accounts of the Federal Reserve and the banking system appear as follows:

**Federal Reserve**

| | | | |
|---|---|---|---|
| U.S. government securities | +900 million | Deposits of banks | +900 million |

**Banking System**

| | | | |
|---|---|---|---|
| Deposit at Fed | +900 million | Demand deposits | +900 million |

The Fed writes checks to private individuals totaling $900 million. The checks are deposited into private banks, which credit the checking accounts of the individuals involved. The banks then send the checks to the Fed, which pays off the banks by crediting the banks' reserve accounts with the Fed by $900 million (bookkeeping entries). Note that the nation's bank reserves have expanded by $900 million. The Fed has paid for its security acquisition by creating new reserves in the banking system.

When the Fed *sells* securities to individuals, firms, or banks, aggregate reserves are withdrawn from the banking system. The security buyers write checks on their accounts in depository institutions. The checks are presented to the Federal Reserve, which collects on the checks by debiting the deposit accounts (reserve accounts) of the banks on which the checks are written. Reserves are reduced on a dollar-for-dollar basis.

The Fed controls the aggregate amount of both reserves and required reserves (the latter by setting the percentage reserve requirement), initiating changes in the amount of excess reserves in banks—reserves above and beyond the amount banks are required to hold. Multiple expansion of deposits results when the Fed injects excess reserves into the banks. By the same token, a deficiency of reserves (negative excess reserves) and multiple contraction of deposits result when the Fed withdraws reserves from the banking system.

This sketch of the Federal Reserve's monetary controls is superficial. In reality, many complications must be considered. Nevertheless, this sketch captures the essence of the mechanism by which the Federal Reserve exerts monetary control. Chapters 15 to 18 provide a more thorough treatment of the Federal Reserve System's role in the money supply process.

**YOUR TURN**

Suppose the percentage reserve requirement set by the Federal Reserve is 15 percent. Now, suppose the Fed purchases $1,000 million worth of U.S. Treasury securities through government securities dealers in New York. Calculate the impact of the Fed's action on:

1. Reserves
2. Required reserves
3. Excess reserves
4. The initial, direct change in the money supply
5. The eventual change in the money supply after all banks have rid themselves of all their excess reserves

## SUMMARY

Modern monetary systems are based on a system of *fractional reserve* banking. In fractional reserve banking, banks maintain only a relatively small percentage of their customers' deposits in the form of reserves—that is, as cash on hand and deposits at the Federal Reserve. Banks earn income by lending or investing their deposit customers' funds rather than holding the funds as reserves. Thus, banks do not hold substantially more reserves than are required. When a bank increases its loans or purchases securities, the bank creates new deposits in the banking system. These bank actions increase the money supply because all measures of the money supply include these deposits. Because each dollar of bank reserves supports several dollars of deposits, new reserves added to the banking system create new deposits that are a *multiple* of the new reserves. Conversely, a contraction of reserves in the banking system leads to a multiple contraction of deposits. The public influences bank reserves by depositing or withdrawing cash from banks. However, the Federal Reserve can easily counteract the effects of the public's actions. The Fed controls the amount of reserves in the banking system, thereby strongly influencing bank lending and investing activity. Therefore, the Fed controls the amount of deposits and the nation's quantity of money.

## YOUR TURN ANSWERS

PAGE 332

**A.** \$1,000,000

**B.** \$1,000,000 × 20% = \$200,000

**C.** \$1,000,000 − \$200,000 = \$800,000

**D.** The amount of its excess reserves, or \$800,000

**E.** Excess reserves × 1/% reserve requirement, or \$800,000 × 5 = \$4,000,000

**F.** \$4,000,000 plus the initial \$1,000,000 = \$5,000,000

**G.** M1 = DDO + $C^P$. DDO increases by \$5,000,000, but $C^P$ declines by \$1,000,000 because your grandmother's old currency was counted as $C^P$ while the money was in the attic but not after the money was deposited in the bank. Hence, the net change in the money supply (M1) is \$4,000,000.

PAGE 334

1. \$1,000 million
2. 15% × \$1,000 million, or \$150 million
3. \$1,000 million − \$150 million, or \$850 million
4. \$1,000 million
5. \$1,000 million × 1/0.15, or \$6,667 million

## KEY TERMS

reserve requirement
required reserves
excess reserves

## STUDY QUESTIONS

1. Suppose you deposit $100 cash into your checking account. Assume the reserve requirement is 12 percent.
   A. What is the effect on your bank's reserves?
   B. What is the effect on your bank's required reserves?
   C. What is the effect on your bank's excess reserves?
   D. By how much is your bank now able to expand its loans?

2. Illustrate the multiple deposit expansion process in the first problem using T-accounts and assuming banks use all their excess reserves to grant loans. Carry the example through Banks A, B, C, and D. At each step of the process, calculate what happens to:
   A. The individual bank's total, required, and excess reserves
   B. The total amount of demand deposits in the banking system
   C. Total reserves in the banking system
   D. Required reserves in the banking system
   E. Excess reserves in the banking system

3. You find $1,000 worth of old coins while you are mountain climbing in Colorado. You promptly deposit the coins in your checking account. If the reserve requirement is 10 percent, how much money did you ultimately create?

4. Suppose the Federal Reserve buys government securities worth $100 million from dealers. Assume the reserve requirement is 10 percent.
   A. Illustrate this transaction with T-accounts for the Fed and all banks.
   B. By how much does the money supply immediately expand?
   C. Banks begin making loans and purchasing securities. When the multiple deposit expansion process is complete, by how much will the money supply have grown?

5. Because you fear terrorist incidents are imminent, you decide to liquidate your $20,000 checking account and bury the currency in a coffee can in your back yard.
   A. Draw the T-account of your bank that results from this transaction.
   B. Does your transaction, by itself, immediately change the money supply?
   C. Draw T-accounts illustrating the multiple deposit contraction your action touches off (assume the reserve requirement is 10 percent). Show three rounds of contraction.
   D. Calculate the ultimate effect of your action on the nation's money supply.

6. Suppose the Fed buys $1 million of securities from dealers and the reserve requirement is 10 percent. If the Fed's action results in an $8 million expansion of deposits, is the banking system in equilibrium? Why or why not?

7. Suppose the banking system has $1,000 million worth of checkable deposits. The reserve requirement is 10 percent.
   A. What ultimately happens to the money supply if the Fed cuts the reserve requirement to 8 percent?
   B. What ultimately happens to the money supply if the Fed increases the reserve requirement to 15 percent?

8. Suppose the reserve requirement is 10 percent. The Fed buys $1,000 million worth of securities from a N.Y. dealer.
   A. What is be the ultimate effect on the money supply?
   B. If all banks maintain 5 percent of their deposits as reserves over and above the Fed's reserve requirement, what is the ultimate effect? (Hint: Draw a few rounds of T-accounts.)

## ADDITIONAL READING

- For alternative explanations of the simple deposit expansion process, see any principles of macroeconomics textbook. For example, see William J. Baumol and Alan S. Blinder, *Macroeconomics: Principles and Policy*, 9th edition (Mason, Ohio: Thomson Learning-South-Western, 2003, Chapter 11, pp. 213–219).

# Chapter 15

# MONEY SUPPLY DETERMINATION: THE MONETARY BASE

As we discussed in Chapter 1, the money supply is an important variable influencing economic activity. Changes in a nation's money supply or "monetary aggregates" (M1, M2, etc.) change the nation's output, employment, and price level. Economists and major players in financial markets monitor the monetary statistics released weekly by the Federal Reserve.

In this chapter and Chapter 16, we develop the tools you need to understand the *money supply process*—the factors that change the nation's quantity of money. Because banks' lending and purchasing of securities creates money (as we demonstrated in Chapter 14), *banks* are clearly involved in the money supply process. The *public* also participates in the money supply process by allocating financial wealth among checking accounts, currency, and other financial assets and by requesting loans from banks. The *Federal Reserve* is the most important player in the money supply process. The Fed dominates the trend growth rate—but not all of the shorter-term movements—of the money supply. In this chapter and Chapter 16, we provide a comprehensive explanation of the elements governing the week-to-week fluctuations and the longer-term trend of the money supply.

## THE MONETARY BASE–MONEY MULTIPLIER FRAMEWORK

The framework we use to analyze determination of a nation's money supply is given by a simple equation expressing the money supply as the product of two fundamental variables. These variables are the *monetary base* and a *money supply multiplier,* which encompasses the multiple deposit expansion process inherent in the fractional reserve banking systems prevailing in nations throughout the world. We can express the relationship as follows:

$$\text{(15-1)} \quad \mathbf{M = m \cdot B},$$

where M is the money supply, m is the money supply multiplier, and B is the monetary base.

Dividing both sides of Equation (15-1) by B, the money supply multiplier can be expressed as follows:

$$\text{(15-2)} \quad \mathbf{m} = \frac{\mathbf{M}}{\mathbf{B}}.$$

Recall from Chapter 2 that several alternative measures of the U.S. money supply, including M1, M2, and M3, exist. M1 includes demand deposits and other checkable deposits in depository institutions (hereafter called "banks") plus currency and coins held by the public outside of banks. M2 and M3 broaden the M1 measure of money by progressively adding the public's holdings of liquid financial assets such as savings deposits, money market mutual fund shares, and overnight repurchase agreements.

**monetary base**
those financial assets that can potentially be used as reserves; bank reserves and currency held by the public

**money supply multiplier**
ratio of the money supply to the monetary base

The **monetary base (B)** consists of bank reserves (R—cash in banks and banks' deposits at the Fed) and currency held by the public ($C^P$). The **money supply multiplier (m)** is the ratio of the money supply (M) to the monetary base (B). For each money supply measure, a corresponding money supply multiplier exists. For example, we can write $m_1 = M1/B$ and $m_2 = M2/B$. This multiplier, the link connecting the monetary base to the money supply, reflects portfolio decisions made by banks and the public. Sometimes Federal Reserve actions influence the multiplier.

Expressing the money supply as the product of a money supply multiplier and the monetary base helps you to understand the sources of changes in a nation's money supply. Any change in the money supply results from a change in B, a change in m, or some combination of B and m. This simple framework permits us to analyze some important issues of monetary policy. For example, what roadblocks make it difficult for the Federal Reserve to accurately control the money supply? Without the Fed's aggressive efforts to hit specific money supply targets, what factors might cause the money supply to change? What are the mechanisms through which the Fed's policy instruments influence the money supply?

We will have a much better handle on these questions after we analyze the factors underlying the monetary base and the money supply multiplier. Accordingly, this chapter examines the monetary base. Chapter 16 analyzes the money supply multiplier. Chapter 17 is an in-depth case study in which we use the base–multiplier framework to analyze the causes of money supply collapse and the Federal Reserve's role in America's greatest economic catastrophe—the Great Depression of the 1930s. Chapter 18 covers the tools of Federal Reserve policy—the instruments the Fed uses to change the money supply, credit conditions, and interest rates.

## MONETARY BASE: FUNDAMENTAL CONCEPTS

We specifically study the monetary base for two reasons. First, a significant body of theory and empirical evidence supports the view that monetary aggregates such as M1 and M2 importantly influence economic activity. Second, the Federal Reserve can accurately control the monetary base and thus strongly influence M1 and M2 levels and growth rates. Hence, an important chain of influence runs from Federal Reserve policy actions to the monetary base to the monetary aggregates to the nation's gross domestic product, income, and price level.

The monetary base forms the foundation on which the superstructure of bank credit and money is built. Figure 15-1 illustrates the relationship of the monetary base to the monetary aggregates. Because each dollar of base money (monetary base) supports several dollars of money, the base is sometimes known as "high-powered money."

The monetary base is an important type of monetary asset supplied primarily by the Federal Reserve. Banks are required to hold specified quantities of the items included in the monetary base in the form of reserves supporting their deposit liabilities. As we noted earlier, banks are in the business of earning a profit. Banks earn

**Figure 15-1** Relationship Between Monetary Aggregates and the Monetary Base

The monetary base provides the foundation for the various money measures (the monetary aggregates).

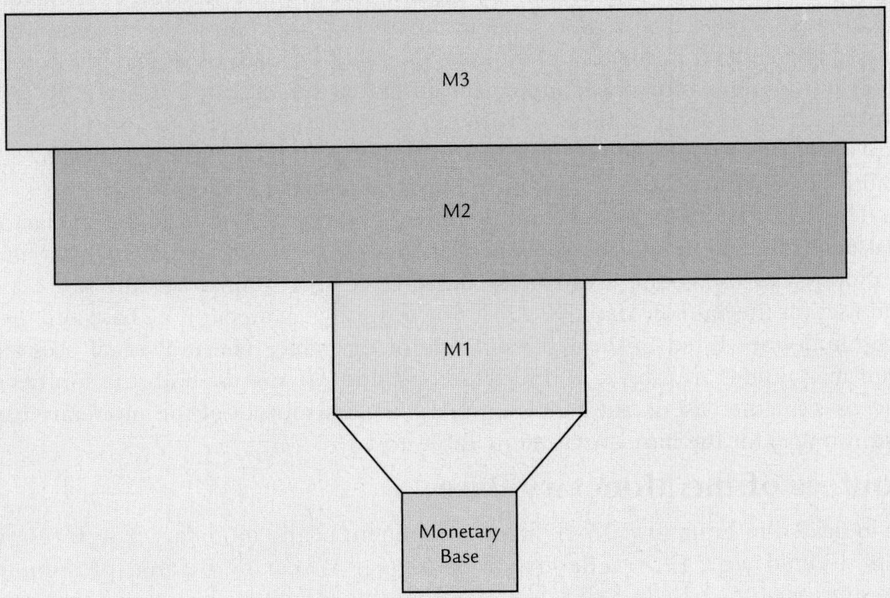


profits by acquiring earning assets such as loans and securities. Bank acquisition of earning assets creates deposits—a major portion of the nation's money supply. Although there are some slips 'twixt the cup and lip, the Fed strongly influences the money supply by accurately controlling the monetary base. Shortly we will see how.

The monetary base consists of the particular liabilities of the *monetary authorities*—the Federal Reserve and the Treasury—that depository institutions can use as reserves.[1] The monetary liabilities of the monetary authorities include (1) deposits held by banks in the Federal Reserve and (2) currency and coins issued by, and residing outside, the Treasury and the Fed—that is, currency and coins held by banks and the general public. This definition of the monetary base is expressed in Equations (15-3) and (15-4).

(15-3) $\mathbf{B = R + C^P}$

where B is the monetary base, R is bank reserves, which consist of bank deposits at the Fed ($F_b$), and currency and coins held by the banks ($C_b$).
Because $R = F_b + C_b$,

(15-4) $\mathbf{B = F_b + C_b + C^P}$.

The monetary base (B) consists of bank deposits at the Fed ($F_b$), cash in banks ($C_b$), and currency held by the public ($C^P$).

[1] Banks' reserves consist of bank deposits at the Federal Reserve and cash residing in banks. The monetary base is the pool of items that can be used as reserves. Today, reserves make up less than 15 percent of the monetary base. The remainder of the base is held by the public as currency ($C^P$).

## Derivation of the Monetary Base

The monetary base, as defined in Equation (15-4), consists of the net monetary liabilities of a consolidated balance sheet of the monetary authorities—the Fed and the Treasury. The Treasury's net monetary liabilities consist of the outstanding currency and coins issued by the Treasury, exclusive of the currency and coins held in the Treasury. Today, the Treasury's net monetary liabilities consist predominantly of coins.[2] The Federal Reserve's net monetary liabilities consist of all Federal Reserve notes outstanding (our paper money) not held in the 12 district Federal Reserve banks plus the reserve deposits of banks at the Federal Reserve banks ($F_b$). As we explain shortly, the Fed accurately controls the magnitude of these net monetary liabilities (the monetary base) by controlling its own balance sheet.

**sources of the base** factors determining the monetary base; includes 10 factors, dominated by Federal Reserve security portfolio

**uses for the base** ways in which the monetary base is allocated or used; bank reserves and currency held by the public

The best method for understanding the monetary base is to examine the factors that determine the base—the **sources of the base**—and the ways in which the base is allocated or used—the **uses for the base.** Table 15-1 summarizes the sources of and uses for the base on March 3, 2004. The individual sources of the base and their magnitudes are listed in the left-hand side of the table. The individual uses and their magnitudes are shown in the right-hand side. We discuss both the sources of and uses for the base in the following sections. Ten sources of the monetary base and two uses for the base are listed in Table 15-1.

## Sources of the Monetary Base

As indicated in Equation (15-4), a key component of the monetary base is reserve deposits held at the Federal Reserve by banks ($F_b$). We can derive an expression for the sources of the base by first using an accounting identity to solve for $F_b$ and then substituting this expression for $F_b$ into Equation (15-4) to solve for the monetary base, B.

Let us begin by returning to the Federal Reserve's balance sheet, first discussed in Chapter 12. The accompanying simplified Fed balance sheet (Table 15-2) indicates the Fed's various assets and liabilities and a symbol designating each item. Keep in mind the simple accounting identity that the Fed's total assets must equal the Fed's total liabilities plus its capital accounts. Then the magnitude of $F_b$ (a key component of the base, located on the liability side of the Fed balance sheet) is equal to the Fed's total assets minus all other of the Fed's liabilities and capital accounts. Therefore, we can write the expression for bank deposits at the Fed ($F_b$) as follows:

$$\text{(15-5)}\quad \mathbf{F_b = P + A + FC_a + CIPC + G + OA - FRN - F_t - F_f - DCI - OLC,}$$

where P is the Fed's portfolio of securities—U.S. government securities and agency securities, A is discount loans or discounts and advances (loans by the Fed to depository institutions), $FC_a$ is the Fed's cash holdings, CIPC is cash items in the process of collection by the Fed, G is the Fed's gold certificate and SDR accounts, OA is other assets of the Federal Reserve, including foreign assets, FRN is Federal Reserve notes outstanding (paper money issued by the Fed), $F_t$ is U.S. Treasury deposits at the Federal Reserve, $F_f$ is foreign and other deposits at the Federal Reserve, DCI is deferred credit items, and OLC is other Federal Reserve liabilities and capital accounts.

[2] In the past, the Treasury issued much of the paper currency. Today, the Federal Reserve issues all paper money in the form of Federal Reserve notes. Some of the paper money issued by the Treasury in the past, though recalled by the government, is still in private collections and thus technically constitutes a portion (less than 0.1 percent) of the monetary base.

**Table 15-1 Sources of and Uses for the Monetary Base on March 3, 2004 (in $ Million)**

| Sources of the Monetary Base | | Uses for the Monetary Base | |
|---|---|---|---|
| *Positive Influences:* | | | |
| *(P)* Federal Reserve security portfolio | 695,382 | $(C_b+C^p)$ Currency in circulation | 714,655 |
| *(A)* Discounts and advances | 26 | $(F_b)$ Depository institution balances at the Federal Reserve | 12,877 |
| *(Fl)* Float | −632 | *(B)* Total uses for the monetary base | 727,532 |
| *(G)* Gold certificate + SDR account | 13,245 | | |
| *(OA)* Other assets | 38,199 | | |
| $(TC_u)$ Treasury currency outstanding | 35,402 | | |
| Total | 781,622 | | |
| *Negative Influences:* | | | |
| $(F_t)$ Treasury deposits at the Federal Reserve | 4,698 | | |
| $(F_f)$ Foreign and other deposits at the Federal Reserve | 10,623 | | |
| $(TC_a)$ Treasury cash holdings | 314 | | |
| *(OLC)* Other liabilities and capital | 38,454 | | |
| Total | 54,089 | | |
| *(B)* Total sources of the monetary base | $727,532 | | |

*Source: Board of Governors Release H.4.1 at* http://www.federalreserve.gov/releases

**Table 15-2 Federal Reserve Balance Sheet**

| Assets | Liabilities |
|---|---|
| U.S. government securities *(P)* | Federal Reserve notes *(FRN)* |
| Loans to banks *(A)* | Deposits at Fed, held by |
| Coin *(FCa)* | A. Depository institutions $(F_b)$ |
| Cash items in process of collection *(CIPC)* | B. U.S. Treasury $(F_t)$ |
| Gold certificate account and SDR account *(G)* | C. Foreign and other $(F_f)$ |
| Denominated in foreign currencies and other assets *(OA)* | Deferred credit items *(DCI)* |
| | Other liabilities and capital accounts *(OLC)* |
| Total assets | Total liabilities and capital |

**float**
difference between cash items in the process of collection and deferred credit items; arises from check collection procedures

If we define Federal Reserve **float** (Fl) as the difference between cash items in the process of collection (CIPC) and deferred credit items (DCI) and substitute float (Fl) for CIPC and DCI in Equation (15-5), we obtain:

$$\text{(15-6)} \quad \mathbf{F_b = P + A + FC_a + Fl + G + OA - FRN - F_t - F_f - OLC.}$$

Equation (15-6) is an expression for the sources of banks' *reserve accounts* at the Federal Reserve ($F_b$). To get the monetary base (B), we simply add to $F_b$ the currency and coins held by banks ($C_b$) and the currency and coins held by the public ($C^P$), as indicated in Equation (15-4). This yields:

$$\text{(15-7)} \quad \mathbf{B = P + A + FC_a + Fl + G + OA + C_b + C^P - FRN - F_t - F_f - OLC.}$$

Now, let $TC_u$ represent Treasury currency outstanding (predominantly coins) and $TC_a$ represent the actual cash held by the Treasury. We simplify Equation (15-7) by recognizing that all the paper money (FRN) and coins ($TC_u$) in existence *by definition must be held in one of four places:* the Fed ($FC_a$), the Treasury ($TC_a$), depository institutions ($C_b$), or the public ($C^P$). The currency and coins literally can be nowhere else, given that $C^P$ includes all the currency and coins that do not reside at the Fed, the Treasury, or depository institutions. We convey this identity as follows:

$$\text{(15-8)} \quad \mathbf{FRN + TC_u = FC_a + TC_a + C_b + C^P.}$$

If we rearrange Equation (15-8) by moving FRN to the right-hand side and $TC_a$ to the left-hand side, we obtain:

$$\text{(15-9)} \quad \mathbf{TC_u - TC_a = FC_a + C_b + C^P - FRN.}$$

Equation (15-9) states that if we subtract the currency issued by the Federal Reserve (FRN) from the total currency and coins held by the Federal Reserve, the banks, and the public, we obtain the total amount of currency and coins issued by the Treasury ($TC_u$) that is not residing in the Treasury itself ($TC_a$).

To arrive at our final expression for the sources of the monetary base, we simply substitute into Equation (15-7) the two terms on the left-hand side of Equation (15-9) in place of the four terms on the right-hand side:

$$\text{(15-10)} \quad \mathbf{B = P + A + Fl + G + OA + TC_u - F_t - F_f - TC_a - OLC.}$$

Equation (15-10) indicates that 10 factors determine the monetary base. These 10 sources of the base include six factors that are positive influences (they supply base money) and four factors that are negative influences (they absorb base money and therefore are preceded by a negative sign). We now have the sources of the monetary base in order, as listed in Table 15-1. On March 3, 2004, the magnitude of the monetary base was $727,532 million, or approximately $728 billion.

We will briefly analyze each of these base determinants. For now, we simply point out that the Federal Reserve portfolio of securities (P)—*a variable totally controlled by the Federal Reserve*—has dominated the behavior of the monetary base in recent decades. By judiciously changing its portfolio of securities (P), the Fed easily dominates both the short-term and long-run behavior of the monetary base and thus controls the nation's quantity of money.

## Uses for the Monetary Base

The right-hand portion of Table 15-1 shows the allocation of the monetary base, or the uses to which the base is put, and the magnitude of each use as of March 3, 2004. The Federal Reserve defines "currency in circulation" as all Treasury currency

## FROM THE FINANCIAL PAGES

### Weekly Federal Reserve Data

On most Thursdays, the Federal Reserve releases newly available and detailed monetary data. The following day, *The Wall Street Journal* publishes these data, revealing the magnitudes of the monetary aggregates, total reserves, the monetary base, and all their sources in a column entitled, "Federal Reserve Data." (Much of these data also can be found each week on the Board of Governors' Web site at http://www.federalreserve.gov/releases/). The portion of *The Wall Street Journal* table entitled "Member Bank Reserve Changes" lists the most recent weekly averages of each of the sources of the monetary base and the *changes* in each source over the most recent week and year (see accompanying table). The table also shows currency in circulation ($C_b + C^p$), which is not a *source* of the monetary base but rather a *use* for the base.

**Federal Reserve Data**

**MONETARY AGGREGATES**

(daily average in billions)

| | 1 WEEK ENDED: | |
|---|---|---|
| | Jun. 14 | Jun. 7 |
| Money supply (M1) sa | 1319.9 | 1308.3 |
| Money supply (M1) nsa | 1305.8 | 1292.9 |
| Money supply (M2) sa | 6275.0 | 6264.6 |
| Money supply (M2) nsa | 6289.1 | 6283.3 |
| Money supply (M3) sa | 9247.4 | 9208.5 |
| Money supply (M3) nsa | 9266.6 | 9233.3 |
| | 4 WEEKS ENDED: | |
| | Jun. 14 | May. 17 |
| Money supply (M1) sa | 1321.3 | 1325.0 |
| Money supply (M1) nsa | 1316.7 | 1326.4 |
| Money supply (M2) sa | 6272.6 | 6251.6 |
| Money supply (M2) nsa | 6251.9 | 6223.3 |
| Money supply (M3) sa | 9212.6 | 9170.9 |
| Money supply (M3) nsa | 9201.0 | 9139.4 |
| | MONTH | |
| | May. | Apr. |
| Money supply (M1) sa | 1319.2 | 1321.7 |
| Money supply (M2) sa | 6269.0 | 6201.5 |
| Money supply (M3) sa | 9192.5 | 9084.3 |

nsa-Not seasonally adjusted. sa-Seasonally adjusted.

**MEMBER BANK RESERVE CHANGES**

Changes in weekly averages of reserves and related items during the week and year ended June 23, 2004 were as follows (in millions of dollars)

| | Jun. 23 2004 | CHG FROM Jun. 16 2004 | WK END Jun. 25 2003 |
|---|---|---|---|
| **Reserve bank credit:** | | | |
| **U.S. Gov't securities:** | | | |
| Bought outright | 685,043 | +63 | +33,083 |
| **Federal agency issues:** | | | |
| Bought outright | ... | ... | −10 |
| **Borrowings from Fed:** | | | |
| Primary credit | 54 | +20 | −268 |
| Secondary credit | ... | ... | ... |
| Seasonal credit | 143 | +8 | +59 |
| Float | −262 | +95 | −284 |
| Other Federal Reserve Assets | 39,208 | +441 | +225 |
| Total Reserve Bank Credit | 748,436 | +2,055 | +30,743 |
| Gold Stock | 11,045 | ... | +1 |
| SDR certificates | 2,200 | ... | ... |
| Treasury currency outstanding | 35,825 | +14 | +782 |
| Total | 797,506 | +2,069 | +31,526 |
| Currency in circulation | 724,759 | +12 | +33,613 |
| Treasury cash holdings | 315 | −9 | −53 |
| Treasury dpts with F.R. Bnks | 7,034 | +839 | −165 |
| Foreign dpts with F.R. Bnks | 103 | −29 | −59 |
| Other dpts with F.R. Bnks | 225 | −27 | +5 |
| Service related balances, adj | 10,293 | −4 | −763 |
| Other F.R. liabilities & capital | 21,707 | +296 | +1,601 |
| Total | 783,157 | −258 | +30,186 |

**RESERVE AGGREGATES**

(daily average in millions)

| | 2 WEEKS ENDED: | |
|---|---|---|
| | Jun. 23 | Jun. 9 |
| Total Reserves (sa) | 45,338 | 46,990 |
| Nonborrowed Reserves (sa) | 45,155 | 46,848 |
| Required Reserves (sa) | 43,409 | 45,412 |
| Excess Reserves (nsa) | 1,929 | 1,578 |
| Borrowings from Fed (nsa)-a | 183 | 143 |
| Free Reserves (nsa) | 1,746 | 1,435 |
| Monetary Base (sa) | 736,999 | 736,644 |

a-Excluding extended credit. nsa-Not seasonally adjusted. sa-Seasonally adjusted

Note first the magnitude of the Fed's government security portfolio on June 23, 2004 (more than $685 billion) relative to the other sources of the monetary base. Note also that while the Federal Reserve purchased only $63 million of government securities (net) in the week ending June 23, 2004, the Fed purchased more than $33 *billion* (net) over the previous 12 months. In most of that period (June 2003–June 2004), the U.S. economy was experiencing difficulty generating jobs even though a couple of years had elapsed since the end of the 2001 recession. The Fed was buying Treasury securities to maintain interest rates at extremely low levels and boost the nation's money supply, with a view toward stimulating job creation.

The portion of the table entitled "Reserve Aggregates" shows the daily averages of various measures of reserves and the monetary base over the two most recent 2-week periods. Note that while total reserves were down by more than $1,500 million ($1.5 billion) in the more recent period, the monetary base *increased* slightly. Can you explain what accounts for the difference?

and coins and Federal Reserve notes outstanding, except those held in the Treasury and the Federal Reserve banks. In other words, *currency in circulation* equals the sum of cash in depository institutions ($C_b$) and currency and coins held by the public ($C^P$). Do not confuse "currency in circulation" with currency and coins held by the public ($C^P$).

By adding the amount of currency in circulation ($714,655 million) to the depository institutions' deposits at the Fed ($12,877 million), we obtain the magnitude of *uses* for the monetary base on March 3, 2004: $727,532 million or approximately $728 billion. This amount precisely matches the magnitude shown in the left-hand portion of Table 15-1 as the total *sources* of the monetary base. To get a feel for the U.S. monetary base and the magnitude of the individual factors influencing the base, see "From the Financial Pages," which shows an important table normally released by the Federal Reserve each Thursday and published in *The Wall Street Journal* on Fridays.

**YOUR TURN**

Suppose you observe in the "Federal Reserve Data" column in this Friday's *Wall Street Journal* that the following changes in the sources of the monetary base occurred in the most recent week: float increased $600 million, discounts and advances fell by $200 million, and Treasury deposits at the Federal Reserve fell by $1,200 million ($1.2 billion).

**A.** Assuming all other factors influencing the monetary base remained unchanged, calculate the change in the monetary base in the week.

**B.** If the Federal Reserve desires to keep the base constant, what must the Fed do with its portfolio of government securities (P)?

## ANALYSIS OF THE TEN FACTORS PRODUCING CHANGES IN THE BASE

By definition, any event producing a change in either bank reserves (R) or currency held by the public ($C^P$) without causing an offsetting change in the other item must change the monetary base.[3] As we saw in Table 15-1 and Equation (15-10), 10 sources of the monetary base exist—that is, 10 factors cause the base to change. We now analyze how changes in each of these factors affects the monetary base. This analysis demonstrates why the base changes over time—in both the short and long run. The analysis also demonstrates that the Federal Reserve easily controls the base. We begin with the most important source of the base, the Fed's portfolio of government securities.

### Federal Reserve Securities Portfolio (P)

This item, the dominant element in the monetary base, is totally determined by the Fed. Today, the Fed's securities portfolio makes up about 95 percent of the base (review Table 15-1), up sharply from about 10 percent in the 1920s and 50 percent in the 1950s.

[3] An example of an offsetting change is an increase in currency held by the public ($C^P$) that drains cash from banks and therefore reduces reserves in a dollar-for-dollar fashion. Thus, other things being equal, increased public demand for currency leaves the monetary base unchanged.

How does the Fed's portfolio of securities influence the monetary base? When the Fed buys securities in the open market, it pays with a check *written on itself.* The securities seller (normally a securities dealer) deposits the check in a bank. The bank sends the check to the Federal Reserve district bank (typically the N.Y. Fed because the dealers and their banks are located in New York), which credits the bank's balance at the Fed. When this bookkeeping entry is made, bank reserves and the monetary base increase by the amount of the transaction.[4] If the Fed purchases $175 million of U.S. government securities in the open market, the T-account mechanics are as follows:

| Federal Reserve System | | | | All Banks | | | |
|---|---|---|---|---|---|---|---|
| U.S. government securities | +175 million | Deposits by banks | +175 million | Deposits at Fed | +175 million | Demand deposits | +175 million |

To recap, the Fed gives the dealer a check in exchange for the securities. The dealer deposits the check in a bank. The bank sends the check to the Fed, which credits $175 million to the dealer's bank reserve account at the Fed ($F_b$). At this moment, both reserves and the monetary base increase by $175 million. Thus, bank reserves and the monetary base are easily manipulated by the Federal Reserve! To increase reserves and the base, the Fed buys securities. To reduce reserves and the base, the Fed sells securities.

The Federal Reserve currently holds a portfolio of U.S. government securities that amounts to more than $700 billion, or about 10 percent of the gross U.S. national debt. The Fed has complete authority to increase or decrease its portfolio as the Fed sees fit. Unlike any other entity or agency in the nation, the Federal Reserve can purchase unlimited amounts of securities and pay for the securities by creating new reserves in the form of bank deposits at the Fed. This unique authority gives the Fed its immense power. The only criterion governing the Fed's decision to buy or sell securities is the current magnitude of aggregate bank reserves and the monetary base relative to the magnitudes the Fed believes is desirable. If the base is smaller than the Fed deems appropriate, the Fed purchases securities, adding to its portfolio and boosting the base. If the Fed desires to reduce the base, it sells securities from its portfolio.[5]

## Federal Reserve Discount Loans—Loans to Banks (A)

Discount loans refer to bank borrowing of reserves from the Federal Reserve, normally to remedy a temporary reserve deficiency. A bank typically borrows by contacting the Fed, requesting a loan, and receiving a bookkeeping entry in which the Fed credits the bank's account at the Fed. Suppose a large bank borrows $10 million from the Fed. The balance sheet mechanics are as follows:

| Federal Reserve | | | | All Banks | | | |
|---|---|---|---|---|---|---|---|
| Discount loans | +10 million | Deposits by banks | +10 million | Deposits at Fed | +10 million | Borrowing (discount loans) | +10 million |

[4] Today, these transactions are actually done electronically, and no checks are used. The Fed pays for the securities by electronically crediting the securities seller's bank reserve account at the Fed.

[5] When the Fed sells securities, dealers write checks to the Fed. The Fed collects on these checks by debiting the reserve accounts of the banks on which the checks are written. (The above T-accounts would exhibit minus signs rather than plus signs.) Bank reserves and the base decline dollar for dollar with Federal Reserve sales of securities. More on this in Chapter 18.

Because bank deposits at the Fed ($F_b$) are included in the definition of both reserves and the monetary base, this borrowing action increases both R and B by $10 million. The lesson is clear. When the volume of discounts and advances increases, both reserves and the monetary base increase by the identical amount. When bank borrowing from the Fed declines, R and B decline by a like amount. We examine discounts and advances more carefully in Chapter 18. For now, we regard the volume of discounts and advances to be determined by bank initiative. The Fed influences banks' decisions to borrow from the Fed by setting the *discount rate*—the interest rate charged banks by the Fed—and establishing and enforcing the rules and procedures under which banks are permitted to borrow.

## Federal Reserve Float (Fl)

*Float* is a phenomenon arising from the Fed's procedures for processing checks. One service the Fed provides banks is clearing of checks involving banks in different cities. Suppose you are a student from Los Angeles, attending school at the University of Colorado at Boulder. Halfway through the term, you write a check on your L.A. bank for $80 to pay a merchant in Boulder for a new sweater. The merchant deposits the check in the local Boulder bank, which sends the check to the district Fed bank in Kansas City for collection.

All checks received by the Fed for processing are classified as items for immediate credit, credit deferred for 1 day, or credit deferred for 2 days. In other words, the Kansas City district Fed bank credits the Boulder bank's reserve account either immediately, 1 day later, or 2 days later. The classification depends on the distance and normal transportation time involved between the bank on which the check was issued (your L.A. bank) and its district Federal Reserve bank. The Fed maintains a prearranged schedule that estimates the normal length of time needed to send your check from the Federal Reserve district bank in San Francisco to your local bank in Los Angeles. When this specified time has elapsed, the Fed credits the reserve account of the Boulder bank in the amount of $80.[6] However, the Los Angeles bank's account at the Fed is not debited until the check arrives at that bank. If the actual check transportation time exceeds the Fed's schedule, the Boulder bank receives $80 in its Fed account before your L.A. bank's account is debited. In this case, float is positive and aggregate reserves in the system (and the monetary base) expand by $80. If the check is transported to your L.A. bank more quickly than the Fed's schedule suggests, float is negative because your bank's account at the Fed is debited *before* the Boulder bank's Fed account is credited.

Float on a given day can easily be calculated by subtracting the Federal Reserve liability, "deferred credit items," from the corresponding Fed asset, "cash items in the process of collection." Because the Fed processes hundreds of thousands of checks on any given day, float can be a relatively large positive or negative magnitude and can exhibit sharp day-to-day fluctuations. Anything that slows transportation of checks—such as a snowstorm or fog that shuts down airports—temporarily boosts float. In addition, seasonal fluctuations in the volume of checks being processed influences the volume of float. The pattern of float (weekly averages of daily figures) during 2003 is illustrated in Figure 15-2.

---

[6] Checks are processed by electronic data processing equipment. Look at the coded numbers in the bottom left-hand portion of your personal checks. The first two digits refer to the Federal Reserve district in which your bank is located (10 represents Kansas City, 12 represents San Francisco, etc.). The third digit designates the Fed office (main or branch) to which the check will be sent for processing. The fourth digit represents the number of days (0, 1, or 2) the credit will be deferred—that is, the number of days that must pass before the recipient bank's reserve account is credited. The last five digits identify your bank to the Fed.

**Figure 15-2** Federal Reserve Float During 2003 (Weekly Averages of Daily Figures, in $ Million)

Float sometimes fluctuates considerably from week to week. Were it not for compensatory open market operations conducted by the Fed, wide weekly fluctuations would lead to volatility in reserves and the base.

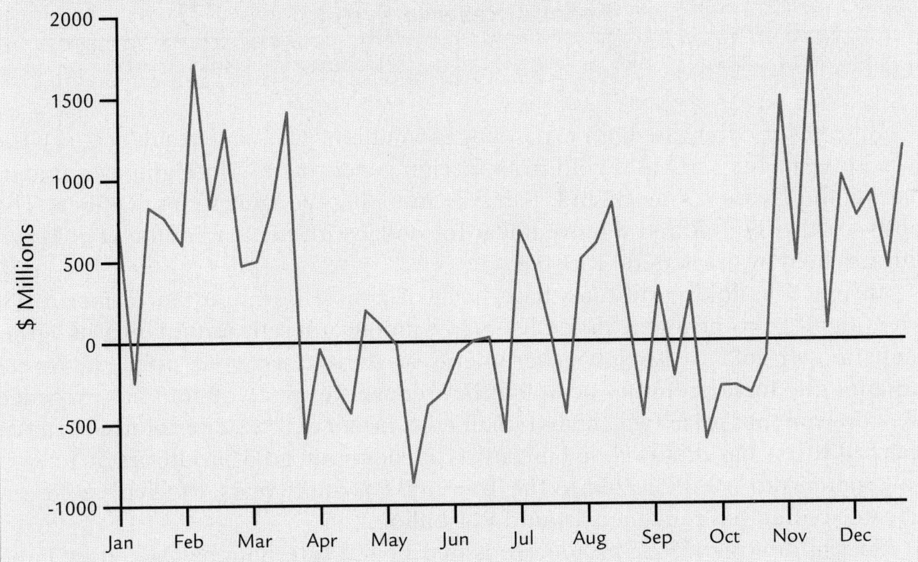

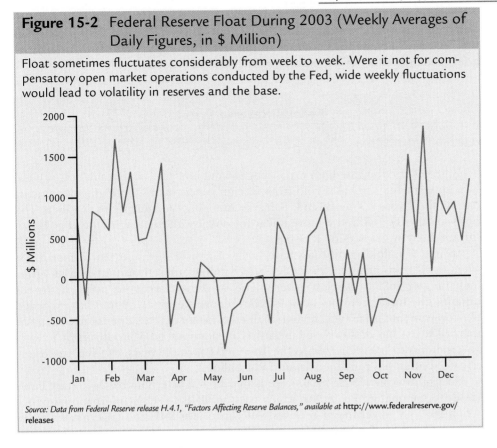

*Source: Data from Federal Reserve release H.4.1, "Factors Affecting Reserve Balances," available at* http://www.federalreserve.gov/releases

Prior to the last 15 to 20 years, float was almost always positive because checks took relatively long to process. In 2003, however, float was *negative* in almost half of the weeks, as indicated in the figure. The structural change in the float pattern results from Fed measures speeding the transportation and processing of checks.

An increase in float raises bank reserves and the monetary base in a dollar-for-dollar fashion. A decline in float reduces R and B. When float rises significantly, the Fed neutralizes the potential effect on R and B by selling securities from its portfolio. When float falls, the Fed purchases government securities in the open market to prevent R and B from falling.

## Fed's Gold Certificates and Special Drawings Rights Accounts (G)

The U.S. Treasury is willing to purchase, at the official government price of $42.22 per ounce, any and all gold offered. If the Treasury purchases gold, either from domestic or foreign sources, the monetary base rises dollar for dollar with the transaction.

Assume the Treasury purchases $66 million worth of gold from domestic miners and pays for the gold with checks drawn on the Treasury's account at the Federal Reserve. The recipients deposit the checks in banks. After the banks send the checks to the district Fed banks for collection, the banks' reserve accounts at the Fed are credited by $66 million. The Fed handles the transaction by a simple bookkeeping entry on the liability side of its balance sheet. The Fed credits the banks' reserve accounts ($F_b$) by a total of $66 million and debits the Treasury's account ($F_t$) by the same amount. Bank reserves and the monetary base thus increase by the amount of the transaction—that is, $66 million.

At this point, the Treasury prints up gold certificates in the amount of $66 million and presents the certificates to the Federal Reserve. The Fed then replenishes the Treasury's Fed deposit account to the level existing prior to the purchase of gold. The final effect of the entire transaction is as follows:

**Federal Reserve System**

| | | | |
|---|---|---|---|
| Gold certificates | +66 million | Deposits by banks | +66 million |

Reserves and the base both expand by $66 million. The same result occurs if the U.S. government purchases gold from foreign governments. Foreign governments deposit the Treasury's checks in U.S. banks, initiating the same series of effects. The upshot is that both R and B move dollar for dollar with the magnitude of gold certificates held by the Federal Reserve.

In practice, gold certificates have been of almost no importance since 1971, when the U.S. government closed its "gold window," thereby terminating its agreement to sell gold to foreign governments at the official gold price. In recent decades, the huge premium by which the free market price of gold has exceeded the government's price (which has remained constant at $42.22 per ounce for more than 30 years) has removed any incentive for domestic gold producers or foreign governments to sell their gold to the Treasury. For many years, the Fed's gold certificate account has remained around $11 billion.

Special drawing rights (SDRs) are issued by the International Monetary Fund (IMF) to national governments, which use the SDRs to settle international debts. When the U.S. government receives SDRs from the IMF, the government issues SDR certificates to the Federal Reserve. The Fed compensates the Treasury by crediting the Treasury's account at the Fed ($F_t$). As we will see shortly, when the Treasury writes checks to spend the funds, both reserves and the base increase. Given the other nine factors determining the base (including $F_t$), an increase in the SDR account [included in G in Equation (15-10)] produces an equal increase in the base.

## Other Federal Reserve Assets (OA)

Other Federal Reserve assets include other items owned by the Federal Reserve, such as buildings, furniture, and equipment. The item also includes the Fed's holdings of foreign assets, which typically are held in the form of foreign government bonds or other safe foreign financial assets, denominated in euros, yen, and so forth. The Fed holds the assets as ammunition to occasionally stabilize exchange rates through direct foreign exchange transactions (see Exhibit 15-1). Suppose the U.S. dollar weakens sharply against the euro. The Fed could sell some of its European bonds for euros and use the euros to purchase dollars in the foreign exchange market. In this instance, foreign exchange dealers in New York write checks (denominated in dollars) to the Federal Reserve to purchase the euros. The Fed collects by debiting the reserve accounts of the dealers' New York banks, thereby reducing aggregate reserves and the monetary base. In this way, a decline in the Fed's holdings of foreign currencies produces a contraction in the base.[7]

[7] On the other hand, suppose the Japanese yen goes into a free fall against the dollar and the Fed wishes to support the yen (hold down the dollar). The Fed can enter the foreign exchange market to purchase yen with dollars. The Fed writes checks to dealers in exchange for the yen and pays the dealers' banks by crediting their reserve accounts at the Fed. Hence, the increase in the Fed's holdings of yen ("other assets") is associated with increases in R and B.

**Exhibit 15-1** Federal Reserve Operations in the Foreign Exchange Market

During 2003 and 2004, the United States exhibited very large international trade deficits. In this period, the Federal Reserve fought high unemployment by maintaining short-term interest rates at the lowest levels in nearly 50 years. Interest rates in the United States fell considerably below levels in Europe. Largely as a result of falling interest rates and rising trade deficits, the U.S. dollar depreciated (fell) sharply against the euro in 2002 and 2003. The pace of the dollar's decline was orderly and was not resisted by U.S. authorities. However, some observers feared that the pace of the dollar's depreciation could increase in subsequent years—that is, the dollar could fall precipitously. Such an event tends to boost inflation and cause other problems for the United States.

What tools does the Federal Reserve have at its disposal to fight an unwarranted or undesired depreciation of the dollar against the euro and other currencies? First, the Fed can boost interest rates. At the margin, raising interest rates attracts foreign funds to the United States, thereby arresting the dollar's decline. But what if U.S. domestic conditions do not warrant higher interest rates? What if unemployment is high and rising? In that event, the Federal Reserve can purchase U.S. dollars directly from foreign exchange dealers in New York, paying for these dollars with euros and other foreign currencies. Recall from Tables 15-1 and 15-2 that "other assets" of the Fed include foreign bonds—for example, bonds issued by European governments and denominated in euros.

To support the dollar, the Fed can sell some of its European bonds for euros and use these euros to buy dollars. When the Fed sells euros for dollars, foreign exchange dealers located in New York write checks, denominated in dollars, to the Federal Reserve. The Fed collects on the checks by debiting the reserve accounts of the N.Y. banks on which the dealers write the checks. Hence, when the Fed supports the dollar by buying dollars with euros, "other assets" of the Fed decline. Bank reserves and the monetary base also decline accordingly.

Holding other factors constant, Fed actions supporting the dollar are *contractionary*—the actions cause the monetary base and the money supply to fall. However, the Fed can purchase government securities on the open market, thus neutralizing the effect of its foreign exchange market activities on the monetary variables. By purchasing securities (increasing P), the Fed *sterilizes* the monetary effects of its foreign exchange market purchases of U.S. dollars. Some economists dispute whether the Federal Reserve exerts appreciable effects on exchange rates by buying and selling dollars if the Fed's foreign exchange transactions are sterilized by open market purchases and sales of government securities.

As a second example, suppose the Fed purchases a posh new table for its Federal Open Market Committee meetings. The Fed writes a check for $80,000. When the furniture dealer deposits the check, the bank in which the check is deposited receives an $80,000 increase in its reserve account at the Fed. Both $F_b$ and the monetary base rise by $80,000. The moral is—when the Fed issues checks to pay for things, regardless of whether the item is government securities, furniture, candy bars, or 2 × 4s from a lumber yard, the Fed pumps funds into the U.S. banking system ($F_b$ increases). Bank reserves and the monetary base increase in a dollar-for-dollar fashion with the Fed's holdings of "other assets."

## Treasury Currency Outstanding (TCu)

The U.S. Treasury mints all U.S. coins. Unless the minting is accompanied by an offsetting transaction, an increase in this item causes an identical increase in the monetary base. The increased Treasury currency ends as either cash in depository institutions (classified as reserves, R) or currency held by the non-bank public (contributing to $C^P$). Either way, the monetary base ($R + C^P$) increases.

The amount of Treasury currency outstanding adapts to the public's need for currency. Suppose the public withdraws an additional \$60 million in coins from banks by drawing down checking accounts. The commercial bank balance sheet impact is as follows:

**All Banks**

| | | | |
|---|---|---|---|
| Cash | −60 million | Demand deposits | −60 million |

The banks are being drained of coins. The Banks wire the Fed and request a \$60 million delivery of coins. The Fed charges the banks for the coins by debiting the banks' reserve accounts ($F_b$). The balance sheet mechanics are as follows:

**All Banks**

| | | | |
|---|---|---|---|
| Cash | +60 million | | |
| Deposits at Fed | −60 million | | |

**Federal Reserve System**

| | | | |
|---|---|---|---|
| Cash | −60 million | Deposits by banks | −60 million |

Now the Fed itself is running low on coins. The Fed contacts the U.S. Treasury and requests \$60 million worth of coins. The Treasury mints \$60 million worth of new coins and ships the coins to the 12 Federal Reserve district banks. The Fed pays for the coins by crediting the Treasury's account at the Fed ($F_t$). The T-accounts appear as follows:

**Federal Reserve System**

| | | | |
|---|---|---|---|
| Cash | +60 million | Deposits by U.S. Treasury | +60 million |

**U.S. Treasury**

| | | | |
|---|---|---|---|
| Deposits at Fed | +60 million | Treasury currency outstanding | +60 million |

In this example, we see that the *public* determines the amount of Treasury currency outstanding. When the public wants more coins, the message is transferred first to the banks, then to the Fed, and finally to the U.S. Treasury. In essence, the Treasury mints or withdraws coins at the public's request. The commercial banks and the Federal Reserve banks act only as agents in the process. If we net out the impact of the entire process on the balance sheet of all banks and the Fed, we get the following:

**All Banks**

| | | | |
|---|---|---|---|
| Deposits at Fed | −60 million | Demand deposits | −60 million |

**Federal Reserve System**

| | | | |
|---|---|---|---|
| | | Deposits by banks | −60 million |
| | | Deposits by U.S. Treasury | +60 million |

Note carefully the impact on the monetary base, $R + C^P$. In this example, the base is *unchanged.* Currency held by the public ($C^P$) increases, but bank reserves (R) decrease by an equal amount. The banks have restored their cash reserves but have reduced their deposits at the Federal Reserve. Looking at the net effect from the point of view of the sources of the base [Equation (15-10)], the impact of the increase in Treasury currency outstanding on the base has been exactly neutralized by a simultaneous change in another determinant—the Treasury's deposits at the Fed ($F_t$). As we will demonstrate, the Treasury normally attempts to keep its balance at the Fed stable over time. When the Treasury returns its Federal Reserve balance ($F_t$) to its original amount, the monetary base increases by the $60 million increase in Treasury currency outstanding.

## Treasury Deposits at the Federal Reserve ($F_t$)

The Federal Reserve is a banker to the federal government. The U.S. Treasury maintains a checking account at the Federal Reserve. U.S. government expenditures are paid for by checks written on the Treasury's account at the Federal Reserve. These Treasury accounts are distributed among the Fed's 12 district banks. When the recipient of a Treasury check deposits the check in a bank account, the Fed clears the check by crediting the bank's account at the Fed ($F_b$) and debiting the Treasury's account ($F_t$) by an equal amount.

Suppose an employee of the U.S. Postal Service receives a $950 paycheck from the U.S. government. The worker deposits the check in a bank, which sends the check to the Federal Reserve. The Fed makes a bookkeeping entry, shifting $950 from the Treasury's account to the account of the postal worker's bank. As a result of these transactions, bank reserves and the monetary base both increase by $950. The relevant T-accounts appear as follows:

| Federal Reserve System | | | | All Banks | | | |
|---|---|---|---|---|---|---|---|
| | | Deposits by banks | +950 | Deposits at Fed | +950 | Demand deposits | +950 |
| | | Deposits by Treasury | −950 | | | | |

Thus, when Treasury deposits at the Fed *decline,* reserves and the base *increase* because checks written by the Treasury end up as deposits in banks and because the Fed clears the checks by crediting the recipient banks' reserve accounts.

Besides the Treasury's account at the Fed, the U.S. Treasury maintains deposit accounts in most of the roughly 7,700 banks in the United States. The accounts are periodically replenished by federal tax receipts and by the proceeds of new Treasury securities sales to the public; hence, these accounts are called **tax and loan accounts.**[8]

**tax and loan accounts**
U.S. Treasury deposits in commercial banks, periodically replenished by federal tax receipts and by the proceeds of new Treasury securities sales to the public

Treasury expenditures are not paid for directly out of tax and loan accounts but rather from the Treasury's account at the Federal Reserve. However, when large payments are scheduled to be made by the Treasury through its Fed account, funds are transferred from the tax and loan accounts to the Treasury's account at the Fed.

[8] The Treasury typically recycles the funds back to the banks on which the public wrote the checks to pay taxes or buy government bonds. Prior to 1978, tax and loan accounts were a free source of funds for banks. Since 1978, the Treasury has required banks to pay interest on such deposits, at a rate 0.25 percentage points below the average federal funds rate for the week.

The net effect is to neutralize the potential expansionary impact of Treasury expenditures on bank reserves and the monetary base.

In the preceding example, when the government paid the postal worker $950, bank reserves and the base increased by that amount. But the Treasury can neutralize the effect of the transaction by transferring $950 from its tax and loan accounts to its account at the Fed. The balance sheet impact of such a transfer is as follows:

**Federal Reserve**

| | | | |
|---|---|---|---|
| | | Deposits by U.S. Treasury | +950 |
| | | Deposits by member banks | −950 |

**All Banks**

| | | | |
|---|---|---|---|
| Deposits at Fed | −950 | Deposits by U.S. Treasury | −950 |

This transaction, coupled with the one in which the postal worker deposited a government paycheck, leaves both reserves and the monetary base unchanged.

The idea behind transferring of government funds between tax and loan accounts and the Treasury's Federal Reserve account is to minimize potentially disruptive swings in the monetary base. Suppose in the week of April 15, as a result of income tax under-withholding, U.S. taxpayers write checks totaling $24 billion to the IRS. If the Treasury deposits the funds in the Treasury's tax and loan accounts, reserves and the base are unaffected. The $24 billion is simply cleared out of reserve accounts of taxpayers' banks and redeposited by the Treasury into banks, which therefore collectively lose no reserves. The monetary base remains constant.

Now, suppose the Treasury tax and loan accounts *did not exist,* and all Treasury funds were kept at the Federal Reserve. In that event, when the Treasury receives the $24 billion in tax receipts, R and B decline by $24 billion when the Fed clears the checks by debiting the Federal Reserve accounts of the banks on which the checks are written. After the Treasury spends the funds, R and B return to their original levels as Treasury checks are deposited in banks. Given the lack of synchronization between Treasury disbursements and receipts of funds, key monetary variables such as reserves, the base, and the monetary aggregates would be subject to large and disruptive short-run fluctuations. These fluctuations would complicate the Federal Reserve's efforts to stabilize the economy. Figure 15-3 illustrates the weekly fluctuations in Treasury deposits at the Fed during 2003.

As you can see from the figure, short-term fluctuations in Treasury deposits at the Fed ($F_t$) can be large. The Fed can prevent these fluctuations from exerting unwanted fluctuations in R and B by judiciously using open market operations.

**YOUR TURN**

Suppose the U.S. Treasury withdraws $2,400 million ($2.4 billion) from its tax and loan accounts and places the funds in its Federal Reserve account prior to spending the funds in a few days.

**A.** What is the impact on bank reserves and the monetary base?

**B.** What must the Federal Reserve do to prevent reserves, the monetary base, and the money supply from changing?

**Figure 15-3** Treasury Deposits at the Federal Reserve in 2003 (Wednesday Figures, in $ Billion)

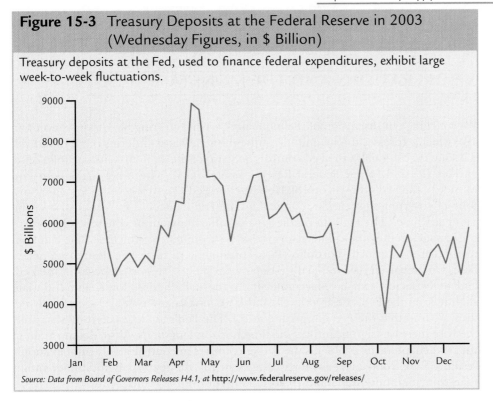

Treasury deposits at the Fed, used to finance federal expenditures, exhibit large week-to-week fluctuations.

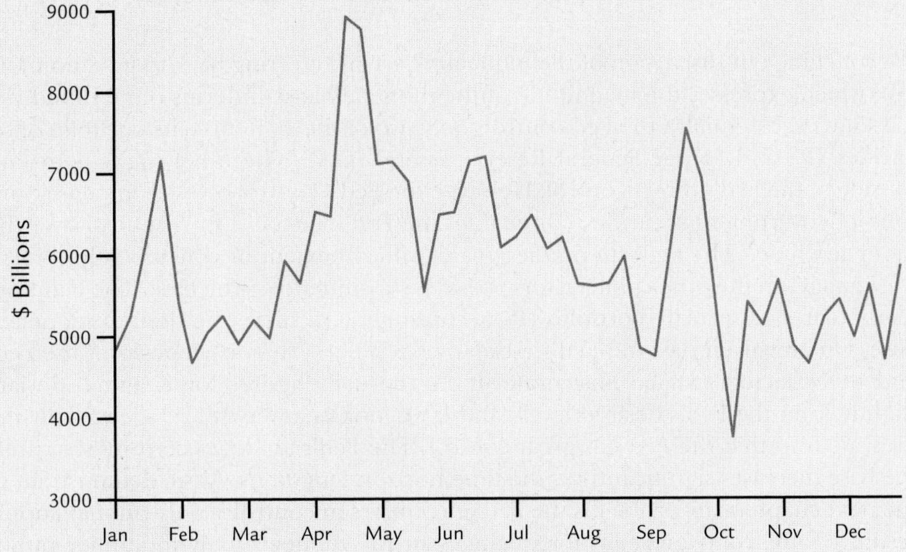


*Source: Data from Board of Governors Releases H4.1, at* http://www.federalreserve.gov/releases/

## Other Factors Absorbing Base Money ($F_f$, $TC_a$, and OLC)

Three other factors (other than $F_t$) *absorb* base money—that is, an increase in factor magnitude *reduces* the monetary base. Foreign central banks and governments maintain deposits at the Federal Reserve, chiefly for financing purchases of U.S. goods and services. Some government agencies, such as the Federal Home Loan Bank, and some international organizations, such as the World Bank, also keep deposits at the Fed. We lump these deposits together and designate them $F_f$.

Changes in these deposits have the same effect on R and B as changes in Treasury Deposits at the Fed ($F_t$). Suppose the German government purchases $40 million of new routers from Cisco Systems. The German government writes a check for $40 million on its Federal Reserve account to Cisco, located in the California Bay area. The Fed clears the check by transferring $40 million from the German government's Fed account to the San Francisco bank account in which Cisco deposits the check. Hence, R and B both increase by $40 million.

Treasury cash holdings ($TC_a$) consists primarily of paper money accumulated by the Treasury in connection with fiscal operations. As the Treasury dispenses this till money, the monetary base rises because the money ends up as either currency held by the public ($C^P$) or cash in depository institutions ($C_b$). By the same reasoning, when Treasury cash increases, the monetary base falls.

The final (negative) source of the base is other liabilities and capital of the Federal Reserve (OLC). Suppose, for instance, the Fed issues additional stock to its owners (commercial banks that are members of the Federal Reserve). The Fed collects payment for these stock shares by debiting the reserve accounts that the banks hold at the Fed. In this way, an increase in OLC reduces reserves and the monetary base. Quantitatively, the changes in this item are relatively small, as are changes in Treasury cash holdings and foreign and other deposits at the Federal Reserve.

## FEDERAL RESERVE OPERATIONS AND THE MONETARY BASE

We conclude our discussion of the monetary base by referring back to Equation (15-10), which expresses the magnitude of the monetary base in terms of its 10 individual sources. Essentially, the Fed controls only two of the 10 items—its portfolio of securities (P) and "other Federal Reserve assets" (OA). The other eight items are outside of the Fed's direct control. However, the Fed's control over its immense portfolio of government securities (P) enables the Fed to achieve firm control over the monetary base.[9] The Fed can predict to a significant extent or concurrently observe the changes in the other nine factors (besides P) influencing the base. The Fed then manipulates its security portfolio (P) accordingly to achieve the desired monetary base. On any given day, the Fed's estimation of float, Treasury deposits at the Fed, and other factors can be inaccurate. If so, the daily figures for R and B deviate slightly from the Fed's desired levels. But if we look at a weekly average of daily figures, we find that the Fed has great control. The Fed's ability to control accurately the base increases significantly as the time horizon lengthens. As we demonstrate in the next chapter, any problems the Fed encounters in controlling the money supply result mainly from unpredictable changes in the money supply multiplier rather than from an inherent inability to accurately control the monetary base.

## SUMMARY

The money supply is the product of a money supply multiplier and the monetary base. Changes in the money supply can result from changes in the multiplier or changes in the base. The Federal Reserve's ability to control the money supply hinges on the Fed's ability to determine the monetary base and forecast the money supply multiplier. Because each dollar of monetary base supports a larger amount of money (M1 and M2), the base is sometimes known as "high-powered money." The base can be analyzed from the viewpoint of its uses or its sources. The base is used as depository institution reserves (R) and currency held by the public ($C^P$). Ten sources of the base exist—that is, 10 factors determine the base. The Fed directly controls only two of the 10 factors. By far the most important factor determining the base is the Fed's portfolio of U.S. government and agency securities. By totally controlling its own security portfolio, the Fed is able to counteract the influence of changes in the other sources of the monetary base, thereby achieving accurate control of the base.

[9] You can compare the Fed's control of the monetary base to engineers' control of a reservoir's water level. Engineers cannot control rainfall, evaporation, and other exogenous factors influencing the reservoir's water level. However, by controlling the rate of outflow at the dam, engineers can accurately control the reservoir's water level.

## YOUR TURN ANSWERS

PAGE 344

**A.** The magnitude of the monetary base varies directly with float and discounts and advances and inversely with Treasury deposits at the Fed [Equation (15-10)]. The net effect of these three factors is to increase the base by $1,600 million ($1.6 billion).

**B.** To offset the influence of these events on the monetary base, the Federal Reserve *sells* $1,600 million ($1.6 billion) of U.S. government securities to securities dealers, thereby reducing its portfolio (P) by that amount.

PAGE 352

**A.** As the Treasury moves these funds to its Federal Reserve account, reserves and the base fall by $2,400 million ($2.4 billion) and $F_t$ rises by the same amount.

**B.** To prevent reserves and the base (and the money supply) from falling, the Fed needs to buy $2,400 million ($2.4 billion) of securities in the open market. The increase in P offsets the effect of the increase in $F_t$ on bank reserves and the monetary base.

## KEY TERMS

monetary base (B)
money supply multiplier (m)
sources of the base
uses for the base
float
tax and loan accounts

## STUDY QUESTIONS

1. Define the monetary base. Why did we select this particular variable for intensive study?
2. Write an equation indicating the 10 sources of the monetary base. Define each variable.
3. "Most of the individual sources of the monetary base are clearly outside Federal Reserve control. Therefore, the Fed is not responsible for the monetary base." Evaluate this statement.
4. Using T-accounts of the Fed and the commercial banks, explain the impact of the following two events on aggregate bank reserves (R) and the monetary base (B):
   - **A.** The Fed sells $3 billion of government securities to dealers.
   - **B.** Bank of America (a commercial bank) sells $3 billion of securities to dealers.
5. Suppose, in a given week, float rises $900 million, Treasury deposits at the Fed rise $1,500 million ($1.5 billion), discounts and advances decline $200 million, and foreign deposits at the Fed increase $150 million. What is the net effect of these changes on the monetary base? What must the Fed do to maintain the base constant during the week? Explain.
6. While reading Friday's *The Wall Street Journal,* you notice that the Fed purchased $3.6 billion of U.S. government securities in the past week. In the previous week, the Fed *sold* $2 billion. Does this more recent Fed transaction necessarily signal a change in the fundamental policy stance of the Federal Reserve? Why or why not?

7. Explain the meaning of Federal Reserve float. Explain how float and the monetary base would change with the following events:
   - A. A tornado shuts down the Atlanta airport for 3 days.
   - B. The Fed increases deferral time on all checks by 1 day.
   - C. Increasing use of the Internet causes more people to pay their bills electronically.

8. Explain carefully how the Treasury uses its two-tier deposit system (in the Federal Reserve and private banks) to minimize the effect of its financial transactions on bank reserves and the monetary base.

9. Calculate the effect of the following events on the monetary base:
   - A. The Treasury writes checks to Social Security recipients for $600 million.
   - B. The Federal Reserve buys a new fleet of cars for $8 million.
   - C. The Treasury transfers $500 million from its tax and loan accounts to its account with the Federal Reserve.
   - D. The Federal Reserve buys $1,400 million ($1.4 billion) of Treasury bills in the open market.
   - E. The Federal Reserve sells $1.5 billion of its German bonds for euros.

10. Recently, a troubled bank borrowed $800 million from the Federal Reserve. Explain the impact of this event on the monetary base.

11. Using T-accounts of the Federal Reserve and the commercial banking system, demonstrate how Federal Reserve purchases of U.S. government securities from dealers would affect:
    - A. Aggregate bank reserves
    - B. The monetary base

12. Go to the Board of Governors Web site at http://www.federalreserve.gov/releases, locate Release H.4.1, and check what happened to the following sources of the monetary base and to the base itself in the most recent week:
    - A. Float
    - B. Treasury deposits at the Federal Reserve
    - C. The Federal Reserve portfolio of securities
    - D. The monetary base

## ADDITIONAL READING

- The two different measures of the monetary base (the Board of Governors' measure and the Federal Reserve Bank of St. Louis measure) can be found on the FRED database at http://www.research.stlouisfed.org/fred2 (click on "Reserves and Monetary Base").
- The *U.S. Treasury Bulletin* contains a wealth of information on Treasury operations (tax and loan accounts, Treasury deposits at the Federal Reserve, and so forth). You can access the relevant Web site at http://www.treasury.bulletin@fms.treas.gov, and you can subscribe to this publication via the Internet at http://www.fms.treas.gov/.
- The *Federal Reserve Bulletin,* available as hard copy at your library or on the Internet at http://www.federalreserve.gov, publishes at least one article per year on recent foreign exchange operations conducted by the Federal Reserve and the Treasury.

# Chapter 16

# MONEY SUPPLY DETERMINATION: THE MONEY SUPPLY MULTIPLIER

As we pointed out at the beginning of Chapter 15, the nation's money supply is expressed as the product of the monetary base and a money supply multiplier that summarizes the multiple deposit expansion mechanism in a fractional reserve banking system.

$$\text{(16-1)} \quad \mathbf{M} = \mathbf{m} \cdot \mathbf{B}$$

$$\text{(16-2)} \quad \mathbf{m} = \frac{\mathbf{M}}{\mathbf{B}}$$

In Equations (16-1) and (16-2), M is the nation's money supply, m is the money supply multiplier, and B is the monetary base. The concepts expressed in Equations (16-1) and (16-2) provide a useful framework for obtaining important insight into the money supply process. Any change in the supply of money must be attributable to a change in the base, a change in the multiplier, or some combination of the two.

In Chapter 15 we established that the Federal Reserve, by exerting *total* control over its portfolio of government securities, maintains a very high degree of control over B. Equation (16-1) implies that if m is a stable and predictable variable whose behavior is independent of B, then the Fed can accurately control the nation's money supply (M) if it desires to do so. Changes in B engineered by the Federal Reserve dominate any changes in the money supply multiplier, allowing the Fed to accurately control the money supply, even over relatively short horizons (for example, 1 month).

On the other hand, if m fluctuates erratically and unpredictably or m changes unpredictably due to monetary base changes engineered by the Federal Reserve, the Fed has difficulty gaining firm short-term control over the money supply. Changes in B produced by the Fed can be dominated by relatively large changes in m. In this case, the chief sources of short-run change in the money supply can be the factors underlying the money supply multiplier. We demonstrate in this chapter that such factors are largely outside of Federal Reserve influence. Some economists regard the money supply as largely *endogenous*—that is, strongly influenced by short-run (1 week, month, or quarter) economic activity. The economists believe that short-run changes in the money supply are caused primarily by changes in the money supply multiplier. The multiplier in turn responds to economic variables such as interest rates, income, and wealth.[1]

---

[1] Even if this hypothesis is valid, the Fed still can control the money supply in the short run if the changes in the multiplier are predictable in advance and are independent of the monetary base. If the Fed knows what the multiplier will be next week, it can set the monetary base at the approximate level required to produce the desired money stock. For example, if the multiplier is expected to be 2.00 and the desired M1 money stock is $1,400 billion ($1.4 trillion), the Fed targets a monetary base of $700 billion.

For each money measure, a corresponding money supply multiplier exists. Hence, $m_1 = M1/B$, $m_2 = M2/B$, and $m_3 = M3/B$. Review Figure 15-1 in the previous chapter, which expresses the relationship between the monetary base and the various monetary aggregates.

Figure 16-1 illustrates the behavior of the monetary base, M1, and M2 from 1960 to 2004. The data are plotted on a logarithmic scale because of the enormous growth of these monetary variables over nearly half a century. Hypothetically, if the multipliers ($m_1$ and $m_2$) connecting the base to M1 and M2 are constants, then M1 and M2 always move exactly in parallel with B. The figure clearly indicates that is not the case. The multipliers change over time. Inspection of the figure indicates that M1 moved pretty much parallel to the base over much of the period, implying a fairly stable $m_1$ multiplier. However, M1 increased much more slowly than B after the late 1980s, implying a significant reduction in the $m_1$ multiplier during that period. M2 increased slightly more rapidly than B over much of the period (the gap between the two lines widens somewhat up to the late 1980s), indicating that $m_2$ increased during that period. The gap has narrowed more recently, indicating that the $m_2$ multiplier has declined.

In this chapter, we examine the meaning of the money supply multiplier and analyze the factors determining the magnitude of this important variable. Essentially, the money supply multiplier summarizes all the forces—other than the monetary base—that influence the money supply. Specifically, the money supply multiplier reflects the public's portfolio decisions on the distribution of financial wealth among currency, demand deposits, and other financial assets. The multiplier also reflects depository institutions' (banks') portfolio behavior in terms of distribution

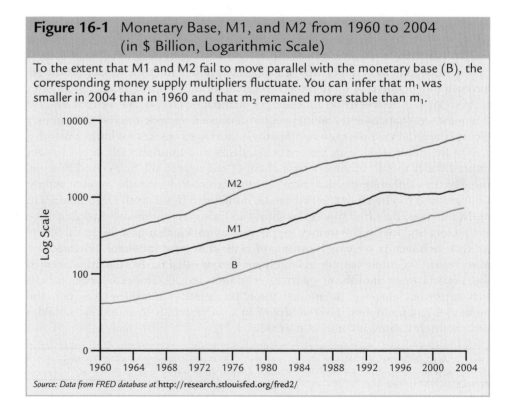

**Figure 16-1** Monetary Base, M1, and M2 from 1960 to 2004 (in $ Billion, Logarithmic Scale)

To the extent that M1 and M2 fail to move parallel with the monetary base (B), the corresponding money supply multipliers fluctuate. You can infer that $m_1$ was smaller in 2004 than in 1960 and that $m_2$ remained more stable than $m_1$.

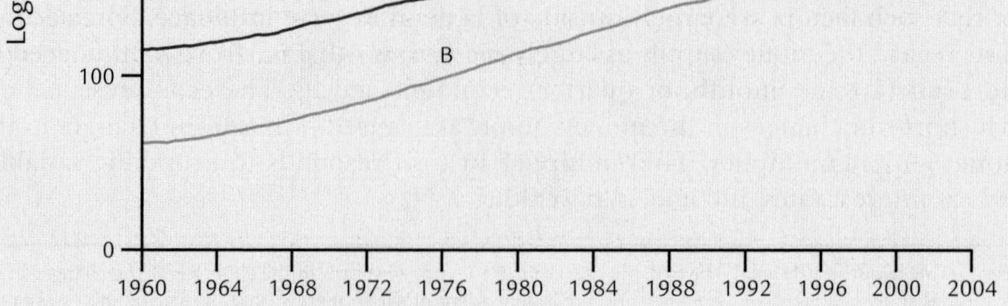


*Source: Data from FRED database at* http://research.stlouisfed.org/fred2/

of assets between reserves (cash and deposits at the Fed) and earning assets such as loans and securities.

The money supply multiplier expresses the magnification factor by which the banking system collectively transforms base money into actual money, much of which consists of demand deposits. Thus, the money supply multiplier is an important behavioral variable in monetary economics.

## MONEY SUPPLY MULTIPLIER: DERIVATION AND APPLICATIONS

We focus chiefly on $m_1$, the ratio of the transactions measure of money (M1) to the monetary base (B). First we derive an expression specifying the variables determining the magnitude of the money supply multiplier. Recall the narrow definition of the money supply in the United States:

$$\mathbf{M1 = DDO + C^P.} \qquad (16\text{-}3)$$

The narrow money supply (M1) consists of demand deposits and other checkable deposits in depository institutions (DDO) plus currency in the public's hands ($C^P$). Because M1 incorporates only items that are actually used to make transactions, this measure of money is sometimes called the "transactions measure" of the money supply.

Let us derive the multiplier for M1, that is, M1/B. From Chapter 15, the definition of the monetary base in terms of its uses or the way in which the base is allocated is:

$$\mathbf{B = R + C^P.} \qquad (16\text{-}4)$$

This expression states that the monetary base (B) equals the sum of bank reserves (R) and currency held by the non-bank public ($C^P$). R includes depository institutions' cash and deposits at the Federal Reserve. $C^P$ includes all currency and coins in existence except currency and coins residing in depository institutions, the Treasury, and the Federal Reserve. If we substitute the expression for M1 given in Equation (16-3) and the expression for B given in Equation (16-4) into Equation (16-2), which defines the money supply multiplier, we obtain:

$$\mathbf{m_1 = \frac{DDO + C^P}{R + C^P}.} \qquad (16\text{-}5)$$

Bank reserves (R) can be broken into two components: required reserves ($R_r$) and excess reserves ($R_e$). *Required reserves* are reserves that banks must hold in order to abide by the Fed's reserve requirements. *Excess reserves* are reserves that banks voluntarily hold above and beyond the required amount, given current and expected future economic conditions.[2]

$$\mathbf{R = R_r + R_e.} \qquad (16\text{-}6)$$

[2] We use the term "banks" generically to include all depository institutions. We assume that banks adjust their actual holdings of excess reserves to the desired amounts instantaneously. This assumption is an exaggeration. However, the adjustment process is rapid in an age of highly developed money markets, computer technology, and instant communication.

Equation (16-6) states that reserves (R) consist of two components: required reserves ($R_r$) and excess reserves ($R_e$). We can express the two component variables as follows:

$$\text{(16-7)} \quad \mathbf{R_r = r_r\,(DDO),}$$

where $r_r = \dfrac{R_r}{DDO}$, and

$$\text{(16-8)} \quad \mathbf{R_e = r_e(DDO),}$$

where $r_e = \dfrac{R_e}{DDO}$.

**required reserve ratio ($r_r$)** ratio of required reserves to DDO (demand deposits and other checkable deposits)

**desired excess reserves ratio ($r_e$)** ratio of banks' desired excess reserves to DDO (demand deposits and other checkable deposits)

Equation (16-7) states that the dollar amount of required reserves ($R_r$) is some fraction ($r_r$) of the amount of demand deposits and other checkable accounts (DDO). The variable $\mathbf{r_r}$ is the **required reserve ratio.** Equation (16-8) states that the dollar magnitude of desired (and actual) excess reserves ($R_e$) is some fraction ($r_e$) of such deposits. The variable $\mathbf{r_e}$ is the banks' **desired excess reserves ratio.** Equation (16-9) indicates that the dollar amount of total reserves (R) is equal to the dollar amount of required reserves ($R_r$) plus the dollar amount of excess reserves ($R_e$). This sum (R), in turn, is expressed as the product of the sum of required and excess reserve ratios ($r_r$ and $r_e$) and the magnitude of checkable deposits (DDO):

$$\text{(16-9)} \quad \mathbf{R = R_r + R_e = (r_r + r_e)(DDO)}$$

We now substitute the expression for R given in the right-hand side of Equation (16-9) into Equation (16-5)—our formula expressing the definition of the money supply multiplier—and obtain the following expression:

$$\text{(16-10)} \quad \mathbf{m_1} = \frac{\mathbf{DDO + C^P}}{\mathbf{(r_r + r_e)(DDO) + C^P}}$$

We now divide both numerator and denominator of Equation (16-10) by DDO and obtain:

$$\text{(16-11)} \quad \mathbf{m_1} = \frac{\mathbf{1 + \dfrac{C^P}{DDO}}}{\mathbf{(r_r + r_e)(1) + \dfrac{C^P}{DDO}}}$$

**currency ratio (k)** ratio of currency held by the public ($C^P$) to DDO (demand deposits and other checkable deposits)

To simplify notation, define **k** as the **currency ratio,** that is, $C^P/DDO$. If we insert this notation into Equation (16-11), we get our final expression for the money supply multiplier $m_1$:

$$\text{(16-12)} \quad \mathbf{m_1} = \frac{\mathbf{1 + k}}{\mathbf{r_r + r_e + k}}$$

Equation (16-12) indicates that the money supply multiplier ($m_1$) is determined by three variables. These variables are the currency ratio (k), the weighted average required reserve ratio ($r_r$), and the banks' desired excess reserve ratio ($r_e$). We carefully examine the behavioral motives and other considerations underlying each of these three variables later in this chapter. For now, we simply note that k is determined by the public, $r_e$ is determined by the banks, and $r_r$ is determined predominantly by the Federal Reserve through the Fed's authority to set and change reserve requirements for depository institutions.

## Comparison of the Money Supply Multiplier with the Naive Deposit Expansion Multiplier

Comparison of this multiplier formulation with the simplified deposit expansion multiplier presented in Chapter 14 is useful.[3] The naive deposit multiplier, which is the reciprocal of the percentage reserve requirement applicable to DDO, was derived based on the following assumptions:

1. As demand deposits change, no change in the public's demand for currency is induced. The public's demand for currency is independent of DDO.
2. As demand deposits change, no change in bank demand for excess reserves is induced. Instead, the bank demand for excess reserves is assumed to always be zero.
3. The percentage reserve requirement applicable to DDO is the same for all deposits (DDO) in all banks. Also, there are no reserve requirements on other bank liabilities besides DDO.

Let us interpret these assumptions in the context of our money supply multiplier expression—Equation (16-12). The first assumption implies that $k = 0$. The marginal propensity of the public to increase currency holdings as DDO increases is assumed to be zero. The second assumption implies that $r_e$ is zero, that is, bankers never want to hold any excess reserves. The third assumption implies that $r_r$ is constant and is simply the percentage reserve requirement set by the Federal Reserve for demand deposits and other checkable deposits. As we note shortly, $r_r$ is a bit more complicated in reality.

Given these three restrictive assumptions and inserting $k = 0$ and $r_e = 0$ into Equation (16-12), our multiplier expression reduces simply to $1/r_r$, the naive deposit expansion multiplier. The simple deposit expansion multiplier is logically valid given the assumptions underlying it. However, these assumptions are unrealistic; therefore, the resulting naive multiplier expression ($1/r_r$) is of limited usefulness in shedding light on real-world monetary phenomena.

The beauty of our money supply multiplier expressed in Equation (16-12) is that this multiplier moves much closer to reality by considering bank behavior concerning excess reserves and the public's behavior toward currency holdings. Of necessity, the multiplier is more complicated than the naive deposit expansion multiplier because it considers the behavior of the public, the banks, and the Federal Reserve in the money supply process. In the naive deposit expansion multiplier, the multiplier remains constant as long as the reserve requirement is unchanged. In this more realistic formulation, the money supply multiplier (and the nation's money supply) changes continuously in response to forces exerted by the public and the banks and to actions taken by the Federal Reserve.

## Role of the Federal Reserve in Influencing the Money Supply Multiplier

The naive deposit multiplier suggests that the Federal Reserve alone determines the multiplier by setting the reserve requirement. The sophisticated multiplier indicates the Federal Reserve influences the multiplier only to the extent the Fed in-

---

[3] Review Table 14-1 and the assumptions and discussion surrounding it.

fluences the three determinants of the sophisticated multiplier—k, $r_r$, and $r_e$. Let's take a look at the Fed's influence over each of these variables.

**The Fed and k.** The Federal Reserve does not directly influence the currency ratio (k). This variable responds entirely to the public's demand for currency and for DDO. The public obtains currency by withdrawing funds from checking and savings accounts. Banks that run short on currency obtain more from the Federal Reserve. Banks pay for the currency by having their reserve deposit accounts at the Fed deducted by the amount of the currency. The Fed obtains paper currency by printing Federal Reserve notes as needed by banks. The Fed obtains coins by requesting the U.S. Treasury to deposit coins with the Fed. The responses of banks, the Fed, and the Treasury are triggered by actions of the public; therefore, the public determines the currency ratio (k).

**The Fed and $r_r$.** The ratio of required reserves ($r_r$) to DDO is dominated by the reserve requirement percentages set by the Fed. In the Fed's current reserve requirement scheme, each bank is subject to a zero reserve requirement on the first $6.6 million (in 2004) of DDO, a 3 percent reserve requirement on DDO between the first figure and an upper threshold level ($45.4 million in 2004), and a 10 percent reserve requirement on all DDO in excess of the upper threshold magnitude. Changes in deposit distributions among banks of different sizes initiate slight changes in $r_r$.[4] Occasionally, the Fed changes the percentage reserve requirement, triggering significant changes in $r_r$. For example, in 1992 the Fed reduced the reserve requirements for all DDO above the upper threshold from 12 to 10 percent.

**The Fed and $r_e$.** The desired excess reserve ratio ($r_e$), directly determined by bank decisions, is only marginally influenced by the Federal Reserve. This variable responds to changes in the costs and benefits of holding excess reserves, as perceived by bank management. The desired excess reserve ratio is sensitive to interest rate levels and expectations about future Federal Reserve policy and other economic phenomena.

**The Fed and the Multiplier: Recap.** To sum up the role of the various parties in influencing the multiplier—the general public essentially determines k, the banks determine $r_e$, and the Fed predominantly (but not totally) determines $r_r$ and the monetary base. Therefore, the money supply at a given time is determined by the public, the banks, and the Federal Reserve. The critical questions debated among professional economists are the following. To what extent is the Federal Reserve capable of accurately controlling short-term (week-to-week, month-to-month) movements in the money supply? Is it important that the Fed be able do so?

Some economists believe that the Federal Reserve can counteract the monetary effects of banks and the general public in any given month. The Fed can establish the money supply very close to a desired target level if it desires to do so. Other economists strongly doubt this proposition. Doubting economists believe short-run instability in k, $r_r$, and $r_e$ produces volatility in the money supply multiplier, making difficult or impractical any Fed move to hit monthly money supply targets.

---

[4] Again, each bank is subject to zero reserve requirements on the first few million dollars of DDO ($6.6 million in 2004), a fact we ignore in order to simplify our multiplier analysis. Now, consider a check cleared from a large bank with $500 million of DDO to a bank with $30 million of DDO (below the threshold magnitude at which the marginal reserve requirement jumps from 3 to 10 percent). This event reduces $r_r$. The latter threshold level and the threshold level at which the reserve requirement increases from 0 to 3 percent are indexed to total transactions accounts (DDO) in the banking system. The threshold changes each year by 80 percent of the percentage change in aggregate DDO in the nation's banks. If aggregate DDO increases 5 percent, the thresholds increase 4 percent.

## **Exhibit 16-1** Multiplier for the M2 Measure of Money (Broad Money)

Our discussion of the money supply multiplier has been couched in terms of the link between the monetary base (B) and the *narrow* measure of money (M1). Beginning around 1980, the link (known as *velocity*) between M1 and the nation's gross domestic product (GDP) loosened considerably. Changes in the nation's GDP expenditures resulting from changes in M1 became much more uncertain. M1 was no longer a suitable variable for the Federal Reserve to control or target in order to stabilize economic activity. Beginning in 1987, the Fed stopped specifying explicit target ranges for M1 in its semi-annual testimony before Congress. Today, the Federal Reserve puts more stake in the behavior of M2 than in M1. Economists of monetarist persuasion have long preferred M2.

M2 includes M1 plus savings and small time deposits, money market mutual fund shares, overnight repurchase agreements, and eurodollars. If we designate all these non-M1 components of M2 as "other monetary assets held by the public (OMA)," we can write the money supply multiplier for M2 as follows:

$$\mathbf{m_2} = \frac{\mathbf{DDO + C^P + OMA}}{\mathbf{R + C^P}}$$

If we divide the top and bottom of the equation by DDO and define k, $r_r$, and $r_e$ as previously discussed, we obtain an expression for the broad money supply multiplier ($m_2$):

$$\mathbf{m_2} = \frac{\mathbf{1 + k + o}}{\mathbf{r_r + r_e + k}}$$

The only difference between the narrow money supply multiplier ($m_1$) and the broad money supply multiplier ($m_2$) is OMA, or the term "o" in the numerator, which is the marginal propensity of the public to acquire "other monetary assets" relative to DDO.

The accompanying graph shows the behavior of the $m_2$ multiplier from 1974 to 2004. As the figure indicates, the $m_2$ multiplier declined sharply in the decade beginning in 1985 (can you explain why?). In the past decade, $m_2$ has fluctuated within a fairly narrow range bounded by 8.0 and 8.7.

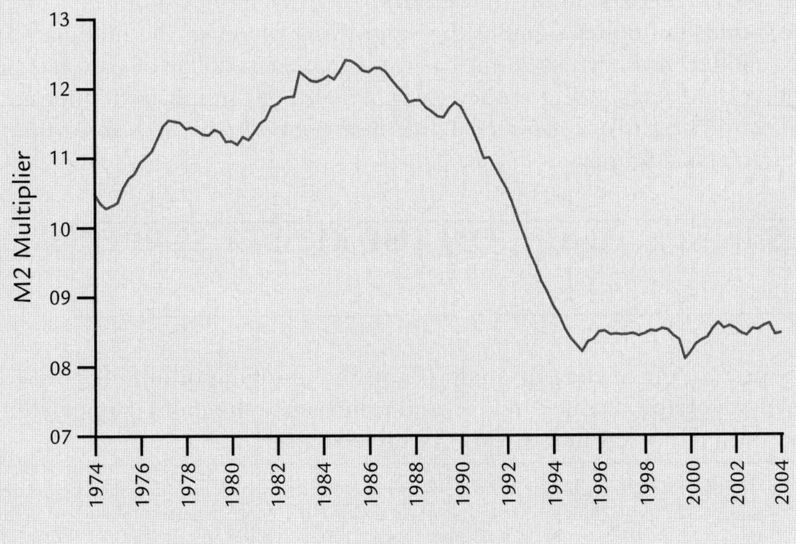

## Arithmetic Examples

Let us now breathe life into these concepts using some hypothetical (but not grossly unrealistic) data. Suppose we make the following assumptions about the relevant aggregate banking variables and reserve requirements.

1. Demand deposits and other checkable accounts (DDO) = \$600 billion.
2. Currency held by the public ($C^P$) = \$600 billion.
3. Reserve requirements for *all* DDO = 10 percent.
4. Reserves = \$61 billion.

We begin by computing $R_r$ and $R_e$ of Equation (16-6). We know that reserves (R) = \$61 billion (this is given). To compute the dollar magnitude of $R_r$, simply take the reserve requirement applicable to DDO times the amount of DDO. We get $R_r$ = 10% (\$600 billion) = \$60 billion. We know that actual (and desired) excess reserves ($R_e$) = R − $R_r$. So $R_e$ = \$ 1 billion.

We now can calculate $r_r$ and $r_e$. From Equation (16-7), $r_r$ = \$60 billion/\$600 billion = 0.10. The volume of required reserves is 10 percent of total checkable deposits. The variable $r_e$ can be computed as $R_e$/DDO. Using Equation (16-8), $r_e$ = \$1 billion/\$600 billion = 0.00167. The desired (and actual) excess reserve ratio is one sixth of 1 percent. To calculate the money supply multiplier we still need to calculate k. Given the data, this is simple:

$$\mathbf{k} = \frac{\$600 \text{ billion}}{\$600 \text{ billion}} = 1.00.$$

We now can calculate the size of the money supply multiplier, as expressed in Equation (16-12).

$$\mathbf{m_1} = \frac{1 + 1.00}{0.10 + 1.00 + 0.0017} \qquad \mathbf{m_1} = 1.815.$$

The money supply multiplier is calculated to be 1.815. Given the propensity of the public to maintain a $C^P$ to DDO ratio of 100 percent, the propensity of banks to maintain an excess reserves to DDO ratio of 0.17 percent, and a ratio of required reserves to DDO held fixed at 10 percent, then a \$1 increase in the monetary base leads to a \$1.82 increase in M1, the narrowly defined money supply.[5]

The money multiplier signifies the magnifying power of the monetary base in creating money. An increase in $m_1$ indicates that each dollar of base has become more powerful in producing money (M1). The money supply multiplier measures the collective magnifying power of the monetary system in transforming base money into actual money.

## IMPACT OF CHANGES IN k, $r_r$, AND $r_e$ ON THE MONEY SUPPLY MULTIPLIER

We now present the arithmetic analyses and the more important economic behavioral analyses of how changes in k, $r_r$, and $r_e$ influence the money supply multiplier and the stock of narrow money (M1) in the economy.

[5] It is important to note that, regarding k and $r_e$, we assume that the *average* and *marginal* propensities are equal. For example, the public holds 100 percent of total DDO in $C^P$ and increases holdings of $C^P$ by 100 percent of any *increase* in DDO. Similarly, banks hold excess reserves in the amount of 0.17 percent of DDO and *increase* excess reserve holdings by 0.17 percent of any *increase* in DDO.

## Impact of a Change in k

Using our original numbers for $r_r$ (0.10) and $r_e$ (0.0017), suppose the currency ratio (k) increases from 1.0 to 1.10. Assuming *all other factors remain unchanged,* we can calculate the multiplier as follows:

$$\mathbf{m_1} = \frac{\mathbf{1 + 1.10}}{\mathbf{0.10 + 0.0017 + 1.10}} = \mathbf{1.748}$$

The increase in the currency ratio reduces the multiplier from 1.815 to 1.748. If the Federal Reserve holds the monetary base constant, the increase in k *reduces* both $m_1$ and M1 by about 4 percent.

So much for the *arithmetic* demonstrating an inverse relationship between the currency ratio and the money supply multiplier. Let's look at the more interesting and important *economic intuition.* Given the size of the monetary base, the increase in currency demanded by the public ($C^P$) comes out of bank reserves (R) as the public withdraws cash from banks. Given the monetary base, the increase in $C^P$ implies an equivalent reduction in bank reserves (R). People withdraw currency from banks, and a larger portion of the (unchanged) monetary base is immobilized and unavailable to banks for lending and buying securities. The portion of the base consisting of reserves (R) decreases. To abide by reserve requirements and maintain desired excess reserve ratios ($r_e$) in the face of reduced actual reserves triggered by the public's withdrawal of cash, banks are forced to liquidate earning assets (loans and securities). As explained in Chapter 14, such bank actions produce a contraction in the nation's DDO and monetary aggregates. M1 declines because individuals who pay off their bank loans and buy the securities sold by the banks pay using checks written on their accounts in depository institutions. This action extinguishes DDO. Therefore, DDO, M1, and $m_1$ must decrease when k rises.[6]

## Impact of a Change in $r_r$

To illustrate the impact of a change in $r_r$, suppose we go back to the original assumptions in which $k = 1.00$, $r_r = 0.10$, and $r_e = 0.0017$. In this case, $m_1$ is 1.815. Now suppose $r_r$ increases from 0.10 to 0.11 because the Federal Reserve raises percentage reserve requirements applicable to DDO. The new multiplier is:

$$\mathbf{m_1} = \frac{\mathbf{1 + 1.00}}{\mathbf{0.11 + 0.0017 + 1.00}} = \mathbf{1.799.}$$

If other factors remain constant, the one percentage point increase in $r_r$ reduces the money supply multiplier from 1.815 to 1.799, a contraction of approximately 1 percent. Note that the magnitude of this impact is considerably smaller than that predicted by the simple or naive deposit expansion multiplier formulation.[7]

The economic interpretation of this phenomenon is straightforward. The increase in required reserves triggered by the Fed's reserve requirement hike does not change actual reserves (R) but does decrease the magnitude of actual excess

[6] Another way to make this point is as follows: one additional dollar of B in the form of $C^P$ supports only \$1 of additional money (in the form of currency), while one additional dollar of B in the form of reserves (R) supports several additional dollars of money (in the form of DDO). An increase in k, by reducing R and increasing $C^P$, means that the existing base supports less money.

[7] In the "naive" deposit expansion multiplier formulation, an increase in reserve requirements from 10 to 11 percent reduces the deposit multiplier from 10 to 9.1, a contraction of about 9 percent. Can you explain why the impact of a change in reserve requirements on the multiplier is smaller in our more sophisticated multiplier framework?

reserves below desired excess reserves. In fact, actual excess reserves initially become negative as banks fall short of the reserve requirement. Banks are forced to liquidate earning assets (reduce loans and securities) to satisfy the new reserve requirements and to restore their excess reserves to meet the desired $r_e$ magnitude.[8] This activity results in contraction of the money stock as government security dealers and the general public write checks to banks (thus extinguishing DDO).

## Impact of a Change in $r_e$

The effect on the money supply multiplier of a change in banks' desired excess reserve ratio ($r_e$) is similar to that of a change in the required reserve ratio ($r_r$). Suppose banks anticipate imminent restrictive monetary policy actions by the Federal Reserve. Banks sharply increase their desired excess reserve ratio from 0.0017 to 0.005. Returning to our original data assumptions for k and $r_r$, we compute the money supply multiplier as follows:

$$\mathbf{m_1} = \frac{\mathbf{1 + 1.00}}{\mathbf{0.10 + 0.005 + 1.00}} = \mathbf{1.810.}$$

The bank scramble to obtain additional excess reserves reduces the money supply multiplier from 1.815 to 1.810, a contraction of only about one fourth of 1 percent. Given a constant monetary base, this precautionary bank action implies a reduction in bank lending and investing (security holdings). Banks reduce loans and sell off securities in order to build up their excess reserves. As the public writes checks to banks, the multiplier (and money supply) decreases. However, $r_e$ is so small today that even a large relative change in $r_e$ magnitude exerts only a modest effect on the money multiplier. The variable ($r_e$) is quantitatively the least important player in the money supply process today.[9]

**YOUR TURN**

Suppose we have the following information about U.S. monetary variables: $C^P$ = \$700 billion, DDO = \$800 billion, the reserve requirement applicable to all DDO is 8 percent, and reserves are \$65 billion. Compute the currency ratio (k), the desired excess reserve ratio ($r_e$), and the money supply multiplier ($m_1$). Also compute the monetary base (B) and the money supply (M1).

## Historical Behavior of the Money Supply Multiplier

Figure 16-2 illustrates the money supply multiplier ($m_1$) since 1984. This multiplier may be calculated in two ways. First, you can simply divide M1 by the monetary base (B). Alternatively, you can calculate the magnitudes of k, $r_r$, and $r_e$ and substitute these values into Equation (16-12), the expression for the money supply multiplier. As we examine the behavior of each of these three important vari-

[8] When banks liquidate loans and securities, they collectively gain no additional reserves. However, such activity reduces required reserves by reducing aggregate DDO. By selling assets, banks collectively can meet reserve requirements and restore their desired $r_e$ position without gaining additional reserves.

[9] However, as we show in the next chapter, $r_e$ behavior was a crucial factor in the great contraction of the money supply in the 1930s. This variable increased dramatically from 1932 to 1935, reaching 8 percent (.08) at the end of 1935. $r_e$ averaged approximately 6 percent from 1934 to 1938—a magnitude about 20 times its size in recent years.

**Figure 16-2** Money Supply Multiplier ($m_1$) Since 1984

The money supply multiplier fluctuates over time in response to changes in k, $r_r$, and $r_e$. The multiplier declined sharply after the late 1980s.

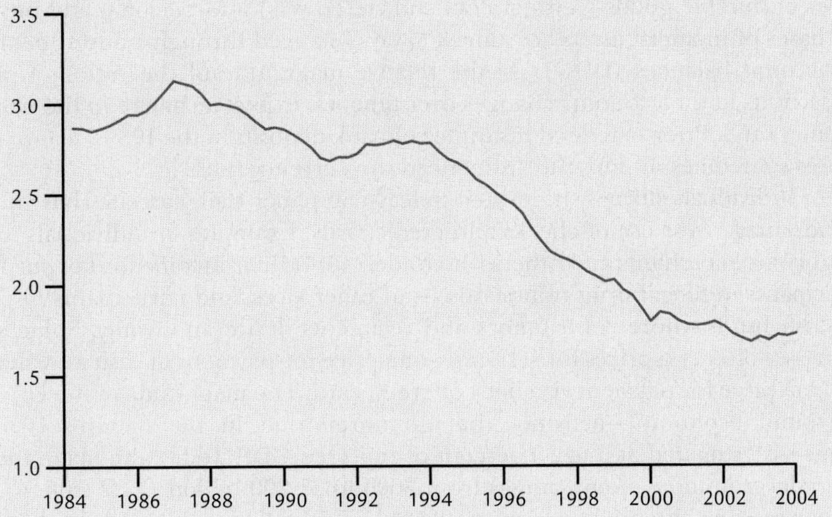

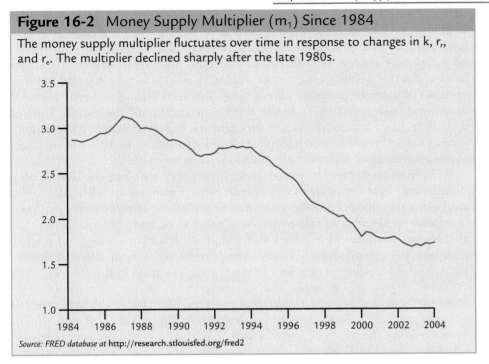

*Source: FRED database at* http://research.stlouisfed.org/fred2

ables, you will understand the causes of the major movements in the multiplier illustrated in this figure.[10]

## ANALYSIS OF THE VARIABLES k, $r_r$, AND $r_e$ UNDERLYING THE MONEY SUPPLY MULTIPLIER

Because the currency ratio, the reserve requirement ratio, and the desired excess reserve ratio influence the money supply multiplier and the money supply, you must understand the factors influencing each of the three variables. We now examine the fundamental determinants of k, $r_r$, and $r_e$.

### Currency Ratio (k)

Because the currency ratio is determined strictly by the public's preferences, the existing ratio of $C^P$ to DDO is largely a function of the costs and benefits of financing transactions with currency relative to the costs and benefits of financing transactions via demand deposits and other checkable accounts (DDO).

Certain considerations favor the use of currency over DDO. The use of currency is more convenient and saves time in small transactions. Also, nearly everyone has been unpleasantly insulted by having a personal check rejected as payment. This

[10] The figure illustrates the ratio of M1 to the monetary base published by the Board of Governors of the Federal Reserve System. The Federal Reserve Bank of St. Louis publishes another measure of the monetary base that adjusts the base for changes in $r_r$. These two measures of the base differ slightly; therefore, the corresponding money supply multipliers differ slightly. Both measures of the base are available at http://research.stlouisfed.org/fred2.

prospect increases as people travel to less familiar surroundings. Historically, the use of currency has escalated during travel and war. Currency is used heavily to finance purchases of inexpensive nondurable goods (candy bars and tennis balls) and inexpensive services (taxi rides and restaurant tips). On the other hand, purchases of durable goods (refrigerators and stereo sets) and personal and business purchases of financial assets are almost always financed through transfer of checking account balances (DDO). As the relative magnitude of the various types of transactions in the economy changes over time, we expect a change in the nation's currency ratio. Prior to federal insurance of bank deposits in the 1930s, fear of bank failures sometimes importantly influenced the currency ratio.

For individuals strongly motivated to leave no paper trail, currency has an obvious advantage over use of checks and credit cards. Examples of individuals in this category are merchants and others who underreport their income for tax purposes, participants in illegal drug transactions and other vices, and participants in political slush funds whose contributors and recipients desire anonymity. Some small businesses offer two prices for services—one price for payment in cash and another (higher) price for payment via check or credit card. The magnitude of the U.S. "underground economy"—activities that go unreported in the nation's GDP accounts—is estimated at 5 to 10 percent of reported GDP. Today, the magnitude of the underground economy ranges from $600 to $1,200 billion ($1.2 trillion). For obvious reasons, the use of currency is favored in the underground economy.

On the other hand, several considerations favor the use of checks, credit cards, and debit cards over the use of currency. Canceled checks and credit card receipts are evidence of payment in the event of claims to the contrary. The extensive list of deductible items in the Internal Revenue Service income tax code provides impor-

**Figure 16-3** U.S. Currency Ratio from 1914 to 2004

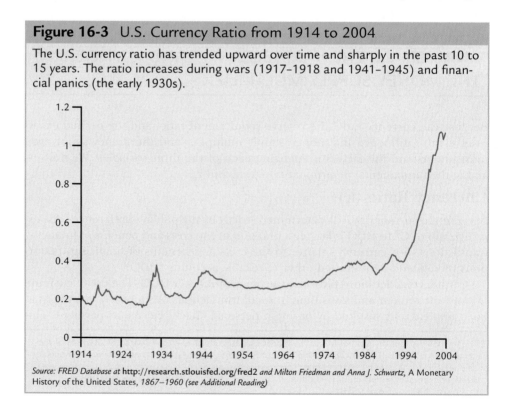

The U.S. currency ratio has trended upward over time and sharply in the past 10 to 15 years. The ratio increases during wars (1917–1918 and 1941–1945) and financial panics (the early 1930s).

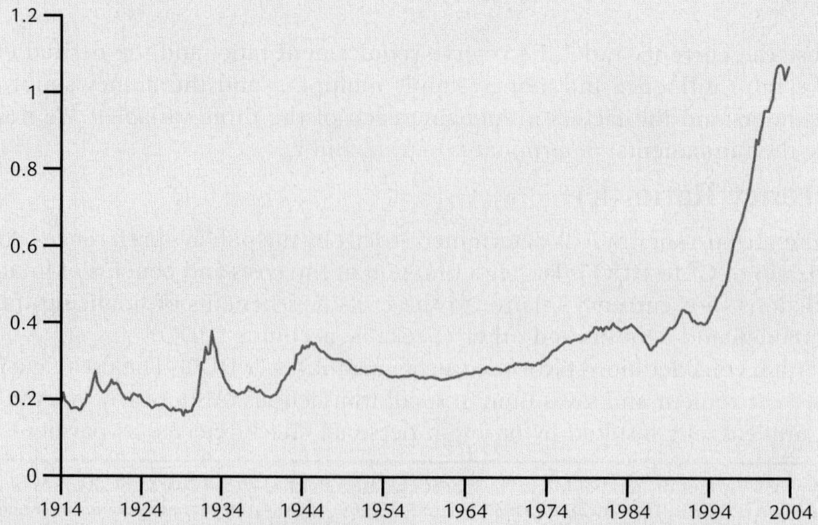


*Source: FRED Database at* http://research.stlouisfed.org/fred2 *and Milton Friedman and Anna J. Schwartz,* A Monetary History of the United States, *1867–1960 (see Additional Reading)*

**Exhibit 16-2** Where Is All That Currency?

In 1959, currency ($C^P$) made up 20 percent of M1 and DDO constituted 80 percent. Today, over half of M1 consists of currency. In 1959, on a per capita basis, currency averaged about $150 per person. Today, the figure exceeds $2,000 per person. Since 1959, currency has increased an average of more than 7 percent per year, while the growth rates for DDO and M1 have been approximately 3.5 percent and 5 percent per year, respectively. In view of the widespread increase in credit card and debit card use since 1959 to pay for transactions formerly rendered in cash, the growth of currency is remarkable. Where is all that currency today?

Some analysts' first reaction is to point to the growth of the "underground economy." The underground economy includes illegal activities, such as drug peddling and prostitution, and legal activities in which cash is used to prevent a paper trail and thereby facilitate tax evasion. Small businesses that employ part-time workers and households that employ "nannies" and gardeners often circumvent federal requirements to pay social security taxes and other worker benefits by simply paying the workers' wages in cash. The workers also benefit from such arrangements by underreporting their income for tax purposes. No one knows for sure the size of the underground economy. But the underground economy has been around for a long time, and this explanation for the tremendous growth of currency may be exaggerated.

A more plausible explanation for the robust growth of currency is foreign demand for U.S. dollars. U.S. banks must report to the government only cash withdrawals exceeding $10,000. The high ceiling facilitates large cash withdrawals from the United States. In 2004, U.S. troops in Iraq found a $600 million cache of U.S. currency. The Federal Reserve estimates that more than 50 percent of U.S. currency today resides outside the borders of the United States. Demand for U.S. dollars abroad stems from a search for stability. U.S. dollars are coveted from Latin American nations exhibiting a propensity toward hyperinflation to war-ravaged nations to former Soviet states. U.S. dollars are viewed as a "hard currency"—the public trusts U.S. dollars will retain value over time and therefore the U.S. dollars are accepted almost anywhere.

One implication of this phenomenon—the link between the reported U.S. money supply and domestic economic activity weakens to the extent that U.S. currency increasingly resides outside the United States. This hypothesis is consistent with the evidence from the past 25 years.

tant incentive for maintaining a record of many types of transactions. The safety factor also enters into the decision about the currency ratio (k). The use of checks and credit cards in purchasing relatively expensive items is partly attributable to the risk of loss or robbery where currency is involved. If you lose your checkbook or credit card, the probability of extensive loss is smaller than if you lose your wallet containing $800 in paper currency.

The history of the currency ratio in the United States since 1914 is illustrated in Figure 16-3.

## Specific Determinants of the Currency Ratio (k)

In analyzing k, recognize that changes in demand for DDO as well as changes in the public's demand for currency ($C^P$) result in changes in the currency ratio. With this fact in mind, we examine some of the specific factors accounting for the historical pattern of the currency ratio illustrated in Figure 16-3.

**Development of Substitutes for DDO.** The currency ratio is increased by factors reducing the public's demand for DDO. The spread of *substitutes* for DDO over the years has increased the currency ratio. The period after World War II witnessed tremendous growth in savings accounts offered by non-bank thrift institutions and the development of corporate and municipal bond markets, the stock market, and the U.S. government securities market. In the post-1960 era, the advent of money market mutual funds, bank repurchase agreements, sweep accounts, and numerous other instruments has induced the public to economize on DDO holdings relative to other financial assets. The opportunity cost of holding DDO increased as new alternatives came on stream, contributing to the general upward trend of the currency ratio in the past 50 years.

**Level of Income Tax Rates, the Underground Economy, and U.S. Currency Holdings Abroad.** The incentive to hide income depends on income tax rate levels. Income taxes were raised sharply during World War II (1940s). An increase in income tax rates increases the incentive to underreport income. Such behavior is facilitated by the use of currency instead of checks and credit cards. Part of the increase in k during past wars derives from the public's desire to hide income and avoid extremely high income tax levels in wartime. Another possible contributing cause of the post-1960 increase in k is the growth of such activities as drug peddling and other illicit activities. Given that the U.S. population includes fewer than 300 million people and that currency ($C^P$) today is more than $600 billion, we can see that *average* currency holdings comes to more than $2,000 per person in the United States. Only a very small portion of the population holds currency in such large amounts, so a major portion of $C^P$ is unaccounted for. A very large portion of $C^P$ is believed to reside outside U.S. borders (Exhibit 16-2).

**Level of Interest Rates.** An obvious (opportunity) cost of holding currency is the interest rate banks pay on DDO. An increase in interest rates payable on DDO reduces the currency ratio if other factors (including market interest rates) are held constant. However, if interest rates payable on DDO rise in line with interest rates in the market, the effect is more complicated. Assuming DDO are closer substitutes for interest-bearing financial instruments (Treasury bills, etc.) than are currency holdings, DDO is reduced relatively more than $C^P$ as market interest rates rise. Hence, an increase in market rates likely *increases* k, assuming rates payable on DDO move in line with interest rates in the open market.

**Level of Income and Wealth.** Expenditures on inexpensive consumer services and nondurable goods tend to be financed significantly with currency. Purchases of more expensive durable goods and services and financial assets are almost always paid for by transferring checking account balances. To understand the effect of income growth on k, you need to ascertain the income elasticity of demand for various types of goods and services. Growth of income and wealth boosts demand for durable goods and relatively expensive services and purchases of stocks, bonds, and mutual funds more than demand for nondurable goods such as candy bars and soda pop. This suggests that income growth increases the demand for DDO more than the demand for currency. In this event, income growth reduces k, other things being equal.

**Other Factors.** The age distribution of the population and other demographic considerations influence the currency ratio. For example, younger people exhibit a much higher currency ratio than older people. As demographic factors change over time, k changes accordingly. Historically, urban dwellers were more accustomed to using banks than were rural people, who relied more heavily on currency. The urbanization movement partially accounts for a long decline in k that occurred from the late nineteenth century to the 1930s. The public's confidence in banks can play a role in the currency ratio, as indicated by the dramatic increase in k during the early 1930s (review Figure 16-3). Once again, a major part of the increase in currency in recent years is attributable to expanded use of dollars abroad. Because of the U.S. dollar's stability and widespread acceptability, the U.S. dollar is increasingly favored as the medium of exchange in other nations, particularly those with relatively unstable governments.

## Importance of k in the Money Supply Multiplier

Figure 16-4 indicates the post-1984 behavior of k and $m_1$, the narrow money supply multiplier. The pattern of $m_1$ is almost a mirror image of k. k has been the most important determinant of the money supply multiplier in recent years. In particular, the persistent rise in k after the early 1990s accounts for most of the corresponding decline in the money supply multiplier.

## Determinants of the Required Reserve Ratio ($r_r$)

The required reserve ratio ($r_r$) is defined as the ratio of the dollar magnitude of required reserves ($R_r$) to total checkable deposits (DDO). The Federal Reserve has authority to impose reserve requirements on other bank liabilities (time deposits, negotiable CDs, eurodollar borrowings, and so forth) as well as on DDO. Over the past 50 years, the Fed has occasionally imposed reserve requirements on such non-DDO bank liabilities. At the present time, however, reserve requirements are levied only on DDO. $r_r$ today depends on the three reserve requirement percentages applicable to DDO (0 percent, 3 percent, and 10 percent). $r_r$ also depends on the DDO threshold levels at which the reserve requirements jump from 0 to 3 percent and from 3 to 10 percent ($6.6 million and $45.4 million, respectively, in 2004) and

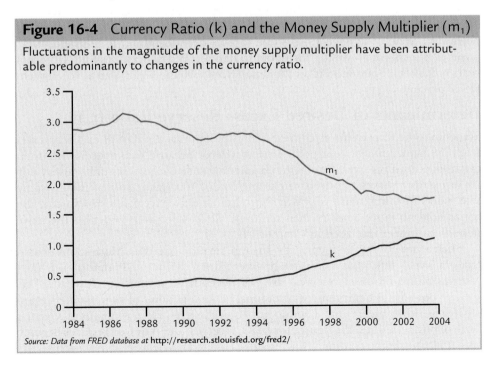

**Figure 16-4** Currency Ratio (k) and the Money Supply Multiplier ($m_1$)

Fluctuations in the magnitude of the money supply multiplier have been attributable predominantly to changes in the currency ratio.

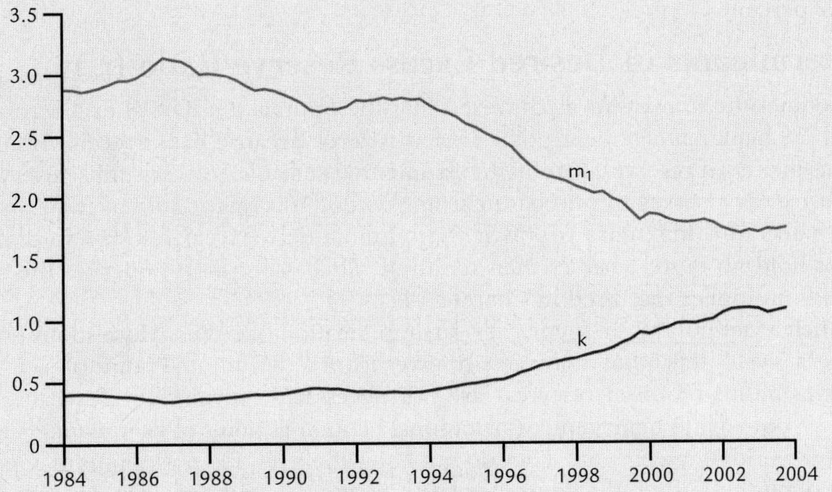


*Source: Data from FRED database at* http://research.stlouisfed.org/fred2/

the distribution among banks of deposits above and below these thresholds. Ignoring the lower threshold (assuming the 3 percent reserve requirement applies to all DDO up to the upper threshold), consider the following formulation:

$$\mathbf{R_r = \%RR_L \times DDO_L + \%RR_H \times DDO_H.}$$

The dollar magnitude of required reserves ($R_r$) equals the reserve requirement percentage for all DDO *below* the threshold ($\%RR_L$) times the amount of such deposits ($DDO_L$) plus the reserve requirement percentage for all DDO *above* the threshold ($\%RR_H$) times the amount of such deposits ($DDO_H$). Because $r_r$ is defined as the ratio of $R_r$ to DDO and because $DDO = DDO_L + DDO_H$, we can write:

$$\mathbf{r_r = \frac{\%RR_L \times DDO_L + \%RR_H \times DDO_H}{DDO_L + DDO_H}}.$$

To simplify, we divide both top and bottom of the expression by $DDO_L$ and obtain:

$$\mathbf{r_r = \frac{\%RR_L + \%RR_H \times Z}{1 + Z}},$$

where $Z = DDO_H/DDO_L$. In this formulation, Z is $DDO_H/DDO_L$, the ratio of deposits in the banking system above the threshold to deposits below the threshold. The variable Z represents the relative *weights* to be accorded the two classifications of deposits in computing $r_r$. The Fed sets $\%RR_L$ (currently 3 percent) and $\%RR_H$ (currently 10 percent). But Z is determined by the allocation of deposits among banks of different sizes. Because Z fluctuates over time, $r_r$ also fluctuates slightly even while the two reserve requirements set by the Fed are fixed. The Fed occasionally changes reserve requirements ($\%RR_L$ and $\%RR_H$), precipitating sharp changes in $r_r$.

The behavior of $r_r$ from 1984 to 2004 is illustrated in Figure 16-5. Note the strong downward spikes in the ratio in 1990 and 1992. The spikes are due to reductions in reserve requirements implemented by the Federal Reserve. The slight downward trend in $r_r$ since 1992 is due to a modest decline in Z, the ratio of deposits in the system above the threshold to deposits below the threshold. In recent years $r_r$ has been bounded within the range from 0.065 to 0.072, that is, 6.5 percent to 7.2 percent.

## Determinants of Desired Excess Reserve Ratio ($r_e$)

Sometimes the impression is conveyed that the optimal amount of excess reserves from the bank management point of view is zero. Because banks receive no interest payments on reserves, you might assume that sensible bankers utilize every dollar of excess reserves to purchase earning assets. You might (mistakenly) assume that banks only maximize profits if they eliminate all excess reserves so that the banks hold no more reserves than required. This assumption underlies the naive deposit multiplier discussed in Chapter 14.

Such a viewpoint is an incorrect oversimplification of reality. More sophisticated analysis reveals that what are excess reserves from a definitional point of view (i.e., reserves minus required reserves) are not necessarily "surplus" or "excessive" reserves from a bank management or rational economic point of view. Bankers operate in a world of uncertainty. They do not know their reserve position until after the close of business, when the figures for DDO, reserves, and required reserves become available. Checks are continually being deposited to and cleared against each bank's

**Figure 16-5** Weighted Reserve Requirement Ratio ($r_r$)

$r_r$ is lower today than in the 1980s, largely due to reductions in reserve requirements implemented by the Federal Reserve in 1990 and 1992.

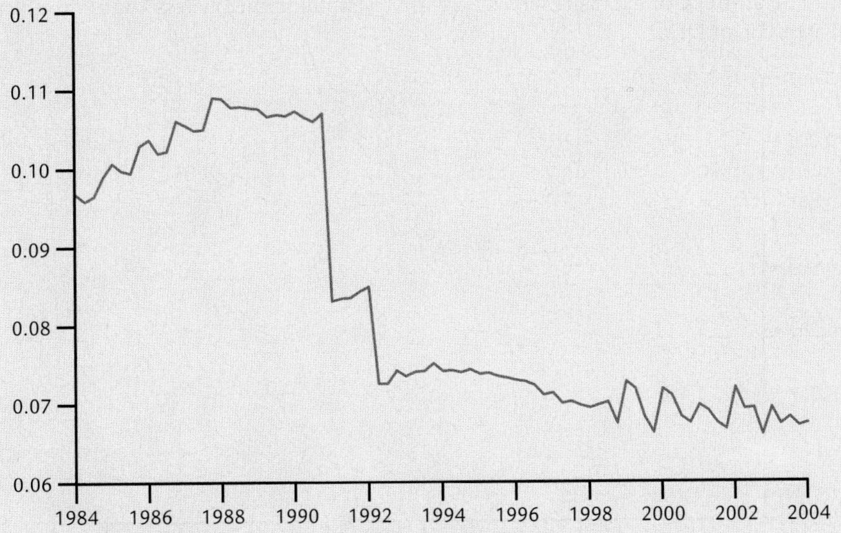

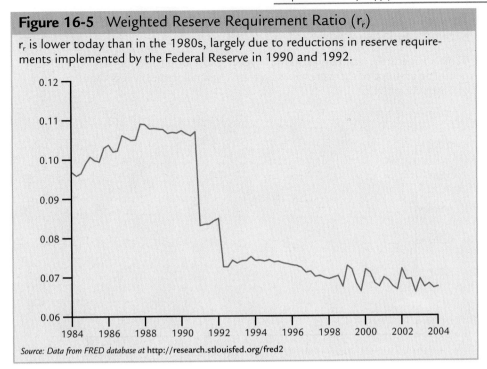

*Source: Data from FRED database at* http://research.stlouisfed.org/fred2

reserve account with the Federal Reserve during the day. Also, currency is continually being deposited and withdrawn from banks during banking hours. Such transactions have a dollar-for-dollar effect on bank reserves. The bank's position at the close of the business day determines whether the bank meets the Fed's reserve requirements. Banks are uncertain of that position until after the bank closes.

Based on past experience, the manager of the bank's reserve position likely has a "feel" for the bank's reserve position in a probabilistic sense. However, managers are not clairvoyant. If the bank comes up short of reserves as a result of larger-than-expected adverse check clearings or currency withdrawals, costs are involved. The bank must sell off securities, "buy" federal funds (that is, borrow excess reserve deposits of other banks at the Fed), or borrow from the Federal Reserve to meet reserve requirements. Transactions costs and other costs are associated with such operations.

In deciding upon the optimal $r_e$ level, bank management must strike a reasonable balance between the opposing costs. The cost of holding excess reserves—an *opportunity cost*—is the interest income forgone. The cost of attempting to get by with potentially inadequate reserves includes the transactions costs and other costs associated with adjusting to frequent reserve deficiencies. Given this general framework, we turn to some specific factors influencing $r_e$. The pattern of $r_e$ since 1984 is illustrated in Figure 16-6.

**Federal Funds Rate or Treasury Bill Yield.** The federal funds market and the Treasury bill market are outlets for adjusting the bank reserve position. Banks with excess reserves often use the reserves to lend in the fed funds market or to purchase Treasury bills. Banks with inadequate reserves typically borrow fed funds or sell Treasury bills. Therefore, the federal funds rate and Treasury bill yield are good indicators of the opportunity cost of holding excess reserves. Holding other factors con-

**Figure 16-6** Behavior of the Desired Excess Reserve Ratio ($r_e$) from 1984 to 2004

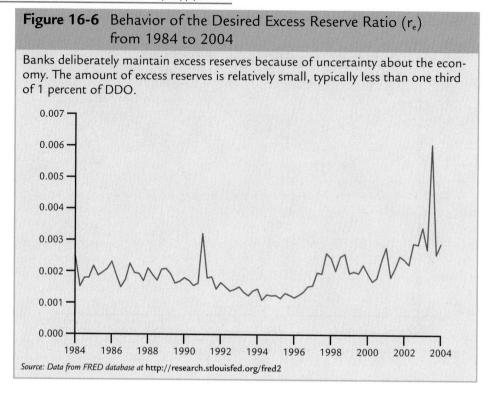

Banks deliberately maintain excess reserves because of uncertainty about the economy. The amount of excess reserves is relatively small, typically less than one third of 1 percent of DDO.

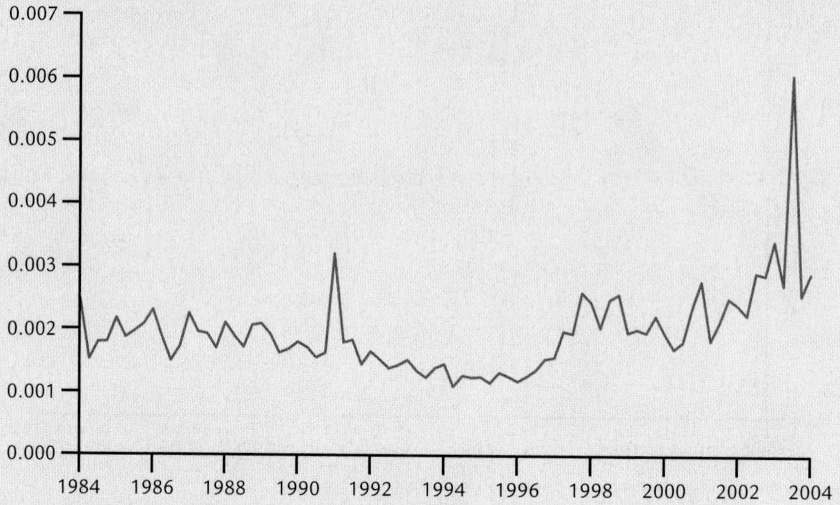


*Source: Data from FRED database at* http://research.stlouisfed.org/fred2

stant, we expect an increase in the fed funds rate and Treasury bill yield to reduce $r_e$. When the fed funds rate and Treasury bill yield decline, the demand for excess reserves increases. In Figure 16-6, the magnitude of $r_e$ was higher in the 1998 to 2004 period of low interest rates than in the 1984 to 1996 period of higher rates.[11]

**Variability of Deposit and Currency Flows.** The prospect of a bank incurring reserve deficiencies depends on the variability of check clearings and currency deposits and withdrawals. If variability increases, the likelihood of a bank becoming reserves deficient increases. Bank exposure to reserve deficiencies increases unless the bank increases the amount of excess reserves on hand. Thus, you expect $r_e$ levels to be higher for banks that experience sharp fluctuations in deposit flows and currency deposits and withdrawals than for banks with more stable reserve positions.

**Expected Federal Reserve Policy.** Bankers react not only to *current* financial conditions but also to *expected* financial and monetary phenomena. If bankers perceive that the economy is moving into a period of increasing inflationary pressures, they expect the Federal Reserve will implement restrictive monetary measures boosting interest rates and restraining economic activity. A prudent bank, anticipating the Fed's restrictive measures, will tighten its lending standards and move its asset structure into a more liquid position. This includes increasing the bank's excess reserve ratio ($r_e$).

[11] A longer-term decline in $r_e$ dating to 1960 (not shown in the figure) can be attributed to financial market developments that have reduced transactions costs in adjusting bank reserve positions. For example, the development of the federal funds market in the 1960s reduced $r_e$. The federal funds market reduced the cost to banks of reserve deficiencies by providing access to a reliable and inexpensive source of funds for banks when needed. In a similar vein, the development of the Treasury bill market and the commercial paper market contributed to a longer-term downward trend in banks' excess reserve positions.

## SUMMARY

The money supply multiplier links the monetary base (B), controlled by the central bank, to the nation's stock of money (M1 and M2). The size of the money supply multiplier changes in response to changes in the currency ratio (k), the average weighted reserve requirement ratio ($r_r$), and banks' desired excess reserve ratio ($r_e$). Because k and $r_e$, in turn, are affected by fundamental economic variables such as interest rates, income, and wealth, these economic variables influence the money supply multiplier and the nation's money supply. In this sense, the money supply is an *endogenous variable,* influenced in the short run by economic forces other than Federal Reserve actions. An important issue in monetary economics involves the stability and predictability of the money supply multiplier. The relative importance of changes in B, k, $r_r$, and $r_e$ in explaining actual historical changes in the supply of money has been documented. Viewed from a long-run perspective, changes in the money supply have resulted predominantly from changes in the monetary base, which is under Federal Reserve control. From a shorter-range perspective, however, changes in the money supply multiplier have at times been more important than changes in the monetary base in accounting for weekly, monthly, and quarterly changes in the money supply. Changes in the currency ratio (k) have been the most important cause of fluctuations in the multiplier during the past 100 years. These findings are *factual* and not subject to serious dispute. However, the evidence from the past does not settle the issue of the *potential* capacity of the Federal Reserve to accurately control the money supply on a weekly, monthly, or quarterly basis if the Fed desires to do so. In recent years, the Fed has not attempted to hit specific money-supply targets. Since the early 1980s, the Fed has instead been preoccupied with controlling short-term interest rates. Economists disagree about the extent to which the Fed's ability to control the monetary base from week to week translates into a similar capacity to exert short-term control over the nation's money supply. Some economists believe short-term movements in the money supply have important implications. Other economists are dubious of this assertion. All economists agree that the longer-term trend of money growth is more important than week-to-week fluctuations, and economists universally agree that the Federal Reserve is responsible for long-term money growth.

## YOUR TURN ANSWERS

PAGE 366

The currency ratio (k) = \$700 billion/\$800 billion = 0.875. The desired excess reserve ratio ($r_e$) = \$1 billion/\$800 billion = 0.00125, and $r_r$ = 0.08. The money supply multiplier can be computed in two ways: by using Equation (16-12) or by simply taking M1/B. Using the M1/B method, the money supply (M1) = \$1,500 billion (\$1.5 trillion). The base = \$65 billion + \$700 billion = \$765 billion. The money supply multiplier ($m_1$) is \$1,500 billion/\$765 billion, or 1.96. Using the Equation (16-12) method, the multiplier is (1 + 0.875)/(0.08 + 0.00125 + 0.875) = 1.96. Both methods yield the same answer.

## KEY TERMS

required reserve ratio ($r_r$)
desired excess reserve ratio ($r_e$)
currency ratio (k)

# STUDY QUESTIONS

1. Write an equation that expresses the money supply multiplier for M1 in terms of its three determinants. Define each of the three variables and explain intuitively why a *decrease* in each of the three variables produces an *increase* in the money supply multiplier.

2. Suppose you are given the following data:
   A. DDO = \$900 billion
   B. $C^P$ = \$600 billion
   C. Reserve requirements for all DDO = 8 percent
   D. Actual reserves = \$73 billion

   Compute k, $r_r$, $r_e$, and $m_1$. Now, suppose k falls to 0.50. Compute the new multiplier. Compute the new multiplier if $r_r$ falls to 7 percent (use k = 0.50).

3. Compare the simple deposit expansion multiplier presented in Chapter 14 with the more sophisticated multiplier developed in this chapter. Explain *intuitively* why the naive multiplier is larger than the sophisticated one developed in this chapter. Begin your analysis by assuming the Fed injects \$1 billion of new reserves into the banks by open market purchases.

4. Suppose that the Fed's reserve requirements for $DDO_L$ and $DDO_H$ are 3 percent and 10 percent, respectively, and that the magnitude of DDO above the threshold is twice as large as the magnitude of DDO below the threshold. Compute both Z (the weight accorded to DDO above the threshold relative to those below the threshold) and $r_r$. Now, suppose DDO above the threshold rise to three times those below the threshold due to mergers of several small banks. Compute the new Z and $r_r$.

5. What actions can the Federal Reserve take to reduce the magnitude of the money supply multiplier without causing a decline in M1?

6. Suppose the U.S. government enacts legislation legalizing the sale and purchase of marijuana, cocaine, and heroin. What would happen to k? What would happen to $m_1$ and M1? What must the Federal Reserve do to keep the money supply from changing in response to this legislation?

7. Analyze the factors influencing the currency ratio (k). What would likely happen to the magnitude of k if:
   A. Congress implements restrictions making money market mutual funds less attractive
   B. Congress abolishes the income tax
   C. The proportion of the U.S. population under age 20 years decreases sharply
   D. Banks adopt universal overdraft facilities, making low-interest loans automatically available to all depositors in the event of overdrawing of DDO accounts

8. Analyze the factors influencing the banks' desired excess reserve ratio ($r_e$). Explain what would happen to the magnitude of $r_e$ if:
   A. The Fed surprises financial markets by sharply boosting the discount rate
   B. The FDIC reduces the deposit insurance ceiling from \$100,000 to \$1,000
   C. Short-term interest rates rise sharply
   D. The economy slumps into a Japanese-style deflationary spiral

9. Suppose the Fed aggressively increases the monetary base (B) to stimulate economic activity. Assume short-term yields decline. Is there any reason to believe this action might induce a change in the magnitude of the money supply multiplier ($m_1$)? Explain.

10. What kind of factors could produce a sustained decline in the currency ratio in the next decade? Explain.

11. "If the Federal Reserve abolished all reserve requirements, the money supply multiplier would be *infinite*—that is, there would be no limit to the expansion of DDO." Critique this statement.

12. Focusing on the behavior of $r_e$, explain why the money supply tends to expand during the economic expansion phase of the business cycle even though the Federal Reserve is holding the monetary base constant.

13. Why might the reported U.S. currency ratio (k) increase in times of political crises in foreign nations?

# ADDITIONAL READING

- The acknowledged pioneer of the monetary base–money supply multiplier framework was Karl Brunner, formerly a professor at UCLA, Ohio State University, and the University of Rochester. For a highly sophisticated (graduate school level) analysis, see Karl Brunner and Allan Meltzer, "Liquidity Traps for Money, Bank Credit, and Interest Rates," *Journal of Political Economy,* January/February 1968. Entire books devoted to the money supply process include Albert Burger, *The Money Supply Process* (Belmont, CA: Wadsworth, 1971), Ralph Bryant, *Controlling Money* (Washington: The Brookings Institution, 1983), and Laurence H. Meyer, ed., *Improving Money Stock Control* (Boston: Kluwer-Nijhoff, 1983). Pertinent empirical articles include Peter Frost, "Short-Run Fluctuations in the Money Multiplier and Monetary Control," *Journal of Money, Credit, and Banking,* February 1977, pp. 165–181, and Robert H. Rasche, "Predicting the Money Supply Multiplier," *Journal of Monetary Economics,* July 1979, pp. 301–25. Also see M. Garfinkel and D.L. Thornton, "The Multiplier Approach to the Money Supply Process: A Precautionary Note," Federal Reserve Bank of St. Louis *Review,* July/August 1991, pp. 47–64.
- On the currency ratio, an important early historical work is Phillip Cagan, *Determinants and Effects of Changes in the Money Stock, 1875–1960* (New York: Columbia University Press, 1965), especially Chapter 4.
- On the role of the underground economy, see Peter Gutmann, "The Subterranean Economy," *Financial Analysts Journal,* November/December 1977, pp. 26–34.
- The classic work on the history of the U.S. money supply and its determinants is Milton Friedman and Anna J. Schwartz, *A Monetary History of the United States, 1867–1960* (Princeton, NJ: Princeton University Press, 1963).

Chapter 17

# THE ROLE OF THE FEDERAL RESERVE IN THE GREAT DEPRESSION OF 1929 TO 1933

Without question, the Great Depression of the 1930s was the worst economic catastrophe in U.S. history. The sheer terror visited upon families by the disaster cannot be expressed in numbers, but the general dimensions of the depression can be sketched with a few pertinent facts. From fall 1929 to spring 1933, the nation's output (gross domestic product [GDP]) fell approximately 50 percent in nominal terms and 30 percent in real terms. The contraction in real GDP was about ten times larger than the most severe post-1930s U.S. economic downturn. Industrial production fell by half. The unemployment rate rose from 3 percent to 25 percent. Stock prices lost more than 85 percent of their value. Approximately 9,000 banks failed, impairing the savings of millions of families. The nation's money supply fell by roughly 30 percent. The price level (consumer price index) fell by 25 percent. Business failures and farm and home foreclosures soared. The great majority of Americans experienced a substantial decline in their standard of living. Over the entire decade of the 1930s, the nation's unemployment rate averaged 18 percent. The unemployment rate did not fall below 10 percent until 1941. Table 17-1 lists some of the important indicators of general macroeconomic conditions in the United States from 1928 to 1938.

**Table 17-1** Key Macroeconomic Indicators from 1928 to 1938

| | Nominal GNP ($ Billion) | Real GNP ($ Billion) | Unemployment Rate (Percent) | Stock Prices* | Bank Failures | Consumer Price Index |
|---|---|---|---|---|---|---|
| 1928 | $98.2 | $98.2 | 4.2% | 153 | 498 | 100.0 |
| 1929 | 104.4 | 104.4 | 3.2 | 201 | 659 | 100.0 |
| 1930 | 91.1 | 95.1 | 8.7 | 161 | 1350 | 97.4 |
| 1931 | 76.3 | 89.5 | 15.9 | 100 | 2293 | 88.7 |
| 1932 | 58.5 | 76.4 | 23.6 | 36 | 1453 | 79.7 |
| 1933 | 56.0 | 74.2 | 24.9 | 79 | 4000 | 75.4 |
| 1934 | 65.0 | 80.8 | 21.7 | 78 | 57 | 78.0 |
| 1935 | 72.5 | 91.4 | 20.1 | 80 | 34 | 80.1 |
| 1936 | 82.7 | 100.9 | 16.9 | 112 | 44 | 80.9 |
| 1937 | 90.8 | 109.1 | 14.3 | 120 | 59 | 83.8 |
| 1938 | 85.2 | 103.2 | 19.0 | 80 | 54 | 82.3 |

*Index of common stock prices for June of each year; 1935 to 1939 = 100.

*Sources: U.S. Department of Commerce,* Historical Statistics of the United States; *Board of Governors of the Federal Reserve System,* Banking and Monetary Statistics *(Washington, DC: National Capital Press, 1943)*

What was the Federal Reserve's role in this economic catastrophe? Should the Fed be held accountable for the fiasco? Or was the Fed an innocent bystander lacking the power to stop the cascade of events that brought down the country? Economists strongly disagree on this issue. In this chapter we examine the diverse viewpoints on the Federal Reserve's role in America's greatest depression. The debate centers on the Federal Reserve's accountability for the behavior of the money supply in the early 1930s and the importance of the money supply in determining economic conditions. Some economists claim the experience of the 1930s illustrates the lack of importance of monetary forces. Other economists insist the episode demonstrates the crucial importance of money in the economy.

## DEBATE OVER THE CAUSES OF THE GREAT DEPRESSION

In explaining the causes of the Great Depression, almost all economists emphasize the role of negative shocks to the nation's aggregate demand for goods and services. The negative shocks reduced real output and the nation's general price level. Some scholars emphasize negative shocks originating from non-monetary sources. For example, economists point to the stock market crash and the blow to consumer confidence caused by devastated financial wealth, an important force pushing down the nation's consumption expenditures. They argue that the nation's 1920s construction boom indicated a significant building decline inevitably would follow.[1] Indeed, in 1933, expenditures on residential structures amounted to only 15 percent of similar expenditures in 1929! Gross investment expenditures on structures and business plants and equipment declined from more than $14 billion in 1929 to less than $3 billion in 1933. Furthermore, *fiscal policy*—federal government tax and expenditure policy—became contractionary in the 1930s. The Revenue Act of 1932 actually raised taxes at a time of massive unemployment! Also, a major contraction in exports resulted partly from the worldwide movement toward economic nationalism triggered by enactment of the infamous Smoot-Hawley Tariff Act of 1930. Non-monetarist economists emphasize that all of these factors were largely unrelated to the Federal Reserve's monetary policy.

Monetarist economists disagree, laying the blame squarely on monetary factors and the Federal Reserve System. In the monetarist view, a normal business cycle contraction was converted into the catastrophe of the Great Depression by the collapse of the nation's banking system and the supply of money. These developments were triggered by banking panics and exacerbated by a series of Federal Reserve blunders. In this view, the Federal Reserve caused the precipitous contraction in the money supply by not acting as "lender of last resort" and by committing a series of other key mistakes. The contraction of the money supply, in turn, accounts for the severe *deflation*—the persistent decline in the nation's general price level. Deflation in the early 1930s set in motion the widespread defaults on business, farm, and household debt that in turn led to the wave of bank failures and the denial of credit to legitimate customers.

We must study the facts more carefully before we can weigh these two opposing points of view. In the next section we look closely at what actually happened to banks and the key monetary variables during the Great Depression.

---

[1] Think about the buildings on your campus, for example. Unless your campus is new, chances are many of the buildings were erected in the 1920s. Few buildings date from the 1930s.

# INTERNATIONAL PERSPECTIVES

## Worldwide Nature of the Great Depression

The Great Depression of the early 1930s was worldwide in scope. None of the major industrial nations escaped the disaster. At least ten countries experienced industrial output contractions of more than 30 percent. The accompanying figure indicates the pattern of industrial production in the world and in four major nations, using annual data from 1927 to 1935. In the figure, the index for each country is based on 1929 = 100. Industrial production peaked in 1929 in all nations. The ensuing relative contraction in industrial production, both in the first year of the depression and from peak to trough (1929–1932), was larger in the United States and Germany than elsewhere around the world. Scholars believe the Great Depression was more severe in the United States and Germany than in any other country.

The causes of the Great Depression are complex. However, the current consensus indicates the *initial* U.S. downturn in 1929 was triggered by restrictive Federal Reserve actions initiated in early 1928 in response to the perceived bubble in U.S. stock prices. As a result of the Fed's restrictive actions, nominal and real U.S. interest rates increased sharply in 1928 and led to a contraction in interest-sensitive expenditures. Building permit applications in 1929 declined by more than 20 percent from peak 1928 levels, and U.S. industrial production peaked in mid-1929. Contrary to popular belief, the U.S. economic downturn began several months before the October 1929 stock market crash.

Powerful forces transmit business cycles across national borders. A U.S. economic downturn reduces U.S. demand for European exports, thereby spreading the U.S. economic recession to European nations. A decline in European output and income feeds back to the United States, reducing European demand for U.S. exports and spreading weakness to the United States. The facts that U.S. exports in the 1920s amounted to less than 6 percent of U.S. GDP and that U.S. exports continued to ex-

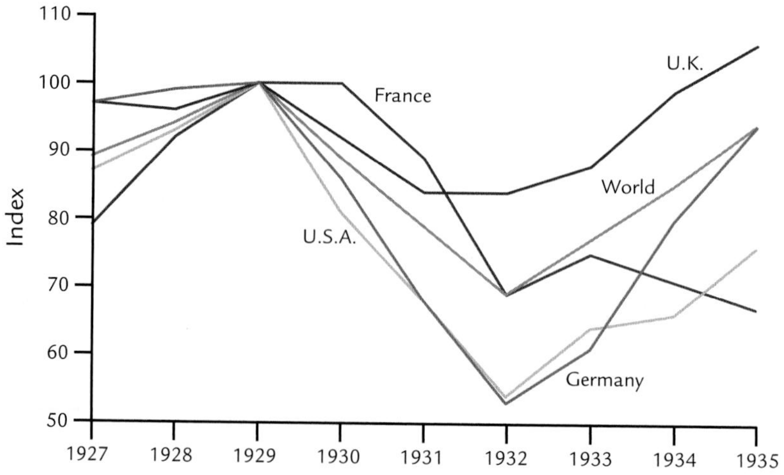

## INTERNATIONAL PERSPECTIVES —*continued*

pand in 1929 suggest the Great Depression did not begin abroad and spread to the United States. A more plausible explanation is that the initial U.S. downturn was transmitted to the rest of the world through two major channels. First, the decline in U.S. income reduced demand for foreign goods. Second, and more importantly, the early portion of the depression was transmitted to the rest of the world in large part through the gold standard. Because gold stocks of foreign nations already were low in the late 1920s, increased U.S. interest rates in 1928 and 1929 forced foreign central banks to boost their own interest rates, hoping to prevent an outflow of financial capital and gold to the United States.

Why was the U.S. contraction deeper than elsewhere? At least three important factors contributed. First, the run-up in stock prices and real investment spending in the United States in the 1920s was larger than elsewhere, leading to a greater "bust" when the "boom" inevitably ended. Second, the number of bank failures and the ensuing loss of wealth, contraction in the money supply, and decline in consumer and business confidence were greater in the United States because foreign banks had more diversified asset portfolios than their U.S. counterparts (most of the U.S. banks that failed were small-town banks with heavy dependence on agricultural loans). Third, unlike Britain and other nations that experienced relatively mild depressions, the United States did not abandon the gold standard until 1933. Britain left the gold standard in 1931, thereby freeing up monetary policy to concentrate on domestic economic problems.

## BANK FAILURES AND MONETARY PHENOMENA: THE FACTS

In this section, we examine certain indisputable facts about bank failures and money supply phenomena. In the following section, we examine the economists' differing interpretations explaining these facts.

### Bank Failures and the Run on Banks

To understand the Great Depression of the 1930s, you must look at the American bank experience in the 1920s. Agriculture played a much more important role in the U.S. economy in the 1920s than it does today. The period from the 1880s to World War I was a "golden age" for agriculture, but the 1920s were a time of considerable distress for farmers. From 1920 to 1921, farm prices declined severely, falling by more than 50 percent on average. Prices of agricultural products recovered somewhat from their lows of 1921, but the 1920s was a decade of falling agricultural prices throughout the world. Farm profits fell, pulling down farm values. Thousands of farmers who had purchased land with borrowed money in the decade prior to 1920 became victims of the falling agricultural prices. These farmers lost their properties through bank foreclosures in the 1920s.

The 1920s decline in agricultural prices that caused farm foreclosures also weakened the balance sheets of thousands of rural banks that had extended loans to farmers. Bank failures were surprisingly frequent in the 1920s given the nation's general prosperity. An average of nearly 600 banks per year failed through the 1920s. These failed banks were located predominantly in the nation's agricultural regions. Almost half of the bank failures of the 1920s occurred in the seven-state north central region of the Great Plains, extending from Kansas and Missouri northward through the Dakotas and Minnesota. Figure 17-1 shows the number of bank failures in the United States each year from 1916 to 1929.

More than 5,800 banks failed in the 1920s, yet their failures did not lead to *contagion effects,* in which serious problems of a few banks set off a mad dash by the public to withdraw cash from other banks. The bank failures of the 1930s, however, were a different story. These failures came in four waves. The first wave began in October 1930. In the Midwest and South, a series of bank failures touched off panic. As fear about the condition of the nation's banking system spread across the country, people began converting their bank deposits into currency. This phenomenon continued into December, when the Bank of United States failed. The Bank of United States failure was especially significant for two reasons. First, the Bank of United States was the largest bank ever to fail in the nation. Second, the bank's name caused some people to conclude (incorrectly) that a huge bank associated with the U.S. government had failed. This uncertainty added to the atmosphere of pandemonium.

The crisis subsided in the winter of early 1931, only to resume again in the spring (the second wave). In May, a major Austrian bank—the Kreditanstalt—failed. The failure of the Kreditanstalt shocked depositors around the world. Shortly thereafter, England abandoned the gold standard in September 1931. The resulting scramble

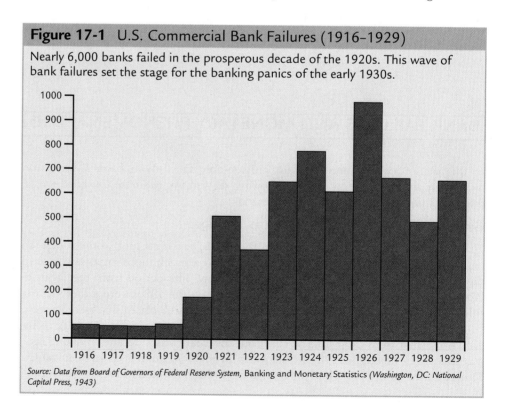

**Figure 17-1** U.S. Commercial Bank Failures (1916–1929)

Nearly 6,000 banks failed in the prosperous decade of the 1920s. This wave of bank failures set the stage for the banking panics of the early 1930s.

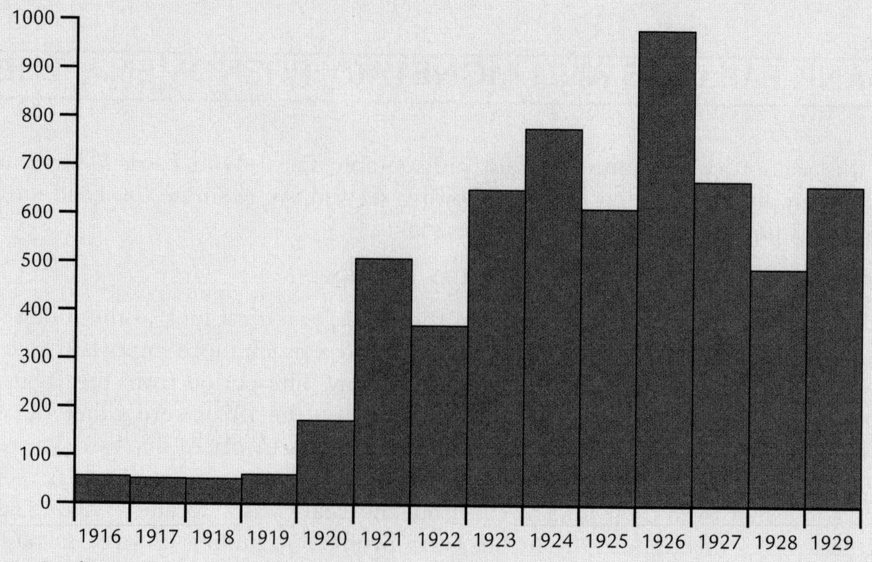


*Source: Data from Board of Governors of Federal Reserve System,* Banking and Monetary Statistics *(Washington, DC: National Capital Press, 1943)*

by foreign nations to convert dollars into gold at the U.S. Treasury caused the Federal Reserve to raise its discount rate by two full percentage points. This dramatic increase came at a time when the U.S. unemployment rate exceeded 15 percent. These events contributed to the crisis atmosphere in which the third run on American banks occurred in the fall of 1931.

The fourth and final panic occurred in early 1933. The weakened condition of the banks after years of price level deflation, the uncertainty associated with the incoming and untested administration of President Franklin D. Roosevelt (FDR), and the general atmosphere of fear produced this final destructive crisis. In the 4 years from 1930 to 1933, more than 9,000 banks in the United States were suspended. In 1933 alone, 4,000 banks failed. On March 6, FDR's third day in office, a "banking holiday" was declared—all banks were closed for 1 week. The public was informed that all banks would be inspected and only the sound banks permitted to reopen. More fundamentally, Congress established the Federal Deposit Insurance Corporation to provide nationwide insurance of bank deposits. For the remainder of the decade (1934–1939), bank failures numbered fewer than 60 in each year (review Table 17-1).

The banking panics of the early 1930s played a key role in the severe contraction in the U.S. money supply.

## Causes of Contraction in the Money Supply

To understand the role of monetary factors in the Great Depression, you must examine some key monetary data. Table 17-2 shows the behavior of the money supply,

**Table 17-2 Monetary Variables During the Great Depression**

| | M1 ($Billion) | B ($Billion) | $m_1$ | k | $r_r$ | $r_e$ |
|---|---|---|---|---|---|---|
| December 1928 | $26.7 | 7.08 | 3.77 | .155 | .105 | −.002 |
| June 1929 | 26.2 | 6.82 | 3.84 | .161 | .104 | .001 |
| December 1929 | 26.4 | 6.94 | 3.80 | .156 | .107 | −.003 |
| June 1930 | 25.1 | 6.62 | 3.79 | .155 | .110 | .000 |
| December 1930 | 24.6 | 7.07 | 3.48 | .172 | .113 | .005 |
| June 1931 | 23.5 | 6.92 | 3.40 | .184 | .116 | .004 |
| December 1931 | 21.9 | 7.32 | 2.99 | .257 | .114 | −.002 |
| June 1932 | 20.2 | 7.39 | 2.73 | .296 | .116 | .010 |
| December 1932 | 20.4 | 7.90 | 2.58 | .297 | .123 | .037 |
| June 1933 | 19.2 | 7.72 | 2.49 | .330 | .126 | .033 |
| December 1933 | 19.8 | 8.25 | 2.40 | .318 | .124 | .057 |
| June 1934 | 21.4 | 9.21 | 2.32 | .279 | .126 | .104 |
| December 1934 | 23.1 | 9.64 | 2.40 | .252 | .124 | .098 |
| June 1935 | 25.2 | 10.55 | 2.39 | .234 | .126 | .118 |
| December 1935 | 27.0 | 11.47 | 2.35 | .222 | .124 | .128 |
| June 1936 | 29.0 | 11.87 | 2.44 | .220 | .122 | .114 |
| December 1936 | 31.0 | 13.15 | 2.36 | .217 | .182 | .078 |
| June 1937 | 30.7 | 13.35 | 2.30 | .218 | .239 | .035 |
| December 1937 | 29.6 | 13.58 | 2.18 | .235 | .243 | .051 |
| June 1938 | 29.7 | 14.48 | 2.05 | .223 | .211 | .118 |
| December 1938 | 31.8 | 15.58 | 2.04 | .222 | .212 | .123 |

*Source: Computed from data in Board of Governors of the Federal Reserve System,* Banking and Monetary Statistics *(Washington, DC: National Capital Press, 1943)*

the monetary base, the money supply multiplier, and the multiplier's determining elements (k, $r_r$, and $r_e$) from the end of 1928 to the end of 1938.[2]

The immediate cause of contraction in the money supply was the collapse of the money supply multiplier ($m_1$). Between the end of 1929 and the end of 1933, $m_1$ fell by more than 35 percent. In the same period, the transactions measure of money (M1) fell from $26.4 billion to $19.8 billion, a decline of 25 percent. The monetary base increased by approximately 19 percent in the same period. The collapse of the money supply multiplier was triggered by the dramatic increase in the currency ratio (k), which resulted from banking panics in which the public withdrew large amounts of cash from their bank deposits. (Remember that federal deposit insurance did not yet exist.) In the latter half of 1933 and in 1934, as the banking panic subsided and the currency ratio declined, bank holdings of excess reserves (and $r_e$) climbed sharply. Excess reserves even exceeded required reserves during a portion of 1935. In other words, banks were holding more than twice as many reserves as required by the Fed! The sharp increases in both k and $r_e$ produced the precipitous contraction in the money supply multiplier in the 1930s.[3] Figure 17-2 illustrates the behavior of the two crucial variables accounting for the money supply collapse.

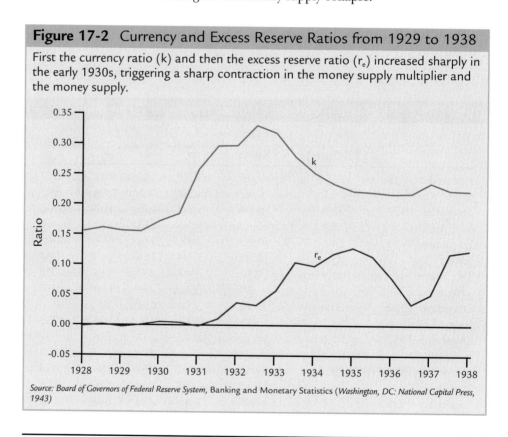

**Figure 17-2** Currency and Excess Reserve Ratios from 1929 to 1938

First the currency ratio (k) and then the excess reserve ratio ($r_e$) increased sharply in the early 1930s, triggering a sharp contraction in the money supply multiplier and the money supply.

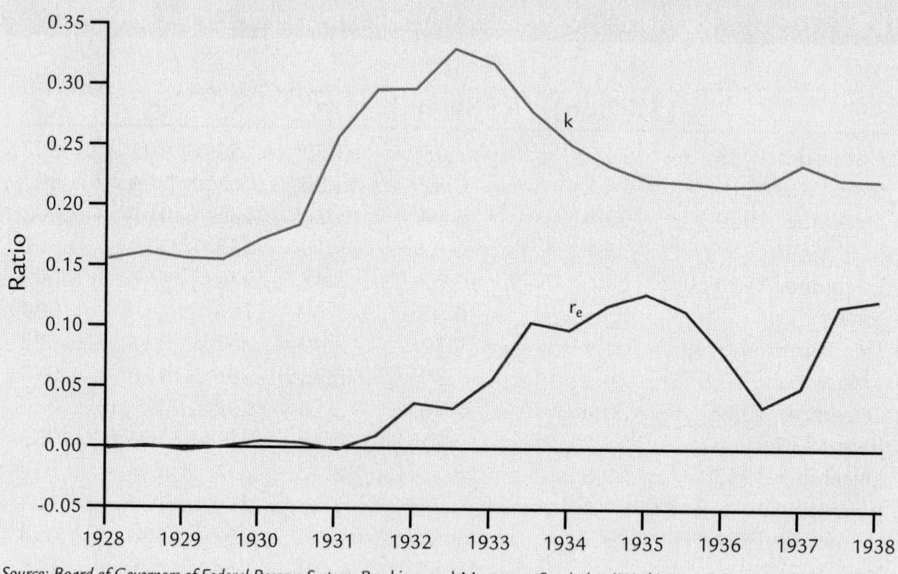


*Source: Board of Governors of Federal Reserve System,* Banking and Monetary Statistics *(Washington, DC: National Capital Press, 1943)*

[2] Here we focus on the narrow (M1) measure of the money supply to simplify the analysis. The broader (M2) measure of money behaved roughly the same as M1 during the 1930s. In fact, M2 fell by a relatively larger amount than M1 from 1929 to 1933 (see Table 17-4). M2 contraction was 37 percent from October 1929 to March 1933, while M1 fell 32 percent in the same period.

[3] An increase in the weighted average required reserve ratio ($r_r$) also contributed to the collapse of the money multiplier (review Table 17-2), although it clearly played a less important role than the increase in the currency (k) and excess reserve ratios ($r_e$). From the end of 1929 to the middle of 1933, $r_r$ increased from 10.7 percent to 12.6 percent. This increase resulted from a shift in deposits from smaller banks to larger banks (which were subject to higher percentage reserve requirements) in response to the public's perception that larger banks were safer than smaller banks.

# INTERPRETING THE FACTS: KEYNESIANS VERSUS MONETARISTS

Figure 17-2 illustrates facts about the elements determining the money supply multiplier. However, economists differ in their interpretation of these facts. One of the interesting things about economics is that eminent economists often are on opposite sides of almost any monetary issue. Sorting out the true explanation of the Federal Reserve's role in the 1930s debacle is particularly difficult because both sides of the issue have compelling arguments. You can find Nobel Laureates who vehemently disagree about the Federal Reserve's role in the Great Depression. Here, we examine the Keynesian and monetarist interpretations.

## The Keynesian View: You Can't Push on a String

The most influential early interpretation of the Great Depression—that advanced by the Federal Reserve itself and supported by the great British economist, John Maynard Keynes—was generally accepted before publication of an influential work by Milton Friedman and Anna Schwartz.[4] In the Keynesian view, the Federal Reserve instituted an "easy money" policy. However, powerful events beyond the Fed's control prevented the Fed from averting the collapse of the money supply and the ensuing economic catastrophe. Keynesians point out that yields on short-term government securities fell from 4 percent in October 1929 to less than 1 percent by mid-1932. The yield remained below 1 percent for the remainder of the decade. The Federal Reserve Bank of New York reduced its discount rate eight times, from 6 percent in October 1929 to 1.5 percent in mid-1931, before raising the rate sharply in late 1931 in response to international economic considerations.[5] Figure 17-3 shows the pattern of the discount rate and the short-term and long-term government security yields in this period.

Between the end of 1929 and the middle of 1938, the monetary base (which the Fed can indisputably control) doubled (review Table 17-2). Excess reserves piled up in banks after mid-1932 and reached massive levels by 1934, when excess reserves amounted to approximately 10 percent of checking accounts. In the conventional (Keynesian) view, these data indicate the Fed's policy actions certainly were not restrictive.

Keynesians absolve the Fed of responsibility for the Great Depression, arguing that "you can't push on a string." The Keynesians' argument—the Federal Reserve can do little once short-term interest rates are pushed to very low levels and banks are flush with excess reserves. If the public is unwilling to borrow from banks and yields on short-term securities are so low that banks are not interested in purchasing securities (note in Figure 17-3 the extremely low level of the Treasury bill yield after 1932), the Fed cannot force banks to use their excess reserves to make loans or purchase securities.[6] Because short-term interest rates had reached extraordinarily low levels by 1932, bank demand for excess reserves was thought to be perfectly elastic with respect to the interest rate. This hypoth-

[4] *A Monetary History of the United States, 1867–1960* (see Additional Readings).

[5] In the 1930s, different discount rates among the various district Federal Reserve banks were not unusual. The New York Fed lowered its discount rate more aggressively from 1929 to 1931 than did the other Federal Reserve banks. From May to September 1931, when the New York Fed posted a 1.5 percent discount rate, the Boston Fed was the only other Federal Reserve bank with a discount rate below 2.5 percent.

[6] Long-term Treasury bond yields were dramatically higher than Treasury bill yields. You may wonder why, if banks weren't attracted to low-yielding Treasury bills, they didn't load up on long-term government bonds. The answer is that long-term bonds are risky because their prices fluctuate significantly over time, as we learned in Chapter 6. Once long-term bonds are purchased, an increase in market interest rates can mean substantial capital losses. Therefore, banks are reluctant to hold large quantities of long-term government bonds.

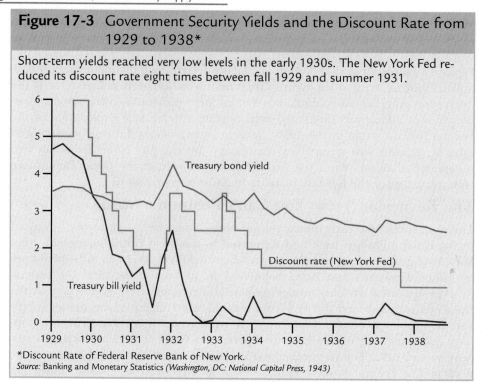

**Figure 17-3** Government Security Yields and the Discount Rate from 1929 to 1938*

Short-term yields reached very low levels in the early 1930s. The New York Fed reduced its discount rate eight times between fall 1929 and summer 1931.

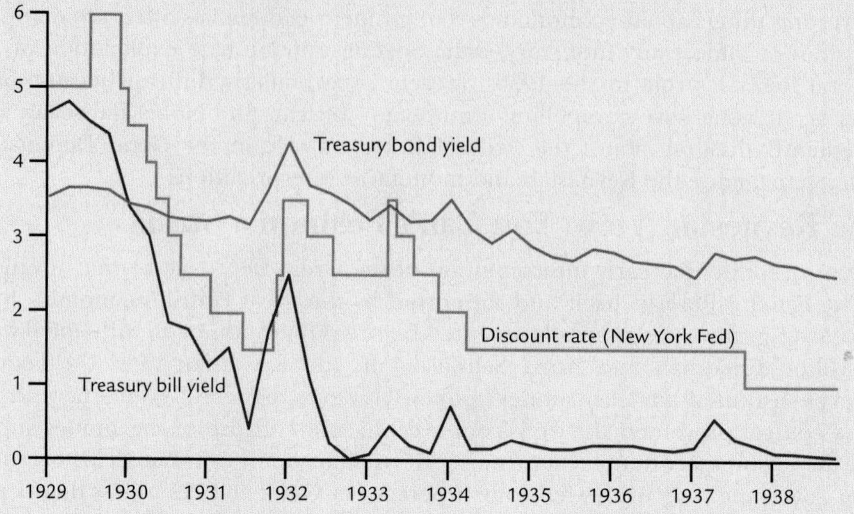


*Discount Rate of Federal Reserve Bank of New York.

*Source:* Banking and Monetary Statistics *(Washington, DC: National Capital Press, 1943)*

**bank liquidity trap** potential situation in which bank demand for excess reserves is perfectly elastic with respect to the interest rate, rendering the central bank incapable of increasing the money supply

esis, known as a **bank liquidity trap,** is a key point of contention between Keynesians and monetarists over the Federal Reserve's accountability for the Great Depression. The Keynesian view of bank demand for excess reserves is illustrated in Figure 17-4.

Keynesians argue that, in this situation, the link between the monetary base and the money supply had been severed. The Fed had lost control over the money supply because banks were unwilling to use additional reserves supplied to them by the Fed to expand loans or invest in securities. Banks did not lend because loan demand by legitimate borrowers was depressed. Banks did not buy securities because yields were extremely low. In this extreme case, the money supply multiplier moves in inverse proportion to changes in the monetary base engineered by the Fed. Had the Federal Reserve aggressively purchased securities in the open market in 1932 and 1933 and quickly doubled the monetary base, the money supply multiplier would have fallen by half as even more excess reserves piled up in banks. Thus, the situation allegedly was beyond the Federal Reserve's control. The Fed did what it could, but only a fiscal policy stimulus (such as increased government spending or a tax cut) could have saved the nation. Monetary policy was impotent: "You can't push on a string."[7]

[7] We focus here on the alleged existence of a bankers' liquidity trap, such that the Federal Reserve cannot induce banks to expand loans and purchase securities. This hypothesis is only one of several advanced by Keynesians supporting the proposition that Federal Reserve policy was inherently impotent in the 1930s. Other factors that allegedly emasculated monetary policy include the proposition that any money stock increase engineered by the Fed would not have pushed down interest rates and the proposition that investment expenditures were not responsive to interest rates in the early 1930s—that is, the investment demand curve was nearly vertical. Keynesians have traditionally held that monetary policy works by changing the money supply, interest rates, and investment expenditures. These propositions suggest that, in a depression situation such as the 1930s, monetary policy was inherently ineffective.

**Figure 17-4** Keynesian View of Bank Demand for Excess Reserves

In the Keynesian view, bank demand for excess reserves becomes infinitely elastic at some low interest rate. Banks willingly hold any and all excess reserves the Fed might supply rather than lending the funds or buying securities.

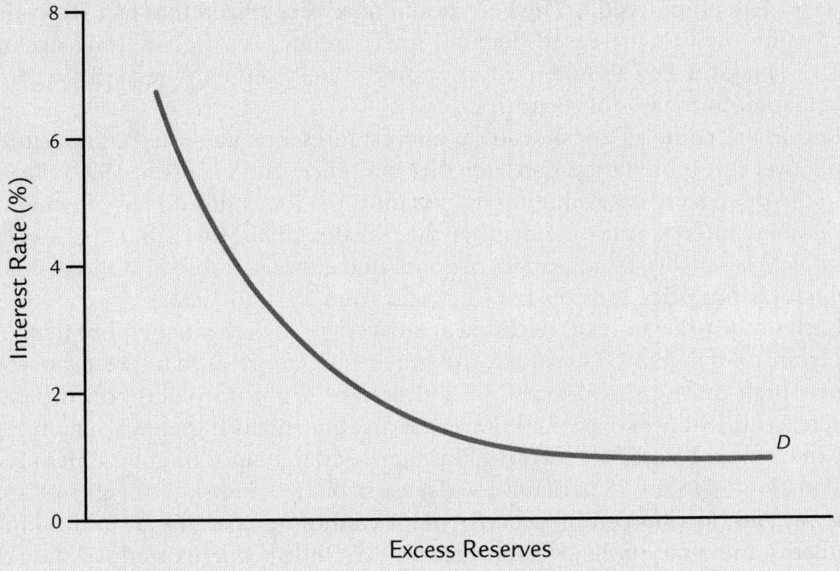

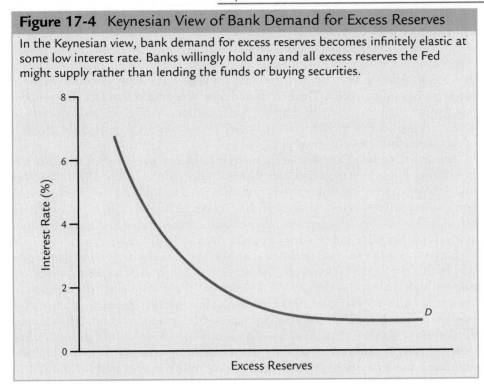

## The Monetarist View: The Fed Didn't Push

Monetarists dispute at almost every turn the Keynesian explanation for the Fed's role in the Depression. Monetarists believe the Fed's monetary policy in the 1930s was not stimulative—as Keynesians assert—but highly contractionary.[8] In the monetarist view, a typical business cycle contraction was converted into the Great Depression by a series of Federal Reserve policy errors. For example, the Fed implemented restrictive policy measures in 1928 and 1929 in response to escalating stock market speculation, even though inflation was nonexistent. The Fed (1) permitted bank reserves to fall sharply during the banking panic; (2) raised the discount rate dramatically in 1931 and maintained the rate at a very high level relative to the Treasury bill yield throughout the 1930s; (3) used open market security sales to counter the effects of gold inflows to the United States that otherwise would have strongly expanded the monetary base; and (4) doubled reserve requirements in three quick steps in 1936 and 1937. Monetarists are convinced the U.S. economy would have experienced only a normal recession rather than the catastrophe that occurred if the Fed had implemented expansionary policy actions in 1930 and 1931.

What evidence can monetarists marshal to challenge the traditional view that Federal Reserve policy was expansionary or "easy" in the Depression? Several arguments seem compelling. First, the monetary base actually did increase in the

[8] In the words of Friedman and Schwartz, "The monetary collapse from 1929 to 1933 was not an inevitable consequence of what had gone before. It was a result of the policies followed during those years. As already noted, alternative policies that could have halted the monetary debacle were available throughout those years. Though the Federal Reserve proclaimed that it was following an easy-money policy, in fact, it followed an exceedingly tight policy" (*A Monetary History of the United States, 1867–1960*, p. 699).

Depression. However, the monetary base consists of two components, reserves (R) and currency held by the public ($C^P$). Faced with a dramatic increase in $C^P$ triggered by the banking panic, the Fed allowed bank reserves (R) to decline by 18 percent between October 1929 and April 1933. Thus, the behavior of the monetary base was misleading because an increasing portion of the base was unavailable to banks for extending credit. The Fed should have recognized that fact. To compensate for the public's increased demand for currency and the resulting decline in bank reserves, the Fed should have aggressively boosted the monetary base through open market purchases of securities.

Keynesians contend low short-term interest rates indicated the Fed's posture was stimulative. But monetarists consider this inference invalid in the 1930s. First, because the price level was changing significantly, the focus should have been on *real,* not *nominal,* interest rates. Remember that, in the 1930s, the U.S. experienced severe *deflation*—that is, falling prices of goods and services. Table 17-3 shows the rates at which various price indexes fell each year from 1930 to 1933.

Each of the price indexes declined at an average annual rate of more than 6 percent from 1930 to 1933. Therefore, the *real* or *inflation-adjusted* interest rate was extremely high during this period.[9] In addition, a "flight to quality" on the part of lenders (security buyers) after 1931 created an abnormally high level of demand for safe, short-term Treasury securities. This increased demand for government securities contributed to the remarkably low Treasury bill yields shown in Figure 17-3. For these reasons, low short-term security yields cannot be taken as an indication of a stimulative monetary policy.[10] Even though very little scope existed for the Fed to push down short-term yields, the Fed could have prevented the disastrously high real interest rates of 1931 and 1932 by aggressively implementing measures to arrest ongoing price deflation.

Monetarists also point out that the Fed sharply tightened its discount window policy in the early 1930s. Bank incentive to borrow from the Fed is not a function

**Table 17-3 Measures of Inflation Rates from 1930 to 1933**

| Price Index | 1930 | 1931 | 1932 | 1933 |
|---|---|---|---|---|
| Consumer price index | −2.6% | −9.0% | −10.1% | −5.4% |
| Producer price index | −9.1 | −15.7 | −10.7 | +1.3 |
| GNP deflator | −2.6 | −9.1 | −10.2 | −2.2 |
| Personal consumption expenditure deflator | −3.1 | −10.6 | −11.7 | −4.0 |

Values given in percent.
*Source:* Economics Report of the President *and* Historical Statistics of the United States

[9] Recall from Chapter 5 that the expected or *ex ante* real rate of interest is given by the equation $r = i - \pi^e$, where r is the expected real rate, i is the nominal interest rate, and $\pi^e$ is the expected rate of inflation. Although we do not know the *expected* real rate, we can calculate the *realized* or *ex post* real rate by subtracting the *actual* inflation rate from the nominal interest rate. Using the 1931 consumer price index inflation rate of negative 9 percent and assuming the interest rate charged by banks on loans was 3 percent, we compute a real rate of 12 percent for 1931—a very high rate indeed.

[10] An indication of the "flight to quality" phenomenon is the increase in spread between the corporate Baa bond yield and the U.S. government bond yield (that is, the risk premium in corporate bond yields) from 2.3 percentage points in mid-1929 to 7.9 percentage points in mid-1932. By 1932, people were avoiding risky securities like the plague. The associated increased demand for safe securities artificially depressed yields on government securities, helping create the illusion that the Fed was pursuing "easy money" policies.

of the discount rate level *per se* but rather of the difference between the discount rate and short-term money market yields. A banker short on reserves does not find the discount window an attractive source of funds if the discount rate is an ostensibly low 1.5 percent while the yield on Treasury bills held by the bank is only 0.3 percent. In that event, the bank's most profitable choice is selling off Treasury bills rather than borrowing from the Fed. Note in Figure 17-3 the huge gap by which the discount rate exceeded the Treasury bill yield throughout the 1930s. To monetarists, this gap suggests a highly restrictive Federal Reserve discount policy in the 1930s.

In 1931, the Fed responded to international crises by raising the discount rate from 1.5 percent to 3.5 percent in two steps. At the time, the U.S. unemployment rate exceeded 15 percent. The Fed also took a tightfisted attitude toward lending to banks. The Federal Reserve sent the banks a letter admonishing the banks on the inappropriateness of increasing bank borrowing from the Fed. Faced with a national panic caused by increasing bank failures, the Federal Reserve apparently forgot its historic function to act as a "lender of last resort." The Fed seemingly forgot that banks collectively can obtain reserves only from the Federal Reserve. The Fed should have reduced the discount rate to zero, opened the discount window full throttle, and encouraged banks to borrow until the panic subsided. Instead, the Fed's defensive actions only aggravated the panic.[11]

Table 17-4 summarizes the evidence supporting the monetarist view of highly restrictive Federal Reserve policy in the early 1930s. Note first the contraction in M1 and M2 from 1929 to 1933. Because monetarists always maintain that the central bank is accountable for the behavior of the money stock, they view the sharp contraction in M1 and M2 as evidence of the Fed's ineptitude. The Fed passively allowed the contraction in bank reserves in the early 1930s, a crucial phenomenon triggered by the public's increased demand for currency. Note also the extremely high real interest rate levels in the early 1930s (look at the Real T-Bill Yield column), which contributed to a massive increase in bankruptcies and foreclosures among debtors in general—particularly among farmers and businesses. Note the unusually large differential by which the Fed's discount rate exceeded U.S. Treasury bill yields after 1931 (also illustrated in Figure 17-3). To monetarists, all of this evidence suggests a highly restrictive Federal Reserve monetary policy.

Finally, monetarists dispute the Keynesian view that the buildup of excess reserves in banks reflected the public's lack of loan demand and banks holding cash rather than purchasing securities because of low security yields. Instead, monetarists claim the buildup of excess reserves was the predictable defensive bank reaction to the earlier banking panics, coupled with banks' lack of confidence in the central bank's willingness to serve its traditional function as lender of last resort. In this view, the buildup of excess reserves reflected a discrete rightward shift in bank demand for excess reserves, as shown in Figure 17-5.

In other words, banks failed to make loans and purchase securities in the early 1930s not because of a lack of viable opportunities but because they felt the need to protect themselves by holding more excess reserves. Had the Fed recognized the bank demand curve for excess reserves was relatively steep (rather than horizontal,

[11] Friedman and Schwartz believe that a good part of the Federal Reserve's ineptitude in the 1930s can be attributed to the untimely death in 1928 of Benjamin Strong, longtime president of the Federal Reserve Bank of New York. His death resulted in a void of intellectual leadership and a struggle for power within the Federal Reserve System in the 1930s. For a fascinating discussion, see *A Monetary History of the United States, 1867–1960,* pp. 411–419. (In fact, you will find it worthwhile to read Chapter 7, "The Great Contraction," in its entirety.)

**Table 17-4** Evidence of a Restrictive Monetary Policy in the 1930s

| | M1 ($Billion)* | M2 ($Billion)* | Bank Reserves ($Billion)* | Inflation Rate (Percent) | Real T-Bill Yield (Percent)† | Discount Minus T-Bill Yield (Percent)‡ |
|---|---|---|---|---|---|---|
| 1929 | $26.3 | $46.0 | $3.20 | 0% | +4.5% | +0.2% |
| 1930 | 25.3 | 45.3 | 3.22 | −2.5 | +4.7 | +0.6 |
| 1931 | 23.8 | 42.6 | 3.26 | −8.8 | +10.0 | +0.9 |
| 1932 | 20.3 | 34.5 | 2.87 | −10.3 | +11.1 | +2.1 |
| 1933 | 19.2 | 30.1 | 2.96 | −5.1 | +5.4 | +2.2 |
| 1934 | 21.2 | 33.1 | 4.69 | +3.4 | −3.1 | +1.4 |
| 1935 | 25.1 | 38.0 | 5.92 | +2.5 | −2.4 | +1.4 |
| 1936 | 29.5 | 43.2 | 6.76 | +1.0 | −0.9 | +1.3 |
| 1937 | 30.6 | 45.2 | 7.93 | +3.6 | −3.1 | +0.9 |
| 1938 | 29.2 | 44.1 | 9.11 | −1.9 | +2.0 | +1.0 |

*Averages of monthly figures for May, June, and July.
†Average monthly T-bill yield minus CPI inflation rate.
‡New York Fed discount rate minus T-bill yield in June.
*Source: Milton Friedman and Anna J. Schwartz,* A Monetary History of the United States, 1867–1960 *(Princeton, NJ: Princeton University Press, 1963, Appendix Tables A-1 and A-2)*

**Figure 17-5** Monetarist Interpretation of Bank Demand for Excess Reserves in the 1930s

In the monetarist interpretation, a relatively steep demand curve for excess reserves shifted rightward in the 1930s, as banks took precautions to protect themselves against further bank runs and inept Federal Reserve policy.

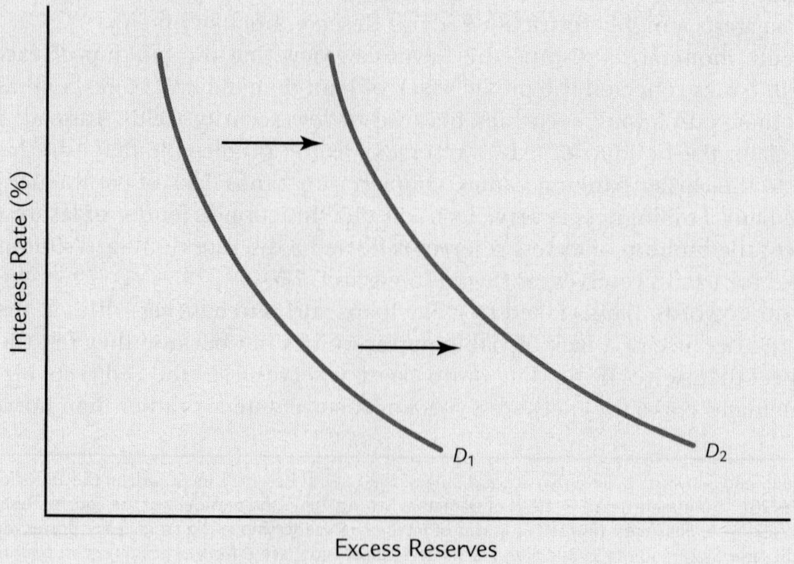

as claimed by the Keynesians), the Fed could have satisfied the increased demand by providing additional reserves or reducing the reserve requirement. Banks would have used the additional funds provided by the Fed to expand loans and purchase securities, quickly halting the contraction in the money supply. In the monetarists' view, the Fed misinterpreted the cause of the buildup of excess reserves in banks and therefore failed to act.

The monetarist view of the Fed's interpretation of excess reserve buildup in banks after mid-1932 is supported by the Fed's decision in 1936 and 1937 to absorb excess reserves by doubling the percentage reserve requirement. The Fed viewed the excess reserves as superfluous and potentially inflationary, and quickly eliminated the excess reserves by sharply boosting reserve requirements. This incredible restrictive action by the Fed helped trigger a second severe contraction—the recession of 1937 to 1938. Note in Table 17-2 the behavior of $r_r$, the money supply multiplier, and the money supply from the middle of 1936 to the end of 1937.

In the monetarist view, the link between the monetary base and the money stock—that is, the money supply multiplier—was not broken, only bent. During the Great Depression, control over the money supply was never out of the Fed's hands. A discrete upward shift in bank demand for excess reserves and corresponding downward shift in the magnitude of the money supply multiplier occurred. The Fed should have recognized this phenomenon and pursued stimulative actions, increasing the monetary base and arresting the monetary contraction, thereby preventing the Great Depression. (Exhibit 17-1 discusses alternative explanations of the Fed's failure to implement aggressive expansionary policies in the early 1930s.)

In sum, monetarists assert the hypothesis "you can't push on a string" was never tested in the 1930s. Monetarists believe the Fed was not pushing at all but in fact was conducting highly restrictive monetary policies. Friedman and Schwartz and other monetarists have established convincing evidence that Federal Reserve policy was tragically misguided in the 1930s. Many Keynesians and other non-monetarists now agree that the Fed made a series of mistakes, although many regard the Fed's sins chiefly as errors of *omission* rather than errors of *commission*. However, many other economists still are convinced that aggressive Fed actions in 1931 and 1932 would have led only to further buildup of excess reserves in the banks—that the link between Fed actions and bank lending and investing had been broken. Thus, the issue is joined! It may never be resolved to the satisfaction of both groups.

In recent years, economic historians studying the Great Depression have placed increasing emphasis on the role of the interwar gold standard in propagating monetary shocks from one country to another, constraining the conduct of central bank policy in many nations, and fostering deflation around the world. In a gold standard regime, a nation's money supply is linked to the value of gold owned by its government. Barring new gold discoveries or an increase in the official price of gold, a central bank may not be able to increase the quantity of money in the nation. Such a regime can lead to deflation if a nation's money supply falls or does not increase in line with trend output growth. The United States adhered to the gold standard from the end of World War I until the end of the Great Depression.

Under regulations of the gold standard, the Federal Reserve was required to maintain gold backing behind its issue of paper currency. "Free gold" refers to gold certificates held by the Federal Reserve above and beyond the amount required as backing behind the paper money issued by the Fed. Free gold was running low in the early 1930s, potentially constraining the Fed's ability to conduct expansionary policies. When England abandoned the gold standard in September 1931, the Fed feared that public speculation of the United States following suit in abandoning the

## Exhibit 17-1 Explanations for the Fed's Behavior in the 1930s

Today, an objective student of the Federal Reserve's actions during the Great Depression can conclude that either the Fed conducted a restrictive or tight monetary policy when faced with a downward economic spiral or the Fed sat back and passively watched the U.S. financial and economic system collapse. At minimum, you can legitimately accuse the Fed of failing to act aggressively to arrest the deflation of prices and the tragic contraction in economic activity. How can you account for the Federal Reserve's failure to act in the 1930s? Several potential explanations exist.

In one view, the Federal Reserve was fooled by its own flawed strategy—its propensity to focus on the wrong indicators of Fed monetary posture. In looking at the low money market yields, low discount rate, and burgeoning quantity of excess reserves after mid-1932, the Fed incorrectly inferred that its policies were expansionary. A related view emphasizes the role of discount window activity as an indicator of monetary policy. Beginning in the 1920s, because banks were believed to be reluctant to borrow, the Fed viewed a large amount of bank borrowing as an indicator that money was "tight." Hence, the Fed interpreted the contraction in discount window borrowing following the 1929 stock market crash as a sign that Fed policy was stimulative, rather than an indication that banks had become more conservative. This theory helps explain why the Fed did not aggressively purchase securities in the 1930s—the Fed wrongly believed it was already in an expansionary policy mode. The Fed's attention was riveted on nominal interest rates, excess reserves, and borrowing at the discount window rather than bank reserves and declining monetary aggregates. Some opponents argue that the Fed was incompetent, its intellectual capital diminished by the death of Benjamin Strong.

Another view emphasizes the inherent conflict between the Fed's dual roles of stabilizing the nation's economy and ensuring the safety and profitability of commercial banks. In the early 1930s, banks engaged in a massive reallocation of their earning assets from loans to short-term government securities. Banks reallocated their assets either because of banks' increased cautionary position or because of a decline in viable loan customers. Interest earned on government securities became a key determinant of bank profits. In early 1932, the Fed finally embarked on a program of aggressively purchasing government securities. As yields on government securities plunged to extraordinarily low levels by mid-1932, the Fed abandoned its short-lived expansionary program out of fear of impairing (the already depressed) bank profits. The Fed became concerned that interest rates were too low for banks to earn a decent profit. In a perverse twist, some members of the Fed seemed to believe occasional depressions help weed out inefficient firms and hold down wages, and thereby play a beneficial "cleansing" role in capitalistic societies.

A third interpretation rests on the requirement (until 1932) for each Federal Reserve bank to hold gold as "backing" for the paper money it issued—Federal Reserve notes. In the early 1930s, "free gold"—gold held by the Fed in excess of its collateral requirements—was precariously low at several Federal Reserve banks. When foreign nations began converting their dollar holdings into gold at the U.S. Treasury in late September and October 1931 in response to England's abandonment of the gold standard and the ensuing atmosphere of uncertainty, the Federal Reserve banks dramatically increased their discount rates. This classic central bank response to international crisis is one indication that the Fed may have been heavily constrained by international economic considerations and thus limited in its ability or willingness to react to domestic economic events. This view has received increasing support among scholars in recent years.

gold standard would lead to an international run on the remaining U.S. gold stock. This fear led the Fed to post its dramatic increase in the discount rate—a traditional central bank signal of the Fed's intention to maintain the gold standard and the existing price of gold. Today, economists view the major industrial nations' adherence to the gold standard in the early 1930s as an important factor in understanding the Great Depression.

## SUMMARY

Economists disagree about the Federal Reserve's role in the Great Depression of the early 1930s. The money supply fell sharply from 1929 to 1933, even though the monetary base increased. The money supply multiplier collapsed because of dramatic increases in the currency ratio (k) and, somewhat later, the excess reserve ratio ($r_e$). The immediate cause of the multiplier collapse was the rush to convert deposits into currency, but economists disagree about whether the Fed had the power to arrest the contraction in deposits and deflation of prices in 1931, 1932, or 1933. The traditional (Keynesian) interpretation holds that a series of non-monetary shocks reduced aggregate expenditures and that, by 1931, the Fed was powerless to stop the downward spiral of events. In the Keynesian view, low short-term interest rates and ample excess reserves in banks suggested an expansionary Fed policy was in place. Because loan demand was depressed and short-term yields were extremely low, banks would willingly hold whatever excess reserves the Fed might have provided through more stimulative actions. In such circumstances, monetary policy is impotent. In the monetarist view, the Keynesian interpretation of events is incorrect. A series of Fed mistakes accounts for the contraction in money and economic activity. Although nominal interest rates were low, severe price level deflation caused by monetary contraction implied that real rates were extremely high—an indication of "tight" monetary policy. Bank demand for excess reserves increased as a predictable response to the banking panics and indications that the Fed would not counter any additional bank runs through expansionary policy measures. Had the Fed aggressively expanded bank reserves to satisfy the increased demand for reserves, banks would have increased their lending and security purchases, thereby increasing the money supply and ending the economic downturn. Monetarists believe the Fed never lost its capacity to increase the money supply. Monetarists blame the severity and duration of the Great Depression on the Fed's failure to implement expansionary policies.

## KEY TERMS

bank liquidity trap

# STUDY QUESTIONS

1. Suppose you are defending the position that Federal Reserve policy was stimulative in the 1930s. What facts would you marshal in support of your position?

2. Suppose you are defending the position that Federal Reserve policy was highly restrictive in the 1930s. What facts would you marshal in support of your position?

3. Explain the intuition underlying the fact that when banks deliberately choose to hold more excess reserves, the money supply multiplier and the supply of money both fall. (If you are unsure, review the relevant portion of the previous chapter).

4. Examine Figure 17-2, which illustrates the currency and excess reserve ratios. Explain in historical context why movements in the excess reserve ratio might duplicate but lag behind movements in the currency ratio.

5. Suppose your great grandfather, whose memory is amazingly clear, was an officer of a major bank during the 1930s. What questions might you pose to him to gain insight into the debate over the causes of the 1930s buildup of excess reserves in the banks?

6. "Because the monetary base increased significantly in the 1930s, it is quite clear that the Federal Reserve cannot be considered a guilty party in the Great Depression." Evaluate this statement.

7. "While it is true that the Federal Reserve made some mistakes in the 1930s, those mistakes were not a major contributor to the Great Depression." Evaluate this statement.

8. In the early 1930s the Fed regarded a high level of discount loans (bank borrowing from the Fed) as a sign of tight monetary policy. Monetarists now view this condition as a sign of stimulative policy. Evaluate the disagreement and explain how the Fed's perception may have produced a policy error on the Fed's part.

9. "The experience of the 1930s confirms the existence of an asymmetry in the power of monetary policy. You can 'pull on a string' but you cannot 'push on a string.'" What does this statement mean? Does the experience of the 1930s confirm this statement?

10. Examine Figure 17-3, which illustrates the Fed's discount rate in the 1930s. In your view, was the Fed's discount window policy generally more restrictive or more stimulative from 1932 to 1936 than from 1929 to 1931? Defend your position.

11. The U.S. economy began to recover in mid-1933 but then suffered a major relapse in the recession from 1937 to 1938. Examine the pertinent tables in this chapter and evaluate the role of the money supply and the Federal Reserve in this second contraction.

12. It seems clear that the Federal Reserve *did* make major policy mistakes in the early 1930s. List some of the mistakes and discuss possible reasons the Fed committed these mistakes.

## ADDITIONAL READING

- The past 20 years have witnessed a renaissance of interest in the economics of the Great Depression of the 1930s. An abundance of recent literature now exists. An important catalyst and point of reference is the monumental work by Milton Friedman and Anna J. Schwartz, *A Monetary History of United States, 1867–1960* (Princeton, NJ: Princeton University Press, 1963).
- An early and brilliant review of this classic book is James Tobin, "The Monetary Interpretation of History," *American Economic Review,* June 1965, pp. 646–695. Recent reviews of the Friedman and Schwartz work include articles by Robert Lucas, Jeffrey Miron, and Bruce Smith in the 1994 issue of *Journal of Monetary Economics,* pp. 5–45. An excellent recent overview of monetary factors and Federal Reserve policy in the 1930s is David C. Wheelock, "Monetary Policy in the Great Depression: What the Fed Did, and Why," Federal Reserve Bank of St. Louis *Review,* March/April 1992, pp. 3–23. See also Wheelock's excellent study of the Fed's misguided discount policy, "Member Bank Borrowing and the Fed's Contractionary Monetary Policy during the Great Depression," *Journal of Money, Credit, and Banking,* November 1990, pp. 409–426.
- An indispensable source is Karl Brunner, ed., *The Great Depression Revisited* (Boston: Nijhoff Publishing, 1981). This book contains articles and comments by Anna Schwartz, Robert Gordon, James Wilcox, Peter Temin, William Poole, James Pierce, and Karl Brunner. Journal articles supporting the monetarist interpretation of the Great Depression include James D. Hamilton, "Monetary Factors in the Great Depression," *Journal of Monetary Economics* 1987, No. 19, pp. 145–169; B.L. Anderson and J.L. Butkiewicz, "Money, Spending, and the Great Depression," *Southern Economic Journal,* 1980, pp. 388–403; and Bennett T. McCallum, "Could a Monetary Base Rule have Prevented the Great Depression?" *Journal of Monetary Economics* 1990, No. 26, pp. 3–26.
- An interesting article that probes into the forces driving the Federal Reserve's behavior in the 1930s is Gerald Epstein and Thomas Ferguson, "Monetary Policy, Loan Liquidation, and Industrial Conflict: The Federal Reserve and the Great Contraction," *Journal of Economic History,* December 1984, pp. 957–983. Individuals critical of the hypothesis that the depression was caused chiefly by monetary factors include Peter Temin, *Did Monetary Forces Cause the Great Depression?* (New York: Norton, 1976), Charles Kindleberger, *The World in Depression* (Berkeley, CA: University of California Press, 1973), and the Tobin piece cited above.
- Recent works placing the U.S. depression in the larger context of the world economy and its institutional framework include Ben Bernanke, "The Macroeconomics of the Great Depression: A Comparative Approach," *The Journal of Money, Credit, and Banking,* February 1995, pp. 1–28, and Barry Eichengreen, *Golden Fetters: The Gold Standard and the Great Depression, 1919–1939* (New York, Oxford University Press, 1992). The above-mentioned Bernanke article and eight other Bernanke journal articles on the 1930s are available in Bernanke's book, *Essays on the Great Depression* (Princeton, NJ: Princeton University Press, 2000).
- Finally, the Spring 1993 issue of the *Journal of Economic Perspectives* contains an excellent symposium on the Great Depression. See especially Christina Romer, "The Nation in Depression," and Charles Calamoris, "Financial Factors in the Great Depression."

# Part FIVE

The Federal Reserve conducts monetary policy to influence key variables such as the growth rate of the gross domestic product (GDP), the unemployment rate, and the nation's price level behavior. The Fed uses certain instruments or tools over which it has absolute control. The most important Fed instrument is open market operations. However, the Fed also can change the discount rate level and reserve requirement levels. Because the link between the Fed's instruments and the Fed's ultimate objectives is uncertain and changes over time, the Fed uses its instruments to control certain variables believed to be more tightly linked to aggregate expenditures and the final policy objectives. These variables are *operating target variables* and *intermediate target variables,* which include short-term interest rates and the various money supply measures. Over the course of Fed history, the Federal Reserve has used many different variables as intermediate target variables. In recent years, the Federal Reserve and other central banks have used short-term interest rates as intermediate target variables.

# Chapter 18

# THE TOOLS OF FEDERAL RESERVE POLICY

**instrument or tool of monetary policy**
variable the Fed controls completely in order to influence such key intermediate variables as short-term interest rates, the monetary base, M1, and M2

The Federal Reserve influences key macroeconomic variables such as national output, the unemployment rate, and price level behavior by controlling certain variables the Fed believes are closely linked to these ultimate objectives. These *intermediate target variables* include short-term interest rates and the monetary aggregates (M1, M2, M3). For example, if the economy is in recession and the Fed wishes to stimulate economic activity, the Fed reduces short-term interest rates and increases the growth rates of the monetary aggregates. The Fed uses certain instruments or tools of monetary policy to bring about the desired changes.

An **instrument** or **tool of monetary policy** is a variable the Fed controls completely and is strongly linked to key intermediate variables such as short-term interest rates, the monetary base, M1, and M2. The Fed uses three general instruments or tools of monetary policy: open market operations, discount window policy, and reserve requirement policy. In this chapter, we analyze these instruments of monetary policy. By far the most important tool is open market operations.

## OPEN MARKET OPERATIONS: FUNDAMENTAL CONSIDERATIONS

**open market operations**
buying and selling of securities in the open market by the central bank (the Fed)

**Open market operations**—the buying and selling of securities in the open market—is the bread-and-butter instrument of Federal Reserve policy. The Fed has the authority to buy or sell U.S. Treasury securities, federal agency securities, banker's acceptances, and certain other securities in the open market. The magnitude and timing of these transactions is entirely up to the Fed's discretion. The Fed implements open market purchases and sales based on the desired impact on short-term interest rates, bank reserves, the monetary base, and the monetary aggregates.

Because the Federal Reserve earns interest income from its portfolio of securities, total revenues earned by the Fed vary in direct proportion to the magnitude of the Fed's portfolio (currently more than $700 billion). However, this consideration plays no role in the Fed's decision to buy or sell securities. Indeed, if it did, the Federal Reserve could not perform the chief function of a modern central bank—to conduct monetary policy in a way that contributes to the stability of aggregate expenditures, economic activity, and the nation's price level.

Suppose the U.S. economy is encountering excessive aggregate expenditures and escalating inflation. The Fed implements a policy of monetary restraint, selling securities in the open market. Assume the Fed sells $225 million in U.S. Treasury bills to a government securities dealer. The Fed receives payment via check written against the dealer's bank checking account. (Actually, Federal Reserve transactions with dealers today are made electronically). When the Fed receives the check, it "collects" on the check by debiting the reserve account at the Fed of the dealer's commercial bank and returns the check to that bank. The commercial bank receives the check and debits the dealer's demand deposit account. The relevant balance sheets exhibit the following changes:

| Federal Reserve System | | | | All Commercial Banks | | | |
|---|---|---|---|---|---|---|---|
| U.S. securities | −225 million | Deposits by member banks | −225 million | Deposits at the Fed | −225 million | Demand deposits | −225 million |

Note that bank reserves and the monetary base move dollar for dollar with the Federal Reserve's security holdings.[1] When the Fed sells $225 million of securities, both reserves (R) and the monetary base (B) decrease by $225 million because aggregate bank deposits at the Fed decrease by $225 million. If the Fed *buys* $660 million of securities, R and B *increase* by $660 million, because the securities sellers receive checks totaling $660 million from the Federal Reserve. In other words, the Federal Reserve pays for these securities by creating new reserves—that is, by crediting the reserve accounts of the security dealers' banks at the Fed. Clearly, the open market operations tool allows the Federal Reserve to dominate the behavior of bank reserves and the monetary base.

Recall from our discussion of the money supply multiplier in Chapter 16 that $M = m \times B$. In a fractional reserve banking system, each dollar change in the monetary base results in a *multiple* change (totaling perhaps $2.00) in the narrow measure of money (M1). In other words, Fed purchase (or sale) of securities triggers a multiple expansion (or contraction) of deposits and the monetary aggregates. Thus, open market operations are a powerful and highly important instrument of Federal Reserve policy. In the next few sections, we discuss the historical accident that elevated open market operations to the premier tool of monetary policy and look at institutional details of open market operations.

## Discovery of Open Market Operations and The Banking Act of 1935

Open market operations were unimportant early in the Federal Reserve System's history. The discount window (where banks borrow from the Fed) was essentially the Fed's only policy tool. In fact, the Fed stumbled upon the use of open market operations by accident in the early 1920s. In the early years of the Federal Reserve's history, the primary source of the Fed's operating revenues was the interest received on the Fed's loans of reserves to commercial banks, known as **discounts loans.** However, the volume of discount loans dropped off sharply in a severe recession in the early 1920s, impairing the Fed's interest revenues. The individual Federal Reserve banks purchased U.S. government securities to supplement dwindling revenues and achieve a steady flow of interest income. The 12 district Federal Reserve banks noticed that interest rates immediately fell and credit conditions eased when they purchased securities. Thus, a new policy tool was born!

**discount loans**
Fed's loans of reserves to commercial banks

[1] Because this transaction increases the dealer's inventory of government securities by $225 million, the dealer likely reestablishes its desired inventory level by selling about $225 million of government securities to the public. In the highly competitive government securities market, a dealer normally accomplishes this by lowering its "ask" price slightly. This reduction in price (increase in yield) induces securities purchases by the public (commercial banks, money market funds, non-financial corporations, and so forth). In this case, the dealer serves as a "middleman" between the Federal Reserve and the public. In other words, the Fed sells to the public via dealers. The final balance sheet changes are exactly as shown above. When the public purchases government securities from dealers, their demand deposits are reduced by $225 million, and the dealers' demand deposits return to the levels that existed prior to the Federal Reserve transaction. Reserve deposits are transferred from the public's banks to the dealers' banks. Therefore, aggregate reserves (and the monetary base) remain down by $225 million. Because dealers are simply middlemen in this process, in essence the Fed sells securities to the general public.

In the early years of the Fed's history, the 12 district Federal Reserve banks were not coordinated, and no coherent national monetary policy existed. In 1923, the Federal Reserve Board in Washington authorized a committee of five Federal Reserve bank "governors"—heads of district Federal Reserve banks (now known as presidents)—to coordinate security purchases and sales for the Federal Reserve System as a whole. The committee, named the *Open Market Investment Committee,* expanded in 1928 to include all 12 district Federal Reserve bank "governors." Individual Federal Reserve banks retained the right to engage in open market operations on their own account and could elect to not participate in the System's purchases and sales.

The Banking Act of 1935 ended this unsatisfactory state of affairs. The Banking Act, essentially a major amendment to the original Federal Reserve Act, shifted a significant amount of power from the individual district Federal Reserve banks to the Board of Governors in Washington, DC. The Banking Act dramatically changed the Committee's composition by revoking voting privileges of seven of the 12 district Federal Reserve bank presidents and adding the seven members of the Board of Governors in Washington. This important act added numerous other provisions that remain in effect today.[2]

## Domain of the Fed's Open Market Activity

Technically, the Federal Reserve's open market operations can be in corporate bonds, common stocks, municipal bonds, or pork-bellies futures rather than U.S. government securities and federal agency securities. No matter what items the Fed purchases, the Fed pays with a check written on itself. When the check recipient deposits the check in a bank, the Fed reimburses that bank by crediting the bank's reserve account at the Fed. Reserves and the monetary base increase by the amount of the transaction because the Fed pays for its purchase by creating new bank reserves in the form of bank deposits at the Fed. The balance sheet impact will always be the same, regardless of the type of asset the Fed purchases.

When the Fed buys Treasury bills and bonds from the *public,* bank reserves and the monetary base increase dollar for dollar. If the Fed's check is deposited in a checking account, M1 and the broader monetary aggregates directly increase by the amount of the transaction. When the Fed buys Treasury bonds and bills from *banks,* reserves and the monetary base expand dollar for dollar, but the money supply is not *directly* or *immediately* affected. The T-accounts associated with a $400 million Fed purchase of U.S. government securities from *banks* is as follows:

| Federal Reserve System | | | | All Commercial Banks | | | |
|---|---|---|---|---|---|---|---|
| U.S. government securities | +400 million | Deposits by member banks | +400 million | Deposits at the Fed | +400 million | | |
| | | | | U.S. government securities | −400 million | | |

Because no demand deposits are initially created, this transaction does not *directly* increase the money supply. However, bank reserves and the monetary base increase

[2] The Banking Act of 1935 also authorized the Board of Governors to change reserve requirements (within congressionally established ranges), granted the Board the final say in setting the discount rates of each of the 12 district Federal Reserve banks, and authorized the Board to determine the budgets of the individual district Fed banks and the salaries of their top officers. The act made the Federal Reserve more independent of the U.S. president by removing both the Secretary of the Treasury and the Comptroller of the Currency (presidential appointees) from the Board of Governors; by lengthening the terms of Board members from 10 to 14 years; and by providing for overlapping appointments to the Board so that one new Board member normally is appointed by the president every 2 years.

dollar for dollar with the Fed transaction. The money supply then increases as banks initiate the multiple deposit–expansion process by acquiring earning assets—that is, loans and securities.

Federal law minimizes the Fed's direct influence on the privately issued securities market by requiring Fed transactions be carried out in U.S. government and agency securities and banker's acceptances. This limitation prevents potential conflicts of interest, favoritism, or "politics" that might occur if the Fed conducted transactions in common stocks, corporate bonds, municipal bonds, or mortgages. Perhaps the most compelling reason to conduct most open market operations in government securities is that no other domestic financial market is so highly developed—no other market possesses as much depth, breadth, and stability as the U.S. government securities market. Such a highly developed market is needed to absorb the huge daily volume of Federal Reserve transactions in an orderly manner. On a typical day, the Fed conducts billions of dollars' worth of open market transactions. Only the U.S. government securities market has the sheer capacity to absorb transactions of that magnitude without experiencing major price fluctuations. In 2004, more than 99 percent of the Fed's security holdings were in the form of U.S. government securities. The remainder of Fed holdings were in federal agency securities. During 2003, the Fed conducted gross transactions of more than $10,000 billion ($10 trillion) worth of U.S. government securities.

During the 1950s, the Fed restricted its open market operations almost exclusively to U.S. government securities of less than 15 months' maturity. This action stemmed from the Federal Reserve's desire to accomplish its reserves and monetary base objectives with minimum impact on security prices and yields. Because the short end of the government securities market is the most highly developed, active, and liquid, Fed transactions in short-term securities have less impact on security prices and yields than comparable transactions in long-term securities. Since the 1950s, the Fed has broadened the range of maturities in which it conducts open market operations. For a period in the 1960s, the Fed even attempted to influence the term structure of interest rates by simultaneously buying and selling different maturities of government securities. In recent years, the overwhelming majority of Federal Reserve open market operations has been conducted in maturities of less than 1 year, but a considerable volume of activity still has been conducted in maturities of 1 to 5 years. Open market operations in long-term instruments are considerably less common.[3]

## EFFECTIVENESS OF OPEN MARKET OPERATIONS

Open market operations is a powerful and efficient monetary policy instrument. This tool influences economic activity through several channels. In this section, we discover that open market operations has distinct advantages over other policy instruments.

### Impacts of Open Market Operations

Open market operations influence the economy through two primary channels: monetary variables (reserves, monetary base, M1, M2) and security prices and yields.

[3] In 2004, approximately one third of U.S. government securities owned by the Federal Reserve had maturities of 1 year or less; approximately half had maturities ranging from 1 to 5 years; and about one sixth had maturities in excess of 5 years. The average maturity of the Fed's government security portfolio was about 3 years. To look at a recent Federal Reserve balance sheet, go to http://www.federalreserve.gov/releases/h41/.

**Impact on Bank Reserves, the Monetary Base, and the Monetary Aggregates.** As we emphasized in Chapter 15, the Fed can exert relatively accurate control over bank reserves (R) and the monetary base (B) by manipulating the Fed's security portfolio. Each dollar of securities the Fed purchases boosts R and B by $1. If the factors governing the money supply multiplier (k, $r_r$, and $r_e$) are relatively stable and independent of the monetary base, then open market operations exert a strong and fairly predictable effect on M1 and other monetary aggregates. These variables, in turn, impact aggregate expenditures on goods and services, thereby influencing economic activity in general.

**Impact on Security Prices and Interest Rates (Yields).** When the Fed buys government securities in the open market, the Fed directly bids up the prices of the securities and therefore reduces their yields. The initial expansion in bank reserves (and excess reserves) directly caused by the Fed's security purchases induces commercial banks to purchase securities, resulting in further price increases and downward pressure on government securities yields. Given that various marketable securities are substitutes for one another, the downward pressure on government security yields spills over to the commercial paper market and other money market instruments, reducing the yields in these other markets. Yields on corporate and municipal bonds and mortgage rates tend to fall, but to a lesser extent. Interest rates in general decline, stimulating expenditures by corporations, municipalities, and individuals. The accompanying reduction in bank lending rates stimulates borrowing and spending by bank customers. Evidence suggests the stock market responds favorably to lower interest rates if other factors are held constant. The resulting capital appreciation in stocks and bonds, by increasing the wealth or net worth of the public and by increasing the value of collateral supporting prospective bank loans, likely has a positive influence on consumption and investment expenditures.

## Advantages of Open Market Operations

The open market operations instrument possesses certain advantages over the other tools of Federal Reserve policy—that is, changes in the discount rate and changes in reserve requirements. The advantages of open market operations include the *precision* with which the Fed influences reserves, the base, and short-term interest rates; the *flexibility* of open market operations; and the fact that the *initiative for change* is totally in the Fed's hands.

**Precision.** Open market operations enable the Fed to exert firm and accurate control over aggregate bank reserves and the monetary base. If the Fed wishes to inject $322 million of reserves into the banking system, the Fed simply purchases $322 million of U.S. government securities. This high degree of accuracy cannot be achieved through changes in the discount rate or reserve requirements. If the Fed wanted to increase bank reserves via discount policy, the Fed would reduce the discount rate. The amount by which this action increases the amount of discount loans (and hence reserves and the monetary base) is highly uncertain.

A similar argument about lack of precision can be made with respect to reserve requirement changes. First, reserve requirement changes influence the money supply through the money supply multiplier rather than through reserves and the monetary base. Even a fairly small change in the percentage reserve requirement produces a relatively large change in required reserves and excess reserves. In principle, the Fed can implement frequent and tiny changes in the reserve requirement—for example, increasing the requirement from 10 to 10.02 percent in a given week. However, frequent reserve requirement changes are inconvenient and costly for banks, and both the banks and the Federal Reserve oppose such a monetary policy strategy. In short, this instrument is blunt and not well suited for frequent use as a Fed policy tool.

**Flexibility.** The Federal Reserve is in the market each day, buying and selling large quantities of U.S. government securities through the Fed's network of dealers. For this reason, the Fed can easily alter the stance of monetary policy and even reverse policy direction through open market operations at a moment's notice, if desired. Because open market operations have no obvious announcement effects, only the most perceptive of observers detect the Fed's policy change.

The same does not hold true for discount rate and reserve requirement changes, which are highly visible to the general public. The media hails Fed increases of the discount rate or reserve requirements as restrictive actions likely indicating further monetary restraint to follow. By announcing increases of the discount rate or reserve requirements, the Fed goes on record indicating the need for monetary restraint. If the Fed abruptly reverses direction through those policy tools and lowers the discount rate or reserve requirements the following week, the Fed publicly admits to a (previous) mistake and is embarrassed. Consequently, the Fed likely will not reverse policy direction through these tools until overwhelming evidence confirms a policy change is essential. For this reason, the discount and reserve requirement instruments are not very flexible in the short run. Reserve requirements are seldom changed (the last change was in 1992). The discount rate is adjusted somewhat more frequently, perhaps a few times each year. In contrast, the Fed conducts enormous transactions in U.S. government securities every business day.

**Source of Initiative.** If the Federal Reserve is to influence economic activity through variables such as reserves, the monetary base, and the monetary aggregates, then changes in those variables must result from deliberate Fed policy decisions rather than outside forces. That is, the *initiative for changes* in reserves should reside with the Fed. Such is the case with open market operations. The Fed can dominate the behavior of aggregate bank reserves and the monetary base by initiating open market operations. The open market operations tool enables the Fed to inject reserves into (or withdraw reserves from) the banking system. However, such is not the case with the discount window instrument. Fluctuations in the volume of bank borrowing (discount loans) and therefore in reserves and the monetary base do not result from conscious Federal Reserve actions. Banks initiate requests for loans at the Federal Reserve, and the Fed passively accommodates such requests. Fluctuations in the volume of discount loans result from changes in bank demand for loans from the Fed rather than from deliberate Federal Reserve actions.

## Early Disadvantages of Open Market Operations

Historically, the Federal Reserve has used its policy instruments to announce changes in the direction or thrust of Fed policies. For example, when England abandoned the gold standard in 1931, the Fed sharply increased its discount rate, mostly to convey to the world the Fed's intention to remain on the gold standard and maintain the existing price of gold (avoid devaluing the dollar). Clearly, changes in the discount rate and reserve requirements are superior to open market operations in signaling policy changes to the public. Today, policy changes need not be conveyed through changes in the discount rate or reserve requirements because the Fed publicly announces at the end of each Federal Open Market Committee (FOMC) meeting the level of the federal funds rate being targeted until further notice.

Some 40 or 50 years ago, open market operations exhibited one important drawback relative to changes in the discount rate and reserve requirements. Because financial markets such as the federal funds market, the market for negotiable CDs and the commercial paper market were not highly developed, open market operations exhibited a pronounced *regional bias*. The effects of open market operations were not dispersed as quickly across the nation as were the effects of changes in reserve requirements and discount rates.

Let's look at the reason for this discrepancy. When the Federal Reserve enters into government security transactions with security dealers, only the dealers' banks are *directly and immediately* affected. Only about 40 primary dealers operate in government securities, and most of the dealers have always been located in New York. Therefore, only a handful of banks initially gain or lose reserves when the Fed buys or sells securities. Decades ago, bankers in Tucumcari, New Mexico, and Tupelo, Mississippi, likely were not quickly affected by a change in direction of Federal Reserve open market operations. Changes in reserve requirements, on the other hand, immediately affect every bank in the United States subject to Fed reserve requirements. Changes in the Fed's discount rate immediately affect every bank that is borrowing (or contemplating borrowing) from the Fed. Discount rate changes provide to every bank in the United States an immediate visible signal or announcement effect on the general thrust of Federal Reserve policy. This signal likely influences the lending decisions of thousands of banks. Thus, the concentration of the early effects of open market operations in select urban areas where government security dealers were located was a disadvantage of the open market operations instrument relative to the Fed's other policy instruments.

## Open Market Operations and the Federal Funds Rate

Today, the effects of the Fed's open market operations are quickly transmitted throughout the nation. To understand this, consider the federal funds market and the market for negotiable CDs, both of which are national in scope. Remember that the *federal funds market* is the market in which banks with more reserves than they need lend their reserve deposits at the Fed to banks that have fewer reserves than desired. This lending and borrowing of reserves by banks is known as "selling" and "buying" federal funds, respectively. The interest rate at which federal funds are bought and sold is the *federal funds rate*. Figure 18-1 depicts the federal funds market and the effect of open market operations on this market.

Bank reserves consist of required reserves and excess reserves. Bank *demand* for reserves stems from the banks' need to meet reserve requirements and the desire to hold excess reserves. The opportunity cost of holding excess reserves declines as the federal funds rate and other short-term rates fall; therefore, banks willingly hold more excess reserves. Because bank demand for excess reserves is inversely related to the interest rate, the demand curve in the figure is downward sloping.

The *supply* of reserves is determined by Federal Reserve policy. When the Fed purchases securities in the open market, bank reserves are boosted in a dollar-for-dollar fashion. Required reserves increase only fractionally, so most of the newly created reserves are *excess reserves*. Government security dealers' banks immediately find themselves with more reserves than they wish to keep. The banks' initial reac-

**Figure 18-1** Federal Reserve Open Market Purchases and the Federal Funds Rate

When the Federal Reserve purchases securities in the open market, the supply of bank reserves increases and the federal funds rate falls.

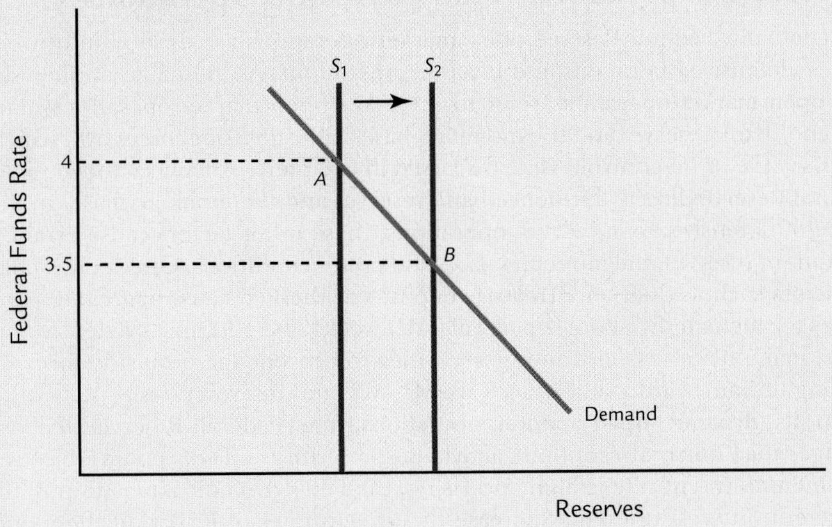


tion is to lend these excess funds in the federal funds market, increasing the supply of federal funds. In the figure, the supply curve shifts rightward from $S_1$ to $S_2$, and the market equilibrium moves from *A* to *B*. The federal funds rate in the figure quickly falls from 4.0 percent to 3.5 percent. Banks in New Mexico and Mississippi immediately gain access to funds (via the federal funds market) at a reduced cost. Bank borrowing in the federal funds market is not restricted—banks can borrow continuously and heavily in this market. The reduced cost of funds permits banks nationwide to lower their interest rates on loans. The *prime rate*—the benchmark rate set by major banks—likely is quickly reduced, leading to corresponding reduced bank lending rates to the public.

Bank reserves decline when the Fed *sells* securities. Required reserves fall by only a small portion of the decline in reserves, so excess reserves fall below desired levels. Dealers' banks find themselves with fewer reserves. The supply of bank reserves decreases. The supply curve shifts left, and the fed funds rate increases. The cost of bank funds increases nationwide, and bank lending rates increase accordingly.

The market for negotiable CDs is now also national in scope. A Federal Reserve open market security purchase increases the funds available to the banking system by boosting reserves and excess reserves. Fewer banks now need to issue negotiable CDs to obtain funds, and the supply of CDs issued by banks (demand for funds) declines. The interest rate on negotiable CDs quickly falls, and banks nationwide have access to funds (by issuing negotiable CDs) at lower cost. As the cost of funds declines, banks reduce their lending rates. In today's economy, the effect of the Fed's open market operations is transmitted across the nation very quickly. The uneven regional influence of open market operations in the first half-century of the Fed's history has been virtually eliminated by the development of our financial markets.

# TECHNICAL ASPECTS OF OPEN MARKET OPERATIONS

## Defensive Operations Versus Dynamic Operations

**defensive open market operations** Fed's open market operations made to "defend" bank reserves and the monetary base against outside forces over which the Fed has little or no control

**dynamic open market operations** operations by which the Federal Reserve deliberately changes the course of economic activity in line with the Fed's policy objectives

Conceptually, Federal Reserve open market operations are divided into two categories: defensive operations and dynamic operations. As the name implies, **defensive open market operations** refer to the Fed's open market operations made to "defend" bank reserves and the monetary base against outside forces over which the Fed has little or no control. As we discussed in Chapter 15, many factors besides the Federal Reserve directly influence bank reserves and the monetary base. In the absence of defensive open market operations, these other factors cause erratic fluctuations in reserves, the monetary base, and credit conditions. On average, changes in factors such as float and Treasury deposits at the Fed cause aggregate bank reserves to fluctuate by about 4 percent each week. The Fed, in its defensive operations, manipulates its portfolio of securities to prevent these outside forces from causing unwanted fluctuations in R, B, M1, M2, and interest rates.

In its **dynamic open market operations,** the Federal Reserve deliberately changes the course of economic activity in line with the Fed's policy objectives. If the unemployment rate is high and rising, the Fed's dynamic aim is to push down short-term interest rates and increase the growth rates of R, B, and the monetary aggregates, thus stimulating economic activity. If the inflation rate is—or is threatening to become—intolerably high, the Fed aims to push up short-term interest rates and restrict the growth rate of the monetary variables.

The modern image of the Fed typically is viewed in the context of the Fed's dynamic aim—the Fed sits at the front of the machine, pushing levers to try to control unemployment, inflation, and other economic evils. Contrary to this modern image, the Fed was created more than 90 years ago with the defensive aim foremost in the minds of its founders. The founders viewed the proposed central bank primarily as an institution that would prevent the fractional reserve banking system from exerting a disruptive impact on the economy.

Recall from Chapter 12 that, prior to the establishment of the Fed in 1913, seasonal credit demands and currency withdrawals caused periodic episodes of credit stringency and occasional panics in which customers rushed to withdraw their money from banks. Such actions forced banks to liquidate loans and securities to meet the depositors' currency demands, precipitating an undesirable contraction of credit availability, deposits, and the money supply. Banks were sometimes forced to close in times of acute stress. The Federal Reserve was established in large part to serve as a "lender of last resort" in times of financial stress. The Fed's founders did not conceive of the institution in its modern, dynamic role of implementing measures to smooth the ups and downs of the business cycle.

In terms of volume of trading, the Fed's defensive operations dwarf its dynamic operations. In 2003, for example, the *net increase* in the Fed's aggregate security portfolio for the year was less than 0.3 percent of the value of total Federal Reserve open market transactions during the year. This balance indicates an overwhelming portion of the Fed's open market operations is defensive in nature.

## Outright Transactions Versus Repurchase Agreements

Federal Reserve open market transactions are classified into two types: *outright transactions* and *repurchase agreements* (and *reverse repurchase agreements*). In general, the Fed uses outright purchases to bring about long-run or permanent growth in reserves and the monetary aggregates. The Fed uses repurchase agreements and reverse repurchase agreements to neutralize the potential impact on reserves and the monetary base of *transitory* changes in R and B resulting from fluctuations in factors outside the Fed's direct control, such as float, Treasury deposits at the Fed, and Treasury currency outstanding. In other words, most of the Fed's defensive open market operations are conducted through repurchase agreements and its close relative—reverse repurchase agreements.

A **repurchase agreement (RP)** is a money market instrument that government security dealers, banks, and other large financial market players use to mobilize temporarily idle funds. The dealers or banks sell securities with an explicit agreement to buy back the securities at a specified date and price. The buy-back date normally is 1 to 15 days in the future. The buy-back price is established at a sufficient premium over the initial price so that the lender's (buyer's) return is equivalent to the yield on collateralized short-term money market loans. The lenders—the initial buyers of these securities from dealers—typically include banks, nonfinancial corporations, and the Federal Reserve System.[4]

**repurchase agreement (RP)**
money market instrument that government security dealers, banks, and other large financial market players use to mobilize temporarily idle funds

From the lender's viewpoint—perhaps a nonfinancial corporation such as IBM with $10 million surplus cash on hand—the RP is a convenient and attractive substitute for demand deposits, which do not pay interest. Firms' expenditures and receipts are not perfectly synchronized over time. Thus, IBM's need for cash balances (money) tends to be uneven, increasing sharply on paydays, dividend dates, and quarterly income tax dates. Pending the arrival of such dates, IBM may conveniently use its bank checking accounts (DDO) to temporarily buy securities from its bank. In the RP arrangement, the bank sells U.S. government securities to IBM and agrees to buy back the securities on the date the firm needs the funds to meet its payroll, pay its dividend, or pay its taxes.

Because paydays, dividend dates, and income tax deadlines cluster on specific dates, U.S. government security dealers face acute stress on dates when they are scheduled to repurchase large amounts of securities. In the absence of Federal Reserve assistance, credit markets would be strained at such times, and yields would increase as dealers scrambled for funds to buy back the securities. To minimize seasonal pressures and contribute to the stability of financial markets, the Fed sometimes enters the market to buy securities under repurchase agreements.

The Fed also engages in RP transactions to defend banks reserves from unwanted fluctuations. For example, as Christmas approaches each year, the public increases its holdings of currency ($C^P$), reducing bank reserves. After Christmas, much of this cash finds its way back into banks, replenishing bank reserves. To provide temporary relief in December, the Fed purchases securities under repurchase agreements. This action temporarily pumps reserves into banks and offsets the effects of the currency drain. After Christmas, the dealers repurchase the securities from the Fed, reducing bank reserves and thereby neutralizing the expansionary effect of the cash that is redeposited into banks by the public.

RP transactions are useful to the Fed when the Treasury conducts heavy financing (borrowing) operations, exerting temporary upward pressure on yields. To help spread the upward pressure on yields over time, the Fed times its RP security purchases for days when the Treasury is borrowing heavily. The Fed purchases inject

[4] Government securities dealers might view the RP as a loan to help finance a large inventory of securities—that is, as an alternative to a regular bank loan. Dealers frequently use this financial instrument because RP rates are lower than bank loan rates.

reserves into the banks, boosting excess reserves and bank demand for securities, thereby moderating the upward pressure on yields. The Fed schedules the date on which dealers repurchase the securities to coincide with a period of light financing by the Treasury.

The Federal Reserve also conducts repurchase agreements in reverse. Temporary events often produce an undesired *increase* in bank reserves and the monetary base. For example, an increase in float or a reduction in Treasury deposits at the Fed temporarily increases R and B on a dollar-for-dollar basis. To neutralize these effects, the Fed engages in a **reverse repurchase agreement (reverse RP),** also known as a **matched sale-purchase transaction.** In a reverse RP, the Fed sells securities to dealers and agrees to buy back the securities at a specific date and price. The reverse RP, or matched sale-purchase agreement, is analogous to the RP but has precisely the opposite effect.

**reverse repurchase agreement (reverse RPs)** or **matched sale-purchase transaction**
transaction in which securities are sold to buyers, who agree to buy back the securities at a specific date and price

Table 18-1 shows the magnitudes of the Federal Reserve's outright transactions, RPs, and reverse RPs in 2003. Note that outright purchases and sales of U.S. government securities were small compared to transactions in RPs and reverse RPs. Gross purchases and sales of U.S. government securities in all forms in 2003 amounted to $6,501.9 billion ($6.5 trillion) and $6,465.3 billion ($6.4 trillion), respectively. The net change in the Fed's portfolio of U.S. government securities for 2003 was (positive) $36.6 billion, or less than half of 1 percent of total Federal Reserve open market transactions. *Other things being equal,* the Fed's open market operations in U.S. government securities increased the U.S. monetary base by $36.6 billion in 2003.

## POLICY DIRECTIVE

The **policy directive** is a key Fed written statement produced by the FOMC at each meeting. The policy directive indicates the intended posture of Federal Reserve policy until the next FOMC meeting. In the next two sections, we discuss how the Fed produces and implements the policy directive.

**policy directive**
written statement indicating the intended posture of Federal Reserve policy until the next FOMC meeting

**Table 18-1** Federal Reserve Operations in U.S. Government and Agency Securities in 2003 ($ Billion)

| | |
|---|---|
| Outright Purchases and Sales | |
| Gross Purchases | 36.9 |
| Gross sales and redemptions | 0.0 |
| Repurchase Agreements | |
| Gross purchases | 1,522.9 |
| Gross sales | 1,518.6 |
| Reverse Repurchase Agreements | |
| Gross purchases | 4,942.1 |
| Gross sales | 4,946.7 |
| Net Change in U.S. Government Security Holdings in 2003 | +36.6 |

*Source: Board of Governors* 2003 Annual Report *at* http://www.federalreserve.gov/

## Arriving at the Policy Directive

Eight times annually (approximately every 6 weeks), the FOMC meets in Washington to formulate the direction and thrust of monetary policy. Discussion at each FOMC meeting covers several areas. First, members give their interpretations of current economic conditions and the likely near-term trend of key economic variables such as output, unemployment, and price level behavior. Second, each member of the FOMC outlines his or her view on what the Fed's dynamic aim should be for both the near-term and the longer-term horizon.

To arrive at a consensus on a specific policy directive, an informal give-and-take discussion ensues. The directive is issued to the **manager of the System Open Market Account,** who is an officer of the Federal Reserve Bank of New York. The manager carries out the directive issued by the FOMC. The directive must be sufficiently specific so that the manager can interpret the FOMC's objective without ambiguity. For many years, the directives were released to the public 45 days after FOMC meetings. In 1995 the Fed began announcing its policy directive immediately after each FOMC meeting. An excerpt from the press release following the FOMC meeting of June 29 to 30, 2004, is given here.

**manager of the System Open Market Account**
New York Federal Reserve bank officer who carries out the directive issued by the FOMC

> The Federal Open Market Committee decided today to raise its target for the federal funds rate by 25 basis points to 1.25 percent.
>
> The Committee believes that, even after this action, the stance of monetary policy remains accommodative and, coupled with robust underlying growth in productivity, is providing ongoing support to economic activity. The evidence accumulated over the intermeeting period indicates that output is continuing to expand at a solid pace and labor market conditions have improved. Although incoming inflation data are somewhat elevated, a portion of the increase in recent months appears to have been due to transitory factors.
>
> The Committee perceives the upside and downside risks to the attainment of both sustainable growth and price stability for the next few quarters are roughly equal. With underlying inflation still expected to be relatively low, the Committee believes that policy accommodation can be removed at a pace that is likely to be measured. Nonetheless, the Committee will respond to changes in economic prospects as needed to fulfill its obligation to maintain price stability.
>
> *Source: http://www.federalreserve.gov/*

A vote of the 12-person committee is taken when a near-consensus on the wording of the directive, including the appropriate target rate for the federal funds rate (or other variable to be controlled), is apparent among members of the FOMC. One or more member votes against the directive is not unusual, although the FOMC vote affirming the above policy action was unanimous.[5] The lack of unanimity is not surprising given varying FOMC member viewpoints on the strength of forces impinging on economic activity and the relative priority of objectives such as price level stability and low unemployment levels.

## Implementation of the Policy Directive

The manager of the System Open Market Account oversees the traders who carry out the Fed's purchases and sales of securities. Early in the morning, before the markets open, the manager reads a report indicating the amount of reserves in the banking system at the close of the previous day's business. He or she also reviews the level of—and recent movements in—the federal funds rate. A declining federal

[5] For example, 57 of the directives drawn up for the 80 FOMC meetings held from 1994 to 2003 were approved unanimously. In 23 cases, one or more members of the FOMC voted against the directive. In the 40 FOMC meetings held from 1999 to 2003, 31 directives were approved without a dissenting vote. See the minutes and votes of FOMC meetings at http://www.federalreserve.gov/default.htm.

funds rate suggests excess reserves are plentiful and pressure on bank reserve positions is easing. A rising federal funds rate suggests the opposite. Together, the information on reserves and the federal funds rate gives the manager a feel for likely money market conditions when the financial markets open.

At 9:00 a.m., the manager contacts several government securities dealers to get their expectations of conditions during the day. At approximately 10:00 a.m., the manager receives a report from the Federal Reserve staff, indicating the expected movement of several important factors influencing bank reserves—float, currency held by the public, Treasury deposits at the Fed, and so forth. If float is expected to rise because of fog or other adverse conditions at several major airports, the manager knows that she must sell securities to offset an undesired expansion in reserves and the monetary base.

At around 10:30 a.m., the manager phones the U.S. Treasury for information that will enable her to fine-tune the Fed staff's preliminary forecast of the change in Treasury deposits at the Fed for the day—a major factor influencing reserves and the monetary base. A Treasury official indicates the government's transactions that will be made that day through the Treasury's account at the Fed. If this information reveals Treasury deposits at the Fed will decrease, the Fed must sell securities to absorb the resulting increase in bank reserves.

Around mid-morning, the manager contacts an official of the Board of Governors and at least one of the five presidents currently serving as voting members of the FOMC to outline intended open market operations for the day. As soon as the manager gets the officials' approval, she reviews the current quotations (prices and yields) of the firms serving as primary dealers in U.S. government securities. The Fed is in electronic contact with the primary government securities dealers through a computer system known as TRAPS (Trading Room Automated Processing System). The Fed seeks to purchase securities at the lowest possible price and sell securities at the highest possible price. If the Fed intends to purchase \$1,800 million (\$1.8 billion) of Treasury bills on the day, the Fed scans the "ask" prices of the various dealers and ranks the prices in ascending order—from low to high. The manager then simply goes down the list and purchases securities until the quota of \$1,800 million is reached. The process typically is completed around noon. On most days, this transaction ends the Fed's trading, although occasionally special developments require Fed action in the afternoon.

## DISCOUNT WINDOW POLICY

**discount window**
facility through which the Federal Reserve district banks lend reserves to depository institutions

In financial market terminology, the **discount window** is a facility through which the Federal Reserve district banks lend reserves to depository institutions. Funds that banks borrow from the Federal Reserve System are known as *discount loans.* The term *discount policy* encompasses both the set of conditions under which banks are permitted to borrow reserves from the Fed's discount window and the interest rate charged banks on such Fed loans, known as the **discount rate.**[6]

**discount rate**
interest rate charged banks on discount loans by the Fed

[6] The term *discount window* derives from the early days of the Federal Reserve when New York bankers would actually go a window at the Federal Reserve Bank of New York to arrange a loan. Today, no such "discount window" exists. When a bank seeks a loan from the Federal Reserve, the bank calls the district Federal Reserve bank and asks the Fed to grant a short-term loan to the bank by crediting the bank's account with the Fed by the desired amount. The transaction is accomplished by a bookkeeping entry, and bank reserves increase dollar for dollar with the amount of the loan.

Today, three classes of credit are extended to banks by the Federal Reserve: primary credit, secondary credit, and seasonal credit. Primary credit is easily the most important. Banks judged to be in good financial condition are permitted to borrow as much as they want through the **primary credit** facility (sometimes referred to as the *standing credit facility*). The rate charged banks that borrow through this primary credit facility is the discount rate, currently set one percentage point above the Fed's target federal funds rate. Typically very little borrowing occurs in this facility because the discount rate is set significantly above the federal funds rate. A bank that is short on reserves normally borrows in the federal funds market instead. Unlike the past, the main function of the discount rate today is to impose an upper limit on potential movements in the federal funds rate. If the federal funds rate initially moved above the discount rate, heavy bank borrowing in the primary credit facility would be used to obtain funds for lending in the fed funds market. Such arbitrage activity by banks would prevent the fed funds rate from remaining above the discount rate.

**primary credit**
discount loans to banks that are in sound financial condition

**Secondary credit** is provided to troubled banks that are experiencing liquidity problems. The interest rate the Federal Reserve charges in the secondary credit facility is 0.5 percentage point above the discount rate. **Seasonal credit** is available to institutions that are subject to strong seasonal fluctuations in loan demand, such as small banks in farming communities and resort areas.

**secondary credit**
discount loans to banks experiencing liquidity problems or other financial problems

## 2003 Federal Reserve Change in Discount Window Policy

A bank deficient in reserves seeks the least costly method of obtaining reserves. The alternatives available to a typical bank include selling short-term securities such as Treasury bills, borrowing reserves from other banks in the federal funds market, and borrowing at the Fed's discount window. Prior to 2003, considerations involved in borrowing from the Federal Reserve included the actual interest cost (the discount rate), costs incurred in the event the public interpreted the bank's borrowing at the Fed as a sign of poor financial condition, and the increased likelihood of the bank's subsequent requests for loans from the Fed being rejected. The decision to borrow at the discount window hinges significantly on the discount rate level relative to money market yields. Prior to 2003, the Fed normally maintained its discount rate *below* the Treasury bill yield and the federal funds rate. The relationship between the Fed's discount rate and the federal funds rate from 1987 to 2004 is illustrated in Figure 18-2.

**seasonal credit**
Federal Reserve loans to institutions subject to strong seasonal fluctuations in loan demand, such as small banks in farming communities and resort areas

**Figure 18-2** Discount Rate and Federal Funds Rate from 1987 to 2004

Prior to 2003, the discount rate almost always was lower than the federal funds rate. This created problems. In 2003, the Fed adopted a procedure of setting its discount rate significantly *above* the federal funds rate and other money market rates.

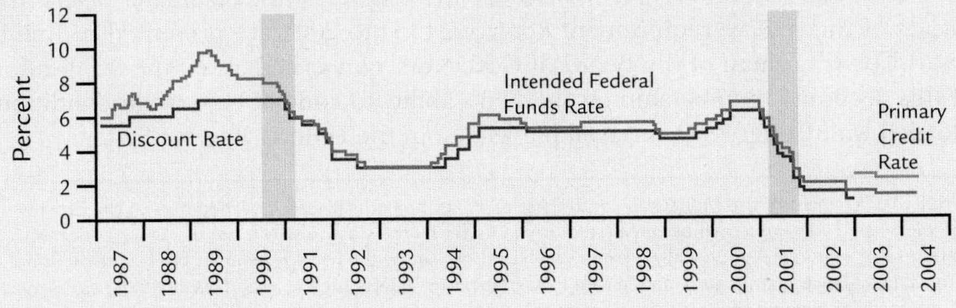

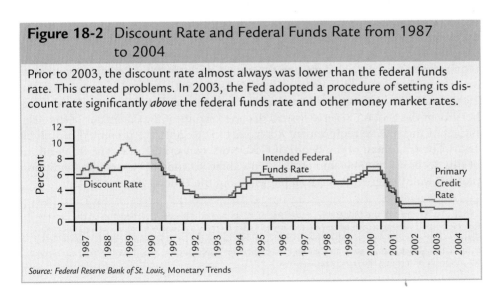

*Source: Federal Reserve Bank of St. Louis,* Monetary Trends

A glance at the figure reveals two facts: the discount rate before 2003 was almost always lower than the federal funds rate, and the gap between the two rates varied significantly over time. The latter finding suggests that the incentive to borrow at the discount window varied over time and was very strong when the spread was large. The Federal Reserve countered banks' incentive to heavily use discount loans through the Fed's "administration of the discount window." Specifically, the Fed limited bank use of the financially tempting discount window by setting and enforcing certain "rules of the game." In general, the Fed informed banks that borrowing for "need" was legitimate, but borrowing for "profit" was not. However, this criterion was highly ambiguous. Economists have long criticized the Fed's conduct of discount window policy (see Exhibit 18-1).

**Lombard system**
system in which the discount rate is set significantly *above* money market yields and use of the discount window is a "right" rather than a "privilege" administered by the central bank

In 2003, the Fed adopted the Lombard discount window system long used by the Bank of England and most other central banks. (Lombard Street in London is the financial center of Britain. Its name derives from the Lombardy region of Italy, the birthplace of banking.) In the **Lombard system,** the discount rate is set significantly *above* money market yields, and use of the discount window is a "right" rather than a "privilege" administered by the central bank. In the past, banks were expected to quickly repay their loans from the Federal Reserve. The new system permits banks to borrow continuously at this facility. The relatively high rate banks pay to borrow at the discount window serves efficiently to limit the use of this facility. Adoption of the Lombard system likely improves the overall conduct of monetary policy.

## RESERVE REQUIREMENT INSTRUMENT

So far, we have analyzed two of the Fed's general tools or instruments—open market operations and discount window policy. The third major instrument of Federal Reserve policy is the authority to change the percentage reserve requirement (within limits set by Congress) applicable to demand deposits and other checkable accounts and certain other liabilities of commercial banks and thrift institutions.

Since 1935, the Federal Reserve has been authorized to set and change the reserve requirements—or required reserve ratios—banks must maintain. The reserve requirements can be considered a "tax" on depository institutions because the requirements force institutions to hold a larger portion of their assets in non–interest-earning form (reserves) than they would voluntarily maintain. Before 1980, reserve requirements for banks that were not members of the Federal Reserve System were lower than those applied to member banks.[7] As interest rates trended upward in the 1960s and 1970s, the magnitude of this "tax" on member banks increased and membership in the Federal Reserve System declined significantly. (Estimates of the magnitude of the reserve requirement tax from 1960 to 2004 are presented in Exhibit 18-2.) The Chairman of the Board of Governors, concerned about the implications of this declining membership on the Fed's ability to control U.S. credit conditions, pleaded with Congress to force all banks to join the Federal Reserve System.

[7] Prior to enactment of the Monetary Control Act of 1980, banks that were not members of the Federal Reserve System were governed by reserve requirements set by the state in which the banks were located. State reserve requirements typically were lower than those set by the Fed for member banks. Furthermore, many states allowed banks to count certain interest-bearing assets, such as U.S. Treasury bills, as reserves for purposes of meeting the reserve requirement.

### **Exhibit 18-1** Federal Reserve's 2003 Adoption of the Lombard Discount Rate Procedure

In early 2003, the Federal Reserve significantly changed the operation of its discount window policy. For many decades, the Federal Reserve set its discount rate *below* Treasury bill yields and other money market rates. From a profit maximization viewpoint, banks were sorely tempted to heavily use this potential source of funds.

Traditional central banking doctrine indicated that two mechanisms limited the amount banks borrowed from the Fed given the bank' obvious temptation to borrow. First, banks were "reluctant" to use the discount window, partly because the public could interpret bank borrowing at the discount window as a sign of banks' financial weakness. Second, the Federal Reserve administered bank requests for discount loans based on the criterion that bank borrowing for "need" was legitimate but borrowing for "profit" was not. Banks could legitimately borrow at the discount window if banks accidentally came up short of reserves at the end of the day. Banks could not borrow to make an arbitrage profit by using funds borrowed from the Fed to purchase higher-yielding Treasury bills and other money market instruments or to make loans to customers.

On deeper analysis, you can see problems with this criterion. Suppose a huge money-center bank frequently comes up short on reserves by tens of millions of dollars at the end of the day because of aggressive management of the bank's reserve position. Such banks hold large portfolios of Treasury bills. If a bank routinely borrows \$50 million from the discount window rather than selling off \$50 million of Treasury bills to cover reserve deficiencies, is the bank borrowing for "need" or for "profit"? You can argue that the bank borrows because the bank profits by borrowing from the Fed rather than liquidating higher-yielding Treasury bills. Some students of central banking argue that the discount window enabled banks to circumvent the intent of monetary policy. If the Fed attempted to implement monetary restraint by open market sales of securities, large money-center banks short on reserves often reacted by increasing borrowing from the Federal Reserve. Reserves taken away by open market operations tended to be replaced by increased bank borrowing at the discount window.

The Bank of England and central banks in Europe traditionally avoided the need to evaluate the legitimacy of bank requests for credit at their discount facility by using the Lombard system. In the Lombard system, the central bank sets its discount rate at a "penalty" level—that is, significantly *above* money market rates. Rather that administering individual bank requests to borrow at the discount window, the central bank proclaims bank borrowing to be a "right" rather than a "privilege." By setting the discount rate appreciably above money market yields, the central bank sharply reduces the likelihood of bank abuse of the discount window. After years of criticism from academic economists, the Federal Reserve finally implemented the Lombard mechanism in early 2003. Today, the Fed sets its discount rate one percentage point above the federal funds target rate (and therefore approximately the same margin above the short-term Treasury bill yield).

This change in the Federal Reserve's discount window procedures likely enhances the Fed's monetary control. For example, when the Fed takes away bank reserves through open market sales of securities, banks now more likely react by liquidating Treasury bills and raising their loan rates rather than increasing borrowing at the discount window.

**Table 18-2 Reserve Requirements for U.S. Depository Institutions**

| Component | Current Reserve Requirement (%) | Federal Reserve Range (%)* |
|---|---|---|
| I. Normal Reserves | | |
| A. Net transactions accounts** | | |
| 1. First $45.4 million | 3 | — |
| 2. Above $45.4 million*** | 10 | 8–14 |
| B. Nonpersonal time deposits | 0 | 0–9 |
| C. Eurocurrency liabilities | 0 | 0–9 |
| II. Supplementary Reserves | 0 | 0–4 |

*The Federal Reserve is authorized by Congress to change reserve requirements within these limits.
**Includes demand deposits, NOW accounts, ATS accounts, telephone transfer accounts, and share drafts. Net transactions accounts exclude the first $6.6 million of transactions accounts (in 2004), which are not subject to reserve requirements.
***This is the 2004 breakpoint. The breakpoint changes in December of each year by 80 percent of the percentage change in total U.S. transactions accounts in the previous fiscal year (June 30–June 30).
*Source:* Federal Reserve Bulletin, *December 2003*

is authorized, under certain conditions, to invoke a supplementary reserve requirement of up to 4 percent on transactions accounts. If the supplementary reserve is invoked, the Fed pays interest on supplementary reserves at a rate that is linked to the rate the Fed earns on its portfolio of securities.

The Monetary Control Act improved the Fed's capacity to exert short-run control of the money supply. By forcing all depository institutions to abide by a uniform set of reserve requirements and replacing the complicated structure of reserve requirements in place before 1980 with a simpler scheme, the legislation reduced short-term instability in $r_r$ (the weighted average reserve requirement) and the money supply multiplier.

## Institutional Aspects of Bank Reserve Management

The Federal Reserve facilitates management of depository institutions' reserve positions through provisions for reserve averaging and use of a carryover allowance.

**Reserve Averaging.** Banks and thrift institutions do not have to meet the required reserve ratio each day but must average the reserves over the *settlement period,* a 2-week period that ends on a Wednesday. Thus, if a depository institution fails to meet the reserve requirement each day until the last day of the settlement period, it still can satisfy the reserve requirement for that period by exhibiting a substantial amount of excess reserves on Wednesday. By the same token, banks that maintain excess reserves over most days in the settlement period may have a deficiency of reserves on the last day(s) of the period. Therefore, Wednesdays are characterized by relatively heavy activity in the federal funds market and Treasury bill market as banks adjust their reserve positions.

**Carryover Allowance.** Reserve deficiencies or excesses for a settlement period, up to a maximum of 2 percent of the dollar amount of required reserves, can be carried over one settlement period. This feature eliminates the need for many depository institutions to scramble at the end of each settlement period either to obtain or to rid themselves of reserves.

## ECONOMIC EFFECTS OF RESERVE REQUIREMENT CHANGES

Let's look at how reserve requirement changes influence the nation's money supply and interest rates. Along the way, we examine the strengths and weaknesses of reserve requirement changes as a Federal Reserve policy tool.

### Influence on the Money Supply and Interest Rates

In Chapter 16, we learned that a change in reserve requirements influences the money supply differently than do open market operations or changes in the discount rate. The latter two instruments derive their influence predominantly by changing the monetary base. Changes in reserve requirements leave the base unaltered but directly change the money supply multiplier. A reduction in reserve requirements increases the money supply multiplier—that is, it increases the total amount of bank credit and money supply that can be supported by a given monetary base. An increase in reserve requirements reduces the money supply multiplier. Let's review two basic expressions of Chapter 16 here, in Equations (18-1) and (18-2).

$$(18\text{-}1)\quad \mathbf{m_1} = \frac{\mathbf{1 + k}}{\mathbf{r_r + r_e + k}}$$

$$(18\text{-}2)\quad \mathbf{r_r} = \frac{\textbf{Required reserves}}{\textbf{DDO}}.$$

Equation (18-1) expresses the money supply multiplier (for M1) in terms of its three fundamental determinants: currency ratio (k), weighted average required reserve ratio ($r_r$), and banks' desired excess reserve ratio ($r_e$). Equation (18-2) defines the weighted average required reserve ratio ($r_r$) as the ratio of the dollar amount of required reserves to the total amount of transactions accounts—demand deposits and other checkable deposits (DDO).

Remember that $r_r$ is affected by check clearing between depository institutions subject to different marginal reserve requirements. For example, when a check written on a $500 million bank is deposited in a $30 million dollar bank, $r_r$ declines. Thus, check clearing among banks of different sizes introduces short-run variation into $r_r$ and the money supply multiplier. Such variation is relatively small, however.

In Chapter 16, we sketched the impact of an *increase* in $r_r$ on the money supply multiplier. Let us now analyze both the arithmetic and the economics of a *reduction* in the required reserve ratio to help us understand the behavioral phenomena causing the change in the money supply multiplier and the money stock.

Suppose that initially $r_r = 0.10$, $k = 0.90$, and $r_e = 0.005$. Using the expression for the money supply multiplier [Equation (18-1)], we compute:

$$\mathbf{m_1} = \frac{\mathbf{1 + 0.90}}{\mathbf{0.10 + 0.005 + 0.90}} = \frac{\mathbf{1.90}}{\mathbf{1.005}} = \mathbf{1.891}.$$

Each dollar of monetary base supports $1.89 worth of money (M1). Now, suppose as a result of an across-the-board reduction of reserve requirements on demand deposits, $r_r$ is reduced from 0.10 to 0.09—that is, from 10 percent to 9 percent. We calculate the new money supply multiplier as follows:

$$\mathbf{m_1} = \frac{\mathbf{1 + 0.90}}{\mathbf{0.09 + 0.005 + 0.90}} = \frac{\mathbf{1.90}}{\mathbf{0.995}} = \mathbf{1.910}.$$

Assuming the currency ratio (k) and the desired excess reserve ratio ($r_e$) are not induced to change by the reduction in $r_r$, the money supply multiplier ($m_1$) rises from 1.89 to 1.91. This represents an approximately 1 percent increase in the money supply multiplier and M1.

In this example, the monetary base is unaltered when the Fed reduces the reserve requirement. Bank reserves also are unaltered. However, a smaller portion of the existing base and reserves is impounded in the form of required reserves, and a greater portion of the base and reserves now qualifies as excess reserves, available to banks for acquiring earning assets in the form of loans and securities. Because actual excess reserves are boosted above desired excess reserves by the reduction in $r_r$, banks expand their loans and security holdings. Demand deposits are thereby created. The money supply increases.

Increased bank loan supply to the public induced by the reduction in $r_r$ triggers a reduction in bank loan rates. Also, the increased bank demand for Treasury securities drives up security prices, thereby reducing security yields. Thus, you expect a reduction in reserve requirements to be followed by a general reduction in interest rates. This expectation is consistent with the monetary authorities' objective in reducing reserve requirements—to increase individuals' and firms' willingness to borrow and spend on goods and services, thus stimulating economic activity.

## Advantages of the Reserve Requirement Tool

Now we outline a few advantages of the reserve requirements tool relative to the other tools of monetary policy.

**Speed of Impact.** Changes in the reserve requirement induce thousands of banks and thrift institutions to rapidly adjust their balance sheets. When the Fed changes reserve requirements, all of these institutions experience an immediate change in their excess reserve position. Therefore, changes in interest rates, credit conditions, and monetary aggregates occur rapidly, perhaps more quickly than when the Fed implements changes through open market operations or changes in the discount rate. However, these latter instruments impact financial markets sufficiently quickly so that speed of impact is not a critical consideration.

**Neutrality.** A related argument is that the reserve requirement instrument has a *neutral* impact on banks—its impact is less discriminatory across depository institutions than the other instruments of Federal Reserve policy. Unlike open market operations and discount rate changes, the impact of reserve requirement changes is spread uniformly across *all* banks and thrift institutions. Use of this instrument may be preferable based on similar effects on many more institutions than are affected by the other instruments.

**Potential Use in an Emergency.** At rare times when other tools cannot accomplish the job, changes in reserve requirements may be needed to neutralize major changes in the monetary base. In the urgent circumstances of war, for instance, the government typically finances an increased level of military expenditures by issuing short-term and long-term securities—by borrowing. To assist the Treasury in financing the war effort, the Fed can purchase larger-than-normal quantities of securities in the open market. This purchase can help the Treasury, but it also paves the way for inflationary expansion of credit and money by directly expanding bank reserves and the monetary base. In this case, the Fed's open market security purchases can be combined with increased reserve requirements to avoid triggering a multiple expansion of deposits in the banking system. That is, as the monetary base expands due to the Fed's security purchases, the money supply multiplier is reduced by the Fed's increased reserve requirements (and $r_r$). In this way, money supply growth is limited to a rate consistent with the Fed's overall objectives.

## Disadvantages of the Reserve Requirement Tool

Most bankers want the Fed to abandon changes in reserve requirements as a monetary policy tool. Many economists agree with the bankers, primarily because in most instances the Fed's objectives can be achieved more easily and smoothly with other policy instruments. A couple of points have been raised supporting the view that reserve requirement levels should remain fixed over time and that the Fed should accomplish its policy objectives through its other policy tools.

**Bluntness.** Given that aggregate DDO today is in the vicinity of $700 billion, a one percentage point reduction (increase) in the reserve requirement would release (absorb) $7 billion of excess reserves. Such magnitudes are simply too large to warrant regular changes in reserve requirements. In fact, use of the reserve requirement tool has been likened to use of an ax by a surgeon. In contrast, open market operations can be calibrated to bring about small and continuous changes in reserves and the monetary aggregates. Thus, open market operations are a much more suitable mechanism for bringing about monetary change.

**Lack of Flexibility.** Suppose the Fed raises the reserve requirement to restrict aggregate expenditures and combat mounting inflationary pressures. Assume that, a couple of weeks later, *falling* expenditures and *rising* unemployment clearly emerge as more serious problems than inflation. Then a *reduction* in reserve requirements is needed. However, given that the Fed had recently *raised* reserve requirements, early reversal of direction constitutes the Fed's admission of error. Some observers believe the Fed would be reluctant to admit the error and would maintain the *status quo* until evidence of a need for monetary stimulus became overwhelming. In this sense, reserve requirement changes do not score highly on the flexibility criterion.

Frequent changes in reserve requirements create uncertainty for banks, and raising reserve requirement levels can trigger liquidity problems for many banks. Partly for these reasons, the Federal Reserve has displayed a much stronger propensity over the years to reduce, rather than increase, reserve requirements. In the past 50 years, The Fed implemented approximately twice as many reserve requirement reductions as increases, and the top reserve requirement rate for DDO has declined from 26 percent in the early 1950s to 10 percent today. The reserve requirement tool is redundant because the Fed's objectives can be amply met through open market operations coupled with discount window policy. Several countries, including Australia, Canada, Switzerland, and New Zealand, have abolished reserve requirements. Although elimination of reserve requirements can hamper the Fed's ability to accurately control the money supply, a strong case can be made for choosing an optimal level of reserve requirements and leaving the reserves requirements at that level indefinitely.

## SUMMARY

A Federal Reserve instrument or tool is a variable over which the Fed has total control. It is linked through intermediate variables such as short-term interest rates and the monetary aggregates to ultimate policy goals—price level stability, reasonably low rates of unemployment, and so forth. The three general tools of Fed policy are open market operations, discount rate changes, and reserve requirement changes. The most important Fed tool is open market operations, chiefly because this flexible tool enables the Fed to exert relatively precise control over bank reserves and short-term interest rates. In addition to open market operations, the Fed has authority to change its discount rate and reserve requirements applicable to all depository institutions (within ranges established by Congress). Together, these tools give the Fed plenty of ammunition to influence bank lending, the monetary aggregates, and short-term interest rates. Discount rate changes are less important as a tool of policy today than in earlier times. The Fed now sets its discount rate at a constant margin above the federal funds target rate and moves the discount rate in lockstep with changes in the fed funds target rate, thus explaining the lesser importance of the discount rate changes. Changing the reserve requirement is potentially a powerful tool of policy but is seldom used because of its bluntness. Open market operations and discount window policy derive their influence through their effect on bank reserves and the monetary base. Changes in reserve requirements impact the money supply multiplier. An increase in reserve requirements reduces the money supply multiplier and the monetary aggregates and boosts interest rates. A reduction in reserve requirements increases the money supply multiplier and the monetary aggregates and reduces interest rates. Reserve requirements can be regarded as a tax on banks, forcing banks to hold more reserves than they would maintain voluntarily. Because a high level of reserve requirements increases banks' incentives to develop new substitutes for demand deposits not subject to reserve requirements, the Fed's ability to control aggregate expenditures is weakened by high reserve requirements. Partly for this reason, central banks around the world in recent years have been reducing or eliminating reserve requirements.

## KEY TERMS

instrument or tool of monetary policy
open market operations
discount loans
defensive open market operations
dynamic open market operations
repurchase agreement (RP)
reverse repurchase agreement (reverse RP) or matched sale-purchase transaction
policy directive
manager of System Open Market Account
discount window
discount rate
primary credit
secondary credit
seasonal credit
Lombard system

# STUDY QUESTIONS

1. Define the term *instrument* or *tool* of Federal Reserve policy. How does an instrument differ from an intermediate target variable?

2. Using T-accounts for the Federal Reserve and for the aggregate banking system, explain how Federal Reserve purchases of $420 million of Treasury bills from dealers affect bank reserves and the monetary base.

3. What is the difference for bank reserves and the monetary base whether the Federal Reserve purchases $1 million worth of government securities from dealers or $1 million worth of automobiles from General Motors? Explain.

4. Suppose the Federal Reserve supports the U.S. dollar by purchasing dollars with the European currency—euros (sells euros for dollars). What will be the impact on U.S. bank reserves and the monetary base, and what could the Fed do (via open market operations) to neutralize the consequences for reserves and the base? Explain.

5. Explain how the federal funds market and the negotiable CD market help transmit the impact of restrictive Federal Reserve open market operations quickly across the entire nation.

6. What are the advantages of open market operations relative to the other instruments of monetary policy? Explain.

7. Assume that, over the course of a given week, the Federal Reserve makes net purchases of $1.8 billion of Treasury securities in the open market. What can we conclude from this information about the Fed's dynamic aim? Explain.

8. Suppose all other factors influencing bank reserves and the monetary base this week are self-canceling and the Fed sells $3,600 million ($3.6 billion) of Treasury notes to dealers. Explain how this Fed action would influence:
   A. Bank reserves, the monetary base, and M1
   B. Security yields and prices

9. Discuss the nature of repurchase agreements and explain two different types of situations that might cause the Fed to buy government securities by repurchase agreements. Do the same with reverse purchase agreements.

10. "The Fed should set reserve requirements at a reasonable level and never change them. The only tool the Fed needs is open market operations." Do you agree or disagree? Defend your position.

11. Suppose you graduate this year and go to work as a loan officer in a small bank in Medicine Lodge, Montana. Assume, during your first week on the job, the Federal Reserve boosts both its discount rate and the federal funds rate by one full percentage point. Explain why this might affect the loan rates your small Montana bank charges its customers.

12. Since early 2003, the Federal Reserve has set its discount rate by formula one percentage point above the federal funds rate. The Fed also has eased restrictions on bank borrowing at the discount window. Explain the factors motivating this change in Fed discount window policy.

13. In what sense are reserve requirements a "tax" on depository institutions? What problems does this "tax" create? Explain. How could this "tax" be eliminated?

14. Explain why the reserve requirement changes enacted in the Monetary Control Act of 1980 enhanced the ability of the Federal Reserve to accurately control the money supply.

15. Explain on a step-by-step basis the mechanism through which an increase in reserve requirements applicable to DDO influences interest rates and the supply of money.

16. Evaluate the Fed's current structure of reserve requirements. Is there room for improvement if the goal is to increase the Federal Reserve's potential control over the nation's money supply?

# ADDITIONAL READING

- On the tools of Federal Reserve policy, see Chapter 3 of *The Federal Reserve System: Purposes and Functions,* 8th edition (Washington, DC: Board of Governors of Federal Reserve System, 1994).
- A report describing Federal Reserve operations in the foreign exchange market is published periodically in the *Federal Reserve Bulletin.* All the directives and discussions of the FOMC are collected each year in the Board of Governors *Annual Report,* published each year in April and available at http://www.federalreserve.gov. Click on "Publications and Education Resources" and then click on "Annual Report." This publication contains a wealth of information on open market operations and other Federal Reserve data.
- An analysis of the proposed changes in discount window policy that were implemented in 2003 is presented in "Proposed Revision to the Federal Reserve's Discount Window Lending Program," *Federal Reserve Bulletin,* July 2002, pp. 313–319.
- A critical view of the Fed's pre-2003 discount window procedures is presented in Anna J. Schwartz, "The Misuse of the Fed's Discount Window," *Federal Reserve Bank of St. Louis Review,* September/October 1992, pp. 58–69.
- On the reserve requirement instrument, excellent general references include Marvin Goodfriend and Monica Hargraves, "A Historical Assessment of the Rationales and Functions of Reserve Requirements," Federal Reserve Bank of Richmond *Economic Review,* March/April 1983, pp. 3–21, and Ann-Marie Muelendyke, "Reserve Requirements and the Discount Window in Recent Decades," Federal Reserve Bank of New York *Quarterly Review,* Autumn 1992, pp. 25–43.
- Finally, on the question of whether reserve requirements should be abolished, see the symposium in the 1999:2 issue of *International Finance.* In this issue, see Benjamin Friedman, "The Future of Monetary Policy: The Central Bank as an Army with Only a Signal Corps?"

# Chapter 19

# CONDUCTING MONETARY POLICY: ULTIMATE GOALS AND INTERMEDIATE TARGETS

In Chapter 18, we analyzed the tools or instruments of monetary policy. The Federal Reserve uses tools such as open market operations and discount rate changes to achieve ultimate goals such as high employment and price level stability. The link between the Fed's policy tools—which the Fed controls *directly* and *precisely*—and its ultimate objectives—which the Fed influences *indirectly,* very *imprecisely,* and with a considerable time lag—is uncertain and variable. The effect of changes in the Federal Reserve's portfolio of government securities or discount rate on the nation's output, employment, and price level may not be seen for at least a year. In conducting monetary policy, the Federal Reserve controls variables that it believes are causally linked to aggregate expenditures, output, and the price level and that it can quickly and accurately influence. The Fed sets target levels for these near-term and intermediate-term variables and uses its tools to hit these targets. Thus, the Fed uses policy tools to influence aggregate gross domestic product (GDP) expenditures and achieve its ultimate goals.

**operating target variables**
near-term variables the central bank controls as part of its strategy to achieve policy goals

**intermediate target variables**
intermediate-term variables the central bank attempts to control in its effort to achieve policy goals

We begin this chapter by briefly sketching Federal Reserve policy *goals.* We discuss the procedure of selecting certain variables to serve as near-term and intermediate-term targets in the conduct of monetary policy. The near-term variables are **operating target variables.** The intermediate-term variables are **intermediate target variables.** We examine the requisite criteria for an ideal target variable. We then analyze the strengths and shortcomings of several variables used as operating and intermediate target variables in the past. We conclude by discussing the Federal Reserve's experience in conducting monetary policy by targeting these variables.

## ULTIMATE GOALS OF MONETARY POLICY

The Federal Reserve's ultimate objectives are to achieve a relatively stable national price level (to keep inflation at low and acceptable levels), maintain a high employment level (low unemployment rate), contribute to long-term economic growth, foster a stable dollar exchange rate *vis-à-vis* other national currencies, and stabilize the nation's financial markets. We briefly discuss each of these objectives.

### Price Level Stability

A major goal of central banks has long been to maintain price level stability. In the United States, the Federal Reserve is considered the guardian of the nation's price level, providing checks and balances on our elected officials' tendency to conduct budgetary policy irresponsibly. In the past 15 years, central banks around the world have placed increased emphasis on achieving price stability. Largely due to greater emphasis on price stability, inflation rates in many countries have been much lower in the past 10 to 15 years than in the 1970s and 1980s. The International Monetary Fund calculates the average annual inflation rate of industrial nations fell from 7 percent in the 1980s to approximately 2 percent from 1996 to 2004.

Price stability maintenance is a crucial policy goal because of inflation's harmful effects. Severe inflation results in misallocation of a nation's resources, thereby reducing economic efficiency. Severe inflation also impairs long-term economic growth and arbitrarily redistributes income and wealth, simultaneously helping some families while hurting others. Here, we briefly outline inflation's adverse consequences.

**Inflation and Resource Allocation.** Inflation reduces economic efficiency in part by creating a discrepancy between behavior that is rational from an individual or business firm viewpoint and behavior that is optimal from society's viewpoint. In a period of inflation, it is rational for each individual and firm to spend additional time on financial affairs, learning how to use futures markets and other means of gaining protection from inflation. During severe inflation, retail stores and other businesses spend time and resources marking up prices. In a country with high inflation, for example, restaurants may print new menus each month.[1] Such behavior is inefficient from society's viewpoint because it diverts scarce resources from socially useful activities.

In a market economy, changes in *relative* prices of goods and services serve a socially beneficial function by allocating resources efficiently. When a good is in short supply, its price increases. Firms step up production of that good, thereby remedying the shortage. For example, economic agents consider increased lumber prices during a period of overall price stability a sign that the relative price of lumber has risen and a lumber shortage exists. Appropriate signals are given, production of lumber is stepped up, and the lumber shortage is alleviated.

In a severe inflation, agents may be uncertain whether an increase in the price of a good is actually an increase in the *relative* price of that good. If lumber prices increase, agents are uncertain whether the increased price results from a lumber shortage or simply general inflationary pressures. Inflation can distort price signals and hinder market efficiency in allocating resources.

**Inflation and Long-Term Economic Growth.** The long-term growth of living standards depends significantly on the rate of technological innovation and business firms' related investment expenditures. Firms' investment expenditures on research and development and other projects with prospective long-term payoffs importantly affect the growth process. Economists believe that severe inflation, by reducing visibility and creating uncertainty, causes firms to postpone or cancel investment projects whose expected payoffs lie in the distant future. Unfortunately, such projects are often the projects that lead ultimately to increased productivity and living standards. If firms are risk averse, severe inflation likely reduces business expenditures on long-term investment projects and therefore is detrimental to long-term economic growth. High inflation may reduce the investment share of the nation's output, slow the growth of the nation's capital stock, and reduce long-term growth of output and income.

**Inflation and Distribution of the Nation's Income and Wealth.** In the near term, inflation is often compatible with high-level aggregate expenditures and national output. However, inflation almost inevitably *redistributes* the nation's in-

[1] Economists have dubbed the various inefficiencies of this sort that result from inflation "menu costs."

# INTERNATIONAL PERSPECTIVES

## Downward Trend in Inflation Throughout the World

The accompanying figure illustrates an important characteristic of economies throughout the world in the past 15 years: declining inflation. The International Monetary Fund's (IMF) measure of "world" inflation fell from more than 25 percent per year in 1990 to less that 4 percent per year in 2003. The IMF's measure of inflation for "industrial nations" declined from slightly more than 5 percent to less than 2 percent per year in the same period.

Several factors contributed to this favorable development. First, very high inflation in nations throughout the world in the 1970s alerted countries to the deleterious effects of inflation and increased nations' resolve to restrain it. Second, the 1991 Maastricht Treaty required nations aspiring to join the European Monetary Union to bring their inflation rates down to very low levels before qualifying for admission. Third, adverse supply shocks of the magnitude witnessed in the 1970s, when crude oil prices increased more than tenfold, have been absent. Finally, beginning with New Zealand in 1990, more than 20 nations have adopted regimes of *inflation targeting*—a policy in which maintaining low inflation is explicitly proclaimed as the overriding objective of central bank policy. As inflation rates in industrial nations trended downward and approached 1 percent per year by the end of the 1990s, economists worried about the possible onset of *deflation*. We will discuss that malady in detail in the remaining chapters of this text.

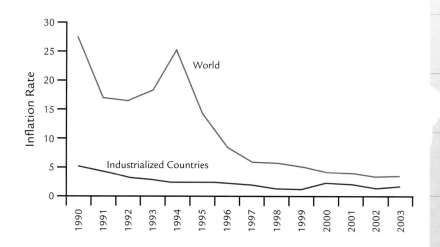

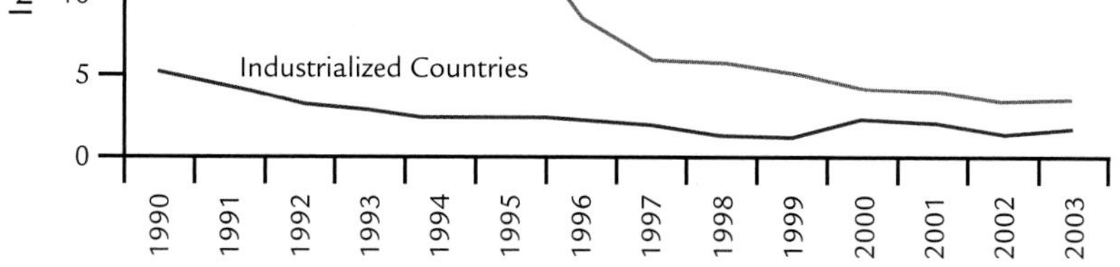

come and wealth unfairly and capriciously. When inflation is severe, wage and salary hikes and interest rates often fail to fully reflect the behavior of the nation's inflation rate. If this happens, *real* wages and *real* interest rates fall. If real wages fall, workers' share of the nation's income declines. If real interest rates fall, borrowers (debtors) benefit at the expense of lenders. Borrowers benefit from the fact that the real value of the incurred debt declines while the interest rate paid on the debt does not compensate for the decline in the debt's real value. The benefits borrowers reap from inflation come at the expense of lenders.

Suppose that, several years ago, your parents purchased a $100,000 home. They paid for 90 percent of the home by taking out a mortgage at 5 percent interest. Assume the inflation rate averaged 7 percent per year over the next 10 years. If the house kept pace with inflation, the house's value approximately doubled over the decade. Your parents experienced a $100,000 gain in the value of the home, while total interest payments (which are tax deductible) amounted to less than $50,000. Your parents benefited from the inflation because they were debtors. Who lost the wealth gained by your parents?—the individuals with funds in the savings institution (which paid them perhaps 3 percent interest) that granted your parents the mortgage loan. In general, the debtor has the advantage during a severe inflation. High-roller and aggressive types eager to incur debt benefit at the expense of thrifty and prudent individuals. Inflation is unfair. It creates tension among various groups in society.

In the past 50 years, U.S. inflation has averaged about 4 percent per year. In the 1970s, severe inflation averaging more than 7 percent per year doubled the U.S. price level in a single decade. In the past decade, however, inflation has been limited to about 2 percent per year, on average. The International Perspectives box outlines worldwide inflation trends since 1990.

## High Employment

Maintaining high output and employment levels is one of the paramount goals of monetary policy. Involuntary unemployment inevitably results in loss of national output and income. Unemployment deprives many families of their chief source of income. High unemployment triggers a host of social problems, such as increased crime and mental illness, and impacts most heavily on the disadvantaged and those at the lower end of the income scale. By reducing output and income, higher unemployment results in lower tax revenues for all levels of government. Public services such as road maintenance, police protection, and education likely are compromised. For these reasons, both the Employment Act of 1946 and the Full Employment and Balanced Growth Act of 1978 (commonly known as the *Humphrey-Hawkins Act)* commit the U.S. government (and the Federal Reserve) to maintaining a high employment level consistent with price level stability.

**Unemployment and Loss of National Output and Income.** When unemployment increases, fewer individuals work and the nation's output declines. Because each dollar of output produced creates a dollar of income earned, higher unemployment implies reduced collective income earned in the nation. In the early 1960s, Arthur Okun, an economist then associated with Yale University, famously quantified the relationship between the nation's unemployment rate and the nation's loss of output in an equation known as **Okun's Law.** A generalized form of Okun's Law is given in Equation (19-1).

**Okun's Law**
equation describing the relationship between the nation's unemployment rate and the nation's loss of output

$$\frac{(\mathbf{GDP} - \mathbf{GDP}^{\text{potential}})}{\mathbf{GDP}} = \mathbf{b}\ (\mathbf{U} - \mathbf{U_N}) \quad (19\text{-}1)$$

On the right-hand side of Equation (19-1), U is the actual unemployment rate and $U_N$ is the **natural rate of unemployment**—the unemployment rate that exists when the labor market is in equilibrium and there is full employment. Economists are uncertain of the precise level of the natural unemployment rate, which changes over time (this topic is discussed in detail in Chapter 20). Today, most economists believe the natural unemployment rate is in the range of 4.0 to 5.5 percent.[2] The left-hand side of Equation (19-1) expresses the nation's relative *output gap*—the difference between actual GDP and potential GDP (the full-employment level of GDP), expressed as a percentage of actual GDP. The parameter b is the percentage loss of output for each one percentage point that the nation's unemployment rate exceeds the natural rate of unemployment. For purposes of illustration, assume $U_N$ is 5 percent and b is 2.0. This particular version of Okun's Law is given in Equation (19-2).

**natural rate of unemployment**
unemployment rate that exists when the labor market is in equilibrium and there is full employment

$$\frac{(\mathbf{GDP} - \mathbf{GDP}^{\mathbf{potential}})}{\mathbf{GDP}} = \mathbf{2\ (U - 5\%)} \qquad (19\text{-}2)$$

Equation (19-2) indicates no loss of output results if the unemployment rate is 5 percent. Actual GDP is at potential in this case. For each percentage point the unemployment rate exceeds 5 percent, the loss of output is 2 percent of GDP. For example, if the nation's unemployment rate is 7 percent, the national loss of output is 4 percent of GDP. In a U.S. economy with GDP of $12,000 billion ($12 trillion), the loss of output is $480 billion, or an average of more than $1,500 per person. Okun's Law demonstrates that unemployment is costly. It shrinks the size of the pie that will be distributed among the nation's inhabitants.

**YOUR TURN**

Assume the economy descends into recession next year, and the unemployment rate increases to 8 percent. Assuming actual GDP is $14,000 billion ($14 trillion), use Okun's Law as expressed in Equation (19-2) to calculate the nation's loss of output and income.

**Other Consequences of Unemployment.** In addition to reducing per capita income, high unemployment unleashes a host of other adverse consequences. First, increased unemployment reduces the nation's income, but the *distribution* of this income loss is borne unequally among the different economic classes in society. Less-educated and lower-income individuals absorb the brunt of the impact because these individuals lose their jobs first when unemployment increases. During economic downturns, unemployment rates typically rise faster among blacks, Hispanics, and other minorities than among whites. High school dropouts are more severely impacted than college graduates. Second, studies indicate high unemployment aggravates a host of social maladies. The incidence of crime, prison incarceration, alcoholism, drug abuse, mental illness, premature deaths, and juvenile delinquency increase with the unemployment rate. Discrimination is more prevalent when unemployment rates are high. Finally, tax revenues received by state and local governments decline when unemployment rises (because aggregate income and the tax base decrease). For this reason, high

[2] In Congressional testimony in early 2004, Fed Chairman Alan Greenspan suggested that the natural unemployment rate may be as low as 4 percent. Most economists place the rate somewhat higher, perhaps around 5 percent.

unemployment typically is accompanied by impaired state and local government services. Funds available for education decline. The national cutback in state funding for education resulting from the 2001 recession and the associated increase in unemployment contributed to the sharply increased tuition levied on college and university students in recent years.

## Long-Term Economic Growth

The long-term growth of a nation's real GDP is important because it determines the fate of living standards over the long haul. Societies that do not increase average output produced per person over time simply cannot sustain increases in living standards. The chief determinants of long-term economic growth are the growth rate of the nation's stock of physical capital and human capital (the skills and education embodied in the work force) and the rate of technological change. Human capital and investment in plants, equipment, and technology are the keys to long-term economic growth.

The Fed's role in this process is relatively simple. The Fed must foster a stable economic environment with low inflation to facilitate low long-term interest rates and high investment expenditure levels. Because inflation creates uncertainty and impairs investment spending, the Federal Reserve must maintain inflation at relatively low levels.[3]

To contribute to long-term growth, the Fed must reduce the frequency, severity, and duration of recessions. Investment spending declines during recessions. If investment spending declines, the nation's future capital stock is permanently lower than it would have been if the recession had been prevented or reduced in severity. Thus, the Fed contributes positively to long-term economic growth by fostering economic stability and preventing severe economic downturns.

## Stable International Exchange Rate

Costs are involved when the U.S. dollar fluctuates sharply in foreign exchange markets. Volatile exchange rates can reduce the volume of international economic activity, harming U.S. export industries and depriving the nation of potential gains from trade. As discussed in Chapter 8, a strongly *falling* dollar boosts U.S. inflation by stimulating demand for U.S. goods, increasing import costs, and reducing the pressure on domestic firms to hold down prices. On the other hand, an excessively *strong* currency can be detrimental to a nation. An overvalued U.S. dollar can price U.S.-produced products out of world markets. An example occurred in 1983 and 1984, when the U.S. dollar appreciated dramatically against the Japanese yen and other currencies. A flood of cheap imported autos and other products caused heavy unemployment in the American automobile industry and other sectors subject to foreign competition. Preventing extreme and unwarranted exchange rate movements is one goal of Federal Reserve policy. The Fed occasionally intervenes directly in the foreign exchange market, aiming to limit exchange rate swings that the Fed deems inappropriate (review Exhibit 15-1 in Chapter 15). Exchange rate concerns can influence the Fed's conduct of monetary policy.

---

[3] The *mix* of monetary and fiscal policy is important to long-term growth because it influences long-term interest rates. Investment expenditures depend on long-term interest rates, especially long-term *real* interest rates. A stimulative fiscal policy (large budget deficits) coupled with restrictive monetary policy (slow or negative money growth) is a bad recipe for long-term economic growth because it produces relatively high long-term real interest rates. The reverse mix—*restrictive* fiscal policy (small budget deficits or budget surpluses) coupled with *stimulative* monetary policy—likely leads to lower long-term real interest rates, greater investment expenditures, and more rapid long-term growth. Therefore, measures that reduce the federal structural budget deficit and thereby allow more stimulative Federal Reserve policy are conducive to improved long-term economic growth.

### Stability of Financial Markets and Interest Rates

As indicated in Chapter 12, the Federal Reserve was *created* in response to periodic bouts of severe instability in U.S. financial markets that culminated in the panic of 1907. By serving its role of lender of last resort, the new central bank intended to stabilize U.S. financial markets in times of severe stress. In the past decade, several incidents may have produced severe financial market instability in the absence of Federal Reserve intervention. The incidents include the 1998 collapse of the Russian financial system and the associated near-collapse of the hedge fund Long-Term Capital Management, the Y2K problem at the beginning of the new millennium, and the terrorist attacks on New York City and Washington, DC, on September 11, 2001. In each case, the Fed stepped in and pumped a large amount of reserves into the U.S. banking system to head off major financial market repercussions. More generally, interest rates must be reasonably stable so that people can plan to purchase a new home, car, or other durable goods that traditionally are financed by borrowing. The Fed fosters interest rate stability mainly by maintaining an economic environment of relatively stable prices and stable output and income growth.

Now that we have sketched the ultimate goals of Federal Reserve policy, we can examine the practice of using intermediate target variables to achieve the Fed's goals.

## INTERMEDIATE MONETARY POLICY TARGETS

The Fed uses variables that respond quickly to its policy tools and strongly influence aggregate spending to attain its policy goals. Assume the Fed desires the nation's nominal GDP to increase at a 6 percent annual rate over the next year to achieve its goals. The Fed can only indirectly influence GDP growth. Suppose the Fed's research staff believes 4 percent growth in M2 would lead to approximately 6 percent growth in nominal GDP. In this case, the Fed selects M2 as the intermediate target variable—that is, the variable whose magnitude the Fed attempts to control in order to achieve its policy goals. The Fed then attempts to deliver 4 percent M2 growth over the following year. Alternatively, suppose the Federal Reserve believes maintaining the federal funds rate at 3 percent more likely would achieve the desired 6 percent growth of nominal GDP. In that event, the Fed selects the federal funds rate as its target variable and sets the target at 3 percent.

At first, specifying targets in terms of the Federal Reserve's policy tools might seem reasonable. Suppose the economy is in a severe recession and the Fed desires to implement a stimulative monetary policy. What would be wrong with Fed policy targeting, say, a 10 percent growth rate of the Fed's portfolio of government securities? Achieving this target with *total precision* is feasible because the Fed has complete control over its own securities portfolio. At first thought, using instrument variables as targets rather than variables over which the Fed exerts less than total influence seems desirable.

The problem with this approach is the uncertain impact of a change in the Fed's portfolio of securities or other tools on aggregate expenditures and GDP. The policy instrument change can be reinforced or counteracted by other factors. During a given week or month, a 10 percent rate of increase in the Fed's security portfolio may be consistent with a zero or even negative growth rate of M1 and M2. On the other hand, a 10 percent growth rate of the Fed's portfolio may result in *excessive* M1 and M2 growth rates. As emphasized in Chapters 15 and 16, many factors besides Federal Reserve policy influence the monetary base, the money supply multiplier, and the monetary aggregates. A similar argument holds for interest rates, which are heavily influenced by business cycle developments, inflationary expectations, and other factors in addition to Federal Reserve policy. Because the Fed is only one of many players influencing crucial variables such as money growth rates and interest rates, the Fed must retain flexibility in using its policy tools to achieve maximum influence over those variables.

## Criteria for an Effective Intermediate Target Variable

A good intermediate target variable must be measurable. That is, accurate data on the variable must be available on a timely basis. In addition, the Fed must be able to accurately control or at least strongly influence the variable. Finally, and most importantly, the variable must have a strong causal link to variables such as aggregate expenditures and nominal GDP. In other words, the variable must be an important determinant of aggregate expenditures.

**Measurability.** Accurate and timely measurability is a prerequisite for a viable intermediate target variable. The Fed cannot shoot for a 4 percent M2 growth rate if frequent and reasonably accurate M2 readings cannot be obtained. Nor can the Fed hit a daily interest rate target if continuous data on the interest rate in question are not available. Interest rates score exceptionally high on the measurability criterion because continuous and accurate readings are available on the federal funds rate, Treasury bill yields, government bond yields, and other interest rates. Furthermore, interest rate data typically are not subject to revision. Because of the difficulty in accurately gauging inflation expectations, *real* interest rates do not fare as well as nominal rates on the measurability criterion. The monetary aggregates (M1, M2, M3) do not score as well as interest rates on the measurability criterion because money supply data are available only with a 2-week delay and are subject to significant revision in following weeks.

**Controllability.** For a particular variable to be a useful intermediate target variable, the Fed must be capable of exerting predominant influence over the variable in the near term. In economists' terminology, a target variable is *endogenous* if the variable is strongly influenced by forces such as the business cycle and inflation expectations. The various potential target variables possess differing degrees of endogeneity. Interest rates are strongly influenced by business cycle forces and the inflation outlook. The Fed can control *short-term* interest rates but has considerably less influence over *long-term* rates, both nominal and real. A variable not strongly influenced by the business cycle and other economic forces is more easily controlled by the central bank. The Fed may have little difficulty dictating the magnitude of such variables, which are "sitting ducks" rather than "moving targets." Ideally, an intermediate target variable can be totally controlled by the Federal Reserve. In reality, the variables proposed as operating and intermediate target variables are influenced by other forces and by Federal Reserve policy.

**Importance.** The behavior of the variable targeted by the Fed should strongly influence aggregate spending and therefore contribute significantly to achievement of policy goals. If the Fed can completely control a particular variable but the variable has no influence on aggregate GDP expenditures and the ultimate objectives of Fed policy, then the variable is *irrelevant.* (The Fed can absolutely control the number of cars in its automobile fleet, but no one proposes the Fed automobile fleet as an intermediate target variable of monetary policy.) If the Fed selects an unimportant variable as the intermediate target, then, at best, the Fed is misallocating time and effort in controlling the variable. Of greater consequence, the Fed may considerably harm the economy if its efforts to control the *irrelevant* variable result in inappropriate movement of *relevant* variables. The Fed may inadvertently cause important variables to move in the wrong direction by focusing on the irrelevant variable. Critics occasionally have attacked the Fed for making precisely this mistake.

## Example of a Flawed Target Variable: Net Free Reserves

To illustrate the potential problems caused by Fed selection of a flawed target variable, consider the Fed's use of **net free reserves (NFR)** as its intermediate target variable in the 1950s and 1960s. NFR is the difference between aggregate excess reserves held by depository institutions and borrowed reserves—that is, the volume of discount loans. Economists once believed they selected a superior target variable by focusing on a variable constructed from *excess* reserves rather than *total* reserves. (A major and fluctuating portion of total reserves is in the form of *required* reserves, which are unavailable for extending additional bank credit, whereas excess reserves are potentially available for extending new loans.) NFR was thought to be an even better target variable than excess reserves because excess reserves include a variable portion of *borrowed reserves*. Banks are reluctant to extend credit based on borrowed reserves. Federal Reserve economists once believed that they had found a superior intermediate target variable by subtracting borrowed reserves from excess reserves.

**net free reserves (NFR)**
difference between aggregate excess reserves held by depository institutions and borrowed reserves (discount loans)

If the Fed desired to initiate a more stimulative policy, the Fed raised its NFR target, perhaps from $1,200 million ($1.2 billion) to $1,500 million ($1.5 billion). The Fed purchased securities in the open market in order to hit the new target. Bank reserves and excess reserves increased. Banks paid off some of their debt at the discount window. NFR therefore increased. Banks now had more NFR and expanded their earning assets—that is, loans and securities. Banks boost the money supply and cause interest rates to fall by buying securities and expanding loans. Thus, economic activity is stimulated when the Fed boosts its NFR target. Such was the reasoning behind the Fed's choice of NFR as its intermediate target variable.

More sophisticated analysis and historical evidence indicate NFR is an unsatisfactory intermediate target variable. The preceding description presupposes that economic activity does not feed back to strongly influence NFR. In other words, the Fed assumes fluctuations in NFR result not from changes in bank *demand* for NFR but rather from changes in NFR *supplied* by the Federal Reserve. This assumption is highly suspect. NFR is a highly endogenous variable. Recall our analysis of bank demand for excess reserves in Chapter 16 and our analysis of discount window borrowing in Chapter 18. Bank demand for excess reserves and discount window borrowing fluctuate with changes in interest rates, economic uncertainty, and other factors.

The magnitude of NFR fluctuates even when the Fed is "standing still"—that is, not pursuing a policy of buying or selling securities or changing the discount rate. Suppose, given a very robust economy, the Fed desires to pursue a restrictive policy of zero money growth in the next 3 months. The Fed attempts to achieve this objective by maintaining an operating target level of $1,200 million ($1.2 billion) for NFR. Suppose initially the Fed is on target at $1,200 million ($1.2 billion), and the economy is in the middle of the business cycle expansion phase. Credit demands and interest rates are rising. As rates rise, banks deliberately reduce their excess reserves ($r_e$ declines). Because banks face rising customer loan demand and the Fed's discount rate traditionally lags behind money market yields in cyclical upswings, the volume of discounts and advances increases. Hence, NFR declines.

As NFR falls below the Fed's target level of $1,200 million ($1.2 billion), the Fed must purchase government securities in the open market to push NFR back to the target level. By purchasing securities, the Fed expands reserves, the monetary base, and the money supply at a time when economic activity is already expanding strongly. The Fed policy of targeting NFR may *destabilize* economic activity. A policy aimed at producing no growth in the money supply fails because the Fed uses NFR as an operating target. Not only does the money supply multiplier increase because of reduced bank demand for excess reserves, but the Fed aggravates the situation by purchasing securities and thus expanding the monetary base. Schematically:

$$\mathbf{Y} \Uparrow \Rightarrow \mathbf{i} \Uparrow \Rightarrow \mathbf{NFR} \Downarrow \Rightarrow \mathbf{Fed\ Portfolio} \Uparrow \Rightarrow \mathbf{Base} \Uparrow \Rightarrow \mathbf{M} \Uparrow.$$

Rising output (Y) pulls up interest rates (i), which causes net free reserves (NFR) to fall below the targeted level. The Fed buys securities (increases its securities portfolio) to stay on its NFR target, increasing the base and money supply (M). Interest rate declines during a recession induce banks to hold more excess reserves. NFR increase. The Fed sells securities to return NFR to the target level. This action reduces the money supply in a time of recession. A Fed policy of targeting NFR becomes *procyclical,* turning stimulative during economic expansions and restrictive in recessions. The Fed abandoned use of NFR as an intermediate target variable in the 1960s, after receiving persistent criticism from monetary economists.

## LINKS BETWEEN POLICY INSTRUMENTS, TARGETS, AND GOALS

Figure 19-1 shows the chain of influence—that is, the linkage through which the Federal Reserve's monetary policy tools work to achieve the Fed's goals. The variables connecting the Fed's policy tools with its goals are divided into two categories: short-range or *operating target variables* and *intermediate target variables.* The basis for this two-tier classification is the order and speed with which these variables respond to Fed policy tools.

Operating target variables respond quickly and strongly to changes in the Fed's policy tools. Intermediate-range variables generally do not respond until after the short-range variables have moved. Intermediate-range variables respond largely *because* of movements in the short-range variables. Operating target variables generally score very high on the *measurability* and *controllability* criteria. On the other hand, intermediate-range variables are more tightly linked to the ultimate goals than are operating variables. Intermediate target variables have a stronger impact on aggregate expenditures and therefore score higher on the *importance* criterion. Because the variables in both groups are significant links in the transmission of monetary policy, they all are candidates for target variables of Federal Reserve policy. We now discuss the merits of these variables as targets of monetary policy.

### Operating Target Variables

In Figure 19-1, operating target variables are positioned in close proximity to the Fed's policy tools. The Fed can exert quick and strong influence over these variables. The Fed can, on a daily basis, push the operating target variables in any desired direction. Based on the controllability criterion, operating variables earn higher grades than intermediate target variables, which generally cannot be influenced as quickly or accurately. On the other hand, operating target variables are less tightly linked to

**Figure 19-1** Links in the Transmission of Federal Reserve Policy

The Fed uses its policy tools to control certain operating and intermediate target variables and ultimately to achieve its long-range goals, such as price level stability.

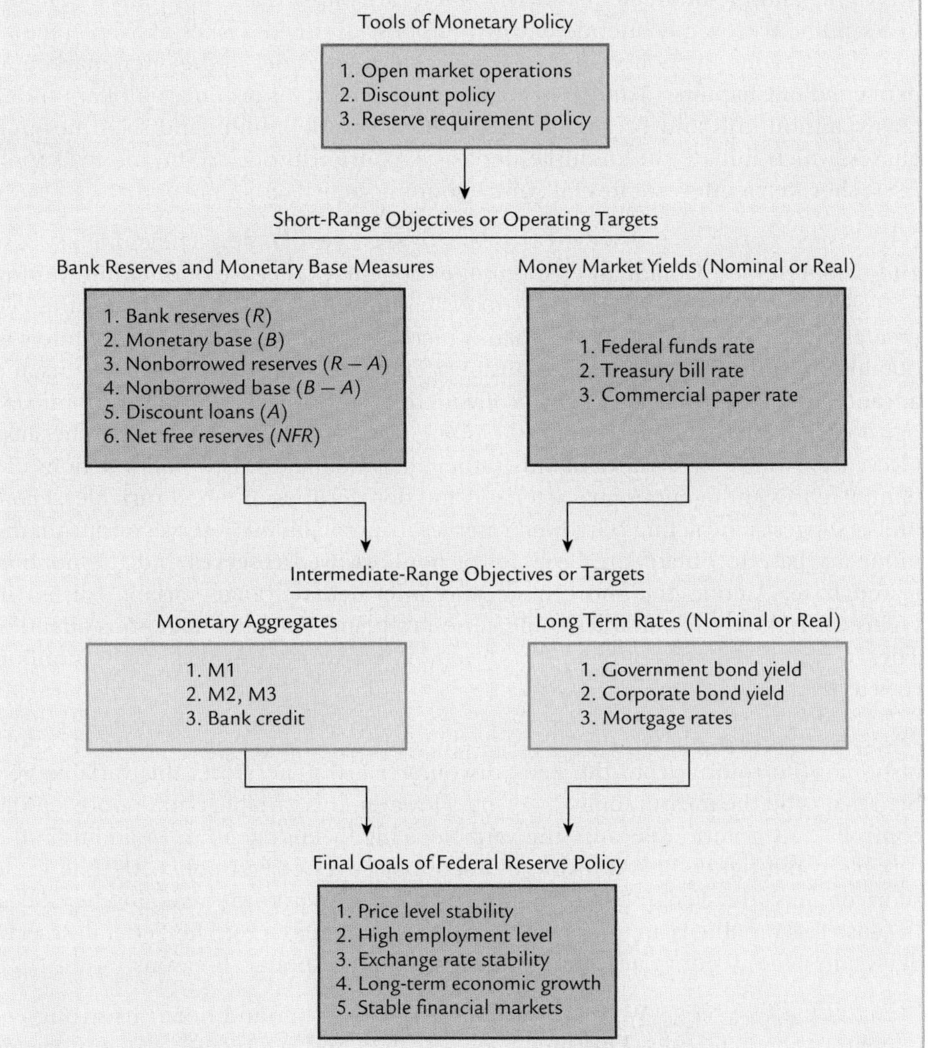


aggregate expenditures and the ultimate goals of monetary policy. Therefore, intermediate-range variables are superior monetary policy targets based on the *importance* criterion. In practice, the Fed has sometimes used a two-tier targeting strategy aimed at operating target variables thought to be consistent with achieving intermediate-range objectives such as M1 or M2 growth rates or medium-term bond yields. For example, the Fed once used a nonborrowed reserves operating target in an effort to hit intermediate M1 and M2 targets. Operating target variables can be divided into two categories: bank reserve or monetary base variables, and nominal and real money market yields—that is, yields on short-term debt instruments.

**Measures of Bank Reserves and the Monetary Base.** These measures are important variables within the transmission linkage. They include bank reserves, the monetary base, nonborrowed reserves, the nonborrowed base, discounts and advances, and NFR. Most of these variables move quickly and predictably when the Fed buys or sells securities in the open market.

**Bank Reserves and the Monetary Base.** The Fed greatly influences bank reserves (R) and the monetary base (B). These variables are an important link in the Fed's influence over economic activity. Suppose the Fed wishes to implement a stimulative economic policy, so the Fed purchases securities in the open market. As explained in Chapters 15 and 18, Fed securities purchases produce a dollar-for-dollar expansion in R and B. The expansion boosts bank lending and securities purchases, which initiate the multiple deposit expansion process. The money supply rises, short-term interest rates fall, and economic activity is stimulated.

**Nonborrowed Reserves and the Nonborrowed Base.** The monetary base and bank reserves contain an element of endogeneity because of discount window borrowing and other factors. Recall that each dollar of bank borrowing at the Fed creates $1 of R and B. In the past, banks increasingly used the discount window to obtain funds during economic expansions. The Fed passively grants discounts and advances, so the monetary base typically increases during periods of economic expansion. That is, total reserves and the monetary base sometimes fluctuate because of cyclical swings in credit demands rather than deliberate Fed policy actions. To eliminate this endogenous characteristic and derive superior target variables, economists suggest subtracting borrowed reserves from total bank reserves and from the monetary base to obtain the variables of **nonborrowed reserves** and the **nonborrowed base.** Among the short-range and intermediate-range variables listed in Figure 19-1, these two variables come closest to being free of endogenous qualities. The Fed can exert accurate control over nonborrowed reserves and the nonborrowed base.

**nonborrowed reserves (R-A)** difference between total reserves held by depository institutions and borrowed reserves (discount loans)

**nonborrowed base (B-A)** difference between monetary base and borrowed reserves (discount loans)

**Discount Loans.** The Federal Reserve has continuous information on depository institution borrowing from the Fed (discount loans). Therefore, this variable gets high marks on the measurability criterion. However, this variable ranks poorly on the controllability criterion because the variable is highly endogenous. In addition, the variable is not tightly linked to the ultimate objectives of Fed policy. Despite these shortcomings, the Fed used discount loans as its operating target in the 1980s. Because this variable is an inferior short-range operating target, the Federal Reserve likely adopted discount rates as an operating target for political reasons.[4]

**Net Free Reserves.** We discussed this variable earlier and noted its strong endogenous characteristic. The link between NFR and aggregate expenditures is highly unstable. NFR scores very poorly on the *importance* and *controllability* criteria. As indicated earlier, use of NFR as an operating target variable can lead to a procyclical money supply pattern. Today, NFR is not considered a viable candidate as a Fed policy target.

**Money Market Yields and Interest Rates.** These variables score very strongly on the measurability and controllability criteria. Continuous readings on nominal interest rates are available throughout each day. Suppose the Fed desires

[4] When the Fed set short-term interest rate targets at extremely high levels in the early 1980s to combat entrenched double-digit inflation, the Fed inevitably became the victim of criticism by some members of Congress and other elected officials. Utilizing a discount loans operating target produces a similar outcome as using a short-term interest rate operating target. The Fed may have used the discount loans target variable in an effort to divert attention from interest rates and thereby minimize Fed exposure to attack by politicians and other critics.

to bring down short-term yields to stimulate economic activity. The Fed purchases U.S. Treasury securities in the open market, driving up the securities' prices and reducing their yields. The Fed transactions increase bank reserves and push excess reserves above desired levels. To the extent that depository institutions use their excess reserves to purchase Treasury bills, further downward pressure is brought upon their yields. This downward yield pressure inevitably spreads throughout the money market.[5]

The decline in money market yields likely impacts positively on aggregate spending. For example, if the commercial paper rate declines due to Fed policy measures, business firms may be encouraged to issue more of these IOU's and use the proceeds to finance expenditures on inventories, materials, or other goods and services. The economic impact of the Fed's policy of driving down money market yields depends considerably on the extent to which the downward pressure is transmitted to *long-term* interest rates. To the extent that financial market agents anticipate the policy stimulus will be sustained, government and corporate bond yields and mortgage rates move downward, stimulating borrowing and spending and exerting an expansionary effect on economic activity.

## Intermediate Target Variables

Intermediate-range variables have a stronger and more predictable effect on aggregate expenditures than do the Fed's short-range operating variables. On the other hand, the Federal Reserve cannot easily control intermediate-range variables. Let's look at the merits of the monetary aggregates and long-term interest rates as intermediate target variables of monetary policy.

**Monetary Aggregates.** In the 1970s and early 1980s, the money supply measures gained widespread acceptance throughout the world as appropriate intermediate target variables for monetary policy. In the late 1960s, the Federal Reserve began conducting open market operations with an eye on the money supply, money market yields, and reserve measures. In the 1970s, the Federal Open Market Committee (FOMC) began specifying certain "tolerance ranges" within which the growth rates of the various money supply measures were to be maintained until the next FOMC meeting. However, the appeal of the monetary aggregates as target variables has diminished in the past 20 years because of increased instability in the link between the monetary aggregates and GDP expenditures.

A problem with using monetary aggregates as intermediate target variables is the lack of timeliness and quality of the data. Weekly data for M1 and M2 become available only with a 2-week delay, and are subject to substantial revision in later weeks. Intra-weekly monitoring and control of the monetary aggregates is not possible. Even if good weekly data were available, short-run volatility in the money multiplier would make accurate control of the money supply over short periods quite difficult. The shortest time horizon over which the Fed can be expected to accurately control the money measures is a monthly or quarterly average of the weekly data. For these reasons, the Fed must consider other operating target variables in planning its day-to-day open market operations.

[5] The various money market instruments are good examples of *substitute goods.* When the price of good *X* (say U.S. Treasury bills) increases, investors increase their demand for substitute goods *Y* and *Z* (commercial paper, banker's acceptances, and so forth). This action assures that much of the price increase on U.S. Treasury bills (*decrease* in yield) is transmitted to the substitute goods (commercial paper, banker's acceptances, etc). This principle is an important cause of the strong propensity for the various money market yields to move together.

**Long-Term Interest Rates.** Economists believe long-term interest rates have a greater impact on spending decisions than do short-term interest rates. That is, long-term rates score higher on the *importance* criterion. Investments in plants and equipment, new homes, and other structures depend on long-term interest rates. Thus, the long-term interest rate is a potential candidate as an intermediate monetary policy target.

Suppose, as part of an anti-recession program, the Fed wishes to bring down long-term interest rates. The Fed purchases securities, preferably bonds, in the open market. As the Fed buys bonds, their prices are bid up somewhat, reducing bond yields. Because Fed securities purchases boost bank reserves, banks begin buying securities, possibly including some long-term bonds. Other things held constant, the Fed's move tends to increase bond prices and reduce bond yields. However, long-term interest rates also depend heavily on factors such as inflation expectations, private credit demands, the outlook for federal budget deficits, and the flow of private saving. The Fed has difficulty exerting control over long-term interest rates because of these other factors. When mortgage rates are relatively high, elected officials sometimes pressure the Fed to reduce these rates with more expansionary policies. Such policies can be counterproductive. More stimulative policies likely increase the nation's inflation rate, such that expansionary policies risk *boosting* long-term interest rates through the Fisher effect.[6] Long-term rates receive high grades on the measurability and importance criteria and a low grade on the controllability criterion.

**Real Versus Nominal Interest Rates.** The *real* interest rate is the difference between the actual (nominal) interest rate and the average inflation rate expected to prevail over the life of the instrument. If the 30-year mortgage rate is 8 percent and inflation is expected to average 3 percent per year over the next 30 years, the real mortgage rate is 5 percent. Economists believe real long-term interest rates critically influence expenditure decisions. Real rates score very high on the *importance* criterion. For this reason, many economists advocate use of real interest rates in place of nominal rates as intermediate targets of monetary policy. For example, what would be wrong with the Fed targeting a real interest rate of 1 percent during a recession? The problem is—although real long-term interest rates are important for determining expenditures, long-term inflation expectations are difficult to ascertain with any degree of confidence. We have a reasonably high degree of confidence in forecasts of expected inflation over the next 6 months or year because of inertia in the inflation process. Also, numerous surveys indicate the short-term inflation outlook. Hence, our estimates of real *short-term* interest rates likely are fairly reliable. However, the inflation rate expected to prevail over the next 30 years is estimated with great uncertainty and is difficult to ascertain. Many uncertain political and economic forces influence long-term inflation trends. Therefore, while *short-term* real interest rates are viable candidates for target variables, *long-term* real rates are not practical. Long-term real interest rates fail the first two criteria for an effective monetary policy target—measurability and controllability.

Exhibit 19-1 provides "grades" in *measurability, controllability,* and *importance* for each of the operating and intermediate target variables. In the next section, we

[6] The populist appeal to the Federal Reserve for "easy money" is a request for the Fed to run on an accelerating treadmill. The harder the Fed tries to bring down long-term interest rates in the short run through stimulative policies, the greater the inflationary pressures and the induced *upward* pull of market forces on long-term interest rates. Ironically, we conclude that the most effective way for the Fed to foster low long-term interest rates is to pursue a protracted policy of *slow* growth of reserves, the monetary base, and the monetary aggregates.

**Exhibit 19-1** Grading Various Proposed Operating and Intermediate Target Variables

The three criteria on which to judge the merits of operating and intermediate target variables are *measurability, controllability,* and *importance.* If we assess grades to the various prospective target variables, we might obtain the following results.

| Variable | Measurability | Controllability | Importance |
|---|---|---|---|
| Bank reserves and the monetary base | B+ | A | B |
| Nonborrowed reserves and nonborrowed base | B+ | A+ | B |
| Discount loans | A | C | D |
| Net free reserves | A− | C | D |
| Short-term interest rates: | | | |
| Nominal | A+ | A | B− |
| Real | B+ | B | B+ |
| Long-term interest rates: | | | |
| Nominal | A+ | C | B |
| Real | D | D | A (or B) |
| Monetary aggregates | B | B | A (or B) |

*Source: Author's "educated guesses"*

Like all grades, these grades contain an element of subjectivity and can be disputed. Economists of different persuasions will assign slightly different grades. On the "measurability" criterion, consensus exists that short-term and long-term nominal (actual) yields get the top grade. On the "controllability" criterion, nonborrowed reserves and the nonborrowed base score highest. However, the key criterion is "importance." Note that we hedged in this category by specifying two grades for both long-term real interest rates and the monetary aggregates. Economists dispute these grades. Monetarist economists assign a higher grade to the monetary aggregates, whereas Keynesian and other non-monetarist economists typically give a higher grade to long-term real interest rates.

look at why a central bank cannot expect to simultaneously hit specific targets for short-term interest rates and the money supply.

## Money Supply Targets Versus Interest Rate Targets

Economic analysis and past experience indicate the Fed cannot simultaneously hit specific targets for the money supply and interest rates. Figure 19-2 demonstrates the conflict.

Assume the supply and demand for money jointly determine the nation's interest rate. The figure shows the supply and demand curves for money. The position of the supply curve, shown here as a vertical line, is determined by the Federal

**Figure 19-2** Market for Money Balances

Given a shifting demand curve for money, the Fed can hit either an interest rate target or a money supply target, but not both. The Fed must choose one target.

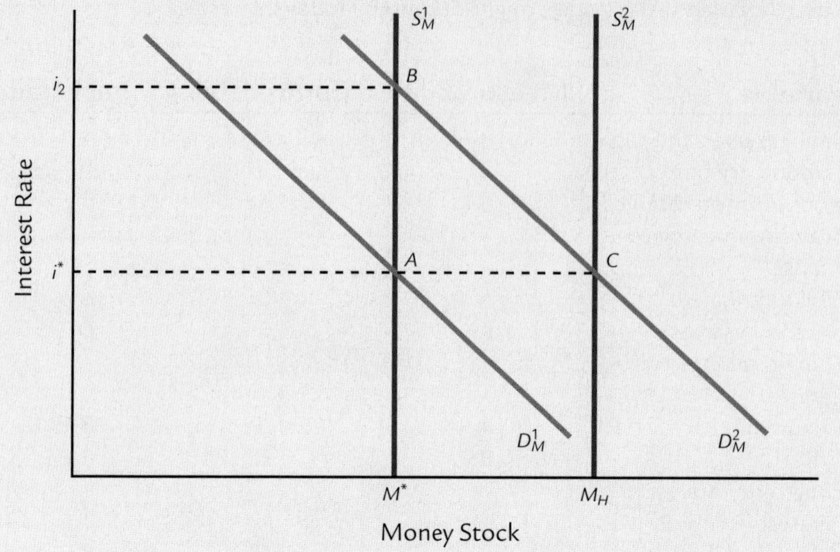

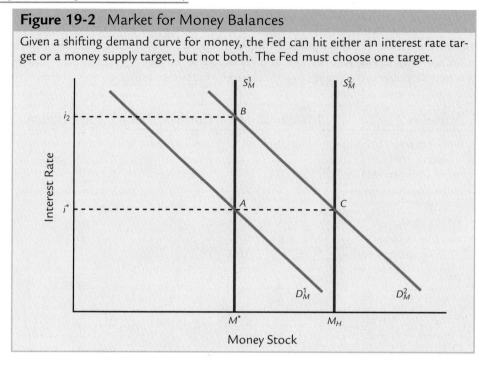

Reserve.[7] For example, the Fed can shift the supply curve rightward by purchasing securities in the open market. The demand curve for money is downward sloping because lower interest rates reduce the opportunity cost of holding money, thereby increasing the amount of wealth people hold in the form of money. The demand curve for money shifts in response to factors such as changes in income and the economic outlook. Increased income shifts the demand curve for money rightward, as individuals and firms hold more money to finance larger planned expenditures. Increased economic uncertainty also increases the demand for money. When uncertainty increases, people sell stocks and bonds and increase their holdings of money—the safest and most conservative of assets.

Assume initially the $S_M^1$ curve and the $D_M^1$ curve intersect at *A*, resulting in an interest rate of i* and a money supply of M*. Assume at first this interest rate and money supply are exactly the levels targeted by the Federal Reserve. Initially, then, the Fed is hitting both its targets. Now assume the nation's income increases significantly during an economic expansion or economic uncertainty increases sharply because of a major terrorist incident. In either case, the demand for money increases—the demand curve shifts rightward to $D_M^2$. If the Fed concentrates on hitting its money supply target and maintains the supply curve at $S_M^1$, we move from *A* to *B* in the figure, with the interest rate rising from i* to $i_2$. In this case, the Fed hits its money supply target M* but misses its interest rate target i*.

On the other hand, suppose the Fed is determined to maintain the interest rate at i*. Faced with the increased demand for money, the Fed must implement expansionary policy actions to boost the supply curve of money from $S_M^1$ to $S_M^2$. We move to *C* in the figure, and the money supply is now $M_H$. Note that the Fed has

[7] A case can be made for drawing the money supply curve as an upward-sloping function of the interest rate. Because both the money multiplier (via bank excess reserve behavior $r_e$) and the monetary base (through discount window activity) likely are positively related to the interest rate, the supply of money may respond positively to interest rates. Here, for simplicity, we assume the supply curve is vertical and shifts in response to Federal Reserve policy actions.

successfully maintained the interest rate at i* but has missed its money supply target. The money supply $M_H$ now exceeds the target level of M*.

In principle, if the Fed could accurately forecast changes in money demand, the Fed could change the interest rate target rapidly enough to be compatible with the stipulated money supply target. As the economy gains strength in an economic expansion, for example, the Fed could aggressively boost the interest rate target to a position consistent with the targeted level of the money supply. In recessions, the Fed could quickly lower the interest rate target to prevent a contraction in the money supply. In theory, a *highly flexible* interest rate target might be consistent with hitting established money supply targets. In practice, however, expecting the Fed to know at any point in time the precise interest rate that is consistent with the desired money supply levels is unrealistic. This problem is compounded by the fact that the FOMC must vote in order to change the targets. The FOMC meets only eight times annually, and disagreements among individual committee members likely slows implementation of target changes.

Occasionally, Fed policy mistakes have stemmed from the conflict between money growth targets and interest rate targets. For example, the Fed often exceeded its money growth targets in the 1970s, as it adhered rigorously to its interest rate targets. This contributed to high inflation in the 1970s.

## Monetarists Versus Nonmonetarists on Appropriate Target Variables

Economists' disagreements about appropriate operating and intermediate target variables for monetary policy follow from disagreements about the factors influencing economic activity. Keynesian and neo-Keynesian economists traditionally have viewed central bank policy as influencing economic activity largely through the central bank's effect on interest rates. Therefore, these economists believe the Fed should set interest rate targets. Some Keynesian and other nonmonetarist economists argue that the Federal Reserve should ignore the monetary aggregates.

Monetarist economists view monetary policy as influencing aggregate expenditures more broadly rather than through specific interest-sensitive sectors such as housing and plant and equipment spending. These economists view an increased money supply as upsetting the equilibrium between actual and desired money holdings. Some of the excess money is spent *directly* on goods and services. In the monetarists' view, much of the economic impact of monetary policy occurs independently of the effect on interest rates. Monetarists traditionally argued that the Fed should target the various measures of the money supply. Therefore, some monetarists would like the Fed to abandon interest rates as targets of monetary policy. They sometimes argue that the Federal Reserve historically, by attempting to control variables such as NFR and interest rates, has destabilized both the money supply and economic activity. Monetarists believe the Fed has often inadvertently conducted *procyclical* policy instead of a *countercyclical* policy. That is, they believe the Fed has amplified, rather than dampened, the severity of business cycles.

# EFFECTS OF FEDERAL RESERVE POLICIES: AN HISTORICAL REVIEW

In the next few sections, we review Federal Reserve targeting policies in the past 65 years and examine the charge that the Fed actually destabilized the U.S. economy during a considerable portion of this period. We begin with the World War II experience.

## Pegging Treasury Bond Yields from 1942 to 1951

To finance World War II, the U.S. Treasury issued a huge volume of debt (Treasury bonds, notes, and bills) during the early 1940s. Given normal market behavior, a major increase in yields would have been required to induce firms and individuals to absorb the extraordinarily large supply of government securities.[8] In addition, the increase in yields would have dramatically increased interest expense to the U.S. Treasury and U.S. taxpayers.[9]

To prevent a major increase in yields, the government appealed to patriotic U.S. citizens to buy Treasury bonds. More importantly, however, the Treasury forced the Federal Reserve to agree to prevent rising interest rates during the financing effort. The agreement stipulated that the Fed would not allow yields on various maturities of government securities to rise above specific levels. Yields were not to rise above 0.375 percent on short-term Treasury bills, 0.875 percent on 1-year notes, and 2.5 percent on long-term government bonds.

To prevent market interest rates from breaking through the artificially low rate ceilings, the Fed had to ensure security prices did not decline below specific corresponding levels. When the Treasury (or public) sold securities, the Federal Reserve was obliged to purchase the securities to keep their prices from falling. Because Fed purchases of securities increase the monetary base and the monetary aggregates, this obligation forced the Fed to sacrifice control over the money supply. The money supply essentially was determined by the amount of securities issued by the Treasury and the public's propensity to hold them. Because low-yielding Treasury securities were not financially attractive to the public, the Fed was forced to purchase an abnormally large quantity of securities during the war. The resulting increases in the Fed's security portfolio, the monetary base, and the monetary aggregates during the war years are shown in Table 19-1.

Note the extraordinary growth of the Fed's security portfolio and the highly inflationary growth rates of the monetary base, M1, and M2 during World War II. As predicted by the analysis in Figure 19-2, the Federal Reserve policy of targeting interest rates at very low levels in the face of increasing demand for money (owing to increasing income and increasing wartime uncertainty) led to rapid growth in the money supply. This rapid growth occurred when government fiscal stimulus resulting from increased wartime expenditures was strongly boosting aggregate GDP expenditures and national output.

The Federal Reserve was remarkably successful in maintaining government security yields at the low target levels during this period. But the cost of maintaining low targets levels was an undesirable and powerful monetary stimulus. The program of wage and price controls in place during the war temporarily disguised and postponed the inflationary consequences of the Fed's bond price support program. When the controls were lifted at the end of the war, prices increased dramatically. By 1948 the wholesale price index stood at twice its 1940 level.

When the war ended, the Treasury insisted that the Fed continue the bond price support program. What if the Fed had withdrawn its support after removal of wage

---

[8] The U.S. national debt increased from roughly $50 billion to $250 billion—that is, by approximately 400 percent—from 1941 to 1945. In other words, the U.S. Treasury incurred about four times as much debt during this 4-year period as it had incurred in the previous 165 years of U.S. history!

[9] To finance the $250 billion national debt at the end of the war in 1945 at (assume) 8 percent interest would have cost $20 billion per year in interest expenses. Given the GDP level at that time, about 10 percent of the nation's aggregate income would have been needed (via taxes) to pay the annual interest on the debt. Such payments would have necessitated substantially higher income tax rates for many years. By keeping interest rates artificially low, the U.S. government shifted a significant part of the financial burden of World War II from U.S. taxpayers to those who purchased government bonds.

**Table 19-1 Annual Growth Rates of the Federal Reserve Security Portfolio, Monetary Base, and Money Supply Measures from 1942 to 1945**

| Year | %ΔFed Portfolio | %ΔMonetary Base | % ΔM1 | %ΔM2 |
|---|---|---|---|---|
| 1942 | +164.5 | +19.6 | +30.0 | +23.1 |
| 1943 | +98.8 | +16.1 | +27.6 | +25.5 |
| 1944 | +16.0 | +17.8 | +13.6 | +16.1 |
| 1945 | +25.9 | +12.2 | +12.9 | +15.4 |

*Sources: Calculated from data in* Federal Reserve Bulletin, *various issues, and Friedman and Schwartz,* A Monetary History of the United States, 1867–1960, *Appendix A, Table A-1*

price controls was accompanied by sharp increases in the reported price indexes? A major increase in *yields* and a corresponding collapse of security *prices* would have occurred—a result highly unfair to patriotic individuals who had purchased government bonds in wartime. A collapse of bond prices also would have raised the likelihood of major losses and financial distress for banks, life insurance companies, and other institutions that had accumulated large blocks of bonds and mortgages.

The Fed continued its bond support program for several years. As time passed, the emergency rationale behind the program diminished, and the fundamental absurdity of the policy became more widely understood. Finally, the Fed pressed for freedom to conduct discretionary monetary policy. In 1951, in a Treasury–Federal Reserve "Accord," the Fed was absolved of responsibility for supporting government security prices.

## The 1950s and 1960s: Targeting "Money Market Conditions" and Net Free Reserves

In the 1950s and 1960s, under the leadership of Federal Reserve Chairman William McChesney Martin, the Fed informally conducted a policy of targeting "money market conditions," with special emphasis on NFR in the banking system and short-term interest rates. As we indicated, a policy of targeting NFR can destabilize the behavior of the monetary aggregates. As output and income expand in a cyclical upswing, interest rates are pulled up by market forces. This rise leads endogenously to decreased bank holdings of excess reserves and NFR, which induces the Fed to buy securities in the open market to remain on its NFR target. This, in turn, increases the monetary base and the money supply, stimulating the economy when it is already expanding.

Targeting money market yields can also lead inadvertently to procyclical money supply behavior and rising inflation, as illustrated in the previous section. In a cyclical upswing, market forces put upward pressure on money market yields. Unless the Fed alertly raises its interest rate target, the Fed must buy securities to remain on its interest rate target. This purchase increases the monetary base and the nation's money supply. Thus, the money supply rises strongly during economic expansion. Schematically, we have the following mechanism:

$$\mathbf{Y} \Uparrow \Rightarrow \mathbf{i} \Uparrow \Rightarrow \textbf{Fed Portfolio} \Uparrow \Rightarrow \textbf{Monetary Base} \Uparrow \Rightarrow \mathbf{M} \Uparrow.$$

Similarly, if inflation is rising, the Fed encounters trouble if interest rates are the target. Rising inflation pulls up inflation expectations, which exerts upward pressure on interest rates through the Fisher effect. To remain on its interest rate target, the Fed must purchase securities. The purchase increases the money supply and exacerbates inflation. Schematically, we have the following mechanism (where $\pi^e$ represents expected inflation).

**Inflation** $\Uparrow \Rightarrow \pi^e \Uparrow \Rightarrow$ **i** $\Uparrow \Rightarrow$ **Fed Portfolio** $\Uparrow \Rightarrow$ **Monetary base** $\Uparrow \Rightarrow$ **M** $\Uparrow \Rightarrow$ **Inflation** $\Uparrow$.

If the Fed is not alert in its conduct of monetary policy, it will destabilize economic activity. As a crude test of the allegation that the Fed conducted *procyclical* (rather than *countercyclical*) policies in the post-World War II period, consider Table 19-2. The table illustrates the behavior of the monetary base—a variable for which the Federal Reserve is clearly accountable—during each economic expansion and recession after 1945.

In the early postwar business cycles, the data reported in the table support the hypothesis of procyclical Fed policy. In the first four business cycles, the monetary base increased during each expansion and actually decreased in each recession. Monetary base growth in the long expansion of the 1960s marginally exceeded growth experienced in the ensuing recession. Beginning in the 1970s, however, the results look much better. In four of the five full business cycles after the1960s, including the three most recent cycles, the Fed boosted the monetary base faster during recessions than during expansions. In response to rising inflation during escalation of the Vietnam War in the late 1960s, academic economists' criticism of the Federal Reserve's policies made the Fed more aware of the potential pitfalls in the Fed's targeting procedures. Apparently the Fed listened to its critics.

## The 1970s: Emergence of Monetary Aggregate Targeting

Shortly after Arthur Burns was appointed Chair of the Board of Governors in 1970, the Federal Reserve announced target ranges for M1 and M2 growth rates. However, the Fed also set target ranges for the federal funds rate. The Fed ostensi-

**Table 19-2** Annual Growth Rate of Monetary Base During Expansion and Recession Phases of Business Cycles (Post-World War II)

| Expansion Phase | | Recession Phase | |
|---|---|---|---|
| **Trough to Peak** | **%ΔB/Year** | **Peak to Trough** | **%ΔB/Year** |
| 10/1945–11/1948 | +2.9 | 11/1948–10/1949 | −10.3 |
| 10/1949–07/1953 | +3.6 | 07/1953–08/1954 | −2.7 |
| 08/1954–07/1957 | +1.3 | 07/1957–04/1958 | −3.2 |
| 04/1958–05/1960 | +0.6 | 05/1960–02/1961 | −3.5 |
| 02/1961–11/1969 | +5.2 | 11/1969–11/1970 | +5.0 |
| 11/1970–11/1973 | +5.5 | 11/1973–04/1975 | +6.5 |
| 04/1975–01/1980 | +7.9 | 01/1980–07/1980 | +6.2 |
| 07/1980–07/1981 | +5.0 | 07/1981–11/1982 | +6.6 |
| 11/1982–07/1990 | +7.7 | 07/1990–03/1991 | +10.5 |
| 03/1991–03/2001 | +6.8 | 03/2001–11/2001 | +10.0 |

*Sources: Calculated from data in* Federal Reserve Bulletin, *various issues, and FRED database at* http://research.stlouisfed.org/fred2/

bly was using the federal funds rate as its *operating* (short-run) target in an attempt to hit *intermediate* targets for M1 and M2 growth. The federal funds target range typically was relatively narrow (for example, 6–6.75%), while the M1 and M2 growth rates were relatively broad (perhaps 4–7% for M1 and 5–8% for M2). Because the FOMC was reluctant to abandon its policy of controlling interest rates, the FOMC instructed the trading desk at the New York Fed to give top priority to hitting the federal funds rate target. If both the fed funds rate and money growth rates threatened to move above their target ranges, the New York Fed would purchase government securities in the open market. As suggested by our analysis in Figure 19-2, this action successfully maintains the fed funds rate within its target band but drives the money growth rate above the target band.

The decade of the 1970s was disastrous for the U.S. economy, as dramatic oil price shocks not only led to a severe recession in 1973 to 1975 but also contributed to two episodes of double-digit inflation (1973–1974 and 1979–1980). As inflation increased in the late 1970s, the charge that the Fed policy of targeting interest rates was fueling the fires of inflation gained increasing credence. In 1978, Congress passed the Humphrey-Hawkins Act, which tightened the Federal Reserve's accountability to Congress and required the Federal Reserve to set and announce money growth targets. In August 1979, President Jimmy Carter appointed Paul Volcker as Fed Chairman. Within weeks, Volcker developed a new plan to attack inflation.

## 1979 to 1982: De-emphasis of Interest Rate Targeting

In October 1979, Volcker's Fed announced a major change in its *modus operandi.* The Fed greatly broadened the target range of the federal funds rate, to a band 4 or 5 percentage points wide, and used narrower intermediate target ranges for M1 and M2 growth. Implicitly, the Fed was de-emphasizing interest rates and placing more emphasis on money growth targets to bring down inflation. To hit the money growth targets, the Fed used nonborrowed reserves as its operating target variable.

The financial markets interpreted Volcker's announcement as the Fed's movement toward more rigorous targeting of growth rates of the monetary aggregates. Some pundits dubbed the new policy a "monetarist experiment." However, money growth was very unstable during this regime. M1 growth deviated from the specified target range in each of the 3 years the regime was in place, and the variance of money growth increased. One interpretation of this experience is that deregulation of financial markets, financial innovations, and a brief episode of credit controls hindered monetary control, such that the Fed could not hit its money growth targets. In this interpretation, the Fed focused on controlling the monetary aggregates but was unable to hit its targets. However, another interpretation is possible.

By October 1979, inflation had been ratcheting upward for 15 years. The annual inflation rate was about 12 percent when Volcker instituted the new policy regime. The new Fed Chairman strongly desired to eradicate the strongly entrenched inflation. He realized that a protracted policy of tight money would be required to accomplish the task. Volcker knew that he would have to push interest rates sharply higher and maintain these high rates for a lengthy period. This action would result in an extended period of high unemployment and particularly severe distress for interest-sensitive sectors of the economy, such as homebuilding. To deflect potential criticism that would make carrying out the disinflation policy politically difficult, Volcker needed to divert public attention from the Fed. Given the announcement that the Fed was de-emphasizing interest rates and focusing on slower money growth to contain inflation, the ensuing rise in interest rates could legitimately be

## Exhibit 19-2 The 1979 to 1982 Targeting Experience: Was It Really a Monetarist Experiment?

Monetarism—a doctrine asserting that slow and steady money growth yields economic results superior to those delivered historically by the Federal Reserve—reached peak popularity levels as both money growth and inflation surged in the late 1970s. Critics of monetarism argued that discretionary monetary policy would outperform the monetarist prescription of slow and stable money growth. Because the Fed had never adhered rigorously to money supply targets, these competing views could not be tested. When the Fed announced in October 1979 that it was de-emphasizing the federal funds rate target, ostensibly to place higher priority on money growth targets, economists eagerly looked forward to the results of this new procedure, which some dubbed "the monetarist experiment."

Effective Federal Funds Rate (Percent)

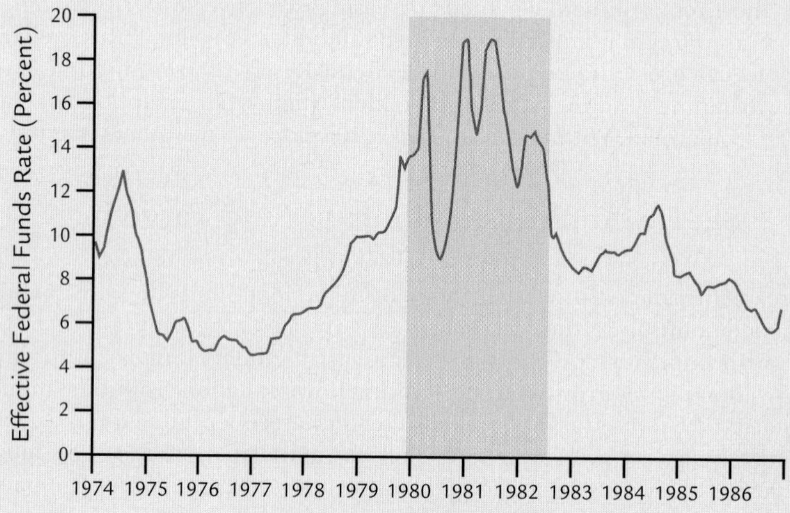


Growth Rate of M1

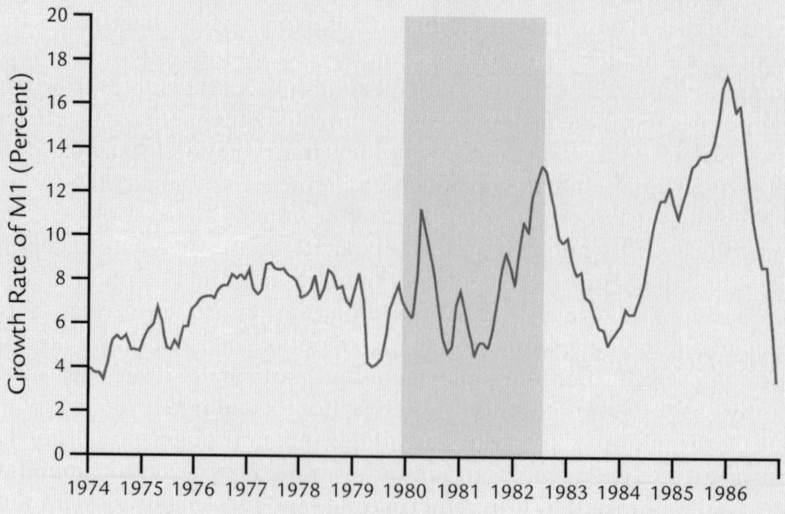

**Exhibit 19-2** The 1979 to 1982 Targeting Experience: Was It Really a Monetarist Experiment?—*cont'd*

But was this episode really a monetarist experiment? The Fed greatly widened the permissible target range of the fed funds rate. But the following data and the accompanying figure raise doubts about whether this episode qualifies as a monetarist experiment.

M1 Target Ranges and Actual M1 Growth Rates

| Year | M1 Target Range | Actual M1 Growth Rate |
|---|---|---|
| 1980 | 4.0–6.5% | 7.4% |
| 1981 | 6.0–8.5% | 5.3% |
| 1982 | 2.5–5.5% | 8.7% |

The data indicate the Fed missed the M1 target range in each of the 3 years the regime was in place. The figure shows the pattern of the federal funds rate and M1 money growth from 1979 to 1982 and the surrounding periods. The evidence indicates the Fed did de-emphasize the fed funds rate, but money growth was highly unstable from 1979 to 1982. The average M1 growth rate was only slightly lower than it was in the preceding 3 years. (Average annual M2 growth, not shown, declined from 12 percent from 1976 to 1978 to 9 percent from 1979 to 1982.)

In retrospect, Chairman Volcker and the FOMC likely were never committed to a monetarism policy. Indeed, they never claimed to be conducting such a policy. Instead, Volcker likely wanted latitude to squeeze entrenched inflation out of the U.S. economy by driving interest rates dramatically higher. He realized that the federal funds rate must be de-emphasized as an explicit target to make the goal politically feasible. In other words, the so-called monetarist experiment was a smokescreen allowing the Fed to administer the harsh medicine required to bring down inflation. The Fed was eminently successful in this venture—the annual inflation rate declined from more than 12 percent in October 1979 to less than 4 percent 3 years later. The nation paid a high price for this victory, however, in the form of the most severe economic contraction since the Great Depression.

blamed on "market forces" rather than on the Fed itself. As the federal funds rate soared as high as 20 percent and more over the next 2 years, the groundwork was put in place to defeat inflation. The Fed allowed interest rates to remain very high for an extended period. The unemployment rate increased over the next 3 years, and inflation came down much faster than expected. (On whether this episode qualifies as a "monetarist experiment," see Exhibit 19-2.)

## October 1982 to the Early 1990s: De-emphasis of Money Supply Targets

By October 1982, the inflation rate had declined to less than 4 percent per year, and the Federal Reserve changed its targeting procedures. The Fed reduced its emphasis on money growth targets and returned essentially to interest rate targeting, initially by using borrowed reserves (discount loans) as an operating target. In such a regime, borrowed reserves rise as credit conditions tighten and interest rates rise.

To keep borrowed reserves at target levels, the Fed purchases securities, thereby increasing reserves and allowing some banks to repay their discount window loans.[10]

The main justification for the Fed's de-emphasis of money supply targeting in late 1982 was the loosening of the relationship between the money supply and economic activity after 1980. The looser link resulted from deregulation of the financial system and emergence of new financial instruments and institutions. In 1987, the Federal Reserve stopped announcing M1 targets but continued announcing M2 targets. The Fed believed the link between M1 and GDP had become totally unreliable, but the link between M2 and GDP appeared to be somewhat more stable. However, the link between M2 and GDP also appeared to break down in the early 1990s. Chairman Greenspan testified to Congress in mid-1993 that the Fed was abandoning all monetary aggregates for purposes of conducting monetary policy. In 2000, Congressional legislation removed the requirement that the Fed report to Congress the target ranges for monetary aggregates.

## Early 1990s to 2004: The Return to Fed Funds Rate Targeting

As indicated, the Fed is no longer required to set money growth targets. Despite the danger of interest rate targeting becoming a procyclical policy, the Federal Reserve has received high marks for its monetary policy since the early 1990s. Apparently the Fed has learned to move its fed funds rate target effectively to become a countercyclical force. Following the 1990 to 1991 recession, the Fed maintained its fed funds target at a relatively low rate of 3 percent for an extended period. This stimulative policy helped the economy in the face of an early 1990s "credit crunch," in which depository institutions tightened their lending standards in response to the severe financial difficulties they experienced in the previous decade. As the economy finally emerged from its doldrums in 1994, the Fed boosted the fed funds rate in a series of steps in the following year to nip incipient inflation pressures. When the collapse of the Russian financial system and the ensuing crisis of Long-Term Capital Management threatened to spill over and cause systemic problems, the Fed aggressively dropped the fed funds rate by 0.75 percentage points in fall 1998. As these dangers passed, the Fed reversed course and boosted its fed funds target in 1999. Many observers credit the Fed with contributing to the longest economic expansion in U.S. history, which extended from March 1991 to March 2001.

The U.S. economy was hammered by a series of negative demand shocks in the early portion of the new millennium. In March 2000, the stock market bubble burst, and the NASDAQ index declined more than 75 percent in the next 2 years (broader stock market indexes fell in half). This shock was followed by the tragic events of September 11, 2001, and then by a series of announcements revealing corporate scandals involving fraudulent reporting of profits. The Fed reacted aggressively to these developments by cutting its federal funds rate target 13 times. From mid-2003 until mid-2004, the Fed maintained the fed funds rate at the extremely low rate of 1 percent, the lowest level in nearly half a century. In the summer and fall of 2004, as the economy finally emerged from the "jobless recovery" of 2002 to 2004 that followed the 2001 recession, the Fed began to move its fed funds rate back toward more normal levels.

---

[10] Just as targeting net free reserves and money market yields may be a procyclical policy, targeting borrowed reserves likely produces similar results. As economic expansion and rising interest rates lead to increased borrowed reserves, the Fed buys securities in the open market to remain on its borrowed reserves target, thus increasing the monetary base and monetary aggregates during an economic expansion.

# SUMMARY

The ultimate goals of Federal Reserve policy are to achieve price level stability, high employment levels, solid long-term growth in real GDP, a stable exchange rate at a level allowing U.S. products to be reasonably competitive with foreign goods, and stable financial markets. Fed policy tools include open market operations, discount window policy, and reserve requirement policy. Because the link connecting policy tools to GDP expenditures and the final policy goals is uncertain and fluctuates over time, the Fed uses operating and intermediate target variables to better achieve its long-term goals. The Fed sets target levels for these variables to move toward this end. A good intermediate target variable meets three standards. The variable can be measured readily and accurately, the variable can be strongly influenced by the Fed, and the variable has an important effect on aggregate expenditures and, therefore, on the ability of the Fed to achieve its goals. Target variables the Fed can most quickly and accurately influence are various measures of bank reserves and short-term interest rates. However, these variables have less influence over aggregate expenditures than the monetary aggregates and long-term interest rates—variables over which the Fed has less control. The Fed can hit either the money supply or the interest rate target, but the Fed typically cannot simultaneously hit both targets. Therefore, the Fed must choose between targeting interest rates and targeting money supply growth. Economists disagree about which are the most appropriate intermediate target variables. The Fed announced target growth rates of the monetary aggregates in the 1970s and early 1980s but has downgraded the use of these aggregates in the past 2 decades. Some evidence suggests the Fed may have inadvertently conducted procyclical policies in the early portion of the post–World War II era, but the Fed's performance has been widely praised in the past couple of decades.

## YOUR TURN ANSWERS

PAGE 427
The percentage loss of output is 2 (8% − 5%), or 6 percent. Taking 6 percent of $14,000 billion, we get $840 billion. Given the U.S. population of some 280 million people, loss of output and income amounts to $3,000 per person.

# KEY TERMS

operating target variables
intermediate target variables
Okun's Law
natural rate of unemployment
net free reserves (NFR)
nonborrowed reserves (R-A)
nonborrowed base (B-A)

# STUDY QUESTIONS

1. Discuss the main goals of monetary policy. Explain why each goal is important.

2. Explain the meaning of an intermediate monetary policy target variable. Explain why the Fed uses a procedure of setting intermediate targets.

3. Explain the three criteria used to determine whether a particular variable is a worthy candidate for an intermediate target variable of monetary policy. Now, based on these criteria, evaluate the following as potential intermediate target variables:
   A. 90-day Treasury bill yield
   B. Real federal funds rate
   C. Real 30-year U.S. government bond yield
   D. Nonborrowed monetary base
   E. Growth rate of M2
   F. Excess reserves

4. Draw a diagram with the interest rate on the vertical axis and the quantity of money on the horizontal axis. Draw supply and demand curves for money and indicate the equilibrium.
   A. Assume the Fed is targeting interest rates, and a severe recession results from a sharp decline in consumer confidence. What will happen to the money supply if the Fed does not change its interest rate target?
   B. What would have happened to interest rates had the Fed been targeting the money supply?

5. Why did the Fed decide to peg government security yields in the 1940s? What were the consequences? Do you believe the Fed's policy was wise? Explain.

6. Explain why, in targeting variables such as the federal funds rate and net free reserves, the Fed may inadvertently destabilize economic activity—that is, the Fed may be conducting procyclical rather than countercyclical policy.

7. Evaluate the merits of discount loans as an intermediate monetary policy target variable.

8. Since 1987, the Fed has been unwilling to set intermediate targets for M1. Evaluate the Fed's decision in the context of the three criteria for a good intermediate target.

9. Firms' decisions on capital expenditures and households' decisions on buying new homes are heavily influenced by the real long-term interest rates. Why then doesn't the Fed use this variable as its intermediate target?

10. The Fed's critics charge that the Fed's policy of targeting money market yields was a procyclical policy in the 1950s and 1960s. How has the Fed avoided that charge in the past 20 years?

11. As the U.S. economy began to strongly generate new jobs in 2004 in the third year of an economic expansion, the Fed was very slow to boost its federal funds rate target above the extraordinarily low rate of 1 percent that it maintained from July 2003 through June 2004. In retrospect, did the Fed make a policy mistake? Justify your answer based on what has happened to the U.S. inflation rate since the middle of 2004 (calculate the annual inflation rate from the consumer price index data on the FRED database at http://research.stlouisfed.org/fred2).

# ADDITIONAL READING

- For more on the consequences of inflation and unemployment, consult any principles of economics textbook. A good general reference on monetary policy targeting is Richard G. Davis et al., *Intermediate Targets and Indicators for Monetary Policy: A Critical Survey,* Federal Reserve Bank of New York, 1990.
- On targeting interest rates, see William Roberds, *What Has the Fed Wrought: Interest Rate Smoothing in Theory and Practice,* Federal Reserve Bank of Atlanta, *Economic Review,* January/February 1992, pp. 25–36.
- On the use of intermediate targets in other countries, see Bruce Kasman, "A Comparison of Monetary Policy Operating Procedures in Six Industrial Countries," *Quarterly Review,* Federal Reserve Bank of New York, Summer 1992, pp. 5–24.
- To learn about the Fed's current targeting practice and the current federal funds rate, see the Board of Governors Web site at http://www.federalreserve.gov/ and look at the most recent *Monetary Policy Report to the Congress.*

# Part SIX

The Federal Reserve affects the nation's output, employment, and price level by influencing aggregate expenditures. Aggregate expenditures consist of consumption, investment, government purchases, and net exports. Monetary policy affects each component. The link between a nation's money supply and a nation's gross domestic product (GDP) is the *velocity of money.* To the extent that velocity is stable and predictable, a strong and predictable relationship exists between changes in the money supply and changes in economic activity. Economists disagree about the stability and reliability of this link. Monetary policy influences GDP through many different channels, and the relative importance of these various channels changes over time. Most economists believe the Federal Reserve can contribute to a more stable economy through discretionary monetary policy. A significant minority of economists disagree, preferring the Fed replace discretionary monetary policy with a monetary policy rule that constrains the decision-making authority of central bankers to react to ongoing economic developments. In the past 15 years, more than 20 nations (though not the United States) have implemented inflation-targeting regimes. In an inflation-targeting regime, maintaining inflation at a specific, pre-announced level (or within a specific range) is proclaimed as the predominant intermediate and long-term objective of monetary policy.

# Chapter 20

# THE AGGREGATE DEMAND-AGGREGATE SUPPLY MODEL

In Part 4, we learned how the money supply is determined, and we studied the Federal Reserve's role in the money supply process. In Part 5, we discussed how the Fed conducts monetary policy. The Fed uses policy tools such as open market operations, aiming for specific levels of intermediate target variables (currently the federal funds rate) to achieve ultimate goals of price level stability and high output and employment levels. In Part 6, we will see how changes in the money supply and interest rates influence economic activity. We examine the link between the nation's money stock and the nation's GDP. Analysis of the relationship between the nation's money supply and economic activity is *monetary theory.*

Before we discuss monetary theory, we examine a simple framework of macroeconomic analysis known as the *aggregate demand and aggregate supply model.* The aggregate demand-aggregate supply (AD/AS) framework is important and useful because interest rate and money supply changes engineered by the Federal Reserve influence economic activity chiefly by influencing the nation's aggregate expenditures—that is, aggregate demand for goods and services. Many factors other than the Fed also influence aggregate demand. Changes in aggregate supply originating from forces beyond the Fed's influence strongly condition the economic environment in which the Fed conducts its policy and thereby influence the Fed's decisions. In this chapter, we develop the AD/AS model. In Chapter 21, we use the AD/AS model to explain major developments in the U.S. economy over the past 75 years, with special emphasis on developments of recent years.

## THE AD/AS FRAMEWORK

Figure 20-1 shows the basic model of aggregate demand and aggregate supply.

The figure shows the nation's price level (P) on the vertical axis and the nation's real output level (Y) on the horizontal axis. The nation's equilibrium price and real output levels are determined by the intersection of the aggregate demand (AD) and aggregate supply (AS) curves. *Changes* in the nation's price level and real output level are caused by *shifts* in the positions of these curves. For example, a rightward shift of the AD curve increases the equilibrium price level and the equilibrium level of real output. A rightward shift of the aggregate supply curve increases the equilibrium level of real output and reduces the nation's equilibrium price level.

The *aggregate* supply and demand curves shown in Figure 20-1 look similar to the familiar supply and demand curves for a particular good, such as wheat. However, these aggregate supply and aggregate demand curves are fundamentally different from the supply and demand curves for individual goods. For example, the expla-

**Figure 20-1** The Aggregate Demand-Aggregate Supply Model

In the aggregate demand-aggregate supply model, the nation's price level (P) and real output (Y) are jointly determined by the aggregate demand for and aggregate supply of goods and services.

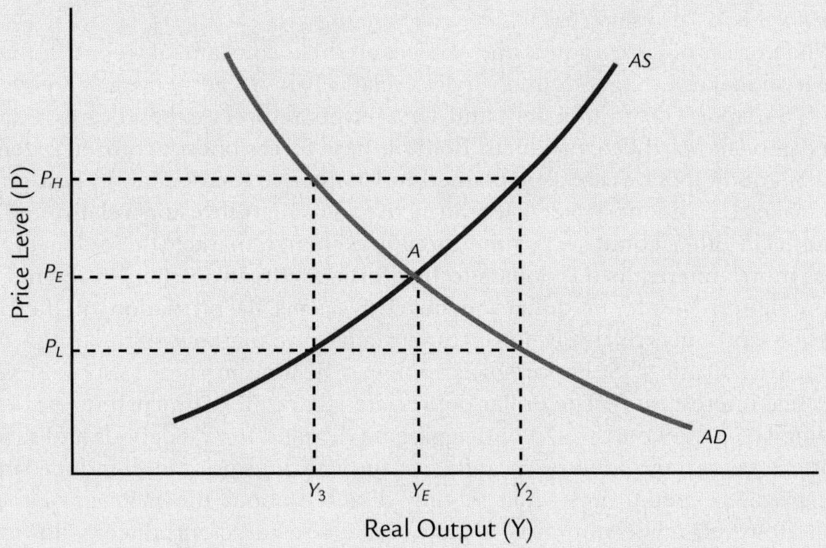

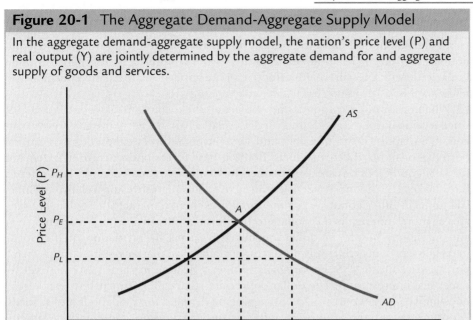

nations for the slopes of the curves are quite different than the explanations for the slopes of the supply and demand curves of an individual product such as wheat.[1]

## The Aggregate Demand Curve

**aggregate demand curve**
relationship between the nation's aggregate price level and the amount of real output (real GDP) demanded, other factors being held constant

The nation's **aggregate demand curve** is the relationship between the nation's aggregate price level and the amount of real output (real GDP) demanded, *other factors being held constant.* The downward slope of the AD curve is attributable to the fact that several of the individual components of aggregate demand are influenced by the nation's price level. The nation's aggregate demand for goods and services consists of four components: consumption demand (C), investment demand (I), government purchases of goods and services (G), and net U.S. exports of goods and services—that is, exports minus imports (NX). Consumption demand, investment demand, and net exports of goods and services are inversely influenced by the U.S. price level.

Let us see why this relationship is true. First, when the money supply (M) is held constant, a decline in the nation's price level (P) boosts the *real money supply* (M/P). Real interest rates decline, stimulating expenditures on consumer durables such as cars and boosting investment spending on plants, equipment, and new structures.

[1] Consider a demand curve for a particular product—wheat. When the price of wheat falls while the prices of corn and rice are held constant, people buy more wheat—they substitute wheat for corn and rice. This *substitution effect* helps explain the downward slope of the demand curve for wheat. But in the case of the aggregate demand curve, the variable on the vertical axis is not the price of a single good but the price of the whole collective basket of U.S. goods and services. When this price declines, no substitution effect occurs (except to the extent that people substitute U.S. goods for foreign goods). Similarly, one reason the wheat supply curve is upward sloping is that an increase in the price of wheat, *ceteris paribus,* causes farmers to plant more wheat (and less corn, rice, and soybeans). When the price of the basket of *all* U.S. goods rises, no such effect is seen. Hence, we must examine alternative explanations for the shapes of the *aggregate* demand and *aggregate* supply curves.

Second, when the price level falls, the *real value* of fixed-principal assets such as government bonds and the nation's money supply increases. If you have $5,000 in a U.S. government bond and the price level falls in half, the real value of your bond doubles to $10,000. The real wealth of the economy's private sector increases when the price level falls. This **wealth effect** of a lower price level increases consumer demand for goods and services (C).

**wealth effect**
effect of a change in the real wealth owned by the private sector on aggregate expenditures

When prices of *foreign* goods and services are held constant, a decline in the U.S. price level makes U.S. goods and services relatively more attractive in foreign markets. U.S. exports are stimulated, and U.S. buyers redirect expenditures from imported goods toward U.S. products. Both of these forces boost net foreign demand for U.S. goods (NX). Also, as explained in Chapter 8, the decline in real interest rates makes U.S. financial assets less attractive to foreign investors relative to financial assets in other countries. In the foreign exchange market, the dollar depreciates as more Americans sell dollars to buy foreign currencies (and foreign assets) and foreigners buy fewer dollars to buy U.S. assets. Depreciation of the dollar makes U.S. products relatively more attractive in world markets, stimulating U.S. exports and reducing U.S. imports. Recapping, a decline in the U.S. price level reduces real interest rates. The dollar depreciates against foreign currencies, thereby boosting U.S. net exports (NX) and aggregate demand for U.S. goods and services. Economists disagree about the *magnitude* of these various price level-induced effects on aggregate expenditures—that is, they disagree about the *steepness* of the AD curve. However, few economists dispute that these forces produce a downward-sloping AD curve, as shown in Figure 20-1.

## The Aggregate Supply Curve

**aggregate supply curve**
relationship between the nation's aggregate price level and the amount of real output firms collectively desire to produce and sell, other factors being held constant

The **aggregate supply curve** is the relationship between the nation's aggregate price level and the amount of real output firms collectively desire to produce and sell, *other factors being held constant.* The aggregate supply curve (AS) in Figure 20-1 is upward sloping. Note that this is a *short-run* aggregate supply curve. In the short run, a higher national price level stimulates aggregate production of goods and services. The upward slope of the short-run AS curve hinges on the existence of certain fixed costs of production in the short run. Wage rates, equipment costs, and raw materials' prices tend to be sticky, changing only infrequently. Wages typically are altered once per year or even less frequently. Firms often contract to purchase raw materials at prices that are fixed for at least 1 year. For example, electric power companies often sign contracts locking in prices of their inputs of coal or natural gas for multiyear periods. Because certain costs remain fixed in the short run, *profit margins*—profits per unit of output—increase as the nation's price level increases. Increased profit margins induce firms to step up production.

As the time period under consideration lengthens, increasingly more input prices adjust to the higher general price level. In the *long run*—a sufficiently long period for *all* input prices to adjust fully to a change in the general price level—the nation's aggregate supply curve is vertical. That is, in the long run the aggregate quantity of output produced is independent of the nation's price level because profit margins do not increase when the price level rises. We discuss the implications of the vertical long-run AS curve for macroeconomic policy later in this chapter.

## Equilibrium Output and the Equilibrium Price Level in the Short Run

In Figure 20-1, the AS and AD curves intersect at *A,* yielding an equilibrium price level of $P_E$ and an equilibrium real output level of $Y_E$. Any other price level produces *disequilibrium,* generating forces that push the economy back to *A.* For example, if the price level initially were at $P_H$ (above $P_E$), aggregate production ($Y_2$) exceeds aggregate expenditures or sales ($Y_3$), resulting in an undesired increase in the nation's inventories. The increased inventories signal firms to cut prices and reduce output in order to return to optimal inventory levels. As the nation's price level declines, production decreases and purchases increase until the economy reached point *A*. On the other hand, if the price level initially were at $P_L$ (below $P_E$), aggregate expenditures and sales ($Y_2$) exceed aggregate production ($Y_3$). Inventories decline involuntarily each period, resulting in numerous product shortages and sales and profit losses to firms. Declining inventories and the shortage of goods and services signal firms to raise prices and increase production. Higher prices cause buyers to reduce their purchases and induce firms to step up production. The economy again returns to point *A* in the figure.

In this elementary but useful model, any changes in the nation's equilibrium price and output levels are attributable to *shifts* in the AD and AS curves. Any increase in the nation's equilibrium output level must be caused by a rightward shift of the AS or AD curve. Any increase in the equilibrium price level must be due to either a rightward shift of the AD curve or a *leftward* shift of the AS curve. Another term for a persistent and continuing increase in the nation's price level is, of course, *inflation*. Therefore, inflation is caused by a persistently rightward shifting AD curve, a persistently *leftward* shifting AS curve, or a combination of the two. Historically, the predominant cause of inflation in all nations has been a persistently rightward shifting AD curve, typically due to rapid growth of a nation's government expenditures and money supply. This phenomenon is known as **demand-pull inflation,** because a rightward-shifting AD curve pulls up the price level. Less common historically is inflation caused by sharp increases in input prices (energy prices, for example), which shift the AS curve leftward. Such inflation is termed **supply-shock inflation** because the "shock" to the AS curve initiates inflation. This type of inflation sometimes is referred to as *cost-push inflation* because the increase in production costs is the initial force that "pushes" up prices. We now examine the various factors that shift the nation's AD and AS curves, producing changes in the nation's real output and price level.

**demand-pull inflation**
inflation caused by a persistently rightward-shifting AD curve, typically the result of rapid growth of a nation's government expenditures and money supply

**supply-shock inflation**
inflation caused by sharp increases in input prices, which shift the AS curve leftward.

## Factors that Shift the Aggregate Demand Curve

A decrease in the nation's price level, to the extent the decrease influences C, I, G, and NX, moves us *along* the AD curve and increases the quantity of output demanded. Any other factor that increases any of the four components of aggregate demand (C, I, G, or NX) *shifts the position* of the AD curve rightward (an *increase* in AD). This shift leads to increases in both real output and the nation's price level. Factors that reduce C, I, G, or NX shift the AD curve leftward (a *decrease* in aggregate demand), resulting in decreases in both output and the price level. To understand why the AD curve shifts around over time, we must discuss the main factors influencing each of the four components of aggregate demand.

**Factors Influencing Consumption(C).** The principal determinants of consumption expenditures (C) include disposable income, wealth, interest rates, and consumer confidence. Increased disposable income resulting from an income tax cut increases consumption expenditures, shifting the AD curve rightward. An increase in stock, bond, or house prices directly increases household wealth, stimulating consumption and shifting the AD curve rightward.[2] Lower interest rates en-

[2] Several studies indicate consumption is induced to change by 2 to 4 percent of the change in wealth. That is, the *marginal propensity to consume wealth* is estimated to range from .02 to .04. However, considerable uncertainty exists about the strength and stability of this wealth effect. The wealth effect stemming from increased house prices may be stronger than the wealth effect resulting from increased stock prices because increased house prices may be perceived as more permanent. For more on this, see Exhibit 23-1 in Chapter 23.

gineered by the Federal Reserve stimulate consumer expenditures on big-ticket items typically bought on credit, such as cars, furniture, and major appliances, shifting the AD curve rightward. Increased consumer confidence due to increased job stability, lower unemployment, or an improving economic outlook stimulates consumption, again shifting the AD curve rightward.

YOUR TURN

From 2000 to 2002, a major decline in U.S. stock prices erased more than $6 trillion ($6,000 billion) of U.S. household wealth. Assume households change consumption expenditures by 2 percent of any change in wealth. Holding other factors constant, analyze the impact of the decline in stock values on the nation's price level and real output.

**Factors Influencing Investment (I).** Investment includes expenditures on new business plants and equipment, construction of new homes and other structures, and changes in the nation's aggregate inventories. Key determinants of investment expenditures include the expected real interest rate, business confidence (perhaps indicated by the expected growth rate of aggregate expenditures or sales), current utilization rate of existing plants and equipment (capacity utilization rate), and federal tax policy toward businesses. Lower real interest rates engineered by the Federal Reserve stimulate several components of investment, including expenditures on plants, equipment, housing, other structures, and inventories, shifting the AD curve rightward. Similarly, improved business confidence increases investment expenditures, shifting AD rightward. An important rationale for investment expenditures is the need to provide additional capacity that can meet expected future market demand. If sales are expected to expand strongly and the current utilization rate of existing plants and equipment is relatively high, firms increase investment spending to provide additional capacity. Hence, an increase in expected sales and/or in the current capacity utilization rate stimulates investment, shifting the AD curve rightward. On the other hand, if expected sales growth is meager and/or the current capacity utilization rate is low, firms anticipate little need for additional capacity, and investment spending is depressed. Finally, tax policy toward the business sector in general and investment spending in particular influences investment decisions. Implementation of more rapid depreciation allowances for income tax purposes, enactment of an investment tax credit, and a reduction in the corporate income tax rate stimulate investment spending, shifting the AD curve rightward.

**Factors Influencing Government Purchases of Goods and Services (G).** Government purchases hinge on political decisions made by federal, state, and local units of government. State and local government purchases (and, to a lesser extent, federal purchases) also depend on available funds (tax revenues) and therefore on the general level of economic activity. Changes in government purchases shift the aggregate demand curve. When government purchases increase, the AD curve shifts rightward. When government purchases decrease, the AD curve shifts leftward.

**Factors Influencing Net Exports of Goods and Services (NX).** Net U.S. exports (exports minus imports, designated as NX) are influenced by the foreign exchange rate, income in foreign nations, trade impediments, and other factors. Suppose the U.S. dollar depreciates against the euro and other major currencies.

U.S. products become cheaper abroad. Other factors being consistent, foreign demand for U.S. exports increases. Because foreign-made products become more expensive in the United States when the dollar depreciates, some former U.S. demand for imported goods is redirected toward U.S. goods and services. Imports decline. Hence, a lower U.S. dollar stimulates net U.S. exports (NX) and shifts the AD curve rightward. Appreciation of the dollar reduces AD in the United States, shifting AD leftward. Other factors that stimulate (NX) and thereby boost AD in the United States include higher income abroad, trade negotiations that reduce trade restrictions imposed by foreign nations, and successful U.S. marketing and promotional campaigns advertising U.S. products.

Table 20-1 indicates several factors that shift the U.S. AD curve rightward, thereby increasing both real output and the price level.

**Table 20.1 Factors that Shift the U.S. AD Curve Rightward**

| Event | Reason Why AD Shifts Rightward |
|---|---|
| 1. Federal Reserve increases bank reserves and money supply | Interest rates fall, stimulating consumption and investment spending |
| 2. Congress enacts income tax cut | Disposable income rises, stimulating consumption spending |
| 3. Consumer confidence rises | Consumption spending increases |
| 4. Business confidence improves; expected returns from investment expenditures increase | Investment expenditures by firms increase |
| 5. State and local government expenditures increase | Increase in government purchases directly increases aggregate demand |
| 6. Income in Europe and Asia increases | U.S. exports increase, boosting U.S. net exports (NX) |
| 7. U.S. dollar depreciates against the euro and other currencies | U.S. exports rise and U.S. imports fall—that is, NX increases |

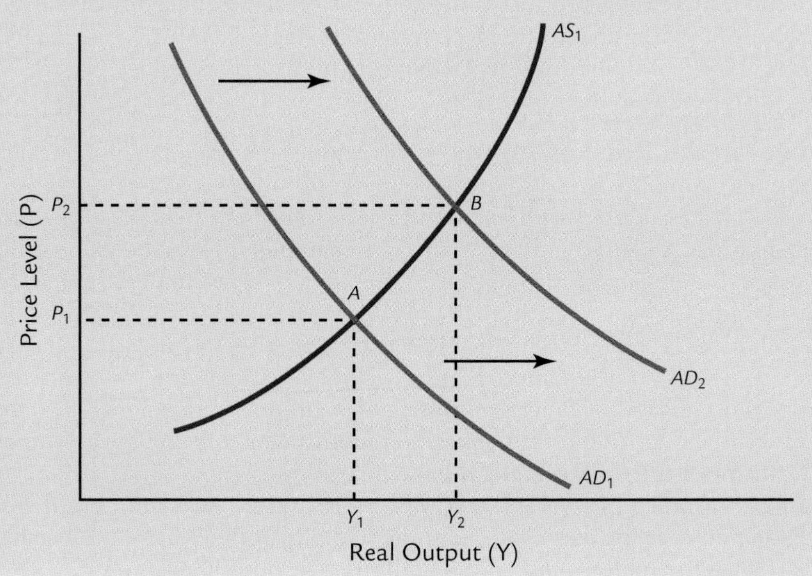

## Factors that Shift the Aggregate Supply Curve

Factors influencing the aggregate supply of U.S. goods and services include the quantity of inputs available (labor, capital, raw materials), the price of these inputs, and the state of technology. Increases in the quantity of inputs and improvements in technology increase aggregate supply—that is, shift the AS curve rightward. Increases in input prices reduce aggregate supply (shift AS leftward). Over the years, the nation's aggregate supply curve has gradually and persistently shifted rightward due to rising population (and labor force), an increasing capital stock, and improving technology. Factors increasing the size or the *productivity*—output per hour of work—of the labor force shift the AS curve rightward.

**Changes in the Quantity of Inputs.** Inputs into the production process include labor, capital, and raw materials. As the labor force grows due to either population growth or an increase in the *labor force participation rate*—the percentage of the working-age population in the labor force—more labor becomes available and the nation's capacity to produce increases. The AS curve shifts rightward. Similarly, as the capital stock grows, any given labor force can produce more output. Labor productivity increases, and the AS curve shifts rightward. *Capital deepening*—increases in the amount of capital goods per worker—stimulates productivity and shifts the AS curve rightward. Policies promoting long-term economic growth typically focus on stimulating investment expenditures to increase and improve the quality of the nation's capital stock. A war or natural disaster that reduces a nation's capital stock and/or its labor force shifts the AS curve leftward. If terrorists in Iraq blow up oil pipelines or destroy electricity-generating plants, the Iraqi AS curve shifts leftward.

**Technological Change.** Improvements in technology increase the amount of output the labor force can produce, shifting the AS curve rightward. For example, the development of personal computers and word-processing software enabled secretaries (and professors) to type examinations and research papers more quickly, boosting output per hour (productivity). The advent of the Internet increased the dissemination of information and accelerated the speed with which information is transmitted, increasing productivity. Economists believe that, historically, technological innovation has been the most important single factor increasing labor productivity and thereby shifting the AS curve rightward. Technology growth is a crucial factor raising worker productivity and living standards.

**Changes in the Price of Inputs.** Other things being equal, increases in input prices (wages, oil prices, and so forth) increase production costs, thereby reducing profit margins associated with each and every (output) price level. Firms reduce output, and the AS curve shifts leftward. For example, if Congress boosts the minimum wage, the AS curve shifts leftward. An increase in raw material prices reduces profit margins associated with each possible price level, and AS shifts leftward. When oil prices increased dramatically in the 1970s, the AS curve shifted sharply to the left. As predicted by the model, industrial nations (including the United States) experienced a period of falling output (and rising unemployment) accompanied by severe inflation. When oil prices fell temporarily in early 2003 with the successful overthrow of the Iraqi regime, the AS curve shifted right.

Table 20-2 indicates several factors that cause a rightward shift in a nation's AS curve (an increase in aggregate supply). Holding other factors constant, such events reduce the nation's price level and raise the output level.

**Table 20.2 Factors that Shift the AS Curve Rightward**

| Event | Reason Why AD Shifts Rightward |
|---|---|
| 1. Labor force increases | Increase in quantity of inputs increases production capability |
| 2. Nation's capital stock increases | Increase in quantity of inputs increases production capability |
| 3. Technological innovations boost worker productivity | Average worker can produce more output per hour |
| 4. Oil prices fall | Lower input prices increase profits associated with each price level, inducing firms to increase output |
| 5. Wages fall | Lower input prices increase profits associated with each price level, inducing firms to increase output |
| 6. Ideal weather results in record crop production | Strong production of food and fiber (cotton, etc.) directly increases output and reduces input prices |

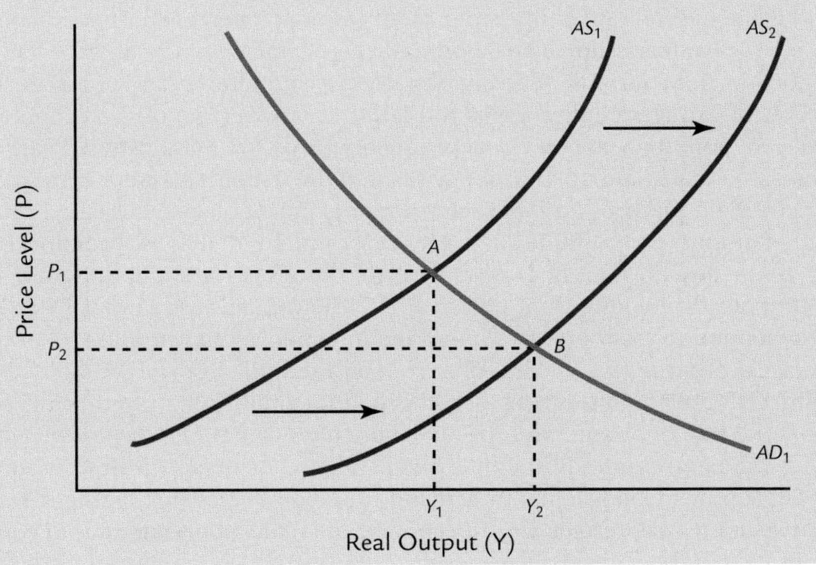


## SHORT-RUN VERSUS LONG-RUN EQUILIBRIUM IN THE AD/AS MODEL

We demonstrated that short-run equilibrium output is determined by the intersection of the nation's short-run AS and AD curves. Depending on the positions of the AS and AD curves, this short-run equilibrium *may or may not* occur at the output level that generates full employment of the nation's labor force. Each possible output level gives rise to a certain level of employment and therefore to a particular unemployment rate. A higher output level is associated with greater employment and therefore a lower unemployment rate. Therefore, some specific output level generates *full employment,* a condition in which the labor market is in equilibrium—

**natural rate of output**
specific output level that generates full employment, where the supply of workers equals the demand for workers

**natural rate of unemployment**
unemployment rate that exists when the economy produces the full employment level of output

**NAIRU (non-accelerating inflation rate of unemployment)**
rate of unemployment at which demand for labor equals the supply, thus maintaining inflation at its existing rate

**recessionary gap**
situation in which equilibrium output falls short of full-employment output and the actual unemployment rate is above the natural rate of unemployment because output falls short of the natural rate of output

**inflationary gap**
situation in which equilibrium output exceeds full-employment output and the actual unemployment rate is below the natural unemployment rate

the supply of workers equal the demand for workers. This hypothetical output level is the **natural rate of output.** The unemployment rate associated with the natural rate of output is the **natural rate of unemployment.** A closely related concept is the **NAIRU (non-accelerating inflation rate of unemployment).** The NAIRU is the rate of unemployment that maintains inflation at its existing rate. Stated differently, NAIRU is the lowest sustainable unemployment rate that does not cause an increase in the ongoing inflation rate. Economists are uncertain of the precise level of NAIRU (which changes over time), but let's assume here for purposes of analysis that NAIRU is 5 percent.

In the *short-run* equilibrium, output may be *below* or *above* (or *at*) the natural rate of output. Correspondingly, the nation's actual unemployment rate at any time may be above or below (or at) the natural unemployment rate. If the actual unemployment rate differs from the natural rate of unemployment and if wages and prices are flexible, adjustments in wages and prices occur. These adjustments cause the actual unemployment rate to move toward the natural unemployment rate. We illustrate these principles in Figure 20-2.

In the top portion of the figure (panel A), assume the short-run aggregate supply curve initially is $AS_1$ and the aggregate demand curve is AD. Short-run equilibrium occurs at *A*, and short-run equilibrium output is $Y_1$. Because output ($Y_1$) falls short of the natural rate of output ($Y_N$), the nation's unemployment rate (7 percent) is *above* the natural rate of unemployment (assume 5 percent). This situation is known as a **recessionary gap.**[3] The labor market is characterized by an excess supply of workers (a labor surplus). Barring obstacles to competitive market forces, an excess supply of workers implies wages will fall. In many sectors of the economy, wages make up more than 60 percent of production costs. We demonstrated earlier that a decrease in wages and other input prices shift the nation's AS curve rightward as firms increase output produced at each price level in response to increased profits per unit of output (review Table 20-2). Hence, point *A* in the figure does not represent a *long-run* equilibrium. Because wages fall, the AS curve shifts rightward to $AS_2$, and the short-run equilibrium moves to *B*. However, because output ($Y_2$) still is below the natural rate of output ($Y_N$) and the unemployment rate still is above 5 percent, wages continue to fall. The AS curve continues to shift rightward until it reaches $AS_3$, with the equilibrium at *C*. At this point, equilibrium output coincides with the natural rate of output, and the actual unemployment rate (5 percent) coincides with the natural rate of unemployment. The labor market is now in equilibrium, with supply of labor equal to demand for labor. Wages stop falling. Given the AD curve, point *C* represents *long-run* equilibrium—the labor market is in equilibrium, output is at the natural output level, and the actual unemployment rate coincides with the natural rate of unemployment.

In panel B of the figure, assume the aggregate supply curve is initially $AS_4$. In conjunction with the aggregate demand curve (AD), we see that the short-run equilibrium is at *D*, and output is $Y_4$. Because output is *above* the economy's natural rate of output ($Y_N$), the actual unemployment rate is *below* the natural unemployment rate of 5 percent. In the figure, output of $Y_4$ corresponds to an unemployment rate of 3 percent. This condition is known as an **inflationary gap.** The labor market exhibits an excess demand (shortage) for workers. At existing wages, the demand for

[3] Be sure you clearly understand the distinction between a *recession* and a *recessionary gap*. A recession is a period of falling output. A *recessionary gap* is the much more common situation in which equilibrium output (*whether rising or falling*) lies below the natural or full employment output level. Output may be rising and yet a recessionary gap exists if equilibrium output lies below the natural output level.

**Figure 20-2** Short-Run Equilibrium Output and the Economy's Self Correcting Mechanisms

If output initially falls short of the natural rate of output ($Y_N$), wages fall, AS shifts right, and output increases **(Panel A).** If output initially exceeds the natural rate, wages rise, AS shifts left, and output falls **(Panel B).** These forces constitute the economy's *self-correcting mechanism.*

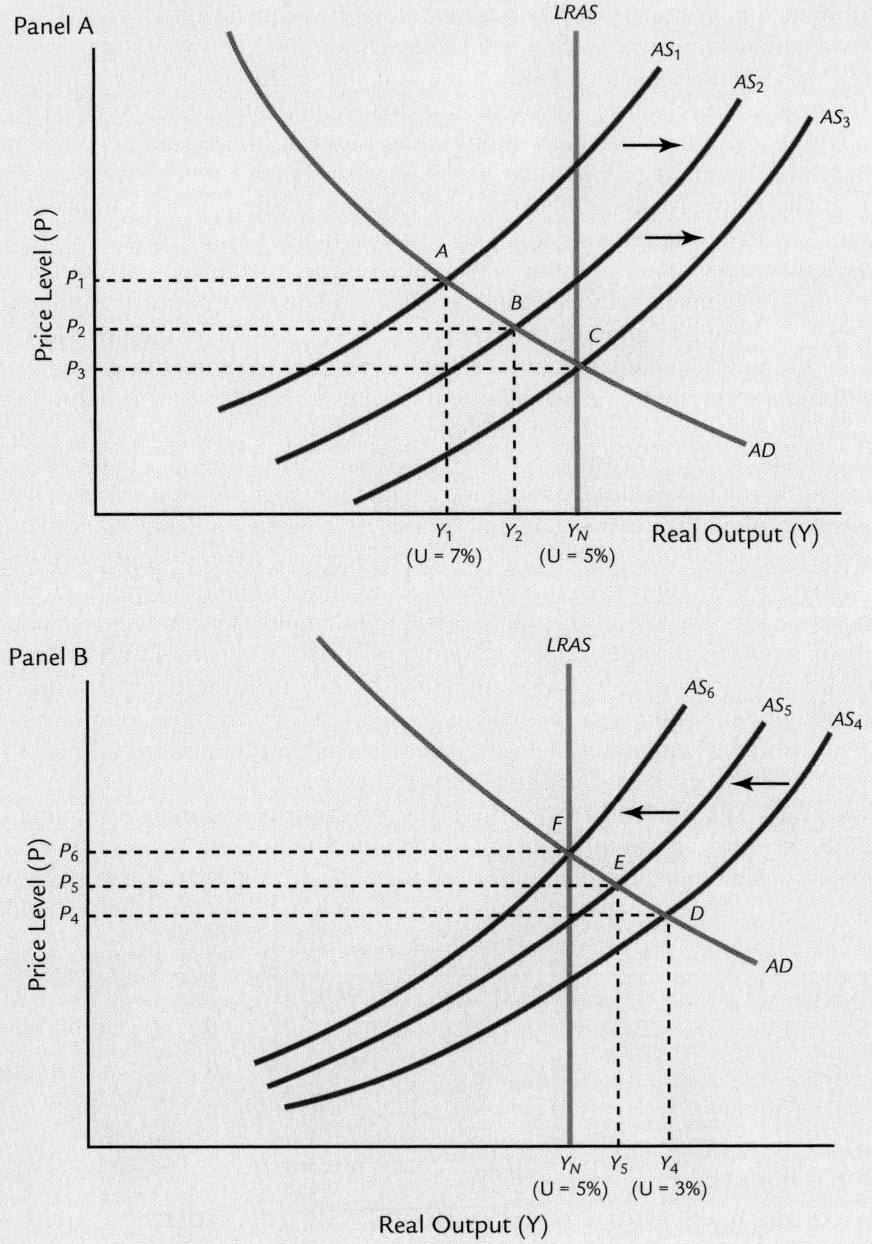

workers exceeds the supply. Wages increase. Hence, point *D* does not represent a *long-run* equilibrium situation. As wages initially rise, the short-run AS curve shifts leftward to $AS_5$. Equilibrium moves to *E* in the figure, with short-run equilibrium output now at $Y_5$. Because output still is above the economy's natural output level, wages continue to rise and the AS curve continues to shift leftward. When the AS curve shifts to $AS_6$, equilibrium output falls to $Y_N$, and the unemployment rate increases to 5 percent, the natural rate of unemployment. Because the labor market is now in equilibrium, point *F* represents a long-run equilibrium.

**self-correcting mechanism**
mechanism that tends automatically to restore full employment conditions through wage and price flexibility

We have demonstrated that, in a market economy where wages and prices move freely in response to the forces of supply and demand, the economy has an inherent **self-correcting mechanism**—a mechanism that tends automatically to restore full employment conditions. When output initially exceeds the natural or full employment output level, wages rise. AS shifts leftward, and the price level rises as we slide upward and leftward along the AD curve. Real output demanded is induced to fall via the wealth effect and other forces discussed at the beginning of this chapter. The process continues until equilibrium output returns to the natural output level. When output initially falls short of the natural or full employment output level, wages fall. AS shifts rightward. As we slide down the AD curve, the price level falls and real output demanded is induced to increase via the forces discussed earlier. The process continues until actual output reaches the natural rate of output, $Y_N$.

**long-run aggregate supply curve (LRAS)**
relationship between nation's price level and real output produced when actual and expected inflation are equal and input prices have fully adjusted to output prices

In this analysis, regardless of the output and price level at which the AD curve intersects the *initial* short-run AS curve, the AS curve shifts until it intersects the AD curve at $Y_N$, the natural level of output. In panel B of Figure 20-2, for example, suppose the economy is in long-run equilibrium at *F*. Now, assume the Federal Reserve lowers interest rates or consumer confidence increases. AD shifts rightward. In the new short-run equilibrium, output exceeds the natural rate of output and the unemployment rate lies below the natural rate of unemployment. Wages rise, and the AS curve shifts leftward. The process continues until the AS curve intersects the new AD curve at $Y_N$. Or, starting at point *C* in the panel A of the figure, assume consumer confidence plunges. The AD curve shifts left, creating a recessionary gap in the near term as output falls below $Y_N$. As wages fall in response to the excess supply of labor, the short-run AS curve shifts rightward until it intersects the new AD curve at $Y_N$. This analysis implies the economy's **long-run aggregate supply curve (LRAS)** is a vertical line through $Y_N$. In the long run, when inflation expectations equal actual inflation and all input prices have adjusted fully to output prices, shifts in the AD curve influence the nation's price level but do not influence output.

## CHALLENGES FACING MONETARY POLICYMAKERS

The AD/AS model is relatively simple but still is useful for understanding some of the challenges confronting the Federal Reserve in conducting monetary policy. We now discuss several of the Fed's challenges.

### Uncertainties about the Positions, Slopes, and Dynamics of the AD and AS Curves

Officials in charge of monetary policy strive to maintain output close to the natural rate of output. That is, they seek to maintain the unemployment rate close to the natural rate of unemployment or the NAIRU. In an ideal but *unattainable* world, the natural and equilibrium output levels always coincide. In the real world, the natural and equilibrium output levels seldom coincide. Monetary and fiscal policies impact the economy in the short run by altering the position of the nation's aggregate demand curve. On the one hand, the Federal Reserve seeks to avoid an inflationary gap by restraining aggregate demand when it threatens to become excessive. On the other hand, the Fed desires to avoid large recessionary gaps and the associated loss of output, income, and jobs by boosting aggregate demand when it is weak. The Fed wants output to approach as closely as possible the natural or full employment output level. That is, the Fed seeks to manage the AD curve in a manner that always maintains equilibrium output approximately equal to $Y_N$.

The Fed's task is daunting—indeed, very nearly impossible. Policymakers are uncertain of the *positions* of both the AD and AS curves at any point in time. Furthermore, the curves constantly shift in response to factors beyond the Fed's control. Factors include changes in consumer and business confidence, highly uncertain wealth effects due to changes in stock and home prices, changes in government expenditures and tax policy, and changes in energy prices and exchange rates, and changing trends in labor force participation rates and productivity growth. Uncertainty also exists about the *dynamics*—the speed with which the nation's price level and real output respond to shifts in the AS and AD curves. In addition, significant time lags occur between implementation of Federal Reserve policy actions and the impact of these actions on the nation's AD curve. Also, the *length* of these lags is variable and uncertain. These facts indicate that even if the Federal Reserve knew the precise NAIRU level at each point in time, the Fed would experience considerable difficulty maintaining the actual unemployment rate close to the NAIRU level.

## Uncertainties About the NAIRU Level and Forces that Cause NAIRU to Change

Life would be considerably easier for monetary policymakers if they knew the NAIRU level and if the NAIRU remained constant over time. For example, if the Fed knows the NAIRU is 4.8 percent and the unemployment rate is currently 6.5 percent, the Fed is confident that policy stimulus is appropriate. Unfortunately, the natural rate of output and NAIRU are uncertain and change over time. Economists simply *don't know* the precise level of NAIRU. A well-known study estimated that the NAIRU was 6.2 percent in 1990, with a 95 percent confidence interval encompassing a NAIRU range of 5.1 to 7.7 percent.[4] This uncertainty poses difficulty for those in charge of monetary policy. The NAIRU level changes over time in response to changing demographics, changing competition in labor and product markets, and other factors. Evidence suggests the NAIRU level has declined significantly since the early 1980s—perhaps by a full percentage point or more.[5] We briefly analyze a few factors that cause the NAIRU level to change over time.

**Changing Demographics and the NAIRU.** Different age groups exhibit different average unemployment rates. Young workers change jobs more frequently than middle-aged workers. In addition, younger workers typically have not attained

[4] This result is reported in the 1997 paper by Staiger, Stock, and Watson cited in the Additional Reading section. Another study reported that, from 1960 to 1997, inflation increased in 90 percent of the quarters in which the (demographically adjusted) unemployment rate was less than 5 percent and decreased in about 85 percent of the quarters in which the adjusted unemployment rate exceeded 7 percent. This finding suggests the NAIRU was in the 5 to 7 percent range in this period. See the paper by Joseph Stiglitz in the NAIRU symposium cited in the Additional Reading section.

[5] In the Federal Reserve's semi-annual testimony on monetary policy before Congress in February 2004, Chairman Greenspan indicated he believed the natural unemployment rate (NAIRU) was around 4 percent.

the same high level of job skills as middle-aged workers. Therefore, unemployment rates normally are higher for 20-year-olds than for 45-year-olds. In the past 40 years, the unemployment rate for workers aged 16 to 24 years averaged more than 12 percent, whereas the unemployment rate for workers older than 25 years averaged less than 5 percent. Because of the differing unemployment rates per age group, changes in the age composition of the labor force trigger changes in the NAIRU. Because of the baby boom extending from 1946 to the early 1960s, young workers flooded into the work force from the mid-1960s through the early 1980s. The portion of the labor force constituted by young workers increased. Any amount of economic stimulus (and inflation) in this period was associated with a higher unemployment rate than in earlier times. The NAIRU increased. In the same period, the labor force participation rate of females increased sharply. In those years, unemployment rates were significantly higher on average for females than for males. The increasing portion of the labor force made up by females thus contributed to the increase in the NAIRU through the early 1980s. After the early 1980s, as the baby boomers moved into middle age and the participation rates of females in the labor force stabilized (and unemployment rates of females declined), the NAIRU decreased. The point is clear: varying demographic conditions cause changes in the NAIRU.

**Changing Competition and the NAIRU.** Increasing competitive forces in labor and product markets likely contributed to the NAIRU decline in the past quarter century. Today, a lower unemployment rate can be achieved without boosting inflation than was possible in the 1980s. Globalization forces have increasingly exposed the U.S. manufacturing sector to foreign competition, as witnessed by declining employment in the manufacturing sector. Immigration of unskilled workers into the United States has increased in recent decades. These factors, along with declining penetration of the work force by labor unions and a downward trend in the real minimum wage level, have resulted in increased restraint on U.S. wages and a decline in the NAIRU. Increasing U.S. exposure to foreign competition has resulted from the *North American Free Trade Agreement (NAFTA),* increased job outsourcing, and other forces. Together with deregulation of airlines, telecommunications, and other sectors, these forces have contributed to enhanced competition in the U.S. economy. The enhanced competition apparently has decreased the pricing power of U.S. companies in product markets. Such forces work to reduce the nation's NAIRU.

**Wage Aspiration Effect, Productivity Growth, and the NAIRU.** Assume that, over time, workers' aspire (and expect) to experience increases in real wages in line with past increases. Based on past experience over many generations, workers feel entitled to achieve living standards that rise in line with the trend rate of productivity growth. Employers are inclined to grant such real wages increases. If the trend growth rate of productivity declines unexpectedly, demands for real wage hikes in line with those of the past are inconsistent with the ongoing inflation rate. Production costs rise more rapidly, inflation increases, and the economy requires a higher unemployment rate to remain in equilibrium. The NAIRU increases. Later, if the growth rate of productivity increases and moves *above* the long-term trend, demands for real wage growth in line with those of the past are consistent with a *lower* inflation rate. In this event, NAIRU declines. Changes in the trend growth of productivity thus lead to changes in the NAIRU. This phenomenon likely helps account for the apparent reduction in the NAIRU level after the mid-1990s, when the trend growth rate of U.S. productivity increased appreciably.

**Hysteresis and the NAIRU.** When unemployment remains high for a sustained period, the work skills of the unemployed likely deteriorate. Also, the confidence and job search skills of unemployed workers decline. Employers may jump to the conclusion (rightly or wrongly) that those who have been unemployed for a substantial period have flaws making them less desirable employees even when good times return. In these ways, sustained high unemployment increases the NAIRU level. On the other hand, in boom times such as the late 1990s, sustained periods of low unemployment reduce the NAIRU level. This idea is known as **hysteresis,** which hypothesizes that the NAIRU level is influenced by the level and duration of the actual unemployment rate. This hypothesis suggests that recessions are doubly costly. Recessions reduce output and income in the near term, but they also increase the NAIRU and thereby impose costs that extend far beyond the recession's end. The hysteresis hypothesis is controversial and probably is more widely accepted in Europe than in the United States.

**hysteresis**
idea that the NAIRU level is influenced by the level and duration of the actual unemployment rate

## THE PHILLIPS CURVE, THE NAIRU, AND MACROECONOMIC POLICY

In 1958, Professor A.W. Phillips of the London School of Economics published a paper that has become one of the most widely cited and important articles in the history of economics. In this paper, Phillips plotted the unemployment rate in England (horizontal axis) against the average rate of change of wages (vertical axis) each year from 1861 to 1957. A strong inverse relationship was reported, and the relationship was robust—it was stable over time. In years in which the national unemployment rate was low, wages increased rapidly. In years in which the unemployment rate was high, wage growth was slow. In fact, wages actually *declined* on average in years when the unemployment rate exceeded 5.5 percent. Phillips established the historical existence of an inverse relationship between the rate of unemployment and the rate of *wage* inflation.

Because wages constitute the major portion of production costs, more rapid wage hikes typically are associated with higher price level inflation rates. Very soon, the **Phillips curve hypothesis** came to be known as the proposition that, *other things being equal,* a lower unemployment rate is associated with a higher price level inflation rate. Thousands of papers have explored the nature of the relationship between unemployment and inflation since Phillips' seminal article. Figure 20-3 illustrates a hypothetical Phillips curve. In the figure, the nation's unemployment rate is on the horizontal axis, and the inflation rate is on the vertical axis.

**Phillips curve hypothesis**
proposition that, other things being equal, a lower unemployment rate is associated with a higher price level inflation rate

Several theoretical rationales have been invoked in support of the Phillips curve hypothesis. The first theory postulates that the bargaining power of labor is high relative to the bargaining power of employers when unemployment rates are low. In tight labor markets, employers find fewer alternative workers available to replace existing workers. Also, profits typically are robust in a strong economy, and a strike would be very costly to firms. Hence, firms grant relatively large wage hikes, which translates into relatively high inflation rates as firms pass increased costs on to consumers. The second theory—as the economy expands and unemployment declines from a high level, the pace of expansion is not uniform across all sectors. A few sectors run into bottlenecks in the form of labor shortages, even when the nation's unemployment rate is relatively high. However, overall wage hikes are modest in such circumstances because most firms face an abundance of qualified workers. As the national unemployment rate declines, increasingly more sectors suffer from shortages of qualified workers. Labor shortages (and large wage increases) occur in

**Figure 20-3** The Phillips Curve

The Phillips curve hypothesis asserts that a *trade-off* exists between unemployment and inflation—that is, lower rates of unemployment are associated with higher inflation rates.

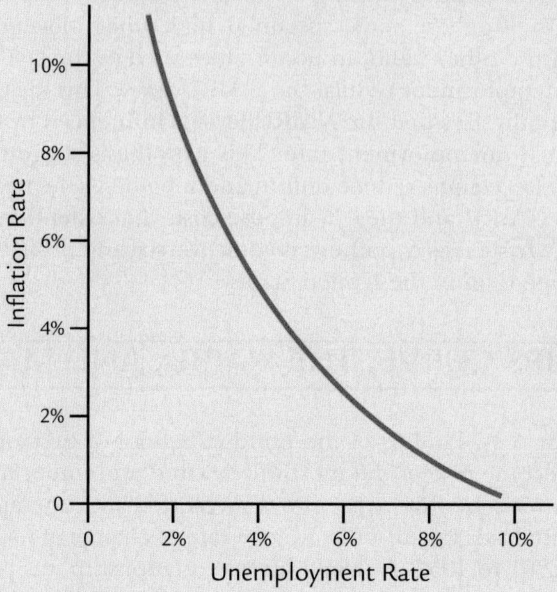

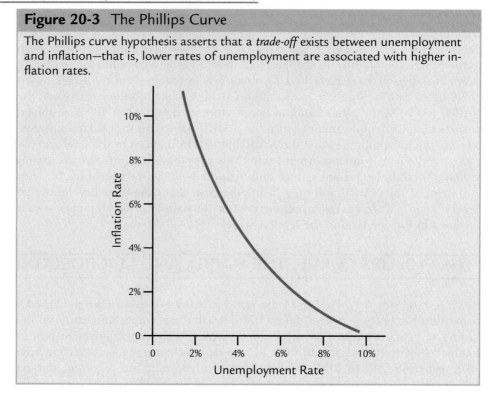

more sectors of the economy, and average wage inflation in the nation increases. When the national unemployment rate is extremely low, *most* sectors face worker shortages. Therefore, the average wage increases are quite large, generating high price level inflation. Additional explanations are available that provide theoretical underpinnings to the Phillips curve hypothesis.

In the first decade or so after Phillips' original article appeared, many economists interpreted the Phillips curve to mean that a nation's policymakers must choose between maintaining low unemployment rates and accepting high inflation on the one hand and living with high unemployment to keep inflation down on the other. That is, the Phillips curve initially was thought of as a *menu of policy choices* facing those in charge of a nation's monetary and fiscal policies. Implicitly, thoughtful consideration of the costs of unemployment and of inflation would permit policymakers to choose the most desirable point along the Phillips curve and seek to operate the economy at that point indefinitely. Today, few economists or policymakers interpret the Phillips curve in this way. Let's explain why. Consider Figure 20-4, which illustrates the AD/AS model in the top panel and the Phillips curve in the bottom panel.

In the top panel of the figure, assume we initially are at *A*, the intersection of $AS_1$ and $AD_1$. The price level and output levels are $P_1$ and $Y_1$, respectively. Assume (unknown to policymakers) this output coincides with the natural rate of output ($Y_N$), so the existing unemployment rate (5 percent) equals the NAIRU. Assume initially no inflation exists. Thus, in the bottom panel of the figure (the Phillips curve framework) the economy is at point *A*, with 5 percent unemployment and zero inflation.

Now, suppose the Federal Reserve, either because of political considerations or because it has underestimated the level of NAIRU, applies monetary stimulus. In

**Figure 20-4** The AD/AS Model and the Phillips Curve

A *family* of short-run Phillips curves exists, one for each level of expected inflation. The long-run Phillips curve is a vertical line at the natural rate of unemployment.

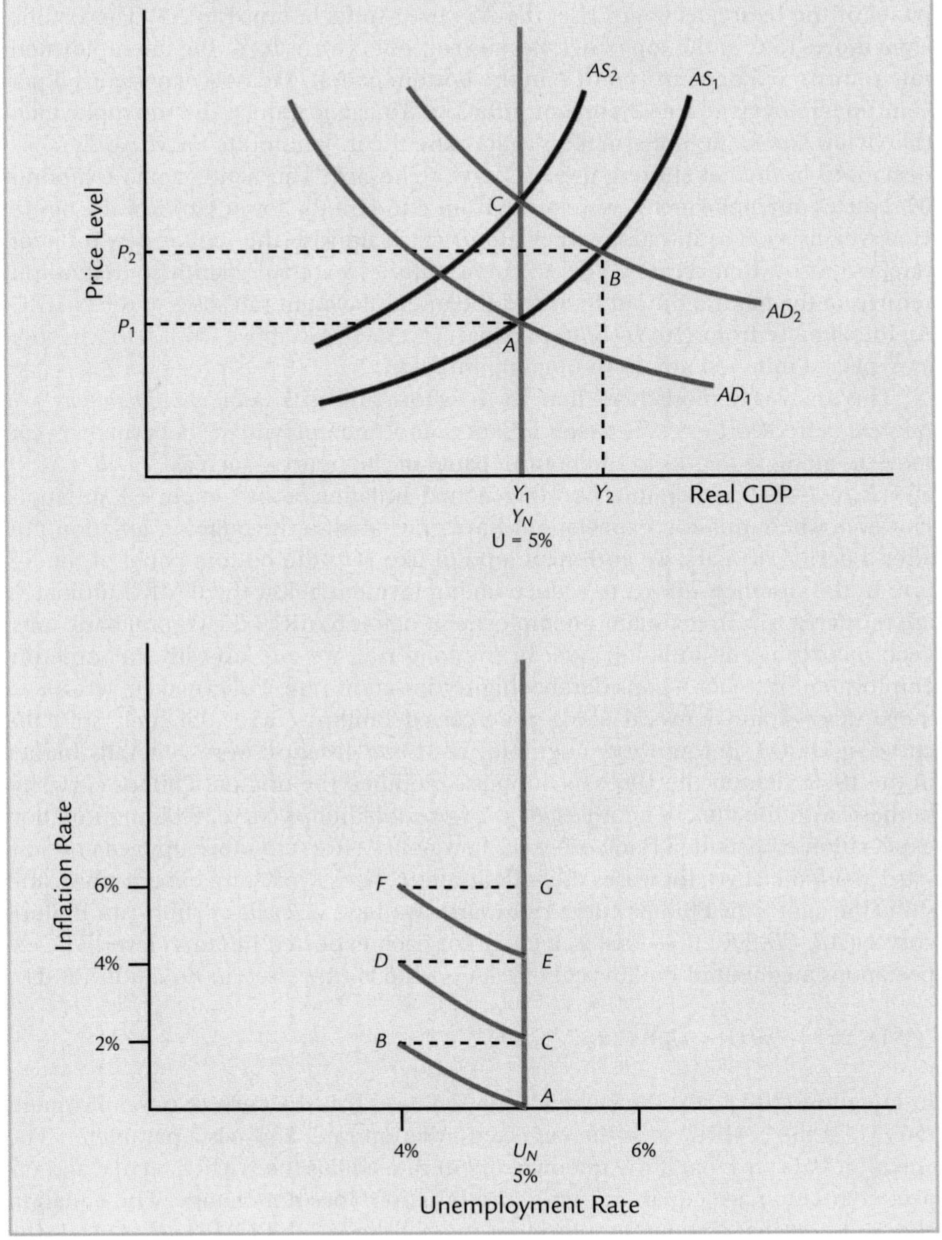

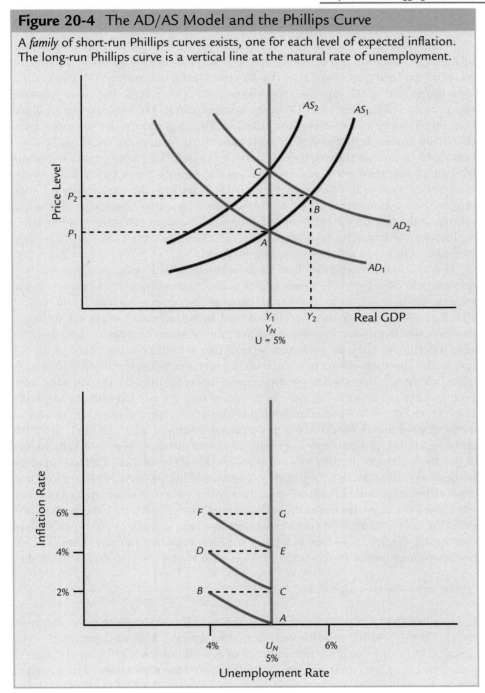

the top panel of the figure, the AD curve shifts right to $AD_2$, boosting the equilibrium price level to $P_2$ and equilibrium output to $Y_2$. Short-term equilibrium is at *B*. Output now exceeds the economy's natural rate of output, and the unemployment rate is below the NAIRU. In the lower panel of the figure, we move from *A* to *B*. The unemployment rate falls to 4 percent, and the inflation rate rises from zero to 2 percent (lower panel) as the price level increases from $P_1$ to $P_2$ (upper panel). In the short run, lower unemployment occurs at the expense of a higher inflation rate. This situation demonstrates the existence of a short-run Phillips curve trade-off.

However, because expectations of inflation are closely tied to recent actual rates of inflation, inflation expectations rise and wage demands increase. In the top panel of the figure, as wages rise, the AS curve shifts leftward to $AS_2$. The equilibrium moves to *C* in the top panel. Because output returns to $Y_1$, the unemployment rate returns to 5 percent (point *C* in the bottom panel). We now experience 5 percent unemployment and 2 percent inflation. To again reduce the unemployment rate below 5 percent, policymakers again raise the inflation rate above workers' expectations by further shifting the AD curve rightward. This action again temporarily reduces unemployment, as we move from *C* to *D* in the lower panel of the figure. However, as soon as inflation expectations catch up with the higher new inflation rate, wage growth increases. The AS curve shifts leftward sufficiently so that output returns to the natural output level and the unemployment rate rises to the NAIRU. An initial move from *C* to *D* (bottom panel) gives way to a move from *D* to *E* as soon as expected inflation adapts to ongoing inflation.

This analysis demonstrates that, in the short run, *with inflation expectations held constant,* a trade-off exists between inflation and unemployment. Policymakers can move us along segments in the bottom panel of the figure—such as *A* to *B, C* to *D,* and *E* to *F*—by persistently boosting actual inflation above expected inflation. However, when inflation expectations have gravitated to the ongoing inflation rate after a period of years, we end up at a point like *G* in the bottom panel of the figure. In this instance, efforts to reduce unemployment below the NAIRU ultimately are unsuccessful. To maintain unemployment below NAIRU, the central bank must keep increasing the inflation rate. In the long run, we end up with the same unemployment rate but a considerably higher inflation rate. Policymakers' efforts to move upward and leftward along a perceived Phillips curve ultimately shift the curve rightward. Because *both* unemployment *and* inflation were generally higher in the 1970s than in the 1960s, economists modified the original Phillips curve hypothesis with the idea of an *expectations augmented* Phillips curve. Holding inflation expectations constant, a trade-off exists, but policy efforts to move upward and leftward along the curve increases the inflation rate, boosts inflation expectations, and shifts the short-run Phillips curve rightward. We have a *family* of short-run Phillips curves (*AB, CD, EF,* . . .)—that is, a curve for each expected inflation level. The expectations augmented Phillips curve relationship is expressed in Equation (20-1).

$$(20\text{-}1) \quad \pi = -\mathbf{a}(\mathbf{U} - \mathbf{U_N}) + \pi^e.$$

In Equation (20-1), $\pi$ is the current inflation rate, U is the current unemployment rate, $U_N$ is the NAIRU, $\pi^e$ is the expected inflation rate, and *a* is a parameter. The equation indicates that if the unemployment rate equals the NAIRU, actual and expected inflation are equal ($\pi = \pi^e$), and inflation does not change. The equation also indicates that if the unemployment rate falls below the NAIRU ($U < U_N$), the inflation rate rises and then exceeds expected inflation ($\pi > \pi^e$). If the unemployment rate is above the NAIRU, the inflation rate falls below expected inflation. The parameter *a* indicates *how much* the inflation rate ($\pi$) changes each year for each percentage point the unemployment rate differs from the NAIRU. Assume, for purposes of illustration, that both actual and expected inflation initially are 2 percent per year, U and $U_N$ both are 5 percent, and *a* is 0.6. The equation indicates that if the unemployment rate falls to and then remains at 4 percent, inflation rises by 0.6 percentage points per year—that is, inflation increases from 2.0 to 2.6 percent after 1 year and to 3.2 percent after 2 years. As long as U is maintained below $U_N$, the inflation rate keeps rising. As long as U is maintained above $U_N$, the inflation rate keeps falling.

In the *long run*, economic rationality suggests expected inflation will gravitate to the actual inflation level. People may initially be fooled by inflation, but eventually they get it right. From Equation (20-1), this means that the unemployment rate will gravitate to the NAIRU. In the long run, no trade-off exists between unemployment and inflation. In Figure 20-4, the long-run Phillips curve is a vertical line at the NAIRU, running through points *A, C, E,* and *G.* The early economists who initially viewed the Phillips curve as a longer-term menu of policy choices implicitly forgot to include the expected inflation term ($\pi^e$) in their consideration of the Phillips curve relationship.[6]

YOUR TURN

Assume, in the context of Equation (20-1), that the NAIRU is 5 percent, the unemployment rate over the next year stays constant at 7 percent, *a* is 0.5, and the inflation rate is currently 3 percent. Calculate the inflation rate that will prevail 1 year from now.

## MONETARY POLICY: RESPONDING TO SHOCKS TO THE AD AND AS CURVES

An important objective of monetary policy is to counteract the undesired consequences of nonpolicy forces producing shifts in the nation's AD and AS curves. The central bank intends to stabilize economic activity by preventing high inflation on the one hand and high unemployment on the other. The task is daunting because of the multitude of uncertainties about the positions of the AD and AS curves, the strength of current forces shifting AS and AS curves, the dynamics of adjustment, the NAIRU level, and other factors.

### Monetary Policy and Aggregate Demand Shocks

Suppose the economy is at full employment when a series of negative aggregate demand shocks occur. The shocks shift the AD curve leftward. First, suppose stock prices fall by 50 percent, impairing consumer and business confidence and reducing household and business wealth. Consumption and investment expenditures decline, shifting the AD curve leftward. Suppose, a few months later, an unprecedented terrorist attack on the United States destroys major buildings in the United States' largest city and kills thousands of individuals. This action reduces U.S.

[6] In a prescient work published in 1968, Milton Friedman indicated the necessity of including the expected inflation term in the equation. From 1963 to 1968, as unemployment declined and inflation increased in the United States, the pattern of unemployment and inflation rates traced out an almost "perfect" downward-sloping Phillips curve (see Exhibit 20-1). Friedman predicted that this situation would not continue—that is, the short-run Phillips curve generated in the 1960s would shift rightward in response to the increased inflation of the 1960s. In Friedman's words, "There is always a temporary tradeoff between inflation and unemployment; there is no permanent tradeoff. The temporary tradeoff comes not from inflation per se, but from unanticipated inflation, which generally means from a rising rate of inflation." Friedman's view soon was borne out by actual developments, as you can see in Exhibit 20-1. See the reference to Friedman's classic article in the Additional Reading section.

household and business confidence, reducing consumption and investment spending. Suppose, less than 1 year later, news of corruption and fraudulent reporting of profits by several major U.S. corporations and the accounting firms that audit them is reported. All of these events, which actually occurred in the first 3 years of the twenty-first century, produce negative shocks to aggregate demand. These negative forces reduce consumption and investment expenditures, shifting the U.S. AD curve leftward.

The Federal Reserve, acutely aware of the impending negative effects of these events on the U.S. economy, responded immediately by implementing stimulative actions to counteract the powerful forces shifting the AD curve leftward. From 2000 to 2003, the Federal Reserve lowered short-term interest rates 13 times in an effort to stem the initial contraction and the ensuing weakness in aggregate demand, output, and employment. Because time elapses before Federal Reserve policy actions influence aggregate expenditures, the Fed was unable to prevent the 2001 recession and the ensuing period of sluggish output growth and rising unemployment. Few economists deny, however, that the Fed's actions reduced the consequences of the series of negative demand shocks. When large, recognizable shocks occur to a nation's AD curve, the central bank's appropriate response is unambiguous. Negative AD shocks necessitate stimulative central bank actions. On the other hand, when unemployment is close to the NAIRU, strong *positive* AD shocks necessitate restrictive central bank actions.

## Dilemma Posed for Monetary Policy by Adverse Supply Shocks

In the 1970s, dramatic increases in world crude oil prices and other forces produced major leftward shifts in the short-run aggregate supply curve in the United States and other industrial nations. Forces shifting the AS curve leftward are known as *negative* or *adverse supply shocks.* These forces create a dilemma for the Federal Reserve and central banks in other nations. Figure 20-5 illustrates the nature of the dilemma.

Assume that, before the oil price hike, the U.S. economy is at *A,* the intersection of $AS_1$ and $AD_1$. The equilibrium price level is $P_1$. The equilibrium output is ($Y_1$), which coincides with the natural or full employment output level ($Y_N$). The economy is enjoying full employment—the unemployment rate equals the NAIRU. Assume initially there is no inflation—the price level has been at $P_1$ for some time. Now, suppose crude oil prices soar. The AS curve shifts leftward to $AS_2$. If the Federal Reserve elects to *not* respond to this supply shock (thereby leaving the AD curve unchanged), the economy moves to point *B* in the figure. The price level increases to $P_2$, and real output falls to $Y_2$. The adverse supply shock produces the worst of all worlds—a recession combined with a significantly higher price level. This phenomenon has been dubbed **stagflation**—the combination of stagnant or falling output and sharply rising prices.

**stagflation**
combination of stagnant or falling output and sharply rising prices

Assume the Federal Reserve commits to maintaining full employment—that is, maintaining output at $Y_1$ (and $Y_N$). The Fed implements expansionary measures to shift the nation's aggregate demand curve rightward, to $AD_2$. The economy moves to point *C* in the figure, output returns to $Y_N$, and the unemployment rate to the NAIRU. In this case, full employment is maintained. Unfortunately, the price level soars to $P_3$, and the nation suffers a period of extremely severe inflation.

On the other hand, suppose the Fed commits to maintaining price level stability—that is, maintaining the nation's price level at $P_1$. The Fed counters the supply shock with *restrictive* monetary policy actions, shifting the AD curve down to

**Figure 20-5** Adverse Supply Shocks and Monetary Policy Alternatives

When adverse supply shocks occur, the AS curve shifts leftward. The Federal Reserve must accept higher inflation, higher unemployment, or both.

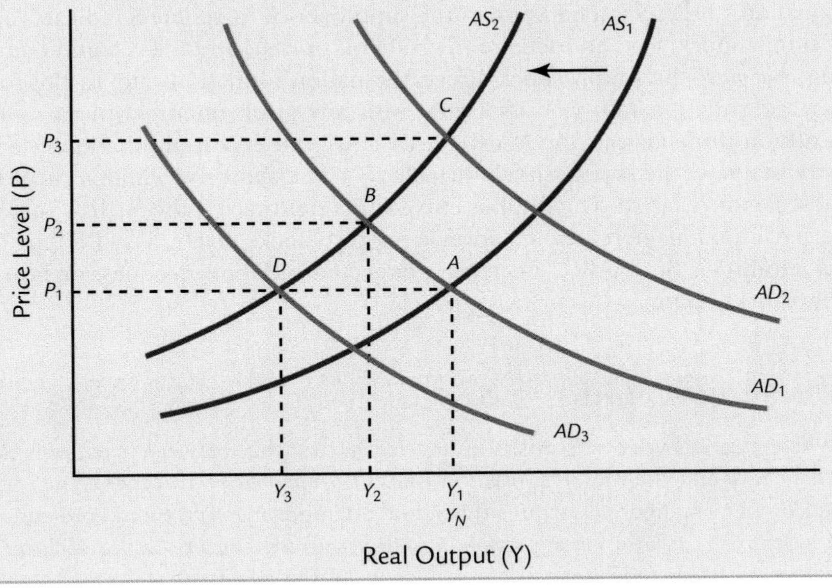

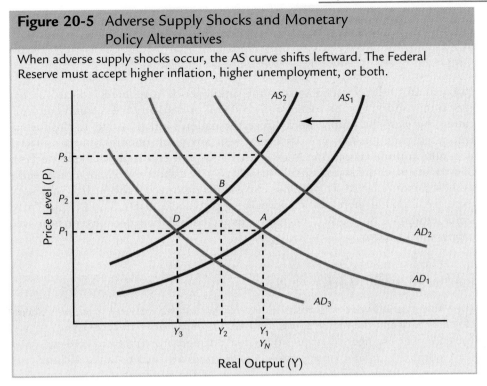

$AD_3$. We move to point *D,* and the price level remains at $P_1$. The supply shock fails to increase the price level. However, output declines to $Y_3$, a severely depressed level. The unemployment rate soars, and financial distress among business firms increases sharply.

This is a no-win situation for the Federal Reserve. Faced with a large adverse supply shock, the Fed can choose extremely high inflation coupled with full employment, extremely high unemployment accompanied by stable prices, or some increase in *both* inflation *and* unemployment. As we will discuss in Chapter 21, the Fed responded to the 1970s oil shocks by steering a middle course. Inflation increased sharply in the 1970s, and the nation suffered two severe recessions in the decade beginning in 1973.

Aggregate supply shocks can be *favorable* or *positive* as well as *adverse* or *negative.* A decline in oil and energy prices, or an unexpected increase in productivity growth for example, shifts the AS curve rightward.[7] A favorable supply shock increases equilibrium output and, by putting downward pressure on prices, enables the Federal Reserve to implement stimulative measures that increase aggregate demand without causing significant inflation. The United States enjoyed the benefits of favorable supply shocks during the boom of the late 1990s, as we will detail in Chapter 21.

[7] Holding wages constant, an increase in productivity shifts AS *rightward.* Holding productivity constant, an increase in wages shifts AS *leftward.* Suppose wages and productivity both have been rising at a rate of 2 percent per year recently, and the AS curve has remained fixed. Now, if productivity accelerates to a growth rate of 4 percent per year while wages continue to rise at 2 percent, the AS curve shifts rightward. Because *unexpected* growth in productivity likely will not be captured in wage hikes, AS shifts rightward.

This analysis of supply shocks suggests that the Phillips curve relation expressed in Equation (20-1) must be modified as follows:

(20-2) $$\pi = -\mathbf{a}(\mathbf{U} - \mathbf{U_N}) + \pi^e + \mathbf{bS}.$$

In Equation (20-2), S is a measure of the supply shock (a *positive* S indicates an *adverse* supply shock, e.g., an increase in crude oil prices), and b is a parameter indicating *how much* the supply shock affects the nation's inflation rate. In this formulation, the inflation rate ($\pi$) associated with any given unemployment rate (U) depends on three factors: the NAIRU level ($U_N$), the expected inflation rate ($\pi^e$), and the status of the supply shock variable (S). The short-run Phillips curve shifts as these factors change. The Phillips curve shifts rightward if the NAIRU increases, expected inflation increases, or adverse supply shocks occur. The Phillips curve shifts leftward if the NAIRU decreases, expected inflation declines, or favorable supply shocks occur.

## Exhibit 20-1 Whither the Phillips Curve?

The Phillips curve hypothesis posits an inverse relationship between a nation's unemployment rate and the nation's inflation rate, *ceteris paribus* (with other things equal). The accompanying figure illustrates the actual unemployment rate and core consumer price index (CPI) inflation rate prevailing each year from 1963 to 2003. A closer look at the overall figure indicates the critical nature of the *ceteris paribus* assumption. The downward-sloping short-run Phillips curve is a shifty animal. In addition to the 1964–1969 period, negatively sloped short-run relationships are notable in the 1976–1979, 1980–1983, 1990–1992, and 2001–2003 periods. However, other factors do *not* remain constant over time. Equation (20-2) indicates the inflation rate associated with any given unemployment rate changes for three reasons—inflation expectations change, NAIRU changes, and positive or negative supply shocks occur. All of these factors alter the position of the short-run Phillips curve.

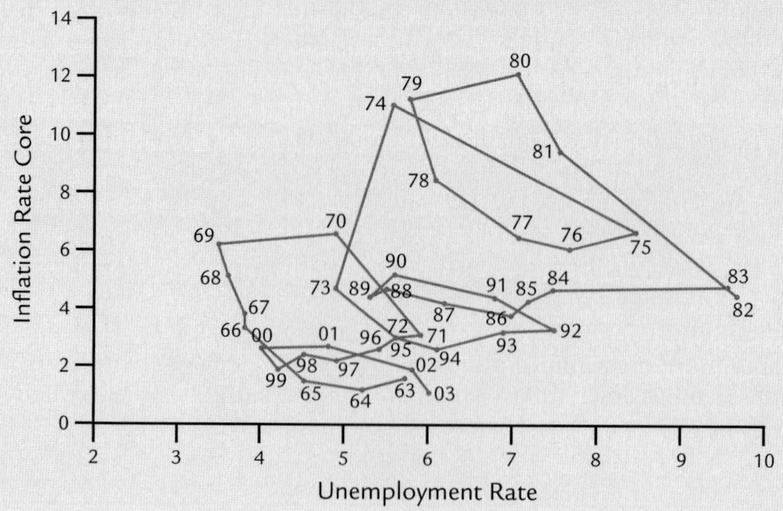


Several episodes occurred during which inflation and unemployment rates moved in the *same direction,* including 1973–1974 and 1979–1980, periods immediately following

## **Exhibit 20-1** Whither the Phillips Curve?—*cont'd*

the dramatic oil price hikes of 1973 and 1979, respectively. From our AD/AS framework, increased oil prices shifts AS leftward, resulting in falling output (hence rising unemployment) and rising prices. Decreased oil prices shift AS rightward, reducing both inflation and unemployment. This relationship helps account for the 1984–1986 pattern of points (oil prices fell sharply in this period).

Changes in inflation expectations shift the short-run Phillips curve. An increase in expected inflation leads to larger wage hikes at any given unemployment rate and hence a higher inflation rate. After the steady acceleration of inflation in the late 1960s, the pattern of points for the early 1970s is to the right of the short-run Phillips curve for the 1960s. And the disastrous 1980–1983 pattern of points followed episodes of double-digit inflation in 1979 and 1980, which clearly boosted inflation expectations (also, the NAIRU was reaching peak levels in the early 1980s due to demographic and other forces). The short-run Phillips curve shifted rightward in the 1970s and again in the early 1980s. The curve then shifted leftward after 1983 for several years in response to declining inflation expectations and other forces.

Finally, note the remarkable pattern of points from 1992 to 1999. Beginning in 1993, in apparent defiance of the Phillips curve hypothesis, *both* inflation *and* unemployment decreased in five of the seven ensuing years. Both inflation and unemployment were sharply lower in 1999 than in 1992. How can you explain this phenomenal U.S. economic performance, which was reflected in a dramatic increase in U.S. stock prices? To reconcile the U.S. economic performance with the Phillips curve hypothesis, you need to invoke (decreasing) inflation expectations, demographics and other forces that were reducing the NAIRU, and favorable supply shocks.

In the first few years of the 1990s, inflation expectations declined as inflation fell from the 5.5 percent rate of 1990. NAIRU drifted downward due to lower birth rates in the late 1960s and much of the 1970s and the resulting 1990s decline in the portion of the labor force made up of young workers. Other forces reducing NAIRU, such as increasing competition in labor and product markets, also were at work. Beginning in 1995, new developments in information technology and other forces contributed to major unanticipated increases in the nation's productivity growth rate. To top matters off, oil prices fell sharply from mid-1997 to the end of 1998. Such favorable supply shocks shift the nation's AS curve rightward, bringing the dual benefits of higher output (hence lower unemployment) and lower inflation.

The downward-sloping Phillips curve reasserted itself after 1999. Check out the inflation and unemployment rates in the most recent calendar year at http://research.stlouisfed.org/fred2. What story can you tell about this year in relation to the 2001–2003 pattern of points on the accompanying graph?

In Chapter 21, we will demonstrate the importance of the AD/AS model by using the model to explain the major events of U.S. macroeconomic history in the past 75 years.

10. Return to Equation (20-1). Assume both the current actual and expected inflation rates are 3 percent. Also assume both U and $U_N$ are 5 percent. Now, suppose stock prices and economic confidence decline sharply and the unemployment rate increases to 8 percent. Assuming *a* of Equation (20-1) is 0.4, what will the nation's inflation rate be in 3 years if the unemployment rate remains at 8 percent?

11. Explain what happens to the position of the nation's short-run Phillips curve if the following events occur:
    - **A.** The Federal Reserve announces its intentions to reduce the inflation rate to zero.
    - **B.** The portion of the population aged 25 to 50 years increases.
    - **C.** Immense oil fields are discovered off the coast of Oregon.

## ADDITIONAL READING

- On the basics of the aggregate demand-aggregate supply model, consult a principles of economics textbook and review the AD/AS chapter. An excellent discussion of the wealth effect resulting from movements in stock prices is provided in James Poterba, "Stock Market Wealth and Consumption," *The Journal of Economic Perspectives,* Spring 2000, pp. 99–120.
- An important study documenting the existence of considerable uncertainty about the NAIRU level is "How Precise Are Estimates of the Natural Rate of Unemployment," by Douglas Staiger, James H. Stock, and Mark W. Watson, in Christina Romer and David Romer, *Reducing Inflation* (Chicago: University of Chicago Press, 1997). An excellent recent paper is Laurence J. Ball and N. Gregory Mankiw, "The NAIRU in Theory and Practice," *The Journal of Economic Perspectives,* Fall 2002, pp. 115–136. Also, the winter 1997 issue of the same journal contains a symposium on the natural rate of unemployment and includes six articles by eminent economists.
- The seminal article on the Phillips curve is A.W. Phillips, "The Relation Between Unemployment and the Rate of Change of Money Wages in the United Kingdom, 1861–1957," *Economica,* 1958, pp. 283–299.
- The entire October 1999 issue of *The Journal of Monetary Economics* is devoted to analyses of the Phillips curve. Milton Friedman's classic paper rejecting the notion of the Phillips curve as a menu of policy choices is Milton Friedman, "The Role of Monetary Policy," *American Economic Review,* March 1968, pp. 1–17.
- For discussion of the recent economic environment, read the most recent *Economic Report of the President,* published in February each year by the U.S. Government Printing Office and available on the Internet at http://www.gpoaccess.gov/eop

Chapter 21

# THE AD/AS MODEL AND POST-1929 U.S. MACROECONOMIC HISTORY

In the long time span since the 1920s, the U.S. economy has experienced lengthy periods of prosperity as well as briefer episodes of severe and widespread hardship. The United States has experienced periods of severe inflation, times of relatively stable prices, and one episode of *deflation*—a period of a persistently falling general price level. America experienced two episodes of *stagflation*—falling output accompanied by rising inflation. More recently, a surge in the growth rate of productivity held down inflation but also contributed to a "jobless recovery" in 2002 to 2003. Fewer Americans were employed in late 2004—after three years of an economic expansion—than in early 2001, immediately before onset of the 2001 recession. The aggregate demand-aggregate supply (AD/AS) framework we developed in Chapter 20 assists us in understanding the most important macroeconomic developments of the past 75 years.

## MACROECONOMIC DEVELOPMENTS FROM 1929 TO 1950

If you searched for the 20-year period in U.S. history that exhibited the most atypical economic conditions, the era extending from the late 1920s through the late 1940s surely ranks at or near the top of the list. The years from the late 1920s through the late 1940s encompassed the largest economic contraction in U.S. history (1929–1933) as well as the most costly war ever waged (1941–1945).

### The Great Depression of the 1930s

We outlined the Great Depression and examined the role of the Federal Reserve in that tragic episode in Chapter 17. In our AD/AS model, a series of negative shocks triggered a persistent leftward shift of the nation's aggregate demand curve from 1929 to 1933. The 1920s experienced a tremendous building boom, suggesting that some reduction in construction activity was inevitable in the 1930s.[1] By 1929 stocks were sharply overvalued (as they were again 70 years later), tripling in price from 1925 to 1929. The Federal Reserve tightened its monetary policy stance in the late

[1] If you attend a college or university established in the 1920s or before, think of all the buildings on your campus erected in the 1920s. To illustrate one example, hundreds of colleges and universities built new football stadiums in the 1920s, naming them "Memorial Stadium" in honor of those who died in World War I. In many of the older campuses around the nation, more new buildings were constructed in the 1920s than in any other decade.

1920s, largely to counter escalating speculation in the booming stock market. These events may have been sufficient to cause a *recession* in the early 1930s but certainly not a severe *depression*—a massive and prolonged contraction of output and employment. However, these events were just the tip of the iceberg of contractionary aggregate demand forces to come.

The stock market crash reduced wealth and impaired consumer and business confidence, thus contributing to major reductions in consumption and investment expenditures. The AD curve shifted persistently leftward from 1929 to 1933, sharply reducing both real output and the nation's price level. (This period was the last episode of general *deflation* experienced in the United States.)

The initial stages of price deflation raised *real* interest rates, triggering widespread bank loan defaults by businesses, farmers, and other debtors.[2] The defaults, in turn, impaired the health of the nation's banks, which were major lenders to businesses, farmers, home buyers, and other borrowers. No federal bank deposit insurance existed at the time. The ensuing initial wave of bank failures led to banking panics as the public attempted to withdraw cash from bank accounts. These panics, coupled with inept Federal Reserve policy, nearly destroyed the nation's banking system. As thousands of banks failed, the life savings of millions of families disappeared. The massive loss of personal savings exacerbated the pervasive atmosphere of gloom, further depressing stock prices, consumption, investment, and aggregate demand for goods and services as the economy spiraled downward.

On the international front, a wave of economic nationalism touched off by enactment of the infamous Smoot-Hawley Tariff Act of 1930 caused a collapse of international trade, wrecking the export industries of the major industrial nations. U.S. authorities stood by passively during the downward-spiraling cascade of events. The government did not utilize either monetary or fiscal actions to combat the massive leftward shift of the nation's AD curve.

The result was the greatest economic catastrophe in U.S. history.[3]

## World War II and Its Immediate Aftermath

Beginning in the late 1930s, U.S. impending involvement in the war being waged by Germany and Japan became increasingly clear. A military buildup that started in the late 1930s in preparation for U.S. involvement in the war escalated dramatically after Japan bombed Pearl Harbor in December 1941. The resulting increase in government purchases (G) stimulated aggregate demand. The fiscal stimulus was reinforced throughout the 1940s by the Federal Reserve. The Fed maintained interest rates at abnormally low levels through heavy open market security purchases to help finance large wartime budget deficits. These Federal Reserve actions rapidly expanded the monetary base and the monetary aggregates (M1, M2, M3). From 1938 through 1945, the nation's aggregate demand curve shifted strongly rightward, sharply expanding real output. By about 1943, actual output exceeded the

---

[2] Suppose that initially inflation is running at a rate of 1 percent per year and the nominal interest rate is 3 percent. The *real* interest rate is 2 percent. Now, assume the price level begins *falling* at a rate of 6 percent annually, and the nominal interest rate falls to 1 percent. The real interest rate is now 7 percent [1% − (−6%)]. Many borrowers find such high real interest rates incompatible with financial viability. Incomes are falling along with prices. Therefore, many borrowers cannot make the interest payments on their loans. Debt defaults increase appreciably in such circumstances.

[3] See Table 17-1 in Chapter 17 for a review of the key U.S. macroeconomic indicators in the 1930s. During 1929 to 1933, the consumer price index declined 25 percent, nominal GDP dropped 46 percent, and real GDP fell 29 percent. This relative contraction of real GDP was almost 10 times that of the most severe recession of the post–World War II era.

natural output level—that is, an inflationary gap had developed. The unemployment rate fell sharply below the non-accelerating inflation rate of unemployment (NAIRU) of the times. However, reported price indexes failed to reflect the buildup of inflationary pressures because rigid wage-price controls were in place. When price controls were removed at the end of the war, prices surged. By 1948, the U.S. price level had nearly doubled relative to the price level in 1940.

## MACROECONOMIC DEVELOPMENTS AFTER 1950

Normal economic conditions finally returned to the United States in the 1950s, after two decades of unique circumstances and economic instability (depression and war). Inflation was subdued, averaging about 2 percent per year throughout the decade. The unemployment rate averaged 4.5 percent. Stock prices appreciated strongly—the S&P 500 index rose approximately 15 percent per year during the 1950s. Between 1952 and 1961, however, the nation experienced three recessions.

### Output and Inflation in the Post-1960 Era

Figure 21-1 shows the behavior of actual gross domestic product (GDP) and *potential* or *natural GDP,* both expressed in real terms, from 1960 to 2004. Actual real GDP *(blue line)* fluctuates over time because of shifts in the nation's AD and AS curves. Potential real GDP *(red line)* trends upward over time. The growth rate of potential real GDP fluctuates with changes in the growth rates of the labor force and productivity.

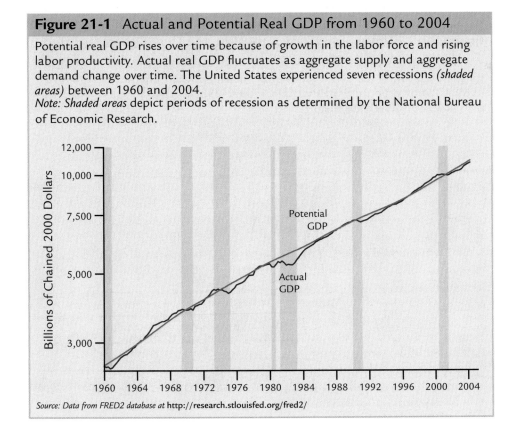

**Figure 21-1** Actual and Potential Real GDP from 1960 to 2004

Potential real GDP rises over time because of growth in the labor force and rising labor productivity. Actual real GDP fluctuates as aggregate supply and aggregate demand change over time. The United States experienced seven recessions *(shaded areas)* between 1960 and 2004.
*Note: Shaded areas* depict periods of recession as determined by the National Bureau of Economic Research.

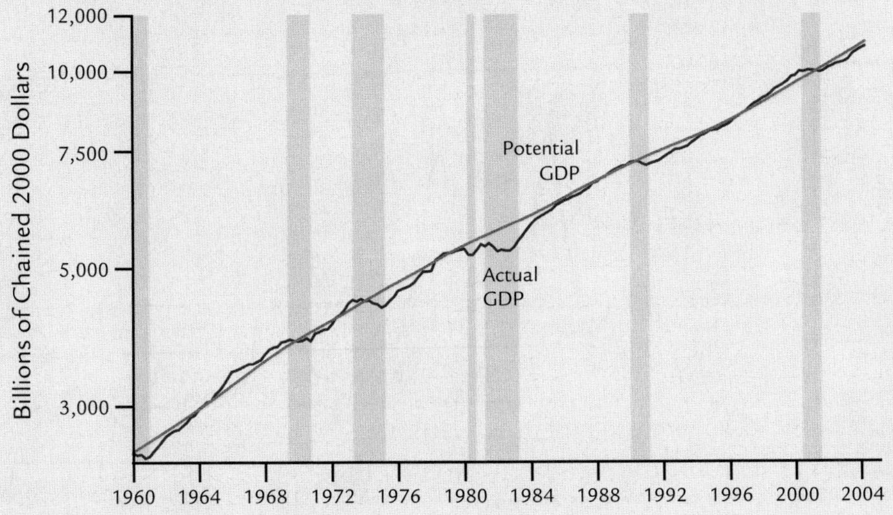


*Source: Data from FRED2 database at* http://research.stlouisfed.org/fred2/

Figure 21-2 shows two measures of the nation's inflation rate over the same 45-year period (1960–2004). The annual rates of change of both the consumer price index (CPI) and the GDP deflator are illustrated. Figures 21-1 and 21-2 reveal considerable information about the macroeconomic history of the United States after 1960. Refer back to these figures as we analyze U.S. economic events of the past half century in the following sections.

## The Early 1960s

**output gap**
situation in which actual GDP is below potential GDP; thus the unemployment rate exceeds the NAIRU

In November 1960, John F. Kennedy was elected president. In his presidential campaign, Kennedy and his advisors had criticized the sluggish U.S. economy of the 1950s under the leadership of President Dwight D. Eisenhower. The Soviet Union had recently launched the satellite Sputnik, and some observers feared the Soviets were on the threshold of surpassing the United States scientifically and perhaps even economically. Note in Figure 21-1 the significant **output gap**—a situation in which actual GDP is below *potential GDP* (a synonym for the natural rate of output)—in 1961 and 1962. The unemployment rate exceeded the economy's NAIRU of the times. Kennedy and his advisors pressed for income tax cuts to stimulate the economy. They also proposed an investment tax credit to foster capital formation, shift the AS curve rightward, and boost long-term economic growth. Following President Kennedy's assassination in late 1963, President Lyndon B. Johnson guided a major tax reduction bill through Congress. The nation's AD curve shifted rightward. The tax reduction stimulated output in 1964 and 1965. By the summer of 1965, the nation's unemployment rate had declined to 4.4 percent, a level that most economists believed was close to the nation's NAIRU at that time. The output gap had been eliminated, as you can see in Figure 21-1. Inflation remained low, as

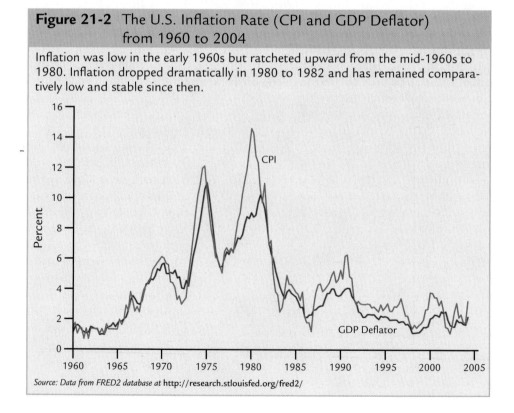

**Figure 21-2** The U.S. Inflation Rate (CPI and GDP Deflator) from 1960 to 2004

Inflation was low in the early 1960s but ratcheted upward from the mid-1960s to 1980. Inflation dropped dramatically in 1980 to 1982 and has remained comparatively low and stable since then.

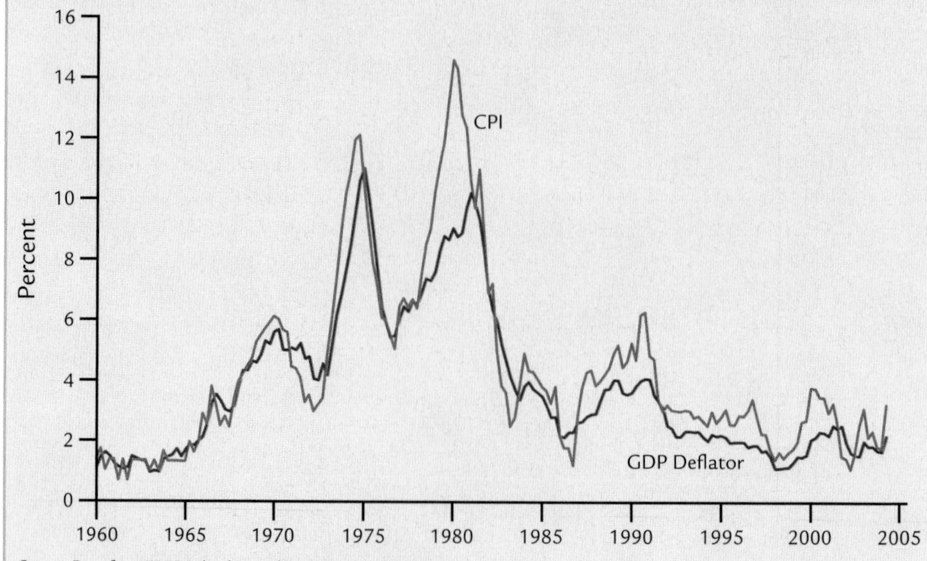


*Source: Data from FRED2 database at* http://research.stlouisfed.org/fred2/

shown in Figure 21-2. The stock market hit an all-time high in 1965. Things looked good. A picture of John Maynard Keynes, the great British economist who was the intellectual architect of activist monetary and fiscal policies, appeared on the cover of *Time* magazine. But the next 17 years were to be a period of great economic instability and disappointment. Stock prices adjusted for inflation in 1982 were less than half the level reached 17 years earlier, in 1965!

## The Vietnam Era: 1965 to 1972

In the summer of 1965, the United States momentously decided to escalate U.S. involvement in the Vietnam War. A major buildup of U.S. forces in Southeast Asia and a large increase in military expenditures ensued. Government purchases increased sharply, shifting the aggregate demand curve rightward. The U.S. economy was already very close to full employment, so the government's failure to cut back non-military expenditures or raise taxes to restrain consumption spending indicated an inflationary gap was certain to develop.[4] The excessive stimulus to aggregate expenditures from 1967 to 1969 reduced the U.S. unemployment rate to approximately 3.5 percent, well below the NAIRU of the times. (Note in Figure 21-1 that actual real GDP was considerably above potential or natural real GDP from 1966 to 1969.) Because of this policy mistake, the U.S. inflation rate steadily escalated from 1.3 percent in 1964 to 5.9 percent in 1969 (Figure 21-2).

After the 1968 presidential election, in which Richard Nixon narrowly defeated Hubert Humphrey, the government made a serious effort to bring down inflation. Restrictive monetary policy actions and a modest income tax hike shifted the AD curve leftward. In November 1969, the U.S. economy entered a mild recession (Figure 21-1). Within 1 year the unemployment rate increased from 3.5 to 6 percent. Inflation, though somewhat reduced, continued to exceed 4 percent throughout 1970, a level that seemed intolerable at the time. Frustrated by inflation's tenacity in the face of a national recession, President Nixon abandoned his free market views. He opted instead for a comprehensive set of wage-price controls in August 1971. The economic rationale for the controls was to bring down *expectations* of inflation, thereby slowing wage hikes and combating the leftward shift of the nation's aggregate supply curve.[5] With the 1972 presidential election approaching, the growth rate of the money supply accelerated, shifting AD rightward. Such an event, in the presence of rigid price controls, creates shortages and bottlenecks, aggravating the eventual increase in the nation's price level (after controls are removed).

## The Economic Nightmare of 1973 to 1982

Nixon's wage-price controls were terminated in early 1973. As predicted by elementary supply and demand analysis, a sharp burst of inflation occurred when price controls were removed in the face of significant excess demand for goods and services. During 1973 and 1974, the inflation rate averaged more than 11 percent

---

[4] In the fall of 1965, President Johnson's economic advisors warned him that inflation would escalate significantly unless non-military government expenditures were cut or taxes were increased. Because Johnson was seeking political support to prosecute the war, he did not request either a tax hike or a cut in government expenditures. His policy mistake was attributable to political considerations, not faulty economic advice.

[5] Recall that a leftward shift of the AS curve pushes up prices and reduces output (thereby raising unemployment). Once inflation becomes heavily entrenched, wages and other input prices anticipate future inflation. This phenomenon shifts AS further to the left, exacerbating inflation and increasing the cost (in terms of lost output) of fighting it. If the announcement of wage price controls could increase the *credibility* of the government's anti-inflation program and thereby reduce the public's expectation of inflation, the controls also would work to reduce wage demands. These actions, in turn, would slow or halt the leftward shift of AS, permitting greater output with less inflation. This was the economic rationale for the wage-price controls.

## **Exhibit 21-1** Oil Prices and Aggregate Supply Shocks

The term *supply shocks* first appeared in the economics lexicon following the dramatic crude oil price increase in 1973. Remember that changes in input prices produce shifts in the aggregate supply curve. Because crude oil is a crucial determinant of energy prices, major changes in the price of crude produce important shifts in the nation's AS curve. The negative consequences of the adverse supply shocks of the 1970s are well known, but supply shocks sometimes are *favorable* or *positive*. When the price of oil drops sharply, we experience a favorable supply shock as the nation's AS curve shifts rightward. A favorable shock event such as an oil price drop has the opposite effect of an adverse supply shock.

Changes in oil prices are not the only source of supply shocks. Significant unexpected changes in the trend of productivity growth or changes in the prices of imported raw materials resulting from large swings in the foreign exchange rate can be considered supply shocks. A severe drought can be an adverse supply shock by increasing the price of food and raw materials such as cotton. However, the most important supply shocks in the past 3 decades have resulted from major changes in oil prices. The demand for crude oil is relatively price-inelastic, so small changes in the oil supply can result in surprisingly large changes in oil price. The accompanying figure illustrates the real price of crude oil (relative to the August 2004 price of $45 per barrel) from 1965 to 2004.

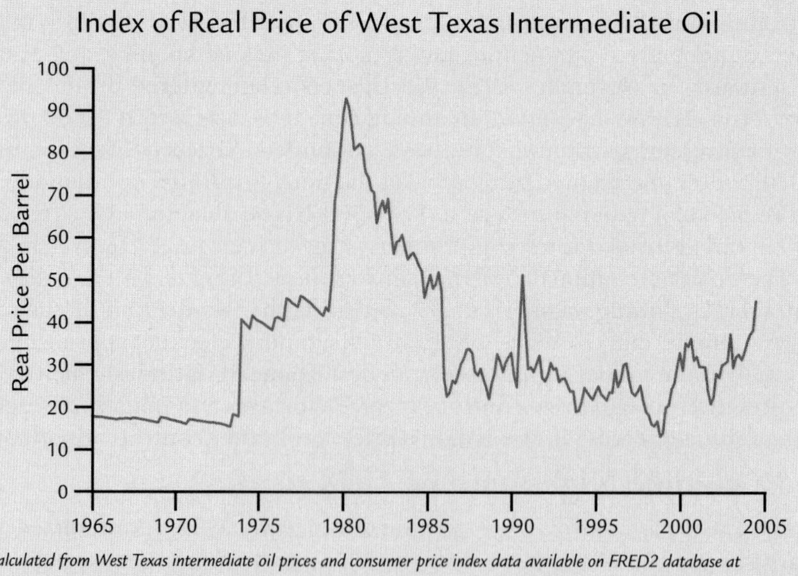


*Source: Calculated from West Texas intermediate oil prices and consumer price index data available on FRED2 database at* http://research.stlouisfed.org/fred2/

Note the handful of sudden and sharp changes in real oil prices. In addition to the infamous spikes in 1973 and 1979 that produced major episodes of stagflation in industrial nations, a few other dramatic episodes are noteworthy. Between November 1985 and March 1986, a brief period of disarray among members of the Organization of Petroleum Exporting Countries (OPEC) cartel resulted in significantly increased oil production in the face of relatively low worldwide demand. Crude oil prices dropped from more than $30 to less than $13 per barrel. The price drop shifted the AS curve right-

**Exhibit 21-1** Oil Prices and Aggregate Supply Shocks—*cont'd*

ward, helping to produce in 1986 the lowest U.S. inflation rate (1.4 percent) in a quarter of a century.

In the summer of 1990, Saddam Hussein confiscated the Kuwaiti oil fields and amassed his Iraqi forces on the Saudi Arabian border. Oil prices spiked again, jumping from \$17 in June to \$35 in October (see figure). The oil price increase may have contributed to the 1990–1991 U.S. recession, although oil prices quickly declined. Following the severe Asian economic contraction initiated by the exchange rate crises that began in July 1997, oil prices plummeted, declining by more than 45 percent between October 1997 and December 1998 (see figure). The oil price decrease shifted the U.S. AS curve rightward, helping the inflation rate decline sharply in 1998, even in the face of a booming economy.

More recently, oil prices in September 2004 were more than double their early 1999 levels. For the first time in U.S. history, gasoline prices moved above \$2 per gallon. The gas price hike helps account for the increased U.S. inflation in 2004. Keep your eye on the price of crude, which has important implications for the U.S. economy.

per year (Figure 21-2). By mid-1973, the unemployment rate had fallen below 5 percent, and real GDP had moved above potential (Figure 21-1). Then the 1973 oil shock shifted the aggregate supply curve sharply leftward as oil prices nearly tripled in the 6-month period beginning in August 1973. The United States experienced its first episode of severe *stagflation*—the simultaneous occurrence of severe inflation and falling output. By most measures, the 1973 to 1975 recession was then the most severe downturn since the Great Depression. Despite the recession, the U.S. inflation rate (CPI) averaged more than 10 percent per year during the 16-month economic contraction.

Inflation slowed to approximately 5 percent during 1975 and 1976 as the rate of increase in oil prices slowed sharply. Jimmy Carter was elected president in November 1976, during a period of economic recovery. The economy expanded in the next 2 years and moved back toward full employment. At the beginning of 1979, the unemployment rate was 6 percent, a level many economists believed was at or slightly below the nation's contemporary NAIRU.[6] The U.S. economy was poised on the brink of another episode of inflation.

In late 1979 and early 1980, a second major oil shock occurred when oil prices zoomed from \$15 to \$40 per barrel. This shock shifted the AS curve leftward, triggering an escalation in inflation and a contraction in output. In 1980, the CPI inflation rate shot above 12 percent (Figure 21-2), and the nation endured the first of two back-to-back recessions (Figure 21-1). The first recession—a brief and mild downturn—lasted only the first half of 1980. The second recession occurred early on President Ronald Reagan's watch. This recession lasted from July 1981 to November 1982, and it was a blockbuster. The Federal Reserve played a crucial role in the economic downturn. The Fed applied severe monetary restraint from 1980 to 1982, pushing short-term interest rates to the highest levels since the Civil War.

[6] Recall from our discussion of the NAIRU in Chapter 20 that demographic forces strongly worked to increase the NAIRU level from the mid-1960s through the early 1980s as baby boomers and female workers entered the labor force in large numbers. By 1982, many economists believe the NAIRU had increased to the 6.0–6.5 percent range. After the early 1980s, the NAIRU drifted downward.

The Fed cracked down in order to attack inflation, which had been running at double-digit levels since late 1978. The resulting downward shift in AD, coupled with the oil shock-induced leftward shift in AS, produced the severe contraction of output from 1981 to 1982 (Figure 21-1). The U.S. unemployment rate peaked at 10.8 percent in late 1982, its highest level since the 1930s.

## 1983 to 1991: The Reagan Expansion and the Era of Supply-Side Economics

In the November 1980 election, Ronald Reagan won a decisive victory over incumbent president Jimmy Carter. In the first Reagan administration (1981–1985), the government instituted a series of measures intended to persistently shift the nation's aggregate supply curve to the *right.* Such policies, if effective, might yield effects opposite to the results of the *adverse* supply shocks of the 1970s—that is, they might boost output and employment and hold down prices. They might work to produce a favorable (leftward) shift in the nation's Phillips curve so that any given unemployment rate is accompanied by a lower rate of inflation. This program became known as **supply-side economics.** An effective supply-side program clearly benefits the nation.

**supply-side economics**
macroeconomic policies designed to increase saving, investment, and work incentives, thereby shifting the aggregate supply curve persistently rightward

No economist quarrels with the *goal* of supply-side economics—implementing policies that produce a persistently rightward-shifting AS curve. Economists' disputes involve the most *effective, efficient,* and *equitable* means of bringing about a rightward-shifting AS curve. To organize your thinking on this issue, reconsider the factors that shift AS rightward. Increases in the quantity of inputs such as labor and capital, decreases in input prices, and increases in technology shift AS to the right. Hence, an enlightened supply-side program should expand the labor force participation rate of the existing population; stimulate saving, investment, and capital formation; hold down the prices of inputs such as raw materials, oil, and capital goods; and promote the search for new technologies.

The Reagan supply-side program featured major reductions in individual and corporate income tax rates, tax incentives aimed at stimulating saving, investment, and labor force participation, and a series of deregulation initiatives to promote competition. The cornerstone of the Reagan program was the large personal income tax cuts implemented in 1981, 1982, and 1983. The tax cuts in total lowered the income tax rates of the average American household by approximately 25 percent. The *supply-side* rationale for the tax cuts was *not* merely to bolster expenditures but rather to increase the *incentive to work and earn income and to increase the economy's productive capacity.* Rather than simply stimulating AD, the tax cuts were intended to shift the AS curve rightward. The Reagan administration believed that marginal income tax rates had become so high by the early 1980s that they significantly impaired the incentive to work and achieve a high income.[7] To the extent that lower income tax rates strengthen the willingness to work hard and develop new technologies, both the supply and productivity of labor should increase, shifting AS rightward. The Reagan program also included the following measures aimed at stimulating investment expenditures: reduced corporate income tax rates, investment tax credits, accelerated depreciation allowances, and reduced capital gains tax rate. Implementation of tax-deductible individual retirement accounts (IRAs) was intended to stimulate household saving, thereby enlarging the pool of funds available to firms for financing new investment expenditures. Such saving and in-

[7] During the 1970s, severe inflation coupled with an un-indexed income tax system steadily pushed most Americans into higher marginal income tax brackets. By 1980, the combined federal and state marginal income-tax rates exceeded 50 percent for a surprisingly large number of families.

vestment incentives, if effective, reduce the consumption share of the nation's output and increase the investment share.

Supporters of the Reagan supply-side policies point to several positive features of economic performance in the 1980s. First, the supply-side measures implemented in the early 1980s were followed by a very long economic expansion that lasted almost 8 years (Figure 21-1). Nearly 17 million jobs were created during Reagan's two terms in office. Inflation declined after 1981 and remained quite low relative to the 1970s (Figure 21-2). The stock market soared to all-time highs in the 1980s, signaling positive sentiment about economic conditions and prospects.

Critics of the Reagan program charge that the program was poorly designed for shifting the AS curve rightward. The tax cuts were not accompanied by reductions in federal expenditures, so large budget deficits ensued. The *national saving rate* (private saving plus government saving) plunged in the 1980s, chiefly because of rising federal budget deficits. Many economists believe real interest rates were very high for several years until the mid-1980s largely because of the large budget deficits. The investment share of national output failed to increase in the 1980s despite the tax breaks targeted toward saving and investment. The trend rate of U.S. productivity growth remained stagnant through the remainder of the decade and did not increase until the mid-1990s.

In the critics' opinion, the strong and lengthy economic recovery from the severe recession of 1981 to 1982 was attributable primarily to a rightward shifting aggregate *demand* curve, not to a rightward shifting aggregate *supply* curve. To support this view, critics point out that productivity growth in the 1980s was even slightly lower than it was in the 1970s. Many of the jobs created in the 1980s paid relatively low wages. In short, the critics claim that the Reagan episode of supply-side economics increased the inequality of the nation's income distribution and failed to produce the desired acceleration of productivity and living standards. These critics derisively termed the Reagan policy *trickle-down economics.*

George Herbert Walker Bush, President Reagan's vice president from 1981 to 1989, became president in early 1989. He inherited an economy in its seventh year of economic expansion and a budget deficit of $250 billion per year (about 4 percent of GDP). The inflation rate was rising (Figure 21-2), which is typical in the latter phase of an economic expansion. The CPI increased 4.6 percent in 1989. In early 1990, Saddam Hussein confiscated the Kuwaiti oil fields and massed his troops on the Saudi Arabian border. Visions of massive oil price hikes and a repeat of the 1970s' nightmare raced through the minds of President Bush and his economic advisors. The initial uncertainty created by this crisis, together with high levels of consumer indebtedness, resulted in a plunge in consumer confidence. The AD curve shifted downward (leftward), tilting the U.S. economy into recession in the summer of 1990 (Figure 21-1).

The Greenspan Federal Reserve implemented expansionary measures, and the recession proved to be relatively mild and brief (see Exhibit 21-2). The recession lasted only 10 months, and the contraction of real output (peak to trough) was only 1.5 percent. The unemployment rate peaked at 7.8 percent, considerably lower than the peaks experienced in the 1973–1975 and 1981–1982 recessions (9.0 and 10.8 percent, respectively).

## 1993 to 2001: The Clinton Years, the Economic Boom, and "New Economy" Debate

The early portion of the recovery from the 1990 to 1991 recession was unusually sluggish (Figure 21-1) and may have accounted for Bill Clinton's narrow 1992 victory over

## Exhibit 21-2 Economic Activity in Recessions

A recession—a period of falling national output—can be touched off by forces producing a leftward shift in either the aggregate demand curve or the aggregate supply curve. Examples of such forces include a decline in consumer confidence and an increase in oil prices, respectively. In general, the economy is in recession when real GDP declines for at least two consecutive quarters. Additional insight into the damage caused by recessions can be gained by looking at several other key indicators. In the accompanying table, the *duration* of each of the nine post-1950 U.S. recessions is indicated. The percentage contraction in real GDP (from peak of the cycle to trough), the largest relative *output gap* (the difference between potential and actual real GDP, expressed as a percentage of actual real GDP), the percentage decline in industrial production, the highest unemployment rate experienced during (or slightly after the end of) the recession, and the percentage decline in after-tax corporate profits also are shown.

Note that industrial production and corporate profits contract much more sharply during recessions than does real GDP. Industrial production declines by a relatively large amount because industrial production excludes the huge and stable service sector, which is included in GDP. Profits drop sharply in recessions because wage and other costs fail to decline commensurate with sales revenues contraction in the short run.

### Indicators of the Severity of Post-1950 Recessions

| Cycle | | | | | | | |
|---|---|---|---|---|---|---|---|
| **Peak** | **Trough** | **Duration (Months)** | **% Decline in Real GDP** | **Largest Output GAP*** | **% Decline in Industrial Production** | **Highest Unemployment Rate** | **% Decline in After-Tax Profits** |
| July 1953 | May 1954 | 10 | −2.8 | 1.0 | −9.1 | 6.1 | −16 |
| August 1957 | April 1958 | 8 | −3.7 | 4.8 | −12.7 | 7.5 | −24 |
| April 1960 | Feb. 1961 | 10 | −1.6 | 4.1 | −8.6 | 7.1 | −24 |
| Dec. 1969 | Nov. 1970 | 11 | −1.0 | 2.2 | −7.0 | 6.1 | −18 |
| Nov. 1973 | March 1975 | 16 | −3.4 | 5.1 | −12.8 | 9.0 | −24 |
| Jan. 1980 | July 1980 | 6 | −2.2 | 3.8 | −7.0 | 7.8 | −18 |
| July 1981 | Nov. 1982 | 16 | −3.0 | 8.6 | −9.6 | 10.8 | −35 |
| July 1990 | May 1991 | 10 | −1.5 | 3.4 | −4.0 | 7.8 | −11 |
| March 2001 | Nov. 2001 | 8 | −0.6 | 1.0 | −5.9 | 6.0 | −41 |
| Average | | 11 | −2.2 | 3.8 | −8.5 | 7.6 | −23 |

* Difference between potential real GDP and actual real GDP, expressed as percentage of actual real GDP.
*Source: Data from FRED database at* http://research.stlouisfed.org/fred

**Exhibit 21-2** Economic Activity in Recessions—*cont'd*

The table indicates that, by most criteria, the two most severe post-1950 U.S. recessions were the downturns from 1973 to 1975 and from 1981 to 1982. Both recessions were preceded by bouts of double-digit inflation (which induced the Federal Reserve to implement highly restrictive monetary policy measures). These two recessions were the *longest* of the post–World War II era. Each recession lasted 16 months. In addition, the output gaps and the unemployment rates reached higher levels in these two recessions than in any other downturns. The two most recent recessions were among the mildest on record, as indicated by the relatively modest declines in real GDP and industrial production. Two alternative hypotheses account for the lesser severity of recent recessions. First, shocks impinging on the economy in the past 20 years have been relatively mild. Second, the Federal Reserve has appreciably improved its recognition of early signals of economic downturns and its implementation of appropriate policies for combatting downturns. Perhaps both of these factors have contributed to our good fortune in recent decades.

incumbent President George H.W. Bush. (At election time in November 1992, the unemployment rate was 7.4 percent.) However, this nascent economic expansion eventually became the longest in U.S. history, lasting exactly 10 years. The unemployment rate declined steadily during this remarkable expansion, dropping below 5 percent in the summer of 1997 and hitting a 30-year low of 3.9 percent in September 2000, near the end of President Clinton's second term. Uncharacteristically, the inflation rate drifted down during the first 7 years of the expansion, reaching a low of 1.8 percent in 1998 before rising in 1999 and 2000 (review Figure 21-2).

All of the productivity measures reported a substantial *acceleration* about midway through the long expansion (review the table in Exhibit 21-3), which also is uncharacteristic of typical business cycles. Normally, productivity growth slows in the second half of an economic expansion. Surging GDP growth produced a sharp increase in federal (and state) tax revenues, ending the 30-year string of federal budget deficits and converting deficits into surpluses (for a few years) beginning in 1998. The improving fiscal outlook helped reduce long-term interest rates, which, together with important new developments in information technology and sharply declining prices of computers, contributed to a major investment boom. Investment spending by firms on software, computers, and other high-tech equipment expanded at double-digit annual rates from 1994 to 2000. A *virtuous cycle* of rising investment spending, productivity, real output, corporate profits, and stock prices accompanied by a strong U.S. dollar, falling inflation, and falling unemployment characterized the remarkable period from 1995 to 2000. The nation's *AS curve* and its AD curve were strongly shifting rightward.

This unusual confluence of favorable events promoted talk of a *new economy*—an economy with much more favorable long-term prospects than had been witnessed for many, many years. Some naïve pundits even suggested that the business cycle had been conquered—that recessions were a relic of the past. These unrealistic sentiments contributed to a speculative bubble in technology stocks during the late 1990s, culminating in an 89 percent increase in the NASDAQ index in 1999 alone! The bubble burst in 2000. The NASDAQ declined more than 75 percent in the next 2 years. Hundreds of Internet and technology stocks lost more than 95 percent of their value in less than 1 year. Business confidence declined. Aggregate

## Exhibit 21-3 Trends in U.S. Productivity Growth

The importance of *productivity growth*—growth of output per hour of work—to the vitality of a nation's economy cannot be overstated. In the long run, barring a longer work week or an increase in the percentage of the population engaged in work, average living standards in the nation cannot rise unless productivity rises. Over several decades, a single percentage point difference in average annual productivity growth remarkably changes the level of living standards achieved.

In the short run, increased productivity growth is an anti-inflation force. Given the ongoing rate of increase in wages, increased productivity growth shifts the nation's aggregate supply curve rightward, which counteracts inflation potentially caused by other factors. The Federal Reserve then can aim for more rapid output growth. The significantly increased trend rate of productivity growth is the principal reason the U.S. economy sustained the longest economic expansion in history from 1991 to 2001, achieved the lowest unemployment rate in 30 years, and maintained an inflation rate substantially below the 40-year average. This productivity performance is indicated in the accompanying table (compare rows 2 and 3).

The table indicates average annual productivity growth rates over various time intervals of three increasingly inclusive measures of the U.S. economy: the manufacturing sector, the non-farm business sector, and the entire business sector. Several observations are noteworthy. First, average productivity growth (via each of the three measures) was substantially higher after 1994 than in the previous quarter century. The improvement of at least 1.5 percentage points per year helps account for several important phenomena that occurred from 1995 to 2000. The phenomena include the sharp increase in the growth rate of real GDP, the dramatic increase in corporate profits and stock prices, the conversion of large federal budget deficits into surpluses, and the remarkable coexistence of falling unemployment and declining inflation. Second, productivity growth in recent decades has been substantially higher in the manufacturing sector than in broader, more inclusive measures of the economy. The service sector, which is generally shielded from foreign competition and in many cases is less amenable to implementation of new technologies and assembly-line production techniques, has exhibited slower productivity growth than the manufacturing sector in the past 35 years.

Productivity exhibits a *cyclical* pattern and a long-term *trend*. If the long-term growth trend is removed from the productivity figures, the cyclical pattern is left. In the first couple of years after a recession ends and economic expansion begins, productivity growth is rapid. Firms expand output to meet rising demand but are cautious about adding to payrolls until they are confident the economic recovery is for real. Firms use existing workers more fully rather than adding more employees, and measured productivity rises. As the expansion continues and management's confidence about sustainability increases, firms add aggressively to their payrolls. Productivity growth slows. Later, the economy peaks and output then turns down. In the first several months of recession, as sales and output decline, firms are hesitant to fire workers. Output drops faster than employment, and productivity declines. As the recession continues and becomes widely recognized, firms aggressively lay off workers, and productivity stops falling.

Clearly, the post-1994 surge in U.S. productivity is a highly favorable development. The crucial question economists debate today is whether we will look back a decade from now and be able to state that the strong productivity performance of this recent period was not just a "flash in the pan."

**Exhibit 21-3** Trends in U.S. Productivity Growth—*cont'd*

Average Annual Productivity Growth Rates in the United States

| Period | Manufacturing Sector | Non-Farm Business Sector | All Business Sector |
|---|---|---|---|
| 1949–1972 | 2.6% | 2.8% | 3.3% |
| **1972–1994** | **2.6** | **1.5** | **1.6** |
| **1995:1–2004:1** | **4.3** | **3.0** | **3.1** |
| 1949:1–2004:1 | 2.9 | 2.3 | 2.5 |

*Source: Data from FRED database at* http://research.stlouisfed.org/fred2/

demand and the rate of growth of output slowed sharply. The nation entered a recession in spring 2001 as the record-length economic expansion came to an end.

An alternative, less optimistic (than the "new economy") explanation for the events that produced the phenomenal economic performance of 1995 to 2000 emphasizes favorable supply shocks that were largely *transitory and fortuitous.* In 1997, perhaps about the time the U.S. economic expansion would have tapped out, oil prices dropped sharply. The oil price drop shifted the AS curve rightward, giving a non-inflationary boost to real output and sustaining the economic expansion. The relatively strong U.S. dollar in the late 1990s helped hold down the U.S. inflation rate. These events, coupled with the surge of productivity growth, permitted Federal Reserve policy to remain unusually accommodative during a business cycle phase when inflation normally begins to rise. The crucial issue in the "new economy" debate involves the "lasting power" of the favorable supply shocks associated with the revolution in information technology and the associated explosion of capital spending of the 1990s. Only time will tell whether the terrific growth rates of productivity experienced from 1995 to 2004 can be sustained over a long period of time.

## The 2001 Recession

As indicated, the economic expansion that extended from March 1991 to March 2001 was of record length. The duration of the expansion likely was prolonged by several fortuitous events—the surge in productivity growth resulting from developments in information technology, a strong dollar in foreign exchange markets, and declining oil prices at opportune times. Historically, recessions have been touched off by a variety of factors. Some recessions have been caused by restrictive Federal policy actions implemented in response to escalating inflation.[8] Other recessions have resulted from a decline in consumer expenditures. The 2001 recession did not result from any of these causes—it clearly resulted from a major contraction in business investment expenditures, as indicated in Figure 21-3.

Figure 21-3 illustrates several characteristics of the U.S. recession that extended from March to November 2001. The figure indicates the behavior of real GDP (panel A) and two of its major components—real household expenditures (panel B) and

[8] Examples include the 1969–1970 and 1981–1982 recessions.

**Figure 21-3** Anatomy of the 2001 Recession and Its Aftermath

The 2001 recession was triggered by a sharp contraction in business investment expenditures. Household purchases of consumption goods and new homes continued to rise strongly during the 2001 recession, which is unlike typical recessions.

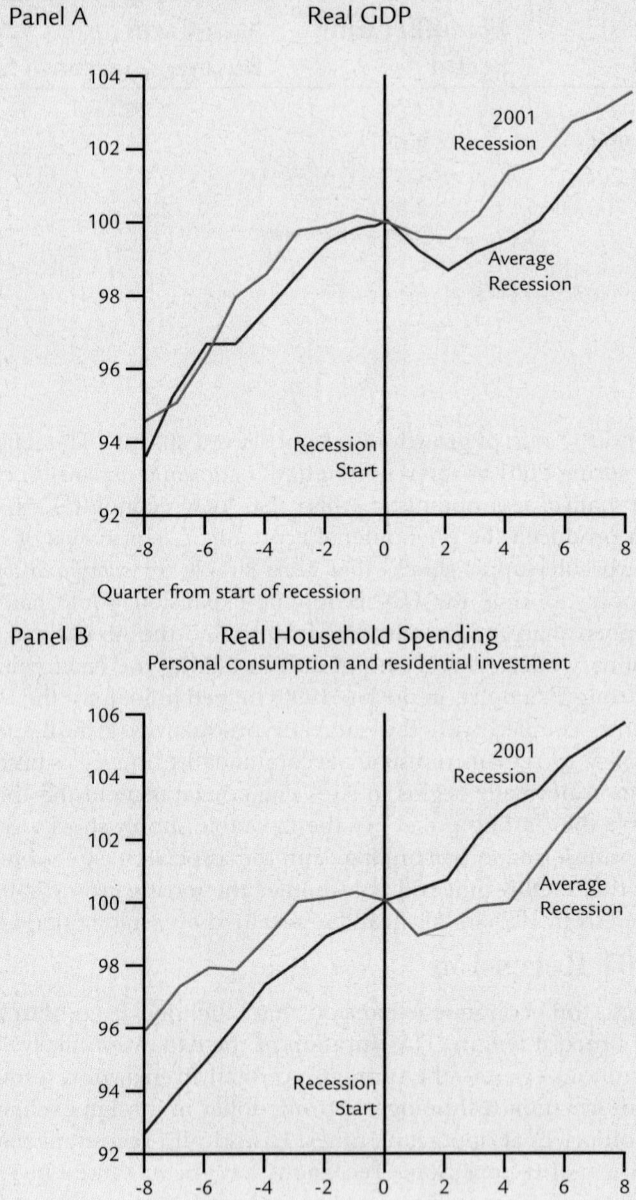

**Figure 21-3** Anatomy of the 2001 Recession and Its Aftermath—*cont'd*

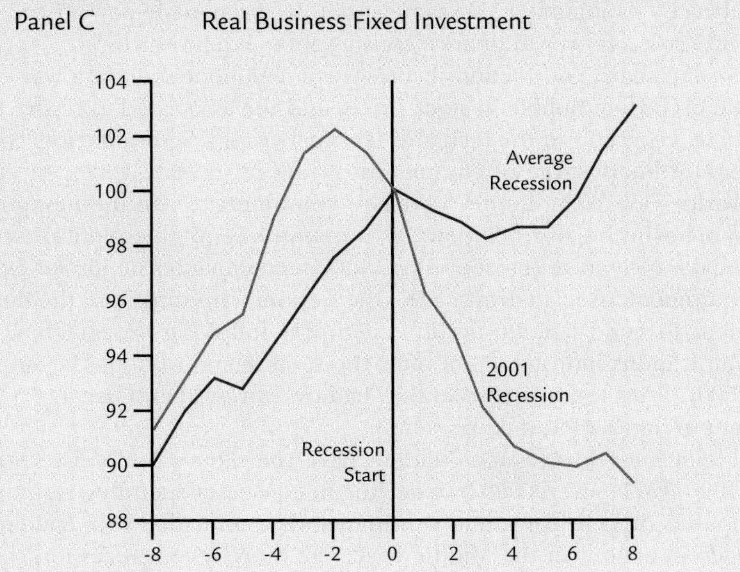


*Source: Federal Reserve Bank of San Francisco*

real business fixed investment expenditures (panel C). In each portion of the figure, the magnitude of the variable being measured is normalized so that the variable is set at 100 at the beginning of the recession (time zero). The magnitude of each variable then is plotted for the period commencing 2 years (eight quarters) prior to, and extending 2 years after, the beginning of the 2001 recession. The behavior of each variable is shown alongside its pattern in the "average" post-1960 recession.

First, note that the 2001 recession was milder than the typical U.S. recession. Real GDP declined less than 1 percent in the 2001 recession, as opposed to about 2 percent in the average recession (panel A). Second, note that real household spending, which includes both personal consumption and residential investment, did *not* contribute to the 2001 recession (panel B). Unlike typical recessions, real household spending continued to rise during the 2001 recession and the ensuing recovery. Finally, note that real business investment began declining at least two quarters before the recession started and fell much more rapidly in the 2001 recession than in the typical downturn (panel C). Real business expenditures continued to fall for more than 1 year after the recession ended. Clearly, the 2001 recession was caused by the sharp contraction in business fixed investment. Because the magnitude of business fixed investment is only about one sixth the magnitude of household spending on consumer goods and new houses, a very sharp *contraction* in the former coupled with the moderate *increase* in the latter explains the modest decline in real GDP in 2001.

What accounts for the divergent behavior of household spending and business fixed investment in 2001 (and beyond)? Several factors sustained household spending. The 2001 reduction in income tax rates and a special IRS tax rebate mailed to taxpayers in 2001 provided fiscal stimulus. Auto manufacturers and other providers of consumer durable goods offered attractive financing deals, sometimes including zero percent financing. Perhaps most importantly, low mortgage rates not only triggered very strong new home sales but also enticed existing homeowners to tap equity in their homes to purchase consumer goods and services. Millions of homeowners were able to take out new, larger mortgages at lower mortgage rates (thereby maintaining the same monthly payments), pay off old mortgages, and have cash left over to finance consumption expenditures.

The sharp contraction in business investment spending was clearly related to the preceding bubble in stock prices and the associated excessive buying of equipment, especially in the tech and telecom sectors. Several factors contributed to the extraordinary surge of equipment buying in the late 1990s: the invention of the World Wide Web; the need for new computers to run the new generation of software beginning with Windows 95; the surge of equipment purchases associated with the dot com craze (most of these dot com companies no longer exist); demand for equipment associated with Y2K (the new millennium); and the demand for equipment to build communications networks following deregulation of the telecommunications industry. Soon after the stock market bubble began to burst (March 2000), firms recognized that they had overinvested and began cutting back sharply on purchases of new equipment.

The moral: recessions seldom have the same profile. The previous recession (1990–1991) was caused by a decline in consumer spending resulting from the precipitous drop in consumer confidence that coincided with Saddam Hussein's belligerent actions in the Middle East. The more recent recession can be blamed on the dramatic cutback in investment expenditures as firms recognized they had overextended themselves during the euphoric days of the late 1990s.

The Federal Reserve reacted swiftly to the ongoing events by aggressively reducing short-term interest rates in 2001. The reduced interest rates and the large and timely income tax cut of 2001 helped render the 2001 recession relatively brief and mild. This situation prevailed despite the shock to consumer confidence imparted by the terrorist attacks of September 11, 2001. Unfortunately, the first 2 years of the ensuing economic expansion were rather anemic, and the nation's unemployment rate continued to drift upward in 2002 and the first half of 2003. The lingering excesses of the bubble of the late 1990s, revelations of numerous corporate scandals involving overstatement of profits and other egregious actions, continued relatively low levels of consumer and business confidence, and general economic weakness abroad contributed to a sub-par economic performance in the first couple of years after the end of the 2001 recession.

## The Jobless Recovery of 2002 to 2004

In the early years of the twenty-first century, American workers discovered productivity growth can be a two-edged sword. On the one hand, a surge in productivity growth shifts the nation's aggregate supply curve rightward, thus serving as an anti-inflation force. It permits a more expansionary monetary policy without increasing inflation. Productivity growth is also the overwhelming source of rising living standards over the long run. On the other hand, rapid productivity growth means firms can expand output strongly without hiring additional workers. If productivity is rising at a (phenomenal) rate of 4 percent per year, firms can accommodate a solid, 4 percent increase in the demand for their products without expanding employment. As a matter of arithmetic, the nation's real GDP must expand more rapidly than productivity growth in order to generate increased employment. Unfortunately, a large speed-up in productivity growth in 2002 and 2003 was not accompanied by a sufficiently robust expansion in the nation's output to warrant employment expansion. As a result, we experienced a "jobless recovery" in those years. The salient facts about productivity growth and employment growth are illustrated in Figures 21-4 and 21-5, respectively.

**Figure 21-4** Productivity Growth in the U.S. Manufacturing and Total Business Sectors from 1990 to 2004

From the mid-1990s through 2004, productivity growth in the United States increased strongly. Employers could squeeze more output out of a given work force, which accounts largely for the jobless recovery of 2002 and 2003.

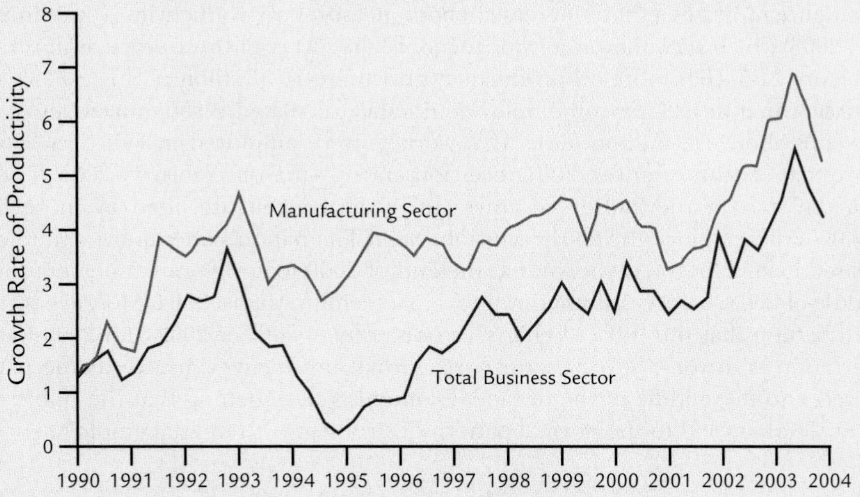


Data plotted are eight-quarter moving averages of productivity growth.
*Source: Data from FRED2 database at* http://research.stlouisfed.org/fred2/

**Figure 21-5** Payroll Employment in the United States (Millions of Workers)

Employment dropped sharply in the 2001 recession and continued to decline in the first 2 years of the ensuing economic recovery. This situation became known as the "jobless recovery."

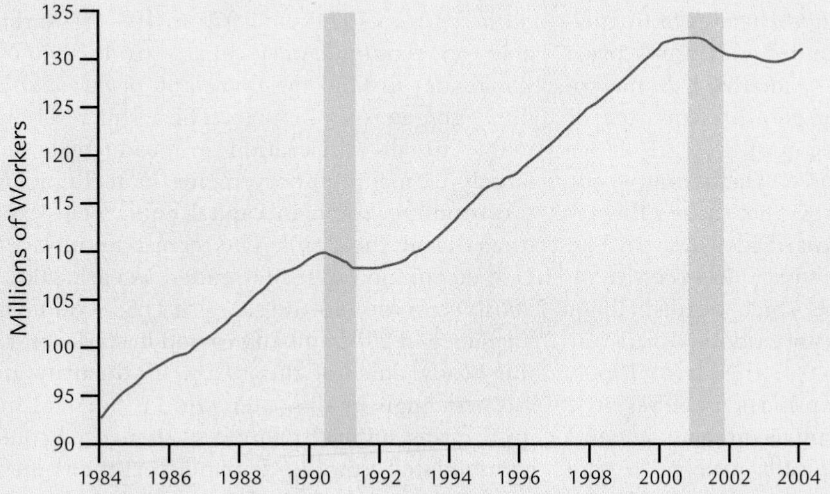


*Data from the survey of employers conducted by the U.S. Bureau of Labor Statistics, available at* http://research.stlouisfed.org/fred2/

In the low-inflation and highly competitive global economic environment of the early twenty-first century, firms increasingly lacked "pricing power." They could not increase profits by raising product prices. To boost profits, firms sought to drive down costs by outsourcing jobs to less expensive foreign workers and introducing measures that increase productivity of existing workers. Figure 21-4 illustrates productivity growth in the U.S. manufacturing sector and the much broader "all business" sector. The figure indicates a sharp increase in both measures of productivity growth in 2002 and 2003, which accounts largely for the jobless recovery of those years, as illustrated in Figure 21-5. (For more on productivity growth, review Exhibit 21-3.)

According to U.S. payroll employment data (calculated through a survey of employers), about 2.2 million fewer U.S. workers were employed in February 2004—more than 2 years after the 2001 recession ended—than in February 2001 (just before the start of the 2001 recession). Total employment declined by more than 500,000 workers since the 2001 recession *ended!* The nation's unemployment rate increased from a low of 3.9 percent at the end of 2000 to a high of 6.3 percent in the middle of 2003, before drifting down to 5.4 percent in August 2004. Most economists were betting that the "off the charts" productivity growth of 2002 and 2003 was an aberration and would give way to more normal productivity growth as the nation moved into the middle of the decade. Economists were betting that the "jobless recovery" would yield to the normal pattern of strong growth in total employment.

## SUMMARY

The aggregate demand-aggregate supply model is a useful framework for analyzing the causes of fluctuations in a nation's output and the nation's price level. The framework is used to analyze U.S. macroeconomic developments in the past three quarters of a century. The Great Depression of the early 1930s was caused by a series of forces (including major Federal Reserve policy mistakes) that caused the AD curve to persistently move leftward (downward). The exigencies of war almost always result in excessive increases in aggregate demand, which result in high inflation rates. Such was the case in both World War II and the Vietnam War of the late 1960s. Historically, most inflation episodes have resulted from a strongly rightward-shifting aggregate demand curve, whereas recessions typically have been triggered by leftward shifts in aggregate demand. In the 1970s, however, the nation experienced two episodes of *stagflation*—periods of declining output (recessions) accompanied by sharply rising prices. The stagflation episodes were caused by major leftward shifts in the aggregate supply curve. The primary culprits were dramatic increases in the price of crude oil in 1973 to 1974 and 1979 to 1980. The remarkable U.S. economic performance from 1995 to 2000 was made possible by important *rightward* shifts in the aggregate supply curve. These shifts were attributable to an acceleration in productivity related largely to major improvements in technology and the resulting boom in capital equipment expenditures during the 1990s. The record-duration 10-year U.S. economic expansion ended in early 2001. The 2001 recession and the sluggish U.S. economic performance in 2002 and 2003 stood in stark contrast to the heady times of the 1990s. Productivity growth was very high in this later period, but real output growth was sufficiently modest that firms could accommodate growing demand for their products without hiring additional workers. Only if real GDP growth exceeds productivity growth will a nation's aggregate employment increase. It will be interesting to look back in 10 years and see if the rate of economic progress experienced from 1995 to 2004 was sustained over the longer time period.

## KEY TERMS

output gap

supply-side economics

## STUDY QUESTIONS

1. Discuss at least four forces that contributed to the disastrous downward shift of the U.S. aggregate demand curve in the Great Depression.

2. What changes in U.S. economic institutions or other developments that have occurred since the Great Depression of the 1930s have reduced the likelihood that we will again experience an economic contraction on the order of magnitude of that occurring in the 1930s? Explain.

3. Update the productivity growth numbers for 1995 to 2004 shown in the table in Exhibit 21-3 using data available at http://research.stlouisfed.org/fred2. Has the superb earlier productivity performance been sustained since the first quarter of 2004? Does your finding shed any light on the "new economy" versus "transitory events" debate?

4. Explain what caused the 2001 recession. Why was the recession a relatively mild downturn?

5. What accounts for the "jobless recovery" of 2002 to 2003? Explain in what sense extraordinary productivity growth can be a two-edged sword.

6. Go to the FRED database (see URL in Question 3) and see what has happened to payroll employment since the beginning of 2004. Also, during President Clinton's time in office (January 1993–January 2001), an average of 250,000 jobs were created per month. Calculate the average monthly growth in jobs since January 2001. What factors do you think account for the difference in average monthly job creation?

[redacted]

## ADDITIONAL READING

- On the oil shocks of the 1970s and the resulting stagflation and policy options, see Alan Blinder, *Economic Policy and the Great Stagflation* (New York: Academic Press, 1979).
- For a sympathetic analysis of the Reagan supply-side program, see Lawrence Lindsey, *The Growth Experiment* (New York: Basic Books, 1990). For a critical view on the same issue, read Benjamin Friedman, *Day of Reckoning: The Consequences of American Economic Policy Under Reagan and After* (New York: Random House, 1988). An excellent and balanced presentation by one of the chief architects of the Reagan program is Martin Feldstein, "Supply-Side Economics: Old Truths and New Claims," *American Economic Review,* May 1986, pp. 26–30.
- On the amazing U.S. economic performance of the 1990s, outstanding sources include Alan Blinder and Janet Yellen, *The Fabulous Decade: Macroeconomic Lessons from the 1990s* (Twentieth Century Fund, 2001) and Joseph Stiglitz, *The Roaring Nineties: A New History of the World's Most Prosperous Decade* (New York: W.W. Norton, 2003). For a discussion of the terrific productivity growth of 1995 to 2003, see Robert J. Gordon, "Exploding Productivity Growth: Context, Causes, and Implications," *Brookings Papers on Economic Activity,* 2003, No. 2, pp. 207–98.
- A discussion of the "virtuous cycle" and the implications of the "new economy" for future business cycles is given by Victor Zarnowitz, "Theory and History Behind Business Cycles: Are the 1990s the Onset of a Golden Age?" *The Journal of Economic*

*Perspectives,* Spring 1999, pp. 69–90. See the Fall 2000 issue of the same journal for a symposium on the role of computers and information technology in the resurgence of productivity growth of the 1990s and beyond.

- For a discussion of the recent economic environment, read the most recent *Economic Report of the President,* published in February each year by the U.S. Government Printing Office and available on the Internet at http://www.gpoaccess.gov/eop/.

# Chapter 22

# MONEY DEMAND AND VELOCITY

In Chapters 20 and 21, we developed the aggregate demand-aggregate supply (AD/AS) model of macroeconomic analysis. We illustrated the model's usefulness in helping us understand the most important U.S. macroeconomic developments in the past 75 years. In the AD/AS model, changes in the nation's real output and price level are initiated by changes in aggregate demand and aggregate supply.

The AD/AS model demonstrates that fluctuations in nominal and real output can result from shifts in either the aggregate supply curve or the aggregate demand curve. However, economists believe most short-term fluctuations are driven predominantly by forces that shift the AD curve. Changes in the nation's money supply are an important cause of shifts in the AD curve. An increase in the money supply shifts AD rightward. A decrease in the money supply shifts AD leftward. However, a multitude of other forces examined in Chapter 20 also initiate shifts in the nation's AD curve. For example, changes in consumer confidence and business sentiment lead to changes in consumption and investment expenditures, shifting the AD curve. Economists disagree about the relative importance of monetary and non-monetary forces in accounting for fluctuations in aggregate demand, real output, and the nation's price level.

Figure 22-1 illustrates the levels and growth rates of both nominal and real gross domestic product (GDP) over the last 40 years. The levels of nominal and real GDP have persistently trended upward (panel A) but not steadily (panel B, which shows the 12-month *rates of change* of nominal and real GDP). Note in panel B, for example, the sharp slowdown in the growth of *nominal* GDP and the contraction in *real* GDP that occurred in the 1973–1975 and 1981–1982 recessions and the smaller decelerations and contractions that occurred in the more recent 1990–1991 and 2001 recessions. Panel B indicates that output has been more stable in the past 20 years than in the first half of the period. Some economists attribute the increased stability to improved conduct of monetary policy. Other economists emphasize the absence of major supply shocks in the more recent period.

**Figure 22-1** Nominal and Real GDP and Their Annual Growth Rates from 1964 to 2004

A: Nominal and real GDP (real GDP is expressed in 2000 dollars). B: Rates of change of nominal and real GDP. Both nominal and real GDP trend strongly upward over time (A). Their growth rates exhibit considerable variability (B).

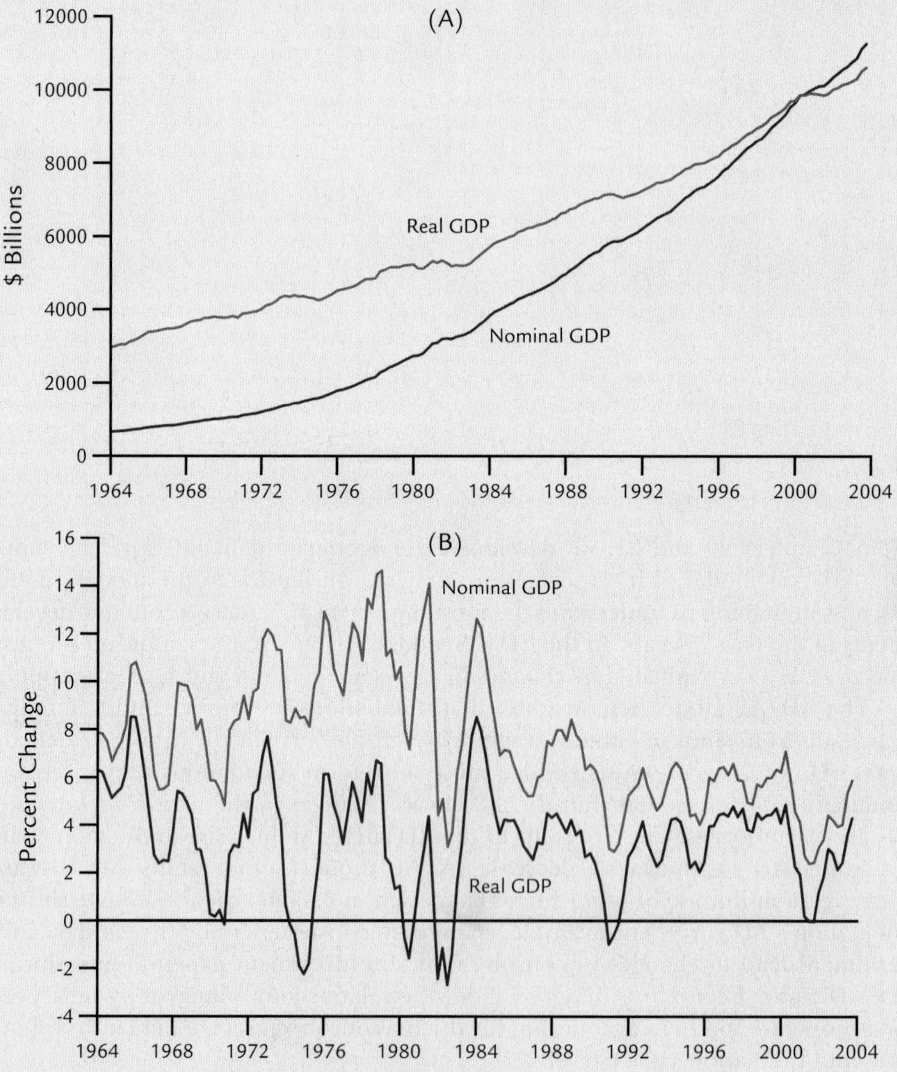


*Source: Data from FRED database at* http://research.stlouisfed.org/fred2/

**velocity of money**
ratio of nominal GDP to the money stock

In this chapter, we examine the link connecting a nation's stock of money to the nation's nominal GDP. The "multiplier" linking the money stock to nominal GDP is the **velocity of money,** or *income velocity.* The multiplier is simply the ratio of nominal GDP to the money stock (GDP/M). The debate over money's role in the economy boils down mostly to a disagreement about the nature of velocity of money and its close relative, the *demand for money.* Some economists, known as *monetarists,* believe velocity is relatively stable and predictable. Other economists, known as *non-monetarists,* view velocity as unstable and extremely difficult to predict.[1] Monetarists believe Federal Reserve-engineered changes in the money supply have a strong and predictable effect on nominal GDP. Non-monetarists are skeptical of this proposition.

## EQUATION OF EXCHANGE AND VELOCITY OF MONEY

A useful way of illustrating the connection between money and economic activity is the famous **equation of exchange.** Developed originally by Professor Irving Fisher of Yale University nearly 100 years ago (see Exhibit 22-1), the equation of exchange is stated as follows:

**equation of exchange** a mathematical identity that sets forth the relationship between the supply of money, velocity, the price level and real output; MV = PY

(22-1) $$\mathbf{MV = PY,}$$

where M is the average money supply in existence in a given year; V is the *income velocity of money* or the number of times the average dollar is spent on GDP—the dollar value of a nation's final goods and services—per year (V = PY/M or GDP/M); P is the average price of all final goods and services purchased during the year, that is, the average price of all goods and services constituting GDP, or an index of such prices relative to some base year; and Y is the number of final goods and services produced in the year or an index of real GDP relative to the base year.

In this formulation, PY is the dollar value of GDP expenditures in a given year (nominal GDP). MV, or the average money supply (M) times the annual rate of turnover of money (V) in purchasing GDP, also represents aggregate spending on these final goods and services in a given year. Again, V is defined (V = PY/M) such that the equation of exchange is an *identity,* true by definition. Suppose Y is $5,000 billion ($5 trillion) and P is 2.0. The current GDP price deflator (the price index) is 200 in relation to some base year = 100. Therefore, aggregate GDP expenditures are $10,000 billion ($10 trillion) per year. If the money supply (M) is $1,250 billion ($1.25 trillion), then the income velocity of money (V) must be exactly eight times per year. That is, to finance annual GDP expenditures of $10,000 billion ($10 trillion), an average money stock of $1,250 billion ($1.25 trillion) must exhibit an income velocity or annual turnover rate of eight times per year. V is easily computed by dividing the annual rate of nominal GDP or (PY) by the average money supply (M) in existence during the year.

By itself, Equation (22-1) tells us *nothing* about real-world behavior. The equation makes no assertions about the causal relationships among its four variables. For example, the equation of exchange does *not* assert that an increase in M causes an increase in P, Y, or PY (nominal GDP). The equation merely expresses the truism or identity that aggregate expenditures viewed from the "money side" (MV) al-

[1] You should be careful when classifying economists into particular categories. Many economists are eclectic—they accept bits and pieces of different theories. Monetarist economists are distinguished from non-monetarist economists by monetarists' general acceptance of the propositions that money demand and velocity are relatively stable and independent of the money supply. Monetarists believe that money supply changes are reflected in fairly predictable expenditures changes, although significant time lags between the change in M and the change in the nation's output and price level exist. In the short run, expenditure changes induced by a change in M can be reflected largely in changes in real output. In the long run, monetarists believe money supply changes are reflected entirely in changes in the nation's price level. The most famous monetarist economist of the past half century is Milton Friedman, formerly of the University of Chicago. William Poole, president of the Federal Reserve Bank of St. Louis and formerly an economics professor at Brown University, is a prominent monetarist who sits on the Federal Open Market Committee.

ways equals aggregate expenditures viewed from the "goods side" (PY). Why, then, should you concern yourself with this equation? Because the equation provides a useful framework for considering money's role in macroeconomic analysis.

Equation 22-1 *does* indicate that if the money supply (M) changes, then one of two things *must* happen:

1. Velocity (V) must change proportionally in the opposite direction so that aggregate GDP expenditures (MV and PY) remain unchanged, or
2. GDP expenditures (that is, PY) must move in the same direction as the supply of money. In other words, if the money supply increases 10 percent, GDP expenditures must increase unless velocity declines 10 percent or more. Equation (22-1) also indicates that if GDP expenditures (PY) are to increase, either M or V (or both) must increase.

At one hypothetical extreme, if V were always constant, then the money supply would be the sole determinant of the level of nominal GDP expenditures. No policy instrument other than the central bank's control of the money supply would be needed to accurately control GDP expenditures. At the other hypothetical extreme, if V fluctuates in a totally unpredictable manner, then Federal Reserve-engineered changes in M would have no *predictable* effect on aggregate GDP expenditures. Controlling the money supply would be a totally ineffective method of influencing GDP. To the extent that velocity is random or unpredictable, the influence of Federal Reserve money supply control on GDP expenditures and general economic activity is compromised. If velocity (V) is not constant but is independent of the money supply and is relatively stable and subject to reasonably good prediction, then a central bank policy of targeting and controlling the money supply is a highly effective method of influencing GDP expenditures.

Let's consider the effectiveness of *fiscal policy* in influencing the economy. If a tax cut or an increase in government expenditures is to stimulate GDP expenditures (MV) given a constant money supply (M), then the fiscal stimulus must necessarily increase V. If the velocity of money is constant or is not influenced by fiscal policy initiatives, then fiscal policy actions are totally ineffective in influencing GDP. On the other hand, if V systematically increases with stimulative fiscal measures and decreases with fiscal restraint, then fiscal policy is a powerful means of influencing GDP. Clearly, the nature and behavior of velocity are important macroeconomic issues.

For each measure of the nation's money supply (M1, M2, M3), a corresponding measure of income velocity exists. The corresponding velocity measures are $V_1$ or (GDP/M1), $V_2$ or (GDP/M2), and $V_3$ or (GDP/M3). Figure 22-2 shows the behavior of these three measures of V since 1964. Note that the velocities are certainly not constant. Economists dispute the stability and predictability of the three income velocity measures.

$V_1$ or GDP/M1 is the velocity of the narrow (M1) measure of money. $V_1$ trended strongly and persistently upward from the mid-1940s until the early 1980s. It then fluctuated without trend for about 15 years before resuming a long-term upward trend. We discuss some reasons for this pattern of $V_1$ behavior later in this chapter. Notice also the pattern of the velocity of the broader measures of money (M2 and M3). Because M2 and M3 are larger than M1, the velocities of these broader measures of money are always lower than the velocity of M1. Because the *growth rates* of M2 and M3 typically exceeded the growth rate of M1 in the past 40 years, the velocities of M2 and M3 exhibited less of an upward trend over the 40-year period than the velocity of M1. While $V_2$ has exhibited a slight upward trend over the full period, $V_3$ shows a modest downward trend.

**Figure 22-2** Three Measures of the Income Velocity of Money from 1964 to 2004

Since 1964, the velocity of M1 has trended strongly upward. The velocities of M2 and M3 have fluctuated with a considerably less pronounced long-term trend.

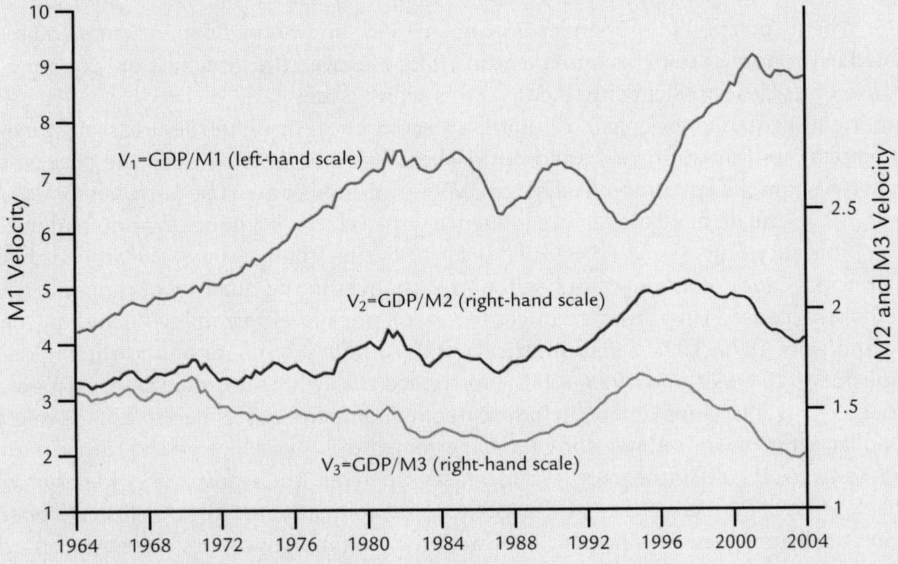


*Source: Data from FRED database at* http://research.stlouisfed.org/fred2/

Because the velocity of money is intimately related to the motives for holding money, the reasons people hold money and the connection between people's motives and velocity are important. The amount of wealth that individuals and firms desire to maintain in the form of money (M1, M2 or M3) is the **demand for money.**

**demand for money** amount of wealth individuals and firms desire to maintain in the form of money

## Velocity of Money and the Demand for Money

Let us return to Equation (22-1). If an individual spends \$8,000 per year on final goods and services and holds an average M1 money balance (currency plus demand deposits) of \$400 throughout the year, then her income velocity (V) must be 20 times per year. That is, if an average money balance of \$400 is to accommodate GDP expenditures of \$8,000 per year, the average dollar must "turn over" or be spent on final goods and services a total of 20 times per year. A precisely equivalent statement is that the individual holds an average money balance equal to one-twentieth of annual GDP expenditures. That is, the ratio of the individual's average money balances to his or her annual GDP expenditures is simply the reciprocal of the individual's income velocity of money.

The same principle holds for the aggregate economy. If a U.S. money supply (M1) of \$1,300 billion (\$1.3 trillion) is associated with annual GDP expenditures (PY) of \$11,700 billion (\$11.7 trillion; so that V is 9), then on average the public holds one-ninth of the dollar value of annual GDP expenditures in the form of money. The amount of money balances held relative to annual GDP is the reciprocal of V, the income velocity of money.

$$\textbf{Because } \mathbf{V} = \frac{\mathbf{GDP}}{\mathbf{M}}, \ \frac{\mathbf{1}}{\mathbf{V}} = \frac{\mathbf{M}}{\mathbf{GDP}}.$$

## Exhibit 22-1 Irving Fisher (1867–1947)

Irving Fisher is considered the foremost American economist of the pre–World War II era (and arguably the greatest of all time). He spent his entire academic career at Yale University. He received his B.S. from Yale in 1888 and earned his Ph.D., also from Yale, 3 years later, at the age of 24 years. Fisher taught mathematics at Yale from 1892 to 1895. When a position in economics opened in 1895, he switched departments and remained in economics until his retirement in 1935. He loved the discipline of economics because of its clear applicability to crucial real-world issues.

Among Fisher's numerous contributions to economics, those in the areas of monetary, capital, and utility theory stand out. Fisher clarified money's role in the economy through his famous equation of exchange, $MV = PY$. In his book *The Purchasing Power of Money* (1911), he detailed the factors influencing the velocity of money (V) and real output (Y). Because Fisher believed velocity and real output change slowly, he argued that the principal cause of inflation and deflation is changes in the quantity of money.

Perhaps because Fisher lived through an era of price-level instability, including the long and slow 1873–1896 deflation, the severe World War I inflation, and the big deflations of 1920–1921 and 1929–1932, he stressed the evils of unstable prices. To prevent severe price level instability, he advocated a "compensated dollar" plan, in which the dollar is tied to a fixed *value* of gold (determined by an index of prices) rather than a fixed *quantity* of gold. If the price level increases 5 percent, the amount of gold required to back $1 rises 5 percent. Given the existence of a gold-standard regime, Fisher's plan automatically produces a 5 percent contraction in the money supply, thereby nipping inflation. Fisher compiled more than 300 documents (books, articles, letters to editors) supporting his proposal from 1912 to 1935.

Brilliant, versatile, and a passionate crusader, Fisher was actively involved in proposed reforms of the times, particularly in the areas of temperance, world peace, eugenics, conservation, and public health (while ill with tuberculosis, he invented a tent for treatment of the disease). He made himself wealthy by devising and marketing a card-index file system in 1910. An indication of the fortune he amassed is that he lost an estimated $8 to $10 million in the Great Depression of the 1930s (more than $100 million in today's dollars).

By applying mathematical and statistical techniques to economics, Fisher made major contributions to the development of economics as a science. Fisher won immortality by having not *one* but *two* important concepts named after him: the *Fisher equation* ($MV = PY$) and the *Fisher effect*—the tendency for a change in expected inflation to produce a corresponding, similar change in nominal interest rates (discussed in Chapter 5).

Note carefully the *units* associated with V and its reciprocal. In the first case, V is the ratio of an annual dollar *flow* (GDP) to an average dollar *stock* (M). Arithmetically, the dollar signs in the numerator and denominator cancel out, leaving a pure number per year. If GDP is $11,700 billion ($11.7 trillion) per year and M is $1,300 billion ($1.3 trillion), then V is 9 *per year.* Now, the reciprocal of V is the ratio of a stock of dollars of money (M) to an annual flow (GDP). Again, the dollar signs cancel out, leaving a number expressed as a fraction of a year. If M is $1,300 billion ($1.3 trillion) and GDP is $11,700 billion ($11.7 trillion) per year, then the reciprocal of V is one-ninth of 1 year, or about 40 days. If the income velocity of money (V) is 9, the average individual or firm retains money balances sufficient to finance expenditures on final goods and services (GDP) for one-ninth of a year, or a bit more than 40 days.

In the next section we look at the *demand for money* and discuss the motives leading individuals and firms to hold a portion of their wealth in the form of money. By understanding the demand for money, you solidify your understanding of velocity.

# DEMAND FOR MONEY

Early in the twentieth century, an influential group of economists at Cambridge University in England analyzed the economic role of money by focusing on the demand to hold money balances. Their approach was a natural result of the widespread familiarity of the concept of demand in economics. Just as economists examine the demand for crude oil and for houses, economist devote much attention to the factors underlying the demand for money balances. Their investigations produced important insights and advances in monetary theory.

Rather than using the equation MV = PY, the Cambridge group and modern economists typically used an expression such as:

$$(22\text{-}2)\quad M_d = kPY, \text{ where } k = \frac{M_d}{PY}.$$

In this formulation, $M_d$ is the *demand* for money rather than the supply of money, and k is the fraction of GDP (or PY) the public *desires* to hold in money balances. If the economy is in equilibrium so that the demand for money ($M_d$) equals the supply of money (M), then k is the reciprocal of the actual income velocity of money, V. In equilibrium, V = 1/k and k = 1/V.

If the demand for money rises relative to GDP (that is, if k rises), then income velocity (V) falls. If people want to *reduce* the fraction of annual GDP expenditures they hold in money (that is, if k falls), then the income velocity of money *increases.* Any theory that explains the behavior of k also explains the behavior of V, and *vice versa.* Given the important role of the variables k and V, you can understand why professional economists have invested many more hours researching the demand for money than, say, the demand for automobiles. In the next section, we discuss the reasons people hold money.

## Motives for Holding Money

Because M1 money (currency and demand deposits) typically earns little or no interest, we might conclude that a typical individual is foolish to habitually maintain an average M1 money balance of $20,000.[2] Why hold wealth in the form of money if other financial and real assets provide substantially higher rates of return? Economists have identified three different motives for holding money, which, in conjunction with institutional factors such as the frequency of paydays, the prevalence of credit cards, and other factors, determine the public's demand for money. The motives for holding money are the transactions motive, precautionary motive, and speculative motive.

**Transactions Demand.** People hold money largely because they need to finance forthcoming expenditures for goods and services that do not coincide

[2] From 1933 to the early 1980s, U.S. law prohibited banks from paying interest on demand deposits. The Depository Institutions Deregulation and Monetary Control Act of 1980 (DIDMCA) ended that prohibition. However, interest rates payable by banks on DDO today are significantly lower than yields on Treasury bills and other short-term securities. Currency ($C^P$) obviously pays no interest. Certain assets included in M2 and M3 (savings deposits, money market mutual fund shares, and so forth) earn competitive rates of interest.

**transactions demand for money**
demand for money to finance expenditures that are not perfectly synchronized with receipt of funds

chronologically with expected income payments. The demand for money to finance ordinary expenditures is the **transactions demand for money.** The principle is easy to illustrate. Suppose a student receives monthly income of $800 from part-time employment supplemented by parental assistance. Assume her monthly expenditures also are $800. Suppose on the first day of each month the student deposits $700 into a checking account and retains $100 in currency. She draws down the initial money balances ($800) at a constant rate throughout the month until the balances are depleted on the last day of the month. She then replenishes the balances at the beginning of the new month.

The heavy line in Figure 22-3 shows the student's spending pattern and money balances.

The student holds a balance of $800 on the first of the month, gradually draws down the balance, and ends the month with no money. If we average her balances on each day of the month, we obtain an average balance of $400. Because the student spends $9,600 during the year on final goods and services and holds $400 of money on average, her income velocity of money is 24 times per year ($9,600/year/$400). That is, on the average day, she holds a money balance equal to 1/24 of her annual expenditures, a balance sufficient to finance 15.2 days of expenditures (365 days/24).

Now suppose the student begins to receive her paycheck and her parents' check on a weekly rather than a monthly basis. To simplify the calculation, assume a month has exactly 4 weeks. On the first day of each week, the student has a balance of $200 in the form of demand deposits and currency. By the end of each week, the funds are exhausted and then replenished. The resulting pattern of the student's money balances is shown by the lighter line in Figure 22-3. Although the student continues to spend $9,600 per year, she now holds an average balance of only $100.

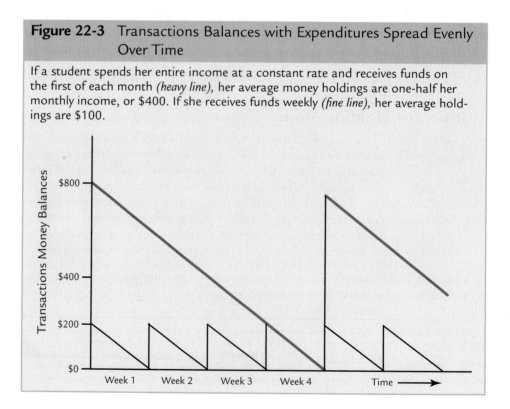

**Figure 22-3** Transactions Balances with Expenditures Spread Evenly Over Time

If a student spends her entire income at a constant rate and receives funds on the first of each month *(heavy line)*, her average money holdings are one-half her monthly income, or $400. If she receives funds weekly *(fine line)*, her average holdings are $100.

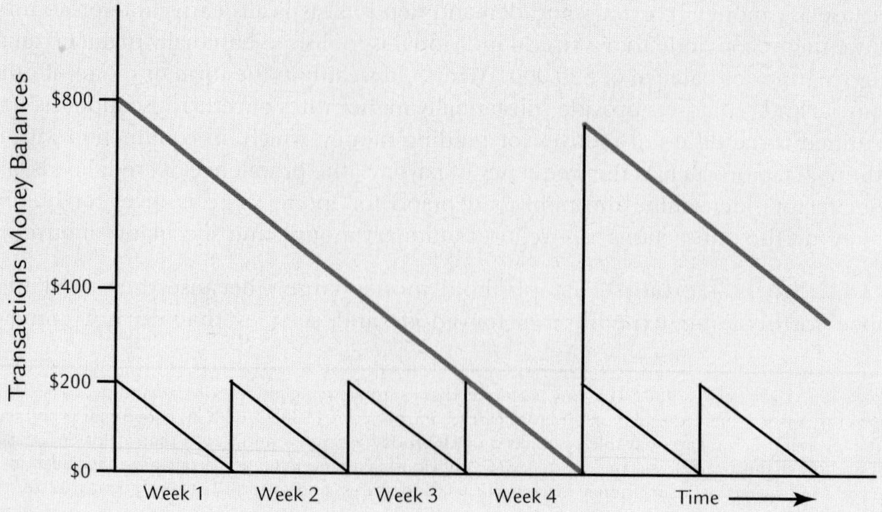

Thus, her velocity is \$9,600/year/\$100, or 96 times per year. On average, she keeps only 1/96 of her annual GDP expenditures in the form of money—that is, enough to finance slightly less than 4 days of expenditures (365 days/96).

The lesson of this example is clear: An increase in the frequency with which income payments are received produces a closer synchronization between receipts and expenditures, reducing the demand for money relative to annual expenditures. When the frequency of paydays increases, money demand falls and the velocity of money rises.[3] In general, *any factor that increases the degree of synchronization between the receipt and disbursement of funds reduces the demand for money and therefore increases velocity.*

Consider a final example, which illustrates the impact of *financial innovations* on the demand for and velocity of money. Return to the assumptions illustrated in Figure 22-3, in which the student receives funds monthly (\$800) and exhibits an income velocity of 24 times per year. Now suppose the student obtains a credit card and runs up a bill of \$400 each month (paying for half of her expenditures with the credit card). On the first day of each month, she spends \$400 to pay the credit card bill from the previous month. Therefore, after the first day of each month, her balance is only \$400. The balance suffices to cover her needs because the student uses her credit card to meet half of her transactions. Suppose the remaining \$400 is used at a constant rate throughout the remainder of the month. Figure 22-4 illustrates the student's spending and money balance pattern.

A quick look at the figure shows that credit card use reduces the average balances the student holds during the month from \$400 to \$200. Assuming the stu-

**Figure 22-4** Transactions Balances of a Credit Card User

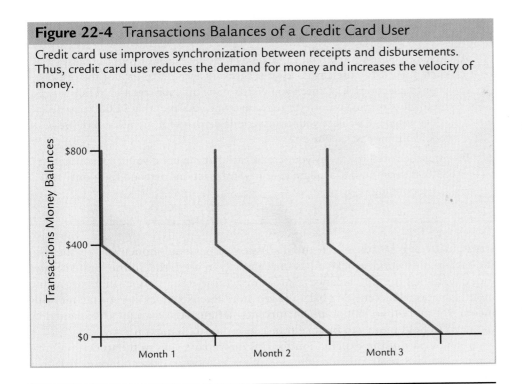

Credit card use improves synchronization between receipts and disbursements. Thus, credit card use reduces the demand for money and increases the velocity of money.

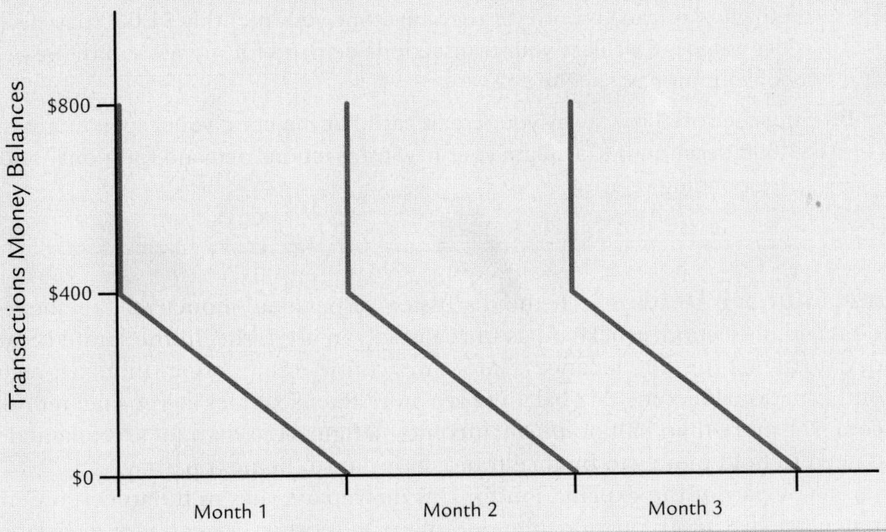


[3] Think about this principle and its implications for money demand and velocity. If income were received just as frequently as it is spent (perfect synchronization), the demand for money would approach zero, and velocity would approach infinity. People hold transactions balances only because their expenditures are not perfectly synchronized with their receipts of funds.

dent's annual expenditures remain at $9,600, the income velocity of her money becomes $9,600/year/$200 = 48/year.

Note that credit card use allowed the student to reduce her average money balances by 50 percent, from $400 to $200. Thus, the velocity of her money doubles. Credit card use raises the velocity of money by reducing the demand for money relative to annual expenditures. The same principle applies to other forms of credit, such as charge accounts, business credit lines, and bank overdraft protection. The proliferation of credit cards and other credit arrangements has been an important contributing factor in the persistent uptrend in the velocity of M1 in the past several decades (review Figure 22-2).[4] These arrangements have increased the *efficiency* of money by reducing the average amount of money required to finance a given amount of monthly or annual expenditures.

Given existing payday schedules, the public's banking habits, and institutional arrangements governing credit use, income level exerts a major impact on the transactions demand for money. As income rises, people increase expenditures, and their transactions demand for money rises accordingly. For example, if the student's monthly income rises from $800 to $1,600, she begins the month with a cash balance of $1,600 instead of $800. Assuming she spends the entire $1,600 evenly throughout the month and does not have a credit card, her average demand for money will be $800 rather than $400. The velocity of her money remains unchanged, however, because her annual expenditures and her average money balances both have increased by 100 percent.

**YOUR TURN**

Assume your monthly income and GDP expenditures are $1,000. You spend your income at a constant rate, and you hold money only for transactions purposes.

**A.** Assume you use your credit card to pay for one-fourth of your purchases each month. You use cash and your checking account to pay for the rest of your transactions. The check you write to pay off your credit card bill clears on the first of each month (at the same time your monthly $1,000 paycheck is deposited). Calculate your transactions demand for money and the velocity of your money.

**B.** Suppose you throw away your credit card but maintain your expenditures at $1,000 per month. Calculate your new transactions demand for money and corresponding velocity.

**Precautionary Demand.** If the discussion of personal money management in the preceding section struck you as unrealistic, you are right! In the United States today, total M1 money balances (M1) are considerably larger than aggregate monthly national income. M2 balances are more than six times larger than monthly income, or more than half of *annual* income—a figure too high to be explained by the need to hold money to finance transactions until the next payday.

A major part of the explanation for this discrepancy lies in the uncertain environment we live in. To provide a margin of error, most of us keep money balances above and beyond the amount we actually expect to use in a given period. Such funds are "precautionary balances." They safeguard against unforeseen events that

[4] Use of debit cards, which enable an individual to make payment by directly debiting his or her checking account, do not influence money demand and velocity.

require unplanned expenditures or result in income loss. Unexpected medical or auto repair bills, an unanticipated markdown of a desired item to a bargain price (tempting its purchase)—these and a thousand other events may prompt expenditures not originally anticipated. Injury, illness, or an economic downturn can disrupt the flow of family income. Maintenance of money balances to meet unforeseen circumstances is the **precautionary demand for money.**[5]

**precautionary demand for money**
maintenance of money balances to meet unforeseen circumstances

**Speculative Demand.** British economist John Maynard Keynes hypothesized that a significant amount of money in the nation as a whole is held to permit capitalization on a good financial opportunity that may arise. In the words of Keynes, the **speculative demand for money** involves money balances held with the intent of "securing profit from knowing better than the market what the future will bring forth."

**speculative demand for money**
money balances held so that a speculative opportunity can be undertaken and financed in the event it should arise

Imagine a situation in which the Standard and Poor's 500 stock market average is 40 percent below its previous high. The economic outlook for the next 3 or 4 years is becoming increasingly favorable. Interest rates and inflation are trending downward, and the outlook for sales and corporate profits is healthy and sustained growth. The time may be at hand to commit funds to the stock market and perhaps also to the corporate bond market. An individual or mutual fund already fully invested in stocks, bonds, and real estate and holding no money balances in excess of the funds needed for transactions and precautionary purposes cannot take advantage of the opportunity. Keynes hypothesized that alert and perceptive individuals and firms desiring to take advantage of good investment opportunities must maintain money holdings in excess of those needed to satisfy transactions and precautionary motives.

Keynes emphasized that the speculative demand for money is volatile because demand depends heavily on the changing nature of the public's expectations. If the stock and bond market outlook becomes increasingly bleak, the speculative demand for money *increases* as people unload securities and hold money instead. As the outlook clears up and becomes more favorable, the speculative demand for money *decreases* as people "take the plunge" and use their money to purchase stocks, bonds, and other assets. The speculative demand for *money* moves in the opposite direction from the speculative demand for *securities* or other non-money assets.

The issue of the existence and nature of the speculative demand for money is an important consideration in assessing the likely stability of the velocity of money—the link between money and GDP expenditures. If a substantial speculative demand for money exists and the demand is highly variable, velocity also will be quite variable and difficult to predict. The nature and indeed the *existence* of a speculative demand for money are controversial. Some economists deny the existence of a significant speculative demand for money, which is one reason these economists view money demand and velocity as relatively stable.

## Demand for Money: Role of Interest Rates

Nobel Laureate Milton Friedman once wrote an equation for money demand as follows:

$$\left(\frac{\mathbf{M}}{\mathbf{P}}\right)_D = \mathbf{f}\ (\mathbf{Y_P}, \mathbf{r_b}, \mathbf{r_e}, \pi^e, \mathbf{u}). \qquad (22\text{-}3)$$

[5] The development of overdraft protection and a variety of "near monies" virtually free of market risk (such as passbook savings accounts and money market mutual fund shares) likely have reduced the relative importance of precautionary M1 balances over the years. The precautionary balances today likely are maintained primarily in *broader* measures of money, such as M2 and M3 rather than in M1, which includes only DDO and $C^P$.

This equation states that the demand for real money balances $(M/P)_D$ of an individual (or the nation) depends on "permanent" or average lifetime income $(Y_P)$, institutional factors including frequency of paydays and use of credit arrangements (encompassed in u), and three variables representing the opportunity cost of holding money. Opportunity cost variables include the rate of return (interest rate) expected from bonds, Treasury bills, and similar instruments $(r_b)$; equities or shares of stock $(r_e)$; and real assets such as gold, silver, and real estate. The expected nominal rate of return from real assets is measured by the expected rate of inflation $(\pi^e)$. Each opportunity cost variable is inversely related to demand for real money balances—that is, an increase in $r_b$, $r_e$, and $\pi^e$ *reduces* the demand for real money balances (M/P).

Because interest-bearing money market instruments are close substitutes for money, the interest rate available on these instruments $(r_b)$ is of special interest. By traditional economic analysis, the quantity of money demanded is a function of its price or cost—that is, the market rate of interest. Money is placed on the same ground as other goods or services whose quantity demanded is inversely related to price. Figure 22-5 shows how the demand for money would look in that case.

The nature of the demand curve shown in Figure 22-5 is one of the important issues in macroeconomics. It is an important consideration in determining whether monetary policy or fiscal policy more strongly and predictably influences the nation's aggregate demand for goods and services and the level of economic activity. Non-monetarist economists believe that the quantity of money demanded is sensitive to the interest rate. They view the curve in Figure 22-5 as relatively flat. They also believe that the *position* of the curve is unstable, shifting back and forth in re-

**Figure 22-5** Relationship Between the Interest Rate and Total Money Balances Demanded

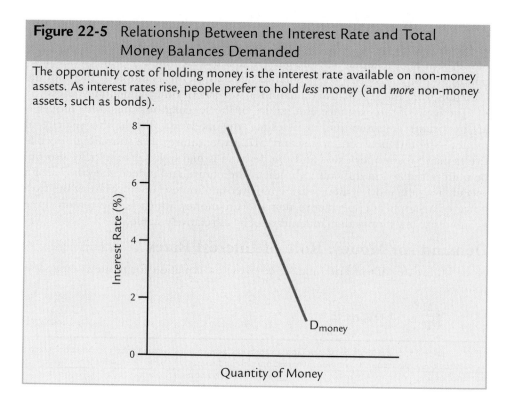

The opportunity cost of holding money is the interest rate available on non-money assets. As interest rates rise, people prefer to hold *less* money (and *more* non-money assets, such as bonds).

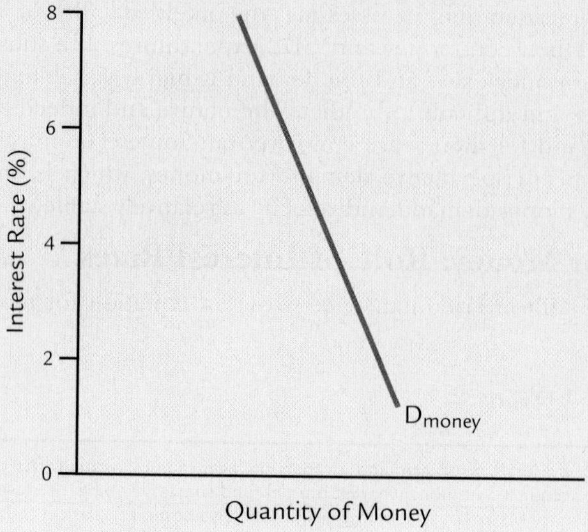

sponse to various events triggering changes in the outlook and therefore in the demand for money. Monetarist economists believe that the curve is very steep (close to vertical)—that is, the demand for money is relatively unresponsive to the interest rate.[6] Further, they believe the curve shifts only slowly and predictably over time, mainly in response to changes in income and *slowly changing* institutional factors. This relationship implies velocity is relatively stable.

We now examine the theoretical basis for the contention that the demand for money is inversely related to the interest rate. We focus on the transactions demand for money—the most important motive for holding money—although all three motives for holding money may respond to the interest rate.

**Interest Rates and the Transactions Demand.** Transactions balances are money balances that must be held in order to bridge the inevitable time gap between the receipt of funds and the funds' later disbursement. If these funds must be held to finance expenditures later in the month, how can their magnitude be related to the interest rate? The answer is that, for the majority of individuals, the interest rate probably is *not* a relevant consideration. However, for wealthy individuals, large corporations, and other organizations exhibiting very large receipts and disbursements of funds, transactions demand for money may be significantly influenced by interest rates.

An example helps to illustrate the principle. Suppose a wealthy individual earns and spends $100,000 each month. Rather than deposit the full $100,000 in a bank checking account on the first of the month, the individual initially deposits $50,000 and uses the rest of the funds to purchase U.S. Treasury bills with 15 days to maturity. At mid-month, as the checking account approaches depletion, he deposits the proceeds from the matured Treasury bills ($50,000 plus interest) into the account. Figure 22-6 illustrates this money-management plan.

The wealthy person earns interest on $50,000 for half of a month by investing half his paycheck in Treasury bills. Does his behavior make sense? Is it rational? That depends on the interest rate and the transactions costs associated with the purchase of the securities, including the inconvenience associated with making the extra transactions.[7] If the interest rate on the Treasury bills in this example is 4 percent and the securities are held for half of each month, the individual grosses $1,000 per year, or $83.33 per month for his trouble. Out-of-pocket transactions costs—primarily the fee charged by the agent who buys the securities—must be deducted from the individual's gross return. Thus, the net return must be weighed against the inconvenience costs and time spent engaging in the transactions. In this case, the transactions seem sensible. In fact, the individual might step up the number of transactions, purchasing $75,000 worth of Treasury bills on the first of the month and retiring $25,000 worth on the first day of weeks 2, 3, and 4 (of a 4-week

---

[6] Interest rate elasticity of demand is the crucial concept in this debate. Non-monetarists often argue that the interest elasticity of the demand for money is fairly high (although not greater than one) in absolute value. Monetarists believe interest elasticity is quite low but by no means zero. Milton Friedman once estimated the interest elasticity of the demand for money to be (minus) 0.1, which implies that a 10 percent increase in the interest rate (e.g., from 6 to 6.6 percent) brings about a 1 percent reduction in the demand for money (e.g., from $1,400 billion to $1,386 billion). Some economists estimate the elasticity is much higher, generally in the (minus) 0.5 to (minus) 0.8 range. See the Laidler book cited in the Additional Reading at the end of this chapter.

[7] Many individuals prefer transferring funds between a bank checking account and a money market mutual fund or using an ATM to transfer funds from a checking account to a savings account rather than buying securities each month.

**Figure 22-6** Transactions Demand of a Wealthy Individual or Business Firm

By making periodic transactions in interest-bearing assets and reducing average money holdings, a wealthy person or a firm can earn higher income. This behavior increases velocity.

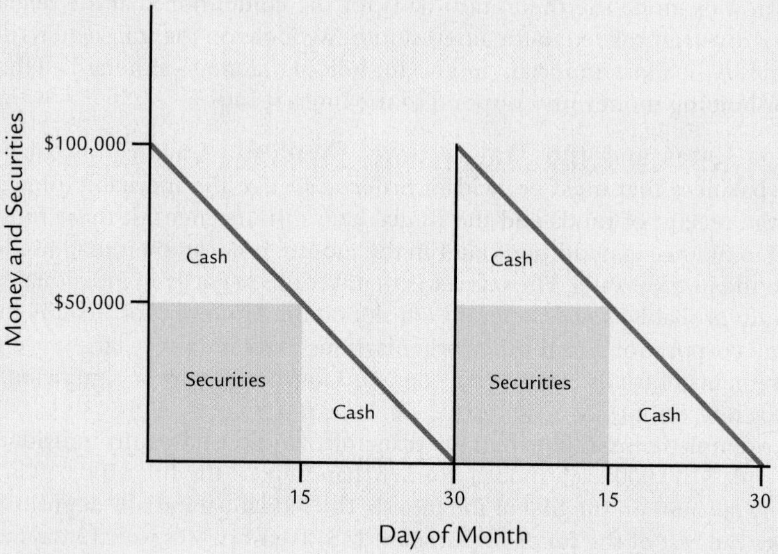

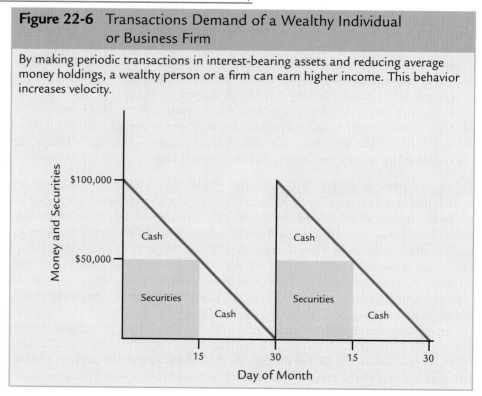

month). The gross return of such a scheme would be $125 per month, or $1,500 per year.[8]

Suppose, on the other hand, the current yield on Treasury bills is only 1 percent. The gross return earned by purchasing $50,000 worth of Treasury bills on the first of each month and liquidating the Treasury bills at mid-month is only $250 per year, or $20.83 per month. After deducting transactions fees, some wealthy individuals might find the net return insufficient to compensate them for the inconvenience. We conclude that for wealthy individuals and for many business firms, the interest rate likely is a significant factor influencing the transactions demand for money and therefore the velocity of money.[9]

A higher interest rate means a lower quantity of money demanded (because more wealth is kept in bonds and other interest-bearing assets) and therefore a higher velocity. Because a large portion of the money in the United States is held by business firms, wealthy individuals, and units of government (whose balances tend to be relatively large), the interest rate may significantly influence the transactions demand (and thus the velocity) of money.

---

[8] Professors James Tobin and William Baumol independently demonstrated that a rational individual or firm increases the number of such transactions as the interest rate rises. Average money balances demanded fall (and V rises) as interest rates rise. See the references to Tobin and Baumol in the Additional Reading at the end of this chapter.

[9] These considerations clearly do not apply to the typical U.S. worker. Suppose a breadwinner earns $1,600 take-home pay per month. On the first of each month, he deposits $800 in a checking and $800 in a savings account. He then transfers $800 from savings to checking on the fifteenth day of the month. Assuming 3 percent interest on savings accounts, the worker earns a piddling $12 per year for his trouble. It is a good bet that the $12 gain will be washed out by the increased service charges levied on his checking account due to the lower average balance kept in the account.

We have seen that the transactions demand for money may be responsive to the market rate of interest. The precautionary and speculative demand for money likely also depend on the interest rate. A higher interest rate increases the cost of holding money and reduces the willingness to hold money. To the extent that demand for money and velocity vary with interest rates, the stability of the link between the money supply (M) and GDP expenditures is weakened because interest rates fluctuate significantly and rather unpredictably over time. Velocity also is subject to a significant *cyclical* influence because interest rates fluctuate systematically over the course of the business cycle.

Let's reinforce our understanding of money demand and velocity by analyzing the historical behavior of the velocity of money in the United States. Our discussion includes analyses of the long-run trends and cyclical and short-term movements in velocity. We begin with an overview of the determinants of the velocity of money.

## DETERMINANTS OF THE VELOCITY OF MONEY

The determinants of velocity are grouped into six categories: institutional factors underlying the synchronization between receipts and expenditures, the state of "financial technology," interest rate levels, the prevailing degree of economic uncertainty, inflation expectations, and income level.

### Institutional Factors

The demand for money and the velocity of money are related to institutional considerations such as the frequency of paydays, payment habits, the use of credit cards, and other institutional factors governing the degree of synchronization between the receipt and disbursement of funds. Improvements in the synchronization of receipts and disbursements caused, for example, by more frequent paydays and increased credit card use reduce the demand for money and increase the velocity of money. Institutional factors tend to evolve slowly over time and increase velocity over the long term.

### Financial Technology

Encompassed within the category of "financial technology" are the availability of substitutes for money, the costs involved in using those money substitutes, and the techniques developed by banks that enable individuals and firms to hold less money. Financial innovations increase the opportunity cost of holding money, thereby reducing money demand and raising velocity. When money market mutual funds (MMMFs) became widely available in the 1970s, the opportunity cost of holding bank checking accounts increased. Because yields on MMMF shares were highly attractive, millions of individuals drew down funds in their bank checking accounts to purchase MMMF shares. The consumers' actions reduced demand for M1 and increased its velocity.[10] The advent of the **sweep account**—a device through which the bank's computer automatically transfers funds (most commonly of business firms) out of customers' checking accounts into interest-bearing financial assets at the end of each day—increased velocity. Development of the overnight repurchase

**sweep account**
device through which the bank's computer automatically transfers funds out of customers' checking accounts into interest-bearing financial assets at the end of each day

[10] Note in Figure 22-2 the surge in M1 velocity from 1975 to 1980 as interest rates escalated sharply. MMMFs are included in M2 but not in M1. When people reduce bank checking account balances to purchase MMMF shares, the velocity of M1 increases while the velocity of M2 is unaltered. (Why? Because M1 declines while M2 does not).

agreement (RP), an instrument through which the bank "purchases" a customer's checking account at the end of business each day and sells the customer interest-bearing government securities in return, increased velocity.[11] Another example is the proliferation of automatic teller machines (ATMs), which reduce the cost of switching funds between savings and checking accounts, thereby reducing demand for M1. All of these innovations reduce the propensity to hold checking accounts and thereby pull up the velocity of M1. Other instruments that provide attractive alternatives to holding money have become available in the past 40 years. Some of the more important instruments include negotiable certificates of deposit (CDs), commercial paper, and Eurodollars. Thus, financial innovations reduce money demand and increase the velocity of money.

## Interest Rates

An increase in interest rates reduces money demand, that is, induces people to hold less of their wealth in the form of transactions, precautionary, and speculative money balances. Because money demand and velocity are inversely related, an increase in interest rates raises velocity. Furthermore, because interest rates exhibit a distinct *procyclical* pattern (rising during economic expansions and falling during recessions), velocity also moves procyclically.

## Economic Uncertainty

Money is the safest asset in that its nominal value remains constant regardless of stock, bond, or real estate prices. If the stock, bond, or real estate market collapses, $10,000 in a checking account is still $10,000. For this reason, any announcement or event that increases the public's perception of potential trouble in the economy increases the demand for money. People become more conservative, selling their stocks and bonds and holding money instead. As a result of the terrorist attacks of September 11, 2001, the stock market fell dramatically as tens of thousands of people rushed to convert their shares of stock into cash. Velocity declined as demand for money increased. Thus, when the economic, political, or military outlook becomes more uncertain, money demand increases and velocity falls. When public confidence improves, people become more aggressive about holding assets other than money. Money demand falls and velocity rises.

## Expected Inflation

Inflation imposes a tax on money, reducing its *real* value at a rate equal to the difference between the annual inflation rate and the interest rate (if any) paid on money. If inflation is 10 percent per year and money pays no interest, then the real value of money declines at a rate of 10 percent per year. Inflation of this magnitude likely appreciably influences the use of money—that is, people reduce their demand for money to escape the inflation tax. Because the value of money depreciates rapidly when inflation is high, people spend money quickly before it depreciates. Historically, during episodes of *hyperinflation* when the implicit tax on money becomes extreme, velocity escalates dramatically as people desperately try to rid themselves of money before its value plunges even more. In recent times, with U.S. inflation running at less than 3 percent annually, inflation expectations likely will not exert much effect on velocity.

[11] The Federal Reserve tabulates its money supply figures from deposit information after banks close, and both overnight RPs and sweep accounts pull funds from DDO at the end of banking hours (and redeposit them into DDO at the opening of business the next day). Thus, reported DDO are reduced by the expanding use of these instruments and reported velocity (GDP/M) is boosted.

## Income

An increase in income typically results in an increase in expenditures by individuals and firms. If a doubling of income were to lead to a doubling of annual expenditures, and if people were induced to hold twice as much money to finance the doubled expenditures level, velocity would be unaffected by the increase in income. The **income elasticity of demand for money**—the ratio of the percentage change in quantity of money demanded to the percentage change in income—would be exactly 1. Therefore, changes in income have no effect on velocity.

**income elasticity of demand for money** ratio of the percentage change in quantity of money demanded to the percentage change in income that induced the change in money demand

In the real world, the income elasticity of demand for money is not necessarily 1. Some economists view money as a *luxury good,* meaning the income elasticity of demand for money is greater than 1.[12] Remember that the more securities and *less* money you hold, the *more* time you must spend managing money balances. An increase in income may increase the value you place on leisure time. Thus, an increase in income may boost money demand not only to accommodate higher expenditures but also to reduce valuable time spent managing your financial affairs. If an increase in income induces a more-than-proportional increased money demand, then higher income leads to lower velocity.

On the other hand, "economies of scale" may exist in cash management, so a doubling of income may require less than a doubling of average money balances to finance the doubled level of expenditures. Individuals with higher incomes and expenditures more likely use credit cards. As income rises, firms more likely develop bank lines of credit. These two phenomena reduce money demand and boost velocity. Higher incomes and expenditures also encourage the sort of intramonthly security transactions analyzed earlier. An increase in income and expenditures can lead to a less-than-proportional increase in money demand and a corresponding increase in velocity. Most empirical studies of money demand estimate the income elasticity of demand for money is less than 1. This implies that the effect of long-run income growth, *ceteris paribus* (other things being equal), is to raise the velocity of money.

**YOUR TURN**

Suppose your econometric research reveals that the income elasticity of demand for money is 1.20. Assuming financial innovations continue at a steady pace and income rises in the next 5 years, but all other factors influencing velocity remain constant, in which direction will velocity move?

# LONG-RUN BEHAVIOR OF VELOCITY

Having analyzed the general forces that influence velocity, we now can discuss the historical behavior of the velocity of money in the United States over the last 130 years. Figure 22-7 shows the velocity of M1 and M2 over a 130-year period.

[12] The income elasticity of demand for any good or service is the percentage change in quantity of the good demanded divided by the percentage change in income that produced the change in demand for the good. If a 10 percent increase in income results in a 15 percent increase in the demand for steak or entertainment, then the income elasticity of demand for these items is 1.5, and those two goods are considered luxury goods. If a 10 percent increase in income results in a 2 percent increase in demand for food and clothing, then those goods are classified as normal goods because their income elasticities of demand are less than 1.

**Figure 22-7** Velocity of M1 and M2 in the United States from 1873 to 2003

The velocity of M1 and M2 exhibit long-term trends and shorter-term cyclical fluctuations.

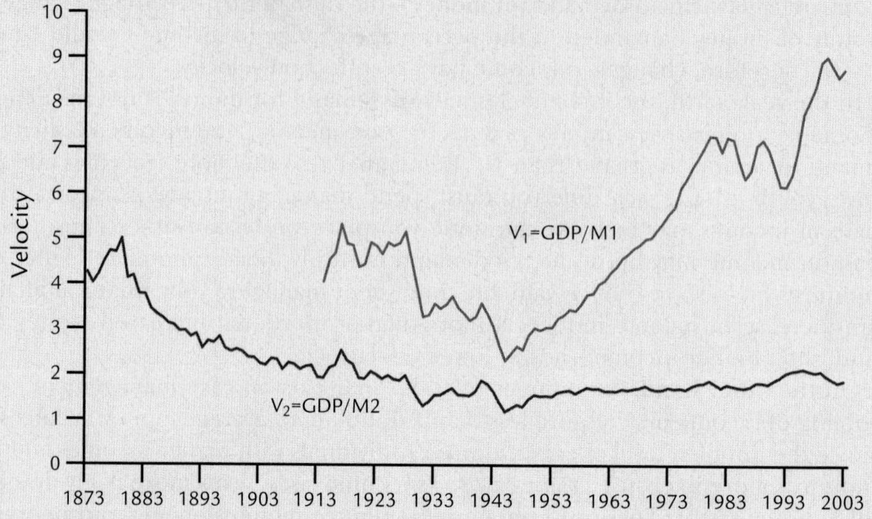

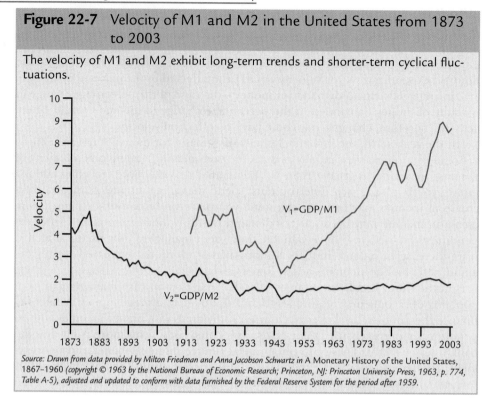

*Source: Drawn from data provided by Milton Friedman and Anna Jacobson Schwartz in* A Monetary History of the United States, 1867–1960 *(copyright © 1963 by the National Bureau of Economic Research; Princeton, NJ: Princeton University Press, 1963, p. 774, Table A-5), adjusted and updated to conform with data furnished by the Federal Reserve System for the period after 1959.*

In the figure, $V_1$ is the income velocity of M1, and $V_2$ is the income velocity of M2. Note that the $V_2$ observations extend from 1873 to the present, while $V_1$ observations extend from 1915 to the present.[13] The two measures exhibit the same turning points and move pretty much in parallel from 1915 through the 1940s. They diverge beginning in the 1950s.

Prior to 1946, the velocities of M1 and M2 exhibit a downward trend.[14] The secular decline in velocity of M1 was followed by a steady and persistent increase, beginning in 1946 and continuing until 1980. $V_1$ increased at an average annual rate of approximately 3 percent during that period. Since 1980, $V_1$ has been less stable, exhibiting a modest downward trend for about 15 years before rebounding sharply in the 1990s. M2 velocity also trended upward after 1946, albeit at a much slower pace than M1 velocity.

Economists have different views about the relative importance of the various forces underlying the long-run behavior of the velocity of money. We examine the theories of two eminent American economists, Nobel laureates Milton Friedman and James Tobin, on the behavior of velocity in the century following the end of the Civil War.

## Friedman Luxury-Good Explanation

Friedman treats the demand for money within the same general framework used to analyze the demand for other goods and services. This treatment suggests the de-

[13] $V_1$ cannot be extended back to 1873 because the recorded data did not distinguish between time deposits and demand deposits until 1915. Therefore, you can compute M2 but not M1 for years prior to 1915.

[14] The velocity of M2 declined from 4.57 in 1869 to a low of 1.16 in 1946—an average compounded negative growth rate of 1.8 percent per year over the 77-year period.

mand for money is a function of the utility or satisfaction derived from holding money, the (opportunity) cost of holding money, and the level of income or wealth. Concerning the relationship between the demand for money and income, Friedman argued that money should be classified as a "luxury" as opposed to a "normal" good. He points out that the long-term trend of per capita income in the United States has been strongly upward. If money is a luxury good and the income elasticity of the demand for money is greater than 1, the demand for money should increase at a faster rate than income over the long run. The long-term trend of velocity should be downward. Friedman hypothesized that money is a luxury good, so a long-run pattern of declining velocity would be expected over the broad sweep of history.

Confronted with the facts illustrated in Figure 22-7, Friedman's theory works quite well up until the end of World War II. Between 1880 and 1946, the only significant interruptions to the downward trend of $V_2$ were World War I and the period from 1932 to 1942. Although $V_1$ has exhibited a major increase since 1946 as the United States experienced substantial growth in per capita income, the upward trend in $V_2$ has been much more modest. Friedman's model predicts a decline in velocity during that period. Of course, money may be a luxury good only up to a certain threshold of income, becoming a normal good after the threshold income level is passed. If so, velocity declines until income reaches the threshold level and increases thereafter.

## Tobin Institutional Explanation

An alternative explanation of the long-term behavior of velocity put forth by James Tobin emphasizes the dramatic changes that occurred in financial institutions, instruments, and markets in the past century.[15] Tobin notes that use of money increasingly replaced barter and payment in kind in the 60-year era preceding World War II. The availability and use of commercial bank checking accounts spread throughout the country, particularly from 1880 to 1915, when the decline in M2 velocity was most steady and distinct. In 1880, mutual savings banks (whose deposits were not included in M1 or M2) were approximately as important a fund repository as commercial banks. Practically all mutual savings banks were located in the northeast. As the U.S. economy expanded westward in the latter part of the nineteenth century and early part of the twentieth century, commercial banking facilities rapidly spread west, while mutual savings banks remained primarily in New York and New England. Savings and loan associations (S&Ls) and other financial intermediaries were relatively undeveloped. Tobin contends that the increasing use of money and the growing availability and acceptance of commercial banks in the 60 years prior to World War II produced a natural increase in the public's M1 and M2 holdings relative to claims on other financial institutions and relative to GDP. In Tobin's view, the increase in "monetization" accounts for the long decline in velocity from 1880 to 1946.

In contrast, the decades following World War II were marked by growth of nonbank thrift institutions such as S&Ls and credit unions. Spurred by the upward trend of interest rates between 1946 and the early 1980s along with tremendous growth in home construction, thrift institutions offered stiff competition for the public's deposits. Thus, the period prior to World War II can be considered the "golden age" of commercial banking growth, but the first several decades after 1946 witnessed the successful penetration of the banking market by S&Ls and other non-

[15] Friedman's velocity hypothesis, Tobin's critique of this hypothesis, and important recent empirical work by Michael Bordo and Lars Jonung and by Pierre Siklos demonstrating the importance of institutional changes are cited in Additional Reading at the end of this chapter.

bank institutions. MMMFs (whose deposits are not included in M1) were invented in the 1970s and grew dramatically for many years. These developments imply a relative decline in the demand for M1 and an increase in the velocity of M1 after 1946.

Many additional institutional changes can be cited in support of Tobin's institutional hypothesis for the post-1945 velocity growth. The post–World War II growth of "financial technology" and the increasing availability of highly liquid, interest-bearing "near-monies" have gradually reduced the relative propensity of individuals, firms, and governments to hold wealth in the form of money. In this period, access to liquid substitutes for money became feasible for millions of individuals. The supply of short-term government securities, especially Treasury bills, expanded dramatically. The network of dealers in U.S. government securities increased efficiency and reduced transactions costs in the government securities market. Savings deposits and CDs increased in variety and were made more attractive, and government insurance of such accounts expanded substantially. The advent of bank overdraft protection reduced the need to hold precautionary balances in checking accounts. The widespread use of credit cards and other credit arrangements gradually improved synchronization of receipts and expenditures. In the mid-1970s, millions of Americans started transferring funds from checking accounts to high-yielding MMMFs and money market deposit accounts. All of these innovations helped raise the velocity of the narrow (M1) measure of money.

Firms and state and local governments have benefited from countless improvements in cash management made possible by a variety of new financial instruments. The new instruments include commercial paper, finance company paper, and short-term U.S. government agency obligations. Use of these instruments has powerfully impacted corporate and governmental liquidity management since the late 1950s. Increased use of trade credit and development of sweep accounts and RPs have reduced the demand for bank deposits by corporations and state and local governments and government agencies. All of these techniques reduce demand for M1 and increase the velocity of M1.

Development of the commercial paper market, the 1961 introduction of negotiable CDs, and the creation of a secondary market in negotiable CDs have influenced cash management not only in corporations and other firms but also in municipal and state governments, pension funds, and nonprofit institutions. They affect money demand and velocity in two ways. First, new markets and instruments increase the range of available interest-bearing liquid assets, raising the opportunity cost of holding money. Second, new instruments induce firms to maintain a less liquid asset structure—including a smaller cash position—than otherwise would have been feasible. Large firms feel more secure knowing they can use instruments such as commercial paper to obtain funds if necessary. Clearly, such financial innovations contributed strongly to the uptrend in M1 velocity in the post–World War II era. (The International Perspectives box discusses long-run velocity patterns in other nations.)

## SHORT-RUN BEHAVIOR OF VELOCITY

Having reviewed the long-run pattern of velocity, we now turn to the *short-term* or *cyclical* pattern of velocity. Suppose a major corporation anticipates increased sales of its product. The firm steps up raw materials purchases in order to build up inventories of finished products. Assume the firm decides the most efficient method for financing the inventory build-up is through issue of commercial paper (short-

# INTERNATIONAL PERSPECTIVES

## International Comparisons of the Long-Run Behavior of Velocity

In an important study, Michael Bordo of Rutgers University and Lars Jonung of the Stockholm School of Economics examined the behavior of the velocity of money in a large number of nations over a period of more than 100 years. Their conclusions were interesting. Almost all nations have exhibited a U-shaped (or V-shaped) pattern of velocity over the years, and institutional factors played an important role in that common pattern. Most nations have exhibited a pattern of velocity quite similar to the U.S. pattern shown in Figure 22-7.

Bordo and Jonung hypothesize that the evolution of a nation's financial sector introduces two competing forces on the long-run trend of velocity. Each force dominates a different stage of economic development. In the first phase of development, metallic coins, barter, and payment in kind are increasing replaced by modern forms of money. In this "monetization" phase, velocity declines as commercial banking proliferates and the public holds more money relative to income or GDP. In the second phase, introduction of substitutes for money such as bonds, shares of stock, and money market instruments reduces the demand for money and therefore increases velocity. Financial innovations such as credit cards and bank overdraft facilities and increasing economic stability boost velocity.

In almost all nations, velocity first declines with increasing monetization and then increases with financial innovations and increased economic stability. The *timing* of trend reversal differs across countries, however. The United States, Canada, Italy, Japan, and the United Kingdom reached the low point in their U-shaped velocity curves around 1946, two decades *after* Sweden, Denmark, Norway, and Germany.

Bordo and Jonung used proxies to represent the influence of certain institutional phenomena. For example, they used the ratio of the non-agricultural labor force to the nation's total labor force as a proxy for monetization because the agricultural sector traditionally has used barter and payment in kind extensively in place of money. They used the ratio of currency to M2 as a proxy for banking penetration in the economy based on the presumption that greater proliferation and use of banks systematically reduces currency use relative to deposits. A moving average of the standard deviation of real GDP served as the proxy for economic stability. In the great majority of instances, the proxy variables were significant determinants of velocity across a sample of 12 industrial nations.

Bordo and Jonung concluded that institutional developments influence money demand and velocity across a large number of countries. Thus, a model that includes institutional variables improves appreciably upon traditional models that consider only the effects of economic variables such as interest rates and income. Velocity is best understood through a full consideration of the long-run evolution of institutional forces.

term business IOUs). The firm prefers this instrument because the instrument's magnitude and maturity can be tailored to meet the firm's needs. By issuing such obligations, the firm attracts funds from lenders—primarily MMMFs and other corporations—in exchange for a competitive rate of return. Because the firm issuing commercial paper transfers the cash payment received from the commercial paper buyer to the raw materials supplier, aggregate demand deposits and the nation's money supply do not change. However, GDP rises as the borrowing firm increases production. Thus, when firms issue commercial paper and use the proceeds to finance increased expenditures, the velocity of money increases.

Assume banks are strapped for funds to meet heavy loan demand during an economic boom. Historically, banks sold some of their holdings of short-term U.S. government securities to make more loans available to business borrowers. Such a move increases the velocity of money because the velocity of the new money made available to businesses tends to be considerably greater than the velocity of the largely idle money that is extinguished when individuals and firms write checks to purchase the securities sold by banks. Banks facilitate an increase in velocity by transferring funds from *inactive* money holders to *active* money spenders.

Suppose, however, banks already depleted their short-term security portfolios. An alternative source of funds tapped by large banks in recent decades is the issue of large-denomination IOUs ($100,000 or more) in the form of negotiable CDs. The principal buyers of large-denomination CDs are corporations having extra cash on hand and seeking a high-yielding liquid asset in which to invest their funds until the funds are needed to meet payrolls, quarterly tax payments, or other scheduled expenditures. Through the instrument of negotiable CDs, banks essentially facilitate the transfer of money from firms not intending to immediately spend the funds to businesses wishing to immediately increase expenditures. The velocity of money increases. Velocity tends to vary cyclically with the amount of negotiable CDs outstanding.

In the next few sections, we will see how short-term fluctuations in velocity challenge the successful conduct of monetary policy.

## Induced Changes in Velocity and the Effectiveness of Monetary Policy

Financial instruments such as commercial paper and negotiable CDs make the conduct of monetary policy more difficult. Suppose the Federal Reserve desires to restrain the economy during a strong cyclical upswing. If the Fed holds the money supply constant over a 6-month period in an effort to cool off aggregate expenditures, firms issue commercial paper and banks issue negotiable CDs to obtain funds. The resulting increase in velocity partially attenuates the Fed's efforts to restrain expenditures. In terms of the $MV = PY$ framework, the increase in V allows aggregate demand for goods and services (MV) to increase despite a constant money supply. The more aggressively the Federal Reserve implements its restraint policy, the greater the propensity of banks and non-bank firms to issue commercial paper and negotiable CDs to obtain funds. The institutions then make the funds available to borrowers desiring to finance expenditures. Instruments such as negotiable CDs and commercial paper weaken the Fed's grip on bank lending and aggregate expenditures.

## "Ratchet Effect" of Financial Innovations

Over time, financial innovations operate on the velocity of money with a ratchet effect. In a period of "tight money" when demand for credit is high relative to the supply and interest rates reach peak levels, the environment is conducive to financial innovations that raise the velocity of money. Federal Reserve restraint stimulates use of commercial paper, negotiable CDs, RPs, and sweep accounts. The financial community becomes familiar with the devices and continues using them, even after financial conditions return to normal. The net result—new financial innovations, as they become available, gradually raise the normal level of the velocity of money. The post-1946 long-term rise in the velocity of M1 likely will continue as long as new financial innovations are introduced.

## Cyclical Behavior of Velocity

The velocity of money displays a systematic procyclical pattern, rising during business cycle expansions and falling (or at least rising at a below-trend rate) during recessions and depressions. This tendency is illustrated in Figure 22-8, which shows the behavior of the velocity of M1 and M2 since 1964. In the figure, periods of recession are shaded, and periods of expansion are unshaded. In the three most recent recessions shown, both $V_1$ and $V_2$ declined. The 1973–1975 recession (an unusual downturn because it was accompanied by rising inflation) marked the first time in 100 years that velocity increased significantly during a U.S. cyclical downturn. If the long-term upward trend from the M1 velocity series is removed, a clear pattern of procyclical variation in velocity remains.

Economists have advanced three explanations accounting for the procyclical behavior of the velocity of M1 and M2. The three hypotheses should not be viewed as mutually exclusive. A combination of factors may have contributed to the pattern illustrated in Figure 22-8.

**Velocity and the Procyclical Pattern of Interest Rates.** Interest rates typically rise during cyclical expansions and fall during cyclical contractions. If the demand for money is significantly influenced by interest rate levels, the results illus-

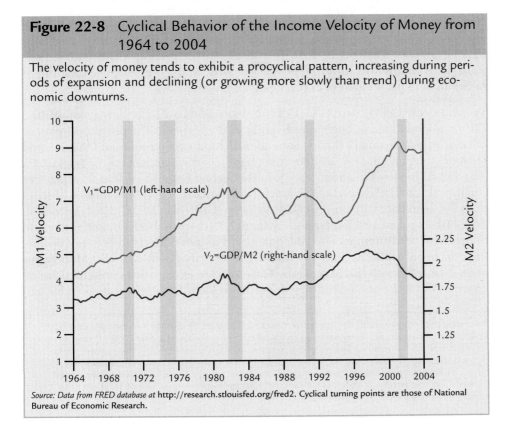

**Figure 22-8** Cyclical Behavior of the Income Velocity of Money from 1964 to 2004

The velocity of money tends to exhibit a procyclical pattern, increasing during periods of expansion and declining (or growing more slowly than trend) during economic downturns.

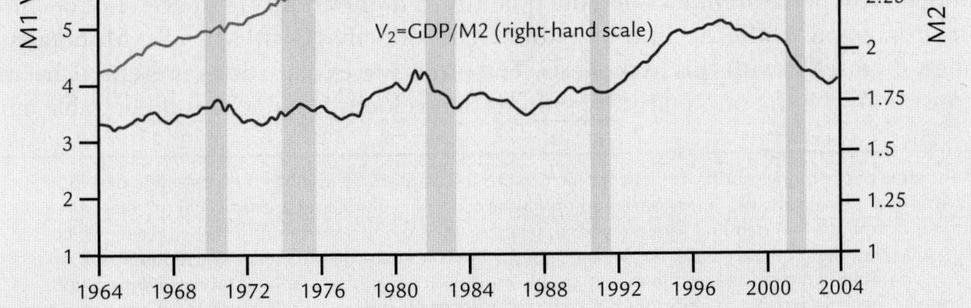


*Source: Data from FRED database at* http://research.stlouisfed.org/fred2. Cyclical turning points are those of National Bureau of Economic Research.

trated in Figure 22-8 are easily explained. As the economy expands in a cyclical upswing, interest rates rise. Money demand is reduced relative to expenditures, thereby raising velocity. Yields decline during recessions, raising the demand for money relative to expenditures and depressing velocity. The validity of this explanation hinges on the interest elasticity of the demand for money. Non-monetarists, who traditionally have viewed the demand for money as relatively sensitive to interest rates, find this hypothesis plausible. Monetarists, who believe money demand is relatively insensitive to interest rates, tend to de-emphasize this hypothesis.

**Velocity and the Non-Monetary Theory of the Business Cycle.** Many non-monetarists believe business cycles are driven largely by changes in consumption, investment, net exports, and the government's fiscal posture that are largely unrelated to money supply phenomena. The supply of money is viewed as *responding passively* and in a lagged fashion to economic activity rather than *actively determining* the behavior of output and employment. In such a framework, the velocity of money naturally exhibits a procyclical pattern.

Assume, near the trough of a recession, government economic stimulus (a tax cut) coincides with improved consumer confidence. The net result is an appreciable rise in aggregate demand for goods and services. The AD curve shifts rightward, and GDP increases. Such cyclical forces likely induce a positive response in the money supply.[16] However, the money supply responds to business conditions somewhat sluggishly. The short-term result is a rise in velocity (GDP/M). In this non-monetarist framework, cyclical downturns also are induced by shifts in consumer expenditures, business investment, net exports, and the government's fiscal posture. If the net effect of such shifts is decreased aggregate demand and GDP, the money supply falls, but only in a lagged and sluggish fashion. Again, simple arithmetic indicates the velocity of money must decline in such circumstances.

These two simple explanations seem reasonable to many non-monetarists but are downplayed by monetarists. Monetarists downplay them because these explanations attribute changes in GDP to changes in interest rates and autonomous shifts in consumption, investment, net exports, and government expenditures rather than to prior changes in the supply of money.

**Velocity and Friedman's Permanent Income Hypothesis.** Milton Friedman developed an ingenious hypothesis that explains the procyclical pattern of velocity. In Friedman's theory, both consumption expenditures and the demand for money depend not on *current* income but on **permanent income,** or *long-run average income* [review Equation (22-3)]. In the second half of a cyclical upswing, *current* income or GDP exceeds *permanent* income or GDP. Therefore, money demand does not keep pace with current GDP. Velocity (GDP/M) rises. During a recession, actual GDP and income fall *below* permanent levels. Again, because money demand depends on permanent income, the quantity of money demanded does not decline in proportion to the decline in actual GDP. Velocity (GDP/M) falls. Monetarists align themselves with this hypothesis. The other two explanations presented are inconsistent with the monetarist hypothesis that velocity is stable and predictable and

**permanent income**
long-run average expected future income

[16] In terms of the money supply framework introduced in Chapters 15 and 16, business cycle developments likely influence both the monetary base and the money supply multiplier in a procyclical manner. As the economy expands and demand for credit escalates, the volume of discount loans may increase, which in turn increases the monetary base. As yields rise in the cyclical upswing, the banks' desired excess reserve ratio ($r_e$) declines, which increases the money supply multiplier. Thus, the supply of money is pulled up by expanded economic activity. In addition, the Fed may purchase securities to remain on its interest rate target, thereby increasing the monetary base and M.

that changes in the money supply are the predominant cause of changes in aggregate expenditures and nominal GDP.

## VELOCITY BEHAVIOR AND MONETARY POLICY

The behavior of velocity has obvious important implications for the conduct of monetary policy. If the velocities of the monetary aggregates (M1, M2, and M3) are stable and predictable and the Fed can hit specific targets for M1, M2, and M3, then targeting these aggregates is a wise and effective method of conducting monetary policy.

Recall that the equation of exchange is MV = PY. This relationship, which literally states that GDP expenditures viewed from the "money side" are identical to GDP expenditures viewed from the "goods side," holds *at any point in time.* To analyze the role of money *over time,* we can differentiate the equation with respect to time and simplify to convert the equation into its dynamic version, as follows:

$$\text{(22-4)}\quad \frac{\left(\frac{dM}{dt}\right)}{M} + \frac{\left(\frac{dV}{dt}\right)}{V} = \frac{\left(\frac{dP}{dt}\right)}{P} + \frac{\left(\frac{dY}{dt}\right)}{Y}, \text{ or}$$

$$\text{(22-5)}\quad \%\Delta M + \%\Delta V = \%\Delta P + \%\Delta Y.$$

This dynamic version of the equation indicates the percentage change in GDP expenditures viewed from the "money side" (%ΔM + %ΔV) equals the percentage change in GDP expenditures viewed from the "goods side" (%ΔP + %ΔY). Put another way, the growth rate of the money supply plus the growth rate of velocity equals the sum of the inflation rate and growth rate of real output.

The Federal Reserve conducts monetary policy, implicitly aiming for a specific growth rate of GDP expenditures (%ΔM + %ΔV and %ΔP + %ΔY). For example, assume the Federal Reserve seeks to achieve 3 percent real output growth (%ΔY) and roughly 2 percent inflation (%ΔP), which the Fed's model indicates is consistent with 3 percent output growth. The Fed then seeks to promote growth of nominal GDP expenditures of approximately 5 percent per year. To arrive at the appropriate growth rate for the money supply, the Fed must forecast or estimate the expected rate of change in velocity during the next year. The whole debate over the desirability of targeting the monetary aggregates boils down to a debate over whether the Fed (or anyone else) can accurately forecast velocity. We conclude this chapter with some food for thought in the form of a graph illustrating the historical pattern of the *12-month rate of change* in velocity of M1 and M2 (Figure 22-9).

You can see from the figure that the rates of change in $V_1$ and $V_2$ were relatively small from 1964 to the end of the 1970s. Velocities were relatively stable. The velocities (particularly M1 velocity) have been significantly more volatile in the more recent period. Intuitively, a more variable velocity should be more difficult to predict or forecast. Therefore, Federal Reserve's adherence to rigid money growth targets likely would have been less successful in stabilizing economic activity after 1980 than in the previous quarter century. It is no coincidence that sentiment for a central bank policy of targeting monetary aggregates reached a high water mark in the 1970s and decreased after the early 1980s.

**Figure 22-9** Twelve-Month Rates of Change in the Velocity of M1 and M2 from 1960 to 2004

Changes in velocity were relatively small from the 1960s through the 1970s. Since 1980, these velocities have been more unstable (especially M1 velocity).

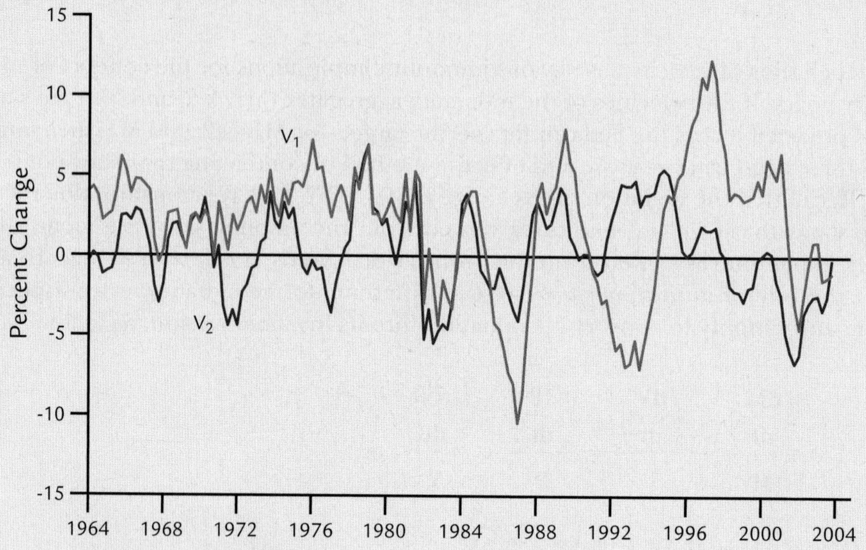


*Source: Calculated from same data used in Figure 22-8.*

## Exhibit 22-2 P-Star Analysis: Search for an Indicator of Future Prices

Maintaining a reasonably stable price level traditionally has been considered the central bank's most important goal. Because monitoring progress toward achieving price level stability is important, the research staff of the Board of Governors of the Federal Reserve constantly searches for reliable indicators of the nation's future price level. Analysts have suggested commodity prices (especially gold and silver), the slope of the yield curve, the recent behavior of the U.S. dollar in foreign exchange markets, and surveys of inflation forecasts of economists as indicators of prospective inflation.

A few years ago, the Fed's research staff thought it had uncovered a superior indicator of the nation's future price level. The indicator was known as the *P-star model,* based largely on monetarist thinking. P-star is an estimate of the nation's future price level implied by the current level of the M2 money supply. M2 is preferred over M1 because, for many years, the velocity of M2 has been more stable and devoid of trends than M1 velocity. To derive P-star, that is, the estimate of the future price level, the Fed's staff began with Fisher's equation of exchange:

$$(1)\ \mathbf{M2 \times V_2 = P^* \times Y.}$$

Solving for the price level (P*), we obtain:

$$(2)\ \mathbf{P^* = \frac{(M2 \times V_2)}{Y}.}$$

## **Exhibit 22-2** P-Star Analysis: Search for an Indicator of Future Prices—*cont'd*

So far we are looking at simple *identities,* which tell us *nothing* about the future price level. Until we specify assumptions about the behavior of $V_2$ and Y, we cannot relate the money stock to the future price level. The key assumptions underlying the development of the P-Star framework were that potential real output (Y) grows at 2.5 percent per year on average and is independent of money supply behavior, and that the velocity of M2 always reverts to its long-term mean (1.73 from 1959 to 1990). To use the model to forecast the future equilibrium price level consistent with any given money supply (M2), you simply plug into Equation 2 the current magnitude of M2 along with the (assumed) eventual velocity of 1.73, take the product of the two, and divide by prospective real output on the specified future date (calculated by assuming 2.5 percent annual real output growth).

The most crucial assumption (and potential flaw) underlying the P-star model is that the velocity of M2 always reverts to its long-term mean within a reasonable time period. The accompanying figure suggests the assumption held true through most of the period until the 1990s. However, during the economic boom of the 1990s, Americans became increasingly attracted to bond and stock mutual funds, which are not included in M2. Hence, demand for M2 declined relative to GDP, and M2 velocity increased strongly for approximately a decade (1987–1997). Because the velocity of M2 rose sharply during the 1990s, the model for several years underestimated the future price level. Formal Fed adoption of this model likely would have resulted in high inflation in the 1990s. After the stock market boom of the 1990s ended, households became more conservative in their financial practices. They became less enamored of stocks and opted for the relatively safe assets included in M2. The increased demand for broad money pulled M2 velocity sharply downward from 1999 to 2004. However, even in mid-2004, M2 velocity still was significantly above its average from 1959 to 1990. The potential errors from taking this indicator seriously are enormous. In recent years, the Fed has downplayed P-star analysis and de-emphasized use of M2 as an indicator of forthcoming economic phenomena.

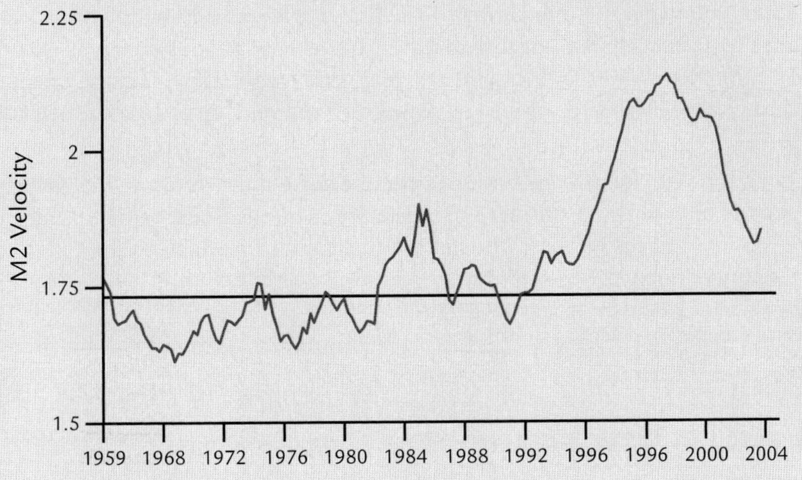

# SUMMARY

The velocity of money—the variable linking a nation's money supply to the nation's nominal GDP—is a key economic variable. Velocity is closely related to the demand for money. People are motivated to *demand money*—to hold a portion of their wealth in the form of money (M1, M2, M3)—primarily to finance expenditures that are not perfectly synchronized over time with their receipt of funds. This demand is the transactions demand for money. Money also may be held for precautionary and speculative purposes. Factors that increase demand for money reduce velocity. Factors that reduce demand for money increase velocity. Some factors that influence money demand and velocity are the frequency of paydays, use of credit cards and other forms of credit, interest rate levels, prevailing degree of economic uncertainty, and evolution of new financial instruments and other forms of financial technology. The latter items enable households and firms to hold fewer money balances relative to expenditures and help account for a long-term upward trend in velocity. Monetarist economists traditionally have viewed the demand for money as relatively stable, which implies central bank-induced changes in the money supply have strong and predictable effects on nominal GDP. Non-monetarist economists traditionally have viewed velocity as unstable and unpredictable, which implies a central bank policy targeting money supply growth rates will not result in a stable or predictable pattern of aggregate expenditures. Given that velocity was more stable from 1946 to 1980 than it has been in the past quarter century, monetarism has lost some of its appeal in the more recent period.

## YOUR TURN ANSWERS

PAGE 506

**A.** Because you begin the month with $750 (since your $250 check to the credit card company clears on the first) and spend the money at a constant rate, your average money balance (transactions demand) is $375. Given your total expenditures of $12,000 per year, the velocity of your money is $12,000/year/$375, or 32 times per year.

**B.** If you stop using the credit card, your average transactions demand is now $500 (you begin the month with $1,000 and gradually draw down the balance to zero at the end of the month). The velocity of your money is now $12,000/year/$500, or 24 times per year. When you stop using the credit card, your demand for money increases and the velocity of your money falls.

PAGE 513

The direction velocity will move is uncertain because the two forces pull velocity in opposite directions. In this case, financial innovations boost velocity, while income growth reduces velocity. The net effect depends on which of the two forces has a stronger impact.

## KEY TERMS

velocity of money
equation of exchange
demand for money
transactions demand for money
precautionary demand for money
speculative demand for money
sweep account
income elasticity of demand for money
permanent income

## STUDY QUESTIONS

1. Write down the equation of exchange and define each of its four terms. Suppose the money supply rises 20 percent. Does the equation of exchange imply that the nation's price level or output level must rise? Explain why or why not.

2. Estimate your own average demand for M1 money over the course of 1 month. Given that information, together with your estimate of your annual GDP expenditures, calculate the income velocity of your M1 money. How many days' worth of GDP expenditures do you hold in the form of M1, on average?

3. Using the equation of exchange, explain why the stability of the demand for money is an important issue underlying the debate between monetarists and non-monetarists over the predictability of the impact of money supply growth in determining the growth of nominal GDP expenditures (PY).

4. Explain why the speculative and precautionary demands for money might be reflected more in the M2 and M3 measures of money than in M1.

5. **A.** Assume, after you graduate, you are paid $3,000 monthly (take-home pay). Assuming you spend your entire income at a constant rate throughout the month and do not use a credit card, calculate your average demand for money and the velocity of your money.
   **B.** Because of outstanding performance, your salary is boosted to $4,000 per month. Assuming you continue to spend your entire income at a constant rate and do not use a credit card, calculate your average money demand and the velocity of your money.
   **C.** A new company policy introduces twice-monthly paychecks. If your spending habits are unchanged, calculate the velocity of your money after the new policy goes into effect.

6. Explain the effect on the velocity of M1 of the following developments:
   **A.** Use of credit cards by individuals under age 25 is banned.
   **B.** New law requires banks to pay interest—equal to the Treasury bill yield—on all DDO.
   **C.** Employers move to a system in which workers are paid only six times per year.
   **D.** Interest rates plunge to 0.1 percent as the economy sinks into a deflationary spiral.
   **E.** Proliferation of ATMs makes withdrawal of cash directly from savings accounts increasingly convenient.

7. Discuss the improvements in "financial technology" that have contributed to the uptrend in the income velocity of M1 money (V1) in the past 40 years.

8. Outline two hypotheses about the cyclical behavior of the velocity of money that are basically inconsistent with the tenets of monetarism.

9. Explain Milton Friedman's explanation for the procyclical pattern of money velocity.

10. Suppose long-term interest rates rise sharply and the yield curve becomes much steeper. Outline the consequences of this development on the velocity of M2.

11. Suppose income elasticity of demand for money is known to be 0.7. Assuming interest rates and financial technology remain unchanged over the next 5 years and income increases at a rate of 3 percent per year, what would you expect to happen to velocity of money? Explain.

12. Explain why many nations have exhibited a "U-shaped" long-term pattern of velocity over the past 150 years.

13. Explain how the introduction of financial instruments such as commercial paper and negotiable CDs may have weakened the Fed's control over GDP expenditures.

14. Suppose the world is stunned by a North Korean declaration of war against South Korea and Japan. What would you expect to happen to the velocity of M2 in the United States? Explain. If the U.S. money supply remains constant, what would happen to U.S. GDP?

15. Suppose, after the U.S. withdraws all personnel from Iraq, the new Iraqi regime finances huge government expenditures by printing money. Inflation skyrockets. Analyze the likely effect on the velocity of Iraqi money.

# ADDITIONAL READING

- The classic discussion of the equation of exchange is provided in Chapters 2 and 4 of Irving Fisher, *The Purchasing Power of Money* (New York: Macmillan, 1911), reprinted in 1963 by Augustus M. Kelley, bookseller in its Reprints of Economic Classics series.
- The three-tier motive for holding money originated by John Maynard Keynes is clearly presented in Chapter 8 of Dudley Dillard, *The Economics of John Maynard Keynes* (Englewood Cliffs, NJ: Prentice-Hall, 1948). This book was reprinted by Greenwood Publishing in 1983.
- On the interest elasticity of the transactions demand for money, classic articles are James Tobin, "The Interest Elasticity of Transactions Demand for Cash," *The Review of Economics and Statistics,* August 1956, pp. 241–247, and William J. Baumol, "The Transactions Demand for Cash: An Inventory Theoretic Approach," *Quarterly Journal of Economics,* November 1952.
- An excellent reference on all aspects of the demand for money is David Laidler, *The Demand for Money,* 5th edition (Upper Saddle River, NJ: Prentice-Hall, 1998). This work presents the various theories of money demand, analyzes the problems encountered is estimating such demand functions econometrically, and surveys the empirical literature on the demand for money. It also contains a comprehensive list of references on the subject.
- Milton Friedman's view on the historical pattern of velocity can be found in Chapter 12 of Anna J. Schwartz and Milton Friedman, *A Monetary History of the United States, 1867–1960* (Princeton, NJ: Princeton University Press, 1963). James Tobin's critique of this view appears in James Tobin, "The Monetary Interpretation of History," *American Economic Review,* June 1965, pp. 646–685.
- An important work lending support to the institutional view of velocity is Michael Bordo and Lars Jonung, *The Long-Run Behavior of Velocity of Circulation: The International Evidence* (New York: Cambridge University Press, 1987). Also see Pierre Siklos, "Income Velocity and Institutional Change: Some New Time Series Evidence," *Journal of Money, Credit, and Banking,* August 1993, pp. 377–392.

# Chapter 23

# THE MONETARY TRANSMISSION MECHANISM: HOW FEDERAL RESERVE POLICY INFLUENCES ECONOMIC ACTIVITY

In Chapters 20 to 22, we developed the aggregate demand-aggregate supply (AD/AS) macroeconomic model and examined the link between a nation's money supply and gross domestic product (GDP) expenditures. The Federal Reserve's monetary policy actions influence economic activity principally through aggregate spending—that is, by shifting the nation's AD curve. If the Federal Reserve increases the money supply and decreases interest rates, the nation's AD curve shifts rightward. This action stimulates real output and increases the nation's price level. If the Fed reduces the money supply and increases interest rates, the AD curve shifts leftward. This action reduces the nation's real output and tends to reduce the nation's price level.

In this chapter, we move beyond the simple notion that changes in the money supply and interest rate levels shift the AD curve. We examine in-depth the **transmission mechanism of monetary policy**—the various avenues or channels through which Federal Reserve policy changes affect aggregate demand and economic activity. Economists broadly agree that monetary policy strongly affects economic activity, but precisely how policy influence is transmitted is uncertain. Different macroeconomic models attribute different degrees of influence to the various channels of monetary policy. The channels change over time in response to changes in institutions, regulations, and financial technology. Monetary policy influences the economy differently today than it did in earlier times. For these reasons, the monetary policy transmission mechanism is actively researched. Numerous papers on the subject have been published over the past 2 decades.

**transmission mechanism of monetary policy**
various avenues or channels through which changes in Federal Reserve policy alter aggregate demand and economic activity

Recall from our discussion in Chapter 20 that aggregate GDP expenditures consist of four components: consumption spending (C), investment spending (I), government purchases of goods and services (G), and net exports of goods and services (NX, or exports minus imports). Monetary policy influences all four components, especially consumption and investment spending and net foreign demand for U.S. goods and services (NX).[1] Figure 23-1 shows the shares of U.S. GDP contributed by C, I, G, and NX in recent decades.

Consumer expenditures constitute more than two thirds of the nation's total GDP expenditures. Consumption share has trended upward in the past 25 years. For almost all of the 44-year period covered in the figure, government purchases contributed the second largest component, typically around 18 to 21 percent of GDP expenditures in the past quarter century. The most variable component of

[1] Monetary policy influences interest rates and thereby local government purchases of goods and services, a large component of G. For example, lower interest rates engineered by the Fed encourage municipalities to issue bonds. Local governments use the funds to finance new expenditures for schools, swimming pools, and so forth. In our discussion in this chapter, however, we ignore the potential effect of monetary policy on G.

**Figure 23-1** GDP Shares Contributed by the Four Components from 1960 to 2004

Consumption spending (C) constitutes about 70 percent of aggregate expenditures. Investment expenditures (I) and government purchases (G) each contributes more than 15 percent. Net exports (NX) are negative.

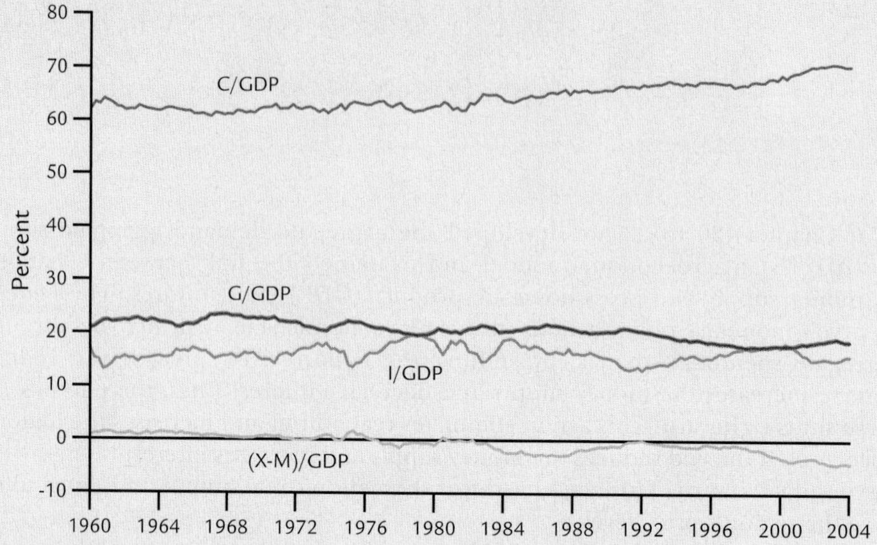


*Source: Data from FRED database at* http://research.stlouisfed.org/fred2/

GDP expenditures is investment spending, which includes residential and nonresidential construction, expenditures for producers' durable equipment (computers, software, machines), and the change in the nation's aggregate inventories. The investment share of GDP fluctuated from 14 to 20 percent. The share increased during the economic boom of the 1990s and declined from 2000 to 2003. Net exports (exports minus imports) have been consistently negative since the mid-1970s. The U.S. trade deficit (the amount by which imports exceed exports) expanded sharply from 1997 to 2004 and was 4.5 percent of GDP in 2004. Although the share of total expenditures constituted by net exports is small, economists believe the international sector has become a very important part of the transmission process of monetary policy.

Theories of the transmission mechanism have evolved. We first sketch the relatively simple early Keynesian and early monetarist views of how monetary policy change affects economic activity. We study in greater detail the various avenues through which monetary policy derives its influence today and examine newer theories and developments of the transmission mechanism.

## EARLY VIEWS OF THE TRANSMISSION MECHANISM

In this section, we examine some early Keynesian and monetarist viewpoints on how Fed policy influences the economy. This discussion lays the groundwork for our discussion of modern views of the monetary transmission mechanism.

**Figure 23-2** Early Keynesian Monetary Transmission Mechanism

In Keynes' scheme, an increase in the money supply reduces interest rates *(panel A)*. The number of profitable investment projects increases, stimulating investment spending and GDP *(panel B)*.

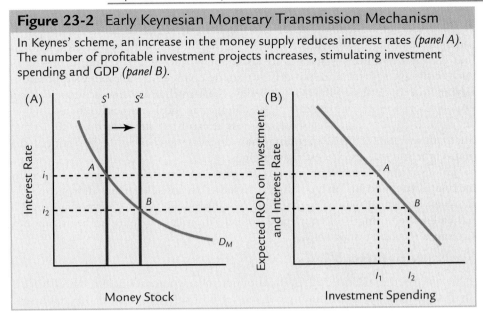

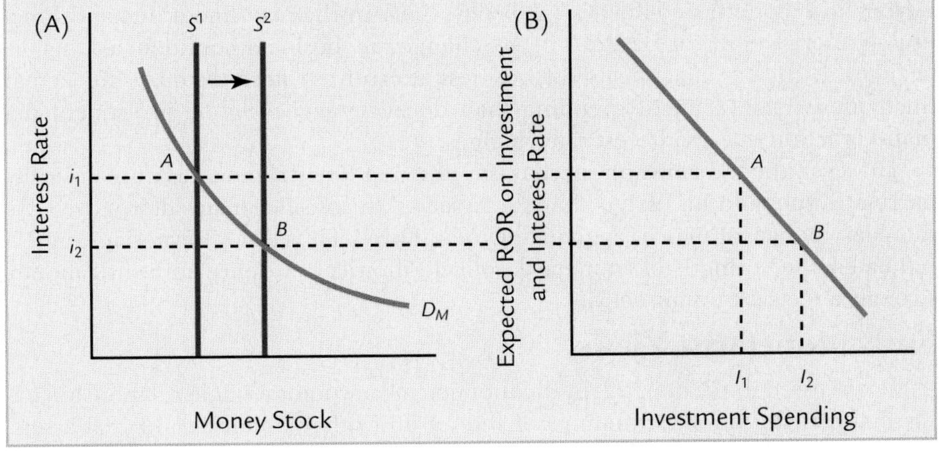


## Early Keynesian Views

In Keynes' original analysis, investment expenditures are determined by the interest rate and the rate of return expected from an additional unit of investment spending. This simple Keynesian framework is illustrated in Figure 23-2. The *investment schedule* (panel B) shows how the expected rate of return on additional investment (ROR) declines as the volume of investment increases. Investment expenditures are profitable whenever the expected rate of return exceeds the market rate of interest. For example, if a potential investment project's expected rate of return is 10 percent per year and the interest rate is 7 percent, the project is profitable. A profit-maximizing firm undertakes the project. A firm that can borrow at 7 percent and use the funds to invest in a project returning 10 percent invests in the project. On the other hand, the same project is *not* profitable if the interest rate is 11 percent.

When the interest rate is placed on the vertical axis alongside the expected rate of return in panel B of the figure, the schedule is an *investment demand function* indicating the amount of investment spending forthcoming at each interest rate. In this framework, monetary policy influences investment expenditures by changing the interest rate and moving along the investment demand schedule.

More precisely, the *expected real* interest rate and the *expected real* rate of return on investment determine the magnitude of investment expenditures. According to Keynes, the interest rate is determined by the supply of and demand for money. Because prices are "sticky"—that is, prices do not respond in the short run to an increase in the money supply—both nominal and real interest rates are influenced by money supply changes. An increase in the supply of money from $S^1$ to $S^2$ in panel A of the figure reduces the nominal and real interest rate from $i_1$ to $i_2$ as we move from point *A* to point *B*. Some investment projects that were unprofitable at higher interest rates now are profitable at reduced interest rates. Businesses move down the investment demand schedule from point *A* to point *B* in panel B of the figure, increasing the nation's investment spending from $I_1$ to $I_2$.

Keynes believed the interest-rate elasticity of investment demand sometimes is low—that is, the investment demand function is relatively steep. In the Keynesian framework, low interest-rate elasticity, coupled with the extremely limited breadth of the Keynesian monetary transmission mechanism, suggests that monetary policy sometimes does not powerfully influence aggregate expenditures. Keynes believed that *fiscal policy* actions—changes in taxes and government expenditures—influence economic activity more powerfully than do changes in the money supply. Both Keynes and modern neo-Keynesians believe *shifts* in the investment demand function (panel B of Figure 23-2) due to changes in business confidence—that is, changes in the "animal spirits" of business executives—account more for actual fluctuations in investment spending than do *movements along* the investment demand function due to interest rate changes.

However, the transmission mechanism posed in Keynes' model is unrealistically narrow. Keynes and his early followers neglected to consider many alternative ways monetary policy influences aggregate expenditures. Thus, early Keynesians underestimated the strength of monetary policy. Empirical evidence indicates money strongly affects economic activity.

### Early Monetarist Views

As we discussed in Chapter 22, in the monetarist viewpoint a stable relationship exists between the public's holdings of money and other financial and real assets. Individuals and firms maintain a broad portfolio of assets, both financial and real. Assets include money, bank CDs, corporate and government bonds, common stocks, physical capital, and durable goods. Based on the returns expected at the margin on such assets, individuals and firms maintain a *portfolio equilibrium* in which money is one of many assets they desire to hold.

Now, assume the Federal Reserve upsets the portfolio equilibrium by increasing the stock of money. Initially, individuals and firms discover they are holding more money than they desire relative to stocks, bonds, durable goods, and so forth. The initial disequilibrium triggers a round of asset substitution. Individuals rid themselves of excess money by acquiring non-money assets such as shares of stock, bonds, cars, television sets, and houses. The economy reaches a new equilibrium when holdings of non-money assets resume their former importance relative to money holdings in portfolios of households and firms. By that time, stock and bond prices have increased, and the amounts of consumer durable goods and houses owned by the public have increased. In this way, money *directly* influences economic activity.

In the monetarist transmission mechanism, changes in the money stock influence economic activity even if interest rates are unaffected. The early Keynesian monetary policy transmission mechanism is *indirect*—it runs from money to interest rates to investment expenditures. The monetarist mechanism is *direct*—it runs from money to expenditures on goods and services and financial assets.[2]

## MODERN VIEWS ON THE TRANSMISSION MECHANISM

Today, economists believe monetary policy influences economic activity through a variety of channels. Several of these channels depend on monetary policy influence on stock and bond prices. First, we examine how monetary policy affects stock and

[2] The difference in the two transmission mechanisms explains why neo-Keynesians are more skeptical than other economists about the universal efficacy of monetary policy. In the neo-Keynesian transmission mechanism, two factors may potentially cause money's influence on economic activity to break down. First, the Federal Reserve may experience difficulty pushing down interest rates. Second, if the investment demand function is highly interest rate inelastic, interest rate changes have little impact on investment and aggregate expenditures. Such breakdowns in monetary policy effectiveness are much harder to rationalize in the monetarists' broader transmission mechanism.

bond prices. Then we discuss how monetary policy influences each of the components of aggregate expenditures.

## Monetary Policy and Stock and Bond Prices

In the monetarist view, the impact of a money supply change on stock and bond prices is direct. A Federal Reserve-initiated increase in the money supply creates a disequilibrium between holdings of money relative to stocks and bonds (and other assets). The disequilibrium prompts individuals to use their excess money to purchase stocks and bonds (and other goods and services), bidding up stock and bond prices. Thus, an increase in the money supply directly raises stock and bond prices. A decrease in the money supply lowers stock and bond prices.

To see other ways a change in the money supply influences stock and bond prices, we should review the present value formula first presented in Chapter 5. Consider the following equation:

$$\text{(23-1)} \quad \mathbf{PV} = \frac{\mathbf{R_1}}{\mathbf{(1+i)}} + \frac{\mathbf{R_2}}{\mathbf{(1+i)^2}} + \frac{\mathbf{R_3}}{\mathbf{(1+i)^3}} + \ldots + \frac{\mathbf{R_n}}{\mathbf{(1+i)^n}}.$$

In this expression, PV is the present value (and price) of an asset such as a stock or bond. The R's are the payments currently expected from the stock or bond in the year indicated by the subscript. For example, $R_3$ is the payment currently expected from the asset 3 years from now. In the denominator, i is the current interest rate used to discount the expected future payments. The present value of any asset expected to yield a flow of payments in the future is calculated by summing the discounted present values of the individual payments expected in each future year.

In the case of corporate, municipal, and government bonds and other debt instruments, the R's are fixed contractually. Barring insolvency of the issuer, no uncertainty exists about the payments to be received each year from bonds. Because the R's earned on bonds are fixed, monetary policy influences bond prices entirely by altering market interest rates. If the Fed reduces interest rates, bond prices rise. If the Fed increases interest rates, bond prices fall.

Corporate equities (shares of stock), unlike bonds, do *not* promise a specific dividend or other payment to stockholders. The R's expected from stocks are highly uncertain. Financial market participants frequently revise the R's as new information about individual companies and the nation's economic prospects becomes available. If the economy is robust and growing, the R's anticipated from common stock likely are positive and sequentially increasing—that is, $R_2 > R_1$, $R_3 > R_2$, and so forth.

We see from this formulation that monetary policy may influence stock prices by influencing either expected payments from stocks (R's) or the market interest rate (i). If an increase in the money supply or lower interest rates consistently stimulates economic activity, announcement of expansionary policy actions may increase the expected payments from stocks (the R's), thereby increasing stock prices. Expansionary actions that do not boost expected payments still may increase stock (and bond) prices by reducing interest rates.[3] *Given other factors,* we conclude that an

[3] However, you must be cautious with the proposition that expansionary monetary actions always increase stock and bond prices. The outcome likely depends on the economic environment at the time of monetary stimulus. In an environment in which economic agents are highly sensitive to the inflation outlook, an acceleration in money growth may trigger an increase in expected inflation, which may lead to *higher* nominal long-term interest rates through the Fisher effect. In that case, bond prices definitely fall. Stock prices also fall unless the positive effect of the monetary stimulus on expected payments (R's) offsets the effect of higher interest rates (i). Most economists agree that, in an environment of very modest inflation, the Fed can lower interest rates through stimulative monetary policy measures. This proposition may not hold in a highly inflationary environment.

increase in the money supply increases stock and bond prices. Holding other factors constant, a decrease in the money supply reduces stock and bond prices.

## Components of GDP Expenditures

Before we analyze the numerous ways monetary policy influences consumption, investment, and net exports, let us examine the relative importance of the various GDP components. Table 23-1 illustrates the proportionate share of GDP constituted by each of the components and subcomponents of GDP expenditures in each decade beginning in 1960.

Consumption spending is by far the largest component of GDP expenditures. Investment expenditures, made up chiefly of producers' equipment (equipment and software) and residential and nonresidential buildings, have contributed approximately 16 percent of total GDP expenditures in recent years. Government purchases today account for approximately 18 percent of GDP, a decrease since the 1960s.[4] State and local government purchases as a share of GDP have increased while federal government purchases has *decreased* sharply. Net exports (NX) have been negative since the mid-1970s. Note, however, the persistent increase in the shares of GDP constituted by exports and imports over the years. The substantially increased role of international trade in the U.S. economy over the past 50 years has important implications for the transmission mechanism of monetary policy.

## Monetary Policy and Consumption Spending

Consumption expenditures have accounted for approximately 70 percent of aggregate expenditures in the United States in recent years (Table 23-1). Consumption spending consists of expenditures on durable goods (cars and TV sets), nondurables (food and clothing), and services (health care and entertainment). Because the income elasticity of demand for consumer services is significantly higher than the elasticity for consumer durables and nondurables, the consumer services share of the nation's output has increased steadily with rising incomes. The nondurables share has declined, while the durables share has remained relatively stable.

Today, economists agree that monetary policy influences total consumption expenditures through several channels. The channels include the effect of a change in (1) *interest rates* on durable goods expenditures, (2) *wealth* on all categories of consumption, and (3) household *liquidity* on durable goods expenditures.

**Monetary Policy, Interest Rates, and Consumer Durable Goods Expenditures.** Table 23-1 indicates consumer expenditures on durable goods constitute approximately 8 percent of aggregate GDP expenditures. Consumer durables such as cars, furniture, and major appliances often are purchased on credit. For example, about 60 percent of new automobile purchases are financed by borrowing. When the Federal Reserve implements expansionary policies that reduce interest rates, monthly payments on new consumer loans are reduced accordingly. Thus, stimulative monetary policies encourage consumer purchases of durable goods. This channel of influence can be summarized as follows (where i represents both nominal and real interest rates):

**M ↑ → i ↓ → Consumer durable goods expenditures ↑ → GDP ↑.**

[4] Government purchases (G) include federal, state, and local government expenditures for goods and services. The component does *not* include *government transfer payments*—government expenditures for which no concurrent good or service is rendered (about half of total government expenditures). Because government transfer payments are reflected in GDP components such as consumption, residential building, and imports, inclusion of government transfer payments in G in national income accounts would be double counting.

**Table 23-1 Shares of GDP by Component**

| | 1960s | 1970s | 1980s | 1990s | 2000:1–2004:2 |
|---|---|---|---|---|---|
| Consumption (C) | 61.8 % | 62.5 % | 64.5 % | 66.7 % | 69.9 % |
| Durables | 8.5 | 8.6 | 8.4 | 7.8 | 8.5 |
| Non-durables | 26.8 | 24.9 | 22.4 | 20.3 | 20.2 |
| Services | 26.4 | 29.0 | 33.8 | 38.6 | 41.2 |
| Investment (I) | 15.5 | 17.0 | 16.8 | 15.7 | 15.9 |
| Residential building | 4.6 | 5.0 | 4.4 | 3.9 | 4.8 |
| Nonresidential structures | 3.7 | 3.9 | 4.2 | 3.0 | 2.8 |
| Equipment and software | 6.2 | 7.3 | 7.7 | 8.3 | 8.2 |
| Change in inventories | 1.0 | 0.8 | 0.4 | 0.5 | 0.1 |
| Government Purchases (G) | 22.4 | 20.9 | 20.6 | 18.8 | 18.2 |
| Federal | 12.3 | 9.1 | 9.4 | 7.2 | 6.2 |
| State and local | 10.1 | 11.8 | 11.2 | 11.5 | 12.0 |
| Net Exports (NX) | 0.3 | −0.5 | −1.9 | −1.3 | −4.1 |
| Exports | 4.9 | 7.5 | 8.3 | 10.6 | 10.0 |
| Imports | 4.6 | 8.0 | 10.2 | 11.9 | 14.1 |

Note: *Figures for each period are averages of quarterly data.*
*Source: Data from FRED database at* http://research.stlouisfed.org/fred2/

According to the consensus in the empirical literature on this subject, however, the effect is relatively small.[5]

**Monetary Policy, Wealth and Consumption Expenditures.** The consensus in macroeconomics is that consumer expenditures depend not only on *current income* but also on *wealth* or *expected average future income.* Holding current income constant, an increase in wealth implies an increase in expected future income or *permanent income.* Thus, an increase in wealth stimulates current consumption.

Stocks (also known as *equities*), bonds, and home equity are important components of household wealth. Monetary policy influences wealth to the extent policy influences stock, bond, and house prices. For example, if the Fed implements stimulative actions that reduce interest rates, stock, bond, and house prices likely rise.

[5] Traditionally, economists have regarded the interest rate as a reward for abstaining from current consumption—that is, the interest rate is a reward for saving. Individuals who save are substituting *future* consumption for *current* consumption. An interest rate change sets off two effects that pull consumption in opposite directions. Assume that real interest rates increase. The rate increase raises the opportunity cost of current consumption by increasing the amount of future goods that can be enjoyed by saving an additional dollar today. Hence, a *substitution effect* occurs. Consumers substitute future consumption for current consumption. Individuals increase current saving. On the other hand, higher interest rates boost the income earned from savings. The greater income earned from savings triggers an *income effect,* which increases the portion of current income spent on consumer goods. In other words, the income effect of higher interest rates reduces saving. If the income effect is equally as powerful as the substitution effect, the net effect of a interest rate increase is unchanged consumption. Only if the substitution effect is stronger than the income effect (an assumption usually made in economic analysis) can we conclude that an increase in interest rates reduces consumption (increases saving).

Wealth increases, stimulating consumption spending. This channel may be summarized as follows:

**M ↑ → i ↓ → Stock, bond, and house prices ↑ → Wealth ↑ → Consumption ↑ → GDP ↑.**

Many economists believe this mechanism contributes appreciably to the power of monetary policy.[6]

**Monetary Policy, Liquidity, and Consumer Durable Goods Expenditures.** Assume you own a portfolio of financial and real assets. The assets differ in their *liquidity*—the ease with which the assets can be converted to money on short notice without appreciable inconvenience and other costs. In general, financial assets such as bank CDs, money market mutual fund shares, bonds, and shares of stock are more liquid than real assets such as houses, cars, and land. If you unexpectedly need cash, you can more easily raise the cash if your portfolio is weighted heavily with financial assets than if your portfolio consists predominantly of illiquid real assets such as real estate and cars.

Big-ticket consumer durables expenditures, then, likely are influenced by the liquidity of the asset portfolios of individuals and firms. The likelihood of financial distress influences consumer confidence and, by extension, consumer purchases of expensive items—that is, consumers may decide to postpone large purchases. Suppose the Fed significantly tightens monetary policy to combat escalating inflation. As interest rates rise, bond prices fall. Stock prices are also likely to decline, reducing the value of financial assets and the share of liquid assets in the overall asset portfolios of individuals. As the liquidity of overall asset portfolios decreases, some individuals likely postpone expenditures on consumer durable goods.

When the Fed implements expansionary policies, interest rates fall. Stock and bond prices rise, and the liquidity of overall asset portfolios increases. As the prospect of financial distress decreases, consumer confidence increases. Expenditures on consumer durables increase, and GDP rises. This channel of monetary influence can be summarized as follows:

**M ↑ → Portfolio liquidity ↑ → Likelihood of financial distress ↓ → Consumer durables expenditures ↑ → GDP ↑.**

This effect applies equally well to purchases of new homes, which are counted in the national income accounts as a form of investment. Expansionary monetary policy actions induce increased stock and bond prices, increase the liquidity of household asset portfolios, reduce households' prospects of financial distress, increase household wealth, and increase individuals' willingness to invest in new housing. This channel is quite similar to the previous example.

**M ↑ → Portfolio liquidity ↑ → Likelihood of financial distress ↓ → Investment in housing ↑ → GDP ↑.**

In summary, monetary policy influences aggregate consumption expenditures and new home purchases by altering interest rates, wealth, and liquidity of households' asset portfolios. Keep in mind that consumption expenditures constitute a

[6] This channel of influence is very important in the Federal Reserve's econometric model. In this model, the influence of monetary policy on consumption through the wealth effect is about the same as that of the money-to-residential-construction channel and four times as much as the influence of the money-interest rate-plant and equipment expenditures channel.

## Exhibit 23-1 Wealth Effect and Consumption Spending

When considering the influence of wealth on consumption expenditures, the single most important asset of the *typical* household is the family home, despite the upward trend in the proportion of U.S. households owning stocks in the past 30 years. The distribution of stock ownership across households is extremely unequal, as indicated in the following table.

**Shares of Aggregate Ownership of Common Stocks, Home Equity, and Net Worth of U.S. Households in 1998**

| Rank in Wealth Distribution | Common Stocks | Housing Equity | Net Worth |
|---|---|---|---|
| Top 1 percent | 48% | 15% | 34% |
| Top 10 percent | 86% | 50% | 69% |
| Bottom 80 percent | 4% | 29% | 19% |

*Source: Survey of Consumer Finances*

Note that the wealthiest 1 percent of U.S. households owns nearly half of all stock market wealth. The wealthiest 10 percent of households owns more than 85 percent. The distribution of ownership of housing equity is less unequal. The wealthiest 10 percent of households owns half of the housing equity. The bottom 80 percent of households owns 29 percent. In studying the effect of stock market wealth on consumption spending, clearly the predominant portion derives from a very small portion of the nation's households. In studying the home equity wealth effect, the behavior of a considerably larger group is involved.

Among empirical studies of the wealth effect, the average estimate of marginal propensity to consume wealth ranges from .02 to .04. A household experiencing a $10,000 increase in wealth increases consumption expenditures by $200 to $400 per year. Using the .02 figure and considering the $10 trillion increase in household stock market wealth during the U.S. bull market of the 1990s, consumption spending at the end of the 1990s was $200 billion (about 2 percent of GDP) higher than would have been the case had stock market wealth remained constant.

However, the magnitude of the wealth effect is highly uncertain. Proponents of the *efficient markets hypothesis* argue that, on average, stock prices correctly anticipate forthcoming changes in economic activity and consumption spending. If the hypothesis is true, changes in consumption spending are correlated with recent changes in wealth *even if the marginal propensity to consume wealth is zero!* Hence, empirical findings purportedly showing the existence of a wealth effect may be spurious. Most economists believe in the wealth effect, but how much of the increase in the consumption share of GDP during the past quarter century was due to the increase in wealth is unclear.

Changes in housing wealth may exert a stronger effect on consumption spending than changes in stock market wealth. Wealth gains due to house price appreciation may be perceived as more "permanent" than similar gains from equities, which can be ephemeral. The continued upward drift of the consumption share of GDP during the stock market meltdown of 2000 to 2002 is consistent with the hypothesis. House prices appreciated strongly in this recent period, offsetting a significant portion of the net loss

*continued*

**Exhibit 23-1** Wealth Effect and Consumption Spending—*cont'd*

of household wealth resulting from the contraction in stock prices (see accompanying figure).

The strength of the wealth effect may depend on whether stocks are held in retirement programs such as IRAs and 401K plans (in which the marginal propensity to consume wealth may be relatively low) or held directly in shares of stock and mutual funds. Finally, for the wealthiest 2 percent of households holding more than half of all stocks and for which the estate tax is a consideration, the marginal propensity to consume wealth may be very high. The opportunity cost of consuming wealth may be low for individuals at the top if the government taxes away perhaps half of any additional wealth at the time of death. Thus, elimination of the estate tax would reduce the magnitude of the wealth effect. Changes in tax legislation are one reason why the wealth effect likely changes over time.

Stock Market Wealth and Home Equity Wealth of U.S. Households*

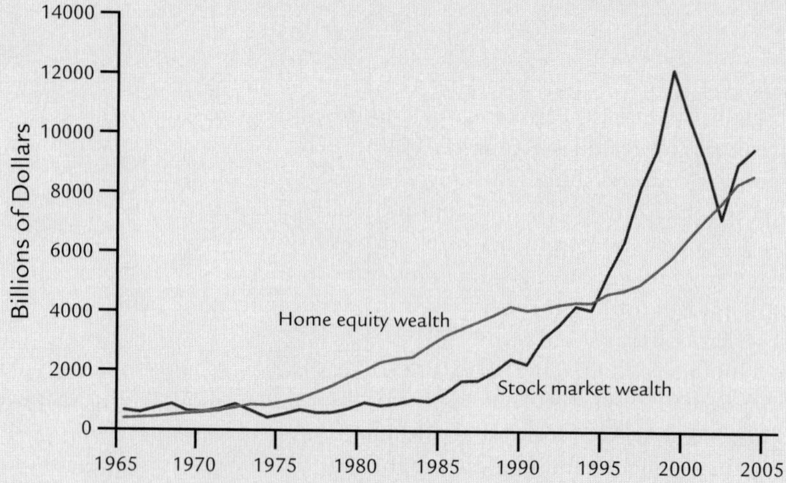


*Stock market wealth shown here excludes value of stocks held in retirement accounts.
*Source: Federal Reserve System,* Flow of Funds Accounts *at* http://www.federalreserve.gov/releases

very large share of GDP. Even fairly modest relative changes in consumption induced by changes in interest rates, wealth, and liquidity can importantly change aggregate consumption expenditures and GDP.

## Monetary Policy and Investment Spending

Table 23-1 indicates that the components of investment expenditures, in order of magnitude, are equipment and software (tractors and computers), residential structures (houses and apartment buildings), nonresidential structures (factories and business buildings), and changes in aggregate business inventories. Monetary policy likely influences each of the four components of investment expenditures.

We can identify four important channels through which monetary policy influences investment spending. The channels are the level of nominal and real interest rates, the availability of bank loans, the role of stock prices in inducing firms to issue new shares of stock, and the role of stock prices in influencing banks to grant loans to prospective buyers of new capital goods. We discuss each of these channels in the following sections.

**Interest Rates and Investment Spending.** The simple Keynesian investment framework outlined earlier in this chapter (the interest rate-investment demand framework) essentially captures this channel. The framework is especially useful for investment in producers' durable equipment such as computers and software and in nonresidential structures. In this framework, firms undertake all investment projects for which the (risk-adjusted) expected real rate of return exceeds the expected real rate of interest. By altering the nominal and expected real rate of interest, monetary policy influences the number of potential investment projects that firms view as profitable. For example, if the Fed reduces interest rates, more projects appear profitable. Firms undertake more of these projects. Investment spending increases.

In the case of new owner-occupied homes (a major share of residential structures), interest rates determine the monthly mortgage payment and therefore the affordability of new homes. If the Fed reduces interest rates, monthly mortgage payments are reduced and more families can afford to purchase new (and more expensive) homes. New home construction is particularly sensitive to interest rates because new home purchases can be postponed if interest rates rise.

The change in the nation's inventories is counted in the national income accounts as a form of investment. Changes in inventories can be voluntary or involuntary. Firms can voluntarily (deliberately) build up inventories if they are optimistic about future sales growth. Or firms may suffer unplanned (involuntary) inventory increases if initial sales forecasts were too optimistic. Costs and benefits are involved in holding inventories. The chief *cost* is the interest expense incurred to finance the inventory, that is, to purchase and hold the goods. The main *benefit* associated with holding larger inventories is the additional sales and customer goodwill gained by maintaining a full complement of goods in stock. If the Fed reduces interest rates, the cost of holding inventories is reduced. Other things being equal, reduced cost of holding inventories leads to a deliberate buildup of inventories—a voluntary increase in inventories that, in turn, stimulates aggregate expenditures by firms. GDP increases.

In summary, this interest-rate channel of monetary policy influence can be described as follows:

$$\mathbf{M} \uparrow \rightarrow \mathbf{i} \downarrow \rightarrow \mathbf{I} \uparrow \rightarrow \mathbf{GDP} \uparrow.$$

**Availability of Bank Credit and Investment Spending.** Large corporations with well-established credit ratings typically choose from several alternative fund sources to finance the purchase of equipment, structures, and inventories. Large corporations can issue commercial paper, bonds, or shares of stock, or they can borrow from banks. Many small firms, however, have no alternative to borrowing from banks. They are not sufficiently large or well established to issue commercial paper, bonds, or stock. Thus, bank loans are crucially important to small firms and individuals with no alternative sources of funds.

When the Fed implements restrictive monetary policy actions, banks tighten their credit standards. Many smaller firms are cut off from funds. Banks deny loans to some smaller firms rather than rationing the limited funds available by allowing the interest rate to move up to market-clearing levels. In other words, banks practice *non-price rationing* of loans. Because many small firms have no alternative sources of funds, the banks' action reduces investment expenditures. Several recent studies have confirmed this phenomenon.

Conversely, when the Fed eases monetary policy by purchasing securities in the open market and expanding bank reserves, banks have additional funds on hand. Banks relax their credit standards and extend loans to firms to which they had previously denied credit. Investment spending increases. The mechanism can be summarized as follows:

**Fed securities portfolio $\uparrow \rightarrow$ Bank reserves $\uparrow \rightarrow$ Bank lending $\uparrow \rightarrow$ I $\uparrow \rightarrow$ GDP $\uparrow$.**

Banks can tighten credit standards on their own initiative, without inducement by restrictive Federal Reserve policy actions. The late 1980s and early 1990s was a period of bank credit tightening (see Exhibit 23-2).

**Tobin's q theory**
theory that monetary policy influences investment spending by altering stock prices and firms' market capitalization relative to replacement cost of capital

**Stock Prices, Firms' Willingness to Issue New Shares of Stock, and Investment Spending.** Professor James Tobin developed a theory of investment known as **Tobin's q theory.** Tobin defined q as follows:

$$q = \frac{\textbf{Market value of firms}}{\textbf{Replacement cost of capital}}$$

In this expression, a firm's market value is the aggregate value the stock market places on the firm's shares of stock, often referred to as the stock's *market capitalization* (number of shares outstanding times the market price per share). The replacement cost of capital is the cost needed to buy the machinery and tools, erect the buildings, and so forth to replicate the firm.

If the stock market places a high valuation on firms, q is high. Firms can issue new stock shares and receive an attractive (high) price for the shares relative to the cost of equipment and buildings the firms are considering replacing or supplementing. Firms likely issue new shares and use the proceeds to buy new plants and equipment. In this case, investment spending is robust. If q is low because stock prices are depressed, firms are reluctant to issue new shares of stock to finance new investment. Investment spending is low.[7]

In Tobin's q theory, monetary policy influences the investment decision by influencing stock prices. Stimulative monetary policy actions reduce interest rates, boost stock prices, raise q, and increase investment expenditures. Schematically,

**M $\uparrow \rightarrow$ i $\downarrow \rightarrow$ Stock prices $\uparrow \rightarrow$ Tobin's q $\uparrow \rightarrow$ Investment spending $\uparrow \rightarrow$ GDP $\uparrow$.**

Tobin's q theory helps explain the enormous contraction in investment spending during the Great Depression of the early 1930s despite extremely low nominal interest rates. By 1933, stock prices were less than 20 percent of their 1929 levels. Tobin's q declined sharply as the market value of firms fell dramatically relative to the replacement cost of capital. Firms were understandably reluctant to issue new shares of stock. Despite extremely low interest rates, net investment in the United States was negative in 1933. In other words, firms did not spend enough on plants and equipment to replace worn-out facilities and tools. The nation's capital stock declined in 1933, an extremely rare occurrence.

---

[7] Suppose a firm is determined to expand. The firm can expand by purchasing an existing firm or by buying new plants and equipment. If stock prices (and q) are low, the firm likely purchases an existing firm. This action does not constitute investment spending because no *new* buildings or equipment are purchased. If stock prices are high, the firm more likely expands through investment expenditures—that is, the firm builds new facilities and buys new equipment.

## Exhibit 23-2 Credit Crunch of the Early 1990s

A *credit crunch* is a sharp reduction in banks' ability or *willingness* to lend to prospective borrowers. Historically, most credit crunches resulted from restrictive Federal Reserve actions. However, evidence suggests the 1990 to 1992 credit crunch resulted from a sharp increase in banks' cautionary behavior unrelated to Federal Reserve policy. In the 18 months following the end of the Gulf War recession—from June 1991 to December 1992—the Federal Reserve pumped up bank reserves by more than 25 percent to jump-start the listless economy. Yet bank loans declined in this period, in sharp contrast to the average annual growth rate of 10.2 percent per year during the 1970s and 1980s. Bank loans typically expand during the early portion of economic expansions. The experience of the early 1990s is unprecedented in post-1950 U.S. history.

Surveys indicate bank loans became more difficult to obtain in the early 1990s. Also, the spread between bank lending rates and banks' cost of funds widened. If the decline in bank lending had resulted from reduced *demand* for loans, the spread should have declined. Clearly banks tightened their credit standards.

Several factors likely contributed to the banks' nervousness. Both individuals and firms had taken on an unprecedented amount of debt in the 1980s, and the increased leverage worried bankers. Also, the late 1980s had witnessed a boom and bust in the real estate sector, resulting in big bank losses. Bank failures were on the rise, and bank regulatory authorities had boosted bank capital standards in response to the deteriorating financial condition of U.S. banks. The recent savings and loan (S&L) debacle and the shocking bankruptcy of the investment banking firm Drexel, Burnham, Lambert in early 1990 were fresh in bankers' minds.

The accompanying figure shows the dramatic slowdown in the growth of bank lending and the corresponding increase in banks' holdings of safe government securities during this period. The bank-induced credit crunch helps account for the unusually slow recovery from the 1990 to 1991 recession and the defeat of incumbent President George H.W. Bush by Bill Clinton in the November 1992 election.

### Commercial Bank Portfolio Management in the Credit Crunch of the Early 1990s (Growth Rate of Bank Loans and Security Holdings)

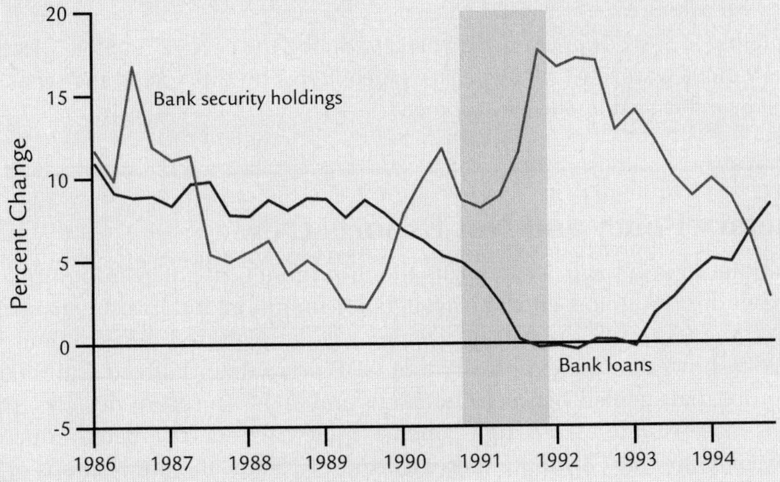


*Source: Data from FRED database at* http://research.stlouisfed.org/fred2/

**Adverse Selection and Moral Hazard, Bank Lending, and Investment Spending.** Monetary policy also influences investment spending in more subtle ways. In Chapters 4 and 11, we learned about the problems associated with asymmetric information in financial markets. *Adverse selection* occurs when individuals most needing loans because of financial difficulties most aggressively seek (and often are granted) loans. Banks are aware of this phenomenon and may deny loans to potential borrowers when banks suspect the problems of adverse selection will be severe. Increases in stock prices and firms' net worth reduce the problem of adverse selection because higher net worth indicates fewer firms are distressed and more firms have adequate collateral to support loans. Financially healthy firms reduce the likelihood of loan defaults, and banks are more willing to grant loans.

Higher net worth reduces the *moral hazard* problem by increasing the prospective cost of failure to a borrowing firm. A firm with a higher net worth has more to lose if things go wrong. Therefore, the firm will be more conservative in requesting loans to finance risky ventures. Expansionary monetary policy—by boosting stock prices and firms' net worth—reduces firms' incentives to undertake highly risky or desperate ventures. Bankers are aware of this improvement in prospective borrowers' net worth and the attendant reduction in the moral hazard problem. Therefore, banks are more willing to grant loans. Investment is stimulated, particularly among small firms. Restrictive monetary policy actions—by reducing stock prices and impairing potential borrowers' balance sheets—increase the moral hazard problem. Bankers are cognizant of the elevated willingness of firms to take long risks. Therefore, banks reduce loans to businesses. Investment spending declines.

In summary, monetary policy influences stock prices, thereby influencing firms' wealth or net worth. Greater wealth or worth, in turn, changes the extent of adverse selection and moral hazard problems, inducing banks to either extend or restrict loans to businesses. In the case of expansionary monetary policy actions, we have the following rather complicated scheme:

**M ↑ → i ↓ → Stock prices ↑ → Net worth ↑ → Adverse selection and moral hazard problems ↓ → Bank loans ↑ → I ↑ → GDP ↑.**

**YOUR TURN**

Suppose U.S. stock prices rise 20 percent during the next 12 months. Discuss the various ways in which aggregate expenditures on U.S. goods and services will be influenced by this development.

## Monetary Policy and Net Exports (NX)

Until about 25 years ago, economists thought monetary policy influenced aggregate expenditures almost entirely through consumption and investment spending. However, the lessons of the past quarter century have altered the economists' view. Table 23-1 shows that the export share of GDP more than doubled and the import share more than tripled between the 1960s and 2004. In recent decades, the U.S. economy has become increasingly "open." Trade barriers have been reduced, and both X/GDP and M/GDP have increased sharply. Thus, the implications of monetary policy for export and import behavior cannot be ignored. Some economists believe the net export channel may be the most powerful channel of monetary influence today.

The key to understanding the influence of monetary policy on net foreign demand for U.S. goods and services (NX) is realizing one fundamental identity—each nation's total transactions with the rest of the world must net out at zero. If the United States imports more goods and services than it exports, the United States must transfer money and securities to the rest of the world. Alternatively stated, if foreign nations acquire more U.S. money and securities (stocks, bonds, and other IOUs) than we acquire from them, then the U.S. must exhibit a deficit in its international trade balance (NX). That is, U.S. imports must exceed U.S. exports. Holding actual flows of money (demand deposits and currency) constant, if net holdings of U.S. assets by foreigners increase by $40 billion in a given year, the U.S. trade deficit must increase by $40 billion.

Monetary policy influences net foreign demand for U.S. goods and services (NX) mostly by influencing U.S. and foreign individuals' and firms' desire to hold U.S. and foreign financial assets. A huge worldwide pool of highly mobile financial capital exists. The funds can be shifted instantaneously to the financial center offering the most attractive expected real rates of return. Monetary policy, by influencing *international capital flows,* influences the exchange rate, which in turn alters net exports.

Suppose the Federal Reserve tightens its monetary policy. U.S. nominal and real interest rates rise. Foreign demand for U.S. interest-bearing financial assets increases, and U.S. demand for foreign financial assets declines. Foreigners must first purchase dollars to purchase U.S. financial assets. The increased foreign demand for dollars (and decreased U.S. demand for foreign currencies) causes the U.S. dollar to appreciate in foreign exchange markets. The value of the U.S. dollar, expressed in units of foreign currencies, rises. U.S. goods become more expensive in foreign markets. Foreign goods become less expensive in the United States. U.S. exports decrease while U.S. imports increase. The U.S. trade surplus (NX) decreases (or the trade *deficit* increases), and aggregate demand for U.S. goods and services declines.

Conversely, if the Fed reduces interest rates, net demand for U.S. financial assets declines. The dollar depreciates. U.S. goods are relatively more attractive to both foreigners and Americans. The decline in the dollar's value stimulates U.S. net exports (NX), boosting aggregate demand for U.S. goods and services. U.S. GDP increases. This channel of monetary policy transmission can be summarized as follows:

$$\mathbf{M \uparrow \rightarrow i \downarrow \rightarrow Exchange\ rate \downarrow (Dollar\ depreciates) \rightarrow (NX) \uparrow \rightarrow GDP \uparrow.}$$

Because the U.S. economy has become more open to international trade since the 1960s and because the post-World War II era of fixed exchange rates gave way to floating rates in the 1970s, changes in NX constitute a more important element in the transmission process of monetary policy today than in earlier times. However, expansion in the worldwide pool of financial capital and the capital's increased mobility may hinder Fed policy effectiveness. For example, as the Fed pushes up interest rates to restrict aggregate demand for U.S. goods and services, inflows of foreign capital moderate the magnitude of the interest rate response. Similarly, when the Fed reduces interest rates via open market security purchases, outflows of financial capital from the United States inhibit the downward movement of U.S. interest rates. Increasing integration of global capital markets may force more vigorous Fed monetary policy actions to achieve a given change in aggregate demand for U.S. goods and services than was the case in earlier times.

# THE MONEY VIEW VERSUS THE CREDIT VIEW

Picture a balance sheet of the aggregate U.S. commercial banking system. Key items on the asset side include cash, deposits at the Federal Reserve, loans, and securities. The liability side of the balance sheet is dominated by checkable deposits (DDO) and savings and time deposits (TD). Large negotiable CDs issued by the nation's larger banks also are listed on the liability side. Under current regulations, banks must maintain reserves (cash and deposits at the Fed) in the amount of a certain percentage of DDO. Currently, non-DDO bank liabilities such as time deposits and large CDs do not have reserve requirements.

**Balance Sheet of All Commercial Banks**

| Assets | Liabilities |
|---|---|
| Cash | DDO |
| Deposits at Fed | TD |
| Loans | Large CDs |
| Securities | |

Almost all economists believe Federal Reserve–induced changes in this balance sheet lead to changes in aggregate expenditures, output, and the price level. However, economists disagree about the details of the process. They disagree about whether we need to look only at the liability side of the balance sheet or look at the asset side as well in order to evaluate the impact of monetary policy. Here, we examine two alternative views of the monetary policy transmission mechanism process: the *money view* and the *credit view.*

## The Money View

**money view**
view that information about the nation's monetary aggregates, obtained from the deposit information on the liability side of the bank balance sheet, is sufficient to predict the impact of monetary policy on aggregate spending and GDP

Monetarist economists have long advocated the traditional **money view.** In the money view, information about the nation's monetary aggregates (M1, M2) obtained largely from the deposit information on the liability side of the bank balance sheet is sufficient to predict the impact of monetary policy on aggregate spending and GDP. Suppose the Fed desires to implement restrictive policy actions, reducing aggregate expenditures to combat inflation. The Fed sells securities in the open market. Essentially, the general public writes checks to the Federal Reserve to purchase the securities. The public does not regard these securities as perfect substitutes for demand deposits. To induce the public to trade their money balances (DDO) for these securities, the Fed must offer higher yields (accept reduced prices) on the securities it wishes to sell.[8] Also, as the checks written to the Fed by the public are cleared, bank reserves decline on a dollar-for-dollar basis. Because required reserves decline only fractionally, banks find themselves holding fewer reserves than they desire. Banks must collectively implement some combination of security sales and loan reductions in order to satisfy reserve requirements. During the bank process of satisfying reserve requirements, the money supply falls and interest rates increase further. The money stock decline and interest rate increases triggered by the Fed's restrictive actions reduces aggregate expenditures through the various channels we have discussed.

[8] If people are to willingly hold fewer DDO, the opportunity cost of holding DDO must increase. A measure of this opportunity cost is the yield that can be obtained on government securities. By offering higher yields (lower prices) on government securities, the Federal Reserve induces the public to hold more securities and less money in the form of DDO.

When the Fed provides new reserves through open market security purchases, banks create new money, either by making additional loans or by purchasing securities from the general public. When the Fed implements restrictive policy actions, banks reduce the money supply by decreasing the number of loans and selling securities. In ignoring the asset side of the balance sheet and focusing only on the liability side (DDO and TD), the "money view" implicitly assumes that the *source* of the money supply change is of little significance. In the money view, an increase in the monetary aggregates (M1 and M2) influences economic activity in approximately the same way, irrespective of whether the money is created through bank lending or through bank security purchases. In other words, the money view ignores the *composition of the asset side* of the bank balance sheet.

## The Lending or Credit View

In recent years, non-monetarist economists have increasingly questioned the "money view." The debate centers on whether the money view's sole concentration on the liability side of the bank balance sheet is a mistake. Today many economists believe that *bank lending,* a crucial item on the asset side of the bank balance sheet, also significantly influences economic activity, above and beyond the role played by *money*. In the **credit view,** an increase in bank loans has a stronger impact on GDP expenditures and economic activity than does an equal amount of bank security purchases, even though both events have the same impact on M1 and M2.[9]

**credit view**
view that an increase in bank loans has a stronger impact on GDP expenditures and economic activity than does an equal amount of bank security purchases, even though both events have the same impact on M1 and M2

Money is created whenever banks grant additional loans. The money supply declines when banks reduce loans. Therefore, you might suspect that the growth of bank loans tracks the growth of M1 and M2 quite strongly over time. If the tracking holds true, ignoring bank loans and focusing on M1 and M2 would make little difference in practice even if bank loans are very important in influencing economic activity. However, Figure 23-3 indicates that the growth rate of bank loans at times differs considerably from the growth rates of the money supply.

Note in the figure that the growth rates of bank lending and M1 are very poorly synchronized. From 1990 to 1993—a recessionary period followed by anemic recovery—M1 growth accelerated strongly while bank loans stagnated. As the economy picked up strength from 1993 to 1995, bank lending accelerated while the growth rate of M1 declined strongly. During the 2001 recession, M1 accelerated while the growth of bank loans slowed sharply. In these instances, bank lending provides a better indicator of economic activity than does M1 growth. Growth rates of bank loans and M2 (not shown) exhibit somewhat higher correlation than growth rates of bank loans and M1. However, several instances when the correlation becomes low or negative occur. In the credit view, bank loans—not the monetary aggregates—drive economic activity.

Two conditions are essential if bank lending is to be an important channel of monetary policy. First, bank loans must be of unique or special importance to borrowers having limited alternative fund sources. In other words, good substitutes for bank loans must be unavailable to a significant group of borrowers. Second, the Fed must be capable of significantly influencing bank lending. From the bank asset management viewpoint, loans and securities must not be perfect substitutes for

[9] In terms of our MV = PY framework of Chapter 22, the "credit view" asserts that money created through bank loans has a higher velocity than does money created through bank security purchases. This follows from the belief that individuals and firms taking out bank loans more likely will spend the proceeds on goods and services than will individuals and firms selling securities to banks. Hence, in the credit view, aggregate expenditures (MV and PY) are stimulated more strongly by an increase in bank lending than by an equal increase in bank security purchases, even though the two bank actions have the same effect on M1 and M2.

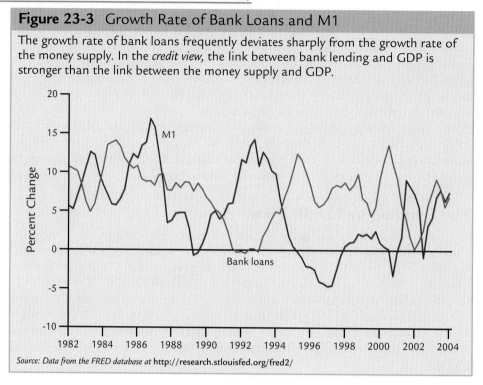

**Figure 23-3** Growth Rate of Bank Loans and M1

The growth rate of bank loans frequently deviates sharply from the growth rate of the money supply. In the *credit view,* the link between bank lending and GDP is stronger than the link between the money supply and GDP.

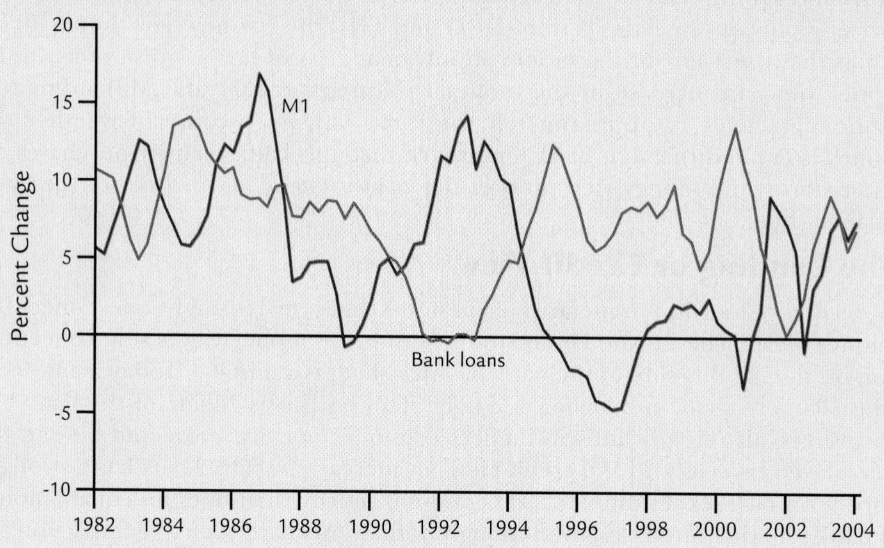


*Source: Data from the FRED database at* http://research.stlouisfed.org/fred2/

each other. Furthermore, from the bank liability management viewpoint, non-reservable sources of funds (such as time deposits and negotiable CDs) must not be close substitutes for reservable sources of funds for banks (DDO).[10]

Banks viewing securities and loans as perfect substitutes may respond to restrictive monetary policy actions by liquidating securities and leaving their loan portfolio intact. In this event, the money supply declines but bank loans do not. Banks viewing non-reservable sources of funds as close substitutes for DDO may respond to loss of DDO and reserves in periods of restrictive Federal Reserve policy by issuing additional negotiable CDs or other non-reservable sources of funds in order to maintain or expand their loans. If banks react in these ways, the Federal Reserve may not be able to control bank lending. A near-consensus exists about the unique or special nature of certain bank loans, but economists disagree about the extent to which the Fed can control bank lending in the short run.

**Are Bank Loans Special?** Because of informational problems in financial markets, alternative forms of finance are imperfect substitutes for individuals and many firms. In fact, alternative sources sometimes are not available to such borrowers. Bank expertise in evaluating and screening loan applicants and in monitoring loan performance enables banks to extend credit to customers (typically individuals and small firms) who find obtaining credit in the open market difficult or impossible. In the *credit view,* bank loans are "special" in that many individuals and smaller firms cannot find other credit sources. Large, established firms with good credit ratings

[10] "Reservable" deposits are deposits subject to reserve requirements. Under current regulations, only DDO are subject to reserve requirements. "Non-reservable" sources of bank funds include savings deposits, small time deposits, negotiable CDs, and eurodollar borrowing.

can borrow in the bond market or commercial paper market. To the extent that such fund sources are close substitutes for bank loans, large firms can maintain desired expenditures even when the Fed tightens credit. However, smaller firms (as well as most individuals) rely entirely on banks for loans and likely are forced to reduce expenditures when the Fed tightens credit and banks respond by reducing lending. In this view, smaller firms absorb the brunt of cutbacks in periods of restrictive Fed policy.[11]

To prevent being denied bank credit in times of monetary stringency, many firms obtain credit lines in advance, in the form of *loan commitments* from banks. Banks are less willing to grant loan commitments to smaller and less established firms. A recent survey indicated 60 percent of firms with more than 50 employees had secured loan commitments, but only 27 percent of smaller firms successfully obtained such commitments. During a period of restrictive monetary policy, small firms without loan commitments are served last or not at all. In summary, a fairly strong consensus exists that bank loans are of crucial importance to a significant class of borrowers.

**Can the Fed Control Bank Lending?** Even given universal agreement that bank loan availability is crucially important to certain borrowers, the lending or credit view breaks down if the Federal Reserve cannot influence bank lending. To the extent that banks respond to restrictive Federal Reserve actions by selling off securities and issuing negotiable CDs and other non-reservable liabilities in order to maintain their supply of loans to the public, the Fed's ability to influence aggregate expenditures is hindered. Studies have shown that banks react at least partly with these actions. A well-known cyclical phenomenon is the rise in the ratio of bank loans to security holdings in business cycle expansions and the decline in the ratio in recessions. Systematically, when economic activity strengthens, banks accommodate increased loan demand by selling securities and issuing negotiable CDs. When economic activity slows and loan demand falls, banks increase their securities holdings and reduce their volume of CDs outstanding. The rates of growth of bank loans and securities from 1982 to 2004 are illustrated in Figure 23-4.

Studies indicate that banks increase issuance of negotiable CDs when economic activity strengthens and the Fed tightens its monetary posture. Banks act to obtain funds that will accommodate their valued customers rather than reduce loans to established customers. Of course, such bank measures in response to restrictive monetary policy actions do not imply Fed policies fail to influence aggregate expenditures. For example, to the extent banks must accept reduced prices for securities they sell to obtain funds to make available to borrowers, banks increase their loan rates. Also, to the extent banks must pay higher interest rates to attract funds through the issue of negotiable CDs, they boost their loan rates to customers. The higher loan rates, in turn, reduce the bank customers' willingness to borrow and spend on goods and services. Hence, bank asset and liability responses to Federal Reserve actions may partially attenuate the effects of monetary policy actions, but few economists deny that monetary policy strongly influences economic activity.

---

[11] A recent study reported that large manufacturing firms with plant and equipment worth more than $1 billion received less than 15 percent of their long-term credit from banks. Firms with capital goods valued between $100 million and $1 billion obtained about 45 percent of long-term credit from banks. Smaller firms obtained approximately 70 percent of their long-term credit from banks. Clearly, small firms are more dependent on banks than are larger firms.

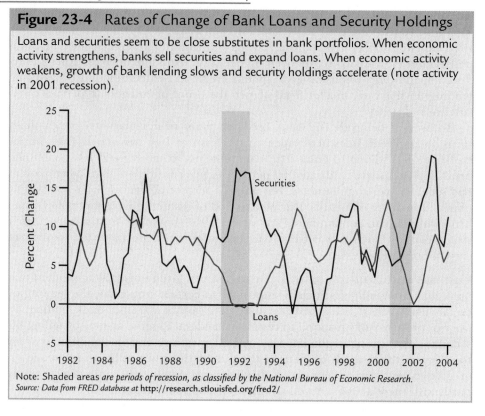

**Figure 23-4** Rates of Change of Bank Loans and Security Holdings

Loans and securities seem to be close substitutes in bank portfolios. When economic activity strengthens, banks sell securities and expand loans. When economic activity weakens, growth of bank lending slows and security holdings accelerate (note activity in 2001 recession).

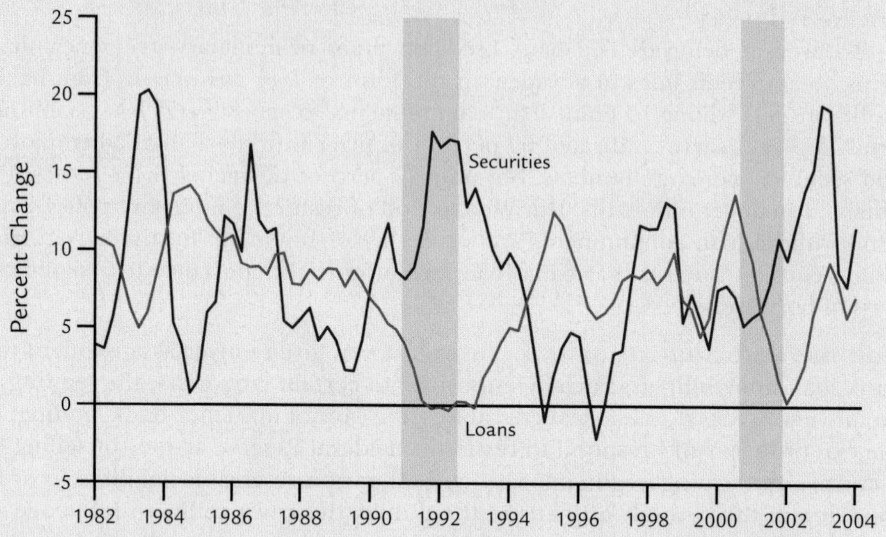


Note: Shaded areas *are periods of recession, as classified by the National Bureau of Economic Research.*
*Source: Data from FRED database at* http://research.stlouisfed.org/fred2/

## CAN MONETARY STIMULUS BE EFFECTIVE WHEN INTEREST RATES ARE ZERO?

In early 2004, the federal funds rate was 1 percent and the economy was sluggish. Some observers worried that the Federal Reserve had only four "bullets" left in its gun. The Fed most commonly changes its fed funds rate target in amounts of 0.25 percent. Four more rate cuts would put the fed funds rate at zero. Given that nominal interest rates are "bounded at zero" (rates cannot be negative as long as people can hold demand deposits or other forms of money without risk), some economists feared the Fed was almost out of ammunition. What if the U.S. economy were to descend into a Japanese-type deflationary quagmire in which output stagnates for an interminable period? With prices falling significantly and nominal interest rates bounded at zero, real interest rates may be too high to generate robust aggregate expenditures. This environment can lead to further price cutting (deflation) and rising unemployment. The accompanying widespread defaults on debt contracts feed the deflationary spiral, exacerbating the problem of high real interest rates. Some observers feared the Federal Reserve would be powerless in such a vicious cycle of deflation, economic contraction, and debt defaults.

Is the Federal Reserve powerless to stimulate economic activity if a zero short-term interest rate is not sufficient to revive aggregate expenditures? You must tread a bit softly on this issue because it involves terrain never before experienced in U.S. history. Yields on short-term Treasury bills were very close to zero in the early 1930s' episode of deflation. However, as we demonstrated in Chapter 17, Federal Reserve policy was far from expansionary in that period, as evidenced by the decline in bank reserves and the dramatic contraction in the U.S. money supply. We cannot be sure of the effect on the economy if the Fed had aggressively purchased securities in the open market and pumped up bank reserves in 1931 and 1932.

Ben Bernanke, an eminent economist and member of the Federal Reserve Board of Governors, addressed this issue in a speech to the National Economists Club. In a slightly tentative tone, Bernanke advanced the hypothesis that the Fed had plenty of tools remaining to extricate the economy from stagnation even if short-term interest rates had reached zero and *deflation* like that experienced in Japan in the past decade had set in.

First, Bernanke pointed out that with short-term rates at zero, long-term rates still might be 2 or 3 percent. Bernanke argued that the Fed could start purchasing long-term government bonds, pushing up bond prices and reducing their yields. Also, Bernanke suggested that the Fed could purchase corporate bonds in an effort to reduce bond yields, although the Fed would have required statutory authority to do so. Long-term interest rates influence household purchases of new homes and business investment spending. Expectations theories of term structure indicate a central bank will have trouble pushing down *long-term* yields unless the bank engineers a reduced outlook for future short-term yields. However, little doubt exists that the Fed can reduce long-term bond yields if the Fed is willing to permit the money supply to expand dramatically. If the Fed announces it will buy unlimited quantities of long-term government bonds at a specific high price (and corresponding low yield), the Fed virtually guarantees these bonds will not sell at lower prices (higher yields) than its announced target price and yield. Who would sell bonds at lower prices than the Fed is paying?

Second, Bernanke pointed out that decisions to buy investment goods (plant, equipment, houses) and consumer durable goods (cars, furniture) depend not on *nominal* interest rates but on *ex ante real* interest rates. As long as the Federal Reserve can engineer an appreciable increase in the nation's price level by pumping up the money supply, the Fed produces sufficiently negative *real* interest rates to stimulate large expenditures. But here, Bernanke should tread a bit softly. Inflation results from rapid increases in aggregate expenditures. Yes, the Fed can engineer a rapid increase in the money supply, but how can we be sure the increased money supply will lead to a robust increase in expenditures in a stagnant economy with interest rates already at zero? The Fed increases the money supply by buying securities from the general public. Suppose the public trades their securities to the Federal Reserve for money because the yield on the securities is negligible. How can we be certain the public will spend the new Fed-injected money on goods and services rather than simply hold the money? How can we be sure the income velocity of the *additional* money created in a zero-interest rate environment is not zero?

If the Fed can move expected real interest rates substantially into negative territory when nominal rates are zero by creating inflation, the Fed likely induces increased expenditures on consumer durables, new construction, and producers' durable goods (computers, etc.). In addition, lower real interest rates in the United States likely lead to depreciation of the U.S. dollar in the foreign exchange market and a corresponding increase in net U.S. exports (NX). The crucial question is whether the Fed can always reverse a deflationary cycle of falling prices and falling output through monetary stimulus. The answer is not obvious, and the proposition has never been tested. As Bernanke admits, the wisest approach is for policymakers to ensure deflation never gets started in the first place. Given the uncertainties associated with monetary policy, in the early years of the twenty-first century most economists recommended that the Fed, if it were to err, should err on the side of monetary stimulus rather than monetary restraint.

# SUMMARY

Monetary policy influences each of the four components of aggregate GDP expenditures: consumption, investment, government purchases, and net exports. Early Keynesian economists restricted monetary policy's influence to the interest rate-investment expenditures channel. In the early monetarists' view, monetary policy influences the economy by creating a disequilibrium between actual and desired money holdings. In this view, an increase in the money supply upsets the equilibrium and directly increases expenditures on real and financial assets. Early monetarists were criticized for failing to indicate more precisely the details

**Figure 23-5** Transmission Mechanism of Monetary Policy

Monetary policy actions influence economic activity through numerous channels.

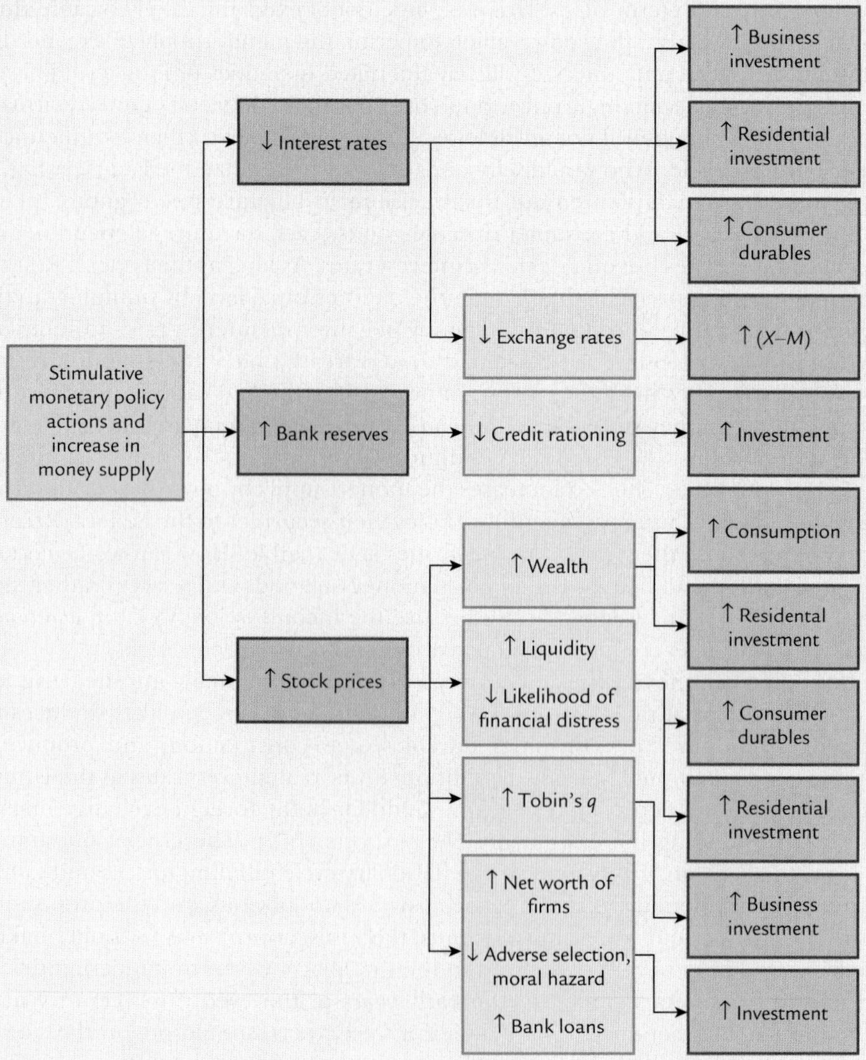

of their transmission mechanism. Today, economists believe monetary policy influences the economy through *numerous* channels. They believe monetary policy works its magic by influencing stock, bond, and house prices (hence, wealth), exchange rates, borrowers' balance sheets, and interest rates. The conduct of monetary policy is complicated by the changing influence of the channels of monetary policy over time. For example, the role of residential construction in the monetary policy transmission process likely has declined in the past 25 years, while the roles of the wealth effect and the international trade balance (X-M) have increased. Figure 23-5 summarizes the various channels through which monetary policy influences aggregate expenditures and economic activity. Study this figure carefully to consolidate your understanding of the various channels of monetary influence discussed in this chapter.

## YOUR TURN ANSWERS

PAGE 540

Because consumption spending depends on wealth as well as disposable income, consumption likely will be stimulated by increased wealth. Because stocks are relatively liquid compared to real assets, consumption likely will be stimulated by the overall increased liquidity of household asset portfolios. Investment expenditures will be stimulated through several channels. Tobin's q is directly increased by the elevation in stock market capitalization, resulting in corporations' increased willingness to issue new shares of stock and use the proceeds to buy new plant and equipment. Because of the improved balance sheets and net worth of prospective borrowers and the resulting reduction in adverse selection and moral hazard problems, bank lending to businesses increases, stimulating investment spending by small firms and other borrowers dependent on banks for loans.

## KEY TERMS

transmission mechanism of monetary policy
Tobin's q theory
money view
credit view

# STUDY QUESTIONS

1. Your company is considering an investment project that will generate after-tax cash flows of $1,000 per year for the next 3 years (the project then will be scrapped, with no salvage value). The cost of the investment is $2,500. Assuming the market interest rate is 10 percent, use the present value formula provided in this chapter to calculate the value of the project. Would you make the investment? If the Fed reduces interest rates to 7 percent, would you make the investment? Explain.

2. Following the terrorist attacks in New York City and Washington, DC, on September 11, 2001, the Federal Reserve immediately engaged in large open market purchases of government securities. What was the Fed seeking to accomplish?

3. "The stock market crash of 1929 was an important contributing element in the Great Depression of the 1930s." On what foundations does this claim rest? Explain.

4. Explain all the ways you can think of that Federal Reserve policy is capable of influencing consumption expenditures.

5. Suppose the Fed sharply reduces the money supply in an effort to combat rising inflation. List and briefly explain all the ways this action might influence investment expenditures on producers' durable equipment (equipment and software).

6. Why might monetary policy actions influence investment spending by small firms differently than investment spending by large firms? Explain.

7. Your firm is experiencing tremendous growth in sales. A major expansion is being contemplated. Before your final commitment, suppose the Fed implements highly restrictive monetary policy actions, and stock prices fall sharply. In terms of Tobin's q analysis, discuss your firm's alternatives and how they might affect your firm's investment decision.

8. In the early 1970s, the United States and other nations moved from a system of fixed exchange rates to a floating-rate system. How do you suppose this move affected the relative importance of the various channels of monetary transmission? How do you suppose it influenced the overall strength of monetary policy? Explain.

9. Suppose the stock market rises 25 percent in the next year. Explain how the following components of GDP expenditures would be affected.
   - **A.** Consumer durables
   - **B.** Consumer nondurables
   - **C.** Consumer services
   - **D.** Residential investment
   - **E.** Investment in new plants and equipment

10. Explain how a Federal Reserve–initiated increase in interest rates affects:
    - **A.** Consumer durables expenditures
    - **B.** Consumer services expenditures
    - **C.** Consumer nondurables expenditures
    - **D.** Residential investment
    - **E.** Nonresidential investment
    - **F.** Inventory investment
    - **G.** Net U.S. exports (X-M)

11. Picture a scenario in which the U.S. consumer price index is falling at a rate of 3 percent per year, real output and employment are declining, and the federal funds rate, discount rate, and Treasury bill yield all are zero. Do you believe the Federal Reserve has sufficient power to boost the economy out of this deflationary slump? Explain why or why not.

# ADDITIONAL READING

- On the monetary transmission mechanism, a good place to start is the Fall 1995 issue of *The Journal of Economic Perspectives,* which includes five articles on the subject. More recently, the May 2002 issue of Federal Reserve Bank of New York *Economic Policy Review* is devoted to "Financial Innovation and Monetary Transmission."
- For an analysis of the change in the ways interest rates influence economic activity, see Gordon H. Sellon, Jr., "The Changing U.S. Financial System: Some Implications for the Monetary Transmission Mechanism," Federal Reserve Bank of Kansas City *Economic Review* 2002, No. 1, pp. 5–35. Also, see Eileen Mauskopf, "The Transmission Channels of Monetary Policy: How They Have Changed," *Federal Reserve Bulletin,* December 1990, pp. 985–1008, and Benjamin Friedman, "The Role of Judgment and Discretion in the Conduct of Monetary Policy: Consequences of Changing Financial Markets," in Federal Reserve Bank of Kansas City, *Changing Capital Markets: Implications for Monetary Policy,* 1993, pp. 151–196. Also, the entire May/June 1995 issue of the Federal Reserve Bank of St. Louis *Review* is devoted to an analysis of the channels of monetary policy.
- An excellent survey on the role of credit is Ben Bernanke, "Credit in the Macroeconomy," Federal Reserve Bank of New York *Quarterly Review,* Spring 1993, pp. 50–70.
- Work supporting the view that credit is an important determinant of economic activity is presented in Ben Bernanke and Alan Blinder, "The Federal Funds Rate and the Channels of Monetary Transmission," *American Economic Review,* September 1992, pp. 901–921, and Anil Kashyap, Jeremy Stein, and David Wilcox, "Monetary Policy and Credit Conditions: Evidence from the Composition of External Finance," *American Economic Review,* March 1993, pp. 78–98.
- Evidence that money dominates bank credit as an indicator of forthcoming economic activity is presented by Christina Romer and David Romer, "New Evidence on the Monetary Transmission Mechanism," *Brookings Papers on Economic Activity,* 1990, No. 1, pp. 149–213. Evidence supporting a strong effect of bank credit on small firms is demonstrated in Mark Gertler and Simon Gilchrist, "Monetary Policy, Business Cycles, and the Behavior of Small Manufacturing Firms," *Quarterly Journal of Economics,* May 1994, pp. 309–340.
- The hypothesis that a bank capital shortage produced the credit crunch of 1990 to 1992 is advanced in Ben Bernanke and Cara Lown, "The Credit Crunch," *Brookings Papers on Economic Activity,* 1992, No. 2, pp. 205–239.
- An excellent overview of the wealth effect is provided by James Poterba, "Stock Market Wealth and Consumption," *Journal of Economic Perspectives* Spring 2000, pp. 99–118. Also see Martha Starr-McCluer, "Stock Market Wealth and Consumer Spending," *Economic Inquiry,* January 2002, pp. 69–79.
- Finally, on the implications of the zero bound on interest rates on the efficacy of monetary policy, read the views of numerous outstanding economists in the excellent conference volume, "Monetary Policy in a Low-Inflation Environment," *Journal of Money, Credit, and Banking,* November 2000, Part 2.

Chapter 24

# DIFFERING VIEWS ON THE APPROPRIATE CONDUCT OF MONETARY POLICY

The Federal Reserve reacted aggressively and immediately to the U.S. economic downturn in the spring of 2001. During 2001 and 2002, the Fed reduced its short-term interest rate target 12 times, dropping the rate from 6.5 to 1.25 percent. In response to the "jobless recovery" of 2002 to 2003, the Fed further reduced the rate to 1 percent in June 2003, the lowest level in 45 years. Many economists applaud the Fed's active efforts to stabilize economic activity, but other economists question the wisdom of the Fed's efforts. How should the Federal Reserve respond to business cycle fluctuations?

Some economists believe the economy is inherently unstable because of frequent shocks to the nation's aggregate demand and aggregate supply conditions. In the absence of active monetary and fiscal policies counteracting these shocks, the economy is subject to undesirable and unnecessary fluctuations in output, employment, and price level. The economists believe the Federal Reserve should "lean against the wind." That is, the Fed should implement stimulative policies when the economy weakens and restrictive measures when the economy overheats and experiences rising inflation. Economists advocating this hands-on approach are **policy activists.**

**policy activists** individuals who believe active use of monetary and fiscal policies contribute positively to economic stability

Other economists believe the economy is inherently stable. They argue that most of the severe inflations and economic contractions resulted from policy mistakes rather than fluctuations in aggregate supply and aggregate demand due to forces beyond the Federal Reserve's control. Furthermore, free market economies contain self-correcting mechanisms that automatically return the nation's equilibrium output level to the natural or full-employment level in a reasonably short interval. These economists dispute the view that monetary policy activism improves the economy. Such economists are **policy non-activists.**

**policy non-activists** individuals who believe active use of monetary and fiscal policies do not lead to increased economic stability

In this chapter, we examine two important issues pertaining to the conduct of monetary policy. First, should monetary policy be active or passive? Second, should the central bank be free to conduct discretionary policy as the central bank sees fit, or should the central bank be governed by a monetary policy *rule* preventing the central bank from implementing discretionary policies? Economists disagree about these issues to a surprising extent.

## SHOULD MONETARY POLICY BE ACTIVE OR PASSIVE?

In Chapter 20, we learned that forces underlying the aggregate demand (AD) and aggregate supply (AS) curves determine the nation's equilibrium output and price level. The resulting equilibrium output level frequently differs significantly from the economy's *natural* or *full-employment output level*—the output level produced when the prevailing unemployment rate equals the economy's non-accelerating inflation rate of unemployment (NAIRU). As discussed in Chapter 20, the NAIRU is the lowest unemployment rate that can be sustained without triggering an increase in the ongoing rate of inflation. The NAIRU level changes with changing demographics and other forces.

Figure 24-1 reviews these concepts. In the left-hand portion of the figure, equilibrium output ($Y_{E1}$) lies below the natural or full-employment output level ($Y_N$). In this instance, a *recessionary gap* exists ($Y_N - Y_{E1}$). Given the aggregate supply conditions, aggregate demand is not strong enough to create full employment; the unemployment rate exceeds the NAIRU. In the right-hand portion of the figure, the equilibrium output level ($Y_{E2}$) exceeds the full-employment output level ($Y_N$), resulting in an *inflationary gap* ($Y_{E2} - Y_N$). Excessive aggregate demand puts upward pressure on the nation's inflation rate; the unemployment rate lies below the NAIRU.

The appropriate prescription for these two situations appears straightforward. When a recessionary gap prevails, why not implement expansionary monetary policy actions that shift AD rightward, boost equilibrium output, and return people to work? When the economy is overheated and an inflationary gap prevails, why not implement restrictive monetary policy measures that shift AD leftward, reduce equilibrium output, and arrest the inflationary pressures? In the context of Figure 24-1, the problem looks simple and unambiguous. However, in reality matters are not so simple. First, economists and policymakers are *uncertain* about many factors: the shapes and positions of the AD and AS curves; the direction and strength of non-policy forces currently shifting the AD and AS curves; and the *dynamics*—that is, the speed with which the curves shift in response to policy actions and non-policy developments, and the speed with which actual output and the price level responds to shifts in the AD and AS curves. Finally, policymakers and professional economists are uncertain about the continuously changing levels of $Y_N$ and NAIRU.

Given all these uncertainties, the Federal Reserve inevitably makes mistakes when it actively conducts monetary policy. Economists supporting policy activism believe the costs of the Fed's occasional mistakes are more than offset by the benefits

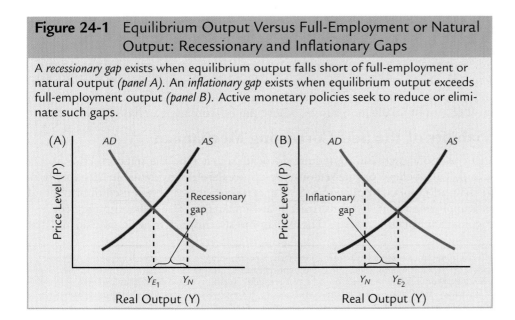

**Figure 24-1** Equilibrium Output Versus Full-Employment or Natural Output: Recessionary and Inflationary Gaps

A *recessionary gap* exists when equilibrium output falls short of full-employment or natural output *(panel A)*. An *inflationary gap* exists when equilibrium output exceeds full-employment output *(panel B)*. Active monetary policies seek to reduce or eliminate such gaps.

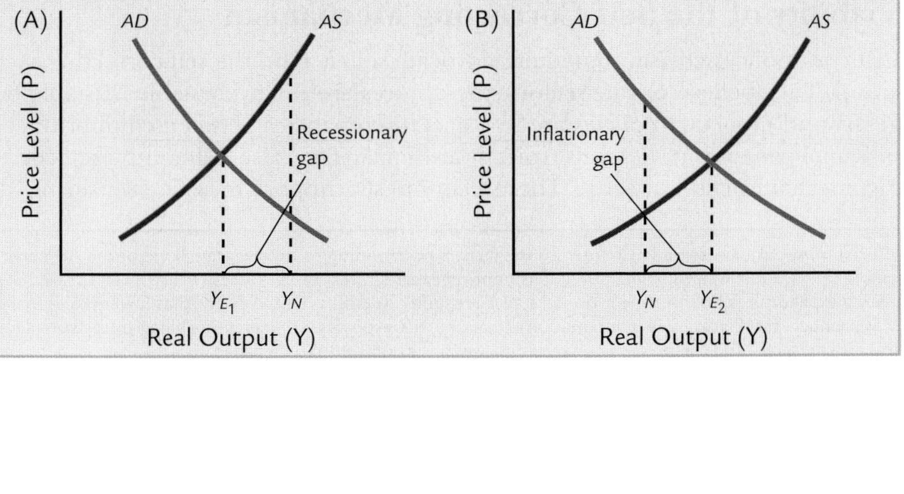

of increased economic stability typically resulting from Federal Reserve policies. Economists who reject policy activism believe most past major economic fluctuations resulted from policy errors. Therefore, they conclude that a non-activist policy is more conducive to economic stability than an activist policy.

Economists advocating abandonment of monetary policy activism defend their position on two grounds. First, they believe the economy contains powerful *self-correcting mechanisms* that, in the absence of Federal Reserve efforts to stabilize the economy, automatically return output to full-employment levels. Hence, they believe active policies are unnecessary. Second, they believe discretionary efforts to manage the AD curve will be ineffective because of the uncertainties just mentioned and for other reasons. They believe monetary policy activism destabilizes output and employment, leading to significantly higher average inflation rates relative to a non-activist policy. We examine these two arguments, beginning with the proposition that stabilization policies are unnecessary because of the economy's self-correcting mechanism.

## Self-Correcting Mechanism

In theory, as we indicated in Chapter 20, free market economies have an inherent tendency toward self-correction that automatically eliminates recessionary and inflationary gaps over time. This mechanism, which stems from wage and price level flexibility, can be reviewed with the aid of Figure 24-1.

Assume output initially is at $Y_{E1}$ in the left-hand portion of the figure. The nation's unemployment rate is 7 percent—well above the NAIRU of perhaps 5 percent. A recessionary gap exists. The existence of involuntary unemployment implies disequilibrium in the labor market. Wages fall because of an excess labor supply at existing wages. The decline in wages shifts the AS curve rightward, and this process continues as long as the unemployment rate exceeds the NAIRU. As the AS curve shifts rightward, the price level declines, and the economy moves down the AD curve.[1] Given unfettered and competitive labor markets, the recessionary gap automatically self-destructs over time.

A similar process causes an inflationary gap to self-correct automatically. In the right-hand portion of the figure, equilibrium output ($Y_{E2}$) exceeds full-employment output ($Y_N$), and the unemployment rate is *below* the NAIRU. An inflationary gap exists. At prevailing wages, the quantity of labor demanded exceeds the quantity of labor supplied. Wages and raw-material prices rise due to the shortage of workers and materials. As long as $Y_E$ exceeds $Y_N$, these forces persistently shift the AS curve leftward. Over time, rising prices reduce wealth and unleash the other effects that move the economy upward to the left along the nation's AD curve. The equilibrium level of output finally moves to $Y_N$, where the inflationary gap has self-destructed.

## Viability of the Self-Correcting Mechanism

Critics of policy activism sometimes advocate reliance on the self-correcting mechanism. They believe private-sector expenditures are relatively stable. If stable budgetary and monetary policies are in place, discrepancies between equilibrium and full-employment output levels typically are small. They also believe the self-correcting mechanism is powerful. These economists support measures ensuring that

[1] Recall from our discussion in Chapter 20 the factors contributing to the negative slope of the AD curve. Falling prices boost wealth, stimulating consumption expenditures. Lower prices reduce interest rates, stimulating expenditures on investment projects and consumer durables. To the extent that lower prices make U.S. products more attractive in international markets, net exports (NX) increase. Falling prices stimulate real expenditures, and the process continues boosting output until $Y_N$ is reached.

wages and other input prices are fully flexible in both directions to facilitate the self-correcting mechanism.

Keynesian economists and other policy activists believe wages and other input prices tend to be "sticky" in the short run, especially on the downside. They believe wages are very resistant or slow to decline, even in periods of substantial unemployment. Economists have developed many theories explaining this stickiness. One explanation relies on the existence of contracts, minimum wage statutes, unions, and other institutional forces that impede the downward flexibility of wages. Another theory argues that workers have a profound psychological resistance to pay cuts. Yet another theory views employers as reluctant to cut wages for fear of alienating and losing their most productive (and marketable) workers. Whatever the cause, the facts indicate that wages *are* sticky. Thus, the self-correcting mechanism may require an intolerably long time to function, especially in recessionary gaps.[2] Largely because of wage stickiness, policy activists call for expansionary monetary policy measures when the unemployment rate appreciably exceeds the NAIRU. They advocate monetary restraint when aggregate demand is excessive and the unemployment rate is below or threatens to fall below the NAIRU.

Policy non-activists believe that—at best—active monetary policy is ineffective in reducing economic fluctuations. More realistically, they believe active monetary policies are *perverse* because the policies result in higher average inflation rates and destabilize economic activity—that is, the policies amplify business cycle swings.

## PROBLEMS CONFRONTING MONETARY POLICY ACTIVISM

Several problems make the successful conduct of active monetary policies more difficult than suggested by glancing at Figure 24-1. Considerable uncertainty exists regarding the *positions, slopes,* and *dynamics* associated with the AD and AS curves and the NAIRU level. Importantly, fairly long lags exist between the time a shock occurs to the nation's AD or AS curve and the time a Federal Reserve policy implemented in response to the shock counteracts the shock's effects. These lags are variable—they change over time. Given these long and variable lags, successful conduct of active monetary policy requires the Fed to forecast the state of the economy a significant distance in the future. But economic developments are impossible to predict. All of these factors render successful monetary policy activism difficult.

### Problems Posed by Lags of Monetary Policy

In the monetarist and other policy non-activist viewpoints, three types of lags make implementation of effective countercyclical policies unlikely. These lags are the recognition lag, the implementation lag, and the impact lag.

**recognition lag**
time that elapses between the point when policy actions ideally would have been implemented (discovered only with hindsight) and the point at which policy-making officials become aware of the need for action

**Recognition Lag.** The **recognition lag** is the time that elapses between the point when policy actions ideally would have been implemented (discovered only with hindsight) and the point at which policy-making officials become aware of the need

[2] Some Keynesians also view the aggregate demand curve as relatively steep, which reduces the efficacy of falling wages as a self-correcting mechanism. If the wealth effect (an important channel through which falling wages and prices stimulate real expenditures) is relatively weak, a big decline in the price level is needed to produce a large enough effect on expenditures to return output to full-employment levels. But deflation (falling prices) introduces other serious problems, for example, debt defaults and associated economic disruptions. Hence, even if prices were *perfectly flexible* on the downside, Keynesians do not consider the so-called *automatic correction mechanism* viable for returning the economy to full employment.

for action. Key economic data (gross domestic product [GDP], industrial production, and so forth) become available only periodically rather than continuously and often are revised months later. The changing data and the imperfect and often conflicting nature of our economic indicators render the recognition lag inevitable. Policymakers (or economists) may not become aware of a recession until several months after the recession has started.

**implementation lag**
time that elapses between the point when a need for policy action is recognized and the point at which the appropriate policy is implemented

**Implementation Lag.** The **implementation lag** is the time that elapses between the point when a need for policy action is recognized and the point at which the appropriate policy is implemented. In the case of monetary policy, the lag normally is quite brief. The Federal Open Market Committee (FOMC) meets approximately every 6 weeks for decision-making purposes. Emergency meetings are called if needed. The Chairman of the Board of Governors sometimes is authorized to adjust monetary policy between meetings as new developments arise. In this aspect, monetary policy is superior to fiscal policy. Implementation lag of fiscal policy tends to be considerably longer because both houses of Congress and the President are involved. Political obstacles often impede implementation of timely fiscal policy actions.

If unemployment is high, elected officials may agree that a tax cut is appropriate but likely disagree on the *design* of the tax cut—that is, whose taxes should be cut the most.

**impact lag**
time that elapses between the point when policy action is implemented and the point at which the policy begins to influence the nation's GDP

**Impact Lag.** The **impact lag** is the time that elapses between the point when policy action is implemented and the point at which the policy begins to influence the nation's GDP. Monetary policy influences GDP with a significant lag because the policy first must influence such variables as interest rates and wealth. Business investment spending, housing construction, and other forms of investment expenditures respond to interest rate changes with a lag. Consumption expenditures respond to changes in wealth and interest rates with a lag. Aggregate expenditures influence production (and GDP) with a slight lag. Monetarists emphasize that monetary policy influences GDP with a long and *variable* lag. The length of this lag is estimated at 6 to 24 months, and the average of these estimates is 9 to 12 months.

**Illustration of Problems Posed by Lags of Monetary Policy.** The problems posed by the three lags can be illustrated through an example. Consider the case of antirecessionary monetary policy illustrated in Figure 24-2.

In the figure, the economy peaks at time $t_0$, and a recession ensues. In retrospect, monetary policy stimulus at time $t_0$ would have been helpful.[3] However, owing to the conflicting evidence suggested by the various indicators and the fact that GDP figures are tabulated only quarterly and revised later, the need for monetary policy stimulus is not clearly established until time $t_1$. The time that elapses between $t_0$ and $t_1$ is the recognition lag.

Unfortunately, expansionary policy measures may not be instituted immediately at time $t_1$. Differing FOMC member viewpoints about the relative costs of unemployment and inflation, political considerations, or bureaucratic inertia may delay implementation of stimulative policies until time $t_2$. The time between $t_1$ and $t_2$ is the implementation lag. Note that the economy is approaching the trough of the business cycle when expansionary policy measures finally are implemented.

---

[3] Because of the impact lag, stimulative policies in a perfect world would be implemented *before* time $t_0$. That would require the Fed to implement actions based on economic *forecasts* rather than actual economic developments. Such a Fed move could prove highly unpopular because the move might involve restrictive actions during a period of fairly high unemployment—in the middle of an economic expansion, for example.

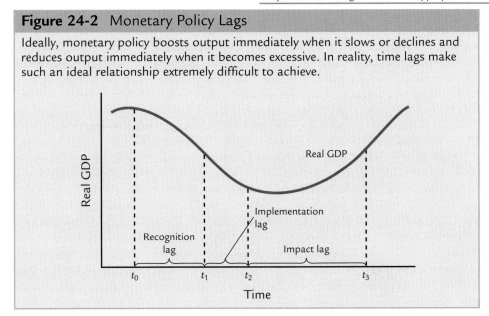

**Figure 24-2** Monetary Policy Lags

Ideally, monetary policy boosts output immediately when it slows or declines and reduces output immediately when it becomes excessive. In reality, time lags make such an ideal relationship extremely difficult to achieve.

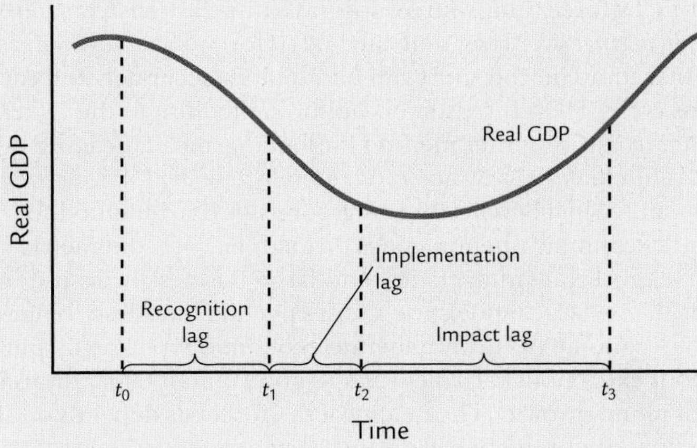


Considerably more time has elapsed by the time expansionary policy actions begin to influence GDP at time $t_3$. The time between $t_2$ and $t_3$ is the impact lag. Note that the stimulative measures begin to take effect after the recession has given way to solid economic expansion. The economy already has gathered momentum, and the need for additional stimulus is dubious. Monetary stimulus that takes effect at time $t_3$ likely accelerates the pace of expansion, possibly causing a rapid climb to full-employment output and triggering inflationary bottlenecks and an ensuing recession. In this way, monetary policy stimulus actually may endanger the economic expansion. Good intentions may produce perverse policies.

We now begin to see the challenges posed to the Fed's conduct of active monetary policy. The genuine possibility exists that active policies will be *procyclical* rather than *countercyclical*—that is, the policies may *amplify* rather than *reduce* cyclical fluctuations. Active policies may shorten economic expansions. The longer and more variable the policy lags, the greater the problems encountered in trying to "fine tune" the economy. Given that the median post-1950 recession lasted only 11 months, a modest error in the timing of monetary policy actions could destabilize the economy.

## Problems Posed by Difficulties of Forecasting

Assume the recognition lag is extremely short, and the Fed implements policies immediately upon recognizing the need for action. Because of the impact lag, for the Fed to effectively implement an activist policy, the Fed must have a reasonably good forecast of economic conditions 6 months to 1 year in the future in the absence of policy action. Unfortunately, predicting future economic conditions is a daunting task given the current state of the forecasting art. Turning points in the business cycle are notoriously difficult to forecast. Economists use several methods to generate information about future economic phenomena. These methods include surveys, use of leading indicators of economic activity, and forecasts generated by macroeconometric models.

Numerous surveys reveal expectations of households, professional economists, and other entities about likely future economic developments. The University of

Michigan conducts a monthly survey of some 500 households to obtain their expectations about inflation, unemployment, and numerous other variables. The Survey of Professional Forecasters, conducted by the Federal Reserve Bank of Philadelphia, obtains quarterly forecasts pertaining to real GDP growth, unemployment, inflation, and other variables. The forecasts are made by individuals who make their living by forecasting. Survey forecasts often are *unbiased* in that they predict correctly *on average* over long time intervals. However, survey forecasts often are considerably inaccurate in the short run and seldom accurately call turning points in the business cycle. Therefore, surveys are of limited use to the Federal Reserve.

*Leading indicators* are another method for looking ahead. Leading indicators are data series that fluctuate in advance of economic activity. Like surveys, leading indicators often fail to signal cyclical turning points. A third method for gleaning insight into future economic phenomena is through macroeconometric models. The Federal Reserve, government agencies, and large business firms use macroeconometric models. These large models use a series of equations describing various components of the economy. You can generate economic forecasts by plugging in assumptions about exogenous variables such as government expenditures, oil prices, and the rate of money growth. The quality of the forecasts depends on the accuracy of the assumptions about the behavior of the exogenous variables.

A few examples illustrate the shortfalls of economic forecasting. First, no one predicted the nation's worst catastrophe—the Great Depression of the 1930s. Irving Fisher, the greatest American economist of the times, made at least two infamous predictions. First, as stock prices reached stratospheric levels in 1929, he claimed that the market had reached a "permanently high plateau." (Four years later, the market had lost more than 80 percent of its value.) Second, about midway through the depression, Fisher erroneously predicted an imminent recovery. About a half century later, the most severe U.S. economic contraction since the Great Depression occurred from 1981 to 1982. Throughout the 1981–1982 recession, the average four-quarter-ahead unemployment rate forecasts of professional economists proved to be too low by at least a full percentage point. In short, economic forecasting is still a relatively primitive and unreliable art.

## HAS THE FEDERAL RESERVE BEEN A DESTABILIZING INFLUENCE?

If the economy is subject to frequent and substantial aggregate supply and aggregate demand shocks and the automatic adjustment mechanisms are slow to function, the case for monetary policy activism is strengthened. If the shocks are relatively minor and the self-correcting mechanisms operate effectively, the case for policy activism is weakened. In practice, the Federal Reserve has long conducted active policy. An interesting and contentious issue is the following: Has the Fed historically been a stabilizing or destabilizing influence? Unfortunately, examining the historical record may not resolve the controversy because identifying the sources of economic fluctuations is difficult. Furthermore, even if the Federal Reserve's historical destabilizing influence on balance is definitively established, you can argue that the Fed has learned from past mistakes and that the Fed's future performance likely will be superior to past performance. Many economists believe the Fed's performance has improved appreciably since the early 1980s.

Studying the pattern of fluctuations in U.S. output over a long period of time is pertinent. Figure 24-3 illustrates the annual rates of change of U.S. real GDP each year from 1890 to 2003.

**Figure 24-3** Annual Rates of Change in Real GDP from 1890 to 2003

Fluctuations in output appear to have been smaller and recessions considerably milder in the past half century than in the previous 60 years.

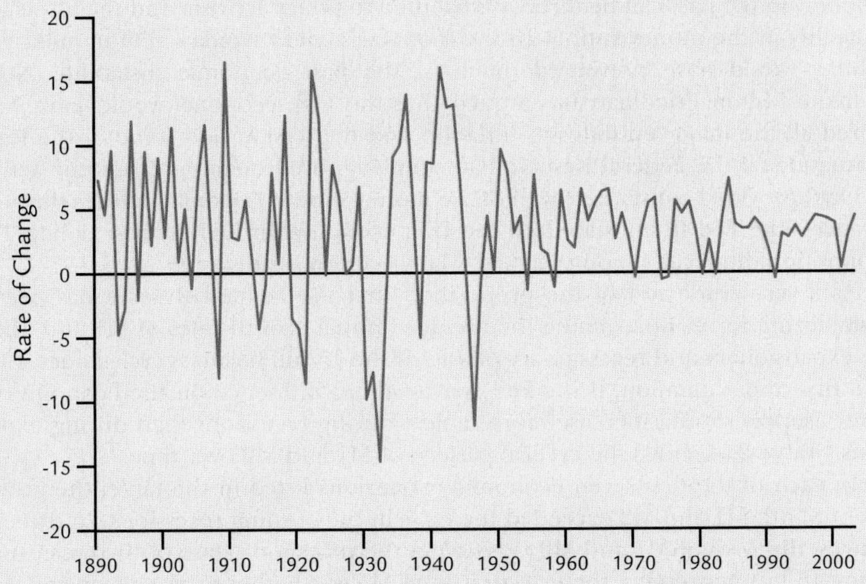

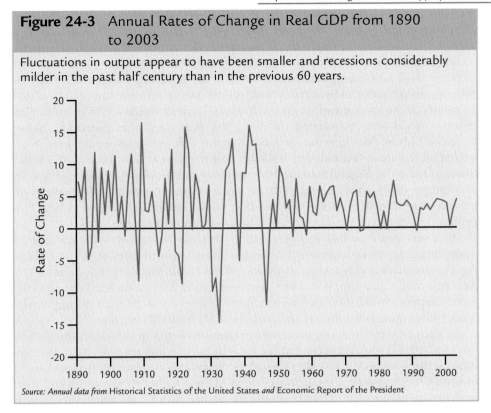

*Source: Annual data from* Historical Statistics of the United States *and* Economic Report of the President

The most striking impressions from a cursory examination of the figure are the increased stability of output and the mildness of recessions (periods of *negative* output growth) in the second half of the period relative to the first half. The advent of Keynesian economics, which advocates policy activism to combat major economic fluctuations, did not occur until after World War II when Congress enacted the Employment Act of 1946. The act committed the government to maintaining high output and employment levels and achieving price stability. For the first time, the U.S. government took explicit responsibility for maintaining prosperity. The Federal Reserve perceived itself as an activist organization only beginning in the 1950s. The Fed then was responsible for "leaning against the wind"—that is, implementing policies to reduce the magnitude of economic fluctuations and combat high unemployment.

Some students of monetary policy attribute the apparent increase in economic stability in the past 50 years partly to the beneficial effects of Federal Reserve policy. However, two general lines of criticism of this viewpoint exist. First, Christina Romer of the University of California and other economists argue that the *apparent* increase in economic stability in the second half of the period reflects not a more stable economy but rather an improvement in the collection and tabulation of economic data.[4] Second, even if the economy actually has become appreciably more stable in the past 50 years, you cannot conclude that the Federal Reserve has been an important contributor. First, higher income tax rates and the enlarged government welfare and unemployment system have worked since the 1930s to increase

[4] Romer argues that faulty construction of early GDP and industrial production series overstates the volatility of economic activity before 1945. See citations to Romer in *Additional Reading* at the end of this chapter.

the power of our *automatic stabilizers*.[5] Furthermore, many important institutional factors have changed over the years. One of the most important factors is federal bank deposit insurance, which has reduced the economy's exposure to disastrous banking panics that contributed to pre-1934 economic instability.

Monetarist economists believe that much of the instability exhibited by the U.S. economy in the past can be directly attributed to policy activism and the associated instability in the money supply. In the monetarist view, avoidance of monetary instability would have prevented much of the past economic instability. Nobel Laureate Milton Friedman has argued that the U.S. economy would have been spared all the major episodes of inflation and depression and some of the lesser fluctuations if the Federal Reserve had simply ignored ongoing economic activity and had provided constant growth of the money supply. Friedman alleges that—on balance—the Fed has destabilized the U.S. economy through activist policy. This proposition, however, is controversial. Many economists disagree.

As a very crude test of the proposition that the Federal Reserve has been a destabilizing force, we examine the average annual growth rates of M1 and M2 in the expansionary and recessionary phases of the 15 full business cycles since 1920. As a first approximation, if the Fed is a *stabilizing* influence on the economy, the money supply should increase more rapidly during recessions than during expansions.[6] Table 24-1 shows the cyclical pattern of M1 and M2 over time.

In each of the first seven economic expansions listed in the table, the growth rates of both M1 and M2 exceeded the rates in the ensuing recessions. In three instances, the *levels* of M1 and M2 *decreased* in the recession phase of the cycle. In 12 of the 15 business cycles, the growth rate of M1 was higher in the expansion than in the ensuing recession. The M2 results are similar, with M2 growing more rapidly during expansions in 11 of the 15 full business cycles (note, however, the apparent improvement in the Fed's performance in the most recent cycle). The difference between the *average* money growth rates during expansions and contractions also is notable. Over the 15 cycles, M1 expanded on average more than *twice as fast* during economic expansions than during recessions. On average, M2 expanded two percentage points faster during expansions than in recessions. Many economists—especially monetarists—consider this evidence an indication of our central bank's inferior record.

However, because money growth is generally believed to influence aggregate expenditures and GDP with a significant time lag, the findings reported in Table 24-1 do not prove the Fed has typically destabilized economic activity. An average of numerous empirical estimates of the length of the impact lag of monetary policy suggests the typical lag is 9 months to 1 year. Figure 24-4 illustrates the relationship between the growth rate of M1 lagged 1 year and the nation's *output gap*—that is,

[5] The federal income tax did not even exist until 1917, and tax rates are higher today than in the first half of the twentieth century. The federal budget is an automatic stabilizer. As economic activity falls, tax revenues decline and income support expenditures increase, automatically swinging the budget toward a deficit and thereby supporting economic activity. As economic activity expands, rising tax revenue and reduced government spending on unemployment and welfare payments automatically move the budget toward surplus, thereby restraining economic activity. The automatic stabilizers are estimated to have reduced fluctuations in the nation's output by perhaps 30 percent relative to fluctuations that would occur in the absence of the stabilizers.

[6] For this proposition to be valid, a couple of assumptions are required. First, the money supply exerts significant influence on economic activity; and second, the influence is experienced after a relatively brief and consistent time lag. If the money supply exerts no influence over economic activity, the Fed cannot be criticized for observed money supply behavior even if the Fed rapidly increased M1 and M2 during business expansions and sharply reduced M1 and M2 during recessions. More importantly, if long and variable lags occur between the time the money supply changes and the time the economy responds to these changes, specifying the appropriate (i.e., stabilizing) cyclical behavior of M1 and M2 becomes quite difficult.

**Table 24-1** Annual Rates of Growth in M1 and M2 During Business Cycles from 1920 to 2001

| Expansionary Phase | | | Recessionary Phase | | |
|---|---|---|---|---|---|
| **Trough to Peak** | **%ΔM1/Year** | **%ΔM2/Year** | **Peak to Trough** | **%ΔM1/Year** | **%ΔM2/Year** |
| July 1921–May 1923 | +5.4 | +7.6 | May 1923–July 1924 | +2.6 | +4.6 |
| July 1924–October 1926 | +4.0 | +5.5 | October 1926–November 1927 | +2.5 | +4.8 |
| November 1927–August 1929 | +0.2 | +0.8 | August 1929–March 1933 | −7.1 | −7.5 |
| March 1933–May 1937 | +12.1 | +10.3 | May 1937–June 1938 | −3.4 | −2.2 |
| June 1938–February 1945 | +19.4 | +16.3 | February 1945–October 1945 | +11.5 | +14.9 |
| October 1945–November 1948 | +2.6 | +3.4 | November 1948–October 1949 | −0.9 | −0.5 |
| October 1949–July 1953 | +4.1 | +4.1 | July 1953–August 1954 | +1.5 | +3.3 |
| August 1954–July 1957 | +1.7 | +2.7 | July 1957–April 1958 | +0.1 | +3.7 |
| April 1958–May 1960 | +1.2 | +2.5 | May 1960–February 1961 | +1.2 | +6.6 |
| February 1961–November 1969 | +4.2 | +7.3 | November 1969–November 1970 | +5.0 | +6.0 |
| November 1970–November 1973 | +6.9 | +11.1 | November 1973–April 1975 | +4.1 | +7.1 |
| April 1975–January 1980 | +7.3 | +10.4 | January 1980–July 1980 | +3.7 | +8.9 |
| July 1980–July 1981 | +8.4 | +9.2 | July 1981–November 1982 | +7.9 | +9.5 |
| November 1982–June 1990 | +7.3 | +7.2 | June 1990–March 1991 | +4.2 | +3.8 |
| March 1991–March 2001 | +2.8 | +4.3 | March 2001–November 2001 | +7.9 | +9.3 |
| Average | +5.8 | +6.8 | Average | +2.7 | +4.8 |

*Sources: Calculated from data in* Federal Reserve Bulletin, *various issues, Milton Friedman and Anna Schwartz,* A Monetary History of the United States, *1867–1960, Appendix A-1, and the FRED database at* http://research.stlouisfed.org/fred2/. Business cycle turning points are National Bureau of Economic Research classifications.

**Figure 24-4** Relationship Between Output Gap and Lagged M1 Growth from 1964 to 2004

Monetarists argue that, prior to the 1980s, Fed policy destabilized output, stimulating GDP when output was strong and retarding GDP when output was weak. After 1980, the Fed's performance looks much better.

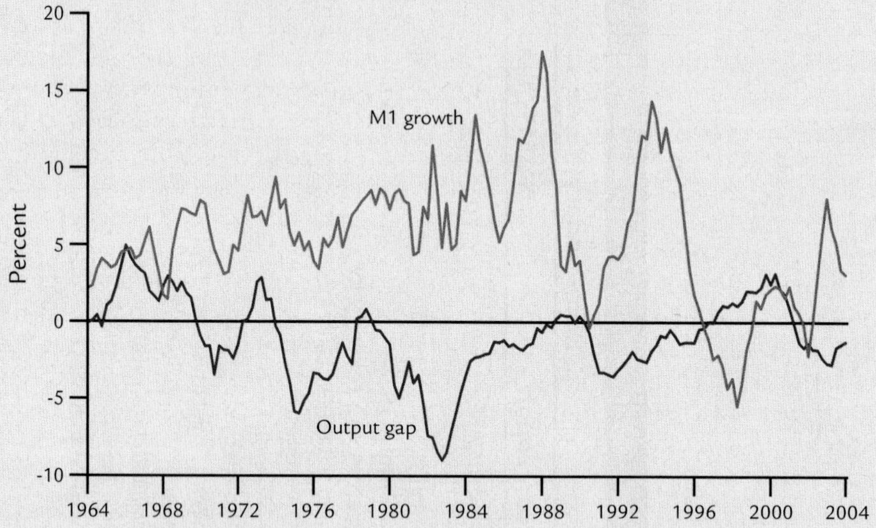


*Source: Data from FRED database at* http://research.stlouisfed.org/fred2/

the difference between actual real GDP and trend real GDP, expressed as a percentage of trend real GDP. In the figure, a positive output gap occurs when real GDP exceeds trend. A negative gap prevails in periods when output lies below trend. In the recessions of 1973–1975, 1981–1982, 1990–1991, and 2001 (and ensuing months), relatively large negative output gaps are evident. A large *positive* output gap occurred in the economic boom of the late 1990s.

Assuming the impact lag of monetary policy is 12 months, with an ideal *(stabilizing)* monetary policy the two series in the figure would be mirror images of each other. The (lagged) money growth rate accelerates when output falls below trend, reaching a peak when the (negative) output gap is largest. Money growth slows when output is above trend, reaching a low point when this (positive) output gap is largest. With *destabilizing* monetary policy, the two series move together over time—that is, the series move in parallel.

Note in the figure that the series seem to fit the latter description through much of the 1960s and 1970s. Some economists believe this (parallel) pattern suggests monetary policy has been *procyclical*—the policy destabilized economic activity during that period. But note the change in the pattern after 1980. The Federal Reserve boosted money growth somewhat to combat the huge recessionary gap of 1982 to 1983 (although the Fed was slow in reacting). In the late 1980s, the Fed slowed money growth sharply to head off incipient inflation as output moved above trend. The Fed then increased money growth to minimize the severity and duration of the 1990 to 1991 recession. In the mid-1990s, the Fed again slowed money growth as the economy moved into years 4 and 5 of an economic expansion. Money growth increased sharply during the 2001 to 2002 recession and anemic recovery. Thus, particularly to monetarist economists, the figure suggests a marked improvement in the Fed's performance during the past 25 years relative to earlier times.[7]

Nevertheless, many economists remain skeptical of monetary policy activism. Because of uncertainties about the economy's structure and the NAIRU level, existence of long and variable lags, and shortcomings in forecasting ability, monetarists and other Fed critics doubt the Fed can consistently stabilize the economy. Also, many economists criticize the Fed's historical propensity to change priorities in response to political forces and other factors. Critics charge the Fed often allowed itself to be diverted from the Fed's *legitimate* goals of promoting economic stability and low inflation. For example, in 1929 the Fed implemented restrictive policy measures in reaction to stock market speculation even though the nation's price level was quite stable. In the early 1930s, the Fed seemed to ignore important domestic considerations such as severe deflation and double-digit unemployment rates. Instead, the Fed conducted policy largely in response to international pressures.[8] In the wartime and early post-war period of 1942 to 1951, the Fed abdicated control over the money supply. To assist the U.S. Treasury in its debt-funding efforts, the Fed maintained interest rates at extremely low levels. The associated expansion of bank reserves and money supply was highly inflationary. A similar phenomenon occurred on a much smaller scale from 1965 to 1969 during the Vietnam War. In the critics' view, policy activism facilitated the Fed's propensity to become sidetracked by various pseudo-objectives. Some economists believe the public would be better served if the Fed were stripped of its authority to implement discretionary monetary policies and instead were governed by a monetary policy rule.

**discretionary monetary policy**
policy in which the central bank is free to assess economic circumstances as they unfold and implement whatever measures the central bank deems appropriate at the time

**monetary policy rule**
arrangement in which the central bank announces in advance specifically how it will respond to ongoing economic developments and commits the central bank to following through on the announcement

## RULES VERSUS DISCRETION IN THE CONDUCT OF MONETARY POLICY

**Discretionary monetary policy** means the central bank is free to assess economic circumstances as they unfold and implement whatever measures the central bank deems appropriate at the time. The Federal Reserve has long conducted discretionary monetary policy. A **monetary policy rule** involves an arrangement in which the central bank announces in advance specifically how the central bank will respond to ongoing economic developments and commits to following through on the announcement. The rules versus discretion debate must be distinguished from the policy activism versus policy non-activism debate. Monetary policy can be governed by a rule and still be either passive or active. In a **passive rule,** the central bank does not respond to ongoing developments. An example is a constant money supply growth rule, in which the central bank simply increases the money supply at the same rate each period, irrespective of contemporary economic events and conditions. In an **active rule (feedback rule),** the central bank changes the level of interest rates or the money growth rate according to strict predetermined formulas

**passive rule**
rule in which the central bank does not respond to ongoing developments; constant money supply growth rule

**active rule (feedback rule)**
rule in which the central bank changes the interest rate levels or the money growth rate by strict predetermined formulas in response to ongoing developments

[7] Several studies using interest rates rather than money growth to assess the Fed's past performance reach a similar conclusion. In the 1960s and 1970s, for example, the Fed typically changed short-term interest rates by an amount less than the change in ongoing inflation. The Fed was "behind the curve" and pursuing a destabilizing policy—one in which real interest rates were allowed to decline when inflation increased and allowed to increase when inflation fell. After 1980, the Fed corrected its mistake. The Fed boosted real rates when inflation was rising and lowered real interest rates when inflation was declining.

[8] In September and October 1931, the Federal Reserve Bank of New York increased the discount rate by two percentage points in response to England's decision to suspend convertibility of foreign currencies into gold. At the time of this massive discount rate hike, the U.S. unemployment rate was more than 15 percent (see Chapter 17).

in response to ongoing developments. Examples of two hypothetical active monetary policy rules (feedback rules) are the following:

(24-1) **Money growth rate = 2% + (Unemployment rate −5%)**

(24-2) **Federal funds rate = 3% + 2(Inflation rate −2%).**

In the first rule, if the nation's unemployment rate is 5 percent (perhaps the Fed's estimate of the NAIRU), the Fed increases the money supply at an annual rate of 2 percent. This rule requires the Fed to increase the annual money growth rate by one percentage point for each percentage point the unemployment rate exceeds 5 percent. If the unemployment rate hits 9 percent, the rule requires the central bank to provide money growth of 6 percent per year. In the second rule, the Fed sets the federal funds rate at 3 percent plus twice the amount that inflation exceeds 2 percent per year (perhaps the Fed's target for inflation). If inflation is running at an annual rate of 5 percent, the rule calls for a 9 percent fed funds rate.

Next, we look at examples of both passive and active rules. In particular, we analyze the constant money growth rule proposal that was popular with monetarist economists for many years and several examples of active rules, including the *Taylor rule,* which requires the central bank to respond to ongoing developments on both the inflation and the unemployment fronts. First, let's look at the case for conducting monetary policy via a rule.

## Case for a Monetary Policy Rule

We might be better off if monetary policy were governed by rule rather than by discretion for several reasons. First, conflict may exist between the objectives of elected officials and central bank policymakers and the objectives of the public. Politicians may use macroeconomic policy (including monetary policy) to further their own political objectives. To the extent that the central bank is not structured to be independent of the legislative and executive branches of government, the conduct of monetary policy likely is influenced by political considerations. Politicians are well aware of the public's tendency to cast their votes based on economic conditions prevailing at election time. If unemployment is high at election time, incumbent politicians know they will pay a price at the polls.

**political business cycle**
manipulation of the economy for political ends

Manipulation of the economy for political ends is the **political business cycle.** Incumbent politicians benefit most from a booming economy and the associated low rate of unemployment at election time. If central bank officials are subject to political influence or are otherwise sympathetic to incumbent politicians, monetary policy can become characterized by unwarranted stimulus in periods leading up to elections and then severe restraint immediately after elections to bring down inflation caused by the pre-election policy stimulus. Thus, discretionary monetary policy contributes to political business cycles. A monetary policy rule followed rigorously prevents the central bank from contributing to a political business cycle.

Even if the central bank is absolutely free of political influence, economists emphasizing the inherent difficulties of conducting successful stabilization policies due to uncertainties, lags, and other factors believe the public would be better served by monetary rule. Monetarists and others who believe the Fed has destabilized economic activity in the past and is likely to do so in the future because of technical reasons believe a monetary rule leads to greater economic stability. Finally, even if our monetary policy officials are extremely competent at economic forecasting and judging the need for policy stimulus or restraint, a case for a policy rule can be made based on the **time inconsistency problem** of monetary policy. *Time inconsistency* refers to the tendency of policymakers to announce a particular policy to influence expectations and then to follow different policies after the expectations have been formed.

**time inconsistency problem**
tendency of policymakers to announce a particular policy to influence expectations and then to follow different policies after the expectations have been formed

An analogy taken from international politics is helpful for understanding the time inconsistency problem facing central banks. Consider government policy towards terrorists who take hostages. Countries have a stated policy against negotiating with terrorists to reduce terrorists' incentive to take hostages. Governments believe the stated policy reduces the incidence of hostage-taking. Once hostages actually are taken, however, the government is under tremendous pressure to negotiate the hostages' release despite stated policy to the contrary. Rational terrorists are aware of the time inconsistency phenomenon and sometimes take hostages. The only way to eliminate the incentive of rational terrorists to take hostages is to remove—perhaps by congressional legislation—government officials' discretion to negotiate with terrorists. Then rational terrorists likely will not take hostages because the terrorists have nothing to gain. Ironically, by tying the hands of public officials in this way, the number of hostages taken and killed almost surely would decline. Elimination of policy discretion in this case yields an improved outcome.

How does this analogy relate to monetary policy? Consider a central bank that desires to achieve both low inflation and low unemployment. Recall the *Phillips curve,* which depicts an inverse short-run relationship between a nation's unemployment rate and the nation's inflation rate, other things being equal. The *position* of the Phillips curve depends on the inflation outlook. The Phillips curve associated with higher expected inflation is located to the right (northeast) of a Phillips curve associated with lower expected inflation. That is, the inflation rate associated with any given unemployment rate will be higher if inflation expectations are higher. (Alternatively stated, the unemployment rate associated with any given inflation rate will be higher if inflation expectations are higher.) For this reason, central banks have a strong incentive to foster low inflation expectations through statements, Fed official speeches, and so forth.

Once the public is conditioned to expect low inflation, however, the central bank may be tempted by political forces to exploit the short-run Phillips curve by implementing stimulative policies that reduce unemployment (and increase inflation). Because informed economic agents are aware of the time inconsistency problem, the central bank has less than full credibility when it makes statements about the inflation outlook and its resolve to fight inflation. We get the surprising result that eliminating monetary policy discretion by implementing a policy rule improves the outcome. Implementation of a credible policy rule eliminates the time inconsistency problem. By increasing the central bank's credibility in its pronouncements about inflation, implementation of the rule improves the terms of the trade-off—that is, it shifts the Phillips curve downward, in the direction of the origin. The nation enjoys lower inflation, lower unemployment, or some combination of the two.

## PASSIVE MONETARY POLICY RULE: THE CONSTANT MONEY GROWTH RULE

In the monetarists' view, unstable monetary policies have been responsible for all of the nation's episodes of severe inflation and major economic contraction since the Federal Reserve's inception in the early part of the twentieth century. For example, monetarists single out the money supply contraction as the predominant force behind the Great Depression. They pinpoint rapid money growth as the culprit involved in the high inflation of the 1970s. Monetarists believe Fed policies have contributed strongly to many of the less severe episodes of inflation and unemployment. Some of the monetarists' claims are contentious. Many who believe the monetarists' claims advocate the constant money growth rule. Adoption of this rule would eliminate the specter of high volatility in money supply growth rates. The rule also would terminate the procyclical pattern of money growth characterizing many past business cycles (review Table 24-1). Monetarists believe the rule would lead to a more stable economic environment than can be expected through discretionary monetary management.

The key issue is whether changes in the *supply* of money are more important sources of economic instability than are changes in the *demand* for money (and velocity, V). If money demand and velocity are inherently stable and short-run changes in aggregate demand for goods and services are therefore more closely related to changes in the *supply* of money than changes in the *demand* for money, the case for the constant money growth rule is enhanced.

Politically conservative economists are attracted to the constant money growth rule. In these economists' view, the various government interventions in the economy inevitably have adverse consequences on balance—that is, the interventions are counterproductive. If a constant money growth rule improves economic stability, intrusive government actions are less justified. For example, fiscal policy measures (changes in government expenditures and federal tax policy) would be required less frequently. If rule implementation enhanced economic stability, instability in the banking industry and other government-supervised or regulated sectors would be reduced, improving the prospects for reducing the government regulatory apparatus. Politically liberal economists are critical of the constant money growth rule. In these economists' view, the economy is subject to numerous shocks whose economic consequences can be attenuated in part through discretionary monetary and fiscal policies. Therefore, liberal economists favor monetary policy discretion and criticize the constant money growth rule.

**YOUR TURN**

Suppose the Fed implements a constant 4 percent money growth rule. Now, assume a series of technological improvements in the payments process causes velocity to increase at a rate of 5 percent per year over the next 5 years. Calculate the growth rate of nominal GDP that would ensue. Also, what would likely happen to the nation's price level?

Critics of the constant money growth rule believe Federal Reserve policy has been an important force contributing to economic stability since the Great Depression. These economists argue that velocity is inherently unstable due to changes in financial technology, economic uncertainty, interest rates, and other factors. These critics believe changes in velocity cannot be forecast. Furthermore, they believe the Fed legitimately has more than one objective—that is, economic stability is not the sole objective of monetary policy. Critics of the constant money growth rule acknowledge the Fed has made numerous mistakes in the past. However, they argue that higher-quality data, better forecasting acumen, and the benefits associated with improved conduct of monetary policy suggest future discretionary monetary policies will be more effective than past policies. Indeed, many economists believe the Fed's performance has improved sharply in the past quarter century.

## ACTIVE MONETARY POLICY RULES (FEEDBACK RULES)

A *passive* monetary policy rule is inflexible. The policy does not permit the central bank to react to ongoing economic developments. The constant money growth rule does not permit the central bank to respond to expected or actual changes in money demand and velocity. If important financial innovations sharply boost velocity, the constant money growth rule likely leads to a temporary increase in inflation. If a negative shock to consumer and business confidence boosts economic uncertainty, adhering to the constant money growth rule likely results in recession. Because money demand has proved to be unstable in the past quarter century, most economists today believe other rules are superior to the constant money growth rule.

An *active* monetary policy rule requires the central bank to respond to ongoing economic phenomena as specified by the particular rule in place. For example, the rule expressed in Equation (24-1) requires the central bank to respond to an increased unemployment rate by boosting the growth rate of the money supply. The rule in Equation (24-2) requires the central bank to respond to an increased inflation rate by raising the federal funds rate. In the remainder of this chapter, we examine three particular types of active or feedback rules: a nominal GDP targeting rule, an inflation targeting rule, and the *Taylor rule*—a rule that requires the monetary authorities to respond to changes in both inflation and unemployment.

### Nominal GDP Targeting Rule

Money demand and velocity appeared relatively stable from World War II through the 1970s. This stable period increased the attractiveness of the constant money growth rule. If the rule locks in money growth at 3 percent per year and velocity trends upward at approximately 2 percent per year with relatively low standard deviation in its growth rate, nominal GDP expenditures (MV) expand at a fairly steady rate centered on 5 percent per year. If potential real GDP trends upward at around 3 percent annually, the rule leads to roughly 2 percent annual inflation, on average. Both the inflation rate and output growth are relatively stable. In this instance, both severe inflation and severe economic contraction are highly unlikely.

However, beginning in the 1980s, money demand and velocity became considerably more unstable. In such an environment, constant money growth likely is associated with unstable inflation and output growth. Because MV represents GDP expenditures, a nominal GDP targeting rule forces the central bank to change money growth in response to ongoing changes in velocity. Suppose a nominal GDP targeting rule in place requires the Fed to aim for 5 percent annual nominal GDP growth. Assume velocity has been trending upward at about 2 percent per year. If the Fed has been increasing the money supply at a 3 percent annual rate and a series of financial innovations boost velocity growth above trend, the Fed would reduce money growth in an effort to remain on its 5 percent nominal GDP (i.e., MV) growth target. The constant money growth rule permits no such flexibility. For this reason, many early advocates of the constant money growth rule switched their allegiance to nominal GDP targeting after velocity became more unstable in the early 1980s.

## Inflation Targeting Rule

Beginning with New Zealand in 1989, central banks in more than 20 nations have initiated inflation targeting regimes. The countries include Australia, Canada, Israel, and the United Kingdom. In most instances, the *central bank* simply announces its inflation targeting intentions. In some cases, *national law* mandates the central bank strive to hit the inflation target. The target typically is expressed as a *range* of inflation rates rather than one specific rate. For example, for several years the Reserve Bank of Australia had an inflation target range of 1 to 3 percent per year. Some countries have rules permitting the central bank to deviate temporarily from the inflation target range if a severe shock occurs (such as a sharp hike in oil prices).

Inflation targeting is designed to circumvent the time inconsistency problem. By providing the central bank with maximum credibility regarding the central bank's commitment to very low inflation, an inflation targeting regime presents central bankers with a favorable Phillips curve—that is, one in which any given unemployment rate can be achieved with minimal inflation.[9] The Federal Reserve has never adopted inflation targeting, but proposals for inflation targeting have been floated occasionally and inevitably will resurface the next time serious inflation occurs in the United States. Chapter 25 analyzes inflation targeting in some depth.

## Taylor Rule

Most economists believe the primary goals of monetary policy include not only maintaining price level stability but also preventing large fluctuations in output and employment. In recent years, the Federal Reserve has directly targeted the federal funds rate in an effort to achieve its policy goals. Two principles are clear. When inflation rises above acceptable rates, the Fed must raise its federal funds rate target, slowing the growth of aggregate demand to reduce the inflationary pressures. When output slows or declines (and unemployment rises to levels appreciably above the NAIRU), the Fed reduces the federal funds rate to stimulate aggregate demand, output, and employment.

In 1993, John Taylor of Stanford University proposed a monetary policy rule in which the Federal Reserve moves its federal funds rate target in response to changes in both inflation *and the output gap*. The output gap measures the relative size of the difference between the nation's actual output and natural or potential output. The specific form of the **Taylor rule** proposed by Professor Taylor is indicated in Equation (24-3).

**Taylor rule**
monetary policy rule in which the Federal Reserve moves its federal funds rate target in response to changes in both inflation and the output gap

$$\text{(24-3)} \quad \textbf{federal funds rate} = \mathbf{2\% + \%\Delta P + 0.5(\%\Delta P - 2\%) + 0.5\,\frac{(Y - Y^*)}{Y}}$$

In this formulation, $\%\Delta P$ is the inflation rate, Y is real GDP, and $Y^*$ is potential or natural real GDP. The last expression in the equation $[(Y - Y^*)/Y]$ is the percentage output gap—the size of the output gap expressed as a percentage of actual output. If you move $\%\Delta P$ to the left-hand side of the equation, you see the Taylor rule requires that the Fed move the *real* federal funds rate in response to changes

[9] In the late 1970s, U.S. inflation was raging and the entrenched expectations of severe inflation had shifted the short-run Phillips curve far to the right (review the figure in Exhibit 20-1). The *Shadow Open Market Committee,* a group of distinguished monetarists formed to "shadow" or critique Fed policy, proposed that the Fed adopt an inflation target (perhaps 2–3 percent per year) backed by the guaranteed resignation of the entire FOMC if inflation ultimately exceeded the target range. Now that is a rule that would have maximum credibility! Not surprisingly, the Fed was unwilling to implement such a rule.

in inflation and changes in the output gap. Note in the equation that a *positive* output gap indicates real GDP exceeds potential real GDP (thus the unemployment rate is *below* the NAIRU). For example, if real GDP exceeds potential real GDP by 2 percent of real GDP (a positive output gap of 2 percent), the Taylor rule requires the Fed to set the real Fed funds rate higher by one percentage point than if real GDP and potential real GDP are equal (a zero output gap).

In the formulation expressed in the equation, the desired inflation rate is assumed to be 2 percent. Given the output gap, the rule requires the Fed to increase real interest rates if inflation moves above 2 percent and reduce real rates if inflation falls below 2 percent. If actual inflation is 2 percent and real GDP is on potential (no output gap), the nominal Fed funds rate is set at 4 percent (the real rate at 2 percent). If inflation increases to 4 percent per year and the output gap remains zero, the Taylor rule requires the Fed to raise the Fed funds rate to 7 percent. Note that the *real* Fed funds rate in this instance is 3 percent—that is 7% − 4%. Importantly, given the size of the output gap, the rule requires the Fed to boost *real* interest rates when inflation rises and reduce *real* rates when inflation falls.

**YOUR TURN**

Suppose the economy is booming, real output exceeds potential output by 2 percent of real GDP, and inflation is running at an annual rate of 5 percent. If the Fed adheres to the Taylor rule, at what level will the Fed set the nominal federal funds rate? The real federal funds rate?

A natural way to interpret the Taylor rule is to view it as a rule that requires the central bank to respond not only to inflation developments but also to unemployment developments (the unemployment rate is inversely and strongly correlated with the output gap as we have defined it). Thus, one might suspect that a pure inflation targeting rule requires the Fed to omit the output gap from Equation (24-3) and focus entirely on the inflation rate.

However, another interpretation of the Taylor rule is possible. The magnitude of the output gap likely is an indicator of *forthcoming* inflation. A positive output gap signals rising inflation and a negative output gap foretells falling inflation.[10] Therefore, you can view the Taylor rule as detailing an operating procedure that facilitates the Fed's ability to achieve an inflation target. In this interpretation, the Taylor rule is consistent with the traditional view that the paramount goal of monetary policy is price level stability.

**Taylor Rule as a Benchmark for Evaluating Monetary Policy.** You can use the Taylor rule as a benchmark for evaluating the posture of monetary policy. If the actual federal funds rate is lower than the rate prescribed by the Taylor rule, monetary policy clearly is more stimulative than if the federal funds rate were at the level indicated by the Taylor rule. In Figure 24-5, the actual U.S. federal funds rate and the federal funds rate prescribed by the Taylor rule are illustrated for 1960 to 2004.

[10] Recall that a positive output gap (actual GDP $>$ potential GDP) implies the unemployment rate is below the NAIRU—inflation is rising. A negative output gap (actual GDP $<$ potential GDP) implies the unemployment rate is above the NAIRU—inflation is declining.

With the aid of hindsight and the Taylor rule, several Federal Reserve policy mistakes committed in the past 40 years can be pinpointed. For example, note in the figure that during escalation of the Vietnam War (1965–1969), the federal funds rate was appreciably *lower* than the rate prescribed by the Taylor rule. This relatively stimulative monetary policy posture and the highly expansionary budgetary policy of the times account for the sharp escalation in inflation in this period. Hence, the Vietnam episode is a clear policy mistake—both monetary and fiscal policy turned highly stimulative given an economy that already had reached full employment by 1965. By 1969, the unemployment rate fell below 3.5 percent—far below NAIRU.

A second policy mistake involves excessive monetary policy stimulus during the year prior to the 1972 presidential election featuring incumbent president Richard Nixon versus George McGovern. Wage and price controls initially implemented in August 1971 were in place. As indicated by the Taylor rule standard, the federal funds rate was relatively low in this period (also, M1 and M2 were increasing at near double-digit rates in the 12 months prior to November 1972). Inflation surged after the controls were removed in 1973, partly due to this policy mistake. The Taylor rule benchmark also helps explain the increased inflation in the late 1970s. In this period, inflation again reached double-digit rates at a time when Taylor rule criteria suggest the federal funds rate was too low—that is, monetary policy was too stimulative. This episode constitutes a third policy error.

By the Taylor rule standard, monetary policy was restrictive in the early 1980s. The restrictive monetary policy helps account for the severe recession of 1981 to 1982 and the associated sharp decline in the inflation rate. However, in view of the severity, duration, and entrenched nature of inflation motivating the Fed's restrictive policies of the early 1980s, this episode cannot clearly be labeled an unam-

**Figure 24-5** Federal Funds Rate and the Rate Prescribed by the Taylor Rule for 1960 to 2004

The Taylor rule can be used as a benchmark for evaluating monetary policy. Such policy was expansionary in the late 1960s and 1970s and was restrictive in the 1980s. In the Greenspan era (1987–2004), the Fed funds rate tracked the Taylor rule fairly closely.

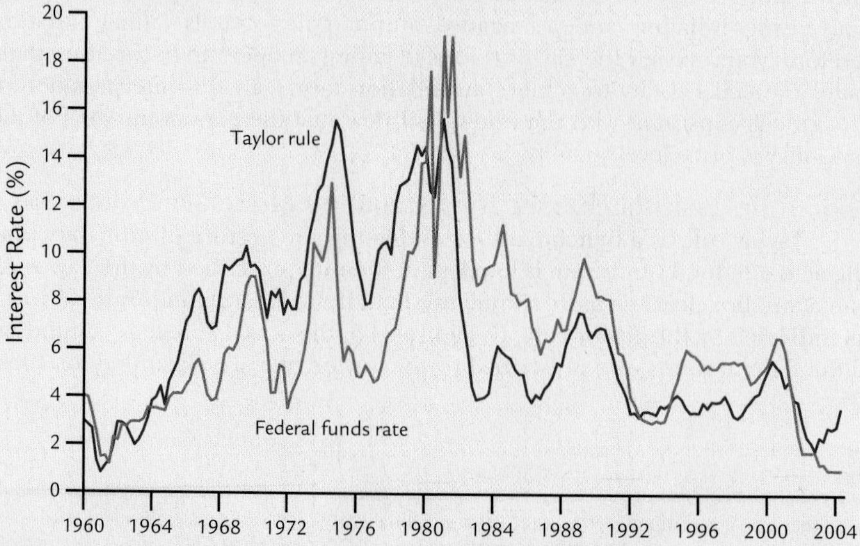


*Source: Taylor rule rate is calculated with Equation (24-3), using the GDP deflator, real GDP, and potential real GDP, available on the FRED database at* http://research.stlouisfed.org/fred2/

biguous policy mistake. If the Taylor rule is used as the standard, monetary policy appears restrictive throughout the 1980s.

Finally, note that actual Fed policy tracked the Taylor rule more closely during Alan Greenspan's tenure at the Federal Reserve (1987–2004) than in earlier periods. (On the Greenspan era, see Exhibit 24-1.) The Fed responded to the shocks associated with the recession that began in March 2001, the terrorist destruction of the World Trade Center in September 2001, and the series of corporate scandals that demoralized U.S. shareholders by aggressively cutting the federal funds rate from 2001 to 2003. The Fed sought to minimize the likelihood of the United States

## Exhibit 24-1 Evaluating the Performance of Alan Greenspan

Fed Chairman Alan Greenspan has been heralded as a genius in conducting monetary policy. Greenspan is so highly regarded that a recent book on Greenspan was entitled *The Maestro.* The performance of the U.S. economy during Greenspan's tenure at the Fed has set a standard worthy of emulation. In the accompanying table, the average growth rate of real output, the average inflation rate, and the average unemployment rate during Greenspan's tenure are compared to those experienced in the nearly 3 decades prior to Greenspan's appointment in August 1987. More importantly, the *standard deviations* (measures of variability) of output growth, inflation, and the unemployment rate also are reported.

Average output growth was somewhat slower in Greenspan's tenure than in his predecessors' terms. However, the Federal Reserve exerts only marginal and indirect influence over the longer-term trend of the nation's output. The Fed is more accountable for output growth *stability.* Note the sharp decline in the standard deviation of output growth after August 1987. Most economists charge the Fed with responsibility for the trend rate of inflation. Under Greenspan's leadership, average inflation was lower by almost two percentage points per year and the variability of inflation declined by about two thirds. The average unemployment rate was somewhat lower, and its standard deviation declined sharply. By all three indicators, the economy was much more stable during Greenspan's regime. The inflation performance was especially noteworthy.

Greenspan cannot be given primary credit for the remarkable recent U.S. economic performance. A strong dose of luck is involved. Unlike the turbulent 1970s when oil prices skyrocketed, no dramatic adverse supply shocks occurred during Greenspan's time at the Fed. Greenspan did not need to battle inherited double-digit inflation, a challenge that faced Paul Volcker (Greenspan's predecessor) when he assumed the chairmanship in 1979. In fact, Greenspan benefited from *favorable* supply shocks that boosted productivity growth around the mid-1990s and helped reduce inflation and sustain the record-length economic expansion (1991–2001). Greenspan also inherited a relatively benign inflation environment in 1987.

Nevertheless, an objective observer must give Greenspan significant credit. His reputation as a consummate student of the multitude of arcane indicators of business cycle activity gives credibility to the view that the increased economic stability under Greenspan was not entirely a matter of luck. The fact that the two recessions experienced during Greenspan's 19-year tenure as Fed chairman were among the shortest and mildest on record, together with the standard deviation measures reported in the table, ensure that Greenspan will likely be remembered as the most effective Fed Chairman in history. Perhaps the ultimate compliment is the absence of talk during Greenspan's tenure of shackling him with a Taylor rule or other means of limiting his authority to conduct discretionary monetary policy.

*continued*

**Exhibit 24-1** Evaluating the Performance of Alan Greenspan—*cont'd*

**Macroeconomic Indicators: Greenspan's Federal Reserve Versus Prior Regimes**

| | Prior Regimes (1960–1987) | Greenspan's Fed (1987–2004) |
|---|---|---|
| Real GDP Growth | | |
| Average | 3.55% | 2.97% |
| Standard deviation | 2.72 | 1.53 |
| Inflation Rate (CPI) | | |
| Average | 5.04 | 3.14 |
| Standard deviation | 3.47 | 1.14 |
| Unemployment Rate | | |
| Average | 6.14 | 5.54 |
| Standard deviation | 1.67 | 0.98 |

*Note:* All values are percentages. Real GDP growth rates are calculated relative to four quarters earlier. Inflation rates are CPI inflation rates, calculated relative to 12 months earlier. All data are from FRED database at http://research.stlouisfed.org/fred2/

following Japan into a deflationary trap by maintaining the federal funds rate substantially below the rate prescribed by the Taylor rule from 2002 to 2004.

**Criticisms of the Taylor Rule.** The Taylor rule is not without shortcomings and critics. First, several alternative measures of inflation and the output gap exist. The federal funds rate prescribed by the Taylor rule differs considerably depending on the price index and output gap measure used. This issue raises practical problems if the Fed wishes to conduct policy via the rule. Second, because of the impact lag of monetary policy, an ideal active policy rule should not use *current* observations for inflation, real GDP, and potential real GDP, but rates that are *expected to prevail* perhaps 9 to 12 months in the future. But using expected rates requires accurate economic forecasting, a task that has proved difficult. Third, the *weights* or *response coefficients* used in the Taylor rule (0.5 both for deviations from the 2 percent inflation target and for deviations from the potential GDP target) were obtained by Taylor in an *ad hoc* fashion. Increasing (decreasing) these response coefficients implies a more (less) aggressive response by the central bank in moving the short-term interest rate. An optimal rule might involve higher or lower response coefficients. Finally, the Taylor rule is very simple—perhaps too simple. The rule requires the Fed to respond to only two variables—inflation and the output gap. Some economists believe a Federal Reserve chairman possessing Alan Greenspan's economic and financial acumen will be able to consistently outperform the Taylor rule (see Exhibit 24-1).

Nevertheless, the Taylor rule contributes importantly to the economic policy dialogue. Implementation of the Taylor rule has the clear advantage of alleviating the time inconsistency problem of monetary policy. Using the Taylor rule as a benchmark provides valuable information for determining policy prospectively and evaluating policy retrospectively. A tremendous amount of research in the past decade has been devoted to the Taylor rule. Some of the past major policy mistakes may be prevented in the future by advances in the science of monetary policy.

# INTERNATIONAL PERSPECTIVES

## Is The Bank of Japan Responsible for Japan's Problems?

One use of the Taylor rule is evaluating central bank policy retrospectively. The accompanying figure shows the short-term interest rate in Japan targeted by the central bank *(blue line)* from 1972 to 2003. The figure also indicates the rate prescribed by the Taylor rule *(red line)*. Several points are noteworthy. During the 1970s, the Bank of Japan maintained short-term rates far below the levels suggested by the Taylor rule. The associated growth in liquidity provided by the Bank of Japan likely contributed to the speculative bubble that pushed Japanese stock and real estate prices to extreme levels, setting the stage for later problems.

Second, after the early 1980s, interest rates in Japan were consistently *higher* than the Taylor rule rate recommends. Although the importance of numerous structural problems contributing to Japan's malaise cannot be minimized, the relatively tight monetary policies in the 1980s and most of the 1990s may have contributed to the deflationary spiral that plagued Japan for almost a decade.

Finally, note the situation the Bank of Japan faces today. Even though the Bank of Japan has maintained the short-term interest rate essentially at zero for several years, the rate prescribed by the Taylor rule is approaching *negative* 10 percent! Even a zero interest rate is far too restrictive by Taylor rule standards. Given that nominal interest rates are "bounded by zero"—that is, they cannot be negative—the ability of the Japanese central bank to extricate the country from its economic morass may be limited. Whether more restrictive monetary policies in the 1970s and more stimulative measures from 1985 to 1995 would have prevented the disastrous situation Japan faced during the early portion of the twenty-first century is debatable.

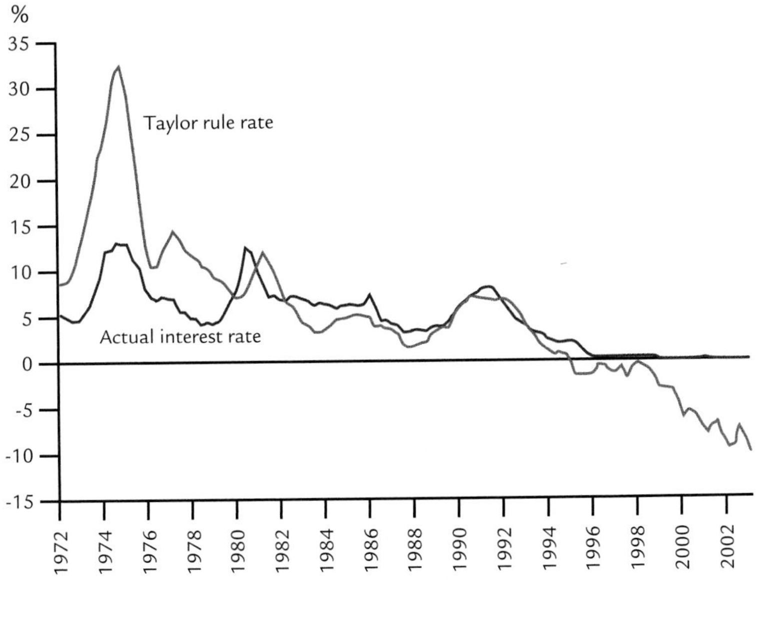

# SUMMARY

The Federal Reserve's efforts to implement active discretionary monetary policy to stabilize economic activity have been criticized for a long time. Critics of the Fed have long charged that discretionary monetary policies almost inevitably fail because of political factors and the Fed's historical propensity to become sidetracked from its legitimate goals of economic stability and relatively stable prices. Furthermore, critics of policy activism believe the Fed will fail even if it focuses strictly on achieving legitimate objectives. This view follows from the various uncertainties about the economy's structure and the long and variable lags characterizing the response of economic activity to changes in the Fed's policy instruments. For these reasons, monetarists have long proposed that the Fed simply abandon efforts to conduct discretionary policies and instead simply increase the money supply each year by a slow and constant rate. Critics of the constant money growth proposal dispute the allegation that the Fed has been a destabilizing influence on balance. They argue that implementation of the rule would handcuff the Fed and prevent the central bank from responding to periodic aggregate supply and demand shocks. Critics believe the unpredictable nature of money velocity renders the constant money growth rule ineffective in stabilizing economic activity. In recent years, economists have moved away from the constant money growth rule, instead proposing *active* or *feedback rules.* In a feedback rule, the central bank responds to ongoing economic developments in a manner specified by the rule in question. A key advantage of a credible monetary policy rule is that it overcomes the problem of time inconsistency plaguing regimes of discretionary monetary policy. By increasing the credibility of the central bank's commitment to its stated objective of price stability, a monetary rule may help achieve a more favorable combination of inflation and unemployment rates. The key question is whether this important advantage of a rule can compensate for abandonment of monetary policy discretion that many economists believe enables a highly competent central bank to respond more effectively to economic developments than any specific rule would allow.

## YOUR TURN ANSWERS

PAGE 566

The growth rate of nominal GDP is the sum of the growth rate of the money supply (M) and the growth rate of velocity (V). In the dynamic version of the equation of exchange, $\%\Delta M + \%\Delta V = \%\Delta P + \%\Delta Y$. Nominal GDP expands at the rate of 9 percent annually. Because real output (Y) can increase only at a maximum rate of perhaps 3 to 4 percent per year in the long run, adhering to this rule likely results in inflation ($\%\Delta P$) of approximately 5 to 6 percent per year on average over the 5-year period.

PAGE 569

The Taylor rule calls for a nominal Fed funds rate of 9.5 percent, that is, $2\% + 5\% + .5(5\% - 2\%) + .5(2\%)$. Given the 5 percent inflation rate, the real Fed funds rate is 4.5 percent ($9.5\% - 5\%$).

# KEY TERMS

policy activists
policy non-activists
recognition lag
implementation lag
impact lag
discretionary monetary policy
monetary policy rule
passive rule
active rule (feedback rule)
political business cycle
time inconsistency problem
Taylor rule

# STUDY QUESTIONS

**1.** Explain why the economy's self-correcting mechanism may be asymmetrical—that is, the mechanism may be more effective in automatically correcting an inflationary gap than a recessionary gap.

**2.** How would an advocate of the constant money growth rule arrive at the appropriate constant growth rate of the money supply? Explain using the dynamic version of the equation of exchange ($\%\Delta M + \%\Delta V = \%\Delta P + \%\Delta Y$).

**3.** Why do you suppose that the growth rate of the supply of money (illustrated in Table 24-1) typically has increased more rapidly during business cycle expansions than during contractions over the past 80 years? Does this fact necessarily indicate the Fed has destabilized the economy? Explain.

**4.** Define the three lags of monetary policy and explain how the existence of the three lags has implications for the debate between policy activists and policy non-activists.

**5.** "If velocity (V) and real output (Y) cannot be projected into the future with any degree of confidence, the case for a constant money growth rule breaks down." Evaluate this statement.

**6.** Consider the three lags of monetary and fiscal policy. Which type of lag would you expect to be the same length for both monetary and fiscal policy? Which types of lags are likely to have different lengths for the two types of policy (monetary and fiscal)? Explain.

**7.** Explain the practical difference between a constant money growth rule and a nominal GDP targeting rule. Explain why many economists who advocated a constant money growth rule 25 years ago became advocates of a nominal GDP targeting rule in the 1980s.

**8.** Suppose we are experiencing stagflation resulting from an adverse supply shock. Assume this shock results in an inflation rate of 6 percent per year and an output gap in which real output is 4 percent below potential. Calculate the federal funds rate called for by the Taylor rule.

**9.** Assume, in the past 12 months, Japan has experienced *deflation* of around 4 percent and an output gap of approximately (negative) 4 percent. Calculate the Japanese short-term interest rate called for by the Taylor rule. Is it possible for the Bank of Japan to deliver this interest rate? Explain.

**10.** **A.** Assume that inflation in the past year was running at an annual rate of 2 percent and actual output was at potential. According to the Taylor rule [Equation (24-3)], what level of the nominal interest rate would the Federal Reserve have targeted? What real interest rate is implied?

**B.** Now suppose inflation heats up to 4 percent while output remains on potential. What nominal interest rate does the Fed now set if the Fed follows the Taylor rule? What real interest rate is implied? Is the Fed "leaning against the wind"? Explain.

**11.** Suppose the central bank of a small underdeveloped country whose rulers are not well informed about economics adopts the following modified version of the Taylor rule: i = 2% + 0.5(Inflation − 2%) + 0.5(Unemployment rate − NAIRU). Is this an appropriate rule? Why or why not?

**12.** Different countries place different priorities on the conflicting objectives of low inflation and low unemployment. By examining the form of the particular version of the Taylor rule adopted by each country below, describe the priorities of countries A, B, and C. Provide an inflation and output gap assumption and calculate the level of interest rates prescribed by the rule for each country to support your conclusions.

Country A: i = 2% + Inflation rate + 0.5(Inflation rate − 2%) + 0.5(% Output gap)

Country B: i = 3% + Inflation rate + 0.7(Inflation rate − 2%) + 0.2(% Output gap)

Country C: i = 1% + Inflation rate + 0.4(Inflation rate – 2%) + 0.7(% Output gap)

**13.** Explain the time inconsistency problem of monetary policy and how its existence strengthens the case for a monetary policy rule over a regime of monetary policy discretion.

**14.** Explain the difference between an active monetary policy rule and a passive rule. Give an example of each rule.

**15.** Using Table 24-1 and Figure 24-4, contrast the Fed's performance in the 2001 recession and the 1973–1975 recession.

**16.** Using the most recent data from the FRED database (see methods and sources associated with construction of Figure 24-5), calculate the most recent federal funds rate that would be prescribed by the Taylor rule. How does your calculated rate compare with today's actual Fed funds rate? What conclusion can you draw from this comparison?

[redacted]

# ADDITIONAL READING

- For a more in-depth discussion of the self-correcting mechanism, see any principles of macroeconomics or intermediate macroeconomics textbook. For an interesting look at economists' forecasting acumen in the Great Depression, see Kathryn Dominguez, Ray Fair, and Matthew Shapiro, "Forecasting the Depression: Harvard versus Yale," *American Economic Review,* September 1988, pp. 595–612.
- An excellent book on monetarism, written during its period of peak popularity, is Thomas Mayer, *The Structure of Monetarism* (New York: Norton, 1980).
- The seminal work on rules versus discretion is Henry Simon, "Rules Versus Authority in Monetary Policy," *Journal of Political Economy,* February 1936, pp. 1–30.
- Milton Friedman's position on the constant money growth rule is set forth in "A Monetary and Fiscal Framework for Economic Stability," *American Economic Review,* June 1948, pp. 245–264, and *A Program for Monetary Stability* (New York: Fordham University Press, 1983). A powerful critique of this viewpoint is provided by Paul Samuelson, "Reflections on Central Banking," in Joseph Stiglitz, ed., *The Collected Scientific Papers of Paul Samuelson,* Volume 2 (Cambridge, MA: MIT Press, 1966, pp. 1361–1386).
- Christina Romer's hypothesis that early estimates of U.S. industrial production and GDP overstate the degree of output instability is presented in "The Prewar Business Cycle Reconsidered: New Estimates of GNP, 1869–1908," *The Journal of Political Economy,* 1989, pp. 1–37, and "Is the Stabilization of the Postwar Economy a Figment of the Data?" *American Economic Review,* June 1986, pp. 314–334.
- The original work analyzing the time inconsistency problem is Finn Kydland and Edward Prescott, "Rules Versus Discretion: The Inconsistency of Optimal Plans," *Journal of Political Economy* 85, 1977, pp. 473–491. These authors were awarded the Nobel Prize in economics in 2004.
- A huge literature on the Taylor rule and related policy rules has emerged since the appearance of John Taylor's seminal article, "Discretion versus Policy Rules in Practice," *Carnegie-Rochester Conference Series on Public Policy,* 1993, No. 39, pp. 193–214. See articles by Taylor and other economists in Taylor's (edited) book, *Monetary Policy Rules* (Chicago: University of Chicago Press, 2001).
- Informative articles on the general topic of monetary policy rules include Sharon Kozicki, "How Useful Are Taylor Rules for Monetary Policy?," *Federal Reserve Bank of Kansas City Economic Review,* 1999, No. 2, pp. 5–33, Lawrence Ball and Robert R. Tchaidze, "The Fed and the New Economy," *American Economic Review,* May 2002, pp. 108–114, and Athanasios Orphanides, "Historical Monetary Policy Analysis and the Taylor Rule," *Journal of Monetary Economics,* July 2003, pp. 983–1022. The latter article contains a comprehensive list of references on the Taylor rule. An interesting article that uses the Taylor rule and other monetary policy rules to demonstrate that Japanese monetary policy was quite restrictive in the 1990s is Bennett McCallum, "Japanese Monetary Policy," Federal Reserve Bank of Richmond *Economic Quarterly,* Winter 2003, pp. 1–31.

# Chapter 25

# INFLATION TARGETING

Milton Friedman once said that inflation is always and everywhere a monetary phenomenon. Economists today agree that the long-run evolution of a nation's price level is predominantly a function of the central bank's behavior. In the near term, a variety of nonmonetary forces can touch off inflation. A severe drought may drive up food prices and the nation's price level over the following 1 to 2 years. Similarly, a sharp increase in crude oil prices may trigger an increased price level. A burst of military expenditures or a sharp depreciation of a nation's currency on foreign exchange markets can cause temporary bouts of inflation. However, the effects of such events on the price level are short lived unless the events are accompanied by accommodative monetary policy. Historically, all serious inflations have been associated with or accompanied by rapid increases in the quantity of money. Because a nation's central bank is responsible for the trend behavior of the money supply, the central bank also is responsible for the long-run behavior of the nation's price level.

Inflation is bad news. Inflation creates inefficiencies that reduce national output in the near term. When inflation is high, economic agents have difficulty recognizing whether an increase in the price of a particular good or service is an increase in the *relative* price of that good or service. Thus, inflation hinders the ability of market economies to allocate resources efficiently. Furthermore, in times of high inflation, individuals and firms devote resources and attention to combatting inflation, diverting time and effort from the production of goods and services. Behavior that is inefficient from society's viewpoint often becomes rational from an individual or firm's viewpoint. Consider the socially wasteful phenomenon of companies reprinting catalogues and brochures monthly rather than annually because rapid price increases quickly render the older publications obsolete.

Second, because inflation creates an atmosphere of uncertainty and low visibility, firms reduce expenditures on research, development, and other capital projects having long-term payoffs. Because such business expenditures are crucial to the development of new technologies and the associated growth of productivity and living standards, high inflation reduces the long-term growth of living standards.

Finally, inflation capriciously and unfairly redistributes the nation's income and wealth. Because severe inflation is seldom fully anticipated, real interest rates and real wages typically fall. The decline in real interest rates means that wealth is redistributed from lenders to borrowers—that is, from creditors to debtors. One of the most objectionable aspects of inflation has been inflation's propensity to transfer wealth from prudent and thrifty individuals of all ages and older retirees living off savings accumulated over a lifetime of hard work to aggressive persons willing to incur large amounts of debt.[1] Inflation is socially divisive.

[1] The consequences of inflation change over time as a nation's institutions adapt to ongoing inflation. For example, social security benefits in the United States have been indexed to the consumer price index (CPI) since the 1970s. If CPI increases by 3 percent in the 12 months ending in October, social security payments also increase 3 percent, beginning the following January. In 1997, the U.S. government introduced an indexed bond whose principal increases each year in line with CPI. For these and other reasons, older individuals are not as severely impacted by inflation today as they were in earlier times.

**Table 25-1** Average Annual CPI Inflation Rates in Selected Industrial Countries from 1970 to 1990

| Country | Average Annual Inflation Rate (%) |
|---|---|
| Germany | 3.8 |
| Japan | 5.2 |
| United States | 6.2 |
| Canada | 6.8 |
| France | 7.9 |
| Australia | 8.9 |
| United Kingdom | 10.1 |
| New Zealand | 11.4 |
| Italy | 11.6 |
| **All Industrial Countries** | **7.0** |

*Source: International Monetary Fund,* International Financial Statistics Annual Yearbook

During the 1970s and 1980s, many countries experienced high inflation rates, as indicated in Table 25-1. Note that the average annual inflation rate for all industrial nations in the world during these 2 decades was 7 percent per year, a rate that approximately doubles a nation's price level each decade. In this period, inflation rates averaged more than 10 percent per year in Italy, New Zealand, and the United Kingdom. Inflation rates were considerably higher in emerging-market economies and less developed countries.

More than 20 nations have implemented an *inflation targeting* strategy since 1990 because of the relatively high inflation in most nations from 1970 to 1990 and the increasing recognition of governments and central banks as the fundamental sources of inflation. The nations include both industrialized countries (Canada, United Kingdom, Australia, Sweden) and emerging-market economies (Chile, Brazil, Mexico, Korea). In this chapter, the meaning of (and rationale for) inflation targeting and the arguments for and against its implementation are discussed. We examine the various practical issues that must be addressed when establishing an inflation targeting regime. We discuss the experience of countries that have implemented inflation targeting regimes and look at the contentious issue of whether the Federal Reserve should implement inflation targeting in the United States.

## INFLATION TARGETING: ITS MEANING AND POTENTIAL BENEFITS

When a nation implements a monetary policy strategy of **inflation targeting,** the nation explicitly identifies very low inflation as the nation's predominant intermediate and long-term objective. The nation announces a specific *numerical inflation target level* (say 2 percent per year) or *band* (say 1–3 percent per year) at or within which the nation commits to maintain inflation. The nation also announces a time frame within which the central bank intends to hit the target. Importantly, the country backs up the announcement with a systematic and credible plan for achieving the inflation target. Monetary authorities must develop a methodology for forecasting inflation that involves a macroeconomic model or a set of indicators containing information about

**inflation targeting**
monetary policy strategy in which a specific low inflation rate (or band of rates) is proclaimed as its predominant intermediate and long-term objective

future inflation. The central bank must implement a forward-looking operating procedure in which the central bank's short-range operating targets (typically short-term interest rates) are adjusted in response to deviations between the central bank's forecast of inflation and the specific inflation target. The central bank normally increases short-term interest rates if inflation appears likely to exceed the target.

Extensive communication between the central bank and the public about the policy process, progress toward hitting the inflation target, and the central bank's intentions is accomplished through various measures. These measures include speeches, written reports issued by monetary authorities, publication of central bank meeting minutes, and periodic testimony of central bank officials before legislative bodies. In some countries, an *escape clause* extending the time horizon for hitting the inflation target is provided in case of extenuating circumstances such as a severe supply shock (for example, a sharp increase in oil prices). In some countries, a penalty is levied against the central bank for failing to achieve the specified inflation target. In New Zealand, an extreme case, the governor of the central bank can be dismissed for missing the inflation target. In other countries (Canada, Israel, Brazil, United Kingdom), the central bank must provide a public explanation or write an open letter to the government accounting for any deviations from the inflation target and disclosing measures being taken to correct the problem.

Many economists advocating inflation targeting consider the strategy a *framework* for monetary policy rather than a monetary policy *rule*. A constant money growth rule or other rule precludes monetary policy discretion. In contrast, most proponents of inflation targeting believe the central bank should be free to pursue important alternative objectives in the near term while being constrained in the long run by the overriding objective of maintaining low inflation. Near-term objectives include preventing major instability in financial markets and exchange rates. Thus, inflation targeting can be described as a policy of "constrained discretion."

## Arguments in Favor of Inflation Targeting

Central banks of industrialized nations have long regarded maintenance of relatively stable prices as their primary—if not *overriding*—responsibility. Certainly the Federal Reserve has regarded price stability as its primary responsibility. The Fed has never used an inflation targeting framework but nevertheless has maintained inflation at low and stable rates averaging about 2.5 percent per year since 1990. Over the years, the Federal Reserve has frequently reminded the public of the crucial importance of price stability and has provided continuing reassurance of the Fed's commitment to maintaining stable prices. What then are the advantages of formalizing a central bank's responsibility for maintaining low inflation through an explicit strategy of inflation targeting? An inflation targeting regime provides a *nominal anchor* for monetary policy, increases the *transparency* of monetary policy and the *accountability* of the central bank, increases the central bank's *credibility* in fighting inflation, and reduces the likelihood of a nation becoming caught in a deflationary spiral.

**Providing a Nominal Anchor for Monetary Policy.** For a society to enjoy reasonably low inflation over the long run and relatively low average rates of unemployment, inflation expectations must be tied down and maintained at a low level. We define an *anchor* as a mechanism or mode of monetary policy that ties down inflation expectations and strongly assures the public that development of serious inflation will not be allowed. In the absence of an anchor, policy actions may drift in response to short-term economic and political developments and become inconsistent with long-range policy goals.

Prior to the advent of inflation targeting in the 1990s, many countries targeted monetary aggregates or exchange rates to anchor the public's expectations. Given the strong and stable link between money growth and inflation in many countries in the early decades after World War II, many countries in the 1970s and 1980s conducted monetary policy by announcing targets for growth rates of monetary aggregates (M1, M2, M3). These money growth targets were set at relatively low rates to convince the public that inflation would be well contained. Among the countries that targeted monetary aggregates were the United States, Germany, Switzerland, Japan, Canada, and the United Kingdom. If actual money growth deviated substantially from announced targets, central bankers typically were required to explain these deviations in testimony before legislative bodies. These reporting procedures diminished the prospects for high inflation and helped anchor the public's expectations about future prices.

In the 1980s and 1990s, most central banks abandoned monetary aggregates as targets because the relationship between these aggregates and the nation's output and price level became more unstable and uncertain, as discussed in Chapter 22. By the 1990s, most countries had replaced the monetary aggregates with short-term interest rates as their short-range operating targets for influencing economic activity. Some nations experiencing relatively low inflation feared that, in the absence of an explicit anchor, an inflationary bias would creep into monetary policy. These countries implemented inflation targeting regimes. Other nations already experiencing high inflation implemented inflation targeting to facilitate disinflation. These countries typically first set their inflation targets moderately high and gradually reduced the target levels after achieving the earlier targets.

Some countries anchor monetary policy using exchange rates, pegging their currency to the U.S. dollar or another strong currency or a basket of currencies. If a nation's currency threatens to depreciate against the currency to which it is pegged, the nation's central bank reduces money growth and raises interest rates to strengthen the local currency. These measures strongly tend to lock in a country's inflation rate to the inflation rate of the larger nation to which the exchange rate is fixed, thereby providing an anchor for monetary policy. The system works well as long as the exchange rate target is compatible with favorable domestic conditions. However, exchange rates can become misaligned, forcing the central bank to conduct policies inconsistent with domestic goals in order to maintain the exchange rate target. This problem caused both the United Kingdom and Sweden to leave Europe's exchange rate mechanism in 1992. The United Kingdom and Sweden promptly implemented inflation targeting regimes to establish a new anchor for monetary policy.

**Increasing the Central Bank's Transparency and Accountability.** A *transparent* monetary policy is a policy in which the public can easily and clearly observe the central bank's actions and intentions. Greater transparency increases monetary policy's effectiveness. If a central bank announces it is implementing an inflation targeting regime and intends to maintain inflation at 2 percent per year on average over the next 3 years, the bank's intentions are much more transparent than if the central bank simply states its goal is to "maintain relatively stable prices over the long run." With increased transparency comes increased accountability. When an inflation targeting central bank misses its target, policymakers must provide an explanation. In some cases, such as a major unanticipated supply shock, failure to hit the inflation target may be justifiable. In cases of monetary mismanagement, the government may hold the central bank accountable.

Advocates of inflation targeting emphasize that such a regime focuses public attention on what a central bank can achieve in the long run. Advocates point out that a central bank *cannot* increase long-run economic growth through expansionary policies. The best possible central bank accomplishment in this regard is maintaining price stability so that the true sources of economic growth (technological innovation, physical and human capital formation, and so forth) can thrive.

The central bank cannot achieve continuous full employment. Uncertainties about nonpolicy factors currently influencing aggregate demand and supply conditions, long and variable lags of monetary policy, and the full-employment rate of unemployment (NAIRU) make the continuous full employment achievement virtually impossible. No reputable economist believes a central bank, no matter how brilliantly managed, can prevent cyclical fluctuations in economic activity and thereby maintain continuous full employment. However, a central bank *can* maintain relatively stable prices in the long run. Advocates of inflation targeting argue that focusing attention on what a central bank can accomplish likely reduces political pressures on the central bank. Thus, inflation targeting reduces the likelihood of a central bank becoming involved in the time inconsistency debacle discussed in Chapter 24.

Advocates believe an inflation targeting regime would spare the United States many of the mistakes committed by the Federal Reserve in the past. Examples include the inflationary monetary stimulus associated with the U.S. intervention in Vietnam in the late 1960s, the inflationary policies of the late 1970s, and the excessive monetary restraint during the Great Depression of the early 1930s. (In the latter episode, the U.S. price level *fell* more than 6 percent per year). In many countries, average inflation rates experienced over a period of years likely will be lower if an inflation targeting regime is in place.

**Increasing Central Bank Credibility.** Implementation of an inflation targeting regime increases the transparency and accountability of the monetary authorities and thereby increases the central bank's credibility. The public's understanding of the central bank's commitment to low inflation increases because the commitment is explicit and specific rather than implicit and vague. The public's understanding is critical because a clear understanding of the central bank's intentions inevitably influences the public's inflation expectations. Several advantages accrue if the public is convinced the central bank is absolutely committed to low inflation. Individuals and firms are more inclined to make long-term commitments based on economic fundamentals rather than the inflation outlook. Risk premiums built into the discount rates that market participants apply to payments expected from bonds and stocks may decrease, boosting asset prices and reducing the cost of capital.[2]

The *Phillips curve* shows that lower unemployment is associated with higher inflation, *given other factors.* In an inflation targeting regime, workers may be content with smaller nominal wage increases because they expect lower inflation. In this case, the short-run Phillips curve is located to the left of the curve that would prevail in the absence of inflation targeting. The nation can enjoy lower unemployment for any given inflation rate (or lower inflation for any given rate of unemployment). A Phillips curve located closer to the origin is unambiguously beneficial to a nation.

---

[2] Higher bond and stock prices reduce the cost of capital, thereby stimulating investment expenditures. Higher bond prices (lower bond yields) reduce the cost to firms of issuing debt (bonds). Higher stock prices reduce the cost to firms of issuing equity (shares of stock). Hence, average annual investment expenditures may be higher if an inflation targeting regime is in place and inflation expectations and long-term interest rates are lower.

As indicated, some nations (Israel, Chile, Brazil, Mexico) have implemented inflation targeting as part of a strategy to bring extremely high inflation rates down to acceptable levels. Disinflation policies almost always involve an important cost to society in the form of a transition period of reduced output and increased unemployment. Economists define the **sacrifice ratio** as the percentage of 1 year's output (GDP) a nation must forgo or "sacrifice" to reduce the inflation rate by one percentage point. If the U.S. sacrifice ratio is 5 and the nation's GDP is $12,000 billion ($12 trillion) per year, the one-time cost of reducing inflation from 4 to 3 percent per year is 0.05 × $12,000 billion, or $600 billion of lost output. Thus, the cost is approximately $2,000 per person in the United States.

**sacrifice ratio**
percentage of 1 year's output (GDP) that a nation must forgo or "sacrifice" in order to reduce its inflation rate by one percentage point

**YOUR TURN**

In the early 1980s under the leadership of Chairman Paul Volcker, the Federal Reserve implemented restrictive measures that reduced the U.S. inflation rate from 12 to 4 percent per year. Assuming the sacrifice ratio was 4 and U.S. GDP was running at a rate of $3,000 billion ($3 trillion) per year, calculate the cost of the disinflation policy.

Advocates believe an inflation targeting regime benefits a society seeking to decrease inflation by lowering the sacrifice ratio, thereby reducing the cost of disinflation policies. The economic rationale for this claim is illustrated in Figure 25-1, which uses our elementary tools of aggregate demand (AD) and aggregate supply (AS) to explain fluctuations in output and the price level.

**Figure 25-1** Potential Role of Inflation Targeting in Reducing the Cost of Disinflation Policy

If an inflation targeting regime increases the central bank's credibility in fighting inflation, the magnitude by which the nation's AS curve shifts leftward because of inflation expectations is reduced. The inflation targeting regime lowers the sacrifice ratio—that is, reduces the cost of disinflation.

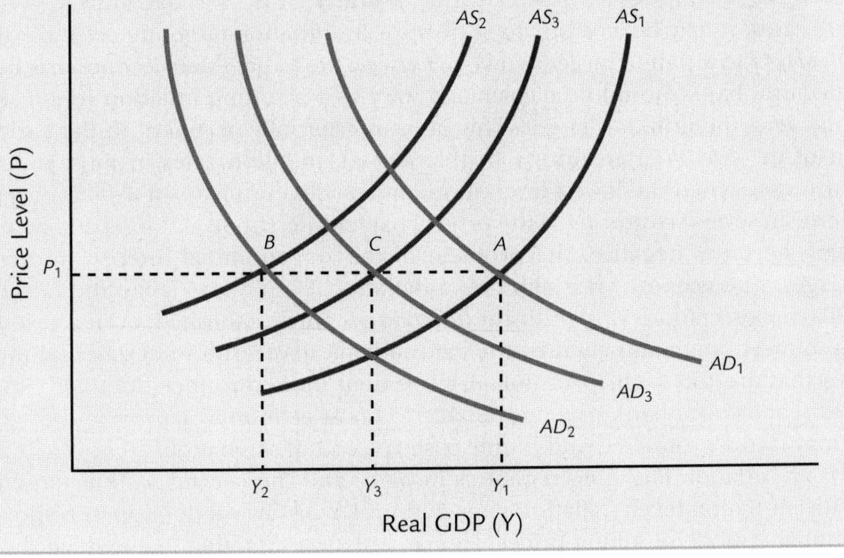

Suppose, at a given point in time, the economy is at point *A* (intersection of $AS_1$ and $AD_1$), output is at $Y_1$, and the price level is at $P_1$. Assume these curves have been shifting about with the result that the nation's price level has been increasing at a rate of 10 percent per year for several years. If inflation expectations are well entrenched, the AS curve persistently shifts leftward as wages rise in response to expected inflation. The AD curve has been shifting rightward as the central bank has sought to maintain high output and employment levels in the face of the leftward-shifting AS curve. (Together, the rightward-shifting AD curve and the leftward-shifting AS curve account for the ongoing 10 percent annual inflation.)

Now, assume the central bank announces its desire and intention to stop inflation. In the absence of an inflation targeting regime, the public is uncertain of the strength of the central bank's commitment to bring down inflation. Wages continue to rise fairly rapidly despite the bank's announcement, shifting the AS curve from $AS_1$ to $AS_2$ in the first year. To stop inflation cold (maintain the price level at $P_1$), the central bank would have to pursue highly restrictive measures shifting the AD curve down from $AD_1$ to $AD_2$. In this case, we move to point *B* in the figure. Equilibrium output falls to $Y_2$ as the price level is maintained at $P_1$. The cost of stopping inflation is high because the reduction in output $(Y_1 - Y_2)$ is large.

Now assume instead the central bank announces implementation of an inflation targeting regime. The explicit target is set at zero and is to be achieved within 1 year, with sanctions applied to the central bank for failing to achieve the target. If the plan convinces the public the central bank is dead serious about stopping inflation, wage hikes will moderate significantly. The AS curve will shift leftward by a lesser amount than in the absence of the inflation targeting regime. Given more modest wage hikes, assume AS shifts from $AS_1$ to $AS_3$ during the ensuing year. In this event, the central bank only needs to shift down the AD curve from $AD_1$ to $AD_3$ to maintain the price level constant at $P_1$. We end up at point *C*, with output at $Y_3$ rather than $Y_2$. The loss of output associated with maintaining the price level at $P_1$ is $(Y_1 - Y_3)$—a smaller loss than in the absence of inflation targeting $(Y_1 - Y_2)$. In this example, introducing an inflation targeting regime reduced the sacrifice ratio. The crucial issue centers on the extent to an explicit inflation targeting regime enhances credibility of the central bank's commitment to reducing inflation.

**Reducing Prospects of Becoming Stalled in a Deflationary Cycle.** In some cases, it may be as costly to society for an inflation-targeting central bank to *undershoot* the inflation target as it is to *overshoot* the target. Many economists believe the central bank should be particularly wary of permitting inflation to fall significantly *below* the inflation target. This point is especially pertinent in the early portion of the twenty-first century. In this period, inflation rates in most industrial countries reached the lowest levels in many decades, and fears of *deflation* began to emerge in several countries. If the central bank undershoots its target and actual inflation becomes negative, the problem of the zero nominal interest rate bound emerges. The economy may slip into a deflationary spiral, as Japan did in the late 1990s. If expectations of significant *deflation* become established, even a zero nominal interest rate maintained by the central bank may result in *ex ante* real interest rates that are too high to stimulate investment and consumer durables expenditures. The central bank may not be able to boost economic activity, and the country may face a protracted and highly costly period of stagnation.

If an inflation targeting regime is in place and the central bank is targeting a positive inflation level, deflation expectations less likely will develop in response to an initial episode of falling prices. Hence, inflation targeting may reduce the likelihood of the economy becoming stalled in a Japanese-type deflationary morass.

**Exhibit 25-1** Should the Bank of Japan Target Inflation or the Price *Level*?

Several eminent economists, including two who have served on the Federal Reserve Board of Governors (Alan Blinder and Ben Bernanke), have recommended that the Bank of Japan (BOJ) adopt a monetary policy regime of targeting the price *level* rather than the *inflation rate.* As we will demonstrate, for countries battling *deflation,* price level targeting likely will be more effective than inflation targeting.

For several years in the late 1990s and early 2000s, Japan's general price level *declined* by approximately 1 percent per year. That is, Japan experienced deflation. Assume the Japanese price index was 100 in the year 2000 and declined to 99, 98, and 97 in 2001, 2002, and 2003, respectively. Suppose an inflation targeting regime had been in place, with an inflation target of 1 percent per year. In 2001, the BOJ would attempt to push up the price index from its 2000 level of 100 to 101. However, as indicated, the actual price index actually declined to 99 in 2001. Maintaining its 1 percent per year inflation target, the BOJ would aim to push the index back to 100 (99.9, to be precise) in the following year (2002). Monetary policy would exhibit approximately the same degree of stimulus in 2002 as in 2001, even though the BOJ undershot its inflation target for 2001.

On the other hand, suppose the BOJ targets the price *level* in a regime in which the target level of the price index is stepped up one point each year—that is, the target is 101, 102, and 103 for 2001, 2002, and 2003, respectively. If the price level fell to 99 in 2001, the BOJ would aim for roughly 3 percent inflation in 2002 to get the price level up to the 102 target. The amount of monetary stimulus prescribed by price level targeting is much greater than that called for by inflation targeting in this case. By the end of 2003, if the price index were 97 and the price level target around 103, the price level targeting procedure would call for roughly 6 percent inflation for 2004, while the inflation targeting regime would prescribe only 1 percent inflation.

The crucial point is as follows. If the central bank is to reduce *ex ante* real interest rates sufficiently to extricate a country from a deflationary spiral, the bank must overcome *deflationary psychology.* For example, if the public expects prices to fall 1 percent per year, the lowest *ex ante* real interest rate the central bank can possibly deliver is +1 percent—the *ex ante* real rate when the nominal interest rate is zero. This real rate may not be low enough to boost interest-sensitive expenditures in a stagnant economic environment. Significantly *negative ex ante* real rates may be required. If the public knows the amount of monetary stimulus provided by the central bank will be progressively stepped up each period as long as the price level continues to fall, deflationary expectations less likely will develop. The rationale for price *level* targeting is eliminating deflation expectations and thereby cutting short the vicious cycle of falling prices, rising real interest rates, declining expenditures, and falling prices. For countries experiencing deflation, price level targeting more likely will achieve the objective than will inflation targeting.

(On the issue of Japanese monetary policy, see Exhibit 25-1, which analyzes a proposal for the Japanese central bank to conduct monetary policy by setting a *price level* target rather than an *inflation* target.)

## Arguments Against Inflation Targeting

Critics of inflation targeting raise several arguments. First and most importantly, setting numerical targets for inflation may reduce the central bank's flexibility to address important objectives of monetary policy other than maintaining low inflation. Second, inflation targeting requires the central bank to adopt a forward-looking monetary policy that uses inflation *forecasts.* But inflation is difficult to forecast, and errors in these forecasts can cause problems for monetary policy in an inflation targeting regime. Third, if output were to become systematically less stable because of overwhelming central bank emphasis placed on hitting the inflation targets, economic planning and decision making of businesses and households could be hindered.

**Inflation Targeting Reduces the Flexibility of Monetary Policy.** Maintaining price level stability is critically important but is not the only monetary policy objective. Monetary policy cannot maintain continuous full employment. However, most economists believe monetary policy *can* reduce instability of output, especially when major shocks occur. Suppose an aggregate demand shock resulting from an event such as a major terrorist attack reduces consumer and business confidence. The Fed can implement expansionary policies that reduce the severity and duration of the resulting economic slowdown or contraction. Similarly, in the event of a large adverse supply shock such as a major increase in oil prices, the Fed can reduce the magnitude and duration of the ensuing economic contraction through expansionary policies. The central bank also can respond to other unexpected crises that occur occasionally. Examples from the past quarter century include the 1984 collapse of the Continental Illinois Bank, the Asian Crisis of 1997, the near-collapse of the hedge fund Long-Term Capital Management in 1998 in the wake of the Russian crisis, and the Y2K problem at the turn of the millennium.

To simplify analysis, assume monetary policy has only two objectives—(1) maintaining inflation at low levels near 2 percent per year and (2) maintaining stability of output and employment at high levels close to full employment. Consider the following societal **loss function,** an equation that indicates the cost or loss to society associated with the twin "evils" of inflation and deviations of output from full employment levels.

**loss function**
equation indicating the cost or loss to society associated with the twin "evils" of deviations of inflation from desired rate and deviations of output from full employment levels

(25-1) $$\mathbf{L = b\,(\%\Delta P - 2\%)^2 + (1 - b)\,(Y - Y^*)^2.}$$

In the equation, L is the loss to society, $\%\Delta P$ is the current inflation rate, Y is current output, and $Y^*$ is the natural or full-employment output level. This equation indicates society is adversely affected (suffers loss) both by deviations of inflation from the desired 2 percent level and by deviations of output from desired high levels. Both inflation and lost output impose costs on society, which are collectively measured by L (loss). The desired inflation rate is assumed to be 2 percent per year, and the desired output level is $Y^*$. Deviations from the desired inflation rate and output level are squared so that deviations on *either* side of the desired rates are shown to be costly, and *large* deviations from the desired levels are shown to be *disproportionately* costly. In the loss function, the relative weights that society places on inflation and lost output are indicated by b and (1 − b), respectively, which add up to 1. If society does not care about inflation, b = 0. If society does not care about lost output, b = 1. If society places equal weights on these two evils, both b and (1 − b) are 0.5.

Maintaining low inflation is *explicitly* emphasized in an inflation targeting regime; maintaining stable output at high levels is not. In an inflation targeting regime, the central bank's loss function may differ from society's loss function because the central bank incurs government-imposed penalties for failing to achieve the specified inflation target. That is, the central bank may exhibit a larger b [and smaller (1 − b)] in its loss function than does society in its loss function. The central bank may place excessive priority on achieving the explicit inflation target relative to the implicit goal of maintaining a high and stable output level. Therefore, output and employment may be more unstable and lower on average than in a monetary policy regime in which inflation targeting is not in place. Critics of inflation targeting suspect the politics of inflation targeting countries encourage the central bank to devote inadequate priority to maintaining output stability at high levels.

The problem more likely occurs in the event of aggregate supply shocks than aggregate demand shocks. Suppose terrorism increases worldwide. Consumer and business confidence decreases. Industrial countries experience downward-shifting AD curves. Because a downward shift in AD leads to downward pressure on the price level, an inflation-targeting central bank that initially was hitting its inflation target is signaled to implement stimulative measures as actual inflation is expected to fall below the target. Monetary stimulus counters the weakness in output and alleviates the downward pressure on the price level. In the case of an AD shock, therefore, targeting inflation is consistent with targeting output stability.

On the other hand, assume we experience a major supply shock in the form of a severe worldwide drought. The AS curve shifts leftward. In this case, the shock boosts inflation and *reduces* output. In the absence of an escape clause, an inflation-targeting central bank is signaled to implement restrictive policies to avoid overshooting its inflation target. The central bank's restrictive policies reduce output more than if the central bank were not targeting inflation. Inflation targeting may be incompatible with maintaining stable and high output levels. Central banks using inflation targeting regimes may experience output instability if important supply shocks occur. To address this issue, several countries using inflation targeting provide the central bank with an escape clause in the event of major supply shocks. Other inflation targeting countries partially address the problem by using a "core" measure of inflation that excludes energy and food prices.[3]

**Inflation Targeting is Hindered by Difficulties in Forecasting Inflation.** Monetary policy influences inflation with a relatively long lag of perhaps 1 year or longer. An effective inflation targeting regime requires that monetary policy be adjusted in response to inflation that is expected to occur *1 year or more in the future.* The regime requires reasonably accurate forecasts of future inflation. Unfortunately, inflation is difficult to forecast, especially over horizons of 1 year or longer. Studies indicate inflation forecasts tend to underestimate inflation when it is relatively high and overestimate inflation when it is relatively low. In the late 1990s, the U.S. inflation rate drifted downward and ultimately reached the lowest levels in 40 or 50 years. Both econometric models and surveys of households and professional economists provided inflation forecasts that consistently were too high. Had the Federal Reserve been operating under a regime of inflation targeting, the Fed would have implemented more restrictive actions than it actually did. The Fed would have restrained the economy and perhaps prevented the above-normal output growth and unusually low unemployment rates enjoyed by the country from 1995 to 2000. By letting the economy rip, the Greenspan Federal Reserve may have engineered an economic performance in the 1990s superior to the performance that would have ensued in an inflation targeting regime.[4]

---

[3] Australia partly circumvents this problem by defining its inflation target in terms of the average inflation rate experienced over the *full business cycle.* It also targets an inflation measure that involves the "core" CPI rather than the "headline" CPI.

[4] On the other hand, Greenspan's critics charge the Fed should have boosted interest rates after 1995 or 1996 to slow or deflate the "bubble" developing in the stock market. The bubble spilled over and contributed to overinvestment in equipment, especially in the technology and telecommunications sectors. After the bubble popped, the United States experienced a protracted period of extremely weak investment spending. Hence, the Fed's critics charge that the Fed could have contributed to economic stability by dealing with the bubble early on. The issue of whether central banks should attempt to pop perceived bubbles is highly contentious.

**Inflation Targeting Increases Uncertainty about Future Output.** Advocates of inflation targeting point out the advantages of low and stable inflation, which facilitates households' and firms' planning and decision making. Critics of inflation targeting argue that the greater *output* instability that likely prevails under inflation targeting could have severe adverse consequences. Agents who believe inflation targeting leads the central bank to place lower priority on stabilizing output at high levels may anticipate increased cyclical instability. Economic planning by households and firms would be hindered, and firms would be reluctant to engage in research and development expenditures and other forms of investments with long-term payoffs.

## PRACTICAL CONSIDERATIONS IN IMPLEMENTING INFLATION TARGETING

Most countries around the globe experienced relatively high inflation rates in the 1970s and 1980s. Some countries (Chile, Mexico) implemented inflation targeting to facilitate efforts to bring down very high inflation rates. Other countries (Australia, United Kingdom) implemented inflation targeting as part of a plan to maintain price stability *after* bringing down inflation through restrictive policies. Figure 25-2 indicates the year inflation targeting was implemented in a sample of 16 nations and the rate of CPI inflation in the 12 months prior to implementation. Four nations in our sample experienced annual inflation rates greater than 15 percent in the year immediately prior to inflation targeting. Seven nations experienced inflation rates less than 5 percent per year.

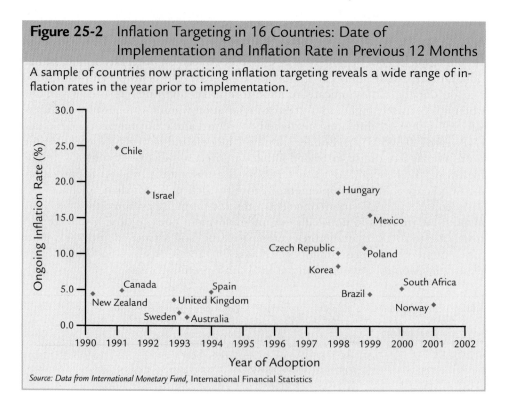

**Figure 25-2** Inflation Targeting in 16 Countries: Date of Implementation and Inflation Rate in Previous 12 Months

A sample of countries now practicing inflation targeting reveals a wide range of inflation rates in the year prior to implementation.

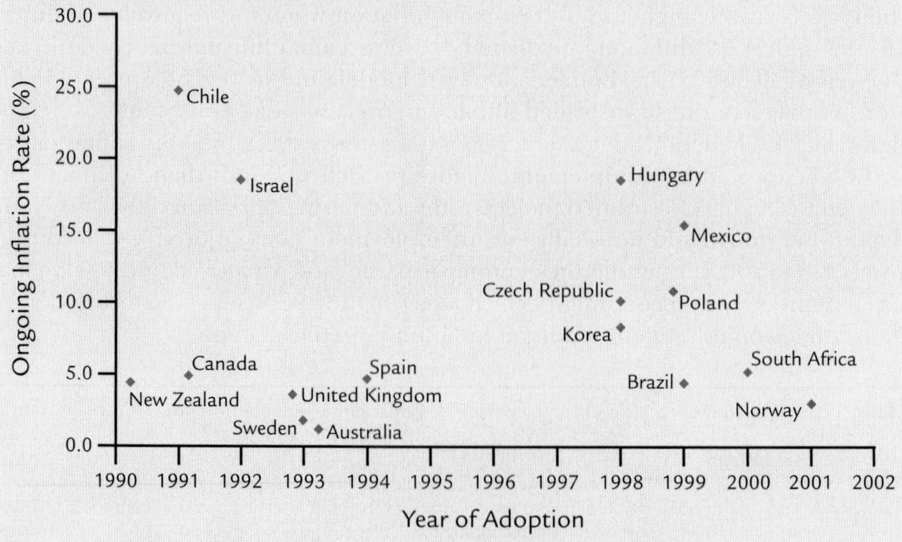


*Source: Data from International Monetary Fund,* International Financial Statistics

A country implementing inflation targeting must make several decisions. Who sets the target—the government or the central bank? Which index of prices should be used to compute the inflation rate to be targeted? (On this issue as it pertains to the United States, see Exhibit 25-2.) Should the inflation target be indicated as a specific *number* or a specific *band* within which inflation is to be maintained? At what specific *level* (or within what specific *band of numbers*) should the inflation target be set? If the target is to be specified as a band, how wide should the band be? Over what specific time frame is the inflation target to be achieved? Should escape clauses permitting the central bank to deviate from the target be included, and, if so, what kinds of circumstances should the escape clauses include? Finally, in order to promote maximum incentive of central bankers to actually achieve the inflation targets and thereby enhance monetary policy credibility, should sanctions be imposed on the central bank if the inflation target is not achieved? If so, what should the sanctions include?

Examining the features actually adopted in countries that have implemented inflation targeting is useful when discussing these issues. Table 25-2 lists a sample of 11 nations that use inflation targeting and some specific aspects of inflation targeting they utilize. The countries listed in the table are arranged chronologically according to when the inflation targeting regimes were implemented.

New Zealand was the first nation to implement inflation targeting. New Zealand initiated the regime in March 1990 after a 20-year period in which inflation averaged 11.4 percent per year (review Table 25-1). Countries that followed New Zealand include Chile, Canada, Israel, the United Kingdom, Sweden, Australia, and many others. The United States and the European Central Bank (ECB) have never implemented an explicit strategy of inflation targeting, although many economists

**Table 25-2 Aspects of Inflation Targeting in Selected Countries**

| Country | Date Introduced | Target Set By | Price Index Targeted | Target Width (2003) | Escape Clauses |
|---|---|---|---|---|---|
| New Zealand | March 1990 | Government and central bank | CPI* | 1–3% | Unusual events |
| Chile | January 1991 | Government and central bank | CPI | 2–4% | None |
| Canada | February 1991 | Government and central bank | Core CPI | 1–3% | Major supply shocks |
| Israel | January 1992 | Government | CPI | 3–4% | None |
| UK | October 1992 | Government | CPI* | 0–2% | None |
| Sweden | January 1993 | Central bank | CPI | 1–3% | None |
| Australia | July 1993 | Government and central bank | Core CPI | 2–3%** | None |
| Czech Republic | January 1998 | Central bank | Core CPI | 1–3% | Major supply shocks |
| Korea | January 1998 | Government | CPI | 2.5–3.5% | None |
| Poland | October 1998 | Central bank | CPI | 1.5–3.5% | None |
| Mexico | January 1999 | Central bank | CPI | 3.0% | None |

*The consumer price index (CPI) targeted by New Zealand and the United Kingdom excludes interest expense on mortgages.
**Australia's target range applies to average rate over a business cycle.

believe the ECB's policy procedure very closely meets the criteria for inflation targeting.

## Who Sets the Target and What Price Index Should be Used?

Note in Table 25-2 that the target in some inflation targeting countries is set by the government (Israel, United Kingdom, Korea). In other countries (Sweden, Czech Republic, Poland, Mexico), the inflation target is selected by the central bank. In New Zealand, Chile, Canada, and Australia, the target is established jointly by the central bank and the government.

The ideal price index for calculating the inflation rate to be targeted should have the following characteristics. The public should be familiar with the index. The index should accurately reflect changes in costs of the market basket consumed by the typical family. The central bank should be capable of controlling the index over the medium and long terms. If the central bank has little control over the chosen price index in the medium term, frequent target misses occur, reducing the central bank's credibility. Many central banks use the consumer price index (CPI) because of the CPI's widespread familiarity. However, because supply shocks beyond the central bank's control significantly influence the CPI, several countries (Canada, Australia, Czech Republic) target the inflation rate derived from a "core CPI" that removes food and energy prices from the index.[5]

## What Is the Appropriate Level or Band for the Inflation Target?

If the central bank chooses to target a specific inflation rate rather than a band of rates, the central bank has less flexibility to react to developments that occur occasionally. Suppose inflation is currently on target but then a severe drought temporarily pushes up inflation. The central bank may be forced into more restrictive actions if it is operating under a specific inflation target rather than a band. On the other hand, the central bank has less credibility with the public when the bank specifies the inflation target as a band, especially a relatively wide band. Hence, a trade-off is involved between central bank flexibility and credibility. Measures giving the central bank more flexibility to pursue alternative objectives in the near term may lower the bank's credibility with the public regarding the bank's commitment to the inflation target.

You may first suppose that the optimal inflation target level is zero (or the optimal *band* is centered on zero—for example, negative 1 percent to positive 1 percent). However, most economists believe the inflation target should not be zero but rather a low positive number or a narrow band encompassing low but positive inflation rates. First, price indexes typically are *upward biased*—that is, they overstate increases in the price level. The upward bias stems from the index's failure to fully consider improving quality of products over time and other factors. Suppose the CPI is biased upward by 1 percent per year.[6] If the index is reporting 1 percent annual inflation, true inflation actually is zero. If the central bank seeks true price stability, the bank should set the CPI inflation target at 1 percent per year.

Second, many economists believe nominal wages display considerable "stickiness" on the downside—that is, actual wages often fail to decline when an excess supply of labor exists in any particular occupation or geographic region. For the

---

[5] A price index (such as CPI) that includes interest expenses incurred by households presents problems for inflation targeting countries. If the central bank raises interest rates to fight inflation and stay on its inflation target, the interest component of the CPI rises, which *increases* the CPI and complicates the central bank's task. For this reason, New Zealand and the United Kingdom use a CPI that excludes interest expenses.

[6] In a 1997 report, the Boskin Commission studied the U.S. CPI and estimated CPI overstated inflation by 0.8–1.6 percentage points per year. The commission recommended measures to reduce the magnitude of this bias. Although the magnitude of the bias has been reduced, a bias is still believed to exist.

## **Exhibit 25-2** Which Measure of Inflation Should a Central Bank Target?

One of the important decisions a nation implementing inflation targeting must make is the *measure* of inflation the nation will target. Ideally, the price index used to calculate inflation most accurately reflects underlying inflationary pressures, responds predictably to central bank policies, and is familiar to the public. In the accompanying figure, the pattern of the 12-month U.S. inflation rate calculated from four different measures of the U.S. price level is illustrated over the course of the decade ending in 2004. The indexes are the CPI, the core CPI, the GDP deflator, and the personal consumption expenditures component of the GDP deflator (PCE).

Several points are noteworthy. The CPI is the most familiar of the U.S. price indexes. However, the CPI contains at least two important flaws militating against CPI as the measure to target if the Fed were to implement inflation targeting. First, the CPI is believed to be *biased upward*—that is, the CPI overstates inflation. Second, the CPI contains volatile food and energy prices. Thus, the CPI exhibits relatively high variability over time, as indicated in the figure. The standard deviation of the rate of change of the CPI exceeds that of the other indexes. Selection of CPI as the target variable could cause the Federal Reserve to react to strictly transitory inflation movements. The core CPI extracts both food and energy prices from the CPI. Therefore, the core CPI growth is believed to more accurately depict the trend of fundamental inflationary forces. The GDP deflator encompasses *all* of the goods and services entering into the nation's GDP. Therefore, the GDP deflator is a broader price index than the other three indexes. Finally, the PCE deflator encompasses prices of the various consumer goods and services weighted in proportion to their role in the nation's GDP. The PCE deflator inflation measure moves very much in parallel with the CPI measure but consistently reports lower inflation than does CPI. Fed Chairman Alan Greenspan pays considerable attention to PCE behavior.

Perhaps the most important point made by the graph is that the inflation rate reported by the four different measures often differs appreciably. In several time periods, the inflation rates reported by indexes differ from one another by more than one full percentage point. If the Fed were to adopt inflation targeting, one of the Fed's most important decisions would be the particular price index to use.

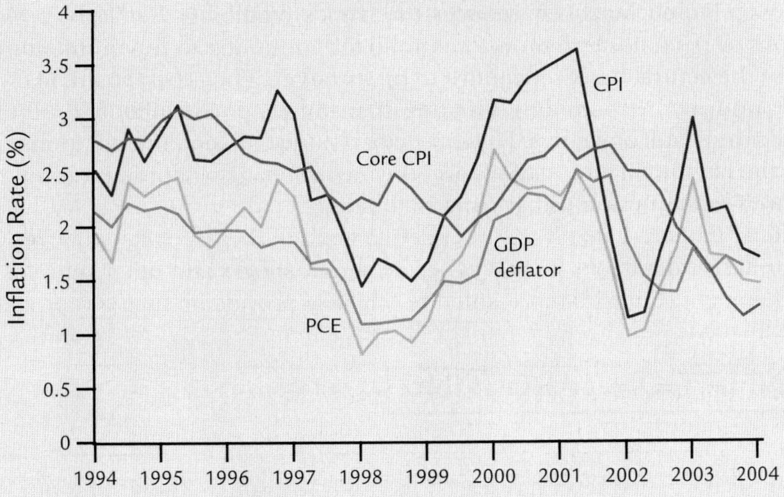

market mechanism to effectively signal the need for reallocation of labor across occupations and regions, real wages must fall in markets with prevailing labor surpluses. If the inflation rate is zero and nominal wages in labor markets are inflexible on the downside, no signals are given. Real wages do not fall in response to high unemployment. In this case, the labor market fails to signal the need for fewer workers in a particular sector or region experiencing labor surpluses. The outcome is inefficient. Positive inflation is needed to bring about reduced real wages so that market signals are given to eliminate the excess labor supply.

Perhaps the most compelling reason for setting the inflation target in positive territory is the highly uncertain environment in which monetary policy is conducted. As suggested in Chapter 24, occasional monetary policy errors are inevitable because of uncertainties and policy lags. Suppose the central bank is successfully maintaining inflation at a zero target level, but then oil prices unexpectedly decline sharply or productivity growth unexpectedly surges. The nation's AS curve shifts rightward. Instead of price stability, the economy experiences *deflation*. As we discussed earlier, monetary policy effectiveness may be significantly weakened in the presence of deflation. The zero bound on nominal interest rates compromises the Fed's ability to push down real rates to stimulate economic activity. The central bank may have difficulty extricating an economy from an episode of falling prices and contracting output. To minimize the likelihood of experiencing such an episode, setting the inflation target in positive territory seems desirable and prudent.

For all of these reasons, no inflation targeting country has set its inflation target at zero. Note in Table 25-2 that the United Kingdom sets its target closest to zero. The United Kingdom uses a band with a midpoint at 1 percent. Mexico has established its target at 3 percent. Most countries use an inflation target band rather than a specific inflation target number.

### Should There be Escape Clauses and Sanctions for Central Bank Failure to Hit Inflation Targets?

As mentioned earlier, a trade-off likely exists between a central bank's flexibility in conducting monetary policy and the bank's credibility as an inflation-fighter. A liberal escape clause increases the central bank's flexibility to pursue objectives other than low inflation but likely reduces the bank's credibility. Similarly, prospective sanctions or penalties levied on a central bank for failing to hit an inflation target increase the central bank's incentive to hit its target. The central bank likely places greater priority on containing inflation than on output stability and other traditional central bank objectives. Powerful sanctions for missing the inflation target increase the likelihood an inflation-targeting central bank will permit output to deviate more frequently and widely from high levels.

Note in Table 25-2 that New Zealand, Canada, and the Czech Republic provide for inflation target deviations in case of severe supply shocks and other unusual events. The other eight countries represented in the table provide no such escape clauses.

## EXPERIENCE WITH INFLATION TARGETING

Economists have used several research methods to evaluate the success or failure of inflation targeting regimes. One method is simply to study the actual behavior of inflation and other important macroeconomic indicators such as output stability or unemployment rates in a nation or sample of nations before and after inflation targeting is implemented. A second procedure is to compare inflation rates and other macroeconomic indicators in a given time period in countries that have versus those that have not implemented inflation targeting. A third method is to attempt to model a nation's economy, with special reference to price level and output behavior, and observe the differences in outcomes if inflation targeting were implemented. Unfortunately, all of these procedures have shortcomings, leading to some disagreement about the actual benefits and costs to countries that have implemented inflation targeting. The disagreement results partly from the newness of inflation targeting. Economists are actively conducting research aimed at resolving the issues surrounding inflation targeting. Here, we focus on the first two research methods.

## Inflation Performance Before and After Inflation Targeting Implementation

If you simply look at inflation rates in nations with inflation targeting regimes before and after implementation of the regime, the regimes clearly seem to have battled inflation very successfully. Inflation rates have come down substantially in virtually all countries that have implemented inflation targeting. This finding is illustrated in Table 25-3, which indicates average CPI inflation rates in our sample of 11 inflation targeting nations in the decade prior to and in the years (through 2002) after implementation of inflation targeting. Note the dramatically reduced inflation in countries that had previously experienced extremely severe inflation (Israel and Poland) and the very significantly decreased inflation in nations that

**Table 25-3 Inflation Performance of Inflation Targeting Countries Before and After Implementation**

| Country | Inflation Targeting Implementation Date | Average Inflation Rate in Prior 10 Years | Average Inflation Rate Since Implementation* |
|---|---|---|---|
| New Zealand | March 1990 | 12.0% | 2.0% |
| Chile | January 1991 | 20.5% | 6.9% |
| Canada | February 1991 | 6.0% | 1.8% |
| Israel | January 1992 | 62.9% | 7.5% |
| United Kingdom | October 1992 | 5.5% | 2.5% |
| Sweden | January 1993 | 6.7% | 1.3% |
| Australia | July 1993 | 6.6% | 2.5% |
| Czech Republic | January 1998 | 9.1%** | 4.6% |
| Korea | January 1998 | 6.2% | 2.5% |
| Poland | October 1998 | 106.6% | 6.2% |
| Mexico | January 1999 | 20.8% | 9.4% |

*Through 2002.
**Data unavailable prior to1994.
*Source: Data from International Monetary Fund,* International Financial Statistics

had previously experienced moderate inflation (Canada, United Kingdom, Sweden, Australia).

Because inflation also came down sharply after 1990 in countries that did *not* institute inflation targeting regimes, the facts shown in Table 25-3 are insufficient to demonstrate the general success of inflation targeting in reducing inflation. Inflation rates throughout the world fell sharply after 1990. Decreased inflation rates resulted from several factors. The factors include the absence of major adverse supply shocks after 1990; the 1993 Maastricht Agreement requiring countries aspiring to become members of the European Monetary Union to bring inflation down to levels close to rates experienced in Germany and other low-inflation countries; and an apparent increase in aversion to inflation in countries around the globe. The average annual "world" inflation rate calculated by the International Monetary Fund (IMF) declined from 16.8 percent in 1981 to 1995 to 5.4 percent in 1996 to 2002. The average annual inflation rate for "all industrial countries" compiled by the IMF declined from 5.2 percent in 1981 to 1990 to 3 percent in 1991 to 1995 and 1.9 percent in 1996 to 2002. Inflation targeting was instituted when conditions were conducive to falling inflation.

A somewhat more revealing research strategy is examining the inflation performance (and output performance) of inflation targeting countries *relative to non–inflation targeting countries* before and after the inflation targeting nations implemented the regimes. Because the United States is the most important nation that does not use inflation targeting, we use the United States as the standard. Table 25-4 indicates the difference between average inflation rates experienced in each inflation targeting country and the United States, *before* and *after* the foreign nation implemented inflation targeting.

For example, New Zealand experienced average annual CPI inflation that was 6.3 percentage points higher than U.S. inflation in the 1980s. However, New

**Table 25-4 Inflation Performance of Inflation Targeting Countries Relative to United States Before and After Inflation Targeting Implementation**

| Country | Inflation Differential in 1980s* | Inflation Differential After Inflation Targeting Implementation* |
|---|---|---|
| New Zealand | +6.3% | −0.5% (1991–2002) |
| Chile | +15.8% | +3.9% (1991–2002) |
| Canada | +0.9% | −0.7% (1991–2002) |
| Israel | +124.0% | +4.7% (1992–2002) |
| United Kingdom | +1.9% | −0.1% (1993–2002) |
| Sweden | +2.3% | −1.1% (1993–2002) |
| Australia | +2.8% | +0.1% (1993–2002) |
| Czech Republic | Data not available | +0.6% (1998–2002) |
| Korea | +2.9% | +1.2% (1998–2002) |
| Poland | +47.3% | +2.4% (1999–2002) |
| Mexico | +66.3% | +6.9% (1999–2002) |

*Average CPI inflation in foreign country – average U.S. CPI inflation.
*Source: Calculated from data in International Monetary Fund,* International Financial Statistics

Zealand's average annual CPI inflation was 0.5 percentage points *lower* than U.S. inflation in the first 11 years after New Zealand implemented inflation targeting. Canada, the United Kingdom, and Sweden also exhibited higher inflation than the United States before the countries introducing inflation targeting and lower inflation than the United States after implementation. Each of the remaining countries in the table experienced an appreciable reduction in its inflation differential *vis-à-vis* the United States after implementing inflation targeting.

## Sacrifice Ratios and Other Considerations

As suggested by our discussion of sacrifice ratios, the inflation targeting countries did not reduce inflation without a transitional cost. In varying amounts and for varying lengths of time, these inflation targeting countries, like non–inflation targeting countries, experienced slower output growth and higher unemployment rates during the transition to low inflation. Evidence of inflation targeting's influence on *sacrifice ratios* is mixed. Some studies show no effect in industrialized nations. However, at least one study shows a significantly reduced sacrifice ratio in emerging economies that initially exhibited high inflation.

Studies focusing on inflation targeting's effect on inflation *expectations* also provide mixed results. Some studies suggest inflation targeting implementation assists in lowering inflation expectations. However, a study that used survey measures of expected inflation found no effect. One study demonstrated that the difference between long-term bond yields in the United Kingdom (an inflation targeting country) and Germany (a non–inflation targeting country) failed to decline in the 1990s after the United Kingdom implemented inflation targeting. This finding suggests inflation expectations fell no more in the United Kingdom than in Germany, thus calling into question the benefits of inflation targeting. Evidence indicates that, holding other factors constant, implementation of an inflation targeting regime in emerging economies reduces inflation expectations. This finding suggests that inflation targeting implementation in emerging economies reduces the sacrifice ratio—the one-time loss of output incurred during transition to the lower inflation rate.

One interesting study attempted to measure the magnitude of the relative weight placed by central bankers on maintaining low and stable inflation versus the weight placed on maintaining output stability—that is, the study attempted to measure b in Equation (25-1).[7] The degree of central bank "inflation aversion" is proportional to the magnitude of b. The study reports that central bank inflation aversion increased in the 1990s in inflation targeting countries after they adopted inflation targeting. However, the study reported that inflation aversion also increased by a similar amount in countries that did not adopt inflation targeting.

As indicated, experience with inflation targeting is relatively new. Ongoing and future research likely will move us closer to a consensus on the consequences of inflation targeting. Because the inflation targeting era has witnessed a relative dearth of adverse supply shocks relative to the previous couple of decades, observing the behavior of output stability and price level stability in inflation targeting and non–inflation targeting countries when such shocks do occur in the future will be particularly interesting. In the meantime, many monetary economists favor inflation targeting, particularly for countries not having a history of relatively stable prices. The favorable impression is reinforced by the fact that few, if any, countries that adopted inflation targeting have abandoned the regime.

[7] See the reference to Cecchetti and Ehrman and other studies pertinent to the inflation targeting debate in the *Additional Reading* at the end of this chapter.

# INTERNATIONAL PERSPECTIVES

## Chile's Experience with Inflation Targeting

Chile is an excellent example of a successful experience with inflation targeting. The country's inflation rate averaged more than 90 percent per year in the 1970s during a time of political upheaval and more than 20 percent per year in the 1980s. Chile began announcing inflation targets in January 1991. Each September, the Central Bank of Chile (CBC) announces inflation targets for the following calendar year.

Because the ongoing inflation rate was approximately 25 percent per year in late 1990 and because the CBC needed to gain credibility, the initial inflation target for the 12 months beginning in January 1991 was set as a 15 to 20 percent band. As inflation fell, the CBC gradually reduced the target band each year until September 1994, when band targets were replaced by point targets. The target level was gradually reduced each year through the 1990s. As indicated in the accompanying graph, the CBC was relatively successful in staying on target. Inflation declined from more than 20 percent in 1990 to 2.3 percent at one point in 1999, the lowest inflation rate in Chile since the 1930s. Inflation averaged just 3.2 percent per year from 1998 to 2003. Having successfully engineered the disinflation, the CBC now specifies its target as a band encompassing inflation rates of 2 to 4 percent per year. Remarkably, Chilean real GDP growth increased sharply in the 1990s despite successful disinflation.

The key reason for Chile's success is that most of the preconditions for a successful inflation targeting regime were instituted *prior* to regime implementation. First, legislation enacted in 1989 granted independence to the CBC for the first time. Second, the Chilean government was fiscally sound. Budget surpluses were exhibited each year from 1991 to 1997. Fiscal surpluses are important because large fiscal deficits almost universally place political pressure on the central bank to help finance ("monetize") the deficits, ultimately leading to high inflation. Third, structural reforms implemented in the 1970s and 1980s led to large capital inflows that maintained a strong currency externally and helped finance domestic investment expenditures that stimulated growth. Fourth, by 1990 Chile had established a rigorous and sound system of banking regulation and supervision.

Once the essential elements were in place and the CBC was granted independence, the CBC implemented a rigorous inflation targeting regime that featured relatively short horizons for hitting the targets and an absence of escape clauses. These features and the country's early success in hitting the inflation targets reinforced the public's perception of the CBC's strong commitment to low inflation. Thus, Chile serves as an excellent role model for emerging economies desiring to reduce high inflation rates to tolerable levels.

## INTERNATIONAL PERSPECTIVES —*continued*

Inflation Targets and Inflation Rates in Chile from 1988 to 2003

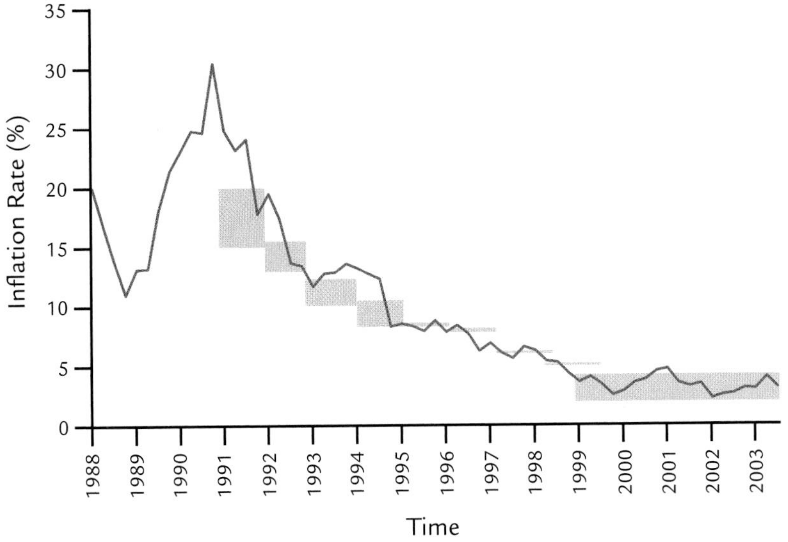


## EVOLUTION OF THE FEDERAL RESERVE'S POLICY MANDATE

When the Federal Reserve was created in the early twentieth century, the Fed's original charter did not mention the Fed's responsibility for maintaining price stability. In fact, the Federal Reserve Act of 1913 contained very little discussion of policy objectives. The only explicit objectives were to "furnish an elastic currency and to afford means of rediscounting commercial paper." The Federal Reserve was founded in response to a series of banking and financial market panics that culminated in the Panic of 1907. Not surprisingly, the Fed's principal initial focus was promoting financial stability. The Fed provided banks a source of liquidity through the Fed's discount window in the event of large-scale bank deposit withdrawals.

In the 1920s and 1930s, proposals imposing a price stability mandate on the Federal Reserve were made to Congress. The Fed opposed such a mandate, and the mandate was not implemented. In response to the catastrophic events of the Great Depression and other developments, Congress enacted the Employment Act of 1946. This act applied to the U.S. government as a whole. Because the Federal Reserve is part of government, the act implicitly applied to the Federal Reserve's conduct of monetary policy. The Employment Act of 1946 identified the government's economic objectives as follows: "to promote maximum employment, production, and purchasing power." Although this language sometimes is interpreted to include price level stability and full employment, the wording suggests an overriding emphasis on maintaining full employment.

A 1978 amendment to the Federal Reserve Act made the Fed's policy mandate considerably more specific. This amendment requires the Fed to "maintain the growth of monetary and credit aggregates commensurate with the economy's long-run potential to increase production, so as to promote effectively the goals of maximum employment, stable prices, and moderate long-term interest rates." Because the Federal Reserve can maintain "moderate" long-term interest rates only by fostering low inflation rates, the language mandating the Fed to maintain "moderate long-term interest rates" is redundant—it is not an independent goal of monetary policy. Hence, the language of the Employment Act suggests a **dual mandate** for the Federal Reserve—that is, to maintain both price level stability and "maximum" employment, which is taken to mean maximum *sustainable* employment.

**dual mandate**
mandate given to the central bank to maintain both price level stability and maximum sustainable employment

## Authority for Implementing Inflation Targeting in the United States

Today the Fed operates under a dual mandate requiring the Fed to strive for both price level stability and full employment. Should the United States adopt a formal inflation targeting regime? This decision is not up to the Federal Reserve but rather to Congress. Several proposals requiring the Fed to implement inflation targeting have been made in Congress, but none has ever been enacted. In the late 1980s and early 1990s, Representative Steven Neal, Chair of the House Banking Committee's Subcommittee on Monetary Policy, introduced bills requiring the Fed to "adopt and pursue monetary policies leading to, and maintaining, zero inflation."[8] In 1995 and 1997, Senator Connie Mack and Representative Jim Saxton introduced bills requiring the Fed to provide an explicit numerical definition of price stability and "maintain a monetary policy that effectively promotes long-term price stability." In 1999, Representative Saxton introduced a revised version of these bills requiring the Fed to state a specific numerical definition of price stability and then to adopt price stability as the "primary goal" of monetary policy. In 1999, Senator Mack introduced a bill that would have abolished the dual mandate and made price stability the sole objective. This bill would have mandated a U.S. inflation targeting regime that would have been one of the strictest regimes in the world. The Federal Reserve has consistently opposed these bills, and none has been enacted by Congress. The issue of whether the United States should adopt inflation targeting is contentious.

## Should the United States Implement Inflation Targeting? The Affirmative View

Advocates of inflation targeting in the United States argue that the U.S. inflation performance since the early 1980s has been exemplary but cannot be considered permanent. This recent period has been marked by strong Federal Reserve leadership, declining worldwide inflation, and the absence of major shocks that contributed to inflation in the past. On the other hand, from 1970 to 1982 the U.S. inflation rate averaged approximately 8 percent per year. Furthermore, advocates of inflation targeting believe the existing evidence demonstrates the effectiveness of inflation targeting. The consensus is that the economic performance of countries that have adopted inflation targeting has been favorable. Inflation has come down in all countries that implemented inflation targeting (dramatically in several cases), and no nation that adopted such a regime has abandoned it.

---

[8] In later versions of this bill, zero inflation was defined as existing "when the expected rate of change of the general level of prices ceases to be a factor in individual and business decision-making." Hence, these versions of the bill did not necessarily imply the Fed must shoot for zero reported CPI inflation.

Proponents of inflation targeting emphasize the benefits of the transparency and accountability that accrue with such a regime. They argue that the outstanding performance delivered by the Fed under the leadership of Paul Volcker and Alan Greenspan from 1979 to 2005 cannot be taken for granted. Remember that, despite safeguards intended to make the Federal Reserve independent of short-term political pressures, few members of the Board of Governors serve more than half of their 14-year terms before stepping down. Many future U.S. presidents likely will have the opportunity to appoint a majority of Board members in a single term and perhaps six or even all seven members during a two-term presidency. If some future members of the Board of Governors are sympathetic to the political career of the incumbent president who appointed them or are influenced by other elected officials, the time inconsistency phenomenon discussed in Chapter 24 could return to plague monetary policy. Political considerations could easily lead the Fed to implement policies in the short run that are inconsistent with the medium-term and long-term goals of price stability. Such developments are less likely to occur in a framework of inflation targeting.

## Should the U.S. Implement Inflation Targeting? The Negative View

"If it ain't broke, don't fix it." Opponents of inflation targeting point out that the Federal Reserve is strongly committed to low inflation and has delivered low inflation in the past 25 years. Furthermore, economists' studies have shown that the revealed aversion to inflation is as high today for the Federal Reserve as for central banks of nations using inflation targeting. In practice, therefore, critics believe Fed adoption of inflation targeting would contribute little or nothing to the actual inflation performance of the United States. Opponents often agree that inflation targeting has benefited countries with a history of chronic and severe inflation, but they believe the United States does not fit the description of a country that would benefit from inflation targeting.

Unlike some supporters of inflation targeting, the regime's critics firmly believe the Federal Reserve is quite capable of reducing output instability touched off by significant aggregate demand and aggregate supply shocks. They believe abandoning the current dual mandate would result in increased instability of the nation's output and higher rates of unemployment on average. If a negative aggregate demand shock occurs, real output may decline quickly but inflation tends to lag—it is slow to come down. If overzealous "inflation hawks" are in charge of monetary policy in an inflation targeting regime, critics fear the Fed would acquiesce in a recession rather than implement an expansionary policy.[9] However, a *forward-looking* Fed should anticipate that the adverse AD shock ultimately will reduce inflation. In this event, an astute inflation-targeting Federal Reserve would implement an expansionary policy as soon as the AD shock occurs—that is, prior to the decline in actual inflation.

Adverse supply shocks pose a serious problem when inflation targeting is in place. In the event of a severe drought, sharp increase in crude oil prices, or unexpected decline in productivity growth, the nation's AS curve shifts left. The shift tends to boost inflation while it *reduces* output. This situation presents a serious dilemma when the Fed is concerned about both inflation and output stability. If the Fed tries to prevent increased inflation, it must implement restrictive policies that

[9] The term *inflation nutter* was coined by Mervyn King, governor of the Bank of England. The term describes a myopic central banker who interprets the inflation target with extreme rigidity, giving no consideration in the near term to the objective of output stability. In reference to Equation (25-1), an inflation nutter exhibits a loss function with $b = 1$.

# ADDITIONAL READING

- For excellent general overviews of inflation targeting, see Ben Bernanke and Frederic Mishkin, "Inflation Targeting: A New Framework for Monetary Policy," *Journal of Economic Perspectives* 1997, No. 11, pp. 97–116, and Guy Debelle, Paul Masson, Miguel Savastano, and Sunil Sharma, "Inflation Targeting as a Framework for Monetary Policy," International Monetary Fund *Economic Issues,* No. 15, 1998. Also, see George Kahn and Klara Parish, "Conducting Monetary Policy with Inflation Targets," Federal Reserve Bank of Kansas City *Economic Review,* 1998, No. 3, pp. 5–32.
- An exceptionally clear analysis of inflation targeting is provided in a talk by former Federal Reserve Board of Governors member Larry Meyer, "Inflation Targets and Inflation Targeting," July 17, 2001, available at http://www.federalreserve.gov/boarddocs/speeches/2001. Other informative speeches available at the same Web site are Ben Bernanke, "A perspective on Inflation Targeting" (March 25, 2003), and Edward Gramlich, "Inflation Targeting" (January 2000).
- A book that includes detailed case studies of inflation targeting and advocates U.S. implementation of inflation targeting is Ben Bernanke, Thomas Labauch, Frederic Mishkin, and Adam Posen, *Inflation Targeting: Lessons From International Experience* (Princeton, NJ: Princeton University Press, 1999).
- A more recent edited volume of articles on inflation targeting is Ben Bernanke and Michael Woodford, *Inflation Targeting* (Chicago: University of Chicago Press for National Bureau of Economic Research, 2003). In this book, Marvin Goodfriend makes the case for the United States implementing inflation targeting in "Inflation Targeting in the United States?" Works analyzing the actual experience of inflation targeting include Francisco D.E.A. Nadal-De Simone, "Inflation Targeters in Practice: A Lucky Lot?" *Contemporary Economic Policy,* July 2001, pp. 239–253, and Frederic Mishkin and Klaus Schmidt-Hebbel, "One Decade of Inflation Targeting in the World: What Do We Know and What do We Need to Know?" NBER Working Paper 8397, July 2001.
- A widely cited empirical study of inflation targeting is Steven Cecchetti and M. Ehrmann, "Does Inflation Targeting Increase Output Volatility? An International Comparison of Policymakers' Preferences and Outcomes," *Central Bank of Chile Working Papers 69* (April 2000), available at http://www.bcentral.cl/esp/estpub/estudios/dtbc/htm/069.htm.
- A recent and outstanding collection of articles on inflation targeting is contained in "Inflation Targeting: Prospects and Problems," Federal Reserve Bank of St. Louis *Review,* July/August 2004.

# Glossary

## A

**active rule (feedback rule)** rule in which the central bank changes the interest rate level or the money growth rate by strict predetermined formulas in response to ongoing developments

**adjustable-peg (Bretton Woods) exchange rate** agreement in which each country's central bank intervenes aggressively in foreign exchange markets to *fix* or *peg* its exchange rate at a predetermined level

**adverse selection** condition in which people who are most undesirable from the other party's viewpoint are the ones most likely to seek to engage in a transaction

**aggregate demand curve** relationship between the nation's aggregate price level and the amount of real output (real GDP) demanded, other factors being held constant

**aggregate supply curve** relationship between the nation's aggregate price level and the amount of real output firms collectively desire to produce and sell, other factors being held constant

**amortized mortgage** mortgage in which part of each monthly payment reduces the principal so that the home is owned free and clear after a period of 15 or 30 years

**appreciation** an increase in value of one nation's currency relative to another currency

**assets** indications of what is owned or claims on external entities

**asymmetric information** condition in which two parties to a transaction have differing information about the intentions of the other party and the likely risks involved

**automatic transfer service (ATS) accounts** type of account in which funds are automatically transferred from savings account to checking account as checks are presented for payment

## B

**balance sheet** statement of assets, liabilities, and net worth at a given point in time

**bank charters** official authorizations to open and operate banks

**bank holding company** corporation that owns a controlling interest in one or several banks but is itself not a bank

**Bank Holding Company Act of 1956** legislation prohibiting bank branching via acquisition of banks by bank holding companies

**bank insolvency** state of financial condition in which the value of a bank's total assets is less than the value of the bank's total liabilities

**Bank Insurance Fund (BIF)** insurance fund created by FIRREA for commercial banks

**bank liquidity trap** potential situation in which bank demand for excess reserves is perfectly elastic with respect to the interest rate, rendering the central bank incapable of increasing the money supply

**Bank of the United States** first national bank chartered in the United States

**banker's acceptance** check, generally written by a business firm, payable at a specific future date and stamped "accepted" by a major bank

**Banking Act of 1933 (Glass-Steagall Act)** legislation separating commercial banking from investment banking, and separating banking from industry

**banking panic** waves of systemic bank runs that lead to contraction of bank lending and economic contraction

**banks** institutions that accept various types of deposits and use the funds primarily to grant loans and purchase relatively safe debt instruments

**barter economy** economy in which goods and services are traded directly for one another

**Board of Governors** seven-person board that dominates the conduct of monetary policy; this board sets reserve requirements and the discount rate, and constitutes the voting majority of the Federal Open Market Committee

**bond** long-term debt instrument issued by a corporation, government, or government agency; a contractual agreement to make certain payments at specified future dates

**brokers** individuals acting as customers' agents, locating a security buyer or seller and charging a commission for the service

**budget deficit** annual amount by which federal government expenditures exceed tax revenues

## C

**CAMELS system** acronym indicating the six categories evaluated to assess a bank's overall financial condition: C (capital adequacy), A (asset quality), M (management), E (earnings), L (liquidity), and S (sensitivity to risk)

**capital accounts (capital)** net worth of a bank, or value of the bank owners' residual claim on the bank's assets

**capital market** market in which *long-term* securities issued by government and private concerns are exchanged

**cash market** transactions in which the buyer pays the seller for the asset up front

**central bank** a nation's monetary authority or agency charged with conducting monetary policy and other duties

**certificate of deposit (CD)** a form of deposit that stipulates that the bearer will receive annual interest payments of a specified amount plus a lump sum equal to the original principal at maturity

**commercial paper** short-term promissory notes issued by major corporations to attract funds for day-to-day business needs

**common stocks** ownership claims against a firm's real capital assets; entitles owner to share in profits of the firm

**Comptroller of the Currency** government agency within the Treasury Department charged with chartering, supervising, and examining national banks

**convergence criteria** specific and stringent standards each nation must meet to achieve membership in the monetary union

**corporate bonds** long-term debt claims against a corporation's assets, claims that may or may not be secured by mortgages and other assets

**cost of capital** cost of raising funds to finance capital expenditures

**Council of Economics and Finance Ministers (ECOFIN)** group consisting of the finance ministers of each of the European Union member countries; group initiates the Executive Board appointment process

**coupon bonds** bonds that promise a finite series of constant annual or semi-annual payments for 10, 20, or 30 years and repayment of principal at maturity

**credit view** view that an increase in bank loans has a stronger impact on GDP expenditures and economic activity than does an equal amount of bank security purchases, even though both events have the same impact on M1 and M2

**currency ratio (k)** ratio of currency held by the public ($C^p$) to DDO (demand deposits and other checkable deposits)

**current yield** yield computed as the annual payment from the instrument (in dollars) divided by the price or initial principal

## D

**dealers** holders of inventories of securities who stand ready to buy or sell at quoted bid and ask prices

**debit card** card with which an individual pays for an item by transferring funds electronically and *immediately* from his/her bank account to the merchant's bank account

**debt instrument** contractual agreement by the issuer to pay a specific amount of money (principal or face value) at a specified future date; contract may include periodic interest payments as well

**default risk** risk that issuer of debt instrument will not make interest payments or pay back the face value when the instrument matures

**defensive open market operations** Fed's open market operations made to "defend" bank reserves and the monetary base against outside forces over which the Fed has little or no control

**deflation** persistent or continuing *decline* in a nation's general price level

**demand deposits** deposits that can be withdrawn in currency or transferred to a third party at the initiative of the owner

**demand for money** amount of wealth individuals and firms desire to maintain in the form of money

**demand-pull inflation** inflation caused by a persistently rightward shifting AD curve, typically the result of rapid growth of a nation's government expenditures and money supply

**Depository Institutions Act of 1982 (Garn–St. Germain Act)** act accelerating deregulation of the S&Ls by authorizing them to engage in additional activities and compete with money market mutual funds

**depreciation** a decrease in value of one nation's currency relative to another currency

**derivative market** trades that are arranged currently with locked-in terms, but settlement and delivery of the instrument are made at a specified future date

**desired excess reserves ratio ($r_e$)** ratio of banks' desired excess reserves to DDO (demand deposits and other checkable deposits)

**discount loans (discounts and advances)** loans made by the Federal Reserve to depository institutions

**discount rate** interest rate charged on loans made by the Federal Reserve to commercial banks

**discount window** facility through which the Federal Reserve district banks lend reserves to depository institutions

**discretionary monetary policy** policy in which the central bank is free to assess economic circumstances as they unfold and implement whatever measures the central bank deems appropriate at the time

**disintermediation** active withdrawal of funds from depository institutions by customers searching for higher yields elsewhere

**district Federal Reserve banks** one Federal Reserve bank exists for each of the 12 Federal Reserve districts in the United States

**dividend yield** annual dividend expressed as a percentage of the stock's price

**divisia aggregates** weighted measures of money used to predict changes in price level and output of goods and services; may eventually replace our current measures of money

**dual banking system** system in which both the federal government and state governments have authority to charter banks

**dual mandate** mandate given to the central bank to maintain both price level stability and maximum sustainable employment

**dynamic open market operations** operations by which the Federal Reserve deliberately changes the course of economic activity in line with the Fed's policy objectives

## E

**Economic and Monetary Union (EMU)** group of European nations that use a common currency (the euro) and have a common monetary policy

**economies of scale** economies formed when the average cost of providing a unit of bank service declines as more units of the service are provided

**economies of scope** economies formed when greater efficiency is achieved by one firm providing a group of services rather than separate specialized firms providing those services

**electronic cash (e-cash)** form of money that facilitates payment for items purchased over the Internet

**electronic checks** form of checks that are processed electronically, circumventing the costly procedure of physically processing and transporting checks

**electronic money system** a system in which money is stored and transferred electronically via cards and computer accounts

**equation of exchange** a mathematical identity that sets forth the relationship between the supply of money, velocity, the price level and real output; $MV = PY$

**equities** financial claims representing ownership in a business entity; gives bearer the right to share in the net income of issuer

**equity multiplier** ratio of financial institution's total assets to capital; indicates magnitude of leverage applied to the rate of return on assets

**equity risk premium** additional rate of return required to compensate prospective investors for risk and induce investors to buy stocks rather than safer government bonds

**euro** single currency used by 12 western European nations

**Eurodollars** deposits in foreign banks or U.S. bank branches in foreign countries, in denominations of U.S. dollars rather than local currencies

**European Central Bank** central bank that conducts monetary policy collectively for Economic and Monetary Union countries

**European System of Central Banks (ESCB)** organization consisting of the European Central Bank and the individual central banks of the European Monetary Union nations

**European Union (EU)** organization dedicated to achieving economic integration and unification of its member countries

**excess reserves** depository institution reserves (cash and deposits at Fed) above the required amount

**exchange traded funds (ETFs)** instruments designed to track a particular stock market index or sector; can be purchased by individual investors like shares of stock

**Executive Board** six-person board that participates on the Governing Council of the European Central Bank in formulating monetary policy

**expected (ex ante) real interest rate ($r_{ex\ ante}$)** difference between nominal interest rate and *expected* inflation rate

## F

**Federal Deposit Insurance Corporation Improvement Act of 1991 (FDICIA)** legislation that recapitalized the nearly insolvent FDIC and redesigned the federal deposit insurance system with the intent of minimizing taxpayer exposure to future losses

**federal funds** unsecured loans, in the form of deposits at the Federal Reserve Banks, made between depository institutions

**federal funds market** market in which banks borrow funds overnight from other banks in the form of deposits at the Federal Reserve

**federal funds rate** rate of interest prevailing on overnight loans between banks of deposits at the Federal Reserve

**Federal Home Loan Bank Board (FHLBB)** organization established by Congress to regulate the savings and loan industry

**Federal Open Market Committee (FOMC)** committee responsible for formulating the general posture of monetary policy; consists of the seven members of the Board of Governors and the 12 presidents of the district Federal reserve banks

**Federal Reserve Act** legislation establishing the Federal Reserve System

**Federal Reserve float** difference between "cash items in the process of collection" and "deferred availability cash items"

**Federal Reserve System (Fed)** the central bank of the United States, charged with conducting monetary policy and other duties associated with our financial system

**Federal Savings and Loan Insurance Corporation (FSLIC)** subsidiary of the FHLBB created to insure savings and loan deposits

**fiat money (credit money)** form of money that derives its value by fiat or government decree rather than through its value as a commodity

**financial futures** purchase of (and payment for) a financial instrument at a specified future date, at a price determined *in advance*

**Financial Institutions Reform, Recovery, and Enforcement Act of 1989 (FIRREA)** legislation abolishing both the FHLBB and the FSLIC and creating The Office of Thrift Supervision, The Bank Insurance Fund, and The Savings Association Insurance Fund

**financial intermediaries** institutions that serve as middlemen for the transfer of funds from individuals, businesses, and other entities with surplus funds to those who borrow

**financial intermediary** institution that obtains funds by issuing secondary claims and uses the proceeds to purchase primary claims, thereby transferring funds from society's savers/lenders to borrowers/spenders

**financial intermediation** flow of funds from savers to deficit spenders by way of financial intermediaries

**Fisher effect** tendency for interest rates to be positively related to the level of inflation expectations

**Fisher hypothesis** strong form of this theory asserts that interest rates move one-for-one with the magnitude of expected inflation; the weak form states that expected inflation significantly influences interest rates

**fixed exchange rates** international financial arrangement in which exchange rates are pegged or held constant by direct government intervention in the foreign exchange market

**float** difference between cash items in the process of collection and deferred credit items; arises from check collection procedures

**floating exchange rates** international financial arrangement in which exchange rates are allowed to change continuously in response to the market forces of supply and demand, with occasional government intervention

**FOMC directive** formal statement indicating the intended conduct of monetary policy until the next meeting of the Federal Open Market Committee and voted on by the FOMC

**foreign exchange market** market in which national currencies are exchanged

**foreign exchange rate** price at which one nation's currency is exchanged for another nation's currency

**forward exchange rate** exchange rate at which forward transactions take place

**forward interest rate** hypothetical future short-term interest rate that equalizes average returns earned on a long-term security and a succession of short-term securities

**forward transactions** purchase and sale of foreign currencies for delivery and payment at a particular future date and a price specified in advance

**fractional reserve banking system** system in which each bank maintains only a small percentage of bank deposit liabilities in the form of reserves

**Free Banking Era** period from 1836 to 1863, characterized by minimal supervision of banking activity

**freely floating exchange rates** system in which governments do not intervene in the foreign exchange market, permitting exchange rates to be driven entirely by free market forces

**full-bodied money (commodity money)** form of money whose value is approximately the same whether it is used as money or for nonmoney (commodity) purposes

## G

**Glass-Steagall Act** law mandating the separation of commercial banking and investment banking

**Governing Council** committee that makes European Central Bank monetary policy decisions

**Governors** heads of the central bank of the 12 individual nations making up the Economic and Monetary Union

**Gramm-Leach-Bliley Financial Services Modernization Act of 1999** legislation allowing securities and insurance firms to purchase banks and permitting banks to participate in securities, insurance, and real estate activities

## H

**hysteresis** idea that the NAIRU level is influenced by the level and duration of the actual unemployment rate

## I

**impact lag** time that elapses between the point when policy action is implemented and the point at which the policy begins to influence the nation's GDP

**implementation lag** time that elapses between the point when a need for policy action is recognized and the point at which the appropriate policy is implemented

**income** flow of earnings, measures as dollars per unit of time

**income elasticity of demand for money** ratio of the percentage change in quantity of money demanded to the percentage change in income that induced the change in money demand

**inflation** persistent or continuing increase in a nation's general price level

**inflation neutrality** condition in which inflation is fully anticipated and compensated for by economic agents, attenuating the potential redistributive effects of inflation

**inflation targeting** monetary policy strategy in which a specific low inflation rate (or band of rates) is proclaimed as its predominant intermediate and long-term objective

**inflationary gap** situation in which equilibrium output exceeds full-employment output and the actual unemployment rate is below the natural unemployment rate

**instrument** or **tool of monetary policy** variable the Fed controls completely in order to influence such key intermediate variables as short-term interest rates, the monetary base, M1, and M2

**interest parity condition** condition in which, in a world of capital mobility, expected returns on assets are equal across countries

**interest rate** cost of borrowing (or the return from lending), expressed as a percent per year

**intermediate target variables** intermediate-term variables the central bank attempts to control in its effort to achieve policy goals

**international capital flows** acquisition of financial and real assets across national borders

**International Monetary Fund (IMF)** organization created in 1944 for the purpose of creating a stable international monetary order

**investment banks** institutions that underwrite new securities issues and trade existing issues

## J

**junk bonds** bonds judged to have a high risk of default, rated Ba or lower by Moody's

## L

**law of one price** principle that a homogeneous good's price will be the same whether purchased at home or abroad if free trade and zero transactions costs prevail

**legal reserves (reserves)** cash and deposits that a bank places in a larger bank (formerly) or Federal Reserve (today)

**legal tender** money that cannot lawfully be refused as payment for goods and services or for discharge of debts; consists of currency and coins

**lender of last resort** provider of temporary cash reserves to the banking system in times of crisis

**liabilities** indications of what is owed or claims that external entities have on a bank or other entity

**limited branching** restrictions limiting banks to a certain number of offices

**liquidity** relative ease with which an asset can be converted into money without significant commissions or other charges, inconvenience, and risk of loss of principal

**liquidity premium theory** theory asserting that the long-term interest rate equals the average of current and expected future short-term interest rates plus a premium to compensate lenders for market risk

**loanable funds model** model in which the supply and demand for funds determine the interest rate

**Lombard system** system in which the discount rate is set significantly *above* money market yields and use of the discount window is a "right" rather than a "privilege" administered by the central bank

**long-run aggregate supply curve (LRAS)** relationship between nation's price level and real output produced when actual and expected inflation are equal and input prices have fully adjusted to output prices

**loss function** equation indicating the cost or loss to society associated with the twin "evils" of deviations of inflation from desired rate and deviations of output from full employment levels

## M

**M1** narrow or transactions measure of money, which includes only currency, demand deposits and other checking accounts in depository institutions, and traveler's checks

**M2** broad measure of money, which includes M1 and several highly liquid financial assets such as savings deposits, money market mutual fund shares owned by individuals, and other instruments

**M3** very broad measure of money, which includes M2 and several additional liquid instruments

**managed float** system in which governments intervene to prevent exchange rate movements perceived to be excessive or strongly at odds with the national interest

**manager of the System Open Market Account** officer of the Federal Reserve Bank of New York responsible for carrying out, through a network of government security dealers, the open market transactions needed to meet the specifications outlined in the Federal Open Market Committee directive

**margin requirements** percentage of the value of securities purchased that the buyer must pay for using his/her own funds, as opposed to borrowed funds

**marginal productivity of capital** rate of return expected by firms from purchase of an additional unit of capital goods

**market capitalization** market value of the aggregate shares of stock outstanding of a corporation or a universe of corporations

**market risk** risk that the price of a financial instrument will fluctuate

**McFadden Act** legislation prohibiting national banks from operating outside their home state and compelling banks to abide by state regulations on intrastate branching

**mean reversion** tendency to ultimately revert to long-term averages

**monetary base** those financial assets that can potentially be used as reserves; bank reserves and currency held by the public

**monetary policy** measures implemented by the central bank that influence the availability of credit, the level of interest rates, and the money supply in the nation

**monetary policy rule** arrangement in which the central bank announces in advance specifically how it will respond to ongoing economic developments and commits the central bank to following through on the announcement

**monetary union** adoption of a single currency by a group of countries

**money** anything that is generally acceptable as payment for goods and services or for settlement of debt; most commonly defined to include currency, coins, and checking accounts in depository institutions

**money market** market in which *short-term* debt instruments—those with maturities less than 1 year—are traded, typically in massive quantities

**money market deposit accounts (MMDAs)** interest-bearing deposits with limited check writing features that permit banks to compete with money market mutual funds

**money supply multiplier** ratio of the money supply to the monetary base

**money view** view that information about the nation's monetary aggregates, obtained from the deposit information on the liability side of the bank balance sheet, is sufficient to predict the impact of monetary policy on aggregate spending and GDP

**moral hazard** risk that one party to a transaction will undertake activities that are undesirable from the other party's viewpoint

**mortgage** long-term loan financing the purchase of real property, secured by a lien on that property

**mortgage-backed security** financial instrument that splits the financing and servicing of mortgages; banks package groups of mortgages, which are sold in security form to large investors

**municipal bonds** long-term debt instrument representing a claim on a city or county

## N

**NAIRU (non-accelerating inflation rate of unemployment)** rate of unemployment at which demand for labor equals the supply, thus maintaining inflation at its existing rate

**National Banking Act of 1863** legislation allowing the charting of national banks, thereby facilitating issuance of a uniform currency

**national debt** stock of government debt outstanding; cumulative sum of past budget deficits less past surpluses

**natural rate of output** specific output level that generates full employment, where the supply of workers equals the demand for workers

**natural rate of unemployment** unemployment rate that exists when the labor market is in equilibrium and there is full employment

**negotiable CDs** large CDs that can be traded through a network of dealers prior to maturity

**negotiable order of withdrawal (NOW) accounts** interest-bearing savings account, on which limited check writing privileges are permitted

**net free reserves (NFR)** difference between aggregate excess reserves held by depository institutions and borrowed reserves (discount loans)

**net worth** amount by which total assets exceed total liabilities

**nominal interest rate** actual interest rate unadjusted for inflation

**nonborrowed base (B-A)** difference between monetary base and borrowed reserves (discount loans)

**nonborrowed reserves (R-A)** difference between total reserves held by depository institutions and borrowed reserves (discount loans)

## O

**Office of Thrift Supervision (OTS)** organization created as a bureau within the Treasury Department to replace the FHLBB

**Okun's Law** equation describing the relationship between the nation's unemployment rate and the nation's loss of output

**open market operations** buying and selling of government securities by the Fed to influence bank lending, interest rates, and the nation's money supply

**operating target variables** near-term variables the central bank controls as part of its strategy to achieve policy goals

**options** contracts that give the owner the right to buy or sell a financial asset at a particular price within a specified time period

**output gap** situation in which actual GDP is below potential GDP; thus the unemployment rate exceeds the NAIRU

## P

**passive rule** rule in which the central bank does not respond to ongoing developments; constant money supply growth rule

**permanent income** long-run average expected future income

**Phillips curve hypothesis** proposition that, other things being equal, a lower unemployment rate is associated with a higher price level inflation rate

**policy activists** individuals who believe active use of monetary and fiscal policies contribute positively to economic stability

**policy directive** written statement indicating the intended posture of Federal Reserve policy until the next FOMC meeting

**policy non-activists** individuals who believe active use of monetary and fiscal policies do not lead to increased economic stability

**political business cycle** manipulation of the economy for political ends

**precautionary demand for money** maintenance of money balances to meet unforeseen circumstances

**preferred habitat theory** theory that borrowers and lenders have strong preferences for particular maturities but may be induced to switch if expected benefits are large

**present value** value *today* of payments to be received in the future

**present value formula** formula expressing the value today of the right to receive a payment or stream of payments in the future

**price/earnings (PE) ratio** ratio of the price of a share of stock to the current annual earnings per share achieved by the corporation

**price-to-book ratio** ratio of the price of a share of stock to the book value of the company

**primary credit** discount loans to banks that are in sound financial condition

**primary market** market in which newly issued securities are exchanged

**prime loan rate** key interest rate posted by large U.S. banks, used as a benchmark for setting bank lending rates

**principal-agent problem** moral hazard problem that occurs when those in control (agents) act in their own interest rather than the interest of the owners or the public (principals)

**productivity** output per hour of work

**purchasing power parity (PPP) theory** theory postulating that exchange rates adjust *completely* to offset the effects of different rates of inflation in two countries

**pure expectations theory** theory in which market forces dictate that the yield on a long-term security of any particular maturity equals the geometric mean (the average) of the current short-term yield and successive future short-term yields currently expected to prevail over the life of the long-term security

## Q

**quotas** nation's restrictions on the volume of imported goods

## R

**rate of time preference** extent to which people prefer present consumption over future consumption

**real interest rate** interest rate after adjusting the nominal interest rate for expected inflation

**realized (ex post) real interest rate ($r_{ex\ post}$)** difference between nominal interest rate and *realized* inflation rate

**recessionary gap** situation in which equilibrium output falls short of full-employment output and the actual unemployment rate is above the natural rate of unemployment because output falls short of the natural rate of output

**recognition lag** time that elapses between the point when policy actions ideally would have been implemented (discovered only with hindsight) and the point at which policy-making officials become aware of the need for action

**representative full-bodied money** paper money that attests to an ownership claim on a commodity such as gold or silver

**repurchase agreement (RP)** money market instrument that government security dealers, banks, and other large financial market players use to mobilize temporarily idle funds

**required reserve ratio ($r_r$)** ratio of required reserves to DDO (demand deposits and other checkable deposits)

**reserve requirements** percentage figure that depository institutions are required to hold in reserves to support deposit liabilities

**reserves** cash on hand and deposits at the Federal Reserve maintained by depository institutions

**Resolution Funding Corporation (RFC)** establishment created by Congress to issue bonds to cover the expenses of financial institution reform

**Resolution Trust Corporation (RTC)** temporary institution created by FIRREA that managed and resolved insolvent thrift institutions and liquidated assets of failed institutions

**reverse repurchase agreement (reverse RPs)** or **matched sale-purchase transaction** transaction in which securities are sold to buyers, who agree to buy back the securities at a specific date and price

**Ricardian equivalence proposition** theory that asserts that agents anticipate future tax liabilities associated with larger budget deficits and increase their saving rates to compensate

**Riegle-Neal Interstate Banking and Branching Efficiency Act of 1994** act revoking the rights granted states to determine branching laws for banks operating within individual states

**risk premium** additional yield contained in financial instruments to compensate lenders for default risk

## S

**sacrifice ratio** percentage of 1 year's output (GDP) that a nation must forgo or "sacrifice" in order to reduce its inflation rate by one percentage point

**Savings Association Insurance Fund (SAIF)** insurance fund created by FIRREA for thrift institutions

**seasonal credit** Federal Reserve loans to institutions subject to strong seasonal fluctuations in loan demand, such as small banks in farming communities and resort areas

**secondary credit** discount loans to banks experiencing liquidity problems or other financial problems

**secondary market** market in which securities are traded after they have been issued

**Securities and Exchange Commission (SEC)** government organization charged with preventing financial abuses such as insider trading of stocks, bonds, and other financial instruments, and failure of corporations to clearly and honestly disclose key financial information

**securitization** transformation of illiquid financial assets into highly marketable capital market instruments

**segmented markets theory** theory that borrowers and lenders are committed to particular maturities, unwilling to switch in response to yield considerations

**self-correcting mechanism** mechanism that tends automatically to restore full employment conditions through wage and price flexibility

**shares** claims of ownership in individual corporations held by stockholders

**sources of the base** factors determining the monetary base; includes 10 factors, dominated by Federal Reserve security portfolio

**speculative demand for money** money balances held so that a speculative opportunity can be undertaken and financed in the event it should arise

**spot exchange rate** exchange rate at which spot transactions take place

**spot transactions** exchange of currencies for immediate or "on the spot" delivery and payment

**stagflation** combination of stagnant or falling output and sharply rising prices

**stored value cards** cards loaded with a predetermined amount of money; used to make payments

**supply-shock inflation** inflation caused by sharp increases in input prices, which shift the AS curve leftward.

**supply-side economics** macroeconomic policies designed to increase saving, investment, and work incentives, thereby shifting the aggregate supply curve persistently rightward

**sweep account** device through which the bank's computer automatically transfers funds out of customers' checking accounts into interest-bearing financial assets at the end of each day

## T

**T-accounts** a device showing the change in the balance sheet resulting from a given event

**tariffs** taxes on imported goods

**tax and loan accounts** U.S. Treasury deposits in commercial banks, periodically replenished by federal tax receipts and by the proceeds of new Treasury securities sales to the public

**Taylor rule** monetary policy rule in which the Federal Reserve moves its federal funds rate target in response to changes in both inflation and the output gap

**term premium** additional yield embedded in long-term debt instruments to compensate lenders for market risk

**term structure of interest rates** relationship *at a given point in time* between the length of time to maturity and the yield on a security

**terms of trade** ratio of the price of the nation's exports divided by the price of the nation's imports, with both prices measured in units of domestic currency

**time inconsistency problem** tendency of policymakers to announce a particular policy to influence expectations and then to follow different policies after the expectations have been formed

**time preference** human propensity to exhibit preference for current consumption over future consumption

**Tobin's q theory** theory that monetary policy influences investment spending by altering stock prices and firms' market capitalization relative to replacement cost of capital

**too big to fail policy** regulatory policy of systematically bailing out very large, troubled financial institutions whose failure might touch off major financial market repercussions

**trade deficit** amount by which the total value of a nation's imports exceeds the total value of its exports

**transactions (checkable) deposits** deposits on which checks can be written with unlimited checking privileges

**transactions costs** value of money and time needed for financial transactions

**transactions demand for money** demand for money to finance expenditures that are not perfectly synchronized with receipt of funds

**transmission mechanism of monetary policy** various avenues or channels through which changes in Federal Reserve policy alter aggregate demand and economic activity

**Treasury bills** short-term IOUs issued by U.S. government, traded at a discount from face value in a well-developed secondary market

**Treasury bonds** IOUs issued by the U.S. government that have original maturity of 10 to 40 years

**Treasury notes** IOUs issued by the U.S. government that have an original maturity of 1 to 10 years

**Treaty on Monetary Union (Maastricht Treaty)** agreement that formed the European Union and set forth the requisite conditions for the creation of the single currency and central bank

**Treaty of Rome** treaty that created the European Economic Community and formed an arrangement in which member countries practice free trade among themselves while maintaining a common tariff or other trade restrictions *vis-à-vis* nonmember nations

## U

**unit banking** system in which a bank is permitted to have only one office, with no branching permitted

**uses for the base** ways in which the monetary base is allocated or used; bank reserves and currency held by the public

## V

**velocity of money** ratio of nominal GDP to the money stock

**virtuous cycle** cycle in which expanding economic activity and rising stock prices lead to increased investment expenditures, thereby further expanding economic activity

## W

**wealth** the value of assets, including money stock and other financial and real assets, minus the value of liabilities

**wealth effect** effect of changes in individuals' net worth on their consumption and saving decisions

## Y

**yield** rate of return on an asset, expressed as a percentage per year

**yield curve** graphical depiction of the term structure of interest rates

**yield to maturity** average annual return including any capital gain or loss realized at maturity when the face value of the bond is redeemed

## Z

**zero coupon bond** bond that provides no annual payments but agrees to return a specific principal at maturity

# Index

## N



## O



## P